ROMANS

VOLUME 33

THE ANCHOR BIBLE is a fresh approach to the world's greatest classic. Its object is to make the Bible accessible to the modern reader; its method is to arrive at the meaning of biblical literature through exact translation and extended exposition, and to reconstruct the ancient setting of the biblical story, as well as the circumstances of its transcription and the characteristics of its transcribers.

THE ANCHOR BIBLE is a project of international and interfaith scope. Protestant, Catholic, and Jewish scholars from many countries contribute individual volumes. The project is not sponsored by any ecclesiastical organization and is not intended to reflect any particular theological doctrine. Prepared under our joint supervision, THE ANCHOR BIBLE is an effort to make available all the significant historical and linguistic knowledge which bears on the interpretation of the biblical record.

THE ANCHOR BIBLE is aimed at the general reader with no special formal training in biblical studies; yet, it is written with the most exacting standards of scholarship, reflecting the highest technical accomplishment.

This project marks the beginning of a new era of cooperation among scholars in biblical research, thus forming a common body of knowledge to be shared by all.

William Foxwell Albright
David Noel Freedman
GENERAL EDITORS

THE ANCHOR BIBLE

ROMANS

◆

A New Translation
with
Introduction and Commentary

JOSEPH A. FITZMYER, S.J.

THE ANCHOR BIBLE

Doubleday

New York London Toronto Sydney Auckland

THE ANCHOR BIBLE
PUBLISHED BY DOUBLEDAY
a division of Bantam Doubleday Dell Publishing Group, Inc.
1540 Broadway, New York, N.Y. 10036
The ANCHOR BIBLE, DOUBLEDAY, and the portrayal
of an anchor with the letters AB are trademarks of
Doubleday, a division of Bantam Doubleday Dell Publishing
Group, Inc.

IMPRIMI POTEST
Reverend Edward Glynn, S.J.
Praepositus Provinciae Marylandiae

NIHIL OBSTAT
Reverend James Walsh, S.J.
Censor Deputatus

IMPRIMATUR
Reverend Msgr. William J. Kane
Vicar General for the Archdiocese of Washington

28 April 1992

The *nihil obstat* and *imprimatur* are official declarations that a book or pamphlet is free of doctrinal
or moral error. No implication is contained therein that those who have granted the *nihil obstat* and
the *imprimatur* agree with the content, opinions, or statements expressed.

Library of Congress Cataloging-in-Publication Data

Bible. N.T. Romans. English. Fitzmyer. 1993.
    Romans : a new translation with introduction and commentary /
Joseph A. Fitzmyer. — 1st ed.
        p.   cm. — (The Anchor Bible ; 33)
    Includes bibliographical references and index.
    1. Bible.   N.T.   Romans—Commentaries.   I. Fitzmyer, Joseph A.
II. Title.   III. Series: Bible. English. Anchor Bible.   1964 ; v.
33.
BS192.2.A1   1964.G3   vol. 33
[BS2663]
220.7'7 s—dc20
[227'.1077]   92-29702
                                                                CIP

ISBN 0-385-23317-5

Piae memoriae

magistrorum meorum

americanorum, belgicorum, romanorum

CONTENTS

◆

Contents

TRANSLATION, COMMENTARY, AND NOTES

Contents

Contents

Contents

Contents

PREFACE

♦

During my days as a student of theology at Eegenhoven-Louvain, Belgium I once picked up the commentary on Paul's letter to the Romans written by M.-J. Lagrange *(Saint Paul: Épître aux Romains)* and read how that famous commentator described his first approach to this difficult Pauline writing: "Le premier contact fut écrasant" (Avant-propos, iii). That brief statement about his experience of trying to interpret Romans has stuck in my mind ever since. Though I have often studied and taught Romans over the years, I still think that any contact with this letter is *écrasant*. It overwhelms the reader by the density and sublimity of the topic with which it deals, the gospel of the justification and salvation of Jew and Greek alike by grace through faith in Jesus Christ, revealing the uprightness and love of God the Father.

Moreover, the role that Romans has played in the history of Christianity manifests that it is the most important of the Pauline writings, if not of the entire NT. The impact that this letter has had on the history of the Christian church is incalculable. Generation after generation of commentators over the ages have sought to interpret it and make it intelligible for people of their age. The commentaries on it in books and articles over the centuries make clear the contribution that the study of this letter has made to the history of Christianity. In fact, one can almost write the history of Christian theology by surveying the ways in which Romans has been interpreted.

The last full-scale commentary on Paul's letter to the Romans written by an English-speaking Roman Catholic was published in 1934 (P. J. Boylan). Since that time there have been a number of short Roman Catholic commentaries on the letter, including my own ("The Letter to the Romans," *JBC*, art. 53; revised, *NJBC*, art. 51). Although there exist recent full-scale commentaries on Romans in English (e.g., the translation of Käsemann's renowned German commentary; Cranfield's monumental two-volume work; and the more recent commentary of Dunn), there is still room for another view of Romans. Advances in the study of Pauline theology, in the clearer distinction generally admitted between Paul's authentic and doubtfully authentic letters, and in the role that Romans has been

xiii

playing in modern ecumenical discussions provide the background for a fresh approach to Romans.

In Roman Catholic biblical studies there has also been the influence of the encyclical of Pope Pius XII, *Divino afflante Spiritu* (1943), and serious concern for historical-critical and literary methods in the study of Scripture has become so manifest that our approach to Romans (and to Pauline theology in general) has come into close contact with that of Protestant commentators.

Rudolf Bultmann, the great German NT scholar of the early part of this century, maintained that there was no presuppositionless exegesis of the Bible. Every commentator somehow manifests his or her confessional stance in interpreting a biblical text. Yet there also exists a corporate exegetical endeavor engaged in by interpreters of different backgrounds, whether Jewish, Protestant, or Roman Catholic. This corporate endeavor tends to produce over a period of time a less subjective approach to a particular biblical writing and also brings to light the often subconscious presuppositions of the individual interpreter. From such presuppositions no one fully escapes. Although this commentary will always be recognized as one written by a Roman Catholic, I hope that my background will not show up too boldly. I hope that this commentary will advance not only the corporate exegetical endeavor, but also the ecumenical dialogues in which Paul's letter to the Romans has been so involved.

My intention has been to write a detailed commentary of classic proportions on Romans for modern twentieth-century Christian readers. It is hoped that the commentary will explain Paul's thought in this important writing and will make it accessible in a not-too-technical form for general readers. I have at times introduced Greek words in transcription into the discussion, where necessary, but always with an English translation, at times with a literal rendering of the Greek in order to present what Paul's text actually says.

Earlier commentators on Romans will be mentioned by their last names and an abbreviated title of their works, which are listed in the general bibliography. In that bibliography the commentators are broken down into groups according to time: patristic period (Greek, Latin, and Syriac writers, listed chronologically); medieval period (Greek and Latin writers, listed chronologically); fifteenth- to eighteenth-century commentators (listed chronologically according to the year of their death); nineteenth- and twentieth-century commentators (ordered alphabetically). It has been my aim to give as complete a list of commentaries on Romans as I have been able to find, something that has not been attempted in recent times. Many medieval commentaries have never been published; they are found in manuscripts in European libraries. In such cases I have listed the title of the commentary, followed by reference to standard source works, where indication is given of the location of such manuscripts. In the specific bibliographies at the end of pericopes authors are listed in alphabetical order. When a strange or unfamiliar name appears in the COMMENTS or NOTES, the reader should consult first the specific bibliography at the end of the pericope; if the information is not found there, then the general bibliography should be consulted, where not only commentaries are listed, but also monographs on Romans as well as on some general Pauline topics. Further bibliography on such topics will at times be found in the list that accompanies the sketch of Pauline teaching in this letter. The index of modern authors offers guidance to the needed information. References to OT books cite the chapter and verse according to the Hebrew or Aramaic text, not that of most English Bibles. This is to be noted in the case of the Psalter, where psalms are always referred to according to the numbering of the Hebrew text, even when the discussion may involve the Greek of the LXX. In case of doubt, one can usually consult the *NAB*, which uses the Hebrew-text numbering.

In the introduction to the commentary the reader will find discussion of the usual questions about the letter's addressees, the authorship of the letter, its Greek text, its date and place of composition, occasion and purpose, unity and integrity, and structure and outline. In addition, there is a synthetic sketch of Paul's teaching in this letter, with a bibliography. During the course of the commentary reference will often be made to this synthesis in order to avoid repetitious treatment of topics that appear frequently in various parts of the letter.

As in my commentary on the Lucan Gospel, I present a fresh translation of the Greek text of each pericope, followed by COMMENTS on the pericope as a whole and then by NOTES on lemmata taken from its individual verses. COMMENT is the term used throughout for the introductory discussion of a pericope, and NOTES are reserved for the detailed treatment of problematic words and phrases introduced as lemmata. At times the discussion of problems in the NOTES may become technical, and the general reader will have to bear with this aspect or learn to pass over them. The overall thrust of the letter will be treated in the COMMENTS. The division of the Pauline texts into pericopes will follow the outline of the letter given in section VIII of the introduction. References, sometimes in parentheses, without the mention of a biblical book's title mean a chapter and verse in Romans; "Rom" will be used only to avoid ambiguity in a particular context. Translations of other biblical passages are my own, except where another standard translation enters the discussion.

I have to express my thanks to many persons who have aided me in recent years while I have been working on this commentary. In particular, I should like to thank Eugene M. Rooney, S.J., the director of the Woodstock Theological Center Library, and his staff; Alan C. Mitchell, S.J., who often helped me to get this text on the word processor; James P. M. Walsh, S.J., who read the manuscript and made many useful suggestions for its improvement; David Berger, the director of the library of Concordia Seminary, St. Louis, who helped with many bibliographical items on old commentaries; Henry Bertels, S.J., the librarian of the Biblical Institute, Rome, who helped with bibliographical items; the Anchor Bible series editor, David Noel Freedman, for his suggestive criticism and helpful

advice; and Michael L. Iannazzi, the in-house editor at Doubleday, and his staff
for their cooperation in bringing the manuscript into book form.

Finally, I dedicate this book to the revered memory of the many persons who
taught me here in the United States, but also in Louvain and in Rome. All but a
few have passed to their reward.

Joseph A. Fitzmyer, S.J.
Professor Emeritus, Biblical Studies
The Catholic University of America
Resident at the Jesuit Community
Georgetown University
Washington, DC 20057

Principal Abbreviations

◆

Aeg	*Aegyptus*
AER	*American Ecclesiastical Review*
AGJU	Arbeiten zur Geschichte des antiken Judentums und des Urchristentums
AGSU	Arbeiten zur Geschichte des Spätjudentums und Urchristentums
AI	R. de Vaux, *Ancient Israel* (New York and London: McGraw-Hill, 1961)
AIPHO	*Annuaire de l'Institut de Philologie et d'Histoire Orientales*
AJA	*American Journal of Archaeology*
AJBI	*Annual of the Japanese Biblical Institute*
ALBO	Analecta lovaniensia biblica et orientalia
AmiCler	*Ami du clergé*
AnBib	Analecta biblica
ANEP	J. B. Pritchard, *The Ancient Near East in Pictures* (Princeton, N.J.: Princeton University Press, 1954)
ANET	J. B. Pritchard, *Ancient Near Eastern Texts* (Princeton, N.J.: Princeton University Press, 1950) and *Supplement* (1968)
Ang	*Angelicum*
AnGreg	Analecta gregoriana
ANRW	H. Temporini and W. Haase (eds.), *Aufstieg und Niedergang der römischen Welt*, Part 2: Principat—Religion 25.1–6 (Berlin and New York: de Gruyter, 1982–88)
ANTF	Arbeiten zur neutestamentlichen Textforschung
Anton	*Antonianum*
AOT	H. F. D. Sparks (ed.), *The Apocryphal Old Testament* (Oxford: Clarendon Press, 1984)
ARG	*Archiv für Reformationsgeschichte*

AsJT	*Asian Journal of Theology*
ASNU	Acta seminarii neotestamentici upsaliensis
AsSeign	*Assemblées du Seigneur*
ATANT	Abhandlungen zur Theologie des Alten und Neuen Testaments
ATR	*Anglican Theological Review*
ATRSup	Supplements to *ATR*
AusBR	*Australian Biblical Review*
AUSS	*Andrews University Seminary Studies*
BA	*Biblical Archaeologist*
B-A	W. Bauer, K. Aland, and B. Aland, *Griechisch-deutsches Wörterbuch zu den Schriften des Neuen Testaments und der frühchristlichen Literatur*, 6th ed. (Berlin and New York: de Gruyter, 1988)
BAC	Biblioteca de autores cristianos
BAGD	W. Bauer, W. F. Arndt, F. W. Gingrich, and F. W. Danker, A *Greek–English Lexicon of the New Testament and Other Early Christian Literature* (Chicago, Ill.: University of Chicago Press, 1979)
BARev	*Biblical Archaeology Review*
BASOR	*Bulletin of the American Schools of Oriental Research*
BBB	Bonner biblische Beiträge
BBET	Beiträge zur biblischen Exegese und Theologie
BCPE	*Bulletin du Centre Protestant d'Études*
BDF	F. Blass and A. Debrunner, A *Greek Grammar of the New Testament and Other Early Christian Literature*, trans. R. W. Funk (Chicago, Ill.: University of Chicago Press, 1961)
BDR	F. Blass and A. Debrunner, *Grammatik des neutestamentlichen Griechisch*, 14th ed., rev. F. Rehkopf (Göttingen: Vandenhoeck & Ruprecht, 1976)
BeO	*Bibbia e oriente*
BETL	Bibliotheca ephemeridum theologicarum lovaniensium
BEvT	Beiträge zur evangelischen Theologie
BFCT	Beiträge zur Förderung christlicher Theologie
BGBE	Beiträge zur Geschichte der biblischen Exegese
BGPTM	Beiträge zur Geschichte der Philosophie und Theologie des Mittelalters
BHT	Beiträge zur historischen Theologie
Bib	*Biblica*
BibLeb	*Bibel und Leben*
BibSF	Biblische Studien (Freiburg im Breisgau)

BibSN	Biblische Studien (Neukirchen)
BJRL	*Bulletin of the John Rylands (University) Library (of Manchester)*
BK	*Bibel und Kirche*
BLit	*Bibel und Liturgie*
BN	*Biblische Notizen*
BNTC	Black's New Testament Commentary
BR	*Biblical Research*
BSac	*Bibliotheca sacra*
BT	*The Bible Translator*
BTB	*Biblical Theology Bulletin*
BU	Biblische Untersuchungen
BullSNTS	*Bulletin of Studiorum Novi Testamenti Societas*
BVC	*Bible et vie chrétienne*
BW	*Biblical World*
BWANT	Beiträge zur Wissenschaft vom Alten und Neuen Testament
BZ	*Biblische Zeitschrift*
BZAW	Beihefte zur ZAW
BZNW	Beihefte zur ZNW
Carth	*Carthaginiensia*
CBQ	*Catholic Biblical Quarterly*
CCConMed	Corpus christianorum, Continuatio mediaevalis
CCER	*Cahiers du Cercle Ernest-Renan*
CCHS	B. Orchard et al. (eds.), A *Catholic Commentary on Holy Scripture* (New York and Edinburgh: Nelson, 1953)
CCLat	Corpus christianorum, series latina
ChrC	*Christian Century*
CII	J.-B. Frey, *Corpus insriptionum iudaicarum*, 2 vols. (Vatican City: Institute of Christian Archaeology, 1936–52)
CIG	*Corpus inscriptionum graecarum*
CIL	*Corpus inscriptionum latinarum*
CJT	*Canadian Journal of Theology*
ClassQ	*Classical Quarterly*
ColMech	*Collectanea mechliniensia*
ComViat	*Communio viatorum*
ConcJourn	Concordia Journal
ConNeot	*Coniectanea neotestamentica*
CQR	*Church Quarterly Review*
CR	Corpus Reformatorum

CRINT	Compendia rerum iudaicarum ad Novum Testamentum
CSEL	Corpus scriptorum ecclesiasticorum latinorum
CSS	Cursus sacrae Scripturae
CTJ	*Calvin Theological Journal*
CTM	*Concordia Theological Monthly* or *CTM* (abbreviation used as the title for a while)
CTQ	*Concordia Theological Quarterly*
CUA	The Catholic University of America
CurTM	*Currents in Theology and Mission*
DB	Deutsche Bibel (see also WAusg)
DBM	*Deltion biblikon meleton*
DBSup	*Dictionnaire de la Bible, Supplément*
DJD	Discoveries in the Judaean Desert (of Jordan)
DKP	K. Ziegler and W. Sontheimer, *Der kleine Pauly*, 5 vols. (Stuttgart: Druckenmüller, 1964–75)
DTT	*Dansk teologisk tidsskrift*
EDNT	H. Balz and G. Schneider (eds.), *Exegetical Dictionary of the New Testament*, 3 vols. (Grand Rapids, Mich.: Eerdmans, 1990–)
EgThéol	*Église et théologie*
EKK	Evangelisch-Katholischer Kommentar zum Neuen Testament
ENTT	E. Käsemann, *Essays on New Testament Themes*, SBT 41 (London: SCM, 1964)
ESBNT	J. A. Fitzmyer, *Essays on the Semitic Background of the New Testament* (London: Chapman, 1971; repr. Missoula, Mont.: Scholars, 1974)
EspVie	*Esprit et vie*
EstBíb	*Estudios bíblicos*
EstEcl	*Estudios eclesiasticos*
EstFranc	*Estudios franciscanos*
EtBib	Études bibliques
ETL	*Ephemerides theologicae lovanienses*
ETR	*Études théologiques et religieuses*
EvQ	*Evangelical Quarterly*
EvT	*Evangelische Theologie*
EWNT	H. Balz and G. Schneider (eds.), *Exegetisches Wörterbuch zum Neuen Testament*, 3 vols. (Stuttgart: Kohlhammer, 1980–83)
Expos	*Expositor*

ExpTim	*Expository Times*
FB	Forschung zur Bibel
FBBS	Facet Books, Biblical Series
FilNeot	*Filología neotestamentaria*
FP	Florilegium patristicum
FRLANT	Forschungen zur Religion und Literatur des Alten und Neuen Testaments
GCS	Griechische christliche Schriftsteller
GLeb	*Geist und Leben*
GNS	Good News Studies
Greg	*Gregorianum*
GTA	Göttinger theologische Arbeiten
GTJ	*Grace Theological Journal*
GTT	*Gereformeerd theologisch Tijdschrift*
HALAT	W. Baumgartner et al. (eds.), *Hebräisches und aramäisches Lexikon zum Alten Testament*, 5 vols. (Leiden: Brill, 1967–)
HBT	*Horizons in Biblical Theology*
HerTS	*Hervormde teologiese Studies*
HeyJ	*Heythrop Journal*
HibJ	*Hibbert Journal*
HJ	*Historisches Jahrbuch*
HJPAJC	E. Schürer, *The History of the Jewish People in the Age of Jesus Christ (175 B.C.–A.D. 135)*, 3 vols., rev. ed. G. Vermes et al. (Edinburgh: Clark, 1973–87)
HNT	Handbuch zum Neuen Testament
HNTC	Harper's New Testament Commentary
HTKNT	Herders theologischer Kommentar zum Neuen Testament
HTR	*Harvard Theological Review*
HTS	Harvard Theological Studies
HUCA	*Hebrew Union College Annual*
HUT	Hermeneutische Untersuchungen zur Theologie
IB	*Interpreter's Bible*
IBS	*Irish Biblical Studies*
ICC	International Critical Commentary
IER	*Irish Ecclesiastical Review*
IGRom	R. Cagnat and G. LaFaye (eds.), *Inscriptiones graecae ad res romanas pertinentes*, 4 vols. (Paris: Leroux, 1906)

IKZ	*Internationale katholische Zeitschrift (Communio)*
Int	*Interpretation*
ITQ	*Irish Theological Quarterly*
JAC	*Jahrbuch für Antike und Christentum*
JBC	R. E. Brown et al. (eds.), *The Jerome Biblical Commentary* (Englewood Cliffs, N.J.: Prentice Hall, 1968)
JBL	*Journal of Biblical Literature*
JBR	*Journal of Bible and Religion*
JChSt	*Journal of Church and State*
JDTh	*Jahrbücher für deutsche Theologie*
JES	*Journal of Ecumenical Studies*
JETS	*Journal of the Evangelical Theological Society*
JJS	*Journal of Jewish Studies*
JP	*Journal of Philology*
JQR	*Jewish Quarterly Review*
JR	*Journal of Religion*
JRS	*Journal of Roman Studies*
JSJ	*Journal for the Study of Judaism in the Persian, Hellenistic and Roman Period*
JSNT	*Journal for the Study of the New Testament*
JSNTSup	Supplements to *JSNT*
JSOT	*Journal for the Study of the Old Testament*
JTCh	*Journal for Theology and Church*
JTS	*Journal of Theological Studies*
JTSA	*Journal of Theology for Southern Africa*
KBW	Katholisches Bibelwerk
KD	*Kerygma und Dogma*
KJV	*King James Version* (of the Bible)
KRS	*Kirchenblatt für die reformierte Schweiz*
LAE	A. Deissmann, *Light from the Ancient East*, 2d ed. (London: Hodder & Stoughton, 1927)
LB	*Linguistica biblica*
LCR	*Lutheran Church Review*
LD	Lectio divina
LexTQ	*Lexington Theological Quarterly*
LQ	*Lutheran Quarterly*
LR	*Lutherische Rundschau*
LS	*Louvain Studies*

LSJ	H. G. Liddell and R. Scott, *A Greek–English Lexicon*, new ed. by H. S. Jones with the assistance of R. McKenzie, 2 vols. (Oxford: Clarendon Press, 1925–40; repr. in one volume, 1966)
LTJ	*Lutheran Theological Journal*
LTP	*Laval théologique et philosophique*
LumVie	*Lumière et vie*
LuthW	Luther's Works, ed. J. Pelikan and H. Lehman (St. Louis, Mo.: Concordia; Philadelphia, Penn.: Fortress, 1958–86)
LW	*Lutheran World*
LWSup	Supplements to *LW*
MarTS	Marburger theologische Studien
MDB	*Le Monde de la Bible*
MeyerK	MeyerKommentar (H. A. W. Meyer, Kritisch-exegetischer Kommentar über das Neue Testament)
MM	J. H. Moulton and G. Milligan, *The Vocabulary of the Greek Testament* (London: Hodder & Stoughton, 1930)
MNT	R. E. Brown et al. (eds.), *Mary in the New Testament* (New York: Paulist Press; Philadelphia, Penn.: Fortress, 1978)
MTS	Münchener theologische Studien
MTZ	*Münchener theologische Zeitschrift*
N-A[26]	E. Nestle and K. Aland (eds.), *Novum Testamentum graece*, 26th ed. (Stuttgart: Deutsche Bibelstiftung, 1979)
NAB	*New American Bible*
NABRNT	*New American Bible, Revised New Testament* (1987)
NCCHS	R. C. Fuller et al. (eds.), *A New Catholic Commentary on Holy Scripture* (London: Nelson, 1969)
NDIEC	G. H. R. Horsley, *New Documents Illustrating Early Christianity*, 5 vols. (North Ryde, N.S.W.: Ancient History Documentary Research Center, Macquarie University, 1981–89)
NEB	*New English Bible*
NedTTs	*Nederlands theologisch Tijdschrift*
NeutForsch	Neutestamentliche Forschung
NGTT	*Nederuits gereformeerde teologiese Tydskrif*
NIBC	New International Bible Commentary
NICNT	New International Commentary on the New Testament

NIDNTT	C. Brown (ed.), *New International Dictionary of New Testament Theology*, 3 vols. (Grand Rapids, Mich.: Zondervan, 1975–78)
NJBC	R. E. Brown et al. (eds.), *The New Jerome Biblical Commentary* (Englewood Cliffs, N.J.: Prentice Hall, 1990)
NJDTh	*Neue Jahrbücher für deutsche Theologie*
NKZ	*Neue kirchliche Zeitschrift*
NorTT	*Norsk teologisk Tidsskrift*
NovT	*Novum Testamentum*
NovTSup	Supplements to *NovT*
NovVet	*Nova et vetera*
NRSV	*New Revised Standard Version* (of the Bible)
NRT	*La Nouvelle Revue théologique*
NTAbh	Neutestamentliche Abhandlungen
NTB	C. K. Barrett, *The New Testament Background: Selected Documents* (London: SPCK, 1956)
NTD	Das Neue Testament deutsch
NTF	Neutestamentliche Forschung
NThStud	*Nieuwe theologische Studiën*
NTL	New Testament Library
NTQT	E. Käsemann, *New Testament Questions of Today* (Philadelphia, Penn.: Fortress, 1969)
NTRG	New Testament Reading Guide
NTS	*New Testament Studies*
NTSR	New Testament for Spiritual Reading
NTTS	New Testament Tools and Studies
OBO	Orbis biblicus et orientalis
OCD	N. G. L. Hammond and H. H. Scullard (eds.), *The Oxford Classical Dictionary*, 2d ed. (Oxford: Clarendon Press, 1970)
PAHT	J. A. Fitzmyer, *Paul and His Theology: A Brief Sketch* (Englewood Cliffs, N.J.: Prentice Hall, 1989)
PCB	M. Black and H. H. Rowley (eds.), *Peake's Commentary on the Bible* (London: Nelson, 1963)
PG	Patrologia graeca (ed. J. Migne)
PIBA	*Proceedings of the Irish Biblical Association*
PJ	*Palästina-Jahrbuch*
PL	Patrologia latina (ed. J. Migne)
PLSup	Patrologia latina, Supplement
PosLuth	*Positions luthériennes*

ProcEGLMBS	*Proceedings of the Eastern Great Lakes Midwest Biblical Society*
PSB	*Princeton Seminary Bulletin*
PVTG	Pseudepigrapha Veteris Testamenti graece
PW	*Paulys Real-Enyclopädie der classischen Altertumswissenschaft*, ed. G. Wissowa (Stuttgart: Metzler; Munich: Druckenmüller, 1893–1978)
QD	Quaestiones disputatae
RAC	*Reallexikon für Antike und Christentum*, ed. T. Klausner (Stuttgart: Hiersmann, 1950–)
RAT	*Revue africaine de théologie*
RB	*Revue biblique*
RBén	*Revue bénédictine*
RBMA	F. Stegmüller, *Repertorium biblicum medii aevi*, 11 vols. (Madrid: Consejo Superior de Investigaciones Científicas, Instituto Francisco Suárez, 1950–80; vols. 8–11, with the assistance of N. Reinhardt; vols. 1–3, repr. 1981)
RBR	*Ricerche bibliche e religiose*
RDT	*Revue diocésaine de Tournai*
RechBib	Recherches bibliques
RefTR	*Reformed Theological Review*
REJ	*Revue des études juives*
RelS	*Religious Studies*
ResQ	*Restoration Quarterly*
RevApol	*Revue apologétique*
RevEcclLiége	*Revue ecclésiastique de Liége*
RevEclBras	*Revista ecclesiástica brasileira*
RevExp	*Review and Expositor*
RevistB	*Revista bíblica*
RevQ	*Revue de Qumran*
RevScRel	*Revue des sciences religieuses*
RevThom	*Revue thomiste*
RGG	*Die Religion in Geschichte und Gegenwart*, 3d ed., ed. K. Galling (Tübingen: Mohr [Siebeck], 1957–65)
RHPR	*Revue d'histoire et de philosophie religieuses*
RHR	*Revue de l'histoire des religions*
RivB	*Rivista biblica*
RivBSup	Supplements to *RivB*
RNT	Regensburger Neues Testament

RomDeb	K. P. Donfried (ed.), *The Romans Debate: Revised and Expanded Edition* (Peabody, Mass.: Hendrickson, 1991)
RömQ	*Römische Quartalschrift*
RRef	*Revue reformée*
RRel	*Review for Religious*
RSPT	*Revue des sciences philosophiques et théologiques*
RSR	*Recherches de science religieuse*
RSV	*Revised Standard Version* (of the Bible)
RTAM	*Recherches de théologie ancienne et médiévale*
RTK	*Roczniki teologiczno-kanoniczne*
RTP	*Revue de théologie et de philosophie*
RTR	*Reformed Theological Review*
SacPag	*Sacra Pagina*, BETL 12–13, ed. J. Coppens et al. (Gembloux: Duculot, 1959)
SANT	Studien zum Alten und Neuen Testament
SBB	Stuttgarter biblische Beiträge
SBFLA	*Studii biblici franciscani liber annuus*
SBJ	*La Sainte Bible de Jérusalem*
SBLDS	Society of Biblical Literature Dissertation Series
SBLMS	Society of Biblical Literature Monograph Series
SBLTT—ECLS	Society of Biblical Literature Texts in Translation— Early Christian Literature Series
SBM	Stuttgarter biblische Monographien
SBS	Stuttgarter Bibelstudien
SBT	Studies in Biblical Theology
SBU	*Symbolae biblicae upsalienses*
SC	Sources chrétiennes
ScCatt	*Scuola cattolica*
ScEccl	*Sciences ecclésiastiques*
ScEspr	*Science et Esprit*
SCM	Student Christian Movement
Scr	*Scripture*
ScrTheol	*Scripta theologica*
SdZ	*Stimmen der Zeit*
SE II, IV, V, VI, VII	*Studia evangelica II, IV, V, VI, VII* (= TU 87 [1964], 102 [1968], 103 [1968], 112 [1973], 126 [1982])
SEA	*Svensk exegetisk årsbok*
SémBib	*Sémiotique et Bible*
SIG	W. Dittenberger, *Sylloge inscriptionum graecarum*, 4 vols., 3d ed. (Leipzig: Hirzel, 1915–24; repr. Hildesheim and New York: Olms, 1960)

SJLA	Studies in Judaism in Late Antiquity
SJOT	*Scandinavian Journal of the Old Testament*
SJT	*Scottish Journal of Theology*
SMSR	*Studi e materiali di storia delle religioni*
SNT	Studien zum Neuen Testament
SNTSMS	Studiorum Novi Testamenti Societas Monograph Series
SNTU	*Studien zum Neuen Testament und seine Umwelt*
SPAW	*Sitzungsberichte der preussischen Akademie der Wissenschaften*
SPB	Studia postbiblica
SPCIC	*Studiorum paulinorum congressus internationalis catholicus 1961*, AnBib 17–18 (Rome: Biblical Institute, 1963)
SPCK	Society for the Promotion of Christian Knowledge
SPIB	Scripta Pontificii Instituti Biblici
SR	*Studies in Religion/Sciences religieuses*
ST	*Studia theologica*
STK	*Svensk teologisk Kvartalskrift*
Str-B	(H. Strack and) P. Billerbeck, *Kommentar zum Neuen Testament aus Talmud und Midrash*, 6 vols. (Munich: Beck, 1926–63)
StudBibTheol	*Studia biblica et theologica*
StudPatav	*Studia patavina*
STV	*Studia theologica varsaviensia*
SUNT	Studien zur Umwelt des Neuen Testaments
SVTQ	*St. Vladimir's Theological Quarterly*
SwJT	*Southwestern Journal of Theology*
TAG	J. A. Fitzmyer, *To Advance the Gospel: New Testament Studies* (New York: Crossroad, 1981)
TAPA	*Transactions of the American Philological Association*
TB	Theologische Bücherei
TBei	*Theologische Beiträge*
TBl	*Theologische Blätter*
TBT	*The Bible Today*
TCGNT	B. M. Metzger, *A Textual Commentary on the Greek New Testament* (London and New York: United Bible Societies, 1971)
TD	*Theology Digest*
TDNT	G. Kittel and G. Friedrich (eds.), *Theological Dictionary of the New Testament*, 10 vols. (Grand Rapids, Mich.: Eerdmans, 1964–76)
TEH	Theologische Existenz heute

TF	*Theologische Forschung*
TGl	*Theologie und Glaube*
ThStud	*Theologische Studiën*
TLZ	*Theologische Literaturzeitung*
TNT	R. Bultmann, *Theology of the New Testament*, 2 vols. (London: SCM, 1952–55)
TorJT	*Toronto Journal of Theology*
TP	*Theologie und Philosophie*
TPINTC	Trinity Press International New Testament Commentary
TPQ	*Theologisch-Praktische Quartalschrift*
TQ	*Theologische Quartalschrift*
TRev	*Theologische Revue*
TrinJ	*Trinity Journal*
TRu	*Theologische Rundschau*
TS	*Theological Studies*
TSAJ	Texte und Studien zum antiken Judentum
TSK	*Theologische Studien und Kritiken*
TTijd	*Theologisch Tijdschrift*
TTKi	*Tidsskrift for Teologi og Kirke*
TToday	*Theology Today*
TTZ	*Trierer theologische Zeitschrift*
TU	Texte und Untersuchungen (Berlin: Akademie Verlag)
TvT	*Tijdschrift voor Theologie*
TynBul	*Tyndale Bulletin*
TynNTC	Tyndale New Testament Commentary
TZ	*Theologische Zeitschrift*
UBS	United Bible Societies
UNT	Untersuchungen zum Neuen Testament
USQR	*Union Seminary Quarterly Review*
USR	*Union Seminary Review*
VC	*Vigiliae christianae*
VCaro	*Verbum caro*
VD	*Verbum domini*
VF	*Verkündigung und Forschung*
VKGNT	K. Aland et al. (eds.), *Vollständige Konkordanz zum griechischen Neuen Testament*, . . . 2 vols. (Berlin and New York: de Gruyter, 1975–83)
VoxRef	*Vox Reformata*
VS	Verbum salutis
VSpir	*Vie spirituelle*
VSpirSup	Supplements to *VSpir*

VT	*Vetus Testamentum*
VTSup	Supplements to VT
WA	J. A. Fitzmyer, A *Wandering Aramean: Collected Aramaic Essays*, SBLMS 25 (Missoula, Mont.: Scholars, 1979)
WAusg	Weimarer Ausgabe, Martin Luther, *Werke*, Kritische Gesamtausgabe (Weimar: Böhlau, 1883–)
WBC	Word Biblical Commentary
WF	Wege der Forschung
WMANT	Wissenschaftliche Monographien zum Alten und Neuen Testament
WTJ	*Westminster Theological Journal*
WUNT	Wissenschaftliche Untersuchungen zum Neuen Testament
WW	*Word and World*
ZAM	*Zeitschrift für Aszese und Mystik*
ZAW	*Zeitschrift für die alttestamentliche Wissenschaft*
ZBG	M. Zerwick, *Biblical Greek*, SPIB 114, trans. J. Smith (Rome: Biblical Institute, 1963); translation of ZGB
ZEE	*Zeitschrift für evangelische Ethik*
ZGB	M. Zerwick, *Graecitas biblica* (Rome: Biblical Institute, 1960)
ZKT	*Zeitschrift für katholische Theologie*
ZNW	*Zeitschrift für die neutestamentliche Wissenschaft*
ZPE	*Zeitschrift für Papyrologie und Epigraphie*
ZRGG	*Zeitschrift für Religions- und Geistesgeschichte*
ZST	*Zeitschrift für systematische Theologie*
ZTK	*Zeitschrift für Theologie und Kirche*
ZWT	*Zeitschrift für wissenschaftliche Theologie*

Grammatical Abbreviations

◆

absol.	absolute		masc.	masculine
acc.	accusative		neut.	neuter
act.	active		nom.	nominative
adj.	adjective		obj.	object
adv.	adverb		opt.	optative
aor.	aorist		pass.	passive
art.	article		perf.	perfect
cl.	clause		pers.	personal
conj.	conjunction		pl.	plural
dat.	dative		prep.	preposition(al)
fem.	feminine		pres.	present
fut.	future		pron.	pronoun
def.	definite		ptc.	participle
dem.	demonstrative		rel.	relative
gen.	genitive		sg.	singular
imperf.	imperfect		subj.	subject
impv.	imperative		subjunct.	subjunctive
indef.	indefinite		vb.	verb
indic.	indicative		voc.	vocative
infin.	infinitive			

OTHER ABBREVIATIONS

◆

1 Clem.	Clement of Rome, *Ep. to*	MS(S)	manuscript(s)
	Corinthians	MT	Masoretic Text
Ag.Ap.	Josephus, *Against Apion*	n.s.	new series (any language)
Ant.	Josephus, *Antiquities*	NT	New Testament
Apoc.	Apocalypse	or.	*oratio*, oration
app. crit.	apparatus criticus	OT	Old Testament
bis	two occurrences	OxyP	Oxyrhynchus Papyrus
cod.	codex	pap.	papyrus
E	English version	repr.	reprinted
	numbering	rev.	revised
ed.	editor, edited by	serm.	*sermo*, sermon
ep.	epistle, *epistola*	T.	*Testament (of)*
fl.	floruit	Tg.	Targum
hom. (in)	*homilia in*, homily on	trans.	translator, translated by
J.W.	Josephus, *Jewish War*	v.l.	*varia lectio*, variant
lit.	literally		reading
LXX	Septuagint	Vg	Vulgata, Vulgate
m.	*Mishna* (tractate named)	VL	Vetus Latina, Old Latin

WRITINGS OF IGNATIUS OF ANTIOCH

Eph.	*Ep. to the Ephesians*
Magn.	*Ep. to the Magnesians*
Phld.	*Ep. to the Philadelphians*
Pol.	*Ep. to Polycarp*
Rom.	*Ep. to the Romans*
Smyrn.	*Ep. to the Smyrnaeans*
Trall.	*Ep. to the Trallians*

WRITINGS OF PHILO OF ALEXANDRIA

De Abr.	*De Abrahamo*
De cherub.	*De cherubim*

De. conf. ling.	*De confusione linguarum*
De congr.	*De congressu quaerendae eruditionis causa*
De Dec.	*De Decalogo*
De migr. Abr.	*De migratione Abrahami*
De mut. nom.	*De mutatione nominum*
De post. Caini	*De posteritate Caini*
De praem. et poen.	*De praemiis et poenis*
De somn.	*De somniis*
De spec. leg.	*De specialibus legibus*
De vita cont.	*De vita contemplativa*
De vita Mos.	*De vita Mosis*
In Flacc.	*In Flaccum*
Leg. ad Gai.	*Legatio ad Gaium*
Leg. alleg.	*Legum allegoriarum liber*
Quod Deus imm.	*Quod Deus immutabilis sit*

Dead Sea Scrolls and Related Texts

CD	Cairo (Genizah text of the) Damascus Document
Mur	Wadi Murabbaʿat texts
p	Pesher (commentary)
Q	Qumran
QL	Qumran Literature
1Q, 2Q, etc.	Numbered caves of Qumran, yielding written materials; followed by abbreviation of biblical or nonbiblical work
1QapGen	*Genesis Apocryphon* of Cave 1
1QH	*Hôdāyôt (Thanksgiving Psalms)* from Cave 1
1QpHab	*Pesher on Habbakuk* from Cave 1
1QM	*Milḥāmāh (War Scroll)* from Cave 1
1QS	*Serek hayyaḥad (Rule of the Community, Manual of Discipline)* from Cave 1
1QSa	Appendix A *(Rule of the Congregation)* to 1QS
4QEn	Enoch texts from Cave 4
11QtgJob	Targum of Job from Cave 11

The numbering of chapters and verses in the OT follows that of the Hebrew MT. This is especially to be noted when reference is made to the Psalter. Even if the discussion concerns the Greek form of a psalm in the LXX, the numbering still follows the Hebrew text. In case of doubt, one can always consult the NAB, which uses the numbering of the Hebrew OT.

TO THE ROMANS: TRANSLATION

◆

1. [1]Paul, a slave of Christ Jesus, called to be an apostle, set apart for God's gospel—[2]which he promised long ago through his prophets in the sacred Scriptures, [3]concerning his Son who was born of David's stock by natural descent, [4]but established as the Son of God with power by a spirit of holiness as of his resurrection from the dead, Jesus Christ our Lord, [5]through whom we have received the grace of apostleship to promote a commitment of faith among all the Gentiles on behalf of his name, [6]among whom you too were called to belong to Jesus Christ—[7]to all the beloved of God in Rome, called to be his dedicated people, grace and peace to you from God our Father and the Lord Jesus Christ.

[8]First of all, I give thanks to my God through Jesus Christ for all of you, because your faith is proclaimed in all the world. [9]Now God, whom I worship with my spirit in the evangelization of his Son, is my witness that I constantly make mention of you.

[10]I beg always in my prayers that somehow, by God's will, I may at length succeed in coming to you. [11]I yearn to see you in order to pass on to you some spiritual gift that you may be strengthened—[12]or rather that we may be mutually encouraged by each other's faith, both yours and mine. [13]I do not want you to be unaware, brothers, of how often I have proposed to come to you though I have been hindered up to now, in order to reap some fruit also among you as among the other Gentiles. [14]Both to Greeks and to barbarians I am indebted, both to the wise and to the unlearned! [15]Hence my eagerness to preach the gospel also to you who are in Rome.

[16]Now I am not ashamed of the gospel. It is God's power (unleashed) for the salvation of everyone who believes, for the Jew first but also for the Greek. [17]For in it is revealed the uprightness of God, through faith and for faith, as it stands written, *The One who is upright shall find life through faith.*[a]

[18]For God's wrath is being revealed from heaven against all the godlessness and wickedness of human beings who by such wickedness stifle the truth: [19]that

3

what can be known about God is manifest to them. For God himself has made it evident for them. [20]Ever since the creation of the world his invisible qualities, his eternal power and divinity, have been perceived by reflection on what he has made. Consequently, such people are without excuse, [21]because, though they knew God, they did not glorify him as God or thank him. Instead, they were reduced to futile thinking, and their misguided minds were steeped in darkness. [22]Pretending to be wise, they became fools [23]and exchanged the glory of the immortal God for an image shaped like a mortal human being, like birds, four-footed creatures, or reptiles.

[24]For this reason God delivered them over to the craving of their hearts for impurity that their bodies might be degraded among them. [25]These people exchanged the truth about God for a lie and reverenced and worshiped the creature rather than the creator—blest be he forever! Amen. [26]For this reason God delivered them over to disgraceful passions. Their women exchanged natural intercourse for that against nature; [27]and their men likewise abandoned natural relations with women and burned with lust for one another—males committing shameless acts with males and being paid in turn in their own persons the wage suited to their deviation.

[28]As they did not see fit to acknowledge God, he delivered them over to a base mentality and to improper conduct. [29]They became filled with every sort of wickedness, evil, greed, and malice; they were full of envy, murder, strife, craftiness, and spite. They became tale bearers, [30]slanderers, God haters, insolent, haughty, and boastful; contrivers of evil, rebels against parents; [31]foolish, faithless, uncaring, and merciless. [32]Though they know full well God's requirement that those who do such things deserve to die, they not only do them but even give approval to those who so act.

2. [1]So you are without excuse, whoever you are who sit in judgment. In judging another, you condemn yourself, since you, the judge, do the same things. [2]Yet we know that God's judgment falls in truth on all who do such things. [3]Do you really think that you will escape the judgment of God, you who sit in judgment on those who do such things and yet do them yourself? [4]Or do you make light of the abundance of his goodness, forbearance, and long-suffering? Do you not realize that what is good about God is meant to lead you to repentance? [5]With your stubborn and impenitent heart you are amassing wrath for yourself on the day of wrath, when God's just judgment will be revealed. [6]For *he will repay everyone according to his deeds:*[b] [7]eternal life for those who by patiently doing good strive for glory, honor, and immortality; [8]but wrath and fury for those who selfishly disobey the truth and are won over to wickedness. [9]There will be distress and anguish for every human being who does evil, for the Jew first and also for the Greek. [10]But there will be glory, honor, and peace for everyone who does good, for the Jew first and also for the Greek. [11]For there is no partiality in God.

[12]All who have sinned apart from the law will also perish apart from the law, and all who have sinned under the law will be judged by the law. [13]For it is not those who listen to the law who are upright before God; rather, those who observe the law will be justified before him. [14]Thus whenever Gentiles who do not have the law observe by nature precepts of the law, they are actually a law to themselves, though not having the law. [15]They show that what the law prescribes has been written on their hearts, as their consciences also bear witness and their thoughts either accuse or defend them—[16]on the day when, according to my gospel, God judges through Christ Jesus the secrets of human hearts.

[17]But suppose you call yourself a Jew, rely on the law, and boast of God, [18]knowing his will and scrutinizing the things that really matter, because you are instructed by the law, [19]and suppose you are persuaded that you yourself are a guide to the blind, a light to those in darkness, [20]a corrector of the foolish, a teacher of the immature, because you have in the law the embodiment of knowledge and truth—[21]then do you who would teach others fail to teach yourself? Do you who preach against stealing steal yourself? [22]Do you who forbid adultery commit it yourself? Do you who abominate idols rob temples? [23]As for you who boast of the law, you dishonor God by the transgression of the law. [24]As it stands written, *Because of you the name of God is blasphemed among the Gentiles.*[c]

[25]Circumcision, indeed, has value, if you observe the law. But if you are a transgressor of the law, your circumcision has become uncircumcision. [26]Again, if an uncircumcised man keeps the precepts of the law, will not his uncircumcision be reckoned as circumcision? [27]He who by nature is uncircumcised yet keeps the law will condemn you, with your written code and circumcision, as a transgressor of the law. [28]One is not a Jew outwardly only; nor is real circumcision external, in the flesh. [29]Rather, one is a Jew in secret, and real circumcision is of the heart, a thing of the spirit, not of the letter. His praise comes not from human beings, but from God.

3. [1]"Then what is the advantage of being a Jew, or what is the value of circumcision?" [2]Much in every way! First of all, Jews were entrusted with the oracles of God. [3]What then? Suppose some Jews were unfaithful? Will their infidelity nullify the fidelity of God? [4]Certainly not! God will be true, though every human being be a liar, as it stands written, *that you may be vindicated in your speech, and win out when you are being judged.*[d]

[5]If our wickedness brings forth the uprightness of God, what are we to say? Is God unjust to bring wrath upon us (I am speaking, of course, in human terms)? [6]Certainly not! Otherwise how is God to judge the world? [7]Again, if through my untruthfulness the truthfulness of God has overflowed to his glory, then why must I still be condemned as a sinner? [8]And why should we not "do evil that good may come of it"—as some people defame us with the libelous charge that we so teach? (The condemnation of such people is not unjust.) [9]What, then, is the situation? Are we (Jews) at a disadvantage? Not at all! For we have already charged that all, Jews and Greeks alike, are under the power of sin.

[10]As it stands written,

> No one is upright, no, not one;[e]
> 11 no one has understanding;[f]
> no one searches for God.
> 12 All have turned away, all have become depraved.
> No one does good, not even one.
> 13 Their throats are open graves;[g]
> with their tongues they have practiced deceit;
> the poison of asps lies behind their lips.[h]
> 14 Their mouths are full of cursing and bitterness.[i]
> 15 Swift are their feet to shed blood.[j]
> 16 Ruin and wretchedness strew their paths.
> 17 The path of peace they have not known.
> 18 Fear of God is not before their eyes.[k]

[19]Now we know that all the law says is addressed to those who are under the law so that every mouth may be silenced and the whole world become accountable to God, [20]since no human being will be justified before[l] him through deeds prescribed by the law; for through the law comes the real knowledge of sin.

[21]But now, independently of the law, the uprightness of God has been disclosed, even though the law and the prophets bear witness to it, [22]the uprightness of God that comes through faith in Jesus Christ toward all who believe, toward all, without distinction. [23]For all alike have sinned and fall short of the glory of God; [24]yet all are justified freely by his grace through the redemption that comes in Christ Jesus. [25]Through his blood God has presented him as a means of expiating sin for all who have faith. This was to be a manifestation of God's uprightness for the pardon of past sins committed [26]in the time of his forbearance, a manifestation of his uprightness also at the present time to show that he is upright and justifies the one who puts faith in Jesus.

[27]Where, then, is there room for boasting? It is ruled out! On what principle? On the principle of deeds? No, but on the principle of faith. [28]For we maintain

that a human being is justified by faith apart from deeds prescribed by the law. [29]But is God the God of Jews only? Is he not also the God of Gentiles? Yes, even of Gentiles! [30]For God who will justify both the circumcised in virtue of their faith and the uncircumcised through their faith is one. [31]Are we, then, nullifying the law by faith? Certainly not! We are rather upholding the law.

4.   [1]What, then, shall we say that Abraham, our forefather according to the flesh, found? [2]If Abraham was justified by deeds, he has reason to boast, but not before God. [3]For what does Scripture say? *Abraham put his faith in God, and it was credited to him as uprightness.*[m] [4]Now when a person labors, wages are not credited to him as a favor, but as what is due. [5]But when one does not labor, yet puts faith in him who justifies the godless, his faith is credited as uprightness. [6]So too David utters a beatitude over the human being to whom God credits uprightness apart from deeds: [7]*Blessed are those whose iniquities have been forgiven, whose sins have been covered up;* [8]*blessed is the man whose sin the Lord does not credit.*[n]

[9]Is this beatitude uttered, then, only over the circumcised, or over the uncircumcised too? We maintain that "faith was credited to Abraham as uprightness." [10]Under what circumstances, then, was it credited (to him)? While he was circumcised or not (yet) circumcised? He was not circumcised, but (was still) uncircumcised! [11]He accepted the sign of circumcision as the seal of uprightness that comes through faith while he was still uncircumcised. Thus he was to be the father of all who believe when uncircumcised, so that uprightness might also be credited to them, [12]as well as the father of those circumcised, who are not only such but who walk in his footsteps along the path of faith that Abraham our father once walked while he was still uncircumcised.

[13]It was not through the law that the promise was made to Abraham or to his posterity that he would inherit the world, but through the uprightness that came from faith. [14]For if the heirs are those who hold to the law, then faith has been emptied of its meaning and the promise nullified. [15]The law brings only wrath; but where there is no law, there is no transgression. [16]For this reason the promise depends on faith, that it might be a matter of grace so as to be valid for all Abraham's posterity, not only for those who adhere to the law, but to those who share his faith. For he is father of us all; [17]as it stands written, *I have made you the father of many nations.*[o] So he is in the sight of God in whom he put his faith, the God who gives life to the dead and calls into being things that exist not. [18]Hoping against hope, Abraham believed, so as to become the father of many nations according to what had been said to him, *So shall your posterity be.*[p] [19]He did not weaken in faith when he considered his own body to be already as good as dead (being about a hundred years old) and the deadness of Sarah's womb. [20]Yet

he never wavered in disbelief about God's promise, but, strengthened in faith, he gave glory to God, [21]fully convinced that God was capable indeed of doing what he had promised. [22]That is why Abraham's faith was credited to him as uprightness. [23]Those words "it was credited to him" were written not only for Abraham's sake, [24]but for ours too. It is also going to be credited to us who believe in him who raised from the dead Jesus our Lord, [25]who was handed over (to death) for our trespasses and raised for our justification.

5. [1]Therefore, now that we are justified through faith, we are at peace with God through our Lord Jesus Christ, [2]through whom we have gained access in faith to this grace in which we now stand and boast of our hope for the glory of God. [3]Yet not only that, but let us also boast of our afflictions, since we know that affliction makes for endurance, [4]endurance makes for character, and character for hope. [5]Such hope does not disappoint, because God's love has been poured out into our hearts through the holy Spirit that has been given to us. [6]While we were still helpless, Christ died at the appointed time for the godless. [7]Rare, indeed, is it that one should lay down one's life for an upright person—though for a really good person one might conceivably have courage to die. [8]Yet God shows forth his own love for us in that, while we were still sinners, Christ died for us. [9]And so, since we are now justified by his blood, we shall all the more certainly be saved by him from the wrath to come. [10]For if, when we were God's enemies, we were reconciled to him through the death of his Son, now that we are reconciled, we shall all the more certainly be saved by his life. [11]Yet not only that—but we boast of God through our Lord Jesus Christ, through whom we have now received reconciliation.

[12]Therefore, just as sin entered the world through one man, and through sin death, and so death spread to all human beings, with the result that all have sinned—[13]up to the time of the law sin was in the world, even though sin is not accounted when there is no law; [14]yet death held sway from Adam until Moses, even over those who had not sinned in a way similar to Adam's transgression—who is a type of the one who was to come. [15]But the gift is not like the trespass. For if many have died because of the trespass of one man, how much more have the grace of God and his gift overflowed to the many because of the grace of one man, Jesus Christ. [16]Moreover, the gift is not like the result of one man's sin; for judgment resulting from one trespass became condemnation, whereas the gift following upon many trespasses brought justification. [17]If by the trespass of one man death came to hold sway through that one man, how much more will those who receive the abundance of God's grace and his gift of uprightness reign in life through the one man, Jesus Christ. [18]So, just as through one trespass condemnation came upon all, through one act of uprightness justification and life came to all human beings. [19]Just as through the disobedience of one man many were

made sinners, so through the obedience of one many will be made upright. ²⁰The law slipped in that trespass might increase; but where sin increased, grace has abounded all the more, ²¹so that, just as sin held sway in death, grace too might reign through uprightness to bring eternal life through Jesus Christ our Lord.

6. ¹What, then, shall we say? "Let us persist in sinning so that grace may abound"? ²Certainly not! How shall we who have died to sin go on living in it? ³Or do you not know that those of us who were baptized into Christ Jesus were baptized into his death? ⁴Through baptism into his death we were indeed buried with him so that, as Christ was raised from the dead by the Father's glory, we too might conduct ourselves in a new way of life. ⁵For if we have grown into union with him through a death like his, we shall also be united with him through a resurrection like his. ⁶This we know, that our old self has been crucified with him so that the sinful body might be rendered powerless and we might no longer be slaves to sin. ⁷For the one who has died has been acquitted of sin. ⁸But if we have died with Christ, we believe that we shall also come to life with him, ⁹since we know that Christ has been raised from the dead and dies no more; death no longer has sway over him. ¹⁰For in dying as he did, he died to sin once and for all; and in living as he does, he lives to God. ¹¹So you too are to consider yourselves dead to sin, but alive to God in Christ Jesus.

¹²Do not, then, let sin hold sway over your mortal body so that you obey its lusts. ¹³Do not put your members at sin's disposal as weapons of wickedness, but instead put yourselves at God's disposal as those who have come to life from death and offer your members to God as weapons of uprightness. ¹⁴Sin is not to have sway over you, for you are not under law but under grace. ¹⁵What, then, does this mean? Should we sin because we are not under law, but under grace? Certainly not! ¹⁶Do you not know that, if you put yourselves at anyone's disposal in obedience, you become slaves of the one you obey—whether of sin, which leads to death, or of real obedience, which leads to uprightness. ¹⁷But thanks be to God, you who were once slaves of sin have wholeheartedly become obedient to the standard of teaching to which you have been entrusted. ¹⁸Freed then from sin, you have become slaves of uprightness. ¹⁹I am putting this in human terms because of your weak human nature: just as you used to put your members slavishly at the disposal of impurity and iniquity, which led to anarchy, so now put them slavishly at the disposal of uprightness, which leads to holiness. ²⁰When you were slaves of sin, you were free from uprightness. ²¹But what benefit did you then have—save things of which you are now ashamed? Things that result in death! ²²But now that you have been freed from sin and have become slaves of God, the benefit you have leads to holiness, which results in life eternal. ²³For the wages of sin are death, but the gift of God is eternal life in Christ Jesus our Lord.

9

7. ¹Or are you unaware, brothers—for I am speaking to those who know what law is—that the law has authority over a human being only as long as one is alive? ²Thus a married woman is bound by law to her husband while he is alive. But if the husband dies, she is released from the law regarding her husband. ³Accordingly, she will be called an adulteress if she gives herself to another man, while her husband is still alive. But if her husband dies, she is free of that law and does not become an adulteress if she gives herself to another man. ⁴So you too, my brothers, have died to the law through the body of Christ that you might give yourselves to another, to him who has been raised from the dead, so as to bear fruit for God. ⁵For when we were living merely natural lives, sinful passions aroused by the law were at work in our members, so as to bear fruit for death. ⁶But now, by dying to what we were once held captive, we have been released from the law so that we might serve God in a new way of the Spirit and not in the old way of a written code.

⁷What then can we say? Is the law sin? Certainly not! Yet I would not have known sin, if it were not for the law. I would not have known what it was to covet, if the law had not said, *"You shall not covet."*q ⁸But sin, using the commandment, seized the opportunity and produced in me every sort of covetousness. Now in the absence of law sin is as good as dead. ⁹Indeed, I once lived in the absence of law, but when the commandment came, sin sprang to life, ¹⁰and I died. The commandment that was meant for life was found to be death for me. ¹¹For sin, using the commandment, seized the opportunity and deceived me; through it sin killed me. ¹²Yet the law is holy, and the commandment is holy, upright, and good. ¹³Did, then, what was good become death for me? Certainly not! Rather, sin, that it might be unmasked as sin, produced death in me by using what was good so that through the commandment it might become sinful beyond all measure.

¹⁴Now we know that the law is spiritual, whereas I am of flesh, sold in bondage to sin. ¹⁵I do not understand what I do. For I do not do what I want to; and what I detest, that I do. ¹⁶Yet if I do what I do not want, I agree that the law is good. ¹⁷But as it is, it is no longer I who do it, but sin that dwells in me. ¹⁸I know that no good dwells in me, that is, in my flesh. I can desire what is good, but I cannot carry it out. ¹⁹For I do not do the good I desire, but instead the evil I do not desire. ²⁰Yet if I do what I do not want, it is no longer I who do it, but sin that dwells in me. ²¹So I discover this principle at work: when I want to do right, evil is ready at hand. ²²For in my inmost self I delight in God's law; ²³but I see another law in my members battling against the law that my mind acknowledges and making me captive to the law of sin that is in my members. ²⁴Wretch that I am, who will rescue me from this doomed body? ²⁵Thanks be to God—(it is done) through Jesus Christ our Lord! So then I myself in my mind am a slave to God's law, but in my flesh a slave to the law of sin.

8. ¹Now then, there is no condemnation for those who are in Christ Jesus. ²For in Christ Jesus the law of the Spirit of life has set you free from the law of sin and death. ³What the law, weakened by the flesh, was powerless to do, God has done: by sending his own son in a form like that of sinful flesh and for the sake of sin, he condemned sin in the flesh, ⁴so that the requirement of the law might be fully met in us who conduct ourselves not according to the flesh, but according to the Spirit. ⁵Those who live according to the flesh are concerned about things of the flesh, whereas those who live according to the Spirit are concerned about things of the Spirit. ⁶Now the concern of the flesh is death, but the concern of the Spirit is life and peace. ⁷Since the concern of the flesh is hostility to God, it is not submissive to God's law; nor can it be. ⁸So those who live by the flesh cannot please God. ⁹Yet you are not in the flesh; you are in the Spirit, if in fact God's Spirit dwells in you. If one does not have Christ's Spirit, one does not belong to Christ. ¹⁰But if Christ is in you, though the body be dead because of sin, the spirit has life because of uprightness. ¹¹And if the Spirit of him who raised Jesus from the dead is dwelling in you, he who raised Christ from the dead will give life even to your mortal bodies through his Spirit that is dwelling in you. ¹²So then, brothers, we are not indebted to the flesh, to have to live according to it. ¹³If you live indeed according to the flesh, you will die; but if through the Spirit you put to death the deeds of the body, you will live.

¹⁴For all those who are led by God's Spirit are children of God. ¹⁵You did not receive a spirit enslaving you again to fear, but you received a Spirit of sonship, one in which we cry, "*Abba*, Father!" ¹⁶The Spirit itself bears witness with our spirit: we are children of God! ¹⁷If children, then heirs too, heirs of God and coheirs of Christ, if we now suffer with him in order also to be glorified with him.

¹⁸I consider the sufferings that we now endure not worth comparing with the glory that is going to be revealed in us. ¹⁹Indeed, creation itself is waiting with anxious expectation for the revelation of the children of God. ²⁰For creation has been subjected to frustration, not of its own choice, but by him who subjected it—with hope—²¹because creation itself too will eventually be freed from its bondage to decay and brought to the glorious freedom of the children of God. ²²Yes, we realize that all creation has been groaning and laboring in pain up to the present time. ²³Not only that, but we ourselves, though we have the Spirit as the firstfruits, are groaning inwardly as we wait for the redemption of our bodies.

²⁴For in hope we have been saved. But a hope that is seen is no hope at all. Who hopes for what he sees? ²⁵But if we hope for what we do not see, we wait for it with endurance.

²⁶Similarly, the Spirit too comes to the aid of our weakness, for we do not know for what we should pray. But the Spirit itself intercedes for us with ineffable

sighs. [27]Yet he who searches our hearts knows what the mind of the Spirit is, because it intercedes for God's dedicated people in accordance with his will.

[28]We realize that all things work together for the good of those who love God, for those who are called according to his purpose. [29]Those whom he foreknew, he also predestined to be conformed to the image of his Son that he might be the firstborn among many brothers. [30]Those whom he predestined, he also called; those whom he called, he also justified; and those whom he justified, he also glorified.

[31]What then shall we say about this? If God is for us, who can be against us? [32]He who did not spare his own Son, but handed him over for all of us—how will he not give us everything else along with him? [33]Who will bring a charge against God's chosen ones? God himself, who justifies? [34]Who will condemn them? Christ Jesus, who died, or rather who was raised, who is at God's right hand and even intercedes for us? [35]Who will separate us from the love of Christ? Will distress or anguish or persecution or famine or nakedness or danger or the sword? [36]As it stands written, *"For your sake we are being put to death all day long; we are considered as sheep to be slaughtered."*[r] [37]Yet in all of it we are more than victors because of him who loved us. [38]For I am convinced that neither death nor life, neither angels nor principalities, neither the present nor the future, nor any powers, [39]neither height nor depth, nor any other creature will be able to separate us from the love of God, which is in Christ Jesus our Lord.

9. [1]I am speaking the truth in Christ; I am not lying, as my conscience bears witness to me in the holy Spirit, [2]that my sorrow is great and the anguish in my heart is unrelenting. [3]For I could even wish to be accursed and cut off from Christ for the sake of my brothers, my kinsmen by descent. [4]They are Israelites, and to them belong the sonship, the glory, the covenants, the giving of the law, the cult, and the promises; [5]to them belong the patriarchs, and from them by natural descent comes the Messiah, who is God over all, blest forever! Amen.

[6]It is not as though the word of God has failed. For not all descendants of Israel are truly Israel; [7]nor because they are offspring of Abraham are they all his children. Rather, *"It is through Isaac that your offspring will be named."*[s] [8]That is, it is not the children of the flesh who are the children of God, but the children born of the promise who are reckoned as Abraham's offspring. [9]For so runs the promise, *"At the time appointed I shall return, and Sarah will have a son."*[t] [10]Not only that, but even when Rebecca had children by one and the same man, our father Isaac,—[11]even before they had been born or had done anything good or evil, in order that God's purpose in election might persist, [12]not because of deeds

but because of his call—it was said to her, *"The older shall serve the younger."*ᵘ ¹³As it stands written, *"Jacob I loved, but Esau I hated."*ᵛ

¹⁴What then shall we say? Is God unjust? Certainly not! ¹⁵For he says to Moses, *"I will show mercy to whomever I will, and I will have compassion on whomever I will."*ʷ ¹⁶So it depends not on human willing or effort, but on God's mercy. ¹⁷For Scripture says to Pharaoh, *"For this very reason have I raised you up, that I might display my power through you and that my name might be proclaimed over all the earth."*ˣ ¹⁸Therefore he has mercy on whomever he wills and hardens the heart of whomever he chooses. ¹⁹Will you therefore say to me, "Then why does God still find fault? Who has ever resisted his will?" ²⁰But who are you, a mere human being, to answer back to God? *Will what is molded say to its molder, "Why did you make me like this?"*ʸ ²¹Has not the potter the right to make out of the same lump of clay one vase for a noble purpose and another for common use? ²²Yet what if God, wishing to display his wrath and make known his power, has endured with much long-suffering those vases of wrath, fashioned for destruction? ²³This he did to make known the riches of his glory for the vases of mercy, which he had fashioned beforehand for such glory.

²⁴Even for us, whom he has called, not only from among the Jews, but also from among the Gentiles, ²⁵as indeed he says in Hosea,

> *"Those who were not my people*
> *I shall call 'my people';*
> *and her who was not loved*
> *I shall call 'my beloved' ";*ᶻ

²⁶and

> *"In the very place where it was said to them,*
> *'You are not my people,'*
> *there they shall be called 'children of the living God.' "*ᵃ

²⁷And Isaiah cries out about Israel,

> *"Should the number of the Israelites be as the sands*
> *of the sea, a remnant shall be saved."*ᵇ
> 28 *"For the Lord will carry out his sentence*
> *on the earth with rigor and dispatch."*ᶜ

²⁹And as Isaiah has predicted,

"If the Lord of hosts had not left us offspring,
we would have fared like Sodom
*and been made like Gomorrah."*ᵈ

³⁰What then shall we say? That the Gentiles who did not pursue uprightness have attained it, an uprightness based on faith, ³¹whereas Israel, which was pursuing a law of uprightness, did not achieve it? ³²Why was this? Because they pursued it not with faith, but as if it were by deeds. They stumbled over "the stumbling stone," ³³as it stands written: *"Look, I am setting in Zion a stone to stumble against, a rock to trip over; and no one who believes in him shall be put to shame."*ᵉ

10. ¹Brothers, my heart's desire and my prayer to God for them is their salvation. ²Indeed, I can testify for them that they have zeal for God; but it is not well informed. ³For being unaware of God's uprightness and seeking to set up their own uprightness, they have not submitted to the uprightness of God. ⁴For Christ is the end of the law so that there may be uprightness for everyone who believes.

⁵For Moses writes thus of the uprightness that comes from the law: *"The one who does these things will find life in them."*ᶠ ⁶But the uprightness that comes from faith speaks thus: *"Do not say in your heart, 'Who will go up to heaven?' "*ᵍ (that is, to bring Christ down); ⁷or *" 'Who will go down into the abyss?' "*ʰ (that is, to bring Christ up from the dead). ⁸But what does it say instead? *"The word is near to you, on your lips and in your heart"*ⁱ (that is, the word of faith that we preach): ⁹if you profess with your lips that "Jesus is Lord," and believe in your heart that God has raised him from the dead, you will be saved. ¹⁰Such faith of the heart leads to uprightness; such profession of the lips to salvation. ¹¹For Scripture says, *"No one who believes in him shall be put to shame."*ʲ ¹²No distinction is made between Jew and Greek: the same Lord is Lord of all, bestowing his riches on all who call upon him. ¹³*"For everyone who calls upon the name of the Lord shall be saved."*ᵏ

¹⁴But how will people call upon him in whom they have not believed? How can they believe in him to whom they have not listened? How can they hear of him unless through a preacher? ¹⁵And how can people preach unless they are sent? As it stands written, *"How timely the arrival of those who bring good news!"*ˡ ¹⁶Yet everyone has not heeded the gospel. But even Isaiah says, *"Lord, who has believed our message?"*ᵐ ¹⁷Faith then comes from what is heard, and what is heard comes through the word of Christ. ¹⁸But I ask, Can it be that they have not heard of it? Of course they have! *"Their voice has gone forth over all the earth, and their words to the bounds of the world."*ⁿ ¹⁹But again I ask, Can it be that Israel did not

14

understand? First of all, Moses says, *"I shall make you jealous of those who are not a nation; and with a foolish nation shall I provoke your anger."*o ²⁰And Isaiah made bold to say, *"I was found by those who were not seeking me; I showed myself to those who were not asking for me."*p ²¹Yet of Israel he says, *"All day long have I held out my hands to a disobedient and defiant people."*q

11. ¹I ask then, Has God rejected his people? Certainly not! I am an Israelite myself, a descendant of Abraham, from the tribe of Benjamin. ²No, *God has not rejected his people,*r whom he foreknew. Do you not know what Scripture says in the passage about Elijah, how he pleaded with God against Israel: ³*"Lord, they have killed your prophets and torn down your altars; and I am left alone, and they are seeking my life."*s ⁴And what was the divine reply to him? *"I have reserved for myself seven thousand men who have not bent the knee to Baal."*t ⁵So too at the present time a remnant, chosen by grace, has come into being. ⁶And if by grace, it is no longer by deeds, for grace would cease to be grace. ⁷So then what? What Israel sought, it did not achieve; the chosen ones achieved it, whereas the others were made obtuse. ⁸As it stands written, *"God granted them stupor of spirit, eyes that see not and ears that hear not—even to this day."*u ⁹David too says, *"May their table be a snare and a trap, a stumbling block and a retribution for them;* ¹⁰*may their eyes be dimmed so that they cannot see! Bend their backs continually!"*v

¹¹Now then I ask, Did they stumble so as to fall irremediably? Certainly not! Yet because of their trespass salvation has come to the Gentiles to make Israel jealous. ¹²Now if their trespass has meant the enrichment of the world, and their loss the enrichment of Gentiles, how much more will their full number mean! ¹³I turn now to you Gentiles: inasmuch as I am the apostle of the Gentiles, I make much of this ministry of mine ¹⁴in the hope that I may stir up my own people to jealousy and save some of them. ¹⁵For if their rejection has meant the reconciliation of the world, what will their acceptance mean? Nothing less than life from the dead! ¹⁶If the firstfruits are holy, so too is the whole batch of dough; if the root is holy, so too are the branches. ¹⁷If some of the branches have been lopped off, you, though a branch from a wild olive tree, have been grafted into their place and have come to share in the rich sap of the olive root. ¹⁸Do not boast over those branches. If you do, remember this: you do not support the root; the root supports you. ¹⁹You may indeed say, "Branches were lopped off so that I might be grafted in." ²⁰True, but they were lopped off because of a lack of faith, whereas you are there because of faith. So do not become haughty for that reason; be fearful. ²¹For if God did not spare the natural branches, perhaps he will not spare you either. ²²Consider then God's kindness and severity; severity to those who have fallen, but kindness to you, if you only remain in his kindness. For you too may be cut off. ²³And those others, if they do not remain in their lack of faith, will be grafted back in. God indeed has the power to graft them in again. ²⁴For if you were cut

from an olive tree that is wild by nature and grafted contrary to nature into a cultivated one, how much more readily will these, the natural branches, be grafted back into their own olive stock!

²⁵I do not want you to be unaware of this mystery, brothers, lest you become wise in your own estimation: a partial hardening of heart has come upon Israel until the full number of the Gentiles comes in; ²⁶and so all Israel shall be saved, as it stands written, *"From Zion shall come the deliverer; he shall turn godlessness away from Jacob. ²⁷This is my covenant with them, when I take away their sins."*ʷ ²⁸As far as the gospel is concerned, they are enemies for your sake; but as far as election is concerned, they are beloved of God because of the patriarchs. ²⁹For irrevocable are God's gifts and his call. ³⁰As you were once disobedient to God but now have been shown mercy as a result of their disobedience, ³¹so too they have now become disobedient so that they too may now be shown mercy as a result of the mercy shown to you. ³²For God has imprisoned all people in disobedience that he might show mercy to all!

33   O the depth of the riches, of the wisdom, and of the knowledge of God!
          How inscrutable are his judgments!
          How untraceable his ways!
34   *Who has known the mind of the Lord?*
          *Who has been his counselor?*ˣ
35   Who has ever given him a gift
          to receive a gift in return?
36   For from him and through him and for him are all things.
          To him be glory forever! Amen.

12.   ¹I urge you, then, brothers, by God's mercy to offer your bodies as living sacrifices, holy and acceptable to God, as a cult suited to your rational nature. ²Do not conform yourselves to this present world, but be transformed by a renewal of your whole way of thinking so that you may discern what is God's will, what is good, acceptable to him, and perfect.

³In virtue of the grace given to me I say to every one of you: Do not think more highly of yourself than you ought to; rather, think of yourself with sober judgment according to the measure of faith that God has apportioned each of you. ⁴For just as we have many members in one body and all of the members do not have the same function, ⁵so we, though many, are one body in Christ, and individually members of one another. ⁶We have gifts that differ according to the grace given to us. If prophecy, let it be used in proportion to one's faith; ⁷or ministry, let it be used in service; or if one is a teacher, let him use it for instruction; ⁸if one is an exhorter, for encouragement; if one is a contributor to

16

charity, let him use it with simple generosity; if one is a leader, with diligence; if one does works of mercy, let it be with cheerfulness.

[9]Love must be unfeigned. You must detest what is evil and cling to what is good. [10]Be devoted to one another with brotherly love; outdo one another in showing honor. [11]Serve the Lord, unflagging in diligence, fervent in spirit, [12]rejoicing in hope, patient in affliction, persistent in prayer. [13]Contribute to the needs of God's dedicated people, and practice hospitality. [14]Bless those who persecute you; bless and do not curse them. [15]Rejoice with those who are rejoicing; mourn with those who are mourning. [16]Think in harmony with one another. Put aside haughty thoughts and associate with the lowly. Do not become wise in your own estimation. [17]Repay no one evil for evil; take thought for what is noble in the sight of all human beings. [18]If it possibly lies in your power, live at peace with everyone. [19]Take no revenge, dear friends, but leave room for God's wrath, for it stands written: *"Vengeance is mine; I will repay,"*[y] says the Lord. [20]But *if your enemy is hungry, feed him; if he is thirsty, give him something to drink. In doing so, you will heap coals of fire upon his head.*[z] [21]Do not be overcome by evil, but overcome evil with good.

13. [1]Let every person be subject to the governing authorities, for there is no authority except from God, and those which exist have been set up by God. [2]Consequently, anyone who resists authority opposes what God has instituted; such opponents will bring judgment on themselves. [3]For rulers are not a terror to good conduct, only to evil. Would you be free from fear of the bearer of authority? Then do what is right, and you will gain his approval. [4]For he is God's servant working for your good. But if you do wrong, then be afraid, for he does not carry the sword for nothing. He is God's servant, an avenger, bringing wrath upon the wrongdoer. [5]Therefore, one must be subject, not only because of such wrath, but also because of one's conscience. [6]For this reason you also pay taxes. Authorities are God's servants, persistently devoted to this very task. [7]Pay all of them their due—taxes to whom taxes are due, revenue to whom revenue is due, respect to whom respect is due, and honor to whom honor is due.

[8]Owe no one a debt, save that of loving one another; for the one who loves another has fulfilled the law. [9]The commandments, *"You shall not commit adultery, You shall not kill, You shall not steal, You shall not covet"*[a]—or any other commandment—are summed up in this one, *"You shall love your neighbor as yourself."*[b] [10]Love does no wrong to a neighbor, for love is the fulfillment of the law.

[11]Do this, then, realizing how critical the moment is—that it is already time for you to be roused from sleep; for our salvation is now closer than when we first

believed. [12]The night is far spent, and day has drawn near. Let us cast off, then, the deeds of darkness and don the armor of light, [13]that we may conduct ourselves with decency as befits the daylight, not in orgies or drunkenness, not in debauchery or sexual excess, not in quarreling or jealousy. [14]Put on rather the Lord Jesus Christ and give no more thought to the desires of the flesh.

14. [1]Welcome among you anyone who is weak in conviction, but not to quarrel about disputable matters. [2]One may be convinced that one may eat anything, but the one who is weak eats only vegetables. [3]Let the one who eats not despise the one who abstains; let the one who abstains not pass judgment on the one who eats, for God has welcomed him. [4]Who are you to sit in judgment on the servant of another? Before his own master he stands or falls. And stand he will, for the master is able to make him stand. [5]One person regards one day as more important than another; yet another regards every day as the same. Each one, however, should be fully convinced of this in his own mind: [6]the one who observes a set day, observes it for the Lord; and the one who eats, eats for the Lord, for he gives thanks to God. The one who abstains, abstains for the Lord and also gives thanks to God. [7]Yet none of us lives for himself, and none of us dies for himself. [8]If we live, we live for the Lord; and if we die, we die for the Lord. So whether we live or die, we belong to the Lord. [9]For this reason too Christ died and came to life again in order that he might exercise lordship over both the dead and the living. [10]Why then do you sit in judgment over your brother? Or why do you despise your brother? We shall all have to appear before God's tribunal, [11]for it stands written, *"As I live, says the Lord, to me every knee shall bend, and every tongue shall give praise to God."*[c] [12]Every one of us, then, will give an account of himself before God.

[13]So let us no longer pass judgment on one another. Make rather this decision, never to put a stumbling block or an obstacle in your brother's way. [14]As one who is in the Lord Jesus, I know and am convinced that nothing is unclean in itself; but for the one who considers something to be unclean, that becomes so for him. [15]If your brother is indeed distressed because of what you eat, you are no longer conducting yourself in love. Let not the food you eat bring ruin to such a one for whom Christ died. [16]Do not let what is good for you be reviled as evil. [17]For the kingdom of God is not eating and drinking, but uprightness, peace, and joy in the holy Spirit. [18]Anyone who serves Christ in this way is pleasing to God and esteemed among human beings. [19]Let us then pursue what makes for peace and for mutual edification. [20]Do not demolish the work of God for the sake of food. All things are indeed clean, but it is wrong for a human being to eat something that creates a stumbling block for another. [21]It is better not to eat meat or drink wine, or do anything that causes your brother to trip, to stumble, or to be weakened. [22]The conviction that you have keep to yourself before God. Blessed,

indeed, is the one who does not condemn himself for what he approves. ²³But the one who has doubts is already condemned if he eats, because the eating does not proceed from conviction. For whatever proceeds not from conviction is sin.

15. ¹We who are strong ought to bear with the failings of those who are weak and not merely suit our own pleasure. ²Each of us should please his neighbor for his good, to build him up. ³For not even Christ suited his own pleasure, but as it stands written, *"The insults of those who insult you have fallen upon me."*ᵈ ⁴And what was written of old was written for our instruction that through endurance and the encouragement of the Scriptures we might have hope. ⁵May God, the source of such endurance and encouragement, grant you a spirit of mutual harmony in accord with Christ Jesus, ⁶so that with one mind and one voice you may glorify the God and Father of our Lord Jesus Christ.

⁷Welcome one another, then, as Christ welcomed you, for the glory of God! ⁸For I tell you, Christ became a servant to the circumcised to show God's fidelity, to confirm the promises made to the patriarchs, ⁹and Gentiles have glorified God for his mercy, as it stands written,

> *"Therefore, I will proclaim you among the Gentiles*
> *and sing praise to your name."*ᵉ

¹⁰Again it says,

> *"Rejoice, you Gentiles, along with his people."*ᶠ
> 11 *"Praise the Lord, all you Gentiles,*
> *and let all peoples sound his praise."*ᵍ

¹²Once again Isaiah says,

> *"There shall appear the Root of Jesse,*
> *the one who rises to rule the Gentiles;*
> *in him the Gentiles shall find hope."*ʰ

¹³So may the God of hope fill you with all joy and peace in believing, so that you may abound in hope by the power of the holy Spirit.

¹⁴I myself am convinced about you, brothers, that you are full of goodness, equipped with all knowledge, and capable of admonishing one another. ¹⁵Yet I write to you quite boldly, partly to remind you in virtue of the grace given to me by God ¹⁶to be a minister of Christ Jesus to the Gentiles, with the priestly duty of preaching God's gospel, so that the offering of the Gentiles might become

acceptable and consecrated by the holy Spirit. [17]Therefore, in what pertains to God I have this boast in Christ Jesus. [18]For I shall not dare to speak of anything save what Christ has accomplished through me for the commitment of the Gentiles, either in word or in deed, [19]by the power of signs and wonders, or by the power of God's Spirit. So I have fully preached the gospel of Christ from Jerusalem all the way around to Illyricum. [20]Thus it has been my ambition to preach the good news where Christ has not been named, lest I build on the foundation of someone else. [21]But as it stands written, *"Those who have had no news of him will see, and those who have not heard of him will understand."*[i] [22]This is why I have so often been hindered from coming to you. [23]But now since I no longer have room for work in these regions and have been longing for many years to come to you, (I plan to do so) [24]as I proceed on my way to Spain. I hope to see you as I travel along and be sped on my way there by you, once I have enjoyed your company for a while.

[25]At present, however, I am making my way to Jerusalem to bring aid to God's dedicated people there. [26]For Macedonia and Achaia kindly decided to make some contribution for the poor among these people in Jerusalem. [27]They kindly decided to do so, and indeed they are indebted to them. For if Gentiles have come to share in the spiritual blessings of Jerusalem Christians, they ought to be of service to them in material things. [28]So when I have completed this task and have delivered this contribution under my own seal, I shall set out for Spain, passing through your midst. [29]I know that, when I arrive among you, I shall be coming with the full blessing of Christ.

[30]I urge you, then, brothers, by our Lord Jesus Christ and by the love of the Spirit, to join me in my struggle by praying to God on my behalf, [31]that I may be delivered from unbelievers in Judea and that my service in Jerusalem may be acceptable to God's dedicated people, [32]and that by God's will I may come to you with joy and be refreshed together with you. [33]May the God of peace be with all of you! Amen.

16. [1]I commend to you our sister Phoebe, a minister of the church of Cenchreae. [2]Please receive her in the Lord in a manner worthy of God's dedicated people and help her in whatever she may require of you; she has been a patroness of many here, and of myself too.

[3]My greetings to Prisca and Aquila, fellow workers of mine in Christ Jesus. [4]They risked their necks for me; not only am I, but all Gentile churches are grateful to them. [5]Greet too the church that meets at their house. Greetings to my dear friend Epaenetus, the first convert to Christ in Asia. [6]Greetings to Mary, who has worked hard for you. [7]Greetings to Andronicus and Junia, my fellow

countrymen, who were imprisoned with me and who are outstanding among the apostles. They were in Christ even before me. [8]Greetings to Ampliatus, my dear friend in the Lord. [9]Greetings to Urbanus, my fellow worker in Christ, and to my dear friend Stachys. [10]Greetings to Apelles, who is approved in Christ's service, and to the household of Aristobulus. [11]Greetings to my fellow countryman Herodion, and to those who belong to the Lord in the household of Narcissus. [12]Greetings to those workers in the Lord, Tryphaena and Tryphosa. Greetings to my dear friend Persis, who has toiled hard in the Lord. [13]Greetings to Rufus, the chosen one of the Lord, and to his mother—whom I call mother too. [14]Greetings to Asyncritus, Phlegon, Hermes, Patrobas, Hermas, and the brothers who are with them. [15]Greetings to Philologus and Julia, Nereus and his sister, Olympas, and all God's dedicated people who are with them. [16]Greet one another with a holy kiss. All of the churches of Christ send you their greetings.

[17]I urge you, brothers, to watch out for those who create dissension and scandal in opposition to the teaching you have learned. Keep away from them. [18]For such people do not serve our Lord Christ, but their own appetites; for by smooth talk and flattery they deceive the minds of the simple. [19]Your commitment, however, is known to all; so I am happy about you. But I want you to be wise about what is good, and innocent about what is evil. [20]The God of peace will soon crush Satan under your feet. The grace of our Lord Jesus be with you!

[21]Timothy, my fellow worker, and Lucius, Jason, and Sosipater, my fellow countrymen, send their greetings to you. [22]I, Tertius, who write this letter, also greet you in the Lord. [23]Gaius, my host, and the whole church here, send greetings too. Erastus, the treasurer of this city, and Quartus, our brother, also greet you.

[25]Now to him who is able to strengthen you according to my gospel and the preaching of Jesus Christ, in accord with the revelation of the mystery kept secret for long ages, [26]but now disclosed and made known by command of the eternal God in prophetic writings so that all of the Gentiles may come to the commitment of faith—[27]to the only wise God, be glory forever through Jesus Christ! Amen.

[a]Hab 2:4	[m]Gen 15:6	[y]Isa 29:16
[b]Prov 24:12 or Ps 62:13	[n]Ps 31:1–2	[z]Hos 2:25
[c]Isa 52:5	[o]Gen 17:5	[a]Hos 2:1
[d]Ps 51:6	[p]Gen 15:5	[b]Isa 10:22–23
[e]Qoh 7:20	[q]Exod 20:17; Deut 5:21	[c]Isa 28:22
[f]Ps 14:1–3	[r]Ps 44:23	[d]Isa 1:9
[g]Ps 5:10	[s]Gen 21:12	[e]Isa 28:16; 8:14–15
[h]Ps 140:4	[t]Gen 18:10	[f]Lev 18:5
[i]Ps 10:7	[u]Gen 25:23	[g]Deut 30:12
[j]Isa 59:7–8; Prov 1:16	[v]Mal 1:2–3	[h]Ps 107:26
[k]Ps 36:2	[w]Exod 33:19	[i]Deut 30:14
[l]Ps 143:2	[x]Exod 9:16	[j]Isa 28:16

[k]Joel 3:5
[l]Isa 52:7
[m]Isa 53:1
[n]Ps 19:5
[o]Deut 32:21
[p]Isa 65:1
[q]Isa 65:2
[r]Ps 94:14
[s]1 Kgs 19:10

[t]1 Kgs 19:18
[u]Isa 29:10; cf. Deut 29:3
[v]Ps 69:23–24
[w]Isa 59:21–22; 27:9
[x]Isa 40:13; cf. Wis 9:13
[y]Deut 32:35
[z]Prov 25:21–22
[a]Deut 5:17–21; Exod 20:13–17

[b]Lev 19:18
[c]Isa 49:18; 45:23
[d]Ps 69:10
[e]Ps 18:50; 2 Sam 22:50
[f]Deut 32:43
[g]Ps 117:1
[h]Isa 11:10
[i]Isa 52:15

INTRODUCTION

◆

I. ROME AND
ROMAN CHRISTIANS

◆

The Letter to the Romans is addressed to the Christians of the capital of the Roman Empire at the time of its composition. Along with Alexandria in Egypt, Corinth in Greece, and Antioch on the Orontes in Syria, Rome was one of the most important cities of the Mediterranean world in the first century A.D. As the capital of the empire, it dominated the eastern Mediterranean area, where Christianity found its matrix. To it Christianity itself was eventually attracted.

Rome was originally a shepherds' village, founded as an offshoot of Alba Longa. In time it surpassed its neighboring tribes because of its geographical position in central Italy, near the sea and in command of the ford of the Tiber River.

Tradition has it that Rome was founded by descendants of Aeneas, Romulus and Remus (at varying dates, but principally in 753 B.C.). By the beginning of the sixth century different shepherd settlements on various hills had coalesced to form one town. Ruled at first by kings (Numa Pompilius, Tullus Hostilius, Ancus Marcius, Tarquinius Priscus, Servius Tullius, and Tarquinius Superbus), it became a republic about 510 B.C., governed by two magistrates called consuls elected each year. By 275 B.C. Rome had gained control of all Italy. During the rest of the third century Rome waged war on Carthage and gradually acquired provinces (Sicily, in 241; Sardinia, 238; Spain, 206). During the next century it began to intervene more in areas of the Mediterranean. Provinces of Spain were reorganized in 197 B.C. In the east, Macedonia became a Roman province in 148 B.C., and the Aegean Confederacy was suppressed with the conquest of old Corinth under Lucius Mummius Achaicus in 146 B.C. Corinth too then became a province. Class struggle and slave wars (135–132, 103–101) marred Rome's subsequent history. Eventually a dictatorship was set up by Marius (107–100), who held repeated consulships, and a reaction to it was stirred up under Sulla, who marched against Rome at the head of Roman legions (88–79). In time (60 B.C.) Rome came to be governed by a triumvirate of generals, Pompey, Crassus, and Julius Caesar. Pompey had conquered the eastern Mediterranean area, subduing Jerusalem and the land of the Jews in 63 B.C. and making it part of the reorganized province of Syria. The triumvirate eventually broke up, and Julius Caesar was assassinated in 44 B.C. After his death C. Octavius (later called Gaius Julius Caesar Octavianus) and Mark Antony vied for power. The latter was defeated in the battle of Actium in September 31 B.C. Then Octavian became the sole master of the Roman world. In 27 B.C. the Roman Senate conferred on him the title *Augustus* (*Sebastos*, "the Venerable"), and he ruled as *Princeps* (actually as a disguised constitutional monarch or benign dictator) until his death in A.D. 14. He was succeeded by Tiberius Caesar (14–37), Gaius Caligula (37–41), Claudius (41–54), and Nero (54–68), emperors of the Julio-Claudian line.

Under *Princeps Augustus* Roman society was greatly improved. Augustus put an end to civil strife at Rome and in the provinces. Of this he boasted in *Res gestae divi Augusti* §3 (*NTB* §1, lines 12–45). Throughout the empire *Pax Augusta*, "the Peace of Augustus," reigned, the era of peace. During Augustus's principate the Roman Senate decreed three times that the doors of the Shrine of Janus, which usually stood open in time of war, be closed. The army was reformed and made the protector of the people. In the Campus Martius, the Senate ordered the construction of an altar, *Ara Pacis Augustae*, dedicated to the goddess Peace, which still stands to this day (in restored condition). Augustus saw to the building of the forum named after him, *Forum Augusti*. He set up *vigiles*, "guards," to prevent fire and instituted urban cohorts as a police force. With friends, benefactors, and supporters like the wealthy Marcus Vipsanius Agrippa and Gaius Maecenas, Augustus sponsored arts and letters. During his reign wrote Vergil (Publius Vergilius Maro, 79–19 B.C.), Horace (65–8 B.C.), Propertius (ca. 47 B.C.–ca. A.D. 2), and Livy (ca. 64 B.C.–A.D. 12), the great writers of the Golden Age of Latin literature. Thus Augustus sought to create a new *populus romanus*, "People of Rome," promoters of civilization at home and throughout the inhabited world.

Augustus's achievements were in large part continued by his successors in the Julio-Claudian dynasty, especially under Claudius. Augustus's constructive work survived even the disaster toward the end of Nero's reign, when half of Rome burned in 64 and revolt marred the peace of the empire.

As Paul wrote his letter to the Christians of Rome, Nero Claudius Caesar was the emperor (54–68). At that time Nero was basking in what a later historian of the fourth century referred to as *Neronis quinquennium*, "the five-year period of Nero" (Aurelius Victor, *Caesares* 5, epit. 12; cf. Lucan, 1.33), the best period of the empire since the death of Augustus. For Nero had not yet become the ambitious and murderous tyrant that he was known to be in the latter years of his rule (from about A.D. 60 on).

Rome, as the capital of the empire, attracted like a magnet large foreign colonies from the provinces of the Mediterranean area. The columbaria of the imperial period of Rome reveal that many persons with foreign names, both slaves and freed, had lived and were buried there. Foreign cults too were brought there:

that of Mithras (as early as the reign of Tiberius), of Isis and Osiris, of Dea Syria (whom Nero himself revered), of Judaism, and of Christianity.

It is not known when Jews first came to Rome. Judas Maccabee is said to have sent envoys to Rome about 160 B.C. to "establish an alliance and peace" with the Romans (1 Macc 8:17–22), to which the Roman Senate agreed, acknowledging "the nation of the Jews" (8:25); compare 2 Macc 11:37. The implication seems to be that Jews were moving between Rome and Jerusalem at this date, and that some were already resident there. The earliest reference to Jews in Rome in a Roman writer seems to be associated with the Roman *praetor peregrinus*, Gnaeus Cornelius Hispalus, who in 139 B.C. "forced the Jews, who tried to contaminate Roman customs with the cult of Jupiter Sabazius, to return to their own homes" (see Valerius Maximus, *Facta et dicta memorabilia* 1.3.3; cf. Stern, *Greek and Latin Authors*, §147b). The reference is probably to Jewish merchants and sojourners accused of proselytism, but whether there was really a connection between Jews and Sabazius is quite debatable; see Lane, "Sabazius." In general, Romans tended to misunderstand the Jews, who were often lumped together with Chaldei and other Asiatics, who were also expelled.

By the first century B.C. Rome possessed a large Jewish community. The number of Jews in Rome has been estimated to have been about fifty thousand, grouped in several synagogues. Many of them had been brought to Rome as slaves by Pompey after his conquests in the east, especially after 63 B.C., when he stormed Jerusalem. Allusions to this enslavement may be found in *Pss. Sol.* 2:6; 17:13–14; cf. Philo, *Leg. ad Gai.* 23 §155. Josephus tells how Pompey took to Rome a member of the Herodian family, "Aristobulus in chains, together with his family" (*Ant.* 14.4.5 §79; *J.W.* 1.7.7 §157). Others would have been merchants who came on business trips and eventually established themselves there. Delegations of Jews from Palestine came to Rome on occasion (*J.W.* 2.6.1 §80; 2.7.3 §111; 2.12.6 §§243–44).

In 59 B.C. Cicero defended Lucius Valerius Flaccus, whose administration of the Roman province of Asia (62–61) had been marked by profligacy and who, in light of an old senatorial decree renewed as late as 63 B.C., had forbidden the Jews of that province to send gold to Jerusalem. In his defense Cicero used anti-Jewish prejudice to support his client: "You know how large a troop they are, how they stick together, how influential they are in political assemblies. . . . for there are plenty of people to stir them up against me and against every good citizen" (*Or. pro Flacco* 28.66–67); and he refers there to the Jews' *barbara superstitio*, "barbarian superstition." Compare Horace, *Satires* 1.4.142–43, who alludes to their known custom of Jewish proselytizing (cf. 1.5.100; 1.9.67–72).

Later Josephus records a letter sent by Julius Caesar to the magistrates, council, and people of Parium about the Jews, in which he notes that "even in Rome Jews were not forbidden" to assemble or live according to their religious customs (*Ant.* 14.10.8 §§214–15). Suetonius records that among the crowd of foreigners who mourned at Caesar's pyre there were "above all the Jews, who even flocked to the place for several successive nights" (*Iulii vita* 84.5). Philo too tells how in the time of Augustus, who supported them, Jews occupied and inhabited "the great section of Rome across the Tiber," and that "most of them were emancipated Roman (citizens)" (*Leg. ad Gai.* 23 §§155–56). He also tells of their "houses of prayer" (*proseuchai*), their celebration of the Sabbath, their training "in their ancestral philosophy," and their collections for sacrifices to be offered in Jerusalem. Josephus (*Ant.* 17.11.1 §300) tells of "more than eight thousand of the Jews in Rome" gathering to support the delegation of fifty Jews who were sent by Judean Jews to Caesar Augustus to complain about Archelaus's autocratic ways (including the summary dismissal of high priests) and to seek autonomy.

Josephus also mentions how the emperor Tiberius in the year A.D. 19 "ordered the entire Jewish community to depart from Rome, and how the consuls conscripted four thousand of these Jews for military service, sending them to the island of Sardinia" (*Ant.* 18.3.5 §§83–84). See also Cassius Dio, *Roman History* 57.18.5a; Tacitus, *Annals* 2.85.4; Suetonius, *Tiberii vita* 36; Juvenal, *Satires* 3.10, 62–63; 6.542–47; 14.96–104. This expulsion of Jews did not, however, decimate their numbers there, because the Herodian family maintained contacts with the imperial household (*Ant.* 18.6.6 §§179–94).

Moreover, from thousands of funerary inscriptions in the catacombs of Rome we learn about the Jewish population there and its groupings into thirteen synagogues (see *CII* 1.lvi–ci and §§1–532; Frey, "Le Judaïsme"; Leon, *The Jews of Rome*, 135–66; Penna, "Les Juifs," 328–30). On these inscriptions the word *synagōgē* denotes not a building, but a grouping of Jews or a "congregation"; the place where they gathered for prayer was called *proseuchē* (*CII* 1.682–84). The *synagōgai* were often named after patrons or protectors: Synagogue of the Agrippesians, Augustesians, Bernaclesians, Calcaresians, Campesians, Elaea, Hebrews, Herodians (or Rhodians), Sekenians, Siburesians, Tripolitans, Volumnesians, and the Arca Libanou.

From such sources we also learn that the Jewish community in Rome was organized; a *synagōgē* was governed by a *gerousia*, "council of elders," presided over by a *gerousiarchēs*. These were the *archontes* of the community; there was also a *phrontistēs*, "administrator" of the community's material goods and supervisor of the dole. Among them were also *hiereis*, "priests," but that was probably a title of honor for members of priestly families, since there was no temple.

After the destruction of Jerusalem in A.D. 70, many Jews were taken prisoner, and the bulk of them were brought to Rome as slaves. Josephus (*J.W.* 6.9.3 §§420–21) records that ninety-seven thousand prisoners were taken by the Romans, even though they were not all Jerusalem Jews.

Especially in the first century A.D. many Roman writers deprecatingly describe the mode of life lived by the Jews of Rome; they displayed much hostility to the Jews; see Wiefel, "Jewish Community," 94–101. Cassius Dio (*Roman History* 37.17.1) reports that "this class [Jews] exists even among the Romans and, though often repressed, has increased to a very great degree."

The Jews of Rome preserved strong links with those of Jerusalem. Marcus Julius Agrippa, who is called "Herod" in Acts 12:1, 6, 21, 23, had lived in Rome at the emperor's court. He enjoyed good relations with the emperor and his court, in particular with Caligula and Claudius, and was eventually made "king" of the tetrarchies of Philip and of Herod Agrippa I by Caligula. Trade between Rome and the east is exemplified in the travels of Prisca and Aquila (see 16:3); and Acts 28:21 suggests that news of Judean Jews traveled to Rome as well as elsewhere. Roman Jews, like others, paid the tax for the Jerusalem Temple and went on pilgrimage to Jerusalem (Philo, *Leg. ad Gai.* 23 §156). Events among the Jewish people of Palestine were certainly known to the Jews of Rome, and what ensued on the death of Herod the Great certainly affected the Jews of Rome as well.

In Acts 2:10 Luke lists among the "Jews and proselytes" gathered in Jerusalem for the Feast of the Assembly (or Pentecost [see the NOTE on 15:24]) "Roman sojourners" (*pace* Brown [*Antioch*, 104 n. 215], *epidēmountes* does not mean "residents" [of Jerusalem]; they were rather pilgrim "sojourners"). Acts 6:9 also knows of a "Synagogue of the Freedmen" (*Libertinōn*), that is, of *liberti*, Jewish slaves who had managed to gain their freedom in the Roman world (see Sanday and Headlam, *Romans*, xxviii). These freedmen could actually have come from anywhere in the Roman Empire, but many of them might well have been descendants of Jerusalem Jews taken to Rome by Pompey as prisoners of war in 63 B.C., who came to form a great part of the Jewish population there. In the rabbinic writings of later date there is mention of rabbis who visited Rome: Gamaliel, Eleazar ben Azariah, Joshua ben Hananiah, and Aqiba ben Joseph (*m. ʿErub.* 4:1; *m. ʿAbod. Zar.* 4:7; *Maʿaś. Š.* 5:9; *Šabb.* 16:8).

If some of the Roman sojourners in Jerusalem were among the three thousand Jews converted to Christianity according to the Lucan account (Acts 2:10–11, 41), they may have formed the nucleus of the Christian community in Rome on their return there. Thus the Roman Christian community would have had its matrix in the Jewish community, possibly as early as the 30s, and thus was made up at first of Jewish Christians and God-fearing Gentiles (or even of *prosēlytoi*, Acts 2:11, also mentioned in Roman Jewish funerary inscriptions), who had associated themselves with Jews of Rome.

The Letter to the Romans itself is actually the earliest document that attests the existence of the Roman Christian community, which Paul knows to have been in existence "for many years" (15:23).

Much later, Eusebius tells of Peter arriving in Rome on the heels of Simon Magus to preach the gospel there in the second year of Claudius (A.D. 42; *Historia Ecclesiastica* 2.14.6; cf. 2.17.1; *Chronicon* 261F [GCS 7.179]; cf. Jerome, *De viris illustribus* 1 [PL 23.638]; Orosius, *Historiae adversus paganas* 7.6 [CSEL 5.446]). The *Catalogus Liberianus*, dating from A.D. 354, also speaks of Peter as the founder of the Roman church, having exercised an episcopate of twenty-five years. This is undoubtedly part of a later legendary tradition that sought to explain where Peter went when he departed Jerusalem "for another place" (Acts 12:17).

Eusebius's notice encounters the difficulty that Paul in Gal 2:7–9 (written ca. 54) knows that Peter was still in Jerusalem for the so-called Council (dated ca. 49) and had apparently not yet left the eastern Mediterranean area; similarly Acts 15:6–7.

A more reliable tradition associated Paul with Peter as "founders" of the Roman community, not in the sense that they first brought Christian faith there, but because both of them eventually worked there and suffered martyrdom there (or in its immediate environs), and because their mortal remains were in the possession of the Roman church (see Ignatius, *Rom.* 4.3; Irenaeus, *Adversus Haereses* 3.1.1, 3.3.2 [SC 211.22–23, 32–33]).

In any case, Paul never hints in Romans that he knows that Peter has worked in Rome or founded the Christian church there before his planned visit (cf. 15:20–23). If he refers indirectly to Peter as among the "superfine apostles" who worked in Corinth (2 Cor 11:4–5), he says nothing like that about Rome in this letter. Hence the beginnings of the Roman Christian community remain shrouded in mystery. Compare 1 Thess 3:2–5; 1 Cor 3:5–9; and Col 1:7 and 4:12–13 for more or less clear references to founding apostles of other locales. Hence there is no reason to think that Peter spent any major portion of time in Rome before Paul wrote his letter, or that he was the founder of the Roman church or the missionary who first brought Christianity to Rome. For it seems highly unlikely that Luke, if he knew that Peter had gone to Rome and evangelized that city, would have omitted all mention of it in Acts.

Most likely the Christian community in Rome began not under any direct evangelization of the area, as it did in parts of the eastern Mediterranean, but through the presence of Jewish Christians and Gentiles associated with them who came to live there and went about ordinary tasks and secular duties. Slaves brought to Rome, merchants who came from other parts of the empire, and other individuals probably carried the Christian gospel there. Neither the Letter to the Romans nor the Acts of the Apostles alludes to any initial evangelization of Rome by a particular missionary, but Paul does send greetings to Andronicus and Junia, whom he recognizes as "my fellow countrymen" and "outstanding among the apostles" (16:7) and who may have been among such Jewish Christians who originally came from Jerusalem. The community undoubtedly also grew by the gradual immigration of Christians themselves, who traveled to the capital during the 40s via the Jewish diaspora. The situation may be paralleled in Alexandria, whither the new faith also spread; we know nothing of its evangelization by an apostle, even though a later tradition associated that with Mark the evangelist (Eusebius, *Historia ecclesiastica* 2.16.1). Ambrosiaster tells us about Roman Christians: "It is evident then that there were Jews living in Rome . . . in the time of the apostles. Some of these Jews, who had come to believe (in Christ), passed on to the Romans (the tradition) that they should acknowledge Christ and keep the law. . . . One ought not to be angry with the Romans, but praise their faith, because without seeing any signs of miracles and without any of the apostles they came to embrace faith in Christ, though according to a Jewish rite" (*ritu licet iudaico,* a phrase found only in cod. K; *In ep. ad Romanos,* prol. 2; CSEL 81.1.5–6). Ambrosiaster speaks of the Gentile Christians of Rome, who were associated with the original Jewish converts of the Roman community.

Writing about A.D. 120, the Roman historian Suetonius, who had been the private secretary of the emperor Hadrian and wrote the lives of the Caesars, reports that the emperor Claudius *Iudaeos impulsore Chresto assidue tumultuantis Roma expulit,* "expelled from Rome Jews who were making constant disturbances at the instigation of Chrestus" (*Claudii Vita* 25.4). This sounds as though some Chrestus were a rabble-rouser or extremist who incited Jews of Rome (so Benko, "The Edict"). Yet how would a pagan Roman rabble-rouser have caused such trouble among Roman Jews as to bring about their banishment?

Chrēstos, "useful, good, valuable," was a common Greek name of slaves and freedmen in the Roman world of the time. *Chrestus* was also used by Romans, both slaves and freed: for instance, P. Aelius Chrestus (A.D. 211; *CIL* 6.10233; 6.6390, 6402, 10046, 14756, 14757; see further the lists of names in *CIL* 6, fasc. 2.237, fasc. 7.5.6324–26); and among Greek-speaking people in the Roman world, *Gemeinios Chrēstos* (P. Grenfell, 1.49:111 [A.D. 220–21]; cf. D. Foraboschi, *Onomasticum alterum papyrologicum* [Milan: Istituto Editoriale Cisalpino, 1971], 342). Suetonius, then, not understanding the name *Christos,* "Christ" or "anointed," seems to have confused it with the commonly used Greek name *Chrēstos,* which would have been pronounced at that time as *Christos* (by itacism, the tendency in the Greek language to pronounce various vowels and diphthongs as *ī*). So Suetonius's text is understood by many modern historians today. This phenomenon was recognized by Tertullian (*Apologeticus* 3.5, CSEL 69.10; *Ad nationes* 1.3, CSEL 20.63) and Lactantius (*Divine Institutions* 4.7, CSEL 19.293–94). Compare Tacitus, *Annales* 15.44.2–4: *Chrestianos . . . auctor nominis eius, Christus.* Justin Martyr also plays on *Christianoi* and *chrēstos* (1 *Apology* 4.5–7, ed. G. Rauschen, FP 2.12–14). See further F. Blass, "XPHCTI-ANOI-XPICTIANOI," *Hermes* 30 (1895): 465–70; M. J. Edwards, ZPE 85 (1991): 232–35.

Suetonius, then, would have been referring to a conflict between Jews and Jewish Christians of Rome in the late 40s; the constant disturbances would apparently have been caused by Jews who opposed those who accepted Jesus as the Messiah or Lord, and who consequently differed in their interpretation of the law and threatened thereby ethnic unity and identity. These disturbances were happening so frequently (*assidue tumultuantis*) that they became the reason for the imperial banishment of Jews and Jewish Christians from Rome. Among the latter would have been Prisca and Aquila, who left Italy for Corinth (Acts 18:2).

Orosius, a fifth-century Christian historian (*Historiae adversus paganos* 7.6.15–16 [CSEL 5.451]), who quotes Suetonius's text, dates the expulsion in the ninth regnal year of Claudius (25 January 49 to 24 January 50). Since Orosius claims that Josephus tells us of this expulsion, whereas the Jewish historian says nothing about it, modern scholars sometimes suspect that Orosius's information is faulty, and some are reluctant to accept his information about the dating of this event too. No one knows where Orosius got his information about the ninth regnal year. In any case, this year remains the most likely (see Jewett, *Chronology*, 36–38; Howard, "The Beginning," 175–77; Lampe, *Die stadtrömischen Christen*, 4–8; Smallwood, *The Jews*, 211–16; Wiefel, "Jewish Community," 93).

Some, however, have attempted to interpret Suetonius's testimony as a reference to a decision made by Claudius in his first regnal year (41), reported by Cassius Dio (*Roman History* 60.6.6): the emperor, noting the increasing number of Jews in Rome, "did not drive them out" but ordered them "not to hold meetings" (see Leon, *The Jews*, 23–27; Lüdemann, *Paul*, 6–7, 165–71; Murphy-O'Connor, *St. Paul's Corinth*, 130–40). Such an interpretation of the texts of Cassius Dio and Suetonius is, however, unconvincing, for Cassius Dio says explicitly that Claudius did *not* banish the Jews (i.e., at that time). Claudius may indeed have expelled Jews later on, as Suetonius affirms. Hence, as Dunn (*Romans*, xlix) notes, "the best solution is probably to see two actions by Claudius, in 41 and 49: the first an early palliative ruling, short-lived and limited in effect; the second more deliberate and drastic after his patience had worn out." (Cassius Dio's history for the year 49 exists only in epitomes and hence is of no help for that year.) See further *Cambridge Ancient History* 10.500–501; Borg, "New Context," 211; Bruce, "Christianity," 314–15; Slingerland, "Suetonius *Claudius* 25.4." They are regarded as two events by Balsdon, Bammel, Frend, Graetz, Hardy, Huidekoper, Jewett, Jones, Meyer, Smallwood, and Wiefel. Moreover, one has not only to prescind from the Lucan hyperbole, "all of the Jews" (Acts 18:2), but ask how recently Aquila and Priscilla would have come from "Italy" (not specifically Rome), for it is not clear that they arrived in Corinth just prior to Paul himself early in 51. In any case, there was a sizable Jewish Christian community in Rome by the year 49.

That there were Jews in Rome prior to Paul's writing of his letter is thus certain. That there were also Jewish Christians there is gathered from the way Paul writes in Romans. But was the Roman Christian community solely of Jewish background, made up of Jewish Christians alone? Because the main theme of Romans deals with justification by faith without the need of observing the Mosaic law and because Paul quotes so abundantly from the OT, a number of modern commentators on Romans have concluded that the Roman community was mostly, if not entirely, composed of Jewish Christians; so Baur, Fahy, Krieger, Leenhardt, Lietzmann, W. Manson, O'Neill, Renan, Ropes, Zahn, and others. The reasons put forth to sustain this thesis are of the following sort: (1) chaps. 1–11 seem to be a debate with a congregation of Jews; (2) in 2:17–3:8 (if not earlier in chap. 2), Paul turns his argument directly against a Jewish interlocutor; (3) in 3:27–31 he defends himself against Jewish objections that his teaching about justification sets the law aside; (4) in 4:1 he refers to Abraham as "our forefather according to the flesh"; (5) in chaps. 9–11, Paul seems to feel it necessary to defend his thesis about the role of Israel in salvation history; and (6) isolated verses, such as 6:16; 8:15; 9:1–5; 10:1–2; and 15:26 seem to imply Jewish Christian readers. Indeed, O'Neill *(Paul's Letter)* would delete all references to Gentiles as glosses and maintain that Romans was written to Jewish Christians.

It is clear, however, that Paul writes to the Roman Christian community as mixed, yet as predominantly of Gentile background. He refers to himself as "the apostle of the Gentiles" (11:13) and addresses his readers as "Gentiles." In his opening paragraphs he includes the Roman Christians among "the other Gentiles" (1:13; cf. 1:5–6; 15:15–16). In 9:3–4; 10:1–2; and 11:23, 28, and 31 Paul speaks to non-Jewish Christian readers about his own people. In 6:17–22 Paul recalls to the readers their former sinful lives as heathens; also 12:1–2 implies a Gentile background of the Roman Christian readers. His statements about "the Jew first, but also the Greek" (1:16; 2:9) show that he is thinking of a mixed community; he seems to view the "weak" of chaps. 14–15 as Jewish Christians (see NOTES on 14:14, 20). *Pace* Munck *(Paul and the Salvation of Mankind,* 200), Paul does not write to the Roman church as "purely Gentile Christian" (a view that Munck may modify in *Christ & Israel,* 5). It is hardly likely that Christianity reached Rome through Gentile missionaries from either Antioch or Jerusalem, *pace* Stuhlmacher ("Purpose," 238). More likely, Jewish Christians, such as Andronicus and Junia, first brought the faith there.

Part of the problem in trying to determine the Christian community to which Paul addresses his letter is that he writes to it with a certain ignorance. He has not founded that church or evangelized the Romans. What little he knows about that community and its problems has undoubtedly come to him by hearsay, such as the problem of the "weak" and the "strong" (14:1–15:13). The best explanation of that distinction is that the "weak" refers to Christians of a Jewish background, and the "strong" to Christians of a Gentile background, who had been influenced at one time by Jews. Hence, as Paul writes, the Roman church was a mixed community, partly of Jewish, but predominantly of Gentile background.

Roman Christians seem to have been in continual contact with the Christians of Jerusalem, and Christianity there seems to have been shaped by that of Jerusalem, as Brown has maintained *(Antioch,* 110). It seems to have been influenced especially by those associated with Peter and James of Jerusalem, in other words, by Christians who retained some Jewish observances and remained faithful to the Jewish legal and cultic heritage without insisting on circumcision for Gentile converts. Such Jewish Christians in Rome would have associated with themselves people of Gentile background, those who were called "Godfearers." This relation would have characterized the Christian community until the time of the banishment of "Jews" from Rome by Claudius. On their return to Rome these Jewish Christians would have found a Christian situation different from what they had left; they would now be a minority in the church that they had shaped at an earlier date. They would undoubtedly have fallen under the ban of Jews themselves, who were still forbidden to assemble in *collegia.* This ban undoubtedly gave rise to the house churches in Rome, of which Paul is aware

(16:5). In any case, Christians of Rome would have continued their contacts with Christians of Jerusalem, as the epistle of Clement of Rome to the Corinthians suggests, in its recognition that "sacrifices are offered . . . only in Jerusalem" (*1 Clem.* 41.2), despite the earlier destruction of the Temple.

It is another question, however, whether there were in Rome judaizers of the sort that Paul had had to combat in the churches of Galatia. In writing, "Why should we not 'do evil that good may come of it'—as some people defame us with the libelous charge that we so teach?" (3:8), Paul is hardly implying that such persons were among Roman Christians, *pace* Edmundson (*Church in Rome*, 18) and Stuhlmacher ("Purpose," 239). That is a charge about antinomianism. It does not ring true that it stems from judaizers in Rome itself. The Pauline statement undoubtedly reflects rather some past experience of Paul. The judaizing problem had to be coped with in earlier situations, but there is no reason to think that it plagued the Roman community too. When Paul now writes to the Romans about justification by grace through faith, he is reflecting on his missionary endeavors of an earlier time. Even if some of Paul's friends were among the Christians of Rome to whom he writes, there were undoubtedly some others who did not agree with him. But even so, this does not mean that the judaizing problem of old still persisted. It is far from certain that charges leveled against Paul in Asia Minor and Greece made their way to Rome. Even Paul's apprehension about the reception of the collection that he will take to Jerusalem sounds much different from the tone in which he wrote Galatians, as he coped with the judaizing problem.

In writing to the Christians of Rome, Paul assumes that they are familiar with the OT, building, as he does, large parts of his argument on the Greek OT. There is, however, no real evidence that the Greek version was known outside of Jewish communities or Jewish Christian communities. The LXX was not known in Greco-Roman literary circles (see Collins, *Between Athens*, 4; Momigliano, *Alien Wisdom*, 91–92). Evidence from Jewish funerary inscriptions in Rome shows that Jews there normally used Greek as their main language, so they would have used the OT in a Greek version. Hence Paul cites the OT from the LXX. Yet even a predominantly Gentile Christian community was certainly familiar with the LXX as well as with other Jewish tenets and practices: the Decalogue, Jewish prayers used in synagogues, messianic expectations, dietary regulations, and details of the Mosaic law affecting daily life.

Luke too was aware of Christians at Rome, for he tells of *hoi adelphoi*, "brothers," coming to meet Paul on his way to Rome at "the Forum of Appius and the Three Taverns" (Acts 28:15). He was referring, of course, to a situation a few years later. But Luke also recounts that Jews of Rome told Paul that they "had received no letters from Judea" about him and that none of the Jewish brethren coming from there "reported or spoke anything evil about him" (Acts 28:21). Implicit in such a Lucan statement is that the Roman Jews had nonetheless heard about Paul; they were anxious to learn his views about the Christian *hairesis*, "which is everywhere spoken against" (28:22).

Yet the number of Roman writers who refer to Christians of Rome in the first century is not numerous. Suetonius (*Claudii Vita* 25) in the second century may refer to them indirectly, as we have seen. Tacitus (*Annales* 15.44) explicitly refers to them as those whom Nero accused of burning Rome and implies that Christianity in Rome had come from Judea:

> To suppress this rumor [that he himself had caused the burning of Rome in 64], Nero created scapegoats. He punished with exquisite cruelty the notoriously depraved group whom the populace called Christians. The originator of the group, Christ, had been executed in the reign of Tiberius by the procurator Pontius Pilate. Yet, in spite of such a temporary setback, this pernicious superstition broke out again, not only in Judea, the origin of this mischief, but even in the City [Rome], whither all degraded and shameful practices collect from all over and become the vogue. First, Nero arrested self-acknowledged members of this sect. Then, on the information they supplied, large numbers [*multitudo ingens*] were condemned, not so much for their arson as for their hatred of the human race. Their deaths were made a farce . . . so that despite their guilt and the ruthless punishment they deserved, there arose pity, for it was felt that they were being sacrificed to one man's brutality rather than to the public interest.

Tacitus thus states that there was a large number of Christians in Rome, that they were distinguished from Jews, and that even pagans related Roman Christianity to an origin in Judea. The first of these items is confirmed by *1 Clement*, which speaks of Christians of Rome as "a considerable multitude" (*poly plēthos*, 6.1). Suetonius even refers to them as *genus hominum superstitionis novae ac maleficae*, "a class of human beings given to a new and mischievous superstition" (*Neronis Vita* 16.2).

In a recent publication, Lampe has presented all of the evidence, literary and archaeological, that bears on Christians dwelling in various parts of Rome and their social history in the first two centuries of this era (*Die stadtrömischen Christen*).

Tacitus (*Annales* 13.50–51) also reports that in the year 58, in view of repeated complaints of the people in the empire about the collecting of indirect taxes by the *publicani*, "publicans," Nero wondered whether he should abolish all indirect taxation and present "the reform as the noblest of gifts to the human race." But senators warned him of the likely consequences of such an action, the fall in imperial revenue and further demands for the abolition of other taxation. Nero, however, recognized that the tax collectors' cupidity was extreme and had to be curbed. So he decreed that regulations for taxation were to be posted publicly and strictly enforced. At Rome the praetor and in the provinces the propraetors and proconsuls were to waive the usual order of trials in favor of actions against the *publicani*. Similarly, Suetonius recounts that Nero "either abolished or lowered the more oppressive taxes" (*Neronis Vita* 10.1). Hence Paul was probably aware of this brewing problem of taxation that also faced the Christians of Rome and included in his letter to them advice on the matter (13:6–7). See Friedrich et al., "Zur historischen Situation."

It was, then, to the Christians of the capital of the Roman Empire that Paul sends this letter. He greets them as "all the beloved of God in Rome, called to be his dedicated people" (1:7). He thanks God for all of them, because their faith "is proclaimed in all the world" (1:8), and he is convinced that they are "full of goodness, equipped with all knowledge, and capable of admonishing one another" (15:14). When Paul was writing, those Christians were subject to Nero during his *quinquennium*, and Paul's words about the duty of Christians to be submissive to governing authorities (13:1–2) would have fallen on receptive ears, because there is no reason to think that Christians of Rome would have been opposed to Nero at this time.

Finally, in this letter Paul appeals to Roman Christians for prayer and help as he prepares for his journey to Jerusalem with the collection taken up among Achaean and Macedonian Christians. He recognizes that Christianity at Rome has been shaped mainly by that of Jerusalem and Judea, especially by that associated with James and Peter, hence by a Christianity that regarded Judaism highly and was still loyal to its customs, even though Roman Christianity proved by this time to be predominantly of Gentile background.

In chap. 16 Paul refers to Roman Christians by name, some who are probably friends or personal acquaintances, others merely known to be dwelling there. Ten have Latin names; eighteen have Greek names; and two may have Hebrew names. He also knows some Christians from the households of two pagans, Aristobulus and Narcissus. Lietzmann noted from the uncommon names, which have been found in different regions of the empire, that "everyone streams to Rome" (*An die Römer*, 125).

Meanwhile, the Roman suspicion of Jews and Jewish *superstitio* continued and developed in various forms of anti-Semitism (see Quintilian, *Institutio oratoria* 3.7.21: *iudaica superstitio*, "Jewish superstition"; Seneca, quoted by Augustine, *De civitate Dei* 6.11, CSEL 39.298; Pliny the Elder, *Natural history* 31.11; Tacitus, *Historiae* 5.1: *adversus omnes alios hostile odium*, "a hostile hatred toward all others"). The accusation of *superstitio* spread from the Jews to the Christians.

BIBLIOGRAPHY

Balsdon, J. P. V. D., *Romans and Aliens* (Chapel Hill, N.C.: University of North Carolina, 1979).

Rome and Roman Christians

Benko, S., "The Edict of Claudius of A.D. 49 and the Instigator Chrestus," *TZ* 25 (1969): 407–18.

Bludau, A., "Die Juden Roms im ersten christlichen Jahrhundert," *Der Katholik* 83 (1903): 113–34, 193–229.

Borg, M., "A New Context for Romans xiii," *NTS* 19 (1972–73): 205–18, esp. 211.

Brown, R. E., "Further Reflections on the Origins of the Church of Rome," *The Conversation Continues: Studies in Paul and John in Honor of J. L. Martyn*, ed. R. T. Fortna and B. R. Gaventa (Nashville, Tenn.: Abingdon, 1990), 98–115.

Brown, R. E. and J. P. Meier, *Antioch and Rome: New Testament Cradles of Catholic Christianity* (New York and Ramsey, N.J.: Paulist Press, 1983), 87–210.

Bruce, F. F., "Christianity under Claudius," *BJRL* 44 (1961–62): 309–26.

———, "St. Paul in Rome," *BJRL* 46 (1963–64): 326–45.

Collins, J. J., *Between Athens and Jerusalem: Jewish Identity in the Hellenistic Diaspora* (New York: Crossroad, 1983).

Edmundson, G., *The Church in Rome in the First Century: An Examination of Various Controverted Questions Relating to Its History, Chronology, Literature and Traditions* (London: Longmans, Green, 1913).

Fahy, T., "St. Paul's Romans Were Jewish Converts," *ITQ* 26 (1959): 182–91.

Frey, J.-B., "Les Communautés juives à Rome aux premiers temps de l'église," *RSR* 20 (1930): 269–97; 21 (1931): 129–68.

———, "Le Judaïsme à Rome aux premiers temps de l'église," *Bib* 12 (1931): 129–56.

Friedrich, J., W. Pöhlmann, and P. Stuhlmacher, "Zur historischen Situation und Intention von Röm 13, 1–7," *ZTK* 73 (1976): 131–66.

Gabba, E., *Dionysius and the History of Archaic Rome* (Berkeley, Calif.: University of California Press, 1991).

Grummond, N. T. de, "Pax Augusta and the Horae on the Ara Pacis Augustae," *AJA* 94 (1990): 663–77.

Hadas-Lebel, M., *Jérusalem contre Rome*, Patrimoines: Judaïsme (Paris: Cerf, 1990).

Horst, P. W. van der, *Ancient Jewish Epitaphs: An Introductory Survey of a Millennium of Jewish Funerary Epigraphy (300 BCE–700 CE)*, Contributions to Biblical Exegesis and Theology 2 (Kampen: Kok Pharos Publishing House, 1991), 86–96.

Howard, G., "The Beginning of Christianity in Rome: A Note on Suetonius, Life of Claudius XXV,4," *ResQ* 24 (1981): 175–77.

Hugedé, N., *Saint Paul et Rome*, Le monde romain (Paris: Desclée de Brouwer/Belles Lettres, 1986).

Janne, H., "Impulsore Chresto," *Mélanges Bidez*, 2 vols., AIPHO 2.1–2 (Brussels: Université Libre de Bruxelles, 1934), 531–53.

Jewett, R., *A Chronology of Paul's Life* (Philadelphia, Penn.: Fortress, 1979).

Johnson, S. E., "Jews and Christians in Rome," *LexTQ* 17.4 (1982): 51–58.

Judge, E. A. and G. S. R. Thomas, "The Origin of the Church at Rome: A New Solution?" *RefTR* 25 (1966): 81–93.

Juster, J., *Les Juifs dans l'empire romain: Leur Condition juridique, économique et sociale*, 2 vols. (Paris: Geuthner, 1914; repr. New York: B. Franklin, n.d.).

Kasher, A., *Jews and Hellenistic Cities in Eretz-Israel: Relations of the Jews in Eretz-Israel with the Hellenistic Cities During the Second Temple Period (332 BCE–70 CE)*, TSAJ 21 (Tübingen: Mohr [Siebeck], 1990).

Keresztes, P., *Imperial Rome and the Christians: From Herod the Great to about 200 A.D.*, 2 vols. (Lanham, Md.: University Press of America, 1989), 1.45–66.

Kraabel, A. T., "The Roman Diaspora: Six Questionable Assumptions," *Essays in Honor of Yigael Yadin*, = *JJS* 33 (1982): 445–64.

Krieger, N., "Zum Römerbrief," *NovT* 3 (1959): 146–48.

Lampe, P., *Die stadtrömischen Christen in den ersten beiden Jahrhunderten*, WUNT 2.18 (Tübingen: Mohr [Siebeck], 1987; 2d ed. 1989).

Lane, E. N., "Sabazius and the Jews in Valerius Maximus: A Re-examination," *JRS* 69 (1979): 35–38.

La Piana, G., "Foreign Groups in Rome During the First Centuries of the Empire," *HTR* 20 (1927): 183–403.

Leon, H. J., *The Jews of Ancient Rome* (Philadelphia, Penn.: Jewish Publication Society of America, 1960).

———, "The Names of the Jews of Ancient Rome," *TAPA* 59 (1928): 205–24.

Lietzmann, H., "Zwei Notizen zu Paulus," *SPAW*, Phil.-histor. Kl. 8 (1930): 151–56; repr. *Kleine Schriften*, TU 68 (1958), 284–91, esp. 290–91.

Lüdemann, G., *Paul: Apostle to the Gentiles: Studies in Chronology* (Philadelphia, Penn.: Fortress, 1984), 6–7, 165–71.

Mackinnon, A. G., *The Rome of Saint Paul* (London: Religious Tract Society, 1930).

———, *The Rome of the Early Church* (London: Religious Tract Society, 1933).

Miller, R. H., "Life Situations in the Roman Church as Reflected in Paul's Letters," *RevExp* 32 (1935): 170–80.

Momigliano, A., *Alien Wisdom: The Limits of Hellenization* (Cambridge: Cambridge University Press, 1975).

———, *Claudius: The Emperor and His Achievement* (Oxford: Clarendon, 1934; repr. New York: Barnes & Noble, 1961).

Murphy-O'Connor, J., *St. Paul's Corinth: Texts and Archaeology* (Wilmington, Del.: Glazier, 1983).

Penna, R., "Les Juifs à Rome au temps de l'Apôtre Paul," *NTS* 28 (1982): 321–47.

Perrot, C., "La Diaspora juive de Rome," *MDB* 51 (Nov.–Dec. 1987): 3–5.

Ramsay, W. M., *The Church in the Roman Empire before A.D. 170*, 2d ed. (London: Hodder & Stoughton, 1893).

Reinach, T., *Textes d'auteurs grecs et romains relatifs au Judaïsme réunis, traduits et annotés* (Paris: Leroux, 1895; repr. Hildesheim: Olms, 1963).

Rengstorf, K. H., "Paulus und die älteste römische Christenheit," *SE II*, TU 87 (1964), 447–64.

Ropes, J. H., "The Epistle to the Romans and Jewish Christianity," *Studies in Early Christianity*, ed. S. J. Case (New York: Century, 1928), 353–65.

Rordorf, W., "Die neronische Christenverfolgung im Spiegel der apokryphen Paulus-akten," *NTS* 28 (1982): 365–74.

Roth, C., *The History of the Jews of Italy* (Philadelphia, Penn.: Jewish Publication Society, 1946).

Rutgers, L. V., "Archaeological Evidence for the Interaction of Jews and Non-Jews in Late Antiquity," *AJA* 96 (1992): 101–18.

Safrai, S. and M. Stern, *The Jewish People in the First Century: Historical Geography, Political History, Social, Cultural and Religious Life and Institutions*, CRINT 1 (Assen: Van Gorcum; Philadelphia, Penn.: Fortress, 1974), 160–70, 180–82.

Saulnier, C., "Il les chassa de Rome," *MDB* 51 (Nov.–Dec. 1987): 8–10.

Schelkle, K.-H., "Römische Kirche im Römerbrief," *Wort und Schrift: Beiträge zur Auslegung und Auslegungsgeschichte des Neuen Testaments*, Kommentare und Beiträge zum Alten und Neuen Testament (Düsseldorf: Patmos, 1966), 273–81.

Schöllgen, G., "Probleme der frühchristlichen Sozialgeschichte: Einwände gegen Peter Lampes Buch über 'Die stadtrömischen Christen in den ersten beiden Jahrhunderten,' " *JAC* 32 (1989): 23–40.

Seston, W., "L'Empereur Claude et les chrétiens," *RHPR* 11 (1931): 274–304.

Simon, M., "Les Juifs à Rome au 1er siècle," *MDB* 18 (1981): 33–34.

Slingerland, D., "Chrestus: Christus?" *New Perspectives on Ancient Judaism*, vol. 4: *The Literature of Early Rabbinic Judaism*, ed. A. J. Avery-Peck (Lanham, Md.: University Press of America, 1989), 133–44.

———, "Suetonius *Claudius* 25.4 and the Account in Cassius Dio," *JQR* 79 (1988–89): 305–22.

Smallwood, E. M., *The Jews under Roman Rule*, SJLA 20 (Leiden: Brill, 1976).

Solin, H., "Juden und Syrer im westlichen Teil der römischen Welt: Eine ethnisch-demographische Studie mit besonderer Berücksichtigung der sprachlichen Zustände," ANRW 2.29.2 (1983), 587–789, esp. 654–724 (on Rome).

Stern, M., *Greek and Latin Authors on Jews and Judaism*, 3 vols. (Jerusalem: Israel Academy of Sciences and Humanities, 1976–84).

Stuhlmacher, P., "The Purpose of Romans," *RomDeb*, 231–42.

Vitti, A. M., "S. Paolo alla volta di Roma," *BeO* 3 (1961): 48–52.

Wiefel, W., "Die jüdische Gemeinschaft im antiken Rom und die Anfänge des römischen Christentums: Bemerkungen zu Anlass und Zweck des Römerbriefs," *Judaica* 26 (1970): 65–88; also earlier in *Wissenschaftliche Zeitschrift Halle, gesellschafts- und sprachwissenschaftliche Reihe* 19.6 (1970): 171–84; "The Jewish Community in Ancient Rome and the Origins of Roman Christianity," *RomDeb*, 85–101.

II. AUTHORSHIP

◆

In 1:1 Paul names himself as the one who writes this letter to the Roman Christians. He is otherwise known in the Christian tradition as "the Apostle Paul."

In 11:1 he identifies himself: "I am an Israelite myself, a descendant of Abraham, from the tribe of Benjamin" (cf. Phil 3:5). He speak of the Jewish people as "my brothers, my kinsmen by descent" (9:3), thus acknowledging proudly his relationship with God's chosen people. Writing as a Christian to Christians, he also proudly recognizes his call to be "the apostle of the Gentiles" (11:13). But he also acknowledges that "both to Greeks and to barbarians I am indebted" (1:14). In other words, Paul writes not only as a Christian of Jewish background, but also as one conscious of his non-Jewish heritage. From his Jewish background he has derived the extensive knowledge of the Scriptures that he displays in Romans; from his diaspora background comes his knowledge of those writings in Greek form and of other Jewish literature preserved in Greek form (e.g., The Wisdom of Solomon).

Without naming Paul as their author, various apostolic Fathers echo phrases from Romans: *1 Clem.* 32:2 (Rom 9:5); 35:5 (1:29–32); Ignatius, *Eph.* 19:3 (6:4); *Magn.* 6:2 (6:17); *Trall.* 9:2 (8:11); *Smyrn.* 1:1 (1:3–4), which shows that Romans was well known at an early date; see further Sanday and Headlam, *Romans*, lxxix–lxxxiii. Marcion is the first to ascribe the letter to Paul (*Apostolicon*; Tertullian, *Adversus Marcionem*, 5.13–14), even though he only recognized parts of it. By the end of the second century the Canon of Muratori (44–53) ascribes to Paul a letter written to the Romans, and from the earliest canonical lists of the Council of Laodicea, Athanasius, and Amphilochus it is always so recognized (see *Enchiridion biblicum*, 4th ed. [Rome: Arnodo, 1961], 6–9). Although the authorship of Romans has been questioned at times in the not-too-distant past, modern students of the letter almost unanimously agree about its Pauline authenticity. It is usually reckoned today among the unquestioned Pauline letters, along with 1 Thessalonians, Galatians, 1–2 Corinthians, Philippians, and Philemon.

In the nineteenth century and the early part of the twentieth a few scholars denied or questioned the Pauline authorship of the entire letter (for a variety of reasons): B. Bauer, Evanson, Loman, van Manen, Schlaeger, Smith, Steck. But Cranfield (*Romans*, 1–2) rightly relegates the denial of the Pauline authorship of Romans "to a place among the curiosities of NT scholarship."

The question, however, has been raised in a new way by O. Roller, who studied the Pauline letters against the background of various ancient modes of epistolography. He raised the question because of 16:22, where Tertius says, "I who write this letter also greet you in the Lord." This greeting clearly reveals that the text of Romans comes from Tertius's pen. Moreover, in Gal 6:11 Paul himself snatches the pen from the hand of someone like Tertius and compares his writing with that of the skilled scribe, "See what big letters I use when I write to you in my own hand." But in what sense did Paul use a scribe like Tertius in the composition of his letters? Did he dictate the whole letter to Tertius, who laboriously wrote it down in longhand? Did he dictate it to Tertius, who wrote it in shorthand and then later reproduced it in a longhand copy? Or did Paul use Tertius as an amanuensis or secretary, to whom he gave his ideas and whom he commissioned with the formulation of them? Roller opted for the last of these modes of letter writing and ascribed the anacolutha in Romans to additions made by Paul himself as he corrected drafts of it.

Certainly, the three modes of ancient letter-writing are well documented by Roller. If his choice of the third mode were correct, it would mean that the question of the Pauline authorship of Romans is raised in a new way. But unless one could show that Tertius was the secretary always used by Paul (in Corinth, in Ephesus, in Macedonia), this view of the mode of writing Romans encounters the difficulty of the uniformity of Pauline style and language in the seven uncontested letters of the corpus. (Roller's work has not gone without serious criticism; see E. Percy, *Die Probleme der Kolosser- und Epheserbriefe*, Acta regiae societatis humaniorum litterarum lundensis 39 [Lund: Gleerup, 1946], 10; W. Michaelis, *Einleitung in das Neue Testament* [Bern: Haller, 1946], 242–44; 2d ed. [1954], 251; J. N. Sevenster, *Do You Know Greek*, NovTSup 19 [Leiden: Brill, 1968], 12.) Furthermore, the importance of the topic treated in Romans and its relation to Galatians would make it unlikely that Paul would have left the formulation of such a writing to a secretary.

Cranfield (*Romans*, 3) has also called attention to the Roman practice of dictation *syllabatim*, "syllable by syllable," which Cicero mentions in his letters (*Ad Atticum* 13.25.3; cf. Lucullus, 119).

Earlier Sanday and Headlam (*Romans*, lx) had opted for dictation of the letter to Tertius, who would have taken it down in shorthand and then written it out in longhand. They argued for this mode of dictation on the basis of the way that Origen's lectures were taken down and subsequently copied, as described in Eusebius, *Historia ecclesiastica* 6.23.2. Tachygraphy or shorthand writing was used in the ancient Greek-speaking world of the eastern Mediterranean area; legend ascribes it to Xenophon, but an example of it, as yet undeciphered, has been found even in Palestine. It occurs in a text written on skin discovered in a

41

Murabba^cat cave, dating from the early second century A.D. (see P. Benoit, "Document").

It is really impossible to say whether Tertius would have taken down the letter from Paul's dictation in either longhand or shorthand; one can argue for either mode. But the ubiquitous *gar*, "for," which is so abundant in Romans (143 occurrences), would seem to argue for a dictated text. The repetition of it sounds like spoken language. Again, J. H. Michael ("A Phenomenon") has called attention to problematic words or phrases that occur in a context in which the same word or phrase again occurs, and the repetition may be owing to dictation.

Another problem is whether Tertius was referring to the writing of Romans as a whole or only to chap. 16. This question, however, is further complicated by the literary problem of chap. 16 in Romans as a whole, the discussion of the text of Romans, the language and style of Romans, and the possibility that the letter is the result of a conflation of writings (see Introduction, section IV).

In the matter of Pauline authorship some commentators, who admit the authenticity of chaps. 1–14, have denied that chaps. 15–16 (Baur, Ryder) or chap. 16 (Knox, "The Epistle," 365–68: "a pseudonymous addition to Romans," probably added by someone in the community at Rome), or the doxology, 16:25–27, can be ascribed to Paul. Again, this matter is affected by the literary question of the last chapters of Romans.

The relationship of the doxology (16:25–27) is the most problematic of all of these parts. Whereas Cambier, Dupont, Feuillet, Frede, Guthrie, Harrison, Höpfl and Gut, Leenhardt, Mariani, Meinertz, Murray, Nygren, Roosen, Schmidt, and Walkenhorst have regarded it as of Pauline authorship, some, while admitting it to be Pauline, think that it originally belonged to another letter: so Bacon, Feine and Behm, Lightfoot, Michaelis, Schumacher, and Wikenhauser. And many commentators have denied its authenticity: Althaus, Barrett, Bartsch, Cranfield, Donfried, Elliott, Gaugler, Jülicher and Fascher, Kamlah, Klijn, Lietzmann, Lührmann, T. W. Manson, Marxsen, Michel, Romaniuk, Schelkle, Schenke, Widmann, and Zuntz; or have been very hesitant about it: Fuller and Minear.

BIBLIOGRAPHY

Bahr, G. J., "Paul and Letter Writing in the First Century," *CBQ* 28 (1966): 465–77.

Bacon, B. W., "The Doxology at the End of Romans," *JBL* 18 (1899): 167–76.

Bauer, B., *Christus und die Caesaren: Der Ursprung des Christenthums aus dem römischen Griechenthums* (Berlin: E. Grosser, 1877; repr. Hildesheim: Olms, 1968).

―――, *Kritik der paulinischen Briefe*, 3 vols. (Berlin: G. Hempel, 1850–52; repr. Aalen: Scientia Verlag, 1972), 3.47–76.

Baur, F. C., *Paulus, der Apostel Jesu Christi*, 2 vols. (Leipzig: Fues-Verlag, 1845; 2d ed., 1866–67; repr. Osnabrück: Zeller, 1968), 1.393–409; *Paul, the Apostle of*

Jesus Christ . . . , 2 vols., 2d ed. (London and Edinburgh: Williams and Norgate, 1876), 1.352–65.

Benoit, P., "Document en tachygraphie grecque," *Les Grottes de Murabbaʿat*, DJD 2, ed. P. Benoit et al. (Oxford: Clarendon, 1961), 275–29 (+ pls. CIII–CV).

Elliott, J. K., "The Language and Style of the Concluding Doxology to the Epistle to the Romans," ZNW 72 (1981): 124–30.

Evanson, E., *The Dissonance of the Four Generally Received Evangelists, and the Evidence of Their Respective Authenticity Examined: With That of Some Other Scriptures Deemed Canonical* (Ipswich: G. Jermyn, 1792), 257–61; 2d ed. (Gloucester, Mass.: J. Johnson, 1805), 305–12.

Kamlah, E., "Traditionsgeschichtliche Untersuchungen zur Schlussdoxologie des Römerbriefes," Ph.D. diss., Universität Tübingen, 1955; see TLZ 81 (1956): 492.

Knox, J., "The Epistle to the Romans," *IB* 9.365–68.

Lambert, W. A., "Did Paul Write Romans? The Evidence of Chaps. XV. and XVI.," LCR 23 (1904): 58–66.

Loman, A. D., "Paulus en de kanon," TTijd 20 (1886): 387–406.

———, "Quaestiones paulinae," TTijd 16 (1882): 141–85; 20 (1886): 42–113.

Manen, W. C. van, *Paulus: II. De Brief aan de Romeinen* (Leiden: Brill, 1891).

———, "Romans (Epistle)," *Encyclopaedia Biblica*, 4 vols., ed. T. K. Cheyne and J. S. Black (New York: Macmillan, 1899–1903), 4.4127–45, esp. 4129–30, 4141.

———, *Die Unechtheit des Römerbriefes* (Leipzig: Strübig, 1906).

Michael, J. H., "A Phenomenon in the Text of Romans," JTS 39 (1938): 150–54.

Renié, J., "Authenticité et integrité de l'épître aux Romains," RevApol 66 (1938): 704–10.

Richards, E. R., *The Secretary in the Letters of Paul*, WUNT 2.42 (Tübingen: Mohr [Siebeck], 1991).

Roller, O., *Das Formular der paulinischen Briefe: Ein Beitrag zur Lehre vom antiken Briefe* (Stuttgart: Kohlhammer, 1933), 14–23, 295–300.

Romaniuk, K., "Autentyczność i jedność literacka listu św. Pawła do Rzymian," *Studia theologica varsaviensia* 12.1 (1974): 31–44.

Ryder, W. H., "The Authorship of Romans xv. xvi.," JBL 17 (1898): 184–98.

Schlaeger, G., "La Critique radicale de l'épître aux Romains," *Congrès d'histoire du christianisme: Jubilé Alfred Loisy*, ed. P.-L. Couchoud, 3 vols. (Paris: Editions Rieder; Amsterdam: Van Holkema & Warendorf, 1928), 2.100–118.

Schmiedel, P. W., "Did Paul Write Romans?—A Reply," HibJ 1 (1902–3): 532–52.

Schmithals, W., "Zur Abfassung und ältesten Sammlung der paulinischen Hauptbriefe," ZNW 51 (1960): 225–45.

Smith, W. B., "Address and Destination of St. Paul's Epistle to the Romans," JBL 20 (1901): 1–21.

———, "Did Paul Write Romans?" HibJ 1 (1902–3): 309–34.

———, "Unto Romans XV. and XVI.," JBL 20 (1901): 129–57; 21 (1902): 117–69.

Steck, R., *Der Galaterbrief, nach seiner Echtheit untersucht: Nebst kritischen Bemerkungen zu den paulinischen Hauptbriefen* (Berlin: G. Reimer, 1888).

III. THE TEXT

◆

The Greek text of Romans on which this translation and commentary have been based is that of K. Aland et al., *Novum Testamentum graece*, 26th ed. (Stuttgart: Deutsche Bibelstiftung, 1979; hereafter N-A[26]). It is dominated by the Hesychian or Alexandrian text-tradition in the transmission of Greek NT writings. It represents the best available form of the Greek text of Romans. It is impossible in a commentary like this one to set forth in detail the reasons for the preference of this form of the text. But a few details must be mentioned because certain decisions about the text of Romans will be made in the course of the commentary, and the reader has a right to know on what the decisions are based, even though one may not comprehend all of the intricacies of this abstruse aspect of NT scholarship.

Parts of the Greek text of Romans are preserved on papyrus codices or leaves; none of them, however, contains the full text. The papyrus texts usually date from earlier centuries than those parchment MSS which have preserved the text in its entirety, though in the case of Romans one parchment fragment may be as early as some of the papyri. Portions of the text of Romans are found on eight papyri, of which three date from the third century; the most important of these is P[46], the Chester Beatty Papyrus II. The following are the eight papyrus texts of Romans (the number in parentheses refers to the folio of the codex; v = verso; r = recto):

Papyrus	Date	Name	Contents
1. P[46]	ca. A.D. 200	Chester Beatty Papyrus II (Dublin): University of Michigan Pap. Inv. 6238 (Ann Arbor)	(8v) 5:17–6:3; (8r) 6:5–14; (11v) 8:15–25; (11r) 8:27–35; (12v) 8:37–9:9; (12r) 9:10–22; (13v) 9:22–32; (13r) 10:1–11; (14v) 10:12–11:2; (14r) 11:3–12; (15v) 11:13–22; (15r) 11:24–33; (16v) 11:35–12:9; (16r) 12:11–

Papyrus	*Date*	*Name*	*Contents*
			13:1; (17v) 13:2–11; (17r) 13:12–14:8; (18v) 14:9–21 (frgs.); (18r) 14:22–15:9 (frgs.); (19v) 15:11–19; (19r) 15:20–29; (20v) 15:29–33; 16:25–27; 16:1–3; (20r) 16:4–13; (21v) 16:14–23; (21r) 16:23.
2. P[27]	3d cent.	Univ. Libr. Add. MS 7211 (Cambridge); OxyP 11.9–12, §1355	8:12–22, 24–27, 33–39; 9:1–3, 5–9
3. P[40]	3d cent.	Univ. Libr. Inv. Pap. gr. 45 (Heidelberg)	1:24–27, 31–2:3; 3:21–4:8; 6:4–5, 16; 9:17, 27
4. P[10]	4th cent.	Harvard Sem. Museum Pap.; OxyP 2.8–9, §209 (Cambridge, Mass.)	1:1–7
5. P[26]	ca. 600	Southern Methodist Univ., Lane Museum; OxyP 11.6–9, §1354 (Dallas)	1:1–16
6. P[31]	7th cent.	John Rylands Libr.; Pap. Ryl. 4 (Manchester, UK)	12:3–8(?)
7. P[61]	ca. 700	New York Univ. P. Colt 5 (New York)	16:23, 25–27
8. P[94]	5th–6th cent.	P. Cairo 10730	6:10–13, 19–22

The most important parchment manuscripts of Romans are those written in uncials or majuscules and dating mainly from the third to the ninth centuries. These are the following seventeen codices or leaves of codices:

Parchment Manuscript	*Gregory Numbering*	*Date*	*Name*	*Contents*
1.	0220	3d cent.	Leland C. Wyman (Boston)	4:23–5:3, 8–13
2. ℵ	01	4th cent.	Cod. Sinaiticus; Brit. Mus. Add. MS 43725 (London)	All of Romans

Parchment Manuscript	Gregory Numbering	Date	Name	Contents
3. B	03	4th cent.	Cod. Vaticanus, Vatican Libr., Gr. 1209 (Rome)	All of Romans
4.	0221	4th cent.	Österr. Nat. Bibl., Pap. G. 19890 (Vienna)	5:16–17, 19; 5:21–6:3
5.	0219	4th or 5th cent.	Österr. Nat. Bibl., Pap. G 36113 (Vienna)	2:21–23; 3:8–9, 23–25, 27–30
6. A	02	5th cent.	Cod. Alexandrinus, Brit. Mus., Royal 1 D. VIII (London)	All of Romans
7. C	04	5th cent.	Cod. Ephraemi rescriptus, Bibl. Nat., Gr. 9 (Paris)	All of Romans, exc. 2:5–3:21; 9:6–10:15; 11:31–13:10
8.	048	5th cent.	Vatican Libr., Gr. 2061 (Rome)	13:4–15:9
9.	0172	5th cent.	Bibl. Laurenziana, PSI 4 (Florence)	1:27–30, 32; 2:1–2
10. Dᵖ	06	6th cent.	Cod. Claromontanus, Bibl. Nat., Gr. 107, 107AB (Paris)	All of Romans, exc. 1:1–7a, 27–30
11.	0209	7th cent.	Univ. of Michigan, MS 8 (Ann Arbor)	14:9–15:2; 16:15–17
12.	044	8th or 9th cent.	Cod. Athous Laurae 172 (Mt. Athos)	All of Romans
13. Fᵖ	010	9th cent.	Cod. Augiensis, Trinity Coll. Libr., B XVII. 1 (Cambridge, UK)	All of Romans, exc. 1:1–3:19

Parchment Manuscript	Gregory Numbering	Date	Name	Contents
14. Gᴾ	012	9th cent.	Cod. Boerneri-anus, Sächische Landesbibl. A 145b (Dresden)	All of Romans, exc. 1:1–5; 2:16–25
15. K	018	9th cent.	Hist. Mus. V. 93, S. 97 (Moscow)	1:1–10:17
16. L	020	9th cent.	Bibl. Angelica §38 (Rome)	All of Romans
17. P	025	9th cent.	Publ. Bibl., Gr. 225 (Leningrad)	1:1–2:14; 3:6–8:32; 9:12–11:21; 12:2–16:28

Among the important minuscule MSS of the Greek NT, the text of Romans, or at least part of it, is preserved in the following twenty-nine codices (in the Gregory numbering): 5, 17, 33, 81, 104, 109, 181, 326, 330, 365, 436, 451, 460, 614, 629, 630, 1241, 1424, 1739, 1841, 1877, 1881, 1962, 1984, 1985, 2127, 2464, 2492, 2495. Although these minuscule MSS date from the ninth century or later, they are sometimes important, being at times copies of earlier good MSS. The two most important among them are 33 and 1739 (the latter is a tenth-century copy of the Greek text of Romans usually thought to represent that used by Origen). For the contents of the minuscules, see N-A²⁶, 703–10; Hatch, *Facsimiles and Descriptions*, passim.

The fundamental books in which to check the data in the preceding lists are Aland, *Kurzgefasste Liste*, 27–33 (papyri), 35–57 (majuscules), 59–202 (minuscules), and 203–318 (lectionaries); idem, *Studien*, 91–136 (papyri); cf. Aland and Aland, *The Text*, passim.

The major text-critical problems of Romans have to do with the address in 1:7 (*tois ousin en Romē agapētois theou*, "to all the beloved of God in Rome") and in 1:15 (*tois en romē*, "who are in Rome"), with the doxology (16:25–27), and with the concluding blessing (16:20b or 16:24 or 16:28).

As for the mention of Rome in the address of 1:7, 15, the words quoted above are omitted in codex G (Boernerianus, a ninth-century Greek and Latin text). They were probably also omitted in codex F (Augiensis, a sister bilingual text of the ninth century), which lacks completely 1:1–3:18. Absence of the mention of Rome in these verses is also deduced from the discussion of the oldest commentators on Romans: Origen (*Commentarius in ep. ad Romanos* 1.8, PG 14.853;

and the marginal scholion on 1:7 in MS 1739), Ambrosiaster (*Ad Romanos* 1.7, CSEL 81.1.19), and Pelagius (see Souter, *Pelagius's Expositions*, 2.9; cf. Hatch, "On the Relationship"; Smith, "Address"; Steinmetz, "Textkritische Untersuchung"; Zuntz, *The Text*, 69–71).

As for the doxology, six forms of the use of it are found in the Greek MSS, ancient versions, and patristic writers:

1. It is omitted entirely in MSS F, G, 629, g; Marcion, Jerome, Priscillian
2. It is added after 14:23 only in MSS L, Ψ, 181, 0209(?), 326, 330, 451, 460, 614, 1241, 1877, 1881, 1984, 1985, 2492, 2495, etc.; the Harclean Syriac; Origen, Cyril, Theodoret, and John of Damascus
3. It is added after 15:33 only in MS P⁴⁶
4. It is added after 16:23(24) only in MSS P⁶¹, ℵ, B, C, D, 81, 365, 436, 630, 1739, 1962, 2127, 2464; d, e, f; Peshitta, Vg, Coptic
5. It is added after both 14:23 and 16:23(24) in MSS A, P, 5, 17, 33, 104, 109; Armenian
6. It is added after both 14:23 and 15:33 (16:1–24 being omitted) in MS 1506

On these readings, see Aland, "Glosse, Interpolation, Redaktion," *Studien*, 35–57; de Bruyne, "Les Deux Derniers Chapitres"; Dupont, "Pour l'Histoire"; Gamble, *Textual History*, 23–24, 96–126; E. Riggenbach, "Die Textgeschichte."

As for the concluding blessing, two basic forms of it are found in different positions:

1. *Hē charis tou kyriou hēmōn Iēsou meth' hymōn*, "the grace of our Lord Jesus be with you!": This form is found at 16:20b in MSS P⁴⁶, ℵ, B, 1881, etc.; some MSS (A, C, Ψ, and the *Koinē* text-tradition) read the same form but add *Christou* after "Jesus." It is omitted from v 20b in MSS D, F, G, and some copies of the Vg
2. *Hē charis tou kyriou hēmōn Iēsou Christou meta pantōn hymōn. Amen*, "the grace of our Lord Jesus Christ be with all of you! Amen": This form agrees with 2 Thess 3:18 and is found after 16:23 as v 24 in MS Ψ and the *Koinē* text-tradition (with varying positions of the doxology affecting the placement). MSS P⁴⁶, P⁶¹, ℵ, A, B, C, 81, 1739, 2464, and some ancient versions (Vg, Coptic) omit this verse entirely
3. The second form of the blessing is found as v 28 in MSS P, 33, 104, 365, in some ancient versions (Peshitta, Bohairic), and in Ambrosiaster; see Gamble, *Textual History*, 127–32. For the Marcionite form of the blessing (*gratia cum omnibus sanctis*), see de Bruyne, "Les Deux Derniers Chapitres"

These three main problems have given rise to further discussion about the forms that the letter has taken in its history, for it may have existed in three different forms, to which some brief attention must be given here.

1. A Short Form of Romans Without Chaps. 15 and 16. Although no extant MS of Romans has preserved the letter without chaps. 15 and 16, evidence for such a form has been found in various sources.

a. Origen, *Commentarius in ep. ad Romanos* 10.43, PG 14.1290. He mentions that Marcion not only dropped the doxology, but "cut away" all that followed 14:23 (*ab eo loco ubi scriptum est 'omne autem quod non est ex fide' dissecuit*). But Origen also knew of texts not contaminated by Marcion that had the doxology after 14:23. Hence, despite modern attempts to label the fourteen-chapter form as Marcionite in origin, it cannot be so simply described; see Gamble, *Textual History*, 22–23, 100–114.

b. Ancient *capitula* or précis of segments of the text of Romans that are found in MSS of the Vg (fifty-one of them occur in the eighth-century codex Amiatinus, of which the fiftieth *capitulum* pertains to 14:15, 17, and the fifty-first to the doxology). They argue for a form of Romans having 1:1–14:23 + 16:25–27. Similar *capitula* in the sixth-century codex Fuldensis presuppose a text of Romans having 1:1–14:23 without the doxology; see Corssen, "Zur Überlieferungsgeschichte"; Hort, "On the End"; Riggenbach, "Die Kapitelverzeichnisse"; Gamble, *Textual History*, 16–18.

c. The *concordia epistularum paulinarum*, a sort of concordance found in some MSS of the Vg, lists subject headings of matter in Romans only from 1:1 to 14:23 and the doxology; see Gamble, *Textual History*, 18–19.

d. Some Latin MSS of the so-called Marcionite prologue of Romans. They designate the place from which the letter was sent as Athens (*ab Athenis*), a designation that would ill suit the reference to Cenchreae in 16:1, if it were present; see D. de Bruyne, "La Finale marcionite."

e. The silence of Irenaeus, Cyprian, and Tertullian, who do not quote at all from chaps. 15 or 16; see Gamble, *Textual History*, 20–22.

Such evidence seems to suggest that Romans existed in some places in a fourteen-chapter form, either alone (without the doxology), or with the doxology, or with the concluding blessing and doxology; see Gamble, *Textual History*, 96–124.

2. A Form of Romans Without Chap. 16. The discovery in this century of Chester Beatty Papyrus II (P[46]), which alone has the doxology between 15:33 and 16:1, raised anew the question about the character of 16:1–23 and especially the question whether Romans ever existed only in the form of 1:1–15:33. Being the oldest text of Romans, dated usually ca. 200, and being a witness of a text tradition related to MSS B and 1739, it bears valuable testimony to the transmission of the text of Romans. It includes chap. 16, but places the doxology before it. But does it possibly bear witness to a text tradition in which Romans consisted only of 1:1–15:33, followed by the doxology, to which the rest of chap. 16 was extrinsically added at some point? No certainty is possible in this matter, and the question about a fifteen-chapter form of Romans remains speculative. But only such a form would explain, according to some commentators, why the doxology got where it is in P⁴⁶. (It should be recalled that folios 1–7 of this codex are missing; it begins with 5:17; see Kenyon, *The Chester Beatty Biblical Papyri*; Sanders, *A Third-Century Papyrus Codex*; and the secondary literature on it.)

3. The Long Form of Romans (1:1–16:27 or 28). This form of Romans is found in every extant Greek MS of the letter that contains the full text. Although the quantity of manuscript testimony would support the placing of the doxology after 14:23, the quality of the ancient witnesses supporting the positioning of it at 16:25–27, the geographical spread of their testimony, and the diversity of the textual traditions represented are decisive for reading it after 16:23. On the basis of textual criticism one might, therefore, conclude that the sixteen-chapter form of Romans is the most original. This conclusion, drawn by textual critics, could, however, change with the discovery of new evidence. It should be recalled that the sixteen-chapter form of Romans differs in various MSS as to the position of the concluding blessing and its wording (see above).

The best that one can say about the original form of Romans from a text-critical viewpoint is that it most likely contained 1:1–16:23 (or only with a remote possibility, 1:1–15:33). The Marcionite form of the text had only 1:1–14:23. At some point the doxology was added to the Marcionite form (1:1–14:23 + 16:24–27), just as it was added elsewhere (either once or twice). Such additions produced the six forms mentioned above. K. Aland ("Der Schluss") has distinguished in the various MSS of Romans 14 different forms of the text and has tried to order them; but that task is highly speculative and does not contribute much to the understanding of the text form of Romans; cf. Lampe, "Zur Textgeschichte." In sum, the text-critical evidence suggests that the fourteen-chapter and fifteen-chapter forms of Romans were only secondary, later abbreviations of the original letter.

The conclusion about the preferred form of Romans as including chap. 16 cannot, however, be decided solely on the textual evidence. It is complicated by the literary question of the unity and integrity of the letter (see Introduction, section IV). Many other minor textual problems in the Greek text of Romans, problems that have to do with individual verses, will be taken up and discussed in the commentary itself.

In 1972 José O'Callaghan startled the world of biblical scholarship with his claim that some of the Greek fragments found in Qumran Cave 7 belonged to NT texts. Subsequently he announced the identification of 7Q9 as containing part of Rom 5:11–12 (see *Los papiros griegos*, 73–74). He read -*agēn* on one line of the fragment, and *ōsp*- on the next (allegedly = *katallagēn* and *hōsper* of 5:11–

12). This identification was immediately contested by the original editor, M. Baillet ("Les Manuscrits"); see Leaney, "Greek Manuscripts," 298–300.

BIBLIOGRAPHY

Aland, K., *Kurzgefasste Liste der griechischen Handschriften des Neuen Testaments*, vol. 1: *Gesamtübersicht*, ANTF 1 (Berlin and New York: de Gruyter, 1963).

———, "Die Entstehung des Corpus Paulinum," *Neutestamentliche Entwürfe*, Theologische Bücherei 63 (Munich: Kaiser, 1979), 302–50.

———, "Der Schluss und die ursprüngliche Gestalt des Römerbriefes," ibid., 284–301.

———, *Studien zur Überlieferung des Neuen Testaments und seines Textes*, ANTF 2 (Berlin and New York: de Gruyter, 1967).

———, and B. Aland, *The Text of the New Testament: An Introduction to the Critical Editions and to the Theory and Practice of Modern Textual Criticism* (Leiden: Brill; Grand Rapids, Mich.: Eerdmans, 1987); *Der Text des griechischen Neuen Testaments* (Stuttgart: Deutsche Bibelgesellschaft, 1982).

Aland, K. et al. (eds.), *Text und Textwert der griechischen Handschriften des Neuen Testaments*, vol. 2: *Die paulinischen Briefe: 1. Allgemeines, Römerbrief und Ergänzungsliste* (Berlin and New York: de Gruyter, 1991).

Baillet, M., "Les Manuscrits de la grotte 7 de Qumran et le Nouveau Testament (suite)," *Bib* 54 (1973): 340–47.

Baljon, J. M. S., *De tekst der brieven van Paulus aan de Romeinen, de Corinthiërs en de Galatiërs als Voorwerp van de conjecturaalkritiek beschouwd* (Utrecht: Kemink & Zoon, 1885).

Bardy, G., "Le Texte de l'épître aux Romains dans le commentaire d'Origène-Rufin," *RB* 29 (1920): 229–41.

Benoit, P., "Le Codex paulinien Chester Beatty," *RB* 46 (1937): 58–82.

Bingen, J., "P94: Romains 6,10–13; 19–22 (P. Cair. 10730)," *Miscel.lània papirològica Ramon Roca-Puig en el seu vuitantè aniversari*, ed. S. Janeras (Barcelona: Fund. S. Vives Casajuana, 1987), 75–78.

Brady, E., "The Position of Romans in P. 46," *ExpTim* 59 (1947–48): 249–50.

Bruyne, D. de, "Les Deux Derniers Chapitres de la lettre aux Romains," *RBén* 25 (1908): 423–30.

———, "La Finale marcionite de la lettre aux Romains retrouvée," *RBén* 28 (1911): 133–42.

Chadwick, H., "Rufinus and the Tura Papyrus of Origen's Commentary on Romans," *JTS* 10 (1959): 10–42.

Corssen, P., *Epistularum paulinarum codices graece et latine scriptos Augiensem, Boernerianum, Claromontanum examinavit inter se comparavit ad communem originem revocavit*, Programma gymnasii leverensis, 2 vols. (Kiel: Fiencke, 1887–89).

————, "Zur Überlieferungsgeschichte des Römerbriefes," ZNW 10 (1909): 1–45; "Nachtrag," 97–102.

Dupont, J., "Pour l'Histoire de la doxologie finale de l'épître aux Romains," RBén 58 (1948): 3–22.

Farrar, F. W., "Various Readings in the Epistle to the Romans," Expos 1.9 (1879): 202–20.

Gamble, H. Jr., The Textual History of the Letter to the Romans: A Study in Textual and Literary Criticism, Studies and Documents 42 (Grand Rapids, Mich.: Eerdmans, 1977).

Hartke, W., Die Sammlung und die ältesten Ausgaben der Paulusbriefe (Bonn: Georgi, 1917).

Hatch, W. H. P., Facsimiles and Descriptions of Minuscule Manuscripts of the New Testament (Cambridge, Mass.: Harvard University Press, 1951).

————, "On the Relationship of Codex Augiensis and Codex Boernerianus of the Pauline Epistles," Harvard Studies in Classical Philology 60 (1951): 187–99.

————, "A Recently Discovered Fragment of the Epistle to the Romans," HTR 45 (1952): 81–85 (on MS 0220).

Hort, F. J. A., "On the End of the Epistle to the Romans," JP 3 (1871): 51–80; repr. in J. B. Lightfoot, Biblical Essays (London: Macmillan, 1893; repr. Grand Rapids, Mich.: Baker, 1979), 321–51.

Hoskier, H. C., "A Study of the Chester-Beatty Codex of the Pauline Epistles," JTS 38 (1937): 148–63.

Junack, K. et al., Das Neue Testament auf Papyrus, 2 vols., ANTF 6 and 12 (Berlin: de Gruyter, 1986–89), 2.1–151.

Kenyon, F. C., The Chester Beatty Biblical Papyri . . . , fascicle 3: Pauline Epistles and Revelation (London: E. Walker Ltd., 1934), 1–9; fascicle 3, Supplement (1937), pls. f. 8v–f. 21r.

Lagrange, M.-J., "La Vulgate latine de l'épître aux Romains et le texte grec," RB 13 (1916): 225–39.

Lampe, P., "Zur Textgeschichte des Römerbriefes," NovT 27 (1985): 273–77.

Leaney, A. R. C., "Greek Manuscripts from the Judaean Desert," Studies in New Testament Language and Text: Essays in Honour of George D. Kilpatrick . . . , NovTSup 44, ed. J. K. Elliott (Leiden: Brill, 1976), 283–300.

Lietzmann, H., "Die Chester-Beatty-Papyri des Neuen Testaments," Kleine Schriften II, TU 68 (1958), 160–69.

————, "Einführung in die Textgeschichte der Paulusbriefe," ibid., 138–59.

————, "Zur Würdigung des Chester-Beatty-Papyrus der Paulusbriefe," ibid., 170–79.

Lightfoot, J. B., "M. Renan's Theory of the Epistle to the Romans," JP 2 (1869): 264–95; repr. Biblical Essays, 287–320.

————, "The Epistle to the Romans," JP 3 (1871): 193–214; repr. Biblical Essays, 352–74.

Metzger, B. M., *The Early Versions of the New Testament: Their Origin, Transmission, and Limitations* (Oxford: Clarendon, 1977), 81, 136, 150, 172–73, 242–44, 345.

―――, "Explicit References in the Works of Origen to Variant Readings in New Testament Manuscripts," *Biblical and Patristic Studies in Memory of Robert Pierce Casey*, ed. J. N. Birdsall and R. W. Thomson (Freiburg im Breisgau: Herder, 1963), 78–95, esp. 88–90; repr. *Historical and Literary Studies: Pagan, Jewish, and Christian*, NTTS 8 (Leiden: Brill, 1968), 88–103, esp. 97–99.

―――, "The Practice of Textual Criticism among the Church Fathers," *Studia patristica* 12, = TU 115 (1975), 340–49; repr. *New Testament Studies: Philological, Versional, and Patristic*, NTTS 10 (Leiden: Brill, 1980), 189–98.

―――, "St Jerome's Explicit References to Variant Readings in Manuscripts of the New Testament," *Text and Interpretation: Studies in the New Testament Presented to Matthew Black*, ed. E. Best and R. M. Wilson (Cambridge: Cambridge University Press, 1979), 179–90, esp. 184; repr. as *New Testament Studies: Philological . . .* , 199–210, esp. 204.

―――, *The Text of the New Testament: Its Transmission, Corruption, and Restoration*, 2d ed. (New York and London: Oxford University Press, 1968; 3d ed. 1991).

Michael, J. H., "A Phenomenon in the Text of Romans," *JTS* 39 (1938): 150–54.

Michelsen, J. H. A., "Kritisch onderzoek naar den oudsten tekst van 'Paulus' brief aan de Romeinen," *TTijd* 20 (1886): 372–86, 473–90; 21 (1887): 163–203.

Murphy, H. S., "The Text of Romans and 1 Corinthians in Minuscule 93 and the Text of Pamphilus," *HTR* 52 (1959): 119–31.

O'Callaghan, J., *Los papiros griegos de la cueva 7 de Qumrán*, BAC 353 (Madrid: Editorial católica, 1974).

Prins, J. J., "Rom. I–VI volgens Tischendorf's Editio VIII," *TTijd* 8 (1874): 510–20.

Riggenbach, E., "Die Kapitelverzeichnisse zum Römer- und Hebräerbrief im Codex Fuldensis der Vulgata," *Neue Jahrbücher für deutsche Theologie* 3 (1894): 350–63.

―――, "Die Textgeschichte der Doxologie Rom. 16,25–27 im Zusammenhang mit den Übrigen, den Schluss des Römerbriefs betreffenden, textkritischen Fragen," ibid. 1 (1892): 526–605.

Rönsch, H., "Italafragmente des Römer- und Galaterbriefes aus der Abtei Göttweig: Textabdruck nebst Einleitung und kritischen Anmerkungen," *ZWT* 22 (1879): 224–38.

Sanders, H. A., *A Third-Century Papyrus Codex of the Epistles of Paul*, University of Michigan Studies, Humanistic Series 38 (Ann Arbor, Mich.: University of Michigan, 1935), 39–57.

Seesemann, H., "Die Bedeutung des Chester-Beatty Papyrus für die Textkritik der Paulusbriefe," *TBl* 16 (1937): 92–97.

Smith, W. B., "Address and Destination of St. Paul's Epistle to the Romans," *JBL* 20 (1901): 1–21.

Steinmetz, R., "Textkritische Untersuchung zu Röm 1,7," *ZNW* 9 (1908): 177–89.

Vogels, H. J., "Der Codex Claromontanus der paulinischen Briefe," *Amicitiae corolla:*

A *Volume of Essays Presented to James Rendel Harris* . . . , ed. H. G. Woods (London: University of London, 1933), 274–99.

———, "Der Einfluss Marcions und Tatians auf Text und Kanon des NT," *Synoptische Studien Alfred Wikenhauser . . . dargebracht* . . . , ed. J. Schmid and A. Vögtle (Munich: Zink, 1953), 278–89.

———, *Untersuchungen zum Text paulinischer Briefe bei Rufin und Ambrosiaster*, BBB 9 (Bonn: Hanstein, 1955), 1–44 (I. "Der Römerbrief").

Walker, W. O., Jr., "Text-Critical Evidence for Interpolations in the Letters of Paul," CBQ 50 (1988): 622–31.

Williams, C. S. C., "P[46] and the Textual Tradition of the Epistle to the Romans," *ExpTim* 61 (1949–50): 125–26.

Zuntz, G., *The Text of the Epistles: A Disquisition upon the Corpus Paulinum*, Schweich Lectures 1946 (London: Oxford University Press, 1953).

IV. UNITY AND INTEGRITY

♦

In discussing the text of Romans, I noted that the question of an original fourteen-chapter, fifteen-chapter, or sixteen-chapter form of Romans could not be settled solely on the basis of textual criticism, since there are literary aspects to be considered. These aspects are complicated by various attempts made in the past to explain the genesis and history of the three different forms. Some mention must be made, at least briefly, of such attempts to explain the alleged shorter forms of Romans, even though I shall ultimately be commenting on the sixteen-chapter form, the only form that has survived in the extant Greek manuscripts. These literary questions have to do with the unity and integrity of Romans but also affect further questions about the occasion and purpose of the letter.

Lightfoot (*Biblical Essays*, 315–20) considered the sixteen chapters (1:1–16:23) to be Paul's original composition, a letter written to the Christians of Rome, a mixed body of Jewish and Gentile converts. Having written 1 Corinthians to correct "errors of Gentile licence" and Galatians to denounce "the deadening effects of Judaic bondage," Paul would have later written in a more comprehensive way this letter of "conciliation—conciliation of claims, conciliation of doctrine, conciliation of practice" and sent it to Rome, as he contemplated a visit to the Christians there. But the short form, in which the last two chapters were omitted, came to Paul as an "after-thought," to make his text "a circular letter or general treatise." He would then have omitted the references to Rome in 1:7, 15 and the personal news in 15:1–16:23(24). Although Lightfoot considered the doxology to be of Pauline authorship, he did not think it was written at the same time as the letter itself. A similar explanation was proposed by Lietzmann (*An die Römer*, 27). As plausible as this explanation may seem at first sight, it has always encountered the objection that Paul himself would thus have cut in two his discussion of the problem of the weak and the strong (14:1–15:13). Moreover, there is no indication that Paul ever made similar general treatises out of other specifically addressed writings.

Adopting an opposite point of view, Lake (*The Earlier Epistles*, 362–65) proposed in 1911 that Paul's original composition was rather the fourteen-chapter form, written as a general letter, which initially had nothing to do with the

Roman community. Later on, Paul would have added the address in 1:7, 15 as well as chap. 15, thus continuing his discussion of the weak and the strong from 14:23 and adding personal news (15:14–33). This form of the letter would have been sent to Rome. (Lake regarded chap. 16 as a letter originally addressed to Ephesus.) This explanation, however, again raises the question about the unity of the discussion of the weak and the strong (14:1–15:13), which seems to make it unlikely that 15:1–13 is an afterthought.

In 1948 T. W. Manson ("St. Paul's Letter") proposed, largely on the basis of MS P⁴⁶, in which the doxology appears after 15:33, that the letter that Paul sent to the Christians of Rome was the pre-Marcionite fifteen-chapter form, whereas the sixteen-chapter form (indeed, as in P⁴⁶, with 16:1–23 following the doxology) represented the letter as known in Egypt, originally addressed to Ephesus. Manson called attention to the Egyptian provenience of P⁴⁶, to Clement of Alexandria as the earliest patristic writer to speak about chap. 16, and to the text of chap. 16 as standing closer to MS B (of Egyptian provenience) than the text of the other chapters in the letter. Manson concluded that Paul had prepared in Corinth one letter (Romans 1–15) and sent it to Rome, and another copy (Romans 1–16) and sent it to Ephesus. For Manson the fourteen-chapter form was the result of Marcion's excision. Manson regarded Romans, then, as "the summing up of the positions reached by Paul and his friends at the end of the long controversy whose beginnings appear in 1 Corinthians" and in Philippians 3. This he sent to Rome with a statement of his future plans. The Corinthian church had heard this "summing up" by word of mouth; the church in Syria and Palestine would hear it soon in the same way, but the church in Asia and the church in Rome would hear it in writing. "Looked at in this way Romans ceases to be just a letter of self-introduction from Paul to the Roman church, and becomes a manifesto setting forth his deepest convictions on central issues, a manifesto calling for the widest publicity" (p. 15). Thus Manson also broached the question of the occasion and purpose of Romans.

In 1954 and 1956 Knox ("A Note"; cf. "Epistle to the Romans," 365–68) reverted to Lake's explanation and called attention to the absence of any reference to Spain in chap. 1, in contrast to that in 15:14–33. Knox regarded Romans 1–15 as an adaptation of an earlier general letter, which had been composed for a Gentile church with which Paul was seeking contact, a letter announcing a visit that thus far had had to be postponed. The plans to go to Spain via Rome (15:14–33) would have adapted the general letter to a form for the church of Rome. (It will be recalled that Knox considered chap. 16 to be a still later non-Pauline addition to Romans; see section II above.)

The views of Lake, Manson, and Knox all treat Romans as having been a general or circular letter in some form.

The latest thorough treatment of the fourteen-chapter hypothesis comes from Gamble (*Textual History*, 96–123). He has examined the various earlier proposals in great detail. The following salient points in his rejection of this hypothesis as the original form of Romans should be noted. First, no address other than "Rome" is attested in any manuscript; hence the destination of a form of Romans to another church is without textual basis. Second, the fourteen-chapter form cuts in two the clearly unified treatment of the strong and the weak (14:1–15:13). Third, the fourteen-chapter form would lack completely the usual epistolary conclusion (see pp. 61–63). Fourth, the fourteen-chapter form cannot be the result merely of Marcion's excision, for Origen himself, who mentions that excision (*Commentarius in ep. ad Romanos* 10:43 [PG 14. 1290]), speaks of "other copies . . . not contaminated by Marcion," in which the doxology appears after 14:23, and still others that have it at the end (i.e., after 16:23 or 24). Fifth, that fourteen-chapter form is not to be regarded as the result of a later liturgical abridgment, which sought to eliminate the personal plans of Paul, considered unsuitable for public reading in a worship service (so Hort, Lagrange); nor was it owing to the early loss of final pages in some codex (so Emmet, Frede). Rather, Gamble argues, the fourteen-chapter form was the result of a later "catholic generalization," in other words, an attempt to make the letter more suitable for a wider and general audience (p. 116). This explanation would account for the omission of "Rome" in 1:7, 15 and for the references in patristic writers to a short form of Romans. So in the long run all the evidence, both textual and literary, is against the proposal that the fourteen-chapter form of Romans was the original Pauline composition.

One cannot discuss the fifteen-chapter form without considering at the same time the literary character of chap. 16. Although MS P[46] seems to support the view that Romans at one time may have existed in a fifteen-chapter form (because the doxology follows 15:33), the literary question is far more complicated.

The Pauline authorship of 16:1–23 is generally admitted today, but the question whether vv 1–23 might have been part of a separate letter of recommendation written by Paul for Phoebe, a deacon of the church of Cenchreae, is quite debated. For those who consider it part of a separate letter, it would have lost its opening prescript in being attached to Romans, would have been sent to the church in Ephesus, and would have been added to Romans by someone other than Paul, probably at the time of the collection of his letters into a corpus toward the end of the first century A.D.

The problem of the ending of Romans was apparently first broached by J. S. Semler in 1769 (*Paraphrasis*, 277–311), and the Ephesian destination of chap. 16 was first proposed by D. Schulz in a book review written in 1829. Since then such a destination has often been discussed and defended; so, with slight variations, commentators Bartsch, Bornkamm, Bultmann, Feine and Behm, Feuillet, Fitz-myer, Friedrich, Georgi, Goodspeed, Harrison, Heard, Henshaw, Jewett, Käse-mann, Kinoshita, Lake, Leenhardt, McDonald, McNeile, T. W. Manson, Marxsen, Michaelis, Moffatt, Munck, Refoulé, Schenke, Schmithals, Schu-macher, Scott, Suggs, Taylor, and Widmann.

The arguments for the Ephesian destination of 16:1–23 are mainly the following: first, the character of 16:1–23 is so different from the rest of Romans, and these verses are abruptly added to 15:33, which reads like a usual Pauline concluding blessing (cf. 1 Cor 16:23–24; 2 Cor 13:11; Phil 4:9). Second, in the order of the text preserved in MS P⁴⁶ (5:17–15:33 + 16:25–27 + 16:1–23), vv 1–23 seem to have been secondarily added to a fifteen-chapter form of Romans with a doxology. Third, early patristic writers such as Irenaeus, Cyprian, and Tertullian do not quote from chap. 15 or 16. Fourth, Rom 16:1–16 reads like a Greco-Roman *epistolē systatikē*, "letter of recommendation," using the verb *synistēmi*, plunging in medias res, and containing greetings. It introduces a person (Phoebe), states her identity (a deacon and leader of the church in Cenchreae), and requests the favorable treatment of her by the recipients (welcome and hospitality); cf. *LAE*, 226–27; Kim, *Form and Structure*, 101, 113–15, 135–42.

Additionally, whereas Romans 1–15 envisages a coming first visit of Paul to Rome and contains no clearly specific references to the Christian community there, vv 3–16 send greetings to twenty-six persons, as well as in a generic way to some groups (households and "brothers"). Indeed, Paul even knows of a house church to which some belong (16:5). He characterizes some of them as dear friends, personal acquaintances, and fellow countrymen (or possibly relatives): Mary, Andronicus and Junia, Ampliatus, Urbanus, Stachys, Herodion, Persis, Rufus and his mother. The greetings sent to Prisca and Aquila (16:3–5) would seem to argue definitively for an Ephesian destination, for they were in Ephesus when Paul wrote 1 Corinthians (16:19) and seem to have been still there when 2 Timothy was written (4:19; cf. Acts 18:18–19, 24–26). Furthermore, Epaenetus is singled out not only as Paul's dear friend (16:5b), but also as his "first convert to Christ in Asia," the Roman province, the capital of which was Ephesus. The long list of persons so greeted would assure Phoebe of a good reception in a town where Paul himself had labored and was well known.

Finally, although Paul has been dealing irenically with a ticklish subject throughout the rest of Romans (justification and salvation of Jew and Greek alike by grace through faith, apart from deeds of the law), his admonition in vv 17–20 comes as a surprise, if it be destined for the same readers as the rest of the letter. It is an authoritarian warning against those who create dissension and scandal, in opposition to the teaching that the addressees have received. It would seem, then, to be more suited for the community at Ephesus, where Paul had labored and had his difficulties (cf. also Acts 20:29–30).

These arguments are sometimes proposed with differing nuances and conclusions. For instance, some commentators would limit the separate letter to the Ephesians to vv 3–20 and ascribe vv 1–2, the letter of recommendation proper, to Paul, who appended it himself to Romans 1–15 and sent it to Rome; vv 3–20 would have been secondarily added later (so Feine and Behm, Leenhardt, Schenke, Michaelis).

Others would make vv 21–23, the greetings sent by Paul's companions, also part of Romans 15; Schenke ("Aporien") and Schmithals ("The False Teachers,"

237 n. 86) would insert them between 15:32 and 15:33. It should also be noted that J. Weiss once conceived the possibility that the Ephesian letter began as early as chap. 12. But the majority of the commentators named above treat vv 1–23 as a unit.

The foregoing arguments present a strong case in favor of 16:1–23 as a separate Pauline letter, originally sent to Ephesus, and later secondarily attached to Romans 1–15. If they are considered valid, then the integrity of the sixteen-chapter form of Romans is called in question. Nevertheless, each one of the arguments has been met with strong counterarguments. And, after all, all the Greek MSS of Romans have the sixteen-chapter form and imply that the sixteenth chapter was sent to Rome.

In response to the first point, the abrupt transition from 15:33 to 16:1 can be matched in Phil 3:1 and 3:2, an abrupt beginning after a farewell. Although many commentators on Philippians postulate a conflation of several letters that Paul may well have written to the church of Philippi (myself included, *JBC*, art. 50, §§7–8), there is no text-critical basis for different forms of Philippians, whereas there is some evidence of the kind for Romans. Moreover, the arguments for the conflation of Philippians are inconclusive, and the unity of Philippians has been defended, which gives one pause in drawing too strong a conclusion from an abrupt transition in Romans at this point. Again, the abrupt change sensed at 16:17 can be matched in 1 Cor 16:20b–22.

As for the second argument, although the order of the text in MS P[46] (5:17–15:33 + 16:25–27 + 16:1–23) may suggest that a fifteen-chapter form of Romans did exist at one time, to which the doxology was secondarily added, this suggestion is not fully convincing because P[46] may be witnessing to nothing more than a text form in which the doxology was moved for some reason to the end of chap. 15 from the end of chap. 16. It is known to have been moved and inserted elsewhere in the text tradition (see section III above); so it could also be here. Hence the order in this, the oldest MS of Romans, does not make one necessarily conclude that 16:1–23 originally had a separate existence. As Kümmel notes (*Introduction*, 224), P[46] gives no absolute proof that Romans ever existed in a fifteen-chapter form.

As for the third point, the silence of the early patristic writers about chaps. 15–16 is significant; but the argument based on it remains an argument from silence, about which one should consult Gamble, *Textual History*, 20. How much weight does it really carry for the Ephesian hypothesis? Similarly, that 16:1–16 reads like a Greco-Roman letter of recommendation does not prove that it could not have been a part of Romans. This Pauline letter makes use of many subforms within its generic epistolary framework (see section VII below). As an appendix to an essay-letter, there is nothing a priori unlikely about a letter of recommendation (see McDonald, "Was Romans?").

The fifth argument, the greetings sent to twenty-six individual Christians of Rome, a place that Paul is preparing to visit for the first time, and about which he seems otherwise to have little specific information (to judge from chaps. 1–15), has always been the most formidable one against the Roman destination of chap. 16. But there are counterarguments that have to be considered. Prisca and Aquila, having left Rome because of the edict of Claudius that expelled Jews (and Jewish Christians) from the capital (see section I above), could have already returned to Rome after the death of Claudius (A.D. 54) and established a house church there (cf. 1 Cor 16:19); through them Paul could have learned about some details in the church of Rome (e.g., about the problem of the strong and the weak, which they would have discovered on their return). This possible connection has to be given serious consideration, since under favorable conditions letters could be sent from Rome to Corinth in less than ten days (Pliny, *Naturalis Historia* 19.1.3–4). Also, Paul could be sending greetings to eastern convert Christians who had since moved to Rome. It is also possible that Paul could be sending greetings to people resident in Rome, but known to him only by hearsay. He would be building up a list of possible contacts for his coming visit, perhaps among people whom he met in the east and who he knows have moved to Rome. It should additionally be noted that in letters Paul sent to churches that he himself had founded and that he has known well, he sends no particular greetings; only collective greetings to addressees are found in 1 Thess 5:26; Phil 4:21; but cf. Col 4:10–17 (if one is disposed to regard Colossians as Pauline). Although it is often said that the greetings from Paul's companions are likewise collective, as in Phil 4:22; 2 Cor 13:13, individual companions are sometimes mentioned, as in 1 Cor 16:19 (Prisca and Aquila); Phlm 23–24 (Epaphras, Mark, Aristarchus, Demas, Luke). Only in Rom 16:3–16, 21–23 does one find the expansive lineup of greetings to individuals and from individuals. Moreover, if he greets Aquila and Prisca, who might be in Ephesus (1 Cor 16:19), why does he not greet others certainly known to be there: Sosthenes (1 Cor 1:1); Apollos, Stephanas, Fortunatus, Achaicus (1 Cor 16:12, 17); Epaphras, Mark, Aristarchus, Demas, or Luke (Phlm 23–24)? As for Epaenetus, nothing demands that he still be in Asia; he could well have moved to Rome, since the mobility of Asiatics to the capital of the empire is well attested (see G. La Piana, "Foreign Groups in Rome During the First Century of the Empire," *HTR* 20 [1927]: 183–403, esp. 194). Even more problematic for the Ephesian hypothesis is the way that Paul characterizes persons to whom the greetings are sent. Would people in Ephesus have to be told about Prisca and Aquila as "fellow workers of mine" (16:3), about Epaenetus as "the first convert to Christ in Asia" (16:5b), or about Timothy as Paul's "fellow worker" (16:21)? Yet this objection is not really strong, for one cannot rule out a bit of legitimate praise or flattery in such Pauline characterizations. Against the Ephesian hypothesis, some of the persons greeted might otherwise be known to have been in Rome. Rufus (16:13) may be the same as the Rufus of Mark 15:21 (i.e., on the supposition that the Marcan Gospel was composed in Italy). Aristobulus (16:10) may be the grandson of Herod the Great and son of Aristobulus IV and Bernice (J.W. 2.11.6 §221 end), and thus the brother of Herod Agrippa I, who is said to have resided in

Rome. Narcissus (16:11) may be the notorious wealthy freedman, former secretary of the emperor Claudius. Although Narcissus was no longer alive, Paul sends greetings to the Christians of his household; see the NOTES on 16:10, 11, 13. Finally, the mixture of Semitic, Latin, and Greek names in the lineup of those greeted, in use even for Jews or Jewish Christians, could well suit the metropolis of Rome as well as that of Ephesus. (On all of these arguments about persons greeted, see Gamble, *Textual History*, 47–55.)

In response to the final argument for the Ephesian destination of 16:1–23, it should be pointed out that the admonition in vv 17–20 is actually of mixed character. Its initial verb, *parakalō*, "I urge" (used elsewhere by Paul: 12:1; 15:30; 1 Cor 1:10; 4:16; 16:15; 2 Cor 2:8; 10:1; etc.), need not be understood as an authoritarian warning, as Bjerkelund (*Parakalô*) has shown. It is a fixed epistolary element, expressive of polite insistence. Moreover, v 19ab takes the edge off some of the sternness of the admonition in vv 17–18 as well as the implication of v 20a ("the God of peace will soon crush Satan under your feet"). The words *didachē* and *skandalon* are found elsewhere in the irenic discussion of Romans (6:17; 14:13; cf. 9:33; 11:9). Yet even so, the admonition remains; and its presence here, if intended for the church of Rome, has been variously explained. It could be that fresh news had been received by Paul as he was completing the writing of the letter, which prompted him to abandon the irenic tone that characterizes the rest of the letter (so Barrett, *Romans*, 284–85). Lietzmann (*An die Römer*, 127) preferred to think that Paul actually wrote this part of the letter in his own hand, as in Gal 6:11–16. That, however, is sheer speculation; Paul nowhere else gives a hint of such an action, as he does in Galatians. But no matter to what community that admonition is addressed, it remains generic and scarcely yields specific information about the problem (unsound teaching?) to which it refers. In fact, in this quality it sounds like the rest of Romans.

Finally, one must ask why a letter addressed to Ephesus would be attached to one addressed to Rome. In the case of the composite 2 Corinthians, the conflation was made of letters all addressed to the same church (see Lampe, "Roman Christians," 216).

None of the foregoing counterarguments can completely undermine those brought forth for the Ephesian hypothesis. By contrast, Gamble (*Textual History*, 57–95) has introduced a new form of argument in support of the Roman destination of 16:1–23. Having studied the style of epistolary conclusions in Hellenistic Greek letters and compared the ending of Romans with the details in such conclusions, he has marshaled strong evidence in support of the Roman destination of chap. 16 and of the original sixteen-chapter form of Romans. In Hellenistic letters one finds as elements of the epistolary conclusion the following items: (1) A final wish, expressed either in a single word (*errōsō*, "farewell," to peers and inferiors, or *eutychei*, "may you prosper," to superiors) or in an expanded sentence (e.g., *errōsthai se euchomai/boulomai*, "I pray for your health"). Such a wish was meant to be the definitive end of the letter, followed only at times by the date. (2) Greetings, sent to others associated with the addressee(s); introduced by some form of the verb *aspazesthai*, "greet" (impv. or 3d sg. indic. with a different subject). (3) A health wish, using the verb *epimelesthai*, "take care of"; this wish is found even at the beginning of a letter in some instances. (4) Date, giving the year, month, and day. (5) Concluding autograph, added in a hand different from the scribe who penned the message, sometimes intended as a mark of authenticity. (6) Postscript, not always present. Two other items are sometimes included: (7) a request for a reply, introduced by *graphe peri*, "write concerning . . ."; and (8) an admonition, often in the form *mē oun allōs poiēsēs*, "do not then do otherwise." The order of the stable elements is usually as follows:

Greetings

Health Wish

Final Wish

Date

to which is sometimes appended the concluding autograph or a postscript.

When Gamble compared these elements with what one finds in the conclusions of Pauline letters, he noted that the following elements emerge: (1) A grace-blessing, which is the Pauline form of the final wish. It includes the mention of "our Lord Jesus (Christ)" in the other six authentic letters of Paul (1 Thess 5:28; Gal 6:18; Phil 4:23; 1 Cor 16:23; 2 Cor 13:13; Phlm 25); see also 2 Thess 3:18. (2) A wish of peace, which usually precedes the grace-blessing (1 Thess 5:23; Gal 6:16; Phil 4:9b; 2 Cor 13:11); see also 2 Thess 3:16; Eph 6:23. This element may reflect Paul's Semitic background, since it is sometimes found in Aramaic letters; but it is usually related there to the opening prescript (see WA, 183–204, esp. 191–93). This wish is absent only in 1 Corinthians and Philemon (cf. Colossians). (3) Greetings, introduced by the verb *aspazesthai* (as an impv. or in the 3d sg. indic. with a different subject). This element is absent in Galatians (and in Ephesians and 1 Timothy). (4) Greeting with a holy kiss, found in three letters of Paul (1 Thess 5:26; 1 Cor 16:20b; 2 Cor 13:12), apart from Rom 16:16. (5) Autographic conclusion (1 Cor 16:21; Gal 6:11; Phlm 19); cf. 2 Thess 3:17; Col 4:18. Moreover, in some letters there are additional items like exhortations, notes about personal movements of Paul, or requests for prayers. The order of the stable elements is usually as follows:

Hortatory Remarks

Wish of Peace

Greetings (with or without the holy kiss)

Grace-blessing

The place of the autographic conclusion varies.

Because of Gamble's study one now has clearly to reckon with a formal epistolary conclusion to a Pauline letter. His study has likewise cast the destination of Romans 16 in another light. To regard 16:1–23 as a letter sent originally to Ephesus would deprive Romans of an epistolary conclusion and make it unique in the Pauline corpus. Gamble even toys with the possibility that Paul may have written 16:1–20ab in his own hand; it would be an unlabeled autographic conclusion. Then Tertius would have added 16:21–23 (and possibly even v 24, if one considers the evidence of some MSS to be strong enough). This last consideration, however, may be too speculative to be convincing.

By and large Gamble's thesis seems valid, but there are some minor details, even problems, that he has glossed over. If one takes the concluding elements in Romans 15–16 as they now stand in the best MSS, one finds the following order:

15:33	Wish of Peace
16:1–2	Recommendation for Phoebe
16:3–15	Greetings to Associates of the Addressees
16:16	Greeting with a Holy Kiss
16:17–20a	Hortatory Remarks
16:20b	Grace-blessing
16:21–23	Greetings from the Companions of Paul
(16:24	Grace-blessing)
(16:15–27	Doxology)

Although Gamble has shown that a recommendation of persons forms at times part of an epistolary conclusion of Greco-Roman letters (*Textual History*, 84–87) and even that one finds a parallel to 16:1–2 in 1 Cor 16:10–11 (the commendation of Timothy), nevertheless vv 1–2 do interrupt the stable order of the conclusion of a Pauline letter that he has sought to establish. Moreover, the hortatory remarks and the grace-blessing (16:17–20) not only depart from the stable order but also split up the greetings into two groups. Gamble himself has acknowledged some of these problems (p. 88), even setting the word "interrupted" in quotation marks (the implication of which is not clear). Nevertheless, though these minor differences should have been more clearly acknowledged, they do not seem to be serious enough to undermine the basic thrust of his thesis. He has, in other words, marshaled a strong argument, previously not considered, for regarding chap. 16 as the conclusion to the letter originally sent to the church of Rome. This is, then, a strong argument also for the unity and integrity of the sixteen-chapter form of Romans. Gamble rightly admits, however, that the letter apart from chap. 16 contains little to show that Paul personally had much concrete awareness of the problems facing the Roman community; this has a bearing on the occasion and purpose of Romans. Thus Gamble with his new arguments joins a list of commentators who have always maintained the integrity of 1:1–16:23 and the Roman destination of 16:1–23, including Althaus, Barrett, Guthrie, Kümmel, Lyonnet, and Sanday and Headlam. In this commentary I shall work with this view of the unity and integrity of Romans, abandoning the Ephesian hypothesis that I once espoused in the brief commentary on Romans in *JBC*, art. 53 §10.

There is also, however, the challenge to the unity and integrity of Romans that Schmithals and Widmann have proposed. Schmithals (*Römerbrief als historisches Problem*) would have us believe that Romans is a conflation of, mainly, two letters with insertions: letter A, Romans 1–11 (without 5:1–11) + 15:8–13, written from Ephesus early on; and letter B, Rom 12:1–15:7 (without 13:1–14) + 15:14–33; 16:21–23. Also according to Schmithals, there are many inserts in Romans 7 and 8 (7:7–25 being a "foreign body"), and 5:2–11 and 13:11–14 belong to the Thessalonian correspondence, whereas 16:1–20 recommends Phoebe to Onesiphorus in Ephesus. He maintains such a conflation because of a tension that he finds in Romans, especially between 1:14–15 and 15:20. Letter A would then have been originally addressed to Roman Gentile Christians, possibly former Godfearers, in light of the Galatian problems; they must be won over to Paul's law-free gospel, because he has been hindered from coming to Rome personally. To these same people Paul later wrote letter B, trying to persuade them to be more considerate of their fellow Christians who still clung to Jewish regulations. Schmithals denies that the Roman church had Jewish Christians, that is to say, Christians who had been ethnically and culturally Jewish. Thus Schmithals distinguishes two occasions and purposes.

That the majority of the Roman Gentile Christians came to Christianity via a connection with Judaism seems highly plausible; but that such Gentile Christians constitute Paul's sole audience is asking too much. Where would the Gentile Christians' Jewish connection have arisen? Such hacking up of Romans is arbitrary and gratuitous. This sort of interpretation of Romans is clever, but unconvincing. Minor exegetical details in the interpretation will be handled at the proper places in the NOTES.

Noting the inner contradictions of Romans 9–11 and the subject of that part of the letter, Widmann maintains that the present form of Romans stems from a redactor, who has added the concluding doxology (16:25–27) and inserted the passage on civil authorities (13:1–7). To such a redactor he also attributes the anti-Jewish verses of 1 Thess 2:15–16, and even the word "Judaism" in Gal 1:13–14, which is allegedly derived from Christian usage of the second century! In Romans Widmann distinguishes two genuine letters: the first letter to Rome (1:1–17; 3:21–4:25; 5:12–6:23; 15:14–21), the theme of which is Paul's account of his evangelization and his theology of universal grace in Christ Jesus (written in Thessalonica in the autumn of 55): to it belong only those paragraphs which fill out the theme announced in 1:16–17; and the second letter to Rome (9:1–6a; 11:1–5, 11–32; 15:22–29), the theme of which is the covenant with Israel, against a self-glorifying

Gentile church (written in Corinth in the winter of 55–56). This letter is marked by the I-sayings of "der Israelit Paulus." It was written to correct misunderstandings of the first letter. These are brief letters characteristic of the Apostle Paul. Into what is now Romans 9–11 two tractates have been inserted: 9:6b–29, written by a predestinationist "Anti-Paulus"; and 9:30–10:21; 11:7–10, a Deutero-Pauline tractate on the Failure of Israel. All of this conflation is the work, finally, of an "anti-Jewish redactor of the Pauline Corpus." (In footnote 11 Widmann claims that he cannot take up the analysis of Romans 7–8 or 12:1–15:7!) Yet this sort of analysis of Romans is no more convincing than that of Schmithals.

Finally, there is the question of smaller secondary glosses introduced into the basically authentic and unified text of Romans. These are said to be found in 1:19–21, 32; 2:1, 16, 17; 3:10–18, 24–26; 4:1, 17, 18–19; 5:1, 6–7, 17; 7:6, 25; 8:1; 9:5; 10:9, 17; 11:6; 12:11; 13:1–7; 14:6; and 16:5, 24. I shall discuss some of these problems at the proper places in the commentary, but for the overall problem that they present, consult Walker, "Text-Critical Evidence."

Short shrift, however, has to be given to the proposals of O'Neill (*Paul's Letter*), who thinks that Paul writes to "Jewish Christian synagogues" to get their support for his plan to found separate Gentile Christian congregations in Rome; he would consider 12:1–15:13 to be non-Pauline and all references to Gentile Christians (1:18–21; 11:13–24; 14:1–23) to be glosses. The same has to be said for the dissection of Romans by C. M. Mead (*Romans Dissected*).

BIBLIOGRAPHY

This list is supplemental to the bibliography on the authorship and text of Romans.

Aland, K., "Glosse, Interpolation und Komposition in der Sicht der neutestamentlichen Textkritik," *Studien zur Überlieferung des Neuen Testaments und seines Textes*, ANTF 2 (Berlin: de Gruyter, 1967), 35–57.

Bultmann, R., "Glossen im Römerbrief," *TLZ* 72 (1947): 197–202; repr. *Exegetica: Aufsätze zur Erforschung des Neuen Testaments*, ed. E. Dinkler (Tübingen: Mohr [Siebeck], 1967), 278–84.

Donfried, K. P., "A Short Note on Romans 16," *JBL* 89 (1970): 441–49; repr. *RomDeb*, 44–52.

Eichholz, G., "Der ökumenische und missionarische Horizont der Kirche: Eine exegetische Studie zu Röm. 1,8–15," *EvT* 21 (1961): 15–27.

Emmet, C. W., "Romans XV and XVI: A New Theory," *Expos* 8.11 (1916): 275–88.

Feine, P., *Die Abfassung des Philipperbriefes in Ephesus mit einer Anlage über Röm. 16,3–20 als Epheserbrief*, BFCT 20.4 (Gütersloh: Bertelsmann, 1916).

Feuillet, A., "Note complémentaire sur le dernier chapître de l'épître aux Romains (xvi, 1–24)," *RB* 57 (1950): 527–29.

Frede, H. J., *Altlateinische Paulus-Handschriften*, Vetus Latina: Die Reste der altlateinischen Bibel 4 (Freiburg im Breisgau: Herder, 1964), 152–58.

Goodspeed, E. J., "Phoebe's Letter of Introduction," *HTR* 44 (1951): 55–57.

Holtzmann, H., "Der Stand der Verhandlungen über die beiden letzten Capitel des Römerbriefes," *ZWT* 17 (1874): 504–19.

Kim, C.-H., *Form and Structure of the Familiar Greek Letter of Recommendation*, SBLDS 4 (Missoula, Mont.: Scholars, 1972).

Kinoshita, J., "Romans—Two Writings Combined: A New Interpretation of the Body of Romans," *NovT* 7 (1964–65): 258–77.

Kling, [C. F.], "Über den historischen Charakter der Apostelgeschichte und die Aechtheit der beiden letzten Kapitel des Römerbriefs, mit Beziehung auf Hrn. Dr. Baur," *TSK* 10 (1837): 290–327.

Knox, J., "A Note on the Text of Romans," *NTS* 2 (1955–56): 191–93.

Kümmel, W. G., *Introduction to the New Testament: Revised Edition* (Nashville, Tenn. and New York: Abingdon, 1975), 314–20.

Lake, K., "Shorter Form of St. Paul's Epistle to the Romans," *Expos* 7.10 (1910): 504–25.

Lampe, P., "The Roman Christians of Romans 16," *RomDeb*, 216–30.

Lightfoot, J. B., *Biblical Essays* (London: Macmillan, 1893; repr. Grand Rapids, Mich.: Baker, 1979).

Lönnermark, L.-G., "Till frågan om Romarbrevets integritet," *SEA* 33 (1968): 141–48.

Lucht, H., *Ueber die beiden letzten Kapitel des Römerbriefes: Eine kritische Untersuchung* (Berlin: Henschel, 1871).

McDonald, J. I. H., "Was Romans XVI a Separate Letter?" *NTS* 16 (1969–70): 369–72.

Mair, A., "Apologetic Argument from the Names in Romans XVI," *Expos* 4.7 (1893): 75–80.

Manson, T. W., "St. Paul's Letter to the Romans—and Others," *BJRL* 31 (1948): 224–40; repr. *RomDeb*, 3–15.

Mead, C. M. (alias E. D. McRealsham), *Romans Dissected: A Critical Analysis of the Epistle to the Romans* (Edinburgh: Clark, 1891).

Michaelis, W., "Die Teilungshypothesen bei Paulusbriefen: Briefkompositionen und ihr Sitz im Leben," *TZ* 14 (1958): 321–26.

Montgomery Hitchcock, F. R., "A Study of Romans XVI," *CQR* 121 (1935–36): 187–209.

Mowry, L., "The Early Circulation of Paul's Letters," *JBL* 63 (1944): 73–86.

Ollrog, W. H., "Die Abfassungsverhältnisse von Röm 16," *Kirche: Festschrift für Günther Bornkamm* . . . , ed. D. Lührmann and G. Strecker (Tübingen: Mohr [Siebeck], 1980), 221–44.

Pope, A. M., "The Genesis of the Roman Epistle," *Expos* 8.21 (1921): 359–65.

Refoulé, F., "A contre-courant: Romains 16,3–16," *RHPR* 70 (1990): 409–20.

Rengstorf, K.-H., "Paulus und die älteste römische Christenheit," *SE II*, TU 87 (1964), 447–64.

Schenke, H.-M., "Aporien im Römerbrief," *TLZ* 92 (1967): 881–88.

Schmithals, W., *Der Römerbrief als historisches Problem*, SNT 9 (Gütersloh: Mohn, 1975).

———, "The False Teachers of Romans 16:17–20," in *Paul & the Gnostics* (Nashville, Tenn.: Abingdon, 1972), 219–38.

Scholten, J. H., "Rom. XV en XVI: Critisch onderzoek," *TTijd* 10 (1876): 1–33.

Schulz, D., Review of the Introductions to the New Testament by J. G. Eichhorn and W. M. L. De Wette, *TSK* 2 (1829): 563–636, esp. 609–12.

Schumacher, R., *Die beiden letzten Kapitel des Römerbriefes: Ein Beitrag zu ihrer Geschichte und Erklärung*, NTAbh 14.4 (Münster in Westfalen: Aschendorff, 1929).

Straatman, J. W., "Het slot van den brief van Paulus aan de Romeinen," *TTijd* 2 (1868): 24–57.

Walker, W. O., Jr., "Text-Critical Evidence for Interpolations in the Letters of Paul," *CBQ* 50 (1988): 622–31.

Widmann, M., "Der Israelit Paulus und sein antijüdischer Redaktor: Eine literarkritische Studie zu Rom. 9–11," *"Wie gut sind deine Zelte, Jaakow . . ."*: *Festschrift . . . von Reinhold Mayer*, ed. E. L. Ehrlich and B. Klappert (Gerlingen: Bleicher, 1986), 150–58.

Young, F. M., "Romans xvi: A Suggestion," *ExpTim* 47 (1935–36): 44.

V. OCCASION AND PURPOSE

◆

If it is usually possible to distinguish the occasion and purpose of other Pauline letters (e.g., of 1 Corinthians), it is not easy in the case of Romans. At first sight, one might think that the distinction would be obvious, because in 1:10–15 and 15:14–33 Paul clearly mentions details about himself and his plans that explain the background and the occasion of the writing of this letter. These sections are so different from the rest of Romans (1:16–15:13—prescinding from the opening prescript and the thanksgiving) that they have given rise over the centuries to a variety of views about the purpose of Romans.

The debate has included questions about whether Romans is a letter or an epistle. The distinction between these forms of writing was made in the early part of this century by Deissmann: "A letter is something non-literary, a means of communication between persons who are separated from each other. Confidential and personal in its nature, it is intended only for the person or persons to whom it is addressed, and not at all for the public or any kind of publicity" (LAE, 218). Its tone, style, and form could be as intimate, free, or familiar as conversation itself. But "An epistle is an artistic literary form, just like the dialogue, the oration, or the drama. It has nothing in common with the letter except its form: apart from that one might venture the paradox that the epistle is the opposite of a real letter. The contents of an epistle are intended for publicity—they aim at interesting 'the public' " (ibid., 220).

Although the Pauline writings form a corpus today, which have often been given the title "epistles," it is far from certain that they were originally intended as such by their author, and this title for Romans in particular has often been queried. Moreover, Deissmann's distinction has in recent times been considered too rigid. Yet this is not the place to engage in a lengthy discussion of forms of epistolary writing (see W. G. Doty, Letters; H. Rahn, Morphologie; H. Cancick, Untersuchungen). In the case of Romans the relation of the occasion to the purpose of the writing is precisely why modern commentators think that it is difficult to decide whether it should be called a "letter" or an "epistle" (in Deissmann's sense). Recently, Stirewalt ("Form and Function") has studied fifteen ancient writings (2 Maccabees, letters of Epicurus, of Dionysius of Halicarnassus, selections from Plutarch, and the Martyrdom of Polycarp) and has shown that in antiquity there was a "Greek letter-essay" that was losing some of the form, phraseology, and structure of the letter proper and acquiring some of the more impersonal style of a monograph. It was destined for particular addressees and treated a specific topic, but it was intended to be read by others than the addressees. This description suits Romans rather well in my opinion, even though I should prefer to label it an "essay-letter," to put stress on its missive character, an aspect that the German term "Lehrbrief" (didactic letter) may better express. But, in reality, does such a description of Stirewalt really improve on Deissmann's definition of an "epistle"? Stirewalt has supplied, indeed, the concrete ancient examples that document Deissmann's definition. Similarly, Jewett's description of Romans as an "ambassadorial letter" is of little help, as Wedderburn has noted (*Reasons*, 9–10).

When one analyzes the contents of Romans as a whole, one notes that there are two sets of features in it that have to be considered when one speaks of the occasion and purpose of this letter. On the one hand, there is the material that tells of Paul's plans; on the other, in the didactic material there are echoes of themes and phrases that Paul has treated in earlier writings (1 Thessalonians, Galatians, Philippians, 1–2 Corinthians). These echoes form part of both the doctrinal and the hortatory sections of Romans. They raise, moreover, the question why Paul wrote such a complicated letter to the Christians of Rome, whom he was planning to visit soon for the first time, a community not founded by him, and one about which he seems to know so little in concrete detail.

When one analyzes the first set of features, the sections in which Paul gives news about his plans (1:10–15; 15:14–33), one learns the following things about his personal apostolic ministry, that is, what ostensibly seems to be the occasion of Romans:

1. Paul's prayerful wish and longstanding proposal to come to the community in Rome, a visit hindered up to now;

2. his desire to evangelize them, or better, as he puts it more diplomatically, to share the Christian life of faith mutually with them; and

3. his indebtedness to Jews and Greeks elsewhere, to the wise and unlearned.

These first three details from 1:10–15 are somewhat vague, but they become more specific when his plans are more concretely formulated in 15:14–33, where he continues:

4. he is conscious that his ministry to Gentiles includes even such Christians as those at Rome;

5. his ministry among Gentiles in the eastern Mediterranean area has come

to a term; he has preached the gospel of Christ from Jerusalem around to Illyricum;

6. this extensive eastern ministry has thus far prevented him coming to Rome;

7. his policy, moreover, has been not to evangelize people among whom other Christian missionaries have labored;

8. he now looks forward to his coming to the Christian community in Rome itself, before he goes on to the west, to Spain;

9. he wants to enjoy life with them there before they speed him on his way westward;

10. but first he must carry to the poor of God's dedicated people in Jerusalem the collection taken up for them among the Christians of Macedonia and Achaia, who have thus acknowledged their debt to the people of the Christian matrix; and

11. he is aware that he may encounter a hostile reaction to himself in Jerusalem on the part of two groups, "unbelievers in Judea" and the dedicated people of God themselves, who may misunderstand his intentions; so he asks the Romans for prayers that his journey to Jerusalem be successful.

Why was Paul eager to go to Spain, having finished his evangelization of the eastern Mediterranean area? He knew that the church was already founded in Rome itself; so part of the western Mediterranean area was acquainted with the Christian gospel. But Spain probably had not yet been evangelized. (Certainly, nothing in Romans suggests that Paul knew that Spain had been evangelized by James, son of Zebedee, who was put to death by Herod Agrippa in A.D. 44 [Acts 12:1-2]. An ancient legendary tradition, dating from about the seventh century, ascribes the evangelization of Spain to this James.) At this time in Spain there was Latin literary brilliance. Martial, the epigrammatist, was born there (A.D. 40–104), as was Lucan, the epic poet (A.D. 39–65). There too lived at this time Columella, a farmer and writer on agricultural matters, and Pomponius Mela, the geographer. Quintilian (ca. A.D. 30–100), the illustrious orator and rhetorician, was a Spaniard, as was Lucius Annaeus Seneca (ca. 4 B.C.–A.D. 65), the philosopher, dramatist, and Nero's prime minister. Such persons would have enhanced the reputation of Spain, and it would have been natural for Paul the Apostle to think of going there to spread the gospel to Gentiles of that area, as he proposes in 15:24.

From such details in Romans one gets a clear idea of the occasion or the background of the writing. But the occasion then gives rise to the question of why Paul wrote such a complicated letter on such an abstruse topic as justification or salvation by faith to a community that he himself had not yet evangelized or founded.

For this reason also some commentators have thought that Romans was originally written as a general letter or an encyclical, not originally intended to be sent specifically to the Christians of Rome. To such commentators its dispatch to Rome came as an afterthought (see section IV above). Yet such an explanation seems hardly adequate.

The other set of features in Romans also has to be considered, namely, the echoes of themes and phrases from earlier Pauline writings. In the following list I have drawn inspiration from Bornkamm ("The Letter," 25–27), who listed sixteen key phrases, which have been expanded in my list. It reveals that Paul has been reflecting on his own preaching of the gospel of justification and salvation through faith in Christ Jesus during his ministry in Asia, Macedonia, and Achaia. These echoes are what gives the reader of Romans the impression that it might be a general or encyclical letter, an essay-letter.

1:1–7	Paul's grace of apostleship	Gal 1:1, 11–17; Phil 3:4–21
	Among all of the Gentiles	1 Cor 9:1; 2 Cor passim
1:16–17	Salvation by faith and the revelation of God's uprightness	Gal 2:15–21; Phil 3:9; 2 Cor 5:21
1:18–3:20	The bondage of all human beings	Gal 3:23–4:7; 4:8–11
1:18	God's wrath revealed	1 Thess 1:9b–10
1:19–20	God's self-manifestation	1 Cor 1:21
3:21–31	Justification by faith, apart from deeds of the law	Gal 2:15–21
4:1–23	Abraham, the model of Christian faith	Gal 3:6–9, 14–18, 19; 4:21–31
4:17	The power of the Creator God	1 Cor 1:28; 2 Cor 4:6
4:24–25	The Lord put to death for our trespasses, raised for our justification	2 Cor 5:15; Gal 2:19–21
5:1–11	God has reconciled us to himself through Christ Jesus	2 Cor 5:18–19
5:12–21	The antithetical typology of Adam and Christ	1 Cor 15:21, 45
5:20	The law made its entrance to increase trespasses	Gal 3:19
6:1–11	Freedom from sin and self through baptism	Gal 3:27
6:14	You are not under law, but under grace	Gal 5:18
7:4	You have died to the law through Christ, to be raised from the dead	Gal 2:19–20; 2 Cor 5:15

71

7:5, 24	Death, sin, and the law	1 Cor 15:56
7:25; 8:1–2	Through Christ one is freed from the law, sin, and death	1 Cor 15:57
8:2	Freed through the Spirit	2 Cor 3:17
8:3	The Father sent his Son	Gal 4:4
8:3	The Son in the likeness of sinful flesh	Phil 2:7
8:9	God's Spirit dwells in you	1 Cor 3:16
8:10	Christ is in you	Gal 2:20; 2 Cor 13:5
8:11	He who raised Christ from the dead will give life to your mortal bodies	1 Cor 6:14
8:14	Those who are led by the Spirit	Gal 5:18
8:14–15	Adoptive sonship, "Abba, Father"	Gal 4:5–6
8:18	Suffering at the present time is a preparation for glory	2 Cor 4:17
8:23	The Spirit as firstfruits	2 Cor 1:22; 5:5
8:23	We groan awaiting the redemption of our bodies	2 Cor 5:2, 4
8:28	All things work together for good of those who love God	1 Cor 2:9
9:3–4	My brothers, my kinsmen by descent, Israelites	2 Cor 11:22
9:23	The riches of his glory	Phil 4:19
10:3	Their own uprightness	Phil 3:9
10:9	Jesus is Lord	1 Cor 12:3; 2 Cor 4:5
10:12	No distinction between Jew and Greek	Gal 3:28
10:17	Faith comes from what is heard	Gal 3:2, 5
11:1	I am an Israelite, a descendant of Abraham, of Benjamin's tribe	2 Cor 11:22; Phil 3:5
11:14	I may save some of them	1 Cor 9:22
11:15	Reconciliation of the world	2 Cor 5:19
11:20	Standing in faith	1 Cor 16:13
11:32	God has imprisoned all people in disobedience	Gal 3:22
11:34	The use of Isa 40:13	1 Cor 2:16
	Many members in one body	1 Cor 12:4–30
12:6	Gifts that differ according to the grace given	1 Cor 12:25
12:9–13	The role of love	1 Cor 13:1–13

12:17	Repay no one evil for evil	1 Thess 5:15
13:9	The law summed up in Lev 19:18	Gal 5:14
13:11–14	Vigilance for the endtime	1 Thess 5:1–11; 1 Cor 15:51–54; cf. 7:29–31
13:14	Put on rather the Lord Jesus	Gal 3:27
14:1–15:13	The strong should be guided by love toward the weak	1 Corinthians 8–10
14:2–3	Scruples about food	1 Cor 10:25–27
14:6	Scruples about days	Gal 4:10
14:8	We live for the Lord	Gal 2:20; 1 Cor 3:23
14:11	Quotation of Isa 45:23	Phil 2:10–11
14:13	Put no obstacle or stumbling block in your brother's way	1 Cor 8:9, 13
14:15	Your brother is one for whom Christ died	1 Cor 8:11
14:17	What the kingdom of God is not	1 Cor 4:20
14:21	Abstention from meat and wine	1 Cor 8:13
15:4	What was written in the OT was written for us	1 Cor 10:1
15:5	God as the source of encouragement	2 Cor 1:3
15:7	Welcome one another as Christ welcomed you	Phlm 17
15:20	Paul's nonintervention	2 Cor 10:15–16; cf. 1 Cor 3:10
15:25	Collection for the poor in Jerusalem	1 Cor 16:1–4; 2 Cor 8:1–6; 9:1–2
15:33	Peace-blessing	1 Thess 5:23; Phil 4:9b; 2 Cor 13:11
16:16	Holy-kiss greeting	1 Cor 16:20; 2 Cor 13:12
16:20b	Grace-blessing	1 Thess 5:28; 1 Cor 16:23

This list of corresponding themes and phrases, extensive though it is, should not be misunderstood. It is not meant that Paul always used the identical language or used the phrase in the same kind of context in which it appears in Romans. But it does reveal the extent to which echoes are found in Romans of details in earlier letters. In this sense it reveals that Romans is an irenic discussion of many of the topics that Paul had written about earlier, often in a more polemical or apologetic tone. For the one thing that Romans is not is a polemical or apologetic writing. It is, for example, quite different from Galatians, which treats much of the same doctrine, but is clearly polemical.

Late medieval, Renaissance, and Reformation writers often characterized Romans as a doctrinal or dogmatic treatise. Thus it was called by Philipp Melanchthon "a summary of all Christian doctrine" ("caput et summa universae doctrinae christianae," *Dispositio orationis in ep. ad Rom. Philippi Melanthonis opera quae supersunt*, ed. C. G. Bretschneider, 28 vols. [Halle: Schwetschke, 1834–60], 15.445; cf. *Comm. in ep. Pauli ad Romanos [anno 1532]*, ibid., 15.495: "continet enim praecipuos et proprios locos doctrinae christianae"; "doctrinae christianae compendium," *Loci communes, 1521*, Werke in Auswahl 2.1, ed. R. Stupperich [Gütersloh: Bertelsmann, 1952], 7). Such a characterization of Romans has often been repeated in modern times: for instance, "the apostle's dogmatic and moral catechism" (Godet); a theological treatise to instruct the Christians of Rome in the central principles of the faith (B. Weiss); the theological self-confession of Paul (Kümmel). It persists in a more sophisticated way in the view of Bornkamm, who writes, "This great document, which summarizes and develops the most important themes and thoughts of the Pauline message and theology and which elevates his theology above the moment of definite situations and conflicts into the sphere of the eternally and universally valid, this letter to the Romans is the last will and testament of the Apostle Paul" ("The Letter," 31; cf. *Paul*, 88–96). This view is also espoused by Wilckens, *Römer*, 47–48.

Even if one were to admit that Romans is Paul's "last will and testament," such a view of Romans gives rise to many difficulties. First, it does not adequately explain chaps. 14–15. Second, noteworthy elements of Pauline theology are absent from Romans, so that it is scarcely a summary of Christian doctrine or even a summary of Pauline theology. Elements of the Apostle's doctrine that are absent include (1) Ecclesiology: there is no teaching about *ekklēsia*, "church," in Romans. Although the word occurs in 16:1, 4, 5, 16, and 23, it has the sense only of a local or house church; it does not appear in chaps. 1–15. Moreover, even in 12:3–8, where Paul speaks of Christians forming "one body in Christ," no mention is made of the community as "church." (2) Eucharist: there is not a hint of it. (3) Eschatology: apart from the isolated remarks about Christians being judged before God's tribunal (2:5–11) or the vigilance required before the end time (13:11–14), there is little about the *eschaton* and nothing about the parousia; cf. 14:10–12.

The break with this sort of interpretation of Romans came with F. C. Baur in 1836, who insisted that this letter had to be interpreted according to the historical circumstances in which Paul wrote it as well as the historical situation of the Roman community at that time, thus shifting the emphasis away from the dogmatic mode. There are diverse ways of formulating the differences in these basic approaches to Romans and to the purpose of its composition. Those who espoused the so-called dogmatic view of Romans tended to insist that Paul wrote the letter for himself, hoping to encapsulate what had been the main thrust of his preaching up to this point, when a new phase in his ministry was about to begin.

Indeed, it was thought that the occasion and purpose of Romans was to be sought with Paul himself. Such a view was easily adapted to the idea that Romans was a general or encyclical letter (in T. W. Manson's sense). This view of Romans also lay behind those who insisted that it was an epistle (in Deissmann's sense).

But it has always encountered the difficulties that Baur originally pointed out. All of Paul's other letters are regarded as ad hoc compositions. That there is a difference in the case of Romans has not been proved; in fact, it has resulted in a failure to take seriously some of the details in the sections that speak of the Apostle's plans. Paul did not write Romans as a monologue. The recent modern respect for Baur's contention has resulted in an interpretation of Romans that has consequently introduced some of the occasion into the discussion of the purpose itself. Much of the "Romans debate" of recent times has been precisely devoted to this aspect of the interpretation of Romans.

Thus Dodd has emphasized Romans as a letter of introduction, which also reckons with the worldwide outreach of the gospel; Paul is indebted to all and plans to visit Rome en route to Spain. Yet such an interpretation does not sufficiently explain why Paul explains his gospel so elaborately. Would Paul have been so unfamiliar to Christians of Rome that he would have to give them a sample of his gospel? Again, his plan to visit Rome is only subordinate to his plan to evangelize Spain. As a letter of introduction, Romans is not adequately explained.

One also has to take seriously Paul's concern about Jerusalem and the reactions that he was likely to encounter there, a reaction from Jews who knew of him as a former Pharisee, a persecutor of the Christian church, and now as an apostate; but also a reaction from the "poor" among the Jewish Christians in Jerusalem, who might have been inclined to misinterpret his gesture. In saying so, however, I do not think with Fuchs (*Hermeneutik*, 191) that Jerusalem was actually the "secret addressee of Romans." That is going too far. Nor is it simply to be regarded as "a brief drawn up by Paul in anticipation of the renewed necessity of defending his gospel in Jerusalem" (Suggs, "The Word," 295; similarly Jervell, "The Letter to Jerusalem"). These possible Jerusalemite reactions lurk in the background of the letter and undoubtedly made Paul write in part as he did in chap. 15, but the Jerusalem connection does not adequately explain the historical situation that led to the writing of Romans as a whole, to addressing it to Rome, or to seeking to handle the problem of the "weak" and the "strong" in Rome. After all, Paul does implicitly side with the "strong" (15:1); for him "the kingdom of God is not eating and drinking" (14:17). Also, his use of the figure of the olive branches and his counsel against smugness destined for Gentile Christian readers hardly suits the Jerusalem connection.

Moreover, one has to take into account Paul's desire to preach the gospel in Rome, especially to the Christians of Gentile background there. He considers them to be part of the apostolate given to him. If he diplomatically rephrases his relation to them in 1:12 ("or rather that we may be mutually encouraged by each other's faith, both yours and mine"), he does repeat at the end of the paragraph his "eagerness to preach the gospel also to you who are in Rome" (1:15). Again, in saying as much, I do not agree with Klein ("Paul's Purpose," 46–48) that Paul regarded Christianity in Rome as a church not yet properly founded, as still in need of "apostolic foundation," and hence not *ekklēsia*, a term he never uses in reference to it. As Donfried has pointed out, that view has little exegetical basis, stands in conflict with 15:14, and was scarcely a situation that Paul could have remedied merely in passing through Rome on his way to Spain. Moreover, Paul clearly regards the Romans to whom he writes as full Christians. He recognizes that the Roman Christians are full of knowledge, capable of instructing one another, and having a faith that is widely acclaimed. That there is division among them Paul realizes and seeks to remedy. Again, Klein's view implicitly ascribes to Paul a rather officious sense of his apostolic authority, undetected elsewhere in his writings.

Klein is right, however, in pointing out that Paul regards the Christians of Rome as predominantly of Gentile background (1:5–6, 13; 15:15–16); but they are also Gentile Christians related to and aware of a Jewish Christianity stemming from Jerusalem. And there were also Jewish Christians from Jerusalem among them. Klein is also right in saying that there is a real tension between Paul's policy of nonintervention in the field in which other Christian missionaries have labored (15:20) and his eagerness to preach the gospel in Rome itself (1:15), a tension pointed out long ago by Sanday and Headlam (*Romans*, 409–10). Klein also refers to 1 Cor 3:10, but that very verse reveals that Paul himself could be viewing his preaching of the gospel in Rome as "building" on the foundation laid by someone else. If, in the case a community that he had apostolically founded, Paul could recognize Apollos's work in Corinth as the "watering" of what he had "planted" (1 Cor 3:6), the Romans could indeed be to Paul both Christian "brothers" (1:13; 7:1, 4; 8:12; 10:1; 11:25; 12:1; 15:14, 30; 16:17) and objects of his "watering."

Further, one might well ask with Donfried whether 15:20 is not so much a statement of Pauline policy as an apology to the Romans for taking so long to come to them, citizens of the capital of the Roman world. One must also recall that there is no real evidence that Roman Christianity has come into being under the influence of any one missionary prior to Paul's writing his essay-letter to them. How Christianity first came to Rome remains a mystery; perhaps not even Paul was aware who first brought it there.

One must also reckon with the importance of chaps. 9–11 in the letter. This part of Romans has often been neglected or treated as a digression or a foreign body. Yet even if Romans is not wholly concerned with the problem of the Jews' relation to the gospel and perhaps it is not even the core of Romans, as Leenhardt (*Romans*, 20) maintains, it is nevertheless a crucial concern of Paul. Indeed, it forms the climax of his doctrinal discussion.

Marxsen (*Introduction*, 92–104) has come closer than most recent commentators to a viable interpretation of the occasion and purpose of Romans in his discussion of the situation of the church in Rome at the time that Paul wrote. He finds Michel's description of the purpose of Romans a good starting point: "What we have in the letter to the Romans is the exegetical demonstration that Paul's preaching confronts both Judaism and paganism in the proper way with the truth of the Gospel" (*Brief an die Römer*, 31). Yet this is not done in a polemical way as in Galatians, where Paul deals with the problem of Gentile Christianity affected by judaizers. That was also a problem for Paul in Jerusalem at the time of the so-called Council, but it is not the contemporary situation in Rome. Giving more recognition to the hortatory section of Romans than most modern commentators, Marxsen thinks that the problem of the "strong" and the "weak" (14:1–15:13) is connected with that of Gentile and Jewish converts; the "strong" are the Roman Christians of Gentile background (among whom former Godfearers would be numbered), and the "weak" are Jewish Christians. The contrast of Jew and Greek runs through Paul's essay-letter and is especially confronted in chaps. 9–11, where the consequences of his doctrine about justification by grace through faith are treated. Now in chaps. 14–15, however, it is rather the contrast between Jewish Christians and Gentile Christians. It is not a question of Jewish Christians trying to impose Jewish customs on the rest; there was no Jewish prohibition of eating meat or drinking wine. That such an issue now emerges reveals that it was no longer the judaizing problem of old being addressed.

Marxsen builds on this foundation and seeks to explain the specific situation in the Roman church in terms of the edict of Claudius, reported by Suetonius, who "expelled from Rome Jews who were making constant disturbances at the instigation of Chrestus," that is to say, Christus (see section I above). The disturbances would have arisen in Jewish congregations of Rome as the result of the intrusion of Christian elements. In other words, it developed into a conflict between Jews and Jewish Christians about whether Jesus was the Messiah, so Jewish Christians had to leave Rome as well as Jews (the arrival of the Christians Prisca and Aquila in Corinth is evidence of this expulsion, Acts 18:1–2). As a result, the Christian community that remained would have been largely of Gentile background (see Brown, *Antioch*, 109). Such a community would have tended to develop more freely and along lines different from those which stemmed from synagogue existence. After Claudius's death in 54, a relaxation of the ban seems to have taken place, and under Nero, whose wife Poppaea Sabina is said to have been favorably disposed toward Judaism, Jews and Jewish Christians would have returned to Rome. The latter would have found a Christian community of a sort different from what had existed there earlier, which would have again given rise to conflict—but conflict no longer of the judaizing sort that vexed the churches of Galatia or of the sort between Jews and Jewish Christians in the time of Claudius. It now became a conflict between Christians of different backgrounds. The "strong" among them would have been those of Gentile background, no longer concerned about dietary or calendaric regulations, over which the "weak," those of Jewish background and closely related to Jerusalem Jewish Christians, still had concern. Paul exhorts all of these Christians of Rome to the proper exercise of love for one another and of care not to be critical of those who differed in their convictions about such things as dietary and calendaric regulations, even as he urged on all of them his understanding of the law-free gospel. He begs them all to pray for him in view of the visit to be made to Jerusalem, where he expects to encounter other Jewish and Jewish Christian reactions to himself. If this suggestion has any validity, then it reveals that Romans as a letter is concerned with a genuine Roman problem, one akin to the problems that faced Paul in his earlier eastern ministry, yet a problem that was different and had its own character. It would explain as well why Paul writes a basically irenic essay-letter to this community that he has still to visit for the first time and that he addresses only in generic terms. So I prefer to adopt and adapt Marxsen's interpretation.

Despite Marxsen's suggestion that the "strong" and the "weak" may be explained in terms of Gentile and Jewish Christian elements in the community of Rome, it has to be recalled that Paul's discussion is lean on specific problems that confront that community. This is undoubtedly the reason why he thinks mainly in terms of Gentile Christians and why the hortatory section is partly addressed (14:1–15:13) vaguely to the "strong" and the "weak." An objection could be addressed to Marxsen's thesis: if Paul were aware of the strife between Jewish and Gentile Christians in Rome, why did he not address that problem more specifically, instead of using merely the vague terms, the "strong" and the "weak"?

According to Paul's thesis, all human beings need the gospel, for all are under sin. "Paul is obviously arguing here in the light of his Jerusalem experiences. His arguments are directed against those who even as Christians still see their real guarantee of salvation in their having been Jews, in their circumcision. The same could have been said as regards Jerusalem at least until the Apostolic Council took place, although perhaps not thought out to the same extent, as circumcision was still taken for granted there" (Marxsen, *Introduction*, 102). Paul does not want the weak at Rome to live like the strong, but he advocates a principle of charity that he had invoked in his dealings with the church of Corinth earlier. Minear *(The Obedience)* has argued in a way similar to Marxsen, but he has made the hortatory section of Romans too dominant in the letter. His interpretation sounds like the tail wagging the dog. For Karris has rightly stressed that Paul's paraenesis in Romans still remains generic, built up mostly on what he had been recommending in the eastern Mediterranean area on the basis of problems encountered earlier ("Romans 14:1–15:13"). Moreover, Minear seriously fails to reckon with chaps. 9–11.

Furthermore, it is not impossible that Paul included his advice about the relation of Christians to civil authorities and about paying taxes in 13:1–7 precisely because he was aware of Nero's reactions to the cupidity of the *publicani* throughout the empire (see section I above). Nero's decision was made in the year 58; it is not possible to say that Paul yet knew of that decision, as he wrote Romans. But he may well have realized the general situation regarding taxation and the *publicani* in the empire, so it may be another example of how Paul has reacted in this letter to the ad hoc situation of Roman Christians.

Paul alone writes Romans; there is no cosender, as in some other Pauline letters. He writes the essay-letter to introduce himself to the Roman Christians, who are mostly unknown to him personally, and sets forth in it his view of the gospel, which he has been preaching in the east, and his reflections upon it, hoping that it will aid the lives of Roman Christians as well, as indeed his coming visit is intended to do. But as Käsemann well recognizes (*Commentary*, 405), "The real problem of the text and therewith the purpose of writing it lies in the combination of Rome, Jerusalem, and Spain, and, if the importance of the last two factors is sufficiently recognized, in the mediating function of Rome." An adequate explanation of the purpose and occasion of Romans has to cope with six factors: (1) the letter form of the writing, its epistolary characteristics; (2) the body of the letter, its doctrinal and hortatory parts; (3) the viewpoint and concrete situation of Paul, the writer; (4) the concrete situation of the Roman community, to which he writes; (5) Paul's attempt to cope with Jewish criticisms of his doctrine; and (6) the fact that Paul speaks at times to Christians of Gentile background (see Wedderburn, *Reasons*, 5).

Hence Paul writes Romans for ad hoc purposes: a letter to introduce himself to the Roman community, to seek support and aid from it for his projected trip to Spain, to ask for prayers and perhaps intercession of the Roman Christians with their colleagues in Jerusalem, so that, when he goes there with the collection, he will be rightly welcomed. But he also writes to handle some concrete problems in the Roman community, about which he has learned, especially about its divided nature. Recognizing that chap. 16 is an integral part of the letter, we see that Paul is also addressing to Christians of the capital of the Roman Empire an elaborate document, in which he propounds his understanding of the gospel not only to get across to them his important missionary reflections on it, which have emerged in his evangelization of the eastern Mediterranean, but also to win support for it from the Roman Christian community, with its traditional links with the Jewish Christian church of Jerusalem, hoping to overcome any mistrust of him that the Jerusalem community might be harboring because of his gospel of justification without the deeds of the law. He writes as an evangelist and a missionary, seeking too to build up the Roman community by his reflections on the gospel of God about Christ Jesus and the new mode of justification and salvation that Jesus brought to all human beings, Jews and Greeks alike. He writes thus to a community that he considers to be predominantly Gentile Christian, but which contains important Jewish Christians; he regards the whole community as particularly close to Jerusalem's church. Paul's letter is not an abstract, dogmatic treatise or a dialogue with Jews who do not accept his gospel; it is rather a didactic and hortatory letter, intended for discussion by the Jewish and Gentile Christians of Rome, for their understanding and for their conduct.

This last element is all-important in explaining why Paul has written Romans as he has. Though he knows of a division existing between Roman Christians, between the "strong" and the "weak," he stresses through the letter the equality of Jew and Greek: "all . . . are under the power of sin" (3:9; cf. 3:19–20); all "who call upon the name of the Lord shall be saved" (10:13). It is for this reason that Paul presents Abraham as "the father of all who believe" (4:11). Paul also accords a priority to the Jews with regard to the gospel (1:16; 2:9–10, 28–29; 3:9), not on an ethnic basis but on a religious one, for he recognizes the prerogatives of Israel (3:1–2; 9:4–5), that God's promises to it are irrevocable (11:29). Into the stock of Israel Gentiles have been grafted (11:18–19). Indeed, chaps. 9–11 are mostly addressed to the Gentile Christians of Rome, to explain to them the problem of Israel and its place in the new economy brought by Christ Jesus, and how they have rightfully come into membership in Israel, the people of God. No explanation of the occasion and purposes of Romans can be given without reckoning with the place that these chapters have in this writing. They are not merely an afterthought, as they have been treated by Bultmann, Dodd, Sanday and Headlam, and others. They are part of the one gospel about which Paul writes to the divided Christians of Rome, the gospel of which he is not ashamed (1:16). Hence his purposes in writing Romans have been multiple.

BIBLIOGRAPHY

This list is supplemental to the bibliography on the unity and integrity of Romans.

Aune, D. E., "Romans as a *Logos Protreptikos*," *RomDeb*, 278–96; fuller form in *Paulus und das antike Judentum*, WUNT 58, ed. M. Hengel and U. Heckel (Tübingen: Mohr [Siebeck], 1991), 91–124.

Barnikol, E., *Römer 15: Letzte Reiseziele des Paulus Jerusalem, Rom und Antiochien: Voruntersuchung zur Entstehung des sogenannten Römerbriefes* (Kiel: W. G. Mühlau, 1931).

———, *Spanienreise und Römerbrief* (Halle an der Saale: Akademischer-Verlag, 1934).

Bartsch, H.-W., "Die antisemitischen Gegner des Paulus im Römerbrief," *Antijudaismus im Neuen Testament? Exegetische und systematische Beiträge*, Abhandlungen zum christlich-judischen Dialog 2, ed. W. P. Eckert et al. (Munich: Kaiser, 1967), 27–43.

———, "Die Empfänger des Römerbriefes," *ST* 25 (1971): 81–89.

———, "Die historische Situation des Römerbriefes," *SE IV*, TU 102 (1968), 281–91; *ComViat* 8 (1965): 199–208; "The Historical Situation of Romans," *Encounter* 33 (1972): 329–39.

———, "Paulus und die Juden: Zur Auslegung des Römerbriefes," *Kirche in der Zeit* 20 (1965): 210–20.

Baur, F. C., "Ueber Zweck und Gedankengang des Römerbriefes, nebst der Erörterung einiger paulinischer Begriffe, mit besonderer Rücksicht auf die Commentare von Tholuck und Philippi," *Theologische Jahrbücher* 16 (1857): 60–108, 184–209.

——, "Ueber Zweck und Veranlassung des Römerbriefs und die damit zusammenhängenden Verhältnisse der römischen Gemeinde: Eine historisch-kritische Untersuchung," *Tübinger Zeitschrift für Theologie* (1836): Heft 3.59–178.

Boman, T., "Die dreifache Würde des Völkerapostels," *ST* 29 (1975): 63–69.

Bornkamm, G., "The Letter to the Romans as Paul's Last Will and Testament," *AusBR* 11 (1963–64): 2–14; repr. *RomDeb*, 16–28.

Borse, U., "Die geschichtliche und theologische Einordnung des Römerbriefes," *BZ* 16 (1972): 70–83.

Bruce, F. F., "The Romans Debate—Continued," *BJRL* 64 (1981–82): 334–59; repr. *RomDeb*, 175–94.

Burney, R. S., "The Purpose of Romans and the Central Theme of the Preaching of Paul," *African Journal of Biblical Studies* (Nigeria) 1 (1986): 136–47.

Campbell, W. S., "Paul's Missionary Practice and Policy in Romans," *IBS* 12 (1990): 2–25; repr. *Paul's Gospel*, 81–97.

——, "Revisiting Romans," *Scripture Bulletin* 12 (1981–82): 2–10.

——, "The Romans Debate," *JSNT* 10 (1981): 19–28.

——, "Romans III as a Key to the Thought and Structure of the Letter," *NovT* 23 (1981): 22–40; repr. *Paul's Gospel*, 25–42; *RomDeb*, 251–64.

——, "Why Did Paul Write Romans?" *ExpTim* 85 (1973–74): 264–69; repr. *Paul's Gospel*, 14–24.

Cancick, H., *Untersuchungen zu Senecas Epistulae Morales*, Spudasmata 18 (Hildesheim: Olms, 1967).

Crafton, J. A., "Paul's Rhetorical Vision and the Purpose of Romans: Toward a New Understanding," *NovT* 32 (1990): 317–39.

Donfried, K. P., "False Presuppositions in the Study of Romans," *CBQ* 36 (1974): 332–55; repr. *RomDeb*, 102–25.

—— (ed.), *The Romans Debate* (Minneapolis, Minn.: Augsburg, 1977); *The Romans Debate: Revised and Expanded Edition* (Peabody, Mass.: Henrickson, 1991 [hereafter cited as *RomDeb*; all references are to the revised edition]).

——, "The Nature and Scope of the Romans Debate," *Romans Debate* (1977), ix–xvii; repr. *RomDeb*, xli–xlvii.

——, "The Romans Debate since 1977," *RomDeb*, xlix–lxxii.

——, "A Short Note on Romans 16," *JBL* 89 (1970): 441–49; repr. *RomDeb*, 44–52.

Doty, W. G., *Letters in Primitive Christianity* (Philadelphia, Penn.: Fortress, 1973).

Drane, J. W., "Why Did Paul Write Romans?" *Pauline Studies: Essays Presented to Professor F. F. Bruce . . .*, ed. D. A. Hagner and M. J. Harris (Exeter, UK: Paternoster; Grand Rapids, Mich.: Eerdmans, 1980), 208–27.

Drummond, J., "Occasion and Object of the Epistle to the Romans," *HibJ* 11 (1912–13): 787–804.

Dunn, J. D. G., "The Formal and Theological Coherence of Romans," *Romans*, lix–lxiii; repr. *RomDeb*, 245–50.

———, "The New Perspective on Paul: Paul and the Law," *Romans* lxiv–lxxii; repr. *RomDeb*, 299–308.

Elliott, N., *The Rhetoric of Romans: Argumentative Constraint and Strategy and Paul's Dialogue with Judaism*, JSNTSup 45 (Sheffield, UK: Sheffield Academic Press, 1990).

Etzold, O., "Von der kirchenbauenden Kraft der Rechtfertigung: Ein Blick auf das Ziel des Römerbriefes," *Beth-El* 25 (1963): 145–53.

Fuchs, E., *Hermeneutik*, 3d ed. (Bad Cannstatt: Müllerschön, 1963).

Gaston, L., "Israel's Misstep in the Eyes of Paul," *Paul and the Torah* (Vancouver: University of British Columbia, 1987), 135–50; repr. *RomDeb*, 309–26.

Genuyt, F., "L'Épître aux Romains: Les Intentions du voyageur, clef de lecture de la lettre," *Sémiotique et Bible* 35 (1984): 12–22.

Grafe, E., *Über Veranlassung und Zweck des Römerbriefes* (Freiburg im Breisgau and Tübingen: Mohr [Siebeck], [1881]).

Guerra, A. J., "Romans: Paul's Purpose and Audience with Special Attention to Romans 9–11," *RB* 97 (1990): 219–37.

Haacker, K., "Exegetische Probleme des Römerbriefs," *NovT* 20 (1978): 1–21.

Harder, G., "Der konkrete Anlass des Römerbriefes," *Theologia viatorum* 6 (1954–58): 13–24.

Jervell, J., "Der Brief nach Jerusalem: Über Veranlassung und Adresse des Römerbriefes," *ST* 25 (1971): 61–73; "The Letter to Jerusalem," repr. *RomDeb*, 53–64.

Jervis, L. A., *The Purpose of Romans: A Comparative Letter Structure Investigation*, JSNTSup 55 (Sheffield, UK: Academic Press, 1991).

Jewett, R., "Following the Argument of Romans," *WW* 6 (1986): 382–89; adapted and expanded, *RomDeb*, 265–77.

———, "Romans as an Ambassadorial Letter," *Int* 36 (1982): 5–20.

Karris, R. J., "The Occasion of Romans: A Response to Professor Donfried," *CBQ* 36 (1974): 356–58; repr. *RomDeb*, 125–27.

———, "Romans 14:1–15:13 and the Occasion of Romans," *CBQ* 35 (1973): 155–78; repr. *RomDeb*, 65–84.

Kaye, B. N., " 'To the Romans and Others' Revisited," *NovT* 18 (1976): 37–77.

Kettunen, M., *Der Abfassungszweck des Römerbriefes*, Annales Academiae Scientiarum Fennicae, hum.-litt. 18 (Helsinki: Suomalainen Tiedeakatemia, 1979).

Klein, G., "Der Abfassungszweck des Römerbriefes," *Rekonstruktion und Interpretation: Gesammelte Aufsätze zum Neuen Testament*, BEvT 50 (Munich: Kaiser, 1969), 129–44; "Paul's Purpose in Writing the Epistle to the Romans," *RomDeb*, 29–43.

Lampe, P., "The Roman Christians of Romans 16," *RomDeb*, 216–30.

Lütgert, W., *Der Römerbrief als historisches Problem*, BFCT 17.2 (Gütersloh: Bertelsmann, 1913).

MacRory, J., "The Occasion and Object of the Epistle to the Romans," *ITQ* 9 (1914): 21–32.

Manson, T. W., "St. Paul's Letter to the Romans—and Others," *Studies in the Gospels and Epistles*, ed. M. Black (Manchester: University of Manchester; Philadelphia, Penn.: Westminster, 1962), 225–41; repr. *RomDeb*, 3–15.

Marcus, J., "The Circumcision and the Uncircumcision in Rome," *NTS* 35 (1989): 67–81.

Marxsen, W., *Introduction to the New Testament: An Approach to Its Problems* (Philadelphia, Penn.: Fortress; Oxford: Blackwell, 1968), 92–109.

Minear, P. S., *The Obedience of Faith: The Purposes of Paul in the Epistle to the Romans*, SBT 2.19 (London: SCM; Naperville, Ill.: Allenson, 1971).

Nestingen, J. A., "Major Shifts in the Interpretation of Romans," *WW* 6 (1986): 373–81.

Noack, B., "Current and Backwater in the Epistle to the Romans," *ST* 19 (1965): 155–65.

Osten-Sacken, P. von der, "Erwägungen zur Abfassungsgeschichte und zum literarisch-theologischen Charakter des Römerbriefs," *Theologia viatorum* 12 (1975): 109–20; repr. *Evangelium und Tora*, 119–30.

Pachali, H., "Der Römerbrief als historisches Problem: Bemerkungen zu W. Lütgert's gleichnamiger Abhandlung," *TSK* 87 (1914): 481–505.

Preisker, H., "Das historische Problem des Römerbriefes," *Wissenschaftliche Zeitschrift der Universität Jena/Thüringen*, Geisteswissenschaftliche Reihe 1.2 (1952–53): 25–30.

Rahn, H., *Morphologie der antiken Literatur* (Darmstadt: Wissenschaftliche Buchgesellschaft, 1969).

Rongy, H., "Le But de l'épître aux Romains," *RevEcclLiége* 22 (1930–31): 165–70.

Roosen, A., "Le Genre littéraire de l'épître aux Romains," *SE II*, TU 87 (1964), 465–71.

Russell, W. B., "An Alternative Suggestion for the Purpose of Romans," *BSac* 145 (1988): 174–88.

Schrenk, G., "Der Römerbrief als Missionsdokument," *Aus Theologie und Geschichte der reformierten Kirche: Festgabe für E. F. Karl Müller-Erlangen . . .* (Neukirchen: Erziehungsverein, 1933), repr. *Studien zu Paulus*, ATANT 26 (Zurich: Zwingli-Verlag, 1954), 81–106.

Smiga, G., "Romans 12:1–2 and 15:30–32 and the Occasion of the Letter to the Romans," *CBQ* 53 (1991): 257–73.

Stirewalt, L. M., Jr., "The Form and Function of the Greek Letter-Essay," *Romans Debate* (1977): 175–206; repr. *RomDeb*, 147–71.

Stuhlmacher, P., "Der Abfassungszweck des Römerbriefes," *ZNW* 77 (1986): 180–93; "The Purpose of Romans," *RomDeb*, 231–42.

———, "The Theme of Romans," *AusBR* 36 (1988): 31–44; repr. *RomDeb*, 333–45.

Suggs, M. J., " 'The Word Is Near You': Romans 10:6–10 Within the Purpose of the

Letter," *Christian History and Interpretation: Studies Presented to John Knox*, ed. W. R. Farmer et al. (Cambridge: Cambridge University Press, 1967), 289–312.

Suhl, A., "Der konkrete Anlass des Römerbriefes," *Kairos* 13 (1971): 119–30.

Theobald, M., "Warum schrieb Paulus den Römerbrief?" *BLit* 56 (1983): 150–58.

Trocmé, E., "L'Épître aux Romains et la méthode missionnaire de l'apôtre Paul," *NTS* 7 (1960–61): 148–53.

Watson, F., "The Two Roman Congregations: Rom. 14:1–15:13," *Paul, Judaism and the Gentiles: A Sociological Approach*, SNTSMS 56 (Cambridge: Cambridge University Press, 1986), 94–105; repr. *RomDeb*, 203–15.

Wedderburn, A. J. M., "The Purpose and Occasion of Romans Again," *ExpTim* 90 (1978–79): 137–41; repr. *RomDeb*, 195–202.

———, *The Reasons for Romans*, Studies of the New Testament and Its World (Edinburgh: Clark, 1988).

Wiefel, W., "Die jüdische Gemeinschaft im antiken Rom und die Anfänge des römischen Christentums: Bemerkungen zu Anlass und Zweck des Römerbriefs," *Judaica* 26 (1970): 65–88; "The Jewish Community in Ancient Rome and the Origins of Roman Christianity," *RomDeb*, 85–101.

Wilckens, U., "Über Abfassungszweck und Aufbau des Römerbriefs," *Rechtfertigung als Freiheit*, 110–70.

Williams, P. R., "Paul's Purpose in Writing Romans," *BSac* 128 (1971): 62–67.

Wuellner, W., "Paul's Rhetoric of Argumentation in Romans: An Alternative to the Donfried–Karris Debate over Romans," *CBQ* 38 (1976): 330–51; repr. *RomDeb*, 128–46.

VI. Date and Place of Composition

◆

Although some commentators have sought to locate the writing of Romans either in Athens (the so-called Marcionite Prologue in some MSS of the Vg) or in Ephesus (Richards, Schmithals) or in Philippi (Michaelis, Taylor) or in Thessalonica (Westberg) or in Macedonia (Suhl), the majority of interpreters maintain that Paul wrote the essay-letter from Corinth, as was already stated in the subscript of MSS B[1] and D[2] (see the NOTE on 16:27).

From the letter itself one gathers that Paul, as he writes, is somewhere in the eastern Mediterranean area. His missionary activity there has come to an end (15:19, 23), and before he makes his planned trip to Spain and his visit to Rome en route, he has to go eastward, to Jerusalem, to bring to the poor of the church there the Achaean and Macedonian collection (15:25–28). The mention of Achaia and Macedonia suggests, therefore, that he is somewhere in Greece, not in Asia Minor (compare 1 Cor 16:1–3, written to Corinth, Greece from Ephesus; 2 Cor 2:12–13; 9:4), which rules out the possibility that Romans was written in Ephesus. Moreover, Paul is the house guest of Gaius (16:23a), undoubtedly the one mentioned as baptized at Corinth (1 Cor 1:14). He sends greetings also from Erastus, treasurer of Corinth (16:23b; cf. 2 Tim 4:20). Thus Corinth becomes the likely town from which Paul wrote this essay-letter.

Paul's presence in or near Corinth is further suggested by 16:1, where he mentions Phoebe, a deacon of the church of Cenchreae, one of the ports of Corinth. This notice, however, depends on how one regards chap. 16 of Romans. If that chapter is, indeed, part of the letter sent to the Christians of Rome, then it would suggest that the letter is being written from Corinth and that Phoebe was the bearer of the letter to Rome. But if chap. 16 is considered rather to be a note originally destined for Ephesus, then it would not follow that Romans was composed at Corinth, or even at Cenchreae. Because I consider chap. 16 an integral part of Romans, part of the letter sent to the Christians of Rome, Corinth is then understood as the place of composition of Romans.

The mention of the collection in 15:25–28 brings Romans into close connection with two letters Paul sent to Corinth (see 1 Cor 16:1–4; 2 Corinthians 8–9), implying that Romans has been written after the Corinthian letters. 1 Corinthians would have been written in the spring of 57 and 2 Corinthians 8–9 in the autumn of that year. Since 1 Cor 16:1 mentions a collection taken up in the churches of Galatia for the poor of Jerusalem, it shows that Romans is also to be regarded as having been written after the letter to the Galatians (cf. Gal 2:10). Galatians itself would have been written toward the beginning of Mission III, when Paul was based in Ephesus, hence about 54 (see *PAHT* §P40–45).

According to the Lucan story of Paul's missionary journeys in Acts, the place of composition would also be Corinth, where he spent the three months of the winter of 57–58 before leaving for Syria (and Jerusalem) via Macedonia at the end of Mission III (Acts 20:2–3). Paul himself notes that his writing of Romans preceded a projected trip to Jerusalem (Rom 15:25–28), which cannot be other than that mentioned by Luke in Acts 20–21, because the details about the collection in 15:25–28 agree with the notice in Acts 24:17, "after a number of years I have come to bring alms and offerings to my nation." Compare Acts 19:21: "When these things were completed, Paul proposed in the Spirit to pass through Macedonia and Achaia and go to Jerusalem, 'After I have been there, I must also see Rome.' " In the spring, then, of 58 Paul spent the days of Unleavened Bread and Passover at Philippi (Acts 20:6), before continuing on to Jerusalem. Although modern commentators are at times skeptical about the Lucan story of Paul's movements, this point of convergence is generally admitted; see Campbell, "Paul's 'Missionary Journeys,'" 87; Kümmel, *Introduction*, 254; Fitzmyer, *According to Paul*, 36–46.

When did Paul write the Epistle to the Romans? The answer depends on how one reconstructs Paul's "life" and the extent to which one admits the validity of the Lucan data from Acts. The Lucan data have to be used critically; they may not take priority over what Paul himself says in his authentic letters. (In the question of the dating of Romans, nothing in Colossians or Ephesians bears upon it, since even for those who maintain the authenticity of these letters, they would stem from a period later than the composition of Romans. As for 2 Thessalonians, which some would ascribe to Paul at a period prior to Romans, there is nothing in it that has to do with a date either of 2 Thessalonians or of any other Pauline letter.) For my reconstruction of Pauline chronology, see *PAHT* §P3–54.

The one "peg" on which most NT interpreters hang their "lives" of Paul is the appearance of Paul before Gallio, the proconsul of Achaia (Acts 18:12–16). What is noteworthy is that even those who are most skeptical about the historical value of the Lucan story of Paul's movements begin with his appearance before Gallio, which Paul himself never mentions in his letters. Yet if one accepts the historical validity of this Lucan item, then Paul would have appeared before Gallio in the summer or early autumn of 52.

The appearance of Paul before Gallio (Acts 18:12–16) would mark the end of Paul's Mission II, during which he would have spent eighteen months in Corinth

(51–52). After that he would have traveled to Jerusalem (implied in Acts 18:22) and begun Mission III after a sojourn in Antioch. During Mission III he would have been based in Ephesus (54–57; cf. 1 Cor 16:8), whence he would have traveled via Troas (2 Cor 2:12) and Macedonia (2 Cor 12:13; cf. 1 Cor 16:5) on his way to Corinth (2 Cor 9:4). There he would have written the Epistle to the Romans sometime during the winter of 57–58, before leaving for Jerusalem via Macedonia, Philippi, Asia Minor, and Caesarea Maritima. Compare Acts 20:2b–6, 13–17; 21:1–8, 15–17.

According to Cranfield (*Romans*, 12), that Romans was written "during the period of winter and early spring in one of the years between late A.D. 54 and early A.D. 59 is certain, but within those limits the opinions of scholars vary." Cranfield thinks it "highly likely that Paul's appearance before Gallio was in A.D. 51" (ibid., 13), while admitting "that any date between mid-50 and mid-54 is theoretically possible." Yet neither of these dates, in my opinion, is possible. If we follow the available evidence about the proconsulship of Gallio, his year of proconsulate would have been 52–53 (no other year!) and Paul would have been haled before him in the summer or early autumn of 52, because Gallio did not say in Achaia for the full year, but, having become sick, returned to Italy in 52 before *mare clausum*, when sea travel on the Mediterranean was impossible (see my article, "The Pauline Letters," 87–89; repr. *According to Paul*, 46).

But if one can be certain about Gallio's proconsulship in 52, there still remains the problem of the absolute date of the procuratorships of Festus and Felix. Unfortunately, there is no way of tying down more certainly the rest of the Lucan chronology of Paul's movements; consequently, scholars differ about the absolute date of the composition of Romans. Most, however, date it to either the mid or the late fifties.

Lüdemann (*Paul*, 263) would date the composition of Romans as early as 51/52 or 54/55—which is impossible (see Dunn, *Romans*, xliv). Barrett (*Romans*, 5) would date the composition to the first three months of 55; similarly Suhl (*Paulus*, 249, 344), Tolbert ("Life"). Cranfield would rather date it to the winter of 55–56 or 56–57; similarly Bornkamm (*Paul*, xii), Dunn (*Romans*, xliii), Jewett (*A Chronology*, 104 and graph), Kümmel (*Introduction*, 311), Lagrange (*Romains*, xx), Pesch (*Römerbrief*, 5), Söding ("Zur Chronologie"), and Zeller (*Brief an die Römer*, 15). Schlier (*Römerbrief*, 2) dates it to the beginning of the year 57 or 58. And Sanday and Headlam (*Romans*, xiii) would date it to the winter of 57–58, as I prefer; so too Black (*Romans*, 20), J. B. Lightfoot (*The Epistle of St. Paul to the Galatians* [Grand Rapids, Mich.: Zondervan, 1967], 40, 43), Michel (*Brief an die Römer*, 27), Wikenhauser and Schmid (*Einleitung*, 455), and Zahn (*Introduction to the New Testament*, 3 vols. in 1 [Edinburgh: Clark, 1917], 1.434).

BIBLIOGRAPHY

Campbell, T. H., "Paul's 'Missionary Journeys' as Reflected in His Letters," *JBL* 74 (1955): 80–87.

Fitzmyer, J. A., "The Pauline Letters and the Lucan Account of Paul's Missionary Journeys," *SBL Seminar Papers 1988* (Atlanta, Ga.: Scholars Press, 1988), 82–89; repr. *According to Paul*, 36–46.

Gilchrist, J. M., "Paul and the Corinthians—The Sequence of Letters and Visits," *JSNT* 34 (1988): 47–69.

Jewett, R. A *Chronology of Paul's Life* (Philadelphia, Penn.: Fortress, 1979).

Knox, J., *Chapters in a Life of Paul*, ed. D. A. Hare, rev. ed. (Macon, Ga.: Mercer University, 1987).

Kümmel, W. G., *Introduction to the New Testament*, rev. ed. (Nashville, Tenn.: Abingdon, 1975), 311–14.

Lüdemann, G., *Paul Apostle to the Gentiles: Studies in Chronology* (Philadelphia, Penn.: Fortress, 1984), 262–63.

Michaelis, W., *Die Gefangenschaft des Paulus in Ephesus und das Itinerar des Timotheos: Untersuchungen zur Chronologie des Paulus und der Paulusbriefe*, Neutestamentliche Forschungen 1.3 (Gütersloh: Bertelsmann, 1925).

———, "Kenchreä (Zur Frage des Abfassungsortes des Rm)," *ZNW* 25 (1926): 144–54.

Murphy-O'Connor, J., *St. Paul's Corinth: Texts and Archaeology*, GNS 6 (Wilmington, Del.: Glazier, 1983).

Richards, J. R., "Romans and I Corinthians: Their Chronological Relationship and Comparative Dates," *NTS* 13 (1966–67); 14–30.

Schmithals, W., *Der Römerbrief als historisches Problem*, SNT 9 (Gütersloh: Mohn, 1975).

Söding, T., "Zur Chronologie der paulinischen Briefe: Ein Diskussionsvorschlag," *BN* 56 (1991): 31–59.

Suhl, A., *Paulus und seine Briefe: Ein Beitrag zur paulinischen Chronologie*, SNT 11 (Gütersloh: Mohn, 1975).

Taylor, T. M., "The Place of Origin of Romans," *JBL* 67 (1948): 281–95.

Tolbert, M. D., "Life Situation and Purpose of Romans," *RevExp* 73 (1976): 391–99.

Westberg, F., *Zur neutestamentlichen Chronologie und Golgathas Ortslage* (Leipzig: Deichert, 1911), 72–73.

Wikenhauser, A. and J. Schmid, *Einleitung in das Neue Testament*, 6th ed. (Freiburg im Breisgau: Herder, 1973), 449–62.

VII. Language and Style

◆

Apropos of the language of the letter to the Romans, Sanday and Headlam (*Romans*, lii) once noted the "rather strange paradox" that a letter addressed to the Christians of Rome, "the capital of the Western or Latin world, should be written in Greek." One might also add that in Romans Paul even acknowledges his debt to "barbarians," in other words, non–Greek-speaking Gentiles (1:14). One can only guess how that terminology might have suited Latin-speaking Roman Christians who would read his letter. Yet for roughly three centuries Greek was the predominant language of the city of Rome, or at least of considerable portions of its inhabitants.

Greek had become the lingua franca of the Mediterranean world, taking the place of Aramaic, after the conquests of Alexander the Great and his hellenization of the region. Although Rome eventually conquered Greece and the rest of the world that had been governed by Alexander's successors, the Macedonian, Lagide or Ptolemaic, and Seleucid *diadochoi*, it was the language of Greece that dominated the Roman Empire for several centuries. The Attic dialect of the Golden Age of Greek literature (fifth–fourth centuries B.C.) had been supplanted by a pan-Hellenic form of Greek that came to be known as *Koinē* ("common" [language]) and that served precisely as the lingua franca in the post-Alexandrian, Hellenistic period.

In the first century B.C. Cicero could write, "Nam si quis minorem gloriae fructum putat ex graecis versibus percipi quam ex latinis, vehementer errat, propterea quod graeca leguntur in omnibus fere gentibus, latina suis finibus, exiguis sane, continentur" ("For if anyone thinks that the glory won by writing Greek verse is less than that given to one who writes in Latin, he is entirely wrong, because Greek letters are read in nearly every nation there is, whereas Latin letters are confined to their own, quite narrow, boundaries," *Pro Archia* 23). A century later the poet Juvenal could complain, "Non possum ferre, Quirites, graecam Urbem; quamvis quota portio faecis Achaei? Iam pridem Syrus in Tiberim defluxit Orontes, et linguam et mores . . . secum vexit" ("I can't stand, Noble Citizens, a Rome of Greeks; and yet how great a portion of our dregs are Achaeans! The Syrian Orontes has long since flowed into the Tiber, bringing with it its patois and its manners!" *Satire* 3.60–65).

Greek so infiltrated even Palestine that funerary inscriptions discovered in the environs of Jerusalem and engraved in Greek outnumber those in Aramaic or Hebrew (see *CII* 1.lxv–lxvi; Fitzmyer, "The Languages of Palestine in the First Century A.D.," *WA*, 29–56; cf. M. Smith, "Aramaic Studies and the Study of the New Testament," *JBR* 26 [1958] 304–13).

Similarly, in Rome the majority of Jews who dwelled there in the first century A.D. were Greek-speaking, as funerary inscriptions in Roman catacombs reveal. Of 534 Jewish inscriptions recovered from Roman catacombs, 405 of them are in Greek, 123 in Latin, 3 in Hebrew, and 1 in Aramaic (and the last four use the Semitic language only in stereotyped phrases); one is bilingual Greek and Latin, another bilingual Aramaic and Greek (see Leon, *Jews of Ancient Rome*, 76; cf. *CII*, 1.lxv–lxvi; Sevenster, *Do You Know Greek?* NovTSup 19 [Leiden: Brill, 1967], 88).

The first Christian writers known to have written in Latin are Apollonius and Victor of Africa (the latter in time became a bishop of Rome); their *floruit* was in the second-to-last decade of the second century A.D. They were followed by Tertullian of Carthage (160–240) and Minucius Felix (fl. 200–240). So it is not surprising that the earliest Christian writers after NT times, Clement of Rome (ca. 96) and Ignatius of Antioch (ca. 115), would still have written in Greek, and even more likely that Christians of Rome in the fifties would be speaking mostly Greek and that Paul would write to them in Greek.

The Greek that Paul writes in Romans is a form of *Koinē*. Although it is not as good as the Greek of Luke or of the Epistle to the Hebrews, Paul does express himself very well at times, for example, in a passage such as Rom 8:31–39 (and in 1 Cor 13:1–13). His Greek is correct, even though it is punctuated at times with anacolutha (2:17–24; 5:6–8, 12–14; 9:22–24), which may be owing to his practice of dictating to a scribe. His use of the Greek language shows not only a good Hellenistic education and dependence on the popular philosophers and rhetoricians of the day, but also on his Jewish training. In fact, Norden went so far as to claim that Paul's style was "as a whole, unhellenic" (*Die antike Kunstprosa*, 499). By this Norden was referring to Paul's Semitic background; but that is certainly an exaggeration, for his prose is not saturated with Aramaisms or Semitisms, as are the Gospels and Acts. Van Unnik's attempt to discover Aramaisms in Paul did not succeed ("Aramaisms").

Paul's Greek is affected by that of the LXX; but it is no worse for that reason than that of many other NT authors or other Hellenistic writers of the period. Septuagintal influence is seen in the postpositive position of the adjective with repeated article, for instance, *tou huiou autou tou genomenou* (1:3; cf. 12:2, 3, 6), and especially in the first place given to the verb in many sentences (1:11, 13, 16, 18, 23, 28, etc.).

Paul writes this essay-letter in the manner of contemporary Greek epistolography. Although he developed his own form of epistolary greeting ("grace and peace to you from God our Father and the Lord Jesus Christ," 1:7) as a substitute for the secular *chairein* (see *NJBC*, art. 45 §8A), he did otherwise use many conventional epistolary formulations: "I urge you, brothers" (12:1; 15:30; 16:17); "I do not want you to be unaware" (1:13; 11:25); "I am happy about you" (16:19). See Eschlimann, "La Rédaction"; del Paramo, "Las fórmulas"; Perry, "Epistolary Form."

Normally, his style has been said to be devoid of artificial rhetoric, but Paul has been under the influence of some contemporary rhetorical style, when he introduces into his essay-letter a number of literary subforms:

1. Diatribe, a dialogical form of argumentation developed by ancient teachers such as Teles, Dio of Prusa, and Maximus of Tyre in the Cynic and Stoic schools of philosophy. It was a pedagogical discourse conducted in a lively debate and in familiar conversational style with an interlocutor; it was peppered with apostrophes, proverbs and maxims, rhetorical questions, paradoxes, short statements, parodies, fictitious speeches, antitheses, and parallel phrases. This subform is used especially in 2:1–6, 17–24; 3:1–9, 27–4:25; 9:19–21; 10:14–21; 11:17–24; 14:4, 10–11 (see Bultmann, *Der Stil*; especially Stowers, *The Diatribe*). According to Schmeller *(Paulus)*, it is also present in 1:18–2:11; 8:31–39; 11:1–24. The diatribe style may also be evident in Paul's use of *mē genoito*, "certainly not!": 3:4, 6, 31; 6:2, 15; 7:7, 13; 9:14; 11:1, 11 (see Malherbe, "*Mē genoito*"), also in *tí oun*, "what then?": 3:1, 9; 4:1; 6:1, 15; 7:7; 8:31; 9:14, 30; 11:7. This form has been contested, however, by Donfried, "False Presuppositions," 211–21, who strangely makes no reference to the work of Stowers or Schmeller. Yet even if there were no such established form, the elements usually called diatribic are certainly part of Greek rhetoric, which Paul utilizes. The debate about Paul and his use of diatribe is far from over. In any case, such a style is particularly apt in a letter to a church that Paul has not founded or even visited.

2. *Testimonia* lists: 3:10–18; 9:25–29; 15:9–12. The name is derived from a work of Cyprian, *Ad Quirinium: Testimoniorum libri tres adversus Iudaeos* (ed. G. Hartel, CSEL 3.1 [1868], 33–184). Cyprian's work was a polemical treatise against the Jews, which culled OT passages on different topics to argue against them. Although this form has been well known from patristic literature, an example of it has turned up in QL, 4QTestimonia, which reveals that the form was already known among Palestinian Jews in pre-Christian times; see E. Lohse, *Die Texte aus Qumran: Hebräisch und Deutsch* (Munich: Kösel, 1964), 249–53; cf. A. Dupont-Sommer, *The Essene Writings from Qumran* (Cleveland, Ohio and New York: World, 1962), 315–19. *Pace* Dunn (*Romans*, 145), neither CD 5:13–17 nor 4 Ezra 7:22–24 is a contemporary parallel to such a catena of OT passages; that of CD 5:13–17 is rather a pesher form of quotation. See my " '4QTestimonia.' "

3. Hymns: 8:31–39; 11:33–36.
4. Letter of recommendation: 16:1–2 (or 16:1–16).
5. Metaphors: see Heylen, "Les Métaphores."
6. Metonymy: ibid.
7. Chiasm: 2:7–10; 3:19; 10:9–10; 11:22; 14:7–9; perhaps also 11:33–36. See Jeremias, "Chiasmus" (but beware of some examples); Lund, *Chiasmus*, 222–23.
8. Analogy: 4:4; 5:7; 6:1–14, 15–23; 7:1–6; 9:20–24; 11:16–24. See Gale, *Use of Analogy*.

Paul's style is more that of an orator than of a writer. It is clear that he has dictated the text of Romans, and in this he is the preacher. "A writer he was not and did not want to be" (von Dobschütz, "Zum Wortschatz," 66). Romans was meant to be read aloud, more as a formal lecture than as a literary essay-letter. And yet, it does not for that reason lack in spontaneity. Romans is "calm in the sense that it is not aggressive and that the rush of words is always well under control. Still there is a rush of words, rising repeatedly to passages of splendid eloquence; but the eloquence is spontaneous, the outcome of strongly moved feeling; there is nothing about it of labored oratory" (Sanday and Headlam, *Romans*, lv).

A mark of Paul's dictation style is his frequent use of the conjunction *gar*, "for." Indeed, it is so common (144 instances) that it becomes tiresome; one cannot always translate it well; see Zedda, "L'Uso di *gar*."

Another rather common feature of Paul's writing is his use of the theological passive to express something that is being done by God; see ZBG §236; cf. C. Macholz, "Das 'Passivum divinum,' seine Anfänge im Alten Testament und der 'Hofstil,' " ZNW 81 (1990): 247–53. Macholz appeals to such OT passages as Gen 42:22, 28; Lev 4:20, 26, 31, 35; 5:6, 10, 13, 16, 18, 26; 2 Kgs 18:30 (= Isa 36:15); Ps 130:4; Dan 9:9; Neh 9:17; and Sir 44:16, 18. As examples of *Hofstil*, he appeals to Num 32:2, 5; 1 Sam 18:17, 19; 25:18, 27; and 2 Sam 21:5–6.

BIBLIOGRAPHY

Adúriz, J., "Régimen de la preposiciones en el vocabulario paulino de pistéuo," *Ciencia y fe* 13 (1957): 157–61.

Aletti, J.-N., "La Présence d'un modèle rhétorique en Romains: Son Rôle et son importance," *Bib* 71 (1990): 1–24.

Aune, D., "Romans as a Logos Protreptikos in the Context of Ancient Religious and Philosophical Propaganda," *Paulus und das antike Judentum*, WUNT 58, ed. M. Hengel and U. Heckel (Tübingen: Mohr [Siebeck], 1991), 91–124; abbreviated, *RomDeb*, 278–96.

Biays, P. M., *Parallelism in Romans*, Fort Hays Studies n.s. 5 (Hays, Ks.: Fort Hays Kansas State College, 1967).

Bjerkelund, C. J., *Parakalô: Form, Funktion und Sinn der parakalô-Sätze in den paulinischen Briefen*, Bibliotheca theologica norvegica 1 (Oslo: Universitetsforlaget, 1967).

Bornkamm, G., "Paulinische Anakoluthe im Römerbrief," *Das Ende des Gesetzes*, 76–92.

Bultmann, R., *Der Stil der paulinischen Predigt und die kynisch-stoische Diatribe*, FRLANT 13 (Göttingen: Vandenhoeck & Ruprecht, 1910; repr. with preface by H. Hübner, 1984).

Credner, K. A., *Beiträge zur Einleitung in die biblischen Schriften*, 2 vols. (Halle an der Saale: Buchhandlung des Waisenhauses, 1832–38), 2.318–28.

Danker, F. W., "Under Contract: A Form-Critical Study of Linguistic Adaptation in Romans," *Festschrift to Honor F. Wilbur Gingrich . . .* , ed. E. H. Barth and R. E. Cocroft (Leiden: Brill, 1972), 91–114.

Dobschütz, E. von, "Zum Wortschatz und Stil des Römerbriefs," *ZNW* 33 (1934): 51–66.

Dodd, C. H., *According to the Scriptures: The Sub-structure of New Testament Theology* (New York: Scribners, 1953), 28–60.

Elliott, N., *The Rhetoric of Romans: Argumentative Constraint and Strategy and Paul's Dialogue with Judaism*, JSNTSup 45 (Sheffield, UK: Academic Press, 1990).

Eschlimann, J.-A., "La Rédaction des épitres pauliniennes d'après une comparaison avec les lettres profanes de son temps," *RB* 53 (1946): 185–96.

Fitzmyer, J. A., " '4QTestimonia' and the New Testament," *TS* 18 (1957): 513–38; repr. *ESBNT*, 59–89.

Fraiken, D., "The Rhetorical Function of the Jews in Romans," *Anti-Judaism in Early Christianity*, vol. 1: *Paul and the Gospels*, ed. P. Richardson and D. Granskou (Waterloo, Ont.: Wilfrid Laurier University, 1986), 91–105.

Gale, H. M., *The Use of Analogy in the Letters of Paul* (Philadelphia, Penn.: Westminster, 1964), 173–215.

Grumm, M. H., "The Gospel Call: Imperatives in Romans," *ExpTim* 93 (1981–82): 239–42.

Gyllenberg, R., "De inledande hälsningsformlerna i de paulinska breven," *SEA* 16 (1951): 21–31.

Harmon, A. M., "Aspects of Paul's Use of the Psalms," *WTJ* 32 (1969): 1–23.

Harmsen, E., "Ueber *eis to* mit dem artikulirten Infinitiv in den Briefen an die Römer und Korinther," *ZWT* 17 (1974): 245–60.

Harris, J. R., "St. Paul's Use of Testimonies in the Epistle to the Romans," *Expos* 8.17 (1919): 401–14.

——, *Testimonies*, 2 vols. (Cambridge: Cambridge University Press, 1916–20).

Hatch, E., *Essays in Biblical Greek* (Oxford: Clarendon, 1889), 204–14.

Heylen, V., "Les Métaphores et le métonymies dans les épîtres pauliniennes," *ETL* 12 (1935): 253–90.

Hübner, H. "Die Rhetorik und die Theologie: Der Römerbrief und die rhetorische Kompetenz des Paulus," *Die Macht des Wortes: Aspekte gegenwärtiger Rhetorikforschung*, ed. C. J. Classen and H.-J. Müllenbrock, Ars rhetorica 4 (Marburg: Hitzeroth, 1992), 165–79.

Jeremias, J., "Chiasmus in den Paulusbriefen," *ZNW* 49 (1958): 145–56.

Jewett, R., "Following the Argument of Romans," *RomDeb*, 265–77.

Kraft, R. A., "Barnabas' Isaiah Text and the 'Testimony Book' Hypothesis," *JBL* 79 (1960): 335–50.

Lagrange, M.-J., "Langue, style, argumentation dans l'épître aux Romains," *RB* 12 (1915): 216–35.

Lofthouse, M. F., " 'I' and 'We' in the Pauline Letters," *ExpTim* 69 (1952–53): 241–45.

Lund, N. W., *Chiasmus in the New Testament: A Study in Formgeschichte* (Chapel Hill, N.C.: University of North Carolina Press, 1942), 222–23.

McGrath, B., " 'Syn' Words in Saint Paul," *CBQ* 14 (1952): 219–26.

Malherbe, A. J., "*Mē genoito* in the Diatribe and Paul," *HTR* 73 (1980): 231–400.

Mattill, A. J., Jr., "Translation of Words with the Stem *dik-* in Romans," *AUSS* 9 (1971): 89–98.

Michel, O., *Paulus und seine Bibel*, BFCT 2.18 (Gütersloh: Bertelsmann, 1929; repr. Darmstadt: Wissenschaftliche Buchgesellschaft, 1972).

Nägeli, T., *Der Wortschatz des Apostels Paulus* (Basel: Baseler Berichthaus, 1904).

Norden, E., *Die antike Kunstprosa vom VI. Jahrhundert v. Chr. bis in die Zeit der Renaissance*, 2 vols. (Leipzig: Teubner, 1898; repr. Darmstadt: Wissenschaftliche Buchgesellschaft, 1958; Stuttgart: Teubner, 1983).

Nygren, A., "Objektives und Persönliches im Römerbrief," *TLZ* 77 (1952): 591–96.

Ortiz Valdivieso, P., *Epistulae beati Pauli Apostoli ad Romanos textum graecum recognovit et stichice disposuit* (Rome: Biblical Institute, 1969).

Paramo, S. del, "Las formulas protocolarias en las cartas del Nuevo Testamento," *EstBíb* 10 (1951): 333–55.

Penna, R., "Aspetti narrativi nella lettera di s. Paolo ai Romani," *RivB* 36 (1988): 29–45.

———, "Narrative Aspects of the Epistle of St. Paul to the Romans," *Parable and Story in Judaism and Christianity*, ed. C. Thoma and M. Wyschogrod (New York: Paulist Press, 1989), 191–204.

Perry, A. M., "Epistolary Form in Paul," *Crozer Quarterly* 26 (1949): 48–53.

Prigent, P., "Quelques Testimonia messianiques," *TZ* 15 (1959): 419–30.

———, *Les Testimonia dans le christianisme primitif: L'Épître de Barnabé I–XVI et ses sources*, EtBib (Paris: Gabalda, 1961).

Probst, H., *Paulus und der Brief: Die Rhetorik des antiken Briefs als Form der paulinischen Korintherkorrespondenz*, WUNT 2.45 (Tübingen: Mohr [Siebeck], 1991).

Rolland, P., *Épître aux Romains: Texte grec structuré* (Rome: Biblical Institute, 1980).

Roosen, A., "Le Genre littéraire de l'Épître aux Romains," *SE II*, TU 87 (1964), 465–71.

Schmeller, T., *Paulus und die "Diatribe": Eine vergleichende Stilinterpretation*, NTAbh n.s. 19 (Münster in Westfalen: Aschendorff, 1987).

Spencer, A. B., *Paul's Literary Style: A Stylistic and Historical Comparison of II Corinthians 11:16–12:13, Romans 8:9–39, and Philippians 3:2–4:13*, Monograph Series, Evangelical Theological Society (Jackson, Miss.: Evangelical Theological Society, 1984).

Stowers, S. K., *The Diatribe and Paul's Letter to the Romans*, SBLDS 57 (Chico, Calif.: Scholars Press, 1981).

———, *Letter-Writing in Greco-Roman Antiquity* (Philadelphia, Penn: Westminster, 1986).

Straub, W., *Die Bildersprache des Apostels Paulus untersucht* (Tübingen: Mohr [Siebeck], 1937).

Thils, G., *Pour Mieux Comprendre Saint Paul*, 3d ed. (Bruges: Desclée de Brouwer, 1942).

Thyen, H., *Der Stil der jüdisch-hellenistischen Homilie*, FRLANT 65 (Göttingen: Vandenhoeck & Ruprecht, 1955).

Turner, N., "The Style of Paul," in J. H. Moulton and W. F. Howard, *A Grammar of New Testament Greek*, 4 vols. (Edinburgh: Clark, 1949–76), 4.80–100.

Unnik, W. C. van, "Aramaisms in Paul," *Sparsa collecta: The Collected Essays of W. C. van Unnik*, part 1: *Evangelia Paulina Acta*, NovTSup 29 (Leiden: Brill, 1973), 129–43.

Vitti, A. M., "L'Eloquenza di S. Paolo nelle sue lettere," *Bib* 21 (1940): 413–25.

Vollmer, H., *Die alttestamentlichen Citate bei Paulus* . . . (Freiburg im Breisgau and Leipzig: Mohr [Siebeck], 1895).

Weiss, J., "Beiträge zur paulinischen Rhetorik," *Theologische Studien* . . . *Prof. D. Bernhard Weiss* . . . *dargebracht* (Göttingen: Vandenhoeck & Ruprecht, 1897), 165–247.

Wuellner, W., "Paul's Rhetoric of Argumentation in Romans: An Alternative to the Donfried-Karris Debate over Romans," *CBQ* 38 (1976): 330–51; repr. *RomDeb*, 128–46.

Zedda, S., "L'Uso di *gar* in alcuni testi di San Paolo," *SPCIC* 2.445–51.

VIII. STRUCTURE AND OUTLINE

◆

The structure of the letter to the Romans is, for the most part, not a matter of much dispute. Practically all interpreters agree on its major divisions, but there is dispute about the role of chap. 5 in the letter as a whole. One can, however, discern the structure most easily by beginning with the end of the letter and working forward.

In its present form, Romans ends with a doxology in 16:25–27. Preceding that is the letter of recommendation for Phoebe in 16:1–23. (Verse 24 is missing in the best Greek MSS.) Before this letter of recommendation one finds the concluding remarks of Paul about his plans, his coming trip to Jerusalem, and his request for prayers, in 15:14–33. Just before that is a hortatory section of Romans in 12:1–15:13, which clearly falls into two parts: (a) 12:1–13:14, in which Paul exhorts the Roman Christians to a proper Spirit-guided life; and (b) 14:1–15:13, in which he gives guidance to the "weak" and the "strong" in the Roman community. Preceding the hortatory section is the doctrinal section in 1:16–11:36, recognized by the majority of interpreters. In this section, chaps. 9–11 are clearly set off from what precedes. The doctrinal section itself is preceded by a proem (1:10–15), a thanksgiving (1:8–9), and an epistolary prescript (1:1–7). In these instances some commentators would treat 1:8–15 as a unit, a minor difference of opinion.

The major problem in chaps. 1–8, however, is how to divide them, and the debate focuses on chap. 5. Almost all commentators recognize 1:16–4:25 as a unit, in which Paul discusses his thesis about the gospel of justification by faith without the deeds of the law. But how is chap. 5 to be related to 1:16–4:25 and to 6:1–8:39, which again almost all commentators recognize as a unit?

Four main views have been proposed regarding it. (1) *Chapter 5 concludes part A.* Thus justification is the subject matter of 1:18–5:21; sanctification, that of 6:1–8:39. This view has been proposed by Calvin, Cerfaux(?), Dunn, Feine and Behm, Godet, Goguel, Huby, Knox, Lagrange, Léon-Dufour, Pesch, Sanday and Headlam, Schlatter, B. Weiss, and Wilckens. (2) *Chapter 5 introduces part B.* Thus justification is treated in 1:18–4:25, and the condition and life of the justified in 5:1–8:39, which some would extend even to 11:36. This view is proposed by Byrne, Cerfaux, Cranfield, Dahl, Dodd(?), Dupont(?), Feuillet(?), Jacono, Jeremias, Käsemann, Kümmel, Lamarche, Lietzmann, Lyonnet, Michel, Minear, Moo, Nygren, Osten-Sacken, Prat, Schlier, Schmidt, Scroggs, Viard, and Wikenhauser and Schmid. (3) *Rom 5:1–11 concludes part A, whereas 5:12–21 introduces part B.* This view is maintained by Black, Bonnard, Feuillet, Leenhardt, and Zahn. (4) *Chapter 5 is an isolated unit.* This view is put forth by Althaus, Barrett, Cambier, Dupont, Kuss, and Taylor. Certainty in such a debate is impossible to achieve. It should also be noted that some commentators (e.g., Achtemeier, Zeller) propose the outline of Romans in such a way as to depart from the normally admitted breaks and divisions of the letter mentioned above.

In this commentary the structure of Romans will reckon with the end of part A of the doctrinal section at 4:25. Thus chap. 5 will be regarded as the beginning of part B of the doctrinal section. The reasons for this interpretation are numerous. For one thing, the paragraph 5:12–21 would be a strange beginning of a new part of the doctrinal section of Romans. 5:1–11 is clearly transitional; it alludes to what has been the topic in 1:16–4:25 ("now that we are justified through faith . . .") and announces the topic that will eventually be developed in chap. 8. But 5:12–21 is related to Romans 6–7, even if it gives the impression of an isolated unit because its themes are not picked up again, save in a vague way in 8:2.

Second, 5:1–11, especially 5:8–11, announces briefly what 8:1–39 will develop at length. (In this regard I differ with Käsemann [*Commentary*, 131], who sees 5:1–21 as "Freedom from the Power of Death," because there is neither a suggestion of freedom in 5:1–11, nor of death; the only "death" mentioned is that of Christ himself.)

Third, the discussion in 1:16–4:25 centers on Jews and Greeks, who are not mentioned in 5:1–8:39. By contrast, 5:4 contains the first mention of the holy Spirit since 1:4, a topic that will be developed in chap. 8 (vv 2, 4, 5, 6, 9, 10, 11, 13, 15, 16, 23, 26, 27). Similarly, in 1:16–4:25 *dikaiosynē*, "uprightness," was the divine attribute that dominated part A; now divine *agapē*, "love," comes to the fore, and it assures salvation. Mentioned briefly in 5:5, 8, it will be treated more fully in 8:28, 35, 37, 39.

Sixth, 1:16–4:25 is dominated by juridical, forensic notions, but in 5:1–8:39 the emphasis is put on the ethical, even the mystical, in that it affects human behavior and union with God; mild polemics give way to hope and exhortation.

In the area of style, divisions within chaps. 5–8 are indicated by variations of a concluding formula, which echoes 1:5: thus 5:21, "grace . . . through Jesus Christ our Lord"; 6:23, "gift . . . in Jesus Christ our Lord"; 7:24–25, "thanks be to God! Through Jesus Christ our Lord"; compare 8:39. The conclusions are doxological, and through this repetition they serve to unite part B.

Finally, in 5:12–7:25, after the introductory paragraph of 5:1–11, three freedoms (from sin and death, from sin and self, and from the law) prepare the way for the discussion of life in the Spirit. All of this discussion forms a unit that cannot really be broken up; see Lyonnet, "Note sur le plan"; Rolland, "L'Ordon-nance."

In the following outline, the arabic numbers that are used on the left refer to the paragraphs in the translation that precedes this introduction. They also appear at the beginning of each pericope in the commentary. Hence, once the structure of the letter is discerned from the uppercase roman numerals (I, II, III) and letters (A, B, C), the arabic numbers are continuous throughout.

BIBLIOGRAPHY

Bizer, E., *Texte aus der Anfangszeit Melanchthons*, Texte zur Geschichte der evangelischen Theologie 2 (Neukirchen-Vluyn: Neukirchener-Verlag, 1966), 9–30 (M.'s outline of Romans).

Bohn, F., "Die Verzahnung des Römerbriefes, Kapitel 1–8," *TSK* 104 (1932): 439–48.

Boismard, M.-E., "L'Épître de Saint Paul aux Romains," *RB* 65 (1958): 432–36.

Bonnard, P., "Où en est l'Interprétation de "l'épître aux Romains?" *RTP* 3.1 (1951): 225–43.

Byrne, B., "Living out the Righteousness of God: The Contribution of Rom 6:1–8:13 to an Understanding of Paul's Ethical Presuppositions," *CBQ* 43 (1981): 557–81.

Campbell, W. S., "The Place of Romans ix–xi Within the Structure and Thought of the Letter," *SE VII*, TU 126 (1982), 121–31.

———, "Romans iii as a Key to the Structure and Thought of the Letter," *NovT* 23 (1981): 22–40.

Dahl, N. A., "Two Notes on Romans 5," *ST* 5 (1951): 37–48.

Dunn, J. D. G., "Paul's Epistle to the Romans: An Analysis of Structure and Argument," *ANRW* 2.25.4 (1987), 2842–90.

Dupont, J., "Le Problème de la structure littéraire de "l'épître aux Romains," *RB* 62 (1955): 365–97.

Etzold, O., "Gedanken zum Aufbau des Römerbriefes," *Bethel* 26 (1934): 67–74.

Feuillet, A., "Les Attaches bibliques des antithèses pauliniennes dans la première partie de l'épître aux Romains (1–8)," *Mélanges bibliques en hommages au R. P. Béda Rigaux*, ed. A. Descamps and A. de Halleux (Gembloux: Duculot, 1970), 323–49.

———, "La Citation d'Habacuc 2,4 et les huit premiers chapitres de l'épître aux Romains," *NTS* 6 (1959–60): 52–80.

———, "L'Histoire du salut dans les lettres aux Galates et aux Romains: La Progression des idées dans la première partie de l'Épître aux Romains (chapîtres 1–8)," *EspVie* 92 (1982): 257–67.

———, "Le Plan salvifique de Dieu d'après l'épître aux Romains: Essai sur la structure littéraire de l'épître et sa signification théologique," *RB* 57 (1950): 336–87, 489–529.

———, "Le Règne de la mort et le règne de la vie (*Rom.*, v, 12–21): Quelques Observations sur la structure de l'épître aux Romains," *RB* 77 (1970): 481–521.

ROMANS

Girardin, B., *Rhétorique et théologique: Calvin, le commentaire de l'épître aux Romains*, Théologie historique 54 (Paris: Beauchesne, 1979), 369–87.

Grayston, K., " 'Not Ashamed of the Gospel': Romans 1,16a and the Structure of the Epistle," *SE II*, TU 87 (1964), 569–73.

Jeremias, J., "Zu Rm 1,22–32," ZNW 45 (1954): 119–21.

———, "Zur Gedankenführung in den paulinischen Briefen," *Studia Paulina in honorem Johannis de Zwaan septuagenarii* (Haarlem: Bohn, 1953), 146–54.

Jewett, R., "Following the Argument of Romans," WW 6 (1986): 382–89.

Léon-Dufour, X., "Situation littéraire de *Rom. V*," RSR 51 (1963): 83–95.

Luz, U., "Zum Aufbau von Röm. 1–8," TZ 25 (1969): 161–81.

Lyonnet, S., "Note sur le plan de l'épître aux Romains," *Mélanges Jules Lebreton I*, = RSR 39 (1951): 301–16.

———, "Notes sur l'exégèse de l'Épître aux Romains," Bib 38 (1957): 35–61, esp. 35–40.

Manson, W., "Notes on the Argument of Romans (Chapters 1–8)," *New Testament Essays: Studies in Memory of Thomas Walter Manson 1893–1958*, ed. A. J. B. Higgins (Manchester: Manchester University Press, 1959), 150–64.

Ortigues, E., "La Composition de l'épître aux Romains (I–VIII)," *VCaro* 8 (1954): 52–81.

Prümm, K., "Zur Struktur des Römerbriefes: Begriffsreihen als Einheitsband," ZKT 72 (1950): 333–49.

Ramaroson, L., "Un 'Nouveau Plan' de *Rm* 1, 16–11, 36," NRT 94 (1972): 943–58.

Refoulé, F., "Unité de l'*Épître aux Romains* et histoire du salut," RSPT 71 (1987): 210–42.

Rolland, P., " 'Il est notre justice, notre vie, notre salut': L'Ordonnance des thèmes majeurs de l'épître aux Romains," Bib 56 (1975): 394–404.

Rossi, B., "Struttura letteraria e articolazione teologica di Rom 1,1–11,36," SBFLA 38 (1988): 59–133.

Ruijs, R. C. M., *De structuur van de brief aan de Romeinen: Een stilistische, vormhistorische en thematische analyse van Rom. 1,16–3,23* (Utrecht: Dekker & Van de Vegt, 1964).

Schmithals, W., "Die Integrität von Kap. 1–15," *Der Römerbrief als historisches Problem*, SNT 9 (Gütersloh: Mohn, 1975), 152–89.

Schnackenburg, R., "Römer 7 im Zusammenhang des Römerbriefes," *Jesus und Paulus: Festschrift für Werner Georg Kümmel . . .*, ed. E. E. Ellis and E. Grässer (Göttingen: Vandenhoeck & Ruprecht, 1975), 283–300.

Spadafora, F., "La lettera ai Romani nel suo svolgimento logico," *Divinitas* 2 (1958): 460–71.

Suibertus a S. Ioanne a Cruce, "De structura idearum in ep. ad Romanos," VD 34 (1956): 68–87.

Thils, G., "Epistolae ad Romanos analysis," *ColMech* n.s. 16 (1946): 288–91.

Viard, A., "Bulletin du Nouveau Testament," RSPT 42 (1958): 324–48, esp. 333–34.

IX. PAULINE TEACHING IN ROMANS

◆

Hic liber est in quo quaerit sua dogmata quisque,
Invenit et pariter dogmata quisque sua.
(This is the book in which each one seeks his own dogmas,
and likewise finds each his own.)

In the letter to the Romans, the most important of the Pauline corpus in the NT, there is a remarkable summary of some Pauline teachings, even though it is not complete. It is not, to repeat Melanchthon's description of Romans, "caput et summa universae doctrinae Christianae" (summary of all Christian doctrine; see section V above), or even a summary of all Pauline doctrine. For some characteristic Pauline tenets are missing from Romans: his teaching on the church, the eucharist, or eschatology (save for fleeting remarks). Yet despite such omissions, Romans contains many characteristic Pauline teachings about God, Christ Jesus, the Spirit, and human beings in their relation to them and in their dealings with one another. So an effort is made here to synthesize these teachings as a means to the proper understanding of Romans as a whole and to the interpretation of individual passages in it. But any synthetic summary is a modern construct; it is no substitute for Paul's own expression of such teachings or for the reading and exegetical study of the letter itself.

Pauline teaching in Romans will be presented under five headings: (A) theology proper, or Pauline teaching about God; (B) christology, or teaching about Christ Jesus and his role in God's salvific plan; (C) pneumatology, or teaching about the holy Spirit; (D) anthropology, or teaching about human beings with and without the influence of Christ; and (E) Christian conduct, or teaching about the call of humanity to Spirit-guided existence.

103

A. THEOLOGY PROPER, TEACHING ABOUT GOD

God. Apart from the debated passage in Rom 9:5, where *theos* may be predicated of Christ (the Messiah), *(ho) theos* occurs elsewhere in Romans only as a designation of the God of the OT, the God of Israel, the God whom Paul himself worshiped as a Jew (11:1) and whom he now serves as "the apostle of the Gentiles" (11:13). In fact, as Morris has shown ("The Theme of Romans," 250), *theos* is the word that is found most frequently in Romans (apart from the symbolic words like the article, *kai, en,* and *autos*); occurring 153 times, it is used more frequently than *de*, the verb *einai*, the preposition *eis*, and even *Christos*, which occurs only 66 times. Indeed, *theos* appears more frequently in Romans than in any other book of the NT save Acts (168 times), which is more than twice as long as Romans (VKGNT 2.130, 300). Significantly, Paul is clearly preoccupied with the activity of God in human history.

For Paul "God is one" (3:30), and he tells of the glory of this "immortal God" (1:23). The name of God is to be praised and glorified (4:20; 15:17) and not "blasphemed among the Gentiles" (2:24, quoting Ezek 36:20). His oracles have been entrusted to the Jewish people (3:2); he is the God of the "covenants" made with Israel (9:4). Yet, Paul insists, he is not "the God of Jews only," but of "the Gentiles too" (3:29), since he is "one" (3:30). He is the God whom Abraham, the forefather of Israel, trusted and "believed" (4:3, 17), "the living God" (9:26), who has not rejected his people Israel (11:1–2).

Paul insists that "what can be known about God is manifest" to human beings (1:19); "ever since the creation of the world his invisible qualities, his eternal power and divinity, have been perceived by reflection on what he has made" (1:20). This God is "the creator" (*ho ktisas,* 1:25), who gives life to the dead and calls into existence things that are not (4:17). "From him and through him and for him are all things" (11:36). Paul refers to God's creative activity when he speaks of the scope of things that can never separate Christians from his love manifested in Christ Jesus: "neither angels nor principalities, neither the present nor the future, nor any powers, neither height nor depth, nor any other creature" can do so (8:38–39). Implicitly he affirms God's dominion over the cosmos, even over the world of spirits, of which human beings stand in awe.

This God is "the Father" (6:4), "the Father of our Lord Jesus Christ" (15:6). Thus Paul's *theo*logy is not independent of his christocentric soteriology. Yet he is also "our Father" (1:7), that is to say, the Father of all Christian people. To him Christians cry "*Abba,* Father" (8:15), for through Christ and his Spirit they have become "children of God," even "heirs of God" (8:16).

But this God also judges human beings (2:3–6) and "will repay everyone according to his deeds" (2:6, quoting Prov 24:12 or Ps 62:13), for he is a God of "severity" (11:22). For Paul, all human beings must stand "before God's tribunal" (14:10, where he quotes Isa 49:18 or 45:3 to prove it); none "will escape the judgment of God" (2:3), "when God's just judgment (*dikaiokrisia*) will be revealed" (2:5). This God is a God of "eternal power and divinity" (1:20), of "wisdom and knowledge" (11:33), a "God of steadfastness and encouragement" (15:5), a "God of fidelity" (15:8; 3:3), of "goodness" (2:4), of "truth" (1:25; 3:4, 7), "truthfulness" (2:2; 3:7), "forbearance" (2:4), "longsuffering" (2:4), "mercy" (11:32), "peace" (15:33; 16:20), and "hope" (15:13), who fills all with love, hope, joy, and peace (15:13). Such are the generic qualities or attributes that Paul predicates of God, but three of them in particular call for further comment: God's love, uprightness, and wrath. Each of these attributes Paul has inherited from his OT background.

The Love of God. *Hē agapē tou theou* is a divine quality mentioned in Deut 7:7; Isa 63:9; Zeph 3:17; Jer 3:13; and Hos 3:1. Paul recognizes that from this love stems the election of Israel (11:28) and the favor shown to the patriarchs. That love has also been "poured out into our [Christian] hearts through the holy Spirit that has been given to us" (5:5, 8). Paul sings of the love of God (8:39), the overpowering gift to Christians, who will never be deprived of the manifestation of it in Christ Jesus. This attribute of God pervades part B of the doctrinal section of Romans (chaps. 5–8) and is the basis of the plan of salvation, assuring humanity of its justification and reconciliation. Paul also speaks of "the love of the Spirit" (15:30), without explaining this concept further.

The Uprightness (or Righteousness) of God. *Dikaiosynē theou* is another quality derived from the OT and used frequently in Romans. The meaning of the phrase is, however, much debated. Is the genitive *theou* subjective or possessive, referring to God's own uprightness, a quality of his being or his activity? Or is it an objective genitive, expressive of the uprightness communicated by God to human beings? Paul seems to use the phrase in both ways: as a subjective genitive (at least in 3:5, if not always in Romans) and as an objective genitive (in 2 Cor 5:21; cf. Phil 3:9). Sometimes, especially in this century, interpreters have tried to combine the two and speak of a genitive of authorship, in other words, an uprightness that comes from God, given to human beings, which becomes the basis of their relationship with God. This reading seems questionable; it is better to take it everywhere in Romans as a subjective or possessive genitive.

The phrase itself, the equivalent of Hebrew *ṣedeq ʾEl/ʾElōhîm* or *ṣidqat ʾEl/ʾElōhîm*, is not found in the OT. The closest one comes to it is *ṣidqat YHWH* (Deut 33:21), which is not quite the same thing, for the RSV renders it "the just decrees of the Lord," and the NRSV translates it "what the Lord deemed right"; the LXX translates, *dikaiosynēn Kyrios epoiēsen*, "the Lord has wrought righteousness." Or again, *ṣidqôt YHWH* (Judg 5:11), which the RSV translates "the triumphs of the Lord," and the NRSV, "the victories of the Lord"; the LXX has *ekei dōsousin dikaiosynas Kyriō*, "there they will grant the Lord righteous acts."

The exact Hebrew equivalent of Paul's phrase occurs, however, in QL: *ṣedeq ʾEl* (1QM 4:6) or *ṣidqat ʾEl* (1QS 10:25; 11:12); see also *T. Dan* 6:10 (in some MSS). This correspondence reveals his dependence on a genuine pre-Christian Palestinian Jewish tradition. Paul did not invent the phrase, even if he uses it in a striking, otherwise unattested sense in 2 Cor 5:21.

In the OT God is, of course, often called *ṣaddîq*, "upright, righteous": for instance, Ps 116:5 ("Gracious is the Lord, merciful and righteous"); Exod 9:27; Jer 12:1; Zeph 3:5. His "uprightness" is often mentioned, as in Pss 35:28; 36:7; 51:16; 103:17; 112:9; Prov 16:10; Isa 46:13; 59:16. In the early books of the OT *ṣedeq* or *ṣĕdāqāh* expresses the quality whereby Yahweh, involved in a lawsuit (*rîb*) with rebellious Israel, judges it and displays his "uprightness" in doing so (Isa 3:13; Jer 12:1; Hos 4:1–2; 12:3; Mic 6:2). It is a quality of God manifested in judicial activity; God "judges" with "uprightness" (Pss 9:9; 96:13; 98:2 ["Yahweh has made known his salvation; in the sight of the nations he has revealed his uprightness," from which Paul has probably derived three of the important ideas of 1:16–17]). In such a context "the triumphs of the Lord" are to be understood as legal or judicial triumphs (cf. Mic 6:5; 1 Sam 12:7).

At times OT scholars maintain that Yahweh's uprightness has a cosmic dimension: creation and all that God has done in the world are to be attributed to this divine quality. Appeal is made to Dan 9:14 ("You, O Lord, are righteous in all that you have done") or Jer 31:35–36 (see Schmid, *Gerechtigkeit*; von Reventlow, *Rechtfertigung*; Müller, *Gottes Gerechtigkeit*). To make this claim, however, they tend to empty the quality of *ṣedeq* of its judicial aspect. Creation and governance of the world are scarcely judicial acts. The alleged "cosmic" dimension has thus been read into texts in which it is not really found.

In the postexilic period, *ṣedeq* as a divine attribute acquired an added nuance: the quality whereby God acquits his people, manifesting toward them a gracious, salvific power in a just judgment. In Isa 46:13, "my uprightness" and "my salvation" stand in parallelism; cf. 51:5, 6, 8; 56:1; 61:10; Ps 40:9–10. In this sense Yahweh is acknowledged to be "upright" (Ezra 9:15; Neh 9:8) and "righteous" in all that he has done (Dan 9:14), namely, in all the ways he has treated rebellious Israel.

Even later, *dikaiosynē* in the LXX sometimes translated other (nonjudicial) covenant qualities of God: his *ʾĕmet*, "fidelity" (Gen 24:49; Josh 24:14; 38:19), his *ḥesed*, "steadfast mercy" (Gen 19:19; 20:13; 21:23). This mode of translation reflects the postexilic connotation of *ṣedeq* more than its original judicial denotation. Indeed, Greek *eleos*, "mercy," is even found to translate *ṣĕdāqāh* in Isa 56:1; cf. Ezek 18:19, 21.

Paul adopts this postexilic understanding of "God's uprightness" in Romans (as a quality, certainly in 3:5, and most likely in 1:17; 3:21–22, 25–26; 10:3[bis]; see the NOTES on these passages). God manifests it toward humanity when through the death and resurrection of Jesus Christ he brings about the vindication and acquittal of sinful human beings. It is a manifestation of God's saving and acquitting power: "God's sovereignty over the world revealing itself eschatologically in Jesus . . . , the rightful power with which God makes his cause to triumph in the world which has fallen away from him and which yet, as creation, is his inviolable possession" (Käsemann, " 'Righteousness of God,' " 180). This description is admissible, provided one does not empty that "rightful power" of the legal or judicial denotation that is proper to it. It is, indeed, "Gottes heilsetzende Macht" (Stuhlmacher), but *exercised in a just judgment*. Käsemann phrases it better when he speaks of it as "God's power working itself out forensically in the sphere of the covenant" (*Commentary*, 79). Yet as such, it is a manifestation of divine "power" and, therefore, of a divine attribute, which idea Käsemann is reluctant to accept. Paul's idea of the justification of sinners is thus rooted in a divine quality, God's uprightness or righteousness. Convinced of God's uprightness, Paul can ask, "Is God unjust?" (9:14), an idea he resolutely rejects. So he depicts God saving human beings in accordance with what is upright and just: manifesting through Christ crucified "that he [God] is upright and justifies the one who puts faith in Jesus" (3:26).

Bultmann was right in denying the apocalyptic connotation of *dikaiosynē theou* that Käsemann sought to derive from the alleged Qumran use of the expression and associate with the Pauline usage of the phrase. Insistence on that connotation has distracted from the importance of Käsemann's view of God's uprightness as his salvific or acquitting power. Sanders (*Paul and Palestinian Judaism*, 305–12) analyzed the main Qumran passages in which *ṣedeq/ṣĕdāqāh* occurs and has shown that such a divine quality is not characteristic of apocalyptic settings; but he stresses too much "uprightness" as a mere synonym of "mercy." The Pauline idea of "God's uprightness" verges indeed on his "mercy," but it is not the same. The judicial or forensic element is lacking in the latter idea, even though it is often used in parallelism with "uprightness." Through his uprightness "God makes his integrity known through his active faithkeeping" and persists "in keeping his covenant intact in spite of human unfaithfulness" (Hays, "Psalm 143," 111).

The Wrath of God. *Orgē theou* is another divine quality inherited by Paul from the OT (Ps 78:31; Isa 13:13; 26:20; 2 Kgs 22:13; Ezra 10:14; 2 Chr 12:12). It expresses not an irrational or irresponsible outburst of rage, a capricious or arbitrary anger against human beings; nor is it to be associated with the Greek idea of angry deities who have to be placated. Rather it denotes the expected divine reaction to human sin and evil. It is linked to monotheism and to the covenantal relationship of God with Israel, expressing the justifiable reaction of a loving and faithful God toward his disobedient people and their proneness to idolatry, to evil, and to sinful conduct. It denotes God's steadfast attitude as a judge of Israel's breach of the covenant (Ezek 5:13; Hos 5:10; 2 Chr 36:16). When the people of Israel chose Aaron as their leader in Moses' absence and worshiped the golden calf, Yahweh sent Moses to that "stiff-necked people," declaring, "Now leave me alone that my wrath may burn against them and that I may consume them. Yet I will make of you a great nation" (Exod 32:10; cf. Isa 30:27–28). Yahweh's wrath was also manifested against neighboring nations that oppressed his people (Isa 10:5–11; Ezek 36:5–6; Jer 51[LXX 28]:11). But God's wrath is also often linked with mercy and loving-kindness, when he is said to be "slow to anger, abounding in steadfast love" (Ps 103:8; Joel 2:13). The prophet Habakkuk prays to the Lord, "In wrath remember mercy" (3:2).

From such a Jewish background Paul derives the notion of God's wrath, which he now associates with God's cosmic judgment. It is the wrath not only of the God of Israel, but of God, the creator of all. Often the genitive *theou* is omitted and has to be supplied in the context (2:5, 8; 3:5; 4:15; 5:9; 9:22; 12:19; 13:4, 5). In the OT the "wrath of God" is often related to "the day of the Lord" (Zeph 1:14–18), and thus it expresses God's eschatological retribution for sin. This too becomes a feature of Paul's eschatological teaching; it will be manifested in the future (at judgment), but it can also manifest itself in the course of human earthly life: it is already being revealed against the godlessness and wickedness of pagans (1:18–32) and of Jews (3:5). But, in another form, it is still awaited (2:6). Paul thus sees God very much involved in the world of free human beings who abuse that freedom.

This is an example of protological thinking that Paul has also inherited from the OT. In such thinking, God is considered responsible for all that happens to his people and his creation, good or evil. For instance, Deutero-Isaiah depicts Yahweh declaring, "I form the light and create darkness, I make peace and create evil; I, the Lord, do all these things" (45:7). Or, again, Amos says, "If evil comes upon a city, has not the Lord done it?" (3:6). In this way the inevitable retribution of human sin is ascribed to God's "wrath." The theological distinction between God's absolute will and his permissive will had not yet entered the history of ideas; it was to wait for the time of Augustine. Meanwhile neither the OT nor much of the NT has corrected this way of thinking. For the beginning of the correction, see Jas 1:13.

Divine Plan of Salvation. With such attributes Paul depicts God not only as a judge of humanity (2:3, 16; 3:6) but also as its savior, of Jew and Greek alike (1:16; 10:1, 10; 13:11). God, the Creator, is presented as the author of a plan or "project" of salvation (*prothesis*, 8:28; 9:11), which accords with his "will" (1:10; 15:32) and his "predestination" of all things (8:28–30). This divine plan is concerned with human history and is now ordered to the salvation of his "people," not only his chosen people of old (11:1–2, quoting Ps 94:14; and 15:10, quoting Deut 32:43), but the Gentiles, those who were "not his people" (9:25–26, quoting Hos 2:1, 25). Paul speaks specifically of the "election" of Israel (11:18) and of the "promises" made to Abraham and to the patriarchs (4:13; 9:4; 15:8). But that plan now embraces also all who are willing to put their faith in Christ Jesus, beginning with "remnant" of Israel, "chosen by grace" (11:5), and including the Gentiles "called" to praise the same God along with Israel (11:10–11). To this predestining plan of God Paul attributes the call, justification, and glorification of all Christians (8:30). Thus Paul describes not only the attributes of God, but also God's initiative and activity on behalf of humanity in and through Christ Jesus. For this very reason God raised Jesus from the dead. The initiative in this process always lies with God, in Paul's thinking.

To this plan of salvation are related phases of human history, as Paul viewed them through Jewish spectacles. He knows of a phase "from Adam to Moses" (5:14; cf. Gal 3:17), the Law-less period when human beings did evil, but when such evil was not imputed as a transgression (5:13–14); then of a phase from Moses to the Messiah, when "the law was added" (Gal 3:19) or "slipped in" (Rom 5:20); in this period there was, in addition to the influence of Adam's sin, the contributing factor of individual sin now reckoned as transgressions and booked because there was a law to violate; finally, the phase of the Messiah, of Christ who is "the end of the law" (10:4), when there is freedom from the law through the grace of Christ (8:1). Now justified human beings, living a life of faith working itself out through love, fulfill what the law requires (13:10). This phase, already begun, when "Christ died at the appointed time for the godless" (5:6), perdures until the coming of "the day" of the Lord (13:11–14).

The Old Testament. Related to this sacred history is the record of the history of Israel itself compiled in the OT. God's "gospel," which Paul preaches, is understood as having been "promised long ago through his prophets in the sacred Scriptures" (1:2). Indeed, even God's uprightness has been disclosed by the witness borne to it "through the law and the prophets" (3:21). Paul quotes the OT time after time in the course of Romans to bolster his view of God's saving activity at work generation after generation as it moves relentlessly toward its goal. In chap. 4 he uses the Genesis story of Abraham to illustrate the theme of justification by grace through faith explained in 3:21–31. In chap. 5 he compares Christ and Adam. In chaps. 9–11 he cites many OT examples to strengthen his argument. In fact, he assures his readers that the "words 'it was credited to him' [Gen 15:6] were written not only for Abraham's sake, but for ours too" (4:23–24). "What was written of old was written for our instruction that through endurance and the encouragement of the Scriptures we might have hope" (15:4).

God's Gospel. Paul ascribes to God himself not only such a salvific plan, but even the "gospel," the good news about that plan now realized in the ministry, passion, death, and resurrection of Jesus Christ, which Paul preaches. *Euangelion*, the specifically Christian word denoting the "good news of Jesus Christ," occurs nine times in Romans, usually to express the content of Paul's proclamation. It is "God's gospel" (1:1), that is, good news that has its origin in God; "the gospel of his Son" (1:9), wherein the genitive is normally understood as objective, in other words, the good news about the Son, even though it may also connote the gospel coming from Christ (15:18–19). It is Paul's one-word summary of the Christ-event, the meaning that the person and lordship of Jesus have for human existence. Paul speaks of it as "my gospel" (2:16), a gospel of which he is "not ashamed" (1:16); he looks on his preaching of it as a cultic, priestly act offered to God (1:9; 15:16).

Euangelion is used seven times in the LXX in the sense of "good news" (2 Sam 18:20, 22, 25, 27; 2 Kgs 7:9) or a "reward for good news" given to a herald (2 Sam 4:10; 18:22 [cf. Homer, *Odyssey* 14.152–53, 166]). The cognate verb *euangelizesthai* occurs in Isa 52:7; 60:6; and 61:1 and may be part of the OT background of the Christian use of "gospel." Such OT passages lie behind Paul's reference to the prophets (1:1), for in the Hebrew division of the Scriptures 2 Samuel and 2 Kings would be part of the Former Prophets and Isaiah part of the Latter Prophets.

Paul sees the gospel as "apocalyptic," revealing God's salvific power and activity for his people and now making known his salvation in a new way through the ministry and lordship of Jesus Christ (1:17). This "gospel" continues the promises made by God of old, "promised beforehand through the prophets in the holy Scriptures" (1:1). It reveals the reality of the new age and makes known a "mystery" hidden for all ages (16:15–26). Even the partial insensibility of Israel to the gospel is part of this "mystery" (11:25). In presenting the gospel as mystery, Paul implies that proclamation of the good news is never fully made known by ordinary means of communication and that its message is apprehended only in faith. Paul's gospel is a "force" *(dynamis)* newly unleashed by God in human history to bring about the salvation of all, Jew and Greek alike (1:16). It proclaims and makes known to all that "Jesus is Lord" (10:9) and announces him as the "Son of God with power . . . as of his resurrection from the dead" (1:4). The gospel thus becomes a norm for Christian conduct and life, summoning human beings to "hear" it (10:16–17) and "obey" it with "a commitment of faith" (1:5). Thus God's gospel is apocalyptic, dynamic, kerygmatic, normative, promissory, and of universal value.

B. CHRISTOLOGY, TEACHING ABOUT CHRIST JESUS AND HIS ROLE IN GOD'S SALVIFIC PLAN

Jesus Christ. In writing Romans, Paul is not addressing a community that he has evangelized or founded. He may presume that Roman Christians know something, perhaps much about Jesus, but they have not yet experienced his personal way of presenting Jesus Christ and his message; they have not yet learned about Paul's gospel or Pauline christology.

The overall teaching about Christ in Romans is easily summed up: Jesus is presented as God's new agent for the justification and salvation of all human beings, Jew and Greek alike, who come to belief in him and in his Spirit, which manifests God's love of all. In Romans Paul can boast that he is not ashamed of the gospel that he preaches because it reveals God's christocentric power now unleashed through the gospel of his Son and his Spirit in the world of human beings, precisely for their salvation (1:16–17).

Paul never hints that he ever knew Jesus of Nazareth. Although there are a few echoes of Jesus' sayings in some letters (1 Cor 7:10–11; 9:14; 11:23–26; 14:37; 1 Thess 4:15–17 [see Alison, Dungan, Keck, Stanley, Stuhlmacher]), Paul passes on nothing in Romans about what the Jesus of history did or said in his earthly life and ministry. He does sum up in a remarkable way, however, the significance of the role that Jesus played in the Father's plan of salvation. Paul gives us little by way of ontological christology; he is interested in the functional aspects of christology, in what Christ Jesus has done for humanity. For this reason Paul's teaching is best characterized as a christocentric soteriology.

Paul's christology in Romans can be synthesized under the following headings: the names and titles used of Jesus; the role ascribed to him; and the effects of the Christ-event.

Names and Titles Used of Jesus in Romans: Jesus. At times Paul refers simply to "Jesus" (3:26; 8:11a), calling him by his heaven-given name *Iēsous*, without alluding to either its origin or its meaning. It was, after all, a common enough Jewish name, borne by many Jews of the time, being used in the OT itself, but now borne by the Palestinian Jew sent by God to announce his gospel of salvation. *Iēsous* is a grecized form of the Hebrew name *Yēšûaʿ* (Ezra 2:2), transcribed in the LXX as *Iēsous*. This name was most likely a postexilic contraction of earlier *Yĕhôšûaʿ*, "Joshua" (Josh 1:1), which means "Yahweh, help!" (= *Yhw* + the imperative *šwʿ*). Paul, however, never plays on the meaning of the name, undoubtedly because Jesus of Nazareth had already become for him "Christ our Lord."

Christ. Paul refers to Jesus as *Christos* and acknowledges his messianic character. When he singles out the seven prerogatives of his former coreligionists, he admits that to the Israelites belong "the sonship, the glory, the covenants, the giving of the law, the cult, the promises, . . . [and] the patriarchs" (9:4). To these seven he adds an eighth: "from them by natural descent comes the Messiah" (9:5). Here Paul uses *Christos* in its basic titular sense, equaling *Māšîaḥ*, "Messiah," denoting him as God's anointed agent for the salvation of his people and as "born of David's stock by natural descent" (1:3). This titular sense is important in this Pauline letter, which has so much to do with the interpretation of the OT, with the election of Israel, and with the relation of Gentile Christians to Israel.

In many passages, however, Paul uses *Christos* as Jesus' second name, "Jesus

Christ" (1:1, 4, 6, 8; 3:22; 5:1, 15, 17, 21; 13:14; 15:6; also in the appended doxology, 16:25, 27). In these instances, Paul speaks of "Jesus Christ" without alluding to the basic messianic denotation of "Christ." He has undoubtedly inherited this double name from the early Christian tradition before him, where it had already become so common. In thus coupling the names Jesus and Christ, Paul signifies that the Messiah whom Israel had awaited for centuries has now come and that it is his task as a commissioned apostle to proclaim that coming of the Messiah (see Dahl, "The Crucified Messiah" and "The Messiahship").

Sometimes, Paul simply refers to Jesus as "Christ," using only his second name, the one that became common after his death and resurrection as a result of the Easter faith among the disciples (5:6; 6:4, 8, 9; 7:4; 8:9, 10, 11, 17, 34[?], 35; 9:1, 3, 5; 10:4, 6, 7; 12:5; 14:9, 15, 18; 15:3, 7, 18, 20; 16:5, 7, 9, 10, 16). In a distinctive way, Paul reverses the double name as "Christ Jesus" (6:3, 11; 8:1, 39; 15:5, 16, 17; 16:3). Only he among NT writers uses this form. (The inverted names occur in Acts 3:20; 5:42; 17:3; 18:5, 28; 24:24, but then only as variant readings, probably introduced by copyists familiar with the Pauline usage.) According to some commentators this inverted form of the double name gives "the title extra emphasis" (so Cranfield, *Romans*, 836). But it may be only a literary variant of no significance.

The Lord. Although *Kyrios* occurs for God in OT passages that Paul quotes, he also uses it of Jesus, retaining it in its titular sense. Christ Jesus has become for him the risen "Lord." He acknowledges, "Jesus is Lord" (*Kyrion Iēsous*, 10:9), using the same formula as in 1 Cor 12:3 and repeating the kerygma used by those who were apostles before him. They used this kerygma as they proclaimed Jesus of Nazareth, God's chosen agent for the salvation of humanity, and carried that proclamation forth from Jerusalem to the eastern Mediterranean world, where it quickly became the confessional affirmation of all Christians. For Paul it meant that "God raised him from the dead" (10:9b). Jesus of Nazareth was thus for Paul not only Christ Jesus, but the *Lord* Jesus Christ.

Paul not only uses *Kyrios* absolutely of Christ (10:9; 14:4, 6, 8; 16:2, 8, 11, 12, 13, 22), but also with various modifiers. Time after time he combines the titles "Jesus Christ our Lord" (1:4; 5:21; 7:25), or "the/our Lord Jesus Christ" (1:7; 5:1, 11; 13:14; 15:30), or "Jesus our Lord" (4:24), or "Christ Jesus our Lord" (6:23; 8:39). He also uses the prepositional phrase *en Kyriō* (14:14; 16:2, 8, 11, 12, 13, 22) to express the relation of various persons or activities to the Lord (see Cerfaux, Foerster, Hahn, Kramer, V. Taylor).

In so using *Kyrios*, Paul acknowledged along with the rest of the early church that the risen Jesus was on a par with Yahweh of the OT, whom Palestinian Jews had come to call "(the) Lord" (contrary to Bultmann's contention that "the un-modified expression 'the Lord' is unthinkable in Jewish usage" [*TNT* 1.51]). In the OT *ʾādôn* usually denotes a human "master, lord" (*ʾădōnî*, "my lord"), and *ʾădōnāy* (lit., "my lords") was used for "Lord" (= God). But *ʾādôn* in Hebrew was on occasion applied to Yahweh (Ps 114:7). Moreover, recently discovered Qumran texts reveal that Palestinian Jews in the last pre-Christian century had begun to refer absolutely to Yahweh as "(the) Lord": 4Q4031 i 28 (*bārûk [hā]ʾādôn, mele[k hak]kôl*, "Blest be the Lord, King of the Universe"; 11QPsᵃ 28:7–8, possibly to be read as *maʿăśê ʾādôn*, "the works of the Lord"), or in Aramaic as *mārêh* or *māryāʾ* (11QtgJob 24:6–7; 4QEnochᵇ 1 iv 5). Even Josephus in the first Christian century used Greek *Kyrios* of God (*Ant.* 20.4.2 §90; 134.3.1 §68). Paul's use of *Kyrios*, then, does not simply identify Jesus with God, but it shows that he regarded him as on a par with God, whom he otherwise still calls *Kyrios* (4:8 [quoting Ps 32:2]; 9:28 [possibly quoting Isa 28:22], 29 [quoting Isa 1:9]; 10:13 [quoting Joel 3:5]; 10:16 [quoting Isa 53:1]; 11:3 [quoting 1 Kgs 19:10], 34 [quoting Isa 40:13]; 12:19 [quoting Prov 25:21]; 14:11 [quoting Isa 49:18]; and 15:11 [quoting Deut 32:43]). In giving the risen Christ the title *Kyrios*, Paul acknowledges that he has become an ever-abiding influence in his life and in the life of all Christians. The risen Christ is *Kyrios*, and Paul is his bonded servant or slave, *doulos* (1:1; see Fitzmyer, "The Semitic Background").

The Son. In Romans Paul also recognizes Jesus' special relationship with the heavenly Father as filial, calling him "his Son" (*ho huios autou*, 1:3, 9; 5:10; 8:3 ["his own Son"], 29, 32). Moreover, he recognizes that Jesus, "born of David's stock by natural descent" (1:3), was also God's "Son," and has been "constituted Son of God with power" as of (his) resurrection from the dead (1:4), in other words, that he has thus become a life-giving force for all who acknowledge him as the risen Lord, and this precisely as "Son." The title "Son of God" has a long history in the ancient Near East and in the OT (see *PAHT* §PT49). In the OT it is used as a mythological title for angels (Job 1:6; 2:1), as a title of predilection for the people of Israel collectively (Exod 4:22; Deut 14:1), as a title of adoption for a king on the Davidic throne (2 Sam 7:14; Ps 2:7), for judges (Ps 82:6), and even for an individual upright Jew (Sir 4:10; Wis 2:18). It is often said to be a messianic title, but there is no evidence in pre-Christian Jewish literature of such usage. Paul himself undoubtedly inherited this title for Jesus from the early Christian community before him. As such, Jesus is regarded as the "one man" who "through his obedience" (5:19) as Son became the source of uprightness for all who believe in him. For God himself did not spare this Son of his, but gave him over to manifest the bounty of his love "for us all" (8:32). For Paul, "God's gospel" clearly centers on his "Son" (1:1, 3, 9). As Cranfield notes (*Romans*, 840), this title indicates "a relationship involving a real community of nature between Christ and God."

Adam of the Eschaton. Although Paul does not refer in Romans explicitly to Christ Jesus as "the last Adam," as he does in 1 Cor 15:45, he admits implicitly that Christ plays such a role, when he refers to Adam as the "type of the one who was to come" (5:14). This image becomes in patristic literature "the Second

Adam," dependent in part on 1 Cor 15:47b, "the second man" (see Athanasius, *Contra Apollinarem* 1.8; PG 26.1105). Thus for Paul Christ has become the Adam or head of a new humanity, the source of "newness of life" (6:4). The phase of salvation history "from Adam to Moses" (5:14) has come to an end, and similarly the phase from Moses to the Messiah, because "Christ is the end of the law" (10:4); but as such, he has become the source of salvation and uprightness for all, Jew and Greek alike, in this newly begun life of the eschaton. His "obedience" stands in contrast to the "disobedience" of Adam (5:19), to Adam's "trespass" (5:14) and "transgression" (5:15).

God. Although the meaning of the passage is debated, Paul may even give Christ the title *theos* in 9:5. Having recognized Jesus the Messiah "according to the flesh" as the eighth prerogative of the Israelites, Paul may add a comma and the appositive, "who is God over all, blest forever." If this is the correct punctuation of the verse (a comma before *ho ōn*, as N-A[26] reads it), then Paul, as early as A.D. 57–58, would have recognized Jesus' divine status. Such a recognition is found nowhere else in Paul's uncontested letters (save possibly in Gal 2:20, which is just as problematic); cf. Col 2:2; 2 Thess 1:12; Titus 2:13. Yet it would mean that for Paul Jesus is not only "Lord" or "Son of God," but in some sense "God." Paul is, of course, aware that Jesus is not *'abbā'* because he knows that Christians under the influence of the Spirit are enabled so to address God the Father (8:15), in imitation of Jesus' own mode of calling on God in prayer (Mark 14:36). Unfortunately, Paul does not explain in what sense he would understand Jesus to be God, and it was left for later theologians to unpack the notion of "God" in such a biblical text. Yet because Paul came to regard Jesus as *Kyrios* and implied thereby that he was on a par with Yahweh of the OT, it is not surprising that he would eventually call him *theos*. Note too how he relates Christ to the activity of the Father (mentioned together in 1:7; 2:16; 5:8) and how he speaks interchangeably of "the love of Christ" (8:35) and of "the love of God" (8:39). This tendency made John Chrysostom comment, "It is thus indifferent to him to call (Jesus) both Christ and God" (*In ep. ad Romanos*, hom. 15.3; PG 60.544). Yet Paul himself still expressed the relation of Christ to God thus: "the God and Father of our Lord Jesus Christ" (15:6).

The Role Ascribed to Jesus in Romans. In Romans Paul not only makes use of traditional christological names or titles, but also alludes in many ways to his soteriological role for, as I have said, Paul's basic teaching is a christocentric soteriology. He is aware of certain important events in the life of Jesus of Nazareth, especially those with vicarious and salvific value. First of all, he shows awareness of who Jesus was, and what he did and suffered. Paul knows that Jesus was descended from David according to the flesh (1:3) and speaks of him as *heis anthrōpos*, "one man" (5:15, 17, 19), thus emphasizing his humanity and what he did as an individual human being in the course of his earthly life on behalf of all. He speaks of Jesus' existence *kata sarka*, lit., "according to the flesh" (1:3; 9:5), emphasizing his human pedigree. Paul never ascribes a salvific meaning to Jesus' birth, ministry, preaching, or miracle working, but he thinks of him as someone brought down from heaven (10:6) and thus implicitly reckons with his preexistence. The same may be implicit in his calling Jesus God's "Son" (1:3; 5:10; 8:3, 32). Paul says of him that he was someone who "did not please himself" (15:3), but was "a servant to the circumcised" (15:8), who "suffered" on behalf of all human beings (8:17). His "obedience" is recorded (5:19), and for Paul "the service of Christ" (14:18; 16:18) consisted in all of these features of his life.

Second, in Romans Paul acknowledges that Jesus was "handed over (to death)" (4:25), that "he died" (5:6, 8; 8:34; 14:15), and that he "shed his blood" (5:9). He not only speaks of "the death of his [God's] Son" (5:10), or of "his death" (6:3, 5, 10), but recognizes that "Christ . . . died for the godless" (5:6), in other words, that Jesus died precisely as the Messiah (contrast Bultmann, *The History of the Synoptic Tradition* [Oxford: Blackwell, 1968], 273 and Dahl, "Crucified Messiah," 23–36). Again, Paul alludes to Jesus' death by crucifixion (6:6) and to his burial (6:4). Indirectly, he tells of things that happened to the earthly Jesus, even though he never narrates his life or ministry as did the evangelists. Sometimes he refers to Jesus' death and its soteriological value by speaking of our justification "by his blood" (5:9); "Through his blood God has presented him as a means of expiating sin" (3:25). What lies behind this notion is Lev 17:11, "the life of the flesh is in the blood; and I have put it for you upon the altar to make expiation for your lives; for it is the blood that makes expiation by reason of the life."

Paul also affirms Jesus' "resurrection from the dead" (1:4; cf. 6:5), thus admitting that he was brought "up from the dead" (10:7) or "was raised" (4:25; 6:9; 8:34). Again, he asserts that Jesus "was raised from the dead by the glory of the Father" (6:4) and "no longer dies" (6:9). Paul ascribes the efficiency of Christ's resurrection to the Father (4:24; 6:4; 8:11; 10:9; 1 Thess 1:10; Gal 1:1; 1 Cor 6:14; 15:15; 2 Cor 4:14; cf. Col 2:12; Eph 1:20); as such, the Father is also the initiator of human salvation through that powerful act. He also speaks of "his life" as the risen Lord (5:10; cf. 14:19), who "lives to God" (6:10) and enjoys "eternal life" (6:23).

Paul sees an intimate connection between Jesus' cross and his resurrection: he "was handed over (to death) for our trespasses and raised for our justification" (4:25). This becomes the basis of Paul's proclamation and explanation of faith: "If you profess with your lips that 'Jesus is Lord,' and believe in your heart that God raised him from the dead, you will be saved" (10:9).

Finally, Paul alludes to Christ's ascension (10:6), acknowledging that he was not only raised from the dead, but is now "at God's right hand" and "intercedes for us" (8:34). Hence Jesus' salvific role is not limited to his earthly life or ministry or even to his death and burial. It continues in his existence as the risen Lord as he exerts his heavenly influence on Christians at all times in prayer to the Father on their behalf. Thus the risen Christ, "established as the Son of God with

115

power," exists "by a spirit of holiness" (1:4) and unites his activity to that of the Father. Again, "the Spirit of life" in Christ Jesus (8:2) exerts its liberating influence on all humanity. Indeed, as "God's Spirit" (8:9) and "the Spirit of him who raised Jesus from the dead" (8:11), "the Spirit itself" also "intercedes for us" and remedies the deficiencies of weak human prayer (8:26). Yet Christ is not only the heavenly intercessor praying to the Father on behalf of human beings, but through Christ God himself is to judge "the secrets of human hearts" (2:16). So the role of the heavenly Christ is double: intercessor and judge.

The foregoing points sum up briefly what Paul in Romans teaches about Christ, about what Jesus was and what he became through his death and resurrection. But Paul also describes the effects of the Christ-event, namely, the effects of what Christ achieved for humanity in his soteriological role, in his life, ministry, death, burial, and resurrection.

The Effects of the Christ-Event. In describing what Christ has achieved for humanity, Paul in Romans makes use of images drawn from his background and applies them to the soteriological work of Jesus. In a sense, Paul is trying to utter the ineffable, to describe what is really indescribable, and that is why he resorts to so many different images. Each one has a symbolic value and differs from the others; each one has, then, to be studied in and for itself that the nuance associated with it be appreciated. It is as if Paul were looking at a many-sided solid figure, which encapsulates those effects; when he looks at it from one angle, he says, "Christ justified us," from another angle, "Christ saved us," or from another, "Christ reconciled us." Each image so used carries its own significance. The images are drawn from Paul's Jewish or Hellenistic background and are applied by him in different ways to various aspects of Christ's salvific role. But, most importantly, they all express the one reality: what Christ Jesus has done for humanity, for Jew and Gentile alike.

The image most frequently used in Romans to express an effect of the Christ-event is "justification" (*dikaiōsis, dikaioun*). On the one hand, Schweitzer years ago termed justification "a subsidiary crater, which has formed within the rim of the main crater—the mystical doctrine of redemption through the being-in-Christ" or a teaching that is "incomplete and unfitted to stand alone" (*Mysticism*, 225–26). On the other, it is undoubtedly going too far to say with Käsemann that for Paul "justification is the heart of the Christian message" ("Some Thoughts," 63). Yet to anyone who reads Romans justification is clearly the effect that claims pride of place, the chief way that Paul expresses the effects of the Christ-event.

"Justification" is drawn from Paul's Jewish background, expressing a relationship between human beings and God, a judicial relationship, either ethical or forensic (i.e., related to human conduct and to law courts: Deut 25:1; cf. Gen 18:25–26). *Dikaios*, "righteous, upright," usually denoted a person who stood acquitted or vindicated before a judge's tribunal (Exod 23:7; 1 Kgs 8:32; Job 31:35–37), and thus in a right relationship with other human beings. Used of Israelites, it denoted their covenantal relationship, their status of "uprightness" achieved in the sight of Yahweh the Judge by the observance of the statutes of the Mosaic law (Pss 7:9–12; 119:1–8). The OT often noted how difficult a status this was to retain (Job 4:17; Ps 143:2; Ezra 9:15). Josephus could imagine nothing "more righteous" than obeying the statutes of the Law (*Ag. Ap.* 2.41 §293). The Essenes of Qumran sang of their sinfulness and sought justification from God alone: "As for me, I belong to wicked humanity, to the assembly of perverse flesh; my iniquities, my transgressions, my sins together with the wickedness of my heart belong to the assembly doomed to worms and walking in darkness. No human being sets his own path or directs his own steps, for to God alone belongs the judgment of him, and from his hand comes perfection of way. . . . If I stumble because of a sin of the flesh, my judgment is according to the righteousness of God" (1QS 11:9–12; cf. 1QH 9:32–34; 14:15–16).

Building on such an OT and Palestinian Jewish understanding of justification, Paul introduces a reference to the historical event of the death of Christ: Christ alone has become the way in which the "uprightness of God" is revealed or made known. Whereas the Qumran teaching about justification involved a dualism of light and darkness, uprightness and iniquity, and a heightened understanding of OT legal regulations, the Pauline teaching knows nothing of the kind. For him Christ is "the end of the law" (10:4), that is to say, the goal toward which it was aimed; whereas in Gal 3:13 Paul calls Christ the "curse of the law," he never says anything like that in Romans. Moreover, the Pauline teaching on justification differs from that of Qumran by reason of the Apostle's insistence on "faith" as the mode whereby all human beings, Jew and Greek, appropriate this justification that Christ Jesus has made possible. Whereas Qumran had taught that justification came about *sola gratia*, Paul goes farther and insists that it is *solo Christo* and *sola fide*, and not by deeds of the law.

When, then, Paul in Romans says that Christ Jesus "justified" human beings "by his blood" (3:25; cf. 5:9), he means that by what Christ suffered in his passion and death he has brought it about that sinful human beings can stand before God's tribunal acquitted or innocent, with the judgment not based on observance of the Mosaic law. Thus "God's uprightness" is now manifested toward human beings in a just judgment, one of acquittal, because Jesus "our Lord . . . was handed over (to death) for our trespasses and raised for our justification" (4:25). This was done for humanity "freely by his grace" (3:24). For God has displayed Jesus in death ("by his blood") as "a manifestation of his [God's] uprightness . . . at the present time to show that he is upright and justifies [= vindicates] the one who puts faith in Jesus" (3:26; cf. 5:1). Thus God shows that human activity, indeed, is a concern of his judgment, but through Christ Jesus he sets right what has gone wrong because of the sinful conduct of human beings. Paul insists on the utter gratuity of this justification, because "all alike have sinned and fall short of the glory of God" (3:23). Consequently, this uprightness does not belong to human beings (10:3), and it is not something that they have produced or merited;

it is an alien uprightness, one belonging rightly to another (to Christ) and attributed to them because of what that other has done for them. So Paul understands God "justifying the godless" (4:5) or "crediting uprightness" to human beings quite "apart from deeds" (4:6; see Käsemann, Kertelge, Lyonnet, Reumann, Schlatter, Schulz).

This effect of the Christ-event was undoubtedly recognized by early Christians even before Paul; at least Rom 4:25 is often regarded as a pre-Pauline affirmation of Christ's role in the justification of human beings, which Paul is here echoing. The distinctive Pauline contribution, however, is his teaching that such justification comes about "by his grace" (3:24) and through "faith" (3:25). Although it is unlikely that the judaizing problem with which Paul had to cope in his experience in eastern Mediterranean churches gave rise to this way of viewing the Christ-event, that problem undoubtedly helped Paul to sharpen his own view of the matter.

The action whereby the God of uprightness "justifies" the sinner has been the subject of no little debate. Does the verb *dikaioun* mean "to declare upright" or "to make upright"? One might expect that *dikaioun*, being a verb belonging to the *-oō* class, would have a causative or factitive meaning, "to make someone *dikaios*" (as *dēloun*, "make clear"; *douloun*, "enslave"; *nekroun*, "mortify"; *anakainoun*, "renew"). But in the LXX, *dikaioun* seems normally to have a declarative, forensic meaning (Schrenk, *TDNT* 2.212–14; cf. D. R. Hillers, *JBL* 86 [1967]: 320–34; cf. N. M. Watson, "Some Observations on the Use of *dikaioô* in the Septuagint," *JBL* 79 [1960]: 255–66). At times the declarative seems to be, indeed, the sense in Paul's letters (e.g., 2:13; 3:4, 20; 8:33); but many instances are ambiguous, and the effective sense seems to be supported by 5:19, "through the obedience of one many will be made upright (*dikaioi katastathēsontai*)."

Again, if Käsemann's emphasis on "God's uprightness" as "power" is correct, this sense of *dikaioun* acquires an added nuance, and the OT idea of God's word as effective would support it (Isa 55:10–11). The debate about the declarative or effective sense of *dikaioun* has been acute ever since the Reformation. Yet it is to be recalled that even Melanchthon admitted that "Scripture speaks both ways" (*Apology* 4.72). Compare too the modern debate about its meaning between (Presbyterian) B. M. Metzger (*TToday* 2 [1945–46]: 562) and (Baptist) E. J. Goodspeed (*JBL* 73 [1954]: 86–91).

From patristic times on, the effective sense of *dikaioun*, "make upright, just, righteous" has been used (*dikaion poiēsai*: John Chrysostom, *In ep. ad Romanos* 8.2 [PG 60.456]; *In ep. II ad Corinthios* 11.3 [PG 61.478]; Augustine, *De Spiritu et littera* 26.45 [CSEL 60.199]: *iusti facti*; 32.56 [CSEL 60.215]: *iusti efficimur*; *Sermo* 131.9: *iustos facit*; 292.6: *iustum facere* [PL 38.733, 1324]). From such statements, McGrath concludes that "righteousness, effected in justification, is regarded by Augustine as *inherent* rather than *imputed*, to use the vocabulary of the sixteenth century" (*Iustitia Dei*, 1.31). He also maintains that this sense of *dikaioun* persisted throughout the early and late medieval period (ibid., 184).

In modern times this sense of *dikaioun* is often called "transformationist." It would mean that the sinful human being is not only "declared upright," as *dikaiousthai* may mean in some instances in Romans, but is "made upright" (as in 5:19). For the sinner's condition has changed: *dikaiousthai* is the opposite of *hamartanein* and *hysterountai tēs doxēs tou theou*, falling short of the glory of God (3:23). Through justification the condition of *doxa* is restored to the sinner. "God's judgment has creative power. Declaring the sinner upright has not only a forensic effect, but as forensic also an 'effective' meaning" (Kertelge, *"Rechtferti- gung,"* 123). Through faith in Christ Jesus the sinner experiences the manifesta- tion of God's uprightness and "becomes" in the concrete "the uprightness of God" (2 Cor 5:21). As a result, the sinner is *dikaios* and stands before God as "upright, acquitted."

Paul also uses the image of "salvation" (*sōtēria, sōzein*). This image is most probably derived from the OT, where it expresses Yahweh's deliverance of Israel, either as its Savior (*môšîac*, Isa 45:15; Zech 8:7; cf. Ps 25:5; Mic 7:7) or by "saviors" raised up to deliver Israel (Judg 3:9, 15; 6:36; 2 Kgs 13:5). It is not impossible, however, that Paul has also been influenced in the use of this image by the contemporary Greco-Roman world, in which gods such as Zeus, Apollo, Artemis, or Asclepius were often called *theos sōtēr* and hailed with a cultic epithet in time of need (illness, travail, sea storms). This title was also given to kings, emperors, and town councils in their roles as benefactors (see H. Volkmann, "Soter, Soteria," *DKP* 5.289–90).

The image expresses deliverance or rescue from evil or harm, whether physical, psychic, national, cataclysmic, or moral. In using it, Paul recognizes that Christians "are being saved" by the cross of Christ. This image is, strikingly enough, used in the very thesis of Romans, where he identifies the "gospel" as "God's power (unleashed) for the salvation of everyone who believes" (1:16). Although Paul realizes that this effect of the Christ-event has already been achieved once and for all, he nevertheless regards its end result as still a matter of the future, having an eschatological aspect (5:9–10; 8:24 ["in hope we have been saved"]; 10:9–10, 13). Indeed, "our salvation is now closer than when we first believed" (13:11). Related to this future aspect is the role of intercession ascribed to the risen Christ in heaven (8:34). Paul himself prays for the salvation of his fellow coreligionists, the Jewish people (10:1), and is convinced that "all Israel will be saved" (11:26).

Another image that Paul uses to describe effects of the Christ-event is "reconciliation" (*katallagē, katallassein*). This image is derived from Paul's Greco-Roman background, for there is no Hebrew or Aramaic word to express the idea in the OT. The LXX uses *diallassein*, which has the same meaning, about a Levite who became angry with his concubine and went to talk to her "to reconcile her to himself" (Judg 19:3), but the Hebrew text says "to cause her to return to him." Compare 1 Sam 29:4, where the Hebrew reads, "He will make him acceptable." In Hellenistic Greek, however, the verbs *katallassein* and *diallassein* are found abundantly (see Dupont, *La Réconciliation*, 7–15).

The words are compounds of the root *all-*, "other," and denote a "making otherwise," in either a secular or a religious sense. In a secular sense, they denote a change in relationship between individuals, groups, or nations and describe relations in social or political spheres. They denote a change from anger, hostility, or alienation to love, friendship, of intimacy; feelings may accompany such a change, but they are not essential (see Matt 5:23–24; 1 Cor 7:11). In a religious sense, Greek literature uses these verbs of the reconciliation of gods and humans (e.g., Sophocles, *Ajax* 744; cf. 2 Macc 1:5; 7:33; 8:29). When Paul applies this image to the Christ-event, he speaks of God or Christ reconciling human beings, who are enemies or sinners, to himself. The initiative lies with God, who through Christ brings it about that human sinners are brought from a status of enmity to friendship: "if, when we were God's enemies, we were reconciled to him through the death of his Son, now that we are reconciled, we shall all the more certainly be saved by his life. Yet not only that—but we boast of God through our Lord Jesus Christ, through whom we have now received reconciliation" (5:10–11).

Paul even extends this effect of the Christ-event to the cosmos as well; he speaks of the "reconciliation of the world" (11:15; cf. 2 Cor 5:19). Thus reconciliation expresses not only an anthropological effect of the Christ-event, but also a cosmic effect.

Another effect of the Christ-event in Romans is described as "expiation" (*hilastērion*). Despite attempts to relate this image to Paul's Hellenistic background (see the NOTE on 3:25), it has almost certainly been derived by him from the Greek OT.

Because *hilastērion* is related to the verb *hilaskesthai*, "appease, propitiate," often used of appeasing angry gods in classical and Hellenistic Greek literature (Homer, *Iliad* 1.386; Strabo, *Geography* 4.4.6; Appian, *Hannibaikē* 27.115; Philo, *De spec. leg.* 1.23 §116; Josephus, *Ant.* 6.6.5 §124), many commentators on Romans think of *hilastērion* in this sense. It would then mean that God has set forth Christ as "appeasing" or as "a means of appeasing" his own anger or wrath.

In the LXX, however, *hilaskesthai* refers either to God's pardon of sin or to a ritual removal of cultic defilement that hinders the communion of a person or an object with God (see Lyonnet, *Sin*, 124–27, 137–46). When *hilastērion* first occurs in the LXX (Exod 25:17), it seems to be an adjective, *hilastērion epithema*, "expiating cover, lid" and translates Hebrew *hakkappōret*. This refers to the "lid" of fine gold, 2.5 by 1.5 cubits, that was erected over the top of the Ark of the Covenant in the Holy of Holies as the base for the two cherubim of Yahweh's throne, that is, for his footstool (Exod 25:17–22). But thereafter it appears twenty-six times as *to hilastērion* (e.g., Exod 25:18–22 [where the article is used, as in the MT]; 31:7; 35:12); it is often accompanied by the Greek definite article (except 1 Chr 28:11, where Hebrew *bêt hakkappōret* becomes *tou oikou tou exilasmou*). Hence it has become a noun signifying "means of expiation" or "place of expiation." Compare Philo, *De Cherub.* 8 §25; *De fuga* 19 §100; *De vita Mos.* 2.20 §95; *T. Sol.* 21:2. In Hebrew *kippēr* means "smear over, wipe away" (see *HALAT*, 470), and the lid was called *kappōret* because it was smeared with the blood of a sacrificed bull by the high priest who entered the Holy of Holies once a year to make expiation for the holy place and for the sins of Israel on *yôm hakkippûrîm*, "the Day of Atonement," which really means "the Day of Expiations" (Lev 16:14–20).

In the Vg, *kappōret* was rendered in most cases *propitiatorium* (whence the translation "propitiatory" in some older English Bibles), but it is translated as *oraculum* in six instances (Exod 25:18, 20b; 40:18 [= Hebrew 40:20]; Lev 16:2b, 13, 15b [in 1 Chr 28:11 *domus propitiationis* occurs]). Now this use of a noun related to the verb *propitiare*, "appease, propitiate," has given *hilastērion* the added nuance of a "means of appeasing God's anger," an understanding that long persisted, especially in the Latin theological tradition.

Luther, however, broke with that tradition and translated *hakkappōret* or *hilastērion* as *Gnadenstuel* (WAusg DB 7.39); and in imitation, the *KJV* rendered it as "mercy seat." Luther's translation caught better the sense of the term used in both Lev 16:2, 11–17 and this Pauline passage. In using this image to describe an effect of the Christ-event, Paul reflects its relation to the Day of Atonement ritual in Leviticus 16: "Through his blood God has presented him as a means of expiating sin for all who have faith" (3:25). God has set forth Christ Jesus on the cross as the "mercy seat" of the new dispensation, the new means of expiating (= wiping away) the sins of human beings. Jesus' death, then, surpasses and supersedes the ritual of expiation in the Temple of old (Leviticus 16). The vicarious nature of expiation is illustrated by 4 Macc 17:22, where the phrase *tou hilastēriou tou thanatou* is used of the death of the seven brothers, averting God's wrath from the nation of Israel. Christ's blood has achieved for humanity once and for all what the Day of Atonement ritual symbolized each year for Israel of old, the wiping away of human sins. In referring to the crucified Christ as the *hilastērion*, Paul is not just comparing him with a cult object or piece of furniture in the Temple of old, but with the place wherein God reveals himself to his people and wherein his expiating power in regard to their sins is made known: "*There* [at the mercy seat] I shall meet with you . . . (and) I shall speak with you about all that I shall give to you as commandments for the people of Israel" (Exod 25:22); *there* too the high priest was to bring the incense and the blood of the bull to make expiation (Lev 16:13).

Pace Lohse (*Märtyrer*, 152), the word *hilastērion* cannot be said to mean the same thing as *tou hilastēriou tou thanatou autōn*, "the propitiation/expiation of their death" in 4 Macc 17:22. First, the reading there is not certain, and Lohse is following the Swete text, MS A: *tou hilastēriou thanatou autōn*, "their propitiating/expiating death." But MS ℵ reads *tou hilastēriou tou thanatou autōn*, "the expiation/propitiation of their death," as in the Rahlfs text. Unfortunately the Göttingen text of 4 Maccabees does not yet exist. Second, in the Pauline text *hilastērion* lacks a modifier, and there is simply no evidence in any Jewish writing of the expression *hilastērion thyma*, allegedly meaning "propitiatory sacrifice," which Lohse and others claim is the meaning of *hilastērion* in Paul's phrase. Although the adjective *hilastērious* occurs in secular Greek writings joined to *thysias*, "propitiatory victims (for the gods)" (*Papyrus Fayum* 337 [second century A.D.]), the entire context of Paul's paragraph has so many allusions to OT motifs that it is highly unlikely that he would mean by *hilastērion* anything like the secular "propitiatory sacrifice" or even the "propitiatory death" of 4 Macc 17:22. Third, it introduces into Pauline vocabulary a term *(thyma)* that Paul never uses for the Christ-event in any of his uncontested letters; he never says that Christ was sacrificed for our sake (contrast Eph 5:2, where *thysia* is so used). That notion enters the later theological tradition, but it is not one that can be traced directly to Paul; it is at best a reformulation of an implication of *hilastērion*, because Christ's "blood" is here implied to be the substitute for the sacrificial blood of the animals in the Day of Atonement rite. Indeed, the notion of Christ's death as a sacrifice is more tributary to Hebrews and to the Deutero-Pauline Eph 5:2 than to the uncontested Pauline letters. See further the refutation of Lohse's views by Stuhlmacher, "Recent Exegesis."

In the LXX, however, *hilastērion* is also used as the translation of Hebrew *ʿăzārāh* (Ezek 43:14, 17, 20 [in 45:19 this Hebrew word is instead rendered by *hieron*]), which is usually translated "ledge," part of the altar of sacrifice, again a place of expiation (the blood to be smeared is called *haima tou exilasmou* [45:19]). (In the late second century A.D. Symmachus translated *tēbāh* of Gen 6:16, (Noah's) "ark," by *hilastērion*, undoubtedly attributing to it the salvific nuance implicit in this Greek word.)

Another image used by Paul is "redemption" *(apolytrōsis)*. Whence does Paul derive this image? It has been related to the emancipation of war prisoners and the sacral manumission of slaves in the Greco-Roman world (see *Ep. Arist.* 12.35; Josephus, *Ant.* 12.2.3 §27; BAGD, 12; Deissmann, *LAE*, 320–23): more than a thousand Delphic inscriptions record that "Pythian Apollo purchased So-and-So for freedom"). That Paul is aware of the social institution of emancipation is clear from 1 Cor 7:20–22; but his Greek vocabulary is notably different from that in the Delphic inscriptions. So it is perhaps better to explain the background of this image in the light of LXX terminology, where the verb *apolytroun* is used for the "redeeming" of a slave (Exod 21:8) and the noun *apolytrōsis* occur (Dan 4:34). Again, the simple forms *lytron*, "ransom," and *lytroun*, "redeem," are used abundantly in the LXX (Exod 6:6; 15:13–16; 21:30; 30:12). Behind this OT usage lies the idea of Yahweh as Israel's *gôʾēl*, "redeemer," the kinsman who had the duty of buying back an enslaved or captive Jewish relative (Isa 41:14; 43:14; 44:6; 47:4; Pss 19:15; 78:35). It referred at first to the freeing of Israel from Egyptian bondage (Deut 6:6–8; Ps 111:9), when Yahweh "acquired" a people as a possession for himself (Exod 15:16; 19:5; Mal 3:17; Ps 74:2); later on, to the return of Israel from Babylonian captivity (Isa 51:11; 52:3–9). Still later, it acquired an eschatological nuance: what God would do for Israel at the end of days (Hos 13:14; Isa 59:29; Ps 130:7–8). This image Paul applies to Christ when he records that Christians are justified freely by his grace "through the redemption that comes in Christ Jesus" (3:24). This image is also used in an eschatological sense and even a cosmic sense, for Paul in 8:21–23 speaks of "creation itself" eventually being freed "from its bondage to decay and brought to the glorious freedom of the children of God," who are groaning inwardly as they "wait for the redemption" of their bodies.

Related to the image of redemption is yet another, "freedom" (*eleutheria*, *eleutheroun*). Although "freedom" sometimes carries the nuance of redemption, it is more properly explained by the Greco-Roman notion of freedom as the social status of citizens in a Greek *polis* or Roman *municipium* (see OCD, 703, 851– 52), a "city" in the Roman world that enjoyed freedom. (The Greek root *eleuthero-* occurs in the LXX, but it is found for the most part in the deuterocanonical and apocryphal Greek writings.) In applying this image to the Christ-event, Paul means that Christ Jesus has conferred on human beings the rights of citizens of a free city or state; he has made them citizens of heaven (see Phil 3:20: "our commonwealth is in heaven"). The freedom to which Paul refers is that from bondage to "sin and death," "self," and "the law" (7:3; 8:1–2). "When you were slaves of sin, you were free from uprightness" (6:20; cf. 6:18). This effect of the Christ-event also has its eschatological aspect, being associated with the status of Christians in "glory" (8:21).

Paul also sees the Christian introduced into a "new way of life" through the Christ-event (6:4–5). Even though he does not use in Romans the image of *kainē ktisis*, "new creation" (see Gal 6:15; 2 Cor 5:17), he means the same thing by *kainotēs zōēs*, "newness of life" (6:4). It is a share in the risen life, by which Christ himself now lives, a life lived in "the glory of God" (3:23b). Because of Christ's status as of his resurrection, Paul regards him as "the firstborn among many brothers" (8:29c), who are "predestined to be conformed" to his "image" (8:29b). Thus Christians enjoy proleptically the very life of the risen Christ, which is nothing else than "eternal life" (5:21; 6:23).

Paul refers to *hagiasmos*, "sanctification," as an effect of the Christ-event only in 6:19 and 22, where he speaks of Christians putting their members at the disposal of uprightness, "which leads to holiness," which in turn "results in life eternal." "Sanctification" is a way of expressing the dedication of Christians to the awesome service of God. This figure is derived by Paul from the OT, where things and persons were often said to be "holy" (e.g., Exod 3:5; 19:14; 26:33; Lev 19:2; Isa 48:2; 62:12; 64:10; 1 Macc 2:54). It was a cultic term that marked off from the secular or profane such persons or things for this service. For Paul, Christ Jesus became "our sanctification" (1 Cor 1:30), namely, the means whereby Christians become "saints" (1:7; 12:13; 15:25, 26, 31; 16:2, 15).

Still another image that Paul uses to describe an effect of the Christ-event is "glorification" (*doxa*, *doxazein*). This image is derived from the OT, where

Hebrew *kābôd* and Greek *doxa* express "glory, splendor," the perceptible manifestation of God's presence, especially in theophanies of the exodus (e.g., Exod 24:16–17; 40:34; Num 14:10; Tob 12:15). Paul uses it to express the destiny of the Christian, that of which sinful human beings have fallen short (3:23). It is also the goal of divine predestination: "Those whom he predestined, he also called; those whom he called, he also justified; and those whom he justified, he also glorified" (8:30). This is also "the glory that is going to be revealed in us" (8:18), associated with the freedom that Christians await (8:21).

Although the image is doubtful, Paul may also speak in Romans of "pardon" *(paresis)* as an effect of the Christ-event. The uncertainty that surrounds the image is exegetical: does *paresis* mean "a passing over" or "a remission or pardon" of a debt due to human sinfulness? See the NOTE on 3:25. The latter seems preferable.

Thus in nine or ten different ways Paul describes in Romans effects of the Christ-event, making use of different figures or images drawn from his Jewish or Hellenistic background. He makes it clear that these effects stem from "the love of Christ" (8:35), and as a result there is now "no condemnation for those who are in Christ Jesus" (8:1), for it has all been achieved through "one act of uprightness" *(dikaiōma,* 5:18).

C. PNEUMATOLOGY, TEACHING ABOUT THE HOLY SPIRIT

The Spirit. The end result of what Christ has done is that all human beings can now live in the "new way of the Spirit" (7:6). Paul affirms that "If one does not have Christ's Spirit, one does not belong to Christ" (8:9) and that newness of life comes from him "who raised Christ from the dead" and who "will give life . . . through his Spirit" (8:11).

In Romans, when Paul speaks of the Spirit, he does not understand *pneuma* as in the Hellenistic world of his time, as the power of thaumaturgy and ecstasy, but rather as an apocalyptic manifestation of the endtime, as in the OT. Whereas in the OT it was often an eschatological manifestation, early Christianity understood it as related to the resurrection of Christ. Paul especially used the idea to express the presence and activity of the risen Lord in his community. Consequently, when Paul uses *pneuma,* he takes over much of the OT idea of "the Spirit of God." There the "Spirit" expresses God's presence to his people, his agents, or his world in a creative, prophetic, quickening, or renovating way (Gen 1:2; Num 24:2; 1 Sam 19:20, 23; 2 Chr 15:1; 24:20; Pss 51:12; 139:7; Isa 11:2; 61:1; Ezek 2:2; 11:5). Although Paul realizes that God is present to Christians in and through Christ Jesus, he never calls him explicitly "the Spirit of God." In 8:9–11 "God's Spirit," "Christ's Spirit," "Christ," and "the Spirit of him who raised Jesus from the dead" are used interchangeably in the Pauline description of God's indwelling. In using *pneuma hagiōsynēs* as something pertaining to the risen Christ (1:4), Paul explains how he has become functionally "the Son of God with power," the transcendent, dynamic source of holiness, in virtue of which he as the risen Lord quickens and vivifies human beings. Thus he is the Adam of the eschaton (1 Cor 15:45); "the Lord is the Spirit" (2 Cor 3:17). "Spirit of holiness" is a Palestinian Jewish equivalent of "holy Spirit" (see the NOTE on 1:4). The risen Lord is thus intimately related to the Spirit as a mode of bringing Christians into God's presence. The Father/God, our Lord Jesus Christ, and the holy Spirit are a threesome that Paul uses to affirm this presence (5:1–5; 8:14–17), though he does not sort out the relation of the three, as later trinitarian theology would attempt.

As in his christology, so too in his references to the Spirit Paul is mainly interested in the function of the latter in human conduct and salvation. If Christ Jesus has brought about the possibility of a new life for human beings, to be lived in him and for God, it is more precisely "Christ's Spirit" that is the dynamic and vital principle of that life. For Paul the Spirit is an energizer, by whose "power" (15:13) Christians are enabled to live in joy, peace, and hope (14:17). Through the Spirit, justified human beings are freed "from the law of sin and death" (8:2) and become "children of God" (8:14). The gift of the Spirit enables them to overcome their weakness in prayer, and it also "intercedes for us with ineffable sighs" (8:26), making us aware of our special relationship with the Father.

Because the love of God has been poured out into the hearts of Christians through the holy Spirit given to them (5:5), they, though sinners, share in that love, which is the source of their reconciliation and salvation (5:8–10). So gifted, Christians are able to conduct themselves not according to the flesh, but "according to the Spirit" (8:4), for that Spirit is actually "dwelling in" them (8:11), enabling them to "put to death the deeds of the body" (8:13). "The Spirit of life" has made Christians free of "the law of sin and death" (8:2). What was impossible for the law to do, God has achieved for those who conduct themselves "according to the Spirit" (8:3–4). Again, the Spirit is the source of "adoption" (*huiothesia*) and "sonship," whereby justified human beings are enabled to call upon God as ᵓ*abbā*ᵓ, Father (8:15).

Strangely enough, Paul never mentions the Spirit in his discussion of Israel's place in the divine plan of salvation (chaps. 9–11). The Spirit is mentioned in 9:1, but only apropos of Paul's own testimony about his sorrow and anguish over his fellow kinsmen by race. (In 11:8 *pneuma* occurs, but then to express a "stupor of spirit" in a conflated quotation of Isa 29:10 and Deut 29:3. It has nothing to do with the holy Spirit.) Yet through "consecration by the holy Spirit" (15:16) Paul offers Gentile converts as an offering acceptable to God.

Paul is also aware of the Spirit's power in his own life and ministry, as he admits that it was in virtue of such power that he could perform "signs and wonders" (15:19) in his ministry among the Gentiles. "By the love of (that) Spirit"

(15:30) Paul urges the Roman Christians to pray for him and his journey to Jerusalem, as he will bring to the poor there the collection taken up among Gentile Christians of Macedonia and Achaia.

Grace. Related to the gift of the Spirit is *charis*, "grace." This term denotes God's "favor," the gratuitous aspect of the Father's initiative in the salvation and justification of human beings (5:15c). It expresses the divine prevenience in the call of Abraham and in the promise made to him and his posterity (4:16), in the call of Paul the apostle (1:4), in the justification of human beings (3:24), and in the election of the remnant of Israel (11:5). This grace comes from the Father through "one man, Jesus Christ" (5:15, 17, 20), and through God's favor thus manifested comes "life through Jesus Christ our Lord" (5:21; cf. 6:4).

At times Paul speaks of *charis* as if it were something "given to," "manifested to," or "received" by humans like a concrete gift (12:3, 6; 15:15). One may debate whether *charis* in such texts is conceived of as something created by God and productive of the good for which it was destined. In any case, such Pauline texts led in time to the patristic and medieval theological idea of "sanctifying grace" and of *gratia creata* as the counterpart of *gratia increata*, the mode in which such later theology spoke of the holy Spirit, the energizing force of such created grace.

This "favor" from God is sometimes joined with *eirēnē*, "peace," in Paul's epistolary greeting (1:70), where one learns that its source is both the Father and the Lord Jesus Christ. Access to such "grace" comes only through "faith" (5:1–2). It is superabundant in comparison with human sin; there is no real equivalence between them (5:17, 20). God's "grace" as the source of new life brings it about that Christians cannot even think of sinning, much less remain in a state of sin (6:1, 14). And so abundant is God's "grace" in justification that all need of "deeds of the law" is eliminated (11:6).

D. ANTHROPOLOGY, TEACHING ABOUT HUMAN BEINGS WITHOUT AND WITH THE INFLUENCE OF THE GOSPEL

Many of Paul's comments reveal the ways in which he has thought of humanity apart from Christ Jesus. He recognizes that, left to themselves, human beings are "sinners" and "under the power of sin" (3:20, 23; 11:32). Part of the reason for that status is the very physical makeup of human beings, for they are "body," "flesh," "soul," "spirit," "mind," and "heart." These are not to be conceived of as organs or parts of the human composite. Rather, for Paul, as for his Jewish peers, these elements express aspects of the unique human totality. This totality is above all *sarkinos*, "carnal," made of flesh *(sarx)*. Yet a human being does not merely have a body; one is *sōma*. It can even be another way of expressing the "self": the human being as a complex, living organism, the subject of activity and the object of one's own actions and those of others (6:12–13). It is also the seat of "deeds" and "lusts" (6:12; 8:13).

Body. The visible, tangible, biological aspect of a human being is designated as *sōma*, usually translated as "body" and regarded as the composite of flesh, blood, and bones (1:24; 4:19). This "body" is dominated by sin (6:6, 12; 7:14, 18) and becomes thereby a sin-ruled self (7:23), a "doomed body" (*sōma tou thanatou*, lit., "a body of death," 7:24; cf. 8:10, 13). As *sōma*, a human being in Paul's view is bereft of Christ, and without God's grace and Spirit the *sōma* can never belong to Christ.

Flesh. In the OT, Hebrew *bāśār*, lit., "flesh," expresses both "body" and "flesh," as there is no ordinarily distinct word for body (*gûphāh* occurs only once, in the sense of "corpse" [1 Chr 10:12]; and *gĕwiyyāh*, which usually means "corpse, carcass," only rarely has the sense of a living body [Dan 10:6; Ezek 1:11, 23]). Yet the LXX, under the influence of the Greek philosophical dichotomy of the body and the soul, distinguished *sōma*, "body," and *sarx*, "flesh." Echoing this LXX usage, Paul sometimes uses *sarx* to denote a human being and to connote his or her natural frailty (6:19). Often it designates natural, material human existence in its weak and earthbound isolated condition: "Those who live according to the flesh are concerned about things of the flesh" (8:5); they "cannot please God" (8:8). Paul does not mean by "flesh" merely the human sexual drive, for he identifies the *egō* itself with *sarx* and finds "no good" in either of them (7:18). Correspondingly, Paul contrasts "flesh" and "spirit" (8:4–9, 13), meaning a human being subject to earthbound tendencies and a human being open to the influence of God's Spirit.

Soul. Similarly, *psychē* denotes not just the vital principle of biological activity, but, as in the OT, a "living being" or "living person" (= Hebrew *nepeš* [Gen 2:7]). When it seems to mean more than "self," it connotes the conscious, purposeful vitality of the self (2:9; 13:1; 16:4).

Spirit. *Pneuma* too can be used not only to denote the holy Spirit, but also that aspect of a human being which is the knowing and willing self. As such, it expresses what is especially apt to receive the Spirit of God (1:9; 8:16).

Mind. For Paul *nous* denotes a human being as a knowing, planning, and judging subject, one whose capacity is for intelligent, conscious, and critical understanding. It is the aspect of a human being as one reflects on God's created world and learns from it about God (1:20, the *nooumena* are the things that a human as *nous* can comprehend). As *nous*, a human being acknowledges God's law (7:23,

25), but the *nous* can also prove worthless and base in not recognizing God for what he is (1:28).

Heart. Similar to *nous* is *kardia*, which often functions in the OT as "mind" and which designates the responsive and emotional reactions of the intelligent and planning self. The heart "grieves" (9:2); it "craves" (1:24); it "doubts and believes" (10:6–10); it can be "steeped in darkness" (1:21); it can be "stubborn and impenitent" (2:5). And yet, prescriptions of the law can be written on the "hearts" of Gentiles (2:15). "Real circumcision" is said to be "of the heart" (2:29), and "God's love" can be "poured out into [the] hearts" of human beings "through the holy Spirit" (5:5). With the "heart" one "believes that God raised" Jesus the Lord "from the dead" (10:9). "Such faith of the heart leads to uprightness" (10:10).

Conscience. Related to *nous* is *syneidēsis*, "conscience" (Latin *con-scientia*), which expresses the ability of the intelligent human being to judge one's actions in retrospect (as right or wrong) or in prospect (as a guide for proper activity). "Conscience" has no counterpart in the Hebrew OT or in QL; it enters the Jewish tradition via the LXX (Job 27:6; Qoh 10:20; Sir 42:18; Wis 17:10; cf. *T. Reub.* 4:3). It is certainly not borrowed by Paul from Stoic philosophy, for from at least the sixth century B.C. on it was a tenet of widespread Greek popular thinking. Initially, *syneidēsis* denoted "co-knowledge," or "consciousness" (of human activity in general); eventually it was applied to the consciousness of moral conduct, at first as "bad conscience," then as "conscience" in general. What Paul teaches about conscience eventually develops in the later rabbinic teaching as *yēṣer hāraʿ* and *yēṣer haṭṭôb*, "evil impulse" and "good impulse." In 2:14–15 Paul recognizes that through the "conscience" Gentiles may perform some of the prescriptions of the Mosaic law and are thus a "law" unto themselves. He also counsels Christians to be subject to governing authorities "because of one's conscience" (13:5).

All of these aspects of a human being characterize the individual. When left to their own devices, individuals do not accomplish good, because of weakness and indwelling sin that dominates them.

Humanity. Apart from such notions about the makeup of human beings, Paul also reckons with people of different ethnic or religious backgrounds. He distinguishes human beings into Jews, Greeks, and barbarians (1:14, 16), namely, his kinsmen by race (9:3), Gentiles who speak Greek, the common language of the Roman Empire, and Gentiles who babble in other, non-Greek languages. He says that he is indebted to all of them (1:14), but he also assesses their status in life as they live without the gospel.

Gentiles. Paul admits that Gentiles, even without the influence of the gospel, do at times "observe by nature" some "precepts of the law" (2:14a), that is to say, the Mosaic law. They are thus "a law to themselves, though not having the [Mosaic] law. They show that what the law prescribes has been written on their hearts" (2:14b–15a). Although this *nomos* has been related at times by commentators to "another law" or "the law of my mind" (7:23), that is probably wrong, for the prime analogate in chap. 7 is the Mosaic law. Paul does not mean that the Mosaic law as such has been written on the hearts of Gentiles, but that through their consciences they are aware of at least some of the do's and dont's of the Mosaic law, for instance, some of the Decalogue. Hence they are in a figurative sense "a law to themselves" (see p. 131, on the different senses of *nomos*). Again, though in 1 Cor 11:14 Paul does argue from *physis*, "nature," it is not easy to be sure that he so argues in Rom 2:14, where the phrase "by nature" may be a contention of others that he is merely quoting for the sake of the argument (perhaps it should be set in quotation marks). Again, in speaking of a law written on the hearts of Gentiles, Paul may be reflecting an OT formulation, echoing Jer 31:33 or Isa 51:7. The upshot is that 2:14–16 is not clearly a passage in which Paul teaches the so-called "natural law," an idea more at home in Greek philosophy and in patristic theology, even though one might have to admit that Paul's teaching about the Gentiles and their knowledge and conscience eventually led to the patristic formulation and understanding of natural law. Perhaps one might say that the patristic teaching about that law is the fuller sense *(sensus plenior)* of what Paul himself teaches. See K.-H. Schelkle, *Paulus Lehrer der Väter*, 81–83.

Paul passes stern judgment on the Gentiles who live without the gospel. As he sees it, they in their godlessness and wickedness "stifle the truth" about God and "his invisible qualities, his eternal power and divinity" (1:18–19). "Though they knew God, they did not glorify him as God or thank him" (1:21). Rather, they "exchanged the glory of the immortal God for an image shaped like a mortal human being, like birds, four-footed creatures, or reptiles" (1:23). Because Gentiles did not come to the proper knowledge of God by reflection on what God had made in creation and because of the idolatry that they practiced instead, Paul sees the bulk of them "delivered" by God to perversion, degradation, and sins of all sorts (1:24–30). Thus against them "God's wrath is being revealed from heaven" (1:18). In this scathing indictment of Gentile godlessness Paul reacts like a Jewish preacher, echoing OT times (see the COMMENT on 1:18–31).

Jews. When Paul speaks of the Jewish people, he refers to them as his "brothers," his "kinsmen by race" (9:3). He recognizes them as "Israelites" (9:4) or collectively as "Israel" (9:6), acknowledging their privileged position in human history governed by God's salvific plan: "the Jew first" (1:16; 2:9–10). This privilege is not only temporal but de jure, because God's gracious activity has been manifested to them beyond all others in the execution of the divine plan of salvation for humanity. That privilege is found in their "election" (11:5); they are "beloved of God because of the patriarchs" (11:28; 15:7). Paul readily admits their classic seven prerogatives as Israelites: "the sonship, the glory, the covenants, the giving of the law, the cult, and the promises; to them belong the patriarchs" (9:4–5), to which he adds an eighth: "from them by natural descent comes the Messiah" (9:5). He grants too that "the oracles of God," namely, the Scriptures, have been "entrusted" to them (3:2). Hence they know what God's will is for humanity; they have the Mosaic law, which continues to be valid for them.

Yet he says about the Jewish people:

> Suppose you call yourself a Jew, rely on the law, and boast of God, knowing his will and scrutinizing the things that really matter, because you are instructed by the law, and suppose you are persuaded that you yourself are a guide to the blind, a light to those in darkness, a corrector of the foolish, a teacher of the immature, because you have in the law the embodiment of knowledge and truth—then do you who would teach others fail to teach yourself? Do you who preach against stealing steal yourself? Do you who forbid adultery commit it yourself? Do you who abominate idols rob temples? As for you who boast of the law, you dishonor God by the transgression of the law. (2:17–23)

So Paul sternly indicts his former coreligionists. In his view the Jewish people have been given the law of Moses and hence must live according to it because that is part of Israel's pact with God: "we know that all that the law says is addressed to those who are under the law" (3:19a). Paul adds, "all who have sinned under the law will be judged by the law" (2:12). Yet he also recognizes that such human beings without the gospel were in bondage not only to sin and death, but also the law itself; they are "under law" (6:14; 3:19). (In Galatians Paul even went farther: they were locked up under the [Mosaic] law, as under custodians and guardians; 3:23–25.) So he describes the lot of the Jews covenanted with God and his law, yet without the gospel.

It is not easy to describe Paul's attitude to the Jewish people and their relation to the gospel. Their failure to accept the good news of Christ Jesus, he knows, does not mean that the divine plan of salvation has failed. Notwithstanding the reaction of Israel, God still is faithful to his word: to the promises made to Israel of old, to his control of human destiny, and to the future of Israel. Paul considers Israel's "rejection" of the gospel to be partial, because some Jews have become Christians, as he himself has; but it is also temporary. In God's providence the reaction of Israel has been one of the reasons that the gospel has been carried to the Gentiles, and that Paul himself has become "the apostle of the Gentiles" (11:13), Jew that he is. Indeed, Paul considers in this letter that he is making known a divine mystery about Israel: that it will all be saved (11:25–26). Debate, however, surrounds his statement about the salvation of all Israel (see the COMMENT on 11:25–27). No little part of that debate is the way Paul looks at the Mosaic law and its purpose in human history.

Paul expresses his sadness when he considers the situation in which his brothers, his kinsmen by race, exist in their failure to accept the Christian gospel. Yet he is aware that Israel's misstep is not contrary to God's direction of history. He realizes too that divine promises were made to Israel because of God's gracious election of it as his people. So he insists that God's word to Israel has not failed (9:6–13), because God in his sovereign freedom can even use indocility to his own purpose, as he did in the case of Pharaoh (9:14–23). Moreover, God does not act arbitrarily, for Israel's call, its infidelity, and the remnant of Jewish Christians were all foreseen in what God himself had announced in the OT (9:24–29). Yet Paul insists that Israel's failure is derived solely from its own refusal to listen to God's gospel, the message about Christ Jesus (9:30–10:21). In seeking to pursue an uprightness based on the law, it has preferred its own way to uprightness and not the uprightness that God himself has chosen to reveal in Christ (10:3). Finally, Paul emphasizes that Israel, in not responding to the preached word, has failed; but its failure is only partial and temporary. Indeed, it has been providential, because justification and salvation have consequently been carried to the Gentiles, who have heard the good news and been grafted into the heritage of Israel itself (11:1–24). Yet the role that Israel still plays in God's salvific plan is part of the mystery that is hidden in God: for "a partial hardening of heart has come upon Israel until the full number of the Gentiles comes in; and so all Israel will be saved" (11:25–26). Paul knows that Israel has been and is the object of divine election: "they are beloved of God because of the patriarchs" (11:28), and God's gifts to Israel and his call are "irrevocable" (11:29). Paul ends his discussion of the "mystery" of Israel with a hymn of praise to God's mercy and inscrutable wisdom (11:33–36).

The Law. Paul's attitude about the law is complicated, but it is neither inconsistent nor contradictory, as Räisänen *(Paul and the Law)* would have us believe. In Romans Paul writes about the law in a far less polemical manner than in Galatians; he is far less negative about it, and his thinking has developed. For some differences, see *PAHT* §PT89–99; cf. H. Hübner, *Law in Paul's Thought*.

At the outset, one must realize that, in speaking of *nomos*, Paul uses the word with different nuances. (1) Sometimes it is generic, "a law" (4:15b, "where there is no law, there is no transgression"; 7:1a, "to those who know what law is"). (2) Sometimes it is used in a figurative or analogous sense, as a "principle" (3:27a; 7:21, 23a), as a way of referring to "sin" (7:23c, 25b) or to "sin and death" (8:2b) or to human nature (2:14d), or even as a way of referring to "faith" (3:27b) and to "the Spirit" (8:2a); in the last two instances he speaks with oxymoron. (3) On occasion he means by it the OT or some part of it: the Psalms (3:19a), the *Tôrāh* (3:31b). (4) Otherwise, in the vast majority of occurrences, *nomos*, with or without the article, refers to the Mosaic law (2:12–14a, 15, 17–18, 20, 23, 25–27; 3:19–21, 27b, 28; 4:13–15a, 16; 5:13, 20; 6:14–15; 7:2–9, 12, 14, 16, 22, 23b, 25;

8:3–4, 7; 9:31; 10:4; 13:8, 9), that set of regulations which were to guide Israel in its covenant with God.

In speaking of the Mosaic law, Paul views human history as a stage on which certain figures perform as actors. Among these struts *Anthrōpos*, "Human Being" (7:1), also called at times *Egō*, "I" (7:9), confronted not only by *Hamartia*, "Sin," *Thanatos*, "Death," (5:12), and *Nomos*, "Law" (7:1, 6), but also by *Charis*, "Grace" (5:21). Paul personifies them all, attributing to them human activity: they "enter," "dwell," "reign," "revive."

The intricate role that *Nomos* plays creates an anomaly in human life. As an actor on the stage of human history, *Nomos* governs *Anthrōpos*, but is depicted as a good actor: "the law is holy, and the commandment is holy, upright, and good" (7:12); "good" (7:16) and "spiritual" (7:14), that is, belonging to the sphere of God and not to that of this-world humanity. It is "God's law" (7:22, 25b; 8:7), having come from him and been destined by him to lead *Anthrōpos* to life, in other words, to enjoyment of the glorious presence of God (7:10). In 9:4 Paul concedes that the giving of the law was one of the prerogatives of Israel, privileged by God with this means of knowing his covenantal will. It was addressed by God to all those who are under its authority and acknowledge it (3:19). Even when human beings reject the law, it continues to be good, for it entrusts "the oracles of God" (3:2) to privileged Israel.

Yet despite this God-given aid, Paul recognizes that his kinsmen by race were as much sinners as the Law-less Gentiles (2:17–24; cf. 1:18–32), for "all alike have sinned and fall short of the glory of God" (3:23). Given this situation, Paul formulates the anomaly that the law creates in human life, boldly stating it when he quotes Ps 143:2, and makes a daring addition to that psalm: "no human being will be justified before him through the deeds prescribed by the law," that is to say, by observing the Mosaic law. Thus Paul states the *negative* role of the law: "What the law . . . was powerless to do" (*to adynaton tou nomou*, 8:3). It was incapable of giving life because it was only an external norm, a list of do's and dont's, possessing in itself no life-giving force.

Yet Paul also depicts *Nomos* as playing a *positive* role in human history. Arriving on the stage in the second act (from Moses to the Messiah), when it "was added" to the promises already made to Abraham in the first act, "The law slipped in that trespass might increase" (5:20). Though good in itself, *Nomos* entered the scene to become the henchman or tool of another actor, *Hamartia*. Because the law supplied no *dynamis*, "energy," whereby *Anthrōpos* could find life in obeying it, ironically enough it became the instrument of Sin, which has unleashed God's wrath on humanity. For "the law brings only wrath" (4:15). Not sinful in itself, it aided and abetted sin: "What then can we say? Is the law sin? Certainly not! Yet I would not have known sin, if it were not for the law," because "in the absence of the law sin is as good as dead" (7:7–8).

In Romans Paul teaches that the law aided sin in three ways: first, the law acted as an "occasion" (*aphormē*) for sin, instructing humanity in the material possibility of doing evil, either by forbidding what was indifferent (e.g., the eating of certain animals, Lev 11:2–47; Deut 14:4–21) or by arousing desires and annoying the conscience with external regulations about "forbidden fruit." This aspect of the law is discussed in 7:5, 8, 11: The *Egō* would not have known "what it was to covet, if the law had not said, 'You shall not covet' " (7:7).

Second, the law acted as a moral informer; it gave human beings "the real knowledge of sin" (*epignōsis hamartias*, 3:20): it made known the true character of moral disorder as a rebellion against God, as a transgression of his will, and as an infidelity to the covenant and its stipulations (e.g., the Decalogue). Paul recognizes that "up to the time of the law sin was in the world, even though sin is not accounted when there is no law" (5:13). Paul would not have denied that people did evil during the first act of human history, from Adam to Moses, but in that Law-less period their evil deeds were not booked against them as open rebellion or transgressions. Humans sinned, indeed, but they "had not sinned in a way similar to Adam's transgression" (5:14), who violated a command of God (Gen 2:17; 3:6, 11). Hence Paul can write generically, "Where there is no law, there is no transgression" (4:15). "In the absence of law sin is as good as dead. Indeed, I [= the *Egō*] once lived in the absence of law, but when the commandment came, sin sprang to life, and I died" (7:8b–10a). So Paul depicts humanity first in the Law-less period and then in the period of *Tôrāh*.

So finally, the law brought "condemnation" upon *Anthrōpos*, who was obliged to obey it (implied in 8:1). In Romans, however, Paul does not explain this "condemnation." Yet it is the same as the "dispensation of condemnation" mentioned in 2 Cor 3:9 (cf. 3:7, "dispensation of death") and the "curse" of Gal 3:10, where Deut 27:26 is quoted (the curse leveled against all those who do not observe the law).

Thus did the law according to Paul introduce an anomaly into human existence. In Romans Paul explains this anomaly by ascribing the inability of *Anthrōpos* to obey the law to its carnal condition: the *Egō* is weak, made of flesh, which is dominated by indwelling *Hamartia*. "I am of flesh, sold in bondage to sin" (7:14). (For the way he explains this notion in Galatians, see *PAHT* §PT95.) Here the evil force, *Hamartia*, introduced into the world by Adam's transgression, has kept *Anthrōpos* in bondage, because the *Egō* is basically "carnal." Although *Anthrōpos* recognizes God's law with the *nous*, "mind," another principle is recognized to be at work within it, which is at war with that law: "it is no longer I (= the *Egō*) that do it, but sin that dwells in me" (7:17). Although the *Egō* with its mind "is a slave to God's law," that is to say, it recognizes that it is bound to that law, yet in the flesh "it is a slave to the law of sin" (7:25). Thus Paul figuratively calls *Nomos* "the law of sin," using an appositional genitive, because of the anomalous and degrading situation to which such humanity is reduced by Sin making use of the law. Thus Paul recognized that the law could, in principle, enable an individual Jew to remain upright in God's sight—in other words, be faithful to the covenant—but the human condition being what it is, the law did not achieve that goal. Indeed, it could not, because of the carnal condition of *Anthrōpos*. This situation is what creates the problem for the Jewish people, who have been living out a works righteousness in their covenantal situation. Paul is not offering a distorting view of Judaism, as is now clear from the discovery of the sense of *ma'ăśê hattōrāh*, "the deeds of the law," in Qumran texts, which reveals that such a view of the law was, indeed, current among some Jews in the Palestine of Paul's day (see the NOTE on 3:20). For Paul the major problem with the law was humanity's inability to observe it.

Paul's solution in Romans for this anomaly created by the Mosaic law in human existence is to substitute for obedience to it faith in Christ Jesus, "who was handed over (to death) for our trespasses and raised for our justification" (4:25). In effect, human beings "have died to the law through the body of Christ" (7:4), that is, through the crucified body of Christ. Again, in 7:24 Paul exclaims, "Wretch that I am, who will rescue me from this doomed body?" His answer: "Thanks be to God—(it is done) through Jesus Christ our Lord" (7:25). He explains further in 8:1–4: "Now then, there is no condemnation for those who are in Christ Jesus. For in Christ Jesus the law of the Spirit of life has set you free from the law of sin and death. What the law, weakened by the flesh, was powerless to do, God has done: by sending his own son in a form like that of sinful flesh and for the sake of sin, he condemned sin in the flesh, so that the requirement of the law might be fully met in us who conduct ourselves not according to the flesh, but according to the Spirit." "God's love has been poured out into our hearts through the holy Spirit that has been given to us" (5:5), and this "Spirit of life" in Christ Jesus (8:2) brings it about that *Anthrōpos* can now stand before God's tribunal "justified," that is, acquitted. So according to Paul the anomaly is resolved. What the law could not achieve (8:3), God himself has brought about in Christ Jesus and in what he has done for humanity.

For this reason Paul can say that Christ is *telos nomou*, "the end of the law" (10:4). This expression might seem to allude to the "end" of the period of *Tôrāh*, the second phase or act of human history. But *telos* can also mean "goal, purpose, finis." In the former sense, Christ would be understood as the termination of all human striving to remain upright in God's sight through the observance of the law. But in Romans it is also likely that *telos* is meant in the sense of the "goal of the law." In other words, what the law was intended to bring about for humanity, namely, covenantal uprightness in God's sight, is now attained through Christ Jesus. This purposive or teleological sense of the law is better suited to the preceding context (9:30–32; 10:3), where the metaphor of a chase or race is used, in which a goal is implied: "the Gentiles who did not pursue uprightness" actually attained it (through faith in Christ Jesus), "whereas Israel, which was pursuing a law of uprightness, did not achieve it." Thus "the requirement of the law" is now "fully met in us who conduct ourselves . . . according to the Spirit" (8:4). All that the law was destined to achieve for human uprightness is now attained through the death and resurrection of Christ Jesus. The goal of the law is attained in and through Christ. This reasoning explains too why Paul speaks of the "uprightness that comes from faith," as he interprets Deut 30:12, 14 in terms of Christ (10:16–20); implicitly he is suggesting that Deuteronomy 30 was already aimed at Christ and the uprightness that comes to human beings through him. Hence, what the law was unable to do God himself has brought about through "his own Son, who was sent by him "in a form like that of sinful flesh" (8:3). Moreover, the love of God that has been poured into human hearts enables them to live in faith that works itself out through human love, and thus Christians fulfill the requirements of the law (see pp. 138–39).

Sin. Paul indicts all humanity that is without the gospel, for they are all without the influence of Christ Jesus. "All alike have sinned and fall short of the glory of God" (3:23). For Paul "sin" is a missing of the mark *(hamartanein)*. This Greek verb retains in Paul's writings its basic meaning, "miss the mark," in other words, to fail to attain a moral goal or standard, as in classical Greek literature (Homer, *Iliad* 5.287; 9.501; *Odyssey* 13.214; 21.155; Aeschylus, *Prometheus vinctus* 26) and the LXX (Judg 20:16; Prov 8:36). But it also connotes transgression against nature, custom, law, or divine will. "To sin" means to commit personal, individual acts in thought or execution from which evil results (*TDNT* 1.296–302, 308–11; *EDNT* 1.65–69).

In his teaching about this pervasive influence of sin in humanity, Paul depends on the teaching of the OT itself, which in a variety of ways asserts the universality, contagion, and ubiquity of human sin (e.g., Gen 6:5; 1 Kgs 8:46; Isa 64:5–7; Job 4:17; 15:14–16; Qoh 7:20; Sir 8:5). Sin creates a solidarity of sinners, of contemporaries (Gen 11:1–9; 2 Sam 14:1–17; Num 16:22), and of successive generations (Ps 79:8; Exod 20:5; 34:7). The etiological story of Genesis 2–3 sought to explain how this sinful condition of humanity first emerged. It tells how Adam and Eve brought sin into the world; yet the etiology of that account teaches that sin has been around as long as humanity has: its genesis and origin are not in God, but from human beings. That story, however, has produced no echo in any of the protocanonical books of the OT, except indirectly in Ezek 28:11–29, the lament over the king of Tyre (where the sin "in Eden, the garden of God," is said to have been "dishonest trading"). In the deuterocanonical books, however, the introduction of sin and death is ascribed to Eve (Sir 25:24, "Sin began with a woman, and because of her we all die"; similarly Wis 2:23–24; *Jub.* 2–5; *2 Enoch* 30:17; *Apoc. Mos.* 14). Only in the *Life of Adam and Eve* (44:2) are the "transgression and sin of all our generations" ascribed to "our parents" (in the plural).

Paul, however, breaks with such a pre-Christian Jewish tradition about Adam and Eve and ascribes to *Adam* not only death (as he does in 1 Cor 15:21–22), but also sin itself: "Just as sin entered the world through one man, and through sin death, and so death spread to all human beings, with the result that all have sinned—up to the time of the law sin was in the world, even though sin is not accounted when there is no law; yet death held sway from Adam until Moses, even over those who had not sinned in a way similar to Adam's transgression—who is a type of the one who was to come" (5:12–14). Paul sees a causal connection between Adam's sin and the sinfulness of all human beings, even though he never explains how that causal connection operates. Later in the same chapter Paul affirms, "Just as through the disobedience of one man many were made sinners *(hamartōloi katestathēsan)*, so through the obedience of one many will be made upright" (5:19). The contrast of antitype and type, Christ and Adam, demands that the sinful status of all human beings be attributed to Adam, just as their condition of uprightness is attributed to Christ alone. In this way Paul introduces his novel teaching about Adam's maleficent influence. It is this sin that dominates the human condition and brings it about that weak, carnal human beings cannot achieve the goal of the law.

Paul also teaches that all human beings have to answer to God for the lives that they lead:

> With your stubborn and impenitent heart you are amassing wrath for yourself on the day of wrath, when God's just judgment will be revealed. For 'he will repay everyone according to his deeds' [Prov 24:12]: eternal life for those who by patiently doing good strive for glory, honor, and immortality; but wrath and fury for those who selfishly disobey the truth and are won over to wickedness. There will be distress and anguish for every human being who does evil, for the Jew first and also for the Greek. But there will be glory, honor, and peace for everyone who does good, for the Jew first and also for the Greek. For there is no partiality in God. (2:5–11)

Such is the human condition: the pagan and the Jew alike are sinners and will one day stand before the divine tribunal. Paul speaks of this condition, prescinding from the gospel of Christ Jesus. Related to the sinful condition is death, the consequence of sin (6:23). Paul thus insists on the impartiality of God, even though he also affirms the priority of the Jew over the Greek, a priority that is rooted in the divine plan of salvation. Yet, despite that priority, both Jew and Greek stand as sinners before God, who deals with them and their conduct in an impartial way. Compare Amos 3:2, "You alone have I favored, more than all the families of the earth; for this reason shall I punish you for all your iniquities."

Humanity in Christ. In Romans Paul does not merely paint a dismal picture of humanity's condition apart from Christ; he also portrays the remarkable life that human beings may lead "in Christ" through faith and baptism and the glorious destiny to which they are called. For God's own salvific initiative and activity have brought it about that human beings can live for God in Christ and through his holy Spirit. They apprehend the effects of the Christ-event above all through "faith in Jesus Christ" (3:22, 26) and are baptized into him; they live, as it were, a

136

symbiosis in union with Christ. And this is true of Jewish as well as Gentile Christians, who in solidarity with one another share this life "in Christ."

Faith. The experience whereby a human being responds to God's saving deed in Christ Jesus and apprehends the effects of the Christ-event is *pistis*, "faith." This is the human response to the gospel, to the "word . . . that we preach" (10:8). It is the response required of Jew and Greek alike: only through faith in Christ Jesus can they be saved.

Faith begins with *akoē*, "a hearing" (10:17), a listening to the gospel or to the word preached about Christ and God's salvific deed wrought in him. This hearing results in an assent of the mind that acknowledges the lordship of Christ in one's existence: "if you profess with your lips that 'Jesus is Lord,' and believe in your heart that God has raised him from the dead, you will be saved" (10:9). That experience may begin with a mental assent or a profession of the lips, but it ends as *hypakoē pisteōs*, often translated as the "obedience of faith," but which means etymologically a "hearing under" (*hypo* + *akoē*), a submissive hearing. It connotes the "submission" or "commitment" of the believer to God in Christ, which is the end result of faith as *akoē* (10:17). Thus for Paul faith is not merely an intellectual assent to the proposition, "Jesus is Lord," but also a vital, personal dedication of the whole person to God in Christ in all his or her relations with God, with other human beings, and with the world. "Faith" is not just a vague attitude of trustfulness or a response without a specific object; it is rather a conviction about the difference that God and the lordship of Christ have made for human history, a confidence in the promises of God and his assisting grace, and a trust upon which Christian hope is built. As *hypakoē*, it is the full acceptance of dedication to God in Christ (6:16–17), to the exclusion of all reliance on self, or of what Paul calls "boasting" (3:27). Faith enables Gentiles to be grafted like wild olive branches onto the cultivated olive tree, the patriarchal stock of Israel, and to share in Israel's promises and destiny. Only the lack of faith brings about the lopping off of Jewish branches (11:20–23). That "faith" is faith in Christ Jesus, and Israel itself will find salvation through it (9:6).

Such faith is a gift of God, just as is the whole salvific process (3:24–25; 6:14; 11:26; 12:3). This is the underlying notion in the discussion of Abraham's faith in chap. 4. In the polemical context in which Paul rejects the idea of justification being achieved by "deeds of the law," he stresses that it comes instead through faith (3:28). The relation of Paul's notion of faith to certitude of salvation is a question that he does not really grapple with; it is a question born of later systematic theological problems.

The full sense of Paul's understanding of faith, however, is not formulated in Romans. For he elsewhere demands further that Christians manifest such faith in conduct, or through deeds of love (*agapē*). As he puts it in Galatians, "In union with Christ Jesus neither circumcision nor the lack of it is of any value, but only faith working itself out through love" (5:6). For the Pauline sense of love, see below. Yet even in Romans Paul will tell the Christians of Rome that "all things work together for the good of those who love God" (8:28) and conversely recalls to them that they are "beloved of God" (1:7). In this setting he exhorts them to conduct that excels in its service to other human beings. For Christian faith involves not only a freedom from law, from the *sarx* self, from sin and death, but also a freedom to serve others in love. Such a notion of faith that blossoms in deeds of love is not to be misunderstood as if it were an attempt to reformulate the medieval idea of *fides caritate formata*, faith shaped by love. That is a philosophical transposition of the Pauline teaching—acceptable or not, depending on whether one agrees with the philosophy involved—but the genuine Pauline idea of "faith working itself out through love" is implicit in Romans; it comes to the fore in his exhortations (12:9; 13:8–10), and especially in his remarks addressed to the "weak" and the "strong" (14:15). He does not equate faith with love; nor does he ascribe to love what he does to faith (viz., justification, salvation), even though he recognizes the necessity of the two working in tandem. For Paul there cannot be any faith without accompanying love, that is to say, deeds that manifest that faith in the concern for God or for other human beings.

When Harnack wrote his famous article on *sola fide*, he recognized that human beings become upright and holy "durch Glaube und Liebesübung" and that for Paul *pistis di³ agapēs energoumenē* was "a strictly unified concept" (*ein streng einheitlicher Begriff* [ZTK 1 (1891): 86–87]), a unity that was often lost sight of in subsequent centuries. He found Clement of Rome rightly reformulating Pauline faith: "All of them [the OT patriarchs and kings] were renowned and highly thought of, not because of themselves or their deeds or the upright acts that they had performed, but because of his [God's] will. And so we too, who have been called by his will in Christ Jesus, are not justified because of ourselves, not even because of our wisdom or understanding or piety or deeds that we have wrought in holiness of heart, but through faith, through which Almighty God has justified everyone from the beginning of the world. To him be glory forever and ever. Amen" (*1 Clem.* 32:3–4). Yet Harnack also noted that the same Clement, having quoted Gen 15:6, says about Abraham, "Because of (his) faith and hospitality a son was given to him in his old age" (10:7), and of Rahab he says, "Because of (her) faith and hospitality Rahab the harlot was saved" (12:1). Thus Clement was a patristic writer who understood the Pauline unity of "faith working itself out through love," but who also began the process of emphasizing the role of faith and deeds separately; compare *1 Clem.* 32:4 (*dikaioumetha . . . dia pisteōs*) and *1 Clem.* 30:3 (*ergois dikaioumenoi*).

Love/Charity. For Paul "love" is neither *eros*, "the love of desire," which is aimed at the possession of the person or thing loved, nor *philia*, "love of friendship," which rejoices in the free response of the beloved, but rather a self-sacrificing openness, an outgoing concern and respect of one person for another in concrete acts or deeds that result in the diminution of the lover's "self" and subordinates the lover's personal ends to that of the one loved. For this reason Paul can exhort the Romans to owe no one a debt, "save that of loving one another; for the one who loves another has fulfilled the law" (13:8). Love sums up all the commandments of the law. "Love does no wrong to a neighbor, for love is the fulfillment of the law" (13:10). In other words, the Christian who lives a life of faith that works itself out through love is found to be fulfilling the objective of the law itself, is found to be achieving its goal.

Hope. Another characteristic of Christian life is hope, *elpis*. It is the outlook produced by faith, enabling Christians to look forward to their destiny, their share in *doxa*, "glory" (see the NOTE on 3:23; "the glory that is going to be revealed in us," 8:18), or their share in "life eternal" (6:22–23), in the risen life of Christ (6:4). For the Father has "predestined" Christians "to be conformed to the image of his Son," the "firstborn among many brothers" (8:29). This is what is meant by Christians who have been "glorified" (8:30), in a proleptic sense. Indeed, Paul stresses that as Christians we "boast of our hope for the glory of God" (5:2); for "in hope we have been saved" (8:24). He cites Abraham as the prime example of one who "believed," while "hoping against hope" (4:18). Indeed, there is a sense in which one can speak of Romans as the gospel of hope. For in 1 Thessalonians Paul used this very feature to distinguish Christians from the rest of humanity that has "no hope" (4:13).

Baptism. Linked to the Christian experience of union with Christ through faith is that of baptism. Indeed, the role of faith is only fully understood when it is linked to Paul's teaching on baptism. This initiatory rite, which incorporates human beings into Christ and the church, already existed in pre-Pauline Christian tradition, but it is Paul who developed its significance. Through baptism the Christian is actually identified with the death, burial, and resurrection of Christ, the main phases of Christ's salvific activity: "Through baptism into his death we were indeed buried with him so that, as Christ was raised from the dead by the Father's glory, we too might conduct ourselves in a new way of life. For if we have grown into union with him through a death like his, we shall also be united with him through a resurrection like his" (6:4–5). Paul's comparison of baptism with the death, burial, and resurrection of Christ is often thought to allude to the early Christian rite of baptism by immersion. Although this mode of baptism may be difficult to certify for the first century A.D., Paul's symbolism is sufficiently preserved if the baptized person is regarded as somehow under the water. Identified with Christ in death, the Christian dies to the law and to sin (6:6, 10; 7:4). Paul goes even so far as to depict Christians as having "grown into union with him" (6:5) so that they now share in his risen life. As a result of such faith and baptism the Christian's "old self has been crucified" with Christ (6:6) and has been "conformed to the image of his [= God's] Son" (8:29). So the Christian has "put

139

on the Lord Jesus Christ" (13:14); having donned him like a robe, he or she has become one with him.

The experience of faith and baptism brings it about that Jewish Christians form a "remnant" among Paul's kinsmen by race. They have accepted Christ, and, to describe them, Paul takes over this idea of the remnant from the OT, especially from Isa 10:22–23 and 1 Kgs 19:18 (see 9:27; 11:4): "So too at the present time a remnant, chosen by grace, has come into being" (11:5).

As for baptized Gentile converts to Christianity, Paul thinks of them as branches of a wild olive tree grafted onto the cultivated olive tree that is Israel (11:17). This is but another way in which Paul regards the unity of Gentile and Jewish Christians in the "one body." The image used is different, but the solidarity of Jew and Gentile "in Christ" thus expressed is the same. So he formulates symbolically the continuity of the Gentile Christian heritage with that of Israel of old. He realizes that some of his kinsmen by race have not accepted the Christian gospel and have as a result lost their places on the stock of Israel of old, into whose places the Gentile Christians have now been grafted. Yet he counsels the Gentile Christians not to grow smug about this situation in which they find themselves, because their faith could become deficient and they too might be lopped off. "For if God did not spare the natural branches, perhaps he will not spare you either" (11:21).

Body of Christ. In Romans Paul uses the phrase *to sōma tou Christou* only once and then to designate the historical "body of Christ," crucified on the cross (7:4). Through his death the Christian has also died to the law. Otherwise, he does not use the phrase in either the ecclesiological or the eucharistic sense, as he does elsewhere (see *PAHT* §PT122). But Paul does say that all baptized believers become "one body in Christ" (12:4). In him, then, Jewish and Gentile Christians are closely united to one another, forming one body. In this way too Christ Jesus has "welcomed" all Christians, the weak and the strong alike (15:7), to be part of this one body. The roles they play in the community may differ, but they are the functions of different members of that one body, and "individually members of one another" (12:5).

Church. In Romans Paul speaks of "church" only in chap. 16 and then uses *ekklēsia* only in the sense of a local church (vv 1, 4, 16, 23) or a house church (v 5); possibly he refers also to such gatherings in vv 10–11 ("the household of Aristobulus" or "of Narcissus"). But none of his discussion transcends this narrow local view, not even in 12:4–8, where he speaks of the roles of Christian individuals in the community and refers to them as making up "one body in Christ" (12:5). *Ekklēsia* is not mentioned in that context (contrast 1 Cor 12:27–28). Significantly, he does not address his letter to "the church at Rome," a formula that he uses in other letters.

In using *sōma* to express the unity of Christians in Christ, Paul is drawing on the common popular philosophy of his day. Interpreters dispute the origin of the Pauline idea (see Bultmann, Dubarle, Hegermann, Hill, and Robinson in the bibliography on pp. 168–69), but the best explanation remains that of Paul's Greco-Roman background, which regarded the *polis* or *res publica* as *sōma* or *corpus* (whence comes the idea of the "body politic"). This notion is found as early as Aristotle, *Politics* 5.2.7; it is also in Dionysius of Halicarnassus, *Roman Antiquities* 6.86.1–2. It became part of Stoic philosophy; see Seneca, *Epistulae morales* 95.52; Cicero, *Orationes Philippicae* 8.5.15: *in rei publicae corpore*; Plutarch, *Coriolanus* 6.3–4. In Plutarch's *Moralia* 426A, there is even the collocation of *sōma* and *ekklēsia*.

E. CHRISTIAN CONDUCT, OR TEACHING ABOUT THE CALL OF HUMANITY TO SPIRIT-GUIDED EXISTENCE

Paul's teaching in Romans includes not only doctrinal matters, such as have been discussed above, but also pastoral exhortations to Christian conduct. For the life that Christians lead through faith and baptism involves not only incorporation into "one body in Christ" so that they are "individually members of one another" (12:5), but they are also "led by God's Spirit" (8:14). Christians are Jewish and Gentile persons who are justified by grace through faith and who live in Christ Jesus (3:24–25); they are no longer "under law but under grace" (6:15). Yet, though already justified and reconciled through the Christ-event, they are still in this world and have to prepare themselves for the day, when "God's just judgment will be revealed" (2:5). Hence, Paul exhorts the Roman Christians: "Do not conform yourselves to this present world, but be transformed by a renewal of your whole way of thinking so that you may discern what is God's will, what is good, acceptable to him, and perfect" (12:2).

In Christ. As a result of the experience of faith and baptism, Paul sees Christians living "in Christ (Jesus)." He uses this phrase or one equivalent to it twenty-nine times in Romans. The phrases are used with different connotations, depending on the context. Sometimes they express the instrumentality of Christ's activity (3:24; 8:39); sometimes they express the intimate relation of Christians and Christ, who live a sort of symbiosis (6:11); sometimes they are a mere synonym for the Christian name (16:7). Modern commentators have variously explained the nature of this symbiosis, understanding it either in a local, spatial sense (Deissmann), in a mystic sense (Schweitzer), or in other dynamic, eschatological, or metaphysical senses. No one sense appears adequate. See *PAHT* §PT121.

Prayer. Among the various activities that Paul considers proper for Christian life is prayer. He recommends such a communing with God. He speaks of "my prayer to God" (10:1) on behalf of his fellow Jews (cf. 11:2) and begs the Roman Christians to "pray to God on my behalf" (15:30) for the success of his trip to Jerusalem. Paul himself often gives thanks to God (1:8; 6:17; 7:25; cf. 14:6) and prays for the harmony of the Roman Christian community (15:5–6, 13). Paul recognizes that the error in pagan life was the failure to thank God and glorify him properly (1:21). For this reason, he urges his readers to pray (12:11–12), to bend their knees before God and sing his praise (14:11, quoting Isa 49:8; 45:23), recognizing that in this is one of the chief ways that the Spirit aids weak Christians (8:26–27). He also implies that they are to "call upon the name" of the Lord (10:12), that is, to address prayer to Christ himself. Paul expresses his prayer in the form of a doxology (1:25).

Christian Conduct. Paul exhorts the Roman Christians to think about one another as "members in one body" (12:5) with different functions or roles (prophecy, ministry, teaching, exhortation, philanthropy, leadership, social work, 12:6–8) and urges that "unfeigned love" must govern all that they do (12:9). This love becomes the guiding idea of the hortatory section, as Paul exhorts the Romans to proper conduct: brotherly love, philanthropy, hospitality, love of enemies, mutual respect (12:10–16a, 20); or warns them against haughtiness, repaying evil, and taking revenge (12:16b–19). Paul gives a concrete example of such respect, when he writes the letter of recommendation for the deacon Phoebe (16:1–23). In part B of the hortatory section, in particular, Paul exhorts the Roman Christians to manifest that love toward one another, the "weak" toward the "strong" and the "strong" toward the "weak" (14:1–15:13). Dietary regulations or calendaric observances are not to stand in the way of such manifestations of love. The strong are to respect those "weak in conviction" (14:1). The ethical list that Paul incorporates in 1:29–31 is a description of pagan conduct; indirectly, it tells what should not characterize Christian conduct.

Attitude about Civil Authorities. Paul also urges the Roman Christians to respect governing authorities, for they "have been set up by God" (13:1); "anyone who resists authority opposes what God has instituted" (13:2). This he recommends not only in view of God's eschatological wrath (13:4–5), but also for the good of one's conscience (13:5). Hence, one must pay all such authorities their due: taxes, revenue, respect, and honor (13:7).

In the admonition that he addresses to the Roman Christians (16:17–20), he manifests his concern for their community, lest dissension, scandal, or strange teaching disrupt their unity and commitment.

At the end of his letter Paul of Tarsus greets the Christians of Rome with the blessing, "the grace of our Lord Jesus be with you" (16:20). So he sums up his theological and christological teaching in the letter that he sends to the capital of the Roman Empire, to the Christians of the church that he has not founded himself, but to those whose "faith is proclaimed in all the world" (1:8).

BIBLIOGRAPHY ON PAULINE TEACHING IN ROMANS

For monographs listed only by title, see the general bibliography, which follows the introduction.

General Studies

Beker, J. C., "Paul's Letter to the Romans as Model for Biblical Theology: Some Preliminary Observations," *Understanding the Word: Essays in Honor of Bernhard W. Anderson*, JSOTSup 37, ed. J. T. Butler et al. (Sheffield, UK: JSOT, 1985), 359–67.

Getty, M. A., "The Apostle of Romans: Paul's Message for Today's Church," *TBT* 91 (1977): 1281–88.

Hamilton, W., "A Theology for Modern Man: A Study of the Epistle to the Romans," *Int* 11 (1957): 387–404.

Hawkins, R. M., "Romans: A Reinterpretation," *JBL* 60 (1944): 129–40.

Hower, R. G., "Romans—Changing Hearts, Changing History," *Evangelical Journal* 7 (1989): 15–24.

Hoyt, H. A., *The First Christian Theology: Studies in Romans* (Grand Rapids, Mich.: Baker, 1977).

Kümmel, W. G., "Die Botschaft des Römerbriefs," *TLZ* 99 (1974): 481–88.

Kürzinger, J., "Die Grundgedanken des Römerbriefes des Apostels Paulus," *BK* 8.4 (1953): 3–11.

Lattey, C., "Relativity in Romans," *CBQ* 5 (1943): 179–82.

Legrand, L., "The Tragedy of Man According to St. Paul," *Jeevadhara* 5 (1975): 135–47.

Lehmann, P., "Contemporary Reflections on the Epistle to the Romans," *JBR* 14 (1946): 158–63.

Martin, J. P., "The Kerygma of Romans," *Int* 25 (1971): 303–28.

Pathrapankal, J., "The Letter to the Romans and Its Message for Our Times," *Jeevadhara* 12 (1982): 129–39.

Quanbeck, W., "Theological Reorientation: The Thought of the Epistle to the Romans," *Int* 14 (1960): 259–72.

Rongy, H., "Les Idées directrices de l'épître aux Romains," *RevEcclLiége* 22 (1930–31): 299–303.

Rossano, O. et al., *Attualità della lettera ai Romani*, Guidati dallo Spirito 25 (Rome: AVE, 1989).

Sampley, J. P., "Romans and Galatians, Comparison and Contrast," *Understanding the Word* (see Beker, above), 315–39.

Ward, W. E., "The Theology of the Epistle to the Romans," *RevExp* 54 (1957): 42–58.

Williams, N. P., "The Message of the Epistles—Romans," *ExpTim* 45 (1933–34): 6–10.

Young, F. M., "Understanding Romans in the Light of 2 Corinthians," *SJT* 43 (1990): 433–46.

God

Baasland, E., "Cognitio Dei in Römerbrief," *SNTU* 14 (1989): 185–218.

Beker, J. C., "The Faithfulness of God and the Priority of Israel in Paul's Letter to the Romans," *Christians among Jews and Gentiles: Essays in Honor of Krister Stendahl on His Sixty-fifth Birthday* (Philadelphia, Penn: Fortress, 1986 [= *HTR* 79 (1986)]), 10–16; repr. *RomDeb*, 327–32.

Betz, H. D., "*Theos*," *EDNT* 2.140–42.

Holtz, T., "Theo-logie und Christologie bei Paulus," *Glaube und Eschatologie: Festschrift für Werner Georg Kümmel . . .* , ed. E. Grässer and O. Merk (Tübingen: Mohr [Siebeck], 1985), 105–21.

Johnson, A. R., *The One and the Many in the Israelite Conception of God*, 2d ed. (Cardiff: University of Wales Press, 1961).

Morris, L., "The Theme of Romans," *Apostolic History and the Gospel: Biblical and Historical Essays Presented to F. F. Bruce . . .* , ed. W. W. Gasque and R. P. Martin (Exeter, UK: Paternoster; Grand Rapids, Mich.: Eerdmans, 1970), 249–63.

Moxnes, H., *Theology in Conflict*.

Villapadierna, C. de, "Concepto de Dios en San Pablo," *XXVIII Semana Bíblica Española (Madrid 23–27 sept. 1968)* (Madrid: Consejo Superior de Investigaciones Científicas, 1971), 253–63.

Divine Attributes: Love

Levie, J., "Le Plan de l'amour divin dans le Christ selon saint Paul," *L'Homme devant Dieu: Mélanges offerts au Père Henri de Lubac*, Théologie 56–58 (Paris: Aubier, 1963–64), 1.159–67.

Mayer, F., *Das absolute Dekret der Liebe nach dem Römerbrief . . .* (Stuttgart: Quell-Verlag, 1951; repr. 1963).

Romaniuk, K., *L'Amour du Père et du Fils dans la sotériologie de Saint Paul*, AnBib 15 (Rome: Biblical Institute, 1961).

Söding, T., "Gottesliebe bei Paulus," *TGl* 79 (1989): 219–42.

Uprightness, Righteousness

Achtemeier, E. R., "The Gospel of Righteousness: A Study of the Meaning of Ṣdq and Its Derivatives in the Old Testament," Ph.D. diss., Columbia University, 1959 (Ann Arbor, Mich.: University Microfilms no. 59-4049, 1959).

Beck, H., "Die *Dikaiosynē Theou* bei Paulus," *Neue Jahrbücher für deutsche Theologie* 4 (1895): 249–61.

Berger, K., "Neues Material zur 'Gerechtigkeit Gottes,'" ZNW 68 (1977): 266–75.

Brauch, M. T., "Perspectives on 'God's Righteousness' in Recent German Discussion," Appendix in E. P. Sanders, *Paul and Palestinian Judaism*, 523–42.

Brunner, H., "Die Gerechtigkeit Gottes," ZRGG 39 (1987): 210–15.

Bultmann, R., *"Dikaiosynē Theou,"* JBL 83 (1964): 12–16.

Cremer, H., *Die paulinische Rechtfertigungslehre.*

Donahue, J. R., "Biblical Perspectives on Justice," *The Faith That Does Justice*, ed. J. C. Haughey, Woodstock Studies 2 (New York: Paulist Press, 1977), 68–112.

Häring, T., *"Dikaiosynē Theou" bei Paulus* (Tübingen: Heckenhauer, 1896).

Hays, R. B., "Psalm 143 and the Logic of Romans 3," JBL 99 (1980): 107–15.

Hellegers, F. R., *Die Gerechtigkeit Gottes im Römerbrief* (Tübingen: Chr. Gulde, 1939).

Holm-Nielsen, S., "Die Verteidigung für die Gerechtigkeit Gottes," SJOT 2 (1987): 69–89.

Käsemann, E., " 'The Righteousness of God' in Paul," NTQT, 168–82; also published as "God's Righteousness in Paul," *The Bultmann School of Biblical Interpretation: New Directions*, ed. J. M. Robinson (New York: Harper & Row, 1965), 100–110.

Klein, G., "Gottes Gerechtigkeit als Thema der neuesten Paulus-Forschung," VF 12.2 (1967): 1–11; repr. in *Rekonstruktion und Interpretation: Gesammelte Aufsätze*, BEvT 50 (Munich: Kaiser, 1969), 225–36.

Knight, G. A. F., "Is 'Righteous' Right?" SJT 41 (1988): 1–10.

Kölbing, P., "Studien zur paulinischen Theologie: *Dikaiosynē Theou* in Röm. 1,17," TSK 68 (1895): 7–51.

Krašovec, J., *La Justice (ṢDQ) de Dieu dans la bible hébraïque et l'interprétation juive et chrétienne*, OBO 76 (Fribourg: Presses Universitaires; Göttingen: Vandenhoeck & Ruprecht, 1988).

Kutter, H., *Gerechtigkeit: Ein altes Wort an die moderne Christenheit* (Jena: Diederichs, 1910).

Ladd, G. E., "Righteousness in Romans," SwJT 19 (1976–77): 6–17.

Lührmann, D., "Die Offenbarung der Gerechtigkeit, Röm 1,17f 3,21ff," *Das Offenbarungsverständnis bei Paulus und in paulinischen Gemeinden*, WMANT 16 (Neukirchen-Vluyn: Neukirchener-Verlag, 1965), 141–53.

Lyonnet, S., "De 'justitia Dei' in epistola ad Romanos," VD 25 (1947): 23–34, 118–21, 129–44, 193–203, 257–63.

Míguez Bonino, J., "The Biblical Roots of Justice," WW 7 (1987): 12–21.

Millás, J. M., "Justicia de Dios: Rudolf Bultmann intérprete de la teología paulina de la justificación," Greg 71 (1990): 259–91.

Minestroni, I., " 'Giustizia' nella lettera ai Romani," RBR 10.2 (1975): 7–33.

Müller, C., *Gottes Gerechtigkeit.*

Oepke, A., *"Dikaiosynē Theou* bei Paulus in neuer Beleuchtung," TLZ 78 (1953): 257–64.

Quell, G. and G. Schrenk, *Dikē, dikaios . . . ,"* TDNT, 2.174–225.

Reicke, B., "Paul's Understanding of Righteousness," *Soli Deo Gloria: New Testament*

Studies in Honor of William Childs Robinson, ed. J. M. Richards (Richmond, Va.: John Knox, 1968), 37–49.

Reumann, J., *"Righteousness" in the New Testament: "Justification" in the United States Lutheran–Roman Catholic Dialogue, with Responses by Joseph A. Fitzmyer, Jerome D. Quinn* (Philadelphia, Penn.: Fortress; New York and Ramsey, N.J.: Paulist Press, 1982).

————, "The 'Righteousness of God' and the 'Economy of God': Two Great Doctrinal Themes Historically Compared," *Aksum—Thyateira: A Festschrift for Archbishop Methodios of Thyateira and Great Britain*, ed. G. Dion (London: Thyateira House, 1985), 615–37.

Reventlow, H., Graf, *Rechtfertigung im Horizont des Alten Testaments*, BEvT 58 (Munich: Kaiser, 1971).

Romaniuk, K., "La Justice de Dieu dans l'épître de saint Paul aux Romains," *Collectanea theologica* 47 (1977): 139–48.

Ropes, J. H., " 'Righteousness' and 'the Righteousness of God' in the Old Testament and in St. Paul," *JBL* 22 (1903): 211–27.

Scheper, J. B., *Justitia Dei and Justificatio (Romans I.17) in Early Latin Literature* (Washington, D.C.: Catholic University of America, 1932).

Schlatter, A. *Gottes Gerechtigkeit.*

Schmid, H. H., *Gerechtigkeit als Weltordnung: Hintergrund und Geschichte des alttestamentlichen Gerechtigkeitsbegriffes*, BHT 40 (Tübingen: Mohr [Siebeck], 1968).

————, "Rechtfertigung als Schöpfsgeschehen: Notizen zur alttestamentlichen Vorgeschichte eines neutestamentlichen Themas," *Rechtfertigung: Festschrift für Ernst Käsemann . . .* , ed. J. Friedrich et al. (Tübingen: Mohr [Siebeck]; Göttingen: Vandenhoeck & Ruprecht, 1976), 403–14.

Soards, M. L., "The Righteousness of God in the Writings of the Apostle Paul," *BTB* 15 (1985): 104–9.

————, "Once Again 'Righteousness of God' in the Writings of the Apostle Paul," *Bible Bhashyam* 17 (1991): 14–44.

Stuhlmacher, P., *Gerechtigkeit Gottes bei Paulus*, FRLANT 87 (Göttingen: Vandenhoeck & Ruprecht, 1965).

Williams, S. K., "The 'Righteousness of God' in Romans," *JBL* 99 (1980): 241–90.

Zänker, O., "*Dikaiosynē Theou* bei Paulus," *ZST* 9 (1931–32): 398–420.

Wrath

Bedenbaugh, J. B., "Paul's Use of 'Wrath of God,' " *LQ* 6 (1954): 154–57.

Hanson, A. T., *The Wrath of the Lamb* (London: SPCK, 1957), 68–111.

Herold, G., *Zorn und Gerechtigkeit bei Paulus: Eine Untersuchung zu Röm. 1,16–18*, Europäische Hochschulschriften 23.14 (Bern and Frankfurt: Peter Lang, 1973).

MacArthur, J., *The Wrath of God* (Chicago, Ill.: Moody, 1982).

MacGregor, G. H. C., "The Concept of the Wrath of God in the New Testament," *NTS* 7 (1960–61): 101–9.

Smith, T. C., "The Wrath of God," *RevExp* 45 (1948): 193–208.

Spieckermann, H., "Dies Irae: Der alttestamentliche Befund und seine Vorge-schichte," *VT* 39 (1989): 194–208.

Divine Plan of Salvation

Allan, J. A., "The Will of God: III. In Paul," *ExpTim* 72 (1960–61): 142–45.

Danell, G. A., "The Idea of God's People in the Bible," *Root of the Vine*, ed. A. Fridrichsen (New York: Philosophical Library; Westminster, London: Dacre, 1953), 23–26.

Dietzfelbinger, C., *Heilsgeschichte bei Paulus? Eine exegetische Studie zum paulinischen Geschichtsdenken*, TEH 126 (Munich: Kaiser, 1965).

Dimmler, E., *Erlösung: Gedanken über den Heilsplan Gottes nach dem Römerbrief* (Kempton: J. Kösel and F. Pustet, 1921).

Feuillet, A., "Le Plan salvifique de Dieu d'après l'épître aux Romains," *RB* 57 (1950): 336–87, 489–529.

Giblet, J., "Notes sur l'idée d'élection dans l'écriture," *Collectanea mechlinensia* 26 (1956): 367–75.

Goppelt, L., "Paulus und die Heilsgeschichte: Schlussfolgerungen aus Röm. IV und I. Kor. X. 1–13," *NTS* 13 (1966–67): 31–42.

Hoeksema, H., *God's Eternal Good Pleasure* (Grand Rapids, Mich.: Reformed Free Publ. Assoc., Kregel, 1979).

Hoppe, T., *Die Idee der Heilsgeschichte bei Paulus: Mit besonderer Berücksichtigung des Römerbriefes*, BFCT 1.30.2 (Gütersloh: Bertelsmann, 1926).

Kümmel, W. G., "Heilsgeschichte im Neuen Testament?" *Neues Testament und Kirche: Für Rudolf Schnackenburg*, ed. J. Gnilka (Freiburg im Breisgau: Herder, 1974), 434–57.

Luz, U., *Das Geschichtsverständnis*, 26–28, 64–84, 269–74.

Maier, G., "Neutestamentliche Prädestinationsaussagen in Rö 9–11," *Mensch und freier Wille: Nach den jüdischen Religionsparteien zwischen Ben Sira und Paulus*, WUNT 12 (Tübingen: Mohr [Siebeck], 1971), 351–400.

Michaelis, W., "Zur Frage der Aeonenwende," *TBl* 18 (1939): 113–18.

Penna, A., "L'Elezione nella lettera ai Romani e nei testi di Qumran," *Divinitas* 2 (1958): 597–614.

Stanley, D. M., "Theologia 'promissionis' apud S. Paulum," *VD* 30 (1952): 129–42.

Weber, E., *Das Problem der Heilsgeschichte*.

Wiederkehr, D., *Die Theologie der Berufung*, 168–87.

God's Gospel

Allo, E.-B., "L'Évolution' de l'"évangile de Paul,'" *Mémorial Lagrange*, ed. L.-H. Vincent (Paris: Gabalda, 1940), 259–67.

Becker, U., "Gospel, Evangelize, Evangelist," *NIDNTT* 2.107–15.

Burrows, M., "The Origin of the Term 'Gospel,' " *JBL* 44 (1925): 21–33.

Davies, J. G., "What Is the Gospel?" *ExpTim* (1969–70): 328–30.

Fitzmyer, J. A., "The Gospel in the Theology of Paul," *Int* 33 (1979): 339–50; repr. TAG, 149–61.

―――, "The Kerygmatic and Normative Character of the Gospel," *Evangelium— Welt—Kirche: Schlussbericht und Referate der römisch-katholisch/evangelisch- lutherischen Studienkommission "Das Evangelium und die Kirche," 1967–1971, Auf Veranlassung des Lutherischen Weltbundes und des Sekretariats für die Einheit der Christen*, ed. H. Meyer (Frankfurt am Main: Lembeck/Knecht, 1975), 111– 28.

Friedrich, G., "*Euangelizomai, euangelion* . . . ," *TDNT* 2.707–37.

Garofalo, S., "San Paolo ai Romani: La potenza dell'evangelo," *Divinitas* 2 (1958): 441–59.

Hultgren, A. J., *Paul's Gospel and Mission: The Outlook from His Letter to the Romans* (Philadelphia, Penn.: Fortress, 1985).

Hunter, A. M., *Gospel and Apostle* (London: SCM, 1975); USA title, *Gleanings from the New Testament* (Philadelphia, Penn.: Westminster, 1975), 142–47.

Macquarrie, J., "What Is the Gospel?—I," *ExpTim* 81 (1969–70): 296–300.

Molland, E., *Das paulinische Evangelion: Das Wort und die Sache*, Avhandlinger utgitt av Det Norske Videnskaps-Akademie i Oslo, II. Hist. Filos. Kl., 1934, no. 3 (Oslo: Dybwad, 1934), 11–12, 41–42.

Petty, O. A., *Did the Christian Use of the Term "to euangelion" Originate with Paul?* (New Haven, Conn.: Norwood, 1925).

Read, D. H. C., "What Is the Gospel?—III," *ExpTim* 81 (1969–70): 359–63.

Schlier, H., "*Euangelion* im Römerbrief," *Wort Gottes in der Zeit: Festschrift Karl Hermann Schelkle . . . dargebracht . . .* , ed. H. Feld and J. Nolte (Düsseldorf: Patmos, 1973), 127–42.

Schniewind, J., *Die Begriffe Wort und Evangelium bei Paulus* (Bonn: C. Georgi, 1910).

―――, *Euangelion: Ursprung und erste Gestalt des Begriffs Evangelium*, BFCT 2.13, 25 (Gütersloh: Bertelsmann, 1927–31; repr. in 1 vol., Darmstadt: Wissenschaft- liche Buchgesellschaft, 1970).

Strecker, G., "*Euangelion*," *EDNT* 2.70–74.

―――, "Literarische Überlegungen zum *euangelion*-Begriff im Markusevangelium," *Neues Testament und Geschichte: Historisches Geschehen und Deutung im Neuen Testament: Oscar Cullmann . . .* , ed. H. Baltensweiler and B. Reicke (Zurich: Theologischer Verlag; Tübingen: Mohr [Siebeck], 1972), 91–104; repr. in *Escha- ton und Historie: Aufsätze* (Göttingen: Vandenhoeck & Ruprecht, 1979), 76–89.

Stuhlmacher, P., *Das paulinische Evangelium: I. Vorgeschichte*, FRLANT 95 (Göttin- gen: Vandenhoeck & Ruprecht, 1968).

―――, "Das paulinische Evangelium," *Das Evangelium und die Evangelien: Vor- träge von Tübinger Symposium 1982*, WUNT 28, ed. P. Stuhlmacher (Tübingen: Mohr [Siebeck], 1983), 157–82.

Pauline Teaching in Romans

Christology: General Studies

Alfaric, P., "Le Jésus de Paul," *Congrès d'histoire du christianisme: Jubilé Alfred Loisy,* ed. P.-L. Couchoud, 3 vols. (Paris: Editions Rieder; Amsterdam: Holkema & Warendorp, 1928), 2.70–99.

Black, M., "The Christological Use of the Old Testament in the New Testament," *NTS* 18 (1971–72): 1–14.

Boismard, M.-E., "La Divinité du Christ d'après Saint Paul," *LumVie* 9 (1953): 75–100.

Brückner, M., *Die Entstehung der paulinischen Christologie* (Strasbourg: Heitz, 1903).

Cerfaux, L., *Christ.*

Cullmann, O., *The Christology of the New Testament,* rev. ed. (London: SCM; Philadelphia, Penn.: Westminster, 1963).

Dungan, D. L., *The Sayings of Jesus.*

Lagrange, M.-J., "Les Origines du dogme paulinien de la divinité de Christ," *RB* 45 (1936): 5–33.

Michel, O., "Der Christus des Paulus," *ZNW* 32 (1933): 6–31.

Neirynck, F., "Paul and the Sayings of Jesus," *L'Apôtre Paul: Personalité, style et conception du ministère,* ed. A. Vanhoye, BETL 73 (Louvain: Peeters/Leuven University, 1986), 265–321.

Schade, H.-H., *Apokalyptische Christologie bei Paulus.*

Schweizer, E. "Dying and Rising with Christ," *NTS* 14 (1967–68): 1–14.

———, *Jesus Christus im vielfältigen Zeugnis des Neuen Testaments,* Taschenbuch 126 (Munich and Hamburg: Siebenstern, 1968), 93–111.

———, "Zur Herkunft der Präexistenzvorstellung bei Paulus," *EvT* 19 (1959): 65–70.

Segundo, J. L., *The Humanist Christology of Paul* (Maryknoll, N.Y.: Orbis; London: Sheed & Ward, 1986).

Stanley, D. M., "Pauline Allusions to the Sayings of Jesus," *The Apostolic Church in the New Testament* (Westminster, Md.: Newman, 1965), 352–70.

Stuhlmacher, P., "Jesustradition im Römerbrief," *TBei* 14 (1983): 240–50.

Thüsing, W., *Per Christum in Deum,* 125–25.

Vögtle, A., " 'Der Menschensohn' und die paulinische Christologie," *SPCIC* 1.199–218.

Names and Titles of Christ

Barrett, C. K., *From First Adam to Last.*

Berger, K., "Zum traditionsgeschichtlichen Hintergrund christologischer Hoheitstitel," *NTS* 17 (1970–71): 391–425, esp. 422–24.

Black, M., "The Pauline Doctrine of the Second Adam," *SJT* 7 (1954): 170–79.

Brandenburger, E., *Adam und Christus: Exegetisch-religionsgeschichtliche Untersuchung zu Röm. 5, 12–21 (1. Kor. 15),* WMANT 7 (Neukirchen-Vluyn: Neukirchener-Verlag, 1962).

Brown, R. E., *Jesus God and Man: Modern Biblical Reflections* (Milwaukee, Wisc.: Bruce, 1967), 10–23.

149

Bruce, F. F., " 'Jesus Is Lord,' " *Soli Deo Gloria: New Testament Studies in Honor of William Childs Robinson*, ed. J. M. Richards (Richmond, Va.: John Knox, 1968), 23–36.

Cerfaux, L., "Kyrios," *DBSup* 5.200–28.

———, "Le Titre 'Kyrios' et la dignité royale de Jésus," *RSPT* 11 (1922) 40–71; repr. *Recueil L. Cerfaux*, BETL 6–7, 18, 3 vols. (Gembloux: Duculot, 1954–85), 1.3–63.

Dahl, N. A., "The Crucified Messiah," *The Crucified Messiah and Other Essays* (Minneapolis, Minn.: Augsburg, 1974), 10–36.

———, "The Messiahship of Jesus in Paul," ibid. 37–47.

Feuillet, A., "Le Nouvel Adam et l'antithèse mort-vie," *Le Christ sagesse de Dieu d'après les épîtres pauliniennes*, EtBib (Paris: Gabalda, 1966), 333–39.

Fitzmyer, J. A., "*Abba* and Jesus' Relation to God," *À Cause de l'Évangile: Études sur les Synoptiques et les Actes offertes au P. Jacques Dupont, O.S.B. . . .* , LD 123 (Paris: Cerf, 1985), 15–38.

———, "*Kyrios, kyriakos*," *EDNT* 2.328–31.

———, "New Testament Kyrios and Maranatha and Their Aramaic Background," *TAG*, 218–35.

———, "The Semitic Background of the New Testament *Kyrios*-Title," WA, 115–42.

Foerster, W., *Herr ist Jesus: Herkunft und Bedeutung des urchristlichen Kyrios-Bekenntnisses*, Neutestamentliche Forschungen 2.1 (Gütersloh: Bertelsmann, 1924).

Hahn, F., *The Titles of Jesus in Christology: Their History in Early Christianity* (London: Lutterworth, 1969).

Hengel, M., "Erwägungen zum Sprachgebrauch von *Christos* bei Paulus und in der 'vorpaulinischen' Überlieferung," *Paul and Paulinism: Essays in Honour of C. K. Barrett*, ed. M. Hooker and S. G. Wilson (London: SPCK, 1982), 135–59.

Howard, G., "The Tetragram and the New Testament," *JBL* 96 (1977): 63–83.

Keck, L. E., " 'Jesus' in Romans," *JBL* 108 (1989): 443–60.

Kramer, W., *Christ, Lord, Son of God*, SBT 1.50 (London: SCM; Naperville, Ill.: Allenson, 1966).

McCasland, S. V., " 'Christ Jesus,' " *JBL* 65 (1946): 377–83.

Schneider, G., "*Iēsous*," *EDNT* 2.180–84.

Schweizer, E., "Ökumene im Neuen Testament: Der Glaube an den Sohn Gottes," *Neues Testament und heutige Verkündigung*, BibSN 56 (Neukirchen: Neukirchener-Verlag, 1969), 39–54.

Scroggs, R., *The Last Adam: A Study in Pauline Anthropology* (Philadelphia, Penn.: Fortress, 1966), 75–82.

Stanley, D. M., *Christ's Resurrection*, 176–80.

Taylor, V., *The Names of Jesus* (New York: St. Martin, 1953).

Vögtle, A., "Die Adam-Christus-Typologie und 'der Menschensohn,' " *TTZ* 60 (1951): 309–28.

White, R. F., "The Last Adam and His Seed: An Exercise in Theological Preemption," *TrinJ* 6 (1985): 60–73.

Wilckens, U., "Christus, der 'letzte Adam,' und der Menschensohn," *Jesus und der Menschensohn: Für Anton Vögtle*, ed. R. Pesch and R. Schnackenburg (Freiburg im Breisgau: Herder, 1975), 387–403.

Death of Jesus

Dunn, J. D. G., "Paul's Understanding of the Death of Jesus," *Reconciliation and Hope: New Testament Essays on Atonement and Eschatology Presented to L. L. Morris . . .* , ed. R. Banks (Grand Rapids, Mich.: Eerdmans, 1974), 125–41.

Feuillet, A., "Mort du Christ et mort du chrétien d'après les épîtres paulinennes," *RB* 66 (1959): 481–513.

Güttgemanns, E., *Der leidende Apostel und sein Herr: Studien zur paulinischen Christologie*, FRLANT 90 (Göttingen: Vandenhoeck & Ruprecht, 1966).

Hahn, W. T., *Das Mitsterben und Mitauferstehen mit Christus*.

Käsemann, E., "The Saving Significance of the Death of Jesus in Paul," *Perspectives*, 32–59.

Ortkemper, F. J., *Das Kreuz in der Verkündigung des Apostels Paulus: Dargestellt an den Texten der paulinischen Hauptbriefe*, SBS 24 (Stuttgart: Katholisches Bibelwerk, 1967).

Weder, H., *Das Kreuz Jesu bei Paulus*.

Wiencke, G., *Paulus über Jesu Tod*.

Resurrection of Christ

Dhanis, E. (ed.), *Resurrexit: Actes du symposium international sur la résurrection de Jésus (Rome 1970)* (Vatican City: Libreria Editrice Vaticana, 1974).

Goguel, M., *La Foi à la résurrection de Jésus dans le christianisme primitif: Étude d'histoire et de psychologie religieuses*, Bibliothèque de l'École des Hautes Etudes, Sciences religieuses 47 (Paris: Leroux, 1933), 27–40.

Lyonnet, S., "La Valeur sotériologique de la résurrection du Christ selon Saint Paul," *Greg* 39 (1958): 295–318; repr. in his *Etudes*, 16–35.

O'Collins, G., "The Resurrection of Jesus: Some Current Questions," *America* 153.18 (1985): 422–25.

Stanley, D. M., *Christ's Resurrection in Pauline Soteriology*, AnBib 13 (Rome: Biblical Institute, 1961; repr. 1976).

Christ's Role in the Father's Plan. Effects of the Christ-Event: Justification

Agnew, F., "Paul's Theological Adversary in the Doctrine of Justification by Faith: A Contribution to Jewish-Christian Dialogue," *JES* 25 (1988): 538–54.

Alison, J., "Justification and the Constitution of Consciousness: A New Look at Romans and Galatians," *New Blackfriars* 71 (1990): 17–26.

Barth, K., "The Justification of Man," *Church Dogmatics* (Edinburgh: Clark, 1956), 4.1.514–642.

Barth, M., *Justification*.

Bornkamm, G., "Die Frage nach Gottes Gerechtigkeit (Rechtfertigung und Theodizee)," *Das Ende des Gesetzes*, 196–210.

Bultmann, R., *TNT* 1.270–85.

Cambier, J., "Justice de Dieu, salut de tous le hommes et foi," *RB* 71 (1964): 537–83.

Conzelmann, H., "Die Rechtfertigungslehre des Paulus: Theologie oder Anthropologie," *EvT* 28 (1968): 389–404.

Cosgrove, C. H., "Justification in Paul: A Linguistic and Theological Reflection," *JBL* 106 (1987): 653–70.

Cremer, H., *Die paulinische Rechtfertigungslehre im Zusammenhange ihrer geschichtlichen Voraussetzungen* (Gütersloh: Bertelsmann, 1899; 2d ed., 1900).

Cully, K. B., "Grace and Justification Today: An Interpretation of the Theme of Romans," *Int* 11 (1957): 421–28.

Daalen, D. H. van, "Paul's Doctrine of Justification and Its Old Testament Roots," *SE VI*, TU 112 (1973), 556–70.

Donfried, K. P., "Justification and Last Judgment in Paul," *Int* 30 (1976): 140–52; fuller form, ZNW 67 (1976): 90–110.

Drysdale, D., "Justification by Grace Through Faith," *IBS* 10 (1988): 114–22.

Froehlich, K., "Justification Language and Grace: The Charge of Pelagianism in the Middle Ages," *Probing the Reformed Tradition: Historical Studies in Honor of Edward A. Dowey, Jr.*, ed. E. A. McKee and B. G. Armstrong (Louisville, Ky.: Westminster/John Knox, 1989), 21–47.

Gross, H., " 'Rechtfertigung' nach dem Alten Testament: Bibeltheologische Beobachtungen," *Kontinuität und Einheit: Für Franz Mussner* (Freiburg im Breisgau: Herder, 1981), 17–29.

Grundmann, W., "Gesetz, Rechtfertigung und Mystik bei Paulus: Zum Problem der Einheitlichkeit der paulinischen Verkündigung," ZNW 32 (1933): 52–65.

———, "Der Lehrer der Gerechtigkeit von Qumran und die Frage nach der Glaubensgerechtigkeit in der Theologie des Apostels Paulus," *RevQ* 2 (1959–60): 237–59; rev. version, "The Teacher of Righteousness of Qumran and the Question of Justification by Faith in the Theology of the Apostle Paul," *Paul and the Dead Sea Scrolls*, ed. J. Murphy-O'Connor and J. H. Charlesworth (New York: Crossroad, 1990), 85–114.

Gyllenberg, R., "Die paulinische Rechtfertigungslehre und das Alte Testament," *ST* (Riga) 1 (1935): 35–52.

———, *Rechtfertigung und Altes Testament bei Paulus* (Stuttgart: Kohlhammer, 1973).

Haufe, C., *Die sittliche Rechtfertigungslehre des Paulus* (Halle an der Saale: Niemeyer, 1957).

Hill, D., *Greek Words and Hebrew Meanings: Studies in the Semantics of Soteriological Terms*, SNTSMS 5 (Cambridge: Cambridge University Press, 1967), 82–162.

Jager, H. J., *Rechtvaardiging en zekerheid des geloofs: Studie over Rom. 1:16,17; en Rom. 3:21–5:11* (Utrecht: Kemink & Zoom, 1939).

Jeremias, J., "Justification by Faith," *The Central Message of the New Testament* (London: SCM, 1965), 51–70.

Käsemann, E., "Justification and Salvation History in the Epistle to the Romans," *Perspectives*, 60–78.

Keck, L. E., "Justification of the Ungodly and Ethics," *Rechtfertigung: Festschrift für Ernst Käsemann* . . . , ed. J. Friedrich et al. (Tübingen: Mohr [Siebeck]; Göttingen: Vandenhoeck & Ruprecht, 1976), 199–209.

Kemp, J. T. van der, *De theodicée van Paulus of de rechtvaarigheid Gods door het euangelium uit het geloof* . . . (Dordrecht: Blussé & Zoon, 1799; 3d ed. 1802).

Kertelge, K., *"Rechtfertigung" bei Paulus: Studien zur Struktur und zum Bedeutungsgehalt des paulinischen Rechtfertigungsbegriffs*, NTAbh n.s. 3, 2d ed. (Münster in Westfalen: Aschendorff, 1967).

Klaiber, W., "Rechtfertigung und Kreuzesgeschehen," *Das Wort vom Kreuz: Geschehen—Denken—Theologie* (Giessen and Basel: Brunnen-Verlag, 1988), 93–126.

Lührmann, D., "Christologie und Rechtfertigung," *Rechtfertigung: Festschrift für Ernst Käsemann* (see above under Keck), 351–63.

Lütgert, W., *Die Lehre von der Rechtfertigung durch den Glauben* (Berlin: Reich Christi-Verlag, 1903).

Lyonnet, S., "Justification, jugement, rédemption, principalement dans l'épître aux Romains," *Littérature et théologie paulinienne*, RechBib 5, ed. A. Descamps (Bruges: Desclée de Brouwer, 1960), 166–84; repr. in his *Études*, 144–62.

McGrath, A. E., *Justification by Faith*.

Marco, A. de, "*Dikaiosynē—dikaiōma—dikaiōsis* in Rm: Linguistica ed esegesi," *Laurentianum* 24 (1983): 46–75.

Moule, C. F. D., " 'Justification' in Its Relation to the Condition *kata pneuma* (Rom. 8:1–11)," *Battesimo e giustizia in Rom 6 e 8*, ed. L. de Lorenzi, Benedictina 2 (Rome: Abbazia S. Paolo fuori le mura, 1974), 177–201.

Moxnes, H., "Honour and Righteousness in Romans," *JSNT* 32 (1988): 61–77.

Müller, K., *Beobachtungen zur paulinischen Rechtfertigungslehre* (Leipzig: Hinrichs, 1905).

Pfleiderer, O., "Die paulinische Rechtfertigung: Eine exegetisch-dogmatische Studie," *ZWT* 15 (1872): 161–99.

Resewski, J., "Ist die altlutherische Lehre von der *iustitia imputata* bei Paulus begründet?" *ZST* 16 (1939): 325–49.

Riggenbach, E., *Die Rechtfertigungslehre des Apostels Paulus: Ein erweiterter Vortrag* (Stuttgart: Gundert, 1897).

Schmitz, R., *Rechtfertigung und Heiligung durch den Glauben: Sünde und Gnade nach dem Römerbrief* (Witten [Ruhr]: Bundes-Verlag, 1960).

Schofield, J. N., " 'Righteousness' in the Old Testament," *BT* 16 (1965): 112–16.

Schulz, S., "Zur Rechtfertigung aus Gnade in Qumran und bei Paulus: Zugleich ein

Beitrag zur Form- und Überlieferungsgeschichte der Qumrantexte," ZTK 56 (1959): 155–85.

Schwarz, G., *Justitia imputata? Eine neue Erklärung der entscheidenden Ausprüche des Apostels Paulus über die Rechtfertigung* (Heidelberg: Winter, 1891).

Sedgwick, P., " 'Justification by Faith': One Doctrine, Many Debates?" *Theology* 93 (1990): 5–13.

Seebass, H. and C. Brown, "Righteousness, Justification," *NIDNTT* 3.352–77.

Seifrid, M. A., *Justification by Faith: The Origin and Development of a Central Pauline Theme* NovTSup 68 (Leiden: Brill, 1992).

Strecker, G., "Befreiung und Rechtfertigung: Zur Stellung der Rechtfertigungslehre in der Theologie des Paulus," *Rechtfertigung: Festschrift für Ernst Käsemann* (see above under Keck), 479–508.

Tobac, E., *Le Problème de la justification dans Saint Paul*, Universitas Catholica Lovaniensis, dissertationes 2.3 (Gembloux: Duculot, n.d.).

Vicentini, J. I., "De necessitate operum in priori parte epistolae ad Rom.," *VD* 36 (1958): 270–83.

Villegas Mathieu, B., "Una visión de la gracia: La justificación en Romanos," *Teología y vida* 28 (1987): 277–305.

Wendland, H.-D., *Die Mitte der paulinischen Botschaft: Die Rechtfertigungslehre des Paulus im Zusammenhange seiner Theologie* (Göttingen: Vandenhoeck & Ruprecht, 1935).

Westcott, F. B., *St Paul and Justification: Being an Exposition of the Teaching in the Epistles to Rome and Galatia* (London: Macmillan, 1913).

Ziesler, J. A., *The Meaning of Righteousness: A Linguistic and Theological Inquiry*, SNTSMS 20 (Cambridge: Cambridge University Press, 1972).

Salvation

Anon, *Salvation by Faith: Aspects of Pauline Soteriology in Romans* (= *Neotestamentica* 15; Stellenbosch: University of Stellenbosch, 1982).

Boring, M. E., "The Language of Universal Salvation in Paul," *JBL* 105 (1986): 269–92.

Carrez, M., "Le Salut dans la littérature paulinienne," *DBSup* 11.689–710.

Clark, T. R., *Saved by His Life: A Study of the New Testament Doctrine of Reconciliation and Salvation* (New York: Macmillan, 1959).

Lindars, B., "The Old Testament and Universalism in Paul," *BJRL* 69 (1987): 511–27.

Lyonnet, S., "The Terminology of 'Salvation,' " *Sin*, 3–78.

McIver, E., "The Cosmic Dimensions of Salvation in the Thought of St. Paul," *Worship* 40 (1966): 156–64.

Moreno, J., "La salvación en la historia (Rom. 1–8)," *Teología y vida* 12 (1971): 3–14.

Mussner, F., "Heil für alle: Der Grundgedanke des Römerbriefs," *Kairos* 23 (1981): 207–14.

Packer, J. I., "The Way of Salvation," *BSac* 129 (1972): 195–205, 291–306.

Schelkle, K. H., *"Sōtēr"* and *"Sōtēria,"* EWNT 3.781–84, 784–88.

Stanley, D. M., "The Conception of Salvation in Primitive Christian Preaching," *CBQ* 18 (1956): 231–54.

Viard, A., "Le Problème du salut dans l'épître aux Romains," *RSPT* 47 (1963): 3–34, 373–97.

——, "Le Salut des croyants d'après l'épître aux Romains," *AmiCler* 72 (1962): 257–59, 346–52, 461–64, 476–78, 497–500, 561–66.

Wagner, W., "Über *sōzein* und seine Derivata im Neuen Testament," ZNW 6 (1905): 205–35.

Reconciliation

Breytenbach, C., *Versöhnung: Eine Studie zur paulinischen Soteriologie*, WMANT 60 (Neukirchen-Vluyn: Neukirchener-Verlag, 1989).

Dupont, J., *"La Réconciliation dans la théologie de Saint Paul*, ALBO 2.32 (Bruges: Desclée de Brouwer, 1953); repr. from *EstBib* 11 (1952): 255–302.

Fitzmyer, J. A., "Reconciliation in Pauline Theology," *No Famine in the Land: Studies in Honor of John L. McKenzie*, ed. J. W. Flanagan and A. W. Robinson (Missoula, Mont.: Scholars, 1975), 155–77; repr. *TAG*, 162–85.

Goppelt, L., "Versöhnung durch Christus," *Christologie und Ethik: Aufsätze zum Neuen Testament* (Göttingen: Vandenhoeck & Ruprecht, 1968), 147–64.

Haacker, K., "Der Römerbrief als Friedensmemorandum," *NTS* 36 (1990): 25–41.

Hengel, M., *The Atonement: The Origins of the Doctrine in the New Testament* (Philadelphia, Penn.: Fortress, 1981).

Käsemann, E., "Some Thoughts on the Theme 'The Doctrine of Reconciliation in the New Testament,' " *The Future of Our Religious Past: Essays in Honour of Rudolf Bultmann*, ed. J. M. Robinson (New York: Harper & Row, 1971), 49–64.

Logan, I., " 'Atonement' in the English Language," *ExpTim* 47 (1935–36): 477–78.

Lührmann, D., "Rechtfertigung und Versöhnung: Zur Geschichte der paulinischen Tradition," *ZTK* 67 (1970): 437–52.

Merkel, H., *"Katallassō,"* EDNT 2.261–63.

Taylor, V., *The Atonement in New Testament Teaching*, 2d ed. (London: Epworth, 1945), 54–101.

Whiteley, D. E. H., "St. Paul's Thought on the Atonement," *JTS* 8 (1957): 240–55.

Expiation

See also the bibliography on 3:21–26.

Bover, J. M., "Quem proposuit Deus 'propitiatorium' (Rom. 3,25)," VD 18 (1938): 137–42.

Deissmann, A., *"Hilastērios* und *Hilastērion:* Eine lexikalische Studie," ZNW 4 (1903): 193–212.

Dodd, C. H., *The Bible and the Greeks* (London: Hodder and Stoughton, 1935), 82–95.

————, "Hilaskesthai, Its Cognates, Derivatives and Synonyms in the Septuagint," *JTS* 32 (1930–31): 352–60.

Fitzmyer, J. A., "The Targum of Leviticus from Qumran Cave 4," *Maarav* 1 (1978–79): 5–23.

Garnet, P., "Atonement Constructions in the Old Testament and the Qumran Scrolls," *EvQ* 46 (1974): 131–63.

Grayston, K., "Hilaskesthai and Related Words in LXX," NTS 27 (1980–81): 640–56.

Janowski, B., *Sühne als Heilsgeschehen: Studien zur Sühnetheologie der Priesterschrift und zur Wurzel KPR im Alten Orient und im Alten Testament*, WMANT 55 (Neukirchen-Vluyn: Neukirchener-Verlag, 1982).

Levine, B. A., *In the Presence of the Lord*, Studies in Judaism and Late Antiquity 5 (Leiden: Brill, 1974), 123–27.

Logan, I., "The Strange Word 'Propitiation,' " *ExpTim* 46 (1934–35): 525–27.

Lohse, E., "Die Gerechtigkeit Gottes in der paulinischen Theologie," *Die Einheit des Neuen Testaments: Exegetische Studien zur Theologie des Neuen Testaments* (Göttingen: Vandenhoeck & Ruprecht, 1973), 209–27.

————, *Märtyrer und Gottesknecht: Untersuchungen zur urchristlichen Verkündigung vom Sühntod Jesu Christi*, FRLANT 64 (Göttingen: Vandenhoeck & Ruprecht, 1955), 149–54.

Lyonnet, S., "Expiation," *DBSup* 3.1–262.

Manson, T. W., "Hilastērion," *JTS* 46 (1945): 1–10.

Moraldi, L., *Espiazione sacrificale e riti espiatori nell'ambiente biblico e nell'Antico Testamento*, AnBib 5 (Rome: Biblical Institute, 1956), 182–221.

Morris, L., "The Biblical Use of the Term 'Blood,' " *JTS* 3 (1952): 216–27.

————, "The Use of hilaskesthai etc. in Biblical Greek," *ExpTim* 62 (1950–51): 227–33.

Nicole, R. R., "C. H. Dodd and the Doctrine of Propitiation," *WTJ* 17 (1954–55): 142–43.

Roloff, J., "Hilastērion," *EDNT* 2.185–86.

Siegman, E. F., "The Blood of Christ in St. Paul's Soteriology," *Proceedings of the Second Precious Blood Study Week* (Rensselaer, Ind.: St. Joseph's College, 1960), 11–35.

Young, N. H., "C. H. Dodd, 'Hilaskesthai' and His Critics," *EvQ* 48 (1976): 67–78.

————, " 'Hilaskesthai' and Related Words in the New Testament," *EvQ* 55 (1983): 169–76.

Redemption

Bandas, R. G., "The Master-Idea of St. Paul's Epistles, or the Redemption," AER 81 (1929): 113–23.

Bartchy, S., *Mallon chresai: First-Century Slavery and the Interpretation of 1 Corinthians 7:21*, SBLDS 11 (Missoula, Mont.: Scholars, 1973).

Buchanan, G. W., "The Day of Atonement and Paul's Doctrine of Redemption," *NovT* 32 (1990): 236–49.

Cerfaux, L., "La Sotériologie paulinienne," *Divinitas* 5 (1961): 88–114.
Gibbs, J. G., *Creation and Redemption: A Study in Pauline Theology*, NovTSup 26 (Leiden: Brill, 1971), 48–58.
Kertelge, K., "*Apolytrōsis*," *EDNT* 1.138–40.
Lyonnet, S., "Redemptio cosmica secundum Rom 8,19–23," *VD* 44 (1966): 225–42.
Marshall, I. H., "The Development of the Concept of Redemption in the New Testament," *Reconciliation and Hope: New Testament Essays on Atonement and Eschatology Presented to L. L. Morris . . .* , ed. R. Banks (Exeter, UK: Paternoster; Grand Rapids, Mich.: Eerdmans, 1974), 153–69.

Freedom

Betz, H. D., "Spirit, Freedom, and Law: Paul's Message to the Galatian Churches," *SEA* 39 (1974): 145–60.
Blankenburger Konferenz, 64th, *Die Freiheit der Kinder Gottes* (Bad Blankenburg, Thür. Wald: Allianz-Kommittee, 1958).
Cambier, J., "La Liberté chrétienne selon saint Paul," *LumVie* 61 (1963): 5–40; revised, *SE II*, TU 87 (1964), 315–53.
Croatto, J. S., " 'Hombre nuevo' y 'liberación' en la carta a los Romanos," *RevistB* 36 (1974): 37–45.
Diezinger, W., "Unter Toten freigeworden: Eine Untersuchung zu Röm. iii–viii," *NovT* 5 (1962): 268–98.
Gerhardsson, B., "Eleutheria ('Frihet') i bibliskt tänkande," *STK* 60 (1984): 119–29.
Grässer, E., "Freiheit und apostolisches Wirken bei Paulus," *EvT* 15 (1955): 333–42.
Güemes, A., "La *eleutheria* en las epístolas paulinas: Examen de textos," *EstBíb* 21 (1962): 37–63; 22 (1963): 219–42.
Jones, F. S., *"Freiheit" in den Briefen des Apostels Paulus: Eine historische, exegetische und religionsgeschichtliche Studie*, GTA 34 (Göttingen: Vandenhoeck & Ruprecht, 1987), 110–37.
Lyonnet, S., "Liberté chrétienne et loi de l'Esprit selon saint Paul," *Christus* 4 (1954): 6–27.
Mussner, F., *Theologie der Freiheit nach Paulus*, QD 75 (Freiburg im Breisgau: Herder, 1976).
Quenum, A. G., "La Liberté chrétienne: L'Enseignement de l'Apôtre Paul dans ses lettres aux Galates et aux Romains," *Euntes docete* 34 (1981): 267–86.
Schlier, H., "Zur Freiheit gerufen: Das paulinische Freiheitsverständnis," *GLeb* 43 (1970): 421–36.
Schnackenburg, R., *Present and Future: Modern Aspects of New Testament Theology* (Notre Dame, Ind.: University of Notre Dame, 1966), 64–80.

Glorification

Brockington, L. H., "The Septuagintal Background of the New Testament Use of *Doxa*," *Studies in the Gospels: Essays in Memory of R. H. Lightfoot*, ed. D. E. Nineham (Oxford: Blackwell, 1957), 1–8.

Dupont, J., "Le Chrétien, miroir de la gloire divine d'après II Cor., III,18," *RB* 56 (1949): 392–411.

Forster, A. H., "The Meaning of Doxa in the Greek Bible," *ATR* 12 (1929–30): 311–16.

Schlier, H., "Doxa bei Paulus als heilsgeschichtlicher Begriff," *SPCIC* 1.45–56.

Pardon

Kümmel, W. G., "*Paresis* and *endeixis:* A Contribution to the Understanding of the Pauline Doctrine of Justification," *JTCh* 3 (1967): 1–13.

Lyonnet, S., "Le Sens de *paresis* en Rom 3,25," *Études*, 89–106.

————, "Propter remissionem praecedentium delictorum (Rom 3,25)," *VD* 28 (1950): 282–87.

The Spirit of God/Christ

Benjamin, H. S., "Pneuma in John and Paul: A Comparative Study of the Term with Particular Reference to the Holy Spirit," *BTB* 6 (1976): 27–48.

Chevallier, M.-A., *Esprit de Dieu, paroles d'hommes: Le Role de l'esprit dans les ministères de la parole selon l'apôtre Paul*, Bibliothèque théologique (Neuchâtel: Delachaux et Niestlé, 1966).

Fransen, I., "La Loi de l'esprit de vie (Rom 1, 1–8, 39)," *BVC* 27 (1959): 20–34.

Fuchs, E., *Christus und der Geist bei Paulus: Eine biblisch-theologische Untersuchung*, UNT 23 (Leipzig: Hinrichs, 1932).

Hamilton, N. Q., *The Holy Spirit and Eschatology in Paul*, SJT Occasional Papers 6 (Edinburgh and London: Oliver & Boyd, 1957).

Hermann, I., *Kyrios und Pneuma: Studien zur Christologie der paulinischen Hauptbriefe*, SANT 2 (Munich: Kösel, 1961).

Hoyle, R. B., *The Holy Spirit in St. Paul* (London: Hodder and Stoughton, 1927; Garden City, N.Y.: Doubleday, Doran, 1928).

Huby, J., "La Vie dans l'esprit d'après saint Paul (*Romains*, ch. 8)," *RSR* 30 (1940): 5–39.

Isaacs, M. E., *The Concept of Spirit: A Study of Pneuma in Hellenistic Judaism and Its Bearing on the New Testament*, Heythrop Monographs 1 (London: Heythrop College, 1976).

Käsemann, E., "The Spirit and the Letter," *Perspectives*, 138–66.

Kevan, E. F., *The Saving Work of the Holy Spirit* (London: Pickering & Inglis, 1953).

Luck, U., "Historische Fragen zum Verhältnis von Kyrios und Pneuma bei Paulus," *TLZ* 85 (1960): 845–48.

Merode, M. de, "L'Aspect eschatologique de la vie et de l'esprit dans les épîtres pauliniennes," *ETL* 51 (1975): 96–112.

Montague, G. T., *The Holy Spirit: Growth of a Biblical Tradition* (New York: Paulist Press, 1976), 127–215.

Pfister, W., *Das Leben im Geist nach Paulus: Der Geist als Anfang und Vollendung des christlichen Lebens*, Studia Friburgensia n.s. 34 (Fribourg: Universitätsverlag, 1963).

Sokolowski, E., *Die Begriffe Geist und Leben bei Paulus in ihren Beziehungen zu einander: Eine exegetisch-religionsgeschichtliche Untersuchung* (Göttingen: Vandenhoeck & Ruprecht, 1903).

Stalder, K., *Das Werk des Geistes in der Heiligung bei Paulus* (Zurich: EVZ, 1962).

Steffen, M., "Das Verhältnis von Geist und Glauben bei Paulus: Ein Versuch zur Charakteristik seiner Frömmigkeit," ZNW 2 (1901): 115–39.

Vos, J. S., *Traditionsgeschichtliche Untersuchungen zur paulinischen Pneumatologie*, Van Gorcum's theologische Bibliotheek 47 (Assen: Van Gorcum, 1973).

Wood, A. S., *Life by the Spirit* (Grand Rapids, Mich.: Zondervan, 1963).

Grace

Arichea, D. C., Jr., "Translating 'Grace' *(charis)* in the New Testament," BT 29 (1978): 201–6.

Berger, K., "*Charis*," EWNT 3.1095–1102.

Cambe, M., "La *Charis* chez saint Paul," RB 70 (1963): 193–207.

Doughty, D. J., "The Priority of Charis: An Investigation of the Theological Language of Paul," NTS 19 (1972–73): 163–80.

Moffatt, J., *Grace in the New Testament* (London: Hodder and Stoughton, 1931; New York: R. Long & R. R. Smith, 1932), 129–296.

Potterie, I. de la, "*Charis* paulinienne et *charis* johannique," *Jesus und Paulus: Festschrift für Werner Georg Kümmel* . . . , ed. E. E. Ellis and E. Grässer (Göttingen: Vandenhoeck & Ruprecht, 1975), 256–82.

Humanity Without Christ: The Human Composite

Jewett, R., *Paul's Anthropological Terms: A Study of Their Use in Conflicting Settings*, AGJU 10 (Leiden: Brill, 1971).

Kümmel, W. G., *Man in the New Testament*, rev. ed. (London: Epworth, 1963), 38–71.

Mehl-Koehnlein, H., *L'Homme selon l'apôtre Paul*, Cahiers théologiques 28 (Neuchâtel: Delachaux et Niestlé, 1951).

Seitz, O. J. F., "Two Spirits in Man: An Essay in Biblical Exegesis," NTS 6 (1959–60): 82–95.

Stacey, W. D., *The Pauline View of Man*.

Body

Gundry, R. H., "*Sōma*" in Biblical Theology: With Emphasis on Pauline Anthropology*, SNTSMS 29 (Cambridge: Cambridge University Press, 1976).

Käsemann, E., *Leib und Leib Christi: Eine Untersuchung zur paulinischen Begrifflichkeit*, BHT 9 (Tübingen: Mohr [Siebeck], 1933).

Robinson, J. A. T., *The Body: A Study in Pauline Theology*, SBT 5 (London: SCM; Naperville, Ill.: Allenson, 1952).

Flesh

Fatum, L., "Die menschliche Schwäche im Römerbrief," *ST* 29 (1975): 31–52.

Lindijer, C. H., *Het Begrip "Sarx" bij Paulus*, Theologisch Bibliotheek 22 (Assen: Van Gorcum, 1952).

Lohmeyer, E., "Probleme paulinischer Theologie, III: Sünde, Fleisch und Tod," *ZNW* 29 (1930): 1–59; repr. *Probleme paulinischer Theologie* (Darmstadt: Wissenschaftliche Buchgesellschaft, 1954), 75–156.

Murphy, R. E., "*Bśr* in the Qumrân Literature and *Sarks* in the Epistle to the Romans," *SacPag* 2.60–76.

Sand, A., *Der Begriff "Fleisch" in den paulinischen Hauptbriefen*, BU 2 (Regensburg: Pustet, 1967).

Schweizer, E., "Die hellenistische Komponente im neutestamentlichen *Sarx*-Begriff," *Neotestamentica: Deutsche und englische Aufsätze 1951–1963* . . . (Zurich: Zwingli-Verlag, 1963), 29–48.

Conscience

Dupont, J., "*Syneidēsis*: Aux Origines de la notion chrétienne de la conscience morale," *Studia hellenistica* 5 (1948): 119–53.

Eckstein, H.-J., *Der Begriff Syneidesis bei Paulus: Eine neutestamentlich-exegetische Untersuchung zum "Gewissensbegriff*," WUNT 2.10 (Tübingen: Mohr [Siebeck], 1983).

Lohse, E., "Die Berufung auf das Gewissen in der paulinischen Ethik," *Neues Testament und Ethik: Für Rudolf Schnackenburg*, ed. H. Merklein (Freiburg im Breisgau: Herder, 1989), 207–19.

Maurer, C., "*Synoida, syneidēsis*," *TDNT* 7.898–919.

Osborne, H., "*Syneidēsis*," *JTS* 32 (1931): 167–79.

Pierce, C. A., *Conscience in the New Testament*, SBT 15 (London: SCM, 1955).

Stelzenberger, J., *Syneidesis im Neuen Testament* (Paderborn: Schöningh, 1961).

Thrall, M. E., "The Pauline Use of *Syneidēsis*," *NTS* 14 (1967–68): 118–25.

Natural Law

Dodd, C. H., "Natural Law in the New Testament," *New Testament Studies* (Manchester, UK: University of Manchester Press, 1953), 129–42.

McKenzie, J. L., "Natural Law in the New Testament," *BR* 9 (1964): 3–13.

Martin, W. C., "The Bible and Natural Law," *ResQ* 17 (1974): 193–221.

The Jewish People

Barth, M., *The People of God*, JSNTSup 5 (Sheffield, UK: Academic Press, 1983).

Berry, E. S., "The Conversion of the Jews," *AER* 89 (1933): 414–17.

Cranfield, C. E. B., "Light from St Paul on Christian-Jewish Relations," *The Witness of the Jews to God*, ed. D. W. Torrance (Edinburgh: Clark, 1982), 22–31; repr. *The Bible and Christian Life: A Collection of Essays* (Edinburgh: Clark, 1985), 34–47.

Davies, W. D., "Paul and the People of Israel," *NTS* 24 (1977–78): 4–39.

Eckert, J., "Paulus und Israel: Zu den Strukturen paulinischer Rede und Argumentation," *TTZ* 87 (1978): 1–13.

Grässer, E., "Christen und Juden: Neutestamentliche Erwägungen zu einem aktuellen Thema," *Pastoraltheologie* 71 (1982): 431–49; repr. *Der Alte Bund im Neuen: Exegetische Studien zur Israelfrage im Neuen Testament*, WUNT 35 (Tübingen: Mohr [Siebeck], 1985), 271–89.

Haacker, K., "Das Evangelium Gottes und die Erwählung Israels: Zum Beitrag des Römerbriefs zur Erneuerung des Verhältnisses zwischen Christen und Juden," *TBei* 13 (1982): 59–72.

Huguet, M.-T., "Mise à l'écart d'Israël?" *Nova et Vetera* 60 (1985): 103–20.

Keane, H., "The Church and the Jewish People: Another Look at the Problem," *Theologia evangelica* (Pretoria) 15.1 (1982): 37–47.

Marquardt, F.-W., *Die Juden im Römerbrief*, Theologische Studien 107 (Zurich: Theologischer-Verlag, 1971).

Munck, J., *Paul and the Salvation of Mankind.*

Penna, R., "L'Évolution de l'attitude de Paul envers les Juifs," *L'Apôtre Paul: Personnalité, style et conception du ministère*, BETL 73, ed. A. Vanhoye (Louvain: Leuven University/Peeters, 1986), 390–421; "Evoluzione dell'atteggiamento di Paolo verso gli Ebrei," *Lateranum* 52 (1986): 1–37.

Radermakers, J. and J.-P. Sonnet, "Israël et l'église," *NRT* 107 (1985): 675–97.

Raith, P., "The Conversion of the Jews: Restoration of Israel and Juda," *AER* 89 (1933): 234–45.

Richardson, P., *Israel in the Apostolic Church*, SNTSMS 10 (Cambridge: Cambridge University Press, 1969), 126–47.

Salvoni, F., "Giudei e christiani: Reflessioni storico-bibliche," *RBR* 12.4 (1977): 7–39.

Sanders, E. P., *Paul and Palestinian Judaism.*

——, *Paul, the Law, and the Jewish People* (Philadelphia, Penn.: Fortress, 1983).

——, "Paul's Attitude Toward the Jewish People," *USQR* 33 (1978): 175–87.

Schlier, H., "Das Mysterium Israels," *Die Zeit der Kirche*, 232–44.

Schmitt, R., *Gottesgerechtigkeit—Heilsgeschichte—Israel in der Theologie des Paulus*, Europäische Hochschulschriften 23.240 (Bern, Frankfurt, and New York: Lang, 1984).

Stendahl, K., "A Response [to Sanders]," *USQR* 33 (1978): 189–91.

——, *Paul among Jews and Gentiles.*

Theobald, M., "Verantwortung vor der Vergangenheit: Die Bedeutung der Traditionen Israels für den Römerbrief," *BK* 37 (1982): 13–20.

Wiefel, W., "Paulus und das Judentum," *Die Zeichen der Zeit* 40 (1986): 142–47.

Zeller, D., *Juden und Heiden.*

The Law of Moses

Bandstra, A. J., *The Law and the Elements of the World: An Exegetical Study in Aspects of Paul's Teaching* (Kampen: Kok, 1964).

————, "Paul and the Law: Some Recent Developments and an Extraordinary Book," *CTJ* 25 (1990): 249–61.

Barclay, J. M. G., "Paul and the Law: Observations on Some Recent Debates," *Themelios* 12 (1986–87): 5–15.

Beck, I., "Altes und neues Gesetz: Eine Untersuchung über die Kompromisslosigkeit des paulinischen Denkens," *MTZ* 15 (1964): 127–42.

Benoit, P., "The Law and the Cross According to St Paul: Romans 7:7–8:4," *Jesus and the Gospel*, vol. 2 (London: Darton, Longman & Todd; New York: Seabury, 1974), 11–39; cf. *Exégèse et Théologie* 2.9–40.

Bläser, P., *Das Gesetz bei Paulus*, NTAbh 19.1–2 (Münster in Westfalen: Aschendorff, 1941).

Bring, R., *Christus und das Gesetz: Die Bedeutung des Gesetzes des Alten Testaments nach Paulus und sein Glauben an Christus* (Leiden: Brill, 1969), 1–72.

————, "Die Erfüllung des Gesetzes durch Christus: Eine Studie zur Theologie des Apostels Paulus," *KD* 5 (1959): 1–22.

Bruce, F. F., "The Curse of the Law," *Paul and Paulinism: Essays in Honour of C. K. Barrett* (London: SPCK, 1982), 27–36.

————, "Paul and the Law of Moses," *BJRL* 57 (1974–75): 259–79.

Bultmann, R., "Christus des Gesetzes Ende," *Glauben und Verstehen: Gesammelte Aufsätze*, 4th ed. (Tübingen: Mohr [Siebeck], 1965), 2.32–58.

Cranfield, C. E. B., "Giving a Dog a Bad Name: A Note on H. Räisänen's *Paul and the Law*," *JSNT* 38 (1990): 77–85.

————, "St. Paul and the Law," *SJT* 17 (1964): 43–68.

Cuenca Molina, J. F., "El judeo-cristianismo y la ley: A propósito del nomismo de las 'Homilias Clementinas,' " *Carthaginensia* 2 (1986): 35–54.

Deidun, T., "E. P. Sanders: An Assessment of Two Recent Works: 1. 'Having His Cake and Eating It': Paul on the Law," *HeyJ* 27 (1986): 43–52.

Dülmen, A. van, *Die Theologie des Gesetzes bei Paulus*, SBM 5 (Stuttgart: Katholisches Bibelwerk, 1968).

Fitzmyer, J. A., "Paul and the Law," *TAG*, 186–201.

Gaston, L., *Paul and the Torah* (Vancouver: University of British Columbia Press, 1987).

Gutbrod, W., "*Nomos*," *TDNT* 4.1036–91.

Hahn, F., "Das Gesetzesverständnis im Römer- und Galaterbrief," *ZNW* 67 (1976): 29–63.

Haufe, C., "Die Stellung des Paulus zum Gesetz," *TLZ* 91 (1966): 171–78.

Hooker, M., "Paul and 'Covenantal Nomism,' " *Paul and Paulinism* (see above under Bruce), 47–56.

Hübner, H., *Law in Paul's Thought* (Edinburgh: Clark, 1984).

Hyldahl, N., "Paulus og loven: Nogle bøger fra det sidste årtis Paulus-forskning," *DTT* 53 (1990): 183–92.

Jewett, R., "The Law and the Coexistence of Jews and Gentiles in Romans," *Int* 39 (1985): 341–56.

Journet, C., "L'Économie de la loi mosaïque," *RevThom* 63 (1963): 5–36, 193–224, 515–47.

Kuss, O., "Nomos bei Paulus," *MTZ* 17 (1966): 173–227.

Ladd, G. E., "Paul and the Law," *Soli Deo Gloria: New Testament Studies in Honor of William Childs Robinson*, ed. J. M. Richards (Richmond, Va.: John Knox, 1968), 50–67, 142–46.

Lambrecht, J., "Gesetzverständnis bei Paulus," *Das Gesetz im Neuen Testament*, QD 108, ed. K. Kertelge (Freiburg im Breisgau: Herder, 1986), 88–127.

Larsson, E., "Paul: Law and Salvation," *NTS* 31 (1985): 425–36.

Martin, B. L., *Christ and the Law in Paul*, NovTSup 62 (Leiden: Brill, 1989).

Maurer, C., *Die Gesetzeslehre des Paulus nach ihrem Ursprung und in ihrer Entfaltung dargelegt* (Zollikon-Zurich: Evangelischer Verlag, 1941).

Moo, D., "Paul and the Law in the Last Ten Years," *SJT* 40 (1987): 287–307.

Osten-Sacken, P. von der, "Das paulinische Verständnis des Gesetzes im Spannungs-feld von Eschatologie und Geschichte: Erläuterungen zum Evangelium als Faktor von theologischen Antijudaismus," *EvT* 37 (1977): 549–87; repr. *Evangelium und Tora*, 159–96.

Penna, R., "Il problema della legge nelle lettere di s. Paolo: Alcuni aspetti," *RivB* 38 (1990): 327–52.

Räisänen, H., *Paul and the Law*, WUNT 29 (Tübingen: Mohr [Siebeck], 1983).

Reicke, B., "The Law and This World According to Paul: Some Thoughts Concerning Gal 4:1–11," *JBL* 70 (1951): 259–76.

———, "Paulus über das Gesetz," *TZ* 41 (1985): 237–57.

Reid, D. G., "The Misunderstood Apostle," *Christianity Today* 34 (1990): 25–27.

Schreiner, T. R., "Paul and Perfect Obedience to the Law: An Evaluation of the View of E. P. Sanders," *WTJ* 47 (1985): 245–78.

Segal, A. F., "Torah and *nomos* in Recent Scholarly Discussion," *SR* 13 (1984): 19–27.

Sloan, R. B., "Paul and the Law: Why the Law Cannot Save," *NovT* 33 (1991): 35–60.

Stegemann, E. W., "Die umgekehrte Tora: Zum Gesetzesverständnis des Paulus," *Judaica* 43 (1987): 4–20.

Stuhlmacher, P., "Paul's Understanding of the Law in the Letter to the Romans," *SEA* 50 (1985): 87–104.

Walvoord, J. F., "Law in the Epistle to the Romans," *BSac* 94 (1937): 15–30, 281–95.

Weder, H., "Einsicht in Gesetzlichkeit: Paulus als verständnisvoller Ausleger des menschlichen Lebens," *Judaica* 43 (1987): 21–29.

Weima, J. A. D., "The Function of the Law in Relation to Sin: An Evaluation of the View of H. Räisänen," *NovT* 32 (1990): 219–35.

Welker, M., "Security of Expectations: Reformulating the Theology of Law and Gospel," *JR* 66 (1986): 237–60.

Wilckens, U., "Zur Entwicklung des paulinischen Gesetzesverständnisses," *NTS* 28 (1982): 154–90.

Winger, M. *By What Law? The Meaning of "Nomos" in the Letters of Paul* (Atlanta, Ga.: Scholars, 1992).

Zeller, D., "Zur neueren Diskussion über das Gesetz bei Paulus," *TP* 62 (1987): 481–99.

———, "Der Zusammenhang vom Gesetz und Sünde im Römerbrief: Kritischer Nachvollzug des Auslegung von Ulrich Wilckens," *TZ* 38 (1982): 193–212.

Sin

Barrosse, T., "Death and Sin in Saint Paul's Epistle to the Romans," *CBQ* 15 (1953): 438–59.

Dubarle, A. M., "Le Péché original dans saint Paul," *RSPT* 40 (1956): 213–54; repr. in *The Biblical Doctrine of Original Sin* (New York: Herder and Herder, 1964), 142–200.

———, "Le Péché originel dans les livres sapientiaux," *RevThom* 56 (1956): 597–619.

Feuillet, A., "L'Antithèse péché-justice dans l'épître aux Romains," *Nova et vetera* 58 (1983): 57–70.

Fiedler, P., "*Hamartia . . . ,*" *EDNT* 1.65–69.

Fraine, J. de, *Adam and the Family of Man* (Staten Island, N.Y.: Alba House, 1965).

Freundorfer, J., *Erbsünde und Erbtod beim Apostel Paulus.*

Haag, H., *Is Original Sin in Scripture* (New York: Sheed & Ward, 1969), 95–108.

Ligier, L., *Péché d'Adam et péché du monde*, 2 vols., Théologie 43, 48 (Paris: Aubier, 1960–61).

Lyonnet, S. and L. Sabourin, *Sin*, 3–30, 46–57.

Malina, B., "Some Observations on the Origin of Sin in Judaism and St. Paul," *CBQ* 31 (1969): 18–34.

Martelet, G., *Libre réponse à un scandale: La Faute originelle, la souffrance et la mort* (Paris: Cerf, 1986).

Moreno, J., "Pecado e historia de la salvación (Rom. 1–3)," *Teología y vida* 13 (1972): 39–54.

Porter, S. E., "The Pauline Concept of Original Sin, in Light of Rabbinic Background," *TynBul* 41 (1990): 3–30.

Ramazzotti, B., "Etica cristiana e peccati nelle lettere ai Romani e ai Galati," *ScCatt* 106 (1978): 290–342.

Röhser, G., *Metaphorik und Personifikation der Sünde: Antike Sündenvorstellungen und paulinische Hamartia*, WUNT 2.25 (Tübingen: Mohr [Siebeck], 1987).

Schottroff, L., "Die Schreckensherrschaft der Sünde und die Befreiung durch Christus nach dem Römerbrief des Paulus," *EvT* 39 (1979): 497–510.

Schweizer, E., "Die Sünde in den Gliedern," *Abraham unser Vater: Juden und Christen im Gespräch über die Bibel: Festschrift für Otto Michel . . .* , ed. O. Betz et al. (Leiden: Brill, 1963), 437–39.

Varo, F., "El léxico del pecado en la epístola de San Pablo a los Romanos," *Scripta theologica* 21 (1989): 99–116.

Wernle, P., *Der Christ und die Sünde bei Paulus* (Leipzig and Freiburg im Breisgau: Mohr [Siebeck], 1897).

Humanity in Christ: Faith

Aletti, J.-N., "L'Acte de croire pour l'apôtre Paul," *RSR* 77 (1989): 233–50.

Bartsch, H.-W., "Der Begriff 'Glaube' im Römerbrief," *Kerygma und Mythos VI-4*, ed. F. Theunis (Hamburg: Evangelischer-Verlag, 1968), 119–27; "The Concept of Faith in Paul's Letter to the Romans," *BR* 13 (1968): 41–53.

Becker, O. and O. Michel, "Faith, Persuade, Belief, Unbelief," *NIDNTT* 1.587–606.

Binder, H., *Der Glaube bei Paulus* (Berlin: Evangelische Verlagsanstalt, 1968).

Boismard, M.-E., "La Foi selon Saint Paul," *Lum Vie* 22 (1955): 65–89.

Bornkamm, G., "Faith and Reason in Paul's Epistles," *NTS* 4 (1957–58): 93–100.

Botha, J. E., "The Meanings of *pisteuō* in the Greek New Testament: A Semantic-Lexicographical Study," *Neotestamentica* 21 (1987): 225–40.

Brandenburger, E., "Pistis and Soteria: Zum Verstehenshorizont von 'Glaube' im Urchristentum," *ZTK* 85 (1988): 165–98.

Bultmann, R. and A. Weiser, "*Pisteuō, pistis . . .* ," *TDNT* 6.174–228.

Butler, C., "The Object of Faith According to St Paul's Epistles," *SPCIC*, 1.15–30.

Campbell, D. A., "The Meaning of *Pistis* and *Nomos* in Paul: A Linguistic and Structural Perspective," *JBL* 111 (1992): 91–103.

Daalen, D. H. van, " 'Faith' According to Paul," *ExpTim* 87 (1975–76): 83–85.

Davies, G. N., *Faith and Obedience in Romans: A Study in Romans 1–4*, JSNTSup 39 (Sheffield, UK: Academic Press, 1990).

Etzold, O., *Gehorsam des Glaubens: Die Botschaft des Römerbriefes an die heutige Christenheit* (Gütersloh: Bertelsmann, 1947; repr. 1951).

Fuchs, E., *Die Freiheit des Glaubens: Römer 5–8 ausgelegt*, BEvT 14 (Munich: Kaiser, 1949).

———, "Sola fide: Der Kampf um einen Stilbruch," *ZTK* 73 (1976): 306–14.

García ab Orbiso, T., "De fide in epistola ad Romanos," *Divinitas* 2 (1958): 576–96.

Hatch, W. H. P., *The Pauline Idea of Faith in Its Relation to Jewish and Hellenistic Religion*, HTS 2 (Cambridge, Mass.: Harvard University Press, 1917).

Hay, D. M., "Pistis as 'Ground for Faith' in Hellenized Judaism and Paul," *JBL* 108 (1989): 461–76.

Heidland, H.-W., *Die Anrechnung des Glaubens zur Gerechtigkeit*, BWANT 71 (Stuttgart: Kohlhammer, 1936).

Kuss, O., "Der Glaube nach den paulinischen Hauptbriefen," *Auslegung und Verkündigung I* (Regensburg: Pustet, 1963), 187–212.

Ljungman, H., *Pistis: A Study of Its Presuppositions and Its Meaning in Pauline Use*, Acta reg. Societatis humaniorum litterarum lundensis 64 (Lund: Gleerup, 1964).

Lohse, E., "Emuna und Pistis—Jüdisches und urchristliches Verständnis des Glaubens," *ZNW* 68 (1977): 147–63.

Lührmann, D., *Glaube im frühen Christentum* (Gütersloh: Mohn, 1976).

Lyonnet, S., "Foi et charité d'après saint Paul," *Foi et salut selon saint Paul (Epître aux Romains 1,16)*, AnBib 42 (Rome: Biblical Institute, 1970), 211–31.

————, "Gratuité de la justification et gratuité du salut: Le Problème de la foi et des oeuvres," *SPCIC* 1.95–110.

Millás, J. M., "La concepción paulina de la fe y la existencia cristiana según la interpretación de Rudolf Bultmann," *EstEcl* 65 (1990): 193–214.

Munck, J., *Paul and the Salvation of Mankind*, 196–209.

O'Rourke, J. J., "*Pistis* in Romans," *CBQ* 35 (1973): 188–94.

Schlatter, A., *Der Glaube im Neuen Testament*, 2d ed. (Stuttgart and Calw: Vereins-buchhandlung, 1896; 5th ed., 1963).

Schnackenburg, R., *Glaubensimpulse aus dem Neuen Testament* (Düsseldorf: Patmos, 1973), 133–38.

Theobald, M., "Glaube und Vernunft: Zur Argumentation des Paulus im Römer-brief," *TQ* 169 (1989): 287–301.

Valloton, P., *Le Christ et la foi: Étude de théologie biblique*, Nouvelle série théologique 10 (Geneva: Labor et Fides, 1960), 39–106.

Wiesinger, [J. T. A.], "Über Glaube und Rechtfertigung," *NKZ* 14 (1903): 587–607.

Love/Charity

Descamps, A., "La Charité, résumé de la loi," *RDT* 8 (1953): 123–29.

Dupont, J., "Imiter la charité du Christ," *AsSeign* 4 (1961): 13–34.

Enslin, M. S., *The Ethics of Paul* (Nashville, Tenn.: Abingdon, 1957), 231–94.

Furnish, V. P., *The Love Command in the New Testament* (Nashville, Tenn.: Abingdon, 1972), 91–131.

Navone, J. J., "Love in the Message of Paul," *Worship* 40 (1966): 437–44.

Perkins, P., *Love Commands in the New Testament* (New York: Paulist Press, 1982), 97–103.

Spicq, C., *Agape in the New Testament*, 3 vols. (St. Louis: B. Herder, 1963–66), 2.15–341.

Viard, A., "La Charité accomplit la loi: Commentaire de Romains 12,9 à 13,10," *VSpir* 74 (1946): 27–34.

Hope

Bové, F., "La esperanza cristiana: Su visión teológico a partir de la Epístola a los Romanos," *Mayéutica* 6 (1980): 133–61.

Heil, J. P., *Romans—Paul's Letter of Hope*, AnBib 112 (Rome: Biblical Institute, 1987).

Hunter, A. M., "The Hope of Glory: The Relevance of the Pauline Eschatology," *Int* 8 (1954): 131–41.

Maillot, A., "L'Épître aux Romains: Épître de l'espérance," *BVC* 84 (1968): 1–96.

Mayer, B., "*Elpis*, etc.," *EDNT* 1.437–41.

Nebe, G., "*Hoffnung*" bei Paulus: Elpis und ihre Synonyme im Zusammenhang der Eschatologie*, SUNT 16 (Göttingen: Vandenhoeck & Ruprecht, 1983).

Neyrey, J. H., "Hope Against Hope," *The Way* 27 (1987): 264–73.

Siber, P., *Mit Christus leben.*

Baptism

Badke, W. B., "Baptised into Moses—Baptised into Christ: A Study in Doctrinal Development," *EvQ* 60 (1988): 23–29.

Beasley-Murray, G. R., *Baptism in the New Testament* (London and New York: Macmillan, 1962), 127–204, esp. 127–46.

Bornkamm, G., *Early Christian Experience*, 71–86.

Bover, J. M., "El simbolismo bautismal en las epístolas de San Pablo," *EstBíb* 4 (1945): 393–419.

Braumann, G., *Vorpaulinische christliche Taufverkündigung.*

Cullmann, O., *Baptism in the New Testament*, SBT 1 (London: SCM; Chicago: Regnery, 1950).

Delling, G., *Die Zueignung des Heils in der Taufe: Eine Untersuchung zum neutestamentlichen "taufen auf den Namen"* (Berlin: Evangelische Verlagsanstalt, 1961).

Dunn, J. D. G., *Baptism in the Holy Spirit*, SBT 2.15 (London: SCM; Naperville, Ill.: Allenson, 1970).

Fascher, E., "Zur Taufe des Paulus," *TLZ* 80 (1955): 643–48.

Flemington, W. F., *The New Testament Doctrine of Baptism* (London: SPCK, 1948).

Hahn, W. T., *Das Mitsterben und Mitauferstehen mit Christus bei Paulus.*

Halter, H., *Taufe und Ethos: Paulinische Kriterien.*

Heitmüller, W., *Taufe und Abendmahl bei Paulus* (Göttingen: Vandenhoeck & Ruprecht, 1903).

Hofer, N., "Das Bekenntnis 'Herr ist Jesus' und das 'Taufen auf den Namen des Herrn Jesu,' " *TQ* 145 (1965): 1–12.

Jacono, V., "Il battesimo in S. Paolo," *RivB* 3 (1955): 348–62.

Klaar, E., *Die Taufe nach paulinischem Verständnis*, TEH 93 (Munich: Kaiser, 1961).

———, "Zum paulinischen Taufverständnis," *ZNW* 49 (1958) 278–82.

Kuss, O., "Zur paulinischen und nachpaulinischen Tauflehre im Neuen Testament," *TGl* 42 (1952): 401–25; repr. *Auslegung und Verkündigung I* (Regensburg: Pustet, 1963), 121–50.

Larsson, E., *Christus als Vorbild*, 48–80.

Leenhardt, F., *Le Baptême chrétien: Son Origine, sa signification*, Cahiers théologiques 4 (Neuchâtel: Delachaux et Niestlé, 1946).

Lohse, E., "Imago Dei bei Paulus," *Libertas christiana: Friedrich Delekat . . .* , ed. W. Mattias, BEvT 26 (Munich: Kaiser, 1957), 122–35.

———, "Taufe und Rechtfertigung bei Paulus," *KD* 11 (1965): 308–24; repr. *Die Einheit des Neuen Testaments: Exegetische Studien zur Theologie des Neuen Testaments* (Göttingen: Vandenhoeck & Ruprecht, 1973), 228–44.

Mollat, D., "Symbolismes baptismaux chez saint Paul," *Lum Vie* 26 (1956): 61–84.

Mussner, F., *Mort et resurrection*, 43–54.

Ortkemper, F. J., "Leben aus dem Glauben: Indikativ und Imperativ bei Paulus und die kirchliche Moralpredigt heute," *BK* 28 (1973): 85–89.

Peterson, N. R., "Pauline Baptism and 'Secondary Burial,' " *HTR* 79 (1986): 217–26.

Rey, B., "L'Homme nouveau d'après s. Paul (Exégèse de Rm 6,4–11; Col 3,5–15; Ep 2,11–12; Ep 4,22–24)," *RSPT* 48 (1964): 603–29; 49 (1965): 161–95.

Schnackenburg, R., *Baptism in the Thought of St. Paul: A Study in Pauline Theology* (Oxford: Blackwell; New York: Herder and Herder, 1964), 30–61.

Schnelle, U., *Gerechtigkeit und Christusgegenwart: Vorpaulinische und paulinische Tauftheologie* (Göttingen: Vandenhoeck & Ruprecht, 1983).

Seidensticker, P., "Taufe und Tod: Das Problem des leiblichen Todes im Römerbrief," *SBFLA* 4 (1953–54): 117–83.

Spicq, C., "La Théologie paulinienne du baptême," *Questions liturgiques et paroissiales* 24 (1939): 130–48.

Tannehill, R. C., *Dying and Rising with Christ*.

Tremel, Y. B., "Le Baptême, incorporation du chrétien au Christ," *Lum Vie* 27 (1956): 81–102.

Voss, G., "Glaube und Taufe in den Paulusbriefen," *Una Sancta* 25 (1970): 371–78.

Warnach, V., "Die Tauflehre des Römerbriefes in der neueren theologischen Diskussion," *Archiv für Liturgiewissenschaft* 5.2 (1958): 274–332.

The Body of Christ

Benoit, P., "L'Église corps du Christ," *Populus Dei: Studi in onore del Card. Alfredo Ottaviani per il cinquantesimo di sacerdozio: 18 marzo 1966* (= Communio 10–11; Rome: no publ., 1969), 971–1028; repr. *Exégèse et théologie* 4.205–62.

Bultmann, R., *TNT* 1.299.

Daines, B., "Paul's Use of the Analogy of the Body of Christ—With Special Reference to 1 Corinthians 12," *EvQ* 50 (1978): 71–78.

Dubarle, A. M., "L'Origine dans l'Ancien Testament de la notion paulinienne de l'église corps du Christ," *SPCIC* 1.231–40.

Havet, J., "La Doctrine paulinienne du 'Corps du Christ': Essai de mise au point," *Littérature et théologie pauliniennes*, ed. A. Descamps, RechBib 5 (Bruges: Desclée de Brouwer, 1960), 185–216.

Hegermann, H., "Zur Ableitung der Leib-Christi-Vorstellung," *TLZ* 85 (1960): 839–42.

Hill, A. E., "The Temple of Asclepius: An Alternative Source for Paul's Body Theology," *JBL* 99 (1980): 437–39.

Judge, E. A., "Demythologizing the Church: What Is the Meaning of 'The Body of Christ'?" *Interchange* 11 (1972): 155–67.

Käsemann, E., *Leib und Leib Christi*.

———, "The Theological Problem Presented by the Motif of the Body of Christ," *Perspectives*, 102–21.

Meuzelaar, J. J., *Der Leib des Messias* (Assen: Van Gorcum, 1961).

Percy, E., *Der Leib Christi (Sōma Christou) in den paulinischen Homologumena und*

Antilegomena, Lunds Universitets Årsskrift n.s. 1.38-1 (Lund: Gleerup, 1942), 29–42.

Ramaroson, L., " 'L'Église, corps du Christ' dans les écrits pauliniens: Simples Esquisses," *ScEspr* 30 (1978): 129–41.

Robinson, J. A. T., *The Body*.

Schlier, H., "Corpus Christi," *RAC* 3.437–53.

Schweizer, E., "The Church as the Missionary Body of Christ," *Neotestamentica: Deutsche und englische Aufsätze 1951–1963* (Zurich: Zwingli-Verlag, 1963), 317–29.

————, "Die Kirche als Leib Christi in den paulinischen Homologoumena," ibid. 272–92.

Wedderburn, A. J. M., "The Body of Christ and Related Concepts in 1 Corinthians," *SJT* 24 (1971): 74–96.

Weiss, H.-F., " 'Volk Gottes' und 'Leib Christi': Überlegungen zur paulinischen Ekklesiologie," *TLZ* 102 (1977): 411–20.

Worgul, G. D., "People of God, Body of Christ: Pauline Ecclesiological Contrasts," *BTB* 12 (1982): 24–28.

Yorke, G. L. O. R., *The Church as the Body of Christ in the Pauline Corpus: A Reexamination* (Lanham, Md.: University Press of America, 1991).

The Church

Banks, R. J., *Paul's Idea of Community: The Early House Churches in Their Historical Setting* (Exeter, UK: Paternoster, 1980; Grand Rapids, Mich.: Eerdmans, 1980), 37–42.

Cerfaux, L., *Church*.

Filson, F. V., "The Significance of the Early House Churches," *JBL* 58 (1939): 105–12.

Gielen, M., "Zur Interpretation der paulinischen Formel *hē kat' oikon ekklēsia*," *ZNW* 77 (1986): 109–25.

Gnilka, J., "Die neutestamentliche Hausgemeinde," *Freude am Gottesdienst: Aspekte ursprünglicher Liturgie: Festschrift für Weihbischof Dr. J. Plöger . . .* , ed. J. Schreiner (Stuttgart: Katholisches Bibelwerk, 1983), 229–42.

Hainz, J., *Ekklesia: Strukturen paulinischer Gemeinde-Theologie und Gemeinde-Ordnung*, BU 9 (Regensburg: Pustet, 1972), 199–203, 236–37, 345–48.

Klaiber, W., *Rechtfertigung und Gemeinde: Eine Untersuchung zum paulinischen Kirchenverständnis*, FRLANT 127 (Göttingen: Vandenhoeck & Ruprecht, 1982).

Klauck, H.-J., "Die Hausgemeinde als Lebensform im Urchristentum," *MTZ* 32 (1981): 1–15.

————, *Hausgemeinde und Hauskirche im frühen Christentum*, SBS 103 (Stuttgart: Katholisches Bibelwerk, 1981).

Menoud, P. H., "Church and Ministry According to the New Testament," *Jesus Christ and the Faith* (Pittsburgh, Penn.: Pickwick, 1978), 363–435.

Peterson, E., "Die Kirche aus Juden und Heiden," *Theologische Traktate* (Munich: Kösel, 1929; repr. 1951), 239–92.

———, *Le Mystère des juifs et des gentiles dans l'église*, Courrier des îles 6 (Paris: Desclée de Brouwer, n.d.).

Przywara, E., "Die Kirche aus Juden und Heiden," *SdZ* 126 (1933–34): 414–15.

Rordorf, W., "Was wissen wir über die christlichen Gottesdiensträume der vorkonstantinischen Zeit?" *ZNW* 55 (1964): 110–28.

Schrage, W., " 'Ekklesia' und 'Synagoge': Zum Ursprung des urchristlichen Kirchenbegriffs," *ZTK* 60 (1963): 178–202.

Christian Conduct

Barrett, C. K., "Ethics and Eschatology: A Résumé," *Dimensions*, ed. L. de Lorenzi (see below), 221–35.

Beker, J. C., "Suffering and Triumph in Paul's Letter to the Romans," *HBT* 7 (1985): 105–19.

Bläser, J., "Der Mensch und die Sittlichkeit nach dem Römerbrief des Apostels Paulus," *TGI* 39 (1949): 232–49.

Bouttier, M., *Christianity*.

———, *En Christ*.

Büchsel, F., " 'In Christus' bei Paulus," *ZNW* 42 (1949): 141–58.

Cerfaux, L., *The Christian*.

Corriveau, R., *The Liturgy of Life: A Study of the Ethical Thought of St. Paul in His Letters to the Early Christian Communities* (Paris: Desclée de Brouwer; Montreal: Ed. Bellarmin, 1970).

Deissmann, A., *Die neutestamentliche Formel "in Christo Jesu"* (Marburg: Elwert, 1892).

Delhaye, P., "Ethique humaine et morale révélée dans l'épître aux Romains," *EspVie* 100 (1990): 65–76, 81–92.

Dupont, J., *Syn Christo: L'Union avec le Christ suivant saint Paul* (Bruges: Abbaye de Saint-André, 1952).

Festorazzi, F., "Originalità della morale cristiana secondo San Paolo," *Dimensions*, ed. L. Lorenzi (see above), 237–59.

Feuillet, A., "Loi ancienne et morale chrétienne d'après l'épître aux Romains," *NRT* 92 (1970): 785–805.

———, "Morale ancienne et morale chrétienne d'après Mt. V. 17–20; comparaison avec la doctrine de l'épître aux Romains," *NTS* 17 (1970–71): 123–37.

Furnish, V. P., *The Moral Teaching of Paul: Selected Issues* (Nashville, Tenn.: Abingdon, 1979; 2d ed., 1985).

———, *Theology and Ethics in Paul* (Nashville, Tenn.: Abingdon, 1968), 68–111.

Gerritzen, F., "Le Sens et l'origine de l'*en Christô* paulinien," *SPCIC* 2.323–31.

Gräbe, P. J., "Die verhouding tussen indikatief en imperatief in die pauliniese etiek: Enkele aksente uit die diskussie sedert 1924," *Scriptura* 32 (1990): 54–66.

Halter, H., *Taufe und Ethos: Paulinische Kriterien für das Proprium christlicher Moral* (Freiburg im Breisgau: Herder, 1977).

Käsemann, E., "Die gottesdienstliche Schrei nach der Freiheit," *Apophoreta: Festschrift für Ernst Haenchen* . . . , BZNW 30, ed. W. Eltester and F. H. Kettler (Berlin: Töpelmann, 1964), 142–55; repr. *Perspectives*, 122–37.

Kuss, O., "Die Formel 'durch Christus' in den paulinischen Hauptbriefen," *TTZ* 65 (1956): 193–201.

Lohmeyer, E., "*Syn Christō*," *Festgabe für Adolf Deissmann* (Tübingen: Mohr [Siebeck], 1927), 218–57.

Lohse, E., "Imago Dei bei Paulus," *Libertas christiana: Friedrich Delekat* . . . , BEvT 26, ed. W. Mattias (Munich: Kaiser, 1957), 122–35.

Lorenzi, L. de (ed.), *Dimensions de la vie chrétienne (Rm 12–13)*, Benedictina 4 (Rome: Abbazia San Paolo fuori le mura, 1979).

Merk, O., *Handeln aus Glauben: Die Motivierungen der paulinischen Ethik*, MarTS 5 (Marburg: Elwert, 1968), 157–73.

Moxnes, H., "Honor, Shame, and the Outside World in Paul's Letter to the Romans," *The Social World of Formative Christianity and Judaism: Essays in Tribute to Howard Clark Kee*, ed. J. Neusner et al. (Philadelphia, Penn.: Fortress, 1988), 207–18.

———, "Honour and Righteousness in Romans," *JSNT* 32 (1988): 61–77.

———, "Paulus og den norske vaeremåten: 'Skam' og 'aere' i Romerbrevet," *NorTT* 86 (1985): 129–40.

Murphy-O'Connor, J., *Becoming Human Together: The Pastoral Anthropology of St. Paul*, GNS 2 (Wilmington, Del.: Glazier, 1982).

Neugebauer, F., *In Christus: "En Christo": Eine Untersuchung zum paulinischen Glaubensverständnis* (Göttingen: Vandenhoeck & Ruprecht, 1961).

Nieder, L., *Die Motive der religiös-sittlichen Paränese in der paulinischen Gemeindebriefen: Ein Beitrag zur paulinischen Ethik*, MTS 1.12 (Munich: Zink, 1956), 23–27, 65–88.

Nielson, J. B., *In Christ: The Significance of the Phrase "In Christ" in the Writings of St. Paul* (Kansas City, Mo.: Beacon Hill, 1960).

Pintard, J., "Sur l'Épître aux Romains et la morale chrétienne," *EspVie* 81 (1971): 473–77.

Potterie, I. de la, "Le Chrétien conduit par l'Esprit dans son cheminement eschatologique (*Rom* 8,14)," *Law of the Spirit in Rom 7 and 8*, Benedictina 1, ed. L. de Lorenzi (Rome: Abbazia San Paolo fuori le mura, 1976), 209–78.

Schettler, A., *Die paulinische Formel "Durch Christus"* (Tübingen: Mohr [Siebeck], 1907).

Schmauch, W., *In Christus: Eine Untersuchung zur Sprache und Theologie des Paulus*, NeutForsch 1.9 (Gütersloh: Bertelsmann, 1935).

Schrage, W., *Die konkreten Einzelgebote in der paulinischen Paränese: Ein Beitrag zur neutestamentlichen Ethik* (Gütersloh: Mohn, 1961).

Schweitzer, A., *The Mysticism of Paul the Apostle*, 2d ed. (London: Black; New York: Macmillan, 1953; repr. New York: Seabury, 1968).

Therrien, G., *Le Discernement dans les écrits pauliniens*, EtBib (Paris: Gabalda, 1973).

Wikenhauser, A., *Pauline Mysticism: Christ in the Mystical Teaching of St Paul* (Freiburg im Breisgau: Herder; New York: Herder and Herder, 1960).

GENERAL BIBLIOGRAPHY

◆

INTRODUCTORY SURVEYS

Rábanos, R., "Boletín bibliográfico de la carta a los Romanos," *Salmanticensis* 6 (1959): 704–70 (968 items).

———, "Boletín bibliográfico de la carta a los Romanos (1960–1980)," *EstBíb* 44 (1986): 325–450 (1,176 items).

Metzger, B. M., *Index to Periodical Literature on the Apostle Paul*, NTTS 1 (Leiden: Brill, 1960), 36–58.

COMMENTARIES

I. PATRISTIC PERIOD

A. GENERAL ITEMS

Cramer, John A. (1793–1848), *Catenae graecorum patrum in Novum Testamentum*, 8 vols. (Oxford: Typographeum academicum, 1840–44; repr. Hildesheim: Olms, 1967), 4.1–529.

Staab, K., *Die Pauluskatenen nach den handschriftlichen Quellen untersucht*, SPIB (Rome: Biblical Institute, 1926).

———, *Pauluskommentare aus der griechischen Kirche: Aus Katenenhandschriften gesammelt und herausgegeben*, NTAbh 15 (Münster in Westfalen: Aschendorff, 1933).

Devreese, R., "Chaînes exégétiques grecques, Saint Paul," *DBSup* 1.1209–24.

1. Greek Writers

B. SPECIFIC ITEMS

Origen (185–ca. 254), "Commentaria in epistolam S. Pauli ad Romanos," *Origenis opera omnia*, 25 vols., ed. C. H. E. Lommatzsch (Berlin: Haude and Spener, 1831–48), vols. 6–7 (1836–37); "Commentaria in epistolam b. Pauli ad Romanos," PG 14.837–1291 (Latin paraphrase of Rufinus); *Explanatio Origenis Adamantii presbyteri in epistolam Pauli ad Romanos divo Hieronymo interprete* (Venice: B. Benalium, 1512), part III; A. Robinson, *The Philocalia* (Cambridge:

Cambridge University Press, 1893), 226–31; K. Staab, "Neue Fragmente aus dem Kommentar des Origenes zum Römerbrief," *BZ* 18 (1928–29): 72–82; C. P. Hammond Bammel, *Der Römerbrieftext des Rufin und seine Origenes-Übersetzung*, Vetus Latina, Aus der Geschichte der lateinischen Bibel 10 (Freiburg im Breisgau: Herder, 1985); idem, *Der Römerbriefkommentar des Origenes: Kritische Ausgabe der Übersetzung Rufins, Buch 1–3*, Vetus Latina 16 (Freiburg im Breisgau: Herder, 1990); "Die fehlenden Bände des Römerbriefkommentars des Origenes," *Origeniana Quarta*, Innsbrucker theologische Studien 19, ed. L. Lies (Innsbruck: Tyrolia, 1987), 16–20; O. Bauernfeind, *Der Römerbrieftext des Origenes nach dem Codex von der Goltz (Cod. 184 B 64 des Athosklosters Lawra)*, TU 44.3 (1923), vii + 119; J. Scherer, *Le Commentaire d'Origène sur Rom. III.5–V.7 d'après les extraits du papyrus n°88748 du Musée du Caire et les fragments de la Philocalie et du Vaticanus gr. 762* . . . (Cairo: Institut Français d'Archéologie Orientale, 1957).

Euthalius the Deacon (fourth century?), "In quatuordecim sancti Pauli apostoli epistolas," PG 85.693–799, esp. 747–52.

Eusebius of Emesa (d. ca. 359), PG 86A.561–62; cf. Staab, *Pauluskommentare*, 46.

Acacius of Caesarea (d. 366), cf. Staab, *Pauluskommentare*, 53–56 (fragments).

Diodore of Tarsus (d. ca. 390), cf. Staab, *Pauluskommentare*, 83–112 (fragments).

Apollinaris of Laodicea (310–392?), cf. Staab, *Pauluskommentare*, 57–82 (fragments).

Didymus the Blind of Alexandria (313–398), cf. Staab, *Pauluskommentare*, 1–6 (fragments).

Severian of Gabala (fl. ca. 400), cf. Staab, *Pauluskommentare*, 213–25; Cramer, *Catenae*, passim.

John Chrysostom (347–407), *Homiliae in epistulam ad Romanos*, ed. F. Field (Oxford: Clarendon, 1849); cf. "*Hermēneia eis tēn pros Rhōmaious epistolēn*," PG 60.391–682 (32 homilies); A *Select Library of the Nicene and Post-Nicene Fathers of the Christian Church*, ed. P. Schaff, 14 vols. (Buffalo, N.Y.: Christian Literature Co., 1886–90) 11.329–564; cf. PG 64.1037–38; 51.155–208 (isolated homilies).

Theodore of Mopsuestia (350–428), "In epistolam Pauli ad Romanos commentarii fragmenta," PG 66.787–876; cf. *Theodori episcopi mopsuesteni in epistolas b. Pauli commentarii: The Latin Version with the Greek Fragments, with an Introduction, Notes and Indices*, 2 vols., ed. H. B. Swete (Cambridge: Cambridge University Press, 1880–1882); cf. PG 66.787–876; Staab, *Pauluskommentare*, 113–72 (fragments).

Cyril of Alexandria (d. 444), "*Hermēneia eis tēn pros Rhōmaious epistolēn*," PG 74.773–856.

Theodoret of Cyrrhus (393–466), "*Hermēneia tēs pros Rhōmaious epistolēs*," PG 82.43–226; cf. J. Sirmond, *Opera omnia*, 4 vols. (Paris: Cramoisy, 1642), 3.1–119.

Gennadius of Constantinople (d. 471), "Fragmenta in epistolam ad Romanos," PG 85.1669–1732; cf. Staab, *Pauluskommentare*, 352–418 (fragments); Cramer, *Catenae*, passim.

John of Damascus (675–749), *"Ek tēs katholou hermēneias Iōannou tou Chrysostomou eklogai eklegeisai, eis pros Rhōmaious epistolēn,"* PG 95.441–570.

2. Latin Writers

A. GENERAL ITEMS

Affeldt, W., "Verzeichnis der Römerbriefkommentare der lateinischen Kirche bis zu Nikolaus von Lyra," *Traditio* 13 (1957): 369–406.

Carlson, C. P., Jr., *Justification in Early Medieval Theology* (The Hague: Nijhoff, 1975).

Denifle, H., *Quellenbelege: Die abendländischen Schriftausleger bis Luther über Justitia Dei (Rom. 1, 17) und Justificatio*, Ergänzungen zu Luther und Luthertum 1 (Mainz: Kirchheim, 1905).

Manitius, M., *Geschichte der lateinischen Literatur des Mittelalters*, Handbuch der Altertumswissenschaft 9.2.1–3 (Munich: Beck, 1911–1931; repr. 1959).

Parker, T. H. L., *Commentaries on the Epistle to the Romans 1532–1542* (Edinburgh: Clark, 1986).

Souter, A., *The Earliest Latin Commentaries on the Epistles of St. Paul: A Study* (Oxford: Clarendon, 1927).

Spicq, C., *Esquisse d'un histoire de l'exégèse latine au moyen âge*, Bibliothèque thomiste 26 (Paris: Vrin, 1944).

Stegmüller, F., *Repertorium biblicum medii aevi*, 11 vols. (Madrid: Consejo Superior de Investigaciones Científicas, Instituto Francisco Suárez, 1950–80; vols. 8–11, with the assistance of N. Reinhardt; vols. 1–3, repr. 1981), esp. vols. 2–5, *Commentaria* (hereafter this work is cited as *RBMA*).

B. SPECIFIC ITEMS

Ambrosiaster (ca. A.D. 366–84), "In epistulam ad Romanos," *Ambrosiastri qui dicitur commentarius in epistulas paulinas*, CSEL 81.1 (1966); see PL 17.47–197; *Divi Ambrosii episcopi mediolanensis operum: Tomus quartus continens explanationes scripturarum* . . . , 4 vols. (Basel: Froben, 1527; repr. 1532); cf. H. J. Vogels, *Das Corpus Paulinum des Ambrosiaster*, BBB 13 (Bonn: Hanstein, 1957), 32–61; *RBMA* §§1249–61.

Pelagius (ca. 354–ca. 420), see A. Souter, *Pelagius's Expositions of Thirteen Epistles of St Paul*, Texts and Studies 9.1–3 (Cambridge: Cambridge University Press, 1922–1931), 2.6–126; repr. by A. Hamann, PLSup 1 (1958), 1110–81; "Commentarii in epistolam ad Romanos," PL 30.669–746 (with interpolations of Pseudo-Jerome [Jean Diacre]); *RBMA* §§3439–52, 6355, 6367.8.

Luculentius (fifth–sixth centuries), "Commentum in cap. XII.1–XIII.8 ad Romanos," PL 72.811–26; *RBMA* §5410.

Augustine of Hippo (354–430), "Expositio quarundam propositionum ex epistola ad Romanos, CSEL 84 (1971), 3–52; cf. 183–85 (= "Retractationes," 22); PL 35.2063–88; "Epistolae ad Romanos inchoata expositio," CSEL 84 (1971), 145–81; cf. 186 (= "Retractationes," 24); PL 35.2087–2106; see P. A. Landes,

Augustine on Romans: Propositions from the Epistle to the Romans: Unfinished Commentary on the Epistle to the Romans, SBLTT—ECLS 23.6 (Chico, Calif.: Scholars, 1982); *RBMA* §§1472–73.

Ps.-Primasius (fl. 551), *In omnes d. Pauli epistolas commentari* (Cologne: Johannes Gymnicus, 1538).

Cassiodorus, Flavius M. A. (487–580), "Complexiones in epistolis apostolorum: Epistola sancti Pauli ad Romanos," PL 70.1321–32; "Expositio s. Pauli epistulae ad Romanos . . . ," PL 68.415–506 (= Ps.-Primasius, actually a reworking of Pelagius's commentary); *Complexiones in epistolas et Acta Apostolorum . . .* (Florence: J. Mann, 1721); *RBMA* §§1897, 6367.3–4.

Bede, Venerable (673–735), see Florus of Lyons (790–860); cf. Denifle, *Quellenbelege*, 23–24; *RBMA* §§1619–31.

3. Syriac Writers

Ephraim Syrus (306–373), *Commentarii in epistolas d. Pauli*, ed. by the Mechitarist Fathers (Venice: Lazarus, 1893); trans. from the Armenian.

II. MEDIEVAL PERIOD

1. Greek Writers

Ps.-Theodulus (ninth century), "In Pauli epistolam ad Romanos commentarius," *Maxima bibliotheca veterum patrum et antiquorum scriptorum ecclesiasticorum . . .* (Lyons: J. Anisson, 1677), 8.587–618.

Photius of Constantinople (810–895), "In epistolam ad Romanos, Fragmenta," PG 101.1233–54; cf. Staab, *Pauluskommentare*, 470–544 (fragments).

Oecumenius of Trikka (Thessaly) (tenth century), *"Paulou epistolē pros Rhōmaious,"* PG 118.323–636; *Hypomnēmata eis tas Neas Diathēkēs: Commentaria in Novum Testamentum: Tractatus in Acta Apostolorum, in omnes Pauli epistolas, in epistolas catholicas omnes*, 2 vols. (Paris: C. Sonn, 1631), 2.195–413; cf. Staab, *Pauluskommentare*, 423–32 (fragments).

Arethas of Caesarea (860–940), cf. Staab, *Pauluskommentare*, 653–59 (fragments).

Theophylact of Okhrid (Bulgaria) (d. ca. 1070), *"Tēs tou hagiou Paulou pros Rhōmaious epistolēs exēgēsis,"* PG 124.335–560; *In omnes D. Pauli epistolas enarrationes, diligenter recognitae, Christophoro Porsena Romano interprete* (Cologne: Eucharius Cervicornus, 1528); cf. A. Lindsell, *Exēgēsis tēn epistolēn tou hagiou Paulou* (London: Typographeum Regium, 1636), 1–162.

Euthymius Zigabenus (early twelfth century), *Commentarius in xiv epistolas Sancti Pauli et vii catholicas*, 2 vols. in one, ed. N. Calogeras (Athens: Perri Bros., 1887), 1.3–185.

2. Latin Writers

Claudius of Turin (d. ca. 830), "Commentarius in epistolam ad Romanos," PL 104.837–40; cf. Denifle, *Quellenbelege*, 12–15; *RBMA* §§1959, 6367.4.

Walafrid Strabo (808–849), PL 113–14; cf. Denifle, *Quellenbelege*, 16–18. See also Anselm of Laon.

Rabanus Maurus (784–856), "Expositio in epistolam ad Romanos," PL 111.1277–1616; cf. "Enarrationum in epistolas b. Pauli libri triginta," *Opera a Pamelio collecta*, ed. G. Clovener (Cologne: A Hierati, 1626); cf. Denifle, *Quellenbelege*, 15–16; *RBMA* §7064.

Sedulius Scotus (d. ca. 858), "Collectanea in omnes b. Pauli epistolas: In epistolam ad Romanos," PL 103.9–128; cf. J. Sichardus, *Collectanea in omnes b. Pauli epistolas* (Basel: H. Petri, 1528); S. Hellmann, *Sedulius Scottus*, Quellen und Untersuchungen zur lateinischen Philologie des Mittelalters 1 (Munich: Beck, 1906), 147–49; *RBMA* §§6567.7, 7607–9.

Florus of Lyons (790–860), "Expositio in epistolas b. Pauli ex operibus St. Augustini collecta," PL 119.279–318; cf. *Divi Augustini in sacras Pauli epistolas . . . per venerabilem Bedam ex innumeris illius codicibus . . . collecta . . .* (Paris: Gering & Rembolt, 1499), fols. 1r–64v; *RBMA* §§2276–77; cf. "Expositio epistolae ad Romanos," *Opera omnia Bedae Venerabilis*, 7 vols. (Cologne: J. W. Friessem, Jr., 1688), 6.31–252.

Haymo of Auxerre (= Ps.-Haymo of Halberstadt) (d. 865), "In epistolam ad Romanos," PL 117.361–508; cf. "Expositio in divi Pauli epistolas," *Maxima bibliotheca veterum patrum et antiquorum scriptorum ecclesiasticorm . . .* (Lyons: J. Annison, 1677), 8.889–946; cf. Denifle, *Quellenbelege*, 18–22; *RBMA* §§3101, 7231; Manitius, *Geschichte*, 1.516.

Rahingus (tenth century), "Glossae in ep. paulinas," cf. Denifle, *Quellenbelege*, 332–34; *RBMA* §7152.

Hatto of Vercelli (924–961), "Expositio epistularum Sti. Pauli: Ep. ad Romanos," PL 134.125–288; cf. C. Buronzo del Signore, *Attonis sanctae Vercellarum ecclesiae episcopi opera* (Vercelli: J. Panialis, 1768), 4–123; cf. Denifle, *Quellenbelege*, 25–27; *RBMA* §§3126, 6367.5.

Tietlandus (d. 964), "Commentarius in epistolam ad Romanos," cf. Denifle, *Quellenbelege*, 27–28; *RBMA* §8267.

Marianus the Scot (1028–1082), "Glossae in ep. paulinas," see *RBMA* §§5457–58.

Lanfranc of Bec, archbishop of Canterbury (1003–1089), "Epistola b. Pauli apostoli ad Romanos," PL 150.105–56; cf. J. A. Giles, *Beati Lanfranci . . . opera quae supersunt omnia . . .* 2 vols., Patres ecclesiae anglicanae 29–30 (Oxford: Parker, 1844), vol. 2: *Commentaria*; *RBMA* §5370; L. d'Achery, *Beati Lanfranci . . . opera omnia* (Paris: I. Billaine, 1648).

Ps.-Bruno (= Ralph of Laon? John of Tours?) (eleventh or twelfth century), "Expositio in epistolae Pauli," PL 153.11–122; cf. Denifle, *Quellenbelege*, 37–39.

Ps.-Paterius (eleventh or twelfth century), "Liber testimoniorum in S. Pauli epistolas," PL 79.1121.

Glosulae Glosularum (twelfth century), cf. Denifle, *Quellenbelege*, 84–88.

Bruno the Carthusian (1032–1101), "In epistolam ad Romanos," PL 153.13–124; cf. Denifle, *Quellenbelege*, 34–36; *RBMA* §1817.

Anselm of Laon (1050–1117), "Glossa ordinaria" (often called "Parva glossatura" and ascribed to Walafrid Strabo), PL 114.469–520; cf. *Biblia latina cum glossa ordinaria Walafridi Strabonis aliorumque, et interlineari Anselmi Laudunensis* (Strasbourg[?]: A. Rusch [?], 1480[?]) 4.[136–52]; cf. Denifle, *Quellenbelege*, 36–37; *RBMA* §§1356, 1359.2, 11832.

Ralph of Laon (d. 1131), "Glosule epistolarum Pauli," cf. Denifle, *Quellenbelege*, 37–39.

Rupert of Deutz (d. 1135), "De victoria verbi Dei," §21, PL 169.1310; cf. Denifle, *Quellenbelege*, 39; *RBMA* §7582.

Peter Abelard (1079–1142), *Commentaria in epistolam Pauli ad Romanos*, Petri Abaelardi opera theologica, CCConMed 11 (Turnhout: Brepols, 1969), 3–340; "Commentarii super s. Pauli epistolam ad Romanos libri quinque," PL 178.783–978; cf. A. Landgraf, *Petri Abaelardi expositiones in ep. s. Pauli ad Romanos abbreviatio* (Lemberg: 1936); *Commentarius cantabrigiensis in epistolas Pauli e schola Petri Abaelardi: 1. In epistolam ad Romanos*, Publications in Mediaeval Studies 2 (Notre Dame, Ind.: University of Notre Dame Press, 1937–45); R. Peppermüller, *Abaelards Auslegung des Römerbriefes*, BGPTM n.s. 10 (Münster in Westfalen: Aschendorff, 1972); cf. Denifle, *Quellenbelege*, 49–52; *RBMA* §6378.

Ps.-Hugh of St. Victor (ca. 1097–1142), "Allegoriae in epistolam ad Romanos," PL 175.879–904; "Quaestiones et decisiones in epistolas d. Pauli: I. In epistolam ad Romanos," ibid., 431–514; cf. Denifle, *Quellenbelege*, 65–74; *RBMA* §3831.

Alulfus of Tournai (d. ca. 1144), "Expositio super epistolam b. Pauli apostoli ad Romanos," PL 79.1291–1308; cf. *Sancti Gregorii Papae I . . . opera omnia . . .* (Paris: C. Rigaud, 1705), 4.787–808; *RBMA* §1208.

Guillaume of St. Thierry (1085–ca. 1148), *Expositio super epistolam ad Romanos*, ed. P. Verdeyen, CCConMed 86 (Turnhout: Brepols, 1989); cf. "Expositio in epistolam ad Romanos," PL 180.547–694; *Exposition on the Epistle to the Romans*, trans. J. B. Hasbrouck, ed. J. D. Anderson (Kalamazoo, Mich.: Cistercian Publications, 1980); cf. Denifle, *Quellenbelege*, 53–54; *RBMA* §3031.

Hervaeus of Châteauroux (Burgidolensis) (1080–1150), "Expositio in epistolam ad Romanos," PL 181.595–814; cf. Denifle, *Quellenbelege*, 54–56.

Bernard of Clairvaux (1090–1153), "Tractatus de erroribus Abaelardii," 6.16; PL 182.1053–72; cf. Denifle, *Quellenbelege*, 52–53.

Gilbert de la Porrée (possibly Gilbert of St. Amand) (ca. 1076–1154), cf. Denifle, *Quellenbelege*, 30–34, 334–46; *RBMA* §10719.

Ralph of Flavigny (ca. 1157), "Commentarius in ep. paulinas," cf. Affeldt, "Verzeichnis," 400.

Peter Lombard (1100–1160), "Collectanea in omnes d. Pauli apostoli epistolas: In epistolam ad Romanos," PL 191.1301–1534 (often called "Magna glossatura"); *Collectanea in omnes d. Pauli apostoli epistolas . . .* (Esslingen: Conrad Fyner, 1473; Paris: I. Badius Ascensius, 1535); cf. Denifle, *Quellenbelege*, 56–64, 346–

58; A. Landgraf, "Ein neuer Fund zur Kommentierung des Paulinenkommentares des Petrus Lombardus," *Bib* 25 (1944): 50–61.

Robert of Melun (1100–1167), "Questiones de epistolis Pauli," cf. R. M. Martin, *Oeuvres de Robert de Melun: II. Questiones (theologice) de epistolis Pauli,* Spicilegium sacrum lovaniense 18 (Louvain: Bureaux de SSL, 1938) 1–170; cf. Denifle, *Quellenbelege,* 75–83.

Robert of Bridlington (d. 1180), "Explanatio in Romanos," cf. B. Smalley, "Gilbertus Universalis, Bishop of London (1128–34), and the Problem of the 'Glossa Ordinaria,' " *RTAM* 7 (1935): 235–62, esp. 248–51, 255; 8 (1936): 23–60, esp. 32–34; "La Glossa Ordinaria: Quelques prédecesseurs d'Anselme de Laon," *RTAM* 9 (1937): 365–400, esp. 367, 372–74.

Peter the Chanter (1130–1197), "Commentarius in ep. paulinas," cf. Denifle, *Quellenbelege,* 88–89.

Pierre de Corbeil (d. 1222), "In ep. ad Romanos," cf. Denifle, *Quellenbelege,* 90–94; *RBMA* §6595.

Stephen Langton (1150–1228), "Glossa in glossam Petri Lombardi: Ep. ad Romanos," cf. Denifle, *Quellenbelege,* 94–106; A. Landgraf, *Bib* 25 (1944): 50–61.

Guerric of St. Quentin (d. 1245), "Postillae super epistolas Paul," cf. Denifle, *Quellenbelege,* 111–17; Spicq, *Esquisse,* 320.

Jean de la Rochelle (d. 1245), "Postilla in epistolas Pauli," cf. Denifle, *Quellenbelege,* 122–30; Spicq, *Esquisse,* 325.

Godfried de Bléneau (d. ca. 1250), "Postilla super epistolas Paul," cf. Denifle, *Quellenbelege,* 131–34; Spicq, *Esquisse,* 320.

Robert Grosseteste (1175–1253), "In ep. ad Romanos," *RBMA* §§7403, 7403.7–8; see E. E. Mather, "Lecturae in epistolam ad Romanos V–XVI Roberto Grosseteste adscriptae," Ph.D. diss., University of Southern California, 1987.

Hugh of St. Cher (1190–1263), "Postilla in epistolas Pauli," *Opera omnia,* 8 vols. (Venice: Pezzana, 1703, 7.2–72; cf. Denifle, *Quellenbelege,* 106–11; Spicq, *Esquisse,* 324; *RBMA* §3727.

Eudes de Châteauroux (Odo Gallus) (d. 1273), "Commentarius in ep. paulinas," cf. Denifle, *Quellenbelege,* 117–21; Spicq, *Esquisse,* 319.

Thomas Aquinas (1225–1274), "Expositio in omnes sancti Pauli epistolas: Epistola ad Romanos," *Opera omnia,* 25 vols. (Parma: P. Fiaccadori, 1852–73; repr. New York: Musurgia, 1948–50), 13.3–156; cf. "Epistola ad Romanos," *Opera omnia,* 34 vols. (Paris: L. Vivès, 1871–82), 20.381–602; *In omnes d. Pauli apostoli epistolas commentaria,* new ed., 3 vols. (Liège: Dessain, 1857–58), 1.5–290; *Super epistolas S. Pauli lectura,* ed. R. Cai, 8th ed., 2 vols. (Turin: Marietti, 1953), 1.5–230; cf. H. Fahsel, *Des hl. Thomas von Aquin Kommentar zum Römerbrief* (Freiburg im Breisgau: Herder, 1927); Denifle, *Quellenbelege,* 135–44.

Peter of Tarantaise (= Pope Innocent V) (1225–1276), "Postillae in ep. paulinas," cf. Denifle, *Quellenbelege,* 144–52; Spicq, *Esquisse,* 327.

Nicholas of Gorran (d. 1295), "Postillae in ep. paulinas," cf. Denifle, *Quellenbelege,* 152–56; Spicq, *Esquisse,* 327.

Pierre Jean Olieu (1248/49–1298), "Postillae in ep. ad Romanos," cf. Denifle, *Quellenbelege*, 156–60; Spicq, *Esquisse*, 328.

Duns Scotus, John (1266–1308), "Circa epistolam Pauli ad Romanos," *RBMA* §4450.

Alexander of Alexandria (1270–1314), "Postilla in epistolam ad Romanos," cf. Denifle, *Quellenbelege*, 179–86; Spicq, *Esquisse*, 343.

Egidio Colonna (Giles of Rome) (1247–1316), "Postilla in ep. ad Romanos," cf. *Aegidii Columnae Romani in epistulam Pauli ad Romanos commentaria* (Rome: A. Bladus, 1555); Denifle, *Quellenbelege*, 173–79; Spicq, *Esquisse*, 320.

Peter Aureoli (1280–1322), *Compendium literalis sensus totius divinae Scripturae*, ed. P. Seeböck (Quaracchi: Collegium S. Bonaventurae, 1896), 244–54; Denifle, *Quellenbelege*, 186–88.

Augustinus Triumphus of Ancona (1243–1328), "Postillae in epistolas Pauli," cf. Denifle, *Quellenbelege*, 161–72; Spicq, *Esquisse*, 343.

Nicolaus de Lyra (1270–1349), *Postilla super totam Bibliam*, 5 vols. (Rome: Conrad Sweynheyn and A. Pannartz, 1471–72); 3 vols. (Nuremberg, 1481; Strasbourg, 1492; vols. 1–2 repr. Frankfurt am Main: Minerva, 1971); *Postillae Nicolai de Lyra in epistolas Pauli, cum additionibus Pauli Burgensis et cum replicationibus Matthaei Doringk* (Mantua: Johann de Putzbach, 1478); *Postilla litteralis* (Antwerp: 1492); cf. Denifle, *Quellenbelege*, 188–94; Spicq, *Esquisse*, 347.

Johann von Hesdin (d. 1367), "In omnes epistolas Pauli," *RBMA* §4555.

3. Syriac Writers

Isho῾dad of Merv (ca. 850), *The Commentaries of Isho῾dad of Merv Bishop of Ḥadatha*, vol. 5.1: *The Epistles of Paul the Apostle in Syriac*, Horae Semiticae 11, ed. M. D. Gibson (Cambridge: Cambridge University Press, 1916), 1–34.

III. FIFTEENTH- TO EIGHTEENTH-CENTURY WRITERS

Anon. (fifteenth century), "Expositio epistolae ad Romanos," cf. Denifle, *Quellenbelege*, 248–52.

Anon. of Kraków (fifteenth century), "Lectura in ep. ad Romanos"; cf. Denifle, *Quellenbelege*, 259–78.

Petrus Tzech of Pulka (d. 1425), "Super epistolam b. Pauli ad Romanos," cf. Denifle, *Quellenbelege*, 235–44.

Augustine de Favaroni of Rome (d. 1443), "Expositio super epistolam Pauli ad Romanos," cf. Denifle, *Quellenbelege*, 220–35.

Valla, Lorenzo (1406–1457), "In ep. ad Romanos," *Opera omnia*, 8 vols. (Basel: H. Petrus, 1540; repr., 2 vols., Turin: Bottega d'Erasmo, 1962), 855–61.

Johann Grössel von Titmaning (d. 1467), "Lectura in epistolam ad Romanos," cf. Denifle, *Quellenbelege*, 244–46.

Denis the Carthusian (Denys Ryckel) (1402–1471), *In omnes beati Pauli epistolas commentaria* . . . (Cologne: P. Quentell, 1553; repr. Paris: M. Dupuys, 1542,

1548); *Elucidissima in divi Pauli epistolas commentaria* (Paris: J. Parvum, 1531); cf. Denifle, *Quellenbelege*, 252–59.

Ficino, Marsilio (1433–1499), *In epistolas d. Pauli* . . . , *Opera omnia*, 2 vols. (Basel: H. Paulus, 1561; repr. 1576 [this edition repr. Turin: Bottega d'Erasmo, 1959]), 1.425–72; cf. Denifle, *Quellenbelege*, 279–86.

Colet, John (ca. 1467–1519), *Enarratio in epistolam s. Pauli ad Romanos: An Exposition of St. Paul's Epistle to the Romans* . . . , trans. J. H. Lupton (London: Bell and Daldy, 1873; repr. Ridgewood, N.J.: Gregg, 1965); cf. Denifle, *Quellenbelege*, 297–300.

Barlecta, Paduarus (sixteenth century), "Epistola ad Romanos," *Concilium Pauli* ([Venice]: S. Bernardini, [1545?]).

Bonade, François (sixteenth century), *Divi Pauli apostoli* . . . *epistulae* . . . (Basel: B. Werthener, 1537), 15–59.

Haller, Wolfgang (sixteenth century), *Christliche / deutliche / und verständliche Erklärung oder Auslegung der Epistel des H. Apostels Pauli an die Römer* (Amberg: M. Foster, 1593).

Lorus, Damianus (sixteenth century), *Epistolae divi Pauli apostoli cum triplici editione ad veritatem graecam* (Venice: I. Antonius de Sabio & Fratres, 1533).

Oecolampadius (Hussgen), Johannes (1482–1531), *In epistolam b. Pauli apostoli ad Rhomanos adnotationes* (Basel: Cratandus; Nuremberg: Petreius, 1525).

Zwingli, Ulrich (1484–1531), "In ep. ad Romanos," *Opera: Completa editio* (Zurich, 1545; repr. 8 vols., ed. M. Schuler and J. Schulthess, Zurich; F. Schulthess, 1829–42), 6.2.76–133.

Cajetan (Thomas de Vio) (1469–1534), *Epistolae Pauli et aliorum apostolorum ad Graecam veritatem castigatae* . . . *iuxta sensum literalem enarratae* (Paris: I. Badius Ascensius & I. Parvus & I. Roigny, 1532), fols. 1–48; (repr. Lyons: Prost, 1639), 5.1–84.

Erasmus, Desiderius (1469–1536), *Novum instrumentum* . . . *una cum annotationibus* (Basel: Froben, 1516) 1–30 (translation), 411–55 (*Annotationes in ep. ad Romanos*); *In epistolam Pauli apostoli ad Romanos paraphrasis, quae commentarii vice possit esse* (Basel: Froben, 1518); *Paraphrases on Romans and Galatians*, Collected Works of Erasmus 42, ed. R. D. Sider (Toronto: University of Toronto, 1984), 1–90; *Erasmus' Annotations on the New Testament: Acts—Romans—I and II Corinthians: Facsimile of the Final Latin Text with All Earlier Variants*, ed. A. Reeve and M. A. Screech, Studies in the History of Christian Thought 42 (Leiden: Brill, 1990); cf. Denifle, *Quellenbelege*, 300–307.

Lefèvre d'Étaples, Jacques (Jacob Faber Stapulensis) (1455–1536), *S. Pauli epistolae XIV ex vulgata editione* . . . (Paris: Stephanus, 1512; 2d ed., 1515); cf. Denifle, *Quellenbelege*, 287–96.

Titelmann, Franciscus (1502–1537), *Elucidatio in omnes epistolas apostolicas, quatuordecim paulinas, & canonicas septem* . . . (Antwerp: M. Hellenius, 1528) sigs. A8ᵛ–50ʳ; repr. Antwerp: J. Steels, 1540), fols. 9ʳ–50ʳ); *Collationes quinque super epistolam ad Romanos beati Pauli apostoli* . . . (Antwerp: W. Vorstermann, 1529), 1–308.

Knöpken, Andreas (1468–1539), *In epistolam ad Romanos* . . . *interpretatio* (Nuremberg: 1524).

Broickwy a Konincksteyn, Anton (ca. 1470–1541), *Enarrationes in epistolam Pauli ad Romanos* (Cologne: Birckmann, 1556).

Valdés, Juan de (d. 1541), *La epistola de san Pablo a los Romanos i la 1. a los Corintios* . . . (Geneva: J. Crespin, 1556; Madrid: de Alegría, 1856); *Juan de Valdés' Commentary upon St. Paul's Epistle to the Romans: Now for the First Time Translated from the Spanish* . . . , (trans. J. T. Betts; London: Trübner, 1883).

Contarini (Contareni), Gasparo (1483–1542), "Scholia in epistolas divi Pauli," *Gasparis Contareni cardinalis opera* (Paris: S. Nivelle, 1571; repr. Farnborugh, Hants.: Gregg International, 1968), 433–47.

Grimani, Marino (1489–1545), *Commentarii in epistolas Pauli, ad Romanos et ad Galatas* (Venice: Aldi Filii, 1542), fols. 1–173.

Haresche, Philibert (d. 1545), *Expositio tum dilucida, tum brevis epistolae divi Pauli ad Romanos* . . . (Paris: J. Parvus & P. Le Preu, 1536).

Luther, Martin (1483–1546), *Vorlesung über den Römerbrief 1515/1516*, ed. J. Ficker, Anfänge reformatorischer Bibelauslegung 1 (prelim. ed., Leipzig: Dieterich, 1908; defin. ed. [WAusg 56] Weimar: Böhlau, 1938); *Divi Pauli apostoli ad Romanos epistola*, Autograph der königlichen Bibliothek zu Berlin, MS theol. lat. qu. 21 (1909); *Nachschriften der Vorlesungen über Römerbrief, Galaterbrief und Hebräerbrief*, WAusg 57, ed. J. Ficker (Weimar; Böhlau, 1939), xi–lxxiv, 1–232; *Vorlesung über den Römerbrief 1515/1516*, ed. E. Ellwein (Munich: Kaiser, 1927); *Vorlesung über den Römerbrief 1515/1516: Lateinisch-deutsche Ausgabe*, 2 vols., ed. M. Hofmann (Darmstadt: Wissenschaftliche Buchgesellschaft, 1960); cf. *Commentary on the Epistle to the Romans: A New Translation*, ed. J. T. Mueller (Grand Rapids, Mich.: Zondervan, 1954); *Luther: Lectures on Romans Newly Translated and Edited*, ed. W. Pauck, Library of Christian Classics 15 (London: SCM; Philadelphia, Penn.: Westminster, 1961); *Lectures on Romans: Glosses and Scholia*, LuthW 25, trans. W. G. Tillmanns and J. A. O. Preus (Saint Louis, Mo.: Concordia, 1972); W. Grundmann, *Der Römerbrief des Apostels Paulus und seine Auslegung durch Martin Luther* (Weimar: Böhlau, 1964).

Sadoleto, Jacopo (1477–1547), *In Pauli epistolam ad Romanos commentariorum libri tres* (Lyons: S. Gryphius, 1535; repr. Venice: J. A. de Nicolinis de Sabio, 1536), 1–231; cf. *Opera quae exstant omnia*, 4 vols. (Verona: J. A. Tumerman, 1737–38), 4.1–370.

Lang, Johann (d. 1548), "Epistola divi Pauli apostoli ad Romanos" (Vat. Palatin. Lat. MS 132, 1r–23v); see R. Weijenborg, "Die Wittenberger Roemerbriefvorlesung des Erfurter Augustiners Johannes Lang: Erstausgabe nach dem Vat. Pal. Lat. 132 mit Einleitung und Kommentar," *Anton* 51 (1976): 394–494.

Gagny, Jean de (d. 1549), *Epitome paraphrastica enarrationum* . . . *in epistolam divi*

Pauli apostoli ad Romanos (Paris: M. Vascosanus, 1533); *Divi Pauli apostoli epistolae brevissimis & facillimis scholiis . . . illustratae* (Paris: S. Colinaeus & Galliotus a Prato, 1539); cf. (with others) *Biblia sacra Vulgatae editionis . . . cum selectissimis litteralibus commentariis* (Venice: M. Fentius, 1756), 25.326–543.

Viguier, Jean (d. 1550), *Ad naturalem et christianam philosophiam . . . his annecti curavimus eiusdem Viguerii commentaria . . . in d. Pauli epistolam ad Romanos* (Paris: C. Fremy, 1558; repr. Antwerp: Steels, 1572).

Bucer, Martin (1491–1551), "In epistolam ad Romanos," *Metaphrases et enarrationes epistolarum d. Pauli apostoli . . .* (Strasbourg: Rihel, 1536; repr. Basel: P. Pernan, 1562), 1–507.

Guilliaud, Claude (1493–1551), *Collatio in omnes divi Pauli apostoli epistolas . . .* (Lyons: S. Gryphius, 1542; repr. Paris: A. Parvus, 1550), 1–107.

Politus, Ambrosius Catharinus (1483–1553), *In omnes divi Pauli apostoli et alias septem canonicas epistolas . . . commentaria . . .* (Rome: 1546; Venice: V. Valgrisius, 1551; Paris: M. Sonnius, 1566), 1–131.

Wild (Ferus), Johann (1495–1554), *Exegesis in epistolam b. Pauli ad Romanos* (Paris: G. Desboys, 1559).

Pellikan (né Kürstner), Konrad (1478–1556), *In omnes apostolicas epistolas, Pauli, Petri, Iacobi, Ioannis et Iudae . . . commentarii . . .* (Zurich: Froschauer, 1539), 1–176.

Bugenhagen, J. (Pomeranus) (1485–1558), *In epistolam Pauli ad Romanos interpretatio . . .* (Hagenau: Setzer, 1527).

Araneus, Clemens (1482–1559), *Expositio . . . super epistolam Pauli ad Romanos . . .* (Venice: N. de Bascarinis, 1547).

Sarcerius, Erasmus (1501–1559), *In epistolam ad Romanos pia et erudita scholia* (Frankfurt am Main: Egenolph, 1541).

Melanchthon, Philip (1497–1560), *Annotationes in epistolam Pauli ad Romanos unam . . .* (Nuremberg: 1522; Strassburg: J. Hervagius, 1523); *Dispositio orationis in epist. ad Rom.*, CR 15, ed. C. G. Bretschneider (Halle an der Saale: Schwetschke & Sons, 1848), 441–92 (originally published Hagenau, 1529); *Commentarii in epistolam Pauli ad Romanos*, ibid., 493–796 (originally published Wittenberg: J. Clug, 1532), repr. *Melanchthons Werke in Auswahl*, ed. R. Stupperich, 7 vols. (Gütersloh: Mohn, 1951–75), 5.25–371. *Epistolae Pauli scriptae ad Romanos enarratio*, in CR 15, 797–1052 (originally published Wittenberg: C. Rhuel, 1556); *Anmerkungen zum Brief an die Römer, nebst einer Vorrede Dr. Martin Luthers*, ed. F. W. Meinel (Erlangen: Heyder, 1828); cf. W. Böhmer, "Eine neue Ausgabe der melanchthonischen Commentare zum Briefe des Paulus an die Römer," ZWT 55 (1862): 335–36. Also *"Rhapsōdiai en Paulou ad Romanos," Texte aus der Anfangszeit Melanchthons*, Texte zur Geschichte der evangelischen Theologie 2, ed. E. Bizer (Neukirchen-Vluyn: Neukirchener-Verlag, 1966), 39–85.

Soto, Domingo de (1494–1560), *In epistolam d. Pauli ad Romanos commentarii* (Antwerp: J. Steels, 1550), 1–413.

Vermigli, Pietro Martire (1500–1562), *In epistolam S. Pauli ad Romanos commentarii* (Basel: P. Pernam, 1558; repr. Heidelberg: A. Cambieri, 1612); *Most Learned and Fruitfull Commentaries . . . upon the Epistle of S. Paul to the Romanes* (London: John Daye, [1568]).

Musculus (Meusslin), Wolfgang (1497–1563), *In epistolam d. apostoli Pauli ad Romanos commentarii* (Basel: H. Petrus, 1555; repr. [1600]).

Seripando, Giralomo (1493–1563), *In d. Pauli epistolas ad Romanos et Galatas commentaria* (Naples: 1601).

Calvin, Jean (1509–1564), *Commentarii in omnes epistolas Pauli apostoli* (Strasbourg: W. Rihel, 1539); cf. "Commentarii in epistolam Pauli ad Romanos," *Opera omnia*, 9 vols. (Amsterdam: J. J. Schipper, 1667–71), 7.1–107; cf. *Commentarius in epistolam Pauli ad Romanos*, ed. T. H. L. Parker, Studies in the History of Christian Thought 22 (Leiden: Brill, 1981); O. Weber, *Auslegung des Römerbriefes und der beiden Korintherbriefe*, Auslegung der heiligen Schrift 16 (Neukirchen-Vluyn: Erziehungsverein, 1960), 7–297; *Commentaries on the Epistle of Paul the Apostle to the Romans*, trans. J. Owen (Edinburgh: Calvin Translation Society, 1844; repr. Grand Rapids, Mich.: Eerdmans, 1948), 39–556; *The Epistles of Paul the Apostle to the Romans and to the Thessalonians*, trans. R. Mackenzie, Calvin's Commentaries 8 (Edinburgh and London: Oliver and Boyd, 1960; repr. Grand Rapids, Mich.: Eerdmans, 1961), 5–328.

Hyperius, Andreas Gerhard (1511–1564), *Commentarii . . . in epistolas d. Pauli ad Romanos et utramque ad Corinthios*, 5 vols., ed. J. Mylij (Zurich: C. Froschauer, 1583?; repr. 1584); *In d. Pauli ad Romanos epistolam exegema . . .* (London: Vautroller, 1577).

Ochino, Bernardino (1487–1564), *Expositio epistolae divi Pauli ad Romanos . . .* (Augustae Vindelicorum: P. Ulhard, [ca. 1545]).

Lonicer (Lonitzer), Johann (1499–1569), *Veteris cuiuspiam theologi graeci succincta in D. Pauli ad Romanos epistolam exegesis . . .* (Basel: R. Winter, 1537).

Brenz, Johann (1499–1570), *In epistolam, quam Apostolus Paulus ad Romanos scripsit . . .* (Basel: P. Queckwa, 1565); *Erklerung der Epistel S. Pauls an die Römer* (Frankfurt: P. Brubach, 1564); *Explicatio epistolae Pauli ad Romanos*, ed. S. Strohm, in *Werke: Eine Studienausgabe*, ed. M. Brecht and G. Schäfer (Tübingen: Mohr [Siebeck], 1986).

Aretius, Benedict (1505–1574), *Commentarii in epistolam d. Pauli ad Romanos . . .* (Morges, Switzerland: J. Le Preux, 1583); *Commentarii doctissimi in omnes epistolas d. Pauli et canonicas . . .* (Bern: J. Le Preux, 1607).

Major, George (1502–1574), *Series et dispositio orationis in epistola Pauli ad Romanos* (Wittenberg: J. Lufft, 1558).

Matthisius, Gerhard (d. 1574), *In epistolam b. Pauli ad Romanos commentaria* (Cologne: P. Horst, 1562).

Bullinger, Heinrych (1504–1575), *In sanctissimam Pauli ad Romanos epistolam . . . commentarius* (Zurich: C. Froschauer, 1533); cf. *In omnes apostolicas epistolas,* divi videlicet Pauli XIIII et VII canonicas, commentarii (Zurich: C. Froschauer, 1537), 3–121.

Osorio da Fonseca, Jeronymo (1506–1580), "In epistolam Pauli ad Romanos . . . ," *Opera omnia,* 4 vols. (Rome: Ferrarius, 1592).

Salmerón, Alfonso (1515–1585), "Commentarii in omnes epistolas B. Pauli & canonicas . . . ," *Opera,* 16 vols. (Cologne: A. Hierat & J. Gymni, 1604), 13:274–719.

Walther, Rudolph (1519–1586), *In d. Pauli epistolam ad Romanos homiliae XCVI* (Zurich: C. Froschauer, 1572).

Olevian, Caspar (1536–1587), *In epistolam Pauli ad Romanos notae,* ed. T. de Bèze (Geneva: Vignon, 1578).

Wigand, Johann (1523–1587), *In epistolam s. Pauli ad Romanos annotationes* (Wittenberg: J. Cratonis, 1580).

Corro, Antonio del (1527–1591), *Dialogus theologicus: Quo epistola divi Pauli ad Romanos explanatur . . .* (London: T. Purfoote, 1574); *A Theological Dialogue: Wherein the Epistle of S. Paul the Apostle to the Romanes Is Expounded* (London: T. Purfoote, 1575); *Epistola beati Pauli apostoli ad Romanos e Graeco in Latinam metaphrastikōs versa . . .* (London: T. Vautroller, 1581).

Selneccer, Nicolaus (1530–1592), *In omnes epistolas d. Paul apostoli commentarius plenissimus . . .* (Leipzig: J. Apel, 1595).

Pasqual, R. (d. 1593), *Praeclarissima commentaria in epistolam b. Pauli apostoli ad Romanos* (Barcelona: J. Cendrat, 1597).

Corner, Christophorus (1518–1594, *In epistolam d. Pauli ad Romanos scriptam commentarius . . .* (Heidelberg: J. Spies, 1583).

Toledo, Francisco de (1532–1596), *In epistol. b. Pauli apostoli ad Romanos commentarii et annotationes . . .* (Mainz: B. Lippius, 1603), 1–673.

Creuzinger (Cruciger), Kaspar (1525–1597), *In epistolam Pauli ad Romanos scriptam commentarius . . .* (Wittenberg: J. Cratonis, 1567).

Stapleton, Thomas (1535–1598), *Antidota apostolica contra nostri temporis haereses in quibus loca illa explicantur, quae haeretici hodie . . . depravarunt* (Antwerp: Keerberg, 1595).

Rollock, Robert (ca. 1555–1599), *Analysis dialectica . . . in Pauli apostoli epistolam ad Romanos* (Edinburgh: Waldegrave, 1593); 2d ed. with new title, *In epistolam s. Pauli apostoli ad Romanos . . . commentarius* (Geneva: Stoer, 1608).

Rungius, David (sixteenth–seventeenth centuries), *Disputationes 18. in epistolam ad Romanos* (Frankfurt: Porsius; Wittenberg: Schurer, 1606).

Winckelmann, Johann (sixteenth–seventeenth centuries), *Notationes in epistolam Pauli ad Romanos* (Frankfurt: Porsius, 1614).

Hemmingsen, Niels (1513–1600), *Commentarius in epistolam Pauli ad Romanos* (Leipzig, 1562; London: Vautroller, 1577); *Commentarius in omnes epistolas apostolorum* (Frankfurt am Main: Corvinus, 1571?, 1579).

Hunnius, Aegidius (1550–1603), *Epistolae divi Pauli apostoli ad Romanos expositio plana et perspicua* . . . (Frankfurt am Main: J. Spies, 1587; rev. ed. [with Hebrews], 1592; rev. ed. [with 1–2 Thessalonians], 1596).

Spangenberg, Cyriacus (1528–1604), *Auslegung der letzten acht Capiteln der Epistel s. Pauli an die Römer* (Strasbourg: S. Emmel, 1566; repr. 1569).

Bèze, Théodore de (1519–1605), *Annotationes maiores in Novum Dn. nostri Iesu Christi Testamentum* (Paris: 1556; repr. Geneva: Estienne(?), 1594), 2.3–152.

Mylius, Georg (1548–1607), *In epistolam d. Pauli ad Romanos* . . . (Jena: T. Steinmann, 1595).

Arminius (Jakob Harmensen) (1560–1609), *De vero et genuino sensu cap. VII epistolae ad Romanos dissertatio* (Leiden: G. Basson, 1612).

Scaino, Antonio (1524–1612), *Paraphrasis in omnes s. Pauli epistolas cum adnotationibus* . . . (Venice: D. Nicolin, 1589).

Estius, Gulielmus (Willem Hessels van Est) (1542–1613), *In omnes divi Pauli apostoli epistolas commentariorum* . . . , 2 vols. (Douai: B. Bedler, 1614–16); "In epistolam beati Pauli apostoli ad Romanos commentarius," *In omnes Pauli epistolas* . . . *commentarii*, 7 vols. in 3, ed. F. Sausen (Mainz: Kirchheim, Schott and Thielmann, 1841–45), 1.1–387.

Ferme, Charles (1566–1617), *Analysis logica in epistolam ad Romanos* (Edinburgh: 1651); cf. *A Logical Analysis of the Epistle of Paul to the Romans*, trans. W. Skae, *and a Commentary on the Same Epistle by Andrew Melville in the Original Latin*, ed. W. L. Alexander (Edinburgh: Wodrow Society, 1850).

Grynaeus, Johann Jacob (1540–1617), *Exegesis epistolae Pauli apostoli ad Romanos* (Basel: S. H. Petrus, 1591).

Willet, Andrew (1562–1621), *Hexapla: "That Is, a Six-fold Commentarie upon the Most Divine Epistle of the Holy Apostle S. Paul to the Romanes* . . . (London: L. Greene, 1611).

Giustiniani, Benedetto (1550–1622), *In omnes b. Pauli epistolas explanationes* (Lyons: H. Cardon, 1612), 68–365.

Melville, Andrew (1545–1622), *Commentarius in divinam Pauli epistolam ad Romanos*, ed. W. L. Alexander (Edinburgh: Wodrow Society, 1849), 385–514, written at St. Andrews, 1601; cf. C. Ferme, *A Logical Analysis* (above).

Pareus (Waengler), David (1548–1622), *In divinam ad Romanos S. Pauli apostoli epistolam commentarius* (Frankfurt am Main: J. Rhodes, 1608; repr. Heidelberg: J. Rosa, 1613, 1620).

Wilson, Thomas (1563–1622), *A Commentarie upon the Most Divine Epistle of S. Paul to the Romanes* . . . (London: W. Iaggard, 1614; repr. 1627, 1653).

Huber, Samuel (1547–1624), *Explicatio capitum 9, 10 & 11 epistolae ad Romanos d. Pauli* . . . (Ob. Ursel: N. Henricus, 1597).

Piscator, Johannes (1546–1625), *Analysis logica epistolae Pauli ad Romanos* . . . (Herbornae Nassoviorum: C. Corvini, 1601; repr. 1608).

Balduin, Friedrich (1575–1627), *Catechesis apostolica: Hoc est, s. apostoli Pauli epistola ad Romanos, commentario perspicuo illustrata* . . . (Wittenberg: S. Selfisch & P. Helwich, 1611; 2d ed., 1620); *Commentarius in omnes epistolas beati apostoli Pauli* . . . (Frankfurt am Main: Zumner, 1608–30; rev. ed. J. Olearius, Frankfurt am Main: C. Rötell, 1654–55).

Crinesius, Christophorus (1584–1629), *Epistola s. Pauli Rom. lingua syriaca* . . . *ex Testamento syr. viennensi desumpta* . . . (Wittenberg: Z. Schürer, 1612).

Vorst, Konrad (1569–1629), *Commentarius in omnes epistolas apostolicas, exceptis secunda ad Timotheum* . . . (Amsterdam: G. Blaeu; Harderwijk: T. Daniel, 1631).

Crell, Johann (1590–1633), *Commentarius in epistolam Pauli ad Romanos*, Bibliotheca fratrum polonorum 3.1 (Amsterdam [Eleutheropoli]: I. Philalethius, 1636).

Contzen, A. (1575–1635), *Commentaria in epist. s. Pauli apostoli ad Romanos* (Cologne: I. Kinck, 1629).

Gerhard, Johann (1582–1637), *Adnotationes ad priora capita epistolae d. Pauli ad Romanos* (Jena: C. von Saher, 1645); *Adnotationes posthumae in epistolam ad Romanos*, 2 vols. (Jena: J. L. Neuenhahn, 1666).

Lapide, C. a (Cornelis C. van den Steen, 1567–1637), *Commentaria in omnes d. Pauli epistolas* (Antwerp: M. Nutius and J. Meursius, 1614); cf. *Commentaria in Scripturam Sacram*, 21 vols., 9th ed., ed. A. Crampon (Paris: Vivès, 1874–79), 18.34–245.

Gomarus, Franciscus (1563–1641), "Analysis et explicatio epistolae ad Romanos," *Opera theologica omnia* . . . (Amsterdam: J. Jansson, 1664), 385–448.

Dieu, Lodewijk de (1590–1642), *Animadversiones in d. Pauli apostoli epistolam ad Romanos* (Leiden: Elzevir, 1646).

Cerda, Juan Luis de la (1560–1643), *In epistolam d. Pauli ad Romanos commentaria* (Lisbon: A. Ribero, 1583).

Grotius (Huig van Groot) (1583–1645), *Annotationes in Novum Testamentum*, 2 vols. (Paris: 1644; repr. Leipzig and Erlangen: Ptochotrophium, 1755–57).

Quistorp, Johann (1584–1648), *Annotationes in omnes Novi Testamenti libros* (Frankfurt am Main and Rostock: J. Wild, 1648), 246–76.

Froidmont, Libert (1587–1653), *Commentaria in omnes epistolas b. Pauli apostoli* . . . (Louvain: H. Nempaeus, 1663).

Calixt, Georg (1586–1656), *In epistolam s. apostoli Pauli ad Romanos expositio literalis* . . . (Brunswick: A. Duncker, 1652).

Ambianensis, Georg (d. 1657), *Trina s. Pauli theologia* . . . *seu omnigena in universas Pauli epistolae commentaria exegetica, tropologica et anagogica*, 3 vols. (Paris: D. Thierry, 1649–50).

Hammond, H. (1605–1660), *A Paraphrase and Annotations upon All the Books of the New Testament* . . . (London: R. Royston, 1653; 5th ed. 1681), 437–509; new ed. in 4 vols. (Oxford: University Press, 1845), 2.1–94, 4.1–85.

Paciuchelli, Angelo (d. 1660), *Expositio in epistolam beati Pauli apostoli ad Romanos* . . . (Munich: J. Jaecklin, 1677).

Launay, Pierre de (1573–1661), *Paraphrase et exposition sur les épistres de saint Paul*, 2 vols. (Charenton: L. Vendosme, 1650).

Szlichting, J. (1592–1661), *Commentaria posthuma in plerosque Novi Testamenti libros,* Bibliotheca fratrum polonorum 7 (Amsterdam: I. Philalethius, 1656), 155–325.

Dickson, David (ca. 1583–1663), *Expositio analytica omnium apostolicarum epistolarum* . . . (Glasgow: G. Anderson, 1645).

Breen (Brenius), Daniel van (1594–1664), "Notae in epistolam ad Romanos," *Opera theologica* (Amsterdam: Cuper, 1666), fols. 3–40.

Weller, Jakob (1602–1664), *Annotationes in epistolam s. Pauli ad Romanos collectae,* ed. J. Schindler (Brunswick: Zilliger, 1654).

Day, W. (d. 1666), *A Paraphrase and Commentary upon the Epistle of Saint Paul to the Romans* (London: S. Griffin, 1666).

Przypkowski, Samuel (1592–1670), *Cogitationes sacrae ad initium evangelii Matthaei et omnes epistolas apostolicas* . . . , Biblotheca fratrum polonorum 10 (Amsterdam: I. Philalethius, 1692).

Godeau, Ant. (1605–1672), *Paraphrase de l'épître de Saint Paul aux Romains,* new ed. (Paris: Veuve Jean Camusat, 1641).

La Payrère, I. de (1594–1676), *Praeadamitae: Sive exercitatio super versibus* . . . *capitis quinti epistolae d. Pauli ad Romanos* . . . (no place: no publ., 1655).

Momma, Willem (1642–1677), *Meditationes posthumae in epistolas ad Romanos et Galatas* (The Hague: Leers, 1678).

Alting, Jacob (1618–1679), "Commentarius theoretico-practicus in caput XI epistolae Pauli ad Romanos," *Opera,* 5 vols. (Amsterdam: G. Borst, 1685–87), 4.11–367 (with "Analysis epistolae ad Romanos," 4.368–88).

Poole, Matthew (1624–1679), *Synopsis criticorum aliorumque s. Scripturae interpretum,* 4 vols. in 5 (London: C. Smith, 1669–76) 4.2.1–330.

Brais, Etienne de (d. 1680), *Uitbreidende ontleding van den brief des Apostels Paulus aan de Romeinen* (Leeuwarden: T. van Dessel, 1738); *Epistulae Pauli ad Romanos analysis paraphrastica cum notis* (Salmurii: J. Lesner, 1670; repr. Frankfurt am Main and Leipzig, 1707).

Varenius, August (1620–1684), *Paulus evangelista Romanorum succincta divinissimae* . . . *epistolae ad Romanos analysi et exegesi repraesentatus* (Hamburg: Liebernickel, 1696).

Fell, John, ed. (1625–1686), *A Paraphrase and Annotations upon the Epistles of St. Paul Written to the Romans, Corinthians, and Hebrews* (Oxford: The Theater, 1675); 2d ed., *A Paraphrase and Annotations upon All the Epistles of St. Paul* (1684; repr. London: R. Smith, 1702).

Letourneux, Nicolas (1640–1686), *Explication literale et morale sur l'épître de saint Paul aux Romains* (Paris: Elle Josset, 1696).

Wittich, Christoph (1625–1687), *Investigatio epistolae ad Romanos ab apostolo Paulo exaratae una cum paraphrasi* (Leiden: C. Boutesteyn, 1685).

Groenewegen, H. (1640–1692), *Keten van de gantsche Godgeleerheid, ofte Uytlegginge van den Zendbrief Pauli aan den Romeynen,* 2 vols. (Amsterdam: D. van der Dalen, 1680; Gorinchen: C. Lever, 1683).

Schmid, Sebastian (1617–1696), *Praelectiones academicae: In VI priora d. Pauli ad*

Romanos epistolae capita: Additae sunt eiusdem auctoris aliquot subs. capitum paraphrases (Hamburg: Schultz, 1694); *Commentarii in epistolas d. Pauli ad Romanos . . .* (Hamburg: Schiller, 1704).

Anon. (seventeenth–eighteenth centuries), *Criticorum sacrorum tomus VII exhibens annotata ad Acta Apostolorum et epistolas Pauli* (Amsterdam: 1698), extracts from Valla, Erasmus, and Grotius.

Engelschall, Johann Christian (seventeenth–eighteenth centuries), *Kurtze und catechetische Erläuterung des Epistel Pauli an die Römer* (Leipzig: Lanckisch, 1707).

Wouters, Martin (eighteenth century), *Dilucidationis selectarum S. Scripturae quaestionum pars sexta: In Acta Apostolorum: item in d. Pauli & Catholicas epistolas* (Louvain: Martin van Overbeke, 1753).

Locke, John (1632–1704, *A Paraphrase and Notes to the Epistle of St. Paul to the Galatians, I & II Corinthians, Romans, Ephesians* (London: A. and J. Churchill, 1707).

Spener, Philipp Jakob (1635–1705), *Auslegung des Briefes Pauli an die Römer . . .* , 3d rev. ed. H. Schott (Halle an der Saale: H. W. Schmidt, 1856).

Fibus, B. (1643–1706), *Via veritatis et vitae . . . per genuinam interpretationem d. Augustini super epistolam ad Romanos . . .* (Cologne: J. W. Friessem, Jr., 1696).

Peguigny, Bernardin de (Bernardinus a Piconio, 1633–1707), *Epistularum b. Paul apostoli triplex expositio*, 6 vols. in 3 (Paris: J. Anisson, 1703; Lyons: Russand, 1834; rev. ed., M. Hetzenauer, Innsbruck: Societas Mariana, 1891); *Explication des épîtres de Saint Paul . . .* (Paris: Pierre-Augustin le Mercier, 1706), 1–379.

Limborch, Philippus van (1633–1712), *Commentarius in Acta Apostolorum et in epistolas ad Romanos et ad Hebraeos* (Rotterdam: B. Bos, 1711), 211–520.

Leeuwen, Gerbrand van (1643–1721), *De sendbrief Pauli aan de Romeynen* (Amsterdam: A. Schoonenburg, 1684); rev. ed., *Het gelove en de betragtinge der heyligen, onder een schriftmatige verhandeling van den sendbrief Pauli aan den Romeynen, uyt de eerste gronden ontdekt*, 2d ed. (Amsterdam: A. Schoonenburg, 1743).

Vitringa, Campegius (1659–1722), *Verklaringe over de agt eerste capittelen van de brief Pauli aan de Romeinen* (Frankfurt am Main: W. Bleck, 1729).

Alexandre, Noël (1639–1724), *Commentarius litteralis et moralis in omnes epistolas sancti Pauli apostoli, et in VII epistolas catholicas*, 2 vols. (Paris: T. Bettinelli, 1768).

Hazevoet, S. (1657–1725), *De Brief van den h. Apostel Paulus aan de gemeente te Romen, ontleedt, verklaart, en betoogt* (Leiden: A. Kallewier, 1725).

Paris, François de (1690–1727), *Explication de l'épître de s. Paul aux Romains*, 4 vols. (Paris: no publ., no date; repr. in 3 vols, Paris: no publ., 1732–33).

Wells, E. (1667–1727), *An Help for the More Easy and Clear Understanding of the Holy Scriptures: Being St Paul's Epistle to the Romans Explain'd . . .* (Oxford: J. Knapton, 1711).

Anton, Paul (1661–1730), *Erbauliche Anmerkungen über die Epistel Pauli an die Römer* (Frankfurt: Berger, 1746).

Duguet, Jacques Joseph (1649–1733), *Explication de l'Épître de saint Paul aux Romains* (Avignon: no publ., 1756).

Rambach, Johann Jakob (1693–1735), *Introductio historico-theologica in epistolam Pauli ad Romanos* . . . (Halle an der Saale: Orphanage, 1727); *Ausführliche und gründliche Erklärung der Epistel Pauli an die Römer* . . . (Bremen: N. Sauermann, 1738).

Turrettini, Jean Alphonse (1671–1737), *In Pauli apostoli ad Romanos epistolae capitula priora xi praelectiones criticae, theologicae et concionatoriae* (Lausanne: M. M. Bousquet, 1741).

R. W. [Robert Witham] (d. 1738), *Annotations on the New Testament of Jesus Christ* . . . , 2 vols. (Douai: Seminary?, 1730–33), 2.5–67.

Wolf, Johann Christian (1683–1739), *Curae philologicae et criticae in iv priores s. Pauli epistolas*, 2d ed. (Hamburg: C. Herold, 1737).

LeGros, Nicolas (1675–1751), *Méditations sur l'épître de s. Paul aux Romains, avec le texte latin et français* . . . , 2 vols. (Paris: Deshayes, 1735).

Oudin, François (1673–1752), *Epistola beati Pauli apostoli ad Romanos explicata* (Paris: Bordelet, 1743).

Bengel, J. A. (1687–1752), "Annotationes in epistolam Pauli ad Romanos," *Gnomon Novi Testamenti* (Tübingen: L. F. Fues, 1742; 4th ed. by J. Steudel; also London: David Nutt, 1855; 8th ed., 1915), 523–604; cf. *Gnomon of the New Testament: Now First Translated into English*, trans. A. R. Fausset, 5 vols. (Edinburgh: Clark 1858), 3.1–198; *Gnomon of the New Testament: A New Translation*, trans. C. T. Lewis and M. R. Vincent, 2 vols. (Philadelphia, Penn.: Perkinpine & Higgins, 1862), 2.9–164; renamed and reprinted, *New Testament Word Studies* (Grand Rapids, Mich.: Kregel, 1971), 2.9–164.

Wettstein, J. J. (1693–1754), *Hē Kainē Diathēkē: Novum Testamentum graecum* . . . , 2 vols. (Amsterdam: Dommer, 1751–52), 2.16–100.

Mosheim, Johann Lorenz von (1694–1755), *Exegetische Einleitung in den Brief Pauli an die Römer* . . . (Blankenburg and Quedlinburg: C. A. Reussner, 1771).

Pyle, Thomas (1674–1756), *A Paraphrase, with Some Notes, on the Acts of the Apostles and upon All the Epistles of the New Testament* . . . , 2 vols. (London: J. Wyat, 1715; repr. London: G. G. & J. Robinson, 1725).

Baumgarten, Siegmund Jakob (1706–1757), *Auslegung des Briefes Pauli an die Römer* (Halle an der Saale: J. J. Gebauer, 1749).

Calmet, H. (1672–1757), "In epistolam Pauli apostoli ad Romanos," *Commentarius literalis in omnes libros veteris et novi testamenti*, 8 vols., trans. J. D. Mansi (Venice: S. Colet, 1754–56), 8.1–120; new ed. in 4 vols. Würzburg: F. X. Rienner, 1787–88), 3.344–553.

Berruyer, Isaac Joseph (1681–1758), *Histoire du peuple de Dieu, troisième partie: Paraphrase littérale des épîtres des apôtres*, 5 vols. (Amsterdam: Neaulme, 1758).

Steinhofer, Friedrich Christoph (1706–1761), *Erklärung der Epistel Pauli an die Römer* (Tübingen: L. F. Fues, 1851).

Taylor, John (1694–1761), A *Paraphrase with Notes on the Epistle to the Romans* . . . (London: J. Waugh, 1745; Dublin: J. Smith, 1746).

Crusius, Christian August (1715–1775), *Erläuterung des Briefes Pauli an die Römer* . . . (Leipzig: Langenheim, 1767).

Elsner, G. M. (1698–1775), *Paulus brief aan de Romeinen, geopend, ontleed, verklaard en tot zyn oogmerk toegepast* (Utrecht: G. T. and A. van Paddenburg, 1763–71).

Zachariae, Gotthilf Traugott (1729–1777), *Paraphrastische Erklärung des Briefes an die Römer* (Göttingen: V. Bossiegel, 1768; repr. 1780; 3d rev. ed.; Göttingen and Leipzig: J. D. G. Brose, 1787).

Schmidt, Christian Friedrich (1741–1778), *Annotationes in epistolam Pauli ad Romanos, philologicae, theologicae et criticae* (Leipzig: Kummer, 1777).

Cramer, Johann Andreas (1723–1788), *Der Brief Pauli an die Römer aufs neue übersetzt und ausgelegt* (Leipzig: Schwickert, 1784).

Küttner, Christian Gottfried (1734–1789), "Hypomnemata in epistolam Pauli ad Romanos," *Hypomnemata in Novum Testamentum* . . . (Leipzig: J. G. I. Breitkopf, 1780), 211–58.

Semler, Johann Salomo (1725–1791), *Paraphrasis epistulae ad Romanos cum notis* . . . (Halle an der Saale: C. H. Hemmerde, 1769).

Morus, S. F. N. (d. 1792), *Praelectiones in epistolam Pauli ad Romanos* . . . , ed. J. T. S. Holzapfel (Leipzig: Schwickert, 1794).

Stuber, Jean Georges (1722–1797), *Épître de S. Paul aux Romains* (Strasbourg: 1788).

MacKnight, James (1721–1800), A *New Literal Translation* . . . *of All the Apostolical Epistles, with a Commentary and Notes, Philological, Critical, Explanatory and Practical*, 4 vols. (Edinburgh: private publ., 1795; 2d ed. London: Longman, Hurst, Ress, and Orme, 1806).

Carpzov, Johann Benedict (1729–1803), *Stricturae theologicae et criticae in epistolam Pauli ad Romanos* . . . (Helmstadt: Weygand, 1758).

Roos Magnus, Friedrich (1727–1803), *Kurze Auslegung des Briefs St. Pauli an die Römer* (Tübingen: L. F. Fues, 1789).

Matthaei, Christian Friedrich von (1744–1811), *D. Pauli epistolae ad Romanos, Titum et Philemonem* . . . (Riga: Hartknoch, 1782).

IV. NINETEENTH- AND TWENTIETH-CENTURY WRITERS

Ordered alphabetically; the more important commentaries are marked by an asterisk.

Abbott, L., *The Epistle of Paul the Apostle to the Romans with Notes, Comments, Maps, and Illustrations* (New York and Chicago: Barnes, 1888).

*Achtemeier, P. J., *Romans*, Interpretation (Atlanta, Ga.: John Knox, 1985).

Agus, J., *Epistola beati Pauli apostoli ad Romanos analytice et logice explicata* (Regensburg: Pustet, 1888).

191

Ahern, B. M., *The Epistle to the Galatians and the Epistle to the Romans*, NTRG 7 (Collegeville, Minn.: Liturgical Press, 1960).

Alford, H., *"Pros Rhōmaious," The Greek Testament* . . . , 4 vols. (Cambridge: Deighton, Bell & Co., 1849–61; repr. 1895), 2.311–472.

Allen, L. C., "The Letter to the Romans," *A New Testament Commentary Based on the Revised Standard Version*, ed. G. C. D. Howley (London: Pickering & Inglis, 1969), 341–72; also published in *The New Layman's Bible Commentary*, ed. G. C. D. Howley et al. (Grand Rapids, Mich.: Zondervan, 1979), 1387–1418.

———, "Romans," *The International Bible Commentary with the New International Version*, ed. F. F. Bruce, rev. ed (Grand Rapids, Mich.: Zondervan; London: Marshall Pickering, 1986), 1316–46.

Althaus, P., *Der Brief an die Römer übersetzt und erklärt*, NTD 6 (Göttingen: Vandenhoeck & Ruprecht, 1935; 11th ed., 1970).

Ammon, C. F. von, *Epistola Pauli ad Romanos*, 2d ed. (Göttingen: Dieterich, 1806).

Andel, J. van, *Paulus' brief aan de Romeinen met de gemeente gelezen* (Kampen: Kok, 1904).

Andersen, Ø., *Fortolkning til Romerbrevet* (Oslo: Lunde Forlag, 1972).

Anon. (Pastors and Professors of the Church and Academy of Geneva), *Épître de St. Paul aux Romains* (Geneva: Bonnant, 1819).

Arndt, W., *Romans* (St. Louis, Mo.: Concordia Mimeo Co., n.d.).

Arnold, A. N. and D. B. Ford, *Commentary on the Epistle to the Romans* (Philadelphia, Penn.: American Baptist Publication Society, 1889).

Asmussen, H., *Der Römerbrief* (Stuttgart: Evangelisches Verlagswerk, 1952).

Baarlink, H., *Romeinen I: Een praktische bijbelverklaring* (Kampen: Kok, 1987).

Bacuez, L., "Épître aux Romains," *Manuel biblique ou cours d'Écriture Saint* . . . , 4 vols. (Paris: A. Roger et F. Chernoviz, 1896–1914), 4.227–98.

Barclay, W., *The Letter to the Romans*, Daily Study Bible (Edinburgh: Saint Andrew; Philadelphia, Penn.: Westminster, 1955; repr. 1978).

Bardenhewer, O., *Der Römerbrief des heiligen Paulus: Kurzgefasste Erklärung* (Freiburg im Breisgau: Herder, 1926).

Barmby, J., *Romans: Exposition*, Pulpit Commentary (New York: A. D. F. Randolph & Co., 1890).

Barnes, A., *Notes, Explanatory and Practical, on the Epistle to the Romans* (New York: Leavitt Lord & Co., 1834; 9th ed. rev. S. Green; New York: Harper & Bros., 1852).

Barnhouse, D. G., *Epistle to the Romans* (Philadelphia, Penn.: Bible Study Hour, 1953).

*Barrett, C. K., *A Commentary on the Epistle to the Romans*, BNTC and HNTC (London: Black; New York: Harper & Bros., 1957; 2d ed. 1991 [references are to the 1st ed.]).

———, *Reading Through Romans* (London: Epworth, 1963; Philadelphia, Penn.: Fortress, 1977).

Bartels, H., *Exegetische Uebersetzung des Briefes St. Pauli an die Römer* . . . (Dessau: A. Reissner, 1879).

*Barth, K., *Der Römerbrief*, 5th ed. (Zollikon-Zurich: Evangelischer-Verlag, 1918; rev. ed. H. Schmitt, Zurich: Theologischer-Verlag, 1985; *The Epistle to the Romans* (London: Oxford University, 1933), English trans. from the 6th German ed.

————, *Kurze Erklärung des Römerbriefes* (Munich: Kaiser, 1956; repr., Munich and Hamburg: Siebenstern-Taschenbuch, 1967); *A Shorter Commentary on Romans* (London: SCM; Richmond, Va.: John Knox, 1959).

Baulès, R., *L'Évangile puissance de Dieu: Commentaire de l'épître aux Romains*, LD 53 (Paris: Cerf, 1968).

Baumgarten-Crusius, L. F. O., *Commentar über den Brief Pauli an die Römer*, ed. E. J. Kimmel (Jena: Mauke, 1844).

Beck, J. T., *Erklärung des Briefes Pauli an die Römer*, 2 vols., ed. J. Lindenmeyer (Gütersloh: Bertelsmann, 1884).

Beelen, J. T., *Commentarius in epistolam s. Pauli ad Romanos* (Louvain: C. J. Fonteyn, 1854).

Beet, J. A., *Commentary on St. Paul's Epistle to the Romans* (London: Hodder and Stoughton, 1877; New York: T. Whittaker, 1891; 10th ed., 1902).

Benecke, W., *Der Brief an die Römer* (Heidelberg: Winter, 1831); *An Exposition of St. Paul's Epistle to the Romans* (London: Longman, Brown, Green, and Longmans, 1854).

Benson, R. M., *Exposition of the Epistle of St. Paul to the Romans* (London: Masters, 1892).

Bernard, D. K., *The Message of Romans* (Hazelwood, Mo.: Word Aflame, 1987).

Besser, W. F., *St. Pauli Brief an die Römer in Bibelstunden für die Gemeinde ausgelegt*, 2 vols. (Halle an der Saale: Mühlmann, 1861).

Best, E., *The Letter of Paul to the Romans*, Cambridge Bible Commentary on the NEB (Cambridge: Cambridge University Press, 1967).

Beveridge, H., *Commentary upon the Epistle of Saint Paul to the Romans* . . . *Edited from the Original English Translation of [Calvin's Commentary by] Christopher Rosdell* (Edinburgh: Calvin Translation Society, 1844).

Biesenthal, J. H. R., *Epistola Pauli ad Romanos, cum rabbinico commentario* (Berlin: Low, 1853).

*Billerbeck, P., *Kommentar zum Neuen Testament aus Talmud und Midrasch*, 6 vols. (Munich: Beck, 1926–63), vol. 3 (4th ed., 1965), 1–320.

Bisping, A., *Erklärung des Briefes an die Römer*, Exegetisches Handbuch 5.1 (Münster in Westfalen: Aschendorff, 1854–58; repr. 1870).

*Black, M., *Romans*, New Century Bible Commentary (London: Marshall, Morgan & Scott; Grand Rapids, Mich.: Eerdmans, 1973; 2d ed. 1989).

Blackman, E. C., "The Letter of Paul to the Romans," *The Interpreter's One-Volume Commentary on the Bible*, ed. C. M. Laymon (Nashville and New York: Abingdon, 1971), 768–94.

Bleibtreu, W., *Die drei ersten Kapitel des Römerbriefs ausgelegt* (Göttingen: Vandenhoeck & Ruprecht, 1884).

Bloomfield, S. T., *"Paulou tou apostolou hē pros Rhōmaious epistolē," Hē Kainē Diathēkē: The Greek Testament with English Notes* . . . , 2 vols., 2d ed. (London: Longman, Rees & Co., 1836), 2.1–97.

Böckel, E. G. A., *Epistola Pauli ad Romanos* (Zurich: 1821).

Böhlig, H., *Aus dem Briefe des Paulus nach Rom: Verdeutscht und ausgelegt* (Tübingen: Mohr [Siebeck], 1914).

Boehme, C. F., *Epistola Pauli ad Romanos graece ex recensione nouissima griesbachii cum commentario perpetuo* (Leipzig: S. L. Crusius, 1806).

Boehmer, E., *Des Apostels Paulus Brief an die Römer ausgelegt* (Bonn: Weber, 1886).

Boer, D. C. den, *De brief van Paulus aan de Romeinen*, 2 vols. (Kampen: Kok, 1986).

Bonnet, L., *"Épître de Paul Apôtre aux Romains," Le Nouveau Testament* . . . , 3 vols., 2d ed. (Lausanne: Bridel, 1875), 3.35–148.

Boor, W. de, *Der Brief des Paulus an die Römer*, Wuppertaler Studienbibel (Wuppertal: Brockhaus, 1962; repr. Berlin: Evangelische Haupt-Bibelgesellschaft, 1976).

Bosanquet, E., *A Verbal Paraphrase of St. Paul's Epistle to the Romans* . . . (London: Burns, 1840).

Bosio, E., *L'Epistola di S. Paolo ai Romani*, Commentario esegetico-pratico del Nuovo Testament (Florence: Claudiana, 1896; repr. Torre Pellice: Claudiana, 1930); in new form, *Epistole di S. Paolo ai Romani, I–II Corinzi* (Turin: Claudiana, 1989).

Bosworth, E. I., *Commentary on the Epistle of Paul to the Romans*, Bible for Home and School (New York: Macmillan, 1919).

Bover, J. M., *Las epístolas de San Pablo: Versión del texto original acompañada de commentário*, 2d ed. (Barcelona: Editorial Balmes, 1950), 1–94.

Bowen, R., *A Guide to Romans* (London: SPCK, 1975).

Boylan, P., *St. Paul's Epistle to the Romans: Translation and Commentary* (Dublin: Gill, 1934; repr. 1947).

Briscoe, D. S., *Romans*, Communicator's Commentary, NT 6 (Waco, Tex.: Word, 1982).

Bromehead, A. C., *A Popular Paraphrase on St. Paul's Epistle to the Romans* (London: Bell & Daldy, 1857).

Brown, D., *Commentary on the Epistle to the Romans Embracing the Latest Results of Criticism* (Glasgow: Collins, 1863).

———, *The Epistle to the Romans with Introduction and Notes* (Edinburgh: Clark, 1883; repr. 1950).

Brown, J., *Analytical Exposition of the Epistle of Paul the Apostle to the Romans* (Edinburgh: Oliphant; New York: R. Carter and Bros., 1857).

Brown, W. L. and G. W. Brown, *Romans: Gospel of Freedom and Grace* (New York: Salvation Army, 1988).

*Bruce, F. F., *The Epistle of Paul to the Romans: An Introduction and Commentary*,

TynNTC 6 (London: Tyndale; Grand Rapids, Mich.: Eerdmans, 1963; 5th ed. 1969; Leicester: Inter-Varsity; Grand Rapids, Mich.: Eerdmans, 1985).

Brunner, E., *Der Römerbrief übersetzt und erklärt*, Bibelhilfe für die Gemeinde, NT 6 (Stuttgart: J. G. Oncken, 1938; repr. 1956); *The Letter to the Romans: A Commentary* (London: Lutterworth; Philadelphia, Penn.: Westminster, 1959).

Burkitt, W., *Expository Notes with Practical Observations on the New Testament*, 2 vols. (Philadelphia, Penn.: John Ball, 1849), 2.3–121.

Burwash, N., *A Handbook on the Epistle of St. Paul to the Romans, Based on the Revised Version and the Revisers' Text* . . . (Toronto: Briggs, 1887).

Buttz, H. A., *The Epistle to the Romans in Greek* . . . , 3d ed. (New York: Eaton & Mains; Cincinnati, Oh.: Jennings & Pye, 1876).

Byrne, B., *Reckoning with Romans: A Contemporary Reading of Paul's Gospel*, GNS 18 (Wilmington, Del.: Glazier, 1986).

Cambier, J., *L'Évangile de Dieu selon l'épître aux Romains: Exégèse et théologie biblique*, vol. 1: *L'Évangile de la justice et de la grace*, Studia neotestamentica, Studia 3 (Bruges: Desclée de Brouwer, 1967).

Carpenter, S. C., *A Paraphrase of Selections from St. Paul's Epistle to the Romans* (London: SPCK, 1948).

Cecchin, F., *Incontrare Cristo oggi: Commento esistenziale alla lettera ai Romani* (Casale Monferrato: Piemme, 1991).

Cerfaux, L., *Une Lecture de l'épître aux Romains* (Tournai: Castermann, 1947).

Ceulemans, F. and G. Thils, "Epistola beati Pauli apostoli ad Romanos," *Epistolae sancti Pauli* (Malines: Dessain, n.d.), 9–116.

Challis, J., *A Translation of the Epistle of the Apostle Paul to the Romans with an Introduction and Critical Notes* (Cambridge: Deighton, Bell and Co., 1871).

Chalmers, T., *Lectures on the Epistle of Paul the Apostle to the Romans*, 2 vols. (Glasgow and New York: R. Carter & Bros., 1842; 2d ed. 1843; Edinburgh: Constable, 1856).

Chamberlain, T., *The Epistle to the Romans with Short Notes Chiefly Critical and Doctrinal* (London: Masters, 1870).

Chase, D. P., *The Epistle, of Paul the Apostle, to the Romans* . . . (London: Rivington, 1886).

Clark, G. W., *Romans and I. and II. Corinthians*, People's Commentary (Philadelphia, Penn.: American Baptist Publ. Society, 1897), viii–xiii, 25–187.

Clarke, A., *The Epistle of Paul, the Apostle, to the Romans* . . . (Cincinnati, Oh.: Joseph Mitchell, 1821; New York: Bangs and Emory, 1826).

———, "The Epistle of Paul the Apostle to the Romans," *The New Testament* . . . *with a Commentary*, 2 vols. (New York: W. & P. C. Smith, Collins & Co., 1823), 2.35–178.

Clausen, H. N., *Pauli Brev til Romerne* (Copenhagen: Gad, 1863).

Colenso, J. W., *St. Paul's Epistle to the Romans: Newly Translated and Explained from a Missionary Point of View* (London: Macmillan, 1861; New York: Appleton, 1863).

Conybeare, W. J. and J. S. Howson, *The Life and Epistles of St. Paul*, 2 vols. (London: Longman, Brown, Green, and Longmans, 1852; New York: T. Y. Crowell, n.d.; repr. New York: Scribner, 1854; Grand Rapids, Mich.: Eerdmans, 1953).

Cooper, B. H., *An Essay Towards a New Translation of the Epistle of St. Paul to the Romans* . . . (London: Hamilton, Adams & Co., 1844).

Cordero, F., *L'Epistola ai Romai: Antropologia del cristianesimo paolino* (Turin: Giulio Einaudi, 1972).

Cornely, R., *Commentarius in s. Pauli apostoli epistulas: I. Epistola ad Romanos*, CSS 3.6 (Paris: Lethielleux, 1896; 2d ed. 1927).

Cowles, H., *The Longer Epistles of Paul: Viz. Romans, I Corinthians, II Corinthians* (New York: Appleton, 1880; repr. 1888).

Cox, R. (alias Clericus), *Horae Romanae: Or an Attempte to Elucidate St. Paul's Epistle to the Romans* . . . (London: Baldwyn, 1823).

*Cranfield, C. E. B., *A Critical and Exegetical Commentary on the Epistle to the Romans*, 2 vols. (Edinburgh: Clark, 1975–79).

———, *Romans: A Shorter Commentary* (Edinburgh: Clark; Grand Rapids, Mich.: Eerdmans, 1985).

Crawford, J. R., *Pros Rhōmaious: The Epistle of Paul the Apostle to the Romans* . . . (London: Longman & Co., 1860).

Crosby, H., "The Epistle of Paul the Apostle to the Romans," *The New Testament in Both Authorized and Revised Versions* (Boston: Alden, 1884), 331–65.

Cumming, J., *Romans* (London: Virtue & Co., 1857).

Curci, C. M., *Il Nuovo Testamento volgarizzato ed esposto in note esegetiche e morali* (Turin: Bocca, 1880), 3.1–95.

Dabney, J. P., "The Epistle of Paul to the Romans," *Annotations on the New Testament*, 2 vols. (Cambridge, Mass.: Hilliard and Brown, 1829), 2.285–328.

Daechsel, T., *Der Brief St. Pauli an die Römer* (Dresden: Ungelenk, 1934).

Dargan, E. C., *An Exposition of the Epistle to the Romans* (Nashville, Tenn.: Sunday School Board, Southern Baptist Convention, 1914).

Davidson, F. and R. P. Martin, "Romans," *The New Bible Commentary Revised*, ed. D. Guthrie and J. A. Motyer (Grand Rapids, Mich.: Eerdmans, 1970), 1012–48.

Delitzsch, F., *Paulus des Apostels Brief an die Römer* . . . *in das Hebräische übersetzt und aus Talmud und Midrasch erläutert* (Leipzig: Dörffling und Franke, 1870).

Deluz, G., *La Justice de Dieu: Explication de l'épître aux Romains* (Neuchâtel and Paris: Delachaux & Niestlé, 1945).

Denney, J., *St. Paul's Epistle to the Romans*, Expositor's Greek Testament, ed. W. R. Nicoll (London: Hodder & Stoughton, 1900), 2.555–725; repr. Grand Rapids, Mich.: Eerdmans, 1983).

De Wette, W. M. L., *Kurze Erklärung des Briefes an die Römer*, Kurzgefasstes exegetisches Handbuch zum Neuen Testament 2.1 (Leipzig: Weidmann, 1835; 4th ed., 1847).

Diderichsen, B. K., *Paulus Romanus: Et analytisk bidrag til Romerbrevets aeldste Historie*, Teologiske Studier 1, DTT II. Afd. (Copenhagen: Gad, 1941).

Diedrich, J., *Der Brief St. Pauli an die Römer* (Leipzig: Dörffling und Franke, 1856).

Discus, A. W., *Commentary on Romans and Hebrews* (Tampa, Fla.: no publ., n.d.).

Dix, M., *An Exposition of the Epistle of Saint Paul to the Romans, According to the Analogy of the Catholic Faith* (New York: private publ., 1862).

*Dodd, C. H., *The Epistle of Paul to the Romans*, Moffatt NT Comm. (London: Hodder & Stoughton, 1932; rev. ed., Fontana Books; London: Collins, 1959).

Doulière, R. F., *La Justice qui fait vivre: L'Épître aux Romains, introduction et commentaire* (Neuchâtel: Chave, 1975).

Drach, D. P. and A. Bayle, "Épître de saint Paul aux Romains," *La sainte Bible avec commentaires*, 41 vols. in 31 (Paris: Lethielleux, 1871), 37.1–116.

Drioux, C. J., "Épître aux Romains," *Le sainte Bible*, 8 vols., 3d ed. (Paris: Berche et Tralin, 1879), 8.11–76.

Drummond, J., "The Epistle to the Romans," *International Handbooks to the New Testament*, 2 vols. (London and New York: Putnam, 1899), 2.243–353.

Dunkin, J. E., *Commentary on Romans* (Joplin, Mo.: College Press, 1986).

*Dunn, J. D. G., *Romans 1–8*, WBC 38A (Dallas, Tex.: Word Books, 1988); *Romans 9–16*, WBC 38B (Dallas, Tex.: Word Books, 1988).

Ebrard, J. H. A., *Der Brief Pauli an die Römer übersetzt und erklärt*, ed. P. Bachmann (Erlangen and Leipzig: Deichert, 1890).

Edwards, J. R., *Romans*, NIBC (Peabody, Mass.: Hendrickson, 1992).

Ellicott, C. J., "Romans," *Ellicott's Bible Commentary in One Volume*, ed. D. N. Bowdle (Grand Rapids, Mich.: Zondervan, 1971), 921–54.

Erdman, C. R., *The Epistle of Paul to the Romans: An Exposition* (Philadelphia, Penn.: Westminster, 1925; repr. 1966).

Eschner, W., *Der Römerbrief: An die Juden der Synagogen in Rom? Ein exegetischer Versuch und die Bestimmung des Bedeutungsinhaltes von dikaioun im NT*, 2 vols. (Hannover: private publ., 1981).

Etzold, O., *Der Römerbrief der Gemeinde neu erschlossen* (Metzingen: Brunnquell Verlag, 1970).

Evans, E., *To the Romans: An Exposition of the Epistle* (London: Mowbray, 1948).

Evans, W., *Romans and I and II Corinthians* (New York: F. H. Revell, 1918).

Ewald, G. H. A., *Die Sendschreiben des Apostels Paulus übersetzt und erklärt* (Göttingen: Dietrich, 1857).

Ewbank, W. W., *A Commentary on the Epistle of Paul the Apostle to the Romans: With a New Translation and Explanatory Notes*, 2 vols. (London: J. W. Parker, 1850–51).

Feine, P., *Der Römerbrief: Eine exegetische Studie* (Göttingen: Vandenhoeck & Ruprecht, 1903).

Fenton, F., *St. Paul's Epistle to the Romans . . .* (Batley: Wildsmith, 1882).

Fillion, L.-C., "Épître aux Romains," *La sainte Bible (texte latin et traduction française) commentée d'après la Vulgate et les textes originaux*, 8 vols. (Paris: Letouzey & Ané), vol. 8 (1904), 19–114.

Findlay, G. G., "Romans," A Commentary on the Bible, ed. A. S. Peake (London and New York: Nelson, 1919), 817–31.

Fischer, E., Der Brief an die Römer: Für evangelische Christen . . . , 6th ed. (Berlin: Union Deutsche Verlagsgesellschaft, 1919).

Fischer, M., Der Römerbrief, Christus heute (Stuttgart: Kreuz-Verlag, 1960).

Fitzmyer, J. A., "The Letter to the Romans," JBC, art. 53 (2.291–331); rev. ed., NJBC, art. 51 (830–68).

Five Clergymen (= J. Harrow, G. Moberly, H. Alford, W. G. Humphrey, C. J. Ellicott), The Epistle of St. Paul to the Romans, after the Authorized Version: Newly Compared with the Original Greek . . . , 2d ed. (London: J. W. Parker, 1858).

Flatt, J. F. von, Vorlesungen über den Brief Pauli an die Römer, ed. C. D. F. Hoffmann (Tübingen: L. F. Fues, 1825).

Forbes, J., Analytical Commentary on the Epistle to the Romans: Tracing the Train of Thought by the Aid of Parallelism . . . (Edinburgh: Clark, 1868).

Ford, J., S. Paul's Epistle to the Romans: Illustrated from Divines of the Church of England (London: Masters, 1862).

Foreman, K. J., The Letter of Paul to the Romans . . . , Layman's Bible Commentary 21 (Richmond, Va.: John Knox, 1961).

Foster, R. V., A Commentary on the Epistle to the Romans (Nashville, Tenn.: Cumberland Presbyterian Publ. House, 1891).

Franzmann, M. H., Romans, Concordia Commentary (Saint Louis, Mo.: Concordia Publishing House, 1968).

Fritzsche, C. F. A., Pauli ad Romanos epistola, 3 vols. (Halle an der Saale: Gebauer, 1836–43).

Fry, J., Lectures, Explanatory and Practical, on the Epistle of Saint Paul to the Romans (London: Ogles, Duncan & Cochran, 1816; 2d ed. 1825).

Fulford, H. W., The Epistles of St. Paul to the Galatians and to the Romans (Cambridge: Cambridge University Press, 1917).

Gärtner, J. M., Der Brief Pauli an die Römer von unächter Lesart befreit, bündig deutsch übersetzt, genügend erklärt (Stuttgart: Chr. Belser, 1872).

Gairdner, W. H, T., Hilfsbuch zum Studium des Römerbriefs (Bethel and Bielefeld: Verlagshandlung der Anstalt Bethel, 1911).

Galizzi, M., Lettera di Paolo ai Romani, 2 vols., Commento al Nuovo Testamento (Turin: Elle di Ci, 1974–75).

Garvie, A. E., Romans: Introduction, Authorized Version, Revised Version with Notes . . . , Century Bible (London: Caxton; New York: H. Frowde; Edinburgh: Clark, [1901?]).

Gaugler, E., Der Römerbrief, pt. 1: Kapitel 1–8, Prophezei (Zurich: Zwingli-Verlag, 1945; repr. 1958); pt. 2: Kapitel 9–15, Prophezei (Zurich: Zwingli-Verlag, 1952).

Gerlach, O. von, "Die Epistel St. Pauli an die Römer," Das Neue Testament nach Dr. Martin Luthers Uebersetzung mit Einleitungen und erklärenden Anmerkungen, 2 vols., 2d ed. (Berlin: Thome, 1840), 2.5–120.

Gess, W, F., *Bibelstunden über den Brief des Apostels Paulus an die Römer*, 2 vols. (Basel: Detloff, 1886–89).

Getty, M. A., *Invitation to the New Testament Epistles I: A Commentary on Galatians and Romans* . . . (Garden City, N.Y.: Doubleday Image Books, 1982).

Gifford, E. H., *The Epistle of St. Paul to the Romans with Notes and Introduction*, Speaker's Commentary (London: John Murray, 1881; repr. 1886).

————, "Romans," *The Holy Bible According to the Authorized Version (A.D. 1611) with an Explanatory and Critical Commentary* . . . , ed. F. C. Cook (London: John Murray, 1886; New York: Scribners, 1890), 3.1–238.

Gill, J., "The Epistle of Paul the Apostle to the Romans," *An Exposition of the New Testament* . . . , 3 vols. (Philadelphia, Penn.: W. W. Woodward, 1811), 2.431–615.

Gillies, J., "The Epistle of Paul the Apostle to the Romans," *The New Testament* . . . *with Devotional Reflections*, 2 vols., 2d ed. (London: Byfield and Son, 1810), 2.127–205.

Gilmer, A. E., *Romans: The Gospel According to Paul (A Study of Romans 1–8)* (Ashland, Oh.: Brethren Publ. Co., 1985).

Glöckler, C., *Der Brief des Apostels Paulus an die Römer erklärt* (Frankfurt am Main: Schmerber, 1834).

*Godet, F., *Commentaire sur l'épître aux Romains*, 2 vols. (Paris: Sandoz & Fischbacher; Geneva: Desrogis, 1879–80; repr. Geneva: Labor et Fides, 1879–81; 3d ed., 1968); *Commentary on St. Paul's Epistle to the Romans*, 2 vols. (Edinburgh: Clark, 1880–81; repr. 1889; Grand Rapids, Mich.: Kregel, 1977).

Godwin, J. H., *The Epistle of the Apostle Paul to Romans: A New Translation, with Notes* (London: Hodder and Stoughton, 1873).

Gore, C., *St. Paul's Epistle to the Romans: A Practical Exposition*, 2 vols. (London: John Murray; New York: Scribners, 1899–1900; repr. 1907).

Govett, R., *The Righteousness of God, the Salvation of the Believer: Or, the Argument of Romans* (Norwich: Fletcher & Sons, 1891).

Greene, O. B., *The Epistle of Paul the Apostle to the Romans* (Greenville, S.C.: Gospel Hour Inc., 1962; repr. 1974).

Greijdanus, S., *De brief van den Apostel Paulus aan de gemeente te Rome*, 2 vols., Kommentaar op het Nieuwe Testament 6.1–2 (Amsterdam: H. A. van Bottenburg, 1933).

Grey, H. G., *St. Paul's Epistle to the Romans*, Readers' Commentary (London: Scott, 1911; New York: Funk & Wagnalls, 1916).

Griffith, G. O., *St. Paul's Gospel to the Romans* (Oxford: Blackwell, 1949).

Grinfield, E. W., "*Paulou tou apostolou hē pros Rhōmaious epistolē*," *Scholia hellenistica in Novum Testamentum* . . . , 2 vols. (London: Pickering, 1848), 1.347–96.

Grosche, R., *Kommentar zum Römerbrief*, ed. F.-J. Hungs (Werl: Dietrich-Coelde-Verlag, 1975).

Grubbs, I. B., *An Exegetical and Analytical Commentary on Paul's Epistle to the Romans*, ed. G. A. Klingman, 2d ed. (Cincinnati, Oh.: F. L. Rowe, 1919).

Gutbrod, K., *Der Römerbrief* (Stuttgart: Quellenverlag der Evang. Gesellschaft, [1946]).

Gutjahr, F. S., *Der Brief an die Römer*, Die Briefe des heiligen Apostels Paulus 3 (Graz; Styria, 1923).

Gutzke, M. G., *Plain Talk on Romans* (Grand Rapids, Mich.: Zondervan, 1976).

Haldane, R., *Exposition of the Epistle to the Romans . . .* , 3 vols. (Edinburgh: Whyte, 1842; repr. New York: R. Carter, 1853); repr. in one vol. as *Commentary on Romans* (Grand Rapids, Mich.: Kregel, 1988).

Halverson, R. C., *God's Way out of Futility: A Concise Discussion of Romans—Its Application to Life Here and Now* (Grand Rapids, Mich.: Zondervan, 1973; repr. with modified title, Palm Springs, Calif.: Haynes, 1981).

Hamilton, F. E., *The Epistle to the Romans: An Exegetical and Devotional Commentary* (Philadelphia, Penn.: Presbyterian and Reformed Publ. Co., 1958).

Harford, G., *The Gospel According to Saint Paul: Being an Expanded Rendering of the Epistle to the Romans* (London: Marshall Bros., n.d. [1913?]).

Harrison, E. F., "Romans," *The Expositor's Bible Commentary with the New International Version of the Holy Bible*, 12 vols., ed. F. E. Gaebelein (Grand Rapids, Mich.: Zondervan, 1976–), 10.1–171.

Harrisville, R. A., *Romans*, Augsburg Commentary on the NT (Minneapolis, Minn.: Augsburg, 1980).

Heil, J. P., *Paul's Letter to the Romans: A Reader-Response Commentary* (New York and Mahwah, N.J.; Paulist, 1987).

Heinfetter, H. (alias F. Parker), *A Literal Translation of St. Paul's Epistle to the Romans on Definite Rules of Translation* (London: Craddock, 1842).

Heising, J. A., *Reflexionen zum Römerbrief*, Die Welt der Bibel (Düsseldorf: Patmos, 1970).

Helm, B., *A Commentary on St. Paul's Epistle to the Romans* (Louisville, Ky.: Pentecostal Publ. Co., 1907).

Hendriksen, W., *Exposition of Paul's Epistle to the Romans*, 2 vols. (Edinburgh: Banner of Truth; Grand Rapids, Mich.: Baker, 1980–81).

Hengel, W. A. van, *Interpretatio epistolae Pauli ad Romanos . . .* , 2 vols. ('s-Herzogenbosch: Muller Bros.; Leipzig: Weigel, 1855–59).

Hinton, J. H., *An Exposition of the Epistle to the Romans on the Principles of Scripture Parallelism . . .* (London: Houlston & Wright, 1863).

Hobart, A. S., *Transplanted Truths: Or, Exposition of Great Texts in Romans* (Philadelphia, Penn.: Judson, 1919).

Hobbs, H. H., *Romans: A Verse by Verse Study* (Waco, Tex.: Word Books, 1977).

Hodge, C., *A Commentary on the Epistle to the Romans . . .* (Philadelphia, Penn.: Grigg & Elliot, 1835; rev. ed., Philadelphia, Penn.: Wm. S. and A. Martien, 1864; often repr., latest: Grand Rapids, Mich.: Eerdmans, 1980).

Hofmann, J. C. K. von, "Der Brief an die Römer," *Die heilige Schrift Neuen Testaments*, 11 vols. (Nördlingen: Beck, 1868), 3.1–633.

Hort, F. J. A., *Prolegomena to St Paul's Epistles to the Romans and the Ephesians* (London and New York: Macmillan, 1895).

Horton, T. G., *Lectures on the Romans* (London: Freeman, 1863).

Huber, P., *Gott für uns: Der Brief an die Römer ausgelegt* (Zurich and Frankfurt am Main: Gotthelf-Verlag, 1962).

*Huby, J. *Saint Paul: Épître aux Romains: Traduction et commentaire*, VS 10, 4th ed. (Paris: Beauchesne, 1940; new ed., rev. S. Lyonnet, 1957).

————, *San Paolo: Epistola ai Romani: Commento*, ed. S. Lyonnet (Rome: Studium, 1961).

Hughes, R. K., *Romans: Righteousness from Heaven* (Wheaton, Ill.: Crossway, 1991).

Hunter, A. M., *The Epistle to the Romans*, Torch Bible Commentary 8.6 (London: SCM, 1955; repr. with subtitle, *The Law of Love*, 1968, 1977).

Hupfeld, F., *Der Römerbrief*, Hilfsmittel zum evangelischen Religionsunterricht 18, 3d ed. (Berlin: Reuther & Reichard, 1914).

Iglesias, E., *La energía que salva (Comentario a la Epístola a los Romanos)* (México: Editorial Jus, 1951).

Jacobs, H. E., *Annotations on the Epistles of Paul to the Romans and I. Corinthians, Chaps. I–VI*, Lutheran Commentary (New York: Christian Literature Co., 1896), 11–328.

Jacono, V., *Le epistole di S. Paolo ai Romani, ai Corinti e ai Galati*, Sacra Bibbia (Turin: Marietti, 1951), 75–251.

Jamieson, R., A. R. Fausset, and D. Brown, *Commentary Practical and Explanatory on the Whole Bible*, rev. ed. H. Lockyer (Grand Rapids, Mich.: Zondervan, 1961), 1138–85.

Jatho, G. F., *Pauli Brief an die Roemer nach seinem inneren Gedankengange erläutert*, 2 vols. (Hildesheim: Gerstenberg, 1858–59).

Jervell, J., *Gud og hans Fiender: Forsøk på å tolke Romerbrevet* (Oslo: Universitetsforlaget, 1973).

Jewett, R., *Romans*, Cokesbury Basic Bible Commentary 22 ([Nashville, Tenn.]: Graded Press, 1988).

Johnson, A. F., *The Freedom Letter: A Contemporary Analysis of Paul's Roman Letter That Changed the Course of Christianity* (Chicago, Ill.: Moody, 1974).

Jowett, B., *The Epistles of St. Paul: To the Thessalonians, Galatians, and Romans*, 2 vols. (London: John Murray, 1855; 2d ed. 1859), 2.1–429.

Jülicher, A., *Der Brief an die Römer*, Schriften des Neuen Testamentes 2, 3d ed. (Göttingen: Vandenhoeck & Ruprecht, 1907; rev. ed. 1917).

*Käsemann, E., *An die Römer*, HNT 8a (Tübingen: Mohr [Siebeck], 1973; 4th ed. 1980); *Commentary on Romans* (Grand Rapids, Mich.: Eerdmans, 1980).

Kalt, E., *Der Römerbrief übersetzt und erklärt*, Herders Bibelkommentar: Die heilige Schrift für das Leben erklärt 14 (Freiburg in Breisgau: Herder, 1937), 1–143.

Kelly, W., *Notes on the Epistle of Paul, the Apostle, to the Romans with a New Translation* (London: G. Morrish, 1873).

Kemp, J. T. van der, *De theodicée van Paulus: Of, de rechtvaardigheid Gods door het euangelium . . . in eenige aanmerkingen op dezelfs Brief aan de Romeinen . . .* , 3 vols. (Dordrecht: A. Blussé, 1799–1802).

Kenyon, D. L., *An Interpretation of the Epistle of Paul the Apostle to the Romans*, 2 vols. (Harrisburg, Penn.: Christian Publications, 1979).

*Kertelge, K., *Der Brief an die Römer*, Geistliche Schriftlesung 6 (Düsseldorf: Patmos, 1971); *The Epistle to the Romans*, NTSR 12 (New York: Herder and Herder, 1972).

Kirk, K. E., *The Epistle to the Romans in the Revised Version*, Clarendon Bible 12 (Oxford: Clarendon, 1937).

Kistemaker, J. H., *Die Sendschreiben der Apostel; Übersetzt und erklärt*, 2 vols. (Münster in Westfalen: Theissing, 1822–23).

Klaiber, W. et al., *Rechenschaft über den Glauben: Römerbrief*, Bibelauslegung für die Praxis 21 (Stuttgart: Katholisches Bibelwerk, 1989).

Klee, H., *Commentar über des Apostel Paulus Sendschreiben an die Römer* (Mainz: Kupferberg, 1830).

Kleinschmidt, F. E., *Der Brief an die Römer erläutert* (Gütersloh: Bertelsmann, 1888).

Klofutar, L., *Commentarius in epistolam s. apostoli Pauli ad Romanos concinnatus* (Laibach: Klein et Kovać, 1880).

Klostermann, E., *Korrekturen zur bisherigen Erklärung des Römerbriefes* (Gotha: Perthes, 1881).

Knight, R., *A Critical Commentary on the Epistle of St. Paul the Apostle to the Romans* (London: Bagster, 1854).

Knox, J., "The Epistle to the Romans," IB 9 (1954): 353–668.

Knox, R. A., "St Paul's Epistle to the Romans," *A New Testament Commentary for English Readers*, 2 vols. (London: Burns Oates and Washbourne, 1953–54), 2.68–125.

Kögel, J., *Der Brief des Apostels Paulus an die Römer*, Zum Schriftverständnis des Neuen Testaments 4 (Gütersloh: Bertelsmann, 1919).

Köllner, W. H. D. E., *Commentar zu dem Briefe des Apostels Paulus an die Römer* (Darmstadt: J. P. Diehl, 1834).

Koppe, J. B., *Novum Testamentum graece perpetua adnotatione illustratum . . . Volumen IV complectens epistolam Pauli ad Romanos*, 3d ed. rev. C. F. Ammon (Göttingen: Dietrich, 1824).

Krehl, A. L. G., *Der Brief an die Römer ausgelegt* (Leipzig: K. F. Köhler, 1845).

Krimmer, H., *Römerbrief*, Edition c—Bibelkommentar B10 (Neuhausen-Stuttgart: Hänssler-Verlag, 1983).

Kruijf, T. C. de, *De Brief van Paulus aan de Romeinen vertaald en toegelicht*, Het Nieuwe Testament (Boxtel: Katholieke Bijbelstichting, 1986).

*Kühl, E., *Der Brief des Paulus an die Römer* (Leipzig: Quelle & Meyer, 1913).

Kümmel, W. G., *Römer 7 und die Bekehrung des Paulus*, UNT 17 (Leipzig: Hinrichs, 1929); repr. in *Römer 7 und das Bild des Menschen im Neuen Testament: Zwei Studien*, Theologische Bücherei, NT 53 (Munich: Kaiser, 1974).

Kürzinger, J., *Der Brief an die Römer* (Echterbibel; Würzburg: Echter-Verlag, 1955).

Kuss, O., *Die Briefe an die Römer, Korinther und Galater*, RNT 6 (Regensburg: Pustet, 1940), 15–111.

*————, *Der Römerbrief übersetzt und erklärt*, 3 parts (chaps. 1–11) (Regensburg: Pustet, 1957–78).

*Lagrange, M.-J., *Saint Paul: Épître aux Romains*, EtBib (Paris: Gabalda, 1916; 4th ed. 1931 [with addenda]; repr. 1950).

Laicus, A *Paraphrastic Translation of St. Paul's Epistle to the Romans* (London: Simpkin & Marshall, 1834).

Lange, J. P. and F. R. Fay, *Der Brief Pauli an die Römer*, 2d ed. (Bielefeld and Leipzig: Belhagen und Klasing, 1868); *The Epistle of Paul to the Romans*, 2d ed. (New York: Scribners, 1870).

Langenberg, H., *Der Römerbrief: Der heilsgeschichtliche Missionsberuf der Gemeinde und der paulinische Lehrtypus* (Hamburg: Achtel, 1962).

Lard, M. E., *Commentary on Paul's Letter to Romans* (Cincinnati, Oh.: Standard Publ. Co.; Lexington, Ky.: Transylvania, 1875; St. Louis, Mo.: Christian Board of Publication, 1914).

Lattey, C. (ed.), *The Epistle of St. Paul to the Romans*, Westminster Version (London: Longmans, Green, 1921).

Laurin, R. L., *Romans: Where Life Begins* (Grand Rapids, Mich.: Kregel, 1988).

Lee, E. K., *A Study in Romans* (London: SPCK, 1962).

*Leenhardt, F.-J., *L'Épître de saint Paul aux Romains*, CNT 6 (Neuchâtel and Paris: Delachaux et Niestlé, 1957; 2d ed. avec un complément, Geneva: Labor et Fides, 1981); *The Epistle to the Romans: A Commentary* (London: Lutterworth, 1961).

Leeuwen, J. A. C. van, *De brief aan de Romeinen: Opnieuw uit den grondtekst vertaald en verklaart*, 2d ed. (Kampen: Kok, 1939).

Lekkerkerker, A. F. N., *De brief van Paulus aan de Romeinen*, 2 vols., De prediking van het Nieuwe Testament (Nijkerk: G. F. Callenbach, 1962–65; repr. 1978).

Lenski, R. C. H., *The Interpretation of St. Paul's Epistle to the Romans* (Columbus, Oh.: Lutheran Book Concern, 1936; repr. Minneapolis, Minn.: Augsburg, 1961).

Liddon, H. P., *Explanatory Analysis of St. Paul's Epistle to the Romans* (London: Longmans, Green and Co., 1893; repr. Grand Rapids, Mich.: Zondervan, 1961).

*Lietzmann, H., *An die Römer*, HNT 8 (Tübingen: Mohr [Siebeck], 1906; 5th ed. 1971).

Lightfoot, J. B., *Notes on Epistles of St. Paul from Unpublished Commentaries* (London: Macmillan, 1895; 2d ed. 1904), 237–305 (notes on passages to the end of chap. 7).

Lilly, J. L., "The Epistle to the Romans," *A Commentary on the New Testament* (Washington, D.C.: Catholic Biblical Association of America, 1942), 410–46.

Lipscomb, D., *A Commentary on the New Testament Epistles: I. Romans* (Nashville, Tenn.: Gospel Advocate Co., 1933).

Lipsius, R. A., "Der Brief an die Römer," *Hand-Commentar zum Neuen Testament*, ed. H. J. Holtzmann et al., 3 vols., 2d ed. (Freiburg and Leipzig: Mohr [Siebeck], 1892–93), 2.2.70–206; "The Epistle to the Romans," *A Short Protestant Commentary on the Books of the New Testament with General and Special Introductions*, 3 vols., ed. P. W. Schmidt and F. von Holzendorff (London: Williams and Norgate, 1882–84), 2.20–197.

Livermore, A. A., *The Epistle of Paul to the Romans: With a Commentary, Revised Translation and Introductory Essay* (Boston: Crosby, Nichols & Co., 1854; repr. Boston: Waller and Wise, 1861).

Lloyd-Jones, D. M., *Romans*, 8 vols. (Grand Rapids, Mich.: Zondervan, 1971–76).

Loewe, H., *Der Römerbrief des Apostels Paulus* (Cologne: C. Roemke, 1927).

Lohmann, E., *An die Heiligen in Rom: Der Brief des Apostels Paulus an die Römer übersetzt und erläutert* (Frankfurt am Main: Orient, n.d.; 2d ed. 1920).

Lorenzi, L. de, *Romani: Vivere nello Spirito di Cristo*, Leggere oggi la Bibbia 2.6 (Brescia: Queriniana, 1983).

Lüthi, W., *Der Römerbrief ausgelegt für die Gemeinde* (Basel: F. Reinhardt, 1955); *The Letter to the Romans: An Exposition* (Edinburgh: Oliver and Boyd; Richmond, Va.: John Knox, 1961).

Luthardt, C. E., *Der Brief Pauli an die Römer ausgelegt* (Nördlingen: Beck, 1886).

*Lyonnet, S., *Les Épîtres de saint Paul aux Galates, aux Romains*, SBJ (Paris: Cerf, 1953; 2d ed., 1959), 45–136.

———, *Exegesis epistulae ad Romanos: Cap. I ad IV*, 3d ed. (Rome: Biblical Institute, 1963); *Cap. V ad VII (except. Rom 5,12–21)* (Rome: Biblical Institute, 1962); *Cap. VIII* (Rome: Biblical Institute, 1962); *Cap. I ad VIII* (Rome: Biblical Institute, 1957).

———, *Quaestiones in epistulam ad Romanos: Prima series* (Rome: Biblical Institute, 1955; 2d ed. 1962); *Series altera* (Rome: Biblical Institute, 1956; 3d ed. with suppl., 1975).

MacArthur, J. F., *Romans 1–8*, MacArthur New Testament Commentary (Chicago, Ill.: Moody, 1991).

McClain, A. J., *Romans: The Gospel of God's Grace*, ed. H. A. Hoyt (Chicago, Ill.: Moody, 1973).

MacEvilly, J., *An Exposition of the Epistles of St. Paul, and of the Catholic Epistles . . .* , 2 vols. (Dublin: Gill; New York: Benziger, 1891), 1.142.

MacGorman, J. W., *Romans, 1 Corinthians*, Layman's Bible Book Commentary 20 (Nashville, Tenn.: Broadman, 1980), 15–95.

Mackenzie, W. D., *Galatians and Romans with Introduction and Notes*, Westminster New Testament (New York: F. H. Revell; London: A. Melrose, 1912), 141–380.

MacKnight, J., *A New Literal Translation from the Original Greek of all the Apostolical Epistles: With a Commentary and Notes . . .* (Edinburgh: private publ., 1795; 2d ed. 1806; New York: M. W. Dodd, 1850), 49–138.

Maddalena, A., *La lettera ai Romani*, 2 vols. (Bologna: Pàtron, 1974–75).

Maier, A., *Commentar über den Brief Pauli an die Römer* (Freiburg im Breisgau: Herder, 1847).

Maillot, A., *L'Épître aux Romains: Épître de l'oecuménisme et théologie de l'histoire* (Paris: Le Centurion; Geneva: Labor et Fides, 1984).

Maly, E., *Romans*, New Testament Message 9 (Wilmington, Del.: Glazier, 1979; repr. 1990).

Manson, T. W., "Romans," *PCB*, 2d ed., 940–53.

Marsh, W., *A Brief Exposition of St. Paul's Epistle to the Romans* (London: Nisbet, 1865).

Martini, A., *Nuovo Testamento secondo la Volgata . . . con annotazioni . . .* , 6 vols., 2d ed. (Rome: Unione Cattolica Romana, 1958), 3.209–341.

Matthias, G. W., *Das dritte Capitel des Briefes an die Römer übersetzt und ausgelegt* (Cassel: T. Fischer, 1857).

Maunoury, A. F., *Commentaire sur l'épître de saint Paul aux Romains . . .* (Paris: Bloud et Barral, 1878).

Mehring, H. J. F., *Der Brief Pauli an die Roemer uebersetzt und erklaert: Erster Theil enthaltend die ersten fuenf Kapitel* (Stettin: T. von der Nahmer, 1859).

Meinhof, H., *Der Brief an die Römer: Eine volkstümliche Erklärung*, Das Wort des Heils (Hamburg: Agentur des Rauhen Hauses, 1919).

Menochius, J. S., *Totius sanctae Scripturae commentarius . . .* , 6 vols. (Lyons and Paris: Rusand, 1825), 6.1–79.

Meyer, H. A. W., *Der Brief an die Römer*, MeyerK 4 (Göttingen: Vandenhoeck & Ruprecht, 1836; 5th ed. 1872); *The Epistle to the Romans*, 2 vols. (Edinburgh: Clark, 1873–74; repr. 1884); *Critical and Exegetical Hand-Book to the Epistle to the Romans*, Meyer's Commentary on the New Testament, 2 vols., rev. W. P. Dickson and T. Dwight (New York: Funk & Wagnalls, 1889).

*Meyer, P. W., "Romans," *Harper's Bible Commentary*, ed. J. L. Mays (San Francisco, Calif.: Harper & Row, 1988), 1130–67.

*Michel, O., *Der Brief an die Römer*, MeyerK 4 (Göttingen: Vandenhoeck & Ruprecht, 1955; 14th ed. 1978).

Mickelsen, A. B., "The Epistle to the Romans," *The Wycliffe Bible Commentary*, ed. C. F. Pfeiffer and E. F. Harrison (Chicago, Ill.: Moody, 1962), 1179–1226.

Miller, J., *Commentary on Paul's Epistle to Romans: With an Excursus on the Famous Passage in James (chap. II:14–16)* (Princeton, N.J.: Evangelical Reform Publ. Co., 1887).

Mills, S. C., *A Hebrew Christian Looks at Romans* (Grand Rapids, Mich.: Dunham, 1968; New York: American Board of Missions to the Jews, 1971).

Moe, O., *Apostelen Paulus's Brev till Romerne: Innledet og fortolket* (Kristiania: Grøndahl, 1917).

Möhler, J. A., *Vorlesung zum Römerbrief*, ed. F. X. Reithmayr (Regensburg: Manz, 1845; repr. Frankfurt am Main: Minerva, 1972; new ed. by R. Rieger, Munich: E. Wewel, 1990).

Moffatt, J., *The Epistle to the Romans*, Literary Illustrations of the Bible 5 (New York: Armstrong & Son, 1905).

Monod, E., *Paraphrase de l'épître de saint Paul aux Romains conformément aux conclusions du commentaire de Frédéric Godet* (Neuchâtel: Delachaux et Niestlé, 1911).

*Moo, D., *Romans 1–8*, Wycliffe Exegetical Commentary (Chicago, Ill.: Moody, 1991).

Moody, C., "The Epistle of Paul the Apostle to the Romans," *The New Testament Expounded and Illustrated* . . . (New York: G. Lane & L. Stott, 1852), 315–59.

Moody, D., "Romans," *The Broadman Bible Commentary*, 12 vols., ed. C. J. Allen (Nashville, Tenn.: Broadman, 1969–72), 10.153–286.

*Morris, L., *The Epistle to the Romans* (Grand Rapids, Mich.: Eerdmans; Leicester, UK: Inter-Varsity, 1988).

Mortier, D. A., *L'Épître de saint Paul aux Romains: Simples commentaires pour la vie chrétienne* (Lille: Société Saint-Augustin; Paris and Bruges: Desclée de Brouwer, 1929).

Moule, H. C. G., *The Epistle of St Paul to the Romans*, Expositor's Bible (New York: Armstrong, 1894).

———, *The Epistle of Paul the Apostle to the Romans with Introduction and Notes*, Cambridge Bible for Schools and Colleges (Cambridge: Cambridge University Press, 1879; repr. 1891, 1894); renamed *Studies in Romans* (Grand Rapids, Mich.: Kregel, 1977).

*Murray, J., *The Epistle to the Romans: The English Text with Introduction, Exposition, and Notes*, NICNT, 2 vols.; London: Marshall, Morgan & Scott; Grand Rapids, Mich.: Eerdmans, 1959–65; repr. 1975).

Mynas, C. M. and A. Gerard, *Épîtres de saint Paul, traduites sur le texte grec* . . . (Paris: Chez les editeurs, 1838).

Myrberg, O. F., *Inledning till Romarbrefvet: Biblisk Afhandling* (Uppsala: W. Schultz, 1868).

———, *Pauli Bref till Romarena i ny öfversättning* (Uppsala: W. Schultz, 1871).

Nash, C. H., *Christ Interpreted: Paul's Letter to Romans* . . . (London: Marshall, Morgan & Scott, 1954).

The Navarre Bible, St. Paul's Epistles to the Romans and the Galatians in the Revised Standard Version and the New Vulgate with a Commentary by the Faculty of Theology, University of Navarre, trans. M. Adams (Dublin: Four Courts, 1990).

Neil, C., *Illustrated Notes on St. Paul's Epistle to the Romans* (London: Dickinson, 1877).

Newell, W. R., *Romans Verse by Verse* (Chicago: Moody, 1938; repr. 1975); *La epístola a los Romanos, versículo por versículo*, trans. R. H. Gould and R. Letona (Los Angeles, Calif.: Casa Bíblica de Los Angeles, 1949).

Newman, B. M. and E. A. Nida, *A Translator's Handbook on Paul's Letter to the Romans*, Helps for Translators 14 (London: UBS, 1973).

Niebergall, F., "Der Brief an die Römer," *Praktische Auslegung des Neuen Testaments für Prediger und Religionslehrer* (Tübingen: Mohr [Siebeck], 1914), 296–342.

Niemann, R., *Des Paulus Brief an die Römer für höhere Schulen ausgelegt* (Gütersloh: Bertelsmann, 1905).

Nygren, A., *Pauli Brev till Romarna*, Tolkning av Nya Testamentet 6 (Stockholm: Svenska Kyrkans Diakonistyrelses Bokförlag, 1944); *Der Römerbrief* (Göttingen: Vandenhoeck & Ruprecht, 1951); *Commentary on Romans* (Philadelphia, Penn.: Muhlenberg, 1949).

O'Connor, W. A., *A Commentary on the Epistle to the Romans* (London: Longmans, Green, 1871).

Odland, S., *Kommentar till Romare brevet: Översättning från Norskan* (Stockholm: Evangeliska Fosterlands-Stiftelsens Bokförlag, 1939).

Olbiols, S., *Epístoles de Sant Pau als Romans i als Corintis*, La Biblia: Versió dels textos originals in comentari 20 (Montserrat: Monestir de Montserrat, 1928), 33–155.

Olshausen, H., *Der Brief des Apostels Paulus an die Römer* (Königsberg: A. W. Unzer, 1835); *Biblical Commentary on the New Testament Adapted Especially for Preachers and Students . . . Containing the Epistle of St Paul to the Romans* (Edinburgh: Clark, 1849; repr. 1854).

————, *Die Briefe Pauli an die Römer und Korinther* (Königsberg: A. W. Unzer, 1837).

*Oltramare, H., *Commentaire sur l'épître aux Romains*, 2 vols. (Geneva: A. Cherbuliez, 1843; Paris: Fischbacher, 1881–82).

O'Neill, J. C., *Paul's Letter to the Romans*, Pelican New Testament Commentaries (Harmondsworth, UK: Penguin, 1975).

Ortloph, J. L. A., *Der Brief Pauli an die Römer übersetzt und ausgelegt*, 2 parts (Erlangen: Deichert, 1965–66).

Otto, C. W., *Commentar zum Römerbrief*, 2 parts (Glauchau: Peschke, 1886).

Otto, E., *Bibelstudien für die gebildete Gemeinde: Erklärung des Briefes Pauli an die Römer* (St. Louis, Mo.: A. Wiebusch & Son, 1883).

Paine, J. A., *Questions on the Epistle to the Romans: With a Theme from Each Verse* (New York: Randolph & Co., 1870).

Pallis, A., *To the Romans: A Commentary* (Liverpool: Liverpool Booksellers Co., 1920).

Parry, R. St J., *The Epistle of Paul the Apostle to the Romans*, Cambridge Greek Testament for Schools and Colleges (Cambridge: University Press, 1912; repr. 1921).

Parry, T., *A Practical Exposition of St. Paul's Epistle to the Romans . . .* (London: Rivington, 1832).

Paulus, H. E. G., *Des Apostels Paulus Lehr-Brief an die Galater- und Römer-Christen* (Heidelberg: Winter, 1831).

Peile, T. W., *Annotations on the Apostolical Epistles . . .* , vol. 1.1: *On the Epistle to the Romans* (London: Rivington, 1848–52; 2d ed. 1853).

Pelly, R. L., *St. Paul to the Romans* (London: SCM, 1917).

Perrot, C., *La carta a los Romanos*, Cuadernos biblicos 65 (Estella [Navarra]: Editorial Verbo Divino, 1989).

Pesch, R., *Römerbrief*, Neue Echter-Bibel 6 (Würzburg: Echter-Verlag, 1983).

Petersen, L. W. S., *Paulus' Brev til Romerne fortolket* (Copenhagen: Hagerup, 1900).

Pettingill, W. L., *Simple Studies in Romans*, 3d ed. (Philadelphia, Penn.: Philadelphia School of the Bible, 1915).

Pharmakides, T., *"Paulou tou apostolou hē pros Rhōmaious epistolē,"* Hē Kainē Diathēkē meta hypomnēmatōn archaiōn ekdidomenē (Athens: A. Angelides, 1842), 3.219–469.

Philippi, F. A., *Commentar über den Brief Pauli an die Römer* (Erlangen: Heyden, 1848–52; 3d ed. Frankfurt am Main: Heider & Zimmer, 1866); *Commentary on St. Paul's Epistle to the Romans*, 2 vols. (Edinburgh: Clark, 1878–79).

Pilch, J. J., *Galatians and Romans*, Collegeville Bible Commentary 6 (Collegeville, Minn.: Liturgical Press, 1983), 28–75.

Platts, J., "The Epistle of Paul the Apostle to the Romans," A *New Self-Interpreting Testament* . . . , 4 vols. (London: Robbins and Co., 1830), 3.3–118.

Plumer, W. S., *Commentary on Paul's Epistle to the Romans* (Edinburgh: Oliphants, 1871; repr. Grand Rapids, Mich.: Kregel, 1971).

Ponsot, H., *Une Introduction à la lettre aux Romains*, Initiations (Paris: Cerf, 1988).

Purdue, E., *A Commentary on the Epistle to the Romans, with a Revised Translation* (Dublin: Oldham, 1855).

Quimby, C. W., *The Great Redemption: A Living Commentary on Paul's Epistle to the Romans* (New York: Macmillan, 1950).

Ramazzotti, B., "Lettera ai Romani: Analisi con note di esegesi," *Il messagio della salvezza: Corso completo di studi biblici*, 6 vols. (Turin: Elle di Ci, 1966–79), 5.206–405.

Reiche, J. G., *Versuch einer ausführlichen Erklärung des Briefes Pauli an die Römer mit historischen Einleitungen und exegetisch-dogmatischen Excursen*, 2 vols. (Göttingen: Vandenhoeck & Ruprecht, 1833–34).

*Reuss, E. W. E., *La Bible, traduction nouvelle avec introductions et commentaires*, 16 multipart vols. (Paris: Sandoz et Fischbacher, 1874–81), vol. 13: *Les Épîtres pauliniennes*, 2 vols. in one (1878), 2.1–31.

Rhymer, J., *Good News in Romans: Romans in Today's English Version* (Cleveland, Oh.: Collins & World, 1975).

Rhys, H., *The Epistle to the Romans* (New York: Macmillan, 1961).

Richardson, J. R. and K. Chamblin, *The Epistle to the Romans*, Proclaiming the New Testament (Grand Rapids, Mich.: Baker, 1963), 7–166.

Richter, G., *Kritisch-polemische Untersuchungen über den Römerbrief*, BFCT 6 (Gütersloh: Bertelsmann, 1908).

Ridderbos, H., *Aan de Romeinen*, Commentaar op het Nieuwe Testament (Kampen: Kok, 1959; repr. 1977).

Riddle, M. B., *The Epistle of Paul to the Romans Explained* (New York: Scribners, 1884).

Ripley, H. J., *The Epistle of the Apostle Paul to the Romans, with Notes Chiefly Explanatory* . . . (Boston: Gould and Lincoln, 1857).

Robertson, A. T., "The Epistle to the Romans," *Word Pictures in the New Testament*, 4 vols. (New York: R. R. Smith, 1930–31), 4.320–430.

Robinson, J. A. T., *Wrestling with Romans* (Philadelphia, Penn.: Westminster, 1979).

Robinson, T., *A Suggestive Commentary on St. Paul's Epistle to the Romans, with Critical and Homiletical Notes*, 2 vols. (New York: Appleton, 1873; repr. London: Dickinson, 1878); repr. as *Studies in Romans: A Suggestive Commentary on Paul's Epistle to the Romans*, 2 vols. in one (Grand Rapids, Mich.: Kregel, 1982).

Rogland, R., *Romans* (Phillipsburg, N.J.: Presbyterian and Reformed Publ. Co., 1988).

Rolland, P., *A l'Écoute de l'épître aux Romains*, Lire la Bible (Paris: Cerf, 1991).

Rosenius, C. O., *Epistelen till de Romare*, 2 vols. (Chicago, Ill.: Engberg & Holmsberg Förlag, 1879).

Rosenmüller, J. G., "Scholia in epistolam Pauli ad Romanos," *Scholia in Novum Testamentum*, 5 vols., 6th ed. (Nuremberg: Felsecker, 1815–31), 3.515–799.

Rousseau, M., *L'Épître aux Romains* (Neuchâtel: Delachaux et Niestlé, 1960).

Rowles, W. P., *St. Paul's Epistle to the Romans* . . . (Nashville, Tenn.: Western Methodist Office, 1835).

Rückert, L. I., *Commentar über den Brief Pauli an die Römer* (Leipzig: Hartmann, 1831; 2d ed. [2 vols.] Leipzig: Volckmar, 1839).

Rutherford, W. G., *St. Paul's Epistle to the Romans: A New Translation with a Brief Analysis* (London: Macmillan, 1900).

Sacco, G., *L'Epistola ai Romani, nella versione della Volgata e nella versione dal greco* (Rome: Lateran Atheneum, 1935).

Sadler, M. F., *The Epistle to the Romans, with Notes Critical and Practical* (London: G. Bell & Sons, 1888; 2d ed. 1889; 3d ed. 1895).

Sales, M. M., *Il Nuovo Testamento commentato*, 2 vols. (Turin: Lega Italiana Cattolica Editrice, 1914), 2.13–103.

Sanday, W., *The Epistle to the Romans with Commentary* (London, Paris, and New York: Cassell, Petter, Galpin & Co., [1877]).

———, *The Epistle to the Romans*, ed. C. J. Ellicott (London: Cassell, [1883?]).

*——— and A. C. Headlam, *A Critical and Exegetical Commentary on the Epistle to the Romans*, ICC (Edinburgh: Clark, 1895; 5th ed. 1902; repr. 1962).

Schaefer, A., *Erklärung des Briefes an die Römer* (Münster in Westfalen: Aschendorff, 1891).

Schaff, P. (ed.), "The Epistle of Paul to the Romans," *A Popular Commentary on the New Testament by English and American Scholars of Various Evangelical Denominations*, 4 vols. (New York: Scribners, 1879–83), 3.10–155.

Schlatter, A. von, *Der Brief an die Römer, ausgelegt für Bibelleser*, Erläuterungen zum Neuen Testament 5 (Calw and Stuttgart: Verlag der Vereinsbuchhandlung, 1895; 8th ed.: Calwer, 1928).

*―――, Gottes Gerechtigkeit: Ein Kommentar zum Römerbrief (Stuttgart: Calwer, 1935; 4th ed. 1965; 6th ed., with preface by P. Stuhlmacher, 1991).

*Schlier, H., Der Römerbrief: Kommentar, HTKNT 6 (Freiburg im Breisgau, Herder, 1977).

*Schmidt, H. W., Der Brief des Paulus an die Römer, Theologischer Handkommentar zum Neuen Testament 6 (Berlin: Evangelische Verlagsanstalt, 1963; 3d ed. 1972).

Schmithals, W., Der Römerbrief: Ein Kommentar (Gütersloh: Mohn, 1988).

Scholz, M. A., "Der Brief des Apostels Paulus an die Christen zu Rom," Die heilige Schrift des Neuen Testaments, 4 vols. (Frankfurt am Main: Varrentrapp, 1828–30), 3.39–118.

Schott, T., Der Römerbrief seinem Endzweck und Gedankengang nach ausgelegt (Erlangen: Deichert, 1858).

Schulte, A., Der Brief an die Römer übersetzt und erklärt (Regensburg: G. J. Manz, 1897).

Schumacher, H., Glaubensgerechtigkeit und Geistesherrlichkeit: Der Römerbrief aus dem Grundtext übersetzt und erläutert (Stuttgart: Paulus Verlag K. Gyer, 1967).

Scott, C. A., "Romans," The Abingdon Bible Commentary, ed. F. C. Eiselen et al. (New York: Abingdon, 1929), 1135–68.

Scott, E. F., Paul's Epistle to the Romans, 2d ed. (London: SCM, 1947; repr. Westport, Conn.: Greenwood, 1979).

Shedd, W. G. T., A Critical and Doctrinal Commentary upon the Epistle of St. Paul to the Romans (New York: Scribners, 1879; repr. Grand Rapids, Mich.: Zondervan, 1967).

Shuttleworth, P. N., A Paraphrastic Translation of the Apostolical Epistles, with Notes (Oxford: W. Baxter, 1829).

Sickenberger, J., Die beiden Briefe des heiligen Paulus an die Korinther und sein Brief an die Römer, Die heilige Schrift des Neuen Testaments [Bonnerbibel] 6 (Bonn: Hanstein, 1919; 4th ed. 1932).

Slade, J., Annotations on the Epistles: Being a Continuation of Mr. Elsley's Annotations . . . , 2 vols. (London: Private publ., 1816; 2d ed. London: Rivington, 1824).

Smink, G. G., Romeinen (Kampen: Kok, 1986).

Stagg, F., Galatians—Romans, Knox Preaching Guides (Atlanta, Ga.: John Knox, 1980).

Stahn, J. and R., Der Brief des Paulus an die Römer: Aus dem Griechischen übersetzt (Halle an der Saale: Von Canstein, n.d. [1920s]).

Stam, C. R., Commentary on the Epistle of Paul to the Romans (Chicago, Ill.: Berean Bible Society, 1981).

Steenkiste, J.-A. van, Commentarius in omnes s. Pauli epistolas ad usum seminariorum et cleri, 5th ed. (Bruges: Beyaert, 1892), 1.42–218.

Stellhorn, F. W., *The Epistle of St. Paul to the Romans* (Columbus, Oh.: Lutheran Book Concern, 1918).

Stenersen, S. J., *Epistolae paulinae perpetuo commentario illustratae*, vol. 1: *Ep. ad Rom* . . . (Oslo: Grøndahl, 1829–34).

Stengel, L., *Commentar über den Brief des Apostels Paulus an die Römer*, ed. J. Beck (Freiburg im Breisgau: Wagner, 1836).

Stifler, J. M., *The Epistle to the Romans: A Commentary, Logical and Historical* (New York: F. H. Revell, 1897; repr. Chicago, Ill.: Moody, 1960).

Stöckhardt, G., *Commentar über den Brief an die Römer* (St. Louis, Mo.: Concordia Publ. House, 1907).

Stolz, J. J., "Paulus an die Römer," *Erläuterungen zum Neuen Testament* . . . , 6 facsicles, 3d ed. (Hannover: Hahn, 1806–11), 3.129–216.

Storr, R., *Der Brief des heiligen Apostels Paulus an die Römer: Ausgedeutet für Menschen unserer Zeit* (Stuttgart: Schwabenverlag, 1950).

Storrer, J., *Der Brief Pauli an die Römer, nach den Gesetzen der Logik bearbeitet und übersetzt* (Buffalo, N.Y.: Haas & Klein, 1890).

Stuart, M., *A Commentary on the Epistle to the Romans with a Translation and Various Excursus* (Andover, Mass.: Gould and Newman, 1827; repr. New York: J. Leavitt, 1832; 4th ed., rev. R. D. C. Robbins, Andover, Mass.: Draper, 1859; repr. 1862).

*Stuhlmacher, P., *Der Brief an die Römer übersetzt und erklärt*, NTD 6, 14th ed. (Göttingen: Vandenhoeck & Ruprecht, 1989).

Summers, T. O., *The Epistle of Paul, the Apostle, to the Romans, in the Authorized Version: With a New Translation and Commentary* (Nashville, Tenn.: Southern Methodist Publ. House, 1881).

Sumner, J. B., *A Practical Exposition of the Epistle of St. Paul to the Romans and the First Epistle to the Corinthians, in the Form of Lectures* (London: J. Hatchard, 1843).

Taylor, V., *The Epistle to the Romans*, Epworth Preacher's Commentaries (London: Epworth, 1956; 2d ed. 1962).

Terrot, C. H., *The Epistle of Paul the Apostle to the Romans: With an Introduction, Paraphrase and Notes* (London: Hatchard and Son; Edinburgh: Black, 1828).

Theofana (Feofan), Bp., *Tolkovanīe . . . poslaniya sv. Apostola Pavla k Rymliyanam*, 2 vols. (Moscow: I. Efimova, 1890).

Theissen, A., "The Epistle to the Romans," *CCHS*, 1045–80; rev. by P. Byrne, *NCCHS*, 1103–42.

Tholuck, F. A. G., *Commentar zum Briefe Pauli an die Römer* (Halle an der Saale: Anton, 1824; 5th ed. 1856); *Exposition of St. Paul's Epistle to the Romans* . . . , 2 vols., Biblical Cabinet 5.12 (Edinburgh: Clark, 1833–36).

———, *Umschreibende Uebersetzung des Briefes Pauli an die Römer* (Berlin: F. Dümmler, 1825; 2d ed. 1831).

Thomas, W. H. G., *Romans: A Devotional Commentary*, 3 vols. (London: Religious Tract Society, n.d.; repr. Grand Rapids, Mich.: Eerdmans, 1911–12?).

Thomson, G. T. and F. Davidson, *The New Bible Commentary*, ed. F. Davidson (Grand Rapids, Mich.: Eerdmans, 1953), 939–66.

Torti, G., *La lettera ai Romani: Testo, traduzione, introduzione e commento*, Studi biblici 41 (Brescia: Paideia, 1977).

Toussaint, C., *Les Épîtres de saint Paul: Leçons d'exégèse, II. L'Épître aux Romains*, 2 vols. (Paris: Beauchesne, 1910–13).

Townsend, G., "The Epistle to the Romans," *The New Testament Arranged in Historical and Chronological Order with Copious Notes . . .* , ed. T. W. Coit (Boston: Perkins and Marevin, 1837), 289–314, 360–64.

Trapp, J., "A Commentary or Exposition upon the Epistle of St Paul to the Romans," *A Commentary on the New Testament*, ed. W. Webster, 3d ed. (London: R. D. Dickinson, 1877), 489–518.

Trenchard, E., *Una exposición de la epístola a los Romanos* (Madrid: E. B., 1976).

Trollope, W., "Romans," *Analecta theologica: Digested and Arranged Compendium of the Most Approved Commentaries on the New Testament*, 2 vols. (London: T. Cadell, 1830–35), 2.324–83.

Turnbull, J., *The Epistle of Paul to the Romans: An Original Translation from the Greek Text* (London: Bagster, 1851).

Turner, S. H., *The Epistle to the Romans in Greek and English: With an Analysis and Exegetical Commentary* (New York: Standford and Swords, 1853; rev. ed. 1855).

————, *Notes on the Epistle to the Romans . . .* (New York: T. and J. Swords, 1824).

Turrado, L., "Epistola a los Romanos," *Biblia comentada: Texto de la Nágar-Colunga*, ed. Profesores de Salamanca, BAC 196, 201, 209, 218, 239, 243, 249, 7 vols. (Madrid: Editorial católica, 1960–65), 6.251–368.

Tyson, W., *Expository Lectures on the Epistle of Paul the Apostle to the Romans* (London: Wesleyan-Methodist Book Room, 1882).

Umbreit, F. W. C., *Der Brief an die Römer auf dem Grunde des Alten Testamentes ausgelegt* (Gotha: Perthes, 1856).

Valpy, E., "Paulou tou apostolou hē pros Rhōmaious epistolē," *Hē Kainē Diathēkē: The New Testament with English Notes Critical, Philological, and Explanatory*, (3 vols., 4th ed. (London: Longman & Co., 1836), 2.296–382.

Vanderlip, G., *Paul and Romans* (Valley Forge, Penn.: Judson, 1967).

Vanni, U., *Lettere ai Galati e ai Romani: Versione, introduzione, note* (Rome: Edizioni Paoline, 1967).

Vaughan, C. J., *Pros Rhōmaious: St. Paul's Epistle to the Romans with Notes* (London, Cambridge, and New York: Macmillan, 1859; rev. ed., 1861); repr. as *Romans* (Grand Rapids, Mich.: Zondervan, 1976).

————, and B. Corley, *Romans*, Study Guide Commentaries (Grand Rapids, Mich.: Zondervan, 1976).

Veldhuizen, A. van, *Paulus en zijn brief aan de Romeinen*, 2d ed. (Groningen: Wolters, 1918).

Viard, A., "Épître aux Romains traduite et commentée," *La sainte Bible*, ed. L. Pirot and A. Clamer, 12 vols. (Paris: Letouzey et Ané, 1935–46), 11.2.7–159.

*———, *Saint Paul: Épître aux Romains*, Sources bibliques, 2d ed. (Paris: Gabalda, 1975).

Vicentini, J. I., "Carta a los Romanos," *La sagrada escritura*, ed. Profesores de la Companía de Jesús, 3 vols., BAC 207, 211, 214 (Madrid: Editorial católica, 1961–62), 2.171–327.

Vine, W. E., *The Epistle to the Romans* (London: Pickering & Inglis, 1935).

Volkmar, G., *Paulus Römerbrief: Das älteste Text deutsch und im Zusammenhang erklärt: Mit dem Wortabdruck der vatikanischen Urkunde* (Zurich: C. Schmidt, 1875).

Walford, W., *Notes on the Epistle to the Romans, with a Revised Translation* (London: Jackson and Walford, 1846).

Walther, J., *Paraphrase de l'Épître aux Romains avec notes et texte en regard* (Lausanne: G. Bridel, 1871).

Wardlaw, R., *Lectures on the Epistle to the Romans*, 3 vols. (Edinburgh: Fullarton, 1861–64).

Webster, W. and W. F. Wilkinson, "Paulou tou apostolou hē pros Rhōmaious epistolē," *The Greek Testament with Notes Grammatical and Exegetical*, 2 vols. (London: Parker, Son, and Bourn, 1855–61), 2.353–459.

Weingart, J. F., *Commentarius perpetuus in Pauli epistolam ad Romanos . . .* (Gotha: Ettinger, 1816).

*Weiss, B., *Der Brief an die Römer*, MeyerK 4 (Göttingen: Vandenhoeck & Ruprecht, 1881; 4th ed. 1899); "The Epistle of Paul the Apostle to the Romans," *A Commentary on the New Testament*, 4 vols., trans. G. H. Schodde and E. Wilson (New York and London: Funk & Wagnalls, 1906), 3.1–146.

———, "Pros Rhōmaious," *Die paulinischen Briefe im berechtigen Text . . .* (Leipzig: Hinrichs, 1896), 20–128.

———, "An die Römer," *Das Neue Testament nach D. Martin Luthers berechtiger Übersetzung mit fortlaufender Erläuterung versehen*, 2 vols. (Leipzig; Hinrichs, 1904), 2.3–79.

Wenger, J. C., *A Lay Guide to Romans* (Scottdale, Penn.: Herald, 1983).

Wenham, A. E., *Ruminations on the Epistle of Paul the Apostle to the Romans* (London: Passmore & Alabaster, 1904).

Wesley, J., *Explanatory Notes upon the New Testament* (New York: Lane & Tippett, 1847; repr. Nashville, Tenn.: Methodist Evangelistic Materials, [1962?]), 358–406.

Whedon, D. D., "The Epistle to the Romans," *Commentary on the New Testament: Intended for Popular Use*, 5 vols. (New York: Phillips & Hunt, 1860–80), 3.283–402.

Whitby, D., "A Paraphrase with Annotations on the Epistle to the Romans," *A Paraphrase and Commentary on the New Testament*, 2 vols., 10th ed. (London: Longman, Hurst, Rees, and Orme, 1808), 2.1–98.

White, J. T., *St. Paul's Epistle to the Romans* (London: Longmans & Co., 1877).

Whitwell, W. A., A Translation of Paul's Epistle to the Romans: With an Introduction and Notes (Boston: W. Crosby and H. P. Nichols, 1848).

*Wilckens, U., Der Brief an die Römer, EKK 6.1–3, 3 vols. (Neukirchen-Vluyn: Neukirchener-Verlag; Einsiedeln: Benziger: 1978–82).

Williams, H. W., An Exposition of St. Paul's Epistle to the Romans (London: Wesleyan Conference, 1869).

Williams, N. P., "The Epistle to the Romans," A New Commentary on Holy Scripture Including the Apocrypha, ed. C. Gore et al. (London: SPCK, 1929), 442–84.

Williams, W. G., An Exposition of the Epistle of Paul to the Romans (Cincinnati, Oh.: Jennings and Pye; New York: Eaton and Mains, 1902).

Wilson, G. B., Romans: A Digest of Reformed Comment (Edinburgh: Banner of Trust, 1977).

Winters, H., Commentary on Romans (Greenville, S.C.: Carolina Christian, 1985).

Woods, F. T., The Epistle to the Romans . . . (London: Cassell, 1927).

Wordsworth, C., "The Epistle to the Romans," The New Testament of Our Lord and Saviour Jesus Christ in the Original Greek with Introduction and Notes, 2 vols., 4th ed. (London: Rivington, 1866), 2.185–273.

Wuest, K. S., Romans in the Greek New Testament for the English Reader (Grand Rapids, Mich.: Eerdmans, 1955).

*Zahn, T., Der Brief des Paulus an die Römer ausgelegt, Kommentar zum Neuen Testament 6 (Leipzig: Deichert, 1910; 3d ed. 1925).

Zedda, S., "Lettera ai Romani," Prima lettura di San Paolo, 3 vols. (Turin: Tecnograph, 1958–60), 2.193–322.

*Zeller, D., Der Brief an die Römer übersetzt und erklärt, RNT (Regensburg: Pustet, 1985).

*Ziesler, J., Paul's Letter to the Romans, TPINTC (London: SCM; Philadelphia, Penn.: Trinity Press International, 1989).

Zimmer, F., Der Römerbrief übersetzt und kurz erklärt (Quedlinburg: F. Vieweg, 1887).

Zorn, C. M., Der Brief an die Römer in Briefen an Glaubensbrüder (Zwickau, Saxony: J. Herrmann, n.d.).

V. MONOGRAPHS ON ROMANS

Aletti, J.-N., Comment Dieu est-il juste? (Paris: Éditions du Seuil, 1991).

Anon., Lectures Doctrinal and Practical on the Epistle of the Apostle Paul to the Romans (Edinburgh: Blackwood; London: Cadell, 1838).

———, Salvation by Faith: Aspects of Pauline Soteriology in Romans, Proceedings of the Seventeenth Meeting of the New Testament Society of South Africa . . . Stellenbosch, 21st–23d July 1981 (Stellenbosch: University, 1982 [= Neotestamentica 15]).

Barnhouse, D. G., Exposition of Bible Doctrines, Taking the Epistle to the Romans as a Point of Departure, 5 vols. (Grand Rapids, Mich.: Eerdmans, 1958; repr. 1982).

Barth, M. et al. (eds.), *Foi et salut selon S. Paul (Épître aux Romains 1,16)*, AnBib 42 (Rome: Biblical Institute, 1970).

Beker, J. C., "Romans," *The Books of the Bible*, 2 vols., ed. B. W. Anderson (New York: Scribners, 1989), 2.229–43.

Blackwelder, B. W., *Toward Understanding Romans: An Introduction and Exegetical Translation* (Anderson, Ind.: Warner, 1962).

Brakel, J. E. van, *De gerechtigheid Gods: Kerngedachten uit de brief van Paulus aan de Romeinen*, "Uit de wijngaard des Heren" (Lochen: De Tijdstroom, n.d.).

Brauch, M. T., *Set Free to Be* (Valley Forge, Penn.: Judson, 1975).

Brockhaus, R., *Gedanken über den Brief an die Römer* ([Wuppertal-]Elberfeld: Brockhaus, 1930).

Bryan, C., *Way of Freedom: An Introduction to the Epistle to the Romans with Study Guide* (New York: Seabury, 1975).

Buddeus, J. F., *Erbauliche Betrachtungen über die Epistel an die Römer* (Jena: J. Meyers sel. Witwe, 1728).

Campbell, W. S., *Paul's Gospel in an Intercultural Context: Jew and Gentile in the Letter to the Romans*, Studien zur interkulturellen Geschichte des Christentums 69 (Frankfurt am Main: Peter Lang, 1991).

Carpenter, S. C., *A Paraphrase of Selections from St. Paul's Epistle to the Romans* (London: SPCK, 1948).

Darby, J. N., *Notes on Romans*, 2d ed. (London: Crocket & Cooper, n.d.).

Davies, G. N., *Faith and Obedience in Romans: A Study in Romans 1–4*, JSNTSup 39 (Sheffield, UK: JSOT, 1990).

Davis, R. L., *Becoming a Whole Person in a Broken World: Studies in the Book of Romans* (Grand Rapids, Mich.: Discovery House, 1990).

Diderichsen, B. K., *Paulus Romanus: Et analytisk Bidrag til Romerbrevets aeldste Historie*, Teologiske Studier 1, *DTT*, II Afd. (Copenhagen: Gad, 1941).

Elkins, G. and T. B. Warren, *The Book of Romans* (Jonesboro, Ariz.: National Christian Press, 1983).

Engelke, F., *Der Brief des Paulus an die Römer und an uns: Sein Gedankengehalt in neuer Sprache für unsere Zeit* (Hamburg; Agentur des Rauhen Hauses, 1928).

Erdös, J. von, *Biblisch-theologische Analyse des Römerbriefs* (Amsterdam: Scheffer & Co., 1891).

Evans, W., *Romans and I and II Corinthians* (New York: F. H. Revell, 1918).

Forrester, E. J., *A Righteousness of God for Unrighteous Men: Being an Exposition of the Epistle to the Romans* (Nashville, Tenn.: Sunday School Board of the Southern Baptist Convention; New York: G. H. Doran, 1926).

Fritzsche, C. F. A., *Ueber die Verdienste des . . . D. August Tholuck um die Schrifterklärung: Ein Sendschreiben an ihn und ein Beitrag zur wissenschaftlichen Erklärung des Briefes Pauli an die Römer* (Halle an der Saale: Gebauer, 1831).

Grenholm, C., *Romans Interpreted: A Comparative Analysis of the Commentaries of Barth, Nygren, Cranfield and Wilckens on Paul's Epistle to the Romans*, Acta

Universitatis Upsaliensis, Studia Doctrinae Christianae Upsaliensia 30 (Uppsala: Almqvist & Wiksell, 1990).

Griffith, A. L., *The Roman Letter Today* (London: Lutterworth, 1960).

Griffith, G. O., *St. Paul's Gospel to the Romans* (Oxford: Blackwell, 1949).

Grossmann, H., *Gedanken über den Römer-Brief* (Kassel: Oncken, 1935).

Harrison, N. B., *His Salvation as Set Forth in the Book of Romans*, 2d ed. (Chicago, Ill.: Bible Institute Colportage Assoc., 1926).

Haussleiter, J., *Der Glaube Jesu Christi und der christliche Glaube: Ein Beitrag zur Erklärung des Römerbriefes* (Erlangen and Leipzig: Deichert, 1891).

Hoyt, H. A., *The First Christian Theology: Studies in Romans* (Grand Rapids, Mich.: Baker, 1977).

Hultgren, A., *Paul's Gospel and Mission: The Outlook from His Letter to the Romans* (Philadelphia, Penn.: Fortress, 1985).

Ironside, H. A., *Lectures on the Epistle to the Romans* (New York: Loizeaux, 1928).

Jüngel, E. and D. Rössler, *Gefangenes Ich, befreiender Geist: 2 Tübinger Römerbrief-Auslegungen* (Munich: Kaiser, 1976).

Kaylor, R. D., *Paul's Covenant Community: Jew and Gentile in Romans* (Atlanta, Ga.: John Knox, 1988).

Keble, J., *Studia sacra: Commentaries on the Introductory Verses of St. John's Gospel, and on a Portion of St. Paul's Epistle to the Romans, with Other Theological Papers* (Oxford and London: J. Parker and Co., 1877).

Kögel, R., *Der Brief Pauli an die Römer in Predigten dargelegt: Ein homiletischer Versuch*, 3d ed. (Bremen and Leipzig: E. Müller, 1891).

Kraemer, R., *Weltweit wirkende Gotteskraft: Erläuterungen und Gedanken zum Römerbrief* (Wernigerode: Koezle, 1920).

Krug, H., *Paulus-Worte für Heute und Jedermann, nach Römer- und Erstem Korintherbrief in Dichtung geschrieben* (Zurich: Panta-Verlag, 1951).

Kürzinger, J., *Der Schritt ins Göttliche: Gedanken aus dem Römerbrief* (Würzburg: Echter-Verlag, 1941).

Kutter, H., *Gerechtigkeit (Röm 1–8)* (Berlin: Evangelische Verlagsanstalt, 1908).

Lackmann, M., *Vom Geheimnis der Schöpfung: Die Geschichte der Exegese von Römer I, 18–23, II, 14–16 und Acta XIV, 15–17, XVII, 22–29 vom 2. Jahrhundert bis zum Beginn der Orthodoxie* (Stuttgart: Evangelische Verlagsanstalt, 1952).

Latham, J. H., *Theories of Philosophy and Religion Compared with the Christian Theory as Set Forth by St. Paul in His Letter to the Romans now Newly Translated, with Notes* (London: Longmans, Green and Co., 1871).

Lee, E. K., *A Study in Romans* (London: SPCK, 1962).

Leeuwen, J.-A. C. van, *De joodsche achtergrond van den Brief aan de Romeinen* (Utrecht: Breijer, 1894).

Longenecker, B. W., *Eschatology and the Covenant: A Comparison of 4 Ezra and Romans 1–11*, JSNTSup 57 (Sheffield, UK: Academic Press, 1991).

Lorenz, O., *Das Lehrsystem im Römerbrief* (Breslau: Woywod, 1884).

Lütgert, W., *Der Römerbrief als historisches Problem*, BFCT 17.2 (Gütersloh: Bertelsmann, 1913).

Lyonnet, S., *Les Étapes de l'histoire du salut selon l'Épître aux Romains*, Bibliothèque oecuménique 8 (Paris: Cerf, 1969).

————, *Études sur l'épître aux Romains*, AnBib 120 (Rome: Biblical Institute, 1989).

————, *Le Message de l'épître aux Romains* (Paris: Cerf, 1971).

————, *La storia della salvezza nella lettera ai Romani*, Historia salutis 3 (Naples: M. d'Auria, 1966).

Mackay, B. S., *Freedom of the Christian: Galatians and Romans*, Bible Guides 16 (London: Lutterworth; New York: Abingdon, 1965), 45–96.

McRealsham, E. D. (= C. M. Mead), *Romans Dissected: A Critical Analysis of the Epistle to the Romans* (Edinburgh: Clark, 1891); *Der Römerbrief beurtheilt und geviertheilt* (Erlangen: Deichert, 1891).

Mangold, W., *Der Römerbrief und die Anfänge der römischen Gemeinde: Eine kritische Untersuchung* (Marburg: Elwert, 1866).

————, *Der Römerbrief und seine geschichtlichen Voraussetzungen neu untersucht* (Marburg: Elwert, 1884).

Maurer, I. S., "Allusions to the Epistle to the Romans in *Paradise Lost*: A Comparison of Their Contents in the Light of Reformation Theology," Ph.D. diss., Catholic University of America, 1981.

Mayer, G., *Der Römerbrief in religiösen Betrachtungen für das moderne Bedürfnis*, 2d ed. (Gütersloh: Bertelsmann, 1913).

Mehring, H. J. F., *Das Sündenregister im Römerbriefe* . . . (Wriezen an der Oder: Roeder, 1854).

Moore, W. E., *Stronger than Rome: The Epistle to the Romans in Dialogue* (Wallington, Surrey, UK: Religious Education, 1963).

Morrison, G. H., *Morrison on Romans and I & II Corinthians*, rev. J. Zodhiates (Chattanooga, Tenn.: AMG Publishers, 1982).

Mounce, R. H., *Themes from Romans* (Ventura, Calif.: Regal Books, 1981).

Moxnes, H., *Theology in Conflict: Studies in Paul's Understanding of God in Romans*, NovTSup 53 (Leiden: Brill, 1980).

Mussner, F., *Mort et resurrection: Sermons bibliques pour le Carême sur les passages de la Lettre aux Romains* (Mulhouse: Editions Salvator; Paris: Casterman, 1968).

Ockenga, H. J., *Every One That Believeth: Expository Addresses on St. Paul's Epistle to the Romans* (New York: F. H. Revell, 1942).

Paisley, I. R. K., *An Exposition of the Epistle to the Romans* (London: Marshall, Morgan & Scott, 1968).

Palmer, E. F., *Salvation by Surprise: Studies in the Book of Romans* (Waco, Tex.: Word Books, 1975).

Pridham, A., *Notes and Reflections on the Epistle to the Romans* (Bath: Binns and Goodwin, [1851]; 3d ed. London: W. Yapp, 1864).

Prümm, K., *Die Botschaft des Römerbriefes: Ihr Aufbau und Gegenwartswert* (Freiburg im Breisgau: Herder, 1960).

Ravasi, G. F., *Lettera ai Romani: Ciclo di conferenze tenute al Centro Culturale S. Fedele di Milano*, Conversazioni bibliche (Bologna: Dehoniane, 1990).

Raven, C. E., *Good News of God: Being Eight Letters Dealing with Present Problems and Based upon Romans I–VIII* (New York and London: Harper & Bros., [1943]; repr. London: Hodder and Stoughton, 1944).

Richter, G., *Kritisch-polemische Untersuchungen über den Römerbrief*, BFCT 12.6 (Gütersloh: Bertelsmann, 1908).

Rolland, P., *Épître aux Romains: Texte grec structuré* (Rome: Biblical Institute, 1980).

Schelkle, K.-H., *The Epistle to the Romans: Theological Meditations* (New York: Herder and Herder, 1964).

———, *Paulus Lehrer der Väter: Die altkirchliche Auslegung von Römer 1–11* (Düsseldorf: Patmos, 1956; 2d ed. 1959).

———, *Wort und Schrift: Beiträge zur Auslegung und Auslegungsgeschichte des Neuen Testaments* (Düsseldorf: Patmos, 1966), 216–26, 227–38, 239–50, 251–72, 273–99.

Schieder, J., *Wider die Verzweiflung: Das Wort des Römerbriefes* (Gütersloh: Rufer-Verlag, 1953).

Schlatter, A. von, *Die Botschaft des Paulus: Eine Übersicht über den Römerbrief* (Velbert im Rheinland: Freizeiten-Verlag, 1928).

Schmithals, W., *Der Römerbrief als historisches Problem*, SNT 9 (Gütersloh: Mohn, 1975).

Schmitz, R., *Rechtfertigung und Heiligung durch den Glauben: Sünde und Gnade nach dem Römerbrief* (Witten [Ruhr]: Bundes-Verlag, 1960).

Simonis, W., *Der gefangene Paulus: Die Entstehung des sogenannten Römerbriefs und anderer urchristlicher Schriften in Rom* (Frankfurt, Bern, New York, and Paris: Peter Lang, 1990).

Smart, J. D., *Doorway to a New Age: A Study of Paul's Letter to the Romans* (Philadelphia, Penn.: Westminster, 1972).

Snider, T. M., *The Continuity of Salvation: A Study of Paul's Letter to the Romans* (Jefferson, N.C. and London: McFarland & Co., 1984).

Sobraquès, S., *Commentaires sur l'Épître aux Romains d'après la traduction de l'épître faite par Edouard Reuss* (Perpignan: Capcir, 1960).

Starkey, L. M., Jr., *Romans: A Revolutionary Manifesto* (Nashville, Tenn. and New York: Abingdon, 1973).

Steele, D. N. and C. C. Thomas, *Romans: An Interpretive Outline: A Study Manual of Romans, Including a Series of Interpretive Notes and Charts on the Major Doctrines of the Epistle* (Philadelphia, Penn.: Presbyterian and Reformed Publ. Co., 1963).

Steinke, P. L., *With Eyes Wide Open: Biblical Studies in Romans for Young People* (St. Louis: Concordia Publ. House, 1974).

Steinmeyer, F. L., *Studien über den Brief des Paulus an die Römer*, 2 vols. (Berlin: Wiegandt und Grieben, 1894–95).

Stott, J. R. W., *Men Made New: An Exposition of Romans 5–8* (Chicago, Ill.: Inter-Varsity, 1966).

Takeda, T., "Israel und die Völker: Die Israel-Lehre des Völkerapostels Paulus in ihrer Bedeutung für uns gojim/ethne-Christen: Ein Weg zur Rezeption Israels als ein Weg zur biblischen Theologie," Ph.D. diss., Freie Universität, Berlin, 1981.

Talbot, L. T., *Addresses on Romans*, 2d ed. (Wheaton, Ill.: Van Kampen, 1936).

Thielman, F., *From Plight to Salvation: A Jewish Framework to Understanding Paul's View of the Law in Galatians and Romans*, NovTSup 61 (Leiden: Brill, 1989).

Tholuck, A., *Umschreibende Uebersetzung des Briefes Pauli an die Römer*, 2d ed. (Berlin: Dümmler, 1831).

Throckmorton, B. H., *Adopted in Love: Contemporary Studies in Romans* (New York: Seabury, 1978).

———, *Romans for the Layman* (Philadelphia, Penn.: Westminster, 1961).

Tyndale, W., *A Compendious Introduccion/Prologe or Preface unto the Pistle off Paul to the Romayns* (no place, no publ., n.d.; repr. Amsterdam: Theatrum Orbis Terrarum; Norwood, N.J.: Johnson, 1975).

Völter, D., *Die Komposition der paulinischen Hauptbriefe: I. Der Römer- und Galaterbrief* (Tübingen: Heckenhauer, 1890).

Wangerin, M. E., *The Lutheran Confessions and St. Paul's Epistle to the Romans* (St. Louis, Mo.: no publ., 1978).

Watson, T., *The Divine Comforts* (= *A Divine Cordial* [1663]; Swengel, Penn.: Reiner, 1964).

Wcela, E. A., *Paul the Theologian: His Teaching in the Letter to the Romans*, God's Word Today 8 (New York: Pueblo, 1977).

Weber, E., *Die Beziehungen von Röm. 1–3 zur Missionspraxis des Paulus* (Gütersloh: Bertelsmann, 1905).

Westcott, F. B., *St Paul and Justification: Being an Exposition of the Teaching in the Epistles to Rome and Galatia* (London: Macmillan, 1913).

Willer, A., *Der Römerbrief—Eine dekalogische Komposition*, Arbeiten zur Theologie 66 (Stuttgart: Calwer, 1981).

Woods, F. T., *The Epistle to the Romans: A Little Library of Exposition—With New Studies* (London: Cassell & Co., [1927]).

Zeller, D., *Juden und Heiden in der Mission des Paulus: Studien zum Römerbrief*, FB 8 (Stuttgart: Katholisches Bibelwerk, 1973; 2d ed. 1976).

Zweynert, G., *Die Übermacht der Gnade: Handreichung zur 30. Bibelwoche im Jahre des Reformationsgedenkens 1967 über ausgewählte Texte aus dem Römerbrief* (Berlin: Christlicher Zeitschriftenverlag, [1967]).

VI. MONOGRAPHS ON GENERAL PAULINE TOPICS

Anderson, H. G. et al., *Justification by Faith*, Lutherans and Catholics in Dialogue 7 (Minneapolis, Minn.: Augsburg, 1985), 58–68.

Barrett, C. K., *From First Adam to Last: A Study in Pauline Theology* (London: Black, 1962), 92–119.

Barth, M., *Justification: Pauline Texts Interpreted in the Light of the Old and New Testaments* (Grand Rapids, Mich.: Eerdmans, 1971).

Baum G., *The Jews and the Gospel: A Reexamination of the New Testament* (London: Bloomsbury; Westminster, Md.: Newman, 1961), 208–65.

Baumgarten, J., *Paulus und die Apokalyptik*, WMANT 44 (Neukirchen-Vluyn: Neukirchener-Verlag, 1975).

Beker, J. C., *Paul the Apostle: The Triumph of God in Life and Thought* (Philadelphia, Penn.: Fortress, 1980).

———, *Paul's Apocalyptic Gospel: The Coming Triumph of God* (Philadelphia, Penn.: Fortress, 1982).

Blank, J., *Paulus: Von Jesus zum Christentum: Aspekte der paulinischen Lehre und Praxis* (Munich: Kösel, 1982).

Boer, W. P. de, *The Imitation of Paul: An Exegetical Study* (Kampen: Kok, 1962).

Bonsirven, J., *Exégèse rabbinique et exégèse paulinienne*, Bibliothèque de théologie historique (Paris: Beauchesne, 1939).

Bornkamm, G., *Early Christian Experience* (London: SCM; Philadelphia, Penn.: Westminster, 1969).

———, *Das Ende des Gesetzes: Paulusstudien*, BEvT 16 (Munich: Kaiser, 1952).

———, *Paul* (New York: Harper & Row, 1971).

Bouttier, M., *Christianity According to Paul*, SBT 49 (London: SCM; Naperville, Ill.: Allenson, 1966).

———, *En Christ: Études d'exégèse et de théologie pauliniennes*, Études d'histoire et de philosophie religieuses 54 (Paris: Presses universitaires de France, 1962).

Braumann, G., *Vorpaulinische christliche Taufverkündigung bei Paulus*, BWANT 82 (Stuttgart: Kohlhammer, 1962).

Bruce, F. F., *Paul, Apostle of the Free Spirit* (Exeter, UK: Paternoster, 1977).

Bultmann, R., *The Old and New Man in the Letters of Paul* (Richmond, Va.: John Knox, 1967).

Byrne, B., *"Sons of God"—"Seed of Abraham": A Study of the Idea of the Sonship of God of All Christians in Paul Against the Jewish Background*, AnBib 83 (Rome: Biblical Institute, 1979).

Cerfaux, L., *Christ in the Theology of Saint Paul* (New York: Herder and Herder, 1959).

———, *The Christian in the Theology of St Paul* (London: Chapman, 1967).

———, *The Church in the Theology of St Paul* (New York: Herder and Herder, 1959).

Cunningham, P. A., *Jewish Apostle to the Gentiles: Paul as He Saw Himself* (Mystic, Conn.: Twenty-Third, 1986).

Dahl, N. A., *Studies in Paul: Theology for the Early Christian Mission* (Minneapolis, Minn.: Augsburg, 1977).

Daube, D., *The New Testament and Rabbinic Judaism* (London: Athlone, 1956).

Davies, W. D., *Paul and Rabbinic Judaism: Some Rabbinic Elements in Pauline Theology*, 4th ed. (Philadelphia, Penn.: Fortress, 1980).

Deidun, T. J., *New Covenant Morality in Paul*, AnBib 89 (Rome: Biblical Institute, 1981).

Dodd, C. H., *New Testament Studies* (Manchester, UK: University of Manchester, 1953).

Dungan, D. L., *The Sayings of Jesus in the Churches of Paul* (Philadelphia, Penn.: Fortress, 1971).

Eichholz, G., *Die Theologie des Paulus im Umriss* (Neukirchen-Vluyn: Neukirchener-Verlag, 1972).

Ellis, E. E., *The Old Testament in Early Christianity: Canon and Interpretation in the Light of Modern Research*, WUNT 54 (Tübingen: Mohr [Siebeck], 1991).

———, *Paul's Use of the Old Testament* (Edinburgh: Oliver and Boyd; Grand Rapids, Mich.: Eerdmans, 1957; repr. Grand Rapids, Mich.: Baker, 1981).

Findeis, H.-J., *Versöhnung—Apostolat—Kirche: Eine exegetisch-theologische und rezeptionsgeschichtliche Studie zu den Versöhnungsaussagen des Neuen Testaments (2 Kor, Röm, Kol, Eph)*, FB 40 (Würzburg: Echter-Verlag, 1983).

Fitzmyer, J. A., *According to Paul: Studies in the Theology of the Apostle* (New York and Mahwah, N.J.: Paulist Press, 1993).

Gager, J. G., *The Origins of Anti-Semitism: Attitudes Toward Judaism in Pagan and Christian Antiquity* (New York and Oxford: Oxford University Press, 1983).

Giblin, C. H., *In Hope of God's Glory: Pauline Theological Perspectives* (New York: Herder and Herder, 1970).

Goppelt, L., *Jesus, Paul and Judaism* (New York: Harper, 1964).

Hanson, A. T., *Studies in Paul's Technique and Theology* (London: SPCK, 1974).

Harder, G., *Paulus und das Gebet* (Gütersloh: Bertelsmann, 1936).

Hemsen, J. T., *Der Apostel Paulus: Sein Leben, Wirken, und seine Schriften*, ed. F. Luecke (Göttingen: Dietrich, 1830).

Jewett, R., *Christian Tolerance: Paul's Message to the Modern Church*, Biblical Perspectives on Current Issues (Philadelphia: Westminster, 1982).

Käsemann, E., *New Testament Questions of Today* (Philadelphia, Penn.: Fortress, 1969).

———, *Perspectives on Paul* (Philadelphia, Penn.: Fortress, 1971).

Kümmel, W. G., *The Theology of the New Testament According to Its Major Witnesses, Jesus—Paul—John* (Nashville, Tenn.: Abingdon, 1973).

Kuss, O., *Paulus: Die Rolle des Apostels in der theologischen Entwicklung der Urkirche* (Regensburg: Pustet, 1971).

Kutter, H., *Gerechtigkeit: Ein altes Wort an die moderne Christenheit* (Jena: Diederichs, 1910).

Lake, K., *The Earlier Epistles of St Paul: Their Motive and Origin* (London: Rivington, 1911), 324–420.

Larsson, E., *Christus als Vorbild: Eine Untersuchung zu den paulinischen Tauf- und

Eikontexten, ASNU 23 (Uppsala: Almqvist & Wiksells; Lund: Gleerup, 1962), 48–80.

Lohmeyer, E., *Probleme paulinischer Theologe* (Stuttgart: Kohlhammer, [1955]).

Longenecker, R. N., *Paul: Apostle of Liberty* (New York: Harper & Row, 1964).

Lührmann, D., *Das Offenbarungsverständnis bei Paulus und in den paulinischen Gemeinden,* WMANT 16 (Neukirchen-Vluyn: Neukirchener-Verlag, 1965).

Lüscher, A., *Mit Christus gekreuzigt* (Langerthal: Pflugverlag, n.d.).

Luz, U., *Das Geschichtsverständnis des Paulus,* BEvT 49 (Munich: Kaiser, 1968).

Lyonnet, S. and L. Sabourin, *Sin, Redemption, and Sacrifice: A Biblical and Patristic Study,* AnBib 48 (Rome: Biblical Institute, 1970).

McGrath, A. E., *Justification by Faith: What It Means for Us Today* (Basingstoke: Marshall Pickering; Grand Rapids, Mich.: Academie Books [Zondervan], 1988).

Manen, W. C. van, *Paulus,* 3 vols. (Leiden: Brill, 1890–96).

Mattern, L., *Das Verständnis des Gerichtes bei Paulus,* ATANT 47 (Zurich: Zwingli-Verlag, 1966).

Meeks, W. A., *The First Urban Christians: The Social World of the Apostle Paul* (New Haven and London: Yale University Press, 1983).

Minde, H.-J. van der, *Schrift und Tradition bei Paulus: Ihre Bedeutung und Funktion im Römerbrief,* Paderborner theologische Studien 3 (Paderborn, Munich, and Vienna: Schöningh, 1976).

Munck, J., *Paul and the Salvation of Mankind* (Richmond, Va.: John Knox, 1959).

Ollrog, W.-H., *Paulus und seine Mitarbeiter: Untersuchungen zu Theorie und Praxis der paulinischen Mission,* WMANT 50 (Neukirchen-Vluyn: Neukirchener-Verlag, 1979).

Osten-Sacken, P. von der, *Evangelium und Tora: Aufsätze zu Paulus,* Theologische Bücherei 77 (Munich: Kaiser, 1987).

Pfitzner, V. C., *Paul and the Agon Motif: Traditional Athletic Imagery in the Pauline Literature,* NovTSup 16 (Leiden: Brill, 1967).

Räisänen, H., *The Torah and Christ: Essays in German and English on the Problem of the Law in Early Christianity,* Suomen Eksegeettisen Seuran Julkaisuja 45 (Helsinki: Finnish Exegetical Society, 1986).

Prat, F., *The Theology of St. Paul,* 2 vols. (Westminster, Md.: Newman, 1936).

Ridderbos, H., *Paul: An Outline of His Theology* (Grand Rapids, Mich.: Eerdmans, 1975).

Sanders, E. P., *Paul and Palestinian Judaism: A Comparison of Patterns of Religion* (Philadelphia, Penn.: Fortress, 1977).

Schade, H.-H., *Apokalyptische Christologie bei Paulus: Studien zum Zusammenhang von Christologie und Eschatologie in den Paulusbriefen,* GTA 18 (Göttingen: Vandenhoeck & Ruprecht, 1981).

Schlier, H., *Besinnung auf das Neue Testament: Exegetische Aufsätze und Vorträge,* vol. 2, 2d ed. (Freiburg im Breisgau: Herder, 1967).

———, *Das Ende der Zeit: Exegetische Aufsätze und Vorträge* (Freiburg im Breisgau: Herder, 1971).

————, *Die Zeit der Kirche: Exegetische Aufsätze und Vorträge*, 5th ed. (Freiburg im Breisgau: Herder, 1972).

Schmithals, W., *Paul & the Gnostics* (Nashville, Tenn.: Abingdon, 1972).

Schnabel, E. J., *Law and Wisdom from Ben Sira to Paul*, WUNT 2.16 (Tübingen: Mohr, 1985).

Schoeps, H. J., *Paul: The Theology of the Apostle in Light of the Jewish Religious History* (London: Lutterworth, 1961).

Segal, A. F., *Paul the Convert: The Apostolate and Apostasy of Saul the Pharisee* (New Haven and London: Yale University Press, 1990).

Siber, P., *Mit Christus Leben: Eine Studie zur paulinischen Auferstehungshoffnung* (Zurich: TVZ, 1971).

Stacey, W. D., *The Pauline View of Man in Relation to Its Judaic and Hellenistic Background* (London: Macmillan, 1956).

Stendahl, K., *Paul Among Jews and Gentiles and Other Essays* (London: SCM; Philadelphia, Penn.: Fortress, 1976).

Studiorum paulinorum congressus internationalis catholicus 1961, 2 vols., AnBib 17–18 (Rome: Biblical Institute, 1963).

Synofzik, E., *Die Gerichts- und Vergeltungsaussagen bei Paulus* (Göttingen: Vandenhoeck & Ruprecht, 1977).

Tannehill, R. C., *Dying and Rising with Christ: A Study in Pauline Theology*, BZNW 32 (Berlin: Töpelmann, 1967), 7–43.

Taylor, M. J. (ed.), *A Companion to Paul: Readings in Pauline Theology* (Staten Island, N.Y.: Alba House, 1975).

Theissen, G., *The Social Setting of Pauline Christianity* (Edinburgh: Clark, 1982).

Thüsing, W., *Per Christum in Deum: Studien zum Verhältnis von Christozentrik und Theozentrik in den paulinischen Hauptbriefen*, NTAbh n.s. 1 (Münster in Westfalen, Aschendorff, 1965).

Travis, S. H., *Christ and the Judgment of God: Divine Retribution in the New Testament* (Basingstoke, UK: Marshall, 1987).

Vanhoye, A. (ed.), *L'Apôtre Paul: Personnalité, style et conception du ministère*, BETL 73 (Louvain: Leuven University, 1986).

Watson, F., *Paul, Judaism and the Gentiles: A Sociological Approach*, SNTSMS 56 (Cambridge: Cambridge University Press, 1986), 88–176.

Wedderburn, A. J. M., "Paul and the Hellenic Mystery-Cults: On Posing the Right Questions," *La soteriologia dei culti orientali nell'impero romano*, ed. U. Bianchi and J. Vermaseren (Leiden: Brill, 1982), 817–33.

Weder, H., *Das Kreuz Jesu bei Paulus*, FRLANT 125 (Göttingen: Vandenhoeck & Ruprecht, 1981).

Wegenast, K., *Das Verständnis der Tradition bei Paulus und in den Deuteropaulinen*, WMANT 8 (Neukirchen-Vluyn: Neukirchener-Verlag, 1962).

Westerholm, S., *Israel's Law and the Church's Faith: Paul and His Recent Interpreters* (Grand Rapids, Mich.: Eerdmans, 1988).

Wiederkehr, D., *Die Theologie der Berufung in den Paulusbriefen*, Studia friburgensia 36 (Fribourg: Universitätsverlag, 1963).

Wiencke, G., *Paulus über Jesu Tod: Die Deutung des Todes Jesu bei Paulus und ihre Herkunft*, BFCT 2.42 (Gütersloh: Bertelsmann, 1939).

Whiteley, D. E. H., *The Theology of St. Paul*, 2d ed. (Oxford: Blackwell, 1974).

Wilckens, U., *Rechtfertigung als Freiheit: Paulusstudien* (Neukirchen-Vluyn: Neukirchener-Verlag, 1974).

Wiles, M. F., *The Divine Apostle: The Interpretation of St Paul's Epistles in the Early Church* (Cambridge: Cambridge University Press, 1967).

Translation,
Commentary, and Notes

◆

INTRODUCTION (1:1–15)

◆

1. ADDRESS AND GREETING (1:1–7)

1 ¹Paul, a slave of Christ Jesus, called to be an apostle, set apart for God's gospel—²which he promised long ago through his prophets in the sacred Scriptures, ³concerning his Son who was born of David's stock by natural descent, ⁴but established as the Son of God with power by a spirit of holiness as of his resurrection from the dead, Jesus Christ our Lord, ⁵through whom we have received the grace of apostleship to promote a commitment of faith among all the Gentiles on behalf of his name, ⁶among whom you too were called to belong to Jesus Christ—⁷to all the beloved of God in Rome, called to be his dedicated people, grace and peace to you from God our Father and the Lord Jesus Christ.

COMMENT

In addressing himself to a church that he did not found and with which he had not yet had any personal contact, Paul had to introduce himself. This is the reason for his lengthy and unusual introductory salutation. In it he explains who he is and the right he feels he has to address the Roman Christians. He addresses them not in his name alone, but in that of his Lord and by his commission.

Verses 1–7 contain Paul's address and greeting to the Christians of Rome, a community that he has not evangelized or yet visited personally. The seven verses form one long sentence in Greek. It is the longest and most solemn introductory salutation in the Pauline corpus, being an expanded adaptation of the usual ancient Greek epistolary *praescriptio* or opening formula: X (nominative) to Y (dative), and a stereotyped infin. *chairein*, "greetings" (see Jas 1:1; Acts 15:23; 23:26). Paul never uses the simple *chairein*, but has his own substitute for it, *charis kai eirēnē*, "grace and peace" (be to you). The elements of the basic formula are found in vv 1 and 7; the rest is Pauline adaptation (see further *NJBC* art. 45, §§6–8; cf. W. G. Doty, *Letters in Primitive Christianity* [Philadelphia, Penn.:

Fortress, 1973], 22). The adaptation of the Greek formula may be under Semitic influence (see J. A. Fitzmyer, "Aramaic Epistolography," *Studies in Ancient Letter Writing*, ed. J. L. White, Semeia 22 (Chico, Calif.: Scholars, 1982, 25–57, esp. 31–35), but the formula is scarcely created in imitation of a "Hebrew greeting-formula" (Lietzmann, *An die Römer*, 22). As Friedrich has shown ("Lohmeyers These"), there is no evidence that this Pauline formula is derived from a liturgical greeting used to open divine worship (see Lohmeyer, "Probleme," 162). The simple form of the greeting found in 1 Thess 1:1 suggests its Pauline creation. (See further Lieu, " 'Grace to You and Peace' "; cf. *Apoc. Bar.* 78:2.)

The Pauline substitute of *charis kai eirēnē* (v 7) for the conventional Greek greeting has often been explained as the combination of Greek *chairein*, for which Paul substitutes *charis*, and the Hebrew greeting *šālôm* or the Aramaic greeting *šēlām*, "peace"; cf. 2 Macc 1:1. It may be so, but the combination "grace and peace" may also echo elements of the priestly blessing uttered by the sons of Aaron over the Israelites (Num 6:24–26), "May the Lord bless you and keep you; may the Lord make his face shine upon you and may he be gracious to you; may the Lord lift up his countenance on you and give you peace." If Paul's greeting echoes this blessing, then "grace" would represent God's merciful bounty or covenantal favor *(ḥēn)* revealed in Christ Jesus, and "peace" would connote the fullness of prosperity and well-being characteristic of God's goodness to Israel of old. For all of this Paul prays: that it may come to the Christians of Rome from God our Father and the Lord Jesus Christ as the sum of evangelical blessings.

Paul alone writes to "all the beloved of God in Rome, called to be his dedicated people." So he greets the Christians of the capital of the Roman Empire. He regards them as predominantly of Gentile background, as vv 6 and 13 make clear; they are among those to whom he has been called to serve as "the apostle of the Gentiles" (11:13; cf. 15:15–19). But the community includes Jewish Christians as well (see Introduction, section I).

Paul expands his opening formula by the addition of three elements: (1) by a triple identification of himself: "a slave of Christ Jesus," "called to be an apostle," and one "set apart for God's gospel" (1:1); (2) by the insertion of a fragment of early kerygmatic preaching (1:3–4); and (3) by the use of terms that foreshadow major ideas in the body of the letter: gospel, grace, apostolate, commitment of faith, the Scriptures, the role of Christ Jesus. The added elements account for the length of the introductory salutation in Romans.

Paul refers to himself as "slave of Christ Jesus." Although "slave" could denote merely his dedicated service as a Christian (cf. 1 Cor 7:22b), it more likely expresses his special commitment or service as a minister of the gospel (see 15:16; Phil 2:22). Such a connotation of the title may be derived from the use of *doulos* in the Greek OT for figures who served Yahweh in a special way: Moses (2 Kgs 18:12), Joshua (Judg 2:8), Abraham (Ps 105:42), David (2 Sam 7:5; Pss 78:70; 89:4), the prophets (Amos 3:7; Zech 1:6), and the psalmist (Pss 27:9; 31:17). Paul would thus be implying that his ministry and service put him in the line of such venerable "slaves" of Yahweh in the OT. It would connote the "submission of an instrument to the will of God" (Käsemann, *Commentary*, 5). Specifically, Paul's submission is to the will of Christ Jesus.

Paul has been "called to be an apostle," that is, called by God (see 1 Cor 1:1) and commissioned as an emissary for an authoritative mission explained in the following phrase. In insisting on his apostolate in this letter, Paul is undoubtedly echoing the struggle that he had to be recognized as *apostolos* among Christians (see 1 Cor 9:1–2; 15:9; 2 Cor 11:5; 12:12; Gal 1:1). Recall the reluctance of Luke, who makes Paul the hero of the second part of Acts, to give him this title—it occurs only in Acts 14:4, 14, and probably as part of a pre-Lucan source. Paul's apostolic status is not the result of a call merely to become a Christian, but of a special call linked to God's revealing to him his Son "that I might preach him among the Gentiles" (Gal 1:16). As an "apostle," Paul was fully aware that he was joining those "who were apostles before me" (Gal 1:17).

Lastly, Paul claims that he has been "set apart for God's gospel." He is alluding to what he wrote in Gal 1:15: how God set him apart from birth (lit., from my mother's womb) and called him to proclaim his Son among the Gentiles. There he used a phrase echoing Isa 49:1 (LXX: "called my name from my mother's womb"—Second Servant Song) or Jer 1:5 (the prophet's inaugural call). Such a designation again implies a self-identification of Paul as one in line with great prophetic forebears in OT history. As a human being, he has been destined from birth for a role in God's salvation history—a service dedicated to God's gospel, the good news about the new mode of salvation open to humanity in Christ Jesus, which he has been sent to preach. See Holtz, "Zum Selbstverständnis."

Although Paul claims that his gospel was promised by God long ago through his prophets in the holy Scriptures, he gives no hint of the places in the OT where it is so encountered. The content of that good news is God's Son, who has appeared in human history as a descendant of David, but who has been established with power by a spirit of holiness (i.e., as a life-giving Spirit, 1 Cor 15:45) as of his resurrection from the dead.

Although it is sometimes contested (e.g., Poythress, "Is Romans"), most modern commentators think that Paul incorporates into his opening prescript a fragment of early Christian proclamation or confession, "a handed-down formula" (Bultmann, *TNT* 1.49). The many attempts to isolate the kerygmatic fragment have been surveyed and analyzed by Jewett ("Redaction and Use"). The confessional or kerygmatic formula was a two-pronged parallel affirmation similar to this:

his Son
born
of David's stock   established
                         as Son of God *with power*

| according to the flesh | according to a spirit of holiness |
| | *as of the resurrection from the dead,* |

Jesus Christ our Lord.
(Italics show probable Pauline additions to the inherited parallel formula.)

The basic formula in vv 3–4 is regarded as pre-Pauline, because it contains the only reference in Paul's uncontested writings to Jesus as Son of David (cf. 2 Tim 2:8), the only use of the vb. *horizein*, "limit, determine, define," the Semitic phrase "a spirit of holiness" (Paul usually speaks of "God's Spirit" or "the holy Spirit"), the contrast of "flesh" and "spirit" in a rare Pauline sense—what Käsemann (*Commentary*, 11) calls a christological, not an anthropological, sense—and the association of sonship with the resurrection (otherwise found in an early kerygmatic fragment in Acts 13:33, where Ps 2:7 is quoted). It also makes use of clauses with opening participial formulation, characteristic of fixed tradition. There is no mention of Christ's death or crucifixion, which is surprising if Paul were freely composing these verses (compare 1 Cor 2:2). In using this kerygmatic formula Paul sums up succinctly the content of "God's gospel," that is to say, he quotes something traditional that he expects will resonate with the Roman Christians. He thus illustrates what he maintained in 1 Cor 15:11: "Whether it was I or they (i.e., other early Christian missionaries), so we preach and so you came to believe."

In v 5 Paul recognizes that the grace given to him to preach God's gospel has come from Jesus Christ himself. His graced apostolate is destined to bring non-Jews to the commitment of Christian faith, among whom he classes the Gentile Christians of Rome itself. They too have been called to belong to Christ Jesus. To all God's dedicated people in Rome he sends his greetings of grace and peace.

NOTES

1:1. *Paul.* The Apostle writes this letter to Roman Christians as its sole author. Rom 16:22 reveals that he is using a scribe, Tertius. In other letters of the corpus, Paul often adds the name of a coauthor—or at least of some companion who joins in the greetings: thus in 1 Thess 1:1 (Paul, Silvanus, and Timothy), Gal 1:1–2 (Paul and all of the brethren), Phil 1:1; 2 Cor 1:1; Phlm 1 (Paul and Timothy), 1 Cor 1:1 (Paul and Sosthenes). Compare the Deutero-Paulines: 2 Thess 1:1 (Paul, Silvanus, and Timothy); Col 1:1 (Paul and Timothy); Eph 1:1 (Paul alone). In the Pastorals, "Paul" is the sole author (Titus 1:1; 1 Tim 1:1; 2 Tim 1:1). When, then, in 1:5 Paul uses the 1st pl. "we," it has to be understood as editorial.

Paulos is the only name that the Apostle uses of himself in his uncontested letters or that is used of him in the Deutero-Paulines and Pastorals. It also occurs in 2 Pet 3:15. *Paulos* is the Greek form of a well-known Roman name, *Paul(l)us,* a cognomen used by the *gentes* Aemilia, Sergii, Vettenii, and others (see F.

Münzer, "Paullus," PW 18.4.2362–63). It is the only thing in Paul's writings that supports the Lucan identification of him as a Roman citizen (Acts 22:25–29). Paul himself mentions neither his Roman citizenship nor his birth in Tarsus of Cilicia, inhabitants of which enjoyed Roman citizenship. Ramsay (*The Cities*, 205) traces Roman citizenship in Tarsus to Pompey's conquest of Cilicia in 64 B.C. Luke alone records Paul's other name, Saul (in the grecized form *Saulos* [Acts 7:58; 8:1, etc.] or in the transliterated Semitic form *Saoul* [Acts 9:4, 17; 22:7, 13; 26:14]). The two names occur together in Acts 13:9, *Saulos de, ho kai Paulos*, "Saul, also called Paul." This reflects the custom of Jews bearing two names, one Semitic, the other Greco-Roman. Paul was his *(cog)nomen*, and Saul was the Semitic *signum* or *supernomen* (see *PAHT* §P3; Cranfield, *Romans*, 48–50; cf. Dessau, "Der Name"; Harrer, "Saul Who also Is Called Paul." In calling himself Paul, he is not simply accommodating himself to the world around him, *pace* Käsemann (*Commentary*, 5).

a slave of Christ Jesus. Paul's first description of himself is *doulos Christou Iēsou* (MSS P²⁶, ℵ, A, G, Ψ, and the *Koinē* text-tradition read *Iēsou Christou*). In the contemporary Greco-Roman world *doulos* meant "slave, born bondman" (LSJ, 447), and slavery was widespread in the Roman Empire; estimates claim three slaves to one free citizen. Slaves often occupied positions of high authority and were entrusted with great financial responsibility. *Doulos* denoted a relation to a "master, owner," usually expressed by *despotēs* (Titus 2:9; 1 Tim 6:1; Diodorus Siculus, *Bibliothēkē historikē* 15.8.2), sometimes by *kyrios* (Matt 10:24–25; John 13:16; Phil 2:7, 11); compare the relation of Hebrew ᶜ*ebed* to ʾ*ādôn* (Deut 23:16; Isa 24:2; Mal 1:6). In the Greek OT the relationship was softened by the use of *doulos* for the special service of officers of kings (1 Sam 22:14–15; 2 Sam 11:13), where it often took on the connotation of *pais*, "boy, servant." A further special connotation is found in the phrase *doulos Kyriou*, "servant of the Lord" (and its equivalents; see the COMMENT above). In using the word *doulos* of himself, Paul desires to stress his total submission and commitment to Christ Jesus, who is his *Kyrios*, "master," but also "Lord." See Sass, "Zur Bedeutung." (The often-used translation "servant" is a heritage from English Bible versions, especially of American background, which sought to avoid the negative connotation of slavery in the American tradition.)

Christos is used by Paul in a nontitular sense (compare 9:5); see Introduction, section IX.B.

called to be an apostle. Lit., "called (as) an apostle," or possibly "someone called (by God), an apostle" (if *klētos* should be understood as a substantive). So Paul describes his commission. The task of proclaiming "Jesus is Lord" was not something that he took upon himself; his call to Christian discipleship became a further call to apostolic office, a commission to preach to the Gentiles (11:13; cf. Gal 1:15–16).

Apostolos, derived from the vb. *apostellein*, "send," means "someone/something sent." In extrabiblical Greek it is not used in a religious sense; there it denotes a naval "expedition" (Lysias, *Or.* 19.21; Demosthenes, *Or.* 3.5; 18.80, 107), a "colony to be sent out" (Dionysius of Halicarnassus, *Antiquitates Romanae* 9.59.2), a "trade-vessel" (Plato, *Epistolae* 346a), or an "envoy, messenger, ambassador" (Herodotus, *History* 1.21; 5.38; Josephus, *Ant.* 17.11.1 §300). It occurs as "messenger" in the NT (Phil 2:25; John 13:16), and is found only once in the LXX (1 Kgs 14:6), where it translates the pass. ptc. *šālûaḥ*, "sent," used of Ahaziah dispatched by God as a stern messenger to the wife of Jeroboam. The NT religious sense of *apostolos* is not easily explained from such an extrabiblical or LXX background. For this reason it has been related to the Palestinian Jewish institution of the first century A.D., in which Jerusalem authorities sent out rabbis as *šĕlûḥîm* (Hebrew) or *šĕlîḥîn* (Aramaic), "commissioned emissaries," empowered to act in their name to settle financial, calendaric, or doctrinal questions among Jews living outside Jerusalem. See Vogelstein, "Development of the Apostolate"; K. H. Rengstorf, *TDNT* 1.407–20, esp. 414–17. Although this Palestinian origin of the Christian apostolate has been questioned at times (e.g., by Klein, *Die zwölf Apostel*; Schmithals, *Office of Apostle*), it still remains the best explanation. It builds on OT data about God sending messengers to his people on religious matters, and specifically on such passages as 2 Chr 17:7–9, where Jehoshaphat "sends" princes, Levites, and priests to teach people in all of the cities of Judah. The Hebrew text uses *šlḥ*, and the LXX *apostellein*. Between the Palestinian Jewish institution of *šĕlûḥîm* and the Christian apostolate intervened the action of the risen Christ commissioning followers to bear witness or preach in his name (Luke 24:47–48; Acts 1:8; cf. Matt 28:19–20; John 20:21). See further Gerhardsson, *Die Boten Gottes*; Campenhausen, "Der urchristliche Apostelbegriff"; Kredel, "Der Apostelbegriff."

set apart. Lit., "having been divided off from." Paul uses the perf. pass. ptc. of *aphorizein*, echoing his use of this verb in Gal 1:15 (see the COMMENT above). He claims that he has been set apart from the rest of Christians by God himself. The OT background for the use of this verb can also be seen in God's singling out Israel as his own people (Lev 20:26) or the setting apart of the tribe of Levi for his special service (Num 8:1). In using the ptc., Paul may be playing on his Pharisaic background (see Phil 3:5e); at least the ptc. is so understood by some commentators (e.g., Michel, *Brief an die Römer*, 68 n. 16; Nygren, *Romans*, 45). *Pharisaios* can be explained as a grecized form of Aramaic *pĕrîšāy*, "separated one." Although Käsemann (*Commentary*, 6) sees no contrast "with Paul's Pharisaic past," it is not wholly out of the question. Paul may be implying that his Pharisaic background was divinely ordained for his eventual evangelical mission.

for God's gospel. See 15:16; cf. 1 Thess 2:2, 8, 9; 2 Cor 11:7. The prep. *eis* expresses purpose, as in 1:5, the purpose for which Paul was set apart. "God's gospel" is not the good news about God (objective gen.), but the good news from God (gen. of origin; BDF §163); its content or object will be set forth in vv 3–4. On *euangelion*, see *PAHT* §§PT31–36. Here at the outset of the letter, Paul emphasizes a theme, "the gospel," that is to be developed at length in the course of it. It sums up the great new reality that God has introduced into human history. "What the gospel is, what the content of the Christian faith is, one learns to know in the Epistle to the Romans as in no other place in the New Testament. Romans gives us the gospel in its wide context" (Nygren, *Romans*, 3).

2. *which he promised long ago through his prophets.* That gospel is not unrelated to what has gone before in salvation history. God himself has already prepared for its coming. Even though Paul does not name any OT prophets and uses only a generic expression, he sees the gospel that he has been preaching as stemming from the God of the OT. Paul was no Marcionite; he saw the NT dispensation growing out of the old. God is still the living and active God who brings forth a new mode of salvation for his people. Cf. 16:26.

in the sacred Scriptures. I.e., in those sacred writings entrusted to Israel of old, "the oracles of God" (3:2), which recorded the promises made to his chosen people. So Paul refers to the OT, in which he found the promises (9:4) that have been realized in the death and resurrection of Jesus Christ (see 1 Cor 15:3–4; cf. the words of the Lucan Paul in Acts 13:32–33).

The phrase *hagiai graphai* is not found in the Greek OT, nor elsewhere in Paul's writings, though he frequently uses the sg. *hē graphē*, "Scripture" (4:3; 9:17; 10:11; 11:2; Gal 3:8, 22; 4:30) or the unmodified pl. *graphai* (15:4; 1 Cor 15:3, 4). Josephus (*Ag.Ap.* 2.4 §45) speaks of *hai hierai graphai*, as does Philo (*De Abr.* 61; *De congr.* 34, 90). Thus Paul betrays his Jewish background in the very mode in which he refers to the writings of old. See G. Schrenk, *TDNT* 1.751.

3. *concerning his Son.* This prep. phrase modifies "God's gospel," expressing its content. The center of that gospel is the Son of God, and his coming is announced as the beginning of a new age.

Huios, "son," is a relational word implying a "father" and a "mother"; used here of God, it denotes that God is Jesus' father—with a significant relationship between them. As Cranfield notes (*Romans*, 58), this phrase controls the two following participial clauses and implies that "the One who was born of the seed of David was already Son of God before, and independently of the action denoted by the second participle"; similarly, Lagrange, *Romains*, 5. For the background of "Son of God," see Introduction, section IX.B and *PAHT* §§PT49–50. Käsemann maintains (*Commentary*, 10) that "the title, except as it refers to Israel or is conferred at enthronement (Ps 2:7), is as rare in Judaism as it is common in Hellenism." Yet its occurrence in a Palestinian Jewish extrabiblical Aramaic text reveals that it was less rare than one may be led to expect; see 4Q246 2:1 (Fitzmyer, "Contribution," 90–94). Bultmann was closer to the truth in maintaining that the title was "already traditional before Paul" (*TNT* 1.50; cf. Hengel, *Son of God*). Again, Käsemann (*Commentary*, 10) goes too far in saying that "no NT author understood the unique divine sonship of Jesus otherwise than in a metaphysical sense." That, however, is precisely what has to be shown because, though Paul implies by the title a significant relationship, one should be reluctant to load it with all of the metaphysical connotation of later patristic writers. Although Paul never speaks of Jesus as an incarnate Son (cf. John 1:14–18), his use of *huios* may imply some sort of preexistent filiation. Cf. 5:10; 8:3, 29, 32; 1 Thess 1:10; Gal 1:16; 2:20; 4:4; 1 Cor 1:9; 15:28; 2 Cor 1:19.

who was born of David's stock. Lit., "born (or coming into being) from the seed of David." The Davidic descent of Jesus is noted elsewhere in the NT (Luke 1:32; 3:31; Acts 2:30; Mark 12:35–37; Matt 1:1, 6, 17; 2 Tim 2:8; Rev 5:5; 22:16; cf. John 7:42). Paul is using the word *sperma* in the figurative sense, as it often appears in the OT (Gen 12:7; 15:13; 2 Sam 7:12; Ps 89:5), and scarcely in the literal sense of semen.

A few MSS (51, 61*, 441, etc.) read and the Peshitta presupposes *gennomenon*, "begotten," instead of *genomenon*, "born," the reading of the best Greek MSS. It has been argued that Paul uses *ginesthai* and avoids *gennan* because he is aware of the virginal conception of Jesus (see J. McHugh, *The Mother of Jesus in the New Testament* [Garden City, N.Y.: Doubleday, 1975], 274–77). But this reading presses the use of *genomenon* too far, for *ginesthai* does have the sense "be born" (see Tob 8:6; Wis 7:3; Sir 44:9). Cf. *MNT*, 37–38; H. E. W. Turner, *ExpTim* 68 (1956–57): 12.

by natural descent. Lit., "according to the flesh," i.e., as far as his human connection is concerned. Cf. 4:1; Gal 4:23. In using *kata sarka*, Paul is asserting Jesus' share in our common humanity. The phrase *kata sarka* stands clearly in parallelism and contrast with *kata pneuma* in v 4. Commentators debate whether this parallelism of phrases was part of the pre-Pauline formulation. Normally, when Paul uses this contrast of "flesh" and "spirit," it has an ethical or anthropological connotation (see 8:4–9, 12–13; Gal 3:2–3; 5:16–19; Phil 3:3; 1 Cor 5:5). Here it has rather a christological connotation, as in 9:3, 5; compare the use of *kata sarka* in 4:1. Because this contrast resembles the usage in other primitive NT passages (1 Tim 3:16; 1 Pet 3:18), it should be regarded as pre-Pauline. *Pace* Dunn ("Jesus—Flesh and Spirit"), *kata sarka* is not used pejoratively; it merely expresses Jesus' human condition and existence.

Thus Paul, writing to Roman Christians whom he has not evangelized, presumes that they will recognize the credal formula about Jesus' descent as an expression of their common and shared belief, a belief that Paul never repeats anywhere else in his writings. See J. P. Meier, *A Marginal Jew: Rethinking the Historical Jesus*, 2 vols., ABRL (New York: Doubleday, 1991–) 1.215, esp. 237 and the literature cited in n. 50.

4. *established.* Or "determined." This ptc. stands in parallelism to *genomenon* (v 3) and expresses the higher condition for which Jesus was destined by the Father. The vb. *horizein*, lit., "set a boundary to, limit, delimit," is rare in Pauline writings. Even though no Greek MSS reads *prooristhentos* (see Cranfield, *Romans*, 61 n. 1), the VL, the Vg, and some Latin writers rendered the ptc. *praedestinatus*, "predestined," which persisted in the western theological tradition. Whereas Eusebius regarded *prooristhentos* as a corruption of the text (*Contra*

Marcellum 1.2 [GCS 4.11]), Epiphanius used it in a quotation of this text
(*Panarion* 54.6.1 [GCS 32.323]). John Chrysostom interpreted *horisthentos* as
"displayed, manifested, acknowledged, judged, confessed" (*deichthentos, apoph-
thantentos, homologēthentos, krithentos; In Ep. ad Romanos* hom. 1.2 [PG
60.397]). Elsewhere in the NT *horizein* means "appoint, determine, establish,
constitute" (Acts 2:23; 10:42; 11:29; 17:26, 31: Heb 4:7), a meaning that should
be used here. In some of these passages it is related to God's foreknowledge or
determination, but of itself it does not connote *predestination*; it suggests rather a
decisive act of divine appointment or establishment. The passive is theological
(ZBG §236): "established" (by God). See further Allen, "Old Testament Background"; G. Schneider, *Horizō," EDNT* 2.531–32.

as the Son of God with power. This phrase parallels the Son's Davidic descent.
The gospel now reveals that Jesus is not merely God's Son, born in a human way
of Davidic lineage, but God's Son as a source of power. Before the resurrection
Jesus Christ was the Son of God in the weakness of his human existence; as of the
resurrection he is the Son of God established in power and has become such for
the vivifying of all human beings.

Debate surrounds the prep. phrase *en dynamei*, "with power." Is it part of the
pre-Pauline formulation or not? For Bultmann (*TNT* 1.49) and Käsemann
(*Commentary*, 12) it is; for Barrett (*Romans*, 18–20) and Schweizer ("Ökumene")
it is not. Much can be said for either position. As it now stands in the Pauline
context, it marks a distinct contrast with Jesus' status as of birth. As Käsemann
notes, it functions like *en doxē* in 1 Tim 3:16 and *en hypsēlois* in Heb 1:3 and
should be regarded as pre-Pauline. Second, does the phrase modify adverbially
the ptc. *horisthentos* or adjectivally the title *huiou theou?* In the former instance,
it would mean "decisively established/determined," i.e., by a mighty act (cf. Mark
9:1; 1 Cor 15:43; 1 Thess 1:5). So the NEB, Goodspeed, and Sanday and Headlam
(*Romans*, 9). In the latter instance, it would mean "Son of God with power," i.e.,
Son as a source of power, Son enthroned in the heavenly sphere of power. So
Käsemann (*Commentary*, 12), Barrett (*Romans*, 20), Cranfield (*Romans*, 62),
Schlier (*Römerbrief*, 24). The second meaning is to be preferred, for the "power"
is that by which God effects Jesus' resurrection and endows him with a source of
life to energize human beings who turn to him as the risen Lord; see 1 Cor 6:14;
Phil 3:10 (see Fitzmyer, " 'To Know Him' "). Good Greek style would call for an
article *(tou)* before the prep. phrase, as Paul often writes (see Mowery, "Articular
Prepositional Attributes"); but Paul also uses prep. phrases adjectivally and
anarthrously elsewhere (6:4, *dia tou baptismatos eis ton thanaton;* 10:6, *hē deēsis
pros ton theon;* Gal 3:11, *ho dikaios ek pisteōs;* 1 Cor 2:7, *theou sophian en
mysteriō;* cf. BDF §272).

The title "Son of God" is not being used in a messianic sense, *pace* Boismard
("Constitué," 17) and Langevin ("Quel Est," 150–51); nothing is intimated in the
text about Jesus' anointed status or agency, and no OT background relates "son of
God" to "Messiah." Nor is the contrast between Jesus' weak human condition and

235

his powerful risen status an indication of his messianic role. Moreover, Paul is not thinking here of an inner-trinitarian relationship of Father and Son, but only of the unique relation of Jesus Christ as Son to God the Father in the salvific process. For Paul the resurrection made a difference in that process, but it did not *make* Christ the Son of God.

by a spirit of holiness. Lit., "according to a spirit of holiness," a phrase that parallels *kata sarka* (v 3). *Kata pneuma hagiosynēs* is found only here in Paul's writings; it does not occur in the LXX. Although it is a literal translation of Hebrew *rûaḥ qōdeš*, when forms of this phrase appear in the OT (e.g., *rûaḥ qodšô*, Isa 63:10–11; *rûaḥ qodšĕkā*, Ps 51:13), they are translated as *to pneuma to hagion*, the expression that Paul sometimes uses for "the holy Spirit" (e.g., 15:16, 19; 1 Thess 4:8; 1 Cor 6:19; 2 Cor 6:6; 13:13). Because *rûaḥ qōdeš* appears in QL (1QS 4:21; 8:16; 9:3; CD 2:12; 1QH 7:6–7; 9:32) and other intertestamental literature (*T. Levi* 18:11, *pneuma hagiosynēs*), this Palestinian Jewish usage argues for the pre-Pauline form of the phrase.

The phrase is not to be understood of the holy Spirit, the Third Person in the Trinity, as if its activity were unleashed through the resurrection of Christ (so patristic writers). This reading is excluded because "the antithesis of *sarx* and *pneuma* requires that they shall be in the same person" (Sanday and Headlam, *Romans*, 9). Nor is it to be taken as a way of referring to Christ's divine nature, whereas *sarx* in v 3 would refer to his humanity, as if Christ were now established in a role fully consistent with the divine nature that had been his all along (so Lagrange, *Romains*, 8; Huby, *Romains*, 46; Fahy; Trinidad). Such an interpretation introduces anachronistically ideas of later theology into the Pauline phrase.

Kata pneuma hagiosynēs, being in contrast to *kata sarka*, describes something that is intrinsic to Christ as of the resurrection. It is not merely his moral holiness, as Käsemann rightly notes (*Commentary*, 11), but that which is opposed to the profane and secular and which "opens up access to God." Because the phrase basically stems from the OT, it should be taken in the OT sense of *pneuma*. See Introduction, section IX.C and *PAHT* §§PT61–66.

as of his resurrection from the dead. Lit., "from resurrection of the dead." The second *ek* is omitted, but the phrase should be understood as in 4:24; 8:11; 10:9; cf. Acts 13:33; Eph 1:20; 1 Pet 1:21. The phrase refers to Christ's resurrection from the dead by the Father's activity. It is debated whether this phrase was part of the pre-Pauline inherited formula; for Bultmann (*TNT* 1.49) and Käsemann it is; but for Barrett (*Romans*, 18–20) it is not. As Käsemann notes (*Commentary*, 12), if it is regarded as a Pauline addition, then the formula loses both precision and concluding emphasis. But does it? The prep. *ek* can denote either time or causality. The former seems preferable, because it signifies the new mode of dynamic existence that Christ enjoys as of the resurrection (see Lietzmann, *An die Römer*, 25); but the latter cannot be excluded completely, because it would designate the resurrection itself as the source of the risen Christ's dynamic influence (see Murray, *Romans*, 11). Dunn (*Romans*, 15), however, insists that the phrase should not be translated "as of *his* resurrection *from* the dead," but rather "as from *the* resurrection of the dead": the phrase seemingly reflects the earliest Christian belief that Jesus' resurrection was actually part of the beginning of the general resurrection prior to the last judgment; cf. Acts 4:2; 23:66, the metaphor of Christ's resurrection as the "firstfruits" (1 Cor 15:20, 23), and the ancient tradition of Jesus' resurrection being accompanied by a more general resurrection (Matt 27:52–53); similarly, Dibelius ("Glaube," 103 n. 14); Bartsch ("Zur vorpaulinischen Bekenntnisformel"); and Hooke ("Translation"). Such a view, however, is strange; it does not echo Pauline teaching otherwise, which sees the resurrection of Christ itself as the source of human justification (4:25). In speaking of the resurrection, Paul refers to God's greatest act, an event in human history, by which Christ Jesus was removed from the world of the dead as "the firstborn among many brothers" (8:29). His resurrection was of the kind that is in prospect for all of the dead. Thus Christ has passed the frontier to become the Son of God in power. In virtue of that power others would also share in the glory of his risen life.

Jesus Christ our Lord. This is often thought to be a Pauline addition to the inherited kerygmatic formula, but it is not clear at all that it is. To Jesus' full name, the title *Kyrios* is added, which expresses par excellence his risen status. It thus rounds out the Pauline description of the content of God's gospel. On the use of *Kyrios*, see Introduction, section IX.B. This formula sums up the message of the letter to the Romans (recall 10:9), making clear the content of God's gospel and emphasizing the role of Christ's resurrection in the Father's plan of salvation for all humanity.

5. *through whom we have received the grace of apostleship.* Lit., "grace and apostleship," a hendiadys, in which the second element specifies the first. The "grace" is further explained in 15:15, where it is ascribed to God as its source rather than to Christ. Cf. 12:3; Gal 1:15–16; 2:9; 1 Cor 3:10. *Charis* is here conceived of as something received, a gift that enables Paul to act as a commissioned emissary for the sake of the evangelization of humanity. Not all who receive grace become apostles, so it has to be understood as a special grace. It is grace in view of Paul's function in the church. In Gal 1:15–16, Paul describes his double call, to be a disciple of Jesus the Christ and to be a proclaimer of him to the Gentiles. "Apostleship" is listed among the spiritual gifts intended for the Christian community (1 Cor 12:28). This "grace of apostleship" has come to Paul from Jesus Christ, from him who is *Kyrios* in his life.

to promote a commitment of faith. Lit., "for an obedience of faith." The prep. *eis* expresses purpose, the purpose of Paul's apostleship. The gen. in *hypakoē pisteōs* is epexegetical or appositional, i.e., faith that manifests itself as obedience, or possibly a gen. of source, "obedience that springs from faith." The phrase occurs again in the final doxology (16:26). Compare 1:8 with 16:19; see also 10:16; 2 Cor 10:6, 15. Because "obedience" often has a pejorative connotation, it is better rendered as "commitment." The relationship of human beings with God can, of course, be expressed as obedience, as it has been in the OT, obedience to the covenant, or obedience to God's law (Dan 3:30 LXX). But Christian faith is much more a commitment to the service of God in Christ and through his Spirit. See Introduction, section IX.D. Friedrich ("Muss *hypakoē pisteōs*"), appealing to the use of *hypakoē*, "answer," in the LXX of 2 Sam 22:36 and in *Gos. Pet.* 42, claims that this phrase should be translated "for the preaching of faith." But that is a farfetched solution, as *hypakoē* does not have a connotation of preaching. Paul seeks by his preaching, indeed, to stir up a commitment that begins with faith in his gospel.

among all the Gentiles. Lit., "among all the nations," but in this Pauline context *ethnē* has to be understood of non-Jews, of *gôyīm* in the specific sense. This reading is consonant with Paul's view of himself as "the apostle of the Gentiles" (11:13; cf. 15:16, 18; Gal 1:15–16). Contrast the way the Lucan Paul describes his apostolate in Acts 9:15, where he includes "the children of Israel."

on behalf of his name. So Paul expresses his personal motivation in promoting faith among the Gentiles; it is not for any personal aggrandizement. The evangelization in which he engages is solely to serve the cause of Christ, the task for which he as "slave" has been called by his "Lord."

6. *among whom you too were called to belong to Jesus Christ.* Lit., "among whom you too (are) called ones of Jesus Christ." So Paul classes the Christians of Rome among the *ethnē*; see further 1:13c. In a broader sense, he affirms the divine call of Gentiles to be Christians; their vocation is to belong to Christ along with Israel. This is the first of three designations of the Roman Christians that Paul uses. In referring to them as *klētoi*, Paul stresses the divine initiative; the Christians of Rome as "called ones" have been the object of divine favor and grace. Their call does not depend on their own will and initiative. See further 8:28–29; 9:24; 1 Cor 1:9; and especially 2 Tim 1:9–10: "who called us with a holy calling, not according to our deeds, but according to his own purpose and the grace that he gave us in Christ Jesus ages ago."

7. *to all the beloved of God in Rome.* Lit., "to all being in Rome, beloved of God." Paul uses of them an OT attribute "beloved" (see Pss 60:7; 108:7). This is Paul's second description of the Christians of the capital of the Roman Empire; he understands them as the special objects of God's love. It has prompted him to send his Son for the sake of their justification and salvation (5:8; 8:32; cf. Col 1:13).

As in v 15 the prep. phrase *en Rōmē* is omitted in MS G and noted as an omission in the margins of MSS 1739, 1908 and in Origen (see Introduction, section III); it is, however, read in all other Greek MSS and is to be retained. The phrase *agapētois theou* is found in MSS P[10,26], ℵ, A, B, C, Ψ, 1739 and in the Latin, Syriac, Coptic, and Armenian versions; it is to be preferred to the variant *en agapē theou*, "in the love of God," the reading of MS G and some VL MSS, which probably arose in connection with the omission of *en Rōmē*. See Manson, "St. Paul's Letter," 5–6.

called to be his dedicated people. Lit., "called (as) saints," as in 1 Cor 1:2. This is Paul's third description of the Christians of Rome. *Hagios* has to be understood in its OT sense, "dedicated, consecrated," i.e., separated from the profane aspects of life for an encounter with the awesome presence of God. Although it may imply modes of ethical behavior, this is not its primary emphasis. It is a description of persons, places, and objects reserved for the awesome cult of Yahweh (Exod 28:2, 36; Pss 2:6; 24:3; etc.). In a particular sense, it is used of Israel of old (Lev 11:44; 19:2; 20:26), a people set apart for a special covenant with Yahweh, to be "holy" as he is holy. Now Paul flatters the Roman Christians by applying to them this venerable designation—in a new sense, as those "called" into association *(koinōnia)* with God's Son, Jesus Christ our Lord (1 Cor 1:9). It is noteworthy that Paul uses of the Roman Christians he greets the same appellative *klētos* that he used of himself in v 1. He was "called" or "a called one" (= a Christian), and so are the Christians of Rome. Both he and they are called to acknowledge the same God and the same Lord, which unites both Paul and the Christians of Rome in their worship of God and Christ and as members of the people of the same God. In this calling their holiness consists.

grace and peace to you. This phrase is the standard Pauline substitute for the secular *chairein* (see 1 Thess 1:1; Gal 1:3; Phil 1:2; 1 Cor 1:3; 2 Cor 1:2; Phlm 3). It is also found in 2 Thess 1:2; Col 1:2; Eph 1:2; Rev 1:4. Note the modification of it in the Pastorals (Titus 1:4; 1 Tim 1:2; 2 Tim 1:2). The modification found in 1 Pet 1:2; 2 Pet 1:2 may be influenced by Dan 4:1 (Theodotion). Paul greets the Christians of Rome by wishing that they will have a share in God's favor and in the peace that comes from him. Such "peace" is not merely an inner composure of the undisturbed human soul. It echoes also the Hebrew idea of *šālôm*, the basic meaning of which is expressed in the root *šlm*, "be complete, full, perfect," connoting the fullness of God's gracious bounty. It may also echo the priestly blessing of the sons of Aaron (see the COMMENT above).

from God our Father and the Lord Jesus Christ. The double source of the blessings of grace and peace is thus formulated, as in Gal 1:3; Phil 1:2; 1 Cor 1:3; 2 Cor 1:2; cf. 2 Thess 1:2; Eph 1:2. Together with the preceding phrase, the greeting in Greek is rhythmical, consisting of three lines with four words each.

For Paul *theos* is clearly the Father; in 15:6 he is hailed as "the Father of our Lord Jesus Christ" (cf. 2 Cor 1:3). In 8:15 Paul will explain in what sense he may be regarded as "our Father" (cf. 1 Cor 1:3; 2 Cor 1:2; Phil 1:2). Yet Paul does not stop there; he juxtaposes to the sovereign source of such blessing (God the Father) the lordship of the risen Christ. The Father and Christ are thus treated on a par as the source of blessings for the Christians of Rome.

BIBLIOGRAPHY

Allen, L. C., "The Old Testament Background of *(pro)orizein* in the New Testament," *NTS* 17 (1970–71): 104–8.

Bartsch, H.-W., "Zur vorpaulinischen Bekenntnisformel im Eingang des Römerbriefes," *TZ* 23 (1967): 329–39.

Beasley-Murray, P., "Romans 1:3f: An Early Confession of Faith in the Lordship of Jesus," *TynBul* 31 (1980): 147–54.

Boismard, M.-E., "Constitué fils de Dieu (Rom., i.4)," *RB* 60 (1953): 5–17.

Bröse, E., "Zur Auslegung von Röm. 1,3–4," *NKZ* 10 (1899): 562–73.

Burger, C., *Jesus als Davidssohn: Eine traditionsgeschichtliche Untersuchung*, FRLANT 98 (Göttingen: Vandenhoeck & Ruprecht, 1970), 25–41.

Cambier, J., *L'Évangile de Dieu*, 177–84.

Campenhausen, H. von, "Der urchristliche Apostelbegriff," *ST* 1 (1947): 96–130.

Chevallier, M.-A., *L'Esprit et le Messie dans le bas-judaïsme et le Nouveau Testament* (Paris: Presses Universitaires de France, 1958), 99–104.

Coggan, D., *The Prayers of the New Testament* (Washington, D.C.: Corpus Books, 1967), 95–96.

Dessau, H., "Der Name des Apostels Paulus," *Hermes* 45 (1910): 347–68.

Díaz Rodelas, J. M., "Rom 1,3–4: Contenido y función de una afirmación cristológico," *Cuadernos bíblicos Institución S. Jerónimo* 8 (1983): 50–81.

Dibelius, M., "Glaube und Mystik bei Paulus," *Botschaft und Geschichte*, 2 vols. (Tübingen: Mohr [Siebeck], 1953–56), 2.94–116.

Dunn, J. D. G., "Jesus—Flesh and Spirit: An Exposition of Romans i. 3–4," *JTS* 24 (1973): 40–68.

Duplacy, J., "Le Fils de Dieu né de la race de David (Rm 1,1–7)," *AsSeign* 8 (1972): 12–16.

Fahy, T., "Romans 1:4," *ITQ* 23 (1956): 412.

Fitzmyer, J. A., "The Contribution of Qumran Aramaic to the Study of the New Testament," *WA*, 85–113.

———, " 'To Know Him and the Power of His Resurrection' (Phil 3:10)," *TAG*, 202–17.

Friedrich, G., "Lohmeyers These über das paulinische Briefpräskript kritisch beleuchtet," *TLZ* 81 (1956): 343–46.

———, "Muss *hypakoē pisteōs* Rom 1:5 mit 'Glaubensgehorsam' übersetzt werden?" *ZNW* 72 (1981): 118–23.

Garlington, D. B., *"The Obedience of Faith": A Pauline Phrase in Historical Context*, WUNT 2.38 (Tübingen: Mohr [Siebeck], 1991).

———, "The Obedience of Faith in the Letter to the Romans. Part I: The Meaning of *hypakoē pisteōs* (Rom 1:5; 16:26)," *WTJ* 52 (1990): 201–24; "Part II: The Obedience of Faith and Judgment by Works," *WTJ* 53 (1991): 47–72.

Gerhardsson, B., "Die Boten Gottes und die Apostel Christi," *SEA* 27 (1962): 89–131.

———, *Die Boten Gottes und die Apostel Christi* (Lund: Gleerup, 1962).

Gyllenberg, R., "Glaube und Gehorsam," *ZST* 14 (1937): 547–66.

Harnack, A. von, "Zu Röm. 1,7," *ZNW* 3 (1902): 83–86.

Harrer, G. A., "Saul Who also Is Called Paul," *HTR* 33 (1940): 19–34.

Hengel, M., *Son of God* (Philadelphia, Penn.: Fortress, 1976).

Holtz, T., "Zum Selbstverständnis des Apostels Paulus," *TLZ* 91 (1966): 321–30.

Hooke, S. H., "The Translation of Romans i. 4," *NTS* 9 (1962–63): 370–71.

Jewett, R., "The Redaction and Use of an Early Christian Confession in Romans 1:3–4," *The Living Text: Essays in Honor of Ernest W. Saunders*, ed. D. Groh and R. Jewett (Lanham, Md.: University Press of America, 1985), 99–122.

Johnson, S. L., Jr., "The Jesus That Paul Preached," *BSac* 128 (1971): 120–34.

Jonge, M. de, "Jesus, Son of David and Son of God," *Intertextuality in Biblical Writings: Essays in Honour of Bas van Iersel*, ed. S. Draisma (Kampen: Kok, 1989), 95–104.

Kirchschläger, W., "Von Christus geprägt: Das paulinische Selbstverständnis als Zeugnis des Osterglaubens," *BK* 36 (1981): 165–70.

Klein, G., *Die zwölf Apostel*, FRLANT 77 (Göttingen: Vandenhoeck & Ruprecht, 1961).

Kredel, E. M., "Der Apostelbegriff in der neueren Exegese: Historisch-kritische Darstellung," *ZKT* 78 (1956): 169–93, 257–305.

Lake, K., "The Twelve and the Apostles," *The Beginnings of Christianity*, pt. 1: *The Acts of the Apostles*, ed. F. J. Foakes Jackson and K. Lake, 5 vols. (London: Macmillan, 1922–33), 5.37–59.

Langevin, P.-E., "Quel Est le 'Fils de Dieu' de Romains 1,3–4?" *ScEspr* 29 (1977): 145–77.

Lieu, J. M., " 'Grace to You and Peace': The Apostolic Greeting," *BJRL* 68 (1985): 161–78.

Linnemann, E., "Tradition und Interpretation in Röm 1,3f.," *EvT* 31 (1971): 264–75.

Lloyd-Jones, D. M., *Romans: An Exposition of Chapter 1: The Gospel of God* (Edinburgh: Banner of Truth; Grand Rapids, Mich.: Ministry Resources Library, 1985).

Lohmeyer, E., "Probleme paulinischer Theologie, I. Briefliche Grussüberschriften," *ZNW* 26 (1927): 158–73.

Lohse, E., "Ursprung und Prägung des christlichen Apostolates," *TZ* 9 (1953): 259–75.

McCasland, S. V., " 'Christ Jesus,' " *JBL* 65 (1946): 377–83.

Manson, T. W., "St. Paul's Letter to the Romans—and Others," *RomDeb*, 3–15.

Montagnini, F., *La prospettiva storica della Lettera ai Romani: Esegesi di Rom. 1–4*, Studi biblici 54 (Brescia: Paideia, 1980).

Mowery, R. L., "The Articular Prepositional Attributes in the Pauline Corpus," *Bib* 71 (1990): 85–92.

Olsson, B., "Rom 1:3f enligt Paulus," *SEA* 37–38 (1972–73): 255–73.

O'Rourke, J. J., " 'Dalla risurrezione dei morti' (Rom. 1,4)," *BeO* 6 (1964): 59.

Parke-Taylor, G. H., "A Note on 'eis hypakoēn pisteōs' in Romans i.5 and xvi.26," *ExpTim* 55 (1943–44): 305–6.

Poythress, V. S., "Is Romans 1³⁻⁴ a *Pauline* Confession after All?" *ExpTim* 87 (1975–76): 180–83.

Ramsay, W. M., *The Cities of St. Paul* (London: Hodder and Stoughton, 1908).

Raschke, C. A., "On Rereading Romans 1–6 or Overcoming the Hermeneutics of Suspicion," *Ex auditu* 1 (1985): 147–55.

Riesenfeld, H., "Kristi andes helighet, Rom 1:4," *SEA* 50 (1985): 105–15.

Ruggieri, G., *Il figlio di Dio davidico*, AnGreg 166 (Rome: Gregorian University, 1968).

Sass, G., "Zur Bedeutung von *doulos* bei Paulus," *ZNW* 40 (1941): 24–32.

Schenk, W., "Die Gerechtigkeit Gottes und der Glaube Christi: Versuch einer Verhältnisbestimmung paulinischer Strukturen," *TLZ* 97 (1972): 161–74.

Schepens, P., "Vocatus apostolus (Rom i, 1–1 Cor i, 1)," *RSR* 16 (1926): 40–42.

Schlier, H., "Zu Röm 1, 3f.," *Neues Testament und Geschichte: Historisches Geschehen und Deutung im Neuen Testament: Oscar Cullmann . . .* (Tübingen: Mohr [Siebeck], 1972), 207–18.

Schmithals, W., *The Office of Apostle in the Early Church* (Nashville, Tenn.: Abingdon, 1969).

Schneider, B., "*Kata pneuma hagiosynēs* (Romans 1, 4)," *Bib* 48 (1967): 359–87.

Schweizer, E., "Ecumenism in the New Testament: The Belief in the 'Son of God,' " *Perspective* 9 (1968–69): 39–59.

———, "Röm. 1, 3f. und der Gegensatz von Fleisch und Geist vor und bei Paulus," *EvT* 15 (1955): 563–71.

Segalla, G., "L'*obbedienza di fede*' (Rm 1, 5; 16, 26) tema della Lettera ai Romani?" *RivB* 36 (1988): 329–42.

Stuhlmacher, P., "Theologische Probleme des Römerbriefpräskripts," *EvT* 27 (1967): 374–89.

Theobald, M., " 'Dem Juden zuerst und auch dem Heiden': Die paulinische Auslegung der Glaubensformel Röm 1, 3f.," *Kontinuität und Einheit: Für Franz Mussner*, ed. P.-G. Müller and W. Stenger (Freiburg im Breisgau: Herder, 1981), 376–92.

Toit, A. B. du, "Faith and Obedience in Paul," *Neotestamentica* 25 (1991): 65–74.

———, "Persuasion in Romans 1:1–17," *BZ* 33 (1989): 192–209.

———, "Romans 1, 3–4 and the Gospel Tradition: A Reassessment of the Phrase *kata pneuma hagiosynēs*," *The Four Gospels 1992: Festschrift Frans Neirynck*, 3 vols., BETL 100, ed. F. van Segbroeck et al. (Louvain: Leuven University and Peeters, 1992), 1.249–56.

Trinidad, I., "Praedestinatus filius Dei . . . ex resurrectione mortuorum (Rom. 1, 4)," *VD* 20 (1940): 145–50.

Vogelstein, H., "The Development of the Apostolate in Judaism and Its Transformation in Christianity," *HUCA* 2 (1925): 99–123.

2. THANKSGIVING (1:8–9)

1 ⁸First of all, I give thanks to my God through Jesus Christ for all of you, because your faith is proclaimed in all the world. ⁹Now God, whom I worship

with my spirit in the evangelization of his Son, is my witness that I constantly make mention of you.

COMMENT

Paul follows his opening greeting to the Christians of Rome with an expression of thanks. In many of Paul's letters the section that follows the opening *praescriptio* is a thanksgiving. Such a section can be found in 1 Thess 1:2–5; Phil 1:3–8 (or 11); 1 Cor 4:9; and Phlm 4–7. In 2 Cor 1:3–11 Paul substitutes a blessing, which is more appropriate to the character of that letter of reconciliation. In Gal 1:6–9 there is no thanksgiving. Paul expresses instead his surprise that the Galatians are so quickly turning to another gospel. Cf. the Deutero-Pauline 2 Thess 1:3–10 and Col 1:3–8; in Eph 1:15–23 the thanksgiving not only follows a blessing but is joined to a prayer of intercession. In thus introducing a thanksgiving, Paul is again following the custom of Greek letters of his time, in which the thanksgiving often had to do with the addressee's good health (see *NJBC* art. 45 §8). It is, however, a matter of debate whether this thanksgiving is formulated only in v 8 (a complete sentence in itself in Greek) or goes on in v 9, which, though it is the beginning of a sentence that ends with v 10, continues the topic of his prayer to God. Many commentators take vv 8–15 as a unit, sometimes calling it the "thanksgiving," but in reality vv 10–15 deal with another topic, Paul's desire to visit the Roman Christian community. But, as Schubert has remarked (*Form*, 5–6), "In Romans we search in vain for the carefully built climax which is so typical of the Pauline thanksgivings." Consequently, I take vv 8–9 as the Pauline thanksgiving in this letter, even though v 9 feeds directly into the subsequent discussion.

In this thanksgiving Paul prays in typically early Christian fashion: to God "through Jesus Christ." He utters his gratitude to the God of the OT whom he still worships, though he writes as a Christian apostle. The reason for his utterance of thanks is that he realizes that the faith of Roman Christians is known worldwide. Moreover, Paul calls God to witness that he constantly makes mention of these Christians, i.e., he remembers them in prayers to the God whom he worships in spirit, as he carries on the evangelical proclamation of his Son. Later (in 15:16) Paul will affirm that his role as "a minister of Christ Jesus to the Gentiles" and "his priestly duty of preaching God's gospel" are really a cultic act. By preaching the gospel, he worships God.

NOTES

1:8. *First of all.* As in 3:2, Paul uses *prōton men* and does not follow up on it; cf. 1 Cor 11:18; also BDF §447.4. The adv. probably has the force of "at the outset."

I give thanks to my God. Paul uses the vb. *eucharistein*, as in 1 Thess 1:2; 1

Cor 1:4; Phil 1:3; Phlm 4; cf. 2 Thess 1:3; Col 1:3; 2 Macc 1:11 (a thanksgiving follows the greeting in the second letter). See H. Patsch, *EDNT* 2.98–88; on the thanksgiving formula, see Patsch, "Abendmahlsterminologie"; and Robinson, "Die Hodajot-Formel." The phrase "my God" is also found in Phil 1:3; 4:19; 2 Cor 12:21; Phlm 4. The sense of it is explained by what Paul admits in v 9b. Actually, it is an OT phrase; see Pss 3:8; 5:3; 7:2; etc., where the LXX reads *ho theos mou.*

through Jesus Christ. Christian prayer is poured forth to God through the mediation of his Son, "who was raised, who is at God's right hand and even intercedes for us" (8:34). Christ acts as the mediator not only of God's activity toward human beings (as in v 5), but also of human praise and honor of God, especially in his status as the risen Lord. Käsemann (*Commentary*, 17) tries to play down this intermediary role of Christ, maintaining that *dia* means only "in virtue of," and that the phrase expresses "the basis and validation of prayer." That it expresses such is admitted, but Paul is supremely aware of Christ's actual and current intermediary role as intercessor in heaven (see 8:34; cf. 7:25; 1 Cor 15:57). For the same mediatory formula, see 2:16; 5:1, 11, 21; 15:30; 16:27; cf. Kuss, "Die Formel," 199; Schettler, *Die paulinische Formel.*

for all of you. Paul does not disclose any awareness of differences that exist in the Roman community; that will emerge in 14:1–15:13. Now he prays for all without distinction. "All" resumes that of v 7. The prep. *peri* has the meaning of "on behalf of" and equals *hyper* (BAGD, 644b).

because your faith is proclaimed in all the world. Paul thanks God for the strong faith of Roman Christians, realizing that they have come to Christian belief because of a gift of God himself. What he calls *pistis*, he will call *hypakoē* in 16:19. Neither here nor elsewhere does Paul give a hint about how Romans came to espouse Christianity; yet he is happy to note that their belief is known everywhere, probably because they dwell in the capital of the Roman world. He is also aware of what that really means: that there is in the capital of the Roman Empire a church, a community that believes in Christ. In saying "in all the world," he indulges in hyperbole, as in 1 Thess 1:8 and 2 Cor 2:14.

9. *God, whom I worship with my spirit.* Paul uses the vb. *latreuein*, which even in classical Greek was used of the service of a deity (Plato, *Apology* 9 §23b) and which is found regularly in the LXX for the religious and ritual worship by the people of Israel of Yahweh (Exod 3:12; 10:7, 8, 26; 12:31; Deut 6:13; 10:12–13). Paul does not mean that he worships God only inwardly. His cultic service is manifested in his evangelical preaching; to proclaim Christ Jesus is for Paul an act of worship that he directs with his spirit to God himself (see 15:15–16). Yet Paul's very prayer for the Christians of Rome is an integral part of his worship of God.

The phrase *en tō pneumati mou* has been variously understood: (1) Strathmann (*TDNT* 4.64) translates it, "through the Spirit of God imparted to me"; similarly Kümmel (*Römer 7 und die Bekehrung des Paulus*, 33). Some commentators even compare Phil 3:3, "who worship by the Spirit of God"; in a way it could be parallel to such a passage, but neither the reading nor the sense of that passage is certain. (2) "In toto corde meo et prompta devotione" or "wholeheart-edly" (Pelagius, *Expositio in Romanos* 1.9). (3) "By that aspect of me that is open to God's Spirit"; so Sanday and Headlam, (*Romans*, 20: "*pneuma* is the organ of service"). The last mentioned is preferable; see 8:5.

in the evangelization of his Son. Lit., "in the gospel of his Son," but *euangelion* is to be understood in the active sense of the preaching of the gospel, i.e., the sphere in which the cult is rendered, as in Gal 2:7; Phil 4:3, 15; 1 Cor 9:14b, 18b; 2 Cor 2:12; 8:18. "Of his Son" is an objective gen.: in the preaching of the gospel about his Son.

is my witness. Paul often invokes God's testimony about his work and his activity (1 Thess 2:5, 10; Phil 1:8; 2 Cor 1:23), even apart from the phraseology used here (e.g., 9:1; 2 Cor 2:17). His formulation echoes OT usage (1 Sam 12:5–6; cf. Gen 31:50; Judg 11:10). In this case, Paul is not using a conventional formula. God's testimony is invoked in juridical fashion because it concerns Paul's prayers on behalf of the Roman Christians, something that they could not verify themselves. He invokes divine testimony, not only because he is certain that his cultic service is wholly dedicated to God, but also because he considers it important that Roman Christians realize that he is constantly praying for them. A similar oath, used in a letter to emphasize the importance of the message, is found in the letter of Simon ben Kosiba to Yeshua͑ ben Galgula (Mur 43:3): *mʿyd ʾny ʿly t šmym*, "I call Heaven to witness against me that . . ." (cf. Deut 4:26; 30:19; 31:28; 1 Macc 2:37).

I constantly make mention of you. As in 1 Thess 1:2 and Phlm 4, Paul uses the middle voice of *poiein* with an abstract noun *mneia*, "remembrance," instead of the vb. *mimnēskesthai*, "remember." In the NT it is used only of remembering someone in prayer (cf. Eph 1:16). This is a good classical Greek expression (BDF §310.1), which occurs in Plato, *Phaedrus* 254a and *Protagoras* 317e, and which Paul uses with other abstract nouns (15:26; cf. Phil 1:4). In using "constantly," Paul again indulges in hyperbole.

BIBLIOGRAPHY

Corriveau, R., *The Liturgy of Life*, 139–48.

Kümmel, W. G., *Römer 7 und die Bekehrung des Paulus*, 33.

Kuss, O., "Die Formel 'durch Christus' in den paulinischen Hauptbriefen," *TTZ* 65 (1956): 193–201.

Lyonnet, S., " 'Deus cui servio in spiritu meo' (Rom 1,9)," *VD* 41 (1963): 52–59; repr. *Études*, 36–42.

Patsch, H., "Abendmahlsterminologie ausserhalb der Einsetzungsberichte," *ZNW* 62 (1971): 210–31.

Robinson, J. M., "Die Hodajot-Formel in Gebet und Hymnus des Frühchristentums,"

Apophoreta: Festschrift für Ernst Haenchen, BZNW 30 (Berlin: de Gruyter, 1964), 194–235.

Schettler, A., *Die paulinische Formel "Durch Christus" untersucht* (Tübingen: Mohr [Siebeck], 1907).

Schubert, P., *Form and Function of the Pauline Thanksgivings*, BZNW 20 (Berlin: Töpelmann, 1939).

Stählin, G., "Zum Gebrauch von Beteuerungsformeln im Neuen Testament," *Donum gratulatorium E. Stauffer* (= *NovT* 5.2–3; Leiden: Brill, 1962), 115–43, esp. 132.

3. PROEM: PAUL'S DESIRE TO COME TO ROME (1:10–15)

1 ¹⁰I beg always in my prayers that somehow, by God's will, I may at length succeed in coming to you. ¹¹I yearn to see you in order to pass on to you some spiritual gift that you may be strengthened—¹²or rather that we may be mutually encouraged by each other's faith, both yours and mine. ¹³I do not want you to be unaware, brothers, of how often I have proposed to come to you, though I have been hindered up to now, in order to reap some fruit also among you as among the other Gentiles. ¹⁴Both to Greeks and to barbarians I am indebted, both to the wise and to the unlearned! ¹⁵Hence my eagerness to preach the gospel also to you who are in Rome.

COMMENT

Paul's prayer of thanksgiving has now become a prayer of petition, at least initially, because the petition becomes part of a preliminary statement about his plans to visit the Christian community of Rome and about the occasion of his writing. Paul insists that he has always wanted to come to the capital of the Roman Empire, the center of the civilized world in his time. Fully aware that this important city has been evangelized already, he thinks that there is still room for his evangelical activity there. He expresses his longstanding desire to come to Rome in terms of passing on to Roman Christians some spiritual gift that will strengthen them in their adherence to Christianity. But having so formulated his reason, Paul diplomatically corrects himself, realizing that he too can profit from the experience to which he looks forward: "that we may be mutually encouraged by each other's faith." Paul does not write so out of any insecurity, mistrust, or suspicion; nowhere in this letter does he hint that the Christians of Rome have heard about him or cherish suspicions about him. It is rather part of Paul's skilled rhetoric, part of his *captatio benevolentiae* (way of capturing the reader's good will). His coming visit will be a source of mutual benefit.

In v 13 Paul states his desire to visit the Christian community of Rome. His evangelical activity in the eastern Mediterranean area up to this time ("from Jerusalem all the way around to Illyricum," 15:19) has not permitted him to make serious plans about coming to Rome or elsewhere in the West. Now the possibility looms before him. His desire is to "reap some fruit" evangelically among the Christian people of Rome, as among other Gentiles to whom he has been sent as an apostle (11:13).

Once again diplomacy (and basic humility) brings Paul to admit that success or achievement in evangelical activity has not been the sole mark of his experience thus far. He has profited from contact with Greeks and barbarians, with the wise and the unlearned, in his evangelization of them. This realization moves him in desiring to come to Rome; contact with Christians in the center of the empire will also aid him. It is not that he still thinks of the Christians of Rome as Gentiles, Greeks, or barbarians. But he does want to extend to them his apostolic effort: "hence my eagerness to preach the gospel also to you who are in Rome." Here at the beginning of the letter Paul prescinds from the principle that he will enunciate in 15:20, his ambition to preach the good news only where the name of Christ has not been known.

So Paul announces the occasion of his writing to the Roman community. The occasion is not yet fully formulated, for there is no mention yet of his plans to go farther to the west, to visit Spain. That will come when he discusses the plans more fully in chap. 15. What Paul now sends to the Christians of Rome turns out to be "the most important theological epistle in Christian history" (Käsemann, *Commentary*, 20). Paul gives no indication here that he thinks that the Roman congregation has been lacking in apostolic foundation, *pace* G. Klein (see Introduction, section V).

NOTES

1:10. *I beg always in my prayers.* Lit., "begging always," the ptc. modifies the subject of the last verb in v 9. Thus Paul adds a petition to his prayer of thanksgiving. Commentators debate whether the phrase "in my prayers" should go with the ptc. *deomenos* or with the end of v 9. It is preferably taken with the ptc., because the adv. "continually" is already used in v 9. Cf. Eph 1:16; 2 Tim 1:3.

that somehow. Lit., "whether perhaps." Paul uses *ei pōs*, an unusual conj. to introduce the obj. cl. dependent on *deomenos*. See BAGD 220a. For Lagrange (*Romains*, 14) it expresses a prayer particularly submissive to the will of God.

by God's will. Cf. 1 Cor 4:19; 16:7. Paul realizes that his coming to Rome may depend on factors beyond his control. In 15:25–32 he will express apprehension about his intervening trip to Jerusalem, prior to his coming to Rome; he may now be hinting at that situation. The "will of God" is a frequently used expression in Pauline letters (12:2; 15:32; 1 Cor 1:1; 2 Cor 1:1; 8:5; Gal 1:41; 1 Thess 4:3; 5:18), imitated in Col 1:1; 4:12; Eph 1:1; 6:6. The way Paul uses it here echoes the expression *tou theou thelontos*, "God willing," found in many papyrus letters of the time (see Deissmann, *Bible Studies*, 252).

I may at length succeed in coming to you. In 15:23–24 Paul will explain further the complications of his desire. Cf. Acts 19:21, where the Lucan Paul expresses a similar desire.

Knox thinks that Paul's failure to mention Spain among his travel plans in chap. 1 reveals that the form of Romans was at first addressed to a larger group of addressees than Roman Christians (see Introduction, section IV). But does such an omission necessarily carry that connotation?

11. *I yearn to see you.* Cf. 1 Thess 3:6; 1 Cor 16:7; Phil 1:27. According to Rengstorf ("Paulus," 453), Paul uses *idein*, "see," to express the contemplated meeting with friends in the Roman community. It reveals that Paul looks forward to meeting old friends again, some of whom he will mention in chap. 16. He does not use *historein*, as he does in Gal 1:18, when he speaks of meeting Cephas for the first time.

in order to pass on to you some spiritual gift that you may be strengthened. The *charisma pneumatikon* is not to be understood as one of those gifts mentioned in 12:6 or in 1 Cor 12:4–10 (gifts granted to members of the church for special functions in it), but more generically as the *pneumatika*, "spiritual blessings," of 11:29 and 15:27. Paul is aware that he comes to Rome not as a church-founding apostle, but as an evangelist who may be able to strengthen the faith that already exists among the Christians there. Does Paul mention the "spiritual gift" because he seeks to assert apostolic authority vis-à-vis the *pneumatikoi* in the Roman community? So Michel, *Brief an die Römer*, 82. That, however, is to introduce a problematic of the Corinthian church (1 Cor 2:14–16) into a context that seems to know nothing of it; see Cranfield, *Romans*, 79. Even if "spiritual gift" were to refer to the charisms of 1 Corinthians 12, Paul would scarcely be thinking of the laying on of hands, *pace* J. K. Parratt, *ExpTim* 79 (1967–68): 151–52. It may be, however, that Paul also indirectly intends his very writing of Romans to be a way of passing on to the Christians of Rome some spiritual gift. That is, his plan to visit Rome also supplies a motivation for his writing of Romans. This is then a way of discharging his apostolic and missionary obligation, as he writes this letter. He is sharing the gospel, as he says in 1 Thess 2:8, and in due time he will share himself. Compare what Paul says in 15:15.

12. *or rather that we may be mutually encouraged by each other's faith.* Lit., "that is, to be coencouraged among you through the faith of one another, yours and mine," a cumbersome qualification of v 11, in which the overloaded syntax of the clause suffers. The corrective infin. *symparaklēthēnai* is parallel to neither *idein hymas*, "to see you," nor *stērichthēnai hymas*, "that you may be strengthened." It is an infin. of purpose, loosely connected with the whole v 11. Paul corrects himself similarly in 7:18; cf. Phlm 12. In any case, it is clear that he does not want to insist on his apostolic authority (1:5) or on any superiority in writing to a community that he has not founded, but seeks rather to stress the mutual

profit that both he and Roman Christians will be to each other. Käsemann (*Commentary*, 19–20) rightly recognizes that this admission divests the planned visit of any official character. But is Paul really hedging about his apostolic authority? Is he still struggling for recognition as an apostle? An affirmative answer to such a question would be to read too much into an otherwise forthright self-correction.

13. *I do not want you to be unaware.* Paul has used this formula in 1 Thess 4:13; 1 Cor 10:1; 12:1 and 2 Cor 1:8; he will use it again in 11:25. It introduces something that he considers important and wishes to make explicit. It is always followed by "brothers." Recall his similar use of *gnōrizō*, "I make known" (Gal 1:11; 1 Cor 12:3; 15:1; 2 Cor 8:1). Cf. Phil 1:12.

The words *ou thelō* are read in MSS P²⁶, ℵ, A, B, C, Dᶜ, K, P, Ψ, 88, 614, 1739, etc. and are to be preferred to *ouk oiomai*, "I do not suppose," of MSS D*, G, and some VL MSS, Ambrosiaster and Pelagius, and to *ouk oismai* of MS Dᵈ, Dᵃᵇˢ.

brothers. Paul uses this title for fellow Christians again in 7:1, 4; 8:12; 10:1; 11:25; 12:1; 14:10, 13, 15, 21; 15:14, 30; 16:14, 17, 23; and often in other letters (1 Thess 1:4; 2:1, 9, 14, 17; etc.). Other NT writers also make use of it, and not just as a form of address (e.g., Acts 1:15–16; 9:30; 10:23; 11:1, 12, 29; 12:17; 14:2; 15:3, 22, 32–33, 40; 17:6, 10, 14; 18:18, 27; 21:7, 17, 20; 28:14–15; 1 Pet 5:12; 2 Pet 3:15). The term *adelphos* has nothing to do in these cases with blood relationship or kinship; it designates the closeness experienced by those who were followers of the risen Christ and a sense of the intimate relations that Paul has with those he so addresses.

Peter addresses Jews assembled in Jerusalem as *adelphoi* (Acts 2:29; 3:21), as does Stephen (7:2, 26); these examples reveal the origin of the term, borrowed from Palestinian Jewish usage. Compare Paul's use of the term in 9:3 (see the NOTE there). The Jewish use of "brother" is probably to be traced to Deut 13:7; 15:1–18. But it was not commonly used until deuterocanonical writings such as Tobit, Judith, and the Maccabees. See, e.g., Tob 5:5, 9, 11; 6:7, 14, where it may mean "kinsman," but more likely has a pietist connotation, which appears also in QL (1QS 6:10, 22; 1QSa 1:18; CD 6:20; 7:1–2; 8:6; 19:18; 20:18; 1QM 13:1; 15:7). Josephus (*J.W.* 2.8.3 §122) uses the term to describe the Essenes. It also occurs in the *praescriptio* of the letter in 2 Macc 1:1, addressing Jews in Egypt as such. See further J. Beutler, "Adelphos . . . ," *EDNT* 1.28–30.

how often I have proposed to come to you. The vb. *proethemēn* shows that Paul's yearning (1:11) has been more than a velleity; it suggests that he has even planned on earlier occasions to visit the community of the capital of the Roman world of his day. Thus he expresses his longstanding, but frustrated, proposal. He insists that his failure to come to the Christians of Rome so far has not been caused by indifference to them.

though I have been hindered up to now. I.e., by his missionary duty and endeavors in the eastern Mediterranean area, as 15:22–24 will explain. *Pace*

Schmithals *(Römerbrief)*, the aor. *ekōlythēn* does not imply that Paul is still "hindered." For that he would have had to use the perfect or the present. The hindrance is now clearly over: that is the force of the aorist. The pass. vb. *ekōlythēn* might be considered theological (ZBG §236); then it would mean that God's employment of him elsewhere for the sake of the gospel was more urgent and that God himself therefore hindered him from coming to Rome.

in order to reap some fruit also among you as among the other Gentiles. I.e., to strengthen the faith of the Roman Christians by his evangelical preaching (1:11, 15). Paul employs *karpos*, "fruit," using an agricultural figure to describe the effects of his coming missionary activity (as in Phil 1:22; cf. 1 Cor 3:6–9), or the return that he might expect from it. *Karpos* is used as in Amos 6:12; Josephus, *Ant.* 20.2.4 §48. *Pace* M. A. Kruger (*WTJ* 49 [1987]: 167–73), the reference in "some fruit" is scarcely so specific as to imply that Paul is already thinking of the collection for the poor of Judea (cf. 15:22–29). Again Paul includes the Christians of Rome among the Gentiles (cf. 1:6).

14. *both to Greeks and to barbarians I am indebted.* So Paul expresses his debt to the non-Jewish world. He is indebted in two senses: (a) He has learned and profited from his Hellenistic education and background as a diaspora Jew, from his Roman citizenship (Acts 22:25–28), and from his missionary experience among all of the Gentiles already evangelized. This could again be his experience among the Romans. (b) He addresses his gospel to all of them, because that is the obligation of his apostolate (1 Cor 9:16), the debt that he owes to all because he is "the apostle of the Gentiles" (11:13). It goes without saying that he is indebted, above all, to Christ who died for his salvation; now because of that, he is also indebted to all those to whom Christ wished to bring salvation. "Obligation to him who died produces obligation to those for whom he died" (Minear, "Gratitude," 44).

Since about 700 B.C. the name *Hellēnes* denoted Greek tribes and city-states united by speech, culture, and religion. After the conquest of Alexander the name was used to denote also non-Greek peoples who spoke Greek and shared Greek culture and education. In the LXX, *Hellēnes* denotes the inhabitants of Yāwān, originally of Ionia, whence this Hebrew name spread to mainland Greece (e.g., Zech 9:13; Dan 8:21; 10:20), and in 1 Macc 1:10 it is used even for the Seleucids. As used by Paul, it would refer to the Greek-speaking people among the *ethnē*, and especially to the cultured people of the Greco-Roman world, particularly in the great cities.

Barbaroi, however, would refer to non-Greek-speaking Gentiles. The adj. *barbaros* is formed onomatopoetically of reduplicated *bar*, which to ancient Greeks imitated the unintelligible sounds of foreign languages; they even likened them to the twittering of birds (Herodotus, *History* 2.57). See 1 Cor 14:11. The phrase, however, expresses more than a difference of language, because *barbaroi* for Greeks of the classical and Hellenistic periods connoted peoples less cultured, among whom they included national enemies such as the Persians and Egyptians;

in the Roman period, Spaniards, Gauls, and Germans would have been included (see H. Windisch, *TDNT* 1.547; cf. H. Balz, *EDNT* 1.197–98; W. Speyer and I. Opelt, "Barbar," *JAC* 10 [1967]: 251–90). Paul never hints in his letters where he might have encountered non-Greek-speaking Gentiles, but Luke depicts him dealing with people who spoke Lycaonian (Acts 14:11). For Paul the Christians of Rome would not have been among the *barbaroi*, because in the first century A.D. Greek was spoken by most Romans. Indeed, he writes his letter to the Christians of Rome in Greek. Is 1:14 the "key" to the whole of Romans? So Pedersen would have us believe ("Theologische Überlegungen"), drawing a parallel between 15:14–33 (Jerusalem, Rome, Spain) and 1:13–17 (Jew, Greek, barbarian). Although the parallel is interesting, the rest of the thesis is most unlikely and farfetched. Hence, v 14 is scarcely the key to the whole of the letter.

both to the wise and to the unlearned. By this second pair Paul scarcely means that the Greeks were "wise" and the barbarians were "unlearned." That would be to assume too rigid a parallelism. There is no reason to think that both pairs refer to the same totality, *pace* Cranfield (*Romans*, 83). Rather, the first pair sums up the Gentiles, the second is a description of all humanity, as Huby rightly saw (*Romains*, 57). Paul moves from a restricted group to a larger one. His experience with all levels of humanity has taught him much, and he alludes to this in 1 Cor 1:26–27. Again, he is obligated to all levels of humanity, precisely as an apostle. No one is excepted from this obligation of his.

15. *hence my eagerness to preach the gospel also to you who are in Rome.* So Paul sums up his preliminary statement. He uses *euangelizesthai* of preaching to those who are already Christians, and, as Cranfield (*Romans*, 86) rightly notes contra Kuss (*Römerbrief*, 20), it does not mean that he has forgotten the diplomatic concession he made in v 12. In 15:20 he will use the verb again in its more basic sense of preaching the gospel to the *ethnē* (see Friedrich, *TDNT* 2.720), but then he may be reflecting on his past missionary activity or possibly uttering there a sort of principle. What Paul says here is not really a contradiction of such a principle, which he really intends to implement in Spain. His preaching in Rome will merely take place *en passant*. It is far from certain, however, that he intends to express here merely a past conclusion from vv 13–14, "hence my eagerness was to preach . . . ," as Stuhlmacher ("Purpose," 237) and Zeller (*Römer*, 39) would take it. There is no verb expressed, and there is no reason not to understand the verse as expressing what is on Paul's mind as he writes. In fact, this phrase explains in part why Paul is already writing to the Roman Christians about his gospel, which he proceeds to summarize in the words of vv 16bc–17. Paul has explained his plans briefly, and he will come back to them in chap. 15; but those plans briefly stated here are closely linked to both the greetings of vv 1–7 and the theme of the entire letter to be set forth in vv 16bc–17.

Paul uses *kata* with the acc. *eme* instead of the possessive gen., as in Acts 17:28; 18:15; 26:3; Eph 1:15 (BDF §224.1), and *to prothymon* as equal to the abstract *prothymia*, "eagerness," as in Josephus, *Ant.* 4.8.13 §213. The phrase *to kat' eme prothymon* functions as the subject and the infin. *euangelisasthai* is the predicate.

Again, the words *tois en Rōmē,* "who are in Rome," are omitted in MS G and the Latin translation of Origen; see the NOTE on 1:7.

BIBLIOGRAPHY

Cocchini, F., "L'esegesi origeniana di *Rom* 1,14: Aspetti di una situazione ecclesiale," *SMSR* 54 (1988): 71–79.

Deissmann, G. A. *Bible Studies,* 2d ed. (Edinburgh: Clark, 1909).

Eichholz, G., "Der ökumenische und missionarische Horizont der Kirche: Eine exegetische Studie zu Röm. 1,8–15," *EvT* 21 (1961): 15–27.

Hengel, M., *Jews, Greeks and Barbarians: Aspects of the Hellenization of Judaism* (Philadelphia, Penn.: Fortress, 1980), 55–66.

Klein, G., "Der Abfassungszweck des Römerbriefes," *Rekonstruktion und Interpretation: Gesammelte Aufsätze zum Neuen Testament,* BEvT 50 (Munich: Kaiser, 1969), 129–44.

Kruger, M. A., "*Tina karpon:* 'Some Fruit' in Romans 1:13," *WTJ* 49 (1987): 167–73.

Minear, P. S., "Gratitude and Mission in the Epistle to the Romans," *Basileia: Walter Freytag . . . ,* ed. H. J. Margull (Wuppertal-Barmen: Rheinische Missionsgesellschaft, 1959), 42–48.

Parratt, J. K., "Romans i. 11 and Galatians iii. 5—Pauline Evidence for the Laying on of Hands?" *ExpTim* 79 (1967–68): 151–52.

Pedersen, S., "Theologische Überlegungen zur Isagogik des Römerbriefes," ZNW 76 (1985): 47–67.

Rengstorf, K.-H., "Paulus und die älteste römische Christenheit," *SE II,* TU 87 (1964), 447–64.

Schrenk, G., *Studien zu Paulus* (Zurich: Zwingli-Verlag, 1954), 81–106.

Stuhlmacher, P., "The Purpose of Romans," *RomDeb,* 231–42.

Trocmé, E., "L'Apôtre Paul et Rome: Reflexions sur une fascination," *RHPR* 72 (1992): 41–51.

I. DOCTRINAL SECTION: GOD'S GOSPEL OF JESUS CHRIST OUR LORD (1:16–11:36)

A. Through the Gospel the Uprightness of God Is Revealed as Justifying People of Faith (1:16–4:25)

◆

4. *Theme Announced:* The Gospel Is the Powerful Source of Salvation for All, Disclosing God's Uprightness (1:16–17)

1   ¹⁶Now I am not ashamed of the gospel. It is God's power (unleashed) for the salvation of everyone who believes, for the Jew first but also for the Greek. ¹⁷For in it is revealed the uprightness of God, through faith and for faith, as it stands written, *the one who is upright shall find life through faith.*

COMMENT

Having uttered his thanksgiving and petition and having made his preliminary statement about his plans to come to Rome, Paul begins the major topic of his letter. Although vv 16bc–17 continue the last statement of v 15 and introduce the topic that will be discussed in vv 18–32, they announce the major theme of the letter and one that will be developed until 11:36. This theme recapitulates the whole doctrinal section, which covers eleven chapters in the letter. The section may be divided into three parts: (A) 1:16–4:25; (B) 5:1–8:39; and (C) 9:1–11:36. But the theme enunciated here also acts specifically as the theme of part A; a secondary theme (for part B) will be introduced in 5:1–11. The climax of the development of this theme comes when Paul discusses how both Jews and Gentiles fit into the salvific plan that Paul is now about to sketch, how Gentile Christians become heirs to the promises made to Israel of old, and how both Jews, and Gentiles are related to the mystery of God's redemption in Christ Jesus.

As Aletti has shown, each part of Romans has a rhetorical construction, and parts A and B especially have their own *propositiones*. The main *propositio*, however, is found in these verses ("La Présence"). The introduction has already mentioned "God's gospel" (1:1) and Paul's role in proclaiming it. Now Paul will explain in greater detail how that gospel concerns God's Son and how a new, unique possibility is extended by it to all humanity to find salvation through him "established as the Son of God with power . . . as of his resurrection from the dead" (1:4). Although this gospel reveals God's uprightness as he justifies people

253

of faith (part A), it also discloses God's love that is poured out through his Spirit and assures salvation and new life for such people (part B). Yet the gospel also manifests that this justification and salvation are available to all, Jews and Greeks alike, through faith, and so it does not contradict God's promises to Israel of old (part C).

Paul takes pride in his role of proclaiming this gospel, as he announces the theme that will be first developed. The gospel is not just a message sent from God; it is a "power" unleashed in the world of humanity that actively accosts human beings, challenging them to accept it through faith in Christ Jesus. That "power" is not unrelated to the power of the risen Christ (1:4), which is thus proclaimed. Moreover, the gospel reveals something about the God who promised it of old (1:2) and who now acts in a new way; it reveals his "uprightness" or "righteousness" for those who accept this gospel in faith. *Dikaiosynē theou* is the phrase that Paul uses to sum up the theme of Romans. It delineates the divine salvific activity at work in Christ Jesus, the power that God himself has let loose in the world of human beings. As Stuhlmacher has put it, "Rom. 3:21–31 shows . . . that we must allow the word [the phrase *dikaiosynē theou*] the breadth which is inherent in it from the Old Testament: according to Paul, the one God acts in and through his one Son, Christ, on behalf of the entire world. Christ is his righteousness in person" ("Theme of Romans," 341). Indeed, it brings new sense to the words that the prophet Habakkuk once uttered, "the one who is upright shall find life through faith" (2:4).

What should be noted in this announcement of the theme of Romans is Paul's formulation of the effect of the Christ-event as "salvation" and not as justification, despite the fact that the main emphasis in part A will be on justification. Four further affirmations in the announced theme are noteworthy: (1) the universality of God's salvation for all who are willing to accept it; (2) the equality of Jew and Greek in this plan of salvation, which, however, admits a priority for the Jew, both de facto (in a temporal, chronological sense) and de jure (according to Paul's view of salvation history: this gospel was announced through *Israel's* prophets, 1:2 [cf. 2:9; 9:1–11:36]); (3) this universality and equality of salvation come through the gospel, a force unleashed by God revealing his *dikaiosynē* and directing human history; and (4) human beings share in this salvation through faith, which can be progressively intensified in dedication to God. Striking in this announcement is the absence of any reference to Christ, the description of whose role is put off until 3:21–26.

The theme thus announced will be developed by Paul in three ways: (1) negatively, what happens to humanity without the gospel (1:18–3:20); (2) positively, in the gospel God's uprightness is manifested through Christ to all sinners and apprehended by faith (3:21–31); and (3) by an illustration drawn from the OT: Abraham was justified by his faith, and not by his deeds (4:1–25).

Paul creates a transition from his introductory remarks by declaring his pride in the task entrusted to him of announcing God's gospel. He thus picks up a theme that he had treated at greater length in 1 Cor 1:17–2:16: to unbelievers the gospel is foolishness. Yet such an attitude cannot deter Paul from proclaiming the gospel. He comes to the capital of the Roman world with a simple message, a message that he knows is foolishness to many.

Paul terminates his theme by quoting Hab 2:4, "the one who is upright shall find life through faith." He thus takes from the OT a key passage that summed up the value of observance of the law for the Jew. But Paul not only quotes it; he makes it the pillar of his thesis about salvation through faith, thus wresting it from the clutches of the law. It is now made part of his gospel and becomes the motto of his view of God's new salvific process, which does not depend on the observance of the law. The quotation from Habakkuk illustrates what Paul wrote in Gal 3:8, "Scripture, foreseeing that God would justify the Gentiles through faith, preached the gospel beforehand to Abraham, saying, 'In you shall all the nations be blessed.'" By quoting Habakkuk, Paul gives a concrete example of what he said in his introductory verses about "God's gospel which he promised long ago through his prophets in the sacred Scriptures" (1:1–2).

NOTES

1:16. *Now I am not ashamed of the gospel.* Paul's admission picks up on v 14. It may be understood both socially and psychologically: though he is coming to the capital of the Roman Empire and comes not as a founder of its Christian community or as one of the Twelve, he is "the apostle of the Gentiles" (11:13) and will proclaim the gospel that he knows is folly to some and a stumbling block to others (1 Cor 1:18, 23), a paradox and a contradiction to the society of the capital of the Roman Empire. Yet he knows that God has chosen what is foolish in the sight of the world to shame the wise (1 Cor 1:27); cf. 1 Cor 4:10. Again, "he shrinks neither from Jewish Christians who may slander him, nor from charismatics who may look down upon him" (Michel, *Brief an die Römer*, 86). Although Paul may suspect that some Roman Christians have been critical of the gospel that he has been preaching, as Wedderburn suggests (*Reasons*, 104), he does not say so. If that were the case, his words here about the gospel would then be even more significant.

Paul's use of *ouk epaischynomai*, "I am not ashamed," may instead echo an early Christian confessional formula (Mark 8:38; Luke 9:26; 2 Tim 1:8) and be only the negative equivalent of *homologein*, "acknowledge, confess." He is aware of the temptation to shame about the gospel because he realizes the hostility that it can arouse, and yet he is more than ready to proclaim it, even proud to do so in Rome. For the gospel is for him not merely a passing on of truths or a report about noteworthy events, but the word in which God's will is presently accomplished. On "gospel," see the NOTE on 1:1 and *PAHT* §§PT31–36.

Some MSS (D^c, Ψ, and the *Koinē* text tradition) add *tou Christou*, "(the gospel) of Christ." This addition corrects the absence of mention of Christ in the announcement of the theme of Romans, but the best Greek MSS (P²⁶, ℵ, A, B, C, D*, E, G, etc.) omit the phrase.

God's power. Whenever the gospel is proclaimed, God's power becomes operative and succeeds in saving. His power thus catches up human beings and through the gospel brings them to salvation. This is the essential, all-important theme that Paul announces: salvation comes to all through faith. In 1 Cor 1:18 Paul predicated *dynamis theou* of "the word of the cross," another way of expressing "the gospel," and in 1 Cor 1:24 he applied it to Christ himself, who is in fact the content of the good news. As used here, the phrase formulates the dynamic character of God's gospel; the word may announce the death and resurrection of Jesus Christ, but the emphasis is on that word as a force or power unleashed in human history. Moreover, because that gospel announces the Christ-event, its power is related to that of the risen Christ himself, "established as the Son of God with power" (1:4). Through him God has unleashed his own power. Cf. 1 Cor 2:5; 6:14; 2 Cor 13:4; Phil 3:10. God's "power" *(dynamis)* is often mentioned in the OT (e.g., Deut 3:24; Josh 4:24; Jer 16:21), and the phrase *dynamis theou* occurs in the LXX (1 Chr 12:23, but in the sense of "an army of God"). Cf. Wis 7:25; 2 Macc 3:24, 38.

for the salvation. The phrase *eis sōtērian* is omitted in MS G, but is to be retained because it expresses the purpose of the gospel as God's power. For "salvation" as an effect of the Christ-event, see Introduction, section IX.B. Paul will speak of it again in 5:9–10; 8:24; 10:9–10 (where it appears in parallelism with "justification"), 13. In 1 Thess 5:9–10 Paul made it clear that this salvation comes through "our Lord Jesus Christ who died for us so that . . . we might live with him." So the eschatological destiny of the Christian is formulated in terms of salvation.

of everyone who believes. Lit., "for everyone believing" or "for every believer." To "believe" is the response of a human being accosted by the gospel: faith in its message, faith in Christ Jesus whom it announces, and faith in God from whom it comes. To believe is to accept the gospel and through it to find life in Christ. It is the necessary, indispensable condition for salvation, *pace* Nygren (*Romans*, 68–69). No one, of course, achieves salvation without faith, which arises only because of the proclaimed gospel of God. Thus the initiative is God's in the salvific process; yet he does not save everyone indiscriminately. Paul realizes that human beings must react to the gospel, and such reaction is a human response, the condition without which God does not save. "Faith" in some form is used by Paul four times in these two verses, thus showing the importance that he puts on it. The phrase also expresses the universal destination of the gospel, a force aimed at *all* humanity.

for the Jew first but also for the Greek. Paul sums up all humanity as "Jew" and "Greek." In this sense "Greek" would include the barbarians of v 14. All, both Jews with their covenantal uprightness and Gentiles with their lack of uprightness, are accosted by the gospel of God's uprightness; they can all react to it in faith. Paul phrases the summation this way because, though he recognizes the quality of the believing Jew and Greek vis-à-vis the gospel, expressed by the correlative *te . . . kai*, he is interested in asserting the privileged status of the Jew in God's salvific plan *(Ioudaiō prōton)*, a privilege that he will repeat in 2:9–10. The priority of the Jew is acknowledged not only because the gospel was first preached to the Jews, but because God promised his gospel through the prophets of old in the sacred Scriptures of the Jews (1:2), thus destining it for his chosen people, and through them for all others. That gospel announced "his Son" (1:3), whom he sent at a set time to that people, "born of a woman, born under the law, to redeem those who were under the law" (Gal 4:4; cf. Rom 11:28–29). The "Greek" is brought in because Paul has already in mind the relation between Jew and Gentile that he will formulate in 11:11–12. He also insists that there is no partiality in God (2:11; cf. 3:22; 10:12), for salvation is open to all. On the name *Ioudaios*, see the NOTE on 2:17; on the name *Hellēn*, see the NOTE on 1:14.

The adv. *prōton* is omitted in MSS B, G, in the Sahidic version, and by Marcion, who would not have admitted the privilege of the Jews; the best Greek MSS, however, read it.

17. *in it is revealed*. So the apocalyptic character of the gospel is enunciated: it has disclosed God's sovereign plan of salvation for all humanity, proceeding from his uprightness and realized in the spread of the gospel that Paul has been preaching. Paul uses the vb. *apokalyptein*, "unveil, reveal," which will appear again in v 18 with a different connotation. Compare 3:21, where a synonym with a slightly diverse nuance, *phaneroun*, is employed. Note the significant echo of the vocabulary of Ps 98:2 in 1:16–17: "Yahweh has made known his salvation *(yĕšûʿātô, LXX sōtērion autou)*, in the sight of the nations he has revealed *(gillāh, LXX apekalypsen)* his uprightness *(ṣidqātô, tēn dikaiosynēn autou)*."

the uprightness of God. Or "the righteousness of God." *Dikaiosynē theou* (or *dikaiosynē autou*, "his uprightness") appears again in 3:5, 21, 22, 25, 26; 10:3(bis). Here *dikaiosynē theou* stands in contrast to *orgē theou*, "the wrath of God" (1:18), an attribute, property, or quality in God. Because that sense is also found in 3:5 and best suits the other verses in chap. 3, that sense is used for all passages in Romans in which this phrase occurs.

Theou is thus understood as a possessive or subjective gen., descriptive of God's upright being and of his upright activity, and not as a gen. of author or origin. When *dikaiosynē* is called an attribute or quality, nothing static is implied; it is an aspect of God's power, whence proceeds his acquitting and salvific activity in a forensic mode.

Paul uses *dikaiosynē theou* in the sense in which God's uprightness is spoken of in postexilic writings of the OT, even though the specific phrase never occurs as such in the LXX. It is the quality whereby God actively acquits his sinful people, manifesting toward them his power and gracious activity in a just judgment (see Isa 46:13 [where "my righteousness," and "my salvation" stand in parallelism];

257

51:5, 6, 8; 56:1; 61:10; Ps 40:9–10). It is now manifested toward humanity because of what Christ Jesus has done for them. See Introduction, section IX.A.

No little part of the problem in explaining the Pauline use of *dikaiosynē theou* has been its English translation. In the VL and in the Vg it appears as *iustitia Dei*, and in many Bibles that depended on the Vg tradition it became "the justice of God," "la justice de Dieu," "la justicia de Dios," "la giustizia di Dio." But "justice of God," though defensible as a translation in itself, has often been understood as God's distributive or retributive justice and sometimes as a quality contrasted with God's mercy, specifically his punitive or vindictive justice. Although this sense has been used in the interpretation of Romans, it is far from what Paul means by *dikaiosynē theou*. Very commonly this phrase has been rendered in English as "the righteousness of God." "Righteousness," however, has a peculiar ring in English, suggesting to many something like self-righteousness, which is the last thing that Paul would mean by it. Instead, E. J. Goodspeed (*The Complete Bible: An American Translation* [Chicago: University of Chicago, 1960], NT, 143) rendered it "the uprightness of God," which captures the sense equally well and which I have adopted in this commentary.

Dikaiosynē theou also occurs in 2 Cor 5:21, where Paul asserts that "we become the uprightness of God." There the gen. is objective, and it clearly expresses the status of uprightness communicated to human beings by God's gracious gift. There it could also be called a gen. of author or origin. That too is the sense of Phil 3:9, where Paul contrasts "my own uprightness" with "the uprightness *from* God that depends on faith" *(tēn ek theou dikaiosynēn epi tē pistei)*; in this case the prep. *ek* is used, and it is not a case of a simple gen. Cf. Rom 5:17, where there is clearly mentioned the "gift of uprightness" given to human beings, but it is not said to be *dikaiosynē theou*; also 1 Cor 1:30, where Christ is said to be our "uprightness" (from God). Hence it is clear that Paul could and did speak of the "uprightness" of human beings as a "gift," and even expressed that gift abstractly as *dikaiosynē theou*, in the sense of an object given and a gen. of author (2 Cor 5:21). Note how the Pauline expression in Phil 3:9 *(tēn ek theou dikaiosynēn)* is paralleled by a LXX phrase in Bar 5:2, *peribalou tēn diploida tēs para tou theou dikaiosynēs*, "put on the robe of uprightness from God." Such expressions make it clear that biblical writers could talk about *dikaiosynē* as something coming from God to humans; but significantly, it is not formulated simply as *dikaiosynē theou*. A simple genitive is not used, as in 2 Cor 5:21, but a prep. phrase that clearly makes God the origin or author. Indeed, Paul's use of *dikaiosynē theou* in 2 Cor 5:21 is unique and has no forebears either in the OT or in intertestamental literature. The instance of *dikaiosynē Kyriou* in *T. Dan* 6:10, "Refrain therefore from all wickedness and cling to the uprightness of (the law of) the Lord," may seem to be such a gen., but the text is not certain, because several MSS add *tou nomou* before *Kyriou*. Pace A. Oepke (*"Dikaiosynē theou,"* 262), the Greek text of the *T. 12 Patr.*, which may indeed be derived from a Semitic original, is not certainly "long before Paul." The Greek text has been interpolated by Christians and the formulations are not certainly all traceable to a Semitic original. The fact that *nomon theou* appears in 6:9 reveals that the phrase *tē dikaiosynē tou nomou Kyriou* may be original; it is the preferred reading of M. de Jonge, *Testamenta XII Patriarcharum*, PVTG 1 (Leiden: Brill, 1964), 51.

Augustine used the objective sense of *iustitia Dei* in *De Trinitate* 14.12.15 (CCLat 50A.443) in addition to the subjective sense: "iustitia Dei, non solum illa qua ipse iustus est, sed quam dat homini cum iustificat impium" (not only that justice by which he himself is just, but also that which he gives to a human being, when he justifies the impious); cf. *De Spiritu et littera* 1.9.15 (CSEL 60.167), where he limits it to the second sense: "iustitia dei, non qua deus iustus est, sed qua induit hominem, cum iustificat impium" (the justice of God, not that by which God is just, but that with which he endows a human being, when he justifies the impious). Also 1.11.18 (CSEL 60.171); *Ep.* 140.72 (CSEL 44.220); *In Johannis evangelium* 26.1 (CCLat 36.260).

Three understandings of the phrase prevailed in the medieval period. One was the attribute, or the subjective sense (most likely the sense of Paul himself in Romans), but in the formulation of Ambrosiaster: "iustitia est dei, quia quod promisit, dedit; ideo credens hoc esse se consecutum quod promiserat deus per profetas suos, iustum deum probat et testis est iustitiae eius" (It is the justice of God, because he has given what he has promised; hence the one who believes that he has acquired that which God had promised through his prophets, shows that God is just and becomes a witness to his justice) (*In ep. ad Romanos* 1.17 [CSEL 81.1.36–37]), i.e., God's fidelity to his promises. In fact, Ambrosiaster often used it in the sense of God's mercy: "ideo autem iustitia dei dicta est, quae videtur esse misericordia, quia de promissione originem habet. . . . Et cum suscipit confugientes ad se, iustitia dicitur, quia non suscipere confugientem iniquitas est" (But [that] is then said to be God's justice which seems to be his mercy, because it is rooted in his promise. . . . And when he welcomes those who take refuge in him, it is said to be justice, because not to welcome those who seek refuge is iniquity; 3.21 [CSEL 81.1.116–17]).

The second medieval interpretation was the attribute as distributive justice (as in popular Pelagianism): "Iustitia enim tua est, ut qui fecerit voluntatem tuam, transeat a morte in vitam, per quam et ego nunc eripi deprecor" (For it is by your justice, that whoever does your will passes from death to life, through which I too now plead to be rescued; Ps.-Jerome, *Breviarium in Psalmos* 70.2; PL 26.1087), i.e., God's rewarding of human beings according to their just deserts. Cf. PL 30.649: "quia sine fide, hoc est sine spe retributionis bonorum operum perficere virtutes nemo poterit" (since without faith, that is, without hope of the recompense of good works, no one can live a virtuous life).

Finally, it was understood as communicated justice, or the objective sense (as Paul uses it in 2 Cor 5:21 and as Augustine understood it [see above]). This meaning was also used by Ps.-Primasius, Claudius of Turin, Haymo, and Thomas Aquinas ("iustitia qua Deus iustus est et qua Deus homines iustificat" [the justice with which God is just and by which he justifies human beings]), but Aquinas also combined with it some of Anselm's ideas, regarding divine mercy as the fullness of justice.

Each of these senses underwent further modification and acquired various nuances in the later medieval period, especially as Ciceronian, Justinian, or Aristotelian understandings of *iustitia* were introduced to modify it. The notions of Augustine and Ambrosiaster were often combined. Especially with interpreters like Hatto of Vercelli the idea of God's retributive justice was stressed. He was followed by Lanfranc, Bruno the Carthusian, Anselm of Canterbury, Ps.-Gilbert de la Porrée, et al. Cf. Denifle, *Quellenbelege*; Holl, "Die *iustitia Dei*"; H. Bornkamm, "Iustitia Dei in der Scholastik und bei Luther"; McGrath, *Iustitia Dei*, 1.51–53.

When Luther came to interpret Romans, he understood *dikaiosynē theou* at first as *iustitia distributiva*, as did the Via Moderna and many Nominalists:

> Iustitia autem dicitur redditio unicuique quod suum est. Unde prior est equitas quam iustitia et quasi prerequisita. Et equitas meriti distinguit, iustitia premiae reddit. Sic Dominus iudicat orbem terrae in equitate (quia omnibus idem est, vult omnes salvos fieri) et iudicat in iustitia, quia reddit unicuique suum premium. (*Dictata super Psalterium [1513–15]*; *Scholia in Psalmos* 9.9; WAusg 55.1.70, 55.2.108–9)

> But justice is said to be the rendering to each one what is his. Hence equity comes before justice and [is], as it were, prerequisite. The equity of merit distinguishes, the justice of reward recompenses. Thus the Lord judges the world with equity (in that he is the same for all: He wants all to be saved) and judges with justice in that he renders to each one his reward.

Such an understanding of *iustitia Dei* was also colored by the medieval dispute about the divine attributes, especially in the school of Ockham (see McGrath, *Iustitia Dei*, 68–70, 121–26).

In time Luther came to understand *dikaiosynē theou* as an objective gen., "die Gerechtigkeit die vor Gott gilt" (the justice that counts before God), i.e., the uprightness that a human being enjoys as a gift from God. In the preface to his Latin writings, composed a year before he died, he explains how he came to this meaning:

> I had been captivated with a remarkable ardor for understanding Paul in the epistle to the Romans. But up until then it was not the cold blood about the heart, but a single saying in chap. 1, "In it the justice of God is revealed," that stood in my way. For I hated that word "justice of God," which, according to the use and custom of all the teachers, I had been taught to understand philosophically of the formal or active justice, as they

called it, by which God is just and punishes sinners and the unjust. Though I lived as a monk without reproach, I felt I was a sinner before God with a most disturbed conscience; I could not believe that he was placated by my satisfaction. I did not love, indeed, I hated the just God who punishes sinners. Secretly, if not blasphemously, certainly murmuring greatly, I was angry with God. . . . Finally by the mercy of God, as I meditated day and night, I paid attention to the context of the words, "In it the justice of God is revealed, as it is written, 'He who through faith is just shall live.' " Then I began to understand that the justice of God is that by which the just lives by a gift of God, namely by faith. This, then, is the meaning: the justice of God is revealed by the gospel, viz. the passive justice with which the merciful God justifies us by faith, as it is written, "The just one lives by faith." Here I felt that I was altogether born again and had entered paradise itself through open gates. There a totally other face of all Scripture showed itself to me. Then I ran through Scripture, as I could from memory, and I found an analogy in other terms too, such as the work of God, i.e., what God does in us, the power of God, with which he makes us strong, the wisdom of God, by which he makes us wise, the strength of God, the salvation of God, the glory of God. (*Preface to Latin Writings [1545]*; WAusg 54.185–86; LuthW 34.336–37)

Cf. *Lectures on Romans* ad 1:17; 3:21; 10:3 (LuthW 25.9, 30–31, 89); *Scholia in Rom.* ad 1:17; 3:21; 10:3 (LuthW 25.9, 30–31, 89); *Scholia in Rom.* ad 1:17 (LuthW 25.151); *Table Talk* 5518 (1542–43) (LuthW 54.442).

The interpretation that Luther thus adopted, "that by which the just lives by a gift of God," was derived from the Augustinian tradition. In adopting this translation, Luther was partly reacting against the idea of *iustitia* as a divine attribute, as medieval theologians had often taught, and partly against the idea that *iustitia* denoted God's punitive activity. But in rejecting the Scholastic notion of attribute and in preferring to interpret *dikaiosynē theou* in the Augustinian sense of a gift coming from God, Luther did away with two things. He not only rightly rejected the punitive idea of *iustitia*, but also the idea of *iustitia* as a divine attribute and, following Augustine, made of it a gift that God communicates to sinful human beings. From such an understanding of *iustitia* he came to his idea of *iustitia aliena* (WAusg 2.491.18 or 39.1.83.24–25) and his oft-quoted definition, "die Gerechtigkeit die vor Gott gilt" (the justice that counts before God), used in his translation of 1:17 (WAusg DB 7.30–31).

The Augustinian sense was also adopted by the Council of Trent as the formal cause of justification (*Decretum de justificatione*, 1547, cap. 7 [DS 1529]). That interpretation of the Pauline phrase in 1:17 has persisted into modern times. It was espoused by Bultmann in *TNT* 1.285 and in his debate with Käsemann ("*Dikaiosynē theou*," *JBL* 83 [1964]: 12–16: "die Gabe Gottes" [God-given, God-adjudicated righteousness]). This meaning is also used by Nygren (*Romans*, 74–

76); Cranfield (*Romans*, 98, though he admits that in 3:5 the gen. "must be subjective" [p. 96]); Cornely (*Commentarius*, 68–69); Lagrange (*Romains*, 19); Michel (*Brief an die Römer*, 89); O'Neill (*Romans*, 38); Ridderbos (*Paul*, 163), et al.

Ambrosiaster's sense also persists today, see Williams ("The 'Righteousness' " 255–89): "God's fidelity to this promise to Abraham"; Kümmel (*Theology*, 195): "God's gracious faithfulness which maintained his covenant."

Among modern interpreters Cremer (*Paulinische Rechtfertigungslehre*) began a new trend when he related Pauline *dikaiosynē theou* to the OT idea of *ṣedeq*, a relational concept denoting the action of partners in a covenant and their behavior as consistent with such a relationship, and characteristic especially of God's relation to Israel, the people of his covenant (his *iustitia salutifera* or *Gemeinschaftstreue*, as expressed in such OT passages as Isa 46:13 or 56:1). As a result, modern interpreters began to return to the idea of *dikaiosynē theou* as a subjective or possessive gen., descriptive not so much of God's being, but of his activity as Savior. Schlatter too realized that *dikaiosynē* in 3:5 had to be understood as the attribute (*Gottes Gerechtigkeit*, 116–22; see also 36). He thus broke with the traditional Lutheran interpretation, which his son Theodor Schlatter acknowledged in the preface to 4th ed. of 1965.

What is debatable, however, is whether the gift idea of *dikaiosynē theou* is suitable anywhere in Romans. In his debate with Käsemann, Bultmann insisted on different senses of the phrase in different places in Paul's letters (subjective gen. in 3:5, 25, objective in 1:17; 10:3). Käsemann rightly sought to use one sense, stressing the power character of God's gift. *Pace* Cranfield (*Romans*, 97, 825), it is not "arbitrary" to insist that *dikaiosynē theou* in Romans has only "one sense." It has rather to be shown that it is right to import the objective sense from 2 Corinthians or the prepositional expression of Phil 3:9 into the interpretation of Romans.

In 1:16–17 the attribute sense or the subjective gen. is just as suitable as the gift idea: for God's uprightness even as an attribute can be the object of the gospel's revelation. In fact, it is more suitable than the gift idea, being immediately paralleled by not only "the power of God" (1:16b), but also "the wrath of God" (1:18), another attribute of divine activity, as Schlatter rightly saw (*Gottes Gerechtigkeit*, 36). Moreover, in 3:26 Paul's argument reaches a climax, when he says, *eis to einai auton dikaion*, "to show that he [God] is upright." Recall also the attributes in chap. 3: *hē pistis tou theou*, "the fidelity of God" (3:3), *hē alētheia tou theou*, "the truthfulness of God" (3:7), which are virtual synonyms of "God's uprightness." For this reason the interpretation of Käsemann, who has followed Schlatter and who has been followed by Stuhlmacher, Kertelge, Lyonnet, and others, is preferable (even if one does not insist on God's rectifying "power" as an attribute). So too it is understood by Dodd (*Romans*, 9–10), Lekkerkerker (*Romeinen*, 1.47–49), Kühl (*Römer*, 41–42), Kümmel (*Theology*, 195–96 [though he uses the sense of Ambrosiaster]), Tobac (*Problème*, 107–21), and Van Daalen ("Revelation").

In 10:3, the one place in which the debate may still continue, it again seems to be the better interpretation, even though some modern interpreters, who otherwise follow Schlatter and Käsemann, prefer to understand the gift idea there, as the NRSV still tendentiously translates the Pauline neutral phrase.

There are, of course, some commentators who try to have it both ways, e.g., Moo (*Romans 1–8*, 70), "a relational concept . . . bringing the aspects of activity [what I have called the attribute sense] and status [what I have called the gift sense] together . . . *the act by which God brings people into right relationship with Himself*" (his italics). Yet even in such a relational explanation, Moo's emphasis falls on God and his activity, on what I prefer to call the attribute sense. Similarly, Althaus (*Römer*, 13), and Lietzmann (*An die Römer*, 30): "a changeable double sense," which Oepke rightly characterizes as one that reveals the embarrassment of the interpreter ("*Dikaiosynē theou*," 259).

through faith and for faith. Lit., "from faith to/unto faith." The meaning of this phrase is debated. For Origen (*In Ep. ad Romanos* 1.15; PG 14.861) it meant: as one passes from the faith of the people of old to the faith of the gospel. This sense is, however, hardly adequate for the Pauline usage. Similarly, for the desperate explanation of Ramaroson (*ScEspr* 39 [1987]: 91): ". . . is revealed from the faith (of Jesus) to the faith (of the Christian)," understanding the first to refer to the faithfulness of Jesus, as some commentators would understand 3:22. But that is to introduce an equivocation into the meaning of two occurrences of the same term.

The double prep. phrase with *ek . . . eis* is found in Ps 84:8, where the preps. express passage from one degree to another, a meaning that Paul uses elsewhere (2 Cor 2:16; 3:18) and which is also possible here: God's economy of salvation is shared more and more by a person as faith grows: from a beginning faith to a more perfect or culminating faith. By the coupling of the two prepositional phrases Paul means that there is room only for faith, not deeds, in the process of justification.

Another possible meaning is "through faith (and) for faith," understanding the prep. *ek* instrumentally and *eis* purposively; this reading would be in line with the development in 3:21–22. "Through faith" would express the means by which a person shares in salvation; "for faith" would express the purpose of the divine plan (cf. Jer 9:2; Plutarch, *Galba* 14.1 §1058E). In either case Paul would be suggesting that salvation is a matter of faith from start to finish, whole and entire. It is not that through Christ and through faith in him human beings are enabled to fulfill the law, but rather that through God's gift of Christ Jesus human beings come to believe in him, belong to him, and share in the uprightness that has been revealed through him and the gospel about him. On "faith," see the NOTE on 1:5 and Introduction, section IX.D.

as it stands written. Lit., "as it has been written," in Scripture. So Paul often explicitly introduces an OT quotation (2:24; 3:10; 4:17; 8:36; 9:13, 33; 10:15; 11:26; 15:3, 9, 21; and elsewhere in his letters). *Kathōs gegraptai* occurs in Dan 9:13 (Theodotion) as the translation of Hebrew *ka᾿ăšer kātûb*, and in 2 Kgs 14:6 as the translation of Hebrew *kakkātûb*. The former of these Hebrew introductory formulas is often found in QL (1QS 5:17; 8:14; CD 7:19; 4QFlor 1–2 i 12; 4QpIsa^c 4–7 ii 18; 4QCatena^a 10–11:1; 4Q178 3:2), showing that Paul's mode of introducing Scripture stands in a good pre-Christian Palestinian Jewish tradition. See Fitzmyer, *ESBNT*, 3–58, esp. 8–9; cf. Horton, "Formulas"; Giblin, " 'As It Is Written,' " 478–79.

The one who is upright shall find life through faith. Paul quotes Hab 2:4 to support the theme that he is announcing. The MT reads *wĕṣaddîq be᾿ĕmûnātô yiḥyeh*, "but the righteous shall live by his fidelity." In the original context the words form part of Yahweh's reply to the prophet's complaint about the continuing oppression of Judah. Chaldean invaders, who are expected and whose god is their might, are contrasted with Judah, whose deliverance lies in fidelity to Yahweh. God tells Habakkuk that at the coming invasion the upright Judahite will find life through his fidelity.

Hab 2:3–4 is quoted and commented upon in 1QpHab 7:5–8:3. Unfortunately the crucial Hebrew words of v 4 are not all preserved in the lemma, but in the pesher on v 4 the words that Paul quotes are understood thus: "The interpretation of it concerns the observers of the law in the house of Judah, whom God shall deliver from the house of judgment because of their striving and their fidelity to the Teacher of Righteousness" (M. Burrows [ed.], *The Dead Sea Scrolls of St. Mark's Monastery*, vol. 1: *The Isaiah Manuscript and the Habakkuk Commentary* [New Haven: A.S.O.R., 1950], pl. lviii). Here a Palestinian Jewish tradition has already understood the prophet's words to promise life not only for observance of the law, but also for fidelity to the person of a Jewish leader. Paul's application of Habakkuk's words to the life brought by Christ Jesus, though dependent on the LXX form, stands within such a Jewish tradition. See Käsemann, *Commentary*, 31–32.

A Greek form of Hab 2:4 is preserved in both the fragmentary text of 8HevXIIgr and the LXX. See E. Tov, *The Greek Minor Prophets Scroll from Naḥal Ḥever (8HevXIIgr)*, DJD 8 (Oxford: Clarendon, 1990), 52–53. In 8HevXIIgr 17.29–30 the Greek text translates the Hebrew exactly: *[kai di]kaios en pistei autou zēset[ai]*, "and (the) upright one will live by his fidelity."

But in the LXX three versions of the Hebrew are found. In MSS S, B, Q, V, W* one reads *ho de dikaios ek pisteōs mou zēsetai*, "but the upright one shall live by my fidelity," i.e., by Yahweh's fidelity to his people. In this instance, the translator read the final *waw* on Hebrew *be᾿ĕmûnātô* as *yodh*, the suffix of the first sg. pers. pron. *(be᾿ĕmûnātî)*. This reading of the LXX is regarded by D.-A. Koch ("Der Text") as the oldest and original form of the Greek version. In MSS A and C, however, one finds rather *ho de dikaios mou ek pisteōs zēsetai*, "my upright one shall live by fidelity," i.e., the one righteous in my [God's] sight. It is not easy to explain how the first pers. pron. came to be shifted to "upright one." Finally, in MS 763* one finds simply, *ho de dikaios ek pisteōs zēsetai*, as it appears in Paul's text. This last reading, however, may be owing to a copyist's harmonization of the LXX with the Pauline reading and is to be regarded as secondary in the LXX tradition.

When Paul quotes Habakkuk's words, he quotes them according to neither the MT nor the best MSS of the LXX. He not only drops the poss. pron. altogether, but understands *pistis* in his own sense of "faith," and "life" not as deliverance from invasion and death, but as a share in the risen life of Christ (see 6:4, 8). In this way Paul cites the prophet Habakkuk to support the theme of his letter.

Because the Pauline phrase *ek pisteōs*, "by/through faith," stands between *ho de dikaios* and *zēsetai*, commentators on Romans have debated what it modifies. Some have taken it with the vb. *zēsetai*, "shall live through faith," as it is understood in Habakkuk, and as I have taken it above. So Althaus, Godet, Huby, Leenhardt, Michel, Moody, Murray, Sanday and Headlam, Schlatter, Schlier, Smith, Wallis, Wilckens, and Zahn. Others relate it to *ho de dikaios* and translate, "he who through faith is righteous shall live." So the *RSV*, Barrett, Barth, Black, Byrne, Cranfield, Feuillet, Kuss, Lagrange, Lietzmann, Nygren, and Pesch. The latter do so, claiming that it is thus more expressive of Paul's thought. Moreover, Nygren (*Romans*, 86–90) and Feuillet even argue that 1:17, thus understood, is the key to chaps. 1–8 in that "he who through faith is upright" is the topic of chaps. 1–4, whereas "shall live" is the topic of chaps. 5–8. But on both scores the matter can be argued either way, and has been so argued. I prefer the first interpretation because Paul has not written *ho de ek pisteōs dikaios*. Cf. *hē de ek pisteōs dikaiosynē* (10:6), which shows that Paul could have written *ho de ek pisteōs dikaios*, if that was what he meant. Moreover, he is not formulating something on his own; he is citing Habakkuk, for whom *beʾĕmûnātô* or *ek pisteōs* modified the verb. *Pace* Cranfield (*Romans*, 102), neither the immediate context nor the structure of the letter requires that "by faith" be taken as a modifier of the subject. Although Paul does speak of *dikaiosynē ek pisteōs* (9:30; 10:6) or (in a participial form) of *dikaiōthentes ek pisteōs* (5:1), he never uses *ho dikaios ek pisteōs*, save here, in a quotation from Habakkuk (see Huby, *Romains*, 69). Again, the thrust of vv 16–17 is such that one expects the emphasis to fall on *ek pisteōs*. The phrase stresses the way a person comes to share in life in Christ or salvation. Paul also cites Hab 2:4 in Gal 3:11, where "by faith" stands in contrast to "by law," and Habakkuk's words are quoted to offset the teaching of Lev 18:5. This evidence seems to confirm what Cavallin ("The Righteous") calls the traditional interpretation, i.e., the sense of Habakkuk.

BIBLIOGRAPHY

Aletti, J.-N., "La Présence d'un modèle rhétorique en Romains: Son Rôle et son importance," *Bib* 71 (1990): 1–24.

Barrett, C. K., "I Am Not Ashamed of the Gospel," *Foi et salut*, 19–50.

Barth, M. et al. (eds.), *Foi et salut selon s. Paul (Épître aux Romains 1,16)*, AnBib 42 (Rome: Biblical Institute, 1970).

Bornkamm, H., "Iustitia Dei in der Scholastik und bei Luther," ARG 39 (1942): 1–46.

Cambier, J., *L'Évangile de Dieu*, 1.11–59.

———, "Justice de Dieu, salut de tous les hommes et foi," RB 71 (1964): 537–83.

Campbell, W. S., "A Theme for Romans?" *Paul's Gospel*, 161–99.

Carlson, C. P., Jr., *Justification in Early Medieval Theology* (The Hague: Nijhoff, 1975).

Carrez, M., "Ambakoum Septante," RHPR 72 (1992): 129–41.

Cavallin, H. C. C., " 'The Righteous Shall Live by Faith': A Decisive Argument for the Traditional Interpretation," ST 32 (1978): 33–43.

Corrigan, G. M., "Paul's Shame for the Gospel," BTB 16 (1986): 23–27.

Daalen, D. H. van, "The Revelation of God's Righteousness in Romans 1:17," *Studia Biblica 1978: Sixth International Congress on Biblical Studies, Oxford 3–7 April 1978*, 3 vols., JSNTSup 2–3, 11, ed. E. A. Livingstone (Sheffield, UK: JSOT, 1979–80), 3.383–89.

Denifle, H., *Die abendländischen Schriftausleger bis Luther über Justitia Dei (Rom. 1, 17) und Justificatio*, Ergänzungen zu Luther und Luthertum 1: *Quellenbelege* (Mainz: Kirchheim, 1905).

Dockery, D. S., "The Use of Hab. 2:4 in Rom. 1:17: Some Hermeneutical and Theological Considerations," *Wesleyan Theological Journal* 22.2 (1987): 24–36.

Dunn, J. D. G., "The Justice of God: A Renewed Perspective on Justification," JTS 43 (1992): 1–22.

Emerton, J. A., "The Textual and Linguistic Problems of Habakkuk ii. 4–5," JTS 28 (1977): 1–18.

Feuillet, A., "La Citation d'Habacuc ii.4 et les huit premiers chapitres de l'épître aux Romains," NTS 6 (1959–60): 52–80.

———, "La Situation privilégiée des Juifs d'après *Rm* 3,9: Comparaison avec *Rm* 1,16 et 3,1–2," NRT 105 (1983): 33–46.

Fitzmyer, J. A., "Habakkuk 2:3–4 and the New Testament," TAG, 236–46.

———, "The Use of Explicit Old Testament Quotations in Qumran Literature and in the New Testament," NTS 7 (1960–61): 297–333; repr. ESBNT 3–58.

Fridrichsen, A., "Aus Glauben zum Glauben, Röm. 1,17," *Walter Bauer Gottingensi viro de Novi Testamenti philologia optime merito sacrum*, ConNeot 12 (Lund: Gleerup, 1948), 54.

Froehlich, K., "Justification Language and Grace: The Charge of Pelagianism in the Middle Ages," *Probing the Reformed Tradition: Historical Studies in Honor of Edward A. Dowey, Jr.*, ed. E. A. McKee and B. G. Armstrong (Louisville, Ky.: Westminster/John Knox, 1989), 21–47.

Giblin, C. H., " 'As It Is Written . . .'—A Basic Problem in Noematics and Its Relevance to Biblical Theology," CBQ 20 (1958): 327–53, 477–98.

Glombitza, O., "Von der Scham des Gläubigen: Erwägungen zu Röm. i 14–17," *NovT* 4 (1960): 74–80.

Güttgemanns, E., " 'Gottesgerechtigkeit' und strukturelle Semantik: Linguistische Analyse zu *dikaiosynē theou*," *Studia linguistica neotestamentica*, BEvT 60 (Munich: Kaiser, 1971), 59–98.

Haacker, K., "Das Evangelium Gottes und die Erwählung Israels: Zum Beitrag des Römerbriefs zur Erneuerung des Verhältnisses zwischen Christen und Juden," *TBei* 13 (1982): 59–72.

Herold, G., *Zorn und Gerechtigkeit Gottes bei Paulus: Eine Untersuchung zu Röm. 1,16–18*, Europäische Hochschulschriften 23.14 (Bern and Frankfurt am Main: Lang, 1973).

Holl, K., "Die *iustitia Dei* in der vorlutherischen Bibelauslegung des Abendlandes," *Festgabe von Fachgenossen und Freunden A. von Harnack . . . dargebracht* (Tübingen: Mohr [Siebeck], 1921), 73–92; repr. *Gesammelte Aufsätze*, vol. 3: *Der Westen* (Tübingen: Mohr [Siebeck], 1928; Darmstadt: Wissenschaftliche Buchgesellschaft, 1965), 171–88.

Horton, F. L., Jr., "Formulas of Introduction in the Qumran Literature," *RevQ* 7 (1967–71): 505–14.

Hvalvik, R., " 'For jøde først og så for greker': Til betydningen av Rom 1,16b," *TTKi* 60 (1989): 189–96.

Janzen, J. G., "Habakkuk 2:2–4 in the Light of Recent Philological Advances," *HTR* 73 (1980): 53–78.

Johnson, S. L., Jr., "The Gospel that Paul Preached," *BSac* 128 (1971): 327–40.

Käsemann, E., "The Righteousness of God in Paul," *NTQT*, 168–82.

———, *Perspectives*, 76–78.

Kertelge, K., "*Dikaiosynē*," *EDNT* 1.325–30.

———, "*Rechtfertigung*," 85–95.

Koch, D.-A., "Der Text von Hab 2:4b in der Septuaginta und im Neuen Testament," *ZNW* 76 (1985): 68–85.

Lyonnet, S., "De 'iustitia Dei' in Epistola ad Romanos 1,17 et 3,21–22," *VD* 25 (1947): 23–34.

———, *Les Étapes*, 25–53.

McGrath, A. E., *Iustitia Dei: A History of the Christian Doctrine of Justification*, 2 vols. (Cambridge: Cambridge University Press, 1986).

———, " 'The Righteousness of God' from Augustine to Luther," *ST* 36 (1982): 63–78.

Marin Heredia, F., " 'De fe en fe' (Rom 1,17a): Intento de comprensión," *Carthaginensia* 3 (1987): 27–36.

Mattill, A. J., Jr., "Translation of Words with the Stem *Dik-* in Romans," *AUSS* 9 (1971): 89–98.

Michel, O., "Zum Sprachgebrauch von *epaischynomai* in Röm. 1,16 (*ou gar epaischynomai to euangelion*)," *Glaube und Ethos: Festschrift für Professor D. Dr. Georg Wehrung . . .* (Stuttgart: Kohlhammer, 1940), 36–53.

Moody, R. M., "The Habakkuk Quotation in Romans 1:17," *ExpTim* 92 (1980–81): 205–8.

Moore, R. K., "Issues Involved in the Interpretation of *Dikaiosynē Theou* in the Pauline Corpus," *Colloquium* 23 (1991): 59–70.

Nielsen, H. K., "Paulus' Verwendung des Begriffes *Dynamis*: Eine Replik zur Kreuzestheologie," *Die paulinische Literatur und Theologie*, ed. E. Pedersen, Teologiske Studier 7 (Aarhus: Aros; Göttingen: Vandenhoeck & Ruprecht, 1980), 137–58.

Oepke, A., "*Dikaiosynē theou* bei Paulus in neuer Beleuchtung," *TLZ* 78 (1953): 257–63.

Olley, J. W., " 'Righteousness'—Some Issues in Old Testament Translation into English," *BT* 38 (1987): 307–15.

Prete, B., "La formula *dynamis theou* in Rom. 1,16 e sue motivazioni," *RivB* 23 (1975): 299–328.

Roberts, J. H., "Righteousness in Romans with Special Reference to Romans 3:19–31," *Neotestamentica* 15 (1981): 12–33.

Schenk, W., "Die Gerechtigkeit Gottes und der Glaube Christi: Versuch einer Verhältnisbestimmung paulinischer Strukturen," *TLZ* 97 (1972): 161–74.

Scott, J. M., "A New Approach to Habakkuk ii 4–5a," *VT* 35 (1985): 330–40.

Smith, D. M., *Ho de dikaios ek pisteōs zēsetai*," *Studies in the History and Text of the New Testament in Honor of Kenneth Willis Clark*, Studies and Documents 29, ed. B. L. Daniels and M. J. Suggs (Salt Lake City, Ut.: University of Utah, 1967), 13–25.

Stuhlmacher, P., *Gerechtigkeit Gottes*, 78–84.

——, "The Theme of Romans," *RomDeb*, 333–45.

Wallis, W. B., "The Translation of Romans 1:17—A Basic Motif in Paulinism," *JETS* 16 (1973): 17–23.

Williams, S. K., "The 'Righteousness of God' in Romans," *JBL* 99 (1980): 241–90.

Woude, A. S. van der, "Der Gerechte wird durch seine Treue leben: Erwägungen zu Habakuk 2:4–5," *Studia biblica et semitica Theodoro Christiano Vriezen . . . dedicata* (Wageningen: Veenman, 1966), 367–75.

Zänker, O., "*Dikaiosynē Theou* bei Paulus," *ZST* 9 (1931–32): 398–420.

THEME NEGATIVELY EXPLAINED: WITHOUT THE GOSPEL GOD'S WRATH IS MANIFESTED AGAINST ALL HUMAN BEINGS (1:18–3:20)

◆

5. GOD'S WRATH MANIFESTED AGAINST PAGANS (1:18–32)

1   [18]For God's wrath is being revealed from heaven against all the godlessness and wickedness of human beings who by such wickedness stifle the truth: [19]that what can be known about God is manifest to them. For God himself has made it evident for them. [20]Ever since the creation of the world his invisible qualities, his eternal power and divinity, have been perceived by reflection on what he has made. Consequently, such people are without excuse, [21]because, though they knew God, they did not glorify him as God or thank him. Instead, they were reduced to futile thinking, and their misguided minds were steeped in darkness. [22]Pretending to be wise, they became fools [23]and exchanged the glory of the immortal God for an image shaped like a mortal human being, like birds, four-footed creatures, and reptiles.

[24]For this reason God delivered them over to the craving of their hearts for impurity that their bodies might be degraded among them. [25]These people exchanged the truth about God for a lie and reverenced and worshiped the creature rather than the creator—blest be he forever! Amen. [26]For this reason God delivered them over to disgraceful passions. Their women exchanged natural intercourse for that against nature; [27]and their men likewise abandoned natural relations with women and burned with lust for one another—males committing shameless acts with males and being paid in turn in their own persons the wage suited to their deviation.

[28]As they did not see fit to acknowledge God, he delivered them over to a base mentality and to improper conduct. [29]They became filled with every sort of wickedness, evil, greed, and malice; they were full of envy, murder, strife, craftiness, and spite. They became tale bearers, [30]slanderers, God haters, insolent, haughty, and boastful; contrivers of evil, rebels against parents; [31]foolish, faithless, uncaring, and merciless. [32]Though they know full well God's requirement that those who do such things deserve to die, they not only do them but even give approval to those who so act.

COMMENT

Paul begins the explanation of the theme announced in vv 16–17 by describing the human condition apart from the influence of the preached gospel (1:18–3:20).

What happens to humanity that is not accosted by the gospel and that does not respond to its challenge? Käsemann (*Commentary*, 33) rightly insists that Paul in this part of Romans is dealing "with humanity as such and not just with representatives of religious groupings." Paul looks at "the totality of the cosmos" when it is left to itself without the gospel. His explanation of the theme proceeds at first negatively or antithetically: without the gospel affecting their lives all humanity is sinful and estranged from God. As a result his wrath is manifested toward them all.

In his Apostolicon, Marcion seems to have excised *theou* in v 18 and 1:19–2:2a: "For wrath is being revealed from heaven against all godlessness and wickedness of human beings who by such wickedness stifle the truth . . . who do such things." So it has been judged on the basis of Tertullian, *Adversus Marcionem* 5.13.2–3 (CCLat 1.702); see A. von Harnack, *Marcion: Das Evangelium vom fremden Gott*, TU 45 (Leipzig: Hinrichs, 1924), 103*. In more recent times, however, Harrison has maintained that the Apostolicon preserved the original text of Paul: "this passage had no place in the text of Romans used by Marcion, being an interpolation added by some scribe writing not in Rome but probably in Ephesus, and belonging to the same circle of Paulinist Christians as the author of the Pastorals" (*Paulines*, 81). But Harrison's view has found little following among interpreters of Romans. The passage is scarcely an interpolation into Paul's text.

It is important to note that Paul is not speaking of human beings and their unrighteousness or their attempts to achieve uprightness in God's sight by observing the law, but rather of God and his reaction to humanity without the gospel. Thus the topic in vv 18–32 is God's wrath as a reaction to human wickedness and unrighteousness, and in 2:1–3:9 it will be God's wrath manifested against the unrighteousness of those who try to achieve it by observance of the law. The status of humanity without the gospel is thus characterized as one under the wrath of God; in contrast the new status will be one under the uprightness of God (3:21–31).

In vv 18–32, though Paul speaks only of "human beings" (*anthrōpoi*, 1:18) and never specifies "Gentiles" or "Greeks," it becomes clear from 2:1 on (or at least from 2:9) that he has been thinking in this first subsection of non-Jewish humanity. Thus he implicitly returns to the division of humanity expressed in 1:16 as "Jew" and "Greek" (= the pagan, heathen, or Gentile). In 2:1–3:9 he will deal with Jewish humanity. His discussion will eventually embrace the totality, for "all, Jews and Greeks alike, are under the power of sin" (3:9).

In this subsection Paul echoes the judgment about the pagan world current among Jews of his day. Nevertheless, he is not saying that every individual pagan before Christ's coming was a moral failure. He speaks collectively and describes a de facto situation. Moreover, he does not limit his discussion merely to contemporary Greco-Roman society, *pace* Huby (*Romains*, 75–77), for he has already made mention of "barbarians" along with "Greeks" (1:14). He has in mind the totality of pagan society. *Pace* Cranfield (*Romans*, 105), Paul's allusions to Ps

106:20 and Jer 2:11 (which refer to incidents in Israel's history) do not mean that he envisages Jewish humanity as well in vv 18–32. He is simply extrapolating from such incidents in the history of the chosen people and applying the ideas to the pagan world.

This first subsection (1:18–32) has been variously characterized. For Michel (*Brief an die Römer*, 96) it is an example of a missionary sermon that Paul often enough delivered before pagans. Käsemann (*Commentary*, 33–34) more plausibly thinks that it is not a "self-contained treatise but the deposit of many debates," yet it can scarcely all be summed up as a "dialogue with the Jews." Michel has rightly seen that v 18 is the topic sentence and that v 32 ("those who do such things deserve to die") presents Paul's summary judgment.

For Paul the condition of pagan humanity results, first, from its failure to recognize God for what he is, to glorify him, and to thank him, when it could readily have done so, had it paid due attention to the traces of him and his qualities evident in the created world. The sin of pagans against God stems from their suppression of the truth about him in their lives, and as a result their misguided minds have become steeped in idolatry. They have turned from the glorification of the immortal God to the worship of images of mortal creatures, human or animal. Thus pagan idolatry has become the "big lie," and pagans have no excuse; their godlessness and wickedness have made them objects of divine wrath.

Second, the condition of pagan humanity results from the moral degradation to which their idolatry has brought them: to the craving of their hearts for impurity. Their idolatry has led to moral perversion: sexual excess (1:24, 26a) and homosexual activity (1:26b–27).

Third, it results also from every sort of improper conduct in which they are ensnared in their dealings with other human beings: their vices are cataloged in vv 29–30. This conduct stems likewise from the folly of their idolatry, and Paul judges that they are aware in reality of God's requirement that people who so act "deserve to die" (1:32). Hence they are inexcusable.

Paul's indictment of pagan humanity is severe. Like the prophets of old, he sees pagans as the object of God's "wrath" (*orgē*). This is to be understood as God's reaction of displeasure at human sinfulness; "God is not mocked; whatever a human being sows, that he also reaps" (Gal 6:7). Wrath is thus an attribute or quality of God, parallel to his uprightness or righteousness in v 17. "In their very existence [i.e., pagans' existence] lies the judgment passed against them" (Michel, *Brief an die Römer*, 96). Paul understands the moral degradation of pagan humanity as a concrete manifestation of God's existence in their earthly lives. As long as God exists, he cannot look with indifference on his creation that is destroyed by human sinning, as his will is disobeyed and ignored. On the OT and Pauline idea of God's wrath, see Introduction, section IX.A.

Three times over Paul depicts God in his wrath "delivering over" (*paredōken*, 1:24, 26, 28) pagan humanity to moral degradation. Thus he expresses vividly and concretely the consequences of pagan sin instead of stating the matter abstractly as cause and effect. When Paul speaks of God's wrath being revealed against the godlessness and wickedness of pagans, it is his inherited way of expressing the inevitability of evil finding its own retribution. As J. A. T. Robinson has put it, " 'Wrath' is the process of inevitable retribution which comes into operation when God's laws are broken. It contains the idea of what happens in the life of a man or society when moral control is loosened. It is what takes over if the situation is allowed to rip. Cf. 1.24, 26, 28, 'God gave them over', he leaves pagan society to stew in its own juice. The retribution which overtakes it, resulting in automatic moral degradation, is what 'comes on' almost like a thermostat when, as it were, the moral temperature drops below a certain point" (*Wrestling*, 18). Another way of putting it is found in Wis 11:15–16: "In return for their foolish, wicked thoughts, by which they went astray and worshiped irrational serpents and worthless animals, you sent upon them a throng of irrational creatures to punish them that they might learn that one is punished by the very things in which one sins."

Paul's argument about the inexcusable situation of pagan humanity has to be understood against the background of such pre-Christian Jewish thinking, especially that in the Wis 13:1–19 and 14:22–31. There the author similarly attributes "ignorance of God" to human beings "foolish by nature" (*mataioi physei*) because "they did not succeed in knowing him who exists from the good things that are seen, and they recognized not the craftsman while paying attention to his works" (13:1). Although the author of Wisdom at first admits that "for such people there is little blame" (13.6), he eventually judges, "But again, they are not pardonable (*oud' autoi syngnōstoi*); for if they were capable of knowing so much that they could investigate the world, how did they not sooner find the Lord of these things?" (13:8–9). The author of Wisdom likewise sees a connection between idolatry and sordid human conduct: "It was not, then, enough for them to go astray about the knowledge of God, but living even in the great strife of ignorance, they designated such great evils as peace" (14:22). The "evils" are then cataloged: child sacrifice, secret mystery celebrations, violated marital unions, murder, adultery, theft, deceit, corruption, sexual perversion, and debauchery (14:23–26). See further Romaniuk, "Le Livre."

The folly of idolatry was often linked to fornication or adultery in the Jewish tradition, and avoidance of it became a topic of exhortation in intertestamental literature as well: the deuterocanonical Letter of Jeremiah; *Sib. Or.* 3:8–45; *2 Apoc. Bar.* 54:17–18; *T. Naph.* 3:4. See further Herold, *Zorn und Gerechtigkeit*, 187–209.

When Paul says that God *paredōken*, "delivered (them) over" (1:24, 26, 28), he is speaking protologically; he is seeking to give a logical explanation of the dire condition of pagan humanity; in a primitive way, which echoes OT thinking, he attributes that condition to an action of God who punishes pagan humanity in his divine wrath.

Käsemann (*Commentary*, 39–41) thinks that this passage "raises the hotly contested issue of a natural theology in Paul" and wonders whether Paul wanted to assert only what Hellenistic Jewish teaching about the knowledge of God did. If so, Käsemann finds, Paul would "be advocating a natural theology which could scarcely be reconciled with his eschatology and christology"; similarly, Reicke ("Natürliche Theologie") and Nygren (*Romans*, 106–7). Such irreconcilability, however, is far from clear.

Granted, that human beings were capable of attaining knowledge of God by reason was an idea born in Greek philosophy centuries prior to the Apostle. Yet Paul does not take over even from Hellenistic Judaism its full teaching about the knowledge of God on the part of pagans. Dunn (*Romans*, 56) more plausibly notes "that some sort of natural theology is involved here." Similarly, Black (*Romans*, 46) speaks of a "natural theology"; also Bornkamm ("Gesetz und Natur," 102). Even if one admits with Käsemann that "God's deity" is "a power that encounters us," concentrates it in lordship, and perceives human guilt, not in ignorance, but in revolt against the known Lord (*Commentary*, 41), is not part of that revolt precisely found—at least among pagans—in the stifling of the truth about God (that they can know him)? Indeed, Paul may even go beyond the teaching in Wisdom when he admits that pagans did have some vague, unformulated knowledge about God. He insists on the power of the gospel to make known God's new mode of salvation for humanity, but here he also affirms that some knowledge of God was within the ken of pagans without the gospel, if they wanted to arrive at it. See Bietenhard, "Natürliche Gotteserkenntnis."

Again, it is far from certain, *pace* Moo (*Romans 1–8*, 99), that v 19, which uses *phaneroun*, "guards against any notion that people have access to knowledge of God through their natural capacities." Hooker ("Adam," 299) also thinks that Paul "is speaking of a definite divine revelation which men have rejected, not a knowledge of God to which men have by their reasoning attained." Yet Paul does *not* mean that "only by an act of revelation from above—God 'making it known'— can people understand God as He is." For precisely this reason he uses a different verb, *phaneroun*, "make evident," for example, in and through material creation itself, as distinct from *apokalyptein*, "reveal," namely, through the gospel. It is important to note this distinction. Paul admits that "God's uprightness" is *revealed* in the gospel, but he also maintains that people can perceive or come to a certain awareness of God's "eternal power and divinity" from reflection on what he has *made evident* in material creation.

To import into this passage the idea of a primitive or natural revelation is to understand it as did the majority of the Greek and Latin patristic interpreters, according to whom all knowledge of God is understood as faith supported by God's grace (see Vandermarck, "Natural Knowledge"). Yet those interpreters were addressing a different audience and a different problem from Paul's, and in reality they have missed the point that Paul himself was making. The same would have to be said about Karl Barth's interpretation of this passage.

273

The problem has to be seen in yet another light. Ever since the Enlighten-ment, when thinkers tried to extol human reason and to substitute for Christian revelation a natural religion or a religion of reason, some commentators have subconsciously reacted by denying the capability of the human mind to attain some knowledge of God. As a result, they have taken refuge in a form of fideism. In doing so, they have been reluctant to admit what Paul himself actually says about natural theology; they deny that God makes himself known in any other manner than in Christ. Preoccupation with the problem that the Enlightenment introduced has thus obscured for them what Paul is actually teaching in this passage. From this problem has come a connotation of "natural theology" that is not Pauline and that does not reckon sufficiently with what Paul, who wrote centuries before the Enlightenment, was really saying. The same would have to be said about what Paul writes in 2:14–16. To characterize it as a "natural morality" would be to import again an Enlightenment connotation that is not Pauline. What Paul may say in these passages about natural theology or natural morality is certainly not a complete treatise on these matters; yet one has to respect the snippets of such teaching that are really there.

Some commentators think that Paul is referring to the Adam narratives of Genesis 2–3: Adam first perverted his knowledge of God and sought to escape the status of a creature; he believed a lie and thus became a pattern for mankind (Adam = man). So Hooker ("Adam"), Wedderburn ("Adam"), and Dunn (*Romans*, 53). But this interpretation reads too much of Genesis into the text. What allusions are alleged to be there are to Genesis 1, not to Genesis 2–3. To invoke "rabbinic tradition," as does Hooker ("Adam," 301), is to invoke literature dating from many centuries later than Paul, especially when it comes from the Babylonian Talmud and *Bereshit Rabbah*. How can they reflect a Jewish exegesis "current as early as the first century A.D."? Hooker (ibid.) recognizes, indeed, that the vbs. *exapesteilen*, "he sent forth," and *exebalen*, "he cast out" (Gen 3:23–24) are "different" from *paredōken*, "he delivered over" (1:24, 26, 28); but, if so, where is the allusion to Genesis? The parallelism between vv 23, 25, 28 and vv 24, 26–27, 28 may be there (Hooker, "A Further Note"), but that still fails to show any influence of "the account of Adam's fall in Genesis" on the Pauline discussion. By way of contrast, see Wis 10:1, where Adam *is* referred to as "the first-formed father of the world, when he alone had been created." Yet Paul has nothing that echoes such a reference to Adam, even though he otherwise alludes to passages in this part of the Book of Wisdom (chaps. 10–19) in his argument. The alleged echoes of the Adam stories in Genesis are simply nonexistent.

Into his indictment of the pagans without the gospel Paul introduces a catalog of vices. Such catalogs occur elsewhere in his letters: 13:13; Gal 5:19–21; 1 Cor 5:10–11; 6:9–10; 2 Cor 12:20–21; and elsewhere in the NT (Col 3:5, 8; Eph 4:31; 5:3–4; 1 Tim 1:9–10; 2 Tim 3:2–5), as well as in the OT, especially in the Greek deuterocanonical and apocryphal writings: Wis 14:23–26; 4 Macc 1:26–27; 2:15. Paul's catalogs differ from those in Exodus 20 and 21; 33:14–26; Leviticus 19;

Deut 27:15–26; and Hos 4:1–2, because such OT catalogs list individual instances of evil conduct and activity, whereas Pauline lists mention the attitudes of mind from which spring the individual acts. In this respect they resemble more the Greek philosophical background of such catalogs (e.g., Plato, *Gorgias* 525; *Republic* 4.441c) and probably also reflect the Stoic school tradition. This Stoic influence also made itself felt in the Palestinian Jewish tradition. One can find in Essene writings (1QS 4:9–11) a comparable list: "To the spirit of perversity belong cupidity and slackness in the service of righteousness, impiety and falsehood, pride and haughtiness, falsity and deceit, cruelty and abundant wickedness, impatience and much folly, burning insolence (and) abominable deeds committed in the spirit of lust, and the ways of defilement in the service of impurity; a blaspheming tongue, blindness of eye and hardness of ear, stiffness of neck and heaviness of heart causing one to walk in all the ways of darkness and malignant cunning." Cf. *PAHT* §PT143 (and the literature cited there).

Why does Paul single out homosexual conduct as an example of such moral perversion? First, it was quite prevalent in the Greco-Roman society in which he lived, even though gay people were a minority and homosexual activity was not regarded as either harmful, bizarre, or illicit (see W. Kroll, "Kinaidos," PW 11.1 [1921], 459–62; "Knabenliebe," ibid., 897–906; "Römische Erotik," *Zeitschrift für Sexualwissenschaft und Sexualpolitik* 17 [1930–31]: 145–78; D. M. Robinson and E. Fluck, *A Study of Greek Love-Names, Including a Discussion of Paederasty and a Prosopographia* [Baltimore, Md.: The Johns Hopkins University Press, 1937; repr. New York: Arno, 1979]; K. J. Dover, *Greek Homosexuality* [Cambridge, Mass.: Harvard University Press, 1978]; H. Licht, *Sexual Life in Ancient Greece* [London: Routledge & Kegan Paul, 1932; repr. New York: AMS, 1974], 411–98). In this regard commentators sometimes think that, because Paul wrote this letter from Corinth, he was influenced in his discussion by the reputation of that city. Corinth was known in antiquity as a rich and opulent town allegedly dedicated to Aphrodite, in whose honor harlotry and even cultic prostitution were supposed to be practiced. The vb. *korinthiazesthai* came to mean "to practice fornication" (Aristophanes, *Fragment* 354; Stephanus Byzantinus [ed. A. Meineke], 374.5–6), and ancient writers often quoted the saying, *ou pantos andros eis Korinthon est⁾ ho plous*, "the trip to Corinth is not for every man" (Strabo, *Geography* 8.6.20); similarly, Horace (*Ep.* 1.17.36): "Non cuivis homini contingit adire Corinthum" (It is not the luck of everyone to go to Corinth). That reputation, however, belonged to ancient Corinth, destroyed in 146 B.C. by the Roman general Lucius Mummius Achaicus. Moreover, it is far from certain that even then, though there were many prostitutes in ancient Corinth, there were hierodules consecrated to Aphrodite. Because of its beauty, it was figuratively called a "city of Aphrodite," but it was in reality dedicated to Poseidon, the god of the sea.

Neo-Corinth, which was founded as a Roman colony (Colonia Laus Iulia Corinthiensis) in 44 B.C. and which Paul evangelized, did not share such a reputation. There is no evidence that the contemporary situation in Neo-Corinth was any worse than other towns in the Greco-Roman world of Paul's time. See Saffrey, "Aphrodite"; Murphy-O'Connor, *St. Paul's Corinth*, 55–57.

Second, Paul sees homosexual conduct as a symbol of the perversion stemming from idolatry. For him it is a way in which human beings refuse to acknowledge the manifestation of God's activity in creation. The human being who fails to acknowledge God and turns from him, who is the source of life and immortality, seeks rather a vicarious expression of it through the misuse of the natural procreative faculty. This faculty thus becomes part of frustrated creation, of which Paul will write in 8:22, part of the abnormal groaning of the universe. Homosexual behavior is the sign of human rebellion against God, an outward manifestation of the inward and spiritual rebellion. It illustrates human degradation and provides a vivid image of humanity's rejection of the sovereignty of God the creator. In this regard one might quote here a passage from *T. Naph.*, which links the sin of Sodom with disregard of the order created by God: "The sun, moon, and stars do not change their order; so you must not change the law of God by the disorder of your deeds. Gentiles, in going astray and forsaking the Lord, have changed their order and gone after stones and wooden objects, led away by spirits of error. But not so (will) you (be), my children. You have recognized in the heaven's vault, in the earth, in the sea, and in all created things the Lord who made them all, so that you should not become like Sodom, which changed the order of its nature" (3:2–4). This relation of deviant homosexual conduct to the order of creation underlies the thinking of Paul himself in this passage.

Attempts have been made time and again to uncover the structure of vv 18–32 by appeal to the threefold use of *(met)ēllaxan*, "they exchanged" (1:23, 25, 26) or of *paredōken*, "he delivered over" (1:24, 26, 28) or of *dioti*, "because," *dio*, and *dia touto* (1:21, 24, 26): so Klostermann ("Die adäquate Vergeltung"); Schulz ("Die Anklage"), Jeremias ("Zu Röm"), Lyonnet ("La Structure"); Bouwman ("Noch einmal"); Popkes ("Zum Aufbau"). But there is little agreement about the structure. It seems best to follow Dunn (*Romans*, 53) and divide the passage (after the topic sentence) according to content in this way: (1) vv 19–23—sin against the truth of God; (2) vv 24–27—sin against nature; (3) vv 28–32—sin against other human beings. For other possible rhetorical elements in the structure of 1:18–3:20, see Aletti ("Rm 1,18–3,20"), who builds on the suggestions of Wuellner ("Paul's Rhetoric of Argumentation in Romans," *Rom Deb*, 128–46), Rolland (*Épître aux Romains*), and Bassler (*Divine Impartiality*).

(Paul does not mean that pagans were de jure incapable of moral rectitude. When Christian theologians teach the need of divine assistance for perseverance in a good, natural life, they go beyond Paul's perspective and have in mind the individual's fallen condition. This refinement appeared with the controversy of Augustine and Pelagius in later centuries. Yet the basis of such teaching is Pauline: humanity cannot do without the gospel. Similarly, when the dogmatic constitution of Vatican Council I *De fide catholica* cited Rom 1:20 in support of its thesis that God *can* be known with certainty by the natural light of human reason from created things [DS 3004], it did not mean that Paul was declaring the same thing. The council was opposing fideism and traditionalism and asserted the *possibility* of such knowledge of God apart from faith and apart from positive revelation. Vatican I was dealing with the capability [*potentia activa*] of the human mind to know God. Paul rather speaks of a de facto situation: God is intellectually perceived and known from created things; he also describes the actual "godlessness and wickedness" of pagan humanity and its failure to acknowledge God properly. From this de facto situation the council moved a step farther and argued for the capability. Thus the further theological question about the human capacity to know God without divine assistance [i.e., without grace] goes beyond Paul's perspective. See further Lyonnet, *Quaestiones*, 1st ser., 78–88.)

NOTES

1:18. *For God's wrath is being revealed from heaven.* The conj. *gar* has been used in the Greek text four times in vv 16–18, which links not only vv 16–18 with one another, but also with v 15. Although Lietzmann (*An die Römer*, 31) and Kuss (*Römerbrief*, 35) regard *gar* here as a mere transitional particle, it is better understood as expressing contrast (so Dodd, *Romans*, 18; Huby, *Romains*, 79; Dunn, *Romans*, 54; Wilckens, *Römer*, 1.101), because "God's wrath" is not only invoked in contradistinction to "God's uprightness" (1:17), but in the development of the argument of 1:18–3:20, the human condition without the gospel stands in contrast to that under the revelation of God's uprightness "through faith and for faith." In thus contrasting God's uprightness and God's wrath, Paul is closely linking the whole section 1:18–3:20 to v 17; the status of uprightness before God is offered to humanity only by that which comes *ek pisteōs eis pistin*.

Paul repeats the vb. *apokalyptetai*, but *pace* Barth, Pallis, Cranfield (*Romans*, 111), and Schenke ("Aporien"), he does not say that God's wrath is revealed "in the gospel." Instead he expresses the cosmic dimension of divine wrath, which makes it manifest to all who perceive God's own reaction to sins of humanity. Käsemann rightly insists that wrath is not "the content of the gospel" or "part of the divine righteousness"; "justifying righteousness and condemning righteousness do not run parallel" (*Commentary*, 35); similarly, Wilckens (*Römer*, 1.103), Michel (*Brief an die Römer*, 97), and Nygren (*Romans*, 106). The reason is that Paul sees these attributes as parallel but distinct and contrary, even though they are both attributes of the one God; that too is why the wrath is being revealed "from heaven" (cf. Ps 14:2). Despite using the same verb as in v 17, Paul is deliberately contrasting the situation of pagan humanity, subject to such wrath revealed, with humanity exposed to the revealing gospel. The prep. phrase *ap' ouranou*, "from heaven," i.e., from God, has to be understood as contrasted with *en autō*, "in it," i.e., in the gospel (v 17).

Although the manifestation of wrath is related eschatologically to the "day" of the Lord in 2:5, Paul here implies that it is already being manifested, using the present tense of *apokalyptein*. He sees it as an element in the ongoing divine governance of the world of human beings without the gospel, in which sin is constantly manifesting itself. Opposed to such wrath revealed toward sinful humanity stands the gospel that reveals the uprightness of God. Cf. 2 Cor 2:15–16. Käsemann (*Commentary*, 35) rightly notes contra Bornkamm ("Revelation," 62–63) that in this context Paul is not thinking of the divine *anochē*, "forbearance" (3:26), before Christ; rather, he is thinking of the pagan world without the gospel. Eckstein ("Denn Gottes Zorn"), in dependence on patristic interpretations (of John Chrysostom, Theodore of Mopsuestia, Gennadius of Constantinople) would understand *apokalyptetai* eschatologically, relating this verse to 2:5. But that is to give a future sense to the pres. tense, which is not clear at all, as Feuillet ("La Connaissance") has noted; cf. Lagrange, *Romains*, 21.

Marcion and MSS 47 and 1908 omit *theou*, "of God," but it is to be retained, even though it is not found elsewhere with *orgē* in Paul's uncontested letters (2:5, 8; 3:5; 4:15; 5:9; 9:22; 12:19; 13:4, 5; 1 Thess 1:10; 2:16; 5:9, where it is often supplied in translations). Cf. Col 3:6; Eph 5:6.

against all the godlessness and wickedness of human beings. So Paul generically formulates the object of divine wrath. In particular, he uses *adikia*, which is the opposite of *dikaiosynē*, "wickedness," as opposed to "uprightness." The pair *asebeia* and *adikia*, "godlessness and wickedness," is found in the LXX (Ps 73:6; Prov 11:5); for Paul it is a hendiadys (both nouns are governed by the adj. *pasan*, "all") summing up the total sinfulness and rampant unrighteousness of pagan humanity: the wrong relationship with their creator. In Deut 9:5 "godlessness" is characteristic of "the nations," and in 3:5 Paul declares that human *adikia* calls forth divine uprightness. It is farfetched to see a distinction between *asebeia* and *adikia*, as does Michel (*Brief an die Römer*, 98–99), as if the former referred to the violation of the first tablet of the Decalogue and the latter to the violation of the second); similarly Str-B (3.31): irreligion and immorality.

who by such wickedness stifle the truth. This truth is set forth in v 19a. The vb. *katechein* appears again in 7:6 in a negative sense, "hold captive." It would mean that human wickedness holds the truth about God captive (Wilckens, *Römer*, 1.105). Pagans, who conduct themselves in wickedness, are seen to rebel against God and the truth about him. Consequently, they hold that truth captive and in effect stifle it. "Truth" could also be understood in the OT sense of God's "fidelity, faithfulness" to his covenant with his people, but it is more likely to be understood in the Greek sense, as it introduces the reality about him that should have come to the knowledge and awareness of pagans and that is expressed in the next verse. Some Latin versions and patristic writers add "of God," but that is a copyist's harmonization based on 1:25.

19. *that what can be known about God is manifest to them.* Or "because what. . . ." The conj. *dioti* can be taken either way, as introducing the object clause of "stifle," or as stating the reason for the stifling.

The phrase *to gnōston tou theou* is problematic. The verbal adj. *gnōstos*, which occurs only here in Paul's letters, usually means "known" in the LXX (e.g., Isa 19:21; Ezek 36:32) and often enough in the NT (e.g., Acts 1:19; 2:14; 15:18; 28:22; John 18:15). It has been so understood here by John Chrysostom and the Vg, "quod notum est Dei" (what is known of God). But *gnōstos* also occurs in the LXX of Gen 2:9 and Sir 21:7 in the sense of "knowable, what can be known" (see also Philo, *Leg. alleg.* 1.18 §60–61). Since the time of Origen, who in the Latin translation of Rufinus (*Commentarius in ep. ad Romanos* 1.16 [PG 14.863]) renders it "quod notum est Dei," but interprets it, "quod . . . assequi possunt," the potential meaning has been preferred, because the former would be tautological in this context, especially with the predicate "is manifest to them." See BAGD, 164; Bultmann, *TDNT* 1.719; BDF §263.2; Cranfield, *Romans*, 113. Hence the phrase literally means "the knowability of God."

Paul thus echoes a strong Jewish tradition about the unknowability of God (see Exod 33:20; Deut 4:12; Sir 43:31; Philo, *De Somn.* 1.11 §65–66; Josephus, *J.W.* 7.8.7 §346; *Ag.Ap.* 2.16 §167), but also the Hellenistic Jewish tradition that he has manifested himself to some degree in what he has created (Wisdom 12–15; cf. *Sib. Or.* 3:8–45). In echoing such a tradition, Paul in effect acknowledges what Greek and Roman philosophers before him had admitted about God, e.g., Plato (*Timaeus* 28A–30C, 32A–35A), Ps.-Aristotle (*De mundo* 6.397b–398b), and Cicero (*Tusculan Disputations* 1.29.70).

What can be known about God "is manifest to them," not through a positive revelation or a so-called natural revelation or through miracles, but through creation itself, as v 20 will explain. The prep. phrase *en autois* is best understood as the equivalent of a simple dat. of indir. obj., "to them" (ZBG §120; cf. Gal 1:16; 2 Cor 4:3; 8:1), even though it could be taken as "in their midst" (and all around them), as Cranfield (*Romans*, 113–14) and Michel (*Brief an die Römer*, 99) prefer. Huby (*Romains*, 82) and Lietzmann (*An die Römer*, 31) understand it more literally as "in them" (= within them, to their interior faculties), but that is less likely. Paul explains the "knowable" in v 20. *Pace* Dunn (*Romans*, 60), the verbal adj. *gnōston* in this verse does not allude to the same word in Gen 2:9; the sense of it there is entirely different.

For God himself has made it evident for them. I.e., in such a way that they can grasp it. So God has freely chosen to make himself manifest. Paul uses *phaneroun*, "make evident, show," a vb. that occurs only once in the LXX (possibly Jer 40:6), once in Philo (*Leg. alleg.* 3.15 §47), and seven times in Josephus (*Ant.* 17.2.4 §38; 17.8.2 §194; 17.11.2 §314; 18.8.7 §294; 19.1.8 §48; 20.4.1 §76; *Life* 45 §231). Yet it becomes in the NT a frequently used word (twenty times in John; twenty-two times in the Pauline corpus) to express what is "made known, public, plain." The fact that Paul uses it here instead of *apokalyptein* is significant. According to Bockmuehl ("Das Verb *phaneroō*"), the Pauline use of *phaneroun* shows that it is not a simple synonym of *apokalyptein*. Paul uses the latter to express revelation, but the former to "make something evident," i.e., perceptible.

Bockmuehl (*Revelation*, 141–42) subsequently confuses the issue by speaking of *phaneroun* in the context of "natural revelation," which is better avoided in the discussion of this Pauline passage.

20. *Ever since the creation of the world.* Lit., "ever since the creating of the world." Although the prep. phrase *apo ktiseōs kosmou* might seem to express the source from which the knowledge comes, it is preferably taken in a temporal sense, as *apo* is used in 2 Cor 8:10; 9:2; Matt 11:12; 24:21; 25:34; Rev 13:8; 17:8. Often in the NT *ktisis* can mean "creature, what is created" (8:19), and so the Vg seems to have taken it here, saying "a creatura mundi," but that again seems to be tautological; so the temporal sense of *apo* is preferred (see Cranfield, *Romans*, 114). Cf. Job 12:7–9; 40:6–42:6; Ps 19:1–6; Isa 40:12–31.

his invisible qualities. Lit., "his unseen things," i.e., the sum of his divine being. Two examples of such qualities are expressed later in the verse. Cf. 1 Tim 1:17; Col 1:15–16; Heb 11:27; Ignatius, *Trall.* 5:2, for the idea of the invisible God, a notion affirmed both in Greek philosophy (Ps.-Aristotle, *De mundo* 6 §399b.20: "being invisible to every mortal being, he is perceived through his very deeds"; Diodorus Siculus, *Bibliothēkē Historikē* 2.21.7) and in the Hellenistic Jewish tradition (Philo, *De vita Mos.* 2.12 §65; *De spec. leg.* 1.3 §20; Josephus, *J.W.* 7.8.7 §346).

his eternal power and divinity. The examples of God's invisible qualities are abstractly expressed. The terms are borrowed from the Hellenistic Jewish wisdom tradition (for *dynamis*, "power," see Wis 13:4; for *aidios*, "eternal," see Wis 2:23; 7:26; for *theiotēs*, "divinity," see Wis 18:9). See *Ep. Arist.* 132: *Monos ho theos esti kai dia pantōn hē dynamis autou phanera genetai*, "There is only one God, and his power is manifest through everything." Cf. H. S. Nash, "*Theiotēs— theotēs*, Rom. i:20; Col. ii:9," *JBL* 18 (1899): 1–34.

have been perceived by reflection. Lit., "being intellectually apprehended are perceived." Although God cannot be seen with human senses, he is perceived in his works by the human mind. *Pace* Käsemann (*Commentary*, 40), Paul does use an oxymoron, playing on two words involving the root *horan*, "see": *aorata*, "unseen things," and *kathoratai*, "are perceived"; i.e., though *in se* invisible, they are nevertheless perceptible by the human *nous*. In the contemplation of the created world and in reflection on it, a human being perceives the great "Unseen" behind it all—the omnipotence and divine character of its Maker. Paul echoes a teaching already found in Wis 13:5, "From the greatness and beauty of created things their original maker is, by analogy, seen (*ho genesiourgos autōn theōreitai*)."

Schjött (ZNW 4 [1903]: 75–78) tried to relate *nooumena* to *ta aorata*, in the sense of "God's unseen thoughts," but Fridrichsen ("Zur Auslegung") rightly rejected such an interpretation, because God's "eternal power and divinity" are hardly his "thoughts," and *nooumena* are scarcely the same as Platonic *noēta*.

on what he has made. Lit., "(by reflection) on (his) works," i.e., on what God has produced in creating the world. Although God is essentially invisible, his qualities are mirrored in the great "works" (*poiēmata*) produced by God. Paul is echoing OT teaching about the created universe being the handiwork of God. See Job 12:7–9; Pss 8:4; 19:2; Isa 40:26, 28; Sir 42:15–43:33. The words *tois poiēmasin* can be understood to modify either *nooumena*, "being intellectually apprehended in what he has made," or *kathoratai*, "are perceived in what he has made." The second seems preferable.

Consequently, such people are without excuse. Lit., "unto their being inexcusable." Paul uses the prep. *eis* with an articular infin. (*to einai*), which usually expresses purpose. For Sanday and Headlam, Barrett, and Michel the Pauline phrase would express a (conditional) purpose: God did not intend that pagans should sin; but if they did, he intended that it would be without excuse. But in *Koinē* Greek such a phrase often has a result or consecutive meaning (BDF §402.2; ZBG §351–52), and this reading is to be preferred, with Cornely, Cranfield, Käsemann, Lietzmann, et al. For the same sort of reasoning, see 3:19.

In this devastating conclusion to his argument in vv 19–20 Paul echoes a current Jewish conviction about the culpability of pagans in not acknowledging and reverencing God as they should have. Compare Wis 13:1–9, esp. v 8, "they are not pardonable." Cf. *Assumption of Moses* 1:13 (AOT, 607).

21. *though they knew God.* After the general principle enunciated in v 20, Paul proceeds to explain the specific sin of pagans. He admits that in some sense such pagans have a vague, unformulated knowledge or experience of God—despite what Jews have normally thought about them (cf. Jer 10:25; Ps 79:6; Wis 14:12–22) and what Paul himself seems to say in 1 Cor 1:21, "the world with all its wisdom did not come to know God." In other words, says Paul here, human wisdom among pagans did not come to a proper knowledge of God. Cf. Eph 1:17. What is denied in these passages is the real, affective knowledge of God that includes love, praise, reverence, and thanksgiving. In this quasi-philosophical discussion the word *gnontes* connotes an inceptive, theoretical sort of information about God, which Paul thinks that pagans could not help but have. The inconsequential character of such knowledge, which did not develop into real religious recognition, is the root of the sin of pagans. Whether Paul means that pagans came to a knowledge of God as "Creator" is not easy to say. He does not use *ho ktisas* in this connection, but later he does refer to *ton ktisanta* in v 25, which may imply that he was thinking of God as Creator here. If so, Paul may be going beyond what was affirmed in Wis 13:5, where knowledge of God as *genesiourgos*, "original author," is mentioned, but not as *ho ktisas*, "creator." Yet note the distinction that Philo (*De somn.* 1.13 §76) makes between *dēmiourgos*, "artificer, craftsman," and *ktistēs*, "creator."

One should contrast this Pauline statement about pagans' knowledge of God with what the Lucan Paul declares in Acts 17:23, "As I passed along and observed your objects of worship, I also found an altar with this inscription, 'To an unknown god.' What then you worship as unknown, this I proclaim to you." The difference is striking, as Vielhauer has pointed out ("On the 'Paulinism' of Acts," 34–37). Worship of an unknown God would imply some knowledge of God, a knowledge that has to be purified, corrected, and expanded, but in Acts the pagans are in no way considered to be inexcusable, as Paul says in v 20. "This means that the natural theology has an utterly different function in Rom. 1 and in Acts 17; in the former passage it functions as an aid to the demonstration of human responsibility and is thereafter immediately dropped; in the latter passage it is evaluated positively and employed in missionary pedagogy as a forerunner to faith" (ibid., 36). Cf. Acts 14:15–17.

they did not glorify him as God or thank him. So Paul formulates the proper knowledge expected of human creatures. Even though they "know God" in some sense, they deny that knowledge by their conduct and behavior. They were expected to "glorify" (*doxazein*) God, i.e., praise and honor him for their existence and for the good things that they have experienced in life; cf. 15:6, 9 ("Praise God, all Gentiles"). They were also to "thank" (*eucharistein*) him for his bounty and his mercy toward them. Thus Paul's complaint is centered not so much on pagan ignorance as on the failure to manifest reverence and gratitude, which should have sprung from the knowledge they had of him. Instead, their reverence was paid to created things. Cf. 2 Esdr 8:60, "It is not that the Most High has wanted any human being to be lost, but that those he created have themselves brought dishonor on their creator's name and shown ingratitude to the one who had put life within their reach." When this honoring and thanking really occurs, God is worshiped precisely as Creator, Lord, and Judge (Käsemann, *Commentary*, 42).

Some commentators (Cornely, *Commentarius*, 86; Feuillet, "La Connaissance naturelle," 218–19; Coffey, "Natural Knowledge," 675) think that, because Paul uses the pres. tense in vv 18–20 and the aor. tense in vv 21–23, he is not referring in the latter to pagans of his own day, but to pagans of old; that he may be sketching the stages through which humanity passed from primitive monotheism to contemporary idolatry. But the contrast between vv 18–20 and vv 21–23 is too strongly drawn in such an interpretation, as Lagrange (*Romains*, 25) rightly notes. The aorists are to be understood as gnomic; they express what pagans of all times have done (see BDF §333).

Instead, they were reduced to futile thinking. This is the reason that pagans are declared "inexcusable"; they indulged in vain and useless speculation. Cf. Eph 4:17, "You must no longer conduct yourselves as do the pagans, in the futility of their minds." Three consequences of their failure are mentioned: the futility of self-sufficient reasoning, the obscuring of their vision in other religious matters, and idolatry. Paul probably alludes to Jer 2:5, which in the LXX reads, "They withdrew far from me and went after futile things (*mataion*) and were reduced to futility (*emataiōthēsan*)." Cf. Ps 94:11, "The Lord knows the thoughts of human beings, that they are vain." Also Wis 13:1; 3 Esdr 7:22–23.

their misguided minds were steeped in darkness. Lit., "their foolish hearts were darkened." Futility in thinking and darkness of outlook characterize the state of such pagans. Cf. Eph 4:18, "They are darkened in their understanding, estranged from the life of God because of the ignorance that exists in them, through the hardness of their hearts." Paul regards this futility of thinking and misguided conduct as manifestations of the wrath of God, not provocations of it. He realizes that only the apocalyptic light of the gospel can penetrate such darkness. On the sense of "heart," see Introduction, section IX. D.

22. *Pretending to be wise, they became fools.* For Paul, the resultant state of the pagan is not wisdom but folly. Cf. Jer 10:14, "Every human being has become a fool without knowledge"; also Wis 11:15.

23. *and exchanged the glory of the immortal God for an image shaped like a mortal human being.* Lit., "they changed the glory of the imperishable God for a likeness of the image of perishable man," i.e., instead of praising and thanking the immortal God, pagans turned in their folly to give honor and glory to mortal creatures. Paul echoes Ps 106:20, "They exchanged their glory for the image of a grass-eating bullock," which alludes to the worship of the golden calf at Sinai (Exod 32:1–34). This rather clear allusion to the golden calf makes highly unlikely an implicit allusion to the Adam narratives. Cf. Jer 2:11; Deut 4:15–18; Wis 11:15. In using of the pagans the same vb. *allassein* as is found in the LXX, Paul implies that their "exchange" was just as guilty as that of the Israelites. He will use the same verb again (compounded with *meta-*) of guilty activity in vv 25, 26. For instances of pagan gods in human form, see *ANEP,* 160–87 (statues and reliefs from ancient Syria, Mesopotamia, Egypt, and Anatolia).

Idols were thus preferred by pagans to what was Israel's "glory," viz., the abiding *doxa* of Yahweh, the radiant external manifestation of his presence in the Tabernacle or Temple, what was called *kĕbôd YHWH* (e.g., Exod 24:17; 40:34–35). In Hebrew *kābôd* basically denoted the weight of esteem or honor that a king or important person enjoyed (1 Kgs 3:13). This concept was extended to Yahweh and to what made him impressive to human beings, the force of his self-manifestation and the radiant splendor of his presence. He was regarded as *melek hakkābôd,* "the king of glory" (Ps 24:8; in the LXX, *ho basileus tēs doxēs*). But "glory" was also ascribed to what God had wrought: the earth was full of his glory (Isa 6:3).

Paul also seems to be echoing Deut 4:16–18, where in the LXX both *homoiōma,* "likeness," and *eikōn,* "image," occur in parallelism. This may account for the awkward syntax of this clause. It is scarcely an allusion to Gen 1:26, *pace* Hooker and Hyldhal ("Reminiscence"). There *eikōn* does occur, but not *homoiōma;* the word is instead *homoiōsis.* Nor does the use of *anthrōpos* necessarily mean that Paul is alluding to Gen 1:26; not every use of that word implies an allusion to such a Genesis passage. How else could he say "human being"? Although Paul alludes to an incident in Israel's history, it becomes for him an example of what happens to the world without the gospel; so he can apply the idea even to pagans. Cf. 1QH 5:36, "According to the mysteries of sin they change the works of God by their guilty transgression."

like birds, four-footed creatures, or reptiles. The idolatry of pagans was directed not only toward human beings, but even toward animals of various sorts. At Ugarit "Father Bull El" was worshiped (*ANET*, 129). In Egypt the god Anubis was worshiped in the form of a jackal, Horus in the form of a hawk, and Atum in the form of a serpent (see *ANEP*, 185–89). Even Jeroboam is said to have introduced the pagan worship of golden calves at Bethel and Dan (1 Kgs 12:28–31). Cf. Wis 12:24, "For they wandered far astray on paths of error, accepting as gods those hideous and contemptible animals, deluded like foolish children." Thus in vv 19–23 Paul singles out the sin of the pagans against God himself and castigates pagan idolatry. Cf. Acts 7:41–42. Paul uses *peteina, tetrapoda kai herpeta*, words that are found in the LXX creation account of Gen 1:20, 24; but again, *pace* Hooker ("Adam," 300), that does not mean that he alludes expressly to the Adam story of Genesis. How else would he express such things?

24. *For this reason God delivered them over to the craving of their hearts for impurity.* Pagan idolatry results in human degradation through lust, perversion, and sins against nature. Although God's wrath will manifest itself definitively at the eschatological judgment, it is already revealing itself in human history. God does not allow the impious pagan to prosper; he gives human beings up to their sin, withdrawing his blessing and allowing moral degradation to pursue its course in sin that disgraces humanity and disturbs human society.

The rhetorical triple use of *paredōken* (see also vv 26, 28) introduced by *dio* in this verse, by *dia touto*, "for this reason," in v 26, and by *kathōs*, "as, because," in v 28 shifts the discussion from the question of guilt to that of punishment or fate. Each example intensifies the punishment. He seeks thereby to establish an intrinsic connection between sin and punishment; impiety brings its own retribution (see Wis 11:15–16, ". . . that they might learn that one is punished by the very things by which one sins"; cf. Ezek 23:28–30; *T. Gad* 5:10). "Paul paradoxically reverses the cause and the consequence: Moral perversion is the result of God's wrath, not the reason for it" (Käsemann, *Commentary*, 47). Thus Paul ascribes the punishment protologically to God's wrath (see Introduction, section IX.A).

that their bodies might be degraded among them. I.e., the lust of pagan hearts results in the degradation of their own bodies. Paul uses the gen. of the articular infin. *tou atimazesthai* to express the result or consequence of the craving for impurity (see BDF §400.2). On the sense of "body," see Introduction, section IX.D. The best reading is *en autois*, and not *en heautois*, found in MS G and the *Koinē* text-tradition. In Hellenistic Greek *autois* had already taken on a reflexive sense in addition to its normal meaning. See BDF §64.1.

25. *These people exchanged the truth about God for a lie.* Lit., "the truth of God," i.e., the truth that God is in himself (so Lietzmann, *An die Römer*, 33). Paul echoes what he wrote in 1:18, 22–23, expressing it more forcefully. Thus idolatry, the consequence of the failure to honor God duly, becomes the source of immorality, for it is the "big lie." What is, is true; what is not, is falsehood (see Jer 10:14; 13:25). It is the denial of the truth that should have been obvious to

them. Cf. Wis 14:22–31. Paul expresses here abstractly what he said in the concrete in 1 Thess 1:9. For the association of "idolatry" and "lie," see Isa 44:19–20. "Truth" refers to the reality revealed about God in the gospel, but also to that manifested in creation; "lie," the deception that smothers the truth. Cf. Philo, *De vita Mos.* 2.32 §171. Again, Paul uses *metallassein* of guilty exchange.

reverenced and worshiped the creature rather than the creator. Thus Paul exposes the "lie," the essence of idolatry, using the prep. *para* with the acc. to express preference, "rather than, instead of, more than," as in 12:3 and 14:5 and in *Ep. Arist.* 139 (see BDF §236.3). The vb. *sebazesthai* denotes general religious veneration, whereas *latreuein* refers to cultic worship. In *Ep. Arist.* 139 the author speaks of Israel in contrast to the pagans as a people *ton monon theon kai dynaton sebomenoi par' holēn tēn pasan ktsin*, "reverencing the only powerful God instead of all creation." Thus Paul sees the pagan world in contrast to his own people.

blest be he forever! Paul betrays his native background in spontaneously uttering in Jewish fashion a doxology at the mention of God the creator (cf. 2 Cor 11:31). See 1 Sam 25:32; 2 Sam 18:28; 1 Kgs 1:48; 8:15; Ps 41:14. Dunn (*Romans*, 64) notes that Paul uses the doxology as a mode of distancing himself from worship that does not recognize that all blessings come from the Creator. The prep. phrase *eis tous aiōnas*, lit., "unto the ages," is derived from the LXX, where it sometimes translates Hebrew *lĕʿôlāmîm* (e.g., LXX 2 Chr 6:2; Job 1:21; Pss 48:14; 72:17; cf. 1 Esdr 5:61; Tob 11:14; 13:1), but where the sg. *eis ton aiōna*, i.e., *lĕʿôlām*, is much more frequent.

Amen. Paul adds the usual Jewish conclusion to a prayer or doxology; cf. 9:5; 11:36; 15:33; 16:24, 27; 1 Cor 14:16. See OT usage in Deut 27:15–26; Ps 106:48; Neh 8:6.

26. *For this reason God delivered them over to disgraceful passions.* Lit., "passions of disgrace." The contrast between "women" and "males" in vv 26–27 shows that the "disgraceful passions" of which Paul speaks are the sexual perversion of homosexual activity. The depravity involved in such conduct is the merited consequence of pagan impiety and idolatry. Having exchanged a true God for a false one (1:25), pagans inevitably exchanged their true natural functions for perverted ones (cf. Philo, *De Abr.* 135; *De spec. leg.* 2.50; 3.37; and *T. Joseph* 7.8).

Their women exchanged natural intercourse for that against nature. Paul is thinking of lesbian conduct (see Hays, "Relations"), or tribadism, as it was called in antiquity. This meaning is suggested by the adv. *homoiōs*, "likewise," with which Paul introduces the corresponding male vice in v 27. So the majority of commentators on Romans have understood the female vice to which Paul refers. A few, however, have interpreted it as " 'unnatural' intercourse *chrēsis para physin* of women with men." So P. J. Tomson, *Paul and the Jewish Law: Halakha in the Letters of the Apostle to the Gentiles*, CRINT 3.1 (Assen: Van Gorcum; Minneapolis, Minn.: Fortress, 1990), 94 n. 157. He apparently derives this interpretation from Str-B 3.68.

For ancient references to lesbian conduct, see Lucian, *Dialogi meretricum* 5.2; *Amores* 28; Plutarch, *Lycurgus* 18; *Apoc. Pet.* 32 (Greek). In describing it as an "exchange" (*metēllaxan*), Paul thus insinuates the guilty nature of such conduct, for he uses of it the same verb as of idolatry in vv 23, 25. The noun *chrēsis*, lit., "use," is often used of sexual "intercourse."

The noun *physis*, "nature," which occurs in the OT only in the Greek deuterocanonical books (Wis 7:20; 13:1; 19:20; cf. 3 Macc 3:29; 4 Macc 1:20; 5:7, 8, 25; 13:27; 15:13, 25; 16:3; *T. Naph.* 3:4–5), occurs here for the first time. Paul will use it again in 2:14, 27; 11:21, 24(ter). In chap. 11 he will employ it in the most basic sense, about olive branches growing *kata physin*, "according to nature," i.e., with no human interference, and others grafted on *para physin*, "against nature," i.e., with human interference. Thus, *kata physin* denotes living or existing in harmony with the native or natural order of things, a peculiarly Greek, especially Stoic, idea (*TDNT* 9.271, 264–65). This Hellenistic philosophical notion has colored Paul's thinking, but in the context of vv 19–23, "nature" also expresses for him the order intended by the Creator, the order that is manifest in God's creation or, specifically in this case, the order seen in the function of sexual organs themselves, which were ordained for an expression of love between man and woman and for the procreation of children. Paul now speaks of the deviant exchange of those organs as a use *para physin*. *Ep. Arist.* 152 implies that such unnatural sexual practices were characteristic of "most of the rest of mankind" or of "whole countries and cities," but not of the Jewish people: "we have been set apart from these things." Indeed, Josephus mentions that "the law [of Moses] knows no sexual connection but the natural intercourse with a wife (*tēn kata physin tēn pros gynaika*), and that only for the procreation of children" (*Ag. Ap.* 2.24 §199). Here the prep. *para* denotes not merely "alongside" or "more than" (which it can mean at times, as in v 25), but "against" or "contrary to" nature. For other instances, see 4:18 (in a play on *ep' elpidi*); 11:24 (the opposite of *kata physin*); 16:17; Josephus, *Ag. Ap.* 2.32 §234 (*para tous heautōn nomous*, "against their own laws"); Thucydides, *Peloponnesian Wars* 6.17.1. Plato's comment is particularly pertinent: *ou para physin tēn tou thēleos pros to arren*, "not contrary to female nature in comparison with male" (*Republic* 5.13 §466d). From such instances it can be seen how wide of the mark Boswell's interpretation of *para* in this verse really is (*Christianity*, 111). Hays ("Relations," 192–99) rightly notes that Boswell's position, which claims that Paul regards homosexual acts as "extraordinary, peculiar," but not "morally reprehensible" (*Christianity*, 114, 112), ignores "the plain sense of the text, which places its explicit reference" to homosexual activity "in direct parallelism with the 'base mind and improper conduct' which the vice list of 1:29–31 elaborates" ("Relations," 196). While that is true, Paul's use of *physis* in 1 Cor 11:14 creates a problem, when he asks, "Does not nature itself teach us that if a man lets his hair grow long, it is a disgrace to him?" In this instance, *physis* hardly refers to the natural order of things, but to social convention. That use of *physis*, however, is said to be "of no theological significance" (*TDNT* 9.273); but it is a problem for the interpretation of 1 Corinthians. Yet what is meant there has little relevance for this context in Romans.

Patristic writers commenting on this verse did not speak of "male homosexuality" or "lesbianism," but they recognized what Paul was referring to. Thus John Chrysostom (*In ep. ad Romanos* Hom 4:1 [PG 60.417]) labeled the unnatural activity of women a "monstrous insanity" (*allokoton lyssan*) and regarded it as more disgraceful "when they seek this sort of intercourse, who ought to have more shame than men." See also Clement of Alexandria, *Paidagogos* 3.3.21.3 (GCS 12.249). *Pace* B. Brooten, Augustine (*De nuptiis et concupiscentia* 20.35 [CSEL 42.289]) did not interpret Paul's words as referring to "unnatural heterosexual intercourse" ("Patristic Interpretations," 287–88). He acknowledged rather that intercourse with a harlot was illicit, but natural. He granted that a husband and wife could have intercourse that was unnatural, but that has nothing to do with this statement of Paul.

Only modern eisegesis could read these words of Paul and understand them as referring to female contraception. See J. C. Ford and G. Kelly, *Contemporary Moral Theology*, 2 vols. (Westminster, Md.: Newman, 1958–64), 2.272, who regard Paul's words as possibly an implicit revelation of the condemnation of contraception! Compare J. T. Noonan, *Contraception: A History of Its Treatment by the Catholic Theologians and Canonists* (Cambridge, Mass.: Belknap, 1965), 43.

27. *and their men likewise abandoned natural relations with women and burned with lust for one another*. Lit., "were consumed in their desire for one another." *Orexis* expresses a human or animal desire, but is often used in a pejorative sense. Not only women in paganism were so affected, Paul recognizes, but men as well. The adv. *homoiōs* indicates that Paul was thinking of female homosexual conduct in the preceding verse; the parallelism with this verse makes it clear. Abandoning heterosexual intercourse, men too indulged in homosexual acts, as is made explicit in the next part of the verse.

males committing shameless acts with males. So Paul euphemistically describes male homosexual activity. In 1 Cor 6:9 such persons are described as *malakoi*, lit., "soft ones" (Vg "molles"), usually interpreted as men or boys who allow themselves to be treated as women (Dionysius of Halicarnassus 7.2.4: *Malakos . . . hoti thēlydrias egeneto pais ōn kai ta gynaixin harmottonta epaschen*, "[he was called] Malakos . . . because, when a boy, he was effeminate and allowed himself to be treated as a woman") cf. BAGD, 488; B-A, 991. There they are also called *arsenokoitai* (Vg "masculorum concubitores"), usually interpreted as "pederasts" (BAGD, 109; B-A, 220). See also 1 Tim 1:10. Paul seems to be the earliest writer to use *arsenokoitai*; and according to Boswell (*Christianity*, 335–53), he may have meant by it no more than active male prostitutes. But Boswell's meaning is not that certain either, for *arsenokoitai* is undoubtedly the Greek translation of Hebrew *miškab zākûr*, "lying with a male," a term used in rabbinic texts based on Lev 18:22. Note how Josephus speaks about male homosexual activity: *tēn [mixin] de pros arrenas arrenōn estygēke, kai thanatos toupitimion ei tis epicheirēseien*, "it [the Mosaic law] has abominated [intercourse] of males with males, and death is the punishment if anyone attempts (it)" (*Ag. Ap.* 2.24 §199), alluding to Lev 18:22, 29; 20:13.

No matter what the meaning of the words is in 1 Cor 6:9, Paul is clearly referring here to the conduct of active male homosexual persons and is merely echoing the OT abomination of such homosexual activity; see Lev 18:22; 20:13; Deut 23:17; 1 Kgs 14:24; 15:12; 22:46; 2 Kgs 23:7; especially the Sodom story (Gen 19:1–28), often alluded to elsewhere in the OT (Judg 19:22–26; Isa 1:9–10; 3:9; Jer 23:14; Lam 4:6). Cf. *Sib. Or.* 3:594–600: "Surpassing, indeed, all humans, they [Jewish men] are mindful of holy wedlock and do not engage in evil intercourse with male children, as do Phoenicians, Egyptians, and Romans, spacious Greece and many other nations, Persians, Galatians, and all Asia, transgressing the holy law of the immortal God."

being paid in turn in their own persons the wage suited to their deviation. I.e., receiving in their own persons the recompense suited to their deviation. Paul echoes the verdict of Wis 11:16, *di' hōn tis hamartanei, dia toutōn kolazetai,* "one is punished by the very things with which he sins." Cf. Wis 12:27. But he speaks of *tēn antimisthian hēn edei tēs planēs autōn,* lit., "the recompense that was due to their misstep," undoubtedly adopting a legal formulation. In using *planē*, Paul regards such homosexual activity as a perversion, a deviation, a wandering astray from what is right (*planan*, "to err, wander astray"). He knows nothing of the modern idea of homosexuality as an inversion, but not a perversion, as such writers as J. J. McNeill (*The Church and the Homosexual* [Kansas City: Sheed Andrews and McMeel, 1976], 55–56) would have us believe.

So Paul describes pagan idolatry that leads to sins against nature; but he does not stop there. He goes on to indict the pagan failure to recognize and glorify God as the source also of sins against other human beings and human society (vv 28–32).

28. *As they did not see fit to acknowledge God.* Lit., "they did not consider it proper to keep God in mind," i.e., by praising him and thanking him. These words are a summary of the accusation in vv 18, 20–21, 23, 25. Paul uses a comparative conj. *kathōs* in a causal sense, "since, as, because" (see BDF §453.2). Cf. Philo, *De dec.* 18 §91, *pēgē de pantōn adikēmatōn atheotēs*, "the source of all wicked deeds is godlessness."

he delivered them over to a base mentality and to improper conduct. Lit., "to a worthless mind to do improper things." The adj. *adokimos* denotes something that has not passed the test. Paul plays on the root *dokim-*, using it in the introductory verb *edokimasan*, lit., "they did not test and judge to be fitting," and the adj. modifying *noun*, an "untested, unsuitable mind," hence worthless. Pagan idolatry leads not only to sexual perversion, but to all sorts of immoral and improper conduct. Paul employs the Stoic expression *ta mē kathēkonta*, lit., "things that are not proper." See 3 Macc 4:16; Philo, *Leg. alleg.* 1.56 (cf. BDF §430.3). On the use of *nous*, see Introduction, section IX.D.

Many Greek MSS add *ho theos* as the subj. of *paredōken*, but it is omitted by MSS ℵ*, A, 0172, not being needed in the context.

29. *They became filled with every sort of wickedness.* Now Paul introduces a catalog of vices, which is in reality an echo of early Christian (pre-Pauline) catechetical teaching. See the COMMENT.

The noun *adikia*, "wickedness," is a generic concept dealing with social behavior, descriptive of one who fails to render due justice to other human beings.

evil, greed, and malice. Generic terms for evil precede more specific expressions in the subsequent phrases. *Ponēria*, "evil," and *kakia*, "malice," are almost synonymous; they occur together in 1 Cor 5:8. *Pleonexia*, "greed," also occurs in that context (5:10). The *Koinē* text-tradition, following MSS L, Ψ, 88, 326, 330, 614, inserts *porneia*, "fornication," before *ponēria*, introduced probably because of a misreading of ΠΟΝΗΡΙΑ as ΠΟΡΝΕΙΑ.

they were full of envy, murder, strife, craftiness, and spite. At first the vices are expressed in abstract form, as here, but soon the list changes and persons are mentioned. The first two words stand in assonance: *phthonou, phonou* (see BDF §488.2).

They became tale bearers. Lit., "whisperers," i.e., carriers of calumny. This and the following vice have to do with relations among human beings.

30. *slanderers, God haters, insolent, haughty, and boastful.* The noun *theostygeis* in classical Greek was used only in the passive sense, "hated by God, abandoned by God," but later in Hellenistic Greek it developed an active sense, "one who hates God." See the use of it in *1 Clem.* 35.3; Ps.-Clem., *Homilies* 1.12. The vice of *hybristēs*, "insolent person," could also refer to God, as in 1 Tim 1:13. But when it is lined up with the two following vices, it more likely refers to dealings with human beings.

contrivers of evil, rebels against parents. The first phrase *epheuretai kakōn*, "contrivers of evil," has a political connotation, whereas *goneusin apeitheis*, lit., "disobedient to parents," refers instead to familial relationships.

31. *foolish, faithless, uncaring, and merciless.* Again assonance governs the first two words: *asynetous, asynthetous*. The first of this pair comes from the wisdom tradition (see vv 21–22); the second expresses faithlessness in a convenantal situation. So ends the catalog of vices that describes the immoral and improper conduct of pagan idolaters.

32. *Though they know full well God's requirement that those who do such things deserve to die.* This clause echoes v 25. It might seem at first to refer to physical death as a punishment for the vices listed, but it is difficult to establish that pagan consciences would recognize death as such a penalty for all these vices. Rather, Paul is probably thinking of "total death" (5:12, 19), the lot of all sinners;

it amounts to exclusion from the kingdom of God (1 Cor 6:10; Gal 5:21). This clause, then, expresses Paul's verdict about the lot of pagan idolaters: "they deserve to die." This is but another way of saying what Paul says in 6:23, "the wages of sin are death." Paul uses *dikaiōma*, which means "what is required by what is right," hence "regulation," "commandment," as he will again use it in 2:26; 8:4 (cf. Heb 9:1, 10; *1 Clem.* 2:8; 58:2). In 5:18 it has a slightly different connotation, denoting rather an "act of uprightness, righteous deed," as in Rev 15:4; 19:8; *Barn.* 1:2.

Instead of the ptc. *epignontes*, MSS B and 1506 read *epiginōskontes*, which has the same meaning; but MSS D*, G, and Latin versions read instead *ouk enoēsan*, "they did not know," which changes the sense of the verse considerably.

they not only do them but even give approval to those who so act. The abysmal state of the pagan without the influence of God's gospel is thus revealed, not only in the failure to honor God and live uprightly, but in the approbation of evil conduct in others. Thus the failure of the pagan to glorify and thank God leads not only to idolatry and sexual perversion, but even to sins against other human beings. The approval of such sins in the conduct of others is just as sinful as if one were doing them oneself.

Instead of *ou monon auta poiousin alla kai syneudokousin tois prassousin*, as translated above, MS B and Latin versions read *ou monon auta poiountes, alla kai syneudokountes tois prassousin*, which eliminates the finite verb, "not only doing them, but also approving those who so act." This is a very old error that has crept into the text, as *1 Clem.* 35.6 reveals in its paraphrase, "Doing these things, they become haters of God: not only those doing them, but also approving those (who do them)." See Cyprian, *Ep.* 67.9; cf. Lietzmann, *An die Römer,* 37.

BIBLIOGRAPHY FOR PART A

Aletti, J.-N., "Rm 1,18–3,20; Incohérence ou cohérence de l'argumentation paulinienne?" *Bib* 69 (1988): 47–62.

Barth, M., "Speaking of Sin: Some Interpretative Notes on Romans 1.18–3.20," *SJT* 8 (1955): 288–96.

Conzelmann, H., "Paulus und die Weisheit," *NTS* 12 (1965–66): 231–44.

Croatto, J. S., "Conocimiento y salvación en Romanos 1,18–3,20: Intento de 'relectura,' " *RevistB* 41 (1979): 39–55.

Daxer, H., *Römer 1,18–2,10 im Verhältnis zur spätjüdischen Lehrauffassung* (Naumburg: G. Pätz/Lippert & Co., 1914).

Elorriaga, C., "La vida cristiana como camino progresivo según Rom 1–8," *Anales Valentinos* (Valencia) 9 (1983): 1–21.

Flückiger, F., "Zur Unterscheidung von Heiden und Juden in Röm 1,18–2,3," *TZ* 10 (1954): 154–58.

Jacques, X., "Colère de Dieu: Romains 1,18–5,11," *Christus* 25 (1978): 100–110.

Lafontaine, R., "Pour une Nouvelle Évangélisation: L'Emprise universelle de la justice de Dieu selon l'épître aux Romains 1,18–2,29," *NRT* 108 (1986): 641–65.

Montagnini, F., *La prospettiva storica de la lettera ai Romani 1–4: Esegesi di Rom. 1–4*, Studi biblici 54 (Brescia: Paideia, 1980).

Oltmanns, K., "Das Verhältnis von Röm 1,18–3,20 zu 3,21ff," *TBl* 8 (1929): 110–16.

Stagg, F., "The Plight of Jew and Gentile in Sin: Romans 1:18–3:20," *RevExp* 73 (1976): 401–13.

Vouga, F., "Römer 1,18–3,20 als narratio," *TGl* 77 (1987): 225–36.

Weber, E., *Die Beziehungen von Röm. 1–3 zur Missionspraxis des Paulus*, BFCT 9.4 (Gütersloh: Bertelsmann, 1905).

1:18–32

Baasland, E., "Cognitio Dei im Römerbrief," *SNTU* 14 (1989): 185–218.

Bartlett, D. L., "A Biblical Perspective on Homosexuality," *Foundations* 20 (1977): 133–47.

Basevi, C., "Exégesis cristiana de los primeros siglos a Rom 1,18–32: El hombre, Dios y la sociedad," *Biblia y hermenéutica: VII simposio internacional de teología de la Universidad de Navarra* (Pamplona: Universidad, 1986), 611–23.

———, "El hombre, Dios y la sociedad según Rom 1,18–32: Un ejemplo de exégesis cristiana de los primeros siglos," *ScrTheol* 17 (1985): 193–212.

———, "El hombre, Dios y la sociedad según Rom 1,18–32: Lectura del texto," *II Simposio Bíblico español (Córdoba, 1985)* (Valencia and Córdoba: Fundación Bíblica Española, 1987), 305–19.

Bassler, J. M., *Divine Impartiality: Paul and a Theological Axiom*, SBLDS 59 (Chico, Calif.: Scholars, 1982).

Bietenhard, H., "Natürliche Gotteserkenntnis der Heiden? Eine Erwägung zu Röm. 1," *TZ* 12 (1956): 275–88.

Bockmuehl, M. N. A., *Revelation and Mystery in Ancient Judaism and Pauline Christianity*, WUNT 2.36 (Tübingen: Mohr [Siebeck] 1990), 133–42.

———, "Das Verb *phaneroō* im Neuen Testament: Versuch einer Neuauswertung," *BZ* 32 (1988): 87–99.

Bornkamm, G., "The Revelation of God's Wrath (Romans 1–3)," *Early Christian Experience*, 47–70.

Boswell, J., *Christianity, Social Tolerance and Homosexuality: Gay People in Western Europe from the Beginning of the Christian Era to the Fourteenth Century* (Chicago, Ill.: University of Chicago, 1980).

Boughton, L. C., "Biblical Texts and Homosexuality: A Response to John Boswell," *ITQ* 58 (1992): 141–53.

Bouwman, G., "Noch einmal Römer 1,21–32," *Bib* 54 (1973): 411–14.

Bouzard, W. C., "The Theology of Wisdom in Romans 1 and 2: A Proposal," *WW* 7 (1987): 281–91.

Brooten, B., "Patristic Interpretations of Romans 1:26," *Studia Patristica XVIII*, ed. E. A. Livingstone (Kalamazoo, Mich.: Cistercian Publications, 1985), 287–91.

Bultmann, R., "Anknüpfung und Widerspruch: Zur Frage nach der Anknüpfung der neutestamentlichen Verkündigung an die natürliche Theologie der Stoa, die hellenistischen Mysterienreligionen und die Gnosis," *TZ* 2 (1946): 401–18.

Castellino, G. R., "Il paganesimo di Romani 1, Sapienza 13–34 e la storia delle religioni," *SPCIC* 2.255–63.

Coffey, D. M., "Natural Knowledge of God: Reflections on Romans 1:18–32," *TS* 31 (1970): 674–91.

Conzelmann, H., "Paulus und die Weisheit," *NTS* 12 (1965–66): 231–44, esp. 236–38.

Cranfield, C. E. B., "Romans 1.18," *SJT* 21 (1968): 330–35.

Dabelstein, R., *Die Beurteilung der "Heiden" bei Paulus* (Bern and Frankfurt: Lang, 1981).

DeYoung, J. B., "A Critique of Prohomosexual Interpretations of the Old Testament Apocrypha and Pseudepigrapha," *BSac* 147 (1990): 437–54.

———, "The Meaning of 'Nature' in Romans 1 and Its Implications for Biblical Proscriptions of Homosexual Behavior," *JETS* 31 (1988): 429–41.

Dresner, S. H., "Homosexuality and the Order of Creation," *Judaism* 159 (1991): 309–21.

Dupont, J., *Gnosis: La Connaissance religieuse dans les épîtres de saint Paul,* Universitas Catholica Lovaniensis diss. ser. 2.40 (Louvain: Nauwelaerts; Paris: Gabalda, 1949).

Eckstein, H.-J., " 'Denn Gottes Zorn wird vom Himmel her offenbar werden': Exegetische Erwägungen zu Röm 1,18" *ZNW* 78 (1987): 74–89.

Feuillet, A., "La Connaissance naturelle de Dieu par les hommes d'après *Rom.* 1,18–23," *LumVie* 14 (1954): 63–80.

Fridrichsen, A., "Zur Auslegung von Röm 1,19f.," *ZNW* 17 (1916): 159–68.

Harrison, P. N., *Paulines and Pastorals* (London: Villiers, 1964), 79–85.

Hays, R. B., "Relations Natural and Unnatural: A Response to John Boswell's Exegesis of Romans 1," *Journal of Religious Ethics* 14 (1986): 184–215.

Herold, G., *Zorn und Gerechtigkeit Gottes bei Paulus,* 187–336.

Hooker, M. D., "Adam in Romans I," *NTS* 6 (1959–60): 297–306.

———, "A Further Note on Romans i," *NTS* 13 (1966–67): 181–83.

Hyldahl, N., "A Reminiscence of the Old Testament at Romans i. 23," *NTS* 2 (1955–56): 285–88.

Iammarrone, L., "L'impensabilità dell'ateismo nei riflessi della Parola di Dio," *Renovatio* 21 (1986): 65–95.

Jeremias, J., "Zu Röm 1,22–32," *ZNW* 45 (1954): 119–21; repr. *Abba,* 290–92.

Jobes, K. H., "Distinguishing the Meaning of Greek Verbs in the Semantic Domain for Worship," *FilNeot* 4 (1991): 183–91.

Johnson, S. L., Jr., " 'God Gave Them Up': A Study in Divine Retribution," *BSac* 129 (1972): 124–33.

———, "Paul and the Knowledge of God," *BSac* 129 (1972): 61–74.

Kamlah, E., *Die Form der katalogischen Paränese im Neuen Testament*, WUNT 7 (Tübingen: Mohr [Siebeck], 1964).

Keck, L. E., "Romans 1:18–23," *Int* 40 (1986): 402–6.

Kertelge, K., " 'Natürliche Theologie' und Rechtfertigung aus dem Glauben bei Paulus," *Weisheit Gottes—Weisheit der Welt: Festschrift für Joseph Kardinal Ratzinger* . . . , 2 vols., ed. W. Baier et al. (St. Ottilien: EOS, 1987), 83–95.

Klostermann, E., "Die adäquate Vergeltung in Rm 1,22–31," *ZNW* 32 (1933): 1–6.

Kottackal, J., *The Salvific Folly of God: A Biblical-Theological Study on the Paradox of God's Folly and the World's Wisdom* (Kottayam, Kerala: Oriental Institute of Religious Studies, 1984).

Łach, J., " 'Albowiem gniew bozy ujawnia się przeciw wszelkiej bezbozno ci' (Rz 1, 18) ['Revelatur enim ira Dei de caelo super omnem impietatem' (Rom 1,18)]," *Ruch Biblijny i Liturgiczny* 40 (1987): 248–52.

Langerbeck, H., "Paulus und das Griechentum: Zum Problem des Verhältnisses der christlichen Botschaft zum antiken Erkenntnisideal," *Aufsätze zur Gnosis* (Göttingen: Vandenhoeck & Ruprecht, 1967), 83–145.

Lührmann, D., *Das Offenbarungsverständnis bei Paulus und in paulinischen Gemeinden*, WMANT 16 (Neukirchen-Vluyn: Neukirchener-Verlag, 1965).

Lyonnet, S., "La Connaissance naturelle de Dieu," *Études*, 43–70.

Moń, R., "Etyka objawoniona a naturalna w Rz 1, 18–32," *STV* 17.2 (1979): 65–80.

Murillo, L., "El veredicto de s. Pablo sobre la religiosidad del paganismo (Rom. I, 18–32)," *Bib* 3 (1922): 301–23, 424–37.

Murphy-O'Connor, J., *St. Paul's Corinth: Texts and Archaeology* (Good News Studies 6; Wilmington, Del.: Glazier, 1983).

Nordhaug, H., "Uråpenbaring og naturlig teologi: Refleksjoner over et spenningsfullt naboforhold hos Paul Althaus," *TTKi* 58 (1987): 35–49.

Novak, D., "Before Revelation: The Rabbis, Paul, and Karl Barth," *JR* 71 (1991): 50–66.

O'Rourke, J. J., "Romans 1,20 and Natural Revelation," *CBQ* 23 (1961): 301–6.

Osten-Sacken, P. von der, "Paulinisches Evangelium und Homosexualität," *Berliner theologische Zeitschrift* 3 (1986): 28–49; repr. *Evangelium und Tora*, 210–36.

Ott, H., "Röm. 1,19ff. als dogmatisches Problem," *TZ* 15 (1959): 40–50.

Owen, H. P., "The Scope of Natural Revelation in Rom. I and Acts XVII," *NTS* 5 (1958–59): 133–43.

Peretto, L. M., "Il pensiero di S. Ireneo su Rom. 1,20," *RivB* 8 (1960): 304–23.

Pohlenz, M., "Paulus und die Stoa," *ZNW* 42 (1949): 69–104.

Popkes, W., "Zum Aufbau und Charakter von Römer 1.18–32," *NTS* 28 (1982): 490–501.

Quirmbach, J., *Die Lehre des hl. Paulus von der natürlichen Gotteserkenntnis und dem natürlichen Sittengesetz*, Strassburger theologische Studien 7.4 (Freiburg im Breisgau: Herder, 1906).

Reicke, B., "Natürliche Theologie nach Paulus," *SEA* 22–23 (1957–58): 154–67.

Romaniuk, K., "Zagadnienie naturalnego poznania Boga według Rz 1,18–33," *RTK* 24.1 (1977): 59–68.

———, "Le Livre de la Sagesse dans le Nouveau Testament," *NTS* 14 (1967–68): 498–514.

Rosin, H., "To gnoston tou theou," *TZ* 17 (1961): 161–65.

Saffrey, H.-D., "Aphrodite à Corinthe: Reflexions sur une idée reçue," *RB* 92 (1985): 359–74.

Salvoni, F., "Ateismo e Paolo (*Romani* 1, 18–25)," *RBR* 11 (1976): 7–41.

S. Marco, E. da, " 'L'ira di Dio si manifesta in ogni genere di empietà e di ingiustizia' (Rom 1,18): (Confronti con Sap cc 13–15)," *SPCIC* 1.259–69.

Schenke, H.-M., "Aporien im Römerbrief," *TLZ* 92 (1967): 881–88.

Schlier, H., "Die Erkenntnis Gottes nach den Briefen des Apostels Paulus," *Besinnung*, 319–39.

———, "Über die Erkenntnis Gottes bei den Heiden (nach dem Neuen Testament)," *EvT* 2 (1935): 9–26; repr. as "Von den Heiden: Römerbrief 1, 18–31," in *Zeit der Kirche*, 29–37.

Schjött, P. O., "Eine religionsphilosophische Stelle bei Paulus: Röm 1,18–20," *ZNW* 4 (1903): 75–78.

Schulz, S., "Die Anklage in Röm. 1, 18–32," *TZ* 14 (1958): 161–73.

Schweizer, E., "Gottesgerechtigkeit und Lasterkataloge bei Paulus (inkl. Kol und Eph)," *Rechtfertigung: Festschrift für Ernst Käsemann* . . . , ed. J. Friedrich (Tübingen: Mohr [Siebeck], 1976), 461–77.

Scroggs, R., *The New Testament and Homosexuality: Contextual Background for Contemporary Debate* (Philadelphia, Penn.: Fortress, 1983).

Segalla, G., "L'empietà come rifiuto della verità di Dio in *Romani* 1,18–28," *StudPatav* 34 (1987): 275–96.

Shields, B. E., "The Areopagus Sermon and Romans 1:18ff: A Study in Creation Theology," *ResQ* 20 (1977): 23–40.

Turner, D. L., "Cornelius van Til and Romans 1:18–21: A Study in the Epistemology of Presuppositional Apologetics," *GTJ* 2 (1981): 45–58.

Vandermarck, W., "Natural Knowledge of God in Romans: Patristic and Medieval Interpretation," *TS* 34 (1973): 36–52.

Vanni, U., "*Homoiōma* in Paolo (Rm 1,23: 5,14: 6,5:8,3: Fil 2,7): Un'interpretazione esegetico-teologica alla luce dell'uso dei LXX—I*a* Parte," *Greg* 58 (1977): 321–45; "2*a* Parte," 431–70.

Vielhauer, P., "On the 'Paulinism' of Acts," *Studies in Luke-Acts: Essays Presented in Honor of Paul Schubert* (Nashville, Tenn.: Abingdon, 1966), 33–50.

Vögtle, A., *Die Tugend-und Lasterkataloge im Neuen Testament exegetisch, religions-und formgeschichtlich untersucht*, NTAbh 16.4–5 (Münster in Westfalen: Aschendorff, 1936).

Wedderburn, A. J. M., "Adam in Paul's Letter to the Romans," *Studia biblica 1978: Sixth International Congress on Biblical Studies, Oxford 3–7 1978*, 3 vols., JSNTSup 2–3, 11 (Sheffield, UK: JSOT, 1979–80), 3.413–30.

Wengst, K., "Paulus und die Homosexualität: Überlegungen zu Röm 1,26 f.," ZEE 31 (1987): 72–81.

Wibbing, S., *Die Tugend- und Lasterkataloge im Neuen Testament und ihre Traditions-geschichte unter besonderer Berücksichtigung der Qumran-Texte*, BZNW 25 (Berlin: Töpelmann, 1959).

GOD'S JUDGMENT MANIFESTED AGAINST JEWS—INDEED, AGAINST ALL HUMAN BEINGS (2:1–3:20)

◆

6. DISCERNMENT AT GOD'S ESCHATOLOGICAL JUDGMENT (2:1–11)

2 ¹So you are without excuse, whoever you are who sit in judgment. In judging another, you condemn yourself, since you, the judge, do the same things. ²Yet we know that God's judgment falls in truth on all who do such things. ³Do you really think that you will escape the judgment of God, you who sit in judgment on those who do such things and yet do them yourself? ⁴Or do you make light of the abundance of his goodness, forbearance, and long-suffering? Do you not realize that what is good about God is meant to lead you to repentance? ⁵With your stubborn and impenitent heart you are amassing wrath for yourself on the day of wrath, when God's just judgment will be revealed. ⁶For *he will repay everyone according to his deeds:* ⁷eternal life for those who by patiently doing good strive for glory, honor, and immortality; ⁸but wrath and fury for those who selfishly disobey the truth and are won over to wickedness. ⁹There will be distress and anguish for every human being who does evil, for the Jew first and also for the Greek. ¹⁰But there will be glory, honor, and peace for everyone who does good, for the Jew first and also for the Greek. ¹¹For there is no partiality in God.

COMMENT

Paul's indictment of his gospel-less contemporaries moves to another dimension. He turns to an imaginary listener or interlocutor, who loudly applauds his description of the pagan's moral failure. Paul reacts and insists that such a person is no better than the pagan, for in spite of a superior moral culture, which may enable the interlocutor to agree with Paul's indictment of the pagan, he does not do what is expected of him by that superior status. He does the same things, evil in all its forms. As a result, he will not escape the outpouring of divine wrath either.

In developing his argument, Paul treats of six topics. First, he enunciates the general principle of God's impartial judgment (2:1–11) and cites the OT to declare that God will recompense all human beings according to their deserts. Second, Paul shows that knowledge and possession of the Mosaic law are no guarantee against the outpouring of divine wrath (2:12–16). Third, he announces that it will be manifested against the Jew as well as the pagan because of the way the Jew lives (2:17–24). Fourth, Paul insists that the Jew is vulnerable in spite of circumcision (2:25–29). Circumcision has value, if one observes the law, but it does not make the real Jew. Fifth, Paul answers objections about the privileges of the Jews (3:1–9). Sixth, Paul affirms that all human beings, Jews and Greeks alike, are sinners and subject to divine wrath. So runs Paul's argument at this point in the letter.

But who is the interlocutor? Paul begins in 2:1 by calling him ō *anthrōpe pas ho krinōn*, lit., "o human being, whoever passes judgment." A similar phrase is used again in 2:3. Just as we noted that Paul's use of *anthrōpōn* in 1:18 created a problem, but eventually had to be understood to refer to "pagans," similarly here; it cannot be taken merely as a reference to humanity in general. In the course of the history of the interpretation of this passage many attempts have been made to identify *anthrōpos*. Thus, for John Chrysostom it was a secular authority (*In ep. ad Romanos* hom. 5.1 [PG 60.423]: *tous archontas*); for Origen it was a Christian bishop (*In ep. ad Romanos* 2.2 [PG 14.873]: *ecclesiarum rectoribus et principibus*, "rectors and princes of the churches"); for Zahn, a pagan philosopher or moralist.

The majority of modern commentators, however, agree that the interlocutor is a Jew who judges himself superior to the pagan because of his people's privileges. In 2:17 the "Jew" is explicitly mentioned, and vv 1–16 merely lead up to that identification. Verses 12–16 show that a knowledge of divine legal prescriptions is not the exclusive possession of the Jew; some prescriptions of the Mosaic law are known even to pagans. In these verses Jews and pagans are implicitly compared. But these verses support what is said in vv 9–10, where Jew and Greek are put on an equal footing before God. Hence vv 1–8 are leading up to and preparing for that discussion. Consequently, vv 1–16 constitute an implicit indictment of Jews, which becomes overt in v 17. Thus Paul forces the Jewish interlocutor to pass judgment on himself. This judgment begins, however, in 2:1 and not with 1:32, as Flückiger ("Zur Unterscheidung") sought to maintain.

In this passage (2:1–11), even before Paul comes to explain his idea of justification by grace through faith in Christ Jesus, which will emerge in 3:21–31, he reckons with the situation that all human beings will have to stand before the divine tribunal and be judged according to their deeds. This is not the only place in his writings in which he speaks of such judgment; cf. 14:10; 2 Cor 5:10; Phil 2:12. Yet the "judgment" of which he speaks in vv 2, 3, and 5 has to be understood against the background of his major thesis about justification by grace through faith (see Käsemann, *Commentary*, 58). Human beings will indeed be judged by God, but in this new phase of salvation history they can share through faith in the justification wrought by the death and resurrection of Christ. It is not that Paul is inconsistent. Nor is it that he is arguing hypothetically, leaving the gospel out of account and proceeding from the presuppositions of the Jews alone. Rather, when in vv 7 and 10 he speaks of "doing good" as the basis on which one will be judged, he is implicitly referring to Christians, whose conduct (good deeds) is to be understood as the fruit of their faith. The Jews are no exception to the teaching of Paul's gospel that no one comes to salvation without God's grace; no one comes to justification on the basis of deeds only. See the COMMENT on 2:12–16.

In this passage not only the subject matter but even the style changes, for Paul now switches from the third person plural to the second person singular, as Paul introduces a subform or *Gattung* into his letter. He indulges in what was called in ancient rhetoric *diatribē*. See Introduction, section VII.

Again there are passages in the Book of Wisdom that illustrate the diatribic argument of Paul. The wrath of God falls on the pagans (Egyptians), but not on Israel: "When they [Israel] had been tried, though only mercifully chastised, they recognized how the wicked [Egyptians], condemned in wrath, were being tormented. Both those afar off and those close by were afflicted. The latter you tested, admonishing them as a father; the former as a stern king you probed and condemned" (11:9–11). Israel takes refuge in its knowledge of God's law: "Even if we sin, we are yours and know your power; but we will not sin, knowing that we are regarded as yours; for to know you is complete uprightness and to recognize your power is the root of immortality" (15:2–3). Even when God judges sternly, he does so with mercy and forbearance: "You have mercy on all people, because you can do all things; you overlook their sins that they may repent" (11:23). When Jews judge others, they should remember God's mercy to them: "that, when we judge, we may think earnestly of your goodness, and, when being judged, we may look for mercy" (12:22). Thus, when Paul addresses his Jewish interlocutor, he thinks in terms of the mode of Jewish existence depicted in the Book of Wisdom.

Bassler (*Divine Impartiality*) considers God's impartiality to be a central theme in Romans 1–2, and v 11 to be pivotal in this passage. She bases her consideration on the repetition of many key phrases of 1:16–18 in 2:5–11 (e.g., "revelation," "wrath," "the Jew first," then "the Greek"), thinking that this emphasis on impartiality is continued until 3:21–26, because Paul's teaching of justification stems from his desire to show that God treats all human beings alike. She is right in stressing divine impartiality, but it is not the central theme of this part of Romans. Her suggestion that 2:11 closes a unit that begins at 1:16 is unconvincing. Her ring construction cuts across an obvious division in the structure of this part of the letter. Rather, vv 1–11 form a transition from the indictment of the pagan in 1:18–32 to the indictment of the Jew in 2:1–3:9. Her explanation does not take into consideration sufficiently the stylistic shift from the third person plural to the second person singular in 2:1. Again, 3:21 clearly parallels 1:17 and thus marks a unit that cannot be disregarded. Thus, though her analysis puts proper emphasis on the Pauline idea of divine impartiality, it does not reckon properly with the overall structure of 1:18–3:26.

NOTES

2:1. *So you are without excuse.* The passage begins with the dialogic particle *dio*, which has its full inferential force here (Stowers, *Diatribe*, 213). Paul alludes to his indictment of the pagan in 1:20, now passing the same judgment on his interlocutor. He recognizes that his interlocutor does not "give approval to those who so act," i.e., who fail to acknowledge God with praise and thanksgiving; but he does acknowledge "God's requirement" (1:32a). According to some commentators (Althaus, Lietzmann, Michel, Schlier) *dio* would have no inferential force, but that force is to be recognized here, because Paul means that those who judge are also those who recognize "God's requirement." It thus concludes from the whole passage that precedes, especially from 1:18–19: because God's wrath is revealed against all human beings and because all have been given some awareness of God, even the one who now judges has to recognize that requirement and so is also "without excuse" before God.

Bultmann ("Glossen") considered v 1 to be a gloss drawing a conclusion from v 3, because of the problematic *dio*. Verse 2 would then be considered to be a conclusion to 1:31, and v 3, introduced by *de*, would start a new consideration. Despite Käsemann's (*Commentary*, 54) concurrence, this is hardly an accurate assessment. Verse 3 presupposes v 1, which acts as the topic sentence in the paragraph, and must be retained, as Wilckens (*Römer*, 1.123) rightly recognizes.

whoever you are who sit in judgment. Lit., "O human being, whoever passes judgment." The phrase is not easily translated, because Paul uses the adj. *pas*, "all, every," before the attributive ptc. *ho krinōn*. Thus he accosts the imaginary interlocutor who applauds what he has been saying about the pagan in 1:18–32. The exclamatory *ō* is used to express emotion (see BDF §146.1b). The same use of *anthrōpos* in an apostrophe is characteristic of diatribes in Epictetus (*Dissertationes* 2.23.36–37; 4.9.5–6; 4.13.10). Paul's use of *krinōn* may echo Wis 12:22, *hina sou tēn agathotēta merimnōmen krinontes*, "so that, when we judge, we may be concerned about your goodness," said of a Jewish critic. The modifying phrase, *pas ho krinōn*, also belongs with *ō anthrōpe* so that it becomes clear that Paul is not just addressing every human being, but specifically that one who scrutinizes pagans and lauds what he (Paul) has been saying about them. The Jew judges in virtue of what is said in Ps 79:6: "Pour out your wrath upon the nations that acknowledge you not, upon kingdoms that call not upon your name."

In judging another, you condemn yourself. Lit., "in that you judge another." This is the topic sentence in the paragraph: You too are a sinner yourself and an object of God's wrath. Thus the self-righteous listener is drawn up short. The dialogic style is seen in the use of the 2d pers. sg. instead of the 3d pers. pl. (see BDF §281). Paul also uses instrumental *en* in a causal sense (see BDF §219.2); or it could mean "in the very act of judging." The vb. *krineis* has the connotation of "condemning" and differs little from *katakrineis*, which is the specific word for condemning, passing a negative verdict.

since you, the judge, do the same things. Though gifted with a superior moral understanding whereby he can agree with Paul's indictment of the pagan, nevertheless the Jew is just as guilty as the pagan for another reason: he does not do what his superior moral understanding bids him to do.

299

2. *Yet we know that God's judgment falls in truth on all who do such things.*
I.e., all who do evil will have to answer for such conduct before God's tribunal.
Paul himself stresses this knowledge (cf. 3:19; 7:14; 8:22, 28, where he similarly
uses *oidamen*, "we know"). It is also possible to understand the passage to mean
"yet we know that God's judgment takes place according to truth for all," as
Lagrange (*Romains*, 43–44) understands it, i.e., judgment is measured by the
truth of reality. Yet condemnation falls on all evildoers "rightly" (= "in truth"),
without respect of persons (2:11). *Pace* Barrett (*Romans*, 44), this verse does not
represent the objection of the interlocutor; it may be "the Jew in Paul himself,"
but it is still Paul who speaks.

The noun *krima* can mean "lawsuit" (1 Cor 6:7) or "decision, judgment"
(Rom 11:33), but it frequently connotes "condemnation, adverse sentence" (3:8;
13:2; Gal 5:10), as here, and like the vb. *krineis* in v 1. Paul speaks in vv 2 and 3
of *to krima tou theou*, "God's judgment." In v 5 he will use the term *dikaiokrisia
tou theou*, "God's just judgment." It is essential not to confuse these terms *krima*
and *dikaiokrisia* with *dikaiosynē theou*; the former express the judgment whereby
God condemns the sinner, whereas the latter is the quality in God whereby he
acquits the sinner in a just judgment. From these verses (2, 3, and 5) it is clear
that Paul reckons with the possible condemnatory judgment of God; they provide
the background for his advice in Phil 2:12: "work out your own salvation with fear
and trembling." Yet even there he adds, "For God is at work in you, both to will
and to work for his good pleasure" (2:13). That addition reveals that in Paul's view
salvation is not accomplished without God's grace. See further the COMMENT on
2:12–16.

MSS ℵ, C, 33, and the Vg read *gar* instead of *de* at the beginning of this
verse; but *de* is the reading of the majority of the best Greek MSS.

3. *Do you really think that you will escape the judgment of God?* Paul realizes
Israel's privilege as God's chosen people; but that is no guarantee against condemnation for lawlessness. Paul may be echoing here *Ps. Sol.* 15:8, "those who
commit lawlessness will not escape the judgment of the Lord" (*to krima Kyriou*).
He begins the clause with an emphatic *sy*, "you," thus seeking to counteract the
conviction of Jews that they are secure in their salvation because of their descent
from Abraham (see Matt 3:9, "Pride yourselves not on the claim, 'We have
Abraham for our father' "). In effect, Paul's argument is based on a claim that
Moses makes: "The nations will hear about all of these statutes and say, 'This
great nation is surely a wise and intelligent people.' For what great nation is there
that has gods so close to it as the Lord our God is to us, whenever we call upon
him? Or what nation is there so great that has statutes and decrees so just as all
this law, which I am setting before you today?" (Deut 4:6–8). Compare too the
later rabbinic conviction, "All Israel has a share in the world to come, as it is
written, 'Your people shall all be righteous, they shall inherit the land forever' (Isa
60:21)" (*m. Sanh.* 10:1). Cf. John 8:33; Gal 2:15.

you who sit in judgment on those who do such things. Paul again uses *ō anthrōpe ho krinōn,* echoing his apostrophe of 2:1. This is the first of two questions that highlight the critic's delusion; once asked, it answers itself.

and yet do them yourself. This is the real point of Paul's accusation of the interlocutor, who is just as much at fault as the pagan indicted in 1:18–32. Paul echoes Isa 57:4, "Of whom do you make fun, at whom do you open wide your mouth and put out your tongue? Are you not rebellious children, a deceitful race?"

4. *do you make light of the abundance of his goodness, forbearance, and long-suffering?* It is a question not only of delusion, but even of contempt: to make light of the delay on God's part to punish sin, which should lead to repentance, is to manifest one's culpable negligence. Compare 2 *Apoc. Bar.* 21:20, "that your power may be made known to those who think that your patience is weakness." Paul invokes three attributes of God, some of which are mentioned in the OT. For *chrēstotēs,* "goodness," see Pss 31:20; 119:65–68; 145:7–9; for *makrothymia,* "long-suffering," see Jer 15:15; cf. Rom 9:22. He may be alluding to Wis 15:1–3, where these qualities of God are mentioned in tandem. For a similar lineup of divine attributes, see 2 Esdr 7:62–69 (132–39).

Do you not realize that what is good about God is meant to lead you to repentance? God's good qualities have a salutary end: they are meant to bring sinners to a recognition of what their status really is. Cf. Wis 11:23, "you overlook their sins that they may repent"; 12:10, 19; 2 Esdr 7:74. Paul uses the neut. sg. substantivized adj. *chrēston* with a def. art. to express an abstraction: goodness in a concrete instance (see BDF §263.2); compare *to prothymon* (1:15); *to perisson* (3:2).

Metanoia actually means a "change of mind," but in time it came to mean "remorse" and, in a religious sense, "repentance, conversion." See H. Merklein, *EDNT* 2.415–19; cf. E. Norden, *Agnostos Theos,* 134–40.

5. *With your stubborn and impenitent heart.* Paul uses the OT term *kardia,* "heart," which is really a synonym for "mind"; see Introduction, section IX.D. "Stubbornness" characterized Israel of old (Deut 9:27; 31:27; cf. Exod 9:35).

you are amassing wrath for yourself on the day of wrath. Lit., "you are treasuring up wrath," i.e., instead of piling up good deeds as a treasure in heaven (cf. Matt 6:20), wrath is being stored up. Paul speaks with irony, as he mentions divine "wrath," a feature of the eschatological day of the Lord. In this wording he echoes an OT association; see Zeph 1:14–15, 18; 2:3; Isa 13:9; 37:3; Lam 1:12; 2:21. See Introduction, section IX.A. Yet is the same wrath that is revealed from heaven against the heathen (1:18).

when God's just judgment will be revealed. Lit., "(and on the day) of the revelation of God's just judgment." Paul uses the compound *dikaiokrisia* only here; it occurs, however, as a variant reading in 2 Thess 1:5 for the fuller form *dikaia krisis.* It is a rare word; cf. LXX Hos 6:5 (Quinta); *Sib. Or.* 3.704; *T. Levi* 3.2; 15.2. Here it has the connotation of God's condemnatory judgment, stressing the equity of the divine sentence to be issued on the day of the Lord. Paul implies that the impenitent Jew fails to realize the relation of the present to the coming judgment of God. *Dikaiokrisia* finds its Qumran Hebrew counterpart in *mišpěṭê ṣedeq*, "just judgments" (1QH 1:23; cf. 1:30; 1QS 4:4), before which the sectarian stood in dread.

6. *For he will repay everyone according to his deeds.* Paul quotes Prov 24:12 or Ps 62:13 to prove his point and to confirm the validity of OT teaching about God's eschatological retribution. He does not simply borrow this affirmation in a moment of ardent rhetoric; it is an important part of his teaching.

7. *eternal life for those who by patiently doing good strive for glory, honor, and immortality.* Cf. 2 Cor 1:6 for a similar use of *hypomonē*, "patient endurance." This is the first Pauline mention of "eternal life," an idea derived from his Jewish tradition (Dan 12:2; 2 Macc 7:9; 4 Macc 15:3; cf. 1QS 4:7); it is life in the *aiōn*, in the "age" to come. See further 5:21; 6:22–23; cf. Gal 6:8. So Paul formulates the destiny of Christian existence, which he will further specify in time as a share in the "glory" of God (3:23; 5:2) and in the life of the risen Christ (6:4), i.e., being "forever with the Lord" (1 Thess 4:17; cf. Rom 5:21; 6:22–23). Three qualities of that destiny are mentioned: *doxa*, "glory," *timē*, "honor," and *aphtharsia*, "imperishability, immortality." The pair *doxa kai timē* occurs in the LXX of Job 40:10 as an expression of what God desires for human beings. It also occurs in the LXX of Ps 29:1 as something that is to be ascribed to God; cf. Ps 96:7.

8. *but wrath and fury for those who selfishly disobey the truth and are won over to wickedness.* Lit., "but for those (who come) from selfishness and disobey the truth and are won over to iniquity (there will be) wrath and fury." The pair *orgē kai thymos* appears often in the LXX: Isa 13:9 (in a context about the "day of the Lord"); 30:30; Jer 7:20; 21:5. The meaning of *eritheia* is debated. Etymologically, it is related to *erithos*, "mercenary's pay." In prebiblical Greek it occurs only twice (Aristotle, *Politics* 5.3 [1302b.4 and 1303a.14]), where it denotes "selfish ambition, selfishness," self-seeking pursuit of public office (Barrett, *Romans*, 47). But it often occurs in contexts of "strife" (*eris*) and was often confused with the latter in popular usage (see Gal 5:20; Phil 1:17; 2:3; 2 Cor 12:20 [consult the apparatus criticus in both of these places]). See H. Giesen, *EDNT* 2.52. Hence some commentators (Lagrange, Lietzmann, Lyonnet) understand it here to mean "rebellious people." Either meaning actually suits the context: such people are not those who patiently pursue the good, and their lot is divine wrath.

9. *There will be distress and anguish for every human being who does evil.* Lit., "for every soul [*psychē*] of man." According to Lagrange (*Romans*, 46–47), these punishments affect specifically the "soul," because of the redundancy of the expression, "soul of man." But that is too Hellenistic an interpretation. Paul is more likely using *psychē* like Hebrew *nepeš* (Lev 24:17; Num 19:20) as an aspect of a human being (see Introduction, section IX.D). Verses 9–10 repeat the same idea as in vv 7–8, but in inverse order. In fact, there may be a chiastic arrangement here, as Grobel has pointed out:

302

a. God will repay everyone according to his deeds (v 6)
   b. eternal life for those who do good (v 7)
      c. wrath and fury for those who disobey (v 8)
      c'. distress and anguish for those who do evil (v 9)
   b'. glory, honor, peace for those who do good (v 10)
a'. no impartiality in God (v 11)

This verse reformulates v 8 in order to introduce the specification that follows. The combination *thlipsis*, "distress," and *stenochōria*, "anguish," is a protological pair, found in Isa 8:22; 30:6; Deut 28:53, 55, 57, expressing divine displeasure shown to human beings in this life (cf. 8:35).

for the Jew first and also for the Greek. Now the Jew is singled out in priority, not because of his status in salvation history (as in 1:16), but because of his privileged, superior moral status, having the advantage of the Mosaic law and knowing God's will thereby. Yet equity for all is stressed.

10. *there will be glory, honor, and peace for everyone who does good.* Again, this verse reformulates v 7 in order to introduce the specification that follows.

for the Jew first and also for the Greek. The same priority and equity are noted again. On the name *Ioudaios*, see the NOTE on 2:17; on the name *Hellēn*, see the NOTE on 1:14.

11. *for there is no partiality in God.* Lit., "for there is no face-uplifting on God's part," i.e., he lifts up the face of both Jew and Greek alike or he looks with equity on both; he has no favorites. This verse provides the basis for what Paul said in v 10 about everyone "who does good" and in v 9 about everyone who "does evil."

The Greek compound noun *prosōpolēmpsia* is found only in Christian writings. It is fashioned on the LXX use of *prosōpon lambanein*, which translates the Hebrew *pānîm nāśāʾ*, "lift up, raise the face" (of someone). Cf. Lev 19:15, *lōʾ tiśśāʾ pĕnê dāl*, "you shall not lift up the face of (the) poor," i.e., you shall not show partiality to the poor; you shall not recompense unfairly because of selfish motives. Cf. Deut 10:17, "For the Lord, your God, is the God of gods, the Lord of lords, the great God, mighty and awesome, who has no favorites, accepts no bribes." In other words, God will not favor the Jew simply because he is a member of the chosen people or because he has the advantage of a superior moral system based on God's own law. Paul makes specific a teaching that is already found in the OT and pre-Christian Jewish literature: Deut 10:17; 2 Kgs 3:14; 2 Chr 19:7; Mal 1:8; Job 34:19; 42:8; Ps 82:2; Wis 6:7; Sir 35:12–13 ("The Lord is the judge; with him there is no partiality"); *Ps. Sol.* 2:18 ("God is a just judge and will not respect anyone" [lit., will not surprise the face]); *Jub.* 5:15; Gal 2:6; Col 3:25; Eph 6:9. It denotes the gracious act of someone who lifts up a person's face by showing him favor. According to ancient Near Eastern customs the greeting to a superior would include the bowing of the head, if not full prostration; and lifting up the face would mean full acceptance of such obeisance.

BIBLIOGRAPHY

Bassler, J. M., "Divine Impartiality in Paul's Letter to the Romans," *NovT* 26 (1984): 43–58.

———, *Divine Impartiality: Paul and a Theological Axiom*, SBLDS 59 (Chico, Calif.: Scholars, 1982).

———, "Luke and Paul on Impartiality," *Bib* 66 (1985): 546–52.

Berger, K., "Die sog. 'Sätze heiligen Rechts' im N.T.: Ihre Funktion und ihr Sitz im Leben," *TZ* 28 (1972): 305–30.

———, "Zu den sogenannten Sätzen heiligen Rechts," *NTS* 17 (1970–71): 10–40.

Bultmann, R., "Glossen im Römerbrief," *TLZ* 72 (1947): 197–202; repr. in *Exegetica* (Tübingen: Mohr [Siebeck], 1967), 278–84.

Cambier, J.-M., "Le Jugement de tous les hommes par Dieu seul, selon la vérité, dans Rom 2:1–3:20," *ZNW* 67 (1976): 187–213.

Carras, G. P., "Romans 2,1–29: A Dialogue on Jewish Ideals," *Bib* 73 (1992): 183–207.

Donfried, K. P., "Justification and Last Judgment in Paul," *Int* 30 (1976): 140–52; fuller form, *ZNW* 67 (1976): 90–110.

Fridrichsen, A., "Quatre Conjectures sur le texte du Nouveau Testament," *RHPR* 3 (1923): 439–42, esp. 440.

Ghiron-Bistagne, P., "L'Emploi du terme grec 'prosopon' dans l'*Ancien* et le *Nouveau Testament*," *Mélanges Edouard Delebecque*, Publications Université de Provence (Aix-en-Provence and Marseilles: Laffitte, 1983), 155–74.

Giesecke, F., "Zur Exegese von Röm. 2,11–16," *TSK* 59 (1886): 173–82.

Grobel, K., "A Chiastic Retribution-Formula in Romans 2," *Zeit und Geschichte: Dankesgabe an Rudolf Bultmann . . .*, ed. E. Dinkler (Tübingen: Mohr [Siebeck], 1964), 255–61.

Johnson, S. L., Jr., "Studies in Romans. Part V: The Judgment of God," *BSac* 130 (1973): 24–34.

Käsemann, E., "Sentences of Holy Law in the New Testament," *NTQT*, 66–81.

Mattern, L., *Das Verständnis des Gerichtes bei Paulus*, ATANT 47 (Zurich: Zwingli, 1966), 123–38.

Morris, T. F., "Law and the Cause of Sin in the Epistle to the Romans," *HeyJ* 28 (1987): 285–91.

Norden, E., *Agnostos Theos: Untersuchungen zur Formengeschichte religiöser Rede* (Leipzig: Teubner, 1913), 134–40.

Pohlmann, H., *Die Metanoia als Zentralbegriff der urchristlichen Frömmigkeit: Eine systematische Untersuchung zum Ordo Salutis auf biblisch-theologischer Grundlage*, UNT 25 (Leipzig: Hinrichs, 1938).

Riedl, J., "Salus paganorum secundum Rom 2," *VD* 42 (1964): 61–70.

Salas, A., "Dios premia según las obras," *La idea de Dios en la Biblia: XXVIII semana bíblica española (Madrid 23–27 sept. 1968)* (Madrid: Consejo Superior de Investigaciones Científicas, 1971), 265–86.

Schlier, H., "Von den Juden: Römerbrief 2,1–29," *Zeit der Kirche*, 38–47.

Snodgrass, K. R., "Justification by Grace—To the Doers: An Analysis of the Place of Romans 2 in the Theology of Paul," *NTS* 32 (1986): 72–93.

Stendahl, K., "Rechtfertigung und Endgericht," *LR* 11 (1961): 3–10; "Justification and the Last Judgment," *LW* 8 (1961): 1–7.

Steinmetz, F.-J. and F. Wulf, " 'Richtet nicht!': Auslegung und Meditation von Röm 2,1, Mt 7,1f. und Röm 8,1," *GLeb* 42 (1969): 71–74.

7. THE LAW AND ITS OBSERVANCE (2:12–16)

2 [12]All who have sinned apart from the law will also perish apart from the law, and all who have sinned under the law will be judged by the law. [13]For it is not those who listen to the law who are upright before God; rather, those who observe the law will be justified before him. [14]Thus whenever Gentiles who do not have the law observe by nature precepts of the law, they are actually a law to themselves, though not having the law. [15]They show that what the law prescribes has been written on their hearts, as their consciences also bear witness and their thoughts either accuse or defend them—[16]on the day when, according to my gospel, God judges through Christ Jesus the secrets of human hearts.

COMMENT

Possession of the law, even that given by God to his chosen people through Moses, will not save such people from divine wrath, unless that law is observed. "Gifts granted to the Jew in salvation history do not protect him against universal judgment" (Käsemann, *Commentary*, 61). By contrast, pagans sometimes manifest a knowledge of some of the precepts of that law, because they have been written on their hearts, as their consciences manifest at times. When, for instance, pagans honor their parents, they do just what the law says, even though they do not have the benefit of the Mosaic decalogue. Hence their harmony with that law is quite different from the Jews who have the Mosaic law, but do not obey it. Pagans thus do, in a natural and forthright way, something that is good and in keeping with the law, because they are a law unto themselves.

In this passage we encounter for the first time Paul's use of *nomos*, "law." It is important to recall that he uses the word in four different senses (see Introduction, section IX.D): in a figurative sense, in a generic sense, as an expression for the whole OT, and especially as the Mosaic law (with or without the def. art.). In fact, the argument in this paragraph proceeds from a vague expression about law to a clear reference to the Mosaic law. The context deals with Gentiles who lived without the benefit of the Mosaic legislation, so "law" in these verses refers to the Mosaic law. If they sin without knowledge of its prescriptions, they will perish without respect to it; their evil and sinfulness brings its own condemnation, even though it is not the condemnation derived from the law. What human beings do will be the criterion by which they will be judged. In this view Paul goes against current Jewish convictions.

Commentators have at times tried to establish a distinction between Paul's use of *ho nomos*, "the (Mosaic) law," and *nomos*, "law" (in general), or even "natural" law; but this distinction is without sound philological support (*pace* ZBG §177; cf. *PAHT* §PT90). Because Paul uses *physei*, "by nature," in v 14, this passage has often been discussed apropos of the so-called natural law. The word *nomos* used in this passage has been related by some commentators to "the law of my mind" (7:23), and together they raise the question whether Paul himself actually teaches something about the natural law. Moreover, because Paul uses the unbiblical and specifically Greek contrast of *physis* and *nomos*, the Greek idea of people being a law unto themselves, and the distinctively Greek ideas of *agraphos nomos* and *syneidēsis* in this paragraph, it would seem that he is tributary to Greek philosophical thinking.

Norden (*Agnostos Theos*, 11 n. 2, 122), Pohlenz ("Paulus"), Dodd ("Natural Law"), Bornkamm ("Gesetz und Natur"), Kuhr ("Römer 2,14f."), and Lietzmann (*An die Römer*, 40–41) are of the opinion that Paul does indeed use the idea of natural law, having been indirectly influenced by Stoic or other Greek philosophy, whereas McKenzie ("Natural Law"), Nygren (*Romans*, 124), Reicke ("Syneidesis," 161), have maintained that he does not. The question is not easily decided. Possibly Paul is reflecting merely elements of the popular Greek philosophy of his day, without really developing a theory of natural law as such. See Introduction, section IX.D; cf. M. Lackmann, *Vom Geheimnis der Schöpfung* (Stuttgart: Evangelisches Verlagswerk, 1952), 285–363. Some commentators have toyed with the idea that "by nature" should be set in quotation marks, which would make Paul use that phrase for the sake of the argument. If that were admitted, then v 14 would be even less of a basis for the discussion whether Paul teaches anything about the natural law. The Second Vatican Council appealed to this passage in its modern teaching on conscience (*Gaudium et spes* §16).

Paul does not ascribe the Gentile's "doing of the law" to a human being's unaided effort (*physei*), because doing the law, even when it is unknown, becomes possible only where "what can be known about God" (1:19) is the basis of human activity, rather than the rebellion that characterizes humanity as a whole (1:18–23).

In this passage, as in 14:7–12, one also encounters a tension between Paul's admission in v 13 that "those who observe the law will be justified before him" and 3:24, "all are justified freely by his grace through the redemption that comes in Christ Jesus," or 3:28, "a human being is justified by faith apart from deeds prescribed by the law." In other words, Paul seems to say that one is justified by faith, but judged by works. The justification of the Christian is accompanied by an assurance of deliverance from the wrath to come (5:9–10; 1 Thess 1:10; 5:9);

the verdict of acquittal has already been pronounced in what Christ Jesus has achieved for humanity, and there is no longer any condemnation of it (8:1, 30–34). But the role of works is still involved, and Paul is thus seen to be tributary to Jewish teaching. Indeed, he uses the traditional teaching to turn it against his Jewish interlocutor and to demolish his smugness based on his privileged position among the chosen people gifted with the Mosaic law. Has Paul thus retained a relic from his pre-Christian Jewish background and failed to incorporate it into his new Christian teaching about justification by grace through faith in Christ Jesus? It might seem so, but it is to be noted that Paul has really reinterpreted that Jewish teaching by adding to it certain modifications of his own (e.g., "what he has done in the body," 2 Cor 5:10) for the sake of his argument. Paul may seem to introduce the motif of judgment according to deeds not to warn the Christian reader as such, but because he wants to undermine the smugness of the Jewish interlocutor. And yet, it is precisely the motif of God's judgment that must be retained for the sake of the message of justification by grace through faith. God has the right to judge the world and to recompense humanity according to its deeds. This Pauline message of judgment is what the Christian needs to hear first (see 3:6), and in the light of that message the message of justification by grace through faith takes on new meaning. It is only in the light of divine judgment according to human deeds that the justification of the sinner by grace through faith is rightly seen. Hence there is no real inconsistency in Paul's teaching about justification by faith and judgment according to deeds. Judgment according to deeds may be a relic of Paul's Jewish background, but it has become an important and integral element in his teaching. See further Watson, "Justified by Faith." Cf. Wilckens, *Römer*, 1.127–31.

Paul introduces mention of God's judgment because he wants to stress the situation of the Jew who seeks uprightness in God's sight through the law. Paul does not want to speak of the pagan's fulfillment of the law as such; he uses such pagan fulfillment to show that the Jew's trust in the law is not well based. The Jew has the law, whereas the pagan does not; but what really matters is the doing of what the law demands. To counteract the confidence of the Jew who *has* the law, Paul uses the pagan who does not have it, yet who sometimes *does* by nature what the law requires. Thus Paul's argument depends on the contrast of the knowledge of the law and the observance of it. In the light of this contrast the question of God's judgment is introduced.

NOTES

2:12. *All who have sinned apart from the law will also perish apart from the law.* Lit., "all who have sinned law-lessly will also perish law-lessly." On the alpha-privative use of the compound adv. *anomōs*, see BDF §120.2. Paul uses the adverb at first in a vague, generic sense, but as the paragraph develops and the contrast sets in between Jews and Gentiles, one realizes that, in referring to the law-less, he is already hinting at those who do not possess the Mosaic law. Hence those who sin apart from the Mosaic law will also perish apart from the Mosaic law. In Gal 2:15 Paul refers to Peter and himself as "Jews by nature" and not "sinners from among the Gentiles." There he plays on the idea that to be *a-nomoi*, "without the (Mosaic) law," was to be *hamartōloi*, "sinners." To be "Law-less" was to be "lawless," a Jewish conviction (see *Jub.* 23:24: "sinful Gentiles"). Paul uses for the first time the vb. *hamartanein*, "miss the mark, sin," meaning that the "Law-less" have missed the mark; they have transgressed the bounds of proper conduct. On his sense of "sin," see Introduction, section IX.D. The aor. tense *hēmarton* is used to express the one-time summation of a person's life from the standpoint of the day of judgment. The fut. vb. *apolountai* expresses the outcome of a life that has been beset with sin (cf. 1 Cor 1:18).

and all who have sinned under the law will be judged by the law. Paul uses *en nomō*, a prep. phrase without the def. art. to correspond to the adv. *anomōs* in the first clause. Again the expression is vague, but he is again hinting at the Mosaic law. In other words, those who live by the guidance of such legislation will find themselves judged according to it. Cf. 3:19. Paul thus insists that there is no distinction between those without the law and those under the law when it comes to the final outcome of sinful conduct or sinful life. Both will either "perish" (*apolountai*) or "be condemned" (*krithēsontai*). The important contrast of "apart from the law" and "under the law" is thus emphasized. That is the basis on which the judgment of God will be based. The vb. *krithēsontai*, "they will be condemned" (i.e., by God), is a theological passive (see ZBG §236). For the first time in this letter Paul has now mentioned *nomos* (see Introduction, section IX.D; cf. H. Hübner, *EDNT* 2.471–77).

13. *For it is not those who listen to the law who are upright before God.* Lit., "it is not the hearers of (the) law. . . ." On the anarthrous form *nomou*, see BDF §258.2; it cannot mean "the hearers of a law." Jews would not find their status of innocence (*dikaioi*) before God simply because they know the prescriptions of the Torah, e.g., from hearing them read every Sabbath in the synagogue (Acts 15:21). Paul uses a well-known hortatory distinction between knowledge and action. Cf. Jas 1:22–23, 25; 4:11.

rather, those who observe the law will be justified before him. Lit., "the doers of (the) law. . . ." For the sake of his argument, Paul adopts a Jewish perspective and implicitly echoes Lev 18:5, "whoever observes these things shall find life," a verse that he quotes explicitly in Gal 3:12. Cf. Acts 10:35. Paul repeats the emphatic teaching of the OT about observing the law (see Deut 4:1, 5–6, 13–14; 30:11–14; 1 Macc 2:67; 13:48; Josephus, *Ant.* 20.2.4 §44). If one were to take the Pauline statement in this part of the verse out of its context, it might seem like a contradiction of what Paul says in 3:20, "no human being will be justified before him through deeds prescribed by the law." In this verse Paul argues *dato, non concesso*, for the sake of his argument.

Paul now uses for the first time the vb. *dikaioun*. It will occur again in 3:4,

20, 24, 26, 28, 30; 4:2, 5; 5:1, 9; 6:7; 8:30, 33. In classical Greek *dikaioun* means "make right" or "deem right." When used with a personal object, it means "do someone justice," usually in the case of someone who is unfair, violent, or wrong; hence it denotes "to pass sentence against, condemn, punish" (e.g., Herodotus, *History* 1.100; 3.29; Aeschylus, *Agamemnon* 393; Plato, *Laws* 11.934b; Thucydides, *Peloponnesian Wars* 3.40.4; Aristotle, *Nicomachean Ethics* 5.9.2 §1136a). This negative sense prevails in classical Greek, and only rarely does one find the positive sense, "to set right an injustice suffered" (e.g., Pindar, *Fragment* 169.3, quoted in Plato, *Gorgias* 484b; Polybius 3.31.9).

When *dikaioun* was used in the LXX to translate Hebrew *hiphᶜil hiṣdîq*, which always means to "acquit, vindicate, declare innocent, justify" (e.g., Exod 23:7; Deut 25:1; Ps 82:3; Isa 5:23; 43:26), the Greek *dikaioun* took on a nuance that it did not normally have in extrabiblical Greek that is not dependent on the Greek OT or the NT. The negative sense is not found in the LXX in any writings that depend on the Hebrew, except perhaps in deuterocanonical Sir 42:2, where *dikaiōsai ton asebē* translates Hebrew *lĕhaṣdîq rāšā*ᶜ and probably means "to pass sentence against the impious." The closest one comes in extrabiblical Greek to the Pauline usage is found in the (second or third century A.D.) *Corpus Hermeticum* (ed. W. Scott) 13.9: *chōris gar kriseōs ide pōs tēn adikian exēlasen . . . edikaiōthēmen, ō teknon, adikias apousēs*, "for aside from judgment see how she has driven out iniquity . . . we have been made righteous, my child, now that iniquity is absent." Here the vb. *dikaioun* connotes some ethical change. See D. Hill, *Greek Words and Hebrew Meanings: Studies in the Semantics of Soteriological Terms*, SNTSMS 5 (Cambridge: Cambridge University Press, 1967), 101–2.

Paul's use of the fut. tense *dikaiōthēsontai* betrays the eschatological, forensic nature of justification expected at the judgment in accordance with the adopted Jewish perspective. See K. Kertelge, "*Dikaioō*," EDNT 1.330–34. See the NOTE on 4:3.

14. *whenever Gentiles who do not have the law observe by nature precepts of the law.* Lit., ". . . do by nature the (things) of the law." Paul's affirmation is couched in a general temporal clause, which thus qualifies what he says. There is no definite article before *ethnē*; so it means "some Gentiles," not necessarily all Gentiles. Again, the phrase *ta tou nomou*, lit., "the (things) of the law," means some of the precepts of the law, not necessarily all that is prescribed by the Mosaic law. Paul does not imply a perfect observance of the Mosaic law by such Gentiles. But what they do, they do *physei*, "by nature, instinctively," in other words, by the regular, natural order of things (BAGD, 869), i.e., prescinding from any positive revelation. Following the guidance of *physis*, Gentiles frame rules of conduct for themselves and know at least some of the prescriptions of the Mosaic Torah. They have *physis* as a guide for their conduct, a guide that is "not only relative or psychological, but absolute and objective" (Michel, *Brief an die Römer*, 118). Thus Paul explains why Gentiles without an explicit knowledge of the Mosaic law will still be punished (2:12). On the meaning of *physis*, see the NOTE

on 1:26. Because the terminology in vv 14–15 is under heavy Greek influence (see the COMMENT above), *physis* has to be taken in the Greek sense: what Gentiles do corresponds to their nature (*TDNT* 9.273–74).

Paul does not mean "by nature" as opposed to "by grace"; so his viewpoint is not that of the later theological problem, whether the pagan's will suffices *physei* to obey the natural law.

Does "by nature" modify what precedes or what follows? Is it "whenever Gentiles who do not have the law by nature," i.e., in virtue of their birth (cf. Gal 2:15; Eph 2:3), or "whenever Gentiles who do not have the law do by nature . . ."? The preferable interpretation is the latter, because Paul would have put *physei* within the participial phrase *ta mē nomon echonta*, if he had meant the former (compare 2:27; Gal 2:15). Both the syntax and the balance of the sentence require that *physei* be taken with what follows, as Leenhardt (*Romans*, 83) and Dunn (*Romans*, 98) have rightly maintained, contra Achtemeier (*Romans*, 45) and Cranfield (*Romans*, 156–57). Cf. 1 Cor 11:14.

Does "Gentiles" refer to Gentile Christians? Augustine so understood it (*De spiritu et littera*, 26.43–28.49 [CSEL 60.196–204]; *Contra Iulianum* 4.3.25 [PL 44.750]); he was followed by Luther (*Scholia in ep. ad Romanos* 2.14 [LuthW 25.185; but see H. Koester, *TDNT* 9.273 n. 220, appealing to WAusg 56.202.16]), and in modern times by Karl Barth, Flückiger ("Die Werke"), Souček ("Zur Exegese"), and Mundle ("Zur Auslegung"). Although Cranfield (*Romans*, 156) prefers it, it remains a highly debatable question. For even though *ethnē* is used of Gentile Christians in 11:13 and 15:9, in those cases it is clear from the context that Gentile Christians are meant; here it is not clear at all, and the thrust of Paul's argument demands that it be understood of Gentiles as such, as Calvin well saw (*Commentary on . . . Romans*, 96). See further Bornkamm ("Gesetz und Natur"), Kuhr ("Römer 2,14f.," 252–61), Kuss ("Die Heiden").

they are actually a law to themselves. Paul uses *nomos* in a figurative sense (see Introduction, section IX.D). Pagans are themselves a way of knowing some of the things prescribed or proscribed by the Mosaic law. On the dative of advantage *heautois*, see BDF §188.2.

For the philosophical background to this notion, see the Stoic Chrysippus in Plutarch, *De Stoicorum repugnantiis* 9.1035C: "It is not possible to find any other beginning or source of justice (*dikaiosynē*) than from Zeus and universal nature (*ek tēs koinēs physeōs*)." Cicero, *De legibus* 1.6.18: "Law is the highest reason implanted in Nature, which commands what ought to be done and forbids the contrary. This reason, when firmly fixed and perfected in the human mind, is Law." Cf. Philo, who also attests such philosophical thinking, *De Abr.* 46 §276: *nomos autos ōn kai thesmos agraphos*, "[the Sage], being himself a law and an unwritten statute"; *Quod omnis probus liber* 7 §46: "Right reason is an infallible law engraved not by this mortal or that, and thus perishable, nor on lifeless scrolls or stelae, and thus lifeless, but by immortal nature on the immortal mind"; *De Iosepho* 6 §29: "This world, the Megalopolis, has one polity and one law, and this is the word of nature, dictating what must be done and forbidding what must not be done." Cf. *1 Enoch* 2:1–5:4.

though not having the law. I.e., not having the benefit of a positive revelation of God's will, not having something like the Mosaic legislation, such as Jews have.

15. *They show that what the law prescribes has been written on their hearts.* Lit., "the deed of the law is written. . . ." Paul uses positively the sg. of the expression that he employs elsewhere in the pl. and in a pejorative sense, *erga nomou*, "deeds of the law" (3:20, 28; Gal 2:16; 3:2, 5, 10 [see the NOTE on 3:20]), or simply *erga* (4:2, 6; 9:12, 32; 11:6). The phrase does not mean "the core of the law" (so Kuss, Lietzmann) or the "epitome of the law" (so Schlier), but the "concrete act demanded by the law" (Käsemann, *Commentary*, 64). As a collective singular, it refers to the "deeds" that the law prescribes. Paul affirms such knowledge as a present, real condition of Gentile awareness. He uses an OT expression, derived from Jer 31[LXX]:33; Isa 51:7, about a law written on human hearts (cf. *2 Apoc. Bar.* 57:2).

Three things thus give witness to the knowledge that the Gentile has about good and evil: (1) the act itself (*ergon*); (2) conscience; and (3) accusing or defending thoughts. All of them show that God's judgment is just, when the Gentile does wrong and so falls under the wrath of God, as does the Jew who does not obey the Mosaic law.

as their consciences also bear witness. Paul repeats the idea in the previous clause now in a different way, making use of a Greek philosophical idea. *Syneidēsis*, "conscience," is the capacity of the human mind to judge one's actions either in retrospect (as right or wrong) or in prospect (as a guide for proper activity). See Introduction, section IX.D.

The ptc. *symmartyrousēs*, lit., "testifying along with," would imply that there is some other witness along with which the conscience bears witness (and an accompanying dative would express the other witness). But it can also mean simply "testifying, bearing witness" (an accompanying dative would then be the object to which the testimony is borne). Because there is no dative in this case, the latter of the two senses is preferred. "To them" would then be implied, i.e., to the Gentiles.

their thoughts either accuse or defend them. Lit., "as their thoughts mutually accuse or defend (them)." This clause describes the role of the conscience in greater detail. The prep. phrase *metaxy allēlōn*, "between one another," is not easily interpreted. It is best understood as referring to the mutual debate of inward thoughts in the Gentile conscience; the debate would concern the pros and cons of conduct (so Cranfield, *Romans*, 162; Käsemann, *Commentary*, 66). Some commentators, however, take it to refer to thoughts that criticize or defend the actions of others, "in their dealings with one another" (so Sanday and Headlam, *Romans*, 61; Lyonnet, *Romains*, 74). But this interpretation seems farfetched.

16. *on the day when, according to my gospel, God judges through Christ Jesus the secrets of human hearts.* Logically, this verse follows 2:13; yet it is instead

stating a conclusion for the whole paragraph, echoing *en hēmera orgēs*, "on the day of wrath," of v 5. Paul does not mean that the Gentile conscience will function only on judgment day, but that it will especially bear witness on that day. "Such self-criticism anticipates the last judgment, as in Wis 1:5–10" (Käsemann, *Commentary*, 66). Paul seeks to explain how it will be that Gentiles who do not have the Mosaic law will yet be judged as if they had some sort of a law. They have, indeed, a law: if not written precepts, at least the law of conscience, and by such a law they will be judged when the living and the dead stand before God's tribunal. Paul's gospel bears witness not to the judgment of humanity by God, which was standard Jewish belief, but to that which God will carry out through Christ. Contemporary Jews sometimes expected Yahweh to exercise judgment through an Elect One, e.g., through Enoch (*1 Enoch* 45:3–6) or Melchizedek (11QMelch) or Abel (*T. Abr.* 13:5). Paul applies this belief to Christ. Cf. Acts 10:42. The prep. phrase *dia Christou Iēsou* refers to the mediation of Christ in his eschatological role. The proclamation of Christ's role in eschatological judgment forms part of Paul's "good news" of salvation. Thus for him it is a salvific judgment, but also one that he declares must be awaited by all human beings. Cf. 2 Cor 5:10; 2 Thess 1:7–10; 2 Tim 4:1; John 5:27; Rev 22:12. There is for Paul no contradiction between justification by faith and judgment by God through Christ. See 14:11–12.

"Christ Jesus" is the order of these names in MSS ℵ* and B; but MSS ℵ¹, A, D, Ψ, and the *Koinē* text-tradition read instead "Jesus Christ."

The idea of God knowing the secrets of the human heart is an OT tradition; see 1 Sam 16:7; 1 Chr 29:9; Ps 139:1–2, 23; Jer 17:10. Cf. 1 Cor 4:5. On God as judge, see 2:2; on the "day" of judgment, see the NOTE on 2:5. The vb. *krinei* could be taken either as present (*krínei*) or as future (*krineî*). The context would supply a future connotation even to the present tense (see BDF §323).

Some commentators suggest that vv 14–15 are parenthetical or even misplaced. See BDF §465.1. Bultmann ("Glossen," 200–201) considered v 16 a secondary gloss introduced into the text. The MS tradition, however, is constant, save for the order of the words *hē hēmera* (MS B) or *hēmera hē* (MS A). Cf. BDF §385.3; H. Sahlin, "Einige"; H. Saake, "Echtheitskritische Überlegungen."

On "my gospel," see the NOTE on 16:25; cf. 2 Tim 2:8.

BIBLIOGRAPHY

Achtemeier, P. J., " 'Some Things in Them Hard to Understand': Reflections on an Approach to Paul," *Int* 38 (1984): 254–67.

Allo, B., "L'Evolution' de l'évangile de Paul' " *Mémorial Lagrange*, ed. L.-H. Vincent (Paris: Gabalda, 1940), 259–67.

Bornkamm, G., "Gesetz und Natur, Röm 2,14–16," *Studien zu Antike und Urchristentum: Gesammelte Aufsätze II*, BEvT 28 (Munich: Kaiser, 1959), 93–118.

Brandt, W., *Das Gesetz Israels und das Gesetz der Heiden bei Paulus und im Hebräerbrief*, Kirche und Erziehung 8 (Munich: Kaiser, 1934).

Briel, S. C., "The Pastor and the Septuagint," *CTQ* 51 (1987): 261–74 [on *dikaioun*].

Dodd, C. H., "Natural Law in the New Testament," *New Testament Studies* (Manchester, UK: Manchester University Press, 1953), 129–42.

Driessen, E., " 'Secundum evangelium meum' (Rom 2,16; 16,25; 2 Tim 2,8)," *VD* 24 (1944): 25–32.

Flückiger, E., "Die Werke des Gesetzes bei den Heiden (nach Röm. 2,14ff.)," *TZ* 8 (1952): 17–42.

Heil, J. P., "Reader-Response and Interculturation in Paul's Letter to the Romans," *EgThéol* 21 (1990): 283–301.

Heinemann, F., *Nomos und Physis: Herkunft und Bedeutung einer Antithese im griechischen Denken des 5. Jahrhunderts*, Schweizerische Beiträge zur Altertumswissenschaft 1 (Basel: Reinhardt, 1945).

Heinemann, I., "Die Lehre vom ungeschriebenen Gesetz im jüdischen Schrifttum," *HUCA* 4 (1927): 149–71.

Hirzel, R., *Agraphos Nomos*, Abhandlungen der königlichen sächsischen Gesellschaft der Wissenschaften, philolog.-histor. Kl. 20.1 (Stuttgart: Teubner, 1900; repr. Hildesheim: P. Gerstenberg, 1979).

Kähler, M., "Auslegung von Kap. 2,14–16 im Römerbrief," *TSK* 47 (1874): 261–306.

König, A., "Gentiles or Gentile Christians? On the Meaning of Romans 2: 12–16," *JTSA* 15 (1976): 53–60.

Kranz, W., "Das Gesetz des Herzens," *Rheinisches Museum für Philologie* n.s. 94 (1951): 222–41.

Kuhr, F., "Römer 2,14f. und die Verheissung bei Jeremia 31,31ff.," *ZNW* 55 (1964): 243–61.

Kuss, O., "Die Heiden und die Werke des Gesetzes (nach Röm 2, 14–16)," *MTZ* 5 (1954): 77–98; repr. in *Auslegung und Verkündigung*, 3 vols. (Regensburg: Pustet, 1963–71), 1.213–45.

———, "Nomos bei Paulus," *MTZ* 17 (1966): 173–227.

Lafon, G., "Les Poètes de la loi: Un Commentaire de *Romains* 2,12–27," *Christus* (Paris) 134 (1987): 205–14.

———, "La Production de la loi: La Pensée de la loi en *Romains* 2, 12–27," *RSR* 74 (1986): 321–40.

Lehmann, A., "Der Bibelvers Röm. 2, 14: Eine kleine Mahnung," *TSK* 50 (1877): 514–18.

Lyonnet, S., " 'Lex naturalis' quid praecipiat secundum S. Paulum et antiquam Patrum traditionem," *VD* 45 (1967): 150–61.

McKenzie, J. L., "Natural Law in the New Testament," *BR* 9 (1964): 1–13.

Märcker, F., "Ueber *ergōn nomou* im Römer- und Galaterbrief," *TSK* 46 (1873): 707–21.

Morison, J., "St. Paul on the Heathen: Romans ii. 12–16," *Expos* 2.7 (1885): 454–66.

Mundle, W., "Zur Auslegung von Röm 2, 13ff.," *TBl* 13 (1934): 249–56.

Pohlenz, M., "Paulus und die Stoa," ZNW 42 (1949): 69–104.

Reicke, B., "Natürliche Theologie bei Paulus," *SEA* 22–23 (1957–58): 154–67.

———, "Syneidesis in Röm. 2, 15," *TZ* 12 (1956): 157–61.

Riedl, J., *Das Heil der Heiden nach R 2, 14–16.26.27*, St. Gabrieler Studien 20 (Mödling bei Wien: St. Gabriel-Verlag, 1965).

———, "Die Auslegung von R 2, 14–16 in Vergangenheit und Gegenwart," *SPCIC* 1.271–81.

Rosman, H., " 'Justificare' est verbum causativum," *VD* 21 (1941): 144–47.

P. C. S., "La ley revelada en orden al juicio divino: Posición de los creyentes judiós y gentiles (Rom. II,12–29)," *EstBíb* 7 (1935): 223–40.

Saake, H., "Echtheitskritische Überlegungen zur Interpolationshypothese von Römer ii. 16," *NTS* 19 (1972–73): 486–89.

Sahlin, H., "Einige Textemendationem zum Römerbrief," *TZ* 9 (1953): 92–100.

Schumann, F. K., "Bemerkungen zur Lehre vom Gesetz," *ZST* 16 (1939): 600–28.

Segal, A. F., "Torah and *nomos* in Recent Scholarly Discussion," *SR* 13 (1984): 19–27.

Snodgrass, K. R., "Justification by Grace—To the Doers: An Analysis of the Place of Romans 2 in the Theology of Paul," *NTS* 32 (1986): 72–93.

Souček, J. B., "Zur Exegese von Röm. 2, 14ff.," *Antwort: Karl Barth* . . . (Zollikon-Zurich: Evangelischer-Verlag, 1956), 99–113.

Walker, R., "Die Heiden und das Gericht: Zur Auslegung von Römer 2, 12–16," *EvT* 20 (1960): 302–14.

Watson, N. M., "Justified by Faith; Judged by Works—An Antinomy?" *NTS* 29 (1983): 209–21.

———, "Some Observations on the Use of *dikaioō* in the Septuagint," *JBL* 79 (1960): 255–66.

Westerholm, S., "*Torah, nomos,* and Law: A Question of 'Meaning,' " *SR* 15 (1986): 327–36.

Yates, J. C., "The Judgment of the Heathen: The Interpretation of Article XVIII and Romans 2:12–16," *Churchman* 100 (1986): 220–30.

8. TRANSGRESSION OF THE LAW BY JEWS (2:17–24)

2 [17]But suppose you call yourself a Jew, rely on the law, and boast of God, [18]knowing his will and scrutinizing the things that really matter, because you are instructed by the law, [19]and suppose you are persuaded that you yourself are a guide to the blind, a light to those in darkness, [20]a corrector of the foolish, a teacher of the immature, because you have in the law the embodiment of knowledge and truth—[21]then do you who would teach others fail to teach yourself? Do you who preach against stealing steal yourself? [22]Do you who forbid adultery

commit it yourself? Do you who abominate idols rob temples? [23]As for you who boast of the law, you dishonor God by the transgression of the law. [24]As it stands written, *because of you the name of God is blasphemed among the Gentiles.*

COMMENT

Again, Paul indulges in rhetorical diatribe, as he addresses a harsh accusation against the Jew (see Introduction, section VII). The imaginary interlocutor is now explicitly so identified. Similarly Epictetus taunts the Stoic philosophers of his day about not being "true Stoics" because they do not live according to the philosophy that they teach (*Dissertationes* 2.19, 19–20; 3.7.17); cf. Stowers, *Diatribe*, 112–13.

Reliance on the Mosaic law and the boast of a special relationship with God give the Jew an advantage: he knows what God's will is and can teach others. The structure of the passage is simple. Israel's boast is set forth in five aspects (2:19–20): Israel is (a) a guide to the blind, (b) a light to those in darkness, (c) a corrector of the foolish, (d) a teacher of children, and (e) the embodiment of knowledge and truth. Having admitted all of these things about his fellow Jews, Paul then counters paratactically with five queries, as he taunts his interlocutor: (a) Though you may teach others, do you teach yourself? (b) Though you preach against theft, do you steal? (c) Though you preach against adultery, do you commit it yourself? (d) Though you abominate idols, do you rob temples? and (e) Though you boast of the law, do you dishonor God by not observing it? Paul ends his queries by quoting Isa 52:5.

These verses could be a throwback to 2:3, showing that the Jews do the "same things" that the Gentiles did. But they are better taken as a continuation of vv 12–13, after the verses about the Gentiles being a law unto themselves. They would then show that Jews cannot claim to be "doers of the law." In either case, Paul's main argument is that the Jew will be judged by God just as the Gentile will be, but with respect to the law; hence the Jew, no more than the Gentile, cannot assume that he will not have to answer to God who judges the deeds of human beings. As Nygren has pointed out (*Romans*, 131), Paul does not speak with irony in these verses. He does not consider the special status of the Jews as something unimportant; he realizes the privileged status of Israel. Because it did have the advantage of the Mosaic law, it could indeed teach others. That law was indeed Israel's boast, but in its failure to observe that law Israel was mistaken, and this is the point that Paul would make, not in irony, but in all seriousness. This is what he has been aiming at since the beginning of the chapter.

NOTES

2:17. *suppose you call yourself a Jew. Ioudaios* was the common contemporary name for a member of the people of Israel, an adherent of OT monotheism, especially in the diaspora. From Maccabean times on it came to be used by Jews themselves instead of the older names "Hebrew" or "Israelite." It was used as a designation of such persons because of their birth, race, or religion. *Hebraios* would denote the Jew as different from *Hellēnistēs*, one who spoke Greek, whereas *Ioudaios* would denote nationality, one different from a *Hellēn*, a citizen of Greece. On "Israelite," see the NOTE on 9:4. Cf. 2 Esdr 6:55–56, "All this I have uttered before you, O Lord, because you have said that it was for us that you created this world. As for the other nations that have descended from Adam, you have said that they are nothing, that they are like spittle, and you have compared their abundance to a drop from a bucket."

rely on the law. Lit., "you have a law to lean upon," without the def. art., as in MSS ℵ, A, B, D*; later MSS add the art., making the reference to the Mosaic law explicit. To such trust and reliance the OT summoned the Jew. Cf. Sir 39:8, "He will boast of the law of the Lord's covenant." Also 2 *Apoc. Bar.* 48:22–24, "In you we trust, for your law is with us, and we know that we shall not fall so long as we keep your statutes. For all time we are blessed in this at least, that we have not mingled with the Gentiles. We are all one famous people, who have received one law from the only One, and the law which is with us will help us; the surpassing wisdom which is in our midst will sustain us." The vb. *epanapauesthai* is found in the LXX of Mic 3:11; Ezek 29:7; 1 Macc 8:11.

and boast of God. Paul is probably alluding here to Jer 9:23, "Let him who boasts boast of this, that he understands and knows me, that I am the Lord. . . ." Paul quotes the same Jeremiah passage again in 1 Cor 1:31 and 2 Cor 10:17. Cf. *Ps. Sol.* 17:1, "For in you, O God, our soul will boast." See also Mic 3:11. Paul detects this tendency among the Jews to boast or glory in the law as the main obstacle to the gospel. That is why he tries to shake the confidence of the Jews, when that mistaken self-confidence is based merely on the knowledge and possession of the law, without the consequent observance of it. Paul knows that sin reigns among Jews in spite of the Mosaic law. See J. Zmijewski, "*Kauchaomai*," EDNT 2.276–79.

MSS ℵ, A, B, D, K, Ψ, etc., read *ei de*, which by itacism has become the inferior reading *ide*, "behold," in the *Koinē* text-tradition. The reason for this change was undoubtedly Paul's failure to conclude the sentence with an apodosis of the condition (in v 21). The inferior reading thus eliminates the anacoluthon and makes the text read as a series of independent clauses (see BDF §467).

18. *knowing his will.* To know God's will concerning his people was a matter of great pride in Jewish piety. Cf. Pss 40:9; 143:10; 2 Macc 1:3–4; Bar 4:4; 1QS 9:23.

scrutinizing the things that really matter. Lit., "assaying the things that differ, the things that excel." The ptc. *diapheronta* is the opposite of *adiaphora*, "indifferent matters, unimportant things." Because the Jew boasts of God and knows his will and his law, he is said to be able to concentrate on and appreciate the matters of life that count for most. Cf. Phil 1:10.

because you are instructed by the law. For the law is the source of all wisdom; "love of her [i.e., wisdom] is the keeping of her laws" (Wis 6:18). Paul alludes to the catechetical traditions of Judaism. The ptc. *katēchoumenos,* "being instructed," is to be understood with the two preceding vbs. *ginōskeis* and *dokimazeis.* See further P. Mourlon Beernaert, *Lumen vitae* 44 (1989): 377–87. Yet precisely in this trust of the law and in the boast about possessing it, the Jew makes his mistake.

19. *suppose you are persuaded that you yourself are a guide to the blind.* I.e., because of your superior law-guided status. Paul uses *hodēgon,* "guide, pathfinder," and is perhaps reflecting the Pharisaic conviction about the law as guiding human beings along the way of life by its halakhah. Cf. Wis 2:12–15; Matt 15:14; 23:16, 24.

a light to those in darkness. The pagans would be in darkness and the law-instructed Jew would be in light. The Jew would be playing the role of the Servant of Yahweh (see Isa 42:6–7; 49:6). "Light" and "darkness" are taken as symbols of ethical conduct; see Isa 9:1; 45:7.

20. *a corrector of the foolish.* Lit., "a schoolmaster of fools," i.e., one who disciplines them. See Sir 37:19.

a teacher of the immature. Lit., "of children, infants," as opposed to *teleioi,* "adults" (Heb 5:13–14). Etymologically, *nēpioi* denotes those who are unable to speak (= *na* + *epos*), the exact equivalent of Latin *in-fans.*

because you have in the law the embodiment of knowledge and truth. The noun *morphōsis* denotes "formation, formulation." Paul recognizes that the law encapsulates all knowledge and truth, a real expression of the divine will. Cf. Sir 24:23–27.

21. *then do you who would teach others fail to teach yourself?* The complex sentence begun in 2:17 is not completed; Paul breaks off and addresses the Jew directly with five pointed questions (vv 21–23). On the asyndetic character of this part, see BDF §454.3; 460.3. For the sentiment that Paul expresses here, compare Ps 50:16–21. The five taunting questions that follow could be punctuated as direct statements; but the dialogic character of the passage makes it likely that they are better understood as questions.

Paul is possibly alluding to the conviction of the Pharisees in his time that knowledge of the law would make the nation holy. Stress on the knowledge of the law came into Judaism at the time of the Babylonian captivity, when the Jews were cut off from the Jerusalem Temple. The Torah became the rallying point among them. At the time of the reform of Ezra and Nehemiah Hellenistic influence introduced among Palestinian Jews the idea that knowledge is virtue. When the Pharisaic movement emerged early in the second century B.C., it developed the idea that it could make the nation holy by instruction in the law. Cf. John 7:49, the Pharisaic disdain for the ʿam hā-ʾāreṣ: "that rabble which knows not the law." For later rabbinic sayings that echo what Paul says here, see Str-B 3.107.

Do you who preach against stealing steal yourself? Cf. Exod 20:15, "You must not steal." Now Paul derives his taunts from the decalogue, from the prohibitions of stealing and adultery.

22. *Do you who forbid adultery commit it yourself?* Cf. Exod 20:14, "You shall not commit adultery."

Do you who abominate idols rob temples? I.e., do you succumb to the idolatry of elevating the Mosaic law to a position of unwarranted devotion and of bestowing on it a permanence it was never intended to have in God's ultimate plan? For Paul, Israel's clinging to the law is the exclusion of Christ and his role in God's plan. Thus Paul uses the vb. *hierosylein* in a figurative sense and shapes to his purpose an accusation that was otherwise made against Israel in other respects. Cf. Acts 19:37; *T. Levi* 14:5, "You will rob the Lord's offerings; from the portions allotted to him you will steal; and before sacrificing to the Lord you will take for yourselves the choicest pieces and share them like common food with whores." The abomination of idols is hinted at in Exod 20:4–6; Deut 5:8–10; 7:25–26; Josephus, *Ant.* 4.8.10 §207. Theft, adultery, and robbing temples occur together in Philo, *De conf. ling.* 163.

23. *As for you who boast of the law, you dishonor God by the transgression of the law.* This is Paul's basic indictment of the Jew; it sums up his taunting queries in one apostrophe. As Sanday and Headlam note (*Romans*, 66), this verse is best not taken as a question, following the preceding questions, but rather as a summary accusation. So too Lagrange (*Romains*, 54), Lietzmann (*An die Römer*, 43). "Boasting of the law" echoes v 17, "relying on the law." Gratefully to boast of the law as the revelation of God's merciful will is right, but to boast of it in order to use it as a means of putting God in one's debt and to regard one's knowledge of it as conferring the right to look down on one's fellow men is altogether wrong. So Cranfield, *Romans*, 179.

24. *As it stands written.* See the NOTE on 1:17. In the Greek text this formula actually stands at the end of the quotation, thus ending the verse.

Because of you the name of God is blasphemed among the Gentiles. Paul quotes Isa 52:5 according to the LXX. In the MT the meaning is that God's name is reviled among the Gentiles because "my people have been taken away for nothing; its rulers scoff, says the Lord, and continually all the day long my name is despised," i.e., God's people has been carried off in exile gratuitously, and their miserable lot evokes the blaspheming of God's name by those who rule over them and scoff at their lot. But the LXX changes the sense, reading *di' hymas dia pantos to onoma mou blasphēmeitai en tois ethnesin*, "because of you my name is continually reviled among the Gentiles." The implication is that the reviling is based on what has been done to the exiled people of God. Paul follows the LXX reading, but he means something different by *di' hymas*, "because of you," i.e., because of what you do or fail to do. Thus Paul applies the words of Isaiah to the transgression of the Mosaic law by the Jews and the scandal caused thereby. Cf. Ezek 36:20. The more the Jews boast of their privileged position and special relation to God, while at the same time failing to obey his will, the more those who do not know God will despise him because of such disobedience. Hence God's wrath must be manifested against the Jews too, and not only against pagans who do not properly know or thank him. Israel's special vocation was to obey God and thereby sanctify his name, but it has become instead the cause of that name being dishonored.

BIBLIOGRAPHY

Forbes, C., "Comparison, Self-Praise and Irony: Paul's Boasting and the Conventions of Hellenistic Rhetoric," *NTS* 32 (1986): 1–30.

Forrester, W. R., "Romans ii. 18," *ExpTim* 36 (1924–25): 285.

Garlington, D. B., "*Hierosylein* and the Idolatry of Israel (Romans 2.22)," *NTS* 36 (1990): 142–51.

Goppelt, L., "Der Missionar des Gesetzes (Zu Röm. 2, 21f.)," *Basileia: Walter Freytag* . . . (Wuppertal-Barmen: Rheinische Missionsgesellschaft, 1959), 199–207; repr. *Christologie und Ethik: Aufsätze zum Neuen Testament* (Göttingen: Vandenhoeck & Ruprecht, 1968), 137–46.

Krentz, E., "The Name of God in Disrepute: Romans 2:17–29 [22–23]," *CurTM* 17 (1990): 429–39.

Olivieri, O., "Sintassi, senso e rapporto col contesto di Rom. 2,17–24," *Bib* 11 (1930): 188–215.

Penna, A., "Testi d'Isaia in S. Paolo," *RivB* 5 (1957): 25–30, 163–79.

Unnik, W. C. van, "Die Rücksicht auf die Reaktion der Nicht-Christen als Motiv in der altchristlichen Paränese," *Judentum, Urchristentum, Kirche: Festschrift für Joachim Jeremias*, BZNW 25, ed. W. Eltester (Berlin: Töpelmann, 1960), 221–34.

9. Circumcision Does Not Make the Real Jew (2:25–29)

2 [25]Circumcision, indeed, has value, if you observe the law. But if you are a transgressor of the law, your circumcision has become uncircumcision. [26]Again, if an uncircumcised man keeps the precepts of the law, will not his uncircumcision be reckoned as circumcision? [27]He who by nature is uncircumcised yet keeps the law will condemn you, with your written code and circumcision, as a transgressor of the law. [28]One is not a Jew outwardly only; nor is real circumcision external, in the flesh. [29]Rather, one is a Jew in secret, and real circumcision is of the heart, a thing of the spirit, not of the letter. His praise comes not from human beings, but from God.

319

COMMENT

At the end of his dialogic confrontation in vv 17–24, Paul adopts a didactic tone and seeks to forestall an objection, "Perhaps we Jews do not observe the law as we should, but at least we are circumcised. In this regard at least we have carried out God's command. Did not God himself set up the covenant with Israel and make circumcision the seal of that covenant, the very shield against God's wrath?" Paul rejects this argument too, because he realizes that the mere possession of the "sign of the covenant" does not guarantee the Jew salvation or spare him from the outpouring of God's wrath. He knows that circumcision and the law are intimately related in the covenant that God has made with his people. Circumcision, then, involves two things: God's promise and the requirement of the law. If the people do not observe the law, then the covenant is broken. Paul thus insists that real circumcision is not that of the flesh, but that of the heart, which manifests the humility of the Jew and his willingness to observe the law. Hence everything to which the Jew appeals to protect him from God's wrath becomes useless; it does not suffice to agree with God's judgment of the pagan or to appeal to God's long-suffering, or even to claim that "the sign of the covenant" was destined to forestall the outpouring of divine wrath. One has to observe the law to be a real Jew, to be a member of the covenanted people of God.

In the background of Paul's thinking about this matter is Jer 9:22–25, where the prophet discourses on boasting in the Lord and the value of circumcision:

> Thus says the Lord, "Let not the wise man boast of his wisdom, let not the strong man boast of his strength, let not the rich man boast of his riches; but let him who boasts boast of this, that he understands and knows me, that I am the Lord who practice steadfast love, judgment, and uprightness in the land; for in these things I take delight, says the Lord. Look, days are coming, says the Lord, when I shall punish all those who are circumcised but yet uncircumcised—Egypt, Judah, Edom, the sons of Ammon, Moab, and all who dwell in the desert who cut the corners of their hair; for all these nations are uncircumcised—and all the house of Israel is uncircumcised in heart."

Moreover, Paul sees the situations reversed, and the result is that the pagan, who does not possess the law and is not circumcised, will stand with the Jew at the judgment and condemn him, i.e., pass judgment on him, just as the Jew tried to do in 2:1. To the contrast of circumcision and uncircumcision Paul now adds the contrast of the letter and the spirit.

To be noted in this passage is the way vv 26–27 reformulate 2:14–15. The uncircumcised pagan, observing prescriptions of the law, is reckoned as equivalently circumcised; he thus shares the destiny of Israel itself. Indeed, Paul eventually plays on the meaning of the name "Jew" itself. In effect, he denies the name to those who may outwardly be Jews, but are not so inwardly. The consequences of his indictment would seem to indicate that Paul regards Jews as cut off from the promises to Israel. To this aspect of the problem he will return in chaps. 9–11.

NOTES

2:25. *Circumcision, indeed, has value.* The lancing and removal of the male foreskin were regarded as "the sign of the covenant" (Gen 17:10–11; *Jub.* 15:28; cf. Rom 4:1), for it incorporated a man into God's chosen people and assured him of life in the age to come. Paul does not deny the value of circumcision or the heritage of Israel connoted by it; but he insists that it means little without the observance of the law (Lev 18:5; Deut 30:16). Circumcision was seen as a mark of loyalty to the covenant. Later rabbinic teaching insisted on the absolute guarantee of a share in the world to come for the circumcised Jew and salvation from the fires of Ge-Hinnom (Str-B 1.119). 1 Macc 1:48, 60–61; 2:46; and 2 Macc 6:10 reveal the importance associated with circumcision. Cf. *Jub.* 15:25. Paul's interlocutor would have agreed with the first part of his declaration, and Paul himself would not have denied that a Jew should be circumcised because of the command laid by God on his people.

As Michel notes (*Brief an die Römer*, 132), the noun *peritomē*, "circumcision," can be understood as designating three things, the act of circumcising, the condition of being circumcised, and community of the circumcised. See Josephus, *Ant.* 20.2.3–4 §34–48.

if you observe the law. Lit., "if you practice the law." Paul insists on the combination of circumcision and observance of the law for one to be a real Jew. Here the Jewish interlocutor might hesitate to agree with Paul, insisting rather on the absolute value of circumcision itself, as did the later rabbinic teaching (Str-B 3.119). But Paul maintains that, because circumcision is "the sign of the covenant," it is a nomistic covenant, and the law has to be observed. Those who are of the "circumcision" must obey the law, for God cannot close his eyes to the transgression and nonobservance of the law. "I testify to everyone who receives circumcision that he is bound to keep the whole law" (Gal 5:3). MS D* and Latin versions read the vb. *phylassēs*, "guard, observe," instead of *prassēs*, "do, practice."

But if you are a transgressor of the law. I.e., if you flout the obligation imposed on you by circumcision itself.

your circumcision has become uncircumcision. I.e., you have become the equivalent of an uncircumcised person; you are no better off than a pagan. Paul's bold declaration, equating a good pagan with a circumcised Jew, would have been an abomination to Pharisaic ears (cf. Gal 5:6). Now he reverses the positions, challenging the Jew about his complacent reliance on circumcision. See also 1 Cor 7:19.

26. *if an uncircumcised man keeps the precepts of the law.* Lit., "if uncircumcision observes the just requirements of the law." Paul uses the abstract noun *akrobystia*, "uncircumcision." Again, Michel (*Brief an die Römer*, 133) observes that this noun can denote three things: the foreskin, the condition of being uncircumcised, and a pagan or pagans. In this case the third sense is intended, and it is not to be understood of Gentile Christians, as Luther, Barth, Godet, or Zahn would have us believe.

Paul reformulates 2:14, now in terms of circumcision. In speaking of "keeping the precepts of the law," Paul makes use of a phrase that occurs often in the OT; see Exod 15:26; Deut 4:4; 6:2; 7:11; 17:19; 1 Kgs 2:3; Ps 119:5; Mic 6:16; Ezek 11:20; 18:9; 20:18.

will not his uncircumcision be reckoned as circumcision? The two words *akrobystia*, "uncircumcision," and *peritomē*, "circumcision," were probably taunt words used, respectively, by Jews and non-Jews to describe their opponents. See Marcus, "The Circumcision," 77–80.

27. *He who by nature is uncircumcised yet keeps the law will condemn you, with your written code and circumcision, as a transgressor of the law.* Lit., "the uncircumcision by nature, (while) fulfilling the law, will judge you as the transgressor with (your) writing and (your) circumcision." Paul speaks of the man who is still in his natural condition, an uncircumcised Gentile, a real Gentile (*TDNT* 9.272). On the phrase *ek physeōs*, see the NOTE on 1:26. Paul uses the prep. *dia* with the gen. to express circumstances (see BDF §223.3). Possession of the written law and circumcision will not spare the Jew, and the uncircumcised pagan who follows his conscience and obeys thereby some of the prescriptions of the law will stand in judgment over the circumcised Jew who violates the law. Thus the uncircumcised pagan will rise at the judgment like the men of Nineveh (Luke 11:32) and condemn the Jew. Paul is not thinking here of Gentile Christians, as Nygren rightly notes (*Romans*, 134, contra Zahn et al.). On the "written code," see 7:6; 1 Cor 3:6.

28. *One is not a Jew outwardly only.* I.e., because circumcision in the flesh is physical and can be detected by other human beings.

nor is real circumcision external, in the flesh. For God deals not with human beings according to outward appearances but "judges the secrets" they cherish in their hearts "through Christ Jesus" (2:16). Cf. Epictetus, *Dissertationes* 2.9.20–21: "Don't you see in what sense each is called a Jew, Syrian, or Egyptian? Whenever we see someone halting between two positions, we usually say, 'He is not a Jew; he is only acting the part.' "

29. *one is a Jew in secret, and real circumcision is of the heart.* Thus Paul expresses the climax of his polemical thesis. He pits against contemporary Jewish religious convictions the principle of the interior motivation of human actions, as he appeals to the OT idea of the circumcision of the heart (Lev 26:41; Deut 10:16; 30:6; Jer 4:4; 9:24–25; Ezek 44:7, 9; cf. 1QpHab 11:13; *Jub.* 1:23; Philo, *De migr. Abr.* 92; *De spec. leg.* 1.6 §305). Paul reminds the Jew who trusts in his

circumcision that the Scriptures themselves emphasize that the important thing is not membership in the chosen people by reason of circumcision, the "sign of the covenant," but rather the circumcision of the heart, the purified motivation of all conduct.

a thing of the spirit, not of the letter. Ta hiera grammata was used by Greek-speaking Jews of their Hebrew Scriptures; it served as the translation of *kitbê haqqōdeš* (e.g., Josephus, *Ant.* 10.10.4 §210; 13.5.8 §167; 20.12.1 §264). Philo, however, uses the sg. *gramma* at times to refer to Scripture or to a single verse of it (*De migr. Abr.* 15 §85; 25 §139; *De congr.* 12 §58). For Paul, the sg. *gramma* refers to the law, especially the Decalogue, and then always in antithesis to *pneuma*, "Spirit" (7:6; 2 Cor 3:6–7). In 2 Cor 3:6 the contrast of the Spirit and the letter is a succinct way of summing up the different realities of the two dispensations, the old and the new. The former was governed by a written code, an extrinsic norm to be observed and esteemed; the latter is vitalized by God's gift of the Spirit, an intrinsic principle reshaping human beings and remolding their conduct. Thus the OT idea of circumcision of the heart takes on a new nuance; it is not just a spiritual circumcision of the human heart, but one that springs from the Spirit of Christ himself. Recall Jer 31:33, "I shall put my law within them; I shall write it on their hearts"; Ezek 36:27, "I shall place my spirit within you and cause you to walk by my statutes."

Such a parallelism has not, however, always been in use. Some patristic interpreters have understood *gramma* to mean the literal sense of Scripture or of the OT, whereas *pneuma* would be its spiritual sense. So Origen, *Contra Celsum* 6.70 (GCS 3.140.16); Athanasius, *Ep. 1 ad Serapionem* 8 (PG 26.549); Gregory of Nyssa, *Contra Eunomium* 3.5, ed. W. Jaeger, *Opera* 2.161; Augustine, *De doctrina christiana* 3.20 (CSEL 80.84). Similarly, some modern commentators deny that Paul, in writing *en pneumati*, is thinking of the holy Spirit; so Lagrange (*Romans*, 57); Prat (*Theology* 2.440).

To be noted is the triple antithesis that Paul introduces: *en tō phanerō*, "outwardly," contrasted with *en tō kryptō*, "in secret"; *en sarki*, "in the flesh," with *kardias*, "of the heart"; and *en grammati*, "of the letter," with *en pneumati*, "of the Spirit." Cf. H. Hübner, "Gramma," *EDNT* 1.258–59.

His praise comes not from human beings, but from God. I.e., the real Jew is an Israelite with a circumcised heart, who will be recognized as such by God and receive praise from him. Such a one cares not for the praise of mortals who might observe his fidelity to the Torah. Paul may be playing on the meaning of the Hebrew name for "Jew," *Yěhûdî*, derived from the patriarchal name Judah (*Yěhûdāh*). In popular etymology it was often explained as the passive of *hôdāh*, "(someone) praised." Thus the person with the circumcised heart is the one "praised" in God's sight, the real Jew. Cf. Gen 29:35; 49:8.

BIBLIOGRAPHY

Burch, V., "Circumcision of the Heart," *ExpTim* 29 (1917–18): 330–31.

Fridrichsen, A., "Der wahre Jude und sein Lob: Rom 2:28f.," *S. Eitrem praesidi suo quinquagesimum natalem celebranti D. D. D. . . . ,* Symbolae Arctoae 1 (Christiana: Erichsen, 1922), 39–49.

Käsemann, E., *Perspectives,* 138–66.

Kamlah, E., "Buchstabe und Geist: Die Bedeutung dieser Antithese für die alttestamentliche Exegese des Apostels Paulus," *EvT* 14 (1954): 276–82.

Lyonnet, S., "La Circoncision du coeur, celle qui relève de l'Esprit et non de la lettre (Rom. 2:29)," *L'Évangile hier et aujourd'hui: Mélanges offerts au Professeur Franz-J. Leenhardt* (Geneva: Labor et Fides, 1968), 87–97; slightly revised, *Études,* 71–88.

McEleney, N. J., "Conversion, Circumcision and the Law," *NTS* 20 (1973–74): 319–41.

Marcus, J., "The Circumcision and the Uncircumcision in Rome," *NTS* 35 (1989): 67–81.

Morreale de Castro, M., "La antítesis paulina entre la letre y el espíritu en la traducción y comentario de Juan Valdés (Rom. 2,29 y 7,6)," *EstBíb* 13 (1954): 167–83.

Schneider, B., "The Meaning of St. Paul's Antithesis 'The Letter and the Spirit,' " *CBQ* 15 (1953): 163–207.

Schrenk, G., "Der Segenswunsch nach der Kampfepistel," *Judaica* 6 (1950): 170–90.

Schweizer, E., " 'Der Jude im Verborgenen . . . , dessen Lob nicht von Menschen, sondern von Gott kommt': Zu Röm 2:28f. und Mt 6:1–18," *Neues Testament und Kirche: Für Rudolf Schnackenburg,* ed. J. Gnilka (Freiburg im Breisgau: Herder, 1974), 115–24.

10. OBJECTIONS TO THIS THESIS ABOUT THE JEWS (3:1–9)

3 [1]"Then what is the advantage of being a Jew, or what is the value of circumcision?" [2]Much in every way! First of all, Jews were entrusted with the oracles of God. [3]"What then? Suppose some Jews were unfaithful? Will their infidelity nullify the fidelity of God?" [4]Certainly not! God will be true, though every human being a liar, as it stands written, *that you may be vindicated in your speech, and win out when you are being judged.*

[5]If our wickedness brings forth the uprightness of God, what are we to say? Is God unjust to bring wrath upon us (I am speaking, of course, in human terms)? [6]Certainly not! Otherwise how is God to judge the world? [7]Again, if through my untruthfulness the truthfulness of God has overflowed to his glory, then why must I still be condemned as a sinner? [8]And why should we not "do evil that good may come of it"—as some people defame us with the libelous charge that we so teach? (The condemnation of such people is not unjust.) [9]What, then, is the situation? Are we (Jews) at a disadvantage? Not at all! For we have already charged that all, Jews and Greeks alike, are under the power of sin.

COMMENT

Paul returns to his diatribe and indulges further in his dialogic discussion with the imaginary Jewish interlocutor (see Introduction, section VII). The passage abounds in rhetorical questions (see BDF §496.1). His preceding exposé might imply that Jews really have no advantage over pagans, despite his willingness to accord them a certain priority or precedence (1:16; 2:9–10). Now he presses his point and argues: despite the divine oracles concerning salvation recorded in their sacred books, despite the "sign of the covenant" that God has set up in circumcision, the wrath of God will burst upon Jews too. And yet, there is room for the Jews in God's new mode of salvation; for them, all is not lost, and they still have an advantage.

The advantage that the Jew has does not rest on what he is or has, but on what God has promised him and what God has done for him. God chose Israel to be his own people and made promises to it that will not be revoked (11:28); through the covenant God established a favored status with the forefathers of the Jews, and that status still stands—a unique place in the history of salvation. Although Paul insists that Jew and pagan alike stand under God's wrath, he does not want to deny the differences between them. In the light of God's promises to Israel, circumcision is seen in a new way. It is now clearly seen that the "sign of the covenant" is likewise the mark of God's promises to Israel. And hence the unfaithfulness of Israel to its part in the covenant in no way undermines the faithfulness of God to his covenant or promises.

These verses (3:1–9) form an integral development in Paul's argument. They are not a digression or something that can be omitted, *pace* Black (*Romans*, 62), Dodd (*Romans*, 46), and Käsemann (*Commentary*, 78). Nor do they lack unity or coherence, as Bornkamm rightly notes ("Theologie"). Despite the contention of Hall, they present a dialogic argument in which Paul pits his teaching about Christian faith against the Torah fidelity of a contemporary Jew. Paul dominates the discussion and, like an ancient teacher using diatribe, guides the discussion with his Jewish interlocutor. Verse 3 poses the leading question that dominates the whole discussion. Verses 1–4 set forth the Jew's advantage in God's fidelity to his covenant, his promises, and his oracles; vv 5–8 handle the objection of antinomianism; and v 9 enables Paul to reformulate his basic thesis in this whole section (in the negative development of his theme): all human beings, both Jews and Greeks, are under the power of sin. Throughout the nine verses the first person plural is to be understood of Paul and the imaginary Jew with whom he is in dialogue; see Stowers, "Paul's Dialogue." What Paul discusses in these verses is in reality a preparation for what he will take up in chaps. 9–11, as Räisänen has rightly noted ("Zum Verständnis"). But these verses are only a part of chapter 3 in the letter, and though in a sense they are introductory to it, the whole discussion of Paul in this chapter is a key to the thought and structure of the rest of Romans, as Campbell has well pointed out ("Romans iii").

Many commentators take the unit to be 3:1–8 and then join v 9 to what follows in 3:10–20. They fail to note, however, the inclusio involved in the use of *tí oun* in vv 1 and 9. Even though Wilckens (*Römer*, 1.172) recognizes this echo in v 9, he still relates v 9 to what follows.

NOTES

3:1. *Then what is the advantage of being a Jew?* I.e., if possession of the law and circumcision mean nothing, what advantage does a member of the chosen people really have over a pagan in regard to salvation? Paul uses the collective singular *tou Ioudaiou*, "the Jew as Jew" (cf. BDF §139).

or what is the value of circumcision? I.e., does "the sign of the covenant" really mean anything in the call of people to Jewish existence?

2. *Much in every way!* Paul immediately concedes that the Jew does have an advantage over the pagan in the matter of salvation.

First of all. Paul recognizes the chosen status of Israel and the promises that have been made to it. But having said *prōton men*, he should have continued with something like *deuteron de*, "and second," etc. Yet he gets distracted and does not continue after having mentioned what this first advantage really is. He will return to the subject in 9:4–5, where he recites the seven prerogatives of Israel in salvation history.

MSS 6 and 1739, as well as Eusebius, read instead *prōtoi gar episteuthēsan*, "for they first were entrusted" (see BDF §447.4). This is a copyist's correction of the problem created by *prōton men*.

Jews were entrusted with the oracles of God. For the diverse senses of *logion* in classical Greek writers, see J. W. Doeve, "Some Notes." The phrase *ta logia tou theou* is not to be limited to the messianic promises, as Sanday and Headlam (*Romans*, 70), Godet, and Cornely, following Ambrosiaster (*Ad Romanos* 3:2 [CSEL 81.94]), have understood it, or to the Mosaic law, as John Chrysostom (*In ep. ad Romanos* 6.4 [PG 60.457]) interpreted it, or to the promises made to the patriarchs, as Lietzmann (*An die Römer*, 45) has taken it. Rather, it is to be taken in the broad sense of the whole of the OT in which the revelation of God's will is set forth, as Lagrange (*Romains*, 60) prefers, and as Philo (*De praem. et poen.* 1 §1; *De vita cont.* 3 §25) and Josephus (*J.W.* 6.5.4 §§311–13) use it. In the LXX the phrase *ta logia tou theou* (Num 24:4, 16; Ps 106:11) denotes the utterances of God made to prophets, which were to be communicated to his people. These included not only revelations and promises, but also rules of conduct by which Israel was expected to live. Yet as elsewhere in the NT (Heb 5:12; 1 Pet 4:11), the phrase refers to the OT in general as God's word about salvation.

Such utterances of God included the blessings promised to the children of Abraham, but were not limited to them. Yet the possession of such oracles constitutes a clear advantage that the Jew has. See Deut 4:7–8, where Moses asks, "What great nation is there that has a god so near to it as the Lord our God is to us, whenever we call upon him? And what great nation is there that has statutes and ordinances so righteous as all this law which I set before you this day!" (Cf. Pss 147:19–20; 103:7. Yet such OT teaching also included a threat of God's punishment despite such privilege: "You alone have I known of all the families of the earth; therefore I will chastise you for all your iniquities" (Amos 3:2).

Noteworthy is the play on the words involving *pistis*: thus *episteuthēsan*, *ēpistēsan, apistia, pistin.*

3. *What then?* Paul expostulates with *tí gar* (see BDF §299.3).

suppose some Jews were unfaithful. Paul uses the vb. *apistein*, which can mean either "refuse to believe" or "be unfaithful" (BAGD, 85). Either or both senses can be intended here, for numerous OT examples could be cited of Israel's historic incredulity (Exod 15:22–16:36 [the reaction of the Hebrews when Moses led them across the Reed Sea to Marah]; Numbers 14 [the murmuring of the Hebrews against Moses and Aaron in the desert]), or of its infidelity (1 Kgs 18:21 [Elijah and the influence of the prophets of Baal at Mount Carmel]; Hos 4:1–2 [Israel's idolatrous adultery]). But only "some" have been unfaithful. Paul does not restrict it in any way temporally. He may be thinking of the "remnant" (9:27; 11:5) that did accept Christ and become the Jewish Christians, so he characterizes the "unbelief" of the rest as a refusal to accept Jesus as the Messiah. Note that he does not say *ēpistēsan tines tō Christō*; nor does he say *ēpistēsan tines tō theō*. Leaving it thus vague, he could intend it either way. He does not excuse the "some" or make light of their failure, but he admits their limited number in order to stress God's preponderant bounty toward them. The "some" will become "all" in v 9. See further Cosgrove, "What If."

Will their infidelity nullify God's fidelity? I.e., will it render God's fidelity ineffective? Even though Israel proved faithless to the God who spoke to it and showed it his favor, his fidelity to it is not undone. As depositaries of the divine oracles, the Jews possessed his protestations of fidelity to the people of his covenant (Exod 34:6–7; Num 23:19; Deut 7:9; Isa 49:7; Hos 2:19–23). Did his fidelity to such promises not depend on Israel's fidelity to him? Cf. 2 Tim 2:13; *Ps. Sol.* 8:28. On *pistis theou*, "God's fidelity," see 1 Sam 21:3 (LXX, not MT); Ps 33:4; *Ps. Sol.* 8:28; cf. Introduction, section IX.A. In this and the coming verses Paul uses different attributes of God, his "fidelity," his "uprightness," his "truth" or "truthfulness." In a sense, one could call them "virtual equivalents" (Williams), because they are attributes of the one and same God, but they have different nuances and different OT backgrounds; they are for that reason better kept distinct.

4. *Certainly not!* God's fidelity is not measured by human fidelity—this idea is basic in Paul's teaching on uprightness. God is always upright and will justify Israel (3:26). The suggestion of God's infidelity is rejected by the indignant negative *mē genoito* (really a negative oath, "Let it not be so!" [BDF §384]). In the LXX (e.g., Gen 44:7, 17) this negative translates Hebrew *ḥălîlāh lî,* "far be it from me!" where it is usually the introduction to a larger statement. Only in

Epictetus (e.g., *Dissertationes* 1.1.13; 1.2.35; 1.5.10; 1.8.15) and in Paul (also 3:6, 31; 6:2, 15; 7:7, 13; 9:14; 11:1, 11.; cf. 1 Cor 6:15; Gal 2:17; 3:21; 6:14) is it used as a negative in a dialogue without being part of a larger sentence. See A. J. Malherbe, "*Mē genoito* in the Diatribe and Paul," *HTR* 73 (1980): 231–40.

God will be true, though every human being be a liar. Lit., "let God become true, but every human being a liar." In using *alēthēs*, Paul plays on its two meanings: "true, honest"; and "faithful, loyal." Although the second meaning is clearly intended in the context (God's fidelity to his promises and oracles), the first cannot be excluded, because of the allusion to Ps 116:11 (LXX 115:2), *pas anthrōpos pseustēs*, "Every human being is a liar." For Paul, though every human being would appear before God as a liar, God's truthfulness and fidelity would shine forth.

The words *alēthēs* or *alētheia* are often used in the LXX to express God's covenantal fidelity (e.g., Ps 89:2, 6, 9, 15, 25, 34). It is the infidelity of humanity that brings out the fidelity of God. Because of human unfaithfulness the divine faithfulness is glorified. Compare the sentiments expressed in the concluding hymn of 1QS 11:9–14: "As for me, I belong to wicked humanity, to the assembly of perverse flesh. . . . If I stumble, God's mercies are always my salvation; and if I stagger because of a sin of the flesh, my judgment stands in the uprightness of God, which exists forever. . . . By his mercy will he bring me near, and with his favor will my judgment come; by the uprightness of his fidelity has he judged me."

as it stands written. See the NOTE on 1:17.

that you may be vindicated in your speech, and win out when you are being judged. Paul quotes the "Miserere," Ps 51:6, but not according to the MT ("that you may be justified in your words, and win out when you are judged"). In the MT the psalmist admits that even when the divine sentence falls on David for his sin with Bathsheba, people will know that God is upright and that divine uprightness has been manifested. But in the LXX, the connotation of "sentence" is lost, and "in your words" refers to "oracles" (as in 3:2), so that even in his infidelity David learns of God's fidelity, "I will not be false to David" (Ps 89:36). Paul cites the psalmist to bear out his contention that Yahweh is ever shown to be faithful to what he has promised, to his utterances. Though human sin is a rebellion against God's will, it serves to magnify divine fidelity and uprightness.

Although Paul cites Ps 51:6 according to the LXX, he changes the mood and tense in the second clause. The first clause has the aor. subjunct. *dikaiōthēs*, as does the second in the LXX; but Paul uses the fut. indic. *nikēseis*. See BDF §369.3. MSS B, G, L, Ψ, 365, 1175, 1739, and 1881, however, read the subjunctive *nikēsēs*; but that is a secondary harmonization of the Pauline text with the LXX reading. Jeremias ("Chiasmus," 154–55) sees a chiastic arrangement in vv 4–8. In v 4 Paul quotes Ps 116:11 and 51:6; v 5 resumes Ps 51:6, and vv 7–8a resume Ps 116:11.

5. *If our wickedness brings forth the uprightness of God.* The diatribe moves

to a logical conclusion that could be drawn from Paul's contention. If David's infidelity did not nullify God's fidelity but rather made it manifest, then human wickedness brings about the manifestation of God's uprightness (again the divine attribute, as the majority of commentators agree for this passage; see the NOTE on 1:17 and Introduction, section IX.A; cf. Schlatter, *Gottes Gerechtigkeit*; Lyonnet, "De 'iustitita Dei' "; Kertelge, "*Rechtfertigung*," 63–70). *Pace* J. Piper ("The Righteousness of God," 15), the divine attribute that Paul speaks of does not "embrace both his [God's] gracious faithfulness to his promises and his punitive judgment upon sin." To admit that would be to upset all the gains of recent decades in the interpretation of Romans. There is no difficulty with the idea of God's fidelity in such a statement; in fact, it shows how closely God's uprightness is related to his fidelity in this passage.

Paul realizes at this point in his argument that a false conclusion could be drawn from what he has said in vv 3–4; so in vv 5–8 he seeks to guard against such a misunderstanding. In doing so, he introduces some of his own experience.

what are we to say? I.e., what can our contention be? Paul often uses the same rhetorical question (see the NOTE on 6:1).

Is God unjust to bring wrath upon us? If human sin magnifies God's uprightness, is it not unjust for God to visit his wrath on human beings? Yet Paul insists that there is no contradiction in the manifestation of divine uprightness and divine wrath. Underlying the objection is the suggestion that, if human wickedness brings forth God's acquitting judgment and fidelity, then God would not be right in inflicting wrath. Because he does not agree with the suggestion, Paul adds the following qualification.

(I am speaking, of course, in human terms.) See 6:19; 1 Cor 9:8; 15:32; Gal 3:15 for similar parenthetic statements (cf. BDF §465.2). Paul seeks by this one to protect himself from seeming to be blasphemous in speaking of infidelity in God. Paul will reject this suggestion because it attributes to God an all-too-human way of phrasing things. See Bjerkelund, " 'Nach menschlicher Weise.' "

6. *Certainly not!* See the NOTE on 3:4. Paul again emphatically rejects the idea of cheap grace for Israel or that God is guilty of injustice. After all, he is the judge of the world.

Otherwise how is God to judge the world? God is the judge of the world and he will scrutinize it, handing down verdicts on human sin and manifesting his wrath against human unrighteousness. Paul echoes a fundamental Jewish belief that regarded Yahweh as the eschatological judge of the world (Isa 66:16; Joel 3:12; Pss 94:2; 96:13). Paul uses the fut. indic. *krineî* as a substitute for a potential optative (see BDF §385.3). Again, the noun *kosmos* here stands for "all human beings."

7. *but if through my untruthfulness the truthfulness of God has overflowed to his glory.* This is really the same objection as that in 3:5, involving merely a third attribute of God. Ought not a human being sin more that God's glory may be the greater? The particle *de* is read in MSS ℵ, A, 81, 365, 1506, etc., and is

preferable to *gar* of MSS B, D, G, Ψ, and the *Koinē* text-tradition because a contrast with v 5 is needed.

then why must I still be condemned as a sinner? I.e., my sin has called forth the truthfulness of God; so why am I still under condemnation or criticism? See 6:1–2.

8. *why should we not "do evil that good may come of it"?* Paul recognizes the sophism for what it is worth, but he does not take pains to refute it, even though it is leveled at him (or at Christians in general). Because he does not refute it, it was often misunderstood later on. Augustine lists it along with 3:28 and 5:20 among the "subobscure opinions of the Apostle not understood even in apostolic times" and considered that the "other apostolic letters of Peter, John, James, and Jude had been especially composed to show definitely that faith without deeds was of no avail, as even Paul himself described, not any nondescript faith, but that as salvific and clearly evangelical faith, the deeds of which proceed from love (Gal 5:6)" (*De fide et operibus* 13.21 [CSEL 41.61–62]).

as some people defame us with the libelous charge that we so teach. In a parenthetic aside Paul simply rejects the allegation (see Cranfield, *Romans*, 185–87).

(The condemnation of such people is not unjust.) Lit., "whose condemnation is just." I.e., their libelous charges merit a condemnation that counters the one in which such people indulge. Here Paul employs *krima*, "judgment," in the negative sense of *katakrima*, "condemnation," as in 2:2–3. See further Fitch, "Note."

9. *What, then, is the situation?* Paul makes use of the elliptical *ti oun*, lit., "what then?" It echoes the phrase in 3:1.

Are we (Jews) at a disadvantage? Not at all! Three problems are encountered in v 9a. One is textual: the preferred reading in critical editions of the NT is *ti oun; proechometha; ou pantōs*, i.e., two questions and an answer, as in MSS ℵ, B, 0219 and the *Koinē* text-tradition). But MSS A and L read the subjunct. *proechōmetha* (as a deliberative question), whereas MSS D, G, Ψ, 104, and some patristic writers have *prokatechomen; perisson*, "Do we have a prior advantage? Abundantly." The last reading was substituted because of the ambiguity in *proechometha*. The second problem is in the punctuation. Should a question mark follow *ti oun* (marking off diatribic expostulation) or not (thus making *ti* the object of the verb, "What advantage then do we have?")? Finally, the voice of the vb. *proechometha* is unclear.

I follow the preferred reading translated in the lemma, and also take *ti oun* to be the expostulation. In the active, *proechein* means "jut out, excel, have an advantage" (see Josephus, *Ant.* 7.10.2 §237). But *proechometha* is a middle-passive form, and many commentators have tried to take it as a middle with active force (so Barrett, Cranfield, Käsemann, Lagrange, Maurer [*TDNT* 6.692–93]; F. Synge, *ExpTim* 81 [1969–70]: 351): "Have we (Jews) any advantage? Not at all!" Although, in general, such a use of the middle voice is possible (see BDF §316.1), no instance of this use is attested for *proechein*. With a minority of commentators (Goodspeed, Lightfoot, Sanday and Headlam, and Stowers), the passive meaning of *proechometha* is to be preferred: "Are we (Jews) excelled (by others)? Not at all!" Such a meaning is not inappropriate after the argument in vv 1–8; in fact, it supplies the climactic question to Paul's dialogue with the Jewish interlocutor, enabling him to assert what he writes in v 9b.

For we have already charged that all, Jews and Greeks alike, are under the power of sin. Lit., "under sin." This is Paul's conclusion and fundamental thesis about the human condition, when humanity is deprived of the challenge that the gospel brings (3:23; 5:12). Thus both Greeks and Jews are indicted. On the name *Ioudaios*, see the NOTE on 2:17; on the name *Hellēn*, see the NOTE on 1:14. The conclusion that Paul draws here, however, has been called "internally inconsistent" and resting "on gross exaggeration" (Sanders, *Paul, the Law*, 125), because it seems to say that all Torah-faithful Jews, especially those who did not accept Jesus as the Messiah, were rebels against God. And if so, how reconcile it with what Paul writes in 2:13?

The noun "sin" is now mentioned for the first time in Romans. Paul personifies it as a master who dominates a slave; it holds humans in bondage to it. See further Introduction, section IX. D.

BIBLIOGRAPHY

Achtemeier, P. J., "Romans 3:1–8: Structure and Argument," *Christ and His Communities: Essays in Honor of Reginald H. Fuller*, ATRSup 11, ed. A. J. Hultgren and B. Hall (Cincinnati, Oh.: Forward Movement Publications, 1990), 77–87.

Bjerkelund, C. J., " 'Nach menschlicher Weise rede ich': Funktion und Sinn des paulinischen Ausdrucks," *ST* 26 (1972): 63–100.

Boers, H., "The Problem of Jews and Gentiles in the Macro-Structure of Romans," *Neotestamentica* 15 (1981): 1–11; *SEA* 47 (1982): 184–96.

Bornkamm, G., "Theologie als Teufelskunst: Römer 3,1–9," *Geschichte und Glaube II: Gesammelte Aufsätze*, vol. 4, BEvT 53 (Munich: Kaiser, 1971), 140–48.

Botschuyver, H. J., "Iets over Rm. 3:7," *NThStud* (Groningen) 2 (1919): 208–9.

———, "Proeve eener vertaling van Rom. 3:4–8," *GTT* 27 (1926–27): 316–27.

Campbell, W. S., "Romans iii as a Key to the Structure and Thought of the Letter," *NovT* 23 (1981): 22–40; repr. *Paul's Gospel in an Intercultural Context*, 25–42.

Canales, I. J., "Paul's Accusers in Romans 3:8 and 6:1," *EvQ* 57 (1985): 237–45.

Cosgrove, C. H., "What If Some Have Not Believed? The Occasion and Thrust of Romans 3:1–8," *ZNW* 78 (1987): 90–105.

Doeve, J. W., "Some Notes with Reference to *ta logia tou theou* in Romans III 2," *Studia paulina in honorem Johannis de Zwaan septuagenarii* (Haarlem: Bohn, 1953), 111–23.

Drejergaard, K., "Jødernes fortrin: En undersøgelse af Rom 3,1–9," *DTT* 36 (1973): 81–101.

Fahlgren, K. H., *Ṣedāḳā*, nahestehende und entgegengesetzte Begriffe im Alten Testament (Uppsala: Almqvist & Wiksell, 1932).

Fitch, W. O., "Note on Romans iii 8*ᵇ*: *hōn to krima endikon esti*," *ExpTim* 59 (1947–48): 26.

Fridrichsen, A., "Exegetisches zu den Paulusbriefen," *TSK* 102 (1930): 291–301, esp. 291–94.

———, "Nochmals Römer 3,7–8," *ZNW* 34 (1935): 306–8.

Griffiths, J. G., "Romans iii. 3," *ExpTim* 53 (1941–42): 118.

Hall, D. R., "Romans 3. 1–8 Reconsidered," *NTS* 29 (1983): 183–97.

Jeremias, J., "Chiasmus in den Paulusbriefen," *ZNW* 49 (1958): 145–56, esp. 154–55.

———, "Zur Gedankenführung in den paulinischen Briefen," *Studia paulina* (see above under Doeve), 146–53, esp. 146–49.

Johnson, S. L., Jr., "Studies in Romans, Part VI: Rite Versus Righteousness; Part VII: The Jews and the Oracles of God; Part VIII: Divine Faithfulness, Divine Judgment, and the Problem of Antinomianism," *BSac* 130 (1973): 151–63, 235–49, 329–37.

Kruijf, T. C. de, "Is Anybody Any Better Off? (Rom 3:9a)," *Bijdragen* 46 (1985): 234–44.

Ljungvik, H., "Zum Römerbrief 3,7–8," *ZNW* 32 (1933): 207–10.

Löfstedt, B., "Notes on St Paul's Letter to the Romans," *FilNeot* 1 (1988): 209–10.

Lyonnet, S., "De 'iustitia Dei' in Epistola ad Romanos 10,3 et 3,5," *VD* 25 (1947): 118–21.

———, "La Notion de justice de Dieu en Rom., III,5 et l'exégèse paulinienne du 'Miserere,'" *SacPag* 2.342–45.

Morison, J., *A Critical Exposition of the Third Chapter of Paul's Epistle to the Romans: A Monograph* (London: Hamilton, Adams, 1866).

Olivieri, O., "Quid ergo amplius Iudaeo est? etc. (Rom. 3, 1–8)," *Bib* 10 (1929): 31–52.

Penna, R., "La funzione strutturale di 3,1–8 nella lettera ai Romani," *Bib* 69 (1988): 507–42.

Piper, J., "The Righteousness of God in Romans 3,1–8," *TZ* 36 (1980): 3–16.

Räisänen, H., "Zum Verständnis von Röm 3,1–8," *SNTU* 10 (1985): 93–108.

Stowers, S. K., "Paul's Dialogue with a Fellow Jew in Romans 3:1–9," *CBQ* 46 (1984): 707–22.

Synge, F. C., "The Meaning of *proechometha* in Romans 3:9," *ExpTim* 81 (1969–70): 351.

Torrance, T. F., "One Aspect of the Biblical Conception of Faith," *ExpTim* 68 (1956–57): 111–14.

11. ALL HUMAN BEINGS, JEWS AND GREEKS ALIKE, ARE SINNERS (3:10–20)

3   ¹⁰As it stands written,

> *No one is upright, no, not one;*
> 11   *no one has understanding;*
> *no one searches for God.*
> 12   *All have turned away, all have become depraved.*
> *No one does good, not even one.*
> 13   *Their throats are open graves;*
> *with their tongues they have practiced deceit;*
> *the poison of asps lies behind their lips.*
> 14   *Their mouths are full of cursing and bitterness.*
> 15   *Swift are their feet to shed blood.*
> 16   *Ruin and wretchedness strew their paths.*
> 17   *The path of peace they have not known.*
> 18   *Fear of God is not before their eyes.*

¹⁹Now we know that all that the law says is addressed to those who are under the law so that every mouth may be silenced and the whole world become accountable to God, ²⁰since *no human being will be justified before* him through deeds prescribed by the law; for through the law comes the real knowledge of sin.

COMMENT

To prove his point that all human beings, Jews and Greeks alike, are enslaved to sin (*hyph' hamartian*, 3:9b), Paul quotes the testimony of Scripture, the testimony of "the oracles of God" (3:2) entrusted to Israel. The catena of ten OT passages that are strung together declares the utter sinfulness of all human beings. The Jewish interlocutor might object that such passages refer to pagans; but Paul silences such an objection at the end by saying "we know that all that the law says is addressed to those who are under the law so that every mouth may be silenced." Thus the Scriptures themselves convict Jews and Greeks of sin. Both are sinners, and the law will not prove to be a shield for the Jews. All human beings must recognize that they stand under the wrath of God as sinners and evildoers.

Paul makes use of a Palestinian Jewish literary form at this point, adopting the subform called *testimonia* (see Instruction, section VII). The OT texts strung together are drawn from the Psalms, Proverbs, Isaiah, and Qoheleth. Although none of them is drawn from the Pentateuch, Paul uses this *testimonia* list to illustrate what "the law says" (3:19). The thesis thus formulated in it—no one is righteous; all human beings sin and do evil—can be compared with 2 Esdr 7:22–

24, even though that passage is itself not a catena of OT texts. See also CD 5:13–17; *As. Mos.* 5:2–6.

It is a matter of debate whether Paul composed this list of *testimonia* himself or adopted an already existing list to prove his point. Dibelius thought that Paul adopted a preexisting list (*TRu* 3 [1931]: 228); similarly Keck, "Function"; van der Minde, *Schrift*, 57. It is hardly a composition of Paul put together ad hoc during his dictation of the letter; it seems rather to be a preexistent list, perhaps derived from some liturgical setting (as the parallel in Justin Martyr, *Dialogue with Trypho* 27.3 would suggest). At any rate, it is a device that amply illustrates Paul's indictment of all humanity. The *testimonia* list acts as a declaration of God's verdict on the world of humanity, and Paul's use of this piece of tradition reveals that it is really the starting point for his reflection on the status of humanity without the gospel, as Keck has shown ("Function"). It is not just an appendage to his argument, but reveals that what he has written in 1:18–3:9 comes to a climax here.

The texts cited are not always quoted exactly from the OT, according to either the MT or the LXX. Is the *testimonia* list structured or not? Some claim that there is a strophic structure: vv 10–12 (2 × 3 lines), vv 13–14 (2 × 2 lines), and vv 15–18 (2 × 2 lines); see Cranfield (*Romans*, 191), who follows Michel (*Brief an die Römer*, 142). That structure, however, is unclear and perhaps debatable, but there is at least a sixfold repetition of *ouk estin*, "there is none." To be noted, however, is the catchword bonding that strings together the different verses; mention is found in them of parts of the body: throat, tongue, lips, mouth, feet (on path), and eyes. The connotation of such elements is that all parts of a human being are involved in sin in God's sight and that the whole human being has participated in evil (Feuillet, "Le Plan salvifique," 350), but Keck ("Function," 155 n. 24) does not think that this detail is "really helpful" in the interpretation of the passage. In citing such texts, Paul uses the Jews' own oracles to demonstrate that they as well as the Gentiles are "under sin."

This paragraph brings to an end the negative development of the thesis that Paul put forth in 1:16–17. The indictment that he levels against all human beings stems from their condition of being without God's gospel about the role of Christ Jesus in human history. Left to their own devices, all human beings can do nothing but become sinners; and so they are in God's sight.

NOTES

3:10. *As it stands written.* See the NOTE on 1:17.

No one is upright, no, not one. The first quotation enunciates Paul's thesis. The list quotes Qoh 7:20, but not exactly. The LXX of Qoh 7:20 reads, *hoti anthrōpos ouk estin dikaios en tē gē,* "since there is no upright human being on earth," which is an exact translation of the Hebrew MT. The addition of *oude heis,* "not even one," enhances the statement of Qoheleth; here the second negative does not cancel out the first, but emphasizes the first part (see BDF §302.2; 432.2). Some commentators, however, think that Paul is quoting Ps 14:3 or even Ps 53:4, but, as Dunn notes (*Romans*, 150), the wording is closer to Qoh 7:20. In admitting as much, however, Dunn strangely says (*Romans*, 149), "As can readily be seen, the LXX is followed in every case." But is it? Note the repeated use of the same idea by the Qumran psalmist; 1QH 9:14 ("No one is righteous in your judgment, and no one innocent in a suit before you"); 4:29–31; 7:17, 28–29; 12:31–32; 13:16–17; 16:11.

11. *no one has understanding; no one searches for God.* The second quotation comes from Ps 14:2 (cf. Ps 53:3). The LXX of Ps 14:3 reads *tou idein ei estin syniōn ē ekzētōn ton theon*, "to see whether there is someone who understands or searches for God," which is a literal translation of the Hebrew MT. The substantivized ptc. is used with the def. art. *ho syniōn, ho ekzētōn* (see BDF §413.1). In Paul's context these words mean that the unrighteousness of human beings in compounded by their folly, their lack of understanding, and their failure to seek out God, their Maker. Such a sentiment of the *testimonia* list echoes 1:21, about the failure of the pagan to honor and thank God; cf. 2 Esdr 7:23, "They even declared that the Most High does not exist." Not only pagan idolatry, but also Jewish self-righteousness are thus indicted.

12. *All have turned away, all have become depraved.* Ps 14:3 is the source of these words, which are a literal quotation of the LXX, *pantes exeklinan, hama ēchreōthēsan*, again an exact translation of the Hebrew MT. Human beings have not only failed to seek God, but in their folly they have all deliberately turned away from him and from the paths he would have them walk. Hence their depravity, which again echoes 1:21b–23.

No one does good, not even one. This is a further citation from Ps 14:3, which in the LXX reads, *ouk estin poiōn chrēstotēta, ouk estin heōs henos*, "there is no one doing good, not even one." The depravity of human beings is compounded by their failure to pursue what is good in human life. MSS B, 6, and 1739 omit the *ouk estin* in the second part of the quotation, differing from the LXX; MSS ℵ, A, D, G, Ψ, and the *Koinē* text-tradition read it.

13. *Their throats are opened graves; with their tongues they have practiced deceit.* The list goes on to cite Ps 5:10, quoted exactly according to the LXX, which is a literal translation of the Hebrew of the MT. In the original the psalmist describes himself as one led by God's demand for uprightness and distinguishes himself from the "workers of lawlessness." For Paul, filthlike contamination and crass deceit pour forth in all that human beings utter. Such a sentiment again echoes 1:29, "filled with every sort of wickedness, evil, greed, and malice."

the poison of asps lies behind their lips. Vicious and deadly utterings come from the lips of human beings. The list cites Ps 140:4, reproducing accurately the reading of the LXX, which is a literal translation of the Hebrew of the MT. In v 13 the move has been from throats to tongues to lips, and it will continue with mouths, feet, and eyes.

14. *Their mouths are full of cursing and bitterness.* Ps 10:7 (= LXX 9:28) is quoted, but not exactly; the LXX reads, *hou aras to stoma autou gemei kai pikrias kai dolou*, "whose mouth is full of cursing, bitterness, and deceit." This reading represents an expansion of the Hebrew original, *pîhû mālē ûmirmôt wātōk*, "and his mouth is full of both deceits and oppression." In other words, human beings emit such violence in their speech, as they scoff at God.

15. *Swift are their feet to shed blood.* Violence proceeds from all human beings, not only in speech, but also in other deeds. Murder and violence again echo 1:29. The list cites Isa 59:7 or Prov 1:16, but the citation does not agree exactly with either OT passage. The LXX of Isa 59:7 reads *hoi de podes autōn epi ponērian trechousin tachinoi ekcheai haima*, "their feet run after evil, swift to shed blood." The LXX of Prov 1:16 reads, *hoi gar podes autōn eis kakian trechousin, kai tachinoi tou ekcheai haima*, "for their feet run after wickedness, and they are swift to shed blood." The LXX version of each passage corresponds to the Hebrew of the MT. In the original the prophet lamented Israel's sins and lack of uprightness. Now for Paul, Isaiah's words are applied to all human beings.

16. *Ruin and wretchedness strew their paths.* Wherever their feet lead them, human beings leave behind destruction and desolation. Isa 59:7b is quoted according to the LXX, which accurately translates the Hebrew of the MT.

17. *The path of peace they have not known.* The list continues with a quotation of Isa 59:8, which in the LXX reads, *kai hodon eirēnēs ouk oidasin*, "the path of peace they do not know," which is an exact translation of the Hebrew original. Paul's text reads *ouk egnōsan*, "they have not known," instead of *ouk oidasin*, "they do not know," a minor change. Such human beings have not known a full and bounteous life, a life characterized by the fullness of blessings from God.

18. *Fear of God is not before their eyes.* Such human beings are not motivated by due reverence for God, the beginning of all wisdom. Ps 36:2b is quoted exactly according to the LXX, which accurately reflects the Hebrew of the MT. In the original, the psalmist is contrasting the lawbreaker and the upright Jew, who stands in awe of God. See Gen 22:12; Deut 6:2; Prov 1:7. Cf. W. F. Beck, "*Phobos*, Rom. 3:18," *CTM* 22 (1951): 511–12.

19. *Now we know that all that the law says is addressed to those who are under the law.* I.e., Jews, who might think that they are exempt from Paul's indictment, actually fall under it as well, because what the law says is applied especially to them. Paul insists that the Jew is mistaken if he thinks that, in trusting in the law, he is exempt from the wrath of God. He uses *nomos* specifically of the Mosaic law, but also generically to refer to the whole OT (cf. 1 Cor 14:21). He has applied the OT quotations in the *testimonia* list to such human beings to whom, first of all, the law applies (2:12), and then to all humanity, because all have been sinners (3:23).

so that every mouth may be silenced. I.e., so that there can be no boasting or vaunting one's innocence or rectitude before others or before God himself. "For

Scripture has consigned all things to sin" (Gal 3:22). Cf. Pss 63:12; 107:42; Job 5:16; 1 Macc 9:55, for the OT motif of "stopping the mouth." The conj. *hina* has the sense of result (see BDF §391.5).

and the whole world become accountable to God. Lit., "may be liable to judgment by God." The activity of the whole *kosmos* is thus held subject to God's judgment. The noun *kosmos* is used in the sense of all mankind, both pagan and Jew alike. In v 19b Paul makes use of a chiasm, a-b-b'-a': *pan stoma*, "every mouth," *phragē*, "be silenced," *hypodikos genētai*, "become accountable," *pas ho kosmos*, "the whole world." The universality of moral failure stemming from gospelless humanity is also emphasized by the threefold use of *pas*, "all, every," in vv 19–20.

20. *Since no human being will be justified before him.* Lit., "since all flesh will not be justified before him." Thus Paul sums up the argument that he began in 1:18. The mention of "justified," however, serves as a transition to the main positive explanation of the theme announced in 1:16–17. Paul now alludes to Ps 143:2, which in the LXX reads, *ou dikaiōthēsetai enōpion sou pas zōn*, "no living being will be justified before you," which almost exactly reproduces the Hebrew of the MT. Paul echoes the psalmist's confession of his unrighteous status before God. The psalm is one of personal lament, in which the psalmist admits his sinfulness and God's transcendent righteousness; he confesses his inability to vindicate himself and appeals for vindication (143:1) through God's "fidelity" (*alētheia*, Hebrew *'ĕmûnāh*) and "uprightness" (*dikaiosynē*, Hebrew *ṣedeq*). These themes become crucial in the development of the argument that Paul is now about to begin, as Hays notes ("Psalm 143"). The fut. *ou dikaiōthēsetai* is to be understood as gnomic (BDF §349.1).

That no human being is upright before God is also an Essene tenet in QL (1QS 11:9–12 [see the NOTE on 3:4]; 1QH 4:29–31 ["I know that uprightness belongs to no human being, or rectitude to any son of man"]; 7:16; 12:19; 13:16–17). Cf. Gen 6:12.

through deeds prescribed by the law. Lit., "through deeds of the law." See the NOTE on 2:15. Paul makes a bold addition to the psalmist's words, accommodating the psalmist's cry for justification to a specific problem: the attainment of uprightness through observance of the law. Cf. Gal 2:16, where Paul argues similarly, making the same addition to Psalm 143, to which he again alludes. *Pace* Gaston (*Paul*, 103; "Works of Law," 42), this phrase is not a "citation from Psalm 143"; it is what Paul adds to the allusion that he makes to that psalm. He means thereby that no one will attain the status of uprightness before God's tribunal by performing deeds mandated by the Mosaic law, or by "all that the law says" (3:19). These are not simply "good deeds," but those performed in obedience to the law and regarded by Jews as the means of preserving their covenantal status before God (modifying Barrett, *Romans*, 70). Or, as Cranfield has put it: No one "will earn justification by . . . obedience to God's requirements" because "*erga nomou* in the sense of such a perfect obedience . . . are not forthcoming" (*Romans*, 198).

Paul uses for the first time the pl. phrase *erga nomou*, "deeds of the law." The sg. appeared in 2:15, and the pl. will appear again in 3:28 and 9:32 (in some MSS); Gal 2:16; 3:2, 5, 10; and in abbreviated form in Rom 3:27; 4:2, 6; 9:[11?], 32. With the gen. of possession *nomou*, the phrase denotes the discrete, concrete actions demanded or required by the law or the human activity dictated by the law ("what the law says" [3:19]); possibly it might also include the mentality of the pious Jew who seeks to observe the law (Lohmeyer, *Probleme*, 57). By contrast, Dunn would understand this phrase as designating "a mode of existence marked out in its distinctiveness as determined by the law, the religious practices which set those 'within the law' (v 19) apart as people of the law" (*Romans*, 154). For Dunn, it would refer specifically to "circumcision and food laws," two obligations that "functioned as boundary markers" to set Jews off from Gentiles" (see also Dunn, "New Perspectives" and "Works of the Law"). This restricted sense of the phrase is hardly correct, for it contradicts the generic sense of "law" about which Paul has been speaking since 2:12 and to which he refers in 3:20b. See further Cranfield, "The Works of the Law."

This anarthrous sloganlike phrase would seem to reflect a Jewish background, and yet it has not been found in the OT. *Pace* Moo (" 'Law,' " 92), the phrase *ta erga* in 2 Chr 17:4; Isa 66:18; and Sir 16:12 is not the same; that OT usage lacks the specific reference to the law. Nor does it occur in the rabbinic literature of later centuries (cf. Str-B 3.160–62). There is a very late midrash called *Ma'ăśê Tôrāh*, but its subject matter sheds little light on the Pauline usage. Cf. R. Heiligenthal, *EDNT* 2.49–51.

The phrase has, however, turned up in QL, which shows that Paul is tributary to a genuine pre-Christian Palestinian Jewish tradition: *ma'ăśê tôrāh* (4QFlorilegium 1:7); *miqṣāt ma'ăśê hattôrāh*, "some deeds of the law" (4QMMT 3:29); cf. *ma'ăśāyw battôrāh*, "his deeds in the law" (1QS 5:21; 6:18); *opera praeceptorum* (2 Apoc. Bar. 57:2). See J. M. Allegro, "Further Messianic References in Qumran Literature," *JBL* 75 (1956): 174–87, esp. 182–86; DJD 5.83–84; E. Qimron and J. Strugnell, "An Unpublished Halakhic Letter from Qumran," *Biblical Archaeology Today: Proceedings of the International Congress on Biblical Archaeology, Jerusalem, April 1984* (Jerusalem: Israel Exploration Society, 1985), 400–407; "An Anonymously Received Pre-Publication of the 4QMMT," *Qumran Chronicle* 2 (1990): appendix, 1–9, esp. p. 9 (line 29). This Qumran Hebrew phrase rules out the suggestions of both Dunn, about a restricted sense of *erga nomou*, mentioned above, and Gaston, that the gen. *nomou* is a subjective gen. ("Works of Law"); cf. Fitzmyer, "Paul's Jewish Background." The Qumran usage makes it clear that "deeds of the law" refers, indeed, to things prescribed or required by the Mosaic law. To the extent that a "works righteousness" would be indicated by the phrase in question, this reading reveals that Paul knew whereof he was speaking when he took issue with contemporary Judaism and its attitude to legal regulations. In 4QMMT the phrase is used precisely in a context mentioning *ṣdqh*, "uprightness," and employs the very words of Gen 15:6 that Paul quotes about Abraham in 4:2c.

for through the law comes the real knowledge of sin. In Paul's view one of the functions of the Mosaic law was to make clear to human beings the *epignōsis*, "real knowledge," of sin, i.e., to unmask its character as a violation of God's law (see 7:7, 13), but also its character as a powerful force active in human life. Before the law was promulgated, human beings did evil, but their wrongs were not recognized as transgressions (4:15; 5:13), i.e., as acts of rebellion against the expressed will of God. If the law declares all people sinners and makes them conscious of their condition, then a fortiori the Jew to whom the law is addressed is just as much an object of God's wrath as the pagan whose moral perversion and degradation reveal his condition. Paul anticipates here the developed discussion about the law that he will undertake in 7:7–8:4. See Sullivan, "Epignosis."

So Paul ends the negative development of his thesis in part A of Romans.

BIBLIOGRAPHY

Blank, J., "Warum sagt Paulus: 'Aus Werken des Gesetzes wird niemand gerecht'?" *EKK Vorarbeiten* 1 (1969): 79–95.

Cosgrove, C. H., "Justification in Paul: A Linguistic and Theological Reflection," *JBL* 106 (1987): 653–70.

Cranfield, C. E. B., " 'The Works of the Law' in the Epistle to the Romans," *JSNT* 43 (1991): 89–101.

Dunn, J. D. G., "The New Perspective on Paul (Manson Memorial Lecture 1982)," *BJRL* 65.2 (1982–83): 95–122.

———, "Works of the Law and the Curse of the Law (Galatians 3.10–14)," *NTS* 31 (1985): 523–42.

———, "Yet Once More—'The Works of the Law,' " *JSNT* 46 (1992): 99–117.

Feuillet, A., "Le Plan salvifique de Dieu d'après l'épître aux Romains," *RB* 57 (1950): 336–87.

Fitzmyer, J. A., "Paul's Jewish Background and the Deeds of the Law," *According to Paul: Studies in the Theology of the Apostle* (New York and Mahwah, N.J.: Paulist Press, 1993), 18–35.

Gaston, L., *Paul and the Torah*, 100–106.

———, "Works of the Law as a Subjective Genitive," *SR* 13 (1984): 39–46.

Harris, R., "St. Paul's Use of Testimonies in the Epistle to the Romans," *Expos* 8.17 (1919): 401–14.

Hays, R. B., "Psalm 143 and the Logic of Romans 3," *JBL* 99 (1980): 107–15.

Hübner, H., "Was heisst bei Paulus 'Werke des Gesetzes'?" *Glaube und Eschatologie: Festschrift für Werner Georg Kümmel . . .* , ed. E. Grässer and O. Merk (Tübingen: Mohr [Siebeck], 1985), 123–33.

Johnson, S. L., Jr., "Studies in Romans. Part IX: The Universality of Sin," *BSac* 131 (1974): 163–72.

Keck, L. E., "The Function of Romans 3:10–18: Observations and Suggestions," *God's Christ and His People: Studies in Honour of Nils Alstrup Dahl*, ed. J. Jervell and W. A. Meeks (Oslo, Bergen, and Tromsö: Universitetsforlaget, 1977), 141–57.

Lafon, G., "Une Loi de foi: La pensée de la loi en *Romains* 3,19–31," *RevScRel* 61 (1987): 32–53.

Lohmeyer, E., "Probleme paulinischer Theologie, II: 'Gesetzeswerke,' " *ZNW* 28 (1929): 177–207; repr. in *Probleme*, 31–74.

Minde, H.-J. van der, *Schrift und Tradition*, 48–52.

Moo, D. J., " 'Law,' 'Works of the Law,' and Legalism in Paul," *WTJ* 45 (1983): 73–100.

Pax, E., "Ein Beitrag zur biblischen Toposforschung (Röm 3,19)," *SBFLA* 15 (1964–65): 302–17.

Porporato, F. X., " 'Non iustificabitur in conspectu tuo omnis vivens' Ps. 142 (143), 2," *VD* 16 (1936): 312–20.

Roberts, J. H., "Righteousness in Romans with Special Reference to Roman 3:19–31," *Neotestamentica* 15 (1981): 12–33.

Roukema, R., "Jews and Gentiles in Origen's Commentary on Romans III 19–22," *Origeniana Quarta*, ed. L. Lies (Innsbruck: Tyrolia, 1987), 21–25.

Schenke, H.-M., "Aporien im Römerbrief," *TLZ* 92 (1967): 881–88.

Schreiner, T. R., " 'Works of Law' in Paul," *NovT* 33 (1991): 217–44.

Sullivan, K., "Epignosis in the Epistles of St. Paul," *SPCIC* 2.405–16.

Tyson, J. B., " 'Works of Law' in Galatians," *JBL* 92 (1973): 423–31.

Vielhauer, P., "Paulus und das Alte Testament," *Studien zur Geschichte und Theologie der Reformation: Festschrift für Ernst Bizer*, ed. L. Abramowski and J. F. G. Goeters (Neukirchen-Vluyn: Neukirchener-Verlag, 1969), 33–62.

Walter, N., "Gottes Erbarmen mit 'allem Fleisch' (Röm 3,20 / Gal 2,16)—Ein 'feminer' Zug im paulinischen Gottesbild?" *BZ* 35 (1991): 99–102.

Wilckens, U., "Was heisst bei Paulus: 'Aus Werken des Gesetzes wird kein Mensch gerecht'?" *EKK Vorarbeiten* 1 (1969): 51–77; repr. in *Rechtfertigung als Freiheit*, 77–109.

THEME POSITIVELY EXPLAINED: GOD'S UPRIGHTNESS IS MANIFESTED TO ALL SINNERS THROUGH CHRIST AND APPREHENDED BY FAITH (3:21–31)

◆

12. ALL SHARE WITHOUT DISTINCTION IN THE JUSTIFICATION, REDEMPTION, AND EXPIATION OF CHRIST JESUS (3:21–26)

3 ²¹But now, independently of the law, the uprightness of God has been disclosed, even though the law and the prophets bear witness to it, ²²the uprightness of God that comes through faith in Jesus Christ toward all who believe, toward all, without distinction. ²³For all alike have sinned and fall short of the glory of God; ²⁴yet all are justified freely by his grace through the redemption that comes in Christ Jesus. ²⁵Through his blood God has presented him as a means of expiating sin for all who have faith. This was to be a manifestation of God's uprightness for the pardon of past sins committed ²⁶in the time of his forbearance, a manifestation of his uprightness also at the present time to show that he is upright and justifies the one who puts faith in Jesus.

COMMENT

Having developed the theme set forth in 1:16–17 in a negative fashion, by showing what happens to humanity without the gospel and under the influence of sin, Paul now proceeds to a positive explanation of that theme. He shows that the void created in human existence without the influence of the gospel cannot be filled by human effort, by pagans following a law that is theirs "by nature" or by Jews following the prescriptions of the Mosaic law. Paul recognizes that a new period in human history has begun with the coming of Jesus Christ, whose mission was to make known in a new way the divine uprightness. Thus God himself has taken the initiative and has restored for humanity the right relationship of it to himself. The gospel proclaiming Christ's passion, death, and resurrection and the effects of those events are thus manifestations of "God's power (unleashed) for the salvation of everyone who believes" (1:16). Paul now explains positively how this is so.

Verses 21–31 make up the first of several important parts of the letter, formulating in effect the essence of Paul's gospel: salvation for all human beings by grace through faith in Christ Jesus and what he has achieved for humanity. Indeed, these verses constitute the kerygmatic proclamation of the divine *Heilsge-*

schehen, in fact, along with what has preceded in this chapter, the "key to the structure and thought of the letter," as Campbell has rightly noted, because they will explain how both Jew and Gentile can be justified and find salvation.

In these verses the theme of the revelation of God's uprightness is developed, as Paul treats of (1) its relation to the Mosaic law (3:21); (2) its universal destination (3:22); (3) its necessity (3:23); (4) its nature and gratuity (3:24a); (5) its mode of revelation (3:24b–25); (6) its finality (3:25b–26); and (7) its consequences (3:27–31). Three, or possibly four, effects of the Christ-event are now formulated in these verses: justification, redemption, expiation, and possibly pardon. It is important to recognize that such effects of the Christ-event are appropriated through faith in Christ Jesus, and only through faith. It is the means whereby human beings experience what Christ has done for all of them.

This section may be treated in two parts: (1) 3:21–26, which at first repeats, in effect, 1:2 and 16–17 with added comments and with v 23 summing up 1:18–3:20; and with vv 24–26 making use of and reinterpreting a pre-Pauline formula about justification, redemption, and expiation; and (2) 3:27–31, which formulates the consequences of Paul's thesis concerning the revelation of God's uprightness. The first part has a proclamatory tone, which repeats basic ideas, whereas the second part indulges in diatribic style and is more polemical.

The pre-Pauline formula about justification, which Paul incorporates and modifies, would have run like this: "being justified freely through redemption (which comes) in Christ Jesus, whom God presented as a means of expiating sin through his blood, as a manifestation of his uprightness for the pardon of past sins committed in the time of his forbearance." According to Bultmann, Higgins, Käsemann, Kertelge ("*Rechtfertigung*," 48–62), and Reumann ("*Righteousness*," 36–38), this would be an early Jewish Christian credal or liturgical formula that Paul adopts. Such formulas are found elsewhere in Romans (1:3–4; 4:25; 10:9; 14:9); see also 1 Thess 1:9–10; 4:14–16; 1 Cor 15:3–5. To be noted is the intrusive character of the verses: a participle (*dikaioumenoi*) introduces the formula instead of a coordinated indicative; the peculiar vocabulary does not appear elsewhere in Pauline writings: *hilastērion*, "means of expiating sin," *paresis*, "pardon," *endeixis*, "manifestation," *proginesthai*, "to be past." (Reumann adds *apolytrōsis*, but he is incorrect [cf. 1 Cor 1:30].) Further, phrases are redundantly repeated: "freely" and "by his grace" (v 24); "a manifestation of God's uprightness" (v 25) and "a manifestation of his uprightness" (v 26). Again, we are confronted with one view of effects of the Christ-event in vv 24–26a and another in v 26b–c. There is also the problem of understanding how God may be said to have pardoned former sins in view of what Paul wrote in 1:18–3:20. His use of this formula makes him seem somewhat inconsistent. For such reasons interpreters, especially Käsemann, judge that Paul has introduced an earlier formula already in use in the Christian tradition. Others (e.g., Lohse, Wengst) try to argue on stylistic grounds for a more Pauline composition, whereas still others (Kuss,

Ridderbos, Schlier) consider it a wholly Pauline composition, which uses traditional language. But the arguments of the latter have not won the day.

In any case, it is generally agreed that Paul has modified the adopted formula by introducing at least three things: (1) *tē autou chariti*, "by his grace," added after "freely" in v 24; some interpreters would even say that he also added *dōrean*, "freely," but that is not clear; (2) *dia [tēs] pisteōs*, "(to be received) through faith," added in the translation given above after "blood" in v 25 (in the Greek text it precedes); and (3) *pros tēn endeixin . . . ,*" for the manifestation of his uprightness also at the present time . . ." (v 26b–c), which expresses God's purpose in the eschatological "now." Again, according to some commentators, Paul would have also added *en tō autou haimati*, "by his blood," but that is not clear either.

If one admits that Paul is using an antecedent tradition in vv 24–26, does it follow that *dikaiosynē theou* in vv 21–22 has a different sense from that in vv 25–26, namely, the latter would be a corrective of the sense in the former? Piper ("The Demonstration") would have us believe that the sense is different. But that reading would introduce an Anselmian distinction into the Pauline text, which does not warrant it.

This is the first place in Romans in which Christ Jesus is introduced by Paul in a significant way. He was mentioned in the letter's prescript (1:1, 4, 6, 7, 8), and thereafter only in passing in 2:16. Now God's new initiative in the salvation of humanity takes shape through the death of Christ on the cross. Paul does not see that initiative manifesting itself in Jesus' teaching or preaching, his proclamation of the kingdom of God, or his healing activity. Instead Paul moves directly to the death of Jesus and describes its effects, using terms from the inherited early Christian formula. He thus concentrates on the most important aspect of Christ's role, his crucifixion and death. Strangely enough, he makes no mention here of the resurrection, for which one must wait until 4:25.

Paul moves from the period of humanity under the law to the new aeon or period of humanity under the gospel, to the *eschaton*, "the last age," which began with Christ and his mission. God's wrath marked the old age, but now God's uprightness marks the new. "The old age has passed away; look, the new has come" (2 Cor 5:17). For this reason Paul begins with the so-called eschatological "now." Whereas formerly God's wrath was revealed from heaven, now his uprightness is revealed in Christ Jesus and the gospel about him; the divine, salvific activity through which God acquits human beings of their sin now dominates human history. But Paul also insists that the uprightness of God now revealed was also announced and prefigured in the law and the prophets, in the Israelite Scriptures of old.

NOTES

3:21. *But now.* The adv. *nyni* is temporal and marks a new stage in salvation history, which moves beyond that of the law and the promises. The period of divine wrath gives way to that of divine uprightness. This is the first use of eschatological "now" in Romans; see further 3:26; 5:9, 11; 6:22; 7:6; 8:1, 18; 11:5, 30, 31; 13:11. For Paul the *eschaton* is at hand, for Jesus, the harbinger of that aeon, has already come and carried out his role for the sake of humanity. "The ends of the ages have met" (1 Cor 10:11), i.e., the term of the old period has met the beginning of the new; hence the *eschaton* has begun. It is also the time in which faith reigns, the "fullness of time" (Gal 4:4).

independently of the law. Lit., "apart from (the) law," i.e., without any recourse to "deeds prescribed by the law" (3:28), to the observance of Mosaic prescriptions or prohibitions. The "law" of which Paul speaks is that which he said in v 20 brings real knowledge of sin. So he insists, this law has nothing to do with the new manifestation of God's uprightness—at least directly (compare Gal 2:19: "for through the law I died to the law that I might live for God").

the uprightness of God has been disclosed. The divine attribute, of which Paul wrote in 1:17 (see the NOTE there) and to which he referred in 3:5, has now been made known in the eschatological and salvific mission of Jesus Christ. It is God's bounteous and powerful uprightness whereby he acquits his sinful people in a just judgment. See Introduction, section XI.A. Cf. Kuss, *Römerbrief*, 115–23; Schlier, *Römerbrief*, 103–4; Wilckens, *Römer*, 1.187. Again Paul uses the vb. *phaneroun*, not in the sense of "reveal" (as with *apokalyptein* in 1:17), but of "making known, making public" in the passion, death, and resurrection of Christ. See the NOTE on 1:19; compare 2 Cor 2:14; 4:2.

even though the law and the prophets bear witness to it. This clause repeats 1:2, which tells of the promise of the "gospel" in the prophets of old. Here Paul uses "law" in a sense different from that at the beginning of the verse. There it denotes the law that constrains human beings to a certain mode of action; here it denotes the Pentateuch, the legal part of the OT. The OT is thus regarded by Paul as a privileged preparation for this new disclosure of God's uprightness (cf. Gal 3:23–25). In fact, the OT still bears witness, for the pres. ptc. *martyroumenē* expresses contemporaneity with the main vb., as 4:23–24 will illustrate. Only here does Paul use *martyrein* of the testimony of Scripture; contrast Acts 10:43; John 5:39. One may ask, Where in the law and the prophets is this testimony found? Although Paul does not cite any passages from the OT, he has already cited the words of Hab 2:4 in connection with the revelation of "the uprightness of God" (1:17). Paul will also use (in chap. 4) the story of Abraham in Genesis as proof of his contention. For "the law and the prophets," as a mode of referring to the whole OT, see the Prologue of Sirach, 2 Macc 15:9; 4 Macc 18:10; Luke 16:16; Acts 13:15; 24:14; 28:23; Matt 5:17; 7:12; 11:13; 22:40 (cf. Käsemann, *Commentary*, 93). A modified form of the phrase is found in 1QS 1:3; 8:15–16; CD 5:21–6:1; 4QDibHam (= 4Q504) 1–2 iii 12–13.

22. *the uprightness of God.* Paul repeats the key phrase *dikaiosynē theou* with an inserted *de* to emphasize that aspect or attribute of God which he now expounds; he repeats it for the sake of clarity because of the distance from its first

occurrence (Moo, *Romans*, 223). *Pace* Dunn (*Romans*, 166), the repetition with the absence of a verb does not confirm that Paul is stressing the dynamic force of the concept, God's action on behalf of those to whom he has committed himself. Rather, he emphasizes that the divine initiative stems from an aspect of God himself. Paul uses the phrase in the same sense that he used in 3:5, to which this verse clearly alludes.

that comes through faith in Jesus Christ. Lit., "through the faith of Jesus Christ." The sense of the gen. is disputed. Some commentators would understand it as subjective (Haussleiter, *NKZ* 2 [1891]: 109–45, 205–30; Kittel, *TSK* 79 [1906]: 419–36; Howard, *HTR* 60 [1967]: 459–65; *ExpTim* 85 [1973–74]: 212–15; Price, *Int* 28 (1974): 272–73; Williams, *JBL* 99 [1980]: 272–78; *CBQ* 49 [1987]: 431–47; Johnson, *CBQ* 44 [1982]: 77–90; Ramaroson, *ScEsp* 39 [1987]: 81–92; 40 [1988]: 365–77; Hooker, *NTS* 35 [1989]: 321–42): "through the fidelity of Jesus Christ," i.e., his obedience to his Father, even to death on the cross. Such interpreters appeal to 3:3 ("the faith of God"), 4:12, 16 ("the faith of Abraham"), where there is mention of the faith *of* an individual, not faith *in* an individual.

While this interpretation might seem plausible, it runs counter to the main thrust of Paul's theology. Consequently, many commentators continue to understand the gen. as objective, "through faith in Jesus Christ," as in 3:26; Gal 2:16, 20; 3:22; Phil 3:9; cf. Eph 3:12. So Luther, *Glossae* 3.22 (WAusg 56.36; LuthW 25.31); *Scholia* 3.22 (WAusg 56.256; LuthW 25.242: "fides in Christum"), Cranfield, *Romans*, 203; Käsemann, *Commentary*, 94; Kuss, *Römerbrief*, 112; Moo, *Romans*, 224–25; Schlier, *Römerbrief*, 105; Wilckens, *Römer*, 1.188. Indeed, as Dunn rightly notes (*Romans*, 166), Paul does not draw attention to Christ's faithfulness elsewhere in the extended exposition of Romans, even where it would have been highly appropriate, especially in chap. 4, where Abraham's *pistis* is the model for the believer. Paul is not thinking of Christ's fidelity to the Father; nor does he propose it as a pattern for Christian conduct. Rather, Christ himself is the concrete manifestation of God's uprightness, and human beings appropriate to themselves the effects of that manifested uprightness through faith in him. Indeed, that divine uprightness is comprehended only by those who have the eyes of faith. For a similar objective gen. with *pistis*, see Mark 11:22 (*echete pistin theou*, "have faith in God"), which stands in contrast to *tēn pistin tou theou* of Rom 3:3; also Acts 3:16a (*en tē pistei tou onomatos autou*, "through faith in his [Jesus'] name [*or* person]"); Phil 1:27 (*tē pistei tou euangeliou*, "for faith in the gospel"); Col 2:12 (*dia tēs pisteōs tēs energeias tou theou*, "through faith in the power of God"); 2 Thess 2:13; Jas 2:1; Rev 14:12; Josephus, *Ant.* 19.1.2 §16 (*pollēn echei pistin tou theou tēs dynameōs*, "furnishes much credibility of God's power"). See further *Diogn.* 11:6; also the appended note in Murray, *Romans* 1.363–74; Moule, *ExpTim* 68 (1956–57): 157, 221–22. Note that in 10:9; 1 Cor 12:3; and 2 Cor 4:5, 14 Jesus Christ is presented as the object of faith. Does the vb. *pisteuein* ever have Christ as the subject in the NT? Not even Heb 12:2 has that connotation.

Furthermore, *pace* Howard (*HTR* 60 [1967]: 461), no argument in favor of the subjective gen. can be deduced from the Vg, even when it translates "per fidem Iesu Christi" or "ex fide Iesu Christi" (Gal 2:16), because the Latin translation is simply a literal version of the Greek and is equally ambiguous. If the Peshitta has translated the phrase in the sense of an objective gen., then that translation is already an interpretation, an interpretation that is old, indeed, but not necessarily what Paul meant by the phrase. Again, *pace* Howard (*ExpTim* 85[1973–74]: 213), one would expect the vast majority of instances of *pistis* with a gen. in nonbiblical literature to be those of a subjective gen., for the word is used with many nuances, but hardly ever with the Christian connotation associated with *pistis* or *pisteuein eis* in Pauline writings. Hence, the instance in Josephus (*Ant.* 19.1.2 §16) shows at least that the objective sense of such a gen. is not impossible. Again, *pace* Johnson (*CBQ* 44 [1982]: 87–89), if Paul meant by *pistis Iēsou Christou* the "faith of Christ" in the sense of the "obedience of Christ," he would have used *hypakoē*, as in 5:19. In 2 Cor 10:5 he even uses *eis tēn hypakoēn tou Christou* precisely in the objective sense, "(to take every thought captive) to obey Christ" (*RSV*). Lastly, *pace* Hultgren ("*Pistis Christou*"), the gen. cannot have both connotations, "both the object and ground of faith." That is idyllic dreaming revealing only the interpreter's embarrassment.

Pistis, "faith," is the mode whereby human beings respond to the challenge of the gospel and appropriate to themselves the effects of the Christ-event. See chap. 10 and Introduction, section IX. D.

toward all who believe. Lit., "unto all those believing." This phrase expresses the universal destination of God's uprightness, being manifested toward all human beings. *Pantas* has the same extension as *pan stoma*, "every mouth," in 3:19. God's uprightness is the sign of the new aeon, just as the law was the sign or mark of the old. Just as God's wrath was revealed as God's power for the punishment of all human beings, so now God's uprightness is made known as his power for the justification of all.

The reading *eis pantas* is found in MSS P[40], ℵ*, A, B, C, P, Ψ, 81, 104, 1739, etc. But the Vg tradition presupposes *epi pantas*, and a number of MSS (ℵ[2], D, F, G, K, and the *Koinē* text-tradition) read a conflated form, *eis pantas kai epi pantas*, "for all and upon all who. . . ."

without distinction. I.e., of Jew or Greek (see 1:14, 16; 2:9–11; 10:12). The opportunity is given equally to all humanity.

23. *For all alike have sinned.* Christian salvation, embracing all human beings, copes with the universality of sin among them. Paul is thinking primarily of two groups of humanity, Jews and Greeks; yet his absolute formulation connotes the idea of "all individuals," i.e., Jews, Greeks, and barbarians. Noteworthy is the continued emphasis on "all" (3:4, 9, 12, 19–20). The characteristic of all humanity is that it is sinful; all are sinners, rebels against God, and their condition can be remedied only by God himself. On the Pauline meaning of *hamartanein*, see Introduction, section IX. D.

and fall short of the glory of God. The vb. *hysterein* means to "come too late, fail to reach," but also to "lack" something (see Ps 23:1; Luke 15:14; 1 Cor 1:7; 8:8); in the middle voice it can mean to "go without, come short of, fail to attain a goal" (governing the gen. [see BAGD, 849]). Thus Paul maintains that all human beings remain, because of their sins, without a share in God's glory, i.e., they have failed to attain the lot that was theirs and so cannot attain their destiny.

On "glory," see the NOTE on 1:23. *Doxa* came to be the way of expressing the enhancing quality of a creature of God as well as the eschatological condition destined for human beings. It is thought of as being communicated to them as they draw close to God (5:2; 8:18, 21; 9:23; 1 Thess 2:12; 1 Cor 2:7; 15:40-41; 2 Cor 3:18; 4:6; Phil 3:21; cf. Col 1:27; 3:4; Eph 1:17; 2 Thess 2:14). Estranged from the intimate presence of God by sin, they have been deprived of that enhancing quality which they should have in this life as well as that for which they are destined eschatologically in the presence of God. Hence they fall short of their share in the glory of God.

It is a matter of debate among commentators whether this "falling short" is only an eschatological condition or Paul thinks of it as a condition already affecting the earthly life of human beings. It is probably both, but it certainly includes the latter, for it is expressed as the present condition of humanity.

Paul is not referring to the contemporary Jewish notion of Adam (and Eve) as robed in glory before their sin. In *Apoc. Mos.* 20:2: Adam says to Eve, "Why have you done this to me and deprived me of my glory?" (AOT, 163); cf. 1QS 4:23; CD 3:20; 1QH 17:15 (*kĕbôd ʾādām*); 3 *Apoc. Bar.* 4:16. Nevertheless, Dunn attempts so to link it (*Romans*, 168), when he says that Paul "refers here *both* to the glory lost in man's fall *and* to the glory that fallen man is failing to reach in consequence." But Paul is not yet expressing himself in the terms he uses in 5:12-21, and even there he corrects the contemporary Jewish understanding of Adam. Hence, a reference to Adam here is eisegetical.

24. *yet all are justified freely.* Lit., "(but) being justified freely." I.e., are "made upright" gratuitously through God's powerful declaration of acquittal. Human beings thus achieve the status of uprightness before God's tribunal which the Jew sought by observing the deeds of the law. Now human beings find that this status is not achieved by something within their own power or measured by their own merits. It comes to humanity through an unmerited dispensation of God himself, who has taken the initiative. The sinful human being is not only "declared upright," but is "made upright" (as in 5:19), for the sinner's condition has changed.

Paul is using the primitive Christian aspect of justification, which comes *dōrean*, "gratis, for nothing" (cf. LXX Exod 21:11, *dōrean aneu argyriou*, "gratis, without silver"). The pre-Pauline term excludes the possibility of meriting justification on one's own; it is a sheer gift of God (*hē dōrea tēs dikaiosynēs*, 5:17; cf. 5:15). He explains it more fully in the phrase that follows. A similar idea is found in QL: "And by your grace you judge them with an abundance of mercy" (1QH 6:9; cf. 7:27).

by his grace. This explanation of *dōrean* has been added by Paul to the adopted formula to emphasize the gratuity of what has been achieved for humanity (cf. 5:15, 17, 20–21; 6:1; 1 Cor 15:10). He is not merely thinking of the OT notion of *hesed*, "steadfast kindness," the gracious root of Israel's covenantal relationship with God, but rather of the new dispensation stemming wholly from a merciful benevolence of God the Father.

It should be superfluous to stress, *pace* Cornely (*Commentarius*, 187), that in using *dōrean* and *tē autou chariti*, Paul is not referring to the efficient cause of justification by the former and the formal cause by the latter (as if *charis* were "sanctifying grace"). That is anachronistic eisegesis, a distinction born of later medieval and Tridentine theology. See Lagrange, *Romains*, 74.

through the redemption that comes in Christ Jesus. Lit., "through the redemption (that is) in Christ Jesus." In using this pre-Pauline formula, Paul mentions a second effect of the Christ-event; human beings are not only "justified" by Christ Jesus, but are also "redeemed" by him. On "redemption," see Introduction, section IX.B. Cf. Wennemer, "*Apolytrōsis* Römer 3,24–25a," *SPCIC*, 1.283–88. Succinctly put, it denotes that Christ Jesus by his death on the cross has emancipated or ransomed humanity from its bondage to sin. Thus Paul extends the redemption achieved by God himself for Israel at the exodus (Ps 78:35) to all humanity. The ransoming has already taken place at the death and resurrection of Christ (3:25), but its definitive phase is still awaited (8:23). Paul uses *en Christō Iēsou*, which could express the mediation of God's redemption "through Christ Jesus," i.e., through the mortal life of Christ (3:25; 4:25; 5:9–10; 2 Cor 5:19, 21), or else the global sphere in which that redemption takes place, "in (the person of) Christ Jesus." As Lagrange has put it (*Romains*, 75), "the merit of the ransom is found in Christ already glorified." All who are "in Christ Jesus" have become partakers of the uprightness that comes from God through him. Through Christ a human being becomes a member of the people that God has acquired for himself, a member of the new people of God. For God has made him the source of life, "our uprightness . . . and redemption" (1 Cor 1:30).

25. *Through his blood.* Lit., "in his blood," i.e., by means of the shedding of his blood on the cross, or by the pouring out of that which signified his life. "For the life of every creature is its blood" (Lev 17:14; cf. 17:10). See Grandchamp, "La Doctrine," 266.

In the Greek text as we now have it, this prep. phrase *en tō autou haimati*, "through his blood," is separated from the vb. *proetheto* by the phrase *dia tēs pisteōs*, "through faith," which Paul has probably added to the inherited formula. Being so separated, it creates a problem for the interpreter. Is the separated phrase to be understood with the vb. *proetheto*, as it has been taken in my translation, or is it meant to modify the subsequent phrase, "for the manifestation of his uprightness through his [Jesus'] blood"? Most likely it is to be taken with the verb, because the first *autou* refers to Jesus ("his blood"), whereas the second refers to the Father ("God's uprightness"). Likewise the parallelism of *eis endeixin* and *pros tēn endeixin* would be somewhat disturbed by the association of the prep. phrase *en tō autou haimati* with the first member. For this reason, I have transposed the order of the phrases in the translation given above in order to achieve a better sense of what Paul seems to mean.

God has presented him as a means of expiating sin. Two problems make the interpretation of this clause difficult. The first is the meaning of the vb. *proetheto*, which has been debated since antiquity. It could mean "God designed him to be" (so Origen, Lagrange, NEB, Cranfield), i.e., God proposed him to himself, as he planned of old a new mode of human salvation. But if stress is put on the prefix *pro-*, then it would mean that "God proposed him," i.e., set him forth or displayed him publicly. Then it would be a reference not so much to the divine plan of salvation as to the crucifixion (cf. Gal 3:1, "before whose eyes Jesus Christ was publicly displayed [*proegraphē*] as crucified"). The vb. is so used in the LXX of Exod 29:23; 40:23; Lev 24:8; 2 Macc 1:8, 15 (the setting out of the shewbread) and is so used in Greek literature (Herodotus, *History* 31.48; Thucydides, *Peloponnesian War* 7.34). This sense has been used by Bruce, Käsemann, Kuss, Michel, and Sanday and Headlam; it is preferred because of other references to divine manifestation in this context. In any case, the effects of justification, redemption, and expiation are ascribed to the Father (*ho theos*), who brings about such effects for humanity through the death of Christ displayed publicly on the cross.

The second problem is the meaning of *hilastērion*, which creates two further problems: (a) is it a masc. sg. adj. (modifying the rel. pron. *hon*) or a neut. sg. noun (in apposition to the rel. pron. *hon*)? If it is understood as an adj., as in the LXX of Exod 25:17 (*hilastērion epithema*, "expiating cover"); Josephus, *Ant.* 16.7.1 §182 (*hilastērion mnēma*, "expiating monument"); or possibly 4 Macc 17:22 (if *tou hilastēriou thanatou autōn*, "their expiating death," is the correct reading there), it would mean that God "(presented Christ) as expiatory." But if it is taken as a noun, it would mean "as a means of expiating (sin)" or "as a place of expiating (sin)." In this regard, the difference in meaning is only slight; either explanation, adjective or noun, is possible and acceptable.

More crucial, however, is (b) the meaning of the word itself. Because *hilastērion* is related to the vb. *hilaskesthai*, "appease, propitiate," often used of appeasing angry gods in classical and hellenistic Greek literature (see Introduction, section IX.B), many commentators think of *hilastērion* in this sense: God has set forth Christ as "appeasing" or as "a means of appeasing" his own anger or wrath. Thus for Cranfield (*Romans*, 201, 214–18), Paul identifies Christ as a "propitiatory sacrifice." See also Morris, "The Meaning"; Lohse, *Märtyrer*, 149–54. But this interpretation of *hilastērion* finds no support in the Greek OT or in Pauline usage elsewhere. (Part of the problem is that Paul uses the word only here; cf. Heb 9:5, where it also is found. Here it is part of the adopted pre-Pauline

349

formula.) Consequently, *hilastērion* is better understood against the background of the LXX usage of the Day of Atonement rite, so it would depict Christ as the new "mercy seat," presented or displayed by the Father as a means of expiating or wiping away the sins of humanity, indeed, as the place of the presence of God, of his revelation, and of his expiating power.

It is, however, sometimes thought that this specific meaning of *hilastērion* as "mercy seat" would have escaped the comprehension of Paul's readers. For if the vb. *proetheto* means "displayed publicly," would not that meaning militate against the sense of Christ as *hilastērion*, hidden in the Holy of Holies of old? For that reason, some commentators would take the word only in a generic sense, as would be known, for instance, from a Cos inscription to Augustus: *ho damos hyper [t]as tou Autokratoros Kaisaros, theou huiou, Sebastou, sōtērias theois hilastērion*, "The people (offer this) as an oblation to the gods for the salvation of Imperator Caesar Augustus, son of God" (W. R. Paton and E. L. Hicks, *The Inscriptions of Cos* [Oxford: Clarendon, 1891; repr. Hildesheim and New York: Olms, 1990], §81; see also §347); cf. Dio Chrysostom, *Orationes* 11.121; *TDNT* 3.320. Schlier (*Römerbrief*, 110–11) prefers this generic sense; yet he still translates the word as "Sühne" or "Sühnemittel."

The Christians of Rome, to whom Paul is writing, almost certainly would have read the OT in Greek, and the LXX use of *hilastērion* would not have been unknown to them. Again, we must not deprive Paul of the possibility of using "mercy seat" in a symbolic or figurative sense, which is precisely what he seems to be doing, even though he insists as well on the public display of Christ crucified.

for all who have faith. Lit., "through faith." This short cryptic phrase, difficult to translate, interrupts the flow of the thought in the borrowed formula. It is not clear with what it should be understood. If it were to be taken with the vb. *proetheto*, it would mean, "whom God presented through faith as a means of expiating sin," which is hardly clear. If, however, Paul has added it to the inherited formula, then it would probably be meant as an expression of the mode in which a person shares in the expiation of sin. Then it would be translated as in the lemma. It is, indeed, crucial to Paul's argument, for even though the most important aspect of Christian salvation is what Jesus did in dying and rising, its benefits are shared in only "through faith," i.e., through a proper response to the gospel. Cf. *Diogn.* 8:6, "But he manifested himself through faith, by which alone it is granted to see God." See further Pluta, *Gottes Bundestreue*.

The Greek MSS are almost equally divided in reading either *dia pisteōs* (P[40], ℵ, C*, D*, F, G, 0219 365, etc.) or *dia tēs pisteōs* (B, C[3], D[2], Ψ, and the *Koinē* text-tradition). The sense is little affected by the omission or addition of the def. art. More crucial is the omission of the whole phrase in MSS A, and a few others along with John Chrysostom.

This was to be a manifestation of God's uprightness. Lit., "for the manifestation (*or* demonstration) of his uprightness." The prep. *eis* with the acc. is used to express purpose (BDF §206.3). The word *endeixis* denotes "demonstration," as in 2 Cor 8:24; Phil 1:28 (cf. Aeschines, *Or. contra Ctesiphonem* 3.219; Aristophanes, *Plutos* 785), not "proof," as Kümmel has shown. Note the similar sense of the cognate vb. *endeiknynai*, "show, display," in 2:15; 9:17, 22). Thus the death of Christ on the cross is seen to fit into the newly revealed divine plan of salvation for humanity. It was to display or make known in a new way God's uprightness, which is to be understood as in 1:17 and 3:21. This is the first of two parallel statements revealing the finality of the cross. Christ's expiatory death makes public the Father's bountiful acquittal, and human uprightness flows from the uprightness of God himself. The Essenes of Qumran also attributed the acquittal of sinners to God's uprightness (1QH 4:37; 11:30–31); indeed, it is rooted in the OT itself (Ps 143:1–2, 11; Ezra 9:13–15; Dan 9:16–18). In QL it is an acquittal awaited in the *eschaton*, but in Pauline thinking the act of acquittal has taken place in the exposure of Christ on the cross. The entire history of God's dealings with humanity has been guided by this manifestation of his uprightness in Christ Jesus, in his foreseen death and resurrection.

for the pardon of past sins committed. Lit., "for the remission of bygone sins," i.e., those that were committed aforetime. The prep. *dia* with the acc. is used either in a causal sense, "because of, for the sake of" (cf. 4:25; 2 Macc 8:15, where *dia* stands parallel to *heneka*), as it is understood in B-A, 362 and BAGD, 181a; or in a prospective or final sense, "with a view to," as in Thucydides, *Peloponnesian Wars* 2.89.4; 4.40.2; 5.53.1; Aristotle, *Nicomachean Ethics* 4.3.31; Plato, *Republic* 7.7 §524c; and Polybius, *History* 2.56.12. See H. G. Meecham, *ExpTim* 50 (1938–39): 564.

The meaning of the rare word *paresis* is debated. It occurs only here in the NT and never in the LXX. Ancient interpreters and the Vg understood it to mean "pardon, remission," a meaning found in extrabiblical Greek for the remission of debts or punishment (Phalaris, *Ep.* 81.1; Dionysius of Halicarnassus, *Antiquitates Romanae* 7.37.2; Athenagoras, *De resurrectione* 16S.68.4; perhaps BGU 624.21; cf. B-A, 1265a; MM, 493). This meaning is preferred by Luther, Calvin, Bultmann (*TDNT* 1.511 [for whom it is a synonym of *aphesis*]), Cerfaux, Käsemann, Kümmel (ZTK 49 [1952]: 145–67; *JTCh* 3 [1967]: 1–13, esp. 4), Lietzmann, Stuhlmacher, et al. Hence Christ's death would have demonstrated the divine uprightness that has remitted the sins of human beings of bygone times, sins that awaited this great Day of Expiation (cf. Acts 13:38–39; Heb 9:15).

Many commentators, however, who follow the translation of Theodore de Bèze (of 1598), prefer to understand *paresis* etymologically in relation to the cognate vb. *parienai*, "pass over, let go," which is so used in Luke 11:42; Heb 12:12 and is found in Sir 23:2; Josephus, *Ant.* 15.3.2 §48. It would then mean "for the sake of the passing over of bygone sins." In this case, Christ's death would now demonstrate God's uprightness in wiping out sins, in contrast to his previous forbearance shown in passing over human sins of the past; so RSV, Althaus, Barrett, Blackman, Boylan, Cranfield, Dodd, Huby, Kuss, Lagrange, Michel,

Prat, and Schlier. This meaning is attested for the noun in Plutarch, *Comparatio Dionis et Bruti* 2, and possibly in Xenophon, *Hipparchicus* 7.10 (see BAGD, 626).

For another, more complicated, but less convincing interpretation, see Lyonnet, *Bib* 38 (1957): 40–61 ("un pardon initial"); *Les Épîtres de Saint Paul aux Galates, aux Romains*, SBJ, ed. (Paris: Cerf, 1959), 83 n.e. ("demi-pardon"); but cf. VD 28 (1950): 282–87.

If *paresis* may indeed be interpreted as "pardon," then this would be a fourth way in which Paul expresses an effect of the Christ-event in this passage. It would be the Pauline equivalent of *aphesis*, "pardon, remission, forgiveness," a term that occurs in the Deutero-Pauline Col 1:24 and Eph 1:7 and in Lucan writings (Luke 1:77; 3:3; 24:27; Acts 2:38). Because the interpretation of this term is debated, it makes one hesitate to say whether Paul in these verses speaks of three or four effects of the Christ-event.

26. *in the time of his forbearance.* Lit.,"in the clemency of God" or "in the delay of God." The temporal sense is derived from the prep. *pro-* of the compound perf. ptc. *progegonotōn*, used in the preceding verse. The noun *anochē* is found in POxy 7.1068:15 in the sense of "delay of days" (*hēmerōn anochēn echō*, "I have a delay of [some] days"). Although up to the coming of Jesus Christ sinful human beings were subject to God's wrath (1:18), that wrath did not always manifest itself in the punishment of sin, because of its eschatological nature. God's tolerance was ultimately based on his plan of salvation, according to which he knew that these sins would be expiated through the death of Christ in due time. Even the expiation of sin on the yearly Day of Atonement made sense only in prefiguring that manifested by the shedding of Jesus' blood on the cross. The time of God's forbearance is now at an end. Cf. 2:4.

It might seem strange that the gospelless world of the pagans subject to God's wrath (1:18) is now said by Paul to have existed in the period of God's forbearance or patience. It is not that God manifested his wrath toward individuals, but not toward pagan humanity as a whole, with which he was patient. Rather, Paul's perspective is that of Jesus Christ and his coming. Looking back on the period before Christ, he has a bipolar perspective: "God's wrath" has been manifested because salvation comes only through Christ Jesus, but "God's forbearance" has also been manifested, displayed toward the Jew as well (2:4). Divine judgment was not yet definitive toward either Jew or Greek. God does not go back on his word; though his wrath abandoned pagan humanity to the consequences of its sinfulness, that wrath is not yet the last word. Nor does God capitulate to human sinfulness. Rather, through Christ Jesus God restores humanity to a right relationship with himself and thus rehabilitates its integrity and order. The proper response to this grace of God, precisely as grace, is only faith. Without any involvement of the law, which however did speak about it in advance, God has manifested to the world his uprightness, his fidelity to human beings, his truth, and his glory. This world no longer bears the splendor of its creation, but is subjected to sin; yet now God's uprightness manifests itself precisely in the justification of sinful human beings who turn to him in faith and thus react to what he has done in the Christ-event. For he has manifested his uprightness in justification, redemption, expiation, and pardon precisely in displaying Christ Jesus on the cross as the agent of such activity toward human beings.

a manifestation of his uprightness also at the present time. This manifestation or demonstration parallels that of v 25. The Christ-event has its effect not only in the past, but also in the present. It takes place in the "eschatological now," a phrase used earlier (see the NOTE on 3:21), but now coupled with *kairos*, "(critical) time," as in 11:5.

to show that he is upright. Lit., "in order that he (God) may be upright." Paul uses *eis* with the acc. of the articular infin. to express purpose (BDF §402.2). Through the public exposure of his Son Jesus on the cross, God has vindicated his claim to be the acquitter and savior of his people (Isa 59:15–20). Thereby he brought humanity into a status of rectitude, innocence, and acquittal. This adjectival use of *dikaion*, referring to God, is the best reason for interpreting *dikaiosynē theou* (1:17; 3:5, 21–22) as an attribute in God. The whole process of acquitting humanity and rendering it upright in his sight is something that proceeds from what God is in himself. The uprightness of God made manifest in Christ Jesus is the very uprightness of God himself.

and justifies the one who puts faith in Jesus. Lit., "and justifying him from (*or* by, through) the faith of Jesus," or "even in justifying." Thus God enables sinful humanity to share by virtue of faith in the very uprightness that he manifests through the death of Christ Jesus. Paul succinctly describes the status of the justified Christian as *ton ek pisteōs*, "the one (who) through faith" becomes a member of Christ and lives a new life in him. Such an uprightness is no longer a status of rectitude achieved by observance of the law, but is *ek pisteōs*, "by faith," and that means "faith in Christ Jesus."

Earlier commentators, who understood *dikaiosynē theou* of God's distributive or vindictive justice, often gave concessive force to the ptc. *dikaiounta*, "in order to be just, even though he justifies. . . ." Blackman (*JBL* 87 [1968]: 204) still toys with the possibility of translating *kai* as *kaiper*, "although." Such an interpretation, however, involves the demand that Jesus died in satisfaction for human sins. This understanding of the clause would tie in with the meaning of *hilastērion* as "appeasing" or a "means of propitiation." The context, however, seems to be all against such an interpretation, which is really born of later theological considerations, especially those of Anselm. Paul is saying instead that the recent divine intervention in human history proves that God is upright; he even makes human beings upright through faith in Christ's expiatory death.

Again, the same problem occurs here about the phrase *ek pisteōs Iēsou* as in v 22: Does it mean "by faith in Jesus," or "by the faith of Jesus," i.e., his fidelity? See the NOTE on 3:22.

The last word (*Iēsou*) is omitted in MSS F, G, the VL, and Ambrosiaster. The omission would mean that God "justifies the one who has faith." A few minor MSS (629) and some ancient versions (Vg^{cl}, Syr^{pesh}) substitute *Christou* for *Iēsou*, or even *Kyriou hēmōn Iēsou Christou*, an insignificant variant.

BIBLIOGRAPHY

See further the bibliography on expiation, pp. 155–56.

Blackman, C., "Romans 3:26b: A Question of Translation," *JBL* 87 (1968): 203–4.

Bleibtreu, W., "Der Abschnitt Röm. 3, 21–26, unter namentlicher Berücksichtigung des Ausdrucks *hilastērion*," *TSK* 56 (1883): 548–68.

Bover, J. M., "El pensamiento generador de la teología de san Pablo sugerido por Rom. 3, 21–26," *Bib* 20 (1939): 142–71.

———, "Quem proposuit Deus 'propitiatorium' (Rom. 3, 25)," *VD* 18 (1938): 137–42.

Bruston, C., "Les Conséquences du vrai sens de *hilastērion*," *ZNW* 7 (1906): 77–81.

Buchanan, G. W., "The Day of Atonement and Paul's Doctrine of Redemption," *NovT* 32 (1990): 236–49.

Cadman, W. H., "*Dikaiosynē* in Romans 3,21–26," *SE II*, TU 87 (1964), 532–34.

Campbell, D. A., *The Rhetoric of Righteousness in Romans 3.21–26*, JSNTSup 65 (Sheffield, UK: Academic Press, 1992).

Campbell, W. S., "Romans iii as a Key to the Structure and Thought of the Letter," *NovT* 23 (1981): 22–40.

Cantalamessa, R., " 'Si è manifestata la giustizia di Dio!': La giustificazione mediante la fede (Rm 3, 21–31)," *Vita consacrata* 22 (1986): 1–11.

Carter, W. C., "Rome (and Jerusalem): The Contingency of Romans 3:21–26," *IBS* 11 (1989): 54–68.

Christie, F. A., "The Judicial and Mystical Idea of Religion: An Exposition of Rom. 3:24 and Gal. 2:20," *BW* 31 (1908): 445–47.

Creed, J. M., "*Paresis* in Dionysius of Halicarnassus and in St. Paul," *JTS* 41 (1940): 28–30.

Dalton, W. J., "Expiation or Propitiation? (Rom. iii. 25)," *AusBR* 8 (1960): 3–18.

Donfried, K. P., "Romans 3:21–28," *Int* 34 (1980): 59–64.

Dunn, J. D. G., "Once More, *Pistis Christou*," *Society of Biblical Literature 1991 Seminar Papers* 30, ed. E. H. Lovering, Jr. (Atlanta, Ga.: Scholars Press, 1991), 730–44.

Fahy, T., "Exegesis of Rom. 3: 25f.," *ITQ* 23 (1956): 69–73.

Fitzer, G., "Der Ort der Versöhnung nach Paulus: Zu der Frage des 'Sühnopfers Jesu,' " *TZ* 22 (1966): 161–83.

Fryer, N. S. L., "The Meaning and Translation of *Hilastērion* in Romans 3:25," *EvQ* 59 (1987): 99–116.

Grandchamp, F., "La Doctrine du sang du Christ dans les épîtres de saint Paul," *RTP* 3.11 (1961): 262–71.

Greenwood, D., "Jesus as Hilasterion in Romans 3:25," *BTB* 3 (1973): 316–22.

Gurlitt, J. F. K., "Studien zur Erklärung der *endeixis tēs dikaiosynēs tou theou*, Röm. 3, 25," *TSK* 13 (1840): 930–1000.

Haussleiter, J., "Der Glaube Jesu Christi und der christliche Glaube: Ein Beitrag zur Erklärung des Römerbriefes," *NKZ* 2 (1891): 109–45, 205–30.

————, *Der Glaube Jesu Christi und der christliche Glaube: Ein Beitrag zur Erklärung des Römerbriefes* (Erlangen and Leipzig: Deichert, 1891).

————, "Eine theologische Disputation über den Glauben Jesu," *NKZ* 3 (1892): 507–20.

Hays, R. B., *The Faith of Jesus Christ*, SBLDS 56 (Chico, Calif.: Scholars Press, 1983).

————, "Pistis and Pauline Christology," *SBL 1991 Seminar Papers* (see above under Dunn), 714–29.

Hebert, G., " 'Faithfulness and 'Faith,' " *Theology* 58 (1955): 373–79.

Herman, Z. I., "Giustificazione e perdono in Romani 3,21–26," *Anton* 60 (1985): 240–78.

Heuschen, J., "Rom 3, 25 in het licht van de OT Zoenvorstelling," *RevEcclLiège* 44 (1957): 65–79.

Hilgenfeld, A., "Der Brief des Paulus an die Römer," *ZWT* 35 (1892): 296–347, 385–407.

Hill, D., "Liberation Through God's Righteousness," *IBS* 4 (1982): 31–44.

Hofius, O., "Sühne und Versöhnung: Zum paulinischen Verständnis des Kreuztodes Jesu," *Versuche, das Leiden und Sterben Jesu zu verstehen*, ed. W. Maas (Munich: Schnell & Steiner, 1983), 25–46.

Hossfeld, F.-L., "Versöhnung und Sünde," *BK* 41 (1986): 54–60.

Howard, G., "The 'Faith of Christ,' " *ExpTim* 85 (1973–74): 212–15.

————, "On the 'Faith of Christ,' " *HTR* 60 (1967): 459–65.

————, "Romans 3:21–31 and the Inclusion of the Gentiles," *HTR* 63 (1970): 223–33.

Hultgren, A. J., "The *Pistis Christou* Formulation in Paul," *NovT* 22 (1980): 148–63.

Jeremias, J., "Das Lösegeld für Viele (Mk. 10,45)," *Abba*, 216–29.

Johnson, L. T., "Romans 3:21–26 and the Faith of Jesus," *CBQ* 44 (1982): 77–90.

Käsemann, E., "Zum Verständnis von Römer 3,24–26," *ZNW* 43 (1950–51): 150–54; repr. in *Exegetische Versuche und Besinnungen*, 2 vols. (Göttingen: Vandenhoeck & Ruprecht, 1960–64), 1.96–100.

Kertelge, K., *Rechtfertigung*, 48–62, 71–84.

————, "Das Verständnis des Todes Jesu bei Paulus," *Der Tod Jesu: Deutungen im Neuen Testament*, ed. K. Kertelge (Freiburg im Breisgau: Herder, 1976), 114–36.

Kittel, G., "*Pistis Iēsou Christou* bei Paulus," *TSK* 79 (1906): 419–36.

————, "Zur Erklärung von Röm. 3, 21–26," *TSK* 80 (1907): 217–33.

Klein, G., "Exegetische Problem in Römer 3,21–4,25: Antwort an Ulrich Wilckens," *EvT* 24 (1964): 676–83; repr. in *Rekonstruktion und Interpretation*, 170–79.

Kolmodin, A., "Undersökning av Rom. 3:21–26," *Teologiska studier tillägnade Erik*

Stave på 65-årsdagen av kolleger och lärjungar (Uppsala: Almqvist & Wiksells, 1922), 232–45.

Kümmel, W. G., "*Paresis* and *endeixis*: A Contribution to the Understanding of the Pauline Doctrine of Justification," *JTCh* 3 (1967): 1–13.

Louw, J., "De wijze van de openbaring de *dikaiosynē tou theou*, Rm 3: 21–24," *NThStud* 2 (1919): 72–76.

Lührmann, D., "Die Offenbarung der Gottesgerechtigkeit, Röm. 1,17f 3,21ff," *Offenvarungsverständnis bei Paulus*, 141–53.

———, "Rechtfertigung und Versöhnung: Zur Geschichte der paulinischen Tradition," *ZTK* 67 (1970): 437–52.

Lutheran World Federation, *Justification Today: Studies and Reports*, LWF Assembly, Helsinki 1963, LWSup 1 (Geneva: Lutheran World Federation, 1965).

Lyonnet, S., "De 'iustitia Dei' in epistola ad Romanos 1,17 et 3,21–22," *VD* 25 (1947): 23–34.

———, "De 'iustitia Dei' in epistola ad Romanos 3,25–26," *VD* 25 (1947): 129–44, 193–203, 257–63.

———, "Gratuité de la justification et gratuité du salut: Le Problème de la foi et des oeuvres," *SPCIC*, 1.95–110.

———, "Notes sur l'exégèse de l'Épître aux Romains," *Bib* 38 (1957): 35–61.

———, "Propter remissionem praecedentium delictorum (Rom 3, 25)," *VD* 28 (1950): 282–87.

———, "Le Sens de *paresis* en Rom 3,25," *Bib* 38 (1957): 40–61; repr. *Études*, 89–106.

Lyonnet, S. and L. Sabourin, "The Sacrificial Function of Blood," *Sin*, 167–84.

———, "The Terminology of 'Expiation' in the Old Testament," ibid., 120–66.

———, "The Terminology of 'Purchasing' or 'Acquisition,' " ibid., 104–19.

Mackay, J. R., "Romans iii.26," *ExpTim* 32 (1920–21): 329–30.

Maier, W. A., "Paul's Concept of Justification, and Some Recent Interpretations of Romans 3:21–31," *Springfielder* 37 (1973–74): 248–64.

Meecham, H. G., "Romans iii.25f., iv.25—The Meaning of *dia* c. acc.," *ExpTim* 50 (1938–39): 564.

Meyer, A., "Der Glaube Jesu und der Glaube an Jesum," *NKZ* 11 (1900): 621–44.

Meyer, B. F., "The Pre-Pauline Formula in Rom. 3. 25–26a," *NTS* 29 (1983): 198–208.

Michaelis, W., "Zur Frage der Aeonenwende," *TBl* 18 (1939): 113–18.

Miller, R. H., "An Exposition of Romans 3:21–31," *RevExp* 30 (1933): 424–31.

Mollaun, R. A., *St. Paul's Concept of "hilastērion" According to Rom. III,25: An Historico-exegetical Investigation*, CUA NT Studies 4 (Washington, D.C.: Catholic University of America, 1923).

Moraldi, L., "Sensus vocis *hilastērion* in R 3,25," *VD* 26 (1948): 257–76.

Morris, L., "The Meaning of *Hilastērion* in Romans iii. 25," *NTS* 2 (1955–56): 33–43.

Moule, C. F. D., "The Biblical Conception of 'Faith,' " *ExpTim* 68 (1956–57): 157, 221–22.

Mussner, F., *Mort et résurrection*, 9–17.

Nygren, A., "Christus der Gnadenstuhl," *In memoriam Ernst Lohmeyer*, ed. W. Schmauch (Stuttgart: Evangelisches Verlagswerk, 1951), 89–93.

————, "Kristus nådastolen," *Professor Johannes Lindblom, Lund, på hans 65-årsdag den 7 juni 1947* (= *SEA* 12, Uppsala: Wretman, 1948), 237–41.

Piper, J., "The Demonstration of the Righteousness of God in Romans 3:25,26," *JSNT* 7 (1980): 2–32.

Pluta, A., *Gottes Bundestreue: Ein Schüsselbegriff in Röm 3:25a*, SBS 34 (Stuttgart: Katholisches Bibelwerk, 1969).

Price, J. L., "God's Righteousness Shall Prevail," *Int* 28 (1974): 259–80.

Pryor, J. W., "Paul's Use of *Iēsous*—A Clue for the Translation of Romans 3:26?" *Colloquium* (Auckland/Sydney) 16 (1983–84): 31–45.

Ramaroson, L., "La Justification par la foi *du* Christ Jésus," *ScEspr* 39 (1987): 81–92.

————, "Trois Études récentes sur 'la foi de Jésus' dans saint Paul," *ScEspr* 40 (1988): 365–77.

Reumann, J., "The Gospel of the Righteousness of God: Pauline Reinterpretation in Romans 3:21–31," *Int* 20 (1966): 432–52.

Rinck, W. F., "Ueber Römer 3, 25 gegen Pastor Gurlitt zu Billwerden," *TSK* 15 (1842): 791–94.

Robbins, R. D. C., "Notes on Acts XIV.16,17; XVII.30, and Rom. III.25,26," *BSac* 36 (1879): 61–71, esp. 68–71.

Robeck, C. M., Jr., "What Is the Meaning of *Hilastērion* in Romans 3:25?" *StudBibTheol* 4 (1974): 21–36.

Robinson, D. W. B., " 'Faith of Jesus Christ'—A New Testament Debate," *RTR* 29 (1970): 71–81.

Rorem, P. E., *Justification by Faith in Qumran? A Study of 1QS xi.2b–16a and the Epistle of the Romans* (Philadelphia, Penn.: STM thesis, Lutheran Theological Seminary, 1975).

Schläger, [G.], "Bemerkungen zu *pistis Iēsou Christou*," *ZNW* 7 (1906): 356–58.

Schlier, H., "Doxa bei Paulus als heilsgeschichtlicher Begriff," *Besinnung*, 307–18.

Schnackenburg, R., "Notre Justification par la foi en Jésus Christ sans les oeuvres de la Loi: Rm 3,21–25a.28," *AsSeign* 40 (1972): 10–15.

Schrage, W., "Römer 3, 21–26 und die Bedeutung des Todes Jesu Christi bei Paulus," *Das Kreuz Jesu: Theologische Überlegungen*, ed. P. Rieger, Forum 12 (Göttingen: Vandenhoeck & Ruprecht, 1969), 65–88.

Schulz, S., "Zur Rechtfertigung aus Gnaden in Qumran und bei Paulus," *ZTK* 56 (1959): 155–85.

Songer, H. A., "New Standing Before God: Romans 3:21–5:21," *RevExp* 73 (1976): 415–24.

Stanley, D. M., *Christ's Resurrection*, 166–71.

Stuhlmacher, P., *Gerechtigkeit*, 86–91.

———, "Recent Exegesis on Romans 3:24–26," *Reconciliation, Law, & Righteousness: Essays in Biblical Theology* (Philadelphia, Penn.: Fortress, 1986), 94–109.

Talbert, C. H., "A Non-Pauline Fragment at Romans 3:24–26?" *JBL* 85 (1966): 287–96.

Taylor, G. M., "The Function of *Pistis Christou* in Galatians," *JBL* 85 (1966): 58–76.

Taylor, V., "Great Texts Reconsidered: Romans 3,25f.," *ExpTim* 50 (1938–39): 295–300; repr. in *New Testament Essays* (London: Epworth, 1970), 127–39.

Theobald, M., "Das Gottesbild des Paulus nach Röm 3,21–31," *SNTU* 6–7 (1981–82): 131–68.

Thornton, T. C. G., "Propitiation or Expiation? *Hilastērion* and *hilasmos* in Romans and 1 John," *ExpTim* 80 (1968–69): 53–55.

Torrance, T. F., "One Aspect of the Biblical Conception of Faith," *ExpTim* 68 (1956–57): 111–14.

Voigt, S., " 'Estâo faltos da glória de Deus' (Rm 3,23)—Ambivalência no pensar e linguajar de Paulo," *RevEclBras* 47 (1987): 243–69.

Völter, D., "Die Verse Röm 3,22b–26 und ihre Stellung innerhalb der ersten Kapitel des Römerbriefs," *ZNW* 10 (1909): 180–83.

Wegenast, K., "Römer 3,24ff." *Das Verständnis*, 76–79.

Wennemer, K., "*Apolytrōsis* Römer 3:24–25a," *SPCIC* 1.283–88.

———, "Gerechtigkeit Gottes (Röm 3,21–26)," *GLeb* 29 (1956): 358–66.

Wengst, K., *Christologische Formel und Lieder des Urchristentums*, SNT 7 (Gütersloh: Mohn, 1972).

Wilckens, U., "Zu Römer 3,21–4,25: Antwort an G. Klein," *EvT* 24 (1964): 586–610; repr. in *Rechtfertigung als Freiheit*, 50–76.

Williams, S. K., "Again *pistis Christou*," *CBQ* 49 (1987): 431–47.

———, "The 'Righteousness of God' in Romans," *JBL* 99 (1980): 241–90.

———, *Jesus' Death as Saving Event*, Harvard Dissertations in Religion 2 (Missoula, Mont.: Scholars Press, 1975).

Wonneberger, R., *Syntax und Exegese: Eine generative Theorie der griechischen Syntax und ihr Beitrag zur Auslegung des Neuen Testamentes, dargestellt an 2. Korinther 5, 2f und Römer 3, 21–26*, BBET 13 (Frankfurt am Main, Bern, and Las Vegas: Lang, 1979).

Young, N. H., "Did St. Paul Compose Romans III:24f.?" *AusBR* 22 (1974): 23–32.

Zeller, D., "Sühne und Langmut: Zur Traditionsgeschichte von Röm 3,24–26," *TP* 43 (1968): 51–75.

Ziesler, J. A., "Salvation Proclaimed: IX. Romans 3:21–26," *ExpTim* 93 (1981–82): 356–59.

13. POLEMICAL DEVELOPMENT OF THIS THEME (3:27–31)

3 [27]Where, then, is there room for boasting? It is ruled out! On what principle? On the principle of deeds? No, but on the principle of faith. [28]For we maintain

that a human being is justified by faith apart from deeds prescribed by the law. [29]But is God the God of Jews only? Is he not also the God of Gentiles? Yes, even of Gentiles! [30]For God who will justify both the circumcised in virtue of their faith and the uncircumcised through their faith is one. [31]Are we, then, nullifying the law by faith? Certainly not! We are rather upholding the law.

COMMENT

The consequences of Paul's assertion about the new manifestation of God's uprightness and especially of the role of faith in human life are now discussed. The style is again that of diatribe. Paul is in debate with an imaginary interlocutor. The whole question of unmerited justification or salvation is now put in terms of "boasting," the human tendency to rely on one's own powers and to think that thereby one can achieve salvation or justification in the sight of God. The question is "faith," the mention of which has occurred four times in the preceding paragraph (twice in v 22, once each in vv 25 and 26). It recurs in this paragraph five more times: in vv 27, 28, 30(bis), and 31. What faith is will be shown in the story of Abraham in chap. 4 and will be explained at greater length in chap. 10. But it is clearly not something that is brought about by human activity; it is not a prerequisite condition to be fulfilled by human beings before God can act (Meyer, "Romans," 1140). Although the Mosaic law might encourage a person to think in terms of boasting, that is not the principle that is now operative in the new dispensation. Indeed, the new dispensation is one that operates on faith for both the Jew and the Gentile. Paul will insist that his teaching on justification by faith, apart from the observance of prescriptions of the law, not only suits God's new plan of salvation through Christ, but upholds the very nature and purpose of the Mosaic law itself. Hence faith excludes all boasting, for either the Greek or the Jew.

Paul now argues about justification in the light of his own Jewish background. He realizes that the Jew in possession of the law (2:23) and fortified by circumcision (2:25–29), "the sign of the covenant," is given a definite relationship to uprightness before God. Yet now that the status of rectitude and uprightness is achieved through Christ Jesus, one may wonder what happens to that wherein the Jew could legitimately take pride. Paul's answer is to say that boasting is excluded, both for the Jew and the Greek, because, though both are sinful human beings in God's sight, they are both brought back into proper relationship with him only through his grace and in virtue of faith in Christ Jesus. Everything in the new aeon now depends on faith, and such faith excludes all boasting, all dependence on one's own merits. The purpose of the law was to silence all boasting (3:19). And yet, the role of faith in human life does not undo the law or prove it ineffective, but instead achieves the very purpose for which the Mosaic law as a set of legal regulations was intended.

Verse 31 serves as the conclusion to Paul's discussion in chap. 3 as a whole, and not merely as a transition or introduction to the story of Abraham in chap. 4, as Cornely (*Commentarius*, 205), Huby (*Romains*, 163), Käsemann (*Commentary*, 105), and Lagrange (*Romains*, 80) have tried to understand it. Indirectly, it does provide such a transition, but its main purpose is to summarize the teaching in 3:21–31.

At 3:28 Luther introduced the adv. "only" into his translation of Romans (1522), "alleyn durch den Glauben" (WAusg 7.38); cf. *Aus der Bibel 1546*, "alleine durch den Glauben" (WAusg, DB 7.39); also 7.3–27 (Pref. to the Epistle). See further his *Sendbrief vom Dolmetschen*, of 8 Sept. 1530 (WAusg 30.2 [1909], 627–49; "On Translating: An Open Letter" [LuthW 35.175–202]). Although "alleyn/alleine" finds no corresponding adverb in the Greek text, two of the points that Luther made in his defense of the added adverb were that it was demanded by the context and that *sola* was used in the theological tradition before him.

Robert Bellarmine listed eight earlier authors who used *sola* (*Disputatio de controversiis: De justificatione* 1.25 [Naples: G. Giuliano, 1856], 4.501–3):

Origen, *Commentarius in Ep. ad Romanos*, cap. 3 (PG 14.952).

Hilary, *Commentarius in Matthaeum* 8:6 (PL 9.961).

Basil, *Hom. de humilitate* 20.3 (PG 31.529C).

Ambrosiaster, *In Ep. ad Romanos* 3.24 (CSEL 81.1.119): "sola fide iustificati sunt dono Dei," through faith alone they have been justified by a gift of God; 4.5 (CSEL 81.1.130).

John Chrysostom, *Hom. in Ep. ad Titum* 3.3 (PG 62.679 [not in Greek text]).

Cyril of Alexandria, *In Ioannis Evangelium* 10.15.7 (PG 74.368 [but alludes to Jas 2:19]).

Bernard, *In Canticum serm.* 22.8 (PL 183.881): "solam iustificatur per fidem," is justified by faith alone.

Theophylact, *Expositio in ep. ad Galatas* 3.12–13 (PG 124.988).

To these eight Lyonnet added two others (*Quaestiones*, 114–18):

Theodoret, *Affectionum curatio* 7 (PG 93.100; ed. J. Raeder [Teubner], 189.20–24).

Thomas Aquinas, *Expositio in Ep. I ad Timotheum* cap. 1, lect. 3 (Parma ed., 13.588): "Non est ergo in eis [moralibus et caeremonialibus legis] spes iustificationis, sed in sola fide, Rom. 3.28: Arbitramur justificari hominem per fidem, sine operibus legis" (Therefore the hope of justification is not found in them [the moral and ceremonial requirements of the law], but in faith alone, Rom 3:28: We consider a human being to be justified by faith, without the works of the law). Cf. *In ep. ad Romanos* 4.1 (Parma ed., 13.42a): "reputabitur fides eius, scilicet sola sine operibus exterioribus, ad iustitiam"; *In ep. ad Galatas* 2.4 (Parma ed., 13.397b): "solum ex fide Christi" [*Opera* 20.437, b41]).

See further:

Theodore of Mopsuestia, *In ep. ad Galatas* (ed. H. B. Swete), 1.31.15.

Marius Victorinus, *In ep. Pauli ad Galatas* (ed. A. Locher), ad 2.15–16: "Ipsa enim fides sola iustificationem dat–et sanctificationem" (For faith itself alone gives justification and sanctification); *In ep. Pauli ad Ephesios* (ed. A. Locher), ad 2:15: "Sed sola fides in Christum nobis salus est" (But only faith in Christ is salvation for us).

Augustine, *De fide et operibus*, 22.40 (CSEL 41.84–85): "licet recte dici possit ad solam fidem pertinere dei mandata, si non mortua, sed viva illa intellegatur fides, quae per dilectionem operatur" (Although it can be said that God's commandments pertain to faith alone, if it is not a dead [faith], but rather understood as that live faith, which works through love").

The phrase occurs also in the writings of Pelagius, *Expositio in ep. ad Romanos* 3:28 (ed. A. Souter, 34 [PL 30.663B–C, 692D; PLSup 1.1129]), who argues against *sola fides*, but his argument shows that the phrase was already current. Similarly, in the writings of the nominalist Gabriel Biel: "Per hanc doctrinam tollitur error et presumptio quorundam carnalium et ociosorum hominum qui in sola fide salvari se putantes; allegant pro se illud Matt. 40 [Mark 16:16], 'Qui crediderit et baptizatus fuerit salvus erit.' Non attendentes quod fides sine operibus mortua est. Hebr. 11 [6:1]" (By this doctrine is removed the error and presumption of some flesh-dominated and idle people who, thinking that they are saved by faith alone, claim for themselves what is said in Matt. 40 [Mark 16:16], 'The one who believes and is baptized will be saved.' They do not note that faith without deeds is dead. Hebr. 11 [6:1])" (*Sermones dominicales de tempore* 1.19C).

The irony of the addition is that the adv. "only" was earlier derived from that "right strawy epistle," Jas 2:24: "You see that a human being is justified by deeds, and not by faith alone" (*ouk ek pisteōs monon*). Once this Jacobean phrase entered the theological tradition, it was eventually used to explain Paul's assertion in 3:28. James' position is usually understood as a refutation not of Paul's teaching, but of an antinomian caricature of his teaching, to which his own generic and sometimes unguarded formulation (e.g., 4:2) was eventually open. Paul was speaking of "deeds of the law" (Jewish deeds in observance of the Mosaic law), whereas James was referring to "deeds" that flowed from faith (Christian deeds). Again, James uses a restricted and narrow sense of *pistis*, seemingly meaning no more by it in the immediate context than an intellectual assent to monotheism (2:19b). Lastly, James understands Abraham as having been justified by his willingness to sacrifice Isaac (a deed), and not by his faith (2:21). See J. Jeremias, "Paul and James,"

ExpTim 66 (1954–55): 368–71; Reumann, *"Righteousness,"* §270–75, 413; Luck, "Der Jakobusbrief und die Theologie des Paulus," *TGl* 61 (1971): 161–79.

Even so, one must further ask whether Luther meant by "only" what his predecessors meant. In the Lutheran tradition the Pauline principle enunciated in 3:28 became "articulus stantis et cadentis ecclesiae," the article by which the church stands or falls. This phrase was apparently first so formulated by V. E. Löscher in an antipietist essay, *Timotheus Verinus* (Wittenberg, 1718); see F. Loofs, "Der articulus stantis et cadentis ecclesiae," *TSK* 90 (1917): 345. But it was based on formulations of Luther himself: "quia isto articulo stante stat Ecclesia, ruente ruit Ecclesia" (because, if that article stands, the church stands; if it fails, the church fails; *Expositio in Psalmos 130.4* [WAusg 40.3.352.3]). Cf. *Promotionsdisp. Pall. u. Tilemann*, pref. (WAusg 39.1.205); *Lect. in Gen.*, 25.31–34 (LuthW 4.400); *Pref. to Acts* (LuthW 35.363). The criteriological principle that it thus became is understandable in systematic theology and creates no difficulty, but one will look in vain for such a use of it in the Pauline writings themselves; it is a theological extension of Paul's teaching that presses beyond what he states.

Sola fide also occurs in canon 9 of the Tridentine "Decree of Justification" of 1547 (DS 1559), where it is said that it cannot be so interpreted as to exclude all human cooperation in the grace of justification or any preparatory dispositions of the will. It is usually recognized today that it is thus formulated against a problematic that differs from what Lutherans then had in mind and is no longer church-divisive (see Wilckens, *Römer*, 1.252). The adv. "only" is not found in the translations of this verse in the commentaries of Barrett, Cranfield, Dunn, Lietzmann, Michel, Schlier, Wilckens, but it is used in the translations of Käsemann, Kuss (in parentheses).

NOTES

3:27. *Where, then, is there room for boasting?* Paul's question recalls 2:17, which tells about the Jew who relies on the law and boasts of his relation to God. Cf. 2:23. By *kauchēsis* Paul means "self-confidence which seeks glory before God and which relies upon itself" (Bultmann, *TDNT* 3.649). Such an act would violate God's impartiality, as Paul asserted in chap. 2 and as he will reiterate here. God's initiative in saving and justifying human beings through the mission of Christ is a matter of grace and precludes any tendency on their part to vaunt human achievements. Here Paul uses the abstract *kauchēsis*, "boasting," whereas in 4:2 he will speak of Abraham's *kauchēma*, concrete basis for "a boast." Yet in 2 Cor 1:12 he uses *kauchēsis* in a concrete sense, and in 2 Cor 5:12 *kauchēma* occurs in an abstract sense. There is no real distinction between them.

Some MSS (F, G) and ancient versions add *sou*, "your" (boasting).

It is ruled out! Lit., "it is locked out." Cf. Gal 4:17, where Paul uses the same verb. Self-confidence and boasting of one's achievements have no place in the new aeon, in the dispensation of divine grace and of faith. God has locked all boasting out. Paul's answer reflects what the OT itself teaches about boasting. Compare 1 Cor 1:29, 31, "so that no flesh might boast before God . . . , as it stands written, 'Let him who boasts boast of the Lord' (= Jer 9:22–23)." Cf. Eph 2:9.

On what principle? Lit., "by what kind of a law," *nomos* being used here in a figurative sense (see Introduction, section IX.D).

On the principle of deeds? Lit., "(by the law) of deeds," i.e., by the deeds that a human being performs and depends on, when one is legalistically inclined. By *nomos tōn ergōn* Paul understands the Mosaic law understood as a demand for obedience in individual acts (so Michel, *Brief an die Römer*, 155). Paul is playing on the different senses of *nomos*. Such an understanding of deeds prescribed by the law has already been discussed in the argument of 2:17–3:20.

No, but on the principle of faith. Lit., "no, but through the law of faith." Thus by an oxymoron Paul contrasts law and faith, which is in reality no law at all. Such a use of *nomos* is unparalleled in other Pauline writings, but in 8:2 he will again indulge in oxymoron and refer to "the Spirit of life" as a law. Cf. Gal 6:2, "the law of Christ." Cf. Lietzmann (*An die Römer*, 52). Paul thus insists that the uprightness that comes to human beings in virtue of faith in Christ Jesus is something alien to them; it is the uprightness of Christ himself that is ascribed to them and that in no way depends on their own merits or striving. It comes to them from God himself as a grace, so all boasting is excluded. Cf. Gal 3:23–25. Faith is now the way to salvation that God has ordained. Friedrich ("Das Gesetz") has tried to give this verse another meaning: in both instances *nomos* would refer to the Mosaic law, but in the first instance as a basis for boasting, whereas in the second it would refer to the law as viewed through the eyes of faith. In this he has been followed by Cranfield (*Romans*, 220) and Wilckens (*Römer*, 245).

28. *we maintain that a human being is justified by faith apart from deeds prescribed by the law.* Lit., ". . . apart from deeds of (the) law." See Gal 2:16, "knowing that a human being is not justified by deeds of (the) law but through faith in Jesus Christ." Paul uses *anthrōpos*, even without an article, as in 1 Cor 4:1 and 7:1, and speaks generically and indifferently of "a human being," making no specific reference to Greek or Jew. But his emphasis falls on *pistei*, "by faith," as Kuss, Bardenhewer, and Sickenberger recognize. That emphasis and the qualification "apart from deeds of (the) law" show that in this context Paul means "by faith alone." Only faith appropriates God's effective declaration of uprightness for a human being. These words repeat what Paul already said in v 20a.

Although talk of avoiding boasting might have seemed strange to the Christians of Rome, whom Paul is addressing in this letter, the basis of his assertion would not be. For that reason Paul includes his audience in his use of *logizometha*, "we maintain, we reckon." As in 6:11; 8:18; and 14:14, by *logizesthai* Paul means, "in judging, we are convinced"; it is a term that expresses the "judgment of faith" (H. W. Heidland, *TDNT* 4.288). So Paul summarizes the main tenet of what he has set forth in vv 21–26, the accepted Christian teaching on justification: God's uprightness has been manifested to humanity apart from any need to observe the prescriptions of the law. Human beings *are* justified through faith; the present is emphasized, in contrast to the eschatological future of 3:20. What Christ Jesus achieved for humanity in terms of justification is already possessed by Christians.

Paul is not speaking about deeds that are the fruit of Christian faith. On "deeds of the law," see the NOTE on 3:20. He never denied, of course, the relation of deeds performed after Christian conversion to salvation (see 2:6; Gal 5:6; Phil 2:12–13). Yet for him such deeds were the fruit of "faith working itself out through love" (Gal 5:6), which was all-important. Such "love" would lead to the performance of deeds, and the wellspring of that love is Christian faith itself, faith in its fullest sense (see Introduction, section IX.D).

What should be noted is the way this Pauline teaching is transposed in the Deutero-Pauline letter to the Ephesians: "By grace you have been saved through faith; and this is not your own doing. It is a gift of God—not because of deeds, lest anyone should boast. For we are his workmanship, created in Christ Jesus for good deeds which God has prepared in advance, that we might walk in them" (2:8–10). Here the Pauline teaching of justification has already been recast as salvation. Cf. Tit 3:5; 2 Tim 1:9; and esp. Acts 13:38–39, the only place in which the Lucan Paul mentions "justification," which is immediately explained by the Lucan theologoumenon of "forgiveness of sins." Later still, Augustine regarded 3:28, with its teaching about faith without deeds of the law, to be among the "subobscure opinions of the Apostle not understood in apostolic times"; he thought that the NT writings, 1 Peter, James, 1 John, and Jude were composed to offset such teaching. See the NOTE on 3:8. He was referring to such passages as Jas 2:14–26 (see the COMMENT above); 1 Pet 2:16–17; and 1 John 3:7–17, esp. 3:10.

Greek MSS ℵ, A, D*, F, G, Ψ, 81, 1739 and the Latin and Syriac versions read *gar*, whereas many MSS (B, C, D^c, K, P, 33, 614) omit it. Its retention seems preferable because v 28 gives a reason for what is said in v 27. Again, MSS F, G, and Latin versions read *anthrōpon dia pisteōs*, "a human being . . . through faith."

29. *is God the God of Jews only?* Compare 10:12. No Jew would have denied that Yahweh was the God of all human beings; but though divine salvation was destined for all, Israel was favored as his covenanted people, as the rabbinic tradition of the Amoraic period (fifth cent. A.D.) stressed (see *Exodus Rabbah* 29:4: "I am God over all earth's creatures, yet I have associated my name only with you; for I am not called 'the god of idolaters,' but 'the God of Israel' "). Paul thus indirectly makes capital of such a Jewish conviction for his own purpose. He calls on it to corroborate his teaching about the exclusion of all boasting. He asks his question, however, to insure what he has just explained against any possible objection that might come from Jewish quarters. This God of "uprightness through faith" is not only the God of the Jewish people. So Paul insinuates the

equal standing of Jew and Gentile. What Paul says here, he will explain at greater length in chaps. 9–11.

Is he not also the God of Gentiles? Yes, even of Gentiles! In asking this question, Paul is alluding to Ps 66:8, which in the LXX reads, *eulogeite, ethnē, ton theon hēmōn,* "Bless our God, o nations." Cf. Ps 117:1, which Paul will quote in 15:11; cf. Ps 47:9; Mal 1:11. In other words, Israel's own psalter and prophets recognized that the "nations" (*ethnē*) were called upon to praise Yahweh and that he is their God too.

30. *For God . . . is one.* Lit., "because one is the God, who will. . . ." The predicate *heis,* "one," is put emphatically in the first position in the sentence; in my translation it is placed at the end of the sentence to bring out its force in English. Compare 1 Cor 8:6, "but for us there is one God, the Father, from whom are all things and for whom we exist." This belief is the cardinal tenet of Israelite faith, "Listen, o Israel! The LORD is our God, the LORD alone!" (Deut 6:4; cf. Deut 32:29; Isa 43:10–12; 44:6; 45:6). Paul thus traces to the monotheism of Israel the unique relationship of all human beings to him. He insists that God not only justifies human beings gratuitously, but also offers that grace to all human beings alike. He thus asserts not only that the same God justifies both Jew and Gentile, but also that he is "one." See Demke, "Ein Gott."

The clause is introduced by *eiper* in many MSS ($\aleph^*$, A, B, C, D¹, 6, 365, 1506, 1739), which could mean "if indeed" or "because, for," as translated above; but in some MSS ($\aleph^2$, D*, F, G, K, Ψ, and the *Koinē* text-tradition) the reading is *epeiper,* "because indeed." See the NOTE on 8:9.

who will justify both the circumcised in virtue of their faith and the uncircumcised through their faith. Paul again contrasts *peritomē,* "circumcision," with *akrobystia,* "uncircumcision" (see the NOTE on 2:25), and *ek pisteōs* (for the former) and *dia tēs pisteōs* (for the latter). In both cases, for Jews and Gentiles, "faith" is the important, operative element. Different as people though they are, they are declared equal before God in the matter of faith. Through faith in Christ Jesus Paul has found that which unites pagan and Jewish humanity, which breaks down the barrier between them, because the demand of observance of the Mosaic law is not the sole way to salvation (see Eph 2:15–16). The fut. *dikaiōsei* is probably to be taken as gnomic, expressing an expected, customary action of God (BDF §349), but it could also be understood eschatologically (cf. 5:19), especially if Paul is echoing here a traditional Christian utterance, as Schlier thinks (*Römerbrief,* 118).

Although the preps. *ek* and *dia* differ, they may be merely a literary variant to suit the contrast, as Augustine (*De Spiritu et littera* 29.50 [CSEL 60.205]) and many modern commentators have understood them; so Dunn, *Romans,* 189; Kuss, *Römerbrief,* 178; Lagrange, *Romains,* 80. See the use of the same preps. in 4:11–12, and compare the use of *dia* and *en* in 5:10; 1 Cor 3:11. A few commentators, however, have tried to see a difference in the use of *ek* and *dia.* The latter might refer to Jesus' expiatory death for the redemption of the Gentiles (see Phil 2:8), whereas *ek pisteōs* is used of the Jews in a more fundamental sense in view of their share in the blessings made to faithful Abraham and may echo Hab 2:4, quoted in 1:17. So Origen, *In ep. ad Romanos* 3.10 [PG 14.955–57]); Theodore of Mopsuestia, *In ep. ad Romanos* 3:30 [PG 66.796]); Gaston (*Paul*, 173), Schlatter (*Gottes Gerechtigkeit*, 155–56); Stowers ("*Ek pisteōs*"); Zahn (*Römer*, 205–6). But Paul certainly does not want to imply a distinction between Jews and Greeks, because for him the all-important thing is faith, which is required of both. *Pace* Gager (*The Origins*, 262), Paul does use "faith" here "as the equivalent of faith in Christ Jesus." It is not merely "a designation of the proper response to God's righteousness, whether for Israel in the Torah or for Gentiles in Christ." As Sanders rightly notes, "the only way to enter the body of those who will be saved is by faith in Christ" (*Paul, the Law*, 196).

31. *Are we, then, nullifying the law by faith?* Paul uses the vb. *katargein*, lit., "render ineffective" (*kata* + alpha privative + *ergon*), "nullify." He draws an obvious conclusion to his teaching about the role of faith in human existence and makes it into an objection from his imaginary interlocutor. He refuses to countenance the dismissal of the Mosaic law, i.e., not just the OT in general, but the Pentateuch, the five books of Mosaic legislation. Paul does not fully answer this objection here, when he is talking about boasting; but he will come back to the topic and will show that in the long run "faith working itself out through love" (Gal 5:6) enables a human being to fulfill the law, because "love is the fulfillment of the law" (Rom 13:10). That love is the fruit of faith itself; and so through faith the law is fulfilled; it is not nullified. In God's providence the Mosaic law was given to Israel to guide it in its relationship with him, but also to curb its tendency to boast in his sight because of the observance of that law. It was destined to silence the boasting of human beings, "that every mouth may be silenced and the whole world become accountable to God" (3:19). So Paul formulates the paradox that justification through faith has introduced into human life. He will return to it in another way in 8:2–4. "The gospel is without doubt God's will and thus nothing other than the very goal of OT law" (Kuss, *Römerbrief*, 178).

Paul does not mean by *nomos* only the OT in a general sense or simply Scripture as story, *pace* Rhyne (*Faith*). He means the Mosaic legal corpus, as it is used in v 31a and in the "deeds of the law" (v 28), i.e., deeds prescribed by the Pentateuch. *Nomos* as Scripture might make sense in v 31c, but it makes no sense in v 31a, as Lambrecht and Thompson rightly note (*Justification*, 48). *Nomos* as a legal corpus has to be retained both here and in chap. 4.

Sometimes interpreters think that underlying Paul's use of *katargein* and *histanein* in this verse is the rabbinic distinction between Hebrew or Aramaic *bṭl* and the causative of *qwm* (so Cranfield, *Romans*, 223–24; Käsemann, *Commentary*, 104), but it is far from certain. There is no evidence that Jewish interpreters of the Mosaic law in Paul's time used this distinction. *Pace* Käsemann (*Commentary*, 104), the rabbinic usage is not presupposed in 4 Macc 5:25, where the vb.

kathestanai refers to God's "setting up" the law; no counterpart of that wording is used; hence the distinction is nonexistent there. Not even Str-B (3.85) refer to it. See Thompson, "Alleged Rabbinic Background."

Certainly not! See the NOTE on 3:4.

We are rather upholding the law. Paul uses the vb. *histanein*, lit., "cause to stand," i.e., making the *nomos* valid. He does not explain how the doctrine of justification by grace through faith upholds the law, but that explanation will emerge in time during the course of his argument in this letter. Chapter 4 will be a partial explanation of this verse, insofar as Paul relates the problem of boasting to the story of Abraham, but he will return to the matter in a theoretical way in chaps. 8, 10, and 13. As chap. 4 will show, *nomos* has to be understood as a reference to the entire Mosaic legislation of the OT, including its ceremonial and cultic aspects, the unity of individual prescriptions that expressed the will of God for Israel. In insisting on faith as the one principle of salvation, and in linking it to the one God, Paul affirms the basic message of the OT, and in particular that of the Mosaic law itself, rightly understood.

BIBLIOGRAPHY

Baeck, L., *Paulus, die Pharisäer und das Neue Testament* (Frankfurt: Ner-Tamid, 1961), 7–37 (= "The Faith of Paul," *JJS* 3 [1952]: 93–100); *The Pharisees and Other Essays* (New York: Schocken, 1966).

Chadwick, H., "Justification by Faith: A Perspective," *One in Christ* 20 (1984): 191–225.

Demke, C., " 'Ein Gott und viele Herren': Die Verkündigung des einen Gottes in den Briefen des Paulus," *EvT* 36 (1976): 473–84.

Diprose, R., "Fede e opere," *Lux biblica* 1 (1990): 75–79.

Corsani, B., "*Ek pisteōs* in the Letters of Paul," *The New Testament Age: Essays in Honor of Bo Reicke*, 2 vols., ed. W. C. Weinrich (Macon, Ga.: Mercer University Press, 1984), 1.87–93.

Friedrich, G., "Das Gesetz des Glaubens Röm. 3,27," *TZ* 10 (1954): 401–17.

Giblin, C. H., "Three Monotheistic Texts in Paul," *CBQ* 37 (1975): 527–47, esp. 543–45.

Grässer, E., " 'Ein einziger ist Gott' (Röm 3,30): Zum christologischen Verständnis bei Paulus," *"Ich will euer Gott werden": Beispiele biblischen Redens von Gott*, SBS 100 (Stuttgart: Katholisches Bibelwerk, 1981), 177–205; repr. in *Der alte Bund im Neuen: Exegetische Studien zur Israelfrage im Neuen Testament*, WUNT 35 (Tübingen: Mohr [Siebeck], 1985), 231–58.

Harnack, A. von, "Geschichte der Lehre von der Seligkeit allein durch den Glauben in der alten Kirche," *ZTK* 1 (1891): 82–178.

Lafon, G., "Une Loi de foi: La Pensée de la loi en *Romains* 3,19–31," *RevScRel* 61 (1987): 32–53.

Lambrecht, J., "Why Is Boasting Excluded? A Note on Rom 3,27 and 4,2," *ETL* 61 (1985): 365–69.

Lambrecht, J. and R. W. Thompson, *Justification by Faith: The Implications of Romans 3:27–31*, Zacchaeus Studies, NT (Wilmington, Del.: Glazier, 1989).

Luck, U., "Der Jakobusbrief und die Theologie des Paulus," *TGl* 61 (1971): 161–79.

Lyonnet, S., "De Rom 3,30 et 4,3–5 in Concilio Tridentino et apud S. Robertum Bellarminum," *VD* 29 (1951): 88–97.

———, "La Justification par la foi selon Rom 3,27–4,8," *Études*, 107–43.

MacArthur, J., *Justification by Faith* (Chicago, Ill.: Moody, 1985).

Peterson, E., *Heis Theos: Epigraphische, formgeschichtliche und religionsgeschichtliche Untersuchungen*, FRLANT 41 (Göttingen: Vandenhoeck & Ruprecht, 1926).

Piguet, J.-C., "La Foi et les oeuvres: Un Dialogue interdisciplinaire," *RTP* 36 (1986): 291–96.

Räisänen, H., "Das 'Gesetz des Glaubens' (Röm 3.27) und das 'Gesetz des Geistes' (Röm. 8.2)," *NTS* 26 (1979–80): 101–17.

Rhyne, C. T., *Faith Establishes the Law*, SBLDS 55 (Chico, Calif.: Scholars Press, 1981).

Stowers, S. K., "*Ek pisteōs* and *dia tēs pisteōs* in Romans 3:30," *JBL* 108 (1989): 665–74.

Thompson, R. W., "The Alleged Rabbinic Background of Rom 3,31," *ETL* 63 (1987): 136–48.

———, "The Inclusion of the Gentiles in Rom 3,27–30," *Bib* 69 (1988): 543–46.

———, "Paul's Double Critique of Jewish Boasting: A Study of Rom 3,27 in Its Context," *Bib* 67 (1986): 520–31.

THEME ILLUSTRATED IN THE LAW: ABRAHAM WAS JUSTIFIED BY FAITH, NOT BY DEEDS (4:1–25)

◆

14. ABRAHAM JUSTIFIED BY FAITH (4:1–8)

4 ¹What, then, shall we say that Abraham, our forefather according to the flesh, found? ²If Abraham was justified by deeds, he has reason to boast, but not before God. ³For what does Scripture say? *Abraham put his faith in God, and it was credited to him as uprightness.* ⁴Now when a person labors, wages are not credited to him as a favor, but as what is due. ⁵But when one does not labor, yet puts faith in him who justifies the godless, his faith is credited as uprightness. ⁶So too David utters a beatitude over the human being to whom God credits uprightness apart from deeds: ⁷*Blessed are those whose iniquities have been forgiven, whose sins have been covered up;* ⁸*blessed is the man whose sin the Lord does not credit.*

COMMENT

In order to show that the justification of all human beings by grace through faith does not undo the law but upholds it, Paul now argues that his thesis was already a principle operative in the OT. He uses the story of Abraham in Genesis, a story drawn from Scripture itself, as an example that illustrates his treatment of the relation of boasting to the observance of the Mosaic law, as put forth in 3:27–31. Paul had appealed to the OT in 3:21, maintaining that his thesis was already announced by "the law and the prophets," but now he has to show that what he has affirmed in 3:21–31, and especially in vv 27–31, is bolstered by the OT itself. When Paul uses *nomos* in this chapter he means by it not just OT as Scripture, but the Mosaic law in Scripture, especially in vv 13, 14, and 16, where it stands in contrast to faith, and in v 15, where it is linked to transgression. Thus Paul's discussion in chap. 4 demonstrates how all human boasting is excluded. If Abraham had no reason to boast in God's sight, neither does any other human being. For precisely that reason Paul opens the discussion in chap. 4 with the conjunction *oun*, "then, therefore," making the discussion of Abraham a fitting conclusion to what he has said in 3:21–31.

In Galatians 3 the story of Abraham provided a major part of Paul's polemical development. In Romans 4 it is introduced more or less as an illustration of 3:27, that if anyone had a reason to boast, it would be Abraham, but also as an answer to the objection formulated in 3:31. Paul had cited, indeed, the testimony of "the law and the prophets" in 3:21 in support of his thesis; now he will show concretely and specifically that his thesis was operative in the story of Abraham. Thus Paul appeals to God's written word, accepted by Jews and Christians alike, as a formulation of divine truth. In writing to a Christian community that he himself has neither visited nor founded, he appeals to something that he knows his readers will not only understand but even accept, the testimony of Scripture.

Paul insists that his thesis concerns not a matter of justice, commutative justice (involved in the payment of wages for work that has been done), but a matter of sheer grace and favor. Abraham was reckoned upright because of his faith in God (4:1–8), not because of anything that he had done, not because of his circumcision (4:9–12), not because of any obedience to a law, but in virtue of a promise made to him by God (4:13–17). As a result, Abraham is the father of all believers, and his faith is the "type" of Christian faith (4:18–25). Because of that grace and favor Abraham is the prime example in the OT of someone who has no reason to boast.

The Genesis story has to be understood against the historical background of Abram as a seminomad wandering in the Syro-Arabian desert. He was part of the nomadic movement usually related to the nineteenth and eighteenth centuries B.C. According to the Yahwist account in Genesis 12, his base is Haran in Upper Mesopotamia, whither he has come with his father Terah from Ur, identified by a late gloss as a town in the land of the Chaldees (who appeared in southern Mesopotamia only centuries later). From Haran Abram is called by God to separate himself from his people and travel to the land of Canaan, first to Shechem, where God promises him, "To your descendants I shall give this land" (Gen 12:7); then to Bethel, where he builds an altar and first calls on the name of Yahweh (12:8); and then to Hebron, Gerar, and Beersheba. Because of a famine in the land of Canaan, Abram descends with his wife Sarai to Egypt. On his return to Canaan he and his nephew Lot divide the land between them. When Lot is carried off by the four foreign kings, Abram goes after them, defeats the kings, and brings Lot back in safety to Canaan. On his return Abram wonders to what purpose he has amassed so much wealth, because he has no heir. Then God appears to Abram and promises him a progeny as numerous as the stars. Abram takes God at his word, and from such belief and trust in God emerges the offspring of Abraham, who is the forefather.

In all of this account Abraham emerges as the paragon of uprightness. The OT picture of Abraham is further embellished in the later pre-Christian Jewish tradition. He is said to be "perfect in all his deeds before the Lord" and "pleasing in uprightness all the days of his life" (Jub. 23:10). "None has been found like him in glory; he has kept the law of the Most High" (Sir 44:19–20), and he did so because God had implanted "the unwritten law" in his heart (2 Apoc. Bar. 57:2).

For Paul's Jewish contemporaries Abraham, the forefather, was an ideal figure; they were his children, his offspring kata sarka, "according to the flesh." Because of him they derived their special relationship with God as the chosen people (Ps. Sol. 9:8–9); with him alone God had made his covenant, and he was considered by God to be "upright" (*ṣaddîq*). And yet, even he had no right to boast of that status in the sight of God. Paul, in interpreting the Genesis story of Abraham, thus removes Abraham from representatives of uprightness achieved by observing the law and makes of him the type of those who through faith are upright.

But what use does Paul make of Abraham in this passage? Is he simply a model or paradigm of faith for the faith of Christians, without any continuity between him and other believers, as Klein would have us believe ("Römer 4")? If Klein were right, there would be no notion of salvation history in Pauline thinking. Against such a denial Wilckens rightly argues ("Die Rechtfertigung Abrahams"). He is correct, for Paul conceives of the God of Christians as already the God who chose Abraham and called him to faith that he might become such a model or paradigm. There is, indeed, continuity between Abraham and Christian believers in a divine plan that embraces human history.

NOTES

4:1. *What, then, shall we say.* On the use of this rhetorical question, see the NOTE on 6:1. It usually occurs without any further modification. Most modern commentators join what follows here to this introductory phrase.

that Abraham, our forefather according to the flesh, found? The Greek text of this verse is not certain. As translated, it agrees with the reading of MSS ℵ*, A, C*, 81, 365, 1506, and of the Coptic versions, which have the word order, *heurēkenai Abraam ton propatora hēmōn kata sarka.* It is the *lectio difficilior*, and asks, What sort of uprightness was Abraham's? So Cranfield, Käsemann, and Wilckens. Some MSS (ℵ¹, C³, D, F, G, Ψ) and Latin versions read *patera*, "father," instead of *propatora*, "forefather," an insignificant variant. Cf. Isa 51:2, which may have influenced the reading here. MSS B, 6, 1739, etc. omit the infin. *heurēkenai: Abraam ton patera hēmōn kata sarka*, which would mean, "What then shall we say about Abraham our forefather according to the flesh?" This is the reading preferred by the *RSV*, *NEB*, Goodspeed, Leenhardt, Lyonnet, and BDF §480.5. Another group of MSS (K, L, P) links the infin. with *kata sarka*, "What shall we say Abraham . . . found according to the flesh?" This reading would imply that Abraham achieved something by natural powers. Besides being weakly attested, it is inconsistent with Pauline teaching. Much can be said for reading either of the first two.

Another interpretation (J. A. Bain, *ExpTim* 5 [1893–94]: 430) has also taken *kata sarka* not with *propatora*, but as modifying the infin. *heurēkenai*: "What shall we say? That we have found Abraham (to be) our forefather, according to the flesh" (i.e., by our own works)? But that is to introduce a consideration that seems wholly wide of the mark and contrary to Paul's basic attitude. The suggestion of R. R. Williams (*ExpTim* 63 [1951–52]: 91–92) to emend *heurēkenai* to *eirgasthai* is even more improbable, for it is conjectural and only compounds the difficulty. See Hays, "Have We."

Paul recalls the traditional Jewish understanding of Abraham as the father of all those circumcised, of those who are Jews "according to the flesh." Abraham was thus the one Jew in history found by God to be "upright." He of all of them might have found reason to boast.

Abraam is the spelling of the forefather's name in all the MSS of Romans. It follows the spelling of his name in the LXX of Gen 17:5, where the name is changed from *Abram* to *Abraam*. The former reflects the Hebrew *ʾabrām*, i.e., *ʾab* + *rām*, "the father (is) exalted." When in the P document it is changed to *ʾabrāhām*, it is explained as meaning *ʾab hămôn gôyīm*, "father of a throng of nations," which accounts for the *h*, but not for the *r*. The change of name symbolizes the divine election of Abraham and especially his call to a role in salvation history. Paul will allude to this change of name and its significance in v 17. The phrase "throng of nations" refers to the descendants of Isaac, Ishmael, and the children of Keturah (Gen 25:1–2). See further M. Liverani, "Un' ipotesi sul nome di Abramo," *Henoch* 1 (1979): 9–18.

our forefather according to the flesh. For this use of *kata sarka*, see the NOTE on 1:3. Paul speaks from his own Jewish background, and his question is indirectly engaging an imaginary Jewish interlocutor. Descent from Abraham was a source of pride for contemporary Jews; see Matt 3:9; Luke 3:8.

2. *If Abraham was justified by deeds*. Paul toys with the question, whether Abraham's status before God might have been merited by his deeds. Paul is reacting to a contemporary Jewish understanding of Abraham and his call. In a sort of midrash on Gen 26:5, "because Abraham obeyed me, keeping my mandate (my commandments, my ordinances, and my instructions)," Sir 44:19–23 extols him especially because "he observed the precepts of the Most High," and "when tested, was found loyal," and "for this reason, God promised him with an oath that in his descendants the nations would be blessed." The order of the items is important: precepts, testing (= found to be upright), then promises of a progeny. So contemporary Judaism embellished the story of Abraham, making him an observer of the Mosaic law even before it was promulgated and ascribing his uprightness, not to his faith, but to his loyalty when tested, i.e., when asked to sacrifice his only son (Gen 22:9–10). Cf. *Jub.* 6:19; 23:10; Wis 10:5; 1 Macc 2:52 ("Was not Abraham found faithful when he was tried; and it was credited to him as uprightness"); 2 *Apoc. Bar.* 57:2; even Jas 2:21. His defeat of the kings (Genesis 14) became in the Jewish tradition a source of merit, as did his testing or trial.

Possibly we have in this verse a mixed conditional sentence, with a contrary-to-fact protasis ("if Abraham had been justified"); one would expect the apodosis to have the imperf. indic. (with or without *an*). But instead of the imperf., Paul uses the present and ends the sentence as a simple real condition. His thoughts get ahead of his expression. See J. Lambrecht, "Unreal Conditions."

by deeds. Paul uses *ex ergōn* only, not *ex ergōn nomou*, "deeds of the law" (see the NOTES on 2:15 and 3:20). Paul goes back to the story in Genesis 15 itself and does not line himself up with the contemporary understanding of Abraham,

which ascribed his uprightness to his testing and observance of the law. Nevertheless, the Pauline tendency to state things generically, as he does here in omitting
"of the law," gives rise to an eventual misunderstanding of his teaching about the
role of deeds in human existence. See the COMMENT on 3:27–31.

he has reason to boast. I.e., perhaps before human beings. But Paul is speaking
on a theoretical level; in theory Abraham's deeds were good and perhaps the basis
of boasting. But Paul eventually rejects this idea too.

but not before God. Thus Paul aligns Abraham with the rejection of boasting
in 3:27. In reality, not even Abraham can boast, because his upright status before
God comes from divine grace and favor. Paul can so conclude, because his
conclusion is based on the premise of 3:27.

3. *For what does Scripture say?* Paul refers to the OT as *hē graphē*, as he will
again in 9:17; 10:11; and 11:2. This use of *hē graphē*, lit., "the writing," as an
abstract designation for Scripture is derived from such LXX passages as 1 Chr
15:15, where the Hebrew *kidbar YHWH*, "by the word of Yahweh," becomes in
the Greek *en logō theou kata tēn graphēn*, "by the word of God in Scripture." Cf.
Ezra 6:18. In the NT this term is frequently used for the OT Scriptures (e.g.,
Mark 12:10; 15:28; Luke 4:21; Acts 1:16; 8:32, 35; John 7:38, 42).

Abraham put his faith in God, and it was credited to him as uprightness. Paul
quotes Gen 15:6; cf. Gal 3:6. The quotation comes not from the MT ("Abram
believed Yahweh, and he credited it to him as uprightness," where one cannot tell
in the ambiguous Hebrew form who is crediting uprightness to whom), but from
the LXX (with the pass. vb. and the prep. phrase *eis dikaiosynēn*). Abraham
believed in Yahweh's promise of a numerous progeny, and this faith was "booked
to his credit" as uprightness (*şĕdāqāh*). By "faith" is meant Abraham's acceptance
of Yahweh at his word and his willingness to trust and abide by it even when he
had no perceptible evidence. It involved his personal confidence and included
hope in a promise that no mere human could guarantee (4:18). For Paul the OT
text, which makes no mention of any deeds, reveals that Abraham was justified,
i.e., was put in a right relationship with God, apart from any deeds; so he could
have no reason to boast before God.

The vb. *elogisthē*, "was credited," is a bookkeeping term figuratively applied
to human conduct (Ps 106:31; 1 Macc 2:52; Phlm 18; similarly *dialogizein*, 2 Sam
19:20); it translates Hebrew *ḥāšab lĕ*. It was thought that the good and evil deeds
of human beings were recorded in ledgers (Esth 6:1; Dan 7:10; *T. Benj.* 11:4;
2 Apoc. Bar. 24:1; *Jub.* 30:17; *Herm. Vis.* 1.2.1). The pass. *elogisthē* is to be
understood as a theological passive; Abraham's faith was counted *by* God as
uprightness, because God sees things as they are. Hence, this manifestation of
Abraham's faith was *de se* justifying. Cf. Jas 2:23.

But in the Jewish tradition after Paul, Abraham's faith was considered to be an
expression of monotheism and a merit (see 4 Ezra 9:7; 13:23; *Mekilta*, Exod 14:15
(356): "Shemaʿyah said, '(God uttered): The faith with which their father Abraham
believed in me, merits that I divide the sea for them, as it says, "And he believed

in Yahweh." ' " Even today, Gen 15:6 is thus interpreted, in terms of the "merit of the fathers," zĕkût ʾābôt: "He put his trust in Jahweh, who accounted it to his merit" (E. A. Speiser, *Genesis*, AB 1 [Garden City, N.Y.: Doubleday, 1964], 110).

In the OT the same cl. *kai elogisthē autō eis dikaiosynēn* is used of Phinehas in Ps 106:31. Phinehas, the grandson of Aaron, put an end to the plague that struck Israel because of its idolatrous infidelity, by killing Zimri, an idolater, and his Midianite mistress, Cozbi (Num 25:6–9, 14–15). In this case, uprightness was credited to Phinehas not because of faith, but because of a deed (the NAB even translates it, "and it was imputed to him for merit"); cf. Sir 45:23–24; 1 Macc 2:26, 54. The contrast between Gen 15:6 and Ps 106:31 was hotly disputed in Reformation times. See Calvin, *Commentary on . . . Romans*, 161; cf. Steinmetz, "Calvin and Abraham."

In his *Novum instrumentum* of 1516, Erasmus departed from the Latin text of the Vg, which read, "Credidit Abraham Deo, et reputatum est illi ad iustitiam" (Abraham believed God, and it was reputed to him unto justice [Douay-Rheims]) and rendered it instead, "Credidit autem Abraham deo & imputatum est ei ad iusticiam" (Abraham believed God & it was imputed to him unto justice). In using "imputatum est" instead of "reputatum est," Erasmus echoed a term common among lawyers of his day and thereby related the vb. *elogisthē* to the Roman legal idea of "acceptilatio" (acceptilation): "Est autem acceptum ferre, debere, sive pro accepto habere, quod non acceperis, quae apud iureconsultos vocatur acceptilatio" (But that is to have to understand as accepted, or to consider as accepted, what you have not accepted, which is called acceptilation among the lawyers, 429). From this use of "imputatum est," Melanchthon, who used Erasmus's NT text, and Lutheran Orthodoxy eventually derived their idea of the forensic understanding of *dikaioun*, or imputed justification. Thus they formulated explicitly what was only implicit in Luther's teaching: "sola autem reputatione miserentis Dei per fidem verbi eius iusti sumus" (only by the accrediting of the merciful God, by faith in his word, do we become just [WAusg 56.287; cf. LuthW 25.24–75]); "extrinsecum nobis est omne bonum nostrum, quod est Christus" (all our good is outside of us, and this good is Christ [WAusg 56.279; cf. LW 25.267]). See further M. D. R. Willink, "Imputed Righteousness," *Theology* 15 (1927): 221–22; J. Resewski, "Ist die altlutherische Lehre von der *iustitia imputata* bei Paulus begründet?" ZST 16 (1939): 325–49; McGrath, *Iustitia Dei*, 2.31; " 'The Righteousness of God' from Augustine to Luther," ST 36 (1982): 403–18.

4. *Now when a person labors, wages are not credited to him as a favor, but as what is due.* Lit., "to the laborer wages are not credited by way of a favor, but by way of a debt." The laborer has a strict right to the profit of his labor; it is a matter of commutative justice. Paul introduces the comparison to illustrate what he said in v 2. Cf. 11:6.

5. *But when one does not labor, yet puts faith in him who justifies the godless.*

Paul contrasts faith with wage-earning labor; justice rules the latter but not the former. The phrase *epi ton dikaiounta ton asebē*, lit., "in the one justifying the godless," is derived from the OT itself (Exod 23:7; Isa 5:23). It does not become a theoretical expression of Abraham's belief. Nor does it mean that Abraham was himself *asebēs*, "ungodly," before he put his faith in Yahweh, even though Jewish tradition considered Abraham a *gēr*, "stranger, sojourner, alien" (Gen 23:4), one called from paganism. For at the moment of Abraham's putting his faith in Yahweh, he had already been called and was scarcely "godless." The phrase is instead a generic Pauline description of God himself: one who justifies the godless, one who acquits the sinner. Thus for Paul, even Abraham was dependent on a God who "justifies the godless." God not merely confirms the good that people may do, but takes the initiative to restore a world that cannot save itself, to bring the godless sinner into a right relation with himself. Cf. Gal 2:16. For the way the later rabbinic tradition understood this phrase used of Abraham and Job, see A. Kolenkow, "Ascription."

his faith is credited as uprightness. Paul thus sums up his basic thesis. He appeals to the example of Abraham who was upright in God's sight neither through the law nor through circumcision. So Abraham became the marking point in human history; before him all humanity was an undifferentiated mass. After him human beings were divided into two groups: the circumcised, the people of God, and the uncircumcised, the godless and idolatrous pagans.

6. *So too David utters.* Paul cites not only the example of Abraham, the Upright One, but also the authority of David, "the man after God's own heart" (1 Sam 13:14). As did his Jewish contemporaries, Paul regards David as the author of the psalms, even though the psalm to be quoted (Ps 32:1–2) is usually considered one of the psalms of personal thanksgiving, dating from a period later than David himself. In the MT it bears the ancient title *lěDāwīd maśkîl*, "of David. A *maskil*" (NAB), and in the LXX *tō Dauid syneseōs*, "of David, (a psalm) of understanding/instruction."

a beatitude over the human being to whom God credits uprightness. Paul uses the technical expression *makarismos*, "macarism, beatitude," which sums up the happy status of the person so acquitted by God, i.e., one who finds a status of rectitude or right relationship before God the Judge. The "beatitude" is expressed in the two verses of the psalm to be quoted.

apart from deeds. Even though there is no mention of *erga* in the psalm to be quoted, Paul boldly adds this phrase. These important words are put in the emphatic final position in the introductory sentence, immediately preceding the words of the psalm itself.

7–8. *Blessed are those whose iniquities have been forgiven, whose sins have been covered up; blessed is the man whose sin the Lord does not credit.* Paul quotes Ps 32:1–2 exactly according to the LXX, which is almost a literal translation of the MT (the LXX omits "to him"). It is a psalm of personal thanksgiving for healing received. Thus another part of the OT, the Writings, is cited to illustrate

Paul's thesis, which began with a pentateuchal passage, Gen 15:6. Paul is probably using the mode of Jewish exegesis that is known in the later rabbinic tradition as *gĕzĕrāh šāwāh* (lit., "equal decision"), according to which identical words, occurring in two different places in Scripture, may be used as the basis for mutual interpretation. Thus the vb. *logizesthai* occurs in Psalm 32 as well as in Gen 15:6, where it is used of Abraham while he was still uncircumcised. Hence Paul cites not only Gen 15:6, but also Ps 32:1-2, in order to show that Abraham, while still uncircumcised, was credited with uprightness and thus became the father of all believing pagans (4:11b) and father as well of all believing Jews (4:12).

The beatitude is uttered on the human being who has been healed, whose sins are forgiven by God (the passive is theological). "Covered up" is merely another way of saying "forgiven," i.e., they are put out of sight by God. The parallel verse makes the same point by stating that God does not book the sin in the ledger of life against a person. The verbs, then, "forgive, cover up, take no account of" simply are literary ways of expressing the same thing, the pardon of sin, which is an obstacle to the status of human rectitude in the sight of God. They express the negative side of the gratuity of divine mercy. Only the Lord can produce such effects, and human beings must trust him and be surrounded by his kindness (Ps 32:10). The words of the psalm do not mean that the sins remain, whereas God's benevolence merely covers them over. Thus both witnesses, Abraham and David, show that the OT itself supports Paul's thesis of graced justification through faith. In this way his teaching not only "upholds" the law (3:31), but shows that Abraham too had no reason to boast.

On *ou mē* with the subjunctive as an emphatic negation, see BDF §365.3.

In the Middle Ages, the "iniquities" of which Paul speaks in citing the OT were interpreted in terms of original sin, and specifically of its *fomes peccati,* . . . *concupiscentia vel concupiscibilitas, sive lex membrorum,* "the tinder of sin . . . concupiscence or possible concupiscence, or the law of the members" (Peter Lombard, "Collectanea," ad 4:7 [PL 191.1368–69]). See the NOTE on 6:12.

BIBLIOGRAPHY

Aletti, J.-N., "L'Acte de croire pour l'apôtre Paul," *RSR* 77 (1989): 233–50.

Bain, J. A., "Romans iv. 1," *ExpTim* 5 (1893–94): 430.

Baird, W., "Abraham in the New Testament: Tradition and the New Identity," *Int* 42 (1988): 367–79.

Berger, K., "Abraham in den paulinischen Hauptbriefen," *MTZ* 17 (1966): 47–89, esp. 63–77.

Bitjick Likeng, P., "La Paternité d'Abraham selon Rom. 4, 1–25," *RAT* 4 (1980): 153–86.

Dietzfelbinger, C., *Paulus und das Alte Testament: Die Hermeneutik des Paulus, untersucht an seiner Deutung der Gestalt Abrahams,* TEH 95 (Munich: Kaiser, 1961).

Dunn, J. D. G., "Some Ecumenical Reflections on Romans 4," *Aksum—Thyateira: A Festschrift for Archbishop Methodios of Thyateira and Great Britain*, ed. G. D. Dragas (London: Thyateira House, 1985), 423–26.

Fahy, T., "Faith and the Law: Epistle to the Romans, Ch. 4," *ITQ* 28 (1961): 207–14.

Goppelt, L., "Paulus und die Heilsgeschichte: Schlussfolgerungen aus Röm. iv und I Kor. x. 1–13," *NTS* 13 (1966–67): 31–42.

Guerra, A. J., "Romans 4 as Apologetic Theology," *HTR* 81 (1988): 251–70.

Hays, R. B., " 'Have We Found Abraham to Be Our Forefather According to the Flesh?' A Reconsideration of Rom 4:1," *NovT* 27 (1985): 76–98.

Heidland, H. W., *Die Anrechnung des Glaubens zur Gerechtigkeit: Untersuchungen zur Begriffsbestimmung von "ḥšb" und logizesthai*, BWANT 4.18 (Stuttgart: Kohlhammer, 1936), 134–56.

Jacob, E., "Abraham et sa signification pour la foi chrétienne," *RHPR* 42 (1962): 148–56.

Jeremias, J., "Zur Gedankenführung in den paulinischen Briefen," *Studia paulina in honorem Johannis de Zwaan septuagenarii* (Haarlem: Bohn, 1953), 146–54, esp. 149–51.

Johnson, B., "Who Reckoned Righteousness to Whom?" *SEA* 51–52 (1986–87): 108–15.

Käsemann, E., "The Faith of Abraham in Romans 4," *Perspectives*, 79–101.

Klein, G., "Exegetische Probleme in Römer 3,21–4,25," *EvT* 24 (1964): 676–83.

————, "Heil und Geschichte nach Römer IV," *NTS* 13 (1966–67): 43–47.

————, "Römer 4 und die Idee der Heilsgeschichte," *EvT* 23 (1963): 424–47; repr. in *Rekonstruktion und Interpretation*, 145–69.

Kolenkow, A., "The Ascription of Romans 4:5," *HTR* 60 (1967): 228–30.

Kraussold, [L.], "Ueber Römer 4, 2," *TSK* 15 (1842): 783–90.

Küssner, [G.], "Studie über Röm. IV.1 sqq.," *ZWT* 34 (1891): 450–64.

Lambrecht, J., "Unreal Conditions in the Letters of Paul: A Clarification," *ETL* 63 (1987): 153–56.

Liverani, M., "Un' ipotesi sul nome di Abramo," *Henoch* 1 (1979): 9–18.

Moberly, R. W. L., "Abraham's Righteousness (Genesis xv 6)," *Studies in the Pentateuch*, VTSup 41, ed. J. A. Emerton (Leiden: Brill, 1990), 103–30.

Moore, R. K., "Romans 4.5 in TEV: A Plea for Consistency," *BT* 39 (1988): 126–29.

Mussner, F., *Mort et resurrection*, 19–29.

Oeming, M., "Ist Genesis 15,6 ein Beleg für die Anrechnung des Glaubens zur Gerechtigkeit?" *ZAW* 95 (1983): 182–97.

Rad, G. von, "Faith Reckoned as Righteousness," *The Problem of the Hexateuch and Other Essays* (New York: McGraw-Hill, 1966), 125–30.

Schmitz, O., "Abraham im Spätjudentum und im Urchristentum," *Aus Schrift und Geschichte: Theologische Abhandlungen Adolf Schlatter . . . dargebracht* (Stuttgart: Calwer-Verlag, 1922), 99–123.

Spohn, W., "Ueber Röm. 4, 2," *TSK* 16.1 (1843): 429–36.

Steinmetz, D., "Calvin and Abraham: The Interpretation of Romans 4 in the Sixteenth Century," *Church History* 57 (1988): 443–55.

Volkmar, G., "Ueber Röm. 4,1 und dessen Zusammenhang," *ZWT* 5 (1862): 221–24.

Wilckens, U., "Die Rechtfertigung Abrahams nach Römer 4," *Rechtfertigung als Freiheit*, 33–49.

Wilken, R. L., "The Christianizing of Abraham: The Interpretation of Abraham in Early Christianity," *CTM* 43 (1972): 723–31.

Williams, R. R., "A Note on Romans iv. 1," *ExpTim* 63 (1951–52): 91–92.

Willink, M. D. R., " 'Imputed Righteousness' (Röm. iv)," *Theology* 15 (1927): 221–22.

15. ABRAHAM JUSTIFIED BEFORE HE WAS CIRCUMCISED (4:9–12)

4 ⁹Is this beatitude uttered, then, only over the circumcised, or over the uncircumcised too? We maintain that "faith was credited to Abraham as uprightness." ¹⁰Under what circumstances, then, was it credited (to him)? While he was circumcised or not (yet) circumcised? He was not circumcised, but (was still) uncircumcised! ¹¹He accepted the sign of circumcision as the seal of uprightness that comes through faith while he was still uncircumcised. Thus he was to be the father of all who believe when uncircumcised, so that uprightness might also be credited to them, ¹²as well as the father of those circumcised, who are not only such but who walk in his footsteps along the path of faith that Abraham our father once walked while he was still uncircumcised.

COMMENT

One of the major elements in the Abraham story of Genesis is the circumcision of himself and his sons in fulfillment of the pact that Yahweh makes with him in chap. 17. Picking up on the argument in 2:25–28, Paul now introduces that item of Abraham's story into his discussion. Obeying that commandment of God might be considered a "deed," because of which Abraham might be thought to have merited his justification, something about which he could boast. But Paul insists that Abraham put his faith in Yahweh's promise and thereby was reckoned upright, even before he was asked by God to adopt circumcision, and therefore independently of it. Thus Abraham had no reason to boast and became the father not only of the circumcised, of the people of Israel, by the adoption of that rite, but also the father of all believers, of those who follow in his footsteps along the path of faith. Thus Paul plays on two aspects of the Abraham story in Genesis. As a Jew himself, "circumcised on the eighth day, of the people of Israel" (Phil 3:5),

Paul implicitly acknowledges his own heritage as belonging to "the circumcision," but he also recognizes the role of Abraham as the father of all believers. Thus no one can cite Abraham's obedience to Yahweh in carrying out circumcision as something over which Abraham could boast. He was indeed loyal to Yahweh's command in adopting such a rite for himself and his descendants, but in Paul's view that was a secondary development; it had nothing to do with his status of uprightness before Yahweh.

One must remember that the Abraham story in Genesis is conflated of various sources. Whereas the story of God's pact with Abraham and his promises in Gen 15:1–21 are derived from the J/E (Yahwist/Elohist) source, that of the covenant of circumcision in Gen 17:1–27 is from the Priestly source. Whether historically the circumcision of Abraham followed or preceded his trust and faith in Yahweh's promise is a question that cannot be answered. In any case, Paul is not introducing a chronological argument, but he is following the literary sequence of the Abraham story in Genesis; so he argues that Abraham was justified by his faith (Genesis 15) *before* he entered into the pact of circumcision with Yahweh (Genesis 17). Hence justification came to Abraham through faith and not by virtue of circumcision, and consequently it comes now to people of faith, and not only to those who are circumcised. Thus the precedent of Abraham in the OT confirms Paul's thesis, that justification by grace through faith apart from the deeds of the law means that both Jew and Gentile stand on an equal basis before the impartial God who judges them. In the case neither of the Jew nor of the uncircumcised Gentile is there any place for boasting. Again, Paul shows how the law of the OT is upheld by his thesis of justification by faith.

Circumcision or the removal of the male foreskin is known to have been practiced by many primitive tribes the world over. The custom came into Israel apparently from Egypt, where it was practiced in the Old Kingdom, as is evident from mummies and wall drawings depicting the operation. The Philistines and pre-Israelite inhabitants of Canaan were apparently not circumcised; nor were the Assyrians or the Babylonians to the east. Among Israel's immediate neighbors it was practiced by Edom, Ammon, and Moab (Jer 9:24–26). Israelite tradition traced the origin of circumcision to the covenant of Abraham with Yahweh. It was normally performed on the eighth day (Gen 17:12; 21:4; Lev 12:3; cf. Luke 1:59; Phil 3:5) originally by the father of the house, but later by a *môhēl*. According to the NT, the naming of the child was associated with the circumcision (Luke 1:59), but this custom is not known to have existed among Palestinian Jews until several centuries later (see Fitzmyer, *Gospel According to Luke*, 380). The rite became of extreme importance at the time of the Babylonian captivity, when Israel lived among the uncircumcised Babylonians. In Hellenistic times, when Jews adopted customs from the Greeks, took part in games of the gymnasia, and played in the nude, they were often subjected to mockery and tried to have the mark of circumcision removed (see 1 Macc 1:14–15; cf. 1:48, 60). Circumcision was held to give access to the world to come. Cf. CD 16:4–6; *Jub.* 15:31–33. In rabbinic times circumcision was the sign of the Abrahamic and Mosaic covenants; Paul himself alludes to this idea in 2:28–29. "The state of uncircumcision is the impurity of all impurities . . . , the mistake of all mistakes" (*Pirqe de Rabbi Eliezer* 29B 4:36). All benefits were believed to come to Israel because it practiced circumcision; because of it Israelites would be saved in the days of the Messiah and preserved from Gehenna. "Abraham will sit at the entrance of Gehenna and will not permit any circumcised Israelite to descend into it." "And what does he do with those who have sinned immoderately in their lives? He removes the foreskins from children who have died before circumcision and puts them on the hardened sinners so that they can descend into Gehenna" (*Gen. Rabbah* 48.8). See Kuss, *Römerbrief*, 94–95.

NOTES

4:9. *Is this beatitude uttered, then, only over the circumcised, or over the uncircumcised too?* The question is elliptical; *legetai*, "is said, is uttered," has to be supplied (BDF §481). Paul himself raises this question because there is no reference to circumcision in the verses of the psalm just cited. He may have been aware that some Jewish teachers considered that the beatitude was reserved for the circumcised Jew. Such a teaching emerges in the later rabbinic tradition (see Str-B 3.203). In any case, Paul insists that the beatitude is not limited to circumcised Jews. It all depends on how the status of uprightness before God is achieved. Because in Abraham's case it came about through faith, and not by deeds of the law, so too the beatitude can be applied to nonobservers of the law, if they too become believers. David's beatitude applies as well to the uncircumcised believer. This Paul will show by citing the example of Abraham himself.

We maintain that "faith was credited to Abraham as uprightness." Faith, and only faith, was the operative element. Again Paul cites Gen 15:6, introducing it with the emphatic *legomen*, "we say," repeating what he said in v 3.

10. *Under what circumstances, then, was it credited?* Paul is again in dialogue with an imaginary interlocutor. He makes use of a rhetorical question (BDF §496.1) and wants to know how Abraham came to be so regarded by God.

While he was circumcised or not (yet) circumcised? Lit., "being in circumcision or in uncircumcision?" Paul asks about the time sequence: Which came first, Abraham's justification or his circumcision?

He was not circumcised, but (was still) uncircumcised! So Paul affirms as he argues from the literary sequence of the Genesis story: Abraham was accounted upright in Genesis 15, but was circumcised in Genesis 17. Therefore, circumcision had nothing to do with his being reckoned upright. It came into Abraham's life only at a later stage.

11. *He accepted the sign of circumcision as the seal of uprightness that comes through faith while he was still uncircumcised.* Paul does not reject circumcision but seeks to order it properly in God's plan of salvation. He plays on a phrase used

in Gen 17:11, where circumcision is called *'ôt běrît*, "the sign of the covenant" (LXX: *sēmeion diathēkēs*), between Yahweh and Abraham's family. In Acts 7:8 it is referred to as *diathēkē peritomēs*, "a covenant of circumcision." Later rabbis, however, regarded it as the sign of the *Mosaic* covenant, for it served to distinguish Israel from the nations (cf. Judg 14:3; 1 Sam 14:6). Significantly, Paul avoids mention of the covenant or pact, and "the sign of the covenant" becomes for him "the seal of uprightness." He seems to have identified the covenant too much with the law and insinuates that God's true covenant was made with people of faith, a faith that imitates that of Abraham while he was still uncircumcised. According to Paul, circumcision was indeed a "seal," a sign given to Abraham and his posterity, but a sign given to Abraham as a person of faith. Because he believed in God, God made a covenant with him, and circumcision became a sign of that covenant, a seal of his uprightness through faith. On *sphragis*, "seal," see Dölger, *Sphragis*; Heitmüller, "*Sphragis*," 40–59.

Thus he was to be the father of all who believe when uncircumcised. When Abraham put his faith in Yahweh and was reckoned justified, he was as uncircumcised as any Gentile. His spiritual paternity is thus established vis-à-vis all believers (Gal 3:7). Circumcision cannot stand in the way of faith. Paul uses an infin. of purpose *eis to einai* (cf. BDF §402.2), thus expressing Abraham's destiny in salvation history. What Paul says about Abraham's faith has to be transferred to "faith in Christ Jesus" in the new aeon. Abraham is the father even of such believers; and all, both Jew and Gentile, must become believers like Abraham.

so that uprightness might also be credited to them. In imitation of the faith of Abraham, uncircumcised Gentiles may also come to enjoy the status of uprightness before God. This status is unmerited and independent of deeds (even of circumcision), depending only on faith.

The adv. *kai*, "also," is omitted in some important MSS (ℵ*, A, B, Ψ, 6, 81, 630, 1506, 1739, etc.), but read in other equally important ones (ℵ², C, D, F, G, and the *Koinē* text-tradition). Again, the def. art. *tēn* before "uprightness" is omitted in some MSS (ℵ, D*, C², 6, 365, 424, 1739). In some others it is replaced by the prep. *eis*; this wording would mean "so that it might be credited to them as uprightness." Other important MSS (B, C*, Dᶜ, F, G, Ψ, and the *Koinē* text-tradition) read *tēn*.

12. *as well as the father of those circumcised, who are not only such but who walk in his footsteps along the path of faith.* Lit., "as well as the father of circumcision, not only for those from circumcision but also for those walking in the footsteps of the faith of our father Abraham, (professed) in uncircumcision." In becoming the forefather of believers, Abraham did not cease to be the forefather of circumcised Jews. But Paul insists that they are to be regarded hereafter as his offspring, when they follow in his footsteps and imitate his faith. Abraham's spiritual paternity is an important aspect of God's salvific plan for all humanity.

The Greek MSS practically all read *tois stoichousin*, but many modern commentators (Sanday and Headlam, Lagrange, BDR §276.2) consider the art.

tois to be anomalous. But in retaining *tois*, I understand v 12 to be speaking of two groups, "those who are circumcised" and "those who follow the example of the faith that our father Abraham had before he was circumcised." In this way the word *peritomē* has two meanings in this verse: "father of the circumcised" would refer to spiritual circumcision, whereas *ek peritomēs* would refer to those physically circumcised. See Swetnam, "The Curious Crux"; Cerfaux, "Abraham."

that Abraham our father once walked while he was still uncircumcised. Paul terminates this paragraph by repeating his view of Abraham, who was a believer while still uncircumcised like any Gentile. Hence he has no right to boast before God. Nor is he an example of one who attained his upright status before God through observance of the law.

BIBLIOGRAPHY

Cerfaux, L., "Abraham 'père en circoncision' des Gentils (*Rom.*, IV,12)," *Mélanges E. Podechard: Études de sciences religieuses* . . . (Lyons: Facultés catholiques, 1945), 57–62.

Dölger, F. J., *Sphragis*, Studien zur Geschichte und Kultur des Altertums 5.3–4 (Paderborn: Schöningh, 1911).

Flusser, D. and S. Safrai, "Who Sanctified the Beloved in the Womb," *Immanuel* 11 (1980): 46–55.

Fox, M. V., "The Sign of the Covenant: Circumcision in the Light of the Priestly ʾôt Etiologies," *RB* 81 (1974): 557–96.

Heitmüller, W., "*Sphragis*," *Neutestamentliche Studien Georg Heinrici* . . . (Leipzig: Hinrichs, 1914), 40–59.

Kölbing, F. W., "Biblische Erörterungen: 2. Über die *klēronomia tou kosmou*, Röm. 4," *TSK* 18.2 (1845): 694–96.

Porporato, F. X., "De paulina pericopa Rom. 4,11–12," *VD* 17 (1937): 173–79.

Sasson, J. M., "Circumcision in the Ancient Near East," *JBL* 85 (1966): 473–76.

Swetnam, J., "The Curious Crux at Romans 4,12," *Bib* 61 (1980): 110–15.

16. AS WITH ABRAHAM, THE PROMISE COMES ONLY TO THE PEOPLE OF FAITH (4:13–25)

4 [13]It was not through the law that the promise was made to Abraham or to his posterity that he would inherit the world, but through the uprightness that came from faith. [14]For if the heirs are those who hold to the law, then faith has been emptied of its meaning and the promise nullified. [15]The law brings only wrath; but where there is no law, there is no transgression. [16]For this reason the promise depends on faith, that it might be a matter of grace so as to be valid for all Abraham's posterity, not only for those who adhere to the law, but to those who

share his faith. For he is father of us all; [17]as it stands written, *I have made you the father of many nations.* So he is in the sight of God in whom he put his faith, the God who gives life to the dead and calls into being things that exist not. [18]Hoping against hope, Abraham believed, so as to become the father of many nations according to what had been said to him, *So shall your posterity be.* [19]He did not weaken in faith when he considered his own body to be already as good as dead (being about a hundred years old) and the deadness of Sarah's womb. [20]Yet he never wavered in disbelief about God's promise, but, strengthened in faith, he gave glory to God, [21]fully convinced that God was capable indeed of doing what he had promised. [22]That is why Abraham's faith was credited to him as uprightness. [23]Those words "it was credited to him" were written not only for Abraham's sake, [24]but for ours too. It is also going to be credited to us who believe in him who raised from the dead Jesus our Lord, [25]who was handed over (to death) for our trespasses and raised for our justification.

COMMENT

Abraham's status of justification before God not only did not depend on his adoption of circumcision, but did not depend even on his observance of the law. Indeed, God's promise to Abraham came independently of the law. Thus Paul draws a third argument from the story in Genesis. He now exploits another element of the Genesis story, the promise made to Abraham for the future that he would have numberless progeny, a progeny not limited to those who would be descended from him physically, but a progeny of believers drawn from all of the nations. The passing on of this benefit of God's promise to Abraham's offspring could not depend on law. Paul realizes that the law could not be the norm of justification, for it would undo the role of faith. The law could not determine who the heirs of the promise would be. Indeed, he levels a baleful accusation against the law, without explaining here what he means by it (he will return to it later in chaps. 7–8). Instead he insists on the role of faith and grace in human life, as it would be lived by Abraham's posterity. Paul stresses God's promise that Abraham would be "the father of many nations," a promise made by the Creator God himself, who is all-powerful and can bring about all things. Not even Abraham's old age or the barrenness of Sarah's womb could be an obstacle to Abraham's faith. Because of that faith he had hope, and never wavered in disbelief about God's promise. That is why uprightness was credited to him. Thus Abraham's example shows how one is to interpret what God has done in Christ Jesus.

From these three examples of Abraham in Genesis Paul draws the lesson that the words in Genesis about Abraham's faith and uprightness have been recorded also for believers of future generations. Such believers are those who put their faith in the Creator God, who makes the dead live, the very one who raised from the dead Jesus our Lord. For he was handed over to death for the sake of the trespasses of such believers, but raised from the dead for the sake of their justification.

Thus "our justification" is the term that concludes part A of the doctrinal section of Romans.

NOTES

4:13. *It was not through the law that the promise was made to Abraham or to his posterity.* I.e., not through the Mosaic law (see the NOTE on 2:12). Paul speaks in the sg. of *hē epangelia*, "the promise," using the term in a collective sense, for in the Genesis story God makes several promises to Abraham: the promise that Abraham's name would be great (Gen 12:2), the promise of inheritance of the land of Canaan (Gen 12:7), the promise of an heir to be born of Sarah (Gen 15:4; 17:16, 19), the promise of a numberless posterity to be descended from him (Gen 12:12; 13:14–17; 17:8; 18:18; 22:16–18). Cf. Sir 44:21. In classical Greek *epangelia* normally means "announcement," but in Hellenistic Greek it took on more of the meaning of "pledge, assurance, promise" (Polybius, *History* 1.43.6; 7.13.2; Diodorus Siculus 1.5.3; 4.16.2; 1 Macc 10:15; Philo, *De mut. nom.* 37 §201; Josephus, *Ant.* 5.8.11 §307); cf. A. Sand, *EDNT* 2.13–16.

that he would inherit the world. This generic promise is not found in Genesis, but the Jewish tradition embellished the promises made to Abraham, and Paul echoes that tradition. The embellishment was based on the universality mentioned in Gen 12:3, "all the families of the earth shall be blessed in you." This universality came to be associated with the "inheritance" (Hebrew *naḥălāh*, Greek *klēronomia*) that Abraham and his offspring were to expect. At first, it meant an inheritance of "the land" as a permanent possession (Exod 32:13; Num 26:52–56; cf. Deut 6:10). In time, Abraham's inheritance was expressed as "the earth" (*Jub.* 19:21) or "the whole world," as in later rabbinic tradition (see Str-B 3.209); cf. 2 *Apoc. Bar.* 14:13; 51:3. Paul is implicitly assailing the Jewish view that all blessings came to Abraham because of his merit in keeping the law, which he was supposed to have known in advance (see the NOTE on 4:2). For Paul the heirs of the promise of inheriting the world are not the observers of the Mosaic law, but the people of faith; for him law and promise have not been interrelated. What Paul says of "inheritance" in the past will become "inheritance" in the Christian futurist eschatology of Eph 1:13–14, 18. See Hammer, "Comparison."

but through the uprightness that came from faith. Lit., "through the uprightness of faith." The gen. *pisteōs* is really epexegetical or appositional (BDF §167), but it has to be understood as the means whereby Abraham achieved his uprightness, i.e., the uprightness based on faith. In 4:11 Paul had set this cardinal tenet in opposition to the claim of circumcision; now he pits it against the Mosaic law itself. God's promises were made independently of the command to observe the Mosaic law.

14. *For if the heirs are those who hold to the law.* Lit., "for if those from the

law (are) heirs." If the only condition for the inheritance of the world were the observance of the law, then faith would have no role in human existence. Faith would be null and void.

then faith has been emptied of its meaning and the promise nullified. Lit., "faith has been emptied and the promise has been rendered ineffective." In other words, God's promise would be no promise at all, because an extraneous condition for such inheritance, foreign to the very nature of a promise, would have been introduced after the fact (cf. Gal 3:15–20). Paul creates a dichotomy: promise, faith, and grace opposed to law, transgression, and wrath.

15. *The law brings only wrath.* This verse is parenthetical, even if it expresses Paul's profound conviction. The prescriptions of the law, because they are not observed, produce transgressions (Gal 3:19) and so promote the reign of sin. Thus the law provokes the retribution described in Romans 2–3. Paul does not really explain this assertion here, but in time it will become clear what he means by it. The "wrath" whereof he speaks is divine wrath (see the NOTE on 1:18). When the law enters in, then there is scope for divine wrath coping with human transgression of it. Law, sin, and wrath become inseparable.

but where there is no law, there is no transgression. A "transgression" implies a word or deed that violates a law that has been set up. So if there is no law, there can be no violation of it (cf. 5:13). This is a cardinal tenet in Paul's view of the law (see Introduction, section IX.D). Without the law, evil may be vaguely apprehended, but it is not regarded as *parabasis*, "transgression" (see 3:20; 5:13). Because transgression, which calls down divine wrath, arises in a legal context, Paul implicitly concludes that the world needs a dispensation independent of law. Wrath is manifested not only against unrighteousness, but also against righteousness sought by observing the law, against law-righteousness. Cf. *Jub.* 33:15–17 for a kindred idea. MSS ℵ*, A, B, C, 81, 104, 945, etc. read *de*, "but," whereas other MSS (ℵ², D, F, G, Ψ, and the *Koinē* text-tradition) read *gar*, "for."

16. *For this reason the promise depends on faith.* Lit., "for this reason (it is) from faith." This cryptic statement picks up the thought of v 13. As the law and the promise cannot exist side by side, the law must yield. Faith is the all-important element, involving God's gracious promise.

that it might be a matter of grace so as to be valid for all Abraham's posterity. Lit., "in order that (it might be) according to grace so that the promise might be valid for all the posterity." I.e., all of Abraham's offspring who live by faith also live by grace; because of faith they experience God's gracious bounty in their lives. Paul uses *eis to* + infin. in a consecutive sense.

not only for those who adhere to the law, but to those who share his faith. The divine promise still holds good for the Jewish people descended physically from Abraham, but now all those who imitate Abraham's faith, whether Jew or Gentile, may find a share in it.

he is father of us all. I.e., without any discrimination. The promises made to the patriarch will be shared by all who share his faith. Paul, as the Apostle of the Gentiles, is here arguing for the equality of Gentiles with the Jews.

17. *as it stands written.* See the NOTE on 1:17.

I have made you the father of many nations. Paul cites Gen 17:5 according to the LXX, which is a paraphrase of the MT, "you will become a father of a throng of nations." See the NOTE on 4:1. Cf. Sir 44:19. He understands "many nations" as a term for Gentiles in general, the children of Abraham through faith. Cf. Gal 3:29. While the promise was made to Abraham in the physical sense in Genesis, Paul now shows that the promise has found a fuller fulfillment: "many nations" has come to include all those who become believers in Christ, who are reckoned as upright through faith. "Scripture, foreseeing that God would justify Gentiles through faith, preached the gospel aforetime to Abraham, saying, 'In you shall all nations be blessed' " (Gal 3:8).

So he is in the sight of God in whom he put his faith. After the argument ends with the citation of the OT, Paul adds a thought, alluding to the colloquy of Abraham with God in Gen 17:15–21. God had promised Abraham a progeny of many nations, but when Abraham looked at his situation, his barren wife and his old age, that promise seemed impossible. How could he become the father of many nations now that his capacity for parenthood was practically dead? And yet, he believed; he took God at his word. He believed the impossible, and from a human point of view it was such. Nevertheless he believed; he put his faith in God.

the God who gives life to the dead and calls into being things that exist not. So Paul characterizes the Creator God. He may be quoting indirectly a Jewish liturgical formula. The first part is similar to *Shemoneh Esreh* 2: "You, O Lord, are mighty forever, you who make the dead live" (NTB, 159). Cf. 2 Cor 1:9; *Joseph and Aseneth* 20:7 (*edoxasan ton theon ton zōopoiounta tous nekrous*, "they glorified God who gives life to the dead"). In Paul's context, however, it refers to the divine power by which the dead womb of barren Sarah came to conceive Isaac (Gen 17:15–21). Remotely, these clauses prepare for 4:24–25.

The second part of the verse is similar to 2 *Apoc. Bar.* 21:4, "you have called (into being) from the beginning of the world things that did not previously exist"; 48:8, "With a word you call to life what was not, and with mighty power you hold back what has not yet come to be" (AOT, 853, 866). Compare Isa 48:13; 2 Macc 7:23, 28–29; 1 Cor 1:28; *Constitutiones Apostolicae* 8.12.7. In this context Paul's words refer to the unborn Isaac. They also connote the influence of God on the numerous Gentiles destined to be called into being as children of Abraham.

18. *Hoping against hope, Abraham believed.* Lit., "who beyond hope in hope believed," i.e., contrary to all human expectation, he expressed his faith with hope. Although Abraham had many motives for despairing of ever having posterity, he believed, confident about what the divine promise inspired in him. Thus Abraham became the model of human believing. Faith is not some inner sanctimoniousness in contrast to external deeds; it is an unwavering reliance on

God's promise, which issues in hope. In the judgment of ordinary humans there was no hope; yet Abraham trusted God's promise, believed, and found hope. When one believes, there is no room for self-reliance.

so as to become the father of many nations according to what had been said to him. Abraham took God at his word and believed in his creative power to do what seemed impossible. Isaac thus became one "born of a promise" (Gal 4:23; cf. Gen 17:16, 19; 18:10).

So shall your posterity be. Paul quotes Gen 15:5 according to the LXX, which is an exact translation of the MT, *kōh yihyeh zarᶜekā*, where *zeraᶜ*, "seed" (in the LXX *sperma*), is used in the sense of "offspring, posterity," the fruit of the seed. The words are drawn from God's promise to Abraham, when he takes him outside and tells him to count the stars of the heavens, if he can. MSS F, G, and a of the VL add: *hōs hoi asteres tou ouranou kai to ammon tēs thalassēs*, "as the stars of the sky and the sand of the sea." But this is a copyist's harmonization of the text with that of the LXX.

19. *He did not weaken in faith when he considered his own body to be already as good as dead.* One might expect that faith would weaken as it was confronted with mounting problems and difficulties of a sort that might make it impossible. Yet Paul insists that Abraham's faith was strengthened. Disregarding Gen 25:1–2, which mentions six other children born to Abraham by Keturah, Paul alludes only to Gen 17:1–21: Abraham fell on his face and laughed when he heard that he, a man of ninety-nine years and with a body near death, would have a son.

MSS ℵ, A, B, C, 81, and 1739 read the positive *katenoēsen*, "(when) he considered." But MSS D, G, K, P, Ψ, 33, and the *Koinē* text-tradition read the negative, *ou katenoēsen*, "he was so strong in faith that he did not consider." The positive reading is preferred because Paul does not mean that Abraham in faith was closing his eyes to reality, "but that Abraham was so strong in faith as to be undaunted by every consideration" (*TCGNT*, 510). See B. Haensler, "Nochmals zu Röm 4,19 (Gn 25,1f)," *BZ* 14 (1916–17): 164–69. MSS ℵ, A, C, D, Ψ, and the *Koinē* text-tradition read the adv. *ēdē*, "already," whereas others (MSS B, F, G, 630, 1739, etc.) omit it.

being about a hundred years old. See Gen 17:1, "when Abram was ninety-nine years old"; cf. 17:17, "a man who is a hundred years old."

the deadness of Sarah's womb. See Gen 17:17, "Shall Sarah who is ninety years old bear a child?" Cf. Heb 11:11, "By faith Sarah too received power to conceive, even when she was past the age, since she considered him faithful who had promised."

20. *Yet he never wavered in disbelief about God's promise.* Paul passes over the fact that Abraham was convulsed in laughter at the thought that he might beget a son. In later Jewish tradition Abraham's "laughter" becomes an expression of his great joy (*Jub.* 16:19). Cf. Heb 6:13, 15. Some commentators take prep. *eis* in a causal sense, "because of God's promise he never wavered" (see Mantey, "The Causal Use of *eis*").

387

strengthened in faith, he gave glory to God. Paul plays upon the contrast of "weakness" (v 19) and "strength." Though "weakened" by the thought of his old age and Sarah's barrenness, Abraham was nonetheless "strengthened" by his faith in God's promise. Abraham did not trust his own powers or his own body; he trusted only God. Paul uses an OT expression, "give glory to God" (1 Sam 6:5; 1 Chr 16:28), to describe Abraham's reaction of grateful recognition to God. His uprightness is now ascribed to this reaction. So Paul describes the believing Abraham as the opposite of the ungrateful pagan of 1:21, 23. Cf. Luke 17:18.

21. *fully convinced that God was capable indeed of doing what he had promised.* Lit., "what had been promised." Paul again reflects on the power of the Creator God; recall 4:17.

22. *That is why Abraham's faith was credited to him as uprightness.* Lit., "why it was also credited to him. . . ." Only through faith does a human being find the status of rectitude before God. For a third time Paul quotes Gen 15:6 (see 4:3, 9). The adv. *kai*, "also," is omitted before the verb in some MSS (B, D*, F, G).

23. *Those words "it was credited to him" were written not only for Abraham's sake.* Paul admits the thrust of the Genesis story, as he acknowledges that Abraham's faith was booked to his credit. Abraham's faith is seen as the type of that of all who would seek to be upright in God's sight. Some MSS (D², 1241, etc.) add "for uprightness."

24. *but for ours too.* Paul now addresses the readers and identifies them with himself as Christians, using the first person plural in doing so. He has cited the story of Abraham to apply it to himself and his readers. He thus employs a feature of midrashic interpretation, modernizing the OT story to apply it to a new situation (see R. Bloch, *DBSup* 3.1263–65). This feature found its formulation in later Jewish midrash: "All that is recorded of Abraham is repeated in the history of his children" (*Gen. Rabbah* 40:8). Thus Abraham's faith is the pattern for Christian faith, because its object is the same: belief in God who promises to make the dead live, who promises to justify the sinner. See further 1 Cor 9:10; 10:11.

It is also going to be credited to us who believe. Uprightness will be booked to the credit of the Christian at the eschatological judgment, provided the Christian has imitated the faith of Abraham. Paul sees an exact correspondence between Abraham's faith and the faith of all Christians.

who raised from the dead Jesus our Lord. Abraham's faith in God, who makes the dead live (4:17), foreshadows Christian faith in God, who in a unique sense has raised Jesus from the dead. Because of faith, Christians are included among the children of the resurrection. Thus faith means not only that we believe in Christ's resurrection, but that we are also removed by his death and resurrection from the realm of sin and death and taken up into the status of uprightness and life. Christ's resurrection is attributed to the Father, as the one who has brought it about; so it is often expressed in Pauline writings (see Introduction, section

IX.B); cf. 1 Pet 1:21. The risen Christ Jesus is hailed as *Kyrios* (see 10:9). This verse and the following one are normally regarded as a Pauline quotation of an early Christian kerygmatic formula.

25. *who was handed over (to death) for our trespasses and raised for our justification.* The clause alludes to Isa 53:4–5, 11–12 and reveals the vicarious character of Christ Jesus' suffering in his role as the Servant of Yahweh who takes away human sin and achieves justification for human beings. In Isa 53:11 (LXX) sins *(hamartias)* and justification *(dikaioun)* are similarly contrasted, and in Isa 53:12 the Servant "was handed over for their sins." The two vbs. are to be understood as theological passives, a periphrasis for God (ZBG §236). Cf. 8:32. This verse is not to be understood as though Paul meant that human trespasses were removed by Christ's death and that human justification was achieved by his resurrection. They are so formulated in a literary parallelism; both effects are to be ascribed to the death *and* the resurrection (cf. A. Charbel, *Revista de Cultura Bíblica* [São Paulo] 12 [1975]: 17–28; J. M. González Ruiz, *Bib* 40 [1959]: 837–58). Paul does not always explicitly relate justification to the resurrection (3:24–26; 5:9–10), as he does here. The dual use of the prep. *dia* makes the parallelism clear.

The sense of the prep. *dia*, however, is disputed. Taylor translates it "because of" in both cases, without further explaining it. Michel is right in rejecting this meaning in the second part, that Jesus was raised up because we were justified through his death (Schlatter). Many commentators distinguish the use, understanding the first *dia* as causal ("because of our trespasses") and the second as final ("for the sake of our justification"); thus Cranfield, Käsemann, Kuss, Leenhardt, Michel, Schlier, and Wilckens. But because the cross and the resurrection are two intimately connected phases of the same salvific event, their juxtaposition is the result of the rhetoric of antithetical parallelism (Käsemann, *Commentary*, 129; cf. A. Charbel, "Ancora su Rom 4,25: Costruzione semitica?" *BeO* 18 [1976]: 28). "If Christ has not been raised, your faith is in vain" (1 Cor 15:17).

Greek Fathers (e.g., John Chrysostom, *In ep. ad Romanos* hom. 9.1 [PG 60.467]; Cyril of Alexandria, *De recta fide Or.* 2.51 [PG 76.1408]) understood the resurrection of Christ as the cause of justification. Many Latin Fathers attempted to integrate the two ideas, death and resurrection, but this attempt unfortunately minimized the causality of the resurrection, for it came to be regarded only as an appendage or even as an exemplary confirmation of Jesus' death, which they considered to be the real cause of the forgiveness of sins and justification (e.g., Ambrosiaster, *In ep. ad Romanos* 4.25 [CSEL 81.149–51]). In this regard, Augustine proved to be the exception among the Latins: "Traditus est propter delicta nostra, et resurrexit propter justificationem nostram. Non dixit, Traditus est propter iustificationem nostram, et resurrexit propter delicta nostra. In eius traditione delictum sonat, in eius resurrectione iustitia sonat. Ergo moriatur delictum, et resurgat iustitia" (He was handed over for our sins and rose for the sake of our justification. He [Paul] did not say, He was handed over for our justification and rose for the sake of our sins. In his being handed over sin is mentioned; in his resurrection justice is mentioned. Therefore let sin die, and let justice rise [*Sermones* 236.1; PL 38.1120]). Peter Lombard repeated Augustine almost verbatim (*In ep. ad Romanos* 4.25; [PL 191.1378]), but it remained for Thomas Aquinas to formulate the causality properly: "mors Christi fuit nobis salutaris, non solum per modum meriti, sed etiam per modum cuiusdam efficientiae . . . ; resurrectionem autem eius, qua rediit ad novam vitam gloriae, dicit esse causam iustificationis nostrae, per quam redimus ad novitatem iustitiae" (the death of Christ was salutary for us, not only by way of merit, but also by way of a certain efficiency . . . ; whereas he [Paul] calls his resurrection, by which he returned to the new life of glory, the cause of our justification, by which we return to the newness of justice [*In ep. ad Romanos* 4.3 (Parma ed., 13.47); cf. *Summa theologiae* 3.56.2 ad 4 (Parma ed., 4.248)]). See Vawter, "Resurrection"; Stanley, "Ad historiam."

The affirmation of the part played by Christ's death and resurrection in the objective redemption of humanity forms a fitting conclusion to part A of the doctrinal section of Romans. See Lyonnet, "La Valeur sotériologique de la résurrection du Christ selon saint Paul," (*Greg* 39 (1958): 295–318; Stanley, *Christ's Resurrection*, 171–73, 261; McNeil, "Raised." As Schlier sums it up (*Römerbrief*, 137):

With this traditional formula, which is derived probably from Hellenistic Jewish Christianity, the goal of the first major division of the Letter to the Romans is reached, and it is shown that the central affirmations of 3:21–31 about the manifestation of God's uprightness in Jesus Christ and about the justification through faith connected with it were already attested in the Scriptures (of the OT), indeed in the case of Abraham. In his uprightness it is a question of uprightness from faith. Circumcision has in no way any relevance to it, and it became only later its seal, with the result that Abraham became the father of believing Jews *and* pagans. Nor did the law have anything to do with it. God's promise was related to *dikaiosynē pisteōs*, to which grace corresponds, whereas law called forth only transgression and the judgment of divine wrath. Abraham, who from that time on was "the father of us all," believed against all likelihood and hoped against all hope and so gave glory to God. His faith is our faith, and his uprightness our uprightness. That is what the Scripture shows about him. It is only that his general faith in the God who gives life to the dead is specified in our faith, which experiences this God in the raising of our Lord Jesus from the dead. The God in whom we believe has already displayed in Jesus Christ the omnipotence of his *charis* and *dikaiosynē*, in which Abraham believed in hope and which he experienced as one who had hope.

BIBLIOGRAPHY

Baulès, R., "La Foi justifiante: Rm 4, 18–25," *AsSeign* n.s. 41 (1971): 9–14.

Delling, G., "Partizipiale Gottesprädikationen in den Briefen des Neuen Testaments," *ST* 17 (1963): 1–59, esp. 31–32.

Ehrhardt, A., "Creatio ex nihilo," *The Framework of the New Testament Stories* (Cambridge, Mass.: Harvard University Press, 1964), 200–23.

Hammer, P. L., "A Comparison of *klēronomia* in Paul and Ephesians," *JBL* 79 (1960): 267–72.

Hofius, O., "Eine altjüdische Parallele zu Röm. iv. 17*b*," *NTS* 18 (1971–72): 93–94.

Holtz, F., "La Valeur sotériologique de la résurrection du Christ selon S. Thomas," *ETL* 29 (1953): 609–45.

Kertelge, K., "Das Verständnis des Todes Jesu bei Paulus," *Der Tod Jesu: Deutungen im Neuen Testament*, ed. K. Kertelge; QD 74 (Freiburg im Breisgau: Herder, 1976), 114–36.

Klaiber, W., "Aus Glauben, damit aus Gnaden: Der Grundsatz paulinischer Soteriologie und die Gnadenlehre John Wesleys," *ZTK* 88 (1991): 313–38.

Kölbing, F. W., "Biblische Erörterungen: 2. Über die *klēronomia tou kosmou*, Röm 4,13," *TSK* 18 (1845): 694–96.

Lafon, G., "La Pensée du social et la théologie: Loi et grâce en Romains 4, 13–16," *RSR* 75 (1987): 9–38.

McNeil, B., "Raised for Our Justification," *ITQ* 42 (1975): 97–105.

Mantey, J. R., "The Causal Use of *eis* in the New Testament," *JBL* 70 (1951): 45–48.

———, "On Causal *eis* Again," *JBL* 70 (1951): 309–11.

Marcus, R., "On Causal *eis*," *JBL* 70 (1951): 129–30.

Mitchell, R. A., "Notes on Romans iv. 25," *ExpTim* 5 (1893–94): 187.

Neill, W., "Paul's Certainties: God's Promises Are Sure—Romans iv. 21," *ExpTim* 69 (1957–58): 146–48.

Patsch, H., "Zum alttestamentlichen Hintergrund von Römer 4,25 und I. Petrus 2,24," ZNW 60 (1969): 273–79.

Romaniuk, K., "L'Origine des formules pauliniennes 'Le Christ s'est livré pour nous,' 'Le Christ nous a aimés et s'est livré pour nous,' " *NovT* 5 (1962): 55–76.

Schenke, H.-M., "Aporien im Römerbrief," *TLZ* 92 (1967): 881–88, esp. 884–85.

Serrano Ursúa, F., "Historia de la salvación a la luz de Rom 4, 23–25," *Estudios Teológicos* (Guatemala City) 4 (1977): 117–44.

Sjöberg, E., "Neuschöpfung in den Toten-Meer-Rollen," *ST* 9 (1955): 131–36.

Stanley, D. M., "Ad historiam exegeseos Rom 4, 25," *VD* 29 (1951): 257–74.

Toit, A. B. du, "Gesetzesgerechtigkeit und Glaubensgerechtigkeit in Rom 4:13–25: In Gespräch mit E P Sanders," *Hervormde Teologiese Studies* (Pretoria) 44 (1988): 71–80.

Vawter, B., "Resurrection and Redemption," *CBQ* 15 (1953): 11–23.

Wegenast, K., "Römer 4,25," *Das Verständnis der Tradition bei Paulus und in den*

Deuteropaulinien, WMANT 8 (Neukirchen-Vluyn: Neukirchener-Verlag, 1962), 80–82.

Wiederkehr, D., *Die Theologie der Berufung in den Paulusbriefen* (Fribourg: Universitätsverlag, 1963), 148–52.

B. THE LOVE OF GOD FURTHER ASSURES SALVATION TO THOSE JUSTIFIED BY FAITH (5:1–8:39)

◆

17. *Theme Announced:* Justified Christians Are Reconciled to the God of Love; They Will Be Saved Through Hope of a Share in the Risen Life of Christ (5:1–11)

5 ¹Therefore, now that we are justified through faith, we are at peace with God through our Lord Jesus Christ, ²through whom we have gained access in faith to this grace in which we now stand and boast of our hope for the glory of God. ³Yet not only that, but let us also boast of our afflictions, since we know that affliction makes for endurance, ⁴endurance makes for character, and character for hope. ⁵Such hope does not disappoint, because God's love has been poured out into our hearts through the holy Spirit that has been given to us. ⁶While we were still helpless, Christ died at the appointed time for the godless. ⁷Rare, indeed, is it that one should lay down one's life for an upright person—though for a really good person one might conceivably have courage to die. ⁸Yet God shows forth his own love for us in that, while we were still sinners, Christ died for us. ⁹And so, since we are now justified by his blood, we shall all the more certainly be saved by him from the wrath to come. ¹⁰For if, when we were God's enemies, we were reconciled to him through the death of his Son, now that we are reconciled, we shall all the more certainly be saved by his life. ¹¹Yet not only that—but we boast of God through our Lord Jesus Christ, through whom we have now received reconciliation.

COMMENT

With this paragraph in Romans one moves into part B of the doctrinal section of the letter. Paul now proceeds from the question of salvation and justification to the consequences of faith in Christ Jesus. Whereas humanity left to itself without the gospel came only under the wrath of God, through the gospel and through the grace of God that it proclaims humanity now finds justification, redemption, expiation, and pardon of its sins. To bolster that position of humanity before God, Paul now explains how, as a result of such justification and salvation, human beings are at peace with God, and now God's love further manifests itself toward them.

393

Having established the justification of human beings by grace and through faith in Christ Jesus, Paul begins to discuss the Christian experience in itself and explains how salvation is assured for the upright. Once justified, the Christian is reconciled to God and experiences a peace that distressing troubles cannot upset, a hope that knows no disappointment, and a confidence that salvation is assured. For not only has God's uprightness been manifested toward humanity, but now his love is poured into hearts through the holy Spirit that is given to human beings. For Christ has died for all humanity to reconcile it to God, and through this reconciliation humanity will find its salvation. The emphasis in the paragraph is on God's love, on Christ Jesus as the mediator of that love, and on reconciliation as the effect produced by that love. Thus once again, three effects of the Christ-event are singled out: justification (5:1, 9), salvation (5:9–10), and reconciliation (5:1, 10–11). Note especially the contrast: justified by his blood, we shall be saved (5:9); reconciled by the death of his Son, we shall be saved by his life (5:10).

Verses 1–5 treat of hope of glory that "we," justified Christians, experience because of the manifestation of God's love for us. Verses 6–11 explain how God's love manifests itself in power to overcome human weakness, sin, and godlessness.

The death of Christ is foremost in Paul's mind as he develops this paragraph: *apethane*, "(Christ) died" (vv 6, 8); *en tō haimati*, "by his blood" (v 9); *dia tou thanatou tou huiou autou*, "through the death of his Son" (v 10). Note too how each clause in vv 6–8 ends with a form of the vb. *apothnēskein*. As he emphasizes the death of Jesus, however, the resurrection is not far from his mind, as one will recall from 4:25. Through both the death and the resurrection of Christ humanity finds its reconciliation with God.

As he presents his argument in this paragraph, Paul argues from experience, from the experience that the Christian has of justification and reconciliation, as the use of the first person plural throughout the paragraph shows clearly. The eschatological implication of the present in which Christians find themselves is thus paradoxical. The grounding of Christian hope is the death and resurrection of Jesus Christ.

Paul referred indirectly to the holy Spirit in 1:4; now he mentions it for the first time. It forms part of the new theme that is being announced in part B of the doctrinal section of Romans. That theme will be developed in chap. 8 (vv 2, 4–6, 9–11, 13, 15–16, 23, 26–27), which will treat extensively of the role of the Spirit as the dynamic force of vitality in Christian life.

The position of chap. 5 in the literary structure of Romans is a matter of no little debate. See Introduction, section VIII.

NOTES

5:1. *Therefore*. The particle *oun* serves to mark a transition to this new section. Paul broaches the consequences of justification by grace through faith. His full discussion of them will begin in chap. 6.

now that we are justified through faith. Lit., "justified from faith," expressed by the aor. pass. ptc., which connotes the once-for-all action of Christ Jesus on behalf of humanity. What is stated at the beginning of this verse is a summation of the latter section of part A, especially of 3:22–26. The mention of *dikaiōsis* in 4:25 is picked up now by the ptc. *dikaiōthentes.* Thus justification forms the basis of the further development of Paul's thought about Christian life and its destiny. Justification seems to be subordinated to reconciliation. Cf. Gal 2:16. On the phrase *ek pisteōs,* see 3:26, 30; 4:16.

we are at peace with God. The first effect of justification is that the Christian experiences peace, a notion that Paul will explain more fully in this paragraph in terms of reconciliation (vv 10–11), especially in v 2. "Peace" is to be understood, not in the sense of peace of mind or conscience about sins forgiven (Kühl, *Römer,* 160), nor only in the negative sense of the absence of war (Deut 20:12; 1 Sam 7:14; 1 Kgs 2:5; 5:26), but in the positive OT sense of *šālôm,* the fullness of right relationship that is implied in justification itself and of all the other bounties that flow from it. See Isa 32:17, "The effect of uprightness *(ma'ăśeh haṣṣĕdāqāh)* will be peace, and the result of uprightness, quiet and trust forever." Cf. Isa 53:5; Ps 85:11; and the NOTE on 1:7.

When human beings enjoy a correct relationship with God, their condition may be one of inner calm and quiet composure, of undisturbed conscience, but the essential thing is the experience of God-given salvation and the hope of glory. Those who are now at peace with God are no longer objects of wrath; for them Christ has removed all wrath. Reconciliation has been provided by God. See 5:10.

The better Greek MSS (ℵ*, A, B*, C, D, K, L, 33, 81, 1175) read *echōmen,* the pres. subjunct., "let us have peace with God," as Kuss, Lagrange, and Sanday and Headlam prefer to read the text. That would introduce a paraenetic nuance, and it has been so understood by patristic writers and others, making it the equivalent of *phylassein eirēnēn,* "keep peace" (with God), i.e., "let us now give evidence of this justification by a life of peace with God." But N-A[26] and most modern commentators prefer the reading *echomen,* the pres. indic., "we have peace" (as in MSS ℵ[1], B[2], F, G, P, Ψ, 0220), regarding the confusion of o with ō as auditory on the part of the copyist. Thus Paul's utterance is a statement of fact expressing an effect of justification, which suits the context better than the hortatory subjunctive. Here Paul is not exhorting human beings to manifest toward God a peaceful attitude, but is instead stating the de facto situation in which they find themselves, one of peace and reconciliation issuing from his grace and mercy and guaranteeing the hope of salvation, for they are no longer under wrath. See Crabtree, "Translation."

through our Lord Jesus Christ. Thus Paul expresses the mediation of Christ the reconciler and mediator in the Father's plan of salvation. In some form or other Paul will make frequent use of such a mediating phrase in 5:2, 9, 11, 17, 21 (cf. 1:5; 2:16); see the NOTE on 1:8. It connotes the present, actual influence of the risen Christ on the lives of Christians as he dispenses the salvation that comes from God himself. This mediating phrase is one of the strong arguments for reading the indic. *echomen* in this verse.

2. *through whom we have gained access in faith*. Or perhaps, "we have also gained access," but the stress on the adv. *kai*, "also," is unlikely, because *kai* is often used with a rel. pron. to indicate the independence of the clause (BDF §393b). The peace that Christians experience is derived from being introduced into the sphere of divine favor by Christ, who has, as it were, escorted them into the royal audience-chamber of God's presence. The noun *prosagōgē* is used in this sense in Xenophon, *Cyropaedia* 7.5.45. Christians are no longer alienated enemies of God, because their relations with him have been altered through the merits of Christ Jesus. Cf. Eph 2:18; 3:12.

Käsemann (*Commentary*, 133) thinks that *prosagōgē*, "access," has a "cultic" sense, "unhindered access to the sanctuary as the place of God's presence," but Dunn (*Romans*, 247–48) more rightly notes that neither this noun nor its verbal counterpart *prosagein* has any such connotation in the LXX. Nor indeed does 1QS 11:13–15, which Dunn admits might have such a cultic connotation.

Some MSS (א*, A, C, Ψ, and the *Koinē* text-tradition) add "in faith," but this reading is omitted by MSS B, D, F, G, so it is not solidly attested. Yet it is to be retained as the "catchword of the last two chapters" (Käsemann, *Commentary*, 133).

to this grace in which we now stand. Through Christ justified Christians enjoy the favor of God; they stand before his tribunal acquitted by the grace of Christ (cf. Gal 1:6). Their status of rectitude is not their own; it does not come from their merits, but from the grace of Christ. To depart from this status would be to "fall from grace" (Gal 5:4) and even to "nullify the grace of God" (Gal 2:21). Recall 3:24. The perfs. *eschēkamen*, "we have gained," and *hestēkamen*, lit., "we have taken our position," express the condition in which Christians now find themselves (see BDF §342.2).

and boast of our hope for the glory of God. Or "we pride ourselves in the hope. . . ." The second effect of justification is confident hope, which dominates this paragraph: the hope of eschatological salvation. That hope is centered on *doxa tou theou*, "the glory of God," which Paul in 3:23 recognized as the destiny of human life, but of which human beings by their sins fall short. Now through the mediation of Christ and his grace they can attain that eschatological destiny. See 8:18, 30; Gal 5:5. Paul's statement is a typical paradox: the Christian who boasts or exults puts that boast in something that is wholly beyond ordinary human powers, in hope. Yet hope is as gratuitous as faith itself; in the long run the boast relies on God himself. Whereas Paul excluded Jewish boasting in 3:27–31 (cf. 2:17, 23), he now establishes the sense in which Christians can really boast. Christ has made it possible that Christians should boast of a share in the glorious life of God himself. With the resurrection of Christ the aeon of the risen life has begun, and Christians may expect a share in it. Cf. Col 1:27; Titus 2:13.

Christians hope for the communicated "glory" of God, still to be attained, even though they have already been introduced into the sphere of "grace." The relation between *charis* and *doxa* should be noted, but it should not be transferred too readily (and without proper distinctions) to the later theological categories of *gratia* and *gloria*.

3. *Yet not only that.* MS D adds *touto*, "that," which is needed in the context but missing in most MSS.

let us also boast of our afflictions. Or "we also take pride in (our) afflictions." Divine grace, the basis of Christian hope, is mighty enough to give confidence even in the face of *thlipseis*, "hardships, troubles, afflictions," that might tend to separate human beings from Christ's love (see 8:35; 1 Cor 4:11–13; 7:26–32; 15:30–32; 2 Cor 1:3–10; 11:23–27). Paul is reflecting on his own experience and knows that justified Christians do not flee from the troubles of this world, in which they still live. Suffering and affliction become precisely the point at which hope is encountered and proves itself. The function of hope in Christian life is to motivate and develop conduct, endurance, and character. The sense of God's love is enough to enable Paul and all Christians to contrast the suffering and affliction with the hope that does not disappoint. In making this claim Paul is modifying slightly his Jewish heritage, for the upright Jew also sensed the value of sufferings: "The just one does not make light of it, when he is chastised by God" (*Ps. Sol.* 3:4). The vb. *kauchōmetha* is either subjunc. or indic. in form; it is difficult to say which is to be preferred in this case.

since we know that affliction makes for endurance. Paul is not advocating some sort of Pelagianism when he says that tribulation produces endurance, endurance character, and character hope, for the basis of it all is divine grace. Hence affliction endured is endured with the aid of God. Paul intends this clause to be understood as a general truth, almost as a proverb. *Hyopomonē* means, lit., "a remaining under" (a problem, suffering), hence "persistent patience." Cf. Jas 1:2–4 for a similar sapiential list of qualities; 1 Pet 1:6–7. See C. Spicq, "*Hypomonē*, patientia," *RSPT* 19 (1930): 95–106; A. M. Festugière, "*Hypomonē* dans la tradition grecque," *RSR* 21 (1931): 477–86.

4. *endurance makes for character, and character for hope.* Whoever patiently persists in trouble and suffering will in the end prove to be *dokimos*, "tested." No matter how strong the affliction, its goal is hope (attained with God's assistance). Thus the growth of moral life initiated by justification becomes the theme of these verses (Käsemann, *Commentary*, 133). Note the climax to which Paul's rhetoric mounts (see BDF §493.3). A similar rhetorical climax can be found in Wis 6:17–20.

5. *hope does not disappoint.* I.e., it does not put one to shame, an allusion to Pss 22:6 and 25:20 ("in you they trusted and they were not put to shame"). Paul stresses that the hope of God's glory is not illusory; it is founded on God's love of human beings. Hence the Christian will never be embarrassed by a disappointed

hope; implicit is a comparison with mere human hope, which can deceive. See Isa 28:16; Heb 6:18–19.

because God's love has been poured out into our hearts. This clause expresses why Christian hope does not disappoint. The certainty of divine love is the guarantee of Christian hope. Paul uses the phrase *hē agapē tou theou* again in 8:39 and in 2 Cor 13:13. It is not "our love of God," as many older commentators, following Augustine (*De Spiritu et littera* 32.56 [CSEL 60.215]), understood it, but "God's love for us" (subjective gen.), as the following phrase makes clear, and as most modern commentators have interpreted it (Cornely, Dunn, Käsemann, Kuss, Lagrange, Nygren, Prat, Schlier, Sickenberger, Zeller).

The image is that of life-giving water being poured out (Isa 44:3). In the OT the "pouring out" of a divine attribute is a commonplace: "mercy" (Sir 18:11); "wisdom" (Sir 1:9); "grace" (Ps 45:3); "wrath" (Hos 5:10; Pss 69:25; 79:6); "the Spirit" (Joel 3:1–2 [cf. Acts 2:17]); "a spirit of kindness and supplication" (Zech 12:10). Paul applies it to God's love, i.e., to the divine energy manifesting itself in an overwhelming embrace of once godless creatures who are smothered with his openness and concern for them. It is the manifestation of God's giving of himself without restraint, in a way unparalleled by any human love. It is impossible for a human being to imagine the dimensions or bounds of divine love; humanity knows of it only because God has graciously willed to pour it out and make it known. Paul insists not simply that we become aware that God loves us, but that in the same experience we receive an assurance of God's love for us, a love that becomes the central motive of our own moral being: we love because he first loved us (1 John 4:19). Because the nature of God himself is love, in giving us love he imparts to us something of his own nature, or, in Pauline language, his Spirit (Dodd, *Romans,* 95).

The perf. *ekkechytai,* "has been poured out," expresses the perduring condition of what has been achieved by Christ Jesus. The human "heart" is singled out as the seat of human love; it is seen as the receptacle for the reception of the poured-out love of God. See Introduction, section XI.D.

through the holy Spirit that has been given to us. The gift of the Spirit is not only the proof but also the medium of the outpouring of God's love (8:15–17; Gal 4:6). The "Spirit" denotes par excellence the divine presence to the justified Christian. Paul does not explain what he means by *pneuma hagion,* taking it for granted that Christians will understand it in the sense in which the term is used in the OT; see Introduction, section IX.C. Paul thinks of the Spirit as "the firstfruits" (8:23) of the glorious destiny of Christians; God "has put his Spirit in our hearts as a guarantee" (2 Cor 1:22), i.e., the first installment of eschatological glory. Compare the Qumran idea of God spreading abroad the holy Spirit: "I thank you, o Lord, for you have supported me with your strength and you have poured upon me your holy Spirit that I may not waver" (1QH 7:6–7).

6. *While we were still helpless.* Or "weak." So Paul describes the enduring condition of the unjustified person: incapable of doing anything to achieve

rectitude in the sight of God. In the Greek text there is an emphatic repetition of the adv. *eti*, "still," which stresses the persistence of the condition. In the face of such persistent weakness and helplessness stands God's action in Christ.

The textual transmission of this verse is hopelessly mixed up; see Sanday and Headlam, *Romans*, 126–27; TCGNT, 512.

Christ died at the appointed time. What has made a difference is the death of Jesus. Paul affirms the historical event in a theological assertion stressing the vicarious character of that death, especially its spontaneous, gratuitous nature. Jesus' death is the mode in which God's love has been manifested. See also 1 John 3:16, "In this we know love, that he laid down his life for us." Paul mentions only the "death," but uses the term in a comprehensive sense, which would include also Christ's resurrection (see the NOTE on 4:25).

The phrase *eti kata kairon* seems to be emphatic, lit., "still, at (that) time," and Paul would be insinuating by it the fitting character of the time when Jesus died for human sinfulness. But some MSS (Ψ and the *Koinē* text-tradition) omit the adv. *eti*, because it is redundant after the proleptic *eti gar*, which is not universally read in the Greek MSS. See BDF §§255.3; 476.1. Yet *kata kairon* may mean nothing more than "then" (see J. Barr, *Biblical Words for Time*, SBT 33 [Naperville, Ill.: Allenson, 1962], 47–81); for J. Baumgarten (*EDNT* 2.233), it means "a past moment in time." It is not easy to decide which connotation better suits the context.

for the godless. So Paul describes the condition of the unjustified; because of sin they were *asebeis*, lit., "without reverence (for God)." Cf. 4:5. For such persons Christ laid down his life. For the expression *apothanein hyper*, see 14:15; 1 Thess 5:10; 1 Cor 15:3; 2 Cor 5:15; 1 Pet 3:18; cf. 2 Macc 7:9; 8:21; 4 Macc 1:8; Josephus, *Ant.* 13.1.1 §§5–6.

The unlikely nature of this gratuitous act calls forth from Paul an aside, which he expresses in the following verse.

7. *Rare, indeed, is it that one should lay down one's life for an upright person.* Lit., "will die," the fut. *apothaneitai* is to be understood as gnomic (see BDF §349.1), expressing what might normally happen. To prove his point, Paul argues a fortiori. Christ not only laid down his life, but did it even for sinful and godless people. "A few may face death for a good man, still fewer for a righteous man, but in the case of Christ there is more even than this; He died for declared enemies of God" (Sanday and Headlam, *Romans*, 127).

though for a really good person one might conceivably have courage to die. Or, if *tou agathou* is neuter, "for a good cause." In any case, Paul quickly corrects himself, allowing that possibly for a really good person, a close relative or a gracious benefactor, one might give up one's natural life (see Clarke, "The Good"; Cranfield, *Romans*, 264–65). The verse is supposed to clarify what Paul said in v 6, but it hardly does so in any clear fashion. Yet it serves to bring out the sheerly gratuitous and unmotivated character of the altruism involved, when Christ died for "the godless." If the neut. is preferred, compare *to agathon ergon* in 13:3–4; cf. Gal 6:10; Dio Chrysostom, *Orationes* 32.50; 46.2–3; Plutarch, *Moralia* 218A.

The adv. *tacha*, "perhaps," is used with the indic. *tolma* instead of a potential optative (BDF §385.1).

This verse is much disputed, whether all of it or only its second part is a later gloss, a qualification, or a correction added by Paul himself to the text written by Tertius, the scribe: Delling, "Der Tod Jesu"; Keck, "Post-Pauline Interpretation"; Landau, "Martyrdom"; Leivestad, "Rom. 5,7"; Sahlin, "Einige Textemendationen"; Wisse, "Righteous Man." None of the suggestions about its shape as a gloss has carried conviction, and clearly one has to wrestle with the Pauline text as it is.

8. *Yet God shows forth his own love for us.* This verse resumes v 6 and surmounts the problematic v 7. It makes clear that there is no quid pro quo in the love manifested: divine love is spontaneously demonstrated toward sinners without a hint that it is repaying a love already shown. The death of Christ is for us, sinners, precisely the proof of God's love for us. Cf. John 3:16; 1 John 4:10. Paul's statement completely rules out any doctrine of the cross that sets God and Christ in contrast to each other (Taylor, *Romans*, 38). God's love is manifested in the love that Christ revealed by his passion and death for the sake of humanity. So Paul establishes the christological basis of all Christian hope.

Because *ho theos* is the Father, whose love is poured out "through the Spirit" (5:5) and now manifested in Christ's death, this triadic text becomes a Pauline starting point for later trinitarian dogma.

in that, while we were still sinners, Christ died for us. This is the formal conclusion that Paul draws from his statement about God's love poured out. Again, the vicarious character of Christ's death is emphasized, "for us." See 14:15. Cf. 1 Cor 8:11; 1 Pet 3:18.

9. *since we are now justified by his blood.* Whereas in 4:25 justification was ascribed to Christ's resurrection, it is now attributed to the shedding of his blood, to his death. For the prep. phrase, *en tō haimati*, to express price, see BDF §219.3. This phrase stands in parallelism with *dia tou thanatou* in v 10. Contrast 5:10, by "his life." Cf. Heb 9:22.

we shall all the more certainly be saved by him. A favor still greater than justification itself will be manifested to the Christian in the eschatological salvation that is to come. Thus Paul draws the conclusion from his argument in the preceding verses. Once again, justification is subordinated to salvation, and the latter is regarded as something begun but still to be consummated or brought to its full expression (10:9, 13; 11:14, 26); yet that consummation is guaranteed. Cf. Reumann, *"Righteousness,"* 82, 213. Paul argues a minori ad maius, as he will again in vv 10, 15, and 17. "By him" is explained in v 10, "by his life."

from the wrath to come. I.e., from the divine wrath to be manifested at the *eschaton*, at the time of judgment. See the NOTES on 1:18; 2:5. Cf. 1 Thess 1:10.

10. *For if, when we were God's enemies.* This verse restates in different words

what was affirmed in 5:8. Sinners are not merely "weak" or "godless," but have actually made themselves "enemies" of God through their sin (8:7). Thus the sinner stands vis-à-vis God in a stance of enmity, hostility, and alienation. Commentators debate whether *echthroi ontes* is to be taken in the passive sense, "hated by God" (Bultmann, Lietzmann [who compares 11:28], Meyer, Murray, Wolter [*Rechtfertigung*, 86]) or in the active sense, "hating God" (Foerster [*TDNT* 2.814], Käsemann, Kuss, Sanday and Headlam, Schlier, Wilckens). But in this case there is no reason it should not be understood of mutual hostility between God and sinners, as Cranfield (*Romans*, 267) and Dunn (*Romans*, 258) have taken it. It aptly expresses the culmination of the human situation of opposition to God, which only God's initiative, based on his love, can remedy.

we were reconciled to him through the death of his Son. The death (and resurrection) of Christ brings about the reconciliation of sinners with God (2 Cor 5:18; cf. Col 1:21–22). This is but another way of stating that sinners are now at "peace" with God (5:1), because reconciliation is the restoration of the estranged and alienated person to friendship and intimacy with God (2 Cor 5:18–21); see Introduction, section IX.B. The mention of "the death of his Son" is not to be pressed in a sacrificial sense, as Käsemann has done, and as Dunn (*Romans*, 259) seeks to make likely. Reference neither to "death" nor to "blood" per se connotes anything sacrificial or cultic; death connotes the giving up of one's life, and blood refers to that. The association of the idea with martyrdom may introduce that nuance. Thus Paul sees justification as a step toward reconciliation, which is a social concept, not sacrificial or cultic.

now that we are reconciled, we shall all the more certainly be saved by his life. The third effect of justification is a share in the risen life of Christ, which is salvation. Although justification and reconciliation are things that happen now, salvation in its full sense is still to be achieved, but it is rooted in a share of Christ's risen life that is communicated in justification. Again, Paul argues a minori ad maius, as in v 9.

11. *Yet not only that—but we boast of God through our Lord Jesus Christ.* The best MSS (ℵ, B, C, D) read the ptc. *kauchōmenoi*, "boasting," instead of the 1st pl. *kauchōmetha*, "we boast," found in MSS L, 104, 365, 630, etc. This is the third climactic boast in the paragraph, following up those in 5:2, 3. The effect of justification is that the Christian even boasts of God himself (1 Cor 1:31), in whom one's salvation is now guaranteed, whereas before one stood in fear of his wrath. Having experienced God's love in what Christ Jesus did for humanity by his death, one can now exult and boast of the very thought of God. See G. Lafont, "La Fierté des sauvés: Rm 5,6–11," *AsSeign* 42 (1970): 12–17.

through whom we have now received reconciliation. Thus Paul repeats the main affirmation of this introductory paragraph.

J. O'Callaghan has claimed that 5:11–12 was partly quoted in fragment 9 discovered in Qumran Cave 7; see "¿Papiros neotestamenticos en la cueva 7 de Qumrān?" *Bib* 53 (1972): 91–100; cf. supplement to *JBL* 91.2 (1972): 1–14. But this is hardly likely; it is undoubtedly a Greek fragment of some LXX text or of some Greek extrabiblical writing. The papyrus fragment is so small that one cannot be certain about the identification of the few letters left on it.

BIBLIOGRAPHY

Boer, M. C. de, *The Defeat of Death: Apocalyptic Eschatology in 1 Corinthians 15 and Romans 5*, JSNTSup 22 (Sheffield, UK: JSOT, 1988), 141–80.

Cerfaux, L., "Description de l'état chrétien de justice," *Une Lecture*, 50–85.

Fuchs, E., *Die Freiheit des Glaubens: Römer 5–8 ausgelegt*, BEvT 14 (Munich: Kaiser, 1949).

Garnet, P., *Salvation and Atonement in the Qumran Scrolls*, WUNT 2.3 (Tübingen: Mohr [Siebeck], 1977).

Grossmann, H., *Gedanken über den Römer-Brief, insbesondere über die Kapitel 5 bis 11* (Kassel: Oncken, [1935]).

Knox, J., *Life in Christ Jesus: Reflections on Romans 5–8* (Greenwich, Conn.: Seabury, 1961; London: SPCK, 1962).

Lamarche, P. and C. Le Dû, *Épître aux Romains V–VIII: Structure littéraire et sens* (Paris: Centre National de Recherche Scientifique, 1980).

Leeuwen, W. S. van, *Eirene en het Nieuwe Testament: Een semasiologische, exegetische Bijdrage op grond van de Septuaginta en de joodsche Literatuur* (Wageningen; Veenman & Zonen, 1940).

Lorenzi, L. de, "La speranza nostro vanto, Rom 5,2c," *Glaube und Eschatologie: Festschrift für Werner Georg Kümmel . . .* , ed. E. Grässer and O. Merk (Tübingen: Mohr [Siebeck], 1985), 165–88.

Minear, P. S., *The Obedience of Faith*, 57–71.

O'Brien, P. T., "Col. 1:20 and the Reconciliation of All Things," *RTR* 33 (1974): 45–53.

Olson, S. N., "Romans 5–8 as Pastoral Theology," *WW* 6 (1986): 390–97.

Osten-Sacken, P. von der, "Die Bedeutung von Röm. 5–7 für die Interpretation von Röm. 8," *Römer 8 als Beispiel paulinischer Soteriologie*, FRLANT 112 (Göttingen: Vandenhoeck & Ruprecht, 1975), 160–225.

Rolland, P., "L'Antithèse de Rm 5–8," *Bib* 69 (1988): 396–400.

Rossano, P., "Il concetto di 'Hamartia' in Rom. 5–8," *RivB* 4 (1956): 289–313.

Stott, J. R. W., *Men Made New: An Exposition of Romans 5–8* (London: Inter-Varsity Fellowship, 1966).

Thomson, G. T., "Exegesis of Romans V–VIII," *EvQ* 15 (1943): 247–51; 16 (1944): 4–8, 81–87.

Rom 5:1–11

Blank, J., "Röm 5,10," *Paulus und Jesus: Eine theologische Grundlegung*, SANT 18 (Munich: Kösel, 1968), 280–87.

Bover, J. M., " 'Gloriamur in spe' (Rom. 5,2)," *Bib* 22 (1941): 41–45.

Clarke, A. D., "The Good and the Just in Romans 5:7," *TynBul* 41 (1990): 128–42.

Crabtree, A. R., "Translation of Romans 5:1 in the Revised Standard Version of the New Testament," *RevExp 43 (1946)*: 436–39.

Delling, G., "Der Tod Jesu in der Verkündigung des Paulus," *Apophoreta: Festschrift für Ernst Haenchen* . . . , BZNW 30 (Berlin: Töpelmann, 1964), 85–96.

Dibelius, M., "Vier Worte des Römerbriefs 5,5. 5,12. 8,10 und 11,30 f.," *SBU* 3 (1944): 3–17, esp. 3–6.

Fatum, L., "Die menschliche Schwäche im Römerbrief," *ST* 29 (1975): 31–52.

Fryer, N. S. L., "Reconciliation in Paul's Epistle to the Romans," *Neotestamentica* 15 (1981): 34–68.

Furnish, V. P., "The Ministry of Reconciliation," *CurTM* 4 (1977): 204–18.

Helewa, G., " 'Fedele è Dio': Una lettura di Rom 5, 1–11," *Teresianum* 36 (1985): 25–57.

—————, " 'Riconciliazione' divina e 'speranza della gloria' secondo Rom 5,1–11," *Teresianum* 34 (1983): 275–306.

Herman, Z. I., "La novità cristiana secondo Romani 5,20–7,6: Alcune osservazioni esegetiche," *Anton* 61 (1986): 225–73.

Hofius, O., "Hilasmos kai katallage: Ho staurikos thanatos tou Christou kata ton Apostolo Paulo," *DBM* 14 (1985): 24–42.

Jacob, R., "Dieu, notre joie: Rm 5,1–5," *AsSeign* 31 (1973): 36–39.

Kaiser, O. and W. G. Kümmel, *Exegetical Method: A Student's Handbook* (New York: Seabury, 1963), 49–58.

Keck, L. E., "The Post-Pauline Interpretation of Jesus' Death in Rom 5,6–7," *Theologia crucis—Signum crucis: Festschrift für Erich Dinkler* . . . , ed. C. Andresen and G. Klein (Tübingen: Mohr [Siebeck], 1979), 237–48.

Kunze, J. A., "Versuch einer Erklärung der Stelle Röm. 5,6 ff.," *TSK* 23.1 (1850): 407–10.

Lafon, G., "La Fierté des sauvés: Rm 5,6–11," *AsSeign* n.s. 42 (1970): 12–17.

Landau, Y., "Martyrdom in Paul's Religious Ethics: An Exegetical Commentary on Romans 5:7," *Immanuel* 15 (1982–83): 24–38.

Leivestad, R., "Rom. 5,7," *NorTT* 57 (1956): 245–48.

Lohse, E., " 'Das Amt, das die Versöhnung predigt,' " *Rechtfertigung: Festschrift für Ernst Käsemann* . . . , ed. J. Friedrich et al. (Tübingen: Mohr [Siebeck]; Göttingen: Vandenhoeck & Ruprecht, 1976), 339–49.

Luck, U., "Weisheit und Leiden: Zum Problem Paulus und Jakobus," *TLZ* 92 (1967): 253–58.

Lührmann, D., "Rechtfertigung und Versöhnung: Zur Geschichte der paulinischen Tradition," *ZTK* 67 (1970): 437–52.

McDonald, P. M., "Romans 5.1–11 as a Rhetorical Bridge," *JSNT* 40 (1990): 81–96.

Mattern, L., "Rö 5,9f.," *Das Verständnis des Gerichtes bei Paulus*, ATANT 47 (Zurich: Zwingli, 1966), 86–91.

Maurer, C., "Der Schluss 'a minori ad maius' als Element paulinischer Theologie," *TLZ* 85 (1960): 149–52.

O'Brien, P. T., "Colossians 1,20 and the Reconciliation of All Things," *RTR* 33 (1974): 45–53.

O'Collins, G. G. and T. M. McNulty, "St. Paul and the Language of Reconciliation," *Colloquium* (Auckland/Sydney) 6 (1973–74): 3–8.

Porter, S. E., "The Argument of Romans 5: Can a Rhetorical Question Make a Difference?" *JBL* 110 (1991): 655–77.

Ridderbos, H., *Paul*, 182–204.

Romaniuk, K., *L'Amour du Père et du Fils dans la sotériologie de saint Paul*, AnBib 15 (Rome: Biblical Institute, 1961), 207–16.

Ruffenach, F., "Caritas Dei diffusa est in cordibus nostris per Spiritum Sanctum, qui datus est nobis (Rom 5,5)," *VD* 12 (1932): 303–4.

Sahlin, H., "Einige Textemendationen zum Römerbrief," *TZ* 9 (1953): 92–100.

Salas, A., "Reconciliados con Dios por la muerte de Cristo (*Rom* 5,10): La penitencia, hoy, vista desde la Biblia," *Biblia y fe* 5 (1979): 47–71.

Stöger, A., "Die paulinische Versöhnungstheologie," *TPQ* 122 (1974): 118–31.

Vicentini, J. I., " 'Déjense reconciliar con Dios': Lectura de 2 Corintios 5,14–21," *RevistB* 36 (1974): 97–104.

Warfield, B. B., "St. Paul's Use of the Argument from Experience," *Expos* 5.1 (1895): 226–36.

Wisse, F., "The Righteous Man and the Good Man in Romans v. 7," *NTS* 19 (1972–73): 91–93.

Wolter, M., *Rechtfertigung und zukünftiges Heil: Untersuchungen zu Röm 5,1–11*, BZNW 43 (Berlin and New York: de Gruyter, 1978).

Wurzinger, A., "In Hoffnung der Herrlichkeit: Eine Meditation zu Röm 5,1–11," *BLit* 37 (1963–64): 75–78.

THEME EXPLAINED: NEW CHRISTIAN LIFE BRINGS A THREEFOLD LIBERATION AND IS EMPOWERED BY THE SPIRIT (5:12–8:13)

◆

18. FREEDOM FROM THE POWER OF DEATH AND SIN (5:12–21)

5 ¹²Therefore, just as sin entered the world through one man, and through sin death, and so death spread to all human beings, with the result that all have sinned—¹³up to the time of the law sin was in the world, even though sin is not accounted when there is no law; ¹⁴yet death held sway from Adam until Moses, even over those who had not sinned in a way similar to Adam's transgression—who is a type of the one who was to come. ¹⁵But the gift is not like the trespass. For if many have died because of the trespass of one man, how much more have the grace of God and his gift overflowed to the many because of the grace of one man, Jesus Christ. ¹⁶Moreover, the gift is not like the result of one man's sin; for judgment resulting from one trespass became condemnation, whereas the gift following upon many trespasses brought justification. ¹⁷If by the trespass of one man death came to hold sway through that one man, how much more will those who receive the abundance of God's grace and his gift of uprightness reign in life through the one man, Jesus Christ. ¹⁸So, just as through one trespass condemnation came upon all, through one act of uprightness justification and life came to all human beings. ¹⁹Just as through the disobedience of one man many were made sinners, so through the obedience of one many will be made upright. ²⁰The law slipped in that trespass might increase; but where sin increased, grace has abounded all the more, ²¹so that, just as sin held sway in death, grace too might reign through uprightness to bring eternal life through Jesus Christ our Lord.

COMMENT

Paul does not immediately continue his discussion with a description of what justified Christians experience as a follow-up of what he set forth in vv 1–11. Rather, he begins his description of the condition of the justified and reconciled Christian by comparing it with the status of humanity before Christ's coming. The Christ-event has had effects on humanity that are superabundant in comparison with the effects of Adam and what he did to the human race. Paul alludes to the history of humanity as affected by Adam and determined by him. Moreover, Paul abandons the "we" style that he has been using (vv 1–11) and casts his argument in the third person, an argumentative comparison of Adam and Christ. In a sense his argument proceeds in three steps: vv 12–14, vv 15–17, vv 18–21.

Paul compares Adam, the first parent, with Christ, the head of the new humanity. Although he does not say so here, he employs the image of Christ as the Adam of the *eschaton*, which he employed in 1 Cor 15:22, 45–48. See Introduction, section IX.B. In this paragraph Paul does not treat Christ as Adam redivivus, but sets Christ up in parallelism and contrast to Adam. He uses this contrast to get across his major concern about the new life that comes in Christ, the freedom from sin and death. As through the one man Adam sin and death came upon Adamic humanity, so through the one man Christ Jesus came eternal life upon Christic humanity. In a sense, this paragraph constitutes the second most important passage in the letter, the first being 3:21–26. The comparison of Adam and Christ sums up in its own way all that Paul has been saying thus far in the letter. "Adam is the head of the old aeon, the age of *death*; Christ is the head of the new aeon, the age of *life*" (Nygren, *Romans*, 210). In making this comparison, Paul establishes once more the basis for Christian hope (5:5): as Adam's sin introduced baleful consequences for all historical humanity, so the justification brought by Christ Jesus has affected those consequences for good and for salvation. Thus Adam and Christ are type and antitype.

But the comparison is not smoothly worked out, for Paul also wants to clarify the dissimilarity and the superabundance of Christ's grace that now reigns instead of sin and death, which had been in control since Adam.

Just as sin came into the world through Adam (and with it death, which affects all human beings), so through Christ came uprightness (and with it life eternal).

So the comparison should run, but Paul felt the need to explain his novel teaching about Adam and broke into the parallelism to assert emphatically that it was Adam's *sin* that has affected all human beings (5:12c–d, 13–14), making them not just mortal, but even sinners. Because of this insertion, anacoluthon appears at the end of 5:14, and Paul's real conclusion of the comparison is expressed only indirectly (when he asserts that Adam was the type of the one who was to come). The comparison involves an antithetical parallelism between the death wrought by Adam and the life brought by Christ. The antithesis is reformulated in 5:15–17, where Paul emphasizes the surpassing quality of what Christ did, when it is compared with Adam's influence. Again Paul argues a minori ad maius. Christ, the new Adam and the new head of humanity, was incomparably more beneficent toward humanity than Adam was maleficent. This idea is repeated again in 5:18–19, and the last verse is an echo of 5:12. In 5:20 the antithesis is again proposed, this time in terms of law. As a result, whatever one wants to think about 5:12 and its problems, the causality of Adam's sin expressed there is reiterated in 5:19. See Bornkamm, "Paulinische Anakoluthe," *Das Ende des Gesetzes*, 76–92, esp. 80–90.

Besides the baneful influence of Adam, Paul also ascribes the mortal condition of humanity to its own sinfulness. "All have sinned" (5:12d), echoing what he has said in 3:9 and 23. Thus Paul ascribes the mortal condition to a dual causality, to Adam and to the sins of individual human beings. For some commentators this elaboration seems to create "confusion."

According to Bultmann ("Adam and Christ," 150, 154), Paul is using in this paragraph a gnostic myth about the original man. The "confusion" about the two causes of man's sin and death "has its basis in that the Adam-Christ parallel, i.e., the thought of two mankinds (or two epochs of mankind) and their determination each by its originator, is a gnostic idea which is conceived cosmologically and not in terms of salvation history. In its purity it becomes evident in I Corinthians 15:21 f." and in "I Corinthians 15:47 f." Similarly Brandenburger, *Adam und Christus*, 168–80; and Schunack, *Das hermeneutische Problem*, 244–47; but see the critique of this gnostic interpretation by Wedderburn, "Theological Structure," 342–44; and Dunn, *Romans*, 272–73.

This is hardly an accurate description of Paul's teaching in this paragraph. If there is a myth behind the discussion, it is not the gnostic myth of the *Urmensch*, but that of Gen 2:4b–3:24, to which Paul alludes, viz., the Yahwist account of the creation of Adam and Eve and of their transgression of the command that Yahweh had laid on them. Paul mentions Adam's "trespass" (5:15, 17) and his "disobedience" (5:19), but prescinds from the dramatic details to utilize the theological truth of the enslavement of human beings to sin and death that they have entailed. The unmistakably etiological character of that story (see Introduction, section IX.D) insinuates that the sin of Adam was the cause of universal misery and sin. Paul ascribes to Adam a baleful influence, one that has affected all human beings, making sinners of them all. For Paul's use of contemporary Jewish tradition about Adam, which builds on the biblical account, see the NOTE on 5:12.

Whereas the main teaching in the paragraph concerns the superabundant life-giving effect of the Christ-event, the parenthetical teaching formulates the origin of sin in human life (so-called Original Sin). Paul is primarily interested in the contrast of the universality of sin and death with the universality of life in Christ; yet he does indicate not only the beginning of such universal phenomena but also the causality of the head (Adam or Christ). Paul does not explain how that baneful effect of Adam takes place; he makes no mention of sin's hereditary character (as Augustine later did). But Paul is aware that not all human sinfulness is owing to Adam alone; he makes this clear in v 12d, as he has already indicted all human beings in 3:9 and 23.

Paul treats Adam as a historical human being, humanity's first parent, and contrasts him with the historical Jesus Christ. But in Genesis itself ʾAdām is a symbolic figure, denoting humanity. (Note the fluctuation between ʾādām, "man" [Gen 1:26; 4:25; 5:1, where it becomes the proper name, "Adam"] and hāʾādām, "the man, the human being" [1:27; 2:7–8, 15–16, 18–23, 25; 3:8–9, 12, 20, 22, 24; 6:1].) Some commentators on Romans have tried to interpret *Adam* in this symbolic sense here (thus Barth, *Romans*, 170–71; Leenhardt, *Romans*, 141; Schlier, *Römerbrief*, 160); but that reading does violence to the contrast that Paul uses in this paragraph between Adam as "one man" and Christ as "one man," which implies that Adam was a historical individual as much as was Jesus Christ. So Paul has historicized the symbolic Adam of Genesis.

What Paul says about Adam's influence on the *death* of all human beings in 1 Cor 15:22 is in line with contemporary Jewish thinking. But what he says here is not. He ascribes to Adam not only death, but also *sin*. That accounts for a break in his thought, the anacoluthon of 5:13–14, marked by dashes in my translation.

Four notorious problems are encountered in the interpretation of v 12d: the meaning of *thanatos*, "death"; the meaning of the phrase *eph' hō*; the meaning of *pantes*, "all"; and the meaning of *hēmarton*, "sinned." See the NOTES for details.

The first three verses of this paragraph (vv 12–14) have been the subject of a centuries-long theological debate, because Paul seems to affirm in this passage the existence of hereditary sin. Indeed, the Roman Catholic exegetical tradition has almost unanimously so interpreted it, especially 5:12, in terms of the universal causality of Adam's sin on the sinfulness of human individuals. This tradition found its formal conciliar expression in the Tridentine *Decretum de peccato originali*, Sess. V, 2–4. Echoing canon 2 of both the Sixteenth Council of Carthage (A.D. 418, DS 223) and the Second Council of Orange (A.D. 529, DS 372), the Tridentine Fathers decreed that "what the Apostle says, 'Through one man sin entered the world, and through that sin, death, and thus death passed to all human beings, in whom all have sinned,' is not to be understood in any other way than as the Catholic church spread all over has always understood it" (DS 1514; cf. 1512). This decree gave a definitive interpretation to the Pauline text in the sense that his words teach a form of the dogma of Original Sin, a rare text that enjoys such an interpretation.

Care must be taken, however, to understand what Paul is saying and not to transform his mode of expression too facilely into the precision of later dogmatic development. Paul, who writes in Greek, does not speak of "original sin," a term that as a translation of Latin *peccatum originale* betrays its western theological origin in the time of Augustine. Trent appealed in its decree to the sense of Paul's words as they were understood in the church's tradition at all times and places. Differences, however, did exist in the tradition regarding details or the understanding of individual words; yet there was agreement on the fact of the sin and on its extent. Nevertheless, those very differences are important, for they show that Paul's formulation has to be understood for what it is. As *Humani generis* 21 (DS 3886) put it, theologians must make it clear in what way (*qua ratione*) the church's teaching is contained in Scripture. In this case Paul's teaching is regarded as seminal and open to later dogmatic development, but it does not say all that the Tridentine decree says.

The story in Genesis 3 is often described as "the Fall" (e.g., Davies, *Paul and*

Rabbinic Judaism, 39), but what that chapter really teaches is the loss of God's trust and friendship by Adam and Eve because of their transgression and disobedience. Yet in that etiological story there is not a hint of a "fall" from grace or original justice, as patristic and later scholastic theologians eventually formulated it. Nor is there in Genesis or anywhere in the OT a hint of the fantastic interpretations that would be given to Adam's "body" or his "glory" found in the rabbinic tradition (ibid., 44–47). There is actually no teaching about a "Fall" in Jewish theology, even though some Jewish writers use that terminology, having borrowed it from their Christian counterparts (e.g., B. Altmann).

"Original Sin" is a Christian idea, which builds on what Paul teaches in this paragraph, as he exploits the implications of the causal connection between Adam's sin and the sinfulness of human beings in the etiological story of Genesis 3. Paul never explains how that causality works or how Adam's sin is transmitted. When Augustine opposed Pelagius, who had been teaching that Adam influenced humanity by giving it a bad example, he introduced the idea of transmission by propagation or heredity. He also introduced the idea of *gratia sanans*, "healing grace," and *gratia elevans*, "elevating grace." With the introduction of those ideas into the debate, the story in Genesis 3 about Adam's sin was then recast in terms of "the Fall": Adam fell from grace, from a supernatural status.

Having quoted 5:12ab, Augustine wrote, "Hoc propagationis est, non imitationis; nam [si imitationis], Per diabolum diceret" (This is [said] of propagation, not of imitation; for [if it (were meant) of imitation], he would have said 'Through the Devil,' " *De peccatorum meritis et remissione* 1.9.10 [CSEL 60.12]). See also *Contra duas epistolas Pelagianorum* 4.4.7 [CSEL 60.527–28], where Augustine argues that "in quo" cannot refer to "death," which in Greek would be masculine, but has to refer to Adam ("restat, ut in illo primo homine peccasse omnes intelligantur," it follows that all are to be understood as having sinned in the first man). Cf. *Sermo 294* 4.15 (PL 38.1344); *Contra Iulianum opus imperfectum* 2.63 (CSEL 85.1.209). See Buonaiuti, "Pelagius"; De Bruyn, "Pelagius's Interpretation"; Lyonnet, "Rom. V,12 chez saint Augustin"; Souter, "Pelagius' Text."

Could the doctrine about Original Sin be considered to be the *sensus plenior* of Rom 5:12–21 or Genesis 3? It would be more difficult to affirm that of Genesis 3 than of Rom 5:12–21. In a sense, it could be said that Original Sin is the *sensus plenior* of Paul's teaching in 5:12–21, but then one must remember that it is such in the western theological tradition. Augustine claims that it is also part of the Greek patristic tradition, and cites the authority of John Chrysostom (*Contra Iulianum* 1.6.27 [PL 44.658–59]), but he does not cite any clear passage that shows that Chrysostom would have used the Greek equivalent of "original" sin. When Greek Fathers mention it, it is merely *hamartia* or Adam's "sin."

In modern times theologians have sought to explain *hamartia* in this Pauline passage as "the sin of the world." That exploits the Pauline terminology in 5:12a ("sin entered the world"), but it is a modern attempt to recast the Latin patristic and scholastic teaching. The extent to which it is correct depends on the extent to which it retains the basic Pauline affirmation of the causality of Adam's sin on human sinfulness. See Ligier, *Péché d'Adam*; Anon., "New Thinking"; Vanneste, "Où en est le problème?"

Above I distinguished "Adam" in Genesis 2–3 as a symbolic figure from "Adam" in 5:12–21 as a historical individual, or as a historicized individual, as he had already become in contemporary Jewish literature. Paul, however, knew nothing about the Adam of history. What he knows about Adam, he has derived from Genesis and the Jewish tradition that developed from Genesis. "Adam" for Paul is *Adam in the Book of Genesis*; he is a literary individual, like Hamlet, but not symbolic, like Everyman. Adam is for Paul what Jonah was for the evangelist Matthew (12:40) and Melchizedek for the author of the Epistle to the Hebrews (7:3). All three have been used as foils for Christ. But they are literary figures who have or have not been historicized, as the case may be.

This distinction impinges on another problem of modern theology, namely, polygenism versus monogenism. Theologians have queried whether Paul was teaching in 5:12–21 a form of monogenism because of his emphasis on Adam as "one man" and his historicization of Adam. Yet this problem stems from Charles Darwin and his books, *The Origin of Species* (1859) and *The Descent of Man* (1871). Polygenism is thus a modern development of teaching about evolution. It goes far beyond Paul's perspective; hence what Paul says in 5:12–21 cannot be used to solve such a problem. See F. Ceuppens, "Le Polygénisme et la Bible," *Ang* 24 (1947): 20–32.

The encyclical of Pius XII, *Humani Generis*, in addressing this problem and opposing the "conjectural opinion" of polygenism stated, "cum nequaquam appareat quomodo huiusmodi sententia componi queat cum iis quae fontes revelatae veritatis et acta Magisterii Ecclesiae proponunt de peccato originali, quod procedit ex peccato vere commisso ab uno Adamo, quodque generatione in omnes transfusum, inest unicuique proprium (cf. *Rom* 5,12–19)" (since it is in no way evident how such an opinion can be reconciled with what the sources of revealed truth and acts of the ecclesiastical Magisterium teach about Original Sin, which stems from a sin truly committed by one Adam and is transmitted by generation to all, [and thus] is present in each person [DS 3897]). The encyclical, however, does not come out against polygenism absolutely, for it says that "it is in no way evident" (in 1950!) how it can be reconciled with the teaching about Original Sin. That is quite different from saying "cum appareat quomodo huiusmodi sententia nequaquam componi queat" (since it is evident that it can in no way be reconciled). (Apparently, the adv. *nequaquam* was originally in the indirect question introduced by *quomodo*, but was moved to modify *appareat* before the encyclical was issued. Cf. J. Levie, *NRT* 72 [1950]: 788–89.)

Except for the formulaic ending in 5:21, Paul does not use the first person plural in 5:12–21, as he does in 5:1–11 and 6:1–8. This fact, plus the unified impression that this paragraph makes in Paul's treatment of Adam and Christ, suggests to some interpreters that Paul may be incorporating here part of a writing composed for another occasion. See Introduction, section VIII.

NOTES

5:12. *Therefore.* The paragraph begins with the phrase *dia touto*, lit., "for this reason," and might seem to introduce a conclusion drawn from v 11, or from 5:1–11, or even from 1:16–5:11. If it were limited to a conclusion drawn from v 11, it would indicate that justification and life have been given to Christians through God's grace. But it should instead be understood as drawing a conclusion from vv 1–11 as a whole (Cranfield, *Romans*, 271): justification, acquired through Christ, and the certainty of salvation and life are the basis of hope, as can be seen in the conquest of sin and death. If the paragraph, however, had actually been composed for another occasion, then the antecedent is lost. Consequently, the phrase may now be merely transitional (compare 2:1; 15:22), introducing a new stage in the thought as a conclusion from the preceding (Schlier, *Römerbrief*, 159; Wilckens, *Römer*, 1.314), or even from all that precedes in the letter thus far (Nygren, *Romans*, 209–12).

just as. The comparison begins with *hōsper*, but the conclusion is not introduced by *houtōs kai*, "so too," as one might have expected and as is done in vv 18 and 19. Instead, we find *kai houtōs*, which Cerfaux (*Christ*, 231–32), Barrett (*Romans*, 109), Kirby ("The Syntax"), and Scroggs (*Last Adam*, 79–80) have tried to take as its equivalent. But if Paul had meant that phrase to introduce the conclusion, he would have written *houtōs (kai)*, as he does later on. For further examples of *kai houtōs*, see 11:26; 1 Cor 7:36; 11:28; Gal 6:2. Cf. Cranfield, "On Some," 326–29. The conclusion to the comparison is implied rather in the last clause of v 14, and not in v 15c (*pollō mallon*. . .), as Englezakis suggests (*Bib* 58 [1977]: 232), nor in v 19, as Black would have it (*Romans*, 79). Rather, anacoluthon is involved.

sin entered the world. I.e., into the cosmos or history of humanity. The words *eis ton kosmon eisēlthen* echo Wis 2:24, "Through the devil's envy death entered the world." Paul alludes to the story recorded in Gen 3:6; cf. 4 Ezra 3:21–22. *Hamartia* is the personified malevolent force, Sin (with capital S), hostile to God and alienating human beings from him; it strode upon the stage of human history at the time of Adam's transgression (6:12–14; 7:7–23; 1 Cor 15:56) and has dominated "all human beings." For the Pauline sense of sin, see Introduction, section IX.D. Paul does not tell us precisely how sin entered the world, save through Adam's "transgression" (5:14), "trespass" (5:15), or "disobedience" (5:19). Through his sin Adam began the common sinning of humanity; he was the author of that malevolent force.

through one man. The phrase *heis anthrōpos* occurs twelve times in this paragraph, thus emphasizing its importance. The "man" is either Adam or Christ, both males, even though Paul uses the generic *anthrōpos*. The contrast between

411

"one man" and the "many" highlights the universality of the influence involved. In this case, the one man is Adam of Genesis 2–3, who is mentioned in v 14 and described as the "type of the one who was to come" and whose "transgression" (5:14) of Yahweh's command unleashed into human history an active evil force, sin. Adam is treated by Paul as the head of the old humanity, and what happened to the head has influenced the body of human beings. Adam is again referred to as "one man" in vv 15–19. Yet one should guard against interpreting "one man" as the *Urmensch*, a term that has too many gnostic connotations for Pauline theology (as Davies rightly notes, *Paul and Rabbinic Judaism*, 45). One can easily recognize the role that Paul ascribes to Adam without introducing those connotations.

It may seem that Paul is tributary to the rabbinic Jewish mode of thinking about Adam. At least so Davies would have us believe (ibid., 53–57): "Paul accepted the traditional Rabbinic doctrine of the unity of mankind in Adam. That doctrine implied that the very constitution of the physical body of Adam and the method of its formation was symbolic of the real oneness of mankind. In that one body of Adam east and west, north and south were brought together, male and female. . . . The 'body' of Adam included all mankind." But Davies should have scrutinized, first of all, the meaning of the rabbinic passages to which he refers (e.g., *m. Sanhedrin* 4:5; *b. Sanhedrin* 38a; *Gen. Rabbah* 8; *Pirqe de Rabbi Eliezer* §11): none of them says a thing about the "inclusion" of all humanity "in" the " 'body' of Adam" in the manner of 1 Cor 15:22. Second, Davies should have paid more attention to the dates of the rabbinic passages to which he alludes; the mishnaic passage comes from the early third century A.D., and the Babylonian Talmud passages are not earlier than the sixth century. Is there any clear reference in pre-Christian Jewish literature to such a notion as the incorporation of all human beings in Adam? Not even Philo has so specific a notion. It seems to appear for the first time in 1 Cor 15:22.

and through sin death. I.e., death, the opposite of life, entered the world of human beings because of sin; see Gen 2:17 and esp. 3:19, where God sentences Adam; cf. 1 Cor 15:21a. *Thanatos,* "death," is also personified as another actor who "enters" on the stage of human history, playing the role of a tyrant (5:14, 17) and dominating human beings. "Death" is not merely physical, bodily death (separation of body and soul), as it has often been interpreted by theologians in the past, but includes spiritual death (the definitive separation of human beings from God, the unique source of life), as 5:21 makes clear (cf. 6:21, 23; 7:5, 10, 13, 26; 8:2, 6; 1 Cor 15:21–22, 26). It is the same as *apōleia,* "destruction" (9:22; cf. 2:12, *apolountai;* 1 Cor 1:18; Phil 1:28; 3:19). Death is thus a personified cosmic force (8:38; 1 Cor 3:22), the "last enemy" to be vanquished (1 Cor 15:56). See de Boer, *Defeat of Death,* 141–80. Ever since Adam the human race has lain in servitude to Sin and Death, personified powers of destruction. Because of the very essence of Sin, derived from Adam, the power of Death has entered the world of humanity.

Paul alludes to contemporary Jewish belief about Adam's influence: see Wis 2:24, quoted above (where *thanatos* has the same sense, "total death"); 2 *Apoc. Bar.* 17:3: "The length of time that he [Adam] lived profited him not, but brought death and curtailed the lives of his descendants"; 23:4: "When Adam sinned, death was decreed against those who were to be born (from him)"; 48:42: "What was it that you, Adam, did to all your posterity? What should be said of Eve who first listened to the serpent? For this multitude is going to corruption"; 54:15: "Though Adam sinned first and brought untimely death on all human beings, yet each one of those who were born of him has either prepared for his own soul (its) future torment or chosen for himself the glories that are to be." 4 Ezra 3:7: "He [Adam] transgressed it [the command of Gen 2:17], and immediately you appointed death for him and his descendants"; 3:21: "The first Adam, burdened with a wicked heart, transgressed (the command) and was overcome, as were also all who were descended from him. So the disease became permanent"; 7:118: "O Adam, what have you done? Though it was you who sinned, the fall was not yours alone, but ours too who are your descendants." But there also emerges in this tradition the awareness that individuals are also responsible for their deaths: 2 *Apoc. Bar.* 54:19: "Thus Adam is not the cause, except for himself only; each one of us is his own Adam."

and so. The adv. *houtōs* is important; it establishes the connection between Adam's sin and that of "all human beings." Death is in part a fate that humanity shares because of Adam, but also an experience stemming from its own guilt, as the rest of the verse makes clear.

death spread to all human beings. So Paul states the universal baleful effect of Adam's sin. Paul uses the vb. *dierchesthai*, "pass through unto" (cf. Mark 4:35). Death's influence has affected all without exception. Cf. 1 Cor 15:21–22 (*en tō Adam pantes apothnēskousin*). From this statement it might seem that all humanity has been doomed to death without any responsibility; but Paul corrects that impression by the addition of the following clause, which asserts in addition to Adam's causality the causality of individual responsibility. Sin brings death not only as punishment (1:32), but also as "wages" (6:23); it is the *telos*, "result" of sin (6:21), that toward which it tends (8:6). See W. Bieder, *EDNT* 2.129–33.

The subject *ho thanatos* is read by MSS ℵ, A, B, C, K, P, 33, 81, 614, 1739 and the *Koinē* text-tradition, but is omitted by MSS D, F, G, 2495 and some MSS of the VL. Its omission affected the controversy between Pelagius and Augustine, when *pantes*, "all," was taken to include infants, a precision that Paul did not envisage. See Augustine, *De natura et origine animae* 4.11.16 (CSEL 60.395). Cf. de Ocaña, "Cristo, segundo Adán."

with the result that. The meaning of the phrase *eph' hō* has been much debated throughout the centuries. It has been understood, first, as introducing a genuine relative clause.

(1) "In whom," with the masc. pron. referring to Adam; it would imply incorporation in him, a meaning based on the VL and Vg translations *in quo* and

commonly used in the western church since Ambrosiaster (*In ep. ad Romanos* 5.12 [CSEL 81:165]: "in Adam . . . quasi in massa"). Augustine, who at first (A.D. 412) explained the antecedent of *quo* as either sin ("peccatum") or Adam ("ille unus homo") in *De peccatorum meritis et remissione* 1.10.11 [CSEL 60.12]), later (A.D. 420) opted for Adam, when he realized that the Greek word for sin was feminine (*Contra duas epistolae Pelagianorum* 4.4.7 [CSEL 60.527]: "in illo homine peccaverunt omnes"). Augustinian interpretations were generally followed by Latin theologians: either "sive in Adamo, sive in peccato" (Peter Chrysologus, Ps.-Primasius, Ps.-Bede, Thomas Aquinas, Denis of Chartres) or "in Adamo" (Sedulius, Fulgentius of Ruspe, Walafrid Strabo, Alexander of Hales, Hugh of Saint-Cher, Bonaventure). The latter interpretation was unknown to the Greek Fathers before John Damascene. Incorporation would not have been an impossible idea for Paul, and it is sometimes further explained by invoking the OT idea of corporate personality or solidarity; so Bruce, *Romans* 126; Ellis, *Paul's Use of the Old Testament*, 58–60; de Fraine, *Adam*, 142–52. Yet if Paul had meant "in whom" (in the sense of incorporation), he would have written *en hō*, as he does in 1 Cor 15:22; cf. Heb 7:9–10. Moreover, *Adam* as the personal antecedent of the rel. pron. is too far removed in the sentence from the pronoun.

(2) "Because of whom," i.e., Adam, all have sinned. So several Greek Fathers: John Chrysostom (*In ep. ad Romanos* hom. 10.1 [PG 60.474]: *ekeinou pesontos*); Theodoret of Cyrrhus (*Interpretatio ep. ad Romanos* 5.12 [PG 82.100]); John Damascene (*In ep. ad Romanos* 5.12 [PG 95.477]: *di' hou*); Theophylact (*Expositio in ep. ad Romanos* 5.12 [PG 124.404]: *pesontos ekeinou*). Similarly Cambier, "Péchés."

(3) "Because of the one by whom" (*eph' hō* would elliptically equal *epi toutō eph' hō*), an interpretation that spells out a possibly elliptical phrase and refers the masc. pron. to Adam. It would thus imply "a relationship between the state of sin and its initiator" (Cerfaux, *Christ*, 232). But it is not clear that the phrase is elliptical, or that the *epi* could tolerate two diverse meanings, "because of" and "by," in such close proximity.

(4) "To the extent that all have sinned," an interpretation that understands *eph' hō* as neuter and equal to *kath' ho*; so Cyril of Alexandria (*In ep. ad Romanos* 5.12 [PG 74.784]). See further J. Meyendorff, "*Eph' hō* (Rom. 5,12) chez Cyrille d'Alexandrie et Théodoret," *Studia patristica* 4, TU 79 (1961), 157–61. Cyril, however, also understood it to mean that all sinned in imitation of Adam: *tēs en Adam parabaseōs gegonamen mimētai*, a meaning that Pelagius also used, even though he understood *eph' hō* as "in quo." Nygren (*Romans*, 214) seems to align himself with this meaning.

(5) "On the grounds of which," or "because of which," an interpretation that takes "death" as the antecedent of masc. *eph' hō* and explains it as the origin of sin (so Galling, Leipoldt, Schlier, and apparently Bultmann [who toys with it in "Adam," 153]). But this meaning is hard to reconcile with 5:21 and 6:23, where death is the result of sin, not its source. It seems to put the cart before the horse.

(6) "Toward which," again with *thanatos* as the antecedent, but expressing the end or goal of human sin. So Héring (*Le Royaume*, 157); Stauffer (*New Testament Theology* [London: SCM, 1955], 270 n. 176). But this meaning is farfetched.

(7) "On the basis of what (law) all sinned," understanding *nomō* from the general context and especially v 13; so Danker, comparing Menander, *Fragment* 531.6–7. But that reading introduces into the sentence a notion that is not clearly envisaged. See Porter, "Pauline Concept."

(8) "On the basis of which" or "under which circumstances," with the antecedent understood as the preceding clauses in the verse; so Zahn (*Römer*, 263–67), who thus stresses the fact and the reason for the universality of sin. Of the relative-pronoun understandings of *ephʾ hō*, this one makes the best sense, and it has extrabiblical parallels.

Second, *ephʾ hō* has been understood as equivalent to a conjunction.

(9) "Since, because, inasmuch as," the equivalent of a causal conj. *dioti*, or as the equivalent of *epi toutō hoti*, as many modern commentators understand *ephʾ hō*, comparing 2 Cor 5:4; Phil 3:12; 4:10 (BAGD, 287; BDF §235.2); so Achtemeier, Althaus, Bardenhewer, Barrett, Bengel, Bonsirven, Brandenburger, Bruce, Bultmann, Byrne, Cranfield, Dibelius, Dodd, Dunn, Gaugler, Huby, Käsemann, Kuss, Lagrange, Lindeskog, Meyer, Michel, Moule, Moo, Murray, Pesch, Prat, Sanday and Headlam, Schlier, Wilckens, and Winer. Montagnini (*Rom 5,12–14*) thinks that *ephʾ hō* is the equivalent of Hebrew ʿal kēn and would translate it as "ecco perché," which is only a refinement of the commonly used "because." This interpretation would ascribe to human beings an individual responsibility for death.

The trouble with this interpretation is that there are almost no certain instances in early Greek literature wherein *ephʾ hō* is used as the equivalent of causal *dioti*. Most of the examples cited by BAGD (287) or B-A (582) are invalid. Thus, *ephʾ hō* in Diodorus Siculus, *Bibliothēkē historikē* 19.98, means "for which reason" (not the conj. "because"); Appian, *Bellum Civile* 1.112: "for which reason"; Synesius, *Ep.* 73: "on condition that" (see 10 below); Aelius Aristides, *Oratio* 53 640D. Only Damascius, *Vita Isidori*, 154 and tenth-century Syntipas, p. 124/5, 127/8 may be relevant. Fourteenth-century Thomas Magister (p. 129, 3) says that *ephʾ hō* with a past verb stands for *dioti*, but gives only the dubious example of Synesius (see 10 below).

Moreover, alleged examples in the Pauline corpus itself, apart from 5:12, are far from certain. In Phil 3:12 *ephʾ hō* means "that for which"; in Phil 4:10, "for whom," or possibly "with regard to which" (Moule, *Idiom Book*, 132). Not even 2 Cor 5:4 does *ephʾ hō* certainly mean "because" (despite the v.l. *epeidē* in minuscule MSS 7*, 20*, 93 and the Vg translation "eo quod"); there it could easily mean "because of that which."

Hence one has to take with a grain of salt the statement of Photius that myriad examples of this phrase in the causal sense can be found (*Quaestio 84 ad*

Amphiloch., PG 101.553). Lyonnet was undoubtedly right: "the alleged current use" of *eph᾿ hō* for *hoti* or *dioti* "has in no way been proved" (*Bib* 36 [1955]: 455).

(10) "In view of the fact that, on condition that," an interpretation that employs the proviso meaning of neuter *eph᾿ hō* understood as a conj. in classical and Hellenistic Greek. So Rothe (*Neuer Versuch*, 17–19); Moulton (*A Grammar of New Testament Greek* [Edinburgh: Clark], 1 [1908], 107); Lyonnet; and Black (*Romans*, 82). Normally, however, *eph᾿ hō*, expressing a proviso, governs an infin. or a fut. indic. (occasionally a subjunc. or opt.). Cf. Plato, *Apology* 17 §29C; Xenophon, *Anabasis* 6.6.22; *Hellenica* 2.2.20; Thucydides, *Peloponnesian War* 1.103.1; 1.126.11; Herodotus, *History* 3.83; 7.158. An example of it with an aor. indic., apart from Phil 3:12, is found in a letter of the fourth-century bishop Synesius (*Ep.* 73 [PG 66.1440]): *eph᾿ hō Gennadion egrapsato*, "on condition that he wrote (an accusation against) Gennadius," which expresses a fulfilled condition.

The last two meanings, both proviso and causal, seem to make Paul say in 5:12d something contradictory to what he says in 5:12abc. In the beginning of v 12 sin and death are ascribed to Adam; now death seems to be owing to human acts. So Lietzmann (*An die Römer*, 62); Bultmann ("Adam," 153); Kuss (*Römerbrief*, 231).

(11) "With the result that, so that," the equivalent of consecutive conj. *hōste*, a meaning found in Plutarch, *Cimon* 8.6.4 ("[Cimon] brought them [the bones of Theseus] back to the city after almost 400 years with the result that the citizenry became most kindly disposed toward him" [*eph᾿ hō kai malista pros auton hēdeōs ho dēmos eschen*]); *Aratus* 44.4.1; *De curiositate* 552E.4–6; Athenaeus, *Deipnosophistae* 2.49d ("It was a custom at banquets that a tablet was handed to the one who had just reclined containing a list of what had been prepared so that he would know what food the cook would provide" [*eph᾿ hō eidenai ho ti mellei opson pherein ho mageiros*]); Cassius Dio, *Historia Romana* 59.19.1–2; 59.20.3; 61.33.8; 63.28.5; 67.4.6; 73.18.2; Diogenes Laertius, *Vitae philos.* 7.173.1–5. For the recent discovery and full discussion of this consecutive meaning, see Fitzmyer, "Consecutive Meaning."

Eph᾿ hō, then, would mean that Paul is expressing a result, the sequel to Adam's baleful influence on humanity by the ratification of his sin in the sins of all individuals. He would thus be conceding to individual human sins a secondary causality or personal responsibility for death. Moreover, one must not lose sight of the adv. *kai houtōs*, "and so" (5:12c), which establishes the connection between the sin of "one man" and the death and sins of "all human beings." Thus Paul in v 12 is ascribing death to two causes, not unrelated: to Adam and to all human sinners. The fate of humanity ultimately rests on what its head, Adam, has done to it. The primary causality for its sinful and mortal condition is ascribed to Adam, no matter what meaning is assigned to *eph᾿ hō*, and a secondary causality to the sins of all human beings. For "no one sins entirely alone and no one sins without adding to the collective burden of mankind." (Byrne, *Reckoning*, 116).

The universal causality of Adam's sin is presupposed in 5:15a, 16a, 17a, 18a, 19a. It would then be false to the thrust of the whole paragraph to interpret 5:12 as though it implied that the human condition before Christ's coming were due solely to individual personal sins.

all have sinned. See the COMMENT on 3:23. The vb. *hēmarton* should not be understood as "have sinned collectively" or as "have sinned in Adam," because they would be additions to Paul's text. The vb. refers to personal, actual sins of individual human beings, as Pauline usage elsewhere suggests (2:12; 3:23; 5:14, 16; 6:15; 1 Cor 6:18; 7:28, 36; 8:12; 15:34), as the context demands (vv 16, 20), and as Greek Fathers understood it (see Lyonnet, *Bib* 41 [1960]: 325–55). Cf. the LXX of Isa 24:6, where one finds a very similar use of the vb. *hamartanein: dia touto ara edetai tēn gēn, hoti hēmartosan hoi katoikountes en tē gē*, "for this reason a curse swallows up the land, because the dwellers on the land have sinned."

13. *up to the time of the law sin was in the world.* Lit., "before there was a law, there was sin." Paul often omits the def. art. before *nomos* (BDF §258.2), but it clearly refers to the Mosaic law. With this clause Paul begins his anacoluthon; he introduces no *houtōs* to follow up on his *hōsper*. His conclusion will be implicit in v 14c. He feels it necessary to stress that it was not just "death" that was inherited from Adam, but "sin" as well. The continuation of the digression produces a further precision. From Adam to Moses, the source of "death" was Adam's sin. Human beings did commit evil (see Gen 6:5–7, to which Paul never alludes), but they were not charged with such evil in the period between Adam and Moses.

sin is not accounted when there is no law. Paul enunciates a general principle that agrees with 4:15 and 3:20 and presupposes the Jewish conception of heavenly books in which human deeds were recorded (see the NOTE on 4:3). He uses again the bookkeeping vb. *ellogeitai*, "charge to someone's account." See Friedrich, "*Hamartia*"; Bouwman, " 'Zonde wordt nit aangerekend . . .' " Cf. Philo, *Quod Deus imm.* 28 §134, for a similar idea, but expressed in Philonic imagery. Sin neither in its grossness nor in its quantity was booked against individuals. There could be no transgression where there was no law.

14. *death held sway from Adam until Moses.* So Paul explains the reign of death; cf. 1 Cor 15:21–22. For the OT background to the imagery of death reigning, see Wis 1:14; Hos 13:14. This statement reveals that Paul viewed human history as divided into periods (see Introduction, section IX.A). He explains the death of human beings between Adam and Moses in terms of what he said in 5:12a and 5:12d, the baleful influence of Adam's *hamartia* and the *hamartanein* of individuals. Augustine conceived of this "reign of death" as the "guilt of sin," which leads human beings to death: "Regnum enim mortis vult intelligi, quando ita dominatur in hominibus reatus peccati, ut eos ad vitam aeternam, quae vera vita est, venire non sinat, sed ad secundam etiam, quae poenaliter aeterna est, mortem trahat" (For the reign of death is meant, when the guilt of sin so

dominates human beings that it does not permit them to come to eternal life, which is true life, but even draws them to the second death, which is eternal as a punishment) (*De peccatorum meritis et remissione* 1.11.13 [CSEL 60.13–14]).

even over those who had not sinned in a way similar to Adam's transgression. Lit., "on the likeness of Adam's transgression." Here *hamartia*, "sin," and *parabasis*, "transgression," are distinguished; the latter is the formal aspect of an evil deed considered as a violation of a law or precept. Adam had been given a precept (Gen 2:17; 3:17), which he violated. Those who lived in the first (Lawless) period, however, did not do evil as he had done, for they violated no precepts. Again, Paul passes over the so-called Noachic legislation (Gen 9:4–6) and discusses only the problem of the Mosaic law. His perspective here has nothing to do with that of 2:14, even though it does not contradict that view. He sees humanity first coming under precepts in an analogous way when the Mosaic law is laid upon it. What Paul here calls Adam's *parabasis*, he will call his *paraptōma*, "trespass," in vv 15, 17, 18 and his *parakoē*, "disobedience," in v 19.

Some MSS (614, 1739*, 2495*), Origen and Ambrosiaster, and some MSS of the VL omit the negative *mē*, so that their text would read, "even over those who sinned." Augustine was aware of this reading; see *De peccatorum meritis et remissione* 1.11.13 (CSEL 60.14). Furthermore, MSS B and 2495 as well as Origen read *en* instead of *epi*, the reading of the majority of the MSS as the prep. governing "the likeness." This is a stylistic variant to avoid the double use of *epi*.

who is a type of the one who was to come. The sentence ends in anacoluthon, as Paul tries to bring his comparison, begun in 5:12, to an end. He sees the first Adam as foreshadowing the future Adam, i.e., Christ, the "last Adam" (1 Cor 15:45), or the Adam of the *eschaton*. Paul calls Adam the *typos* of Christ, who is thus the *antitypos*, i.e., what corresponds to the "type." On *typos*, see the NOTE on 6:17. Here Paul uses it in a specific sense, "pattern, model" (as in Exod 25:40; Acts 7:44; Heb 8:5; Diodorus Siculus 14.41.4). Although Adam prefigures Christ as the head of humanity, the resemblance between type and antitype is not perfect; it is antithetical. Differences exist, and the rest of the paragraph brings them out; the antitype reproduces the type in a sense, but in a more perfect way. Without the Adam-Christ typology, Paul expresses the same idea in 2 Cor 5:14: "He died for all, that those who live might live no longer for themselves, but for him who for their sake died and was raised." See Muddiman, "Adam"; Byrne, " 'The Type.' " It is hardly likely that *tou mellontos* is to be taken as neut., *pace* Biju-Duval ("La traduzione").

15. *But the gift is not like the trespass.* I.e., there is no comparison between what Christ graciously did for humanity and what Adam did. Even though Paul admitted that Adam was the "model" for Christ, yet there is a great difference, which is why he begins this verse with an emphatic *alla*, "but." Verses 15 and 16 have a similar structure: v 15a and v 16a declare the difference between the gift and the trespass, but v 15b and v 16b express the basis for the declaration. The Greek text of vv 14–16 also has a string of nouns that end in *-ma: homoiōma*,

paraptōma, charisma, dōrēma, krima, katakrima, dikaiōma; they have obviously been chosen for rhetorical assonance, but it cannot be reproduced in English (see BDF §488.3). Moreover, in vv 15–17 the argument proceeds a minori ad maius.

if many have died because of the trespass of one man. Lit., "the many," i.e., the mass of humanity, another way of saying "all" (cf. 5:18, where Paul uses instead *pantas;* 12:5; 1 Cor 10:17). To this end Paul makes use of the Greek rhetorical contrast of "the one" and "the many." The use of substantive *hoi polloi* in the LXX is rare (see Dan 12:4) and should not be confused with the ubiquitous anarthrous *polloi* (cf. Isa 53:11–12). Adam's trespass of God's precept has affected all humanity. The contrast also lies between the consequence or result of Adam's trespass and the prevenience of God's grace.

how much more have the grace of God and his gift overflowed to the many. See the NOTE on 3:24. Paul argues a minori ad maius (as in 5:9–10; 11:12, 24; 2 Cor 3:9, 11) and expresses himself in antithetical and step parallelism: the grace of God and his free gift have come to humanity in superabundance. The "free gift" is God's benevolent favor, assuring justification and reconciliation to all who believe in Christ Jesus.

because of the grace of one man, Jesus Christ. Thus Paul identifies Christ as the mediator of God's saving grace (compare 1 Tim 2:5). Lest the comparison with Adam seem an affront to Christ, Paul stresses the surpassing quality of Christ's influence on humanity. The first mode of expressing that superabundance is the manifestation of God's favor far in excess of any mercy that sin might otherwise have evoked. See J. M. Bover, "In Rom. 5, 15."

16. *the gift is not like the result of one man's sin.* Lit., "and not like (what comes) through one man sinning is the gift." So Paul recasts the idea of v 15a in other words, in order to stress the superabundance of the "gift." Recall 2 Cor 8:9, "You recognize the grace of our Lord Jesus Christ: though he was rich, yet for your sake he became poor so that by his poverty you might become rich." Cf. 4 Ezra 7:118–19.

Greek MSS D, F, G, and some ancient versions read *hamartēmatos,* "and not as through the sin of one (man) is the gift," an obvious correction to get rid of the troublesome *hamartēsantos* of the majority of the MSS.

for judgment resulting from one trespass became condemnation. A verb like *egeneto,* "became," has to be supplied. What Adam did in sinning resulted not merely in *krima,* "judgment," but in *katakrima,* "condemnation," when a verdict had to be given. "Condemnation" is the penalty of death, of eternal death passed as a verdict on all human beings. On the related sense of *krima* and *katakrima,* see the NOTE on 2:3.

the gift following upon many trespasses brought justification. The vb. *edothē* has to be understood. The sense: God's gift was given, having been evoked or called forth by many offenses, and it has meant acquittal. Cf. Isa 53:11b–12. The second mode contrasts the verdict of condemnation for one sin, which fell on all human beings, with the justification (or verdict of acquittal) for all those condemned not only through Adam's transgression but also through their own offenses. Again, the contrast occurs between "the one" and "the many." The verse stresses the incomparably greater character of the gift of grace and justification, when it is compared with the trespass of Adam and the sins of human beings. *Dikaiōma* is the end product of God's *charisma* and gracious activity in Christ Jesus. It will be described in v 18 as *dikaiōsis zōēs*, lit., "the justification of life," i.e., justification that brings life.

17. *If by the trespass of one man death came to hold sway through that one man.* Again, Paul poses the problem in different words. Verse 17 is a parallel to v 15b, and in a sense to v 16b. One has to understand what he said in vv 15a and 16a as the thesis, which he is explaining. It is not only that all have sinned (5:12d), but much more the trespass of one man, Adam, has affected all in a mortal way. This is the fate common to all because of Adam, and Christians share in it as long as they live, unless they are under the grace of Christ.

how much more will those who receive the abundance of God's grace and his gift of uprightness reign in life through the one man, Jesus Christ. The third mode contrasts death as the effect of the offense of one man (Adam) with the gift of upright life obtained through one man (Christ). Again in the stress on "one man" lies the similarity of Adam and Christ, but the latter has exerted the more beneficent causality. Note the repeated *pollō mallon*, "how much more," and the emphasis on *tēn perisseian tēs charitos*, "the abundance of grace." Whereas in v 14 Paul spoke of the reign of death, now he replaces that with the reign of life, i.e., justified Christians enjoy the regal freedom of life eternal (cf. 1 Cor 4:18). See Rom 6:12–13; Rev 20:4. So Paul concludes his discussion of the incomparability of the gracious act of God in Christ Jesus.

The gen. *tēs dōreas*, "gift," is read in MSS P⁴⁶, ℵ, A, C, D, G, K, P, and the *Koinē* text-tradition, but is changed to the acc. in MSS 88, 104, 1984, and 1985 (to be parallel with *perisseian* and to avoid too many gens.) and omitted in MS B and the Sahidic version.

18. *just as through one trespass condemnation came upon all.* Or "through the trespass of one man." In view of the preceding context, in which the pron. *henos* refers to "one man," it might seem better to preserve that sense and take it here as masc. Still, Paul may be varying his formulation and intending *henos* to be neuter, "through one offense . . . so through one act of uprightness." The clauses are elliptical and depend on the context for their intelligibility (see BDF §481). In other words, Paul reiterates his idea of Adam as the type of the one who was to come (v 14c).

So . . . through one act of uprightness. Or "through the justifying act (*or* righteous deed) of one man." Paul reiterates the effect of Adam's sin: condemnation to eternal death for all. *Dikaiōma* may also have the connotation of a verdict that is just, as the word is understood in the LXX of 1 Kgs 3:28. Verses 18–19 introduce another topic in the antithetical parallelism of Paul's argument. The contrast is now clearly expressed by *hōsper . . . houtōs*, "just as . . . so."

justification and life came to all human beings. Lit., "for the justification of life," a gen. of apposition, or possibly of direction or purpose (BDF §166). It is the justification that includes life or that leads to life. The gracious act manifesting God's gift of uprightness (5:17) not only cleared human beings of guilt but also granted them a share in "life." Recall 4:25b. "Justification and life" come to "all," both Jews and Greeks, through the upright act of Christ Jesus. Paul will repeat this idea in 11:32 in terms of God's great and impartial mercy. This new "life" is explained more fully in chap. 8. See Street, "On the Use."

19. *Just as through the disobedience of one man many were made sinners.* The climax of the comparison is reached here; it echoes 5:12 and formally enunciates the basic contrast of Adam and Christ. The formal effect of Adam's transgression (Gen 3:6), now labeled *parakoē*, "disobedience," was to make humanity not only liable to punishment, but actually sinners. Thus Paul reformulates what he said in 5:12. The vb. *katesthatēsan* means "were made, were caused to be, were constituted" (compare Jas 4:4; 3:6). See BAGD, 390: "be made, become"; B-A, 792; J.-A. Bühner, *EDNT*, 2.225: "refers to the eschatological judicial act of installation in the realm of righteousness or sin." "There is no philological ground for the common suggestion that the element of judgment predominates rather than the actual fact. The state itself is always presupposed" (A. Oepke, *TDNT* 3.445). As Lagrange (*Romans*, 111) notes, the vb. *kathistanai* indicates more than a juridical assessment. Cf. Danker, "Under Contract," 105–7; de Zwaan, "Rom 5:19"; Korošak, " 'Costituti peccatori,' " Yet so astute a commentator as Taylor has remarked, "No one can be made a sinner or made righteous" (*Romans*, 41). But that is exactly what Paul says, and he is not speaking of personal sinful acts alone. Adam's disobedience placed the mass of humanity in a condition of sin and estrangement from God; the text does not imply that they became sinners merely by imitating Adam's transgression; rather, they were constituted sinners by him and his act of disobedience.

so through the obedience of one many will be made upright. This is the climax in the paragraph: the influence of Christ is overwhelming and knows no bounds. Cf. Phil 2:6–8. Jesus' obedience to the will of his Father has had an effect on the destiny of all human beings. "His whole life was determined by this obedience, and this obedience has won lawful and theological significance for the humanity of the eschatological period" (Michel, *Brief an die Römer*, 191). For the contrast of *parakoē*, "disobedience," and *hypakoē*, "obedience," see 2 Cor 10:6. The fut. *katastathēsontai* does not refer merely to the eschaton; with Lagrange (*Romans*, 112) and Zahn it is better taken as a logical future, *pace* Schrenk (*TDNT* 2.191), Kuss (*Römerbrief*, 239), Schlier (*Römerbrief*, 175), and Lietzmann. In this entire paragraph Paul understands justification as something present. The formal effect of Christ's obedience has been to make humanity upright in the sight of God at the judgment seat. Paul may be alluding here to Isa 53:11–12, though Käsemann (*Commentary*, 157) sees no reason "to introduce the motif of the Suffering Servant into the text. The important thing is only the antithesis to Adam's disobedience and therefore again the antithetical correspondence of primal time and end-time."

Elsewhere the process of justification seems to be regarded as past (5:1, 9); if the fut. tense were to refer to the eschatological judgment, the final phase of that process would be achieved in glory, as in 3:30; cf. Gal 5:5. The many will be constituted righteous through Christ's obedience because God has in Christ identified himself with sinners and taken upon himself the burden of their sin; hence they will receive as a free gift from God that status of uprightness which Christ's perfect obedience alone has merited (to paraphrase Cranfield, *Romans*, 291).

20. *The law slipped in that trespass might increase.* As in Gal 3:19, the Mosaic law during the period that it reigned over humanity is regarded as a means of multiplying offense in the religious history of humanity. Cf. Rom 4:15. It does so by supplying human beings with a "knowledge of sin" (3:20; cf. 7:13). As in the case of *Hamartia* and *Thanatos*, so now *Nomos* is personified and treated as an actor on the stage of human history. Instead of being a source of life for the Jews, according to Lev 18:5, it proved to be an informer against them and accuser, bringing condemnation (see Introduction, section IX.D). It is now said to have "slipped in," i.e., it entered into human history and became a new factor in human existence. Again Paul relates the position of the Mosaic law to the Christ-event, as he did in 3:31. Here it is not his major problem, but it is subordinately related to his topic. On Augustine's understanding of this Pauline statement, see the NOTE on 3:8.

where sin increased, grace has abounded all the more. The basic Pauline thesis is repeated once again, now in the context of law. As Paul will explain in chap. 7, the law, though good in itself, had dire effects in that through it sin increased in the world; but now through Christ grace has abounded in contrast and all the more. Cf. 1 Tim 1:14.

21. *just as sin held sway in death, grace too might reign through uprightness.* So Paul contrasts sin and death with grace and uprightness and thus sums up the thought of the entire paragraph. Through grace and uprightness humanity is now freed of sin and death. Cf. 6:23. Paul now personifies "grace" and sees it as a personal force ruling over human beings.

to bring eternal life through Jesus Christ our Lord. Thus the mediation of Christ (see the NOTE on 5:1), the head of reconciled humanity, is stressed at the end of the first subdivision of this part of the letter. The risen *Kyrios* brings to humanity a share in "eternal life," in the risen and glorious life of the Son of God, in which vitality is derived from his Spirit. The adj. "eternal" indicates the quality of that life rather than its duration; it is the life of glory with God himself.

This section, which we call chapter 5, like the next three, ends with "through Jesus Christ our Lord," with an affirmation of the lordship of Christ Jesus, who has overthrown all other lords that try to dominate human existence. Because

Christ Jesus alone is Lord in human life, he alone "holds sway" or "reigns," and his mediation is recognized.

BIBLIOGRAPHY

Aberle, [M. V.], "Exegetische Studien 1) Ueber Röm. 5, 12–14," *TQ* 36 (1854): 453–70.

Anon., "New Thinking on Original Sin," *Herder Correspondence* 4.5 (1967): 135–41.

Anon., "Ueber *eph' hō*, bei Römer 5, 12," *TQ* 13 (1831): 397–444.

Ayles, H. H. B., "Romans v. 18," *ExpTim* 20 (1908–9): 189–90.

Barclay, W., "Great Themes of the New Testament: III. Romans v. 12–21," *ExpTim* 70 (1958–59): 132–35, 172–75.

Barth, K., *Christ and Adam: Man and Humanity in Romans 5*, SJT Occasional Papers 5 (Edinburgh and London: Oliver and Boyd, 1956).

Biffi, G. and G. Lattanzo, "Una recente esegesi di *Rom.* 5,12–14," *ScCatt* 84 (1956): 451–58.

Biju-Duval, D., "La traduzione di Rm 5,12–14," *RivB* 38 (1990): 353–73.

Black, C. C., II, "Pauline Perspectives on Death in Romans 5–8," *JBL* 103 (1984): 413–33.

Boer, M. C. de, *The Defeat of Death: Apocalyptic Eschatology in 1 Corinthians 15 and Romans 5*, JSNTSup 22 (Sheffield, UK: JSOT, 1988).

Bouwman, G., " 'Zonde wordt nit aangerekend, wanneer er geen wet is': Een onderzoek naar de structuur van Rom. 5, 12–14," *TvT* 17 (1977): 131–44.

Bover, J. M., "In Rom. 5, 15: Exegesis logica," *Bib* 4 (1923): 94–96.

Brandenburger, E., *Adam und Christus: Exegetisch-religionsgeschichtliche Untersuchung zu Römer 5, 12–21 (I. Kor. 15)*, WMANT 7 (Neukirchen-Vluyn: Neukirchener-Verlag, 1962).

Bruston, C., *Le Parallèle entre Adam et Jésus-Christ: Étude exégétique sur Romains V, 12–21* (Paris: Fischbacher, 1894).

Bultmann, R., "Adam and Christ According to Romans 5," *Current Issues in New Testament Interpretation: Essays in Honor of Otto A. Piper*, ed. W. Klassen and G. F. Snyder (New York: Harper & Bros., 1962), 143–65; trans. from "Adam und Christus nach Rm 5," *ZNW* 50 (1959): 145–65.

Buonaiuti, E., "Pelagius and the Pauline Vulgate," *ExpTim* 27 (1915–16): 425–27.

Byrne, B., " 'The Type of the One to Come' (Rom 5:14): Fate and Responsibility in Romans 5:12–21," *AusBR* 36 (1988): 19–30.

Cambier, J., "Péchés des hommes et péché d'Adam en Rom. v. 12," *NTS* 11 (1964–65): 217–55.

———, "Péché et grâce," *L'Évangile de Dieu*, 1.279–338.

Campeau, L., " 'Regnavit mors ab Adam usque ad Moysen' (*Rom.* 5,14)," *ScEccl* 5 (1953): 57–65.

Caragounis, C. C., "Romans 5.15–16 in the Context of 5.12–21: Contrast or Comparison?" *NTS* 31 (1985): 142–48.

Castellino, G. R., "Il peccato di Adamo: Note a Genesi III e a Romani V 12–14," *BeO* 16 (1974): 145–62.

Ceuppens, F., "Le Polygénisme et la Bible," *Ang* 24 (1947): 20–32.

Condon, K., "The Biblical Doctrine of Original Sin," *ITQ* 34 (1967): 20–36.

Cranfield, C. E. B., "On Some of the Problems in the Interpretation of Romans 5.12," *SJT* 22 (1969): 324–41.

Dahl, N. A., "Two Notes on Romans 5," *ST* 5 (1952): 37–48, esp. 42–48.

Danker, F. W., "Romans V. 12: Sin Under Law," *NTS* 14 (1967–68): 424–39.

———, "Under Contract," *Festschrift to Honor F. Wilbur Gingrich*, ed. E. H. Barth and R. E. Cocroft (Leiden: Brill, 1972), 91–114.

De Bruyn, T. S., "Pelagius's Interpretation of Rom. 5:12–21: Exegesis Within the Limits of Polemic," *TorJT* 4 (1988): 30–43.

Dietzsch, A., *Adam und Christus: Röm. V, 12–21: Eine exegetische Monographie* (Bonn: Marcus, 1871).

Dole, I., "Paraphrase of Rom. V. 12–21," *BSac* 45 (1888): 518–20.

Englezakis, B., "Rom 5,12–21 and the Pauline Teaching on the Lord's Death: Some Observations," *Bib* 58 (1977): 231–36.

Feuillet, A., "Le Règne de la mort et le règne de la vie (Rom. v, 12–21)," *RB* 77 (1970): 481–521.

Fitzmyer, J. A., "The Consecutive Meaning of *eph' hō* in Romans 5. 12," *NTS* 39.3 (1993).

Fondevila, J. M., "La gracia capital de Adán y el capítulo quinto de la carta a los Romanos," *SPCIC* 1.289–300.

Fraine, J. de, *Adam and the Family of Man* (Staten Island, N.Y.: Alba House, 1965), 142–52.

Freundorfer, J., *Erbsünde und Erbtod beim Apostel Paulus: Eine religionsgeschicht-liche und exegetische Untersuchung über Römerbrief 5, 12–21*, NTAbh 13.1–2 (Münster in Westfalen: Aschendorff, 1927).

Friedrich, G., "*Hamartia ouk ellogeitai*, Röm 5,13," *TLZ* 77 (1952): 523–28.

Godet, F., "The Logical Arrangement of Rom. V. 15–17," *Expos* 4.1 (1890): 285–95.

González de Carrea, S., "Exégesis e interpretación de Rom 5,12–21," *El pecado original: XXIX semana española de teología (Madrid, 15–19 sept. 1969)* (Madrid: Consejo Superior de Investigaciones Científicas, 1970), 43–67.

González Ruiz, J. M., "El pecado original según San Pablo," *EstBíb* 17 (1958): 147–88.

Grelot, P., "Péché originel et rédemption dans l'épître aux Romains," *NRT* 90 (1968): 337–62, 449–78, 598–621; repr. *Péché originel et rédemption examinés à partir de l'épître aux Romains: Essai théologique* (Paris: Desclée, 1973).

Grundmann, W., "Die Übermacht der Gnade: Eine Studie zur Theologie des Paulus," *NovT* 2 (1958): 50–72.

Hamilton, W., "The Punctuation and Rendering of Romans v. 12–14," *ExpTim* 24 (1912–13): 234–35.

Henry, D. M., "Romans v. 20," *ExpTim* 5 (1893–94): 426–27.

Héring, J., *Le Royaume de Dieu et sa venue: Étude sur l'espérance de Jésus et de l'apôtre Paul,* new ed. (Neuchâtel: Delachaux et Niestlé, 1959), 155–59.

Herman, Z. I., "La novità cristiana secondo Romani 5,20–7,6: Alcune osservazioni esegetiche," *Anton* 61 (1986): 225–73.

Hoekstra, S., "Proeve van verklaring der woorden: *eph' hō pantes hēmarton,* Rom. 5:12ᵇ," *TTijd* 2 (1868): 63–74.

Hulsbosch, A., "Zonde en dod in Rom. 5,12–21," *TvT* 1 (1961): 194–204.

Hünefeld, E., *Römer 5,12–21 von neuem erklärt* (Leipzig: Strübig, 1895).

Jacob, R., "La Nouvelle Solidarité humaine: Rm 5:12–19," *AsSeign* 14 (1973): 32–38.

Jüngel, E., "Das Gesetz zwischen Adam und Christus: Eine theologische Studie zu Röm 5, 12–21," *ZTK* 60 (1963): 43–74; repr. in *Unterwegs zur Sache: Theologische Bemerkungen,* BEvT 61 (Munich: Kaiser, 1972), 145–72.

Kertelge, K., "Adam und Christus: Die Sünde Adams im Lichte der Erlösungstat Christi nach Röm 5,12–21," *Anfänge der Christologie: Festschrift für Ferdinand Hahn zum 65. Geburtstag,* ed. C. Breytenbach and H. Paulsen (Göttingen: Vandenhoeck & Ruprecht, 1991), 141–53; in shortened form in *IKZ* 20 (1991): 305–14; in English in *Communio (International Catholic Review)* 18 (1991): 502–13.

Kirby, J. T., "The Syntax of Romans 5. 12: A Rhetorical Approach," *NTS* 33 (1987): 283–86.

Kline, M. G., "Gospel until the Law: Rom 5:13–14 and the Old Covenant," *JETS* 34 (1991): 433–46.

Klöpper, A., "Die Bedeutung und der Zweck des Abschnitts Röm. 5,12–21," *TSK* 42.2 (1869): 496–514.

Korošak, B. J., " 'Costituiti peccatori' (Rom 5,19)," *Euntes docete* 40 (1987): 157–66.

Lafont, G., "Il n'y a pas de commune mesure!: Rm 5,12 et 15," *AsSeign* 43 (1969): 13–18.

———, "Sur l'Interprétation de Romains V, 15–21," *RSR* 45 (1957): 481–513.

Léon-Dufour, X., "Situation littéraire de *Rom.* V," *RSR* 51 (1963): 83–95.

Ligier, L., " 'In quo omnes peccaverunt': Actes ou état?" *NRT* 82 (1960): 337–48.

———, *Péché d'Adam et péché du monde,* 2 vols. (Paris: Aubier, 1960–61), 2.212–89.

Lombard, H. A., "The Adam-Christ 'Typology' in Romans 5:12–21," *Neotestamentica* 15 (1981): 69–100.

Losada, D., "El texto de Rom. 5,12–21: Un análisis estructural," *RevistB* 36 (1974): 27–36.

Lyonnet, S., "À propos de Romains 5,12 dans l'oeuvre de saint Augustin: Note complémentaire," *Bib* 45 (1964): 541–42.

———, "Augustin et Rm 5,12 avant la controverse pélagienne: À propos d'un texte de saint Augustin sur le baptême des enfants," *NRT* 89 (1967): 842–49.

———, "Le Péché originel et l'exégèse de *Rom.,* 5,12–14," *RSR* 44 (1956): 63–84.

————, "Le Péché originel en Rom 5,12: L'Exégèse des pères grecs et les décrets du Concile de Trente," *Bib* 41 (1960): 325–55.

————, "Péché," *DBSup* 7 (1966): 524–67.

————, "Das Problem der Erbsünde im Neuen Testament," *SdZ* 180 (1967): 33–39.

————, "La Problématique du péché originel dans le Nouveau Testament," in *Il mito della Pena*, ed. E. Castelli (Rome: Istituto di Studi Filosofici, 1967), 101–8; repr. in *Études*, 178–84.

————, "Rom. V,12 chez saint Augustin: Note sur l'élaboration de la doctrine augustinienne du péché originel," *L'Homme devant Dieu: Mélanges offerts au P. Henri de Lubac*, Théologie 56 (Paris: Aubier, 1963) 1.327–39.

————, "Le Sens de *eph' hō* en Rom 5, 12 et l'exégèse des Pères grecs," *Bib* 36 (1955): 436–56 (= *TD* 5 [1957–58]: 54–57); repr. in *Études*, 185–202.

————, "Le Sens de *peirazein* en Sap 2,24 et la doctrine du péché originale," *Bib* 39 (1958): 27–36.

————, "L'Universalité du péché et son explication par le péché d'Adam," *Les Étapes*, 55–111.

Mariani, B., "La persona di Adamo e il peccato originale originante secondo S. Paolo: Rom 5, 12–21," *Divinitas* 2 (1958): 486–519.

Marmorstein, A., "Paulus und die Rabbinen," ZNW 30 (1931): 271–85.

Mascellani, E., *Prudens dispensator verbi: Romani 5, 12–21 nell'esegesi di Clemente Alessandrino e Origene*, Pubblicazioni della Facoltà di Lettere e Filosofia dell'Università di Milano 134 (Florence: La Nuova Italia, 1990).

Miguens, M., "A Particular Notion of Sin," AER 167 (1973): 30–40.

————, *El pecado que entró en el mundo: Reflexiones sobre Rom. 5, 12–14*, (Jerusalem: Franciscan Press, 1972).

Milne, D. J. W., "Genesis 3 in the Letter to the Romans," RTR 39 (1980): 10–18.

Montagnini, F., *Rom. 5,12–14 alla luce del dialogo rabbinico*, RivBSup 4 (Brescia: Paideia, 1971).

Muddiman, J., "Adam, the Type of the One to Come," *Theology* 87 (1984): 101–10.

Müller, H., "Die rabbinische Qal-Wachomer-Schluss in paulinischer Typologie: Zur Adam-Christus-Typologie in Rm 5," ZNW 58 (1967): 73–92.

Murray, J., "The Imputation of Adam's Sin," WTJ 18 (1955–56): 146–62; 19 (1956–57): 25–44, 141–69; 20 (1957–58): 1–25.

Mussner, F., *Mort et résurrection*, 33–41.

Neenan, W. B., "Doctrine of Original Sin in Scripture," ITQ 28 (1961): 54–64.

Ocaña, F. M. de, "Cristo, segundo Adán, según san Pablo, y los niños que mueren sin bautismo," *EstFranc* 65 (1964): 339–50.

Oemmelen, H. J., *Zur dogmatischen Auswertung von Rom [sic] 5,12–14 (Ein neuer Versuch)* (Münster in Westfalen: Aschendorff, 1930).

Pérez Fernández, M., "El numeral *heis* en Pablo como título cristológico: Rom 5,12–19; Gal 3,20; cfr. Rom 9,10," *EstBíb* 41 (1983): 325–40.

Philipose, J., "Romans 5:20: Did God Have a Bad Motive in Giving the Law?" BT 28 (1977): 445.

Picard, E.-E., *Essai exégétique sur Rom. V, 12–21* (Strasbourg: Veuve Berger-Levrault, 1861).

Porter, S. E., "The Pauline Concept of Original Sin, in Light of Rabbinic Background," *TynBul* 41 (1990): 3–30.

Raponi, S., "Rom. 5,12–21 e il peccato originale," *Divinitas* 2 (1958): 520–59.

Renwart, L., "Péché d'Adam, péché du monde," *NRT* 113 (1991): 535–42.

Rey, B., *Créés dans le Christ Jésus: La création nouvelle selon saint Paul* (Paris: Cerf, 1966), 64–76.

Robinson, H. W., "The Hebrew Conception of Corporate Personality," *Werden und Wesen des Alten Testaments*, ed. P. Volz et al., BZAW 66 (Berlin: Töpelmann, 1936), 49–62.

Romaniuk, K., "Nota su Rom. 5,12 (A proposito del problema del male)," *RivB* 19 (1971): 327–34.

Rothe, R., *Neuer Versuch einer Auslegung der paulinischen Stelle Römer V, 12–21* (Wittenberg: Zimmermann, 1836).

Sahlin, H., "Adam-Christologie im Neuen Testament," *ST* 41 (1987): 11–32, esp. 28.

Schlier, H., *Vom Menschenbild des Neuen Testaments: Der alte und der neue Mensch,* BEvT 8 (Munich: Kaiser, 1942), 26.

Schunack, G., *Das hermeneutische Problem des Todes im Horizont von Römer 5 untersucht,* HUT 7 (Tübingen: Mohr [Siebeck], 1967).

Segalla, G., "La struttura circolare di Romani 5,12–21 e il suo significato teologico," *StudPatav* 8 (1981): 377–80.

Souter, A., "Pelagius' Text of Romans v. 12, with Comment," *ExpTim* 28 (1916–17): 42–43.

Spadafora, F., "Rom. 5,12: Esegesi e riflessi dogmatici," *Divinitas* 4 (1960): 289–98.

Stanley, D. M., "The Last Adam," *The Way* 6 (1966): 104–12.

———, "Paul's Interest in the Early Chapters of Genesis," *SPCIC* 1.241–52, esp. 247–50.

Street, O., "On the Use of the Preposition *eis* in the Phrases *eis katakrima* and *eis dikaiōsin zōēs* in Rom. 5: 18," *BSac* 10 (1853): 522–27.

Szlaga, J., "Chrystus jako nowy Adam w Listach Pawła Apostoła," *RTK* 22 (1975): 85–96.

Vanneste, A., "Où en est le problème du péché originel?" *ETL* 52 (1976): 143–61.

Vanni, U., "L'Analisi letteraria del contesto di Rom. V,12–14," *RivB* 11 (1963): 115–44.

———, "Rom. 5,12–14 alla luce del contesto," *RivB* 11 (1963): 337–66.

Vitti, A., "Christus-Adam," *Bib* 7 (1926): 121–45, 270–85, 384–401.

Voigt, S., "*Homoiôma* (Rm 5, 14) e pecado original: Uma releitura exegética," *RevEclBras* 41 (1981): 5–18.

Weaver, D., "The Exegesis of Romans 5:12 among the Greek Fathers and Its Implications for the Doctrine of Original Sin: The 5th–12th Centuries," *SVTQ* 29 (1985): 133–59, 231–57.

————, "From Paul to Augustine: Romans 5:12 in Early Christian Exegesis," *SVTQ* 27 (1983): 187–206.

Wedderburn, A. J. M., "The Theological Structure of Romans v. 12," *NTS* 19 (1972–73): 339–54.

Weder, H., "Gesetz und Sünde: Gedanken zu einem qualitativen Sprung im Denken des Paulus," *NTS* 31 (1985): 357–76.

Widenhofer, S., "Zum gegenwärtigen Stand der Erbsündentheologie," *TRev* 83 (1987): 353–70.

Zwaan, J. de, "Rom 5:19, Jacobus 3:6, 4:4 en de Koinê," *ThStud* 31 (1913): 85–94.

FREEDOM FROM SELF THROUGH UNION WITH CHRIST (6:1–23)

◆

19. FREEDOM FROM SIN AND SELF THROUGH BAPTISM (6:1–11)

6 ¹What, then, shall we say? "Let us persist in sinning so that grace may abound"? ²Certainly not! How shall we who have died to sin go on living in it? ³Or do you not know that those of us who were baptized into Christ Jesus were baptized into his death? ⁴Through baptism into his death we were indeed buried with him so that, as Christ was raised from the dead by the Father's glory, we too might conduct ourselves in a new way of life. ⁵For if we have grown into union with him through a death like his, we shall also be united with him through a resurrection like his. ⁶This we know, that our old self has been crucified with him so that the sinful body might be rendered powerless and we might no longer be slaves to sin. ⁷For the one who has died has been acquitted of sin. ⁸But if we have died with Christ, we believe that we shall also come to life with him, ⁹since we know that Christ has been raised from the dead and dies no more; death no longer has sway over him. ¹⁰For in dying as he did, he died to sin once and for all; and in living as he does, he lives to God. ¹¹So you too are to consider yourselves dead to sin, but alive to God in Christ Jesus.

COMMENT

Paul's description of the Christian experience proceeds a step farther. Justified and reconciled persons have been endowed with new life through Christ (5:12–21), who now reigns supreme instead of sin and death. The assurance and hope of salvation, of which chap. 5 spoke, mean that Christian life and conduct not only involve the fulfilling of duties, but even demand it. The new life brought by Christ entails a reshaping of human beings. Through baptism, they are identified with Christ's death and resurrection, and their very being or "self" is transformed. So the outlook of newly justified persons has been freed of sin and selfishness and is such as to exclude sinful conduct from their ken. Chapter 7 will carry the description of this freedom still farther (freedom from the law). In effect, Paul explains the relation of Christian conduct to the status of justification and reconciliation.

As an introduction to his explanation, Paul takes up a question broached in 3:5–8: Why not do evil so that good may come of it? If God brings about the salvation of the sinner gratuitously through Christ, then why should one not go on sinning? If human wickedness elicits from God his uprightness (his gracious and bounteous power to acquit), then why not give God greater scope for the manifestation of it? Such an idea Paul rejects vehemently: if one is in union with Christ, one is "dead to sin and alive to God." This answer forms the climax of the paragraph (v 11).

Thus Paul picks up the contrast of death and life from 5:21 and describes it in further detail. The new life that the justified and reconciled person enjoys is a freedom from sin and self. Paul indulges in a reductio ad absurdum in vv 2, 4c, 11, 12, and 14, as he argues: once a person is in Christ, how can he or she even think of doing evil?

In effect, Paul is resuming an argument that he used in Gal 2:19–20, where he described Christian life: "For through the law I died to the law, that I might live to God. I have been crucified with Christ; it is no longer I who live, but Christ who lives in me. The very life that I now live in the flesh, I live by faith in the Son of God who loved me and gave himself over for me." In these verses of Galatians Paul enunciated the principle of integrated Christian life, one in which the ontological reality (I am in Christ) has to surface to the psychological level (I live in Christ). Now Paul recasts that idea and contrasts the indicative (you are a Christian!) with the imperative (become the Christian that you have been enabled to become!): you have died to sin, so put to death the old self! You have been raised with Christ, so live a new life with him! Thus, the physical life that a justified person lives has to be lived out consciously in faith.

Into his answer to this question and his main topic of death to sin and life under grace, Paul introduces a secondary topic, a discussion of baptism. Verses 1–11 constitute the main discussion of baptism by Paul in his letters; see also 1 Cor 6:11; 10:1–2; 12:13; 2 Cor 1:22; and Gal 3:27–28 (cf. Col 2:11–12; Eph 1:13; 4:30; 5:14, 26; Titus 3:5). For a synthesis of his teaching on baptism, see *PAHT*, §§PT112–15. Here it should be recalled that for Paul baptism tears a person from one's native condition ("in Adam"), from one's native proclivity ("in the flesh"), and from one's ethnic background ("under the law"). It thus incorporates the person of faith "into Christ" so that one lives "in Christ" and "for God" in order that one may be one day "with the Lord" (1 Thess 4:17).

Hamartia, the noun "sin," occurs in vv 1–2, 6–7, 10–14, 16–18, 20, 22–23, and the vb. *hamartanein* in v 15. It is to be understood again as personified Sin, an actor on the stage of human history, the character that would enslave even Christians as a result of Adamic influence.

The problem that this passage creates in Pauline teaching is the relation of baptism to faith. Several times already Paul has stressed the need of a person to respond to the gospel of Christ in faith (1:16–17; 3:25–26). But now Paul seems to regard the response as baptismal, as an incorporation into Christ through a deed to be performed. Yet Paul himself never addresses this problem directly; he takes it for granted that Christians who put their faith in Christ undergo baptism. In Paul's view baptism is not just a supplement to faith, for in baptism the risen

Kyrios exercises dominion over Christians who by their faith recognize his lordship and live their lives as a consequence of faith in him, acknowledging thereby their obedience to this *Kyrios*.

Whence does Paul derive his teaching about baptism? There is nothing in the OT that would give rise to it; nor can one detect an influence of such Palestinian Jewish teaching as that of the Essenes of Qumran, who practiced indeed ritual washings. The baptism of John the Baptist may have been related to these Essene washings (see Fitzmyer, *Gospel According to Luke*, 453–54). But there is simply no discernible connection between such washings and the Pauline view of baptism.

Was Paul influenced in his thinking about baptism by contemporary pagan mystery cults? Since the time of Tertullian, Christian baptism has been compared with washings in the cults of Isis and Mithras and in Apollinarian and Eleusinian games (*De baptismo* 5.1 [CCLat 1.280]). Consequently, commentators have often wondered whether Paul was so influenced, because one of the characteristic tenets of such cults was the mystical identification of the initiate with a god believed to die and rise again, as a result of which the initiate was said to be reborn. So W. Bousset, *Kyrios Christos* (Nashville, Tenn.: Abingdon, 1970), 158–72, 223–27; R. Reitzenstein, *Hellenistic Mystery-Religions: Their Basic Ideas and Significance* (Pittsburgh, Penn., Pickwick, 1978), 20–21, 40–42, 78–79, 85–86. There are, indeed, superficial resemblances with such cults. But there are also striking differences that make it unlikely that Paul was tributary to such thinking, the chief of which is Paul's idea of Christians as identified with the historical crucifixion, death, and burial of Jesus of Nazareth. Paul is not here talking about a Christ-mysticism; and union with Christ is not the result of mystical experience induced by contemplation of his death and resurrection. For it is not through some human endeavor that this union takes place. It is, rather, the action of God himself on the baptized that brings about the union with Christ. See Wagner, *Pauline Baptism and the Pagan Mysteries*; Kennedy, *St. Paul*; Wedderburn, "Soteriology"; Gäumann, *Taufe*; Dunn, *Romans*, 308–11.

Paul has undoubtedly derived his teaching about baptism from the early Christian tradition that existed before him. Such a tradition would also have recorded the way Jesus himself had referred to his own death as a baptism (Mark 10:38–39; Luke 12:50). From such traditional notions and from the early Christian awareness that all believers were bonded together by the experience of grace and the Spirit, it would not have been difficult for Paul to derive his idea that "through one Spirit we have all been baptized into one body" (1 Cor 12:13). If this is a valid analysis, then there is little reason to appeal to the mystery cults as the source of the Pauline interpretation of Christian baptism.

The division of chap. 6 is controverted, because the latter part of it (vv 12–23) is not well integrated into the letter as a whole; it reads like a digression from 5:12–21; 6:1–11; and 7:1–25. Some interpreters divide the chapter according to its content:

1. 6:1–11, freedom from sin and self through union with Christ by baptism into his death, burial, and resurrection; and

2. 6:12–23, a baptismal exhortation: freedom for commitment to uprightness, sanctification, and God.

This division is also governed by the consideration that Paul uses indicatives in vv 1–11 and imperatives in the following verses. It brings to the fore the importance of the conj. *oun*, "then, therefore" in v 12. So the chapter is divided by the *RSV*, Black, Dunn, Grelot, Huby, Käsemann, Kuss, Lagrange, and Murray. The first part may be subdivided into two sections: (a) vv 1–4, union with Christ through baptism equals death to sin and self; and (b) vv 5–11, death to self.

Other interpreters, however, divide the chapter according to the rhetorical questions in vv 1 and 15:

1. 6:1–14, contrast of death and life related to sin; and

2. 6:15–23, contrast of slavery and freedom, related to law and grace.

So Achtemeier, Barrett, Byrne, Cranfield, Frankemölle, Leenhardt, Moo, Nygren, Price, and Wilckens. In either case one should note the parallelism in vv 5–8 and 9–10, the baptism-event ‖ the Christ-event.

NOTES

6:1. *What, then, shall we say?* Paul often uses this transitional rhetorical question: cf. 3:5; 4:1; 7:7; 8:31; 9:14, 30. Sometimes it is part of Paul's diatribe style. Here it introduces a mistaken conclusion that could be drawn from what he has said in 5:12–21. Paul realizes that what he has said may be controversial.

"Let us persist in sinning so that grace may abound." Or "are we to persist in sin?" if the subjunctive is taken as an emphatic future. The imaginary objection echoes 3:5–8. There it was a question of God's truthfulness and the faithlessness of Israel. Now the question is posed with reference to 5:20 and the mention of God's grace with reference to all human beings. If uprightness comes from faith, not deeds, why does one, even a Christian, have to worry about evil acts? Will not further sinning elicit from God further manifestations of his upright acquittal of such sins and further manifestations of his grace? *Hamartia* is understood as the "act of sinning." The noun *charis* picks up the mention of "grace" in 5:20.

2. *Certainly not!* A resolute rejection of the idea in the rhetorical question. See the NOTE on 3:4.

How shall we who have died to sin go on living in it? Paul's counterquestion resumes the thought of 5:12–21. Underlying his remark is the teaching of Gal 2:20, "It is not I who live, but Christ who lives in me." Cranfield (*Romans*, 299–300) well summarizes four senses in which the Pauline idea of "dying to sin" and "rising to life" can be understood: (1) the juridical sense: justified Christians have died to sin in God's sight, when Christ died for them vicariously (cf. 2 Cor 5:14); (2) the baptismal sense: by baptism justified Christians have ratified God's decision on their behalf and the bestowal of his seal on them individually; (3) the moral sense: justified Christians are called to freedom and to mortify their sinful bodies; (4) the eschatological sense: justified Christians will die and will finally be raised to eternal life at Christ's coming. Cf. Col 3:3, 13; 1 Pet 4:1. Paul presupposes an understanding of what death and resurrection meant for Christ himself. Through Christ's death the ruling power of sin was broken; all of the dominions and powers of the old aeon were cast out, and in the resurrection of Christ the new aeon was begun. In sharing in that death and resurrection of Christ, Christians are delivered from the dominion of sin and are transferred to the realm of his glorious, risen life.

Origen commented: "To obey the cravings of sin is to be alive to sin; but not to obey the cravings of sin or succumb to its will, this is to die to sin. . . . If then anyone, chastened by the death of Christ, who died for sinners, repents in all these things . . . , he is truly said to be dead to sin through the death of Christ" (*In ep. ad Romanos* 5.7 [PG 14.1035–36]).

3. *do you not know.* Roman Christians, instructed in apostolic catechesis, should be acquainted with the sublime effects of baptism. See 7:1, where Paul again uses *ē agnoeite*, in that case to pass on further information.

that those of us who were baptized into Christ. Cf. Gal 3:27. The vb. *baptizein* means primarily "dip into, wash." It is found in Josephus (*J.W.* 1.22.2 §437; 2.18.4 §476; *Ant.* 4.4.6 §81) in the sense of "plunge (into)." In the NT *baptizein* refers either to Jewish ritual washings (Mark 7:4; Luke 11:38), or to the baptism of John the Baptist (Matt 3:24–25; John 1:25, 28), or to Christian baptism (Gal 3:27). The prep. *eis* used with it may suggest immersion as the means of baptism. Yet it is not certain that early Christian baptism was so administered (see Rogers, "Baptism and Christian Archaeology"; Stommel, "Christliche Taufriten"). Or the phrase *eis Christon* may reflect an image drawn from bookkeeping, being an abbreviation of a fuller expression *eis to onoma Christou*, "to the name, account, of Christ." Baptism would be regarded as establishing Christ's proprietary rights over the baptized person, and the name of the baptized person would be booked in the ledger to the account of Christ. In any case, the prep. *eis* expresses an aspect of the relationship of the Christian to Christ, occurring most often with words denoting "faith" or "baptism" and connoting the *initial* movement of introduction or incorporation by which one is born to life "in Christ." See *PAHT* §§PT117–21.

were baptized into his death. The rite of Christian initiation introduces human beings into a union with Christ suffering and dying. Paul's phrase is bold; he wants to bring out that the Christian is not merely identified with the "dying Christ," who has won victory over sin, but is introduced into the very act by which that victory is won. The background of Paul's affirmation is the early

Christian kerygma, embedded in 1 Cor 15:3–5: "that Christ died for our sins according to the Scriptures, that he was buried, that he was raised on the third day according to the Scriptures, and that he appeared to Cephas. . . ." For this reason the Christian is said to be "dead to sin" (6:11), associated with Christ precisely at the moment in which he died and formally became Savior, the one who frees from sin. It is not just that baptized Christians are symbolically "with Christ"; Paul means that they actually experience a union with him.

Cf. Apuleius, *Metamorphoses* 11:21, in which the initiate describes his experience and which is supposed to resemble what Paul says here about baptism into Christ's death. See Lietzmann, *An die Römer*, 65–68. Cf. N. Gäumann, *Taufe*, 41–46.

4. *Through baptism into his death we were indeed buried with him.* The baptismal rite symbolically represents the death, burial, and resurrection of Christ; the person descends into the baptismal bath, is covered with its waters, and emerges to a new life. In that act one goes through the experience of dying to sin, being buried, and rising to new life, as did Christ.

Paul uses one of his favorite compound vbs., *synthaptein*, a compound of *syn-*, "with" (i.e., "coburied"). As a result of the coburial, the Christian lives in union with the risen Christ, a union that finds its term when the Christian will one day "be with Christ" (*syn Christō*) in glory. Cf. 8:32; 1 Thess 4:17; Col 2:12.

so that, as Christ was raised from the dead by the Father's glory. The purpose clause, introduced by *hina*, recalls the objection of v 1; echoing it, it counteracts the question. The comparison introduced by *hōsper* and *houtōs kai* reminds the reader of the similar comparison of 5:12–14, which contrasted the epochs of Adam and Christ. The words *ēgerthē Christos ek nekrōn* are formulaic (see 6:9; 7:4; 8:34; 1 Cor 15:12, 20; 2 Tim 2:8). The efficiency of the resurrection is again ascribed to the Father (see the NOTE on 4:24), and specifically to his *doxa*, "glory." As in the OT (Exod 15:7, 11; 16:7, 10), where exodus miracles are ascribed to Yahweh's *kābôd* (see the NOTE on 3:23), so too is the raising of Christ. In 2 Cor 4:6 Paul describes the "glory" of the Father shining on the face of the risen Christ and investing him with "power" (Rom 1:4; cf. 1 Cor 6:14; 2 Cor 13:4) that is "life-giving" (1 Cor 15:45). This power in turn transforms the Christian (2 Cor 3:18), who is glorified together with Christ (Rom 8:17). Cf. 1 Pet 1:3. For the relationship between God's "glory" and his "power," see Fitzmyer, " 'To Know Him and the Power of His Resurrection' (Phil 3:10)," *TAG*, 202–17.

we too might conduct ourselves in a new way of life. Lit., "we too might walk in newness of life," i.e., in a new life, identified with the risen life of Christ. Baptism brings about Christians' identification with the glorified Christ, enabling them to live actually with the life of Christ himself (cf. Gal 2:20; 1 Pet 3:21). Thus a "new creation" is involved (2 Cor 5:17). The aor. subjunc. is ingressive (BDF §337.1).

Another favorite Pauline verb is *peripatein*, "walk about," borrowed from the OT (e.g., Exod 18:20; 2 Kgs 20:3; 22:2; Ps 86:11; Prov 8:20; 28:18), to designate the conscious ethical conduct of the Jew according to the law. Paul uses it of Christians. Identified with Christ in baptism, they are enabled to lead a new conscious life that can know no sin. As Dunn has noted (*Romans*, 316), this bearing on conduct tells against the language being derived from the Greek mysteries.

5. *For.* Verses 5–8 affirm of the baptized Christian what Paul will say of Christ himself in vv 9–10. The latter verses supply the christological basis for the affirmations about Christian life.

if we have grown into union with him. Lit., "if we have become grown-together with," and the pron. "him" is supplied as the logical complement of *symphytoi,* "grown together with." Paul's bold image is derived from the idea of grafting: a young branch grafted onto a tree grows together with it in an organic unity and is nourished by its life-giving sap. So Paul expresses the communication of Christ-life to Christians. For the use of *symphytos,* see Aristotle, *Historia Animalium* 5.32.17; *Topica* 6.6; Theophrastus, *De causis plantarum* 5.5.2; Cyril of Jerusalem, *Catecheses* 20.7 (PG 33.1084). The conj. *ei* means "if," but is used in the sense of "because."

through a death like his. Lit., "(in) a likeness of his death." The noun *homoiōma* denotes not merely the abstract idea of "likeness," but the concrete image that is made to conform to something else (cf. LXX of Exod 20:4; Deut 4:16–18; 5:8 for a similar use of the concrete meaning). Hence the relationship between baptism and the death of Christ. The dat. *homoiōmati* might seem at first to be dependent on the compound adj. *symphytoi,* "if we have been conformed to the image of his death . . . ," i.e., have grown into union with the deathlike rite. Grammatically, this interpretation is possible and has been so taken by Black (*Romans*, 88), Dunn (*Romans*, 316), Käsemann, Kuss, Lietzmann, Mussner, Sanday and Headlam, and Wilckens. But the construction is problematic: can one grow together with a likeness? The expression is probably elliptical, and the dat. is better taken as a dat. of instrument, referring to baptismal washing as the means of growing together; that means is baptism, a likeness to Christ's death (so the *RSV,* BAGD 567; BDF §194.2; Kühl, *Römer,* 204; and many other commentators). For Paul, the Christian is normally thought to be united with Christ himself or "his body," but not with an "image" of the salvation-event. Cf. 8:29 (*symmorphous tēs eikonos tou huiou autou*); Phil 3:10 (*symmorphizomenos tō thanatō autou*).

we shall also be united with him through a resurrection like his. Lit., "we shall then be (grown together with him) through (a likeness) of the resurrection." Because the context describes the present experience of the Christian, the fut. *esometha* has to be understood as gnomic, expressing a logical sequel to the first part of the verse, for baptism identifies a person not only with Christ's act of dying, but also with his rising. Though future, it describes a share in the risen life of Christ that the justified Christian already enjoys, as a result of the Christ-event. Thus the relationship of baptism to the resurrection, which was not stated in v 4, is now made explicit. See Camelot, "Resuscités"; Gächter, "Zur Exegese"; Kuss, "Zum Röm 6,5a."

The best Greek MSS read *alla*, "but," at the beginning of this clause, but MSS F and G have instead *hama*, "together," which has resulted from the confusion of two capital lambdas, written too close together, with a capital M. This scribal error accounts for the translation in the Vg, *simul et resurrectionis erimus*.

6. *This we know, that our old self has been crucified with him.* Lit., "our old man" *(ho palaios hēmōn anthrōpos)*, i.e., the self we once were, the self that belongs to the old aeon, the self dominated by sin and exposed to wrath. Paul uses the adj. *palaios* to characterize the condition of human life prior to baptism and conversion, i.e., humanity in its Adamic condition (7:6; 1 Cor 5:7–8; cf. Col 3:9; Eph 4:22). That self has been cocrucified *(synestaurōthē)* with Christ, i.e., it has been identified with the very act by which Christ himself died. Thus Paul echoes what he said in Gal 2:19. The contrast of "old man" and "new man" is an echo of the early Christian baptismal instruction (so Michel, *Brief an die Römer*, 207).

so that the sinful body might be rendered powerless. Lit., "the body of sin might be made ineffective." Paul indulges in a rhetorical description of the body inclined to sinning. The "body of sin" is not merely the material part of a mortal human being, as opposed to the soul, but the whole person considered as earth-oriented, not open to God or his Spirit, and prone to sin. In 7:24 he will call it the "body of death." In each case the gen. expresses the element that dominates the earth-oriented, natural human being. Cf. Gal 5:24; Col 1:22 *(sōma tēs sarkos)*; Wis 1:4 *(en sōmati katachreō hamartias*, "in a body enslaved to sin").

and we might no longer be slaves to sin. Thus Paul formulates the real answer to the imaginary objection of v 1. The destruction of the sinful "self" through baptism and incorporation into Christ means liberation from enslavement to sin. Sin is again personified and envisaged as a master that dominates the "body," or the "old man." It rules in human life with an alien power that overcomes. Once liberated from that master, Christians can no longer focus their sights on sin. Paul uses the gen. of the articular infin. to express result (BDF §400.8).

7. *the one who has died has been acquitted of sin.* Cf. Sir 26:29. Two main explanations are current for the difficult vb. *dedikaiōtai*, though C. Toussaint *(Romains*, 182–83) has listed seven different interpretations. Pallis *(To the Romans*, 86) regarded this verse as an interpolation, but commentators usually reckon with the verse as genuinely Pauline.

Understood in a forensic sense, *dikaioun* would mean that from the standpoint of Jewish law a dead person is absolved or "freed," for sin no longer has a legal claim or a case against such a person. It is said to have the meaning of *dikaioun* that is often given to it (rightly?) in Acts 13:38. Possibly, too, Paul is echoing a Jewish universal legal principle, formulated thus in the late Babylonian Talmud: "When one dies, one is freed of the obligation of the law and its precepts" (*b. Shabb.* 151a; see Str-B 3.232). K. G. Kuhn ("Rm 6,7: *ho gar apothanōn dedikaiōtai apo tēs hamartias*," ZNW 30 [1931]: 305–10) argued similarly on the basis of *Sifre Num.* §112: "All who die obtain expiation for their sin through death" (commenting on Num 15:31). Although the death envisaged was meant to be martyrdom, it was physical death in any case of which there is mention in *Sifre.* Whereas such physical death was considered expiatory, Paul would have transferred the meaning to the death by which the Christian dies in baptism. G. Schrenk, *TDNT* 2.218; and Michel, *Brief an die Römer,* 207 argue similarly. Cf. 4 Macc 6:29. Yet one may wonder whether Paul himself ever regarded the physical death of a person as expiatory of sin. Perhaps then the Jewish dictum is not operative.

The other, more likely explanation seeks to interpret the vb. *dikaioun* not as "free," but as "justify, acquit" in the genuine Pauline sense, and *hamartia*, not in the sense demanded above (something like "obligation to the Torah"), but in its Pauline sense, an act against the will of God (so Lyonnet, *Romains,* 89; Cranfield, *Romans,* 310–11): the one who has died has lost the very means of sinning, "the body of sin," so that one is definitively without sin; one has been freed of the fleshy, sin-prone body. In either case, a change of status has ensued; the old condition has been brought to an end in baptism-death, and a new one has begun. See 1 Pet 4:1; Cyril of Alexandria, *In ep. ad Romanos* 6.6 (PG 74.797); Lyonnet, "Qui enim"; cf. Scroggs, "Romans vi. 7: *ho gar apothanōn dedikaiōtai apo tēs hamartias*," NTS 10 (1963–64): 104–8, who argues in the right vein, but who questionably interprets Jesus' death as that of a martyr.

Kearns ("The Interpretation") would rather emphasize that "the one who has died" is primarily Christ himself, and only secondarily (and by consequence) the baptized person. He cites 8:34; 2 Cor 5:15; 1 Thess 5:9–10 as indications that Paul otherwise predicates *apothnēskein* of Christ (cf. also 1 Pet 4:1). Thus the baptized would share in the acquitting death of Christ. Perhaps, but such an interpretation renders v 10 somewhat tautologous, as Dunn (*Romans,* 321) notes.

8. *if we have died with Christ.* So Paul reformulates what he said in v 5: death with Christ through baptism. As in v 5, the conj. *ei* is to be understood in the sense of "because." On "with Christ," see Fitzmyer, *PAHT* §§PT117–21.

we believe that we shall also come to life with him. Paul emphasizes faith in a life begun through death to sin. The new life of the Christian is not the object of sensible perception or immediate consciousness; it is perceived only with the eyes of faith, in token of which baptism has been undergone. Here Paul comes closest to an explanation of the relation of faith to baptism. He now thinks primarily of the future, definitive form of new life *syn Christō,* "with Christ" (1 Thess 4:17). Yet he knows that Christians already enjoy proleptically a share in that life (see 2 Cor 4:10–11). 2 Cor 5:17 is the best commentary on this verse: "If anyone is in Christ, he is a new creation; the old has passed away, look, the new has come." Cf. Phil 3:10–12; 2 Tim 2:11. Future life with Christ is the object of faith, whereas the resurrection of Christ is the object of Christian knowledge (in v 9).

9. *since we know that Christ has been raised from the dead and dies no more.*
To the certainty of baptismal faith, Paul now joins knowledge, knowledge that
Christ "has been raised" by the Father (see the NOTE on 4:24), and is therefore
no longer under the domination of death. The "being raised" that Paul mentions
is not simply a return to earthly life, which would be still subject to death, but
eschatological resurrection, the rising to "eternal life," or life in the glorious
presence of the Father (see 2:7; 5:21).

death no longer has sway over him. I.e., having become *Kyrios* at his exaltation
(Phil 2:9–11), Christ now reigns over the condition of mortality, and of human
life itself. Again Paul personifies death and recognizes its tyrannous power, but he
denies that that is exercised over the risen Christ.

10. *in dying as he did, he died to sin once and for all.* Lit., "the death he
died, he died to sin." Paul uses a sort of cognate acc. (BDF §154). Christ's death
was a unique event, never to be repeated; he died "once and for all" *(ephapax)*,
and through it he entered the definitive sphere of his glory as *Kyrios* and became
a life-giving spirit (1 Cor 15:45; cf. 1 Pet 3:18). In so doing, he died to sin,
"though he knew not sin" (2 Cor 5:21). Jesus came in the likeness of sinful flesh
(8:3) and broke sin's domination by his own death and resurrection, and not only
sin's, but even death's domination. This victory over death is the foundation for
the liberation of the baptized Christian. Christ was raised from the dead not
merely to publicize his good news or to confirm his messianic character, but to
introduce human beings into freedom, a new mode of life, with a new principle
of vital activity, the Spirit. Thus Paul formulates the christological basis of the
answer that he gives in v 6 to the objection in v 1.

and in living as he does, he lives to God. As of the resurrection, Christ enjoys
a new relation to the Father, into which he also introduces those who are baptized
(Gal 2:19–20). Christ's new life is theocentric, and into it he also introduces the
Christian who lives in him.

11. *So you too are to consider yourselves dead to sin.* Paul now applies all that
he has just said to Christians. The vb. *logizesthe* is the impv., "consider!"—the
word that introduces the following paraenetic paragraph; it is also the second
impv. in the letter (see 3:4 for the first, *ginesthō*). It seeks to elicit the act of faith,
which accepts the salvific event embodied in baptism. This is the conclusion of
Paul's argument, as he expresses his view of the problem of the integration of
Christian life. Ontologically united with Christ through faith and baptism,
Christians must deepen their faith continually to become more and more
psychologically aware of that union. Thus consciously oriented to Christ, Christians can never again consider sin without a rupture of that union. For they are
"dead to sin." It is not just that they are to imitate Christ (because he has died to
sin, so you too); Christians are also to arm themselves with the mentality that they
are dead to sin; for that is what has happened to them in the baptismal experience.
A parallelism similar to "dead to sin" and "alive to God" can be found in 4 Macc
7:19: *pisteuontes hoti theō ouk apothnēskousin, hōsper oude hoi patriarchai hēmōn*

Abraam kai Isaak kai Iakōb, alla zōsin tō theō, "believing that to God they would not die, even as our patriarchs Abraham, Isaac, and Jacob did not die, but would be alive to God"; cf. 16:25. MSS P⁴⁶, A, D, F, et al. omit the infin. *einai*, whereas MS Ψ and the *Koinē* text-tradition and Latin versions read it, but place it after *nekrous men*, where it should be logically; but the *lectio difficilior* (of MSS ℵ, B, C, P⁹⁴, 81, 365, 1506, 1739, and many ancient versions) places *einai* between *heautous* and *nekrous*. The omitted *einai* seems to have been the original form (cf. 1 Cor 4:1; 13:11).

alive to God in Christ Jesus. The paragraph ends with the significant phrase of union, a brief description of Paul's view of the relation of Christians to the risen *Kyrios*. This is the first occurrence of this important Pauline phrase of union in the letter; see also 8:1; 12:5; 16:3, 7, 9, 10; cf. 1 Thess 2:14; Gal 1:22; 2:4; 3:28; 5:6; 1 Cor 1:2, 30; 4:10; 15:18–19; 2 Cor 5:17; 12:2; Phil 1:1; 4:7; Phlm 23. "In Christ," Christians are united with the risen body of Christ through the holy Spirit and thereby share in the vitality of his life in glory. In this way they are "alive to God," i.e., they live for him and live in his presence through baptism into the risen Christ. Cf. 2 Cor 5:15. See also Schweizer, *NTS* 14 (1967–68): 1– 14; Wedderburn, "Some Observations." Paul also uses the prep. phrase to express Christians doing something "in Christ": 9:1; 15:17; cf. 1 Thess 4:16; 1 Cor 4:15, 17; 15:31; 16:24; 2 Cor 2:17; 12:19; Phil 4:21; Phlm 20. The *Koinē* text-tradition, following MSS ℵ, P⁹⁴, C, K, P, 33, 1739, etc., add the words *tō Kyriō hēmōn*, "our Lord."

BIBLIOGRAPHY ON CHAPTER 6 AS A WHOLE

Alvarez Verdes, L., *El imperativo cristiano en San Pablo: La tensión indicativo-imperativo en Rom 6: Análisis estructural* (Valencia: Institutión San Jerónimo, 1980).

Bauer, J. A., *A Study of "homoioma" in Romans 6:5* (St. Louis, Mo.: Concordia Seminary, 1969).

Clerc, D., "Notes à propos de Romains 6, 1–14," *BCPE* 37 (1985): 5–10.

Deissmann, A., *Die neutestamentliche Formel "in Christo Jesu"* (Marburg: Elwert, 1892).

Descamps, A., "La Victoire du chrétien sur le péché d'après Rom., vi, 1–23," *RDT* 6 (1951): 143–48.

Frankemölle, H., *Das Taufverständnis des Paulus: Taufe, Tod und Auferstehung nach Röm 6*, SBS 47 (Stuttgart: KBW, 1970).

Gäumann, N., *Taufe und Ethik: Studien zu Römer 6*, BEvT 47 (Munich: Kaiser, 1967).

Grelot, P., "Une Homélie de saint Paul sur le baptême: Épître aux Romains, ch. 6, 1–23," *EspVie* 99 (1989): 154–58.

Kaye, B. N., *The Argument of Romans with Special Reference to Chapter 6* (Austin, Tex.: Schola, 1979).

Kertelge, K., "Der neue Lebenswandel nach Rö 6," *"Rechtfertigung,"* 263–75.

Kürzinger, J., "Zur Taufaussage in Röm 6," *Universitas: Dienst an Wahrheit und Leben: Festschrift für Bischof Dr. Albert Stohr* . . . , 2 vols. (Mainz: Matthias-Grünewald, 1960), 1.93–98.

Kuss, O., "Zum Röm 6,5a," TGl 41 (1951): 430–37; repr. *Auslegung und Verkündigung I* (Regensburg: Pustet, 1963), 151–61.

LaSor, W. S., "Discovering What Jewish Miqvaot Can Tell Us about Christian Baptism," *BARev* 13.1 (1987): 52–59.

Légasse, S., "Être baptisé dans la mort du Christ: Étude de Romains 6,1–14," *RB* 98 (1991): 544–59.

Lorenzi, L. de (ed.), *Battesimo e giustizia in Rom 6 e 8*, Benedictina, Sezione biblico-ecumenica 2 (Rome: Abbazia S. Paolo fuori le mura, 1974).

Moo, D. J., "Romans 6:1–14," *TrinJ* 3 (1982): 215–20.

Polhill, J. B., "New Life in Christ: Romans 6–8," *RevExp* 73 (1976): 425–36.

Price, J. L., "Romans 6:1–14," *Int* 34 (1980): 65–69.

Schelkle, K.-H., "Taufe und Tod: Zur Auslegung von Römer 6, 1–11," *Vom christlichen Mysterium: Gesammelte Arbeiten zum Gedächtnis von Odo Casel O S B*, ed. A. Mayer et al. (Düsseldorf: Patmos, 1951), 9–21.

Schlier, H., "Die Taufe nach dem 6. Kapitel des Römerbriefes," *Zeit der Kirche*, 47–56.

Schnepel, E., *Die Chance des Lebens: Römerbrief / Kapitel 6* (Stuttgart: Junge Gemeinde, 1962).

Schwarzmann, H., *Zur Tauftheologie des hl. Paulus im Röm 6* (Heidelberg: Kerle, 1950).

Süss, T., "Le Problème de Rom 6," *PosLuth* 7 (1959): 16–37.

Venn, J., *St. Paul's Three Chapters on Holiness, or an Attempt to Ascertain the Exact Meaning of the 6th, 7th, and 8th Chapters of St. Paul's Epistle to the Romans* (London: J. Nisbet, 1877).

Vicentini, J. I., "Una afirmación paradójica: 'Ya está todo hecho; pero queda todo por hacer.' Comentario a Romanos 6," *RevistB* 36 (1974): 289–98.

Warnach, V., "Taufe und Christusgeschehen nach Römer 6," *Archiv für Liturgiewissenschaft* 3.2 (1954): 284–366.

Wendland, H.-D., *Vita e condotta dei cristiani: Riflessioni su Rom. 6* (Brescia: Paideia, 1976).

Wuest, K. S., "Victory over Indwelling Sin in Romans Six," *BSac* 116 (1959): 43–50.

On Rom 6:1–11

Ben Pechat, M., "The Paleochristian Baptismal-Fonts in the Holy Land: Formal and Functional Study," *SBFLA* 39 (1989): 165–88.

Bonnard, P., "Mourir et vivre avec Jésus-Christ selon saint Paul," *RHPR* 36 (1956): 101–12.

Bornkamm, G., "Baptism and New Life in Paul: Romans 6," *Early Christian Experience*, 71–86.

Byrne, B., "Living out the Righteousness of God: The Contribution of Rom 6:1–8:13 to an Understanding of Paul's Ethical Presuppositions," *CBQ* 43 (1981): 557–81.

Cambier, J., "La Liberté des baptisés (Rm 6,3–11)," *AsSeign* 60 (1963): 15–27; abridged in n.s. 21 (1969): 42–47.

Camelot, T., "Resuscités avec le Christ," *VSpir* 84 (1951): 353–63.

Clerc, D., "Notes à propos de Romains 6, 1–14," *BCPE* 37 (1985): 5–10.

Cremer, F. G., "Der 'Heilstod' Jesu im paulinischen Verständnis von Taufe und Eucharistie: Eine Zusammenschau von Röm 6,3f und 1 Kor 11,26," *BZ* 14 (1970): 227–39.

Cuivillier, E., "Évangile et traditions chez Paul: Lecture de Romains 6,1–14," *Hokhma* 45 (1990): 3–16.

Dress, D. M., "Taufpredigt über Röm 6, 3–11," *EvT* 2 (1935): 421–23.

Dunn, J. D. G., "Salvation Proclaimed: Romans 6:1–11: Dead and Alive," *ExpTim* 93 (1981–82): 259–64.

Du Toit, A. B., "Dikaiosyne in Röm 6: Beobachtungen zur ethischen Dimension der paulinischen Gerechtigkeitsauffassung," *ZTK* 76 (1979): 261–91.

Eckert, J., "Die Taufe und das neue Leben: Röm 6,1–11 im Kontext der paulinischen Theologie," *MTZ* 38 (1987): 203–22.

Fazekaš, L., "Taufe als Tod in Röm. 6,3ff.," *TZ* 22 (1966): 305–18.

Frid, B., "Römer 6,4–5: *Eis ton thanaton* und *tō homoiōmati tou thanatou autou* als Schlüssel zu Duktus und Gedankengang in Röm 6,1–11," *BZ* 30 (1986): 188–203.

Gächter, P., "Zur Exegese von Röm 6,5," *ZKT* 54 (1930): 88–92.

Gewiess, J., "Das Abbild des Todes Christi (Röm 6,5)," *HJ* 77 (1958): 339–46.

Hagen, W. H., "Two Deutero-Pauline Glosses in Romans 6," *ExpTim* 92 (1980–81): 364–67.

Hahn, W. T., *Das Mitsterben und Mitauferstehen mit Christus bei Paulus: Ein Beitrag zum Problem der Gleichzeitigkeit des Christen mit Christus* (Gütersloh: Bertelsmann, 1937).

Howard, J. K., " '. . . into Christ': A Study of the Pauline Concept of Baptismal Union," *ExpTim* 79 (1967–68): 147–51.

Kearns, C., "The Interpretation of Romans 6,7," *SPCIC* 1.301–7.

Kennedy, H. A. A., *St. Paul and the Mystery Religions* (London: Hodder & Stoughton, 1914).

Klaar, E., "Röm 6,7: *ho gar apothanōn dedikaiōtai apo tēs hamartias*," *ZNW* 59 (1968): 131–34.

Kuhn, K. G., "Rm 6,7: *ho gar apothanōn dedikaiōtai apo tēs hamartias*," *ZNW* 30 (1931): 305–10.

Kuss, O., "Zu Röm 6:5a," *TGl* 41 (1951): 430–37; repr. *Auslegung und Verkündigung*, 3 vols. (Regensburg: Pustet, 1963–71), 1.151–61.

Langevin, P.-E., "Le Baptême dans la mort-résurrection: Exégèse de Rm 6,1–5," *ScEccl* 17 (1965): 29–65.

Légasse, S., "Être baptisé dans la mort du Christ: Étude de Romains 6, 1–14," *RB* 98 (1991) 544–59.

Lohmeyer, E., "*Syn Christō*," *Festgabe für Adolf Deissmann* . . . (Tübingen: Mohr [Siebeck], 1927), 218–57.

Lyonnet, S., " 'Qui enim mortuus est, justificatus est a peccato' (Rom 6,7)," *VD* 42 (1964): 17–21.

Moo, D. J., "Exegetical Notes: Romans 6:1–14," *TrinJ* 3 (1982): 215–20.

Morgan, F. A., "Romans 6:5a: United to a Death like Christ's," *ETL* 59 (1983): 267–302.

Moule, C. F. D., "Death 'to Sin,' 'to Law,' and 'to the World': A Note on Certain Datives," *Mélanges bibliques en hommage au R. P. Béda Rigaux*, ed. A. Descamps and A. de Halleux (Gembloux: Duculot, 1970), 367–75.

Mussner, F., "Zur paulinischen Tauflehre in Röm 6:1–6," *Praesentia Salutis: Gesammelte Studien zu Fragen und Themen des Neuen Testaments* (Düsseldorf: Patmos, 1967), 189–96.

——, "Zusammengewachsen durch die Ähnlichkeit mit seinem Tode: Der Gedankengang von Röm 6,1–6," *TTZ* 63 (1954): 257–65.

Neugebauer, F., *In Christus, en Christō: Eine Untersuchung zum paulinischen Glaubensverständnis* (Göttingen: Vandenhoeck & Ruprecht, 1961).

Ogara, F., " 'Complantati . . . similitudini mortis eius, simul et resurrectionis erimus,' " *VD* 15 (1935): 194–203.

Pelser, G. M. M., "The Objective Reality of the Renewal of Life in Romans 6:1–11," *Neotestamentica* 15 (1981): 101–17.

Preez, J. du, "Rom 6:3–4 in die diskussie vor die vorm van die christelike doop," *NGTT* 25 (1984): 270–76.

Quanbeck, W. A., "Justification and Baptism in the New Testament," *LW* 8 (1961): 8–15.

Rogers, C. F., "Baptism and Christian Archaeology," *Studia biblica et ecclesiatica*, 5 vols., ed. Members of the University of Oxford (Oxford: Clarendon Press, 1885–1903), 5.239–361.

Sawyer, V. S., "In Christ: The Life of Victory: An Expository Development of Romans 6:1–14," *Calvary Baptist Theological Journal* 3.2 (1987): 50–73.

Schäfer, F. G., "Der 'Heilstod' Jesu im paulinischen Verständnis von Taufe und Eucharistie: Eine Zusammenschau von Röm 6,3f und 1 Kor 11,26," *BZ* 14 (1970): 227–39.

Schlarb, R., "Röm 6:1–11 in der Auslegung der frühen Kirchenväter," *BZ* 33 (1989): 104–13.

——, *Wir sind mit Christus begraben: Die Auslegung von Römer 6,1–11 im Frühchristentum bis Origenes*, BGBE 31 (Tübingen: Mohr [Siebeck], 1990), 207–60.

Schnackenburg, R., "Die Adam-Christus-Typologie (Röm 5:12–21) als Voraussetzung für das Taufverständnis in Röm 6:1–14," *Battesimo*, ed. L. de Lorenzi, 37–55.

———, "Todes- und Lebensgemeinschaft mit Christus: Neue Studien zu Röm 6,1–11," *MTZ* 6 (1955): 32–53.

Schweizer, E., "Dying and Rising with Christ," *NTS* 14 (1967–68): 1–14.

Scroggs, R., "Romans vi. 7: *ho gar apothanōn dedikaiōtai apo tēs hamartias*," *NTS* 10 (1963–64): 104–8.

Stanley, D. M., *Christ's Resurrection*, 181–86.

Stommel, E., "Das 'Abbild seines Todes' (Röm. 6,5) und der Taufritus," *RömQ* 50 (1955): 1–21.

———, " 'Begraben mit Christus' (Röm. 6,4) und der Taufritus," *RömQ* 49 (1954): 1–20.

———, "Christliche Taufriten und antike Badesitten," *JAC* 2 (1959): 5–14.

Stricker, S., "Der Mysteriengedanke des hl. Paulus nach Röm 6,2–11," *Liturgisches Leben* 1 (1934): 285–96.

Wagner, G., *Pauline Baptism and the Pagan Mysteries: The Problem of the Pauline Doctrine of Baptism in Romans VI.1–11, in the Light of Its Religio-Historical "Parallels"* (Edinburgh and London: Oliver & Boyd, 1967).

Wedderburn, A. J. M., "Hellenistic Christian Traditions in Romans 6?" *NTS* 29 (1983): 337–55.

———, "Some Observations on Paul's Use of the Phrases 'in Christ' and 'with Christ,' " *JSNT* 25 (1985): 83–97.

———, "The Soteriology of the Mysteries and Pauline Baptismal Theology," *NovT* 29 (1987): 53–72.

Wikenhauser, A., *Pauline Mysticism*, 109–32.

Zeller, D., "Die Mysterienkulte und die paulinische Soteriologie (Röm 6, 1–11): Eine Fallstudie zum Synkretismus im Neuen Testament," *Suchbewegungen: Synkretismus—kuturelle Identität und kirchliches Bekenntnis*, ed. H. P. Siller (Darmstadt: Wissenschaftliche Buchgesellschaft, 1991), 42–61.

20. FREEDOM FOR COMMITMENT (6:12–23)

6 [12]Do not, then, let sin hold sway over your mortal body so that you obey its lusts. [13]Do not put your members at sin's disposal as weapons of wickedness, but instead put yourselves at God's disposal as those who have come to life from death and offer your members to God as weapons of uprightness. [14]Sin is not to have sway over you, for you are not under law but under grace. [15]What, then, does this mean? Should we sin because we are not under law, but under grace? Certainly not! [16]Do you not know that, if you put yourselves at anyone's disposal in obedience, you become slaves of the one you obey—whether of sin, which leads to death, or of real obedience, which leads to uprightness. [17]But thanks be to God,

you who were once slaves to sin have wholeheartedly become obedient to the standard of teaching to which you have been entrusted. [18]Freed then from sin, you have become slaves of uprightness. [19]I am putting this in human terms because of your weak human nature: just as you used to put your members slavishly at the disposal of impurity and iniquity, which led to anarchy, so now put them slavishly at the disposal of uprightness, which leads to holiness. [20]When you were slaves of sin, you were free from uprightness. [21]But what benefit did you then have—save things of which you are now ashamed? Things that result in death! [22]But now that you have been freed from sin and have become slaves of God, the benefit you have leads to holiness, which results in life eternal. [23]For the wages of sin are death, but the gift of God is eternal life in Christ Jesus our Lord.

COMMENT

The following verses, 12–23, are not well integrated into the letter and seem to be a résumé of a baptismal exhortation that Paul may at times have preached, but that he now incorporates into the letter in order to draw out practical conclusions from the preceding exposition on baptism. These verses are laden with hortatory language. They answer the question, In what sense are Christians to consider themselves slaves who owe obedience? Paul plays on the idea that a slave is one owned by a master, to whom the slave is expected to render obedient service. Hence the question is asked, Are baptized Christians slaves to sin or to uprightness? In what sense can Christians be slaves to God who acquits?

The relation of this paragraph to the preceding is best summarized in the ideas of the indicative and the imperative. In vv 1–11 Paul set forth what was meant to have died with Christ in baptism; now in vv 12–23 he sets forth the consequences of the new life that the baptized Christian lives. He says to the baptized: you have been identified with Christ in his death and resurrection; now become the Christian so united with him that you can become. Manifest in your lives the lordship of Christ who has justified you and freed you from the power of sin. Paul does not turn to imperatives or exhortations when he cannot sustain his declarations; instead he utters his imperatives on the basis of the truth of the indicative declarations.

Lietzmann (*An die Römer*, 71) has well summed up the meaning of this paragraph:

[These verses] constitute a unified development of Paul's thought that is not to be missed. Words do not slip like honey from Paul's lips; he struggles rather for expression, using ever new applications and images to show how, despite the setting aside of the law and the setting up of faith as the sole salvific principle, ethical conduct is not an *adiaphoron*, but the necessary, indispensable attestation of the new Christian condition. . . . Paul is not a man of halfway measures; he grasps the new religion at its deepest roots and hence stands unshakably on an antinomistic platform: where life in the Spirit is operative, there is no longer room for legal prescriptions. The person to whom God has given his Spirit is no longer approached by him from without with casuistic legal demands. Whoever walks by the Spirit does of himself what God's precepts would demand because the Spirit is pointing the way for him.

While what he says is true, one should realize that in this paragraph Paul has not yet introduced the Spirit, as Lietzmann has. Paul speaks, rather, of the dominion of the risen Christ over baptized, justified Christians who must constantly appropriate in their conduct the effects of what Christ has done for them. He calls for the obedience of Christians not to Sin, but to Christ and his call of grace. In thus obeying, Christians verify in their lives the gift of divine grace and thus become what they have been enabled to become. Such obedience thus manifests also the union with Christ of which Paul speaks, a "participation in the reign of Christ as the gift of the eschatological act of salvation. This means, however, that in reality the gift is the Giver himself, just as the pneuma means nothing other than the earthly manifestation of the exalted Lord in his community" (Käsemann, *Commentary*, 174–75).

In this paragraph the Pauline teaching on *eleutheria*, "freedom," surfaces in vv 18, 20, and 22. Freedom is an effect of the Christ-event, not the same as *apolytrōsis*, "redemption" (3:24; see the NOTE there). The contrast between slavery and freedom is drawn from the Greco-Roman world, in which freedom denoted the privileged condition or social status of citizens in a *polis* or *municipium*. Another effect of the Christ-event also surfaces in this paragraph: *hagiasmos*, "sanctification," or the dedication of the Christian to God and his awesome service. See Introduction, section IX.B. As Käsemann (*Commentary*, 172–74) rightly notes, "sanctification" is not to be conceived in this letter as somehow the consequence of justification; it is simply saying the same thing under a different image: as does justification, so sanctification also transfers the baptized Christian to the dominion of Christ.

The paragraph may be subdivided into three parts: (1) 6:12–14: Paul exhorts Christians to become aware of their status: having died to sin, they are no longer to let it hold sway over them; (2) 6:15–19: under the reign of grace Christians cannot be unconcerned about their conduct, because they are in bondage to uprightness and sanctification; and (3) 6:20–23: freed from sin and death, Christians have become slaves to uprightness and to God himself. Whereas sin leads only to death, the grace of God leads to life eternal.

As in earlier sections of this part of Romans, Paul personifies sin and death, but now also law and grace. They are all treated as masters who dominate slaves. Slaves are also transferred from one master to another, from sin to Christ. Such is the figure that Paul employs in these verses.

NOTES

6:12. *Do not, then, let sin hold sway over your mortal body.* Lit., "let not sin continue to reign," Paul uses the 3d sg. pres. impv. *mē basileuetō* and the pres. impv. in v 13 *mēde paristanete*, but then the aor. impv. *parastēsate* in an ingressive sense (BDF §337.1). In other words, because the new life (6:4) that you live "in Christ Jesus" (6:11) is beginning, you may not continue to let sin reign in you. Christians may still be in "the sinful body" (6:6) and may be seduced or swayed by "its cravings." The "body of sin" denotes the state in which even baptized Christians may find themselves; with such a body they too can still be subject to the dominion of sin. Paul does not mean that Christians have become sinless or incapable of sin through faith and baptism. They are still human beings, and have in themselves the effects of Adamic sin. That sin can even dominate them. Hence his exhortation that they are not to allow sin to hold sway over them or even the body of sin that they are. Here again *hamartia* is the personified active force that came into human history with Adam, has reigned over human beings up to the time of Jesus' coming, and seeks to continue to reign, by enticing Christians too. See 6:19; 12:1.

What Paul says of "sin" in this passage came to be understood as *concupiscentia*, "concupiscence," or the *fomes peccati*, "the tinder of sin," in the Augustinian tradition (*Contra duas epistolas Pelagianorum* 1.13.27 [CSEL 60.445]). The Council of Trent said that "the Apostle sometimes calls [it] sin" and refers to this very verse, but explained that in itself it is not sin, but "comes from sin and tends toward sin" (DS 1515). Yet, as Lagrange notes (*Romains*, 153), that might be an exact theological transposition, but it is a precision not yet found in the Pauline text. For a Lutheran transposition of the Pauline teaching, see N. A. Dahl, "In What Sense Is the Baptized Person 'simul justus et peccator' according to the New Testament," *LW* 9 (1962): 219–31.

so that you obey its lusts. Or "its cravings" (*epithymiais*). Paul recognizes that sin can still entice baptized Christians, leading them to succumb to its domination. If one obeys such cravings that come from sin, one allows sin itself to reduce one to bondage, and one thereby loses the freedom from sin achieved in Christ Jesus.

This is the preferred reading (of MSS ℵ, A, B, C*, P⁹⁴), but in P⁴⁶, D, G, Irenaeus, and Tertullian one reads instead *autē*, "(obey) it," i.e., sin. This wording might be more logical in the context, but the variant does not change the sense much. MSS C³, Ψ, and the *Koinē* text-tradition read *autē en tais epithymiais*, "(obey) it in (its) cravings," again a minor variant.

13. *Do not put your members at sin's disposal as weapons of wickedness.* I.e., as weapons (*hopla*) for the promotion of wrongdoing or evil. The expression is a military figure, as the second part of the verse also suggests. See 13:12; 2 Cor 6:7; 10:4. Cf. 2 *Apoc. Bar.* 29:3.

instead put yourselves at God's disposal as those who have come to life from death and offer your members to God as weapons of uprightness. I.e., put the body's members at God's disposal in the service of upright conduct and in the war against evil. The vb. *paristanein* is sometimes employed in a cultic or sacrificial sense (12:1; Polybius, *History* 16.25.7), but here it is used in a military sense (Polybius, *History* 3.109.9). Parts of "the body of death" are referred to as *melē*, "members," i.e., limbs and organs, which are to become "weapons," the "arms of uprightness," an allusion to OT terminology (Isa 11:5: "let uprightness be the girdle of his waist"; 59:17: "uprightness as a breastplate"). Christians are supposed to become weapons in God's service, not in that of evil and sin. See 5:21. They are urged to let uprightness dominate their lives and submit themselves to something that does not belong to them; such uprightness is not under their control, but they are to let it dominate them. The contrast of "wickedness" and "uprightness" is also found in QL (1QS 3:20–21: *ʿawel* and *ṣedeq*); but there *ṣedeq*, "uprightness," is closely linked with observance of the law, whereas for Paul it has assumed all of the connotations of "new life" in Christ. Hagen ("Two Deutero-Pauline Glosses") thinks that v 13 is a gloss because it interrupts vv 12 and 14, has a change of person and tense in the verbs, and shifts the theological perspective. But his argument is scarcely convincing, for it deprives Paul of the right of literary license.

See J. H. Michael, "The Text of Romans vi. 13 in the Chester Beatty Papyrus," *ExpTim* 49 (1937–38): 235: *[eis to hyp]akouein autē kai pa[ristanai ta mel]ē hymōn hopla adikias [tē hamartia],* "[so that you o]bey it and pu[t your membe]rs at sin's disposal (as) instruments of wickedness."

14. *Sin is not to have sway over you.* I.e., it is no longer to be the *kyrios* that it was in unregenerate human life, because it is related to death. Again, sin is conceived of as a personified power; cf. E. Lohmeyer, *ZNW* 29 (1930): 2–8: "the mythical exaltation of sin." Here Paul uses *hamartia* anarthrously (BDF §258.2), and the fut. *kyrieusei* expresses a categorical prohibition of it (BDF §362), not a mere "temporal future," *pace* Dunn (*Romans*, 339), who refers to the same place in BDF.

you are not under law but under grace. The "law" is never far from Paul's mind; now he links it again momentarily with sin, as he did in 5:20–21. He will develop its relation to sin more extensively in chap. 7, where it will be clear that he is thinking of the Mosaic law. So too here, *pace* Murray. The new Christian condition can be called "uprightness," but it is not per se associated with "law." It is, rather, the effect of God's benevolent favor (see 3:24; cf. Gal 5:18). The *kyrios* of Christian life is not legalism of any sort, but the prompting Spirit of God, whence comes grace. Again, Paul personifies "law" and "grace" as masters dominating human life. Contrast the expressions *hypo nomon* and *hypo charin* with the phrase *hyphʾ hamartian* of 3:9 to detect the real sense of the prep. *hypo:* "under (the power of)." Where the Christian lives by faith that works itself out through love, that Christian is living by grace, and life is no longer viewed as existence "under law," even the possibility of it (5:20). This attitude does not

447

imply that the Mosaic law has been abolished or has no validity, for Paul does not say that Jewish Christians need not observe it. His point is rather that "in Christ Jesus" even their perspective is that of "grace." What was demanded by the law is now attained through grace. In chap. 8 Paul will relate this concept to life in the Spirit.

15. *What, then, does this mean?* Lit., "what, then?" This rhetorical ellipse will appear again in 11:7; for the full form, see 4:1 and the NOTE on 6:1. Josephus uses the same ellipse in *J.W.* 2.16.4 §364, as does Xenophon in *Memorabilia* 4.2.17.

Should we sin because we are not under law, but under grace? So Paul reformulates the question of 6:1, now in terms of law and grace. Because there is no legal restraint for conduct, should Christians do what they want, even willful and deliberate acts of evil? The preferred reading is *hamartēsōmen* (aor. subjunct.); but some minor MSS (6, 614, 629, 630, 945, etc.) read the fut. indic. *hamartēsomen*, "shall we sin," and a few others (F, G) along with some Latin versions have the aor. indic. *hēmartēsamen*, "we have sinned." The former is an intelligible variant, but the latter is puzzling.

Certainly not! Again, Paul resolutely rejects the suggestion. See the NOTE on 3:4, and compare 6:2.

16. *Do you not know that, if you put yourselves at anyone's disposal in obedience, you become slaves of the one you obey?* Paul uses a rhetorical question to emphasize a fact, as in 11:2; 1 Cor 3:16; 5:6; 6:2–3, 9, 15–16, 19; 9:13, 24. The military figure of 6:13 gives way to one drawn from the social institution of slavery, which better suits the idea of law. In the Mediterranean world of Paul's day many persons sold themselves into slavery as a means of support, especially in urban centers. See Meeks, *First Urban Christians,* 20–23. Such an institution would imply a change of "masters" *(kyrioi),* and Christians, who through baptism become "slaves of Christ" (see the NOTE on 1:1), have him as their *kyrios* (cf. 1 Cor 6:11; John 8:34). Because baptized Christians may consider themselves free from sin, the danger of succumbing to its domination is all the greater. In obeying its enticements, they would thus enslave themselves to it as to a tyrannous master.

whether of sin, which leads to death, or of real obedience, which leads to uprightness. The one who obeys a master is enslaved to that master; hence the Christian must choose between obedience to sin (which leads to death) and obedience to God (which leads to uprightness of life). Yet what underlies Paul's comparison is not so much "slavery" as such, but service. He insists on the freedom of the Christian from the law (Gal 5:1); but he never conceives of it as license, a freedom to sin (Gal 5:13). It is rather a service of God to which the Christian is now dedicated, and it will include service of one's fellow human beings. The parallel is not perfectly expressed, but the sense is clear. Cf. Matt 6:24.

The words *eis thanaton,* "to death," are read in MSS ℵ, A, B, C, G, K, P, Ψ, 33, 81, 330, 614, etc., but are omitted in MSS D and 1739, as well as some versions. The omission was probably an oversight, because the phrase is needed for the sense.

17. *thanks be to God*. Paul utters his thanks to God as he reflects on the present condition of Christians. Cf. 7:25; 1 Cor 15:57; 2 Cor 2:14; 8:16; 9:15 for other examples of this Pauline mode of thanksgiving.

you who were once slaves to sin have wholeheartedly become obedient to the standard of teaching to which you have been entrusted. This part of v 17 and v 18 are sometimes regarded as a non-Pauline gloss (Bultmann, *TLZ* 72 [1947]: 200 [III/2]; he would eliminate the whole clause [6:17b] and restore a balanced couplet: "Thanks be to God! You were slaves of sin, but [now] freed from sin, you have become slaves of uprightness"). But there is little doubt about the Pauline authenticity of these verses (see Cranfield, *Romans*, 323).

The difficulty is that the Greek sentence in v 17 is elliptical: *hoti ēte douloi tēs hamartias hypēkousate de ek kardias eis hon paredothēte typon didachēs*, lit., "because you were slaves of sin, but you became obedient from (the) heart to which pattern of teaching you were handed over." It could mean *hoti hymeis hoi ēte douloi tēs hamartias hypēkousate . . . eis ton typon didachēs (eis) hon paredothēte* or *tō typō eis hon*, "because you, who were slaves of sin, became obedient to the pattern of teaching to which you were handed over." Or it could mean *hoti ei kai ēte douloi tēs hamartias hypēkousate eis ton typon didachēs hō paredothēte*, "because, though you were slaves of sin, you became obedient to the pattern of teaching to which you were handed over." Thus the ellipsis stands for a rel. cl. or a concessive cl., and the attracted rel. *hon* could even mean *hos paredothē hymin*, "which was entrusted to you" (see BDF §294.5). The impf. *ēte* is descriptive or durative and stands in contrast to the aor. *edoulōthēte* in v 18 (BDF §327).

The crucial word, however, is *typos*, which basically means "visible impression" (of a stroke or die), "mark, copy, image." But it was also used to designate a "compendium" or "terse presentation" of some topic (Plato, *Republic* 414a, 491c). Coupled with *didachē*, "teaching," it would seem to be used by Paul in the latter sense. He seems to refer thereby to a succinct baptismal summary of faith to which converts freely entrusted themselves after they had renounced all enslavement to sin. In this interpretation, however, the vb. *paredothēte*, "handed over," would refer not to the transmission of traditional doctrine (cf. 1 Cor 11:23; 15:3), but to the transfer of slaves from one master to another, without a pejorative connotation (see 1 Cor 5:5; Rom 1:24; Acts 14:26; 15:40). The allusion would be to the custom in the Hellenistic world by which the transfer of slaves was often accomplished with their consent. The *typos didachēs* would refer to the gospel or more specifically to a baptismal instruction based on the gospel to which the baptized readily entrusted themselves as a form of uprightness. Thus Christian "teaching" would include not only the proclamation about God's work in Christ Jesus, but also the "pattern" according to which Christians are to live. In 12:2 Paul will exhort Christians not to be conformed to this world, but rather to renew their thinking according to such a pattern of life. The phrase would then foreshadow the later idea of *symbolum fidei*, "symbol of faith," or even "the rule of faith," as Moffatt ("Interpretation") actually translates the phrase. Cf. 16:17. Note the similar expressions in Iamblichus, *Vita Pythagorica* 16.70 (*paideuseōs ho typos*, "pattern of instruction"); 23.103 (*ton typon tēs didaskalias*, "pattern of teaching").

A difficulty is sensed in the verse because *paradidonai* is the classic verb for "handing on" a traditional teaching, and such teaching could be designated by *typos*. If taken in this sense, *paredothēte* would mean that the baptized has become obedient to a teaching associated with baptism that imparts a certain form or pattern of life marked by tradition.

Still other explanations have been proposed. For instance, Lattey ("A Note") emphasizes the pejorative sense of *paradidonai*, "hand over" (as to death or imprisonment) and understands *typon didachēs* as rites or doctrines of paganism. Then vv 17a and 17b would refer to the old status, whereas v 18 would be a description of Christian freedom: "Thanks be to God because, (though) you were sinners and became obedient from the heart to the pattern of teaching to which you were handed over, now . . ." (v 18). Burkitt ("On Romans") took up Lattey's explanation and modified it by referring v 17a to life in paganism (= sinners), v 17b to life under Jewish law (= moral life), and v 18 to truly Christian life. Cf. Borse, " 'Abbild' "; Fridrichsen, "Zu Röm. 6, 17": "you became obedient to the form of teaching, for the learning of which you were given over."

18. *Freed then from sin, you have become slaves of uprightness.* This verse makes explicit the idea contained in the preceding verses, and in fact in the whole paragraph. Through baptism and in Christ Christians have been transferred from the dominion of sin to the dominion of uprightness. They are slaves whose masters have changed. For the first time in Romans Paul speaks of Christian liberty, which from now on becomes an operative notion (6:20, 22; 7:3; 8:2, 21; see Introduction, section IX.B). Actually, he has been speaking of some form of freedom since 5:12. Now he emphasizes the character of Christian life as an emancipation from the tyranny of sin.

19. *I am putting this in human terms because of your weak human nature.* Lit., "I speak (in) a human (way) because of the weakness of your flesh." Cf. 3:5; Gal 3:15; 1 Cor 9:8; also 1 Cor 3:1. Paul means that his referring to the Christian's devotion to uprightness as "slavery" is a very human way of putting it. So he apologizes for such a statement that he makes in a letter being sent to the Christians of Rome, whom he does not know personally. He assumes that they are like other Christians whom he knows and has encountered. He apologizes for using an image drawn from a contemporary social institution (slaves and masters) to describe the Christian reality, but he wants to be sure that his talk about Christian liberty is not misunderstood. It is not a license, a freedom to do what one wills, but a freedom to dedicate oneself to Christ, motivated by faith and

love, which proceeds "from the heart" and which is open to seeking the good of others.

This sort of expression (*anthrōpinon legō*) is not found in the LXX or in other NT writings; it is practically unknown in secular Greek literature and seems therefore to be a Pauline coinage. For later rabbinical counterparts, see Str-B 3.136–39. Cf. Bjerkelund, " 'Nach menschlicher Weise"; Daube, *New Testament and Rabbinic Judaism*, 394–400 (but beware of Daube's naïveté: "Paul avails himself of a phrase, which must have been technical in the Rabbinic Judaism of his epoch." Why "must have been"? The rabbinic counterpart dates only from centuries later).

Again, Hagen ("Two Deutero-Pauline Glosses") considers v 19 a gloss.

just as you used to put your members slavishly at the disposal of impurity and iniquity. Lit., "as you offered your members as slaves to impurity and iniquity" (or "lawlessness"). These were once the tyrants in life; they may seem to be typically pagan vices, but Qumran Essenes repudiated the same in their Jewish confrères (1QS 3:5; 4:10, 23–24). MSS F, G, and Latin versions read the infin., *douleuein*, "(offered your members) to serve slavishly." But the best Greek MSS, including now P⁹⁴, read the adj. *doula*. MS A, however, reads *hopla*, "(offer your members as) weapons."

which led to anarchy. I.e., to (still more) lawlessness.

now put them slavishly at the disposal of uprightness. So Paul exhorts the Christians of Rome to live out the meaning of justification in their lives.

which leads to holiness. Or "sanctification." This is the second effect of the Christ-event that Paul mentions in this paragraph; see Introduction, section IX.B. The end result of baptism is the dedication of the baptized or the consecration of them to God in Christ Jesus, which Paul explains in 1 Thess 4:3–7: those who are thus united with Christ's death and resurrection are called *hagioi*. They belong to the new aeon, the eschaton inaugurated by Christ Jesus. "You were washed, you were made holy, you were justified in the name of the Lord Jesus Christ and in the Spirit of our God" (1 Cor 6:11). Thus the cultic term of "sanctification" is given an eschatological nuance and involves "the daily task of the living out of justification" (Käsemann, *Commentary*, 183). Cf. 1 Pet 2:24.

20. *When you were slaves of sin, you were free from uprightness.* A play on the words "slave" and "free" in this and the following verse stresses that one can be deluded by what one thinks is freedom. Verses 20–23 emphasize the incompatibility of the two ways of life.

21. *what benefit did you then have?* The punctuation of this verse is disputed. It could mean, "What profit did you then get out of the things you are now ashamed of?" The sense, however, is little affected in either case.

save things of which you are now ashamed, things that result in death. Lit., "of which things you are now ashamed, for their end is death." The important affirmation is that death results from such sinful conduct as impurity and iniquity;

not just physical death, but total death. See the NOTE on 5:12. Paul uses the noun *telos* in the sense of goal, as in v 22.

22. *now that you have been freed from sin and have become slaves of God.* Paul repeats the major topic of this exhortation.

the benefit you have leads to holiness, which results in life eternal. Being enslaved to God means a dedication to him that brings with it a withdrawal from the profane and from the attachment to sin. Such dedication does not remove one from this world, but makes one live in it as one dedicated to God and his service. The goal of such dedication is "life eternal," a share in the sphere of divinity (see the NOTES on 2:7; 5:21). Although such life has already begun in a sense, its "end" is yet to come. Cf. 1 Pet 1:9; Heb 12:14.

23. *the wages of sin are death.* Paul reverts to a military figure and uses *opsōnion*, "ration (money)," paid to a soldier. Underlying the figure is the idea of regularly recurrent payment. The more one serves sin, the more pay in the form of death one earns. Such "wages" are paid out as death to those who serve sin. Cf. 8:6, 13. See H. Heidland, *TDNT* 5.592; Caragounis, "*Opsōnion.*"

the gift of God is eternal life. In contrast to the "wages of sin" that are due (4:4), "eternal life" is graciously bestowed on Christians by God himself. There is no quid pro quo, and God's prevenient grace eventually brings about an assimilation of Christians to the life of God himself (5:21; 2 Cor 3:18). But that "grace" is here called *to charisma tou theou*, and Paul thus refers to *the* charism par excellence given to Christians, which comes through Christ Jesus. In 12:6–8 he will discuss its secondary analogates.

in Christ Jesus our Lord. Again Paul uses the concluding formula; see the COMMENT on 5:1–11. Paul insists that the "gift" of eternal life is something that comes to Christians through the mediating death and resurrection of Christ Jesus; it is "a gift that is tied up with the work of Christ" (Michel, *Brief an die Römer*, 216). See F. Neugebauer, *In Christus*, 87.

BIBLIOGRAPHY

Agersnap, S., "Rom 6, 12 og det paulinske imperativ," *DTT* 43 (1980): 36–47.

Beare, F. W., "On the Interpretation of Romans vi. 17," *NTS* 5 (1958–59): 206–10.

Bjerkelund, C. J., " 'Nach menschlicher Weise rede ich': Funktion und Sinn des paulinischen Ausdrucks," *ST* 26 (1972): 63–100.

Borse, U., " 'Abbild der Lehre' (Röm 6, 17) im Kontext," *BZ* 12 (1968): 95–103.

Bouttier, M., "La Vie du chrétien en tant que service de la justice pour la sainteté: Romains 6:15–23," *Battesimo*, ed. L. de Lorenzi, 127–54.

Burkitt, F. C., "On Romans vi 17–18," *JTS* 30 (1929): 190.

Caragounis, C. C., "*Opsōnion*: A Reconsideration of Its Meaning," *NovT* 16 (1974): 35–57.

Dahl, N. A., "In What Sense Is the Baptized Person 'simul justus et peccator' According to the New Testament," *LW* 9 (1962): 219–31.

Fridrichsen, A., "Zu Röm. 6, 7," *ConNeot* 7 (1942): 6–8.

Hagen, W. H., "Two Deutero-Pauline Glosses in Romans 6," *ExpTim* 92 (1980–81): 364–67.

Käsemann, E., "Römer 6, 19–23," *Exegetische Versuche und Besinnungen*, 2d ed. (Göttingen: Vandenhoeck & Ruprecht, 1960), 1.263–66.

Kürzinger, J., "*Typos didachēs* und der Sinn von Röm 6,17f." *Bib* 39 (1958): 156–76.

Lattey, C., "Note on Rom. vi 17,18," *JTS* 29 (1927–28): 381–84; 30 (1928–29): 397–99.

Lyall, F., "Roman Law in the Writings of Paul—The Slave and the Freedman," *NTS* 17 (1970–71): 73–79.

Malan, F. S., "Bound to Do Right," *Neotestamentica* 15 (1981): 118–38.

Marcus, J., " 'Let God Arise and End the Reign of Sin!': A Contribution to the Study of Pauline Parenesis," *Bib* 69 (1988): 386–95.

Moffatt, J., "The Interpretation of Romans 6:17–18," *JBL* 48 (1929): 233–38.

Schweizer, E., "Die Sünde in den Gliedern," *Abraham unser Vater: Juden und Christen im Gespräch über die Bibel: Festschrift für Otto Michel . . .* , AGSU 5, ed. O. Betz et al. (Leiden: Brill, 1963), 437–39.

Trimaille, M., "Encore le 'typos didachès' de Romains 6,17," *La Vie de la parole: De l'Ancien au Nouveau Testament: Études d'exégèse et d'herméneutique bibliques offertes à Pierre Grelot . . .* (Paris: Desclée, 1987), 269–80.

FREEDOM FROM THE LAW (7:1–25)

◆

21. FREEDOM FROM THE LAW
BY THE DEATH OF CHRIST (7:1–6)

7 ¹Or are you unaware, brothers—for I am speaking to those who know what law is—that the law has authority over a human being only as long as one is alive? ²Thus a married woman is bound by law to her husband while he is alive. But if the husband dies, she is released from the law regarding her husband. ³Accordingly, she will be called an adulteress if she gives herself to another man, while her husband is still alive. But if her husband dies, she is free of that law and does not become an adulteress if she gives herself to another man. ⁴So you too, my brothers, have died to the law through the body of Christ that you might give yourselves to another, to him who has been raised from the dead, so as to bear fruit for God. ⁵For when we were living merely natural lives, sinful passions aroused by the law were at work in our members, so as to bear fruit for death. ⁶But now, by dying to what we were once held captive, we have been released from the law so that we might serve God in a new way of the Spirit and not in the old way of a written code.

COMMENT

Paul began his description of the new situation of the justified Christian by explaining how Christ has put an end to the reign of sin and death (5:12–21) and how the "new life in Christ Jesus" means a reorientation of the self so that one could no longer even think of sinning (6:1–23). In 6:14–15 he introduced the relation of the law to the new freedom enjoyed by the Christian, haunted by the problem that the law posed in human life. What role did it still have, if any? Earlier in Romans he betrayed a preoccupation with this problem (3:20, 31; 4:15; 5:13, 20), but now he tries to face it squarely. What is the relation of law to sin? How can law be the minister of death and condemnation (2 Cor 3:7, 9)? What is the Christian's relation to the law? Beause of sin and consequent alienation from God human beings had fallen under the wrath of God; sin ruled over them, and the law seems to have contributed to this situation and thus seems to have become a force leading to death itself. How could this be? In 1 Cor 15:56 Paul had written, "The sting of death is sin, and the power of sin is law." Paul thus saw sin exerting its influence in human life through the law. When such powers as death, sin, and law dominate human existence, it is exposed to wrath, and salvation is nigh impossible. Paul has already shown that through Christ Jesus human beings have been freed from sin, self, and death; now he wants to show how that freedom also liberates from law. Paul's ideas on the law are complicated, and this chapter becomes the most difficult in the letter to understand.

The majority of Paul's teaching on the law is contained in this chapter, yet one should also relate to it what he says in 8:1–7; 9:31; 10:4–5; 13:8–10; Gal 2:16–6:13; 1 Cor 9:20; 15:56. See Introduction, section IX.D.

In chap. 7, vv 1–6 form the introduction to Paul's answer to the questions raised above, as he asserts the Christian's freedom from the law, whereas vv 7–25 formulate the answer itself, the relation of law to sin. In the introductory verses Paul interweaves two arguments. The first is that law binds only the living (7:1, 4a); consequently, Christians who have died "through the body of Christ" are no longer bound to observe the law. And the second is that a wife is freed by the death of her husband from the specific prescription of the law binding her to him. Christians are like the Jewish wife whose husband has died. As she is freed from "the law of the husband" through death, so Christians have died "through the body of Christ" and they are freed from the law (7:2, 3, 4b). The second argument is only an illustration of the first, and not a perfect one at that.

It should not be forced into an allegory, as Sanday and Headlam once proposed (*Romans*, 172, 174): the wife = the true self (Ego); the (first) husband = the old state of man; the "law of the husband" = the law condemning the old state; the new marriage = union with the risen Christ; crucifixion = death of the husband; resurrection = remarriage. For Paul's argument is different; it is the same person who dies and is freed from the law. He uses the illustration for one point only: the law's obligation ceases when death occurs, or death ends the dominion of law. Because Christians have experienced death in and through Christ, the law has no more claim on them. So Paul argues in these verses.

One of the major problems in this chapter is, Of what law does Paul speak? Does *nomos* in 7:1a refer to the same law as in v 1b and the subsequent verses?

According to some commentators, *nomos* in *ginōskousin gar nomon lalō* (7:1a) would refer to (1) "law" in general, or "the legal order," because of the absence of a def. art.: so Bultmann (*TDNT*, 1.259–60), Goodspeed, Käsemann (*Commentary*, 187), Lyonnet (*Exegesis* [1961], 64), Prat (*Theology* 1.225 n. 2), Sanday and Headlam (*Romans*, 172), and Taylor (*Romans*, 45); (2) Roman law, because Paul is writing to Romans, noted for their famous law; so B. Weiss, Jülicher, Kühl (*Römer*, 224), and Lagrange (*Romains*, 160–61); or (3) Mosaic law, as the immediate context (vv 2, 3, 4b), as well as 5:20 and 6:14, seem to demand: so Althaus, Bardenhewer, Barrett, Bover, Cornely, Cranfield, van Dülmen, Huby, Kümmel, Kürzinger, Kuss, Leenhardt, Lietzmann, Lipsius, Michel, Minear, Murray, Schlatter, Schlier, Sickenberger, Viard, Wilckens, and Zahn.

As for *nomos* in 7:1b and in vv 2–6, 7–14, 22–23, and 25 it has been interpreted as (1) the natural law, to which Paul seems to refer to 2:14: so Origen (*In ep. ad Romanos* [PG 14.1032]), Reuss; (2) all law given from the beginning, including the command imposed on Adam, because Paul uses *entolē*, "commandment" (7:13) and alludes to Gen 3:13 (7:11): so Didymus the Blind, Ephraim, Gennadius, Methodius (*De resurrectione* 2.1–8 [GCS 27.329–45]), Severian of Gabala, Theodore of Mopsuestia, Theodoret of Cyrrhus, Cajetan (*In ep. Pauli ad Romanos* 7 [1532, 21]); Dibelius, Holtzmann, Lagrange (*Romains*, 168, 399), Lietzmann, Lyonnet (*Exegesis* [1961] 74–78), Preuschen and Bauer, and Prümm; or (3) Mosaic law, as Paul normally understands *nomos* elsewhere: so all of those listed under 3 above.

None of the reasons provided in favor of 1 or 2 shows that Paul had a concept of law wider than that of the Mosaic law. Thomas Aquinas (*In ep. ad Romanos* 7.1 [Parma 13.66]) rejected the natural law explanation, recognizing that Paul, in speaking absolutely of "the law," elsewhere means the law of Moses. Moreover, the other reasons may attest the belief of some Jews that the Mosaic law was itself already known to Abraham or to people of earlier times (e.g., Noah). But Paul clearly does not share this belief; he never mentions Adam in this connection, and many of his statements elsewhere counter such an interpretation (4:13; 5:12–14; Gal 3:17–19). He is, rather, worried about the conclusion that might be drawn from some of his remarks about the Mosaic law: that it might seem to be sinful itself, because it "slipped in" to increase offenses (5:20), furnishes "knowledge of sin" (3:20), and "brings wrath" (4:15).

As Leenhardt has noted (*Romans*, 177), if Paul's argument were based on a pagan juridical principle such as would be implied in the first interpretation given to 7:1a, it would lose much of its demonstrative force. That would seem, then, to rule out the understanding of *nomos* in v 1a both as law in general or as Roman law. Again, it seems to be stretching a point to argue that *entolē* in v 13 refers to the "commandment" given to Adam, even if Sir 45:5(6) uses the same expression of the commandments given to Moses (see Sir 17:4–11), because *entolē* in vv 11 and 13 is used more to bring out the formal aspect of law as a positive command than to allude to the command laid on Adam. Moreover, the precept quoted in v 7b comes from Exod 20:17, not from Gen 2:17 or 3:3. Hence it seems better to understand *nomos* at least from v 1b on as referring to the Mosaic law, and the same seems to be intended in v 1a as well.

NOTES

7:1. *are you unaware?* See the NOTE on 6:3. Cf. 11:25.

brothers. This is the first use of *adelphoi* in an address to Roman Christians since 1:13 (see the NOTE there). In so using this address, Paul implies that the topic he is about to take up is a sensitive one, for which he wants to win over his readers' mutual understanding (*captatio benevolentiae*); so Schlier, *Römerbrief*, 214.

I am speaking to those who know what law is. Lit., "who know law," *nomos* being anarthrous. Paul refers to the Mosaic law elsewhere without using the def. art. (2:12, 13, 14, 23, 25; 3:20, 21, 28, 31; 4:13; 5:13, 20; etc.), so the anarthrous use here may be explained in the same way. In any case, the term "the law" in v 4 makes this usage clear; see the COMMENT above and BDF §258.2. Paul can assume some knowledge of the Mosaic law among the Christians of Rome because, although he regards them as predominantly Gentile Christians, they have been converts who earlier were related to Jews, especially those who had come from Jerusalem; he also presupposes them to be acquainted with the OT in Greek. The clause does not imply that Paul considers the Christians of Rome to be predominantly Jewish.

the law has authority over a human being only as long as one is alive. Lit., "the law lords it over a human being for so long a time as one lives," i.e., the law keeps one in bondage to the obligation to observe it for the duration of the life of a human being. See 6:7, where Paul expresses the idea in a slightly different way. A conclusion from this statement is drawn in v 4a. Now *ho nomos* is understood as the Mosaic law, because of the illustration that Paul uses in the following verses, 2 and 3, which is taken from that law. Paul's statement as such, however, is not found in the OT, but it agrees with the principle enunciated in later rabbinic literature, e.g., in *m. Qidd.* 1:1: "she acquires freedom by a writ of divorce or by her husband's death." Cf. *b. Šabb.* 30a; see Str-B 3.232, 234. Paul uses of the law the vb. *kyrieuein*, which he also used in 6:9 and 14 of sin and death, thus drawing the law into the threesome that tyrannize human existence apart from Christ. Paul does not say that the law itself dies or has died, nor does he say that for the Christian the law has been repealed or is nonexistent. The law is still in effect, indeed, but it is the Christian who has died to it.

2. *a married woman.* What was said of *anthrōpos* in v 1b is now made specific according to Mosaic law in its regulations about a married woman. Paul uses the Hellenistic phrase *hypandros gynē*, lit., "a woman under-(her)-husband," as a way of speaking of a "married woman" (cf. Polybius, *History* 10.26.3; Artemidorus 1.78 [74.6]). It is also found in the LXX (Num 5:20, 29 [= Hebr. *tahat ʾîš*]; Prov 6:24, 29; Sir 9:9; 41:23).

is bound by law to her husband while he is alive. See 1 Cor 7:39. By OT law a wife was considered the chattel or property of her husband, and he had rights over her that could be violated by her or by another man (cf. Gen 20:3, *wĕhî bĕʿûlat baʿal*, lit., "she is ruled over [or owned] by [her] owner/master"). Hence every extramarital sexual act of hers was regarded as adultery (Exod 20:14, 17; 21:22; Lev 20:10; Num 30:10–16; Deut 22:22); cf. *AI* 26.

if the husband dies, she is released from the law regarding her husband. Lit., "she has been annulled from the law of the husband," i.e., from the specific Mosaic legislation binding a wife to her owner (husband) as long as he lives. Once he dies, then the wife is freed from obligation to her husband and can marry whomever she wills. For further Pauline instances of *katargein* with the prep. *apo*, see 7:6; Gal 5:4.

3. *she will be called an adulteress if she gives herself to another man, while her husband is still alive.* Lit., "if she becomes (the property) of another man," or

"belongs to another man." The Greek expression is a dat. of possession derived from the LXX of Lev 22:12; Deut 24:2; Hos 3:3 (see BDF §189.2). The woman who gives herself to another violates the rights of her husband (owner), and for that reason she is branded as *moichalis*. The freedom of the wife to have relations with another comes with her husband's death; it has nothing to do here with divorce. The fut. *chrēmatisei* is gnomic (BDF §349.1). *Moichalis*, "adulteress," is a term found in the LXX (Ezek 16:38; 23:45; Hos 3:1; Mal 3:5; Prov 18:22a), but not in extrabiblical Greek in pre-Christian times. It does occur in *T. Levi* 14:6 and is a term, then, that reflects Jewish and Christian views of marriage.

if her husband dies, she is free of that law and does not become an adulteress if she gives herself to another man. Lit., "so that she does not become an adulteress in belonging to another man." Paul expresses this with the gen. of the articular infin. (BDF §400.8).

4. *So you too, my brothers, have died to the law.* Lit., "you have been put to death." It is not "the law of the husband," but the Mosaic law as such to which Christians have died. Paul concludes from the specific to the generic. He emphasizes only one aspect of relationship to the law, that which happens when death occurs. Again, Paul introduces the address, "brothers"; see the NOTES on 1:13; 7:1.

through the body of Christ. I.e., through the crucified body of the Jesus of history, as Paul also teaches in Gal 2:19–20. Christians have been made dead to the law's condemnation through the body of Christ by God's merciful decision: they died in his death, in that the death that he died was for all humanity (see 2 Cor 5:14–15; cf. Col 1:22 and Cranfield, *Romans*, 336). This understanding of "body of Christ" as the physical, historical body of Jesus has been used since Origen (PG 14.1073–74). *Pace* Dunn (*Romans*, 362), there is no reason to stress the def. art in *tou Christou*, as if Paul were to mean "the body of *the* Christ," for Paul makes something of the etymology of *Christos* in 9:5 *alone*, of all his writings.

Theodore of Mopsuestia (PG 66.805) understood it of both the physical and the mystical body of Christ, whereas Tertullian interpreted it to mean the body of Christ, "which is the church," in dependence on Eph 1:23 (*De Monogamia* 13.3 [CCLat 2.1248]). Similarly, J. A. T. Robinson, *The Body: A Study in Pauline Theology*, SBT 5 (London: SCM, 1952), 47; Dodd; and Nygren. Yet these last two interpretations hardly suit the Pauline context, introducing an ecclesial consideration into the text that otherwise lacks any reference to it. Paul has already taught that in baptism the Christian has been identified with Christ (6:4–6), sharing in his death, burial, and resurrection. When Jesus died for all "in the likeness of sinful flesh" (8:3), then all died (2 Cor 5:14–15). Clearly, the phrase has nothing to do with the eucharistic "body of Christ," despite the marginal note in N-A[26].

that you might give yourselves to another. Lit., "that you may belong to another." Paul uses *heterō*, "to another," as a dat. of possession (BDF §§188.2,

189.2), picking up the LXX phrase about a second husband (see the NOTE on 7:3); cf. 6:11, 22: dead to sin and alive to God in Christ Jesus; Gal 2:19–20.

to him who has been raised from the dead. I.e., to the glorified Christ, who as *Kyrios* becomes a sort of "second husband" and is the master of the Christian henceforth. See the NOTE on 4:25 for the formulaic mode of referring to the resurrection.

so as to bear fruit for God. The union of the risen Christ and the Christian has just been depicted in terms of marriage. Paul continues the figure: such a union is expected to produce the "fruit" of reformed life dedicated to God. "The believer is free to contract a new union with his Risen Lord, and obtain new progeny through this fresh marriage" (Black, *Romans,* 94). Cf. Col 1:10; Thüsing, " 'Fruchtbringen für Gott,' " *Per Christum in Deum,* 93–101.

5. *when we were living merely natural lives.* Lit., "when we were in the flesh," i.e., when the "flesh" still had the upper hand and we were living under the law or in the past without Christ. For a similar use of *en sarki,* see 2 Cor 10:3. That mode of life will be contrasted with life in "the Spirit" (7:6; cf. 8:9). Note the transition to the first person plural.

sinful passions. Lit., "the passions of sins," i.e., the propensity to sin following upon strong sensory impressions, which come from sin itself; so Paul now phrases what he described in 6:12 as "the cravings" of the mortal body. *Pathēmata* normally means "sufferings" (as in 8:18), but now it is used in the pejorative sense of "emotions, passions," as in Gal 5:24 (cf. Plutarch, *Moralia* 1128E).

aroused by the law. Lit., "those of the law," i.e., cravings for what was sinful were awakened by the law, which acted as an occasion of sin (see 7:7b). Cf. 1 Cor 15:56.

were at work in our members. I.e., became active in our very being; see 6:13.

so as to bear fruit for death. I.e., the opposite of what was expected of the life of a Christian. Paul restates what he said in 6:21–23.

6. *But now.* I.e., in the new aeon of the Christian dispensation (see the NOTE on 3:21). This eschatological "now" will be resumed in the *nyn* of 8:1, as Paul begins to explain what is meant by service in the new life of the Spirit.

by dying to what we were once held captive. Or "by dying to which," i.e., the law, as it is not clear whether *en hō* is masc. (referring to the law) or neut. (referring generically to all that has held one captive). The pron. "what" could refer to the dominance of the passions just mentioned, but it may be only another reference to the law in this paragraph. See Gal 3:23, "locked up under the law, kept in restraint." Cf. 5:20–21; 6:11, 18, 22.

The best MSS (ℵ, A, B, C, K, P, Ψ, 22, 81, 614, 1739) and several ancient versions read *apothanontes,* "dying," whereas the Western text-tradition (MSS D and G and VL MSS) reads *tou thanatou,* which would depend on the preceding phrase *tou nomou,* "the law of death." This substitution of *tou thanatou* for the ptc. is a copyist's harmonization of this text with 8:2. On the reading *apothanontos,* see TCGNT, 514.

we have been released from the law. I.e., by having died to it through the body of Christ (7:4; cf. Gal 2:19). Paul will take up this notion again in 8:1–2.

that we might serve God in a new way of the Spirit. Lit., "that we might serve in a newness of spirit." "God" is supplied as the object of "serve." At first it might seem that *en kainotēti pneumatos,* "a newness of spirit," means only "with a renewed spirit," but the contrast expressed in the following cl. makes it clear that Paul is referring to the holy Spirit. The "Spirit" is the dynamic principle of new life received in baptism (6:4); it will be more fully explained in chap. 8. This sense is also suggested by the contrast with *sarx,* "flesh" in 7:5.

and not in the old way of a written code. Lit., "not in the oldness of (the) letter," *gramma* being used as a way to refer to the OT as the legislation of the "old covenant." (2 Cor 3:6–8 is an excellent commentary on this verse). Thus "Spirit" is contrasted not only with "flesh" (v 5), but also with the "letter" of the old law. We serve not a written code, but God himself with the new dynamic principle of the Spirit. See the NOTE on 2:29 and the bibliography listed there on Spirit and letter (Kamlah, Morreale de Castro, Schneider).

BIBLIOGRAPHY ON CHAPTER 7 AS A WHOLE

Althaus, P., *Paulus und Luther über den Menschen: Ein Vergleich,* Studien der Luther-Akademie 14, 3d ed. (Gütersloh: Bertelsmann, 1958).

Bader, G., "Römer 7 als Skopus einer theologischen Handlungstheorie," *ZTK* 78 (1981): 31–56.

Borchert, G. L., "Romans, Pastoral Counseling, and the Introspective Conscience of the West," *RevExp* 83 (1986): 81–92.

Blank, J., "Gesetz und Geist," *The Law of the Spirit,* ed. L. de Lorenzi, 73–127; repr. *Paulus: Von Jesus zum Urchristentum* (Munich: Kösel, 1982), 86–123.

Bornkamm, G., "Sin, Law and Death: An Exegetical Study of Romans 7," *Early Christian Experience,* 87–104.

Bultmann, R., "Romans 7 and the Anthropology of Paul," *Existence and Faith* (Cleveland, Oh.: World Publ. Co. 1960), 147–57.

Conzelmann, H., *An Outline of the Theology of the New Testament* (New York: Harper & Row, 1969), 228–35.

Cruvellier, J. M. E., *L'Exégèse de Romains 7 et le mouvement de Keswick* ('s-Gravenhage: Pasmans, 1961).

Davies, D. M., "Free from the Law: An Exposition of the Seventh Chapter of Romans," *Int* 7 (1953): 156–62.

Ellwein, E., "Das Rätsel von Römer 7," *KD* 1 (1955): 147–68.

Engel, M. R., *Der Kampf um Römer, Kapitel 7: Eine historisch-exegetische Studie* (Gotha: Verlagsbureau, 1902).

Giese, E., *Römer 7 neu gesehen im Zusammenhang des gesamten Briefes* (Marburg and Lahn: Mauersberger, 1959).

Grelot, P., "La Vie dans l'Esprit (d'après Romains 7–8)," *Christus* (Paris) 29 (1982): 83–98.

Hommel, H., "Das 7. Kapitel des Römerbriefs im Licht antiker Überlieferung," *Theologia viatorum* 8 (1961–62): 90–116; repr. *Sebasmata*, 2 vols. (Tübingen: Mohr [Siebeck] 1983–84), 2.141–73 (mit Nachträge).

Jonas, H., "Philosophical Meditation on the Seventh Chapter of Paul's Epistle to the Romans," *The Future of Our Religious Past: Essays in Honour of Rudolf Bultmann*, ed. J. M. Robinson (New York: Harper & Row, 1971), 333–50.

Kertelge, K., "Exegetische Überlegungen zum Verständnis der paulinischen Anthropologie nach Römer 7," *ZNW* 62 (1971): 105–14.

Kohlbrügge, H. F., *Das siebte Kapitel des Römerbriefes, in ausführlicher Umschreibung*, BibSN 28 (Neukirchen-Vluyn: Neukirchener-Verlag, 1960).

Krummacher, E. W., "Über das Subject in Röm. 7: Eine exegetisch-psychologische Untersuchung," *TSK* 35.1 (1862): 119–36.

Kümmel, W. G., *Römer 7 und die Bekehrung des Paulus* (Leipzig: Hinrichs, 1929).

Kürzinger, J., "Der Schlüssel zum Verständnis von Röm 7," *BZ* 7 (1963): 270–74.

Langevin, P.-E., "Exégèse et psychanalyse: Lecture psychanalytique de *Romains* VII et VIII," *LTP* 36 (1980): 129–37.

Lekkerkerker, A. F. N., "Romeinen 7, een belijdenis der gemeente," *NThStud* 23 (1940): 99–109.

Lorenzi, L. de (ed.), *The Law of the Spirit in Rom 7 and 8*, Benedictina, Biblical-Ecumenical Section 1 (Rome: Abbazia S. Paolo fuori le mura, 1976).

Lyonnet, S., "L'Histoire du salut selon le chapitre VII de l'Épître aux Romains," *Bib* 43 (1962): 117–51; repr. in *Études*, 203–30.

MacGorman, J. W., "Romans 7 Once More," *SwJT* 19 (1976–77): 31–41.

Mitton, C. L., "Romans 7 Reconsidered," *ExpTim* 65 (1953–54): 78–81, 99–103, 132–35.

Morrison, B. and J. Woodhouse, "The Coherence of Romans 7:1–8:8," *RTR* 47 (1988): 8–16.

Packer, J. I., "The 'Wretched Man' in Romans 7," *SE II*, TU 87 (1964), 621–27.

Pretorius, H. S., *Bijdrage tot de Exegese en de Geschiedenis der Exegese van Romeinen VII* (Amsterdam: H. A. van Bottenburg, 1915).

Rétif, A., "À propos de l'Interprétation du chapitre VII des Romains par Saint Augustin," *RSR* 33 (1946): 368–71.

Sanders, E. P., "Romans 7 and the Purpose of the Law," *PIBA* 7 (1983): 44–59.

Schmitz, R., *Fleisch und Geist unter besonderer Berücksichtigung von Römer 7 und 8* (Witten [Ruhr]: Bundes-Verlag, 1962).

Schnackenburg, R., "Römer 7 im Zusammenhang des Römerbriefes," *Jesus und Paulus: Festschrift für Werner Georg Kümmel . . .* , ed. E. E. Ellis and E. Grässer (Göttingen: Vandenhoeck & Ruprecht, 1975), 283–300.

Segal, A. F., "Romans 7 and Jewish Dietary Law," *SR* 15 (1986): 361–74.

Trocmé, E., "From 'I' to 'We': Christian Life According to Romans, Chapters 7 and 8," *AusBR* 35 (1987): 73–76.

Umbreit, F. W. C., "Des Apostels Paulus Selbstbekenntnis im siebentem Kapitel des Briefes an die Römer: Exegetisch beleuchtet," *TSK* 24.2 (1851): 633–45.

Yagi, S., "Weder persönlich noch generell—zum neutestamentlichen Denken anhand Röm vii," *AJBI* 2 (1976): 159–73.

On Rom 7:1–6

Derrett, J. D. M., "Fresh Light on Romans vii. 1–4," *JJS* 15 (1964): 97–108; repr. *Law in the New Testament* (London: Darton, Longman & Todd, 1970), 461–71.

Diezinger, W., "Unter Toten freigeworden: Eine Untersuchung zu Röm. iii–viii," *NovT* 5 (1962): 272–98.

Gale, H. M., *The Use of Analogy in the Letters of Paul* (Philadelphia, Penn.: Westminster, 1964).

Käsemann, E., "The Spirit of the Letter," *Perspectives*, 138–66.

Little, J. A., "Paul's Use of Analogy: A Structural Analysis of Romans 7:1–6," *CBQ* 46 (1984): 82–90.

Murray, J., "Divorce: Fifth Article," *WTJ* 11 (1948–49): 105–22.

Stanley, D. M., *Christ's Resurrection*, 186–88.

Tannehill, R. C., *Dying and Rising*, 43–47.

22. ROLE OF THE LAW IN HUMAN LIFE (7:7–13)

7 ⁷What then can we say? Is the law sin? Certainly not! Yet I would not have known sin, if it were not for the law. I would not have known what it was to covet, if the law had not said, *"You shall not covet."* ⁸But sin, using the commandment, seized the opportunity and produced in me every sort of covetousness. Now in the absence of law sin is as good as dead. ⁹Indeed, I once lived in the absence of law, but when the commandment came, sin sprang to life, ¹⁰and I died. The commandment that was meant for life was found to be death for me. ¹¹For sin, using the commandment, seized the opportunity and deceived me; through it sin killed me. ¹²Yet the law is holy, and the commandment is holy, upright, and good. ¹³Did, then, what was good become death for me? Certainly not! Rather, sin, that it might be unmasked as sin, produced death in me by using what was good so that through the commandment it might become sinful beyond all measure.

COMMENT

In vv 7–13 Paul moves on to answer the questions about the relation of the law to sin. He will explain what is meant by serving under the written code. In vv 1–6 Paul has asserted that through the death of Christ human beings are freed from the law, but now he wants to explain why the law is not one of the enslaving powers. He will, indeed, deny that the law is simply sin and will show that it is in itself holy, upright, and good, but will insist that sin, which dwells in a person, makes use of the law as a henchman or a tool to accomplish its own ends. Again it is the law given to Moses for the Jewish people of which Paul speaks in this part of Romans. Paul implies that the effect of the law is to give human beings knowledge of sin, not only of the abstract notion of sin, but of sin as a dynamic overlord that induces a spirit of rebellion against God and of disobedience to his commandments. By manifesting what God prohibits or commands, the law gives sin the opportunity to goad the Ego into active rebellion. Yet the law gives the Ego no ability to avoid what God prohibits or to do what he commands.

Verses 7–25 are an integral part of Paul's discussion; they have been called an "excursus" on the law, but they are hardly to be regarded as an intrusion that interrupts 7:6 and 8:1, or, worse still, a "foreign body," as Schmithals would have us believe. Similarly, O'Neill thinks that 7:14–25 is not authentically Pauline.

Verses 7–25 have been called an "apology for the law" (Kümmel, *Römer 7,* 11; similarly Lagrange, *Romains,* 166; Lyonnet, *VD* 40 [1962]: 164; Bornkamm, "Sin, Law and Death"). Käsemann (*Commentary,* 192) agrees that the apologetic character of the passage is evident in vv 7a, 12, 13a, and 14, but the power of sin is emphasized even more, especially in vv 14–25, where Torah recedes and the focus is on anthropology. But Bornkamm presses even further and recognizes vv 7–13 as a "confession in which the history of man and my way into lostness and death is portrayed."

Because vv 7–13 act as a confession, Paul casts his argument in the past tense, whereas in vv 14–25 it is formulated in the present tense, which is more properly regarded as the "apology for the law." Whether the past tense used in vv 7–13 is a sign of Paul's pre-Christian past, as some have maintained, is debatable. It is more likely a device that Paul uses to describe humanity under the domination of the Mosaic law. It was the time of the domination of the powers of sin and death. It is the aeon on which the *egō* looks back and from which the *egō* seeks to distance itself. The description in the present tense in vv 14–25 is undoubtedly so composed for the sake of vividness; past events are vividly recalled.

In these verses (7–13) Paul also switches to the first person singular, and this shift has historically posed an exegetical problem: the identification of the *egō* in vv 7–25. Instead of using *anthrōpos,* "human being," or *tis,* "someone," or even "we," Paul chooses to speak of Ego, somewhat as he does in 1 Cor 8:13; 13:1–3, 11–12; 14:6–19; and Gal 2:18–21. This rhetorical device "is encountered not only in the Greek world but also in the OT psalms of thanksgiving when divine deliverance from guilt and peril of death is confessed" (Käsemann, *Commentary,* 193). It is also used, perhaps in a gnomic sense, in the Qumran *Hodayot* (e.g., 1QH 2:7–30; 3:20–21; 4:30; 16:11; fragment 6:6), if it does not refer to the Teacher of Righteousness, as some hold.

The Ego has been understood in at least five different senses. (1) *Autobiographically.* Paul is said to be referring to his own youthful experience as he grew up and was confronted by the demands of the Mosaic law, which crushed him and led to his conversion on the road to Damascus. So Bruce, Deissmann, Dodd, Gundry, Jeremias, Kühl, Packer, Weinel, Zahn, and seemingly Moo. But this interpretation is unconvincing, for it contradicts what Paul says of his own psychological background and pre-call experience with the law in Phil 3:6 and Gal 1:13–14. It also misunderstands Paul's perspective, namely, his reflection on the stages of human history, which he now, as a Pharisee called to Christ, seeks to sort out. See Stendahl, "The Apostle Paul"; Kümmel, *Römer* 7.

(2) *Psychologically*. The *egō* is understood of a young Jewish boy passing from youthful innocence to adolescent experience and the requirements of the Mosaic law (what is called today *bar miṣwāh*, about the age of twelve): so Bardenhewer, Billerbeck, Bläser, Cornely, Davies, Franzmann, and Knox. But such an interpretation again misses Paul's perspective, which is not limited to adolescent problems, and it would make the interpretation of v 9 very difficult. What would it mean for a circumcised Jewish youth to say that he "once lived in the absence of law"?

(3) *As Adam*. The *egō* is understood to be Adam, the father of the human race, confronted with the "command" of Gen 2:16–17. So Methodius of Olympia, Theodore of Mopsuestia, Cajetan, Dibelius, Feuillet, Leenhardt, Lietzmann, Lyonnet, Michel, and Pesch. But this interpretation, though it gives the passage a more comprehensive perspective (which it needs), and though Paul may allude to Gen 3:13 in 7:11, is really eisegetical. It does not explain why Paul would refer to Adam as *egō* or introduce him into a text wherein he is not mentioned; contrast 5:12; 1 Cor 15:45. Certainly, v 9 does not demand such an interpretation, and the precept quoted in 7:7b is from Exod 20:17 or Deut 5:21, not from Gen 2:17.

(4) *As a Christian*. The *egō* is understood to mean Paul's own experience as a Christian believer faced with new obligations in his life as a convert. So Augustine, Thomas Aquinas, Luther, Calvin, Althaus, Barth, Giese, Nygren, to an extent Cranfield, Packer, and seemingly Dunn. But then one must ask, Why all the references to the *Mosaic* law? Such an interpretation tends to make of Paul a young Luther. Moreover, it is clear that in chap. 8 Paul speaks of the Christian living the life of the Spirit; here it is far from clear that he is speaking of the same person. The discussion is more generic.

(5) *In a cosmic-historical dimension*. Paul speaks rhetorically of the *egō*, using a figure of speech to dramatize in an intimate personal way the experience common to all unregenerate human beings faced with law and relying on their own resources to meet its obligations. He views unregenerate humanity with Jewish spectacles and depicts it faced with the Mosaic law and seeking to achieve the status of uprightness by observing such a law. So many of the Greek Fathers, especially Diodore of Tarsus (Staab, *Pauluskatenen*, 47), John Chrysostom (*In ep. ad Romanos*, hom. 12.5 [PG 60.501]), and Cyril of Alexandria (*In ep. ad Romanos* 7.7 [PG 74.801]); also Ambrosiaster, *In ep. ad Romanos* 7.7: "sub sua quasi persona generalem agit causam" (under his own quasi-person he treats of the general issue [CSEL 81.223]); among modern commentators Stauffer (*TDNT*

2.358–59), Schrenk (*TDNT* 2.551), Achtemeier, Benoit ("The Law"), Black, Bornkamm ("Law and Death," 93–94), Bover, Huby (*Romains*, 239), Käsemann (*Commentary*, 192), Kümmel, and seemingly Schlier (*Römerbrief*, 232).

The trouble with all such interpretations is that they tend to trivialize Paul's insight. The confrontation of the Ego with sin and the law is not considered by Paul on an individual, psychological level, but from a historical and corporate point of view. Paul views humanity as it was known to him through Jewish and Christian eyes, without Christ and in Christ (see Stauffer, *TDNT* 2.340–60, esp. 358–62). Some of Paul's generalizing statements in this passage are susceptible of application to experiences beyond his own immediate perspective. What he says in vv 7–25 is undoubtedly the experience of many Christians faced with divine, ecclesiastical, or civil law; when these verses are read in such a light, few will fail to appreciate their significance. But in attempting to understand what Paul meant, it is important to keep *his* perspective in mind, which is that of unregenerate humanity faced with the Mosaic law—but as seen by a Christian, as Kuss (*Römerbrief*, 482–83) has rightly noted. (For some problems that this interpretation raises, see Nygren, *Romans*, 287–92. Whether they are all as cogent as Nygren claims may be questioned.)

In this passage Paul once again personifies sin and the law and treats them as actors on the stage of human history.

Paul's description of the Ego here echoes in various ways the conviction of the Essene sectarian, who is described in QL as an utter sinner.

As for me, I belong to wicked humanity, to the assembly of perverse flesh; my iniquities, my transgressions, my sins together with the wickedness of my heart belong to the assembly doomed to worms and walking in darkness. No human being sets his own path or directs his own steps, for to God alone belongs the judgment of him, and from His hand comes perfection of way. . . . And I, if I stagger, God's grace is my salvation forever. If I stumble because of a sin of the flesh, my judgment is according to the righteousness of God, which stands forever. . . . In His mercy He has drawn me close (to Him), and with His favors will He render judgment of me. In His righteous fidelity He has judged me; in His bounteous goodness He expiates all my iniquities, and in His righteousness He cleanses me of human defilement and of human sinfulness, that I may praise God for His righteousness and the Most High for His majesty. (1QS 11:9–15)

As for me, I know that righteousness belongs not to a human being, nor perfection of way to a son of man. To God Most High belong all the deeds of righteousness, whereas the path of a human is not set firm. . . . And I said, It is because of my transgression that I have been abandoned far from Your covenant. But when I recalled Your mighty hand along with the abundance of Your mercy, then I was restored and I stood up; my spirit strengthened my stance against blows, because [I] have based myself on Your graces and on the abundance of Your mercy. For You expiate iniquity to clean[se a human be]ing from guilt by Your righteousness. (1QH 4:30–38)

This description comes to the fore especially in the *Hodayot* (e.g., 1:21–34; 3:19–36; 6:6–12; 7:16–18; 9:8–18; 10:2–12; 12:24–34; 13:13–19; 16:10–12; 18:12–15, 22–29), and in the Manual of Discipline (1:24–2:1; 10:10–13). The great difference between the two views of such a human situation is that the Qumran sectarian is convinced that he finds salvation in the Torah, whereas Paul insists that the Christian finds salvation in grace through faith in Christ Jesus.

NOTES

7:7. *What then can we say?* See the NOTE on 6:1.

Is the law sin? So the crucial question is posed. It is a conclusion that one could draw from 6:14–15, 19. Paul argues rhetorically, as he did in 4:1 and 6:1, and brings the law into direct relation to sin.

Certainly not! Again, Paul rejects the implication of the rhetorical question. See the NOTE on 3:4. The law is not sin; it is a power that is opposed to sin. Yet it is intimately related to sin and may bring it about that sin occurs. Sin would not be what it is if law did not exist. Paul has already intimated as much in 5:20–21.

I would not have known sin, if it were not for the law. Paul casts his argument as an awareness or real knowledge of the Ego. Recall 3:20b, "through the law comes the real knowledge of sin." Paul does not mean that it is only through the law that a human being comes to know right and wrong; it is, rather, that the law brings it about that sin is unmasked as a transgression of the will of God. Sin would not have become the power that it is in human life, if it were not for the law and the knowledge of sin that it brought into being.

The condition is contrary to fact, even without *an* in the apodosis (BDF §360.1); the negative in the protasis in *mē* (BDF §428.2).

I would not have known what it was to covet, if the law had not said, "You shall not covet." So Paul epitomizes the Mosaic law, quoting the climax of the decalogue in Exod 20:17 or Deut 5:21 ("Nor shall you covet your neighbor's wife; you shall not covet your neighbor's house, his field, his manservant, or his maidservant, his ox, his ass, or anything that belongs to your neighbor"). This epitome expresses the essence of the law, which sought to teach human beings not to let themselves be drawn by created things rather than by the Creator. Through such a commandment the sluggish moral conscience becomes aware of the possibility of the violation of the will of God so made known. Coveting is related to sin as the commandment is to the law. Cf. 4 Macc 2:5–6.

8. *sin, using the commandment, seized the opportunity.* Lit., "sin seizing the

opportunity through the law," i.e., sin made use of the law as a henchman to achieve its own purpose. It has made an ally of what should have been its mortal enemy. Again, Paul personifies sin, as he will law/commandment, covetousness, and death. The "commandment" may sound like an allusion to the injunction laid on Adam in Gen 2:16, but it really refers to a specific prohibition of the Mosaic law just cited. One should recall Paul's view of salvation history (see Introduction, section IX.A): from Adam to Moses people did evil, but they did not violate precepts, as did Adam (5:14). Their evil deeds became violations when the law "was added" (Gal 3:19). Then the law became "the power of sin" (1 Cor 15:56) in human life, because it provided the *aphormē*, lit., "jump start," i.e., "occasion, opportunity," for formal sin. Paul uses *aphormēn lambanein*, "take the opportunity," as does Polybius, *History* 3.7.5; 3.32.7.

produced in me every sort of covetousness. I.e., because the law made known all sorts of possibilities of doing evil. Cf. Jas 1:14.

Now in the absence of law sin is as good as dead. Lit., "without the law sin is lifeless," i.e., a corpselike being, powerless to make the evildoing of humanity a flagrant revolt against God's will (4:15; 5:13b). Without the law human beings in their wickedness were not in open rebellion against God.

9. *I once lived in the absence of law.* Lit., "I was once alive without the law." Here *egō* clearly has a universal meaning; it is "with difficulty referred to the person of the apostle" (BDF §281), because he was a circumcised Jew even before puberty, even before he became aware of the law's demands on him. Hence the *egō* must refer to human beings, who existed before Christ's coming and before the law was added, who were living lives in ignorance of the real nature of their evil conduct. The expression "dead, lifeless," used of sin in v 8, probably suggested to Paul the contrast "I was alive"; but the main stress is on the phrase "without the law." The life so lived was not one of union with God in Christ, but it was not an open rebellion against God in formal transgression. See A. Orbe, "S. Metodio."

the commandment came. I.e., when the Mosaic law "was added" (Gal 3:19) or entered human history and made people aware of their evil conduct as transgressions against the will of God.

sin sprang to life. With the intervention of the law, the human condition before God changed, for "desires" now became "coveting," and the pursuit of such coveting a revolt against God. If the vb. *anezēsen* were taken literally, "came to life again," it would be difficult to see how this phrase could apply to Adam, but it may mean only "sprang to life" (BAGD, 53). Sin "was alive" in Adam's transgression; it "sprang to life" again in the transgressions of the Mosaic law. Sin sprang to life in the sense that the law aroused it to activity, and thereby the law became a power in human life that could lead to death.

10. *and I died.* The evil conduct of humanity was now recognized as open rebellion, and it thrust humanity under the domination of death. The "death" meant here is not that of Gal 2:19, whereby Christians die to the law through

Christ's crucifixion, so that it no longer has a claim on them. This death is instead the condition resulting from sin as a violation of the law. Through formal transgressions, human beings are consigned to the domination of *Thanatos* (5:12, 15, 17a, 21). Cf. Jas 1:15.

The commandment that was meant for life. The Mosaic law promised "life" to those who would obey its prescriptions: "by the observance of which one shall find life" (Lev 18:5, quoted by Paul in Gal 3:12; Rom 10:5; cf. Deut 4:1; 6:24; *Ps. Sol.* 14:1). Although the prescriptions of the Mosaic law were intended by God to oppose sin and teach human beings about sin, that "the whole world might become accountable to God" (3:19), it became instead, through being used by sin, a means to deliver them to death.

was found to be death for me. Lit., "was found (to be) for me a commandment for/unto death," i.e., the commandment of the law was used by sin as an instrument to bring me to death. The law itself did not kill, but it became the instrument used by sin to bring human beings to death. It was not only an occasion of sin (7:5) or a moral informer (7:7), but, in effect, leveled a condemnation to death against the one who did not obey it (Deut 27:26; cf. 1 Cor 15:56; 2 Cor 3:7, 9; Gal 3:10). This was the paradox that emerged with the revival of sin: "in the desire which sin has produced in me I show that I am deceived and am a child of death. The statement (v. 8) about the conduct of the 'I,' its reaction to the 'commandment,' is now radically transformed into a statement about the being of the 'I' itself" (Bornkamm, "Sin, Law and Death," 91).

11. *sin, using the commandment, seized the opportunity.* Paul repeats even more clearly what he said in v 8a. The prep. phrase *dia tēs entolēs*, lit., "through the commandment," has to be understood with *aphormēn labousa*, "taking the opportunity"; Paul does not mean that sin deceived me through the law, as Lietzmann well saw (*An die Römer*, 74). Sir 17:7, echoing Deut 30:15, 19; 45:5(6), speaks of the law given to Moses as *entolai*, "commands," the very word used by Paul here and in 7:8, 13. This occurrence shows that *entolē* can be used of individual items in Mosaic legislation.

deceived me. I.e., as it did Adam. As God's commandment gave the tempting serpent the opportunity to deceive Eve, and through her Adam himself, so sin used the opportunity of the law to deceive the *egō* and entice it to go after forbidden fruit. Paul alludes to Gen 3:13, where the words *ēpatēsen me*, "deceived me," also occur, but it is not as clear as in 2 Cor 11:3. The deception developed when human autonomy was confronted with the divine demand for submission. As the serpent did, so sin enticed the *egō* thus confronted to assert its autonomy and make itself "like God." Cf. Gen 2:17; Heb 3:13. Thus the *egō* is the one deceived and killed by sin, the human being caught in the illusion of life who has long since forfeited life (Bornkamm, "Sin, Law and Death," 95).

The late *Tg. Ps.-Jonathan* interprets Gen 2:15 to mean that God put Adam in Eden to observe the law's commandments: so too Theophilus of Antioch, *Ad Autolycum* 2:24 (PG 6.1092); Ambrose, *De Paradiso* 4 (CSEL 32.282). But this reading is eisegetical and hardly what Paul meant; there is no evidence that he would be thinking of such an idea.

through it sin killed me. I.e., consigned me to the domination of death.

12. *Yet the law is holy, and the commandment is holy, upright, and good.* Cf. 7:16; 1 Tim 1:8; 4 Ezra 9:38. Because the law was God-given and intended to give life to those who would obey it (7:10, 14; Gal 3:24), it never commanded human beings to do evil. Nor was it a means to evil; in itself it was good.

13. *Did, then, what was good become death for me?* So Paul expresses the anomaly of the law. Although it was meant to be *nomos,* a good influence in human life, it produced the opposite effect; it became an anomalous influence, the "power of sin" (1 Cor 15:56) in human life.

Certainly not! Again, Paul vehemently rejects the suggestion that a God-given institution was the direct cause of spiritual death (see the NOTE on 3:4).

Rather, sin, that it might be unmasked as sin, produced death in me. Lit., "that it might appear (as) sin," i.e., that its true character might be shown, as a rebellion against God. *Nomos* did not cause the "death" of the Ego, but it proved to be the occasion of it, playing a secondary role, quite accidentally. The real culprit was sin, the direct cause of death (5:12, 17a, 20; 6:23). Hence the law was not the equivalent of sin (cf. 2 Cor 3:7; 1 Cor 15:56). So Paul answers the question posed in v 7.

by using what was good. I.e., by using the God-given commandment as its tool.

so that through the commandment it might become sinful beyond all measure. Lit., "so that sin might become sinful in the extreme through the commandment," i.e., that the true colors of sin might be shown for what they are. So Paul points his finger at the real culprit in human life, indwelling sin.

BIBLIOGRAPHY

Achelis, E., "Ueber das Subject in Röm. 7: Eine biblisch-theologische Untersuchung," *TSK* 36.2 (1863): 670–704.

Benoit, P., "The Law and the Cross According to St Paul, Romans 7:7–8:4," *Jesus and the Gospel,* vol. 2 (London: Darton, Longman & Todd, 1974), 11–39.

Bergmeier, R., "Röm 7,7–25a (8,2): Der Mensch—das Gesetz—Gott—Paulus—die Exegese im Widerspruch?" *KD* 31 (1985): 162–72.

Blank, J., "Der gespaltene Mensch: Zur Exegese von Röm 7,7–25," *BibLeb* 9 (1968): 10–20; repr. in *Schriftauslegung in Theorie und Praxis,* Biblische Handbibliothek 5 (Munich: Kösel, 1969), 158–73.

Bover, J. M., "Valor de los terminos 'Ley,' 'Yo,' 'Pecado,' en Rom. VII," *Bib* 5 (1924): 192–96.

Braun, H., "Römer 7,7–25 und das Selbstverständnis des Qumran-Frommen," *ZTK* 56 (1959): 1–18; repr. in *Gesammelte Studien zum Neuen Testament und seiner Umwelt* (Tübingen: Mohr [Siebeck], 1962), 100–19.

Brun, L., "Rm. 7, 7–25 ennu engang," *SEA* 12 (1948): 51–68.

Cambier, J., "Le 'Moi' dans Rom. 7," *The Law of the Spirit*, ed. L. de Lorenzi, 13–72.

Campbell, D. H., "The Identity of *egō* in Romans 7:7–25," *Studia Biblica 1978: Sixth International Congress on Biblical Studies, Oxford 3–7 April 1978*, 3 vols., JSNTSup 2–3, 11, ed. E. A. Livingstone (Sheffield, UK: JSOT, 1979–80), 3.57–64.

Cassirer, H. W., *Grace and Law: St. Paul, Kant, and the Hebrew Prophets* (Edinburgh: Handsel; Grand Rapids, Mich.: Eerdmans, 1988).

Crespy, G., "Exégèse et psychanalyse: Considérations aventureuses sur Romains 7:7–25," *L'Évangile hier et aujourd'hui: Mélanges offerts au Prof. Franz-J. Leenhardt* (Geneva: Labor & Fides, 1968), 169–79.

Dahl, N. A., "The Missionary Theology in the Epistle to the Romans," *Studies in Paul*, 70–94.

Dobschütz, E. von, "Wir und ich bei Paulus," *ZST* 10 (1933): 251–77.

Dunn, J. D. G., "Rom 7:14–25 in the Theology of Paul," *TZ* 31 (1975): 257–73.

Espy, J. M., "Paul's 'Robust Conscience' Re-examined," *NTS* 31 (1985): 161–88.

Fuchs, E., "Existentiale Interpretation von Römer 7,7–12 und 21–23," *ZTK* 59 (1962): 285–314; repr. in *Glaube und Erfahrung: Zum christologischen Problem im Neuen Testament* (Tübingen: Mohr [Siebeck], 1965), 364–401.

Fung, R. Y. K., "The Impotence of the Law: Towards a Fresh Understanding of Romans 7:14–25," *Scripture, Tradition and Interpretation: Essays Presented to Everett F. Harrison . . .*, ed. W. W. Gasque and W. S. LaSor (Grand Rapids, Mich.: Eerdsmans, 1978), 34–48.

Gundry, R. H., "The Moral Frustration of Paul Before His Conversion: Sexual Lust in Romans 7:7–25," *Pauline Studies: Essays Presented to Professor F. F. Bruce . . .*, ed. D. A. Hagner and M. J. Harris (Exeter, UK: Paternoster; Grand Rapids, Mich.: Eerdmans, 1980), 228–45.

Hahn, F., "Das Gesetzesverständnis im Römer- und Galaterbrief," *ZNW* 67 (1976): 29–63.

Jarrell, W. A., "Romans 7:7–25, The Experience of Sinners," *RevExp* 5 (1908): 586–97.

Joest, W., "Paulus und das lutherische simul Iustus et Peccator," *KD* 1 (1955): 269–320.

Karlberg, M. W., "Israel's History Personified: Romans 7:7–13 in Relation to Paul's Teaching on the 'Old Man,' " *TrinJ* 7 (1986): 65–74.

Kümmel, W. G., *Das Subjekt des 7. Kapitels des Römerbriefs* (Altenburg [Thür]: Pierer, 1929).

Lambrecht, J., "Man Before and Without Christ: Rom 7 and Pauline Anthropology," *LS* 5 (1974–75): 18–33.

Luck, U., "Das Gute und das Böse in Römer 7," *Neues Testament und Ethik: Für Rudolf Schnackenburg*, ed. H. Merklein (Freiburg im Breisgau: Herder, 1989), 220–37.

Lyonnet, S., "Quaestiones ad Rom 7,7–13," VD 40 (1962): 163–83.

———, " 'Tu ne convoitera pas' (Rom. vii 7)," *Neotestamentica et patristica: Eine Freundesgabe, Herrn Professor Dr. Oscar Cullmann . . . überreicht,* NovTSup 6, ed. W. C. van Unnik (Leiden: Brill, 1962), 157–65.

Maillot, A., "Notule sur Romains 7/7–8 ss," *Foi et vie* 84.6 (1985): 17–23.

Martin, B. L., "Some Reflections on the Identity of *egō* in Rom. 7:14–25," *SJT* 34 (1981): 39–47.

Milne, D. J. W., "Romans 7:7–12, Paul's Pre-conversion Experience," *RTR* 43 (1984): 9–17.

Modalsli, O., "Gal. 2,19–21; 5,16–18 und Röm. 7,7–25," *TZ* 21 (1965): 22–37, esp. 31–37.

Moo, D. J., "Israel and Paul in Romans 7.7–12," *NTS* 32 (1986): 122–35.

Morris, T. F., "Law and the Cause of Sin in the Epistle to the Romans," *HeyJ* 28 (1987): 285–91.

Newman, B. M., "Once Again—The Question of 'I' in Romans 7.7–25," *BT* 34 (1983): 124–35.

Orbe, A., "S. Metodio y la exégesis de Rom. 7,9a: 'Ego autem vivebam sine lege aliquando,' " *Greg* 50 (1969): 93–137.

Packer, J. I., "The 'Wretched Man' in Romans 7," *SE II*, TU 87 (1964), 621–27.

Räisänen, H., "Zum Gebrauch von *epithymia* und *epithymein* bei Paulus," *ST* 33 (1979): 85–99.

Rios, E. de los, "Peccatum et lex: Animadversiones in Rom. 7,7–25," *VD* 11 (1931): 23–28.

Roquefort, D., "Romains 7/7s selon Jacques Lacan," *ETR* 61 (1986): 343–52.

Snyman, A. H., "Stilistiese tegnieke in Romeine 7:7–13," *NGTT* 27 (1986): 23–28.

Stendahl, K., "The Apostle Paul and the Introspective Conscience of the West," *HTR* 56 (1963): 199–215; repr. *Paul among Jews,* 78–96.

Strelan, J. G., "A Note on the Old Testament Background of Romans 7:7," *LTJ* 15 (1981): 23–25.

Trocmé, E., "From 'I' to 'We': Christian Life According to Romans, Chapters 7 and 8," *AusBR* 35 (1987): 73–76.

Varo, F., "Hermenéutica paulina del Antiguo Testamento en Rom 7,7–12," *Biblia y hermenéutica: VII simposio internacional de teología de la Universidad de Navarra* (Pamplona: Universidad, 1986), 439–51.

Watson, N. M., "The Interpretation of Romans VII," *AusBR* 21 (1973): 27–39.

Weber, R., "Die Geschichte des Gesetzes und des Ich in Römer 7,7–8,4: Einige Überlegungen zum Zusammenhang von Heilsgeschichte und Anthropologie im Blick auf die theologische Grundstellung des paulinischen Denkens," *Neue Zeitschrift für systematische Theologie und Religionsphilosophie* (Berlin) 29 (1987): 147–79.

Wenham, D., "The Christian Life: A Life of Tension? A Consideration of the Nature of Christian Experience in Paul," *Pauline Studies: Essays Presented to Professor*

F. F. Bruce . . . , ed. D. A. Hagner and M. J. Harris (Exeter, UK: Paternoster; Grand Rapids, Mich.: Eerdmans, 1980), 80–94.

Westphal, A., *De epistulae Pauli ad Romanos septimo capite (7–25): Commentatio critico-theologica* (Toulouse: Chauvin, 1888).

Wiesler, K., *Der Abschnitt Röm, 7,7–25 exegetische und biblisch-theologisch erörtert* (Greifswald: Bamberg, 1875).

Ziesler, J. A., "The Role of the Tenth Commandment in Romans 7," *JSNT* 33 (1988): 41–56.

23. COMPLAINT AND CRY OF HUMAN BEINGS ENSLAVED BY THE LAW (7:14–25)

7   [14]Now we know that the law is spiritual, whereas I am of flesh, sold in bondage to sin. [15]I do not understand what I do. For I do not do what I want to; and what I detest, that I do. [16]Yet if I do what I do not want, I agree that the law is good. [17]But as it is, it is no longer I who do it, but sin that dwells in me. [18]I know that no good dwells in me, that is, in my flesh. I can desire what is good, but I cannot carry it out. [19]For I do not do the good I desire, but instead the evil I do not desire. [20]Yet if I do what I do not want, it is no longer I who do it, but sin that dwells in me. [21]So I discover this principle at work: when I want to do right, evil is ready at hand. [22]For in my inmost self I delight in God's law; [23]but I see another law in my members battling against the law that my mind acknowledges and making me captive to the law of sin that is in my members. [24]Wretch that I am, who will rescue me from this doomed body? [25]Thanks be to God—(it is done) through Jesus Christ our Lord! So then I myself in my mind am a slave to God's law, but in my flesh a slave to the law of sin.

COMMENT

Paul's explanation is not yet complete; he now probes more deeply. Verses 14–25, the third section in chap. 7, prolongs what Paul has said in the preceding section. He finds that the problem is not with the law, but with human beings themselves. The trouble is that they are carnal, made of flesh that is weak, and prone to succumb to attacks of sin, which dwells within them. Because of such indwelling sin, human beings fail to achieve what God desires of them. Yet not all in human beings is sin; there is also the mind (*nous*), which does recognize God's law and does acknowledge what it desires of humans. But the "mind" itself is not empowered to resist the seductions of sin. Eventually, Paul recognizes the wretched state of human beings and acknowledges that only "through Jesus Christ our Lord" (7:25) can this situation be remedied, through divine grace and the power of the Spirit (8:2–3).

Whereas vv 7–13 were a confession, in which the Ego recognized its deception by sin, which made use of the law, now vv 14–25 become an apology for the law itself. For this reason it is expressed in the present tense. Paul uses it to show the uselessness of any attempt to fulfill demands of legal righteousness apart from God's grace. The problem is not with the law itself, but with the human condition; hence the emphasis in this paragraph on anthropology. Paul deserts his confessional approach, to adopt a more philosophical stance. He now finds that the difficulty lies in the very makeup of human beings.

Paul describes the moral experience of the Ego faced with the law, depicting it as a battle between the Ego of flesh dominated by sin and the spiritual law of God. It is a battle from which the Ego cannot separate itself, for the Ego is no outsider to this battle, nor is it a neutral observer. The Ego finds itself on both sides and is torn by the division. In 7:24 Paul allows the Ego to utter a cry of frustration, but in 7:25a he also allows it to sing thanks for the hope of liberation that has come through Christ Jesus.

Paul thus insists that the Christian is free from the law, and not just free from self, sin, and death. It is not through observance of the law that one becomes upright in God's sight. The law sought to bring humanity to a status of rectitude before God, but also to convict it of sinful activity and to make sin appear in its true colors as a transgression of God's will. Thus the law can, indeed, stop every mouth and make all human beings realize their sinful condition and guilt before God. It is, however, God himself who justifies and gives life, through Christ Jesus. It is entirely a matter of what God does through Christ; thus human beings are justified independently of the law. Even the Christian, if judged according to the law, would be shown to be a sinner, someone who falls under God's wrath. But the uprightness that the Christian has as a result of being in Christ is not the uprightness of the law. "Thanks be to God," it comes about "through Jesus Christ our Lord!"

Thus Paul terminates his discussion of the three freedoms achieved for humanity by Christ Jesus.

NOTES

7:14. *Now we know that the law is spiritual.* Because of its God-given origin (7:23) and its purpose of leading human beings to "life" (7:10) and to God, the law does not belong to the world of earthbound, natural humanity. As *pneumatikos*, the law belongs to the sphere of God, to the sphere of the Spirit of God; it is an expression of God's will. It is thus opposed to what is *sarkinos*, "carnal, belonging to the sphere of flesh."

Most of the Greek MSS read *oidamen*, but some interpreters (e.g., Hofmann, Philonenko, Reicke, Semler, Wilckens, Zahn) follow MSS 33 and a few others and divide the word to read *oida men*, "Now I know." This wording would seem to match *egō de* in the following clause. But the real contrast is between the law and the Ego, and the usual Pauline expression is *oidamen* (see 2:2; 3:19; 8:22, 28; 1 Cor 8:4; 2 Cor 5:1, 16). Hence *oidamen* is the preferred reading.

I am of flesh. Lit., "but I am carnal, made of flesh," i.e., of *sarx*, that aspect of the human person which is native and not oriented to God, but inclined toward limited, earthbound horizons. It is not evil in itself, but is powerless to do good. In contrast to the spiritual origin and destiny of the law, the Ego possesses a nature in which sin is entrenched because of Adam. Paul's use of *pneumatikos* and *sarkinos* plays on his contrast of *pneuma*, "Spirit," and *sarx*, "flesh," as factors in the conduct of human life. This use of the adj. *pneumatikos* resembles that in 1 Cor 2:13, but is not identical with it, because there it is contrasted with *psychikos*, which, however, has almost the same connotations as *sarkinos*. See instead 8:4–6; 2 Cor 3:1. Cf. the Qumran expression *ʾănî lĕbāśār yādaʿtî* [. . .], "I, (a being) of flesh, know [. . .]."

Some MSS (א² and the *Koinē* text-tradition) read *sarkikos* instead of *sarkinos*, but the difference is minor. Cf. Parsons, "*Sarkinos, sarkikos.*"

in bondage to sin. Lit., "sold under sin," i.e., sold as a slave to Sin, the master (Adam's sin and personal sin derived from it). Cf. Isa 50:1 LXX, *tais hamartiais hymōn eprathēte kai tais anomiais hymōn exapesteila tēn mētera hymōn*, "because of your iniquities you were sold, and because of your transgressions I repudiated your mother." Also 4QDibHam (= 4Q504) 1–2 ii 15: *[hn bᶜ]wwnwtynw nmkrnw wbpšᶜynw qrtnw*, "[Look, because of] our [in]iquities we have been sold, but despite our transgressions you have called us." A still better parallel is found in 11QPsᵃ 19:9–10: *lmwt hyyty bḥṭʾy wᶜwwnwty lšʾwl mkrwny*, "To death I belonged because of my sins, and my iniquities sold me to Sheol."

15. *I do not understand what I do.* I.e., as one sold under sin, I am a mystery to myself. See 7:18; 8:7. The mystery stems from a conflict in the inmost depths of a human being, the cleavage between reason-dominated desire and actual performance. So imperious is indwelling sin that the Ego acts without realizing what it is doing.

The Vg translates the vb. *ou ginōskō* correctly, *non intellego*, but Augustine (*Expositio quarundam propositionum ex ep. ad Romanos* 36 [CSEL 84.19]) understood it as *non approbo*, "I do not approve." In this interpretation he has been followed by Barrett and Cranfield.

I do not do what I want to. The vb. *thelein*, as in classical Greek, expresses not a deliberate decision of the free will *(boulesthai)*, but a velleity, an inclination of the natural affective instinct. See 1 Cor 7:7.

what I detest, that I do. The Ego's moral aspiration and performance are not coordinated or integrated. Often quoted in this connection are the plaintive words of the Roman poet Ovid, *Video meliora proboque, deteriora sequor*, "I perceive what is better and approve of it, but I pursue what is worse" (*Metamorphoses* 7.20–21). Cf. Epictetus, *Dissertationes* 2.26.4: *ho thelei ou poiei kai ho mē thelei poiei*, "what he wants he does not do, and what he does not want he does." Also Euripides, *Medea* 1077b–80. The Essenes of Qumran explained the same inner conflict by maintaining that God had put two spirits in human beings to rule until the time of his visitation, a "spirit of truth" and a "spirit of perversity," and they were in conflict (1QS 3:15–4:26). Paul, however, attributes the rift not to God or any such spirits, but to human beings themselves and the sin that dwells in them.

16. *if I do what I do not want, I agree that the law is good.* Lit., "I agree with the law that it is good *(kalos).*" See 7:12. The desire to do what is right is an implicit recognition of the goodness and excellence of what the law prescribes. As far as willing is concerned, the Ego is at one with the law.

17. *But as it is.* Lit., "but now," expressing a contrast.

it is no longer I who do it, but sin that dwells in me. Hamartia came into the world to "reign" over humanity (5:12, 21), and by lodging itself within human beings it has enslaved them. Thus the Ego alone is not the proper subject of such evil conduct; it is the Ego dominated by indwelling sin. Paul again clearly personifies sin. This verse is the corollary of v 16a. Paul may almost seem to absolve human beings of responsibility for sinful conduct (see 7:20); but it is still human sin (5:12d). See Searight, "Rom 7:17."

18. *I know that no good dwells in me, that is, in my flesh.* The added qualification is important, for Paul finds the root of the difficulty in the human self considered as *sarx,* the source of all that is opposed to God and his desires for human beings. From the Ego as *sarx* proceed the detestable things that one does. But the Ego as the true willing self becomes a self that has fallen victim to "flesh" dominated by "sin."

I can desire what is good, but I cannot carry it out. Lit., "for to will the good lies at hand to me, but to carry (it) out does not." In this sentence and following two verses Paul repeats what he has said in vv 15–17 from a different point of view. Again, he contrasts velleity and capability. Action never comes to correspond to what the Ego wants because of the inescapable flesh condition of all human conduct.

The sentence ends with the negative *ou,* and copyists have added a verb to fill out the elliptical clause: *ouch heuriskō,* "I do not find (the capability)," in MSS D, F, G, Ψ and the *Koinē* text-tradition; *ou ginōskō,* "I do not know (how to)," in MSS 88, 2127, etc. See Browning, "Studies."

19. *I do not do the good I desire.* See 7:15b.

instead the evil I do not desire. See 7:15c. Cf. Culler, "Exposition."

20. *if I do what I do not want, it is no longer I who do it, but sin that dwells in me.* A repetition of vv 17–18. In the battle between God's will set forth in the law and evil conduct, the Ego wants to stand on the side of God; yet it realizes that indwelling sin is the cause of its wickedness.

21. *So I discover this principle.* From experience the Ego learns how things stand. Paul uses *ho nomos* in the generic sense of "principle," as in 3:27 and 7:23, and plays on different senses of *nomos* (see Introduction, section IX.D). It is the "law of experience" or the experienced "pattern" of one's activity, which is

explained in the two subsequent clauses. In this verse Paul is not referring by *nomos* to the Mosaic law, to which he will return in the next verse.

when I want to do right, evil is ready at hand. See 7:18b.

22. *in my inmost self I delight in God's law.* Lit., "according to the inner man." This may seem like the Christian speaking, but, as the following verses make clear, the "mind" *(nous)* of unregenerate humanity utters this conviction. Though dominated by sin when considered as "flesh," the Ego still experiences that it desires what God desires. The mind or reason recognizes the ideal proposed by the law, God's will expressed in Mosaic legislation.

23. *I see another law in my members battling against the law that my mind acknowledges.* Lit., "the law of my mind." The *nomos* in which the reasoning self finds delight, the Mosaic law, is opposed by another *nomos* that ultimately makes the self a captive (6:13, 19). The latter *nomos* or "principle" is none other than indwelling sin (7:17), which enslaves a human being so that the willing self that delights in God's law is not capable of observing it. *Ho nomos tou noos mou* is not the law of 2:14b, or the *recta ratio* or *lex naturalis* of scholastic philosophers, but "God's law" (7:22), manifested in its prime analogate, the Mosaic law. This law the mind recognizes as God's will. Cf. 2 Cor 10:3. But Paul describes indwelling sin as *heteron nomon*, "another law," i.e., a principle that battles against God's law.

making me captive to the law of sin that is in my members. I.e., the law used by sin to entice the Ego. Recall 7:7, which prevents one from simply identifying law and sin. Paul now calls it "the law of sin," because it is the law that occasions sin (4:15a), the law that increases the transgression. Cf. 8:2; Gal 5:17; 4 Ezra 7:72.

The best MSS (ℵ, B, D, G, K, P, Ψ, 33) read the prep. *en* before *tō nomō tēs hamartias*, "(making me captive) in/by the law of sin." But *en* is omitted in MSS A, C, L, and many minuscules of the *Koinē* text-tradition.

24. *Wretch that I am.* Lit., "miserable human being that I am!" The agonizing cry of the Ego weighted down with the burden of sin and prevented from achieving what it would; it is a desperate cry to God for help. As long as human life persists, the tension between the old aeon and the new exists, between existence in Adam and existence in Christ. Paul here introduces a lament into his letter. Cf. Rev 3:17.

who will rescue me from this doomed body? Lit., "this body of death." See the NOTE on 6:6. Threatened by defeat in the conflict between willing and execution, the Ego finds no relief in its own native resources. Spiritual death is the only outcome of the sinful condition (see 6:16 and 8:10). Cf. Pss 14:7 and 53:7 for the form of question Paul uses.

25. *Thanks be to God!* Using a thanksgiving utterance, Paul formulates the Ego's gratitude to God, as it realizes what has been achieved in Christ Jesus for humanity. He anticipates the fuller answer given in 8:1–4.

The text tradition is not uniform here. The preferred reading is the exclamation *charis de tō theō*, found in MSS ℵ¹, C², Ψ, 33, 81, 104, 365, etc. But in

MSS D, F, G and in the Vg, the answer to the question in v 24 is *hē charis tou theou* or *hē charis Kyriou*, "the grace of God/the Lord," i.e., God's grace will rescue the Ego. This is an inferior reading. Some MSS (ℵ*, A, and the *Koinē* text-tradition) and Syriac versions have *eucharistō tō theō*, "I thank God," a variant of the preferred reading. The exclamation is preferred because of 6:17 (see the NOTE there). See R. Banks, "Romans 7.25a: An Eschatological Thanksgiving," *AusBR* 26 (1978): 34–42.

(it is done) through Jesus Christ our Lord! The gratitude may be expressed "through Jesus Christ our Lord" (using the refrain of this part of Romans [see the COMMENT on 5:1–11]). Or it may be preferable to understand the sentence as elliptical, separating the exclamation from the initial short answer to the question of v 24 that follows. In either case, the answer is that Christ supplies what is lacking to feeble human nature, and for this reason God is to be thanked.

I myself in my mind am a slave to God's law. Paul recognizes that the reasoning self willingly submits to God's law (7:22) and stands in contrast to the carnal self, the person enslaved to sin. In using *autos egō*, he may even refer the teaching of the preceding paragraphs to himself, as Origen is said to have recognized (BDF §281).

but in my flesh a slave to the law of sin. See the NOTE on 7:23b. The carnal Ego (7:14) is enslaved to the "principle" of sin, the body in which sin dwells and which sin possesses.

Moffatt, in his translation of the NT, moved v 25b up to precede v 24. That is certainly a more logical place for it, as Dodd recognized (*Romans*, 114–15): "it is scarcely conceivable that, after giving thanks to God for deliverance, Paul should describe himself as being in exactly the same position as before." Hence he prefers the order vv 22, 23, 25b, 24. Similarly Müller ("Zwei Marginalien") argues for the order 22, 23, 25b, 24, 25a; 8:2, 1, 3; also J. Wilson, *ExpTim* 4 (1892–93): 192. But such an order is found in no MS of Romans; hence the place of v 25b after 25a is, as it were, the *lectio difficilior*, to be retained. Bultmann, however, regarded v 25b and 8:1 as marginal glosses that have been introduced into the text (*TLZ* 72 [1947]: 197–99); in this matter he admits that he is following Jülicher. Again, it is a logical suggestion, but suspect for that very reason.

BIBLIOGRAPHY

Althaus, P., "Zur Auslegung von Röm. 7,14ff.: Antwort an Anders Nygren," *TLZ* 77 (1952): 475–80.

Banks, R. "Romans 7:25a: An Eschatological Thanksgiving?" *AusBR* 26 (1978): 34–42.

Beld, A. van den, "Romans 7:15–25 and the Problem of *Akrasia*," *RelS* 21 (1985): 495–515; cf. *Bijdragen* 46 (1985): 39–58.

Bonwetsch, N. "Römer 7,14ff. in der alten Kirche und in Luthers Vorlesungen über den Römerbrief," *NKZ* 30 (1919): 135–56.

Browning, W. "Studies in Texts—Romans vii,18f.," *Theology* 52 (1949): 22–25.

Byskov, M. "Simul iustus et peccator: A Note on Romans vii. 25b," *ST* 30 (1976): 75–87.

Culler, M. L. "Exposition of Romans, Chap. 7:19," *LQ* 33 (1903): 98–105.

Dockery, D. S. "Romans 7:14–25: Pauline Tension in the Christian Life," *GTJ* 2 (1981): 239–57.

Dunn, J. D. G. "Rom 7:14–25 in the Theology of Paul," *TZ* 31 (1975): 257–73; also in *Essays on Apostolic Themes: Studies in Honor of Howard M. Ervin* . . . , ed. P. Elbert (Peabody, Mass.: Hendrickson, 1985), 49–70.

Garlington, D. B. "Romans 7:14–25 and the Creation Theology of Paul," *TrinJ* 11 (1990): 197–235.

Huggins, R. V., "Alleged Classical Parallels to Paul's 'What I Want to Do I Do not Do, but What I Hate, That I Do' (Rom 7:15)," *WTJ* 54 (1992): 153–61.

Kapteijn, K. J. "Het lichaam dezes doods," *GTT* 10 (1909): 113–26.

Keuck, W. "Dienst des Geistes und des Fleisches: Zur Auslegungsgeschichte und Auslegung von Rm, 7,25 b," *TQ* 141 (1961): 257–80.

———, "Das 'geistliche Gesetz': Röm 7,14a in der Auslegung der griechischen Väter," *Wort Gottes in der Zeit: Festschrift Karl Hermann Schelkle* . . . dargebracht . . . , ed. H. Feld and J. Nolte (Düsseldorf: Patmos, 1973), 215–35.

Lafon, G. "Un Moi sans oeuvre," *RSR* 78 (1990): 165–74.

Mandeville, H. *An Essay on the Interpretation of Romans, Chap. VII. 14–25; with a General Survey of Chapters III, IV, V, VI, VII and VIII* (Utica: Bennett & Bright, 1837).

Mauro, P. *The "Wretched Man" and His Deliverance, Romans VII* (London: Roberts, 1910).

Merrill, T. F. "Achard of Saint Victor and the Medieval Exegetical Tradition: Rom 7:22–25 in a Sermon on the Feast of the Resurrection," *WTJ* 48 (1986): 47–62.

Müller, F. "Zwei Marginalien im Brief des Paulus an die Römer," *ZNW* 40 (1941): 249–54, esp. 249–52.

Parsons, M. C. "*Sarkinos, sarkikos* in Codices F and G: A Text-Critical Note," *NTS* 34 (1988): 151–55.

Philonenko, M. "Sur l'Expression 'vendue au péché' dans l'"épître aux Romains,' " *RHR* 203 (1986): 41–52.

Rosenau, H. "Der Mensch zwischen Wollen und Können: Theologische Reflexionen im Anschluss an Röm 7,14–25," *TP* 65 (1990): 1–30.

Rüger, H. P. "Hieronymus, die Rabbinen und Paulus: Zur Vorgeschichte des Begriffspaars 'innerer und äusserer Mensch,' " *ZNW* 68 (1977): 132–37.

Schmithals, W. *Die theologische Anthropologie des Paulus: Auslegung von Röm 7,17–8,39* (Stuttgart: Kohlhammer, 1980).

Searight, H. B. "Rom 7:17: A Short Study in Religious Psychology," *USR* 23 (1911–49): 144–49.

Selmer, L. "Rom. 7,14–25," *NorTT* 26 (1925): 88–104.

Smith, E. W. "The Form and Religious Background of Romans VII 24–25a," *NovT* 13 (1971): 127–35.

Tomlinson, J. "Interpretation of Romans 7:14–25," *LQ* 11 (1881): 558–64.

Varo, L. "La lucha del hombre contra el pecado: Exégesis de Rom, 7,14–25," *ScrTheol* 16 (1984): 9–53.

Voorwinde, S. "Who Is the 'Wretched Man' in Romans 7:24," *VoxRef* 54 (1990): 11–26.

Wilson, J. "Romans vii. 24–viii. 2: A Rearrangement, *ExpTim* 4 (1892–93): 192.

24. CHRISTIAN LIFE EMPOWERED
BY THE SPIRIT OF GOD (8:1–13)

8 [1]Now then, there is no condemnation for those who are in Christ Jesus. [2]For in Christ Jesus the law of the Spirit of life has set you free from the law of sin and death. [3]What the law, weakened by the flesh, was powerless to do, God has done: by sending his own Son in a form like that of sinful flesh and for the sake of sin, he condemned sin in the flesh, [4]so that the requirement of the law might be fully met in us who conduct ourselves not according to the flesh, but according to the Spirit. [5]Those who live according to the flesh are concerned about things of the flesh, whereas those who live according to the Spirit are concerned about things of the Spirit. [6]Now the concern of the flesh is death, but the concern of the Spirit is life and peace. [7]Since the concern of the flesh is hostility to God, it is not submissive to God's law; nor can it be. [8]So those who live by the flesh cannot please God. [9]Yet you are not in the flesh; you are in the Spirit, if in fact God's Spirit dwells in you. If one does not have Christ's Spirit, one does not belong to Christ. [10]But if Christ is in you, though the body be dead because of sin, the spirit has life because of uprightness. [11]And if the Spirit of him who raised Jesus from the dead is dwelling in you, he who raised Christ from the dead will give life even to your mortal bodies through his Spirit that is dwelling in you. [12]So then, brothers, we are not indebted to the flesh, to have to live according to it. [13]If you live indeed according to the flesh, you will die; but if through the Spirit you put to death the deeds of the body, you will live.

COMMENT

Paul now introduces the counterpart of his discussion in chaps. 5–7. He has developed in a negative way the theme announced in 5:1–11, by explaining the freedoms that have come in Christ Jesus: freedom from sin and death (5:12–21); from sin and self (6:1–23); and from the law (7:1–25). Those who have put faith in Christ Jesus and have been baptized into his death, burial, and resurrection have become justified Christians, not only liberated from such evils, but also empowered to live a new life as the result of God's love manifested in the freeing acts of Christ Jesus. Moreover, they are now able to live this life "for God," whose love is poured out through the dynamic principle of such life, the Spirit of God himself. Chapter 8 is a literary unit that develops positively the new theme at this point in the letter. It begins by answering in fuller form the question posed in 7:24, "Who will rescue me from this doomed body?" The answer: Christ has rescued human beings from enslavement and made it possible for them to live "according to the Spirit" (8:1–4). This answer repeats the theme of 5:1–11 in a more explicit way: Christian existence is dominated by the Spirit, not by the flesh (8:1–13). Then in the following paragraphs Paul will further explain how Christians become children of God, adopted and destined for the glory of God's intimate presence, and will extol God for the manifestation of such love through Christ.

Chapter 8 discusses many topics about the new life that Christians lead in the Spirit. Although it constitutes a unit, for the sake of discussion it is necessary to subdivide it: (a) 8:1–13: Christian life empowered by the Spirit; (b) 8:14–17: the Christian as a child of God, destined for glory; (c) 8:18–23: the first of the three things that testify to this destiny—creation groaning in travail; (d) 8:24–25: the second—Christian hope; (e) 8:26–27: the third—the Spirit; (f) 8:28–30: the destiny of the Christian called to glory; and (g) 8:31–39: a laudatory hymn to the love of God manifested in Christ Jesus.

This part of Romans introduces the formal treatment of the influence of God's Spirit in Christian life. Paul has mentioned the Spirit so far only three times in this letter, but will mention it nineteen times in chap. 8 alone. He referred to its influence indirectly in 1:4, and more directly in 5:5 and 7:6. Now he takes up the topic of the Spirit explicitly.

In speaking of *to pneuma*, "the Spirit," Paul tends to treat it as it appears in the OT (see Ezek 36:26, "a new Spirit"; Isa 44:3). There, it is a mode of expressing God's outgoing activity and presence to the world and his people in a creative, prophetic, quickening, or renovating way (recall Gen 1:2; Pss 51:11; 139:7; Isa 11:2; Ezek 37:1–14). This is also the basic meaning that Paul attributes to *to (hagion) pneuma*, which is not yet understood as a personal being, distinct from the Father and the Son, as it was to become in later Christian trinitarian theology of the patristic period. There it is clearly regarded as the third person of the Trinity, but that is a logical development beyond Paul's way of thinking and speaking. He may, indeed, personify the Spirit, that is to say, personify the activity and presence of the OT sense, but it is not yet conceived of as a person in his theology. It is for Paul a way of expressing the dynamic influence of God's presence to justified Christians, the manifestation of his love for them, and the powerful source of their new life in Christ. It is the vivifying power of the risen Christ himself (1 Cor 15:45). Thus "God's Spirit" has also become for Paul "Christ's Spirit."

In the latter part of this paragraph (vv 9–13) the reality of the Christian experience is expressed in different ways that should be noted: Christians are said to be (a) "in the Spirit" (9b)—locally, or in union with; (b) "the Spirit dwells in you" (9c)—the personified Spirit; (c) one "has the Spirit of Christ" (9d) as an inward possession; (d) one "belong(s) to him" (Christ, 9d); (e) "Christ is in you" (10a); (f) "the Spirit of him who raised Christ . . . dwells in you" (11); and (g) "through his Spirit dwelling within you" (13). Such expressions may seem confusing at first, because they are not clearly distinguished one from the other, but they forestall an overfacile interpretation of how the Christian is united with Christ or God. The verses also contain a clear triadic text, which becomes a basis in later trinitarian theology for the indwelling in the Christian of the three persons of the Trinity. The Christian is, indeed, related not only to Christ, but to the Father and the Spirit as well.

In a sense, chap. 8 is the third most important part of the letter, equaling the discussion of justification itself in 3:21–31. It forms a certain peak in Paul's whole discussion, because it seeks to bring out the reality of the new aeon and of the new life that human beings can now lead in union with Christ and through his Spirit. It also stresses how God's love is poured out on his human creatures. Divine love is seen as the counterpart of divine uprightness.

NOTES

8:1. *Now then.* Again Paul introduces the eschatological "now"; see the NOTE on 3:21. It picks up immediately on 6:21 and 7:6: through faith and baptism the Christian is alive in a new aeon. The conj. *ara*, "then," draws a conclusion from chaps. 5–7 (BDF §451.2), restating the message of 5:18–21 especially. Some commentators have regarded v 1 (together with 7:25b) as displaced (Müller) or even as an added gloss (Bultmann); but that reading is hardly called for, as Dunn (*Romans*, 415–16) and Schlier (*Römerbrief*, 236) rightly recognize. Paul is obviously beginning a new topic, as he passes to this discussion of the new aeon. Perhaps the transition is not as smooth as it might be. But the aeon of sin, death, and law has come to an end. In a sense, 8:1–17 corresponds to 7:1–6, because the Christian through identification with the crucified Christ is freed from the law.

there is no condemnation for those who are in Christ Jesus. Paul utters a victory cry: through Christ Jesus the Christian has vanquished all of the forces of evil, especially the force of the law in human life. "Condemnation" is no longer leveled by the law against those not observing its specific prescriptions; nor is there condemnation resulting from sin (5:16, 18), from the sin that came through Adam. *Katakrima*, "condemnation," which occurs in the NT only here and in 5:16 and 18, means the same as "the curse" of Gal 3:10, which is derived from Deut 27:26 ("cursed be the one who fails to fulfill the provisions of this law"; cf. Deut 28:58–61). So *Nomos* as the judge of human conduct has passed judgment on those who violate its precepts. Such a curse or condemnation was leveled by the Mosaic law itself on those who were subject to it, and it clung to unregenerate human beings torn in two, because they were "flesh" and dominated by sin (5:16–18); yet they still had a "mind" that recognized God's law as good. This condition, however, no longer affects justified Christians, who do not live under such a dispensation of "condemnation" (2 Cor 3:7), but live in union with Christ. In this regard Paul is emphatic; he places the neg. adj. *ouden*, "no," at the beginning of the sentence.

The prep. phrase *en Christō Iēsou* can be understood either instrumentally (they live by Christ), or locally (in a sphere of his influence), or even mystically (in symbiosis with him). To be "in Christ" means to live as someone freed from sin, death, self, and the law, and consequently from wrath. As Paul will explain, it is to live by the Spirit of God. The phrase echoes that of 5:18–21. "In Christ Jesus" a person lives by the uprightness of God that has been revealed in Christ and under the guidance of his Spirit, as Paul will explain in the following verses. Hence the Christian is no longer under the domination of the flesh and sin.

The Greek MSS A, D¹, Ψ, 81, 365, and 629, followed by the Vg, add *mē kata sarka peripatousin*, "who walk not according to the flesh." But that is not the reading in the best MSS (א*, B, D*, F, G, 6, 1506, 1739, etc.) and is clearly derived from 8:4. Still other MSS (א¹, Dᶜ, K, P, 33, 88, 614 and *Koinē* text-tradition) add the same phrase, but also *alla kata pneuma*, "but according to the Spirit."

2. *in Christ Jesus.* It is not easy to say with what this phrase is to be taken. For Dodd (*Romans*, 118), Lagrange (*Romains*, 191), Michel (*Brief an die Römer*, 250), it is to be taken with *tēs zōēs*, "life in Christ Jesus," and not with the vb. *eleutherōsen*, whereas Sanday and Headlam (*Romans*, 191), Cranfield (*Romans*, 374–75), and Dunn (*Romans*, 418) argue for understanding it with the verb. Kuss (*Römerbrief*, 490) readily admits that it cannot be decided. Schlier (*Römerbrief*, 239) thinks of even a third possibility: to take it with the phrase, "the law of the Spirit of life"; this is a variant of the first interpretation. Taking it with the verb seems preferable. In any case, it is the risen person of Christ Jesus that makes the difference. Having become a "life-giving Spirit" (1 Cor 15:45) through his passion, death, and resurrection, he it is who brings about this freedom for humanity. Verse 2 states the basis of what was asserted in v 1, but it also states the relation of the Spirit to law, sin, and death.

the law of the Spirit of life. The gen. ("life") indicates that which the Spirit guarantees (compare 6:4 and 7:6); "life" and "peace" are the concern of the Spirit (8:6). Through the Spirit of Christ comes life to the mortal bodies of human beings (8:11). In union with Christ, then, Christians come under the "law" of the Spirit that gives life. Thus qualified, *nomos* no longer refers to the Mosaic law. Paul indulges in oxymoron as he now applies *nomos* to the Spirit, which in his understanding is anything but "law." Rather, the law of the Spirit is nothing other than the "Spirit of God" (8:9a, 14) or the "Spirit of Christ" (8:9b) in its ruling function in the sphere of Christ (Käsemann). It is the dynamic "principle" of the new life, creating vitality and separating humans from sin and death, indeed, supplying the very vitality that the Mosaic law could not give. It is the life-giving Spirit of God himself, which "dwells" in the justified Christian (8:9). Paul's expression alludes directly to 7:23, where he spoke of "the law of sin that is in my members." The Spirit has thus become the sphere in which the Christian now lives through union with Christ. See Gal 2:20; 5:25. The Spirit shapes the life of the Christian and becomes the pledge of the glory that is the Christian destiny. As death held sway in the old aeon, so now the Spirit gives life and dominates those who are "in Christ Jesus." On the Spirit, see Introduction, section IX.C.

Paul does not understand the law of the Spirit as the Torah restored by the Spirit (*pace* Cranfield, "Paul and the Law," 166 [he has now changed his opinion]; Fuchs; Lohse, *Ho nomos*; Schmidt), as will become clear in the following verses. Cf. Jas 1:25 for another way of expressing the "perfect law."

has set you free. The freedom that comes from the Spirit in Christ Jesus liberates from the conditions that follow in the next phrase. "Freedom" is again considered as an effect of the Christ-event. Recall 6:18, 20, 22; see 2 Cor 3:17; compare Gal 5:1, 13.

N-A²⁶ reads *se*, "you," as do MSS ℵ, B, F, G, 1505, and 1739*, but MSS A, C, D, the *Koinē* text-tradition, and Latin versions read *me*, "me." Although the extrinsic testimony in support of these readings is almost equal, *se* is often regarded as a copyist's error, a dittography derived from the vb. *eleutherōsen*. But *me* is just as likely a copyist's change, as an answer to the question of 7:24. It is not easy to say which fits the context better. And *hēmas*, "us," read by MSS Ψ and the Bohairic Coptic version, is clearly a secondary modification in the transmission. *Se* is a literary variant for *hēmas*. In any case, Paul clearly means the justified Christian.

from the law of sin and death. Again *nomos* may be used in a figurative sense, "principle." Although Paul explained that the law in itself is not sin, but is used by sin to lead human beings to death, so now he is contrasting the Spirit with *nomos* so used. Possibly, then, *nomos* could be understood in the proper sense. Although the latter meaning cannot be excluded, *pace* Räisänen ("Das Gesetz"), the former explanation is preferable. Paul is really referring to the condition dominated by the two powers, sin and death. In any case, one should not miss the collocation here of the three key words: law, sin, and death. They sum up the discussion of chaps. 5–7. The tyranny exercised by sin and ending in death is broken; the person who is in Christ is freed of them, freed too of the condition described in 7:23–24.

3. *What the law, weakened by the flesh, was powerless to do.* Lit., "the impossible of the law, in which (or since [BAGD, 261b]) it was weak because of the flesh," i.e., "the one thing that the law could not do" (BDF §263.2 [= *ho tō nomō adynaton ēn*, §480.6]). An infin. such as *poiein*, "to do," has to be understood to clear up the ellipse that Paul writes in this sentence. *To adynaton*, "the impossible," is best understood as a nominative absolute in apposition to the

rest of the sentence, "as for the impotence of the law, God condemned. . . ." *Pace* Cranfield (*Romans*, 378), it cannot be an acc. in apposition to *katekrinen tēn hamartian*; if so understood, it would have to be in apposition with *tēn hamartian*, which is impossible. As for the minor question whether *adynaton* should be understood in an active sense, "incapable" (so Tertullian, *De carnis resurrectione* 46 [CSEL 47.94]: "quod invalidum erat legis") or in a passive sense, "impossible" (so Origen, *In ep. ad Romanos* 6.12 [PG 14.1093]: "quod impossibile erat legi"), see Sanday and Headlam, *Romans*, 192. The latter is preferable, because it better expresses the antithesis.

The clause *en hō ēsthenei dia tēs sarkos* is problematic. The *en hō* could be taken modally, "in which, wherein" (so Sanday and Headlam [*Romans*, 192]; Käsemann (*Commentary*, 216]), or it could be understood causally (= *en toutō hoti*), "because" (so Lagrange [*Romains*, 193]; Cranfield, *Romans*, 379; BDF §219.2). The latter seems to be preferable. Paul uses the vb. *asthenein*, "be weak," or the noun *astheneia*, "weakness," in different senses: physical weakness (2 Cor 11:29), intellectual weakness (Rom 6:19), moral weakness (5:6), weakness of faith (4:19), weakness of conviction (14:1–2), weakness of conscience (1 Cor 8:12). In this case, it is the weakness of the law, its failure to overcome the power of sin. A similar weakness is ascribed in particular to the flesh (as dominated by sin) or "because of the resistance of the flesh" (BAGD, 181).

Paul indulges in a kerygmatic assertion, insisting that God himself has brought about what the law could not do. He regards the Mosaic law as incapable of putting human beings in a state of rectitude before God or of freeing them from sin or death. The good that the law might have done was rendered ineffective by the weak human self dominated by indwelling sin (7:22–23). Although the law supplied the knowledge of sin and told human beings what to do and what not to do, it supplied no power to surmount the opposition to it coming from the human inclination to evil and sin. Paul sees that the problem is not with the law as such, but with human flesh dominated by sin.

God has done. Lit., "by sending . . . , God . . . has condemned sin," but a finite vb. like *epoiēsen*, "has done," has to be supplied in English to fill out the ellipse. Paul readily admits that God has been able to bring about through Christ what the law could not do, namely, bring human beings into a status of rectitude before God. It all depends, then, on God's initiative and intervention, and in no way on mere observance of the law. The contrast in the sentence is between *ho theos*, "God," and *nomos*, "the law." Cf. Heb 7:18.

by sending his own Son. See 8:32. This participial clause explains how God has done it; two further modifications follow. The emphatic phrase "his own Son" is stronger than "Son of God" and highlights the divine relationship of Jesus to the Father and the divine origin of the task to be accomplished by one in close filial relationship with God. Implied is the unique bond of love between the two that is the source of human justification and salvation. Also implied is the preexistence of Jesus as Son, as in 1:3; Phil 2:5; and Gal 4:4. Christ's mission and task were to accomplish what the law could not do.

For Hellenistic Greek parallels of gods sending messengers or heralds on certain missions, see Epictetus, *Dissertationes* 3.23; Plutarch, *De Alexandri Magni fortuna* 1.6 §329c. For OT parallels of God sending messengers, see Gen 24:40; Judg 9:23; Isa 6:8; Ezek 2:3; Wis 9:10.

Commentators query whether there is an allusion here to Gen 22:2, to Abraham's willingness to sacrifice his only son, Isaac. If there is such an allusion (and it is undoubtedly more eisegetical than exegetical; see the NOTE on 8:32), it would give a sacrificial nuance to the sending.

in a form like that of sinful flesh. Lit., "in the likeness of the flesh of sin." What is affirmed here is the soteriological assumption of the human condition by the Son. This is the closest expression in Pauline writings to the idea of incarnation, which is otherwise a Johannine way of expressing the coming of Christ. The "sending" might thus refer to the whole redemptive incarnation, but it is better understood of its climax in the cross and resurrection (3:24–25; Gal 3:13; 2 Cor 5:19–21). The emphasis, however, falls on *homoiōma*, "likeness" (recall 5:14; 6:5), and on *hamartia* rather than on *sarx*. Paul's description is not docetic, implying that the Son only appeared to be in a form like that of sinful flesh, but was actually born as a human. He was sent as a man, born of a woman, born under the law (Gal 4:4).

The word *homoiōma* creates something of a problem. It is usually understood as "likeness, copy," or "form" (J. Schneider, *TDNT* 5.191), expressing an identity that is not a full identity (cf. Phil 2:7: *en homoiōmati anthrōpōn*). Branick, however, understands it as meaning that Christ "comes as the full expression of that sinful flesh. He manifests it for what it is. Sinful flesh is fully visible in the flesh of Christ" ("Sinful Flesh"). His reading depends on the studies of Vanni ("Homoiōma"). Branick's interpretation might be tolerable if he stressed that his interpretation does not imply that Jesus sinned, a point that the NT elsewhere denies. For Paul avoids saying that Jesus came *with sinful flesh*, just as in 2 Cor 5:21 he qualifies his statement that God made Christ "sin" for us, by adding "who knew no sin" (cf. Heb 4:15). As Origen noted (*In ep. ad. Romanos* 6.12 [PG 14.1094]), we human beings have "the flesh of sin," but the Son had the "likeness of sinful flesh." He came in a form like us in that he became a member of the sin-oriented human race; he experienced the effects of sin and suffered death, the result of sin, as one "cursed" by the law (Gal 3:13). Thus in his own self he coped with the power of sin. Paul's use of the phrase *sarx hamartias* denotes not the guilty human condition, but the proneness of humanity made of flesh that is oriented to sin. Compare the Qumran expression, *ʾǎnî laʾǎdam rišʿāh ûlěsôd běśar ʿāwel,* "I belong to wicked humanity and to the company of iniquitous flesh" (1QS 11:9; cf. 1QM 4:3). Cf. Dunn, *Romans,* 128; Morgan Gillman, "Another Look."

for the sake of sin. I.e., to deal with sin (Cranfield), or to conquer sin

(Goodspeed), or to take away, expiate sin (BAGD 644); cf. Gal 1:4; 1 Pet 3:18; Num 8:8. Such was the purpose of the sending of the Son. He entered the realm of sin itself in order to bring judgment against it; cf. Heb 2:17. He suffered all of the consequences that sin brought into human life: the law, suffering, and death. But he was able to redeem humanity from the curse of the law, becoming himself a curse (Gal 3:13). Because he became subject to the powers that were hostile to human life, he was able to overcome them. *Peri hamartias* thus expresses the mission on which the Son was sent. Cf. 6:10; 1 Cor 15:3; 2 Cor 5:21.

Some commentators, however, take *peri hamartias* to mean "for the sake of (being) a sin-offering," i.e., as a sacrifice for human sin, because *hamartia* often occurs in the LXX in this sense (e.g., Lev 4:24; 5:11; 6:18; Ps 40:6; cf. 2 Cor 5:21). So Sanday and Headlam (*Romans*, 193), Käsemann (*Commentary*, 216), Moo (*Romans*, 512), Wright ("The Meaning"), and Greene ("A Note"). Although the image would be different, the underlying idea would still be the same. Through Christ's mission humanity's sin has been taken away.

Thornton, however, finding neither of these meanings to be without difficulty, suggests instead that this phrase be taken not with what precedes, but with what follows ("The Meaning"). He translates: "God, sending his own son in the likeness of sinful flesh, condemned sin in the flesh, on the very grounds of its sinfulness." *Peri*, he claims, has such a judicial meaning in the NT (John 8:46; 16:8; Acts 23:6; 24:21; 25:9, 20; Jude 15), and he finds that John Chrysostom (*In ep. ad Romanos* hom. 13.5 [PG 60.514]) and Theodoret of Cyrrhus (*Interpretatio ep. ad Romanos* 8.3 [PG 82.129]) use this very interpretation.

he condemned sin in the flesh. The phrase *en tē sarki* has to be taken with the vb. *katekrinen*, "he condemned in the flesh," thus explaining how and in what respect God issued the decisive verdict against sin, in that realm where sin reigned and dominated. The phrase does not mean that only the effects of sin found in the flesh itself were condemned; that would be to restrict the condemnation too much. By the death Christ underwent on the cross, the death he underwent as a human, he executed the sentencing of sin, which could only touch him as human. The vb. *katekrinen* expresses a negative "sentence" and its execution, viz., condemnation. Sin is again personified, now as a power that has dominated unregenerate human life (5:12; 8:2) but despoiled of such power because it has been condemned "in the flesh" of Christ. But how?

Commentators part ways in explaining how. Some would understand "in the flesh" to mean simply "by the (innocent, sinless) flesh" (of Christ). So Augustine, *Contra duas ep. pelag.* 3.6.16 (CSEL 60.504–5). Others would understand it of the incarnation, when the Father by sending the Son "in the flesh" implicitly passed sentence on sin. It would have been a condemnation in principle, in that the Son assumed flesh (= the human condition) without sin and lived a sinless life; so some Greek Fathers: Irenaeus, *Adversus haereses* 3.20.2; Athanasius, *Or. contra Arianum* 1.51 (PG 26.120); Theodore of Mopsuestia (Staab, *Pauluskatenen*, 134); and some modern commentators: Büchsel, *TDNT* 3.951–52; Cranfield, *Romans*, 383; Kühl (*Römer*, 256–58); Lagrange, *Romains*, 194; Zahn. Still others would understand it more specifically of the crucified "flesh" of Christ: the Father passed definitive judgment against sin in that the death that Christ died on the cross "in the flesh" sentenced to impotence sin that reigned in human flesh, which could touch him only in the flesh that he had in common with all human beings (see 6:6–11; 7:4); so (with differing nuances) Origen, *In ep. ad Romanos* 6.12 (PG 14.1095); John Chrysostom, *In ep. ad Romanos* hom. 13.4 (PG 60.514); Theodoret of Cyrrhus; Thomas Aquinas; Benoit, Dunn (*Romans*, 422), Kuss, Sanday and Headlam (*Romans*, 193–94), and Käsemann. Because elsewhere Paul associates the redemptive activity of Jesus with his passion, death, and resurrection, the phrase is better understood in this last sense. Cf. Col 1:22.

In any case, Paul means that the Father has thus broken the dominion of sin and its consequences over human beings. In this way was destroyed the force that Adam's sin unleashed in the world (5:12). See Giavini, "Damnavit."

4. *so that the requirement of the law.* In vv 4–7 Paul uses a catechesis to draw a conclusion from his kerygmatic affirmation in v 3. Through the power of the Spirit, the divine principle of new life, the uprightness that the law demanded is finally attained. Paul takes over a formula current in the Jewish tradition about the legal claim of the Mosaic law, applying it indirectly to what the will of God requires. What the law required of Jews was the status of uprightness before God's tribunal by observance of the law. The key word is *dikaiōma*, the meaning of which is disputed. It can mean "act of right," as opposed to *adikēma*, "act of injustice," or the "amendment" of a wrong, a "judgment, penalty." Here it most likely means "regulation, requirement, commandment" of the law, i.e., what the law ideally required (as in 1:32; 2:26); cf. BAGD, 198; K. Kertelge, EDNT, 1.335. At this point in Romans Paul does not spell out more explicitly the mode that that fulfillment of the law takes; he will return to it in 13:8–10. Here "the requirement of the law" is the Pauline way of expressing the goal or purpose of the law, that for which the law was promulgated as a legal claim on humanity.

might be fully met. Lit., "might be fulfilled." This is a theological passive (ZBG §236). "The fulfillment spoken of here is in no sense something achieved by Christians themselves; it is something which God, the author of all, works in us through the Spirit as a consequence of the Christ-event. There is a fulfillment of the moral demand, . . . [but this] righteousness is entirely the creation of God operating through the Spirit" (Byrne, *CBQ* 43 [1981]: 569). One has to insist on this meaning of the passive verb and disagree with B. M. Newman and E. A. Nida (*A Translator's Handbook on Paul's Letter to the Romans*, Helps for Translators 14 [London and Stuttgart: United Bible Societies, 1973], 147), who prefer to translate this verb actively, "that we might fully accomplish." This seems to mean that the Spirit through the effects of the Christ-event brings it about that Christians can observe the Mosaic law, i.e., by their deeds can fulfill the requirements to attain a status of uprightness before God. But that is to miss Paul's point about God's gratuitous intervention. It is God himself who brings about the fulfillment of the law through Christ and the Spirit.

in us who conduct ourselves not according to the flesh, but according to the Spirit. Lit., "who walk not." The law proposed an ideal but did not enable human beings, creatures of flesh, to achieve it; now all that is changed. The Spirit enables them to surmount the seductions of the flesh and arrive at the goal that the law once proposed. For Christians are now no longer under the law, but under grace. In the long run, Paul means that the basic purpose of the law, to bring human beings to a status of rectitude before God, is fulfilled by what Christ Jesus has done for them. The uprightness in the sight of God that they now achieve is one that is not their own, achieved by their own deeds or merits, but one that is attributed to them because of what Christ Jesus had done for them. The Greek ptc. with the negative *mē* gives a proviso or conditional sense to the expression, "provided we walk not according to the flesh." It thus insinuates, however, that Christian living is not something that flows automatically from faith and baptism; cooperation with God's Spirit is required. Paul again uses *peripatein* in the Jewish sense of "walk, conduct one's life"; see the NOTE on 6:4. It is a mystery why Lagrange (*Romans*, 195) insists here that *pneuma*, opposed to *sarx*, can only mean "the spiritual principle of our actions, grace, and not the Holy Spirit." That seems to be a refinement born of a later theological perspective. Paul is clearly speaking of the Spirit, and the contrast of "flesh" and "Spirit" is developed in vv 5–13. Cf. Gal 5:16–26. The prep. phrase *en hēmin* indicates that we as Christians are the sphere in which God's Spirit now operates, freeing us from self-centeredness and achieving for us the goal of the law itself. Thus has God through Christ Jesus and his Spirit destroyed the power of flesh and sin, and he has done so in order that his upright demand, expressed by law, might find fulfillment.

5. *Those who live according to the flesh are concerned about things of the flesh*. I.e., those whose motivation in life is a self-centered interest; their aspirations are all self-oriented. Verses 5–8 support what Paul said in v 4, giving the basis for the imperative contained therein. He explains the contrast of *sarx* and *pneuma* in greater detail. The first mode of contrast concerns the outlook or mindset of a person, the way one thinks and desires (*phronein*, the same verb that Paul uses in 12:3,16; Phil 1:7; 2:5; 3:19; 1 Cor 13:11; cf. the use of it in 1 Macc 10:20; Josephus, *Ant.* 14.15.10 §450). For Paul it describes the mind, thoughts, and desires of a person focused on what is carnal, what is of flesh. Such a one cares really not for God or for others, but is self-centered. In v 4 Paul spoke of those "who walk according to the flesh"; now he probes more deeply and speaks of *hoi kata sarka ontes*, lit., "those who are according to the flesh," those whose very being is dominated ontologically by *sarx*. He refers to unregenerate human beings, and their outlook is wholly that of *sarx*, so that they cannot help but do "the deeds of the flesh" (see Gal 5:19).

those who live according to the Spirit are concerned about things of the Spirit. I.e., those who are baptized, live "in Christ Jesus" (8:1), and are open to the promptings of the Spirit. Their aspirations are inspired, and they take the side of the Spirit. Their lives manifest the "fruits of the Spirit" (Gal 5:22–23). Because Christ lives in Christians, they are no longer motivated by the things of the flesh. A thoroughgoing change has taken place in the Christian's whole existence because of faith and baptism. Sin may still try to dominate the flesh, but it does not dominate the self, thanks to the indwelling Spirit. Such a person is now ruled by God's Spirit.

6. *the concern of the flesh is death.* See 6:21; 8:13. The second mode of contrast concerns the result of aspirations. All of the strivings and orientation of unregenerate human beings, left to themselves, are focused on death (total death; see the NOTE on 5:12). Compare Gal 5:21, "*People who do such things have no share in the kingdom of God.*" *Phronēma*, "concern, striving," occurs in the NT only here and in vv 7 and 27, but it occurs here because of the verb *phronein* used in v 5.

the concern of the Spirit is life and peace. Radically opposed to the concern of the flesh is that of the Spirit, which is eternal "life" and "peace," i.e., life with God (8:2; cf. Gal 6:8) and friendship with God (5:1–2; 14:17). Paul implies that the tendency of unregenerate humanity is to enmity with God; he will formulate this notion explicitly in v 7. But through Christ's Spirit, human beings find reconciliation and peace with God, for he is, as Paul calls him, *ho theos tēs eirēnēs*, "God of peace" (15:33; cf. 1 Thess 5:23; 1 Cor 14:22; 2 Cor 13:11; Phil 4:9), and his dominion is one of peace (14:17). Compare the Deutero-Pauline ideas in 2 Thess 3:16; Col 3:15; Eph 2:14.

7. *Since the concern of the flesh is hostility to God.* The third mode of contrast concerns one's attitude about God. This verse and the following one explain why "the concern of flesh is death." Flesh-oriented humanity finds itself in the condition of hostility, enmity, estrangement in God's sight, hence opposed to the life that is his. See 5:10; Jas 4:4. Flesh rises up in active opposition to what God desires.

it is not submissive to God's law. The fourth mode of contrast concerns the law, the concrete expression of God's will. This verse recasts 7:22–25, but goes farther in asserting that earth-minded human beings fundamentally refuse to observe God's law, lacking the power to transcend the inner conflict, when confronted by the law. Thus hostility to God becomes open transgression of the law's commands.

nor can it be. Lit., "for it can not either" (BDF §452.3). I.e., such lack of submission is not merely a question of fact, but even of ability or potentiality, given the basic constitution of unregenerate humanity or of the flesh dominated by indwelling sin, which lacks the power to transcend that inner situation.

8. *those who live by the flesh cannot please God.* Lit., "those who are in the flesh," a repetition of the idea expressed in v 5. The root of the problem is that they are not open to the promptings of the Spirit. Paul chooses a neutral way of expressing the goal of human life: to please God. It is a goal aspired to by both

Jews and Christians (cf. 2 Cor 5:9), yet it cannot be attained by one who is "in the flesh," i.e., dominated by indwelling sin; one must be "in the Spirit," i.e., must live "according to the Spirit" (8:5).

9. *Yet you are not in the flesh.* The status of the justified Christian is not that of the unregenerate human being. Here Paul formulates the indicative of Christian existence. On it he will base his imperative: Live like a Christian. So Paul counsels Roman Christians directly, using the 2d pl. pron. *hymeis.* He wants them to realize that even their earthly life is one now ruled by God's Spirit.

you are in the Spirit, if in fact God's Spirit dwells in you. Or possibly "you are in the spirit," if *en pneumati* refers to the human complex; so Sanday and Headlam, *Romans,* 196. But such an anthropological understanding of *pneuma* in these verses seems to be against the thrust of Paul's context, as Michel notes (*Brief an die Römer,* 254). See 1 Cor 3:16; 1 John 3:24. The Spirit, as the new principle of Christian vitality, is derived from God, the same source as all other manifestations of salvation. Through faith and baptism justified Christians are not only "in the Spirit" (see BDF §219.4), but the Spirit is now said to dwell in them. Both modes express the same reality. The vb. *oikein en* denotes "a settled permanent penetrative influence" (Sanday and Headlam, *Romans,* 196), because God has not only sent his Spirit (Gal 4:6), given it to Christians (Rom 5:5), even as a "pledge" or "guarantee" (*arrabōn,* 1 Cor 1:22; 5:5), and made them "drink of" it (1 Cor 12:13). As a result, Christians "live by the Spirit" (Gal 5:16) and "are led" by it (Gal 5:18). Indeed, the very body (*sōma*) of Christians is said by Paul to be "the temple of the holy Spirit within you" (1 Cor 6:19; cf. 2 Cor 6:16). It should also be noted how "to live according to the Spirit" (v 5) has now become to have "God's Spirit dwelling with you" (v 9a), and that will soon become "having Christ's Spirit" (v 9b). All of these are different modes of expressing "the Spirit of life in Christ Jesus" (v 2). Such persons are said to "belong to Christ" (1 Cor 1:12; 3:23; 15:23; 2 Cor 10:7; Gal 3:29; 5:24), i.e., they are *Christianoi.* The converse of this state is now spelled out in v 9b.

Paul uses the conj. *eiper,* which can mean "if, in fact," or even "because" (BAGD, 220). Cf. 3:30.

If one does not have Christ's Spirit, one does not belong to Christ. Attachment to Christ is only possible through the "spiritualization" of human beings. This is no mere external identification with the cause of Christ, or even a grateful recognition of what he once did for humanity. Rather, Christians who belong to Christ are those empowered to "live for God" (6:10) through the vitalizing influence of his Spirit.

10. *if Christ is in you.* Or if "the Spirit" dwells in you (8:9); cf. Gal 2:20; 2 Cor 5:17; 13:5; Col 1:27. These are for Paul different, generic ways of expressing the basic union of Christians with Christ. Christ dwells in Christians as his Spirit becomes the source of the new experience, empowering them in a new way and with a new vitality.

though the body be dead because of sin, the spirit has life because of uprightness. Paul plays on the two meanings of *pneuma*; in 8:9 it meant the Spirit of God, but he is aware of its sense as "spirit," that aspect of the human being which can be contrasted with "flesh" (see Introduction, section IX.D). Without the Spirit, the source of Christian vitality, the human "body" is like a corpse because of the influence of sin (5:12; cf. 6:6; 7:24; [Col 2:11]); but in union with Christ the human "spirit" lives, for the Spirit resuscitates the dead human body through the gift of uprightness (see Leenhardt, *Romans,* 209; cf. M. Dibelius, *SBU* 3 [1944]: 8–14). Cf. 1 Pet 4:6.

11. *if the Spirit of him who raised Jesus from the dead is dwelling in you.* As in 8:9, *pneuma* is the Spirit of the Father, to whom the efficiency of the resurrection is again attributed (see the NOTES on 4:24; 6:4; cf. 1 Cor 6:14). The power vivifying the Christian is thus traced to its ultimate source, for the Spirit is the manifestation of the Father's presence and life-giving power in the world since the resurrection of Christ and through it. It is the "Spirit of life" (8:2; cf. 1 Cor 15:45; see also Eph 1:19–20). And this "life" is nothing other than "justification" (5:18) and "uprightness" (5:21).

he who raised Christ from the dead will give life even to your mortal bodies. The fut. tense expresses the role of the vivifying Spirit in the eschatological resurrection of Christians. At his resurrection Christ became through the Father's glory (6:4) the principle of the raising of Christians, not only now, by supplying new life to mortal bodies (6:11), but also in the eschaton (1 Thess 4:14; Gal 6:8; Phil 3:10, 21; 1 Cor 6:14; 2 Cor 4:14). See Haskins, "Romans viii.11." Paul speaks no longer of "the body of sin" (6:6) or "the body of death" (7:24), i.e., of the body as subject to these dominating influences, but of *to thnēton sōma,* "the mortal body," i.e., of the body that can be so dominated. It is God himself who vivifies that body through the Spirit, and if the "Spirit" is "life," then it will vivify even the mortal body at the coming resurrection. Indeed, it is described as that power which has already even effected the resurrection of Christ himself.

MSS ℵ*, A, C, and 81 add *Iēsoun* to "Christ," probably under the influence of the first part of the verse.

through his Spirit that is dwelling in you. Whereas in 7:17 Paul admitted that sin dwelled in unregenerate human beings, now he affirms that the Spirit of God itself dwells in them. This indwelling Spirit is thus the driving force and the source of new vitality for Christian life. The life-giving Spirit has an OT background in Ezek 37:14. In v 9 Paul spoke of the Christian being "in the Spirit," now of the Spirit as "dwelling in" the Christian; again he is searching for ways to describe the ineffable union of the Christian with Christ and his vivifying Spirit. In all of this one must recall the role of both faith and baptism. Christ and his Spirit dwell in Christians because of faith that justifies.

Modern editors of the Greek NT read *dia* with the gen., which expresses the instrumentality of the Spirit in the resurrection of human beings (so MSS ℵ, A, C, 81). Another reading, strongly attested, is *dia* with the acc., which would stress the dignity of the Spirit, "because of the Spirit" (so MSS B, D, G, Ψ, and the Vg). In either case "his" refers to Christ (ZBG §210; BDF §31.1), for it is the Spirit as related to the risen Christ that is the vivifying principle.

12. *So then.* Paul now draws a conclusion from what he has said so far in this chapter. Despite the introductory *ara oun*, vv 12–13 form that conclusion and provide a transition to what follows. Some commentators think that v 12 begins the new topic; so Cranfield, Dunn, Käsemann, Kuss, Murray, Sanday and Headlam, and Schlier. It seems better, however, to take vv 12–13 with 1–11, because the content of vv 12–13 is closer to that of the foregoing verses, and that of vv 14ff. is different; so Byrne, Lipsius, Moo, and Wilckens. In any case, Paul, in drawing a conclusion, begins his discussion of the consequences of this condition of the indwelling of Christ and his Spirit.

brothers. Again Paul expresses his intimate relation with the Christians of Rome. See the NOTE on 1:13. In using it again, he stresses the urgency of the situation in a personal way.

we are not indebted to the flesh. Christians united with Christ do not have to depend on the aspirations of the flesh. Paul describes the consequences at first negatively: Christians are not obligated, like *opheiletai*, "debtors," to that power. Freedom from the power of dominating sin and death through justification results in consequences for the present and eschatological existence of Christians. The new salvific situation has consequences and demands that change their relation to *sarx*. It is no longer the norm of Christian life. Christian life is always one that is indebted, but that debt is no longer owed to "flesh"; it is, rather, owed to God and his Spirit.

to have to live according to it. See 8:5; cf. Gal 6:8; Eph 4:22–24. Paul uses the gen. of the articular infin. to express result (BDF §400.2). Christians are not doomed to a flesh-oriented existence; rather, they live according to the Spirit.

13. *If you live indeed according to the flesh, you will die.* I.e., it is still possible for even justified Christians to conduct themselves as self-oriented and flesh-guided individuals; such persons will not escape condemnation to death, which is the "wages of sin" (6:23; cf. 8:6). Paul does not use the simple fut., but *mellete apothnēskein*, "you are going to die, you are bound to die," i.e., you must die, because that is the natural consequence of "flesh" dominated by sin and death (recall 8:6).

if through the Spirit you put to death the deeds of the body, you will live. If the justified Christian responds to the promptings of the Spirit and cooperates with prevenient divine grace, even the "deeds" of the "body" will lead to eternal life. Paul uses *sōma*, "body," as the synonym for *sarx*, "flesh," which some MSS even introduce as a correction (D, F, G, 630). Hence his implied exhortation: Make use of the Spirit received, and mortify the deeds of the body, for this is the debt owed to Christ Jesus who has graced you with his Spirit. Cf. Col 3:5–6; Eph 4:22–24. Paul is not speaking here only of ascetic practices, even though such practices may not be inadvisable, but of the inevitable consequence in Christian life of adaptation of oneself to the influence of the Spirit and divine grace. The consequence involves the selfless pursuit of upright and justified conduct. "The deeds of the body" are no longer the norm of life, when that is lived "through the Spirit." Surrender to the guiding Spirit that frees brings it about that "the deeds of the body" are mortified. The consequence thereof is *zēsesthe,* "you will live," i.e., with the life of the risen Christ and his Spirit, a life that is given to Christians and guaranteed to lead to eternal glory, their destiny. In vv 8–9 Paul stressed: You as Christians are in the Spirit and alive with the Spirit of Christ. Now in vv 12–13 he presses further: You must realize that you are not obligated to your old selfish strivings, but you must through the Spirit react against them. The former lead only to death, but the latter guarantees life.

BIBLIOGRAPHY ON CHAPTER 8

Byrne, B., "Prophecy Now: The Tug into the Future," *The Way* 27 (1987): 106–16.

Coetzer, W. C., "The Holy Spirit and the Eschatological View in Romans 8," *Neotestamentica* 15 (1981): 180–98.

Dodd, C. H., "*Ennomos Christou,*" *Studia paulina in honorem Johannis de Zwaan septuagenarii* (Haarlem: Bohn, 1953), 96–110; repr. *More New Testament Studies* (Grand Rapids, Mich.: Eerdmans, 1968), 134–48.

Faessler, M., "Lecture de Romains 8," *BCPE* 37 (1985): 5–42.

Fuchs, E., "Der Anteil des Geistes am Glauben des Paulus: Ein Beitrag zum Verständnis von Römer 8," *ZTK* 72 (1975): 293–302.

Gatzweiler, K., "Le Chrétien, un homme renouvelé par l'Esprit," *AsSeign* n.s. 18 (1971): 6–10.

Grelot, P., "La Vie dans l'Esprit (*d'après* Romains 7–8)," *Christus* 113 (1982): 83–98.

Herman, Z. I., "Saggio esegetico sul 'già e non ancora' soteriologico in Rm 8," *Anton* 62 (1987): 26–84.

Horton, T., *Forty Six Sermons upon the Whole Eighth Chapter of the Epistle of the Apostle Paul to the Romans . . .* (London: Parkhurst, 1674).

Hubmer, F., *Die dreifache Freiheit der Erlösten nach Römer 8* (Stuttgart-Hohenheim: Hänssler, n.d.).

Keck, L. E., "The Law and 'the Law of Sin and Death' (Rom 8:1–4): Reflections on the Spirit and Ethics in Paul," *The Divine Helmsman: Studies on God's Control of Human Events, Presented to Lou H. Silberman,* ed. J. L. Crenshaw and S. Sandmel (New York: Ktav, 1980), 41–57.

Kuhn, K. G., "New Light on Temptation, Sin, and Flesh in the New Testament," *The Scrolls and the New Testament,* ed. K. Stendahl (London: SCM; New York: Harper & Bros., 1957), 94–113.

Loane, M. L., "The Eighth Chapter of the Epistle to the Romans," *EvQ* 13 (1941): 214–18.

———, *The Hope of Glory: An Exposition of the Eighth Chapter of the Epistle to the Romans* (London: Hodder and Stoughton, 1968), 11–74.

Lohse, E., "Zur Analyse und Interpretation von Röm. 8,1–17," *The Law of the Spirit*, ed. L. de Lorenzi, 129–66.

Lyonnet, S., "Christian Freedom and the Law of the Spirit According to Paul," *The Christian Lives by the Spirit*, ed. I. de la Potterie and S. Lyonnet (Staten Island, N.Y.: Alba House, 1971), 145–74.

———, *Les Étapes*, 161–213.

Mattern, L., *Das Verständnis des Gerichtes bei Paulus*, ATANT 47 (Zurich and Stuttgart: Zwingli, 1966), 91–96.

Müller, M., "Ånden og Loven: Pagtsteologi i Romerbrevet," *DTT* 52 (1989): 251–67.

Osten-Sacken, P. von der, *Römer 8 als Beispiel paulinischer Soteriologie*, FRLANT 112 (Göttingen: Vandenhoeck & Ruprecht, 1975).

Paulsen, H., *Überlieferung und Auslegung in Römer 8*, WMANT 43 (Neukirchen-Vluyn: Neukirchener-Verlag, 1974).

Schnackenburg, R., "Leben auf Hoffnung hin: Christliche Existenz nach Röm 8," *BLit* 39 (1966): 316–19.

Schwantes, H., *Schöpfung der Endzeit: Ein Beitrag zum Verständnis der Auferstehung bei Paulus*, Arbeiten zur Theologie 1.12 (Stuttgart: Calwer-Verlag, 1963), 43–52.

Sillevis Smitt, P. A. E., *Verzekerdheid: Veertien i eerredenen over Romeinen VIII* (Amsterdam and Pretoria: Höveker & Wormser, n.d.).

Sisti, A., "La vita nello Spirito (Rom. 8, 12–17)," *BeO* 10 (1968): 197–206.

Thomas, C., "Spirit Activity in the Church: A View from Romans 8," *TBT* 25 (1987): 160–62.

Tibbe, J., *Geist und Leben: Eine Auslegung von Römer 8*, BibSN 44 (Neukirchen-Vluyn: Neukirchener-Verlag, 1965).

Vledder, E. J. and A. G. van Aarde, "A Holistic View of the Holy Spirit: This View Experienced as Exciting in Romans 8, but Alarming in 1 Corinthians 12," *HerTS* 47 (1991): 503–25.

Wood, A. S., *Paul's Pentecost: Studies in the Life of the Spirit from Romans 8* (Exeter, UK: Paternoster, 1963).

On Rom 8:1–13

Adinolfi, M., "L'Invio del figlio in *Rom* 8,3," *RivB* 33 (1985): 291–317.

Anderson, F. L., "How God Gets the Law Fulfilled: Rom. 8:1–4," *BW* 30 (1907): 118–22.

Baulès, R., "Vivre selon l'esprit: Rm 8,9.11–13," *AsSeign* n.s. 45 (1974): 10–15.

Benoit, P., "The Law and the Cross According to St Paul: Romans 7:7–8:4," *Jesus and the Gospel*, vol. 2 (London: Darton, Longman & Todd, 1974), 11–39.

Branick, V. P., "The Sinful Flesh of the Son of God (Rom 8:3): A Key Image of Pauline Theology," *CBQ* 47 (1985): 246–62.

Bratsiotis, P. I., "Hermēneutikon sēmeiōma eis to chōria, Rhōm. Th' 3 kai I' 1," *Theologia* 12 (1934): 85.

Breytenbach, C., "Oor die vertaling van *peri hamartias* in Romeine 8:3," *HerTS* 45 (1989): 30–33.

Cranfield, C. E. B., "The Freedom of the Christian According to Romans 8.2," *New Testament Christianity for Africa and the World: Essays in Honor of Harry Sawyerr,* ed. M. E. Glasswell and E. W. Fasholé-Luke (London: SPCK, 1974), 91–98.

———, "St. Paul and the Law," *SJT* 17 (1964): 43–68.

Dibelius, M., "Vier Worte des Römerbriefs," *SEA* 9 (1944): 1–17, esp. 8–14.

Fahy, T., "Romans 8:3–4," *ITQ* 25 (1958): 387.

Gatzweiler, K., "Le Chrétien, un homme renouvelé par l'Esprit: Rm 8,8–11," *AsSeign* 18 (1971): 6–10.

Fortna, R. T., "Romans 8:10 and Paul's Doctrine of the Spirit," *ATR* 41 (1959): 77–84.

Giavini, G., " 'Damnavit peccatum in carne': *Rom.* 8,3 nel suo contesto," *RivB* 17 (1969): 233–48.

Greene, M. D., "A Note on Romans 8:3," *BZ* 35 (1991): 103–6.

Haskins, N. R., "Romans viii.11," *ExpTim* 6 (1894–95): 190.

Hermann, I., *Kyrios und Pneuma,* 65–66.

Jones, F. S., *"Freiheit,"* 122–29.

Lohse, E., "*Ho nomos tou pneumatos tēs zōēs*: Exegetische Anmerkungen zu Röm 8,2," *Neues Testament und christliche Existenz: Festschrift für Herbert Braun . . . ,* ed. H. D. Betz and L. Schottroff (Tübingen: Mohr [Siebeck], 1973), 279–87; repr. *Die Vielfalt des Neuen Testaments* (Göttingen: Vandenhoeck & Ruprecht, 1982), 128–36.

Lyonnet, S., "Le Nouveau Testament à la lumière de l'Ancien, à propos de Rom 8,2–4," *NRT* 87 (1965): 561–87.

———, "Rom 8,2–4 à la lumière de Jéremie 31 et d'Ezéchiel 35–39," *Mélanges Eugène Tisserant,* 7 vols. (Vatican City: Vatican Library, 1964), 1.311–23; repr. in *Études,* 231–41.

Morgan Gillman, F., "Another Look at Romans 8:3: 'In the Likeness of Sinful Flesh,' " *CBQ* 49 (1987): 597–604.

Moule, C. F. D., " 'Justification' in Its Relation to the Condition *kata pneuma* (Rom 8:1–11)," *Battesimo,* ed. L. de Lorenzi, 177–87.

Mussner, F., *Mort et résurrection,* 55–65.

Osten-Sacken, P. von der, "Befreiung durch das Gesetz," *Evangelium und Tora,* 197–209.

Overbeck, F., "Ueber *en homoiōmati sarkos hamartias,* Röm. 8,3," *ZWT* 12 (1869): 178–212.

Räisänen, H., "Das 'Gesetz des Glaubens' (Röm. 3.27) und das 'Gesetz des Geistes' (Röm. 8,2)," *NTS* 26 (1979–80): 101–17.

Richard, P., "O fundamento material da espiritualidade (Rm 8,1–17 e 1 Cor 15,35–38)," *Estudos bíblicos* 6 (1985): 73–85.

Sandt, H. W. M. van de, "Research into Rom. 8,4a: The Legal Claim of the Law," *Bijdragen* 37 (1976): 252–69.

————, "An Explanation of Rom. 8,4a," ibid., 361–78.

Schelkle, K. H., " 'Ihr seid geistliche': Eine Predigt," GLeb 35 (1962): 241–44.

Schweizer, E., "Was meinen wir eigentlich wenn wir sagen, 'Gott sandte seinen Sohn . . .'?" NTS 37 (1991): 204–24.

————, "Zum religionsgeschichtlichen Hintergrund der 'Sendungsformel' Gal 4,4f. Rm 8,3f. Joh 3,16f. 1 Joh 4,9," ZNW 57 (1966): 199–210; repr. Beiträge zur Theologie des Neuen Testaments: Neutestamentliche Aufsätze (1955–1970) (Zurich: Zwingli, 1970), 83–95.

Spence, R. M., "Romans viii.3," ExpTim 9 (1897–98): 479–80.

Stalder, K., Das Werk des Geistes, 387–487.

Stanley, D. M., Christ's Resurrection, 189–92.

Thompson, R. W., "How Is the Law Fulfilled in Us? An Interpretation of Rom 8:4," LS 11 (1986): 31–40.

Thornton, T. C. G., "The Meaning of kai peri hamartias in Romans viii. 3," JTS 22 (1971): 515–17.

Thurneysen, E., "Predigt über Römer 8,1," EvT 2 (1935): 1–8.

Twisselmann, W., Die Gotteskindschaft der Christen nach dem Neuen Testament, BFCT 41.1 (Gütersloh: Bertelsmann, 1939).

Vanni, U., "Homoiōma in Paolo (Rm 1,23; 5,14; 6,5; 8,3; Fil 2,7): Un'interpretazione esegetico-teologico alla luce dell'uso dei LXX," Greg 58 (1977): 321–45, 431–70.

Winzer, J. F., Explanatur locus Paulli ad Romanos epistolae Cap. VIII, 1–4 (no place: no publ., 1828).

Wright, N. T., "The Meaning of peri hamartias in Romans 8:3," Studia Biblica III, JSNTSup 3 (Sheffield, UK: JSOT, 1980), 453–59.

Zeller, E., "Zum Röm 8,3: en homoiōmati sarkos hamartias," ZWT 13 (1970): 301–7.

Ziesler, J. A., "The Just Requirement of the Law (Romans 8:4)," AusBR 35 (1987): 77–82.

THEME DEVELOPED: CHRISTIAN LIFE, LIVED IN FREEDOM BESTOWED BY THE INDWELLING SPIRIT, HAS ITS DESTINY IN GLORY (8:14–39)

◆

25. THROUGH THE SPIRIT THE CHRISTIAN BECOMES A CHILD OF GOD, DESTINED FOR GLORY (8:14–17)

8 ¹⁴For all those who are led by God's Spirit are children of God. ¹⁵You did not receive a spirit enslaving you again to fear, but you received a Spirit of sonship, one in which we cry, *"Abba,* Father!" ¹⁶The Spirit itself bears witness with our spirit: we are children of God! ¹⁷If children, then heirs too, heirs of God and coheirs of Christ, if we now suffer with him in order also to be glorified with him.

COMMENT

Paul proceeds a step further in his explanation of the theme of 5:1–11, as he teaches about the influence of the Spirit in Christian life. The Spirit not only enables one to put to death the deeds of the body and gives new life, it also sets up for human beings the relationship to God of an adopted child and heir. This adoption further enables Christians to call upon God as "Father" and is a token of the eschatological destiny that awaits them. This is the first appearance of the theme of adopted sonship in Romans, and it serves to express better the relationship of Christians to God. "According to the flesh" Christians are children of Adam, but those "led by the Spirit" are children of God and heirs of a divine inheritance. This too is the present lot of Christians; they *are* children of God, they *are* heirs. But that condition also has its eschatological consequences. The risen Christ is the firstborn of the resurrection, and through him Christians now share and will share eventually in a fuller form of that life in glory. They are fellow heirs with the risen Christ himself.

Although the idea of "adoption" *(huiothesia)* is not derived by Paul from the OT—the word itself does not even occur in the LXX—the notion of adoptive sonship of Christians is a development of the OT idea of God's election of Israel as his chosen people. Deut 4:34 formulates well the OT idea: "Did any god ever attempt to go and take a nation for himself out of the midst of another nation, by trials, by signs, by wonders, by war, by a mighty hand and outstretched arm, and by great terrors, according to all that the Lord your God did for you in Egypt before your very eyes?" As a result, "Israel is my firstborn" (Exod 4:22); cf. Isa 1:2; Jer 3:19–22; 31:9; Hos 11:1. That character of Israel as the chosen people of God now yields to the further specification of Christians as the adopted children of God. They are no longer just a "people"; through the gift of the Spirit they have been taken into the very *familia* of God's own household. Through faith and baptism they have been adopted into filial relationship with Jesus Christ as brother and with God as Father. In a sense they have now become "the Israel of God" (Gal 6:16).

This paragraph is parallel to Gal 4:6, "that you are sons of God, God has sent the Spirit of his Son in our hearts." But there is a difference. In Gal 4:6 the introductory conj. *hoti* is ambiguous: It could mean "the fact that" and describe the factual ontological status of Christians (i.e., something other than the Spirit may constitute the sonship); or it could mean "because" and thus state that the gift of the Spirit is the basis of adoptive sonship. Here in Romans 8 Paul clears up that ambiguity: Spirit-led Christians are children of God. The gift of the Spirit *constitutes* the sonship, and it is thus the basis of *huiothesia*.

As he did in Gal 4:6, Paul preserves in 8:15 the Greek transliteration of the Aramaic word for "father," *abba*. He has undoubtedly inherited the formula *abba, ho patēr* from the early tradition of Greek-speaking Christians, which existed before him. The Aramaic cry *'abbā'*, used by Jesus in the moment of his supreme earthly confidence in God (Mark 14:36), was cherished by early Christians in memory of Jesus himself, *pace* Wilckens (*Römer* 2.137 n. 574). Many NT interpreters regard the Aramaic *'abbā'* as an instance of *ipsissima vox Iesu*. It is noteworthy that this Aramaic expression is not preserved in a magic or miracle context, and so it cannot be regarded as the retention of *barbarikē rhēsis*, "a barbarian mode of speech," as some interpreters have claimed for the Aramaic words used in miracle stories of the gospel tradition. The formula became a mode of addressing God even in Gentile Greek-speaking Christian communities, and a distinctive one at that, with the added Greek translation *ho patēr*.

Such a mode of address for God, *'abbā'*, is unattested in the OT. Not even passages such as Deut 14:1, "You are children of the Lord, your God," express the same idea, for those passages express the *corporate* relationship of Israel to God (see also Exod 4:22; Hos 11:1; Isa 1:2; Jer 3:22; Wis 18:13), not that of the upright *individual* Israelite or Jew. That usage, however, may occur in Ps 89:27, where David is quoted saying *'ābî' attāh, 'ēlî*, "You are my Father, my God," or in the Alexandrian Book of Wisdom (2:16), where it is used, not as a mode of address, but as a description. The Hebrew form *'ābî*, "my Father," has now turned up in some Qumran texts: 4Q372 1:16, *'by w'lhy*, "my Father and my God"; 4Q460 5:6, *'by w'dwny*, "my Father and my Lord" (see E. Schuller, *RevQ* 14 [1989–90]: 349–76). Cf. Wis 14:3; Sir 23:4; 3 Macc 6:3, 8, where the Greek vocative *pater* is used similarly. Yet such sonship, either corporate of Israel or individual, is not related to the Spirit in the OT, as Christian sonship is in 8:16. The Pauline use of the phrase could reflect some liturgical usage, but such usage may have built on a recollection of Jesus' own usage. In any case, "Paul is surely not speaking here of a mere liturgical usage. The 'cry' **Abba!** is adduced as evidence that **we are children of God,** not as evidence that such was the official doctrine of the Church expressed in its liturgy" (Dodd, *Romans,* 129 [his emphasis]).

NOTES

8:14. *all those who are led by God's Spirit are children of God.* Lit., "sons of God." The mortification of the deeds of the body mentioned in 8:13 does not really constitute Christian life, necessary though it may be for the living of it. The Spirit instead animates and activates Christians, making them children of God. Being "led by the Spirit" is Paul's way of expressing what later theologians would call prevenient grace, the initiative that God's favor takes in guiding Christian life. Käsemann thinks that one should not translate the vb. *agontai* merely as "are led," but rather as "driven by the Spirit," because it is taken "from the vocabulary of the enthusiasts of 1 Cor 12:2" (*Commentary,* 226). But that interpretation is far from certain, for, as Schlier notes (*Römerbrief,* 251 n. 4), Paul uses the vb. *agesthai* also in Gal 5:18, where "being led by the Spirit" is parallel to "walk according to the Spirit" (5:16). In any case, it is the Pauline way of expressing the active influence of the Spirit in Christian life, i.e., the reaction of Christians to the leading of the Spirit; Christians are under the vital guidance of God's Spirit, which leads them when they allow it and thereby mortify the deeds of the body. The pron. *hosoi,* "whoever," is to be understood in an inclusive sense (with Cranfield, Schlier), but some commentators take it in a restrictive sense, "only those who" (so Lagrange, *Romains,* 201), i.e., those who do as v 13 suggests. Dunn (*Romans,* 450) prefers to keep it ambiguous, "as many as," and Käsemann (*Commentary,* 227) takes it both ways. The term "sons" (of God) appears again in vv 19 and 23 (cf. Gal 4:6–7), but in vv 16–17 Paul will use *tekna,* "children," which reveals the inclusive sense of *huioi.* Yet *huioi* more accurately expresses the relationship because of its legal relation to "heirs." Into the hearts of such "sons" God has sent the Spirit of *his* son (Gal 4:6) to establish that intimate relationship to himself. This status is initiated through faith and baptism (see Gal 3:26–27; 4:6); it is activated and realized through the indwelling Spirit (8:14), and is the guarantee of eschatological filiation (8:19, 23).

15. *You did not receive a spirit enslaving you again to fear.* Verses 15–16 provide the proof of what is said in v 14, being introduced by *gar,* "for." Paul again plays on the meaning of *pneuma,* "spirit/Spirit." Christians have received the Spirit (of Christ or of God), but this is not a "spirit" in the sense of a disposition or mentality that a slave would have, which would connote anxiety and fear of a master, the attitude that Paul has described in chap. 7 (especially 7:6; cf. Gal 4:3b). Animated rather by God's Spirit, Christians cannot have an attitude of slavery, for the Spirit sets one free. See 2 Cor 3:17. Christians have thereby won out over the anxiety of death and the fear of slavery. Paul does, indeed, speak at times of Christians as "slaves" (6:16; 1 Cor 7:22), but that is a

way of expressing their relations to the risen Christ as *Kyrios*, "Lord, Master." Moreover, he may even use it with oxymoron, to make a rhetorical point. In reality, he here considers Christians as children adopted into the *familia* or household of God, not merely as slaves, but as adopted sons and heirs. Cf. Gal 4:7. They are now empowered by the Spirit and thus enabled to call upon God as Father. Cf. 8:2 ("the law of the Spirit of life has set you free"); 2 Tim 1:7.

you received a Spirit of sonship. Lit., "a spirit of adoptive sonship," or possibly, "the Spirit of adoptive sonship." Because Paul has been playing on the word *pneuma*, it is not easy to decide in this case which nuance is intended; perhaps both. The Spirit received constitutes adoptive sonship, putting Christians in a special relationship to Christ, the unique Son, and to the Father.

The word *huiothesia*, "adoption," was a technical term in the Greco-Roman world, expressing the legal assumption of a person into the status of sonship in a natural family. Paul has borrowed the word from current Greco-Roman legal language and applied it to both Jews and Christians (see Schoenberg, "*Huiothesia*"; Lyall, "Roman Law"; Theron, " 'Adoption' "; L. Wenger and A. Oepke, RAC 1.99–112). The term, however, is used loosely of Israel in a corporate sense of "sonship" in 9:4, with special reference to its prerogative of election, of its being chosen by God to be his people (see the NOTE there).

Huiothesia is not found in the LXX, probably because adoption was not a normal institution among the Jews. *Pace* Rossell ("New Testament Adoption"), there is practically no evidence of it in the OT. Normally, one could not be taken into a Jewish family in order to continue the line of the adopter. Although a form of adoption seems attested in Gen 15:2; 48:5; Jer 3:19; and 1 Chr 28:6, these are instances of either slaves in the *familia* or other cases about which we know little in detail. For otherwise either polygamy (on which see Deut 21:15–17) or Levirate marriage (Deut 25:5–10) was the substitute for it. Philo of Alexandria knows of the institution, but does not use the word *huiothesia*; he refers to the institution to express figuratively the relation of the wise man to God (*De somn.* 2.41 §273). Later rabbinic Judaism was aware of men who brought up the children of other parents (Str-B 3.340), but it is far from clear that such children ever had filial rights.

For Paul *huiothesia* denotes a special status: because of faith baptized Christians have been taken into the family of God, have come under the *patria potestas*, "paternal authority," of God himself, and have a legitimate status in that family, not simply that of slaves (who belonged, indeed, to the ancient *familia*), but of sons. "Sonship is the expression for the freedom of the baptized person, who needs to recognize no other tie but the will of God, for the understanding that God has committed himself to humanity, and for the trust that grows out of this fatherhood" (Michel, *Brief an die Römer*, 260). The attitude of Christians, then, should correspond to the status that they enjoy. Cf. Gal 4:5, where such adoption has as its purpose the freeing of Christians from the law. See also Eph 1:5, where the eternal destiny of such sonship is envisioned.

one in which we cry, "Abba, *Father!*" I.e., the one in whom Christians are enabled so to cry. Although the vb. *krazein* is used often in the LXX of various situations in which one calls upon God in prayer (e.g., Exod 22:22; Pss 3:5; 17:6; 18:7; 30:3; 34:18; 88:2, 10; 107:13), it also means "cry aloud" in proclamation (Rom 9:27). This may be the sense intended here: through the Spirit Christians proclaim that God is Father. If understood in the former sense, it would be an example of the prayer mentioned in v 26. Cf. Gal 4:6, where Paul says that God has sent the Spirit of his son into our hearts, which itself cries "Abba, Father." The upshot is that Christians cry "Abba, Father" because the Spirit so enables them and cries with them.

The Aramaic emphatic state *ʾabbāʾ*, lit., "the father," was used as a vocative, "Father!" Compare the vocative use of the emphatic state *malkāʾ*, "O King" (Dan 2:4, 29, 31, 37, etc.). When *ʾabbāʾ* was taken up in Greek-speaking communities, it was not translated by the proper Greek voc. *páter* (see Luke 11:2), but its literal Greek translation, *ho patēr*, was added. The combination became a liturgical formula in Greek-speaking Christian communities. Compare *talitha* = *to korasion*, "maiden" (Mark 5:41). For instances of the def. art. with the nom. used as a vocative in the Greek language, see Homer, *Iliad* 1.231; Xenophon, *Cyropaedeia* 6.2.41; Aristophanes, *Frogs* 521; *Acharnians* 243; *Birds* 665–66; also the LXX of Pss 5:11; 36:8; 44:2; 54:3 (*ho theos* for *thee*). Cf. BDF §147.3. See further Fitzmyer, "*Abba*"; cf. Barr, " 'Abba, Father' "; Haenchen, *Der Weg*; Jeremias, "Abba." *Pace* Schlier (*Römerbrief*, 253–54), Aramaic *ʾabbāʾ* does not mean "our Father" (= *ʾabbûn[ā]*) in either mishnaic or targumic texts, an oft-repeated error.

16. *The Spirit itself bears witness with our spirit.* The compound vb. *symmartyrein* means either "testify along with" or simply "testify, certify." If the latter meaning were preferred, then it would mean that the Spirit makes Christians aware of adoptive sonship, "testifies to our spirit that. . . ." This meaning would put more emphasis on the role of the Spirit. But the former meaning reckons more with the compounded *syn-*. Paul would not mean that an unregenerate person, without the influence of the dynamic and vitalizing Spirit, could come to the knowledge of adoptive sonship, so that the Spirit would just concur with the human spirit recognizing this relationship. The preceding context makes it clear that the vital dynamism of the Spirit constitutes the sonship itself and bestows the power to recognize such a status. Now Paul goes further and stresses that the Spirit concurs with the Christians as they acknowledge in prayer or proclamation this special relation to the Father. Thus Paul goes beyond what he said about adoptive sonship in Gal 4:6. The Christian cry is likewise the cry of the Spirit. The inspired *Abba* cry reveals that Christians are children of God and destined for glory.

we are children of God! I.e., *tekna theou*, as in vv 17, 21; 9:8; and Phil 2:15. This is the fundamental affirmation of Christian awareness, of Christians led by the Spirit and taught by God's own Spirit. The expression is also found in Johannine literature (John 1:12; 11:52; 1 John 3:1, 2, 10; 5:2). See Gal 3:26.

17. *If children, then heirs too, heirs of God.* Paul uses *klēronomoi*, the word

employed in the LXX of Judg 18:7 [MS B]; 2 Sam 14:7, translating Hebrew *yôrēš*, and meaning to "give title to a possession." It implies a status in society based on descent from a father in a household. In this case, God himself is considered to be the father and the adopted son shares in his estate as an heir. The Christian, as such an adopted son, is not only admitted into God's family, but by reason of the same gratuitous adoption receives the right to become master of his Father's estate. Despite having no natural right to it, he acquires title by adoption through the Spirit (cf. Gal 3:29; 4:7). The heritage is sometimes expressed as *aphtharsia*, "incorruption" (1 Cor 15:50), as *basileia theou*, "the kingdom of God" (1 Cor 6:9, 10; 15:50; Gal 5:21), or as *doxa*, "glory" (Rom 8:21). Here Paul is content to say that we are heirs, which he further modifies in the next phrase.

and coheirs of Christ. Christ, the unique Son, is the heir in the first sense and has already received a share of the Father's estate (glory); Christians are destined one day to share that estate as coheirs (see the NOTE on 3:23). Cf. Heb 1:2. Recall that Jesus' words in the parable of the wicked tenant farmers implied that he himself was "heir" (Mark 12:7; Matt 21:38; Luke 20:14).

if we now suffer with him in order also to be glorified with him. In a surprising way, a connection is now asserted between the Christians' status and Christ's passion and resurrection. The double use of verbs compounded with the prep. *syn-*, "with," expresses once again the share that Christians have in these phases of Jesus' redemptive activity. They share "with Christ" both his death and his resurrection. Through faith and baptism Christians have grown together with Christ (6:5) and partake of his passion, suffering, and death. Paul does not play down the cooperation of Christians with Christ. In earthly life it is important that they share in the sufferings of Christ himself. Because of it, they are guaranteed a share likewise in his risen glory, in the destiny of Christ himself, who is in the glorious presence of the Father. The way to glorification, or to a share in God's glory, is through suffering in this life. See 3:23; 5:2–3; 6:4; cf. Gal 3:29; 4:7; also the Deutero-Pauline 2 Tim 2:12; and 1 Pet 4:13; 5:1. In different ways the suffering of Christians builds up to eschatological glory. The sufferings now endured (9:18) must always be seen as a participation in the suffering of Jesus himself, in what he has already suffered. Christian suffering is never an individual, lonely experience; Jesus has suffered before, and Christian suffering is only the overflow of his (see Col 1:24). But through such "suffering with Christ" the participation in his glorification is already assured.

Paul uses again *eiper*, this time in its proper sense of "if indeed," "if, in fact" (see BDF §454.2), in a sense slightly different from 8:9 (see the NOTE there). Cf. 3:30.

BIBLIOGRAPHY

Barr, J., " 'Abba, Father' and the Familiarity of Jesus' Speech," *Theology* 91 (1988): 173–79.

———, "'Abbā Isn't 'Daddy,' " *JTS* 39 (1988): 28–47.

Baulès, R., "Fils et héritiers de Dieu dans l'Esprit: Rm 8,14–17," *AsSeign* n.s. 31 (1973): 22–27.

Becker, J., "Quid locutio *palin eis phobon* in Rom 8, 15 proprie valeat," *VD* 45 (1967): 162–67.

Bieder, W., "Gebetswirklichkeit und Gebetsmöglichkeit bei Paulus," *TZ* 4 (1948): 22–40.

Byrne, B., *"Sons of God,"* 85–126.

Cambier, J.-M., "La Liberté du Spirituel dans Rom. 8.12–17," *Paul and Paulinism: Essays in Honour of C. K. Barrett*, ed. M. D. Hooker and S. G. Wilson (London: SPCK, 1982), 205–20.

Camilleri, N., "Teologia pneumatica della prudenza cristiana: 'Quicumque enim Spiritu Dei aguntur, hi sunt filii Dei' (Rom. 8,14)," *SPCIC* 1.175–85.

Crook, J., "Patria potestas," *ClassQ* n.s. 17 (1967): 113–22.

Fahy, T., "St. Paul: Romans 8: 16–25," *ITQ* 23 (1956): 178–81.

Fitzmyer, J. A., "*Abba* and Jesus' Relation to God," *À cause de l'Évangile: Études sur les Synoptiques et les Actes offertes au P. Jacques Dupont, O.S.B. à l'occasion de son 70ᵉ anniversaire*, LD 123, ed. R. Gantoy (Paris: Cerf, 1985), 15–38.

Grassi, J. A., "Abba, Father," *TBT* 21 (1983): 320–24.

Grundmann, W., "Der Geist der Sohnschaft: Eine Studie zu Röm, 8,15 and Gal 4,6 zu ihrer Stellung in der paulinischen Theologie und ihren traditionsgeschichtlichen Grundlagen," *In Disciplina Domini: In der Schule des Herrn*, Thüringer kirkliche Studien 1 (Berlin: Evangelische Verlagsanstalt, 1963), 172–92.

Haenchen, E., *Der Weg Jesu*, 2d ed. (Berlin: de Gruyter, 1968), 492–94, n. 7a.

Helewa, G., " 'Fedele è Dio': Una lettura di Rom 8, 14–39 (I)," *Teresianum* 37 (1986): 3–36; (II), 38 (1987): 3–49.

———, " 'Sofferenza' e 'speranza della gloria' in Rom 8,17," *Teresianum* 39 (1988): 233–73.

Hester, J. D., *Paul's Concept of Inheritance: A Contribution to the Understanding of Heilsgeschichte*, SJT Occasional Papers 14 (Edinburgh and London: Oliver and Boyd, 1968).

James, J. C., "*Abba ho patēr*," *ExpTim* 26 (1914–15): 428–29.

Jeremias, J., "Abba," *TLZ* 79 (1954): 213–14.

———, *Abba: Studien zur neutestamentlichen Theologie und Zeitgeschichte* (Göttingen: Vandenhoeck & Ruprecht, 1966), 15–67.

Lyall, F., "Roman Law in the Writings of Paul—Adoption," *JBL* 88 (1969): 458–66.

McCasland, S. V., " 'Abba, Father,' " *JBL* 72 (1953): 79–91.

Maddalena, A., "La duplice testimonianza per i figli di Dio," *Forma futuri: Studi in onore del Cardinale Michele Pellegrino*, ed. T. Alimonti et al. (Turin: Bottega d'Erasmo, 1975), 3–7.

Marchel, W., "Abba, Pater! Oratio Christi et christianorum," *VD* 39 (1961): 240–47.

———, *"Abba, Père!": La Prière du Christ et des chrétiens: Étude exégétique sur les origines et la signification de l'invocation à la divinité comme père, avant et dans le Nouveau Testament*, AnBib 19 (Rome: Biblical Institute, 1963), 181–91.

Nicol, W., "Hoe direk lei die Gees? 'n dogmatiese en eksegetiese ondersoek rondom Romeine 8:14," *Skrif en Kerk* (Pretoria) 7 (1986): 173–97.

Obeng, E. A., "Abba Father: The Prayer of the Sons of God," *ExpTim* 99 (1987–88): 363–66.

Ogara, F., " 'Ipse Spiritus testimonium reddit spiritui nostro, quod sumus filii Dei' (Rom. 8,12–17)," *VD* 16 (1936): 200–208.

Pathrapankal, J., "The Spirit of Sonship in Romans Chapter 8," *Bible Bhashyam* 2 (1976): 181–95.

Rensburg, J. J. J. van, "The Children of God in Romans 8," *Neotestamentica* 15 (1981): 139–79.

Romaniuk, C., "Spiritus clamans (Gal 4,6; Rom 8,15)," *VD* 40 (1962): 190–98.

Roosen, A., "Testimonium Spiritus (Rom 8, 16)," *VD* 28 (1950): 214–26.

Rossell, W. H., "New Testament Adoption—Graeco-Roman or Semitic?" *JBL* 71 (1952): 233–34.

Schoenberg, M. W., "*Huiothesia*: The Word and the Institution," *Scr* 15 (1963): 115–23.

Scott, J. M., *Adoption as Sons of God: An Exegetical Investigation into the Background of "Huiothesia" in the Pauline Corpus*, WUNT 2.48 (Tübingen: Mohr [Siebeck], 1992).

Taylor, T. M., " 'Abba, Father' and Baptism," *SJT* 11 (1958): 62–71.

Twisselmann, W., *Die Gotteskindschaft der Christen nach dem Neuen Testament*, BFCT 41.1 (Gütersloh: Bertelsmann, 1939).

Van Gemeren, W. A., "ʾAbbāʾ in the Old Testament?" *JETS* 31 (1988): 385–98.

Wolter, M., "Der Apostel und seine Gemeinden als Teilhaber am Leidengeschick Jesu Christi: Beobachtungen zur paulinischen Leidenstheologie," *NTS* 36 (1990): 535–57.

26. THREE THINGS TESTIFY TO THIS NEW DESTINY: CREATION GROANING IN TRAVAIL (8:18–23)

8 [18]I consider the sufferings that we now endure not worth comparing with the glory that is going to be revealed in us. [19]Indeed, creation itself is waiting with anxious expectation for the revelation of the children of God. [20]For creation has been subjected to frustration, not of its own choice, but by him who subjected it—with hope—[21]because creation itself too will eventually be freed from its bondage to decay and brought to the glorious freedom of the children of God. [22]Yes, we realize that all creation has been groaning and laboring in pain up to the present time. [23]Not only that, but we ourselves, though we have the Spirit as the firstfruits, are groaning inwardly as we wait for the redemption of our bodies.

COMMENT

Paul has terminated his description of the new Christian life empowered by the Spirit. Now he calls upon three things to assure the Christian that what he has just described is indeed the reality. Three things bear testimony to this new existence: the groaning of material subhuman creation in travail, the hope that Christians have, and the Spirit itself.

Paul finished his discussion in the last paragraph with the mention of suffering. Now he passes from that stage, realizing that such suffering in this life has its counterpart in the incomparable glory awaited by those who so suffer. The first assurance for this situation is derived by Paul from the state of physical nature or physical creation. Paul looks at the state of God's created subhuman world at the present time and sees the suffering that it endures. He is thinking of the present aeon (see the NOTE on 3:21), the period between Christ's death and resurrection and his coming in glory. Creation is now held in bondage to corruption, decay, and death, and from this fact he draws a comparison with the status of Christians still in this life. If creation is indeed in bondage, it shares the lot of humanity; but it has been subjected to such a state of futility with hope, hope for liberation from death, decay, and corruption. So too the Christian, who suffers and is weighted down by the trials of this earthly life, eagerly awaits the redemption of the body and the liberation from such conditions. This is the glorious destiny to which the justified Christian is called.

In the development of this topic, Paul alludes to Gen 3:17–19 and 5:29, where the earth has been cursed because of Adam's sinful transgression. But he is also thinking of the OT promises about "a new heaven and a new earth," the apocalyptic promises in Trito-Isaiah (Isa 65:17; 66:22). In intertestamental literature such promises were transferred to the messianic age: *1 Enoch* 45:4–5 (the earth will be transformed for the upright along with the Chosen One); *Jub.* 4:26; *2 Apoc. Bar.* 31:5–32:6; *4 Ezra* 7:11, 30–32, 75. This notion is also found in Rev 21:1 and 2 Pet 3:13 in the NT and is echoed in later rabbinic literature (see Str-B 3.247–55): the world, created for humanity and the service of it, was drawn into Adam's ruin; the blessings given to him (fertility of the soil, fecundity of trees, brilliance of stars, friendliness of animals, limitation of insects) were all lost, because Eve gave Adam (= humanity) to eat of the forbidden fruit. Paul is tributary to such Jewish thinking. He realizes that through Adam came not only sin and death (5:12–14), but "bondage to decay" and the "slavery of corruption," which affect all *material* creation, even apart from humanity (8:19–23).

An effect of the Christ-event now reappears in v 23 as *apolytrōsis*, "redemption" (see the NOTE on 3:24), but it is not limited to human beings. It is no longer considered from an anthropological point of view; it is now recast in cosmic terms. Human bodies that are said to await such redemption (8:23) are merely part of the entire material creation, which is itself groaning in travail until such redemption occurs. For the Christ-event is expected to affect not only human beings, but all material or physical creation as well. And yet, it is strange that in all of these verses (18–23) there is no mention of Christ Jesus.

NOTES

8:18. *I consider the sufferings that we now endure not worth comparing with the glory that is going to be revealed in us.* Or "to us." Paul reminds the Roman Christians that, though suffering is a sign of authentic Christian experience, it is only a transition to the assured glory that awaits them in the *eschaton*. Although Christians have been freed from the baleful influence of sin and death, in being received into the new life of the risen Christ through his Spirit, mortality is still part of the human lot, and it often brings suffering, as it did in the case of Christ Jesus himself. In union with Christ, however, Christians must undergo suffering. Yet that suffering is not merely part of the human condition or the earthly lot of humanity, but a sign of identification with Christ and a necessary stage of the transition to the eternal glory, which he now enjoys. Thus "sufferings" act as the foil to *doxa*, "glory" (see the NOTE on 3:23). Such sufferings are not contrary to justification by grace through faith, but can be grace-filled, and Paul expects Christians to cooperate with such grace in order to attain such glory. In v 35 Paul will spell out what such sufferings are. See Phil 1:20; 2 Cor 4:10–11, esp. 4:17 ("this slight momentary affliction is preparing us for an eternal weight of glory beyond all comparison"); 2 *Apoc. Bar.* 15:8. Such glory is for Paul the inexpressible, transcendent condition of God's presence, which is still to be revealed, the unseen and transcendent status of peace, freedom, and joy that Christians await.

19. *creation itself is waiting with anxious expectation for the revelation of the children of God.* Lit., "the anxious expectation of creation awaits the revelation of the sons of God." Paul indulges in apocalyptic language, depicting all creation as a person waiting for a momentous occasion. He discloses his view of the created world, which in its chaotic state manifests its cosmic struggle and is striving toward the very goal set for humanity itself. *Pace* Schlatter (*Gottes Gerechtigkeit*, 274), Paul does not mean by *pasa hē ktisis* the "homogeneous, closed circle, which humanity is." The meaning of *ktisis* has been debated since the time of Augustine (*De diversis quaestionibus octoginta tribus liber* I 67.1 [CCLat 44A.164–65]). From the context *ktisis* must mean *pasa hē ktisis*, "all creation" (8:22), but creation distinct from humanity, as v 23 suggests (see Cranfield, *Romans*, 414; Wilckens, *Römer* 2.153). Hence Paul is affirming a solidarity of the nonhuman world with the human world in the redemption that Christ has wrought. In its own way it echoes Yahweh's promise to Noah of the covenant to be made "between myself and you and every living creature" (Gen 9:12–13). So here *ktisis* denotes "material creation" apart from human beings. Wis 1:14 sums it all up well: "For he created all things that they might exist, and wholesome are the creatures of the world; there is in them no destructive drug, no domain of Hades on earth." Created for human beings (Wis 2:6), it was "cursed" because of Adam's sin (Gen

3:15–17); since then material creation has been in a state of abnormality or frustration, being subject to corruption and decay. Yet Paul sees it sharing in the destiny of humanity, somehow freed of its proclivity to decay. The "revelation of the children of God" expresses the corporate destiny of Christians to be made manifest at the parousia (see 1 Thess 3:13; Gal 5:5). This eschatological condition is now made the object of an apocalyptic affirmation.

Although *apokaradokia*, a substantive (coined by Paul?), occurs only in Christian writers, it is often translated as "eager expectation," as in Phil 1:20 (where it is linked to *elpis*, "hope"). It may actually express a more negative, dubious expectation, as Theodore of Mopsuestia noted (Staab, *Pauluskommentare*, 137): *Karadokein legetai to elpizein, apokaradokein de to apelpizein*, "*Karadokein* means to hope, *apokaradokein* to despair." But as Paul uses the word, it is figurative, derived from the outward conduct of a person, who with curiosity but uncertainty stretches the neck and cranes forward to see what some coming event or object might be like. See Schläger, "Das ängstliche Harren"; Bertram, "*Apokaradokia*"; Denton, "*Apokaradokia*."

"The revelation of the sons of God" refers to glorified Christians, the coheirs of the risen Christ, justified Christians in the glorious presence of the Father. That destiny was hinted at in 3:23 (see the NOTE there). That status is what all Christians long for, and Paul now associates all material subhuman creation with them in such a longing.

20. *creation has been subjected to frustration.* Or "emptiness, futility, purposelessness" (*mataiotēs*). It denotes the state of ineffectiveness of something that does not attain its goal or purpose; concretely, it means the chaos, decay, and corruption (8:21) to which humanity has subjected God's noble creation. In 2 Kgs 17:15 *mataios* is related to Hebrew *hebel*, "vanity, futility." *Mataiotēs* is a broader concept than *phthora*, "corruption, decay," of which Paul speaks in v 21, but there is no need to introduce the idea that material creation was subjected to "futile and transitory cosmic powers," *pace* Lietzmann (*An die Römer*, 85). Paul speaks of "corruption," even though he did not have in mind what modern industry and technology have done and are doing to the universe and Earth's ozone layer. Yet his words somehow ring true even in this century with its ecological concerns. In a sense, *mataiotēs* connotes what *pseudos*, "lie," meant in 1:25. Actually, *mataiotēs* has been subject to many differing minor interpretations over the centuries; see Cranfield, *Romans*, 413. Paul refers to this condition of material creation because he wants to explain why it too is longing with anxious expectation. This clause does not offer that explanation, but it is preparing for the coming phrase, which does.

not of its own choice. I.e., not through its own fault. Subhuman material creation, as it proceeded from the hand of the Creator God, was not marked with the frustration and futility of which Paul speaks. Its present situation stems not from its own natural inclination or purpose.

by him who subjected it. Who is the subject of this ptc. *hypotaxanta*: Adam, sinful man, God, Christ, or Satan? That exegetical question is complicated by the referent in the phrase itself, by the next phrase "in/with hope," and by the conj. *hoti/dioti* at the beginning of v 21.

The prep. *dia* in *dia ton hypotaxanta* might have the causal meaning it often has in Pauline writings (see 2:24; Gal 4:13; Phil 1:15), "because of him who subjected (it)." This phrase might then refer to Adam, whose transgression caused the cursing of the ground and subjected material creation to disorder. Cf. 4 Ezra 7:11–12: "I made the world for their sake, but when Adam transgressed my ordinances, what had been made was judged: the ways of this world were made narrow, sorrowful, and toilsome"; so (with some variations) John Chrysostom (*In ep. ad Romanos* hom. 14.5 [PG 60.530]); Balz (*Heilsvertrauen*, 41), Foerster (*TDNT* 3.1032), Godet, Jülicher, Lampe ("New Testament Doctrine"), Lipsius, Lyonnet, Viard, and Zahn.

The phrase "in/with hope," which is not found in the Genesis story (3:17–18), would then be understood as elliptical, standing for "(yet it was) with hope." The preferred conj. in v 21 would then be *dioti* (read by MSS ℵ, D*, F, G, 945), "because creation itself. . . ." But then the question arises, How could Adam have subjected material creation to futility "in/with hope," according to Paul's addition to the Genesis story?

Other commentators (Cornely, Cranfield, Dodd, Käsemann, Kühl, Lagrange, Leenhardt, Levie, Lietzmann, Michel, Pesch, Sanday and Headlam, and Schlier) interpret the prep. *dia* in the sense of agency, "by him who subjected (it)," which would refer neither to Adam nor to Satan (the serpent), but to God, who cursed the ground and to whom Paul now ascribes the "hope" (not mentioned in Genesis). Cf. 1 Cor 15:27, where "God" is also the subject of "subjected." Then the clause in v 21, introduced by the conj. *hoti* (read by MSS P⁴⁶, A, B, C, D², etc.), would express the object of that hope, "that (creation itself . . .)." The latter interpretation seems to make better sense, even though the use of *dia* + the acc. to denote agency is rare, but not unattested (see BAGD, 181; cf. Sir 15:11; 3 Macc 6:36; *Ep. Arist.* 292; John 6:57; Rev 12:11). Paul would be saying that God, though he cursed the ground because of Adam's sin, still gave it a hope of sharing in human redemption or liberation. On the punctuation of this phrase, see Hill, "The Construction," 296–97.

with hope. Or "in hope." See the preceding NOTE. Cranfield (*Romans*, 414), Michel (*Brief an die Römer*, 267), and Schlier (*Römerbrief*, 261) would make this phrase modify the finite vb. *hypetagē*, "has been subjected," but that reading is unlikely because the phrase is too far removed from that verb. It has to be understood with the ptc. that precedes *hypotaxanta*, as the RSV has taken it. This "hope," however, should not be facilely identified with Gen 3:15, *pace* Cranfield (*Romans*, 414), which expresses not victory, but lasting enmity between the serpent and its offspring and the woman and her offspring. Paul is actually the first biblical writer to introduce the note of hope apropos of the story in Genesis 3. According to him, God did not leave the frustrated creation in a hopeless situation. Creation could not free itself from the corruption and decay that beset it, but the "hope" meant is that it will be freed by its association with the destiny of justified Christians.

The anomalous form *eph> elpidi* (of MSS P⁴⁶, ℵ, B*, D*, F, G, Ψ) is corrected to *ep> elpidi* in MSS P²⁷, A, B², C, D², and the *Koinē* text-tradition. Cf. BDF §14.

21. *because.* Or "that." See the NOTE on 8:20. The oldest and best MSS (P⁴⁶, A, B, C, 33, 81, 614, 1739, etc.) read *hoti.* The reading *dioti* in some MSS (ℵ, D*, F, G) probably developed by dittography (*elpidi hoti* becoming *elpidi dioti*). This verse explains the hope.

creation itself too will eventually be freed from its bondage to decay. I.e., not just moral corruption, but the reign of dissolution and death found in material creation. Physical creation is thus not to be a mere spectator of humanity's liberation and triumphant glory, but is also to share in it by being released from its own material corruption and decay. *Phthōra* denotes not only perishability and putrefaction, but also powerlessness, lack of beauty, vitality, and strength that characterize creation's present condition. Freedom from such a condition is seen by Paul as an attendant aftermath of the glorification of the sons of God.

brought to the glorious freedom of the children of God. Lit., "for the freedom of the glory of the children of God." The freedom is not yet a possession of Christians; it is, rather, the characteristic of the status of eschatological glory, awaited in the *eschaton.* That freedom and glory have not yet been made manifest, but Christ Jesus has entered his glory, and those who believe in him live in the power of his risen, glorious life; they are thus freed proleptically from the powers of sin, death, and corruption, but as yet their "life is hid with Christ in God" (Col 3:3).

22. *all creation has been groaning and laboring in pain up to the present time.* Lit., "groans with (us) and labors in pain with (us)." Or perhaps, "every creature has. . . ." Paul makes use of vbs. compounded with the prep. *syn-* to designate the harmony of the groaning of creation together with humanity in its longing for a glorious destiny. He seems to borrow a mode of expression from contemporary Greek philosophers who often compared the vernal rebirth of nature to a woman's labor. Thus Heraclitus Stoicus, "When [after the winter's cold] the groaning earth gives birth in travail to what has been formed within her (*Quaestiones Homericae* 39 [p. 58.9]). See BAGD, 793; A.-M. Dubarle, *RSPT* 38 (1954): 445–65. In such groaning and travail Paul sees the eschatological expectation of material creation, awaiting the glory of Christian humanity. See Montgomery Hitchcock, " 'Every Creature.' " Whether there is a reference here to the "woes" of the messianic times is debatable. The idea of *ḥeblô šel māšîaḥ,* "woes of the Messiah," is known from later rabbinic literature (Str-B 1.950), but whether it was current in the first century or known to Paul is hard to say.

23. *Not only that, but we ourselves.* This contrasting phrase makes it clear that Paul has been speaking of material creation in the preceding verses. Not only

material creation bears testimony to the Christian destiny, but Christians themselves do so by the *hope* that they have, a hope based on the gift of the holy Spirit already possessed, to be treated more explicitly in vv 24–25.

though we have the Spirit as the firstfruits. Lit., "the firstfruits of the Spirit," the gen. being appositional so that it refers to the work of the Spirit in us, i.e., the foretaste of glory. As in 8:9b, Christians "have" the Spirit, i.e., they possess it as an indwelling gift poured into their hearts (5:5).

The Spirit is compared with *aparchē*, "firstfruits" of the harvest, the flawless first part of harvested food, vegetables, and fruit that, when offered to God, were considered dedicated and holy, and thus betokened the consecration of the whole harvest, which could then be put to the use of Israel (Lev 22:12; 23:15–21). But "firstfruits" was often used in the sense of "earnest money," a guarantee of what was to come, like *arrabōn*, 2 Cor 1:22; 5:5 (cf. G. Delling, *TDNT* 1.486; A. Sand, *EDNT* 1.116–17). In this sense Paul understands the Spirit as the "firstfruits" of the glory that is the Christian destiny. The Spirit, which has been received, is thus the guarantee or pledge of the glory assured for Christians. Though thus assured, they still have to wait, as long as they are alive "in the flesh," for the full payment. See 11:16; 1 Cor 15:20–23 (cf. Num 15:18–21; Exod 23:19; 25:2–3; 36:6; Lev 19:23–25; Deut 12:6, 11, 17; 18:4; 26:2–10).

On *aparchē*, compare Arrian, *Cynegeticus* 33.1; Theopompos, 115 (fragment 334); Cornutus, 28 (p. 55/9); Aelius Aristides, 45 (p. 136D); Porphyry, *De Abstinentia* 2.61. Cf. H. S. Jones, *JTS* 23 (1922): 282–83; R. Taubenschlag, *Opera minora* 2 (1959), 220–21; Oke, "A Suggestion."

are groaning inwardly. Lit., "and we too groan in ourselves." The prep. phrase *en heautois* could mean "within us" or "with reference to ourselves." The nuance would differ slightly, but it would mean in expectation of the glorious destiny awaiting Christians. The "groaning" expresses the association of them with the groaning of physical creation; it is, in reality, but another way of expressing the "sufferings" of 8:18.

as we wait for the redemption of our bodies. I.e., the physical aspect of human existence that now shares in the "bondage of decay" will be "redeemed" from that condition and share in the glory awaited. Paul does not mean that Christians long for the liberation of their bodies from corporeality, but refers to the liberation from "this doomed body" or "this body of *death*" (7:24), in which they presently live. That body of death has to give way to the "spiritual body" of risen life: "when the perishable puts on the imperishable, and the mortal puts on immortality" (1 Cor 15:54). It is also possible that *sōma* here is being used only in the sense of "self." On "redemption," see the NOTE on 3:24 and Introduction, section IX.B.

The transmission of the Greek text of this verse is problematic. MSS P[46], D, F, G, and 614 omit the noun *huiothesian*, "adoptive sonship." Although it is difficult to explain how it got into the text of most of the other Greek MSS, it is preferably omitted. Christians are already adopted children of God (8:15), made so by the Spirit already received. With such "firstfruits" or guarantee, they look forward to the full share of glory, the redemption of the body. However, *huiotheian* is retained in the critical texts of N-A[26], Merk, and UBSGNT[3] as the *lectio difficilior*, and is preferred by Swetnam ("On Romans"). If retained, it would then mean, "as we wait for adoptive sonship, the redemption of our bodies," and Paul would then be referring to a phase of adoptive sonship still to be revealed: though we are already children of God, our full status of sonship has not yet been made manifest. One could also translate v 23, as does Swetnam, "We groan inwardly, *arriving at sonship by inference, as the redemption of our body*" (106). But cf. Benoit, " 'We Too Groan Inwardly . . .' "; De la Calle Flores, "La 'huiothesian.' "

BIBLIOGRAPHY

Balz, H. R., *Heilsvertrauen und Welterfahrung: Strukturen der paulinischen Eschatologie nach Römer 8,18–39*, BEvT 59 (Munich: Kaiser, 1971).

Bartnicki, R., "Współczesna a patrystyczna interpretacja Rz 8, 19," *STV* 16.1 (1978): 49–65.

Beker, J. C., "Suffering and Triumph in Paul's Letter to the Romans," *HBT* 7.2 (1985): 105–19.

Benoit, P., " 'We Too Groan Inwardly as We Wait for Our Bodies to Be Set Free,' Romans 8:23," *Jesus and the Gospel*, vol. 2 (London: Darton, Longman & Todd; New York: Seabury, 1974), 40–50.

Bertram, G., "*Apokaradokia*," ZNW 49 (1958): 264–70.

Biedermann, H. M., *Die Erlösung der Schöpfung beim Apostel Paulus: Ein Beitrag zur Erklärung der religionsgeschichtlichen Stellung der paulinischen Erlösungslehre*, Cassiciacum 8 (Würzburg: Rita-Verlag, 1940).

Bindemann, W., *Die Hoffnung der Schöpfung: Römer 8,18–27 und die Frage einer Theologie der Befreiung von Mensch und Natur*, Neukirchener Studienbücher 14 (Neukirchen-Vluyn: Neukirchener-Verlag, 1983).

Blair, H. A., "Romans 8,22f., and Some Pagan African Intuitions," *SE IV*, TU 102 (1968), 377–81.

Brinkman, B. R., *Creation and Creature: Some New Testament Texts and Tendencies* (Chipping Norton, UK: Heythrop College, 1958; = *Bijdragen* 18 [1957]: 129–39, 359–74).

Bultmann, R., "Römer 8, 18–27," *Marburger Predigten*, 60–70.

Calle Flores, F. de la, "La esperanza de la creación, según el apóstol Pablo (Rom 8, 18–22)," *La esperanza en la Biblia: XXX semana bíblica española (Madrid, 21–25 sept. 1970)* (Madrid: [Librería científica Medinaceli], 1972), 169–86.

———, "La 'huiothesian' de Rom. 8,23," *EstBíb* 30 (1971): 77–98.

Christoffersson, O., *The Earnest Expectation of the Creature: The Flood-Tradition as Matrix of Romans 8:18–27* (Stockholm: Almqvist & Wiksell, 1990).

———, "På jakt efter den rätta bakgrunden till Rom 8:18ff," *SEA* 50 (1985): 135–43.

Collison, J. G. F., "Biblical Perspectives on Stewardship of Earth's Resources," *Bangalore Theological Forum* 18 (1986): 153–60.

Colunga, A., "El cielo nuevo y la tierra nueva," *Géneros literarios en los evangelios, Otros estudios: XVII semana bíblica española (24–28 sept. 1956)* (Madrid: Librería científica Medinaceli, 1958), 293–302.

Cranfield, C. E. B., "Some Observations on Romans 8:19–21," *Reconciliation and Hope: New Testament Essays on Atonement and Eschatology Presented to L. L. Morris . . .*, ed. R. Banks (Grand Rapids, Mich.: Eerdmans, 1974), 224–30; repr. in *The Bible and Christian Life* (Edinburgh: Clark, 1985), 94–104.

Cullmann, O., "La Délivrance anticipée du corps humain d'après le Nouveau Testament," *Hommage et reconnaissance: Recueil de travaux publiés à l'occasion du soixantième anniversaire de Karl Barth*, Cahiers théologiques, hors série 2 (Neuchâtel: Delachaux & Niestlé, 1946), 31–40.

Debrunner, A., "Über einige Lesarten der Chester Beatty Papyri des Neuen Testaments," *ConNeot* 11 (1947): 33–49, esp. 34–35.

Denton, D. R., "*Apokaradokia*," *ZNW* 73 (1982): 138–40.

Dubarle, A.-M., "Le Gémissement des créatures dans l'ordre divin du cosmos (*Rom.* 8, 19–22)," *RSPT* 38 (1954): 445–65.

———, "Lois de l'univers et vie chrétienne: Rm 8,18–23," *AsSeign* 46 (1974): 11–16.

Francis, D., "Terrestrial Realities: Their Liberation," *Jeevadhara* 8 (1978): 148–58.

Gerber, U., "Röm. VIII 18 ff als exegetisches Problem der Dogmatik," *NovT* 8 (1966): 58–81.

Gibbs, J. G., *Creation and Redemption: A Study in Pauline Theology*, NovTSup 26 (Leiden: Brill, 1971), 34–47.

Gieraths, H. K., "Knechtschaft und Freiheit der Schöpfung: Eine historisch-exegetische Untersuchung zu Röm 8,19–22," Ph.D. diss., Universität Bonn, 1950.

Goguel, M., "Le Caractère et le rôle de l'élément cosmologique dans la sotériologie paulinienne," *RHPR* 15 (1935): 335–59.

Hall, J., "Christian Redemption: Human Fulfillment," *Worship* 39 (1965): 551–58.

Hill, E., "The Construction of Three Passages from St. Paul," *CBQ* 23 (1961): 296–301.

Hommel, H., "Das Harren der Kreatur," *Theologia viatorum»* 4 (1952): 108–24; repr. in *Schöpfer und Erhalter: Studien zum Problem Christentum und Antike* (Berlin: Lettner, 1956), 7–22; repr. in *Sebasmata*, 2 vols. (Tübingen: Mohr [Siebeck], 1983–84), 2.127–40.

Käsemann, E., *Perspectives*, 122–37.

Kehnscherper, G., "Romans 8:19—On Pauline Belief and Creation," *Studia Biblica 1978: Sixth International Congress on Biblical Studies, Oxford 3–7 April 1978*, 3 vols., JSNTSup 2–3, 11, ed. E. A. Livingstone (Sheffield, UK: JSOT, 1979–80), 3.233–43.

Köster, F., "Sendschreiben an die Herren Consistorialräthe D. Reiche in Göttingen und D. Meyer in Hannover über die seufzende Creatur, Röm. 8,18–28," *TSK* 35.2 (1862): 755–64.

Lambrecht, J., "The Groaning Creation: A Study of Rom 8:18–30," *LS* 15 (1990): 3–18; cf. *Collationes* 19 (1989): 292–310.

————, "Present World and Christian Hope: A Consideration of Rom. 8: 18–30," *Jeevadhara* 8 (1978): 29–39.

Lampe, G. W. H., "The New Testament Doctrine of *Ktisis*," *SJT* 17 (1964): 449–62.

Lewis, E., "A Christian Theodicy: An Exposition of Romans 8:18–39," *Int* 11 (1957): 405–20.

Lyonnet, S., "Redemptio 'cosmica' secundum Rom 8,19–23," *VD* 44 (1966): 225–42; repr. (French) in *Études*, 242–54.

————, "La Rédemption de l'univers," *LumVie* 9.48 (1960): 43–62.

Mack, [M. J.], "Ueber das Elend, die Sehnsucht und die Hoffnung der Creatur: Erklärung der Stelle im Briefe Pauli an die Römer Cap. VIII. V. 16–25," *TQ* 15 (1833): 601–38.

Mackenzie, G., " 'The Earnest Expectation of the Creature,' " *ExpTim* 5 (1893–94): 333–34.

Menezes, F., "Christian Hope of Glory, Rom 8:18–30," *Bible Bhashyam* 5 (1979): 208–25.

Montgomery Hitchcock, F. R., " 'Every Creature,' Not 'All Creation,' in Romans viii. 22," *Expos* 8.11 (1916): 372–83.

Moore, B., "Suffering: A Study on Romans 8:19–30," *Pulpit and People: Essays in Honour of William Still on His 75th Birthday*, ed. N. M. de S. Cameron and S. E. Ferguson (Edinburgh: Rutherford House, 1986), 141–48.

Nicolau, M., " 'Toda la creación gime y esté con dolores de parto hasta el presente' (*Rom.* 8, 22)," *Salmanticensis* 20 (1973): 643–54.

Obeng, E. A., "An Exegetical Study of Rom. 8:26 and Its Implication for the Church of Africa," *DBM* 18 (1989): 88–98.

Ogara, F., " 'Exspectatio creaturae revelationem filiorum Dei exspectat' (Rom. 8,18–23)," *VD* 18 (1938): 193–201.

Oke, C. C., "A Suggestion with Regard to Romans 8:23," *Int* 11 (1957): 455–60.

Petrausch, J., "An Analysis of Romans viii,19–22," *IER* 105 (1966): 314–23.

Philip, G., "Creation Waiting for Redemption: An Expository Study of Romans viii. 19–22," *ExpTim* 5 (1893–94): 315–19, 415–16, 509–12.

Potter, R., " 'The Expectation of the Creature,' " *Scr* 4 (1949–51): 256–62.

Rhijn, C. H. van, "Rom. VIII, 23," *ThStud* 23 (1905): 377–78.

Rimbach, J. A., " 'All Creation Groans': Theology/Ecology in St. Paul," *AsJT* (Singapore) 1 (1987): 379–91.

Rische, J. H., *"Waiting in Hope," an Exegetical Study of Romans 8:19–22* (St. Louis, Mo.: Concordia Seminary, 1970).

Rupprecht, J. M., "Betrachtung der Stelle Röm. 8, 18–23: Mit besonderer Rücksicht auf die Erklärung derselben von Prof. Zyro," *TSK* 24.1 (1851): 214–36.

Schläger, G., "Das ängstliche Harren der Kreatur," *NorTT* 19 (1930): 353–60.

Schlier, H., "Das, worauf alles wartet: Eine Auslegung von Römer 8,18–30,"

Interpretation der Welt: Festschrift für Romano Guardini . . . , ed. H. Kuhn et al. (Würzburg: Echter-Verlag, 1965), 599–616; repr. in *Das Ende der Zeit,* 250–70.

Schwantes, H., *Schöpfung der Endzeit,* Arbeiten zur Theologie 1.12 (Stuttgart: Calwer-Verlag, 1962), 43–52.

Scott, R., "The Earnest Expectation of the Creature: Romans viii. 19," *ExpTim* 5 (1893–94): 265.

Sisti, A., "La speranza della gloria (Rom. 8, 18–23)," *BeO* 10 (1968): 123–34.

Stacey, W. D., "God's Purpose in Creation—Romans viii. 22–23," *ExpTim* 69 (1957–58): 178–81.

Stanley, D. M., *Christ's Resurrection,* 192–95.

Swetnam, J., "On Romans 8,23 and the 'Expectation of Sonship,' " *Bib* 48 (1967): 102–8.

Viard, A., "Expectatio creaturae (Rom., viii, 19–22)," *RB* 59 (1952): 337–54.

Vögtle, A., *Das Neue Testament und die Zukunft des Kosmos* (Düsseldorf: Patmos, 1970), 183–208.

———, "Röm 8,19–22: Eine schöpfungstheologische oder anthropologisch-soteriologische Aussage?" *Mélanges bibliques* . . . *Béda Rigaux* (Gembloux: Duculot, 1970), 351–66.

Whitehouse, W. F., *The Redemption of the Body, Being an Examination of Romans VIII. 18–23* (London: Stock, 1892).

Wolter, M., "Der Apostel und seine Gemeinden als Teilhaber am Leidensgeschick Jesu Christi: Beobachtungen zur paulinischen Leidenstheologie," *NTS* 36 (1990): 535–57.

Wulf, F., "Von der Sehnsucht des Christen," *GLeb* 44 (1971): 391–94.

Zahn, T., "Die seufzende Creatur, Röm. 8, 18–23 mit Rücksicht auf neuere Auffassungen," *JDTh* 10 (1865): 511–42.

Zyro, [F. F.], "Neue Erklärung von Röm. 8, 18–25," *TSK* 18.1 (1845): 103–16.

———, "Neue Erörterung der Stelle Röm. 8, 18–25," *TSK* 24.2 (1851): 645–66.

27. THE FACT OF CHRISTIAN HOPE (8:24–25)

8 [24]For in hope we have been saved. But a hope that is seen is no hope at all. Who hopes for what he sees? [25]But if we hope for what we do not see, we wait for it with endurance.

COMMENT

The second thing that testifies to the new life that justified Christians live in the power of the Spirit is the fact of Christian hope. Perhaps it seems like a strange argument, but Paul knows that Christians justified by faith and baptized into Christ live in hope of the eternal salvation already achieved for them by Christ

Jesus. In 1 Thess 4:13c he wrote about those "who have no hope," i.e., pagans whose whole orientation is to this world. Christians are not like that, so he can cite the fact that Christians hope as another argument to bolster up his description of the new life lived by Christians in union with Christ. If Christians have "hope," it must be founded on something, and that is the sign of adoptive sonship. This hope gives Christians the vitality to endure the sufferings that lead to glory.

This argument furthers the idea of the "hope" expressed in vv 20 and 23. In v 20 Paul spoke of physical creation being subjected to frustration "with hope." In v 23 he also spoke of Christians "groaning" along with the groaning of frustrated material creation. That Christian groaning and waiting were rooted in hope. Now he picks up the argument of hope explicitly and uses it as a further testimony to the status of Christians who live in the Spirit. Hope is had with reference to what is not seen, what is not in sight. The destiny for which Christians groan is as yet unseen; so they live in hope for what is unseen and eternal (2 Cor 4:18).

Paul recasts his thinking about the difference between the two aeons, the reign of sin and death, and the reign of the Spirit. Christians may still be in the former aeon in a sense, as may be manifest in the sufferings they still undergo, but they also experience in faith the longing for the glory that is to be. This longing manifests itself in Christian hope.

NOTES

8:24. *in hope we have been saved.* Although Paul usually speaks of salvation as eschatological, as something still awaited (see 5:9, 10; 9:27; 10:1, 9, 10, 13; 11:11, 14, 26; 13:11; 1 Thess 2:16; 5:9; Phil 2:12; 1 Cor 3:15; 5:5; 7:16; 9:22; 10:33), he now casts his expression in the past tense, using the aor. pass. *esōthēmen*, "we have been saved." Thus salvation is recognized as an effect of the Christ-event, already achieved (*ephapax*, 6:4); but the aorist may also be gnomic, expressing a general truth (BDF §333). But he adds to it a dative of manner, "in/by hope" (BDF §198.4), thus preserving an eschatological nuance, for "salvation" is not yet fully attained. Thus Paul combines the two aspects of salvation: "we are saved," because of what Christ Jesus has already done for humanity, but we still await the full achievement of that status. See 1 Thess 1:3: "the steadfastness of hope in our Lord Jesus Christ."

a hope that is seen is no hope at all. If the object of hope is within sight, it ceases to be an object of hope. Paul argues from the very nature of "hope."

Who hopes for what he sees? See 2 Cor 4:18, "we look not for the things that are seen, but for things that are unseen." The preferred reading of this poorly transmitted text is *ho gar blepei tís elpizei* (P⁴⁶, B*, 1739, 1908), translated in the lemma. Other MSS (D, G) read *ho gar blepei tis, tí kai elpizei*, "for how can anyone even hope for what he sees." In the long run the sense is little affected. Instead of *elpizei*, some MSS (ℵ*, A, 1739ᵐᵍ) and Syriac and Coptic versions read *hypomenei,* "for who waits patiently for what he sees?" (see BDF §442.14). Cf. *TCGNT,* 517–18.

25. *if we hope for what we do not see.* Cf. 2 Cor 5:7, "we walk by faith, not by sight." Paul realizes that Christian hope is based on faith itself. See also Heb 11:1. "The faith and hope of the Christian reach forward toward that which lies beyond the veil, toward that which does not yet appear" (Nygren, *Romans,* 334–35).

we wait for it with endurance. See Gal 5:5, "through the Spirit, by faith, we wait for the hope of uprightness," i.e., the definitive status of rectitude in the sight of God the Judge. Hope enables Christians then to bear with "the sufferings" they now endure (8:18), but it also makes them witnesses to the world of a lively faith in the resurrection (1 Cor 2:9).

BIBLIOGRAPHY

Broer, I. and J. Werbick (eds.), *"Auf Hoffnung hin sind wir erlöst" (Röm 8,24): Biblische und systematische Beiträge zum Erlösungsverständnis heute,* SBS 128 (Stuttgart: Katholisches Bibelwerk, 1987).

Cambier, J., "L'Espérance et le salut dans Rom. 8, 24," *Message et mission: Recueil commémoratif du Xe anniversaire de la Faculté de Théologie,* Publications de l'Université Lovanium de Kinshasa (Louvain and Paris: Nauwelaerts, 1968), 77–107.

Carrez, M., "La Signification actuelle pour l'histoire du salut du visible et de l'invisible dans la pensée paulinienne," *Oikonomia: Heilsgeschichte als Thema der Theologie: Oscar Cullmann . . . gewidmet,* ed. F. Christ (Hamburg-Bergstedt: Reich, 1967), 109–17.

Lacan, M.-F., " 'Nous sommes sauvés par l'espérance' (*Rom* VIII, 24)," *À la rencontre de Dieu: Mémorial Albert Gelin* (Le Puy: Mappus, 1961), 331–39.

Murphy, J. J., "The Anchor of Hope: Rom viii. 24; Hebrews vi. 19," *Expos* 2.5 (1883): 435–42.

Schlier, H., "Über die Hoffnung," *Besinnung,* 135–45.

Weeda, W. H., "Rm. 8:24a: Want wij zijn in hope zalig geworden," *NThStud* 1 (1918): 169–70.

28. EVEN THE SPIRIT (8:26–27)

8   26Similarly, the Spirit too comes to the aid of our weakness, for we do not know for what we should pray. But the Spirit itself intercedes for us with ineffable sighs. 27Yet he who searches our hearts knows what the mind of the Spirit is, because it intercedes for God's dedicated people in accordance with his will.

COMMENT

The third testimony to the new life and glorious destiny of Christians is borne by the Spirit itself. Human aspirations risk being inefficacious because of the natural weakness of the flesh dominated by sin and subject to death, but the Spirit aids by its intercession, transcending the weak human condition. The Spirit brings it about that Christian prayer is properly presented to the Father. Without the aid of the Spirit, even the prayer of justified and reconciled Christians can fail. Even in their intimate life with God Christians are weak, and as a remedy for this weakness the Spirit intervenes with assistance. In this passage Paul's discussion of the role of the Spirit in Christian life comes to its climax.

Paul mentioned earlier that Christians "groan" together with the groaning material creation (8:23); now he affirms that the Spirit too groans with Christians who have hope and long for the glory of the risen life. It is not that the Spirit itself hopes for such glory, but that it enables Christians by its assistance to formulate the proper prayer of hope. In doing so, the Spirit bears testimony to the status of Christian life and its destiny.

What Paul says about the Spirit in this passage has to be understood not only against the OT background of the quickening influence of God's Spirit in human life (see Isa 32:15–18; 44:3–5; Ezek 36:26–27; Joel 3:1–2), but also in light of the role of the Spirit in human life as understood in the Palestinian Judaism now known from QL. Through God's Spirit the sectarian hopes to be purified of sin: "to cleanse me by your holy Spirit and to bring me near to you by your grace according to the bounty of your loving kindness" (1QH 16:12; cf. 1QS 4:21). The sectarian also acknowledges the help given him by God's Spirit: "I thank you, Lord, for . . . you have shed your holy Spirit upon me that I might not stumble" (1QH 7:6); "I, the Master, know you, my God, by the Spirit that you have given me, and by your holy Spirit I have listened faithfully to your marvellous counsel" (1QH 12:11–12). Through the same Spirit the sectarian recognizes his servant-hood: "I am your servant, and I know by the Spirit that you have given me [that your words are truth] and all your deeds are uprightness" (1QH 13:18–19). But, more to the point, the Qumran sectarian also learns to pray to God through the Spirit: "I know that a human being is not upright apart from you, and I implore you by the Spirit that you have given [to me] to perfect forever your [fa]vors unto [your ser]vant" (1QH 16:11–12).

NOTES

8:26. *the Spirit too comes to the aid of our weakness.* God's Spirit not only makes known to Christians the weakness that they experience but also helps to remedy the condition itself. It brings aid to comfort and strengthen justified human beings, enabling them to make the real boast (in contrast to 3:27). Paul uses the double compound vb. *syn-anti-lambanetai*, "comes to mutual aid," i.e., the Spirit prays along with our feeble utterings in our attempts to commune with God, above all to call upon him as *"Abba,* Father" (8:15).

we do not know for what we should pray. Lit., "for that for which we should pray as is fitting we do not know." Not "do not know how to pray as we ought," as the *RSV* renders it. The human condition vis-à-vis God the Creator and Father of all is recognized by Paul: human beings do not acknowledge his eternal power and divinity; nor do they honor and thank him as they ought (1:20–21). Although Paul initially made this claim of pagans, he would also say the same of justified human beings, who really never come to praise and thank their Creator as they should. "Weakness" is characteristic of the human condition, including the mortality of the body, the tendency of the flesh, all of which creates the problem why human beings do not commune with God as they should. Because of such weakness Christians know not *for what* they should pray or *how* they should pray, as Origen interpreted this verse (*De oratione* 2.1 [GCS 3.299]: *peri tou tina tropon euchesthai dei, kai tina epi tēs euchēs legein pros theon,* concerning in what way one must pray and for what one should address God in prayer). Christians who ask of God only what might seem good for them, yet receive only the contrary, may be said not to know for what they should pray; hence their weakness and need of the Spirit as someone to intercede for them and sustain them lest they lose heart. But the Spirit also makes clear to Christians for what they should pray.

The phrase *katho dei,* lit., "according to what is fitting," is an expression familiar in Stoic philosophy, along with *hōs dei* (see Epictetus, *Dissertationes* 3.23.21).

the Spirit itself intercedes for us with ineffable sighs. Paul recognizes the assistance of the "indwelling Spirit" (8:11) as being that of intercession with the Father on behalf of weak Christians. It pleads their cause with the Father, but it also helps them to formulate their prayer. Paul thus recognizes the Spirit's "ineffable sighs" as the source of all genuine Christian prayer. Such assistance is not limited to the prayer of petition, but would include all manner of communing with God, be it doxology in adoration, blessing, praise, thanksgiving, penitent confession, supplication, or, above all, acknowledgment of God as Father (8:15) and of Jesus as Lord (1 Cor 12:3b). For Paul, genuine Christian prayer is addressed to God the Father, through Christ his Son, in the holy Spirit. Cf. Jude 20, "praying in the holy Spirit"; Eph 6:18, "praying at every moment in the Spirit." See Stendahl, "Paul at Prayer," 156–57.

The idea of "intercession" attributed by Paul to the Spirit (only here in the NT) is based on OT ideas: intercession is ascribed to Abraham (Gen 18:23–33), Moses (Exod 8:8, 12, 28–30), priests (Lev 16:21–22; Num 6:23–27), kings (2 Sam 12:16); prophets (1 Kgs 18:22–40), angels (Tob 12:12; cf. *T. Lev.* 3:5, 6), upright persons in the afterlife (2 Macc 15:12–16; cf. *As. Mos.* 11:14–17). But nowhere in the OT or in pre-Christian Jewish writings does one find the idea of the holy Spirit as an intercessor. It is, then, a Pauline novelty. See Obeng, "The Origins."

Moreover, the *stenagmoi alalētoi,* "ineffable sighs," of the Spirit have nothing to do with *human* sighs in prayer, even those which Paul himself calls *arrēta rhēmata*, "inexpressible words" of some human being in ecstatic rapture (2 Cor 12:4). The "sighs" are those of the Spirit and cannot be expressed in human terms. The "us" designates all Christians, not simply so-called charismatics, for the intercession of the Spirit with ineffable sighs is not to be confused with so-called glossolalia or speaking in tongues (*pace* Origen [*In ep. ad Romanos* 7.6 (PG 14.1120)]; Godet [*Romans*, 2.102]; Käsemann [*Commentary*, 241]; Kühl [*Römer*, 298]; Kuss [*Römerbrief*, 643]; Lietzmann [*An die Römer*, 86]; Zahn [*Römer*, 412–13]). As Cranfield says about Käsemann (*Romans*, 423), "he has offered little in the way of positive argument in support of" such an interpretation.

It is far from clear that Paul means anything like speaking in tongues; he speaks of prayer (blessing God, thanking God), which is not necessarily the same thing. The phenomenon of tongues, however, so often a source of division in the Christian community, is reckoned with by Paul himself, as 1 Cor 14:14–16 makes clear: "If I pray in a tongue, my spirit prays but my mind is unproductive. What then is it? I shall pray with the spirit, and I shall pray with the mind too, since otherwise if you bless (God) with the spirit, how can anyone in the position of an outsider say 'Amen' to your thanksgiving, since the outsider does not know what you are saying?" Paul insists, "In church, I should rather speak five words with my mind, to instruct others too, than ten thousand words in a tongue" (1 Cor 14:19). (Note how in this passage of 1 Corinthians Paul speaks not of "the Spirit," but of "my spirit.")

In genuine Christian prayer, however, "the holy Spirit itself sighs within us, with us, for us, and even over us; thus through his Spirit God himself assists in supporting the needs of his creatures" (Michel, *Brief an die Römer*, 273).

The Greek MSS ℵ², C, K, P, Ψ, 33, 614, the *Koinē* text-tradition, and Latin, Syriac, and Coptic versions add *hyper hymōn*, "for us," whereas MSS ℵ*, A, B, D, F, G, 6, 81, 945, 1506, 1739, and 1881 omit the phrase. It may be a copyist's added phrase.

27. *who searches our hearts.* An OT phrase for God (1 Sam 16:7; 1 Kgs 8:39; 1 Chr 28:9; Pss 7:11; 17:3; 139:1), though the vb. *eraunan* is used in none of the passages in the LXX. See 1 Cor 4:5; Acts 1:24; 15:8; Rev 2:23.

knows what the mind of the Spirit is. No Christian understands this groaning of the Spirit; it is God, the searcher of hearts, who alone understands the "ineffable sighs," the "aspiration" or "striving" (*phronēma*) of the Spirit itself, i.e., the language of Spirit-assisted prayer. See 1 Cor 2:10.

MacRae (*HTR* 73 [1980]: 227–30) understands this verse differently, taking the one "who searches hearts" to refer to the Spirit: "the one who searches hearts [the Spirit] knows what the (human) spirit has [i.e., should have] its mind set on because it is according to (the mind of) God that he intercedes for the saints." This interpretation is not impossible, but is there any evidence elsewhere for the idea of the Spirit as one "who searches hearts"?

because it intercedes for God's dedicated people. Lit., "for the saints." By its intercession the Spirit of God overcomes the weakness of praying Christians, those who are in God's sight "saints," i.e., dedicated to him and his worship. *Hagioi* is a designation for all Christians, not just a special group of them, the beatified or canonized (see the NOTE on 1:7).

Greek MS 33 and a few others read *hēmōn*, "(for) us."

in accordance with his will. Lit., "according to God." It was part of the divine plan of salvation that the Spirit should play such a dynamic role in the aspirations and prayers of Christians and in their longing for glory. That plan is now briefly sketched in vv 28–30.

BIBLIOGRAPHY

Armogathe, J. R., "Gemitibus inenarrabilibus: Note sur *Rom* 8,26," *Augustinianum* 20 (1980): 19–22.

Bieder, W., "Gebetswirklichkeit und Gebetsmöglichkeit bei Paulus: Das Beten des Geistes und das Beten im Geiste," *TZ* 4 (1948): 22–40.

Boyd, R. F., "The Work of the Holy Spirit in Prayer: An Exposition of Romans 8:26,27," *Int* 8 (1954): 35–42.

Cambier, J., "La Prière de l'Esprit, fondement de l'espérance: Rm 8,26–27," *AsSeign* n.s. 47 (1970): 11–17.

Dietzel, A., "Beten im Geist: Eine religionsgeschichtliche Parallele aus den Hodajot zum paulinischen Gebet im Geist," *TZ* 13 (1957): 12–32.

Gaugler, E., "Der Geist und das Gebet der schwachen Gemeinde: Eine Auslegung von Röm. 8, 26–27," *IKZ* 51 (1961): 67–94.

Goedt, M. de, "The Intercession of the Spirit in Christian Prayer (Rom. 8. 26–27)," *Concilium* 79 (1972): 26–38.

Goltz, E. von der, *Das Gebet in der ältesten Christenheit: Eine geschichtliche Untersuchung* (Leipzig: Hinrichs, 1901), 89–122.

Grimm, W., "Ueber die Stelle Röm. 8,26. 27," *ZWT* 26 (1883): 456–60.

Käsemann, E., *Perspectives*, 122–37.

MacRae, G. W., "A Note on Romans 8:26–27," *HTR* 73 (1980): 227–30.

Mitchell, C. C., "The Holy Spirit's Intercessory Ministry," *BSac* 139 (1982): 230–42.

Niederwimmer, K., "Das Gebet des Geistes, Röm. 8,26f.," *TZ* 20 (1964): 252–65.

Obeng, E. A., "An Exegetical Study of Rom. 8:26 and Its Implication for the Church in Africa," *DBM* 18 (1989): 88–98.

———, "The Origins of the Spirit Intercession Motif in Romans 8.26," *NTS* 32 (1986): 621–32.

———, "The Reconciliation of Rom. 8.26f. to New Testament Writings and Themes," *SJT* 39 (1986): 165–74.

———, "The Spirit Intercession Motif in Paul," *ExpTim* 95 (1983–84): 360–64.

O'Brien, P. T., "Romans 8:26, 27: A Revolutionary Approach to Prayer?" *RTR* 46 (1987): 65–73.

Rickards, R. R., "The Translation of *tē astheneia hēmōn* ('in our weakness') in Romans 8.26," *BT* 28 (1977): 247–48.

Schniewind, J., "Das Seufzen des Geistes: Rö. 8, 26. 27," *Nachgelassene Reden und Aufsätze*, ed. E. Kähler (Berlin: Töpelmann, 1952), 81–103.

Stendahl, K., "Paul at Prayer," *Int* 34 (1980): 240–49; repr. *Meanings: The Bible as Document and as Guide* (Philadelphia, Penn.: Fortress, 1984), 151–61.

Vallauri, E., "I gemiti dello Spirito santo (*Rom*. 8,26s.)," *RivB* 27 (1979): 95–113.

Wedderburn, A. J. M., "Romans 8:26—Towards a Theology of Glossolalia?" *SJT* 28 (1975): 369–77.

Zorn, R. "Die Fürbitte im Spätjudentum und im Neuen Testament," Ph.D. diss., Universität Göttingen, 1957.

29. THE CHRISTIAN CALLED AND DESTINED FOR GLORY (8:28–30)

8 [28]We realize that all things work together for the good of those who love God, for those who are called according to his purpose. [29]Those whom he foreknew, he also predestined to be conformed to the image of his Son that he might be the firstborn among many brothers. [30]Those whom he predestined, he also called; those whom he called, he also justified; and those whom he justified, he also glorified.

COMMENT

God not only listens to the ineffable sighs of the Spirit, who assists the praying of Christians, he also listens to them as they pray. Moreover, God sees to it that their very lives, their aspirations, their sufferings, and all that they do contribute to the good of those who pray in this way. Now Paul introduces a formal affirmation of Christian destiny, the basis for the hope that he has discussed in vv 17–27. In 3:23 he had said that without the gospel all human beings have sinned and fall short of the glory of God. Now through the gospel God has not only manifested his uprightness and his salvific power in Christ Jesus, but even reveals how his purpose, his plan of salvation, destines all justified Christians for a share of glory in his presence. All are called in accord with this divine plan of salvation. As this plan works itself out in reality, it orders all things in conformity with it.

Paul may have finished his discussion of the role of the Spirit in Christian life and may be moving on to the place that Christians now play in the salvific plan conceived of old by God the Father. Verse 28 is problematic in that one cannot be sure whether the discussion about the Spirit comes to an end with it. It is certainly a transitional verse to what follows in vv. 29–30. The problem is mainly one of textual criticism, on which see the NOTES.

One encounters in these verses the first mention of "predestination," which Paul will again mention in chap. 9. The combination of the Pauline verses on this topic in these chapters led to a preoccupation with them in the predestinarian controversies of later centuries. What Paul asserts here in this regard is stated from a corporate point of view. He does not have in mind the predestination of individuals (either to glory or to damnation). Such an interpretation of these chapters began with Augustine in his controversy with Pelagians, and it has distracted interpreters of Romans from the main thrust of Paul's discussion in these chapters ever since. Here in chap. 8 it is not his major preoccupation, even though part of Paul's teaching about it is initially formulated as he exposes his thinking on God's salvific plan.

Paul begins by affirming that everything that happens to Christians in earthly life is somehow governed by God's providence. Nothing in this life can harm Christians, whether it be suffering or the attack of hostile evil powers, for all of these things can contribute to the destiny to which Christians are called, and they are now referred to as "those who love God."

NOTES

8:28. *We realize that all things work together for the good of those who love God.* The pron. *panta*, "all things," may refer to the sufferings of vv 17–18, but in all likelihood it includes all of the items mentioned in vv 18–27: sufferings, destiny in glory, the groaning of creation, Christian hope, and perhaps even the Spirit (depending on how the verse is translated). All such factors in Christian life are brought into harmony for those who love God, because they are all elements in the divine plan of salvation. In 5:5, 8 Paul spoke of God's "love" for justified and reconciled human beings; he will speak of it again in v 39. Now he speaks of their love of God, using the same vb. *agapan* (as in 1 Cor 2:9; 8:3; cf. Eph 6:24). In effect, "those who love God" becomes a Pauline definition of a Christian. When he so speaks, he scarcely means that Christians can rest their confidence in themselves in loving God, assured that all that happens to them will work for good. Rather, the reason that all things work for good is not found in Christians themselves, but in God, who takes the initiative and sees that all things will work for good. Michel (*Brief an die Römer*, 275) thinks that Paul, using *oidamen*, "we know, realize," is introducing a traditional Jewish formula, paralleled in *Pss. Sol.* 4:25; 6:6; 10:3; 14:1 ("Faithful is the Lord to those who love him"). To "love God" is an OT idea, first enunciated in the Decalogue (Exod 20:6; Deut 5:10) and often thereafter (e.g., Deut 6:5; 7:9; 10:12; Pss 31:24; 97:10; Sir 1:10; 2:15–16; 47:22). Cf. *1 Enoch* 108:8; Jas 1:12c. "The love of God, which is commanded in Scripture, is nothing less than the response of a man in the totality of his being to the prior love of God. It thus includes the whole of true religion" (Calvin, quoted by Cranfield, *Romans*, 424–25).

"For the good" is also a traditional Jewish expression; cf. Sir 39:25, 27 (*tauta panta tois eusebesin eis agatha,* "For the godly all of these things are for good"). Concretely, it would mean here for the salvation of all, or for their glorification.

The verse, however, is not without its problems. The addition or omission of *ho theos,* "God," as the subj. of the vb. in various MSS has resulted in four different interpretations of this verse:

(1) If *ho theos* is read (as in MSS P⁴⁶, A, B, 81) and the vb. *synergei* is taken intransitively with an indir. obj. ("works together with"), then the verse means "God cooperates in all things (*panta,* adv. acc.) with those who love God." This statement is seen as the realization of God's salvific plan on behalf of those who love him. (P⁴⁶ reads the sg. *pan,* instead of the plural *panta,* read by the rest of the MSS.) For parallels to this use of *synergein,* see Jas 2:22; *T. Reub.* 3:6; *T. Issach.* 3:7; *T. Gad* 4:7. "All things" would refer to sufferings, material creation, and all of the items mentioned at the beginning of this note. This is the meaning preferred by Goodspeed, Huby, Kühl, Lietzmann, and Schlier.

(2) If *ho theos* is read, and the vb. *synergei* is taken transitively with *panta* as the dir. obj., then the verse would mean "God makes all things work together for the good of those who love (him)." This interpretation is preferred by many because the subject of the following verbs is also "God." So Sanday and Headlam (*Romans,* 215); Lagrange (*Romains,* 213–14). But the transitive use of *synergein* is otherwise unknown. The examples from *T. Gad* or *T. Issachar* (see above), which are sometimes cited in this sense, are invalid; and the same has to be said of the alleged instance in Xenophon, *Memorabilia* 3.5.16, *pace* Lagrange.

(3) If *ho theos* is omitted (the better reading, as in MSS ℵ, C, D, G, K, P, 33, 614, 1739, the *Koinē* text-tradition, the Vg, and many patristic writers) and *panta* is taken as the subj. of intransitive *synergei,* then it would mean "all things work together for those who love God." God's purpose and plan are what is really behind all that happens to Christians; he is in control of human history. Although this interpretation is very popular (e.g., Vg, Ambrosiaster, Althaus, Barrett, Cornely, Michel, Sickenberger, Zahn), Lagrange finds it difficult: "Things do not enable human beings really to cooperate in view of salvation, though they can be useful" (ibid.). But it still remains the preferable interpretation.

(4) If *ho theos* is omitted (as above) and *synergei* is again taken as intransitive, but with the Spirit as subject, then "It (the Spirit) works together with all things for those who love God"; so Best, Black, and Wilson. The Spirit has been mentioned in v 27 so that it could be the subject of the vb. *synergei* in this verse; similarly Daniell, who, however, takes the vb. *synergei* as transitive. This reading raises the question of the relation of v 28 to the preceding or the following verses, mentioned in the COMMENT.

In view of the fluctuation in the text tradition, it is not easy to be certain about which interpretation is better. Any one of them would suit the context. The verse, however, seems better related to the following. As translated above, according to interpretation 3, the verse would underscore "the transcendent power of Him who helps us. His power, His authority, is such that all things, even the action of those who are disobedient and set themselves against Him, must subserve His will. To say that all things assist believers is thus—in a *biblical* context—a heightening of the statement that God assists them; for it is to assert not only that He assists them, but also that His help is triumphantly and utterly effective" (Cranfield, *Romans*, 428–29). Compare *Pss. Sol.* 4:25, "May your mercy, Lord, be upon all those who love you." Compare Plato, *Republic* 10.12 §§612e–613a: "Shall we not agree that all that comes from the gods turns out for the best for him who is dear to the gods . . . ? This, then, we must conclude about the just man *(peri tou dikaiou andros)*, that whether he is beset by penury or sickness or any other supposed evil, for him these things will in the end prove good, whether in life or in death."

for those who are called according to his purpose. Lit., "for those called according to a design." *Kata prothesin*, without a personal pron., can only refer to God's eternal plan, described in vv 29–30 from the divine perspective; see 9:11, *hē kat' eklogēn prothesis tou theou.* Some Greek Fathers, however, understood the phrase to refer to the "choice, decision" made by human beings in response to the call of God (so Origen, *In ep. ad Romanos* 7.7 [PG 14.1122]; John Chrysostom, *In ep. ad Romanos* hom. 15.2 [PG 60.541]; Theodoret of Cyrrhus, *Interpretatio ep. ad Romanos* 8.30 [PG 82.141]). But it is instead to be regarded as the divine plan of election conceived in eternity (cf. Eph 1:4) and moving in time to its realization, which will become definitive only in eternity itself, in the realm of glory. So Augustine rightly interpreted it (*Expositio quarundam propositionum ex ep. ad Romanos* 47 [CSEL 84.30]), but the phrase, "called according to (his) purpose," must not be restricted only to such individual Christians as are predestined to glory. Its application to individual predestination stems from the interpretation of Augustine (*De correptione et gratia* 7.14 [PL 44.924–25]; *De praedestinatione sanctorum* 16.32 [PL 44.983–85]). Paul's view is, by contrast, corporate, and the phrase is the complement to "those who love him," i.e., all who have responded to the divine call (see 1:6; 1 Cor 1:2). Human love of God is, then, the result of his initiative, his prevenient call to such love. They are "called" by the gospel and its preachers, but even before that by divine prevenience. Behind the love that justified human beings have for God is God's loving call and prior choice of them, which far surpasses that human love in significance.

Paul uses *prothesis*, "setting forth, presentation," which can also mean "plan, purpose, resolve" (BAGD, 706). It is used here of the projected divine plan of salvation (see 9:11; cf. Eph 1:11; 3:11; 2 Tim 1:9).

Klētoi, "called," is a term Paul often uses for Christians (1:6–7; 1 Cor 1:24). They have been called by God's plan to be followers of Christ his Son and now stand in that vocation.

29. *Those whom he foreknew, he also predestined.* This verse begins the explanation of the preceding. Paul relates that call of human beings by God to a destiny of salvation. He stresses the divine prevenience of the process of salvation, setting it forth in five steps, but his anthropomorphic language should not be too

facilely transposed into the *signa rationis* of later theological systems of predestination. Paul uses, in the first step, *proginōskein*, a cpd. vb. that recurs in 11:2
and reflects the OT use of *yādaʿ*, as in Gen 18:19; Jer 1:5; Amos 3:2; and Ps 1:6,
meaning to "know" as to "know with affection, predilection"; it is not a purely
speculative knowledge but refers not only to God's knowledge prior to the human
love of God, but even to his eternal foreknowledge. Cf. Gal 4:9; especially 1 Cor
8:3, "If one loves God, one is known by him." Compare the similar use of *yādaʿ*
in QL: "Before you created them, you knew all their deeds forever, [for without
you no]thing is made and apart from your will no(thing) is known" (1QH 1:7–8);
"before they were fashioned he knew their deeds" (CD 2:8).

In the second step, he uses *proorizein*, which means "decide beforehand,
predestine" (BAGD, 709a), referring to God's gratuitous election (to the status to
be described in the next phrase); cf. 1 Cor 2:7; Eph 1:5, 11, and see the NOTE on
1:4. Compare the predestination of QL: "From the God of knowledge comes all
that is and will be; before they exist, he has established their entire plan, and
when they come to be as is determined for them, it is according to his glorious
design that they fulfill their task" (1QS 3:15–16). Cf. 1QS 11:10–11, 17–20.

to be conformed to the image of his Son. According to the divine plan,
Christians are destined to reproduce in themselves an image of Christ by a
progressive share in his risen life (see 8:17; Gal 4:4–6; Phil 3:20–21); "all of us,
with unveiled face, are beholding the glory of the Lord (and) being changed into
his likeness from one degree of glory to another" (2 Cor 3:18; cf. 4:4b–6). In other
words, through faith and baptism the sinner becomes a Christian, who bears the
shape or form of God's own Son. Christians are not just adopted children (8:15),
but are being continually transformed or metamorphosed into an *eikōn*, "image,
likeness," of the Son of God. Paul's expression is redundant: conformed to an
image, i.e., to share in the formative image of his Son. This transformation
comes about through the power that enables the Son to subject all things to
himself (1 Cor 15:27, 49). Behind Paul's expression lies the OT idea of human
beings created *katʾ eikona theou*, "according to the image of God" (Gen 1:26–27;
Sir 17:3; Wis 2:23), now adapted to the Son in this salvific process. This clause
and the following make Pauline predestination quite different from that of
Qumran theology.

that he might be the firstborn among many brothers. This clause states God's
purpose in the election of Christians to be conformed to the likeness of his Son.
The transforming power is the "glory" of the risen Christ, which changes
Christians, making them look like Christ and shaping them as members of the
same family. The noun *prōtotokos*, "firstborn," implies Christ's preeminence, but
also the sharing of the status of sonship with numerous Christians. Cf. Col 1:15,
18; Heb 1:6; 2:10; Rev 1:5.

30. *Those whom he predestined, he also called.* So Paul explains v 28b. The
third step is a "call" to faith in the gospel and to baptism into Christ; this is the
beginning of the execution of the plan of salvation history. Paul indulges in

rhetorical climax (see BDF §493.3). Cf. 1 Thess 2:12; 2 Thess 2:13–14. Compare the Qumran idea of qĕrûʾê ʾēl, "those called by God" (1QM 3:2; 4:10–11), or bĕḥîrê ʾēl, "the elect of God" (1QpHab 10:13).

those whom he called, he also justified. The fourth step is the aftermath of the call to faith and baptism: the status of rectitude in God's sight. Again Paul recalls for his readers the basic proposition of the letter. See the NOTES on 2:13; 3:24; 5:1, 9. Cf. 1 Cor 6:11, "You have been washed, you have been sanctified, you have been justified in the name of the Lord Jesus Christ and in the Spirit of our God." Behind the call of God lies his uprightness summoning human beings to rectitude in his sight.

those whom he justified, he also glorified. The fifth step is another effect of the Christ-event: glorification (see Introduction, section IX.B). God's plan, involving his foreknowledge, predestination, call, and justification, is aimed at the term of glorification, at the final destiny for all who put faith in Christ Jesus. Cf. 1 Thess 2:12: "summoning you unto his kingdom and glory." This effect is again spoken of as past: glorification has come to be as an effect of what Christ Jesus suffered for humanity "once and for all" (6:10). Paul speaks of it now in a proleptic sense: but it is the glorification "that is going to be revealed in us" (8:18), guaranteed by divine decision. Lagrange (*Romains*, 217) and Huby (*Romains*, 311) interpret the aor. *edoxasen* as expressing "an anticipation of certitude," echoing Thomas Aquinas's *certitudo futuri*; but Schlier (*Römerbrief*, 273) more rightly understands it not only as a gracious anticipation, but as a present experience. Cf. 2 Cor 3:18, 4:4b–6, which tells of the gradual glorification of the Christian even in this life.

In these last two verses, what is expressed is the absolute sovereignty of God, the transcendence of his goodness, which cannot be subordinated to any of his creatures, or to any of their deeds. In the salvific order of things, God is love, the prevenient love that has its source in him alone; it is not a response, it is an élan (Huby, *Romains*, 313).

BIBLIOGRAPHY

Allo, E.-B., "Encore *Rom.* VIII, 28–30," *RSPT* 13 (1924): 503–5.

———, "Versets 28–30 du chap. VIII *ad Rom.* (La question de la prédestination dans l'ép. aux Romains)," *RSPT* 7 (1913): 263–73.

Bauer, J. B., " '. . . *tois agapōsin ton theon*': Rm 8,28 (I Cor 2,9; I Cor 8,3)," *ZNW* 50 (1959): 106–12.

Black, M., "The Interpretation of Romans viii 28," *Neotestamentica et patristica: Eine Freundesgabe, Herrn Professor Dr. Oscar Cullmann . . . überreicht*, NovTSup 6 (Leiden: Brill, 1962), 166–72.

Blackman, E. C., "A Further Note on Romans viii 28," *ExpTim* 50 (1938–39): 378–79.

Cambier, J., "Dieu veut sauver les élus: Rm 8,28–30," *AsSeign* n.s. 48 (1972): 10–15.

Cassien, [Bp.], "Le Fils et les fils, le frère et les frères," *Paulus-Hellas-Oikumene: An Ecumenical Symposium*, ed. P. I. Bratsiotis (Athens: Student Christian Association of Greece, 1951), 35–43.

Cranfield, C. E. B., "Romans 8.28," *SJT* 19 (1966): 204–15.

Daniell, E. H., "Romans viii. 28," *ExpTim* 61 (1949–50): 59.

Dinkler, E., "Prädestination bei Paulus: Exegetische Bemerkungen zum Römerbrief," *Festschrift für Günther Dehn zum 75. Geburtstag am 18. April 1957 dargebracht* . . . , ed. W. Schneemelcher (Neukirchen-Vluyn: Erziehungsverein, 1957), 81–102; repr. *Signum crucis* (Tübingen: Mohr [Siebeck], 1967), 241–69.

Dobschütz, E. von, "Prädestination," *TSK* 106 (1934–35): 9–19.

Doignon, J., "La Première Exégèse augustinienne de Rm 8,28 et l'unité formulée 'more tulliano' des quatre vertus dans l'amour," *Cristianesimo nella storia* 4 (1983): 285–91.

Durand, A., "Le Christ 'premier-né,' " *RSR* 1 (1910): 56–66.

Evdokimov, P., "L'Amour fou de Dieu (*Rom* 8, 28–30)," *La Bible, chemin de l'unité*, ed. G. Casalis et F. Refoulé (Paris: Cerf, 1967), 55–67.

Fahy, T., "Romans 8:29," *ITQ* 23 (1956): 410–12.

Grayston, K., "The Doctrine of Election in Romans 8,28–30," *SE II*, TU 87 (1964), 574–83.

Griffiths, J. G., "Romans viii. 28," *ExpTim* 49 (1937–38): 474–76.

Guelluy, R., "L'Image du Christ dans le chrétien," *RDT* 8 (1953): 147–51.

Hanson, A. T., *The Image of the Invisible God* (London: SCM, 1982).

Hiebert, D. E., "Romans 8:28–29 and the Assurance of the Believer," *BSac* 148 (1991): 170–83.

Hommel, H., "Denen, die Gotten lieben . . . : Erwägungen zu Römer 8,28," *ZNW* 80 (1989): 126–29.

Jervell, J., *Imago Dei: Gen 1,26f. im Spätjudentum, in der Gnosis und in den paulinischen Briefen*, FRLANT 76 (Göttingen: Vandenhoeck & Ruprecht, 1960), 271–84.

Kürzinger, J., "*Symmorphous tēs eikonos tou huiou autou* (Röm 8,29)," *BZ* 2 (1958): 294-99.

Laetsch, T., "Sermon Study on Rom. 8:29–32," *CTM* 13 (1942): 40–51.

Larsson, E., *Christus als Vorbild: Eine Untersuchung zu den paulinischen Tauf- und Eikontexten*, ASNU 23 (Uppsala: Almqvist & Wiksells, 1962), 293–307.

Leaney, A. R. C., " 'Conformed to the Image of His Son' (Rom. viii. 29)," *NTS* 10 (1963–64): 470–79.

Loane, M. L., *The Hope of Glory: An Exposition of the Eighth Chapter in the Epistle to the Romans* (London: Hodder and Stoughton, 1968).

McCasland, S. V., " 'The Image of God' According to Paul," *JBL* 69 (1950): 85–100.

McFatridge, F. V., "The Called According to His Purpose," *RevExp* 48 (1951): 416–23.

Manz, K. G., "*Synergei eis agathon*," *CTM* 6 (1935): 615.

Mayer, B., *Unter Gottes Heilsratschluss: Prädestinationsaussagen bei Paulus* (Würzburg: Echter, 1974), 136–66.

Michaelis, W., "Die biblische Vorstellung von Christus als dem Erstgeborenen," *ZST* 23 (1954): 137–57.

Osburn, C. D., "The Interpretation of Romans 8:28," *WTJ* 44 (1982): 99–109.

Pack, F., "A Study of Romans 8:28," *ResQ* 22 (1979): 44–53.

Poellot, L., "The Doctrine of Predestination in Rom. 8:28–39," *CTM* 23 (1952): 342–53.

Prat, F., "Terms Referring to Predestination," *Theology* 1.433–37.

Rey, B., *Créés dans le Christ Jésus: La Création nouvelle selon saint Paul* (Paris: Cerf, 1966), 164–80.

Ross, J. M., "Pánta synergeî, Rom. VIII.28," *TZ* 34 (1978): 82–85.

Thüsing, W., *Per Christum in Deum*, 121–34.

Wiederkehr, D., *Theologie der Berufung*, 153–68.

Wilson, J. P., "Romans viii.28: Text and Interpretation," *ExpTim* 60 (1948–49): 110–11.

Wischmeyer, O., "*Theon agapan* bei Paulus: Eine traditionsgeschichtliche Miszelle," *ZNW* 78 (1987): 141–44.

Wood, H. G., "God's Providential Care and Continual Help—Rom. viii. 28," *ExpTim* 69 (1957–58): 292–95.

Wulf, F., " 'Der Erstgeborene unter vielen Brüdern' (Röm 8,32)," *GLeb* 43 (1970): 466–69.

30. Hymn to the Love of God Made Manifest Through Christ Jesus (8:31–39)

8 [31]What then shall we say about this? If God is for us, who can be against us? [32]He who did not spare his own Son, but handed him over for all of us—how will he not give us everything else along with him? [33]Who will bring a charge against God's chosen ones? God himself, who justifies? [34]Who will condemn them? Christ Jesus, who died, or rather who was raised, who is at God's right hand and even intercedes for us? [35]Who will separate us from the love of Christ? Will distress or anguish or persecution or famine or nakedness or danger or the sword? [36]As it stands written, *"For your sake we are being put to death all day long; we are considered as sheep to be slaughtered."* [37]Yet in all of it we are more than victors because of him who loved us. [38]For I am convinced that neither death nor life, neither angels nor principalities, neither the present nor the future, nor any powers, [39]neither height nor depth, nor any other creature will be able to separate us from the love of God, which is in Christ Jesus our Lord.

COMMENT

Having discussed various aspects of the new life in union with Christ and his Spirit and the reasons that provide a basis for Christian hope, Paul concludes part B of the doctrinal section with a rhetorical, even hymnic, passage about the love of God made manifest in Christ Jesus. He has shown that through Christ Christians have been freed from sin and death, self, and the law, from those forces in life which tend to drag human beings down and doom them to frustration, even destruction. One after another these forces have been conquered by Christ Jesus, and his gospel has revealed how "The one who is upright shall find life through faith" (1:17). Paul now sums up his discussion in a concluding paragraph, in which he sings of the gift of divine love made known to humanity in Christ Jesus. In a jubilant hymn of praise to the love of God in Christ Jesus, Paul notes how victory has been gained for humanity over all things that might conceivably oppose it.

No little emotional language and rhythmic phrasing mark the paragraph. The "elevated eloquence" (Cranfield, *Romans*, 434) is noteworthy. Barrett and Käsemann relate the passage to the "rhetorical style of diatribe"; others speak of its "poetic beauty" (Dodd, Jülicher, Kühl); and some consider it hymnic (Huby, Leenhardt, Schlier).

In this way, Paul terminates his discussion of what Christ Jesus has done for humanity, attributing it all to the prevenient love of God. He makes it clear that no creature can bring about the separation of the justified Christian from God, so secure is the union of the Christian with Christ because of that love.

The structure of the passage can be seen from the following:

a. 8:31a: Introductory rhetorical question

b. 8:31b–32: God, who is for us, did not spare his Son

c. 8:33–34: God and Christ are on our side

d. 8:35–37: What can separate us from the love of Christ?

e. 8:38–39: Nothing can separate us from the love of God manifest in Christ Jesus.

Lagrange speaks of four strophes, two by two: 31b–32, 33–34 (these base the Christian's confidence on God's plan realized in Christ); 35–37, 38–39 (what can separate us from God's love?).

The setting for the passage is that of a lawcourt, as in Job 1–2 and Zechariah 3, in which a prosecutor accuses a justified Christian. But the Christian does not have to fear a prosecutor: "with the Lord on my side I fear not" (Ps 118:6). Paul develops this aspect of the case against the justified Christian by a series of prosecutor's questions. Often they answer themselves.

Verses 31b–35 emphasize the theocentric and christocentric aspects of salvation and justification. Verse 36 establishes them on the basis of Ps 44:23; verse 37 draws a conclusion, and vv 38–39 explain the cosmic dimension of the struggle. On the parallelism used in the passage, see BDF §490.

The punctuation in vv 33–34 is problematic. Some Greek MSS, which have punctuation, treat all of the clauses as rhetorical questions. Since the time of Augustine, many commentators have taken the sentences as questions (see BDF §496.2). The RSV makes vv 33b and 34b statements, as do Cranfield, Dunn, Huby, Käsemann, Michel, and Wilckens; but Achtemeier, Barrett, Lietzmann, and Schlier take them all as questions, which seems to be the better solution. Cf. Isa 50:8.

This passage is one of the rare places in Romans in which Paul speaks of the scope of God's creative activity, as he indirectly affirms his dominion over the cosmos, with its "height" and "depth," and over the world of spirits, with "angels," "principalities," and "powers." All is summed up in "any other creature" (8:39), as Paul acknowledges that none of them, for their supposed sway over human existence, can separate Christians from the love of God that is made manifest in what he has done for them in Christ Jesus.

NOTES

8:31. *What then shall we say about this?* To the transitional rhetorical question (see the NOTE on 6:1) Paul adds a phrase, *pros tauta*, in which the pron. "this" refers not only to vv 28–30, the immediate context, but also to vv 18–30, if not to chaps. 5–8 as a whole. God's *love*, first mentioned in 5:5, is now seen to be the basis for all that was said in those chapters. His love brings it about that a Christian lives such a new life in Christ.

If God is for us, who can be against us? Paul's phraseology evokes a law-court setting. Indeed, his question answers itself. God himself has come to the aid of Christians and manifested his love on behalf of them. No one, then, can undo that. An answer like "No one" would be too weak. All of the Pauline emphasis falls on the idea of "God for us." *Ho theos* is clearly the one God of Israel, not just "some god." According to Käsemann (*Commentary*, 247), Paul is referring not to "a concept of God" but to "the saving act centered in the death of Jesus, [which] characterizes God for us." Yes, but centered in the death and resurrection of Christ. Thus it pleased God to "save those who believe" (1 Cor 1:21). This makes him *theos hyper hēmōn*, "God for us." With God on our side, the forces that are marshaled against us amount to nothing. They cannot prevail; they too can only work for our good.

32. *He who did not spare his own Son.* See 5:8; 8:3. So Paul emphasizes the aspect of "God for us"; he expresses it negatively in order to bring out the divine concern. God gave the best that he could, "his own Son," and in this way we were bought "at a price" (1 Cor 6:20). Recall John 3:16, "God so loved the world that he gave his only Son so that everyone who would believe in him might not

perish, but have life eternal." The phrase *tou idiou huiou* designates Jesus as Son of God in the proper, and not in the adoptive, sense. In not sparing his own son, God the judge has thus already pronounced sentence in favor of Christians, his adopted children; hence there is no reason to expect anything different from him hereafter.

Most Greek MSS read *hos ge* (which is emphatic, "he who" or "the same one who," even with a causal nuance, "seeing that he"; see BDF §439.3; A. W. Argyle, *JTS* 4 [1953]: 214–15); but MSS D, F, and G read *hos oude tou idiou huiou*, "who did not spare even his own Son."

Ever since Origen (*In Genesim hom.* 8 [PG 12.208]), an allusion has been seen here to Gen 22:16, Abraham not sparing to sacrifice Isaac, his only son (the Greek of which uses the same vb., *ouk epheisō tou huiou sou tou agapētou di' eme*). See further Irenaeus, *Adversus haereses* 4.5.4. Käsemann refers to it as "the typological prototype of Abraham" (*Commentary*, 247), but considers the allusion to be "possible," yet "hardly certain." Barrett (*Romans*, 172): Paul "makes no serious use of it." Cranfield, however, calls it an "intentional echo" (*Romans*, 208); Moo (*Romans*, 582): a "probable" allusion; Wilckens (*Römer*, 2.172): "it cannot be contested"; Dahl ("The Atonement," 16): "the allusion is unambiguous"; similarly, Dunn, Lyonnet, Michel, Ridderbos, and Zahn. Other commentators, however, do not even mention the allusion (Huby, Lagrange, Lietzmann, Nygren); still others are not convinced at all (Kuss, Schlier).

A reason for hesitating about the allusion is that the same verb is also found in the LXX of 2 Sam 18:5 (*pheisasthe moi tou paidariou tou Abessalom*, "spare me the young boy Absalom"), in David's instruction to commanders who led his troops against Absalom. But the real problem is whether Jewish teaching about the ʿAqēdāh (lit., the "binding" [of Isaac]) was already understood with a vicarious soteriological connotation in pre-Christian Judaism. Was Isaac ever seen as a prototype of the Messiah? Of a Messiah who suffered vicariously for his people?

There is, indeed, reference to the sacrifice of Abraham (Genesis 22) in 4 Macc 7:14, but there is no mention of the vicarious, soteriological, or expiatory understanding of that sacrifice. The same has to be said about 4 Macc 13:12; 16:20; 18:11; *Jub.* 17:15–18:19. *Pace* Swetnam (*Jesus and Isaac*, 10), Isaac in 4 Maccabees is not "implicitly the model for a martyr's death offered in atonement for the sins of Israel." Where in the texts is there such an atoning implication? Moreover, even Josephus's recasting of the Genesis story (*Ant.* 1.13.1–4 §§222–36) includes no such understanding of the sacrifice that Abraham was willing to make. Nor do we find it in Philo, *De Abr.* 35 §198, *pace* Hayward ("Present State," 137 n. 57); nor in Pseudo-Philo, *Liber antiquitatum biblicarum* 18:6; 32:2–4; 40:2. These texts do present Abraham's willingness to offer his son in sacrifice, at times even to admit that he was "to be sacrificed for piety's sake" (4 Macc 13:12); and that God rewarded Abraham. But the vicarious aspect of it, that Isaac was to be sacrificed on behalf of Israel or on behalf of someone else, is never mentioned. It should be obvious that, even if a martyrdom motif were at times associated with the sacrifice, it would still not be vicarious. But that vicarious connotation of the ʿAqēdāh has yet to be shown to be pre-Christian. Segal ("He Who Did Not Spare," 183) has finally put the matter in proper perspective, writing, "The amoraic traditions of the death and ashes of Isaac and his subsequent resurrection can be reasonably understood as an attempt to enrich Judaism with a figure that was as colourful as the one known to Christian exegesis." That amoraic tradition dates from roughly A.D. 200 to 500. The vicarious soteriological understanding of the ʿAqēdāh emerged in rabbinical writings of later centuries: *Gen. Rabbah* 56:8–10; *Pirqe de Rabbi Eliezer* 31; *Tg. Neofiti I*, Gen 22:14. Hence Abraham's willingness to sacrifice vicariously his only son is hardly an idea that Paul might have known in his Jewish past and thus alluded to. As the Pauline allusion is not clear, there can be no certainty about it. Allusion to Abraham's sacrifice in Christian literature is found as early as *Barn.* 7:3, where it is already expressed in a comparison with Christ. Cf. Ps.- Tertullian, *Adversus Iudaeos* 10:6 (CCLat 2.1376). See also Levi, "Le Sacrifice d'Isaac"; Spiegel, *The Last Trial*; Vermes, *Scripture and Tradition*; Daly, "The Soteriological Significance"; Davies and Chilton, "The Aqedah" (the "conception is post-Tannaitic").

handed him over for all of us. The clause, expressing the vicarious character of Jesus' death, is probably traditional, taken over by Paul from primitive catechesis (4:25); it might even be a liturgical or baptismal confessional statement, even though nothing clearly so marks it. In any case, Paul attributes to the Father the initiative for the salvific plan realized in the death (and resurrection) of Christ Jesus and the vicarious effect of it all. Compare the LXX of Isa 53:6, 12, whence the terminology of the vicarious handing over is derived. Paul has already used the vb. *paradidonai* in 4:25 in the same sense (cf. Gal 2:20); but it has a different nuance, "hand over" to degradation (cf. 1 Cor 5:5), in 1:24, 26, 28 (see the NOTE on 1:24), and still another nuance ("hand over" to another master) in 6:17. But it is also the verb that he uses to "pass on" a tradition (1 Cor 11:2, 23; 15:3).

how will he not give us everything else along with him? Anacoluthon invades the argument. The rhetorical question emphasizes the eschatological character of God's gracious act: will he not, then, grace us in all things along with Christ? *Ta panta* is not more narrowly specified; but it must refer to everything pertaining to eschatological salvation. Christian destiny is again expressed as *syn autō*, "with him." Cf. Heb 7:25.

33. *Who will bring a charge against God's chosen ones?* I.e., who will impeach those who are God's elect? Again the rhetorical question implies the answer, "No one." The vb. *enkalesei* is a forensic term (see Sir 46:19; Wis 12:12). There may be an allusion to Isa 50:8–9, "He who vindicates me is at hand; who is it that prosecutes me?" (*engizei ho dikaiōsas me. tís ho krinomenos moi?*). This is part of Servant Song III (50:4–11), where the author, using juridical language, depicts the Servant expressing confidence in God as his vindicator. Paul applies the allusion to God's "elect" (*eklektoi*), the "called" of vv 28, 30. According to

Barrett (*Romans*, 173), "Satan must be meant" as the accuser, in a reference to the last judgment. But this reading misses the point of Paul's rhetoric, as Käsemann (*Commentary*, 248) rightly recognizes. The implication is that no one can bring a charge against the Christian so defended by God.

God himself, who justifies? I.e., the God who vindicates the Christian who puts his faith in Christ Jesus. Again, the rhetorical question implies, "No." If the phrase were punctuated as a statement, then the answer would be ironic. The justifying God and God the judge would be the same.

34. *Who will condemn them?* Lit., "who is the one to condemn?" The ptc. *ho katakrinōn* could be either present or future. The logic of the rhetoric seems to call for the fut. ptc. (see BDF §251.2), as the argument moves forward (from charge to condemnation). Cf. Job 34:29; 1 Pet 3:13.

Christ Jesus, who died? The rhetorical question again answers itself. The argument moves from God to Christ. The one to condemn us cannot be the Christ who assumed human form "for the sake of sin" (8:3), who offered himself in death for our sake (4:25), and who now intercedes for us with the Father.

rather who was raised, who is at God's right hand and even intercedes for us? Attention is shifted from the death of Christ to his resurrection (see 4:24–25), to which Paul adds a rare reference to Christ's exaltation (without mentioning the ascension). He thus alludes to the operative phases of the objective redemption: death, resurrection, exaltation, heavenly intercession. On "was raised," see the NOTE on 4:25. For the OT anthropomorphism of God's right hand, see Ps 110:1; Isa 63:10; *Ps. Sol.* 13:1. In the OT it is an image that expresses enthronement and majestic power. Implicitly it refers to Christ's exaltation (see Phil 2:9). Cf. Acts 2:33; 5:31; Col 3:1.

The risen, exalted Christ still presents his supplication to the Father on behalf of the Christian elect. So not only the Spirit intercedes for Christians (8:26–27), but also the heavenly Christ. Cf. 1 John 2:1, where Christ is depicted as the Paraclete; Eph 1:20. Such an exalted intercessor cannot assume the role of an accuser or one who will condemn us.

In Heb 7:25 and 9:24 this intercession is linked with Christ's priesthood, a notion not found in Pauline writings. Cranfield (*Romans*, 439) quotes Pelagius, who conflates the two ideas: Christ "as true and eternal high priest, intercedes as he continually shows and offers that human nature which he assumed as a pledge to his Father" (*Expositio in Romanos* [ed. A. Souter, 70]).

MSS ℵ*, A, C, Ψ, 33, 81 and Coptic and Ethiopic versions add *ek nekrōn*, "from the dead," but that is almost certainly a copyist's explanatory addition. The shorter reading is found in MSS P27.46, ℵ2, B, D, G, K, 1739 and the *Koinē* text-tradition.

35. *Who will separate us from the love of Christ?* The gen. *Christou* is subjective, i.e., the love that Christ has for us, as vv 37 and 39 make clear. All that Christ has done for us stems from his love of us. Nothing can separate Christians from Christ who has manifested such love for them. Cf. 2 Cor 5:14–

15 and Gal 2:20 for other statements about Christ's love, i.e, his self-surrender on behalf of humanity. The argument moves from the idea of an accuser to a divider, someone or something that would try to sever the link between Christians and Christ.

The reading *theou tēs en Christō Iēsou*, "(the love) of God that is in Christ Jesus," read by MS B and Origen, is almost certainly a copyist's harmonization with v 39, as is the simple *theou* (instead of *Christou*) in MSS ℵ, 326, 330 and the Sahidic version. *Christou* is found in MSS A, C, D, G, K, Ψ, 33, 614, 1241, 1739, and the *Koinē* text-tradition.

Will distress or anguish or persecution or famine or nakedness or danger or the sword? None of the dangers or troubles of earthly life can make the true Christian forget the love that Christ has made known in his death and resurrection. For similar lists of troubles in human life, see 1 Chr 21:12; 2 Chr 20:9; 32:11. The "sufferings" of 8:18 are thus detailed (cf. 5:3; 2 Cor 11:26–27; 12:10). They may be part of the human condition: "for you yourselves know that this is our lot" (1 Thess 3:3). But they are nothing in comparison with the glory that is the destiny of Christians called to be "with the Lord" (1 Thess 4:17).

36. *As it stands written.* See the NOTE on 1:17.

For your sake we are being put to death all day long; we are considered as sheep to be slaughtered. Paul quotes Ps 44:23, word for word according to the LXX, save for the introductory conj. *hoti*, which agrees instead with the MT. Psalm 44 is a psalm of community lament, bemoaning the injustice done to faithful Israel by its enemies, recalling its loyalty to Yahweh, and seeking his aid and deliverance, e.g., at the time of the Maccabees. The psalm is cited by Paul to show that the tribulations that Christians encounter are what have always characterized God's people. They are not proof of God's not loving the persecuted; rather, such things are a sign of his love. Hence, nothing that Christians may suffer will separate them from God any more than Israel's suffering as sheep to be slaughtered could separate it from Yahweh's fidelity to it. Cf. 2 Cor 4:10–11.

37. *Yet in all of it we are more than victors.* Lit., "we are supervictors," i.e., victors in court, because we have been vindicated and justified in a superabundant way by what Christ has done for sinful humanity. Cf. 2 Cor 12:9, "My grace is sufficient for you, for power is perfected in infirmity." Because of Christ all of the powers that drag human life down (sin, death, self, law, enmity, and those factors mentioned in v 35) have been overcome; in this sense too Christians have become more than victors.

because of him who loved us. The empowering love of Christ is again emphasized; because of it Christians are more than vindicated. God's election and the love of Christ are the factors that count for Christians in all of their sufferings. The triumph over all such earthly troubles is brought about by the love and grace of Christ.

38. *I am convinced.* Paul adds his personal conviction as the conclusion to the hymn. Cf. 14:14; 15:14.

that neither death nor life. No natural, cataclysmic, or cosmic power or adversary can rupture the union of Christ and the Christian. No extreme can separate. Neither death and its anguish nor life and its dangers or temptations can create such a separation. Paul indulges in rhetorical merismus, expressing the totality of such adverse and threatening opposition by mentioning its extremes. Cf. 1 Cor 3:22.

neither angels or principalities. Spirits probably of different kind, order, or rank, such as both Jews and Gentiles of Paul's day often considered to be cosmic powers or supramundane rulers of this world. Because they are lined up like "death" and "life" or "height" and "depth," which express extremes, it may be that these too are supposed to express extreme kinds or ranks of spirits. The pair *pasa archē kai pasa exousia* occurs also in 1 Cor 15:24, but they are here separated and used in the plural. Cf. the Deutero-Pauline usage in Col 1:16; Eph 1:21; 3:10; 6:12. Whether they are to be understood as good or bad spirits is not clear; in any case such beings, supraterrestrial though they be, will not be able to separate Christians from God's love. Cf. Phil 2:10c. "Historians of culture and religion have been unable to define these powers in detail, give a precise description of their nature and functions, or fix their exact provenance, although Babylonian (astrological), Iranian, and similar elements, mediated through Gnostic systems and reshaped in Jewish apolcalyptic, are recognizable" (K. Weiss, *EDNT* 1.162–63); cf. H. Schlier, *Principalities and Powers in the New Testament,* QD 3 (New York: Herder and Herder, 1964).

neither the present nor the future. I.e., time personified, or the present age with its instability and any future age with its uncertainty. Paul might be thinking of the period of Roman history in which he lived and of what might be imminent.

nor any powers. I.e., probably still other spirits, now designated as *dynameis,* a term used for heavenly beings in some MSS of the LXX of Isa 34:4. Cf. Philo, *De mut. nom.* 8 §59.

The *Koinē* text-tradition, following MSS K, L, and most minuscules, put *dynameis* before *oute enestōta,* "neither the present," thus collocating the "powers" with "angels or principalities" (as in 1 Cor 15:24; Eph 1:21), undoubtedly a copyist's modification of the text.

39. *neither height nor depth.* I.e., cosmic forces. These are probably terms derived from ancient astrology designating the greatest proximity or remoteness of a star from the zenith, by which its influence was supposed to be measured. Even such astrological forces cannot separate Christians from divine love. For *bathos* as an astronomical term, see Vettius Valens (ed. W. Kroll), 241.26; for *hypsōma,* see Plutarch, *Moralia* §§149a, 782e.

nor any other creature. Lit., "any other kind of creature," for Paul uses the adj. *hetera,* not simply *allē,* i.e., any other conceivable being, even invisible or unknown to human beings. The reason for Paul's absolute assurance is that God is on the side of Christians, and divine influence is not affected by created forces. For a similar concluding generalization, see 13:9.

will be able to separate us from the love of God, which is in Christ Jesus our Lord. The love of God poured out in the Christ-event is the basis of Christian life and hope. No created being or force can unsettle that foundation. In all of the uncertainty of human, earthly life there is something fixed and certain, Christ's love and God's election. These are unshakable; and Christians must learn to trust in them and take them for granted. The "love of God which is in Christ Jesus" echoes (perhaps as a sort of *inclusio*) a similar phrase in v 35. The whole ending of the hymn sums up the theme of part B of the doctrinal section: what Christ has done for humanity is a concrete manifestation of God's love. Once again Paul ends the chapter with the refrain noted earlier (see the COMMENT on 5:1–11).

BIBLIOGRAPHY

Argyle, A. W., "Romans 8,32," *JTS* 4 (1953): 214–15.

Baulès, R., "L'Amour souverain de Dieu: Rm 8,31b–34," *AsSeign* 15 (1973): 31–36.

Brock, S., "Genesis 22: Where Was Sarah?" *ExpTim* 96 (1984–85): 14–17.

Caird, G. B., *Principalities and Powers: A Study in Pauline Theology* (Oxford: Clarendon, 1956), 75–79.

Carpus, "Life and Death as Antagonists of Love: Romans viii. 38, 39," *Expos* 1.3 (1876): 119–23.

Dahl, N. A., "The Atonement—An Adequate Reward for the Akedah? (Ro 8: 32)," *Neotestamentica et Semitica: Studies in Honour of Matthew Black*, ed. E. E. Ellis and M. Wilcox (Edinburgh: Clark, 1969), 15–29; repr. *The Crucified Messiah and Other Essays* (Minneapolis, Minn.: Augsburg, 1974), 146–60.

Daly, R. J., "The Soteriological Significance of the Sacrifice of Isaac," *CBQ* 39 (1977): 45–75.

Davies, P. R. and B. D. Chilton, "The Aqedah: A Revised Tradition History," *CBQ* 40 (1978): 514–46.

Delling, G., "Die Entfaltung des 'Deus pro nobis' in Röm 8,31–39," *SNTU* A.4 (1979): 76–96.

Dibelius, M., *Die Geisterwelt im Glauben des Paulus* (Göttingen: Vandenhoeck & Ruprecht, 1909).

Fiedler, P., "Röm 8,31–39 als Brennpunkt paulinischer Frohbotschaft," *ZNW* 68 (1977): 23–34.

Hayward, R., "The Present State of Research into the Targumic Account of the Sacrifice of Isaac," *JJS* 32 (1981): 127–50.

Hengel, M., "Psalm 110 und die Erhöhung des Auferstandenen zur Rechten Gottes," *Anfänge der Christologie: Festschrift für Ferdinand Hahn zum 65. Geburtstag*, ed. C. Breytenbach and H. Paulsen (Göttingen: Vandenhoeck & Ruprecht, 1991), 43–73.

Hickling, C. J. A., "Paul's Reading of Isaiah," *Studia Biblica 1978: Sixth International Congress on Biblical Studies, Oxford 3–7 April 1978*, 3 vols., JSNTSup 2–3, 11, ed. E. A. Livingstone (Sheffield, UK: JSOT, 1979–80), 3.215–23.

Jeffrey, G. J., "The Love of God in Christ—Rom viii. 38, 39," *ExpTim* 69 (1957–58): 359–61.

Le Déaut, R., "La Présentation targumique du sacrifice d'Isaac et la sotériologie paulinienne," *SPCIC* 2.563–74.

Levi, I., "Le Sacrifice d'Isaac et la mort de Jésus," *REJ* 64 (1912): 161–84.

Lilley, J. P., "The Invincible Love," *ExpTim* 5 (1893–94): 518–21.

Lyonnet, S., "L'Amour efficace du Christ: Rm 8,35.37–39," *AsSeign* 49 (1971): 12–16; repr. *Études*, 260–63.

———, "Dieu 'n'a pas épargné son propre Fils, mais l'a livré' (Rom 8,32)," *Études*, 255–59.

Meile, E., "Isaaks Opferung: Eine Note an Nils Alstrup Dahl," *ST* 34 (1980): 111–28.

Münderlein, G., "Interpretation einer Tradition: Bemerkungen zu Röm. 8, 35f." *KD* 11 (1965): 136–42.

Penna, R., "Il motivo dell' ʿaqedah sullo sfondo di Rom. 8,32," *RivB* 33 (1985): 425–60.

Roberts, A., "Interpretation of Romans viii. 33, 34," *Expos* 5.3 (1896): 380–91.

Romaniuk, K., "L'Origine des formules pauliniennes 'Le Christ s'est livré pour nous,' 'Le Christ nous a aimés et s'est livré pour nous,' " *NovT* 5 (1962): 55–76.

Schille, G., "Die Liebe Gottes in Christus: Beobachtungen zu Rm 8,31–39," *ZNW* 59 (1968): 230–44.

Schmidt, K. L., "Die Natur- und Geisteskräfte im paulinischen Erkennen und Glauben," *Eranos-Jahrbuch* 14 (1946): 87–143.

Schnackenburg, R., *Glaubensimpulse aus dem Neuen Testament* (Düsseldorf: Patmos, 1972), 133–38.

Schoeps, H. J., "The Sacrifice of Isaac in Paul's Theology," *JBL* 65 (1946): 385–92; *Paulus: Die Theologie des Apostels im Lichte der jüdischen Religionsgeschichte* (Tübingen: Mohr [Siebeck], 1959), 144–52.

Schwartz, D. R., "Two Pauline Allusions to the Redemptive Mechanism of the Crucifixion," *JBL* 102 (1983): 259–68.

Segal, A. F., " 'He Who Did Not Spare His Own Son . . .': Jesus, Paul and the Akedah," *From Jesus to Paul: Studies in Honour of Francis Wright Beare*, ed. P. Richardson and J. C. Hurd (Waterloo, Ont.: Wilfrid Laurier University, 1984), 169–84.

Simcock, J. M., "Note on Romans viii.39," *Expos* 2.8 (1884): 239–40.

Snyman, A. H., "Style and Meaning in Romans 8:31–9," *Neotestamentica* 18 (1984): 94–103.

———, "Style and the Rhetorical Situation of Romans 8.31–39," *NTS* 34 (1988): 218–31.

Spiegel, S., *The Last Trial* (New York: Random House, 1967).

Swetnam, J., *Jesus and Isaac: A Study of the Epistle to the Hebrews in the Light of the Aqedah*, AnBib 94 (Rome: Biblical Institute, 1981).

Tisdale, L. T., "Romans 8:31–39," *Int* 42 (1988): 68–72.

Vermes, G., *Scripture and Tradition in Judaism*, SPB 4 (Leiden: Brill, 1961), 193–227.

Wengst, K., *Christologische Formeln und Lieder des Urchristentums*, SNT 7 (Gütersloh: Gütersloher Verlagshaus, 1972), 55–56, 61.

Wilcox, M., " 'Upon the Tree'—Deut. 21:22–23 in the New Testament," *JBL* 96 (1977): 85–99, esp. 98–99.

Wink, W., *Naming the Powers* (Philadelphia, Penn.: Fortress, 1984), 47–50.

Wood, J. E., "Isaac Typology in the New Testament," *NTS* 14 (1967–68): 583–89.

Worden, T., "Christ Jesus Who Died or Rather Who Has Been Raised up (Rom. 8:34)," *Scr* 10 (1958): 33–43; 11 (1959): 51–59.

Wulf, E., " 'Er hat seinen Sohn nicht geschont' (Röm 8,32): Zeitgemässe Gedanken zum Weihnachtsgeheimnis," *GLeb* 34 (1961): 407–9.

C. THIS JUSTIFICATION AND SALVATION THROUGH FAITH DO NOT CONTRADICT GOD'S PROMISES TO ISRAEL OF OLD (9:1–11:36)

◆

31. PAUL'S LAMENT ABOUT HIS FORMER CORELIGIONISTS (9:1–5)

9 ¹I am speaking the truth in Christ; I am not lying, as my conscience bears witness to me in the holy Spirit, ²that my sorrow is great and the anguish in my heart is unrelenting. ³For I could even wish to be accursed and cut off from Christ for the sake of my brothers, my kinsmen by descent. ⁴They are Israelites, and to them belong the sonship, the glory, the covenants, the giving of the law, the cult, and the promises; ⁵to them belong the patriarchs, and from them by natural descent comes the Messiah, who is God over all, blest forever! Amen.

COMMENT

Having developed in chap. 8 the secondary theme announced in 5:1–11, Paul concluded part B of the doctrinal section of Romans. He now turns to another part (C), in which he takes up a specific problem that his gospel of uprightness through faith in Christ has raised: the relationship of Israel to this mode of justification or salvation. In more than one way Paul has been preparing for this discussion all along, and especially in 3:1–9 and 21–31.

The argument in this part of Romans becomes heavily scriptural, as Paul tries to relate his gospel to the teaching of the OT. In announcing and developing the themes of parts A and B, Paul has appealed to the OT (1:17; 2:24; 3:4, 10–18, [20]; 4:3, 7–8, 17, 18, 22; 7:7; 8:36). In doing so, he has sought to show that his teaching on justification by faith was actually "upholding the law" (3:31). Yet his teaching about the new way of attaining the status of uprightness or rectitude must have encountered the obvious objection that the mass of his own fellow coreligionists had resisted his gospel, had rejected the power of God that it unleashed for the salvation of all, Jew and Greek alike, and had not acknowledged the freedom that it announced. Paul himself admitted that the gospel was a message of salvation "for the Jew first" (1:16; cf. 2:9–10; 3:9), but this had become the classic problem of the rejection of Israel (so formulated in 11:15, *apobolē autōn*, "their rejection"). What does this "rejection" mean in view of the election of Israel and of the irrevocable promises made by God to his chosen people of old and to its patriarchs (11:28–29)? The descendants of those who have been the

539

recipients of such promises have not taken up the new divine challenge and thus seem to remain outside the stream of this salvation, whereas Greeks or Gentiles rush into it. In 4:13–14, 16, 20 Paul referred to those promises explicitly; but there they were applied to Abraham's justification by faith and contrasted with the law. Now Paul returns to them in 9:4, 8–9 and relates the "promise(s)" to his thesis in a fresh way. He will now explain in what sense "the rejection of Israel" is understood.

Although Abraham appears in 9:7 and 11:1, most of the development and appeal to the OT in these chapters will refer to other OT figures (Isaac and Esau, Moses and Pharaoh, prophets like Hosea and Isaiah), and even to Sodom and Gomorrah. Thus the appeal to the OT is more complicated than the argument was in chap. 4 and does not depend on the story of one patriarch.

The function of Romans 9–11 in the structure of the epistle as a whole is debated. To some commentators (e.g., Lyonnet), this part serves as a scriptural illustration of part B, somewhat as the discussion of Abraham's justification in chap. 4 served as an OT illustration of 3:21–31. Thus, chaps. 9–11 are to chaps. 5–8 as chap. 4 is to chaps. 1–3. But nowhere in chaps. 9–11 does the "Spirit" appear (save in 9:1 and 11:8, and then in an entirely different sense!), and the whole argument moves in a direction quite different from the thrust of chaps. 5–8. Similarly, the theme of "life" disappears (save in 11:15, which is a problem apart), and *doxa* occurs only in 9:23, a verse that does refer to the predestination of 8:28–30. Moreover, the function of "illustration" does not explain well the bulk of chaps. 9–11.

For other interpreters (e.g., Dodd [*Romans*, 148]; Benoit [*RB* 65 (1958): 432]), this part is seen more rightly as a third step in the development of Paul's major theme (1:16–17). Though an authentic Pauline composition, these chapters are nevertheless regarded by them as a "foreign body" in the letter, added perhaps by a later editor. They are a "compact and continuous whole, which can be read quite satisfactorily without reference to the rest of the epistle" (Dodd). Or they are regarded as "a kind of supplement" (Beare, *St. Paul*, 103). Again, these chapters are sometimes thought to interrupt the continuity between chaps. 5–8 and chaps. 12–15. Similarly, with varying nuances, Bultmann (*TNT* 2.132); Sanday and Headlam (*Romans*, 225); Davies (*NTS* 24 [1977–78]: 14–15 n. 3); Refoulé (*RSPT* 71 [1987]: 219–42). The reasons, however, for so regarding Romans 9–11 are scarcely convincing.

Still other analyses of chaps. 9–11 have isolated one or another item in them and concentrated on such ideas as Paul's teaching on predestination, or his theodicy, or philosophy of history, analyses that Nygren (*Romans*, 354–55) does well to refute, for they fail to relate the chapters as a unit to the letter as a whole.

The differences that one detects in these chapters of Romans have even made some commentators speak of "inner contradictions" in the letter (e.g., Widmann, "Der Israelit," 150). Yet that surely is too strong a way of phrasing the matter. It scarcely calls for a solution of the problem by invoking a redactor.

Centuries ago Calvin succinctly stated the connection of Romans 9–11 with the preceding chapters: "If this [the teaching of chaps. 1–8] be the doctrine of the Law and the Prophets, why is it that the Jews reject it?" (*Comm. in Rom.* 9.1). The same question must have been put to Paul himself many times by his contemporaries.

This part of Romans has to be understood as the climax of the doctrinal section, as Stendahl, in dependence on J. Munck (*Christ & Israel*), has rightly insisted (*Paul among Jews and Gentiles*, 3–4, 85). Although Stendahl oversimplifies a bit, especially with reference to 11:11 and 14, his analysis is on the right track, because the issue that now emerges in Romans is the "gospel as promise" versus the law; or, to put it another way, the uprightness of God versus the promises of God. Again, part C deals not with judaizers (the problem in Galatians), but with Jews and their relation to the gospel; these chapters are not, then, polemical but apologetic, seeking to explain how the Jewish people fit into the new plan of God. The salvation-history perspective that Stendahl advocates has also to be recognized, *pace* Käsemann, who has taken issue with Stendahl on this point. Yet Käsemann (*Perspectives*, 75) is right when he says that the "doctrine of justification dominates Rom. 9–11 no less than the rest of the epistle." Indeed, it is the key to salvation history. The failure of the mission to the Jews raised the question of the faithfulness of God to his promises; Paul then sees the need to justify God's activity in Christ Jesus. In effect, when one reflects on earlier parts of the letter, one can see that Paul was really preparing for this discussion all along. See further Müller, *Gottes Gerechtigkeit*, 27–33; Zeller, *Juden und Heiden*, 109–13; Beker, "The Faithfulness of God," 11.

Because it was to a great extent Paul's mission to the Gentiles that was responsible for the Christian church becoming predominantly Gentile, his own involvement raised problems for him with reference to his former coreligionists. In a sense he had been involved in the "rejection" of Israel. Hence his agonized cry with which this part of Romans begins (9:1–3), a cry that is repeated in his prayer of 10:1. This personal element may also account for the way that this part of Romans becomes more epistolary in its formulation, as Paul once again addresses the Romans as "brothers" (10:1; 11:25) and appeals to the testimony of his conscience (9:1; cf. 1:9). What he says in these chapters serves as the background for the description of his plans in 15:25–32. As Davies has stressed, "these chapters reveal a Paul conscious of an emerging anti-Judaism among Gentile Christians that could draw on the endemic hostilities of the Graeco-Roman pagan world to help it. He is determined to combat this" (*NTS* 24 [1977–78]: 22). To put it another way, what Paul says in chaps. 9–11 is intimately bound up with his personal missionary activity.

Matthew in his Gospel also treats the problem of the relation of Israel to God's new mode of salvation. But unlike Paul, who writes a treatise about it, Matthew in his narrative account of the Jesus movement tries to explain to a mixed

ROMANS

community of Christians why it is that the Gentiles are rushing into the kingdom of heaven and Israel is not. See Matt 8:11–12; 27:24–25.

The reader of Romans 9–11 encounters difficulty in reading these chapters because of three things: (1) Paul's habit of isolating and discussing one aspect of a problem without worrying about ramifications that arise in the mind of the reader (especially of the modern reader since the Holocaust). (2) Paul introduces an unparalleled number of OT texts into his discussion. Sometimes they distract from his main argument and break up the line of thought because of their length. They function like a Homeric simile, which usually has only one point of comparison. But they also interlace Paul's argument in a way that binds it into a unit; see Aageson, "Scripture and Structure." (3) Paul has a tendency to generalize, when speaking of the election and predestination of Israel. His emphasis is on corporate Israel despite the examples of individuals that he uses. The reader, then, has to learn to read Paul for what he is saying and resist the temptation to read later problems into his text.

It is undoubtedly in this part of Romans that the epigram cited at the head of the sketch of Pauline teaching (Introduction, section IX) is most applicable. Caird cited it in this connection and comments,

Augustine, Aquinas, and Calvin have found in this passage one of the main supports of their doctrine of double predestination; Origen, Chrysostom, and Arminius have used it to confirm their belief that man's destiny rests on his own free response to God's grace; and the universalists have seized on it as one of the few Biblical texts which give grounds for belief in universal salvation. The irony is that all have been sound in their affirmations, though grievously at fault in their failure to appreciate the strength of the other two positions. For Paul actually contrives . . . to hold all three beliefs at the same time. (*ExpTim* 68 [1956–57]: 324)

Marcion reacted negatively to this part of Romans, retaining of it only 10:1–4 and 11:33–34. This means that the first excerpt ended with the affirmation that Christ is the end of the law, and on its heels followed a doxology addressed to God. This also means that in Marcion's form of the letter there was no discussion of God's uprightness and the fate of Israel. See A. von Harnack, *Marcion: Das Evangelium vom fremden Gott*, TU 45 (Leipzig: Hinrichs, 1924), 108*–9*.

Part C of Romans may be subdivided into twelve sections: 9:1–5; 9:6–13; 9:14–23; 9:24–29; 9:30–33; 10:1–4; 10:5–13; 10:14–21; 11:1–10; 11:11–24; 11:25–32; and 11:33–36. Chapter 9 has five subdivisions. In 9:1–5 Paul speaks not as a Jew (*pace* Michel, *Brief an die Römer*, 291) but as a Jewish Christian, as "the apostle of the Gentiles" (11:13); yet even as such he begins with an expression of his anguish at the plight of the Jewish people, his "brothers" and "kinsmen," who have not accepted Jesus as God's Messiah. His sadness is poignant because he is aware of Israel's prerogatives as God's people. He acknowledges the classic septet

542

of them and adds even an eighth. But in expressing this anguish, he briefly states the problem that confronted him in preaching the gospel. The pathos of this introductory paragraph corresponds to the emotional conclusion of this section in 11:33–36, as Michel (*Brief an die Römer*, 288) rightly recognized.

Paul has been concerned to teach about God as the source of human justification and salvation; now his concern will be instead with God who has granted prerogatives to the Jews, made them his people, and given them irrevocable promises, but who now calls the Gentiles to faith as well. Justification was offered to Israel; now it is offered to both Jews and Gentiles on the basis of faith in Christ Jesus, in whom the promises have seen fulfillment, yet without deeds of the law. Divine freedom and grace are now manifested toward both Jew and Gentile, but Paul tries to cope with the fact that despite its privileges and his efforts to evangelize his own people, Israel has not reacted as Paul thinks it should have. Now Paul reflects on that sad situation.

It is striking that among the seven prerogatives of Israel that Paul lists here, he does not mention the "election" of Israel. That aspect of Israel's vocation will finally be mentioned in 11:28.

NOTES

9:1. *I am speaking the truth in Christ.* Paul speaks out at first positively and sincerely as a Christian, without any resentment against the Jewish people, who may have caused him trouble or charged him with apostasy or infidelity (2 Cor 2:17; 12:19). He speaks too as a Jew, but also as "the apostle of the Gentiles" (11:13). He utters a solemn oath and expresses the truth as he sees it (cf. 2 Cor 12:6), and that truth is expressed in what follows in v 2.

I am not lying. In a parenthetic statement, Paul negatively formulates his affirmation and echoes the emphatic protestation that he made in 2 Cor 11:31 ("God knows that I do not lie"). Cf. 1 Tim 2:7, where the combination of speaking the truth and not lying also occurs.

as my conscience bears witness to me in the holy Spirit. Again, in a parenthetic statement, Paul invokes the Spirit as the guide of his own secret thoughts about his former coreligionists. On "conscience," see the NOTE on 2:15. The parallelism of "in Christ" and "in the holy Spirit" is noteworthy; both are called to testify to his sincerity and apostolic declaration. Michel (*Brief an die Römer*, 291–92) calls attention to the multiple parallels that Paul uses here: Paul and Christ, conscience and the holy Spirit, truth and not lying, sorrow and anguish.

2. *my sorrow is great and the anguish in my heart is unrelenting.* Thus Paul records for posterity his attitude regarding his fellow Jews. He is not an apostate without sympathy for his brothers and kinsmen. Rather, he is deeply pained at the thought of Israel's failure to accept the gospel. Indirectly, he is recommending to his readers that they too should be reacting similarly to this continuing disbelief

of the chosen people of old. The two nouns *lypē*, "sorrow," and *odynē*, "pain, anguish," are also found in Isa 35:10 and 51:11.

3. *I could even wish to be accursed*. Lit., "I myself would wish that I might be anathema," i.e., separated from Christ by a curse, or consigned to damnation or divine wrath. *Anathema* is the condemnation that Paul leveled against anyone who "has no love for the Lord" (1 Cor 16:22). The vb. *euchesthai* means basically "pray," but the sense of it as "wish" is attested from the fifth century B.C. on. But it might mean, "I myself would pray," if Paul is indeed alluding to Moses' prayer in Exod 32:32. Because there is no particle *an* used with the impf. *ēuchomēn*, it is not easy to say in what sense Paul means his prayer or wish. It is hardly meant to express a past continuous action ("I was wishing") or a conative ("I was trying to pray"); most likely it should be taken as a wish that cannot be fulfilled or that is unattainable (see BDF §359.2); the particle *an* should then be understood. Thus Paul expresses his awareness of playing, as did Moses, a decisive role in God's salvation history in view of his people.

Greek *anathema = anatetheimenon*, "something set up," = classical Greek *anathēma*, a "votive offering" set up in a temple or shrine of some god. In the LXX *anathema* regularly translates Hebrew *ḥerem*, "something devoted to the divinity," whether in the sense of consecration or of taboo. In the latter sense, see Lev 27:28; Num 21:3; Deut 7:26; Josh 6:17; 7:12; Judg 1:17; Zech 14:11. This too is the sense of *anathema* in the NT (see Gal 1:8–9). See Davis, "Anathema"; Morison, "Anathema"; Voigt, "Paulo."

and cut off from Christ. The prep. phrase *apo tou Christou* actually depends on *anathema*; *apo* is used to express separation or alienation (see BDF §211). Paul would willingly undergo the worst possible fate that he could imagine for the sake of his fellow Jews. In this he echoes Moses' prayer for the unruly Israelites (Exod 32:32): "to be blotted out of the book of life," that they may be forgiven. John Chrysostom noted the pathos of this wish in contrast to Paul's hymn in 8:35–39: "What do you mean, Paul? Cut off from Christ? From your Beloved? From him, from whom neither kingdom nor hell could separate you, or things seen, or things understood, or any other such things—do you now pray to be accursed and cut off from him?" (*In ep. ad Romanos* hom. 16.1 [PG 60.549]).

Greek MSS D and G read *hypo*, "by," instead of *apo*, "from."

for the sake of my brothers. Paul used *adelphoi* of fellow Christians: 1:13 (see the NOTE there). Now, in a unique instance, he uses it of his former coreligionists. Actually, it is being employed in the more original sense (= fellow Jew), a term later adopted by Christians. The word is being used in a human sense, for by his faith in Christ Paul has become a member of a new family.

my kinsmen by descent. Lit., "my relatives according to the flesh." This added phrase explains further the sense in which Jews are Paul's "brothers." *Kata sarka* expresses the natural, human connection, as in 1:3; 4:1; 8:1; 9:5; 11:14; 1 Cor 10:8. Paul writes *syngeneis*, lit., "relatives," in the broad sense of tribesmen, members of the same background and culture, as also in 16:7, 11, 21 (cf.

Josephus, *J.W.* 7.8.1 §262; also *Ant.* 12.8.3 §338 for the combination of the term with *adelphoi*). Paul recognizes that Jews are still fellow members of God's chosen people, despite their failure to accept the gospel. "Unbelieving Israel is within the elect community" (Cranfield, *Romans*, 459). Paul insists that it still has a place in God's plan. Cf. LXX Esth 4:17d: "I would have been willing to kiss the soles of his feet to save Israel" (see P. Bratsiotis, *NovT* 5 [1962]: 299–300).

4. *They are Israelites*. Instead of the common ethnic or political title *Ioudaioi*, "Jews" (see 3:28–29; cf. Mark 15:2, 9, 12, 26), Paul readily makes use of the honorific title "Israelites" bestowed of old by Yahweh himself on a patriarch of his people. The name of Jacob was changed to "Israel," interpreted as "striven with God" (Gen 32:29). Paul does not say that "they were Israelites," but "who are Israelites." The tense is significant. Jews still have, then, the right to boast of such an ancestral heritage associated with a God-given name. From earliest times "Israel" was regarded as a sacred name, at first for the confederacy (Judg 5:2, 7), the community united in the cult of Yahweh. Later it became the designation of the Northern Kingdom. After the deportation of Israelites in the Assyrian Captivity (722 B.C.), it was applied to Judah, the Southern Kingdom (Mic 3:1; Isa 5:7), in the hope that a restored Israel might be realized. In the postexilic period it became the self-designation of the Jewish people aware of its status as the holy and chosen people of God. See Isa 65:9, 15, 22; Sir 17:17; *Jub.* 33:20. Cf. 2 Cor 11:22. See further Kugelman, "Hebrew, Israelite"; H. Kuhli, *EDNT* 2.204–5. But it is questionable whether Paul understands "Israelites" to designate merely "a particular category within the people" of Israel, as Refoulé would have it (". . . et ainsi," 170).

To such Israelites belong seven historic, God-given prerogatives, polysyndetically expressed (BDF §460.3). Compare Josephus's statement about the *doxas tōn Ioudaiōn*, what they think "concerning God, his essence, and the laws" (*Ant.* 20.12.1 §268).

to them belong the sonship. The first prerogative is *huiothesia*, but not in the Hellenistic sense of adoptive sonship, as Paul uses it of Christians in 8:15 (see the NOTE there). Paul adopts *huiothesia* from current Hellenistic usage and employs it in a figurative sense of the "sonship" of Israel, chosen by Yahweh as his "firstborn son" as of the exodus from Egypt (Exod 4:22; cf. Deut 14:1; Isa 1:2; Jer 3:19–22; 31:9; Hos 11:1), to whom he constantly expressed his fatherly affection (Deut 1:31; 8:5; 14:1; Isa 1:2; Wis 2:13, 16; 16:26), and from whom he expected filial obedience (Deut 14:1; Mal 1:6). This corporate status of Israel as son was a matter of divine favor. Yet later rabbinic literature lacks a term corresponding to *huiothesia*, as Str-B (3.261) admits.

It should be clear that Paul is speaking of the "sonship" of historical, ethnic Israel, of "the ideal Israel, faithful, such as was conceived in God's plan" (Benoit, *RB* 89 [1982]: 591), not of "the Israel of God" (Gal 6:16), or of the "ultimate destiny to be bestowed . . . on an Israel of the end-time," *pace* Byrne, "Sons of

God," 140). For the other privileges, even that of "glory," are not privileges of Israel of the future, but of that of the past, hence of ethnic Israel.

the glory. The second prerogative is the resplendent manifestation of Yahweh's presence to Israel at the exodus and the crossing of the Reed Sea (Exod 15:6, 11), in the desert (Exod 16:10; 40:34), and in the Jerusalem Temple (1 Kgs 8:11). In 11QTemple 29:8, God says, "I shall sanctify my [t]emple with my glory"; see the NOTE on 3:23. That glory also attended the forming of the Mosaic pact (Exod 34:30; cf. 2 Cor 3:7). It persisted in Israel's belief that Yahweh dwelled among his people; his glory was reflected in the beauty of the Temple. Ancient commentators, however, sometimes understood *doxa* in the Hellenistic sense of Israel's honor or reputation in the world; so Apollinaris of Laodicea (Staab, *Pauluskommentare,* 66); Gennadius (ibid. 398.23–24). Again, later rabbinic literature lacks a corresponding term for this clear OT idea; see Str-B 3.262.

covenants. The third prerogative. If the pl. *diathēkai* is read, as in MSS ℵ, C, K, Ψ, 33, 81, 614, 1739, the *Koinē* text-tradition, and in Latin, Syriac, and Coptic versions, then the "covenants" would be those made with Israel's ancestors: with Abraham (Gen 15:18; 17:2, 7, 9), with Isaac (Gen 26:3–5; Exod 2:24), with the three patriarchs (Exod 6:4–5; Lev 26:42), with Moses (Exod 24:7–8; Sir 44:12, 18 [which use the pl.]), and with David (2 Sam 23:5). A covenant with Jacob at Bethel is also mentioned in 11QTemple 24:10, which alludes to Gen 28:13–15, where there is, however, no mention of *běrît.* For the pl. *diathēkai,* see also Wis 18:22; 2 Macc 8:15; cf. BDF §141.8.

But important MSS (P46, B, D, F, G, etc.) read the sg. *diathēkē,* "covenant," which would then refer to the Mosaic covenant, the pact made at Sinai. Yet because of the plural that is often used, the later rabbinic tradition spoke of *habběrîtôt,* "the covenants," and distinguished three phases of the Mosaic covenant: Horeb, Plains of Moab, and Gerizim and Ebal (see Str-B, 3.262). Alternatively, Roetzel ("*Diathēkai*") understands pl. *diathēkai* to refer not to relationships Yahweh established with the patriarchs at different times, but to the ordinances, commandments, or oaths that Yahweh in his grace gave to Israel. That reading, however, seems to be stretching a point. See da Fonseca, "*Diathēkē—*Foedus an Testamentum?"

the giving of the law. Lit., "the legislation." The Greek noun *nomothesia* could mean either the active giving or promulgation of the law or passively the collection of laws. The latter is what is probably meant, as in 4 Macc 5:35; 17:16; Philo, *De Abr.* 1 §5; *De Cherub.* 26 §87. Later rabbinic tradition spoke of it as *mattan tôrāh,* "the giving of the law" (Str-B 3.262). Hence, the fourth prerogative was the *tôrāh,* the expression of God's will given to Moses to instruct the people (Exod 20:1–17; Deut 5:1–22), "the holy God-given law" (2 Macc 6:23). Paul regarded it as "the oracles of God" (3:2), by which Israel was enabled to "know his will" (2:18), for *tôrāh* literally means "instruction." Israel had as its instructor God himself, and because of that *tôrāh* Israel possessed an unparalleled wisdom, an educative force and guide for its life.

the cult. The fifth prerogative was the awesome worship *(latreia)* of Yahweh in the Temple, that ordained by Yahweh himself (Exodus 25–31; cf. Josh 22:27; 1 Chr 28:13) and so different from the idolatrous worship of Israel's neighbors, which often included prostitution and human sacrifice. Although the noun *latreia* is used a few times in the LXX (e.g., Exod 12:25–26; 13:5; 1 Macc 2:22), the vb. *latreuein* is reserved for the cult of Yahweh (e.g., 3:12c; 4:23; 7:16; cf. Heb 9:1). Later rabbinic tradition spoke of it as *hāʿăbôdāh*, lit., "the service" (Str-B 3.262).

the promises. The sixth prerogative consisted of the promises made by Yahweh to Abraham (Gen 12:2; 13:14–17; 15:4; 17:4–8, 16, 19; 21:12; 22:16–18), Isaac (Gen 26:3–5), Jacob (28:13–14), Moses (Deut 18:18–19), and David (2 Sam 7:11–16). Recall 4:13–21; the promises were regarded by Paul as still in effect and irrevocable (11:29). Strangely enough, the noun *epangelia* is not used in the LXX in the religious sense of God's historic promises to Israel; the vb. *epangellein*, however, is so used in deuterocanonical 2 Macc 2:18, in a context that refers to *klēronomia*, "inheritance." Cf. 3 Macc 2:10; *Ps. Sol.* 12:6; *T. Jos.* 20:1. Later rabbinic tradition spoke of the promises as *hahabṭāḥôt*, lit., "the assurances." See Str-B 3.206–9.

5. *to them belong the patriarchs*. The seventh prerogative was Israel's ancestral heritage, for it still worshiped the God of its *fathers*, Abraham, Isaac, and Jacob (see 11:28; cf. Exod 3:13; 13:5). See Josephus, *Ant*. 14.10.22 §255: "Abraham, who was the father of all the Hebrews." Cf. 4:1, 12, 16; 9:10; Acts 7:2, 12, 15. Later rabbinic tradition spoke of them as *ʾābôt* (Str-B 3.263).

and from them by natural descent comes the Messiah. I.e., God's anointed agent for the salvation of his people. To the seven prerogatives that sum up Israel's historic privileges Paul himself adds an eighth, the climax of them all. See 1:3 for Paul's awareness of Jesus' descent from David; cf. the Lucan and Matthaean genealogies (Matt 1:1–17; Luke 3:23–38). Again, Paul uses *kata sarka*, as in 1:3 (see the NOTE there). Paul realizes that God had chosen Israel to be the stage on which he would enact the salvation of humanity through Christ Jesus, through Jesus as the Messiah, i.e., God's anointed agent of salvation. This rare instance in Paul's writings in which *Christos* has the titular sense of "Messiah" may find a lonely parallel in 1 Cor 1:23, "we preach Christ crucified" or "a crucified Messiah."

"Messianism" was a product of late thinking in pre-Christian Judaism in Israel; it developed out of a promise of a future David (Jer 36:30; 30:9; 23:5–6; 33:15; Hos 3:5; Ps 132:17), but was not formally enunciated in terms of a "Messiah" until Dan 9:25 (*māšîaḥ nāgîd*, "an anointed one, a prince"), shortly before it emerged also in Qumran theology (see 1QS 9:11, with its mention of three expected figures: a "prophet" [like Moses, Deut 18:18] and "the Messiahs of Aaron and Israel," a priestly and a political Messiah). See N. A. Dahl, "The Messiahship of Jesus in Paul," *The Crucified Messiah and Other Essays* (Minneapolis, Minn.: Augsburg, 1974), 37–47.

who is God over all, blest forever! I.e., over all and for all, Jews and Greeks alike, or over all things, if *pantōn* should be taken as neuter. Cf. Eph 4:6 for similar statement of God's preeminence. Such preeminence Paul accords to Jesus, the Messiah.

This part of the verse is problematic. "The interpretation of Rom. ix. 5 has probably been discussed at greater length than that of any other verse in the N.T." (Sanday and Headlam, *Romans*, 233). Part of the problem stems from the punctuation of the verse. Because the earliest MSS of the Pauline epistles were without word dividers or punctuation (uncials written in *scriptio continua*), one cannot appeal to ancient forms of the text, even though a few MSS have at times traces of punctuation. For the punctuation of this part of the verse, four main possibilities have been proposed:

(1) A comma before the participial phrase *ho ōn*: ". . . comes the Messiah, who is God over all blest forever!" This reading was preferred by the vast majority of interpreters of Romans in the first eight centuries (actually from Irenaeus [*Adversus haereses* 3.16.3] to Erasmus [in his *Paraphrases*]); likewise many modern commentators and critical texts (Althaus, Asmussen, Bardenhewer, Best, Bisping, Bruce, Brunner, Cornely, Cranfield, Cullmann, Gutjahr, Huby, Jacono, Kühl, Lagrange, Leenhardt, Lyonnet, Metzger, Michel, Murray, Nygren, Pesch, Plumer, Prümm, Reithmayr, Ridderbos, Sanday and Headlam, Schlatter, Schlier, Schmidt, Sickenberger, Tholuck, B. Weiss, Zahn; Bover, Merk, N-A[26], UBSGNT[3], von Soden, Vogels). This punctuation makes Paul proclaim Christ as preeminent among the prerogatives of Israel, even as God (though not *ho theos*), and blest forever. See Michel, *Brief an die Römer*, 296, for references to patristic writers who were aware of the problem that this application to Christ created, esp. in the time of Arius; cf. Lyonnet, *Quaestiones . . . series altera* (1962): 26–30.

(2) A period before the participial phrase: ". . . comes the Messiah. God who is over all (be) blest forever!" So MSS A, C, Eusebius, Erasmus (who introduced the modern discussion of the punctuation and seems to have favored it); Abbott, Barrett(?), Black, Bultmann, Burkitt, Byrne, Cerfaux, Dodd, Dunn, Feine, Gaugler, Goodspeed, Harrisville, Jülicher, Käsemann, Kümmel, Kuss, Lietzmann, Lipsius, Maillot, P. W. Meyer, Michel, Oltramare, Robinson, Taylor, Wilckens, Zeller; N-A[25], *RSV*, *NEB*. This reading makes Paul assert the natural descent of Christ from Israel, and then because of it utter a doxology addressed to God as preeminent in the manner of Jewish doxologies. Christ is thus the climax of the prerogatives of the Israelites as Messiah, and Paul praises God for it. To many commentators this interpretation is called for by 1 Cor 15:27–28.

(3) A comma after "Messiah" and a period after "over all": ". . . comes the Messiah, who is over all. God (be) blest forever!" So Reuss (*Épîtres* 2.86–88), the marginal note in *NEB*. This version would make Paul acknowledge the natural descent of Christ and assert his preeminence among Israel's prerogatives, and then praise God in a doxology because of it.

(4) An inversion of *ho ōn* and a different breathing, *hōn ho*: "(and) to whom

(belongs) the one over all, God, blest forever!" This conjecture was mentioned as possible by J. Szlichting (a sixteenth-century Socinian, who did not use it himself); it was used by S. Crellius (in a commentary on the Johannine Gospel, 1726), by the early K. Barth, by Dodd, Harder, Lorimer, Strömmann, J. Weiss, Wettstein, and La Bible de Centenaire. Bartsch ("Röm. 9,5") argues for it on the basis of a comparison with *1 Clem.* 32.4. This reading would make Paul assert that Christ by natural descent is a prerogative of Israel, but that God is the one who is preeminent and blest forever, in effect, Israel's ninth prerogative.

The last two intepretations are improbable and have little to commend them; the choice lies between (1) and (2). Preference for (1) is mainly based on four considerations. (a) The first is the normal sense of this half-verse in its context; the phrase *to kata sarka*, "by natural descent," calls for some contrast that would be expressed by the rest of the verse referring to Christ. Barrett (*Romans*, 178), who otherwise uses a period, admits as much. (b) Is a doxology in place in a paragraph otherwise expressing sorrow and regret? Käsemann (*Commentary*, 260) thinks that it is appropriate. (c) The normal wording of a doxology is not used; "blest" should precede *theos*. Compare *bārûk YHWH*, "Blest be the Lord" (e.g., Gen 9:26; 24:27; Exod 18:10; 1 Sam 25:32; Ps 41:14; in the LXX, *eulogētos Kyrios* [*ho theos*]). The exception in the LXX of Ps 67:19 (*Kyrios ho theos eulogētos*) is, however, only apparent, for it is a gloss added to the real doxology in 67:20 (*eulogētos Kyrios* [see the MT]). In Paul's writings such a doxology is never joined asyndetically with what precedes or with the subject expressed first; it usually continues from what precedes as an integral part of the sentence (see 1:25; 11:36; Gal 1:5; 2 Cor 11:31; cf. Eph 3:21; 2 Tim 4:18; 1 Pet 4:11; Heb 13:21). (d) The use of *theos* to refer to Christ is compatible with Paul's teaching, even though the appellation is not found elsewhere, save possibly Gal 2:20, which is also problematic. Yet other statements of Paul make this attribution not unjustifiable (see 1 Cor 8:6; 12:3; esp., as Käsemann admits [*Commentary*, 259], "Christ the preexistent heavenly being to whom *isa theō* of Phil 2:6 applies"). Cf. Col 2:2; 2 Thess 1:12; Titus 2:13 for a possible extension of his thought in Deutero-Pauline letters. Even though *eulogētos* may be elsewhere reserved for *theos* (= the Father), if Paul really does call Jesus *theos* here, it would then be understood as an extension of the Father's title to the risen Christ. Again, if a doxology is eventually addressed to Christ in the NT, as it is in Rev 1:6; 5:13; 7:10; 2 Pet 3:18 (and possibly even in 1 Pet 4:11; 2 Tim 4:18), it is not impossible that Paul would use *eulogētos* of Christ even outside a doxology. For reasons in favor of the doxology addressed to God, see Kuss, "Zu Römer 9,5." Cf. 1 John 5:20.

In any case, one cannot argue apodictically about this problem; cf. *TCGNT*, 520–23; also Cullmann, *Christology*, 311–14; Cranfield, *Romans*, 464–70; Kuss, *Römerbrief*, 679–96; Michel, *Brief an die Römer*, 296-98; Sanday and Headlam, *Romans*, 234.

Amen. Paul adds the usual ending to a prayer. See the NOTE on 1:25.

BIBLIOGRAPHY ON CHAPTERS 9-11

Aageson, J. W., "Scripture and Structure in the Development of the Argument in Romans 9-11," *CBQ* 48 (1986): 265-89.

———, "Typology, Correspondence, and the Application of Scripture in Romans 9-11," *JSNT* 31 (1987): 51-72.

Beasley-Murray, G. R., "The Righteousness of God in the History of Israel and the Nations: Romans 9-11," *RevExp* 73 (1976): 437-50.

Beker, J. C., "The Faithfulness of God and the Priority of Israel in Paul's Letter to the Romans," *HTR* 79 (1986): 10-16.

———, "Romans 9-11 in the Context of the Early Church," *PSB* Sup 1 (1990): 40-55.

Benoit, P., "Conclusion par mode de synthèse," *Die Israelfrage*, ed. L. de Lorenzi, 217-43.

———, "La Question juive selon Rom. IX-XI d'après K. L. Schmidt," *RB* 55 (1948): 310-12; repr. in *Exégèse et théologie* 2.337-39.

Betz, O., "Die heilsgeschichtliche Rolle Israels bei Paulus," *TBei* 9 (1978): 1-21.

Beyschlag, W., *Die paulinische Theodicee Römer IX-XI: Ein Beitrag zur biblischen Theologie* (Halle an der Saale: Strien; Berlin: Rauh, 1868).

Blackman, E. C., "Divine Sovereignty and Missionary Strategy in Romans 9-11," *CJT* 11 (1965): 124-34.

Bleienstein, H., "Israel in der Heilsgeschichte nach Römer 9-11," *ZAM* 6 (1931): 165-70.

Boers, H., "The Problem of Jews and Gentiles in the Macro-Structure of Romans," *Neotestamentica* 15 (1981): 1-11; repr. *SEA* 47 (1982): 184-96.

Bover, J. M., "La reprobación de Israël en Rom 9-11," *EstEcl* 25 (1951): 63-82.

Broer, I., "Die Juden im Urteil der Autoren des Neuen Testaments: Anmerkungen zum Problem historischer Gerechtigkeit im Angesicht einer verheerenden Wirkungsgeschichte," *TG1* 82 (1992): 2-33.

Caird, G. B., "Predestination—Romans ix.-xi.," *ExpTim* 68 (1956-57): 324-27.

Campbell, W. S., "The Freedom and Faithfulness of God in Relation to Israel," *JSNT* 13 (1981): 27-45; repr. in *Paul's Gospel*, 43-59.

Cerfaux, L., *Une Lecture*, 87-107.

Corley, B., "The Jews, the Future, and God (Romans 9-11)," *SwJT* 19 (1976-77): 42-56.

Corsani, B., "I capitoli 9-11 della lettera ai Romani," *BeO* 14 (1972): 31-47.

Cuenca Molina, J. F., "De la ley del Sinai a la ley de Cristo," *Carthaginiensia* 3 (1987): 37-55.

Dahl, N. A., *Studies in Paul*, 137-58.

Davies, W. D., "Paul and the People of Israel," *NTS* 24 (1977-78): 4-39.

Davis, W. H., "Anathema—Romans 9:3," *RevExp* 31 (1934): 205-7.

Dettori, L., "La divinità di Gesù Cristo," *Lux biblica* 1 (1990): 81-85.

Dinkler, E., "The Historical and the Eschatological Israel in Romans, Chapters 9-

11: A Contribution to the Problem of Predestination and Individual Responsibility," *JR* 36 (1956): 109–27.

——, "Prädestination bei Paulus: Exegetische Bemerkungen zum Römerbrief," *Festschrift für Günther Dehn* . . . , ed. W. Schneemelcher (Neukirchen: Erziehungsverein, 1957), 81–102; repr. *Signum Crucis* (Tübingen: Mohr [Siebeck], 1967), 241–69.

Doekes, G., *De beteekenis van Israëls val: Commentaar op Romeinen IX–XI* (Nijverdal: Bosch, 1915).

Ellison, H. L., *The Mystery of Israel: An Exposition of Romans 9–11* (Grand Rapids, Mich.: Eerdmans, 1966; Exeter, UK: Paternoster, 1976).

Evans, C. A., "Paul and the Hermeneutics of 'True Prophecy': A Study of Romans 9–11," *Bib* 65 (1984): 560–70.

Evans, D. D., " 'The Mystery of Israel': A Reply to E. Flesseman-van Leer and David W. Hay," *CJT* 4 (1958): 30–36.

Fabris, R., "La 'gelosia' nella Lettera ai Romani (9–11): Per un nuovo rapporto tra ebri e cristiani," *Rassegna di Teologia* 27 (1986): 15–33.

Feuillet, A., "Les Privilèges et l'incrédulité d'Israël, d'après les chapitres 9–11 de l'épître aux Romains: Quelques suggestions pour un dialogue fructueux entre Juifs et Chrétiens," *EspVie* 92 (1982): 481–93, 497–506.

Fiedler, P., "Israel und unsere Hoffnung: Bibeltheologische Überlegungen zum Israel-Abschnitt im Synodenbeschluss 'Unsere Hoffnung,' " *Wer Tora vermehrt, mehrt Leben: Festschrift für Heinz Kremers* . . . , ed. E. Brocke and H.-J. Barkenings (Neukirchen-Vluyn: Neukirchener-Verlag, 1986), 15–24.

Fischer, J. A., "Dissent Within a Religious Community: Romans 9–11," *BTB* 10 (1980): 105–10.

Flesseman-van Leer, E., "The Significance of the Mystery of Israel for the Church," *CJT* 3 (1957): 5–14.

Fransen, I., "Le Dieu de toute consolation: Romains 9,1–11,36," *BVC* 49 (1963): 27–32.

Gaston, L., *Paul and the Torah*, 135–50.

Getty, M. A., "Paul and the Salvation of Israel: A Perspective on Romans 9–11," *CBQ* 50 (1988): 456–69.

——, "Paul on the Covenants and the Future of Israel," *BTB* 17 (1987): 92–99.

Giblin, C. H., *In the Hope of God's Glory*, 264–310.

Goedt, M. de, "La Destinée d'Israël dans le mystère du salut d'après l'épître aux Romains, IX–XI," *VSpirSup* 11 (1958): 443–61.

Gooch, P. W., "Sovereignty and Freedom: Some Pauline Compatibilisms," *SJT* 40 (1987): 531–42.

Gorday, P., *Principles of Patristic Exegesis: Romans 9–11 in Origen, John Chrysostom, and Augustine*, Studies in the Bible and Early Christianity 4 (New York and Toronto: E. Mellen, 1983).

Guerra, A. J., "Romans: Paul's Purpose and Audience with Special Attention to Romans 9–11," *RB* 97 (1990): 219–37.

Güttgemanns, E., "Heilsgeschichte bei Paulus oder Dynamik des Evangeliums: Zur strukturellen Relevanz von Röm 9–11 für die Theologie des Römerbriefes," *Studia linguistica neotestamentica*, BEvT 60 (Munich: Kaiser, 1971), 34–58.

Haacker, K., "Das Evangelium Gottes und die Erwählung Israels," *TBei* 13 (1982): 59–72.

Hawkins, R. M., "The Rejection of Israel: An Analysis of Romans IX–XI," *ATR* 23 (1941): 329–35.

Hay, D. W., "The Mystery of Israel: A Reply to Dr. E. Flesseman-van Leer," *CJT* 3 (1957): 97–101.

Hofius, O., "Das Evangelium und Israel: Erwägungen zu Römer 9–11," *ZTK* 83 (1986): 297–324.

Hübner, H., *Gottes Ich und Israel: Zum Schriftgebrauch des Paulus in Römer 9–11*, FRLANT 136 (Göttingen: Vandenhoeck & Ruprecht, 1984).

Johnson, E. E., *The Function of Apocalyptic and Wisdom Traditions in Romans 9–11*, SBLDS 109 (Atlanta, Ga.: Scholars Press, 1989).

Journet, C., "Sur la Conversion d'Israël (À propos de saint Paul, Rm 9–11)," *NovVet* 64 (1989): 146–51.

Käsemann, E., *NTQT*, 183–87.

Klappert, B., "Traktat für Israel (Römer 9–11)," *Jüdische Existenz und die Erneuerung der christlichen Theologie*, Abhandlungen zum christlich-jüdischen Dialog 11, ed. M. Stöhr (Munich: Kaiser, 1981), 58–137.

Klumbies, P.-G., "Israels Vorzüge und das Evangelium von der Gottesgerechtigkeit in Römer 9–11," *Word und Dienst* 18 (1985): 135–57.

Kümmel, W. G., "Die Probleme von Römer 9–11 in der gegenwärtigen Forschungslage," *Die Israelfrage*, ed. L. de Lorenzi, 13–33.

Longenecker, B. W., "Different Answers to Different Issues: Israel, the Gentiles and Salvation History in Romans 9–11," *JSNT* 36 (1989): 95–123.

Lorenzi, L. de (ed.), *Die Israelfrage nach Röm 9–11*, Benedictina, Biblisch-ökumenische Abt. 3 (Rome: Abbazia di San Paolo fuori le mura, 1977).

Losada, D. A., "La cuestión de Israel en Rom. 9–11," *RevistB* 43 (1981): 54–80.

Lübking, H.-M., *Paulus und Israel im Römerbrief: Eine Untersuchung zu Römer 9–11*, Europäische Hochschulschriften 23.260 (Bern, New York, and Frankfurt am Main: Lang, 1986).

Lüdemann, G., *Paulus und das Judentum*, TEH 215 (Munich: Kaiser, 1983).

Luz, U., *Das Geschichtsverständnis des Paulus*, BEvT 49 (Munich: Kaiser, 1968), 19–37, 64–84, 267–300.

Lyonnet, S., "Le Rôle d'Israël dans l'histoire du salut selon Rom 9–11," *Die Israelfrage*, ed. L. de Lorenzi, 42–47, 161–67, 174; repr. *Études*, 264–73.

Maier, F. W., *Israel in der Heilsgeschichte nach Röm. 9–11*, Biblische Zeitfragen 12.11–12 (Münster in Westfalen: Aschendorff, 1929).

Maillot, A., "Essai sur les citations vétérotestamentaires contenues dans Romains 9 à 11, ou comment se servir de la Torah pour montrer que le 'Christ est la fin de la Torah,' " *ETR* 57 (1982): 55–73.

Mayer, G., "La Réponse juive à la thèse paulinienne de la caducité de la loi mosaïque en Romains IX–XI," *CCER* 31 (1983): 135–41.

Moltmann, J., "Israel's No: Jews and Jesus in an Unredeemed World," *ChrC* 107 (1990): 1021–24.

Morison, J. "Anathema from Christ: Romans ix.3," *Expos* 1.6 (1877): 177–85.

Moxnes, H., *Theology in Conflict*, 78–107, 216–30.

Müller, C., *Gottes Gerechtigkeit und Gottes Volk: Eine Untersuchung zu Römer 9–11*, FRLANT 86 (Göttingen: Vandenhoeck & Ruprecht, 1964).

Muller-Duvernoy, C., "L'Apôtre Paul et le problème juif," *Judaica* 15 (1959): 65–91.

Munck, J., *Christ & Israel: An Interpretation of Romans 9–11* (Philadelphia, Penn.: Fortress, 1967).

———, "Israel and the Gentiles in the New Testament," *BullSNTS* 1 (1950): 26–38.

———, *Paul and the Salvation of Mankind*, 247–81.

Mussner, F., "Die Psalmen im Gedankengang des Paulus in Röm 9–11," *Freude an der Weisung des Herrn: Beiträge zur Theologie der Psalmen: Festgabe . . . von Heinrich Gross*, SBB 13, ed. E. Haag and F.-L. Hossfeld (Stuttgart: Katholisches Bibelwerk, 1986), 243–63.

———, "Warum ich mich als Christ für die Juden interessiere," *"Wie gut sind deine Zelte, Jaakow . . .": Festschrift . . . von Reinhold Mayer*, ed. E. L. Ehrlich and B. Klappert (Gerlingen: Bleicher, 1986), 191–95.

Noack, B., "Current and Backwater in the Epistle to the Romans," *ST* 19 (1965): 155–66.

Oesterreicher, J. M., "Israel's Misstep and Her Rise: The Dialectic of God's Saving Design in Romans 9–11," *SPCIC* 1.317–27.

Osten-Sacken, P. von der, "Römer 9–11 als Schibbolet christlicher Theologie," *Evangelium und Tora*, 294–314.

Perrot, C., "Le Mystère d'Israël," *MDB* 51 (1987): 33–34.

Plag, C., *Israels Weg zum Heil: Eine Untersuchung zu Römer 9 bis 11*, Arbeiten zur Theologie 1.40 (Stuttgart: Calwer, 1969).

Prado, J., "La iglesia del futuro, según san Pablo," *EstBíb* 22 (1963): 255–302.

Räisänen, H., "Paul, God, and Israel: Romans 9–11 in Recent Research," *The Social World of Formative Christianity and Judaism: Essays in Tribute to Howard Clark Kee* (Philadelphia, Penn.: Fortress, 1988), 178–206.

———, "Römer 9–11: Analyse eines geistigen Ringens," *ANRW* 2.25.4 (1987): 2891–2939.

Refoulé, F., "Cohérence ou incohérence de Paul en Romains 9–11?" *RB* 98 (1991): 51–79.

———, "Unité de l'*Épître aux Romains* et histoire du salut," *RSPT* 71 (1987): 219–42.

Robinson, D. W. B., "The Salvation of Israel in Romans 9–11," *RTR* 26 (1967): 81–96.

Satran, D., "Paul among the Rabbis and the Fathers: Exegetical Reflections," *PSB* Sup 1 (1990): 90–105.

Schlier, H., *Zeit der Kirche*, 232–44.

Schmidt, K. L., *Die Judenfrage im Lichte der Kapitel 9–11 des Römerbriefes* . . . , Theologische Studien 13 (Zollikon-Zurich: Evangelischer-Verlag, 1943).

Schwarz, R., "Israel und die nichtjüdischen Christen im Römerbrief (Kapitel 9–11)," *BLit* 59 (1986): 161–64.

Segal, A. F., "Paul's Experience and Romans 9–11," *PSB* Sup 1 (1990): 56–70.

Senft, C., "L'Election d'Israël et la justification (Romains 9 à 11)," *L'Évangile hier et aujourd'hui: Mélanges offerts au Professeur Franz-J. Leenhardt* (Geneva: Labor et Fides, 1968), 131–42.

Siegert, F., *Argumentation bei Paulus gezeigt an Röm 9–11*, WUNT 34 (Tübingen: Mohr [Siebeck], 1985).

Stanley, D. M., "Theologia 'promissionis' apud S. Paulum," *VD* 30 (1952): 129–42.

Stendahl, K., *Paul among Jews and Gentiles and Other Essays* (Philadelphia, Penn.: Fortress, 1976).

Theobald, M., "Kirche und Israel nach Röm 9–11," *Kairos* 29 (1987): 1–22.

Trocmé, E., "Comment le Dieu d'Abraham, d'Isaac et de Jacob peut-il être à la fois fidèle et libre? (Épître aux Romains, chap. 9 à 11)," *Foi et Vie* 89.1 (1990): 7–10.

Van Buren, P. M., "The Church and Israel: Romans 9–11," *PSB* Sup 1 (1990): 5–18.

Vicent, R., "Derash homilético en Romanos 9–11," *Salesianum* 42 (1980): 751–88.

Villiers, J. L. de, "The Salvation of Israel According to Romans 9–11," *Neotestamentica* 15 (1981): 199–221.

Vischer, W., "Le Mystère d'Israël: Une exégèse des chapîtres ix, x et xi de l'épître aux Romains," *Foi et Vie* 64 (1965): 427–87.

Walter, N., "Zur Interpretation von Römer 9–11," *ZTK* 81 (1984): 172–95.

Watson, F., *Paul, Judaism and the Gentiles*, SNTSMS 56 (Cambridge: Cambridge University Press, 1986).

Weber, E., *Das Problem der Heilsgeschichte nach Röm. 9–11: Ein Beitrag zur historisch-theologischen Würdigung der paulinischen Theologie* (Leipzig: Deichert, 1911).

Welker, M., "Righteousness and God's Righteousness," *PSB* Sup 1 (1990): 124–39.

Westhelle, V., "Paul's Reconstruction of Theology: Romans 9–14 in Context," *WW* 4 (1984): 307–19.

Widmann, M., "Der Israelit Paulus und sein antijüdischer Redaktor: Eine literarkritische Studie zu Röm. 9–11," *"Wie gut sind deine Zelte"* (see above), 150-58.

Winkel, J., "Argumentationsanalyse von Röm 9–11," *LB* 58 (1986): 65–79.

Worgul, G. S., Jr., "Romans 9–11 and Ecclesiology," *BTB* 7 (1977): 99–109.

Zeller, D., "Israel unter dem Ruf Gottes (Röm 9–11)," *IKZ* 2 (1973): 289–301.

Zerwick, M., "Drama populi Israel secundum Rom 9–11," *VD* 46 (1968): 321–38.

Chapter 9

Babcock. W. S., "Augustine and Paul: The Case of Romans IX," *Studia Patristica* XVI, ed. E. A. Livingstone (Berlin: Akademie Verlag, 1985), 473–79.

Beck, J. T., *Versuch einer pneumatisch-hermeneutischen Entwicklung des neunten Kapitels im Briefe an die Römer: Nebst einem Anhange* (Stuttgart: Hoffmann, 1833).

Brandenburger, E. "Paulinische Schriftauslegung in der Kontroverse um das Verheissungswort Gottes (Röm 9)," *ZTK* 82 (1985): 1–47.

Fahy, T., "A Note on Romans 9:1–18," *ITQ* 32 (1965): 261–62.

Goedbloed, W. J., "Een moeilijk hoofdstuck uit den Romeinenbrief," *GTT* 31 (1930–31): 228–41.

Lyonnet, S., "De doctrina praedestinationis et reprobationis in Rom 9," *VD* 34 (1956): 193–201, 257–71; repr. (French) in *Études*, 274–97.

Mahan, A., *Lectures on the Ninth of Romans: Election and the Influence of the Holy Spirit* (Boston, Mass.: Peirce, 1851).

Morison, J., *Exposition of the Ninth Chapter of the Epistle to the Romans* (London: Hodder and Stoughton, 1888).

Parmentier, M., "Greek Church Fathers on Romans 9," *Bijdragen* 50 (1989): 139–54; "Part II," 51 (1990): 2–20.

Piper, J., *The Justification of God: An Exegetical and Theological Study of Romans 9:1–23* (Grand Rapids, Mich.: Baker, 1983).

Rese, M., "Israel und Kirche in Römer 9," *NTS* 34 (1988): 208–17.

Schnieder, P., "The Meaning of 'Israel' in the Writings of St. Paul," *Face to Face* (New York) 10 (1983): 12–16.

Rom 9:1–5

Bernard, J., "Le Mystère de la foi: Rm 9,1–5," *AsSeign* n.s. 50 (1974): 16–21.

Byrne, B., "*Sons of God*," 79–84.

Bratsiotis, P., "Eine exegetische Notiz zu Röm. ix 3 und x 1," *NovT* 5 (1962): 299–300.

Cerfaux, L., "Le Privilège d'Israël selon Saint Paul," *ETL* 17 (1940): 5–26.

Cottier, G., "Sur la théologie d'Israël," *Nova et Vetera* 60 (1985): 98–102.

Dahl, N. A., "Die Messianität Jesu bei Paulus," *Studia paulina in honorem Johannis de Zwaan septuagenarii* (Haarlem: Bohn, 1953), 83–95.

Davis, W. H., "Anathema—Romans 9:3," *RevExp* 31 (1934): 205–7.

Dreyfus, F., "Le Passé et le présent d'Israël (Rom 9, 1–5; 11, 1–24)," *Die Israelfrage*, ed. L. de Lorenzi, 131–92.

Epp, E. J., "Jewish-Gentile Continuity in Paul: Torah and/or Faith? (Romans 9:1–5)," *HTR* 79 (1986): 80–90.

Fonseca, L. G. da, "*Diathēkē*—Foedus an Testamentum?" *Bib* 8 (1927): 31–50, 161–81, 290–319, 418–41; 9 (1928): 26–40, 143–60.

Gábriš, K., "Das Gewissen—normiert durch den Heiligen Geist: Bibelarbeit über Röm. 9,1–5," *ComViat* 27 (1984): 19–32.

Grässer, E., *Der alte Bund im Neuen: Exegetische Studien zur Israelfrage im Neuen Testament*, WUNT 35 (Tübingen: Mohr [Siebeck], 1985), 17–20.

Kamlah, E., "Wie beurteilt Paulus sein Leiden? Ein Beitrag zur Untersuchung seiner Denkstruktur," *ZNW* 54 (1963): 217–32.

Kugelman, R., "Hebrew, Israelite, Jew in the New Testament," *The Bridge* 1 (1955): 204–24.

Michel, O., "Opferbereitschaft für Israel," *In memoriam Ernst Lohmeyer*, ed. W. Schmauch (Stuttgart: Evangelisches Verlagswerk, 1951), 94–100.

Morison, J., "Anathema from Christ: Romans ix.3," *Expos* 1.6 (1877): 177–85.

Mussner, F., "Der Messias Jesus," *SNTU* A.6–7 (1981–82): 5–19.

Rese, M., "Die Vorzüge Israels in Röm. 9,4f. und Eph 2,12: Exegetische Anmerkungen zum Thema Kirche und Israel," *TZ* 31 (1975): 211–22.

Roetzel, C., "*Diathēkai* in Romans 9,4," *Bib* 51 (1970): 377–90.

Schlier, H., "Doxa bei Paulus als heilsgeschichtlicher Begriff," *Besinnung auf das Neue Testament: Exegetische Aufsätze und Vorträge* (Freiburg im Breisgau: Herder, 1964), 307–18.

Stählin, G., "Zum Gebrauch von Beteurungsformeln im Neuen Testament," *NovT* 5 (1962): 115–43, esp. 133–34.

Veldhuizen, A. van, "Rom. 9:2: *hoti lypē moi estin megalē kai adialeiptos odynē tē kardia mou*," *ThStud* 28 (1910): 130.

Voigt, S., "Paulo deseja ser anátema por seus irmâos judeus (Rom 9,3): Proposta de uma interpretaçâo diferente," *RevEclBras* 33 (1973): 298–323.

Punctuation and Interpretation of Rom 9:5

Abbott, E., "On the Construction of Romans ix. 5," *JBL* 1 (1881): 87–154.

———, "Recent Discussions of Romans ix. 5," *JBL* 3 (1881): 90–112.

Baljon, J. M. S., "Rom. IX:5^{b}," *ThStud* 4 (1886): 232–34.

Bartsch, H. W., "Röm. 9,5 und 1. Clem. 32,4: Eine notwendige Konjektur in Römerbrief," *TZ* 21 (1965): 401–9.

Bröse, E., "Wird Christus Röm. 9,5 *Theos* genannt?" *NKZ* 10 (1899): 645–57.

Brown, R. E., *Jesus God and Man: Modern Biblical Reflections* (Milwaukee, Wisc.: Bruce, 1967), 20–23.

Burkitt, F. C., "On Romans IX 5 and Mark XIV 61," *JTS* 5 (1903–4): 451–55.

Champion, L. G., "Benedictions and Doxologies in the Epistles of Paul," Ph.D. diss., Universität Heidelberg, 1934.

Cullmann, O., *Christology*, 312–13.

Dettori, L., "La divinità di Gesù Cristo," *Lux Biblica* (Rome) 1 (1990): 81–85.

Durand, A., "La Divinité de Jésus-Christ dans S. Paul, Rom. ix, 5," *RB* 12 (1903): 550–70.

Dwight, T., "On Romans ix. 5," *JBL* 1 (1881): 22–55.

Faccio, H. M., *De divinitate Christi iuxta S. Paulum: Rom. 9:5* (Jerusalem, 1945).

Grimm, W., "Ueber die Doxologie in Röm. 9,5," *ZWT* 12 (1869): 311–22.

Günther, E., "Zur Exegese von Röm. 9,5," *TSK* 73 (1900): 636–44.

Harmsen, E., "Ueber die Doxologie in Röm. 9, 5," *ZWT* 15 (1872): 510–21.

Kuss, O., "Zu Römer 9,5," *Rechtfertigung: Festschrift für Ernst Käsemann* . . . , ed. J. Friedrich et al. (Tübingen: Mohr [Siebeck], 1976), 291–303.

Lattey, C., "The Codex Ephraemi Rescriptus in Romans ix. 5," *ExpTim* 35 (1923–24): 42–43.

————, "The Codex Vaticanus on Romans ix. 5," *ExpTim* 34 (1922–23): 331.

Lorimer, W. L., "Romans ix. 3–5," *NTS* 13 (1966–67): 385–86.

Metzger, B. M., "The Punctuation of Rom. 9:5," *Christ and Spirit in the New Testament: In Honour of Charles Francis Digby Moule*, ed. B. Lindars and S. S. Smalley (Cambridge: Cambridge University Press, 1973), 95–112; repr. *New Testament Studies: Philological, Versional, and Patristic*, NTTS 10 (Leiden: Brill, 1980), 57–74.

Preuschen, E., "Nochmals Rö 9,5," *ZNW* 9 (1908): 80.

Roozemeyer, J. H. L., "Nog eens: Rom. IX:5[b]," *ThStud* 4 (1886): 397–99.

Strömmann, C., "Röm 9,5," *ZNW* 8 (1907): 319–20.

ISRAEL'S FAILURE: IT IS NOT CONTRARY TO GOD'S DIRECTION OF HISTORY (9:6–29)

◆

32. GOD'S PROMISES TO ISRAEL STEM FROM HIS GRATUITOUS ELECTION OF IT AS HIS PEOPLE; HENCE HIS WORD HAS NOT FAILED (9:6–13)

9 ⁶It is not as though the word of God has failed. For not all descendants of Israel are truly Israel; ⁷nor because they are offspring of Abraham are they all his children. Rather, *"It is through Isaac that your offspring will be named."* ⁸That is, it is not the children of the flesh who are the children of God, but the children born of the promise who are reckoned as Abraham's offspring. ⁹For so runs the promise, *"At the time appointed I shall return, and Sarah will have a son."* ¹⁰Not only that, but even when Rebecca had children by one and the same man, our father Isaac—¹¹even before they had been born or had done anything good or evil, in order that God's purpose in election might persist, ¹²not because of deeds but because of his call—it was said to her, *"The older shall serve the younger."* ¹³As it stands written, *"Jacob I loved, but Esau I hated."*

COMMENT

What Paul has said in vv 1–5 begins to point up the problem. If God has indeed endowed Israel with such prerogatives, does not Israel's failure to react to the gospel and to the new message about salvation and justification by faith really mean that God's purpose too has failed? Have not God's promises to Israel ended in nothing as far as the Jews are concerned? To answer such questions Paul explains how God has dealt with Israel.

Paul's first explanation of the problem that caused his anguish stresses God's role in the predicament. It all started with God. His promises to Israel all stem from his gratuitous election of it as his people; hence his word has not failed. Paul insists: Israel's rejection does not mean that God's word has failed. Through the examples of Isaac, born to Abraham and Sarah, and of Jacob, born to Isaac and Rebecca, Paul will illustrate his thesis of God's gracious election.

Paul develops his argument at this point by making a distinction between *Israēl* and *hoi ex Israēl*, between "Israel" and "those from Israel," between Abraham's *tekna*, "children," and his *sperma*, "offspring." Paul also distinguishes different kinds of divine election, as he tries to explain what election really means. What distinguishes the kinds is the purpose for which God has chosen individuals and groups. From the examples used in this paragraph Paul seeks to show that the way God deals with contemporary Jews is the way he has dealt with the patriarchs of old. It may seem that God, in so dealing, is really unjust; but Paul will not tolerate that implication.

The problem, which Paul's distinction in this paragraph creates, is seen when one considers it in the light of 11:25–27. Here Paul distinguishes between *Israēl* and *hoi ex Israēl*, between Abraham's "children" and his "offspring," implying that "Israel" and the "children of Abraham" are the ones who as heirs of the promise partake of this new mode of salvation. But in 11:25–27 he maintains that "all Israel will be saved." The problem, then, is the sense in which he uses "Israel." Because the use seems to be contradictory in these passages, Paul has been accused of inconsistency or incoherence. This problem will be more fully discussed apropos of 11:25–27. But the reader is alerted to the problem and should read the intervening verses in the light of it.

The paragraphs that follow in this chapter (vv 6–29), coupled with Paul's assertion in 8:28–30, have been the subject of a long history of interpretation with regard to free will and predestination by Gnostics, Origen, John Chrysostom, Augustine, Abelard, Thomas Aquinas, Calvin, Arminius, and more modern interpreters. For a brief survey of this history, see Sanday and Headlam, *Romans*, 269–75.

NOTES

9:6. *It is not as though the word of God has failed.* God's "word" refers to the promises made to Israel and its patriarchs (9:4, 9; 4:13–21), and they have not depended on what Israel has done and have not been thwarted even by the reaction of Paul's kinsmen to salvation history and its new agent, Christ Jesus. Cf. 3:2, "the oracles of God," which declare and make known God's will and his set purpose. The promises made to Israel have been faithfully kept; God has proved true to them. The purpose that God had for Israel has not become a dead letter. So Paul formulates his proposition about God's promises, mercy, and grace in this passage, 9:6–29. Cf. Num 23:19; Isa 55:10–11; 2 Cor 2:17; 4:2.

For *ekpiptein* in the sense of "fail, wither, come to nothing," see Sir 34:7; Job 14:2; Isa 40:7; 1 Cor 13:8 (some MSS); Jas 1:11. For the grammatical construction of the sentence, see BDF §304; 480.5.

not all descendants of Israel are truly Israel. Lit., "not all those from Israel are Israel." If "Israel" be understood to designate a nation like Ammon, Edom, or Moab, then, because the majority of the nation has not accepted the gospel, God's word seems to have come to naught. God promised that Israel would be the recipient of blessings, but now that Gentiles are becoming the recipients, it might seem that God's promises vacillate. If Paul's argument in Romans 1–8 depends on God's promises, then maybe it is all as shaky as they are. No, replies Paul, one has to distinguish the meaning of "Israel." The OT promises were not made to the ethnic or historical-empirical Israel, those of physical descent or of flesh and blood, but to the Israel of faith. If God were bound by physical descent, his promises would not have been freely made. They were made instead to the Israel that would come to faith. Thus Paul vindicates God's part in history by an ethnological argument.

Elsewhere in Romans (9:27, 31; 10:19, 21; 11:2, 7, 25) as well as elsewhere in his letters (1 Cor 10:18; 2 Cor 3:7, 13; Phil 3:5), Paul clearly has "Israel" in the ethnic sense in mind: *Israēl kata sarka*, as he does in the first instance in this verse. The problem is to determine the sense of it in the second instance, and then again in 11:26. In 9:4 he calls the Jews "Israelites," but now he insists that "Israel" has a restricted eschatological meaning. Thus the argument of 2:28 ("Who is the real Jew"?) surfaces again, in a new way. In the ethnic sense, all Jews are Israelites; but in the restricted sense, "Israel" means the Jews of faith.

One might be tempted to identify Israel in the restricted sense with "the Israel of God" (Gal 6:16); that would then include Gentile Christians as well, i.e., the church, which seems to have been the meaning Paul intended by "Israel" there (see W. Gutbrod, *TDNT* 3.387–88: in the immediately preceding context the distinction of circumcision and uncircumcision is declared to be of no account). This is the meaning given to "Israel" in the second instance in this verse by Dinkler (*JR* 36 [1956]: 116), Aageson (*JSNT* 31 [1987]: 55: "Jews and Gentiles who do [believe]"); Ellis (*Paul's Use*, 137); Ponsot (*RB* 89 [1982]: 414).

Does Paul mean it so here? It seems, rather, that "Israel" in the second instance refers to Jewish Christians, to those of ethnic Israel who have put faith in Christ. Having made this distinction, Paul discusses ethnic Israel, seeking to refine its relation to God's election. Cf. Dahl, "Der Name Israel"; Sanders, *Paul, the Law*, 174; H. Kuhli, *EDNT* 2.202–4.

7. *nor because they are offspring of Abraham are they all his children.* Lit., "nor because they are all the seed of Abraham (are they all his) children." Physical descent alone does not insure inheritance, for Abraham had many offspring (*sperma Abraam*): Ishmael, born of Hagar (Gen 16:15); Isaac, born of Sarah (Gen 21:2), and six others born of Keturah: Zimran, Jokshan, Medan, Midian, Ishbak, and Shuah (Gen 25:2); nor should one forget the house boy, Eliezer of Damascus (Gen 15:2). Ishmael, born of Hagar, and the children of Keturah were physical descendants of Abraham, but only the one born of the promise (Gen 18:10), Isaac, was the real "seed" or descendant. The patriarchal promise of salvation was transmitted only through Isaac (Gen 21:12). As Paul had distinguished "Israel" from those "who are from Israel," so now he distinguishes "the children of Abraham" from "Abraham's seed (offspring)." To the former belong the divine promises. For the expression "the seed of Abraham," see Isa 41:8; Ps 105:6; 2 Chr 20:7; 3 Macc 6:13; cf. Rom 4:13, 16, 18; 11:1; Gal 3:16, 19, 29; 2 Cor 11:22.

"*It is through Isaac that your offspring will be named.*" Paul quotes Gen 21:12 word for word according to the LXX, which corresponds to the MT. Isaac has been chosen because he was born in accordance with a promise. The real offspring of Abraham will be born of Isaac's lineage. Through that lineage the promises of God will be continued and will find their fulfillment. Cf. Heb 11:18, where Gen 21:12 is also quoted. Recall Gen 21:8–11, the background of the saying quoted.

8. *it is not the children of the flesh who are the children of God.* Abraham's true progeny are those born to him in virtue of a promise, not by a connection *kata sarka*, i.e., by physical descent (see the NOTES on 1:3; 9:4). Recall the children of the flesh mentioned in the NOTE on v 7. Cf. Gal 4:23, and the allegory used there to illustrate this verse. Cf. *Jub.* 16:17: "All his other sons would be Gentiles and would be reckoned with Gentiles, although one of Isaac's sons would become a holy offspring, not to be reckoned with Gentiles; he would become the portion of the Most High, and all his descendants would be settled in that land which belongs to God, so as to be the Lord's special acquisition."

Paul now reverts to the terminology of 8:21, implying that Christians, Jewish and Gentile, are the true children of Abraham. "Children of God" refers to those related to God by the bonds that have been the privilege and characteristic of the chosen people (Sanday and Headlam, *Romans*, 242).

the children born of the promise are reckoned as Abraham's offspring. Paul is not thinking of the generic promise made to Abraham that he would have a numberless progeny (Gen 15:5), but more specifically of the progeny to be born of Sarah and thus of his son and heir, Isaac (Gen 18:10, 14), as v 9 reveals. Cf. 9:4; 4:13; 15:8; Gal 4:23. Again Paul uses the important vb. *logizein;* in 4:3 it appeared in the quotation of Gen 15:6; thereafter in 4:6, 8. It is thus expressive of the divine freedom of election. God chose to reckon Abraham as upright; now he chooses to reckon the children of Abraham born of the promise as the real offspring of Abraham. It is not that God had no care for Ishmael or the other children of Abraham, but they were not destined for the inheritance of Abraham, as was Isaac, born of Sarah.

9. *so runs the promise.* Lit., "this word is (one) of promise." Paul puts the predicate *epangelias*, "of promise," in the first position in the sentence to emphasize it, for it is the all-important factor in the story of Isaac. For had it depended on *sarx* alone, Isaac would never have been born to barren Sarah.

At the time appointed I shall return, and Sarah will have a son. So the promise specifically is made with reference to the birth of Isaac from Sarah. Paul quotes and conflates Gen 18:10, 14, using words from the LXX. Although the quotation is not exact, it captures the spirit of the Genesis story. The phrase *kata ton kairon touton*, lit., "according to this time," undoubtedly means "about this time next year." In the LXX the phrase is supposed to translate Hebrew *kāʿēt ḥayyāh*, lit., "at the time (when it is) living," i.e., the term of pregnancy. See Gruber, "The Reality."

10. *even when Rebecca had children by one and the same man, our father Isaac.* Lit., "but even Rebecca, having a pregnancy from one (man), Isaac our father." The grammar is at fault here. Paul fails to use a finite verb, expressing his idea only by a participial phrase *koitēn echousa*, "having a pregnancy," which

561

is followed in v 11 by a gen. absol., in which the pl. subject, "children," is not expressed, but understood. The result is that the participial phrase, *Rebekka . . . echousa*, becomes a nom. absol., to which the pron. *autē*, "to her," in v 12 eventually refers.

Another example confirms Paul's contention: God freely bestows favor on whom he wills. In this case it is no longer a choice among mothers, Sarah or Hagar (allegorized in Gal 4:21–31) or Keturah, but between sons of the same mother, between the twins Jacob and Esau, begotten of the same father; hence both born to the patriarch Isaac and his wife Rebecca. Yet God favored not the older twin, Esau, but the younger, Jacob, making a choice that freely conditioned Israel's history (Gen 25:21–26). Paul sensed that his first argument might not be too valid, because only Isaac was born to Abraham of his real wife, whereas Ishmael was born to Sarah's handmaid in the time of her sterility and the others to Keturah. So only Isaac was his real heir. Paul passes over the other offspring, because he is interested only in the child born of the "promise." Now he makes use of a clearer example. Through God's choice only Jacob becomes the heir to the promise. Paul shows that God's word has not failed; his election has descended to ethnic Israel through the favored Jacob. So Paul again emphasizes God's gratuitous election. In using "our father Isaac," he identifies himself with ethnic Israel.

11. *before they had been born or had done anything good or evil.* Lit., "(the children) not yet being born or having done anything . . ." (the gen. absol. that lacks the subject). The choice of Jacob was entirely gratuitous and depended not on merits or demerits; this clause is crucial to Paul's argument, for the call of Gentiles to Christian faith is equally gratuitous. It depends not on what persons have done or not done.

in order that God's purpose in election might persist. Lit., "that the purpose of God according to election might continue," i.e., that the gratuity of the whole salvific plan might go on. Jacob was favored in order to make known the execution of a divine plan proceeding according to gratuitous election. See 11:5–6, 28; Eph 1:11.

12. *not because of deeds but because of his call.* Lit., "because of the one calling (him, i.e., Jacob)." The fundamental thesis of Romans is applied to Israel's patriarchal heritage. Through God's prevenient favor Rebecca conceived twins, and the younger was called by God to be Isaac's heir. Cf. 4:17. All Paul says is that it was "not because of deeds," and says nothing about the basis on which the call was made, either God's foreknowledge, as John Chrysostom understood it (*In ep. ad Romanos* hom. 16.6 [PG 60.557]) or God's predestination, as Calvin did (*Commentary on Romans* [trans. J. Owen], 349).

it was said to her. The pron. *autē* refers to Rebecca (see the NOTE on v 10), who was perturbed at the struggle of the two twins within her (Gen 25:22); God's reassurance was given to her: "Two nations are in your womb, two peoples are quarreling while still within you; but one shall surpass the other . . ." (Gen 25:23a–c).

"The older shall serve the younger." Paul quotes Gen 25:23d according to the LXX, which gives an interpretation to the ambiguous, oracular Hebrew of the MT, which reads, *wĕrab yaʿăbōd ṣāʿîr*. This phrase could mean, "and (the) great(er) will serve (the) small(er)," or it could mean, "and (the) small(er) will serve (the) great(er)." The LXX interpretation adapts the meaning to the context. So Esau, the elder twin, became the servant of his younger brother, Jacob. Esau married Mahalath, the daughter of Ishmael (Gen 28:9) and became the ancestor of Edom, and of the later Idumaeans (Josephus, *Ant.* 12.8.1 §328). The latter were never considered real Jews, even though John Hyrcanus I defeated them (ca. 108 B.C.), forcing them to be circumcised and follow the Mosaic law. Josephus calls them "half-Jews" (*Ant.* 13.9.1 §257; 14.15.2 §403). How different then was their destiny from that of Israel.

13. *As it stands written.* See the NOTE on 1:17.

"Jacob I loved, but Esau I hated." Paul quotes Mal 1:2–3 according to the LXX, but with a change of word order. By this statement Malachi records Yahweh's love of Israel and then gives reasons for the five great reproaches that follow on this protestation of love. The divine choice raises the question of justice, or theodicy. But Paul uses the quotation to stress Israel's role in the salvific plan in contrast to Edom's. Jacob and Esau are the representatives of their ethnic groups and are tools in the execution of the divine plan of salvation. God is sovereign and freely chooses Jacob as such a tool. The aorists are taken as gnomic (see BDF §333).

Esau I hated. I.e., "loved less," according to an ancient Near Eastern hyperbole. It expresses the lack of gratuitous election of Esau and the Edomites (Idumaeans). See Gen 29:30–31: "he loved Rachel more than Leah . . . ; when the Lord saw that Leah was hated . . ."; cf. Deut 21:15–17; compare Luke 14:26 ("hate") with Matt 10:37 ("love more"). There is no hint here of predestination to "grace" or "glory" of an individual; it is an expression of the choice of corporate Israel over corporate Edom.

BIBLIOGRAPHY

Aletti, J.-N., "L'Argumentation paulinienne en Rm 9," *Bib* 68 (1987): 41–56.

Berger, K., "Abraham in den paulinischen Hauptbriefen," *MTZ* 17 (1966): 47–89, esp. 77–86.

Brooks, J. A., "The Influence of Malachi upon the New Testament," *SwJT* 30 (1987–88): 28–31.

Dahl, N. A., "Der Name Israel," *Judaica* 6 (1950): 161–70.

Dobschütz, E. von, "Prädestination," *TSK* 106 (1934): 9–19.

Eborowicz, W., "Ad Romanos 9,11 et la critique augustinienne de la théorie du péché de l'âme préexistante," *SE* V, TU 103 (1968), 272–76.

Ellis, E. E., *Paul's Use of the Old Testament* (Grand Rapids, Mich.: Baker, 1957; repr. 1981).

Gaston, L., "Israel's Enemies in Pauline Theology," *NTS* 28 (1982): 400–423.

Gruber, M. I., "The Reality Behind the Hebrew Expression k^ct hyh," *ZAW* 103 (1991): 271–74.

Gueuret, A., "Épître de Paul aux Romains: Analyse des contenus du ch. 9,6–13," *Sémiotique et Bible* 34 (1984): 15–28.

Hanson, A. T., *Studies in Paul's Technique*, 87–103.

Montagnini, F., "Elezione e libertà, grazia e predestinazione a proposito di Rom. 9, 6–29," *Die Israelfrage*, ed. L. de Lorenzi, 57–97.

Stegner, W. R., "Romans 9.6–29—a Midrash," *JSNT* 22 (1984): 37–52.

Steudel, J. C. F., "Nachweisung der in Röm. C. 9 liegenden Sätze als zu Gunsten eines unbedingten Rathschlusses Gottes nicht deutbarer," *Tübinger Zeitschrift für Theologie* (1836): Heft 1.3–95.

Wiskerke, J. R., *Geroepen Volk: Een studie over Rom. 9:10–29* (Goes: Oosterbaan & Le Cointre, 1967).

33. GOD'S SOVEREIGN FREEDOM EVEN USES INDOCILITY TO HIS PURPOSE (9:14–23)

9 [14]What then shall we say? Is God unjust? Certainly not! [15]For he says to Moses, *"I will show mercy to whomever I will, and I will have compassion on whomever I will."* [16]So it depends not on human willing or effort, but on God's mercy. [17]For Scripture says to Pharaoh, *"For this very reason have I raised you up, that I might display my power through you and that my name might be proclaimed over all the earth."* [18]Therefore he has mercy on whomever he wills and hardens the heart of whomever he chooses. [19]Will you therefore say to me, "Then why does God still find fault? Who has ever resisted his will?" [20]But who are you, a mere human being, to answer back to God? *Will what is molded say to its molder, "Why did you make me like this?"* [21]Has not the potter the right to make out of the same lump of clay one vase for a noble purpose and another for common use? [22]Yet what if God, wishing to display his wrath and make known his power, has endured with much long-suffering those vases of wrath, fashioned for destruction? [23]This he did to make known the riches of his glory for the vases of mercy, which he had fashioned beforehand for such glory.

COMMENT

In this section of chap. 9 Paul draws a further proof of God's gratuitous promise and mercy to Israel in salvation history. What has happened to Israel is "not because of deeds but because of his call" (9:12), i.e., it is not contrary to

God's direction of history, for Israel's call and indocility were foreseen. Paul now cites the manifestation of such mercy in the story of Moses and Pharaoh: how God called Moses and used indocile Pharaoh. He also uses the OT image of a potter who fashions vases for noble or menial uses to express the same idea. Again, the Apostle draws his examples from well-known OT figures and images to stress God's sovereign choice. The argument seems to raise the question of theodicy; in effect, Paul is answering an implied objection, "If all this is true, is not God unjust?" He insists that God does not gauge things by human standards. He does not try to argue the question of theodicy; he simply rejects it.

The dealings of Moses with Pharaoh are recounted in Exod 3:10–12:36. There the opposition of the Egyptian pharaoh to the Hebrews and their desire to depart from Egypt is narrated. Yet even the indocility of Pharaoh, who hardened his heart against the Hebrews, is used to manifest God's freedom and sovereignty. God can even use the pagan pharaoh to his purpose.

The image of the ancient potter recalls the invention of pottery, which was one of the great steps forward in human history. It emerged in the Neolithic age about 4400 B.C., when the first pottery was handmade, coarse, and plain. About a thousand years later the potter's wheel was invented, which enabled one to shape perfectly circular, geometric pottery. A round table on a vertical pole, which a boy or a slave would turn, served the potter, who deftly shaped the forms. In time a device was invented so that the potter could turn the wheel herself with her foot. A lump of clay was thrown on the wheel, and the wheel was spun rapidly; the result was a perfectly circular object, shaped at the will of the potter.

It was not long, however, before the ancients, watching this phenomenon of the clay taking shape under the fingers of an expert potter, who in a matter of seconds shaped all sorts of forms, derived the idea of a potter god. The creator god was depicted in ancient Egypt as a potter working the wheel and fashioning human beings out of clay (see *ANEP*, §569). This is the image that stands behind the creation of Adam by Yahweh in Gen 2:7. The potter thus became the human springboard from which ancients arose to the idea of a god who not only fashioned the earth and all that is in it but who controls and governs it all at his will and choice.

In the OT the image of God as a ceramist is often found. It expresses God's sovereign power, dominion, and freedom in acting. This image serves the prophet Jeremiah: "I went down to the potter's house and there he was, working at the wheel. Whenever the clay object that he was making turned out badly in his hands, he tried again, making of the clay another object of whatever sort he wanted. Then the word of the Lord came to me, 'Can I not do to you, O house of Israel, as this potter has done?' says the Lord. 'Indeed, as is clay in the hand of the potter, so are you in my hand, house of Israel' " (Jer 18:3–6). Cf. Isa 29:16; 45:9; 64:7; Lam 4:2; Wis 15:7; 1QS 11:22.

Paul uses this OT image to inculcate the idea that a creature cannot really ask

God to account for his ways. Hence the fact that Israel has reacted as it has to God's new mode of salvation argues in no way that God has lost control of Israel.

Verses 14–19 are the problematic part of this passage. Origen (*In ep. ad Romanos* 7.16 [PG 14.1143–44]) ascribes these verses to an imaginary interlocutor who objects to what Paul has written. In this reading he was somewhat followed by John Chrysostom (*In ep. ad Romanos* hom. 16.7 [PG 60.558]) and other Greek patristic commentators. Augustine, however, departed from that interpretation, attributing vv 14–19 to Paul himself and insisting that deeds do not precede grace, but follow it (*Opus imperfectum contra Iulianum* 1.141.50–55 [CSEL 85.1.159–60]). See further the COMMENT on 9:6–13.

In this passage Paul again indulges in diatribe; see the COMMENT on 2:1–11 and Introduction, section VII.

NOTES

9:14. *What then shall we say?* I.e., about God's promise and gracious election? About God's ways of dealing with contemporary Israel in the light of what he did for it in the past? On such an introductory rhetorical question, see the NOTE on 6:1.

Is God unjust? Lit., "Injustice is not with God, is it?" Again a diatribic objection is entertained. God might seem to be involved in *adikia*, "injustice," in choosing one brother over the other, Jacob over Esau, or in choosing Gentiles as his people after centuries of service from the Jews, whom he originally declared to be his chosen people and whose prerogatives still stand. Cf. 2:11 for a similar statement about God's impartiality.

Certainly not! See the NOTE on 3:4. Again, Paul resolutely brushes aside the suggestion, denying the propriety of even asking the question. Cf. Deut 32:4, "all his ways are justice."

15. *he says to Moses.* The lawgiver of Israel was mentioned in 5:14; he will appear again in 10:5, 14. He is quoted now to bolster Paul's rejection of the suggestion about God's injustice. See *ESBNT*, 3–58. Moses who was above all the recipient of God's revelation also proclaimed God's mercy. It is of his nature to be merciful.

"I will show mercy to whomever I will, and I will have compassion on whomever I will." Paul cites Exod 33:19 according to the LXX, which corresponds to the MT (with a slight change of tenses). This is Yahweh's answer to Moses after the incident of the golden calf (Exodus 32), when Moses prayed to God on behalf of Israel and begged him to relent and not punish the Hebrews. In spite of such infidelity Yahweh could still manifest his mercy, favoring Israel as his chosen people. In this theophany to Moses, God thus displayed himself once again as a God of mercy; he might have manifested his distributive justice against the Hebrews in punishing them, but revealed instead that his mercy was utterly free. Yet no one, not even Israel, could stake a claim on God's mercy. Through Israel

he would continue to make his will and his mercy known to humanity. These words, addressed originally to Moses, are cited by Paul in order to underscore Yahweh's freedom of merciful activity; he does not act arbitrarily, as Israel itself knows. The quotation acts as a summary of what vv 6–13 have affirmed about God's gracious mercy. It thus forms the answer to the objection raised. This verse is summarized in v 18.

To see these words addressed to Moses as a reflection of Yahweh's words in Exod 3:14, "I am who am," as do Karl Barth and Cranfield (*Romans*, 483), is surely eisegetical.

16. *So it depends not on human willing or effort, but on God's mercy.* Lit., "(it is) not, then, of the one willing or running, but of God showing mercy." Paul's conclusion is so formulated because God's "mercy" is mentioned in the OT verse quoted. Without it all human effort is in vain; no one can claim merciful treatment from God. For God's mercy depends on God alone. It is not a question of human activity, achievement, merit, or worth, or even of heritage, but solely of God being merciful. Paul uses his athletic figure of "running" to express effort and striving toward a goal; he will allude to it again in vv 30–31. Recall 9:11; also Gal 2:2; 5:7; 1 Cor 9:24–26; Phil 2:16; 3:12–14; cf. Titus 3:5; 2 Tim 4:7; *As. Mos.* 12:7. See Derrett, "Running"; Noack, "Celui"; Pfitzner, *Paul and the Agon Motif.*

17. *Scripture says to Pharaoh.* Whereas the transcendent God of Israel spoke to Moses directly (9:15), he speaks to the heathen indirectly, through Scripture. For a similar use of *hē graphē*, "Scripture," see Gal 3:8, 22 (see the NOTE on 4:3). "Pharaoh," who maltreated the Hebrews during their stay in Egypt, represents all who resist God, yet even he plays a role in God's manifestation of his mercy, grace, and power.

In Hebrew, "Pharaoh" appears as *Parʿōh*, an attempt to write Egyptian *pr-ʿ*, "Great House." The word served both as a title (Jer 46:2) and as a name (Gen 39:1) in the OT. The Pharaoh of the oppression and exodus cannot be identified with certainty, but the stories about the building of the supply cities of Pithom and Ramsese (Exod 1:11) point to Ramesses II (1279–1212 B.C.). In the LXX the name appears as *Pharaō*, the form that Paul uses.

"For this very reason have I raised you up, that I might display my power through you and that my name might be proclaimed over all the earth." Paul quotes Exod 9:16 according to the LXX in MS A, which is close to the MT ("cause you to see my power"). The words are derived from Moses' speech to Pharaoh after the sixth plague, that of the boils. The heathen Pharaoh was thus an object of God's design and choice, chosen as an instrument for the execution of the salvific plan for the Hebrews, just as Moses himself was. Pharaoh was "raised up," either from the illness of the plague (see Jas 5:15) or in the sense that God introduced him into human history for a definite purpose (cf. Hab 1:6; Zech 11:16). His very obstinacy was a means that God used to deliver the Hebrews from Egyptian bondage. Ultimately, the hardhearted Pharaoh contributed to the

proclamation of God's name in the world. When human beings react against God, they think that they are acting on their own and believe that they are thus limiting God's power or thwarting his plans; but actually he is in that reaction making them obdurate against him, as he did the Pharaoh. God's freedom and sovereignty in the choice of instruments to achieve his end are made manifest. Thus Pharaoh became an instrument whereby God's power *(dynamis)* was manifested and his name *(onoma)* proclaimed.

18. *Therefore he has mercy on whomever he wills and hardens the heart of whomever he chooses.* Paul summarizes v 15, again asserting the sovereignty and freedom of God's activity with different human beings in order that his will might be accomplished.

In the OT the hardening of Pharaoh's heart is ascribed at times to God (Exod 4:21; 7:3; 9:12; 10:20, 27; 14:8, from the LXX of which Paul derives the vb. *sklērynein,* "harden") and at times to Pharaoh himself (Exod 7:14; 8:11, 15, 28, where the vb. *barein* is usually used). The "hardening of the heart" by God is a protological way of expressing divine reaction to persistent human obstinacy against him, a sealing of a situation arising, not from God, but from a creature that rejects divine invitation. It brings out God's utter control of human history. The exodus of the Hebrews from Egypt was a phase in their salvific history, and Pharaoh who opposed the departure of the Hebrews was a figure setting the stage for God's intervention on behalf of his people. Recall the similar use of Cyrus the Persian king, who is even called *māšîaḥ,* "(God's) anointed one," in Isa 45:1.

19. *Will you therefore say to me?* A diatribelike objection: why blame me, if I, a Jew, do not accept God's offer in Christ?

Then why does God still find fault? I.e., if God can make use of indocility to achieve his purpose, why should he complain about human beings who are obstinate? Recall 3:7; 6:1–2, 15. Is not such a person, like obstinate Pharaoh, an instrument that God can use nonetheless to accomplish his designs? Does not Scripture itself provide the perfect example of God's ability to do so?

Who has ever resisted his will? Or possibly, "Who resists," for the perf. tense often expresses a present (BDF §340–41). It is not "who can resist," as the RSV has it (also Barrett [*Romans,* 187]; Byrne [*Romans,* 187], Michel [*Brief an die Römer,* 236]). If God is sovereign in his choice and use of his power, who then has ever thwarted his designs? Cf. Wis 11:21; esp. 12:12b, "who can oppose your judgment?"

20. *who are you, a mere human being, to answer back to God?* Lit., "Now then, O man/human being, who are you . . ." (see BDF §146.1b; 450.4 for the strong corrective particle *menounge,* "nay, rather," used here). Paul is not trying to silence his imaginary objector; rather, he seeks to put the discussion on its proper level. God's control of the world cannot be judged by the myopic view of a human creature. Cf. Isa 45:9; Job 34:36.

Will what is molded say to its molder, "Why did you make me like this?" Paul quotes Isa 29:16 according to the LXX, which in general corresponds to the MT.

The latter, however, uses the vb. *ʿśy*, "make," whereas the LXX has *plassein*, "form, fashion." Cf. Isa 45:9–11, to which much of Paul's phraseology is similar; also 64:8; Jer 18:6; Wis 15:7; 1QS 11:22; 1QH 1:21; 3:23–24; 4:29; 10:3; 12:26, 32; 18:12.

did you make me like this? Not "why did you make me a clay pot?" but "why did you make me an unshapely pot rather than a beautiful vase?" The function of the molded object is emphasized. See Job 9:12, "Who can say to him, 'What are you doing?' " Cf. Job 10:9; Sir 33:13; 38:29–30.

21. *Has not the potter the right to make out of the same lump of clay.* The freedom of the potter exemplifies God's sovereign freedom to choose Israel and destine it for fidelity to his covenant. The Greek word *phyrama*, which also occurs at 11:16; Gal 5:9; 1 Cor 5:6–7, was translated into Latin as *massa*, from which came the pejorative term *massa damnata* in the predestinarian controversies of the Augustinian period (Augustine, *Ep.* 190.3–9 [CSEL 57.144]).

one vase for a noble purpose and another for common use? Lit., "one vessel for honor, another for dishonor," i.e., one for an exalted use, another for a menial use. The last phrase does not mean "destined for destruction or damnation." Cf. 2 Tim 2:20, where the difference in vases is likewise mentioned, but from the aspect of human responsibility. Here Paul will play on different meanings of the Greek noun *skeuos*, which means, generically, a "thing, object" (used for any purpose); but also (specifically) "vessel, jar, dish," and it can even designate (figuratively) a "tool, instrument" (whether the body, a person, perhaps a wife [cf. 1 Thess 4:4]). Paul will play on the last sense, having used it of a vessel.

22. *what if God, wishing to display his wrath and make known his power.* The ptc. *thelōn*, "wishing," is taken in two different ways by interpreters: (1) causally, "because he wished" (so Jerome, Thomas Aquinas, Barrett, Cranfield, Kühl, Kuss, Michel)—God would then wish to display the awesome nature of his wrath in a final overthrow (e.g., of the Pharaoh); or (2) concessively, "though he wished" (so Black, Cornely, Dunn, Gifford, Gutjahr, Käsemann, Leenhardt, Lyonnet, Moffatt, Sanday and Headlam, B. Weiss, Zahn). The latter is preferred because of the phrase "with much long-suffering" in the next clause, i.e., though wrath might have led God to make known his power, his loving-kindness restrained him. God gave Pharaoh time to repent. Similarly, God in his providence has found a way, through the death of Jesus Christ, to pardon past sins and those of the present (3:25–26). Indirectly, Paul echoes the ideas of 2 Chr 36:15–16: "The Lord, the God of their fathers, sent persistently to them by his messengers, because he had compassion upon his people and on his dwelling place; but they kept mocking God's messengers, despising his words, and scoffing at his prophets, till the wrath of the Lord rose against his people unremittingly."

has endured with much long-suffering those vases of wrath. Paul uses a phrase from Jer 50:25, "vases of wrath," which suits the pottery context (9:21); it also occurs in Isa 13:5 (LXX in some MSS). A "vase of wrath" would be one toward which wrath was displayed, a useless pot to be discarded. Paul now plays on the figurative sense of *skeuos*. Pharaoh was such a vase, an "object" toward which divine wrath could be displayed, but such an object became an "instrument" of God's long-suffering. Cf. Wis 12:10, 20–22. For the gen. of quality ("of wrath"), see BDF §165.

fashioned for destruction. The perf. ptc. *katērtismena* expresses the state in which such "vessels" find themselves, "suited, fitted out" for the rubbish heap, but Paul does not say by whom they were so fashioned. Rather, he seeks to express God's radical incompatibility with rebellious, sinful human beings. It also expresses a nuance of predestination (damnation), but Paul's formulation is more generic than the example with which he began, which is why his words were used in later predestinarian controversies. One should not, however, lose sight of his corporate perspective.

23. *This he did to make known the riches of his glory.* Lit., "and in order to make known. . . ." Paul adds a purpose cl. but fails to conclude the condition he began in v 22, thus creating an anacoluthon; see Bornkamm, "Paulinische Anakoluthe," 90–92. Paul adds this clause in order to forestall an objection, because he realizes that God has tolerated such vases of wrath in order to manifest his mercy to those whom he has called. Those chosen for a role in salvation history have been destined by God for a share in his abundant glory (see the NOTES on 3:23, 29); this destiny is not limited to the Jewish people. But, as 11:22 will show, it is not an absolute predestination. If God has been patient, it is because he wants to allow Israel time to come to the acceptance of Christ so that he might manifest his mercy to it all the more. See 10:12; 11:33; Phil 4:19; cf. Eph 1:18; 3:16; Col 1:27.

Some MSS (B, 326, 436, 1739) and some ancient versions omit the opening conj. *kai*.

for the vases of mercy, which he had fashioned beforehand for such glory. "Vases of mercy" is a phrase Paul has fashioned to parallel "vases of wrath." As v 24b shows, they include Christians from Judaism as well as from paganism. Recall 8:28–30, which serves as an explanation of this part of the verse.

BIBLIOGRAPHY

Beale, G. K., "An Exegetical and Theological Consideration of the Hardening of Pharaoh's Heart in Exodus 4–14 and Romans 9," *TrinJ* 5 (1984): 129–54.

Bornkamm, G., "Paulinische Anakoluthe," *Das Ende des Gesetzes*, 76–92, esp. 90–92.

———, "Predigt über Römer 9,14–24," *Festschrift für Ernst Fuchs*, ed. G. Ebeling et al. (Tübingen: Mohr [Siebeck], 1973), 91–96.

Démann, P., "Moïse et la loi dans la pensée de saint Paul," *Moïse, l'homme de l'alliance*, ed. H. Cazelles (Paris: Desclée, 1955), 189–242.

Derrett, J. D. M., " 'Running' in Paul: The Midrashic Potential of Hab 2,2," *Bib* 66 (1985): 560–67.

Dion, H.-M., "La Notion paulinienne de 'richesse de Dieu' et ses sources," *ScEccl* 18 (1966): 139–48.

Ellingworth, P., "Translation and Exegesis: A Case Study (Rom 9,22ff.)," *Bib* 59 (1978): 396–402.

González Ruiz, J. M., "Justicia y misericordia divina en la elección y reprobación de los hombres (Nota sobre Rom. 9, 19–23)," *EstBíb* 8 (1949): 365–77.

Hanson, A. T., "Vessels of Wrath or Instruments of Wrath? Romans ix. 22–3," *JTS* 32 (1981): 433–43.

Jeremias, J., "Zur Gedankenführung in den paulinischen Briefen," *Studia paulina in honorem Johannis de Zwaan septuagenarii* (Haarlem: Bohn, 1953), 146–54, esp. 146–49.

Montagnini, F., "Elezione e libertà, grazia e predestinazione a proposito di Rom 9:26–29," *Die Israelfrage*, ed. L. de Lorenzi, 57–86.

Noack, B., "Celui qui court: *Rom*. IX, 16," *ST* 24 (1970): 113–16.

Pfitzner, V. C., *Paul and the Agon Motif: Traditional Athletic Imagery in the Pauline Literature*, NovTSup 16 (Leiden: Brill, 1967), 135–38.

Piper, J., "Prolegomena to Understanding Romans 9:14–15: An Interpretation of Exodus 33:19," *JETS* 22 (1979): 203–16.

Plumptre, E. H., "The Potter and the Clay: Jer. xviii. 1–10; Rom. ix. 19–24," *Expos* 1.4 (1876): 469–80.

Schelkle, K. H., *Paulus Lehrer der Väter*, 336–61.

Weber, V., *Kritische Geschichte der Exegese des 9. Kapitels, resp. der Verse 14–23, des Römerbriefes bis auf Chrysostomus und Augustinus einschliesslich* (Würzburg: Becker, 1889).

34. GOD DOES NOT ACT ARBITRARILY: ISRAEL'S CALL, INFIDELITY, AND REMNANT ARE FORESEEN IN WHAT GOD ANNOUNCED IN THE OLD TESTAMENT (9:24–29)

9 [24]Even for us, whom he has called, not only from among the Jews, but also from among the Gentiles, [25]as indeed he says in Hosea,

> "Those who were not my people
> I shall call 'my people';
> and her who was not loved
> I shall call 'my beloved' ";

[26]and

> "In the very place where it was said to them,
> 'You are not my people,'
> there they shall be called 'children of the living God.' "

²⁷And Isaiah cries out about Israel,

> *"Should the number of the Israelites be as the sands*
> *of the sea, a remnant shall be saved."*
> 28 *"For the Lord will carry out his sentence*
> *on the earth with rigor and dispatch."*

²⁹And as Isaiah has predicted,

> *"If the Lord of hosts had not left us offspring,*
> *we would have fared like Sodom*
> *and been made like Gomorrah."*

COMMENT

It is a matter of debate among commentators whether v 24 should go with vv 14–23 or vv 25–29. The problem is caused by a Pauline anacoluthon. Verse 24 would seem to be a conclusion from the preceding verses, but then Paul does not really draw a conclusion in the proper sense. His conclusion should be something like this: how, then, can we speak of injustice in God, if he chooses vases of mercy and, though he wanted to display his anger to vases of wrath, he withholds it in long-suffering and manifests his glory to vessels of mercy? Instead of drawing such a conclusion, Paul merely insists on God's freedom of election and his patience in waiting for instruments that he might use to manifest their utility.

Paul stresses that God does not act arbitrarily, because Israel's call, infidelity, and remnant are all part of what has been announced in the OT itself. There God's plan (8:28) foresaw not only Israel's call and election, but also its infidelity. Having shown in 9:6 the free choice of Abraham's real descendants (children of faith, not merely those of physical descent), he now proceeds to show that God's merciful foresight included not only Israel's infidelity but the call of the Gentiles too, for God had promised Abraham, "All the nations of the earth shall be blessed in you" (Gen 18:18). What the Gentiles need is the call to life. They get it by incorporation into Israel, the chosen people of God.

After the anacoluthon in v 24, Paul cites a string of OT passages to emphasize God's free choice of Gentiles now called to justification by grace through faith in Christ. Again, Paul makes use of a *testimonia* list (see 3:10–20 and the COMMENT there) to illustrate God's plan. In this list conflated quotations are derived from Hosea and Isaiah, mentioned explicitly in vv 25, 27, and 29. So Paul uses the OT to show who make up the real "Israel" (9:6).

NOTES

9:24. *Even for us, whom he has called, not only from among the Jews, but also from among the Gentiles.* This verse resumes the formulation of v 23, "to make known the riches of his glory for the vases of mercy . . . even for us, whom. . . ." Paul recognizes that he as a Jewish Christian is not alone as a "vase of mercy," but that Gentile Christians have also been the object of God's gracious call. They too have become "vases of mercy." Only here and in 10:12 does Paul use the name *Ioudaioi*, "Jews," in this part of Romans. See NOTE on 2:17.

25. *as indeed he says in Hosea.* I.e., in the Hosea part of the Twelve Minor Prophets (*Dōdekaprophēton*). So Paul introduces explicitly the citation from the prophet; see Fitzmyer, *ESBNT*, 3–58; cf. C. Burchard, "Römer 9,25 *en tō Hōsēe*," *ZNW* 76 (1985): 131. A similar mode of citing Scripture is found in the later *m.* ᵓ*Abot* 3:7, "It is written in David," quoting 1 Chr 29:14! Cf. Rom 11:2; Mark 1:2; 12:26; Luke 20:37.

"*Those who were not my people I shall call 'my people'; and her who was not loved I shall call 'my beloved.'*" The quotation is taken from Hos 2:25, but it agrees in wording with neither the MT nor the LXX nor any ancient version; it is influenced by the LXX form of Hos 1:9. Yet the sense is preserved: "not my people" become "my people," i.e., Gentiles, not part of the chosen people, have become God's people, the object of his choice and loving affection. Hosea's words were uttered about the Northern Kingdom of Israel that had been covenanted with Yahweh, but that had rejected the pact by its harlotry (= idolatry); the restoration of the ten tribes after their harlotry was promised by Hosea. Paul freely adapts the prophetic utterance to the coming of the Gentiles to faith. They illustrate God's election and the divine choice of those who were otherwise unworthy to become privileged ones. See 1 Pet 2:10; *Jub.* 2:19. Paul also plays on the double sense of the vb. *kalein*, "call," which can mean either "name" or "elect," i.e., call to a definite role or task.

26. "*In the very place where it was said to them, 'You are not my people,' there they shall be called 'children of the living God.'*" Paul quotes Hos 2:1 according to the LXX, which is almost the same as the MT; some MSS add *ekei*, "there," which Paul uses. The prophet's words refer to the call to Israel to return, and the "place" probably is to be understood as Jerusalem. But the words are now transferred by Paul to the call of the Gentiles, and there really is no need to try to specify the "place," which just happens to be part of the quotation. More important, the OT passage cited echoes Paul's own designation of Christians as "children of God" (8:21), now applied to Gentile Christians. Whereas Paul quoted Hosea's promise apropos of the Gentiles, he will next quote Isaiah's admonition apropos of Israel.

27. *Isaiah cries out about Israel.* Paul adds the testimony of one of Israel's major prophets to the words of a minor prophet. To introduce the quotation, Paul again uses the vb. *krazein*; see the NOTE on 8:15.

"*Should the number of the Israelites be as the sands of the sea, a remnant shall be saved.*" Paul cites Isa 10:22, almost according to the LXX, but abridges it and introduces a phrase, *ho arithmos tōn huiōn Israēl*, "the number of the sons of Israel," from the LXX of Hos 2:1. The reason for this mode of quotation is partly that the sense of the MT of Isaiah is somewhat unclear, and partly that he has just used Hos 2:1 in the preceding verse. Paul extracts from the Isaian verse the kernel, "a remnant shall be saved." Some "seed" will become children of Abraham (9:7–8). Through all of Israel's history a ray of hope has always gleamed; God's mercy has always been manifested to some and will continue to be. The words about the remnant were used originally by Isaiah about those preserved from the Assyrian captivity; as Israel survived that captivity in the days of Isaiah, so too now. Paul applies the words to Jews called to accept Christ, and the remnant becomes those who actually did accept him, viz., Paul and fellow Jewish Christians. That there is such a remnant depends not on human claims, but on divine election, God's free mercy in calling. In this remnant Paul sees the promises of God carried forward and extended to the eschatological Israel. See 11:5.

The Essenes of Qumran also spoke of themselves as a remnant: "For I know that in a short time you will raise up survivors among your people and a remnant within your inheritance" (*šĕʾērît bĕnaḥălātĕkāh*, 1QH 6:7–8). They are the *bĕhîrê ʾēl*, "chosen ones of God" (1QpHab 10:13); *bĕhîrê yiśrāʾēl*, "chosen ones of Israel" (4QFlor 1:19; 1Q37 1:3).

28. *"For the Lord will carry out his sentence on the earth with rigor and dispatch."* Lit., "for the Lord, finishing and cutting short (his) decree, will do (this) on the earth." Paul loosely conflates the beginning of Isa 10:23 with a form of Isa 28:22b. The result is that his quotation agrees with neither the MT of the latter ("I have heard from the Lord, the God of hosts, the destruction decreed for the whole earth") nor the LXX ("I have heard from the Lord of hosts what has been accomplished and limited, what he will do for the whole earth"). The meaning of the pres. ptcs. *syntelōn kai syntemnōn*, derived from the LXX of Isa 10:23, in Paul's form is disputed. They also occur in 28:22 as perf. pass. ptcs., "accomplished and limited." In Paul's form they seem to mean "finishing (definitively) and cutting short" (his decree). See BAGD, 792b. The text cited from Isaiah sounds like a judicial decision that God has made on behalf of the remnant, not on behalf of all Israel. The two ptcs. may refer to God's promise that will see fulfillment, but only to a limited degree (so Lipsius, B. Weiss); or they may indicate that God's promise will be fulfilled only for a limited Israel: salvation will be trimmed down (so Dunn, Jülicher, Schlier, Sickenberger, Wilckens); or they may indicate God's "closing the account and shortening (the time)," i.e., by not prolonging the period of his long-suffering (so Althaus, Schmidt, Zahn, the RSV). Either of the first two meanings seems preferable, referring the ptcs. to the remnant. The two vbs. *syntelein* and *syntemnein* also occur together in the perf. tense in the LXX of Dan 5:26–28. The quotation is intended to explain why "a remnant will be saved." This idea creates a problem when it is related to what Paul will say in 11:25–27.

Some MSS (ℵᶜ, D, G, K, P, Ψ, 33, 88, 326, 614, 1241 and the *Koinē* text-tradition) fill out the quotation by inserting after *syntemnōn* the words *en dikaiosynē, hoti logon syntetmēmenon,* "in uprightness, because (the Lord will make) a work shortened," verbatim from the LXX of Isa 10:23. This insertion, however, cannot be original; it upsets the loose quotation of Isaiah that Paul actually uses.

29. *as Isaiah has predicted.* I.e., has spoken in advance. The second Isaian quotation corroborates the first.

"If the Lord of hosts had not left us offspring, we would have fared like Sodom and been made like Gomorrah." Paul quotes Isa 1:9 according to the LXX, which corresponds to the MT. The offspring makes the difference; they are the remnant, hence Israel has not become like Sodom and Gomorrah, cities destroyed by God's wrath (Gen 19:24–25). The preservation of even a remnant is a manifestation of grace (Cranfield, *Romans*, 502); in this way Paul, by quoting the Isaian verse, goes beyond the affirmation of the quotation in v. 28. The prophet speaks of the punishment of faithless Israel. The burden of these quotations is that the OT, the book that gives Israel a basis for its hope, has itself testified that Israel would fare as did Sodom and Gomorrah of old, except for a remnant that would preserve its name and its offspring.

BIBLIOGRAPHY

Battle, J. A., Jr., "Paul's Use of the Old Testament in Romans 9:25–26," *GTJ* 2 (1981): 115–29.

Bornkamm, G., "Paulinische Anakoluthe," *Das Ende des Gesetzes*, 90–92.

Jeremias, J., "Der Gedanke des 'Heiligen Restes' im Spätjudentum und in der Verkündigung Jesu," ZNW 42 (1949): 184–94.

Watts, J. W., "The Remnant Theme: A Survey of New Testament Research, 1921–1987," *Perspectives in Religious Studies* 15 (1988): 109–29.

W. te G. v. d., "Een afgesnedere zaak doen op aarde: Rom. 9:28," *GTT* 4 (1903): 173–75.

ISRAEL'S FAILURE: IT IS DERIVED FROM ITS OWN REFUSAL (9:30–10:21)

♦

35. ISRAEL HAS STUMBLED IN ITS PURSUIT OF UPRIGHTNESS (9:30–33)

9 [30]What then shall we say? That Gentiles who did not pursue uprightness have attained it, an uprightness based on faith, [31]whereas Israel, which was pursuing a law of uprightness, did not achieve it? [32]Why was this? Because they pursued it not with faith, but as if it were by deeds. They stumbled over "the stumbling stone," [33]as it stands written: *"Look, I am setting in Zion a stone to stumble against, a rock to trip over; and no one who believes in him shall be put to shame."*

COMMENT

Paul has concluded the first step in his treatment of Israel's place in God's new dispensation of salvation: what has happened to Israel does not mean that God has been unfaithful to his promises to it. God is still displaying his grace and mercy to it. Now Paul begins the second step, arguing that the cause of Israel's failure is not to be found in God, but in Israel itself. What has happened to Israel is not contrary to God's direction of human history, for its infidelity was already foreseen in the Scriptures of old. Rather, its situation is derived from its own misstep. In other words, in chap. 9 Paul has so far considered the problem of Israel from the standpoint of God; now he begins to consider it from the standpoint of Israel. Paul reveals here the reasons for his sorrow and anguish (9:2): pagans who have not even been trying to attain rectitude before God have reached that goal by faith and trust, whereas Israel, which was pursuing such a goal, has failed to do so. Pagans have responded to "God's gospel" (1:1), whereas most of God's own people have resisted it. What has gone wrong has caused Paul's sorrow and anguish.

In this section Paul considers the problem of Israel and the Gentiles from both the human and the divine viewpoint. Israel's misstep was in some sense part of God's plan, but in reality it remains the fault of Israel. The tension between these viewpoints is realized by Paul, who in these chapters is facing the age-old problem of God's foreknowledge and human responsibility and freedom. Paul does not have a clear-cut solution to this problem; he is interested only in safeguarding the faithfulness of God and in laying the blame where it should be laid.

Verses 30-33 are transitional to chap. 10, where the second step in his argument is mainly developed. From here to the end of chap. 10 the argument

576

moves in four stages: (1) Israel has preferred its own way of uprightness to God's way (9:30–33); (2) Paul expresses his sorrow that Israel has failed to recognize Christ as the end of the law, through whom uprightness has now been made attainable (10:1–4); (3) the old way of attaining uprightness was difficult and arduous, whereas the new way is easy, within the reach of all and proclaimed to all, as Scripture shows (10:5–13); and (4) Israel has not taken advantage of this opportunity offered by the prophets and the gospel; so the responsibility lies with it (10:14–21).

NOTES

9:30. *What then shall we say?* A diatribe-like rhetorical question advances the argument to a new stage. See the NOTE on 6:1.

That Gentiles who did not pursue uprightness have attained it. Paul stresses the irony of the situation in that some (not all) Gentiles have succeeded in the matter of uprightness by putting faith in Christ. They have sought this "harmonious relation with God from which alone life and salvation can spring. This relation was not a concern of the Gentile world, though its inharmonious and sinful life bore witness—to those who had ears to hear—to the lack of it. It was only under the preaching of the Gospel that they had discovered faith, stumbling upon it unexpectedly" (Barrett, *Romans*, 193). Recall 2:14. For such pagans the status of rectitude in the sight of God the Judge had not really been a *goal* to attain. The vb. *diōkein* means "hasten, run (after), press on" (to a goal); the figure is that of the racecourse, runners trying to reach the goal; cf. Phil 3:12, 14; Sir 11:10; 27:8; Lam 1:13. The "pursuit" of uprightness is an expression that Paul derives from the OT, from Prov 15:9, where it is contrasted with the "paths, ways" of the godless. See also Deut 16:20; Isa 51:1 *(rōdēp ṣedeq)*; Wis 6:4. The pair of vbs. *diōkein*, "pursue," and *katalambanein*, "attain," is found in Exod 15:9; Sir 11:10; 27:8.

This part of the verse, beginning with *hoti*, is problematic. It is here taken as a second question, explaining *tí oun eroumen* in v 30a. This reading would make the rest of the verse conform to Paul's usual practice of following up such an initial rhetorical question by a second one (as in 9:14). It makes, however, the introduction of the appositive in the following phrase somewhat difficult. An alternative would be to take this clause to be the answer to the initial rhetorical question, as Sanday and Headlam (*Romans*, 278–79) prefer.

an uprightness based on faith. Lit., "an uprightness from faith." The rectitude that the Gentiles have attained is derived from faith in Christ Jesus and corresponds to the mode of uprightness revealed in Paul's gospel. The full meaning of "faith" will be developed by Paul in chap. 10. See esp. 10:2–3. Note too that the contrast of uprightness here echoes what Paul has written in Phil 3:9.

31. *whereas Israel, which was pursuing a law of uprightness, did not achieve it?* Lit., "did not catch up with the law." The verse thus expresses the anomaly of

Israel vis-à-vis the mode of attaining uprightness in the sight of God. See 11:7. But Paul's sentence is not clear; he undoubtedly means something like, "Israel was pursuing uprightness of the law, (but) did not achieve (such) uprightness," i.e., did not reach the goal. Instead he inverts the words, using a phrase from Wis 2:11, and speaks of a "law of uprightness." Thus in vv 30–31 Paul uses both *dikaiosynē* and *nomos* in a double sense.

The meaning of the phrase "a law of uprightness" has, however, been diversely understood. Since John Chrysostom (*In ep. ad Romanos* hom. 16.10 [PG 60.563]), many commentators have taken it to mean "the uprightness of/from the law" (*tēn ek tou nomou dikaiosynēn*), but that interpretation is abandoned today. The phrase could mean "the law that teaches uprightness" (so Thomas Aquinas; Huby, *Romains*, 360; Lagrange, *Romains*, 249), or "the law that demands uprightness" (Schlier, *Römerbrief*, 307), or "the law that promises uprightness" (so Schlier, ibid.; Cranfield, *Romans*, 508 n. 1; Käsemann, *Commentary*, 279; Meyer, "Romans 10:4," 62; Rhyne, *CBQ* 47 [1985]: 489). It hardly means, however, the law "misused if treated as a means of attaining" uprightness, as Barrett would have it (*Romans*, 193). By this phrase Paul undoubtedly means a law that would lead Israel to uprightness. So he characterizes the Mosaic law, which he never says has been mistakenly identified by Israel; yet he does say that Israel has not caught up with "the law." The problem is not with Israel's goal, viz., "uprightness," but with the way in which it sought to pursue it, as vv 16 and 32 make clear. For uprightness before God depends not on human will or exertion; it depends on God's mercy.

There is also the problem of the meaning of "the law" that Israel did not "catch up with." For Cranfield (*Romans*, 508), it would mean the object of Israel's pursuit; similarly Michel (*Brief an die Römer*, 321 n. 5): eschatological goal (of the law). But Origen (*In ep. ad Romanos* 7.19 [PG 14.1155]) understood it as the law "of the Spirit," in other words, the gospel; similarly Zahn (*Römer*, 470): "the law of faith." The latter meaning is impossible.

Because of this inconcinnity, some MSS (ℵ², Ψ, and the *Koinē* text-tradition) and Latin and Syriac versions read *nomon dikaiosynēs*, "(they did not catch up with the) law of uprightness." Yet most of the better MSS (P⁴⁶, ℵ*, A, B, D, F, G, 6, 81, 1739, etc.) read simply *nomon*. See 2:13; 11:7.

32. *why was this?* Lit., "for what reason?" Again, an imaginary interlocutor's question advances the argument beyond Paul's unexpected assertions in the previous verses.

Because they pursued it not with faith, but as if it were by deeds. Lit., "because not with faith, but as by deeds." Some verb has to be supplied with these phrases. I have used *ediōxan*, following Cranfield (*Romans*, 509); but Käsemann (*Commentary*, 277) uses "did not live," a verb that does not occur in the context. The vb. *diōkein*, however, creates something of a problem with the first phrase, because the uprightness of faith is a gift and is not really the object of pursuit. But that is precisely the problem: what verb can govern the two phrases in some identical sense?

Again, the two phrases could be an introduction to the statement that follows in the coming clause: "because they pursued . . . deeds, they stumbled. . . ." As Cranfield (*Romans*, 509) rightly notes, the pursuit of the goal was not wrong, but the mode of doing so had become inadequate. The contrast of *pistis*, "faith," and *erga*, "deeds," surfaces again; see 3:20, 28 and the NOTES on 2:15 and 3:20. By "faith" Paul must mean faith in Christ, as patristic writers generally understood it (also Schlier, *Römerbrief*, 308; Refoulé, *RB* 92 [1985]: 179). Other commentators often understand it, however, as faith in God (e.g., Cranfield, *Romans*, 510; Lyonnet, *Quaestiones* ser. 2 [1962], 82). The real explanation of this problem will be given by Paul in 10:2, where he will speak of Israel's "zeal for God," which is, however, "not well informed." How could Israel believe in Christ, if it were determined to pursue its goal "by deeds"? Cf. Isa 51:1; Wis 6:4.

Some MSS (‭א‬ᶜ, D, K, P, Ψ, 33, 81, 614, and the *Koinē* text-tradition) add *nomou*, "of the law," after *ergōn*. That, however, is a copyist's harmonization of the text with 3:20 and 28. The shorter form of the text is found in MSS P⁴⁶, ‭א‬*, A, B, G, and 1739, as well as some ancient versions.

They stumbled over "the stumbling stone." Lit., "they have run into the block (stone) that causes one to stumble." Running ahead madly in pursuit of a certain kind of uprightness, Israel has failed to see the obstacle on its rough road. It has failed to acknowledge Christ, him who is the meaning and goal of the law (10:4), which notion Paul anticipates here. This seems to be the sense of the following verse, in which Paul explains his position by quoting the OT.

Nevertheless, some commentators (P. W. Meyer, "Romans 10:4," 64; Barrett, "Romans 9,30," 112) refer it to the Torah itself, because there is no mention of Christ in the context. True, that understanding of the stumbling stone might fit this context, but then it gives to the law still another (questionably) negative role. So it seems better to stay with the usual interpretation: they stumbled over the gospel. Cf. 1 Cor 1:23.

According to Gager, Israel has stumbled because it has not "accepted the legitimacy of Paul's gospel to and about the Gentiles" (*The Origins of Anti-Semitism*, 252). Once again such an interpretation unduly restricts Paul's meaning. Israel has stumbled over the gospel of God's uprightness (1:16), which proclaims faith in Christ Jesus, "that a human being is justified by faith apart from deeds prescribed by the law" (3:28; cf. 3:21–26; 10:5–13).

33. *as it stands written.* See the NOTE on 1:17.

"Look, I am setting in Zion a stone to stumble against, a rock to trip over; and no one who believes in him shall be put to shame." Paul begins to quote Isa 28:16, but not exactly according to the LXX, and then introduces phrases from the LXX of Isa 8:14. The result is a conflation that disregards the contexts of the original and makes the OT say almost the opposite of what it actually does say. Paul thus accommodates Isaiah's meaning to his own literary purpose.

According to the MT of Isa 28:16, the stone laid by Yahweh in Zion (the eastern hill of Jerusalem on which the Temple was built) was a symbol of salvation for those who trusted in him, and not in the arrogant rulers of Jerusalem: "Look, I am laying a stone in Zion, a stone that has been tested, a cornerstone valuable as a sure foundation; as for the one who trusts, it will not shake." As Paul uses it, however, he makes the stone to be trusted into *lithon proskommatos*, "stone of stumbling," a phrase derived from Isa 8:14, where Yahweh himself is so described for the disobedient two houses of Israel. What was meant to be a basis of security has become a stumbling block. Now, however, Paul makes the "stone" refer to Christ, and neglect of him makes the stone a stumbling block for the vast majority of Israel. Yet those who believe in him (the remnant and the Gentiles) will not come to grief over that stone. Paul thus adds a christological dimension to the stumbling of Israel; it is not merely disobedience to Yahweh, but now disobedience to the gospel of his Son. For those who pursue uprightness by their own deeds, *hoi ek nomou*, Christ has become the stone over which they stumble, whereas for those who believe, *hoi ek pisteōs*, he has become the cornerstone set up by God himself, on which they can build without fear of failure, shame, or stumbling. Thus Christ himself has become the source both of stumbling and of faith.

The prep. phrase *ep' autō*, derived from the LXX of Isa 28:16, refers directly to masc. *lithon*, "stone," but because that stone is understood to be "Christ," it is usually translated, "(believes) in him"; it could also be "(trusts) in it," or even "in him," meaning God himself (so Meyer, *Romans*, 1157). See 10:11. In any case Paul quotes the Hebrew Scriptures, which themselves announce the stumbling stone, which is Christ. So Paul quotes against the Jews the authority of their own Scriptures.

Other NT writers have also made use of or alluded to Isa 28:16: 1 Pet 2:6–8; Matt 21:42; Luke 20:17; Eph 2:20; 2 Tim 2:19. See Oss, "The Interpretation."

The Qumran sect also applied Isa 28:16 to itself, looking on its community as a temple: "This is the tested wall, the precious cornerstone; its foundations will not tremble; it will not shake from its place" (1QS 8:7–8). In the fourth-century *Tg. of Isaiah* the "stone" of the MT becomes "a king in Zion, a mighty king, heroic and awesome." Thus it is understood in a personal sense, perhaps even in a messianic sense, if that is what is implied by "king" in this late Jewish text. Paul had earlier interpreted it in a personal sense without specifying Christ as Messiah. *Pace* Evans ("Paul"), it is highly unlikely that "this targumic tradition" of such a late date would have suggested such an interpretation to the Apostle.

Some MSS (K, P, Ψ, 33, 88, 326, 614, 1739 and the *Koinē* text-tradition) add *pas*, "all," after *kai* in the second part of the quotation, which makes the quotation conform with the way it is quoted in 10:11. But MSS ℵ, A, B, D, G, 81, 1881 and ancient versions omit *pas*.

BIBLIOGRAPHY

Barrett, C. K., "Romans 9:30–10:21: Fall and Responsibility of Israel," *Die Israelfrage*, ed. L. de Lorenzi, 99–130.

Black, M., "The Christological Use of the Old Testament in the New Testament," *NTS* 18 (1971–72): 1–14.

Bring, R., "Paul and the Old Testament: A Study of the Ideas of Election, Faith and Law in Paul, with Special Reference to Romans 9:30–10:30 [*sic*]," *ST* 25 (1971): 21–60.

Cranfield, C. E. B., "Romans 9:30–10:4," *Int* 34 (1980): 70–74.

———, "Some Notes on Romans 9:30–33," *Jesus und Paulus: Festschrift für Werner Georg Kümmel* . . . , ed. E. E. Ellis and E. Grässer (Göttingen: Vandenhoeck & Ruprecht, 1975), 35–43.

Dülmen, A. van, *Die Theologie des Gesetzes bei Paulus*, SBM 5 (Stuttgart: Katholisches Bibelwerk, 1968), 123–27.

Evans, C. A., "Paul and the Hermeneutics of 'True Prophecy': A Study of Romans 9–11," *Bib* 65 (1984): 560–70.

Flusser, D., "From the Essenes to Romans 9:24–33," *Judaism and the Origins of Christianity* (Jerusalem: Magnes, 1988), 75–87.

Gordon, T. D., "Why Israel Did not Obtain Torah-Righteousness: A Translation Note on Rom 9:32," *WTJ* 54 (1992): 163–66.

Luz, U., *Das Geschichtsverständnis*, 157.

Meyer, P. W., "Romans 10:4 and the 'End' of the Law," *The Divine Helmsman: Studies on God's Control of Human Events, Presented to Lou H. Silberman*, ed. J. L. Crenshaw and S. Sandmel (New York: Ktav, 1980), 59–78.

Müller, K., *Anstoss und Gericht: Eine Studie zum jüdischen Hintergrund des paulinischen Skandalonbegriffs* (Munich: Kösel, 1969).

Oss, D.A., "The Interpretation of the 'Stone' Passages by Peter and Paul: A Comparative Study," *JETS* 32 (1989): 181–200.

Refoulé, F., "Note sur Romains ix, 30–33," *RB* 92 (1985): 161–86.

Roberts, J. J. M., "Yahweh's Foundation in Zion (Isa 28:16)," *JBL* 106 (1987): 27–45.

Schreiner, T., "Israel's Failure to Attain Righteousness in Romans 9:30–10:3," *TrinJ* 12 (1991): 209–20.

Via, D. O., Jr., "A Structuralist Approach to Paul's Old Testament Hermeneutic," *Int* 28 (1974): 201–20.

Veldhuizen, A. van, "Rom. 9:30–33," *ThStud* 29 (1911): 439.

36. UPRIGHTNESS COMES FROM FAITH IN CHRIST, WHO IS THE END OF THE LAW (10:1–4)

10 ¹Brothers, my heart's desire and my prayer to God for them is their salvation. ²Indeed, I can testify for them that they have zeal for God; but it is not well informed. ³For being unaware of God's uprightness and seeking to set up their own uprightness, they have not submitted to the uprightness of God. ⁴For Christ is the end of the law so that there may be uprightness for everyone who believes.

COMMENT

Chapter 10 now investigates these two aspects of the reversal that Paul has mentioned in 9:30–33, the different modes of pursuing uprightness. Paul concentrates on the problem of the Jews, beginning with a renewed expression of his sorrow (cf. 9:1–3). He repeats in vv 2–3 what he had said in 9:30–33, now formulating it in terms of uprightness and obedience and not of the race/pursuit and failure. He is again saddened by Israel's failure to recognize God's real mode of attaining uprightness in his sight, through faith in Christ Jesus, who is "the end of the law," i.e., its goal. Real zeal for God has become in effect disobedience; pursuit of their own mode of uprightness has meant the neglect of God's uprightness. So the paragraph echoes in its own way the theme of part A (1:16–17), as it resumes mention of "the uprightness of God."

The major problems in the passage are the sense of *dikaiosynē theou* in v 3 and that of Christ as *telos nomou*, on both of which see the NOTES below.

NOTES

10:1. *Brothers.* So Paul again addresses the Christians of Rome. See the NOTES on 1:13 and 9:3.

my heart's desire and my prayer to God for them. I.e., for the people of Israel last mentioned in 9:31. Recall Paul's emotional reaction expressed in 9:1–3. His emotion probably accounts for the asyndeton here, as a new chapter begins (see BDF §463). What he now says is a foreshadowing of what he will say in 11:26. Paul uses *eudokia*, a word that occurs almost only in Jewish and Christian Greek literature. In the LXX it translates Hebrew *rāṣôn*, "good pleasure," but, *pace* Sanday and Headlam (*Romans*, 282), Paul uses it in the sense of "desire," as in Ps 145:16 ("you satisfy the desire of every living thing"); Sir 39:18; 1:27; 18:31. Cf. 2 Thess 1:11; also LXX Esth 4:17d.

is their salvation. Lit., "for salvation," the object of Paul's prayer. He thus explicitly includes the Jewish people in God's plan of salvation (cf. 1 Thess 5:9; Rom 1:16). He prays that his former coreligionists may eventually share in the eschatological deliverance prepared by God himself (see the NOTE on 8:24). Of this deliverance he is sure; see 11:26. God has not absolutely rejected his people (11:1).

Instead of *autōn*, "their," some MSS (K, 81, 326, 614, 1241 and the *Koinē* text-tradition) read *tou Israēl*, "(the salvation) of Israel." Many of the same MSS also add *estin*, "is." But the short reading is found in the better MSS (P⁴⁶,ℵ*, A, B, D, G, 1739).

2. *Indeed, I can testify for them.* Paul recalls his own Jewish identity and his own zealous fervor as a Jew (Gal 1:13–14; Phil 3:6; cf. Acts 22:3).

they have zeal for God. In postexilic and late pre-Christian Judaism *zēlos*, "zeal," for God, his law, or his Temple was considered the characteristic of the faithful Jew. See Ps 69:10; 1 Macc 2:26–27, 58; Jdt 9:4 for a similar use of *zēlos*. Paul recognizes this quality of his former coreligionists: they are not hypocrites. They know God indeed and are devoted to his service, seeking to live in accordance with his will; but they do not recognize that quality in him which really matters. In Gal 1:14 Paul characterized himself as "extremely zealous for the traditions of the Fathers."

but it is not well informed. Lit., "not according to real knowledge" *(epignōsis)*. It is not an enlightened zeal, one with the knowledge that recognizes the actual relationship of humanity to God as it has now been revealed in Christ Jesus. The zeal has been understood instead as Torah obedience and has failed to recognize that uprightness comes from God through Christ. That aspect of God is summed up in his "uprightness," as v 3 explains. Paul used *epignōsis* of sin in 3:20b (see the NOTE there).

3. *being unaware of God's uprightness.* I.e., being ignorant of that divine uprightness *(tēn theou dikaiosynēn)* which has been revealed in the gospel (1:17) and manifested against all human wickedness (3:5, 21) apart from the law and its observance, Jews have not come to a real knowledge of what divine uprightness is all about. This participial clause explains the foregoing.

Although the *RSV, NRSV,* and many commentators (e.g., Cranfield, *Romans*, 515; Lietzmann, *An die Römer*, 95; Nygren, *Romans*, 379) understand the phrase as "the righteousness that comes from God," that reading imports into Romans a meaning of the phrase from Phil 3:9, where the prep. *ek* is actually used, but which is not found here. 2 Cor 5:21 shows that Paul can use the phrase "the uprightness of God" in the sense of a gift communicated to human beings and coming from God. But it is far from clear that it is so meant anywhere in Romans, let alone here; see Lyonnet, "De 'iustitia Dei.' " Paul is speaking of a misunderstanding of "*God's* uprightness," the divine attribute or quality that is made known by the gospel (1:17, see the NOTE there). The Jewish people have failed to recognize this quality of God and have missed the real meaning of his acquitting power; hence they have refused to submit to it.

Pace Gager, Paul does not mean that "Jews have failed to understand the redemption of Gentiles in Christ as the expression of God's righteousness, a righteousness revealed as promise in Abraham and as fulfillment in Christ" (*Origins of Anti-Semitism*, 249). That interpretation restricts the meaning of "God's uprightness" unduly.

seeking to set up their own uprightness. This clause explains the present ignorance of Paul's former coreligionists. "Their own uprightness" is contrasted with "God's uprightness" and refers to uprightness sought after by "deeds of the law" and by boasting in the law.

Although some important Greek MSS (A, B, D, P, 81, 365, 1739, etc.) omit *dikaiosynēn*, others (P⁴⁶, ℵ, F, G, Ψ, and the *Koinē* text-tradition) read it. The sense is obvious even it if is omitted; so there is little difference of meaning.

they have not submitted to the uprightness of God. I.e., to that aspect of God which is now revealed by the gospel about Christ and faith in him. Paul uses the 2d aor. pass. *hypetagēsan*, but in a middle sense. See BDF §76.2. The use of the 3d pl. aor. here echoes that of *prosekopsan* in 9:32.

4. *For Christ is the end of the law.* Lit., "for end of law is Christ," the anarthrous *telos nomou* serves as the predicate of the sentence. The meaning of this sentence is disputed. In Greek *telos* can mean (1) "termination, cessation," as in Luke 1:33; Heb 6:11; 1 Pet 4:7; (2) "last part, conclusion, last act (of a drama)," as in 1 Cor 10:11; 15:24; or (3) "goal, purpose, *finis,*" as in 6:21–22; 1 Tim 1:5; 1 Pet 1:9; and most likely 2 Cor 3:13; 11:15; Phil 3:19. Cf. Plutarch, *Moralia* 780E: *dikē . . . nomou telos estin*, "justice is the goal of the law" (see BAGD, 811). Meaning (2) is irrelevant, and the dispute centers on whether Christ is the "termination" of the Mosaic law or its "goal." For a thorough study of *telos*, its meaning and history, see Badenas, *Christ the End of the Law*.

In meaning (1), *telos* is taken temporally, the end of the period of *tôrāh*, and Christ is understood as the termination of all human striving to achieve uprightness in the sight of God through legal observance; the law of Moses would have come to an end (so *NEB*, Augustine, Althaus, Bammel, Bultmann, Dodd, Gaugler, Gutbrod, Käsemann, Lagrange, Lietzmann, Linss, Martin, Michel, Mussner, Pesch, Robinson, Sanday and Headlam, and Schlier). Cf. Heb 8:13. Although Paul never uses such a clause in Galatians, this sense of it would agree with what he says in Gal 4:2–6 (see *PAHT* §PT96.1). But does that sense suit the present context and discussion in Romans? See 3:31; 7:12, 14a; 8:2–4; 13:8–10.

Other commentators (John Chrysostom, Karl Barth, Bartsch, Bring, Campbell, Cerfaux, Cranfield, Flückiger, Howard, P. W. Meyer, Rhyne, Schaefer, Sickenberger, Wilckens) prefer meaning (3). Christ would then be the goal of the law, that at which it was aimed or for which it was intended. This meaning is preferred because of the relation of 10:4 to 9:31–33, where the "pursuit" of uprightness by Gentiles implies a "goal" to be reached. Again, the "zeal" of 10:2 suggests this sense, and it is undoubtedly for this reason that Paul insisted in 3:31 that his gospel of justification by grace through faith "upholds" the law. For Pauline faith that "works itself out through love" (Gal 5:6), which is "the fulfillment of the law" (Rom 13:10), explains how Paul not only regards Christ as the *telos* of the law, but also looks on uprightness through faith in him as the way to fulfill the law and uphold all that it stood for. *Pace* Käsemann (*Commentary* 283), it is not "ridiculous to stress the logical connection with the metaphor of the race in 9:31f." In stressing it, one does not "overlook 9:32f.," for "pursuit" is expressed there too. Christ is the goal of the law because through him humanity can reach what was the goal of the law, viz., uprightness in the sight of God.

Some commentators try to take *telos* in both senses of "end" and "goal": Achtemeier, Barrett, Black, Bring, Bruce, Dunn, Hellbardt, Leenhardt, Schneider, and Zeller. But is that possible? One sense seems to imply the denial of the other. Some ancient commentators understood *telos* as *teleiōsis* or as *plērōma*, "fulfillment, completion" (see 13:10); so Origen, Erasmus. But *telos* never seems to have that meaning.

Nomos is here understood as the Mosaic law, as in most places in Romans (see the NOTE on 2:13); so Origen, John Chrysostom, Erasmus, Calvin. Yet some commentators have understand it generically as "principle": "Law as a method or principle of righteousness had been done away with in Christ" (Sanday and Headlam, *Romans*, 284).

Verses 2, 3, and 4 all begin *gar*, "for"; v 2 gives the basis for Paul's concern about the fate of his people, his positive explanation of their situation (v 2b), and the negative explanation (v 2c). The latter is explained in v 3, and v 4 then gives a further explanation of what has been said in v 3. In this verse Paul insists that Christ is the goal of the law, and uprightness is accredited to all who believe what God wants them to believe, i.e., God's way of uprightness.

so that there may be uprightness for everyone who believes. Lit., "unto uprightness for everyone believing." The prized status of uprightness before God is now available to everyone through *faith*, the subject of vv 5–20. Or as Rhyne puts it, the Jews "should have accepted God's righteousness because in Christ the law in its promise of righteousness reaches its goal, so that God's righteousness may be available to everyone who believes" (*CBQ* 47 [1985]: 393). Cf. 1:16.

Mussner ("Christus, des Gesetzes Ende") understands this verse to mean that Christ is the end of the law for the uprightness of those who believe in Christ, but not for Jews, who can still come to uprightness through the law. He makes this claim in view of his interpretation of 11:25–26; see the COMMENT there.

BIBLIOGRAPHY

Baarda, T., "Het einde van de wet is Christus: Rom 10:4–15: Een midrasj van Paulus over Deut. 30:11–14," *GTT* 88 (1988): 208–48.

Badenas, R., *Christ the End of the Law: Romans 10.4 in Pauline Perspective*, JSNTSup 10 (Sheffield: JSOT, 1985).

Bammel, E., "*Nomos Christou*," *SE III*, TU 88 (1964), 120–28.

Bratsiotis, P., "Eine exegetische Notiz zu Röm. ix 3 und x 1," *NovT* 5 (1962): 299–300.

Bring, R., "Die Erfüllung des Gesetzes durch Christus: Eine Studie zur Theologie des Apostels Paulus," *KD* 5 (1959): 1–22.

———, "Das Gesetz und die Gerechtigkeit Gottes: Eine Studie zur Frage nach der Bedeutung des Ausdruckes *telos nomou* in Röm. 10:4," *ST* 20 (1966): 1–36; repr. in *Christus und das Gesetz: Die Bedeutung des Gesetzes des Alten Testaments nach Paulus und sein Glauben an Christus* (Leiden: Brill, 1969), 35–72.

Bultmann, R., "Christus des Gesetzes Ende," *Theologische Abhandlungen*, BEvT 1, ed. E. Wolf (Munich: Kaiser, 1940), 3–27; repr. in *Glauben und Verstehen: Gesammelte Aufsätze*, 4 vols. (Tübingen: Mohr [Siebeck], 1933–65), 2 (1952), 32–58.

Cambier, J., *L'Évangile de Dieu*, 184–93.

Campbell, W. S., "Christ the End of the Law: Romans 10:4," *Studia biblica 1978: Sixth International Congress on Biblical Studies, Oxford 3–7 April 1978*, 3 vols., JSNTSup 2–3, 11, ed. E. A. Livingstone (Sheffield, UK: JSOT, 1979–80), 3.73–81; repr. in *Paul's Gospel*, 60–67.

Dunn, J. D. G., " 'Righteousness from the Law' and 'Righteousness from Faith': Paul's Interpretation of Scripture in Romans 10:1–10," *Tradition and Interpretation in the New Testament: Essays in Honor of E. Earle Ellis . . .* , ed. G. F. Hawthorne with O. Betz (Grand Rapids, Mich.: Eerdmans; Tübingen: Mohr [Siebeck], 1987), 216–28.

Flückiger, F., "Christus, des Gesetzes *telos*," *TZ* 11 (1955): 153–57.

Gaston, L., *Paul and the Torah* (Vancouver: University of British Columbia, 1987).

Hellbardt, H., "Christus, das Telos des Gesetzes," *EvT* 3 (1936): 331–46.

Howard, G. E., "Christ the End of the Law: The Meaning of Romans 10:4ff.," *JBL* 88 (1969): 331–37.

Jewett, R., "The Law and the Coexistence of Jews and Gentiles in Romans," *Int* 39 (1985): 341–56.

Kertelge, K., *"Rechtfertigung" bei Paulus*, 95–99.

Langevin, P.-E., "Sur la Christologie de Romains 10,1–13," *LTP* 35 (1979): 35–54.

Linss, W. C., "Exegesis of *telos* in Romans 10:4," *BR* 33 (1988): 5–12.

Lyonnet, S., "De 'iustitia Dei' in epistola ad Romanos 10,3 et 3,5," *VD* 25 (1947): 118–21.

Martin, B. L., "Paul on Christ and the Law," *JETS* 26 (1983): 271–82.

Müller, C., *Gottes Gerechtigkeit*, 33–38, 72–75.

Mussner, F., " 'Christus, des Gesetzes Ende zur Gerechtigkeit für jeden, der glaubt' (Rom 10, 4)," *Paulus—Apostat oder Apostel* (Regensburg: Pustet, 1977), 31–44.

Refoulé, F., "Romains, x, 4: Encore une fois," *RB* 91 (1984): 321–50.

Reumann, J., *"Righteousness,"* 87–90.

Rhyne, C. T., *Faith Establishes the Law*, SBLDS 55 (Chico, Calif.: Scholars Press, 1981), 95–116.

———, "*Nomos dikaiosynēs* and the Meaning of Romans 10:4," *CBQ* 47 (1985): 486–99.

Sand, A., "Gesetz und Freiheit: Vom Sinn des Pauluswortes: Christus, des Gesetzes Ende," *TGl* 61 (1971): 1–14.

Sanders, E. P., *Paul, the Law*, 36–43.

Sanders, J. A., "Torah and Paul," *God's Christ and His People: Studies in Honour of Nils Alstrup Dahl*, ed. J. Jervell and W. A. Meeks (Oslo: Universitetsforlaget, 1977), 132–40.

Schneider, E. E., "Finis legis Christus, Röm. 10,14," *TZ* 20 (1964): 410–22.

Sloyan, G. S., *Is Christ the End of the Law?* (Philadelphia, Penn.: Westminster, 1978).

Stuhlmacher, P., "Das Ende des Gesetzes: Über Ursprung und Ansatz der paulinischen Theologie," ZTK 67 (1970): 14–39; repr. in Versöhnung, Gesetz und Gerechtigkeit (Göttingen: Vandenhoeck & Ruprecht, 1981), 166–91.

―――, Gerechtigkeit Gottes, 91–99.

37. THE NEW WAY OF UPRIGHTNESS, OPEN TO ALL, IS EASY AND NEAR AT HAND, AS SCRIPTURE SHOWS (10:5–13)

10 ⁵For Moses writes thus of the uprightness that comes from the law: "*The one who does these things will find life in them.*" ⁶But the uprightness that comes from faith speaks thus: "*Do not say in your heart, 'Who will go up to heaven?'* " (that is, to bring Christ down); ⁷or " *'Who will go down into the abyss?'* " (that is, to bring Christ up from the dead). ⁸But what does it say instead? "*The word is near to you, on your lips and in your heart*" (that is, the word of faith that we preach): ⁹if you profess with your lips that "Jesus is Lord," and believe in your heart that God has raised him from the dead, you will be saved. ¹⁰Such faith of the heart leads to uprightness; such profession of the lips to salvation. ¹¹For Scripture says, "*No one who believes in him shall be put to shame.*" ¹²No distinction is made between Jew and Greek: the same Lord is Lord of all, bestowing his riches on all who call upon him. ¹³"*For everyone who calls upon the name of the Lord shall be saved.*"

COMMENT

In vv 5–20 Paul enters into a discussion of the meaning of faith, as he seeks to explain what this new mode is, by which human beings can acquire the status of rectitude before the divine tribunal. Paul contrasts the ease of this mode with the arduous task of observing the deeds of the law, the difficult task of law-uprightness.

Here I follow what Cranfield (*Romans*, 521) calls "the usual explanation": Verse 5 is related to v 4 and explains the futile character of the pursuit of an upright status before God on the basis of works, which is contrasted with the mode of justification by faith described in vv 6–8. Because Christ is the goal of the law, a status of uprightness is available to all who believe in him (v 4); for, while justification by works is the futile pursuit, which Moses indicates (v 5), Scripture has all along set forth the glorious possibility of justification by faith (vv 6–8). Thus vv 5–8 would be an explanation of v 4. Cranfield himself, however, prefers to understand Lev 18:5, as used by Paul, to refer to Christ: Christ would be *ho poiēsas auta anthrōpos*, "the one who does these things," i.e., by his obedience, and has thus found "life" in the resurrection (*Romans*, 521–22). Yet that is an eisegetical solution, which solves nothing; hence the "usual explanation" is retained here.

This section offers a scriptural proof for what was asserted in v 4, but the argument from the OT is complicated, because Paul contrasts two OT passages. Having cited Lev 18:5 explicitly, he does not do the same for Deut 30:11–14. Rather, he quotes parts of it and alludes to the rest, commenting in midrashic fashion on clauses of it that he does cite. As Dunn has noted (" 'Righteousness' "), the two OT passages, when taken in their original contexts, say and emphasize the same thing—the "doing" of the law—but Paul understands the Leviticus passage to be speaking of "uprightness that comes from the law" and the Deuteronomy passage as that which "comes from faith." He thus sets them in opposition. The problem is to understand his logic, if there is any.

The latter passage to which Paul alludes runs as follows in the original: "For this command that I enjoin on you today [to keep the commandments and statues written in the book of the law] is neither too mysterious nor too remote for you. It is not up in the heavens, that you should have to say, 'Who will go up into the heavens to get it for us and tell us about it, so that we may carry it out?' Nor is it across the sea, that you should have to say, 'Who will cross the sea to get it for us and tell us about it, that we may carry it out?' No, it is something very near to you, already in your mouths and in your hearts; you have only to carry it out." Paul makes no mention of the crossing of the sea, but instead introduces an allusion to Ps 107:26, "They [the waves of the sea, mentioned in v 25] mounted up to the heaven; they sank to the depths; their hearts melted away in their plight." But he is not content to introduce the allusion to this psalm, thus substituting for the horizontal contrast (heaven/across the sea) a vertical contrast (heaven/depths), which better expresses the extremes. He also comments midrashically on clauses of Deuteronomy, which he cites, introducing Christ or faith in Christ. So he clearly intends to be commenting on the Deuteronomy passage.

The use of this OT passage creates a difficulty, for in the OT it refers ex professo to the Mosaic law, but Paul applies it to the gospel. Paul, however, does not quote OT in the sense of following what Moses has said. In his argument to establish *dikaiosynē ek pisteōs*, he merely borrows phrases from Deuteronomy and applies them to Christ. Hence he is not interpreting the OT in the strict sense. He is instead using clauses from the Deuteronomy passage as it is also used in Bar 3:29–30; Philo, *De post. Caini* 24 §§84–85.

Paul thus introduces his fundamental assertion about Christian faith (see Introduction, section IX.D). Faith begins with a confession of the lips that "Jesus is Lord," but demands the concomitant recognition of the heart that God has raised him from the dead. This is not a mere external or public affirmation, but the inmost and profound dedication of a person to God in the Lord Jesus. What Paul acknowledges here has become the affirmation par excellence of Christian faith. By his resurrection Christ has become the firstfruits of a new mode of life; he has become the "life-giving Spirit" (1 Cor 15:45). Thus to confess Christ as Lord and to believe in him as the risen Lord is one and the same thing.

Into this paragraph Paul has again introduced some pre-Pauline phraseology, esp. in v 9, where the formula "Jesus is Lord" is used, also employed in 1 Cor

12:3. This seems to have been a confessional formula, if not a kerygmatic formula, of the pre-Pauline tradition.

NOTES

10:5. *For Moses writes.* I.e., in the Pentateuch or the Books of Moses we read. Cf. 2 Cor 3:15, "whenever Moses is read"; Rom 10:19, "first, Moses says." Cf. 1 Cor 9:9; Acts 3:22. Paul quotes the lawgiver of the Hebrews (cf. the formula in Josephus, *Ag. Ap.* 1.26 §250, as he quotes Manetho). The conj. *gar* indicates that v 5 (or possibly vv 5–8) is an explanation of v 4. Paul turns to the OT to explain his understanding of faith.

of the uprightness that comes from the law. Lit., "the uprightness from the law." The acc. *tēn dikaiosynēn* is adverbial: "concerning the uprightness." This reading takes the conj. *hoti* as introducing the quotation from Lev 18:5 (so N-A²⁶, Merk, UBSGNT), whereas N-A²⁵ and other critical editions read *hoti* after the vb. *graphei*, which would mean, "For Moses writes that the one who does uprightness that comes from the law. . . ." The first reading is to be preferred, as in MSS P⁴⁶, B, D², E, F, G, and the *Koinē* text-tradition. Cf. BDF §474.5c. See Lindemann, "Die Gerechtigkeit."

"The one who does these things will find life in them." Lit., "the man (*anthrōpos*) who does these things shall live by them." Paul quotes Lev 18:5, as he does in Gal 3:12, but instead of the rel. pron. *ha* of the LXX he adds the dem. pron. *auta* (missing in MS ℵ*, a copyist's harmonization of the Pauline text with the LXX). Thus Paul argues: according to Moses the lawgiver the observance of the Torah's prescriptions is the way to life that God has promised to his people; "life" is guaranteed for those who pursue covenantal uprightness. This verse was often regarded as "the law of life" (Sir 17:11; 45:5; cf. Bar 4:1; Philo, *De congr.* 16 §§86–87). Implied in the quotation is the arduous nature of the condition. See 2:13.

6. *But the uprightness that comes from faith speaks thus.* A contrast is introduced between the two aeons or the two ways of attaining uprightness in God's sight. Personified uprightness is contrasted with the lawgiver, Moses. "Whereas he demands action understood as achievement, she demands reception of the word. Whereas he characteristically writes, she speaks with the living voice of the gospel, with which there is doubtless an allusion to the relation of *pneuma* and *gramma* in 2:27ff.; 7:6; 2 Cor 23:6ff." (Käsemann, *Commentary*, 284). For a similar personification of Wisdom, see Prov 1:20–33; of the Law, see Rom 7:1, 7. But Paul is not bluntly disagreeing with Moses; he recognizes the validity of the Mosaic dictum and undoubtedly would consider it valid for Jewish Christians. He realizes, however, that in this new aeon uprightness announces a new mode.

As will become apparent in v 9, for Paul this *pistis* involves belief in the death and resurrection of Jesus Christ. Hence, *pace* Mussner (*Tractate*, 34), it cannot be vaguely understood as "Israel's *emunah*," even if it be said that that *emunah* "turns now totally toward the Christ who comes again" (at the parousia); see further the COMMENT on 11:25–32.

"Do not say in your heart, 'Who will go up to heaven?'" Paul quotes part of Deut 9:4 ("do not say in your heart") and of 30:11 ("who will go up to heaven"), conflating clauses. Actually, the quotation is not explicitly introduced, as it is in v 5; hence it is more of an allusion than a quotation. To illustrate his point, Paul argues as did Moses in Deut 30:11–14. Just as Moses tried to convince the Israelites that the observance of the law did not demand that one scale the heights or cross the seas, so Paul plays on Moses' words, applying them in an accommodated sense to Christ himself. The heights have been scaled and the depths have been plumbed, for Christ has come down to the world of humanity and has been raised from the dead. To attain the status of uprightness before God, no one is being asked to bring about an incarnation or a resurrection; one is asked only to accept in faith what has already been done for humanity and to associate oneself with Christ incarnate and raised from the dead. Cf. Bar 3:29; Prov 30:4.

that is. Paul uses this exegetical phrase in vv 6, 7, and 8. Note the similar Qumran introductory formula, when Scripture is quoted: *hy² h⁽t ²šr hyh ktwb ⁽lyh*, "that is, the time about which it is written" (CD 1:13; cf. CD 7:15; 10:16; 16:15; 1QS 8:14–15; 1QpHab 12:3–4; 4QFlor 1:11). *Pace* McNamara (*Palestinian Targum,* 72), this formula is not the same as *pišrô ⁽al*, which means, lit., "the interpretation of it concerns. . . ." That introductory formula has a different function, being normally used in *pesharim*.

to bring Christ down. An indirect allusion to the incarnation of Christ; this is the closest one comes in the Pauline letters to such an idea, which is otherwise a Johannine theologoumenon. Paul gives a midrashic explanation of Deuteronomy. In this explanation "Christ" is substituted for the "word" of the Torah. Paul means that a person asked by God to be upright is not being asked by him to bring about the incarnation of Christ.

7. *"Who will go down into the abyss?"* This is an allusion to Ps 107:26 ("they go down to the abyss"), which Paul substitutes for the crossing of the seas in Deut 30:13. The substitution is made because Paul wants to allude to the resurrection of Christ. In the LXX *abyssos* often refers to the "deep sea, depths of the sea," in contrast to the sky and the earth (Deut 8:7; Pss 33:7; 77:17); in time it also developed into the name for the netherworld or Tartarus (Ps 71:20; Job 41:23–24). This double meaning made it possible for Paul to use it in its original meaning and allude to Christ's resurrection from the dead.

A similar form of Deut 30:13 is found in the late *Tg. Neofiti 1:* "Nor is the law beyond the Great Sea that one should say, 'Would that we had someone like Jonah the prophet who would descend to the depths of the Great Sea and bring it up for us and make us hear its commandments that we might carry them out.'" Given the similarity of Deut 30:12–13 (*mî ya⁽āleh lānû haššāmayĕmāh wĕyiqqā-ḥehā lānû . . . mî ya⁽ăbor-lānû ²el ⁽ēber hayyām . . .*) to Ps 107:26 (*ya⁽ălû šāmayim yērĕdû tĕhômôt*), a similarity that is even more pronounced in the LXX, it is not surprising that the contrast of "heavens" and "sea" would be introduced into the targumic rendering of *Neofiti 1*. References to Pseudo-Philo, *Liber antiquitatum biblicarum* 15:6 and 4 Ezra 3:18 are useless illustrations of the targumic rendering, because they are so different. They in no way indicate that this conflation of texts was already known in pre-Christian Judaism or to Paul in his pre-Christian days. For this reason, one cannot agree with McNamara that "Paul knew of this paraphrase of the text of Dt and adapted it for his own purpose. The text of the PT as Paul found it was very apt for the doctrine Paul expresses in Rm 10,6–8" (*Palestinian Targum*, 77). See York, "The Dating."

that is, to bring Christ up from the dead. An allusion to the resurrection. Cf. Ps 71:20; Wis 16:13. Again, Paul means that a person asked by God to be upright is not being asked by him to bring about the resurrection of Christ.

8. *But what does it say instead?* Paul stresses this part of his allusion to Deuteronomy by singling out the important counsel of Moses. Some MSS (D, F, G, 33, 104, 365, etc.) add *hē graphē*, "what does Scripture say"; cf. BDF §130.3.

"The word is near to you, on your lips and in your heart." Paul quotes Deut 30:14, from which he draws his conclusion.

that is, the word of faith that we preach. Paul thus implies that faith is the expected human reaction to the preached word, the gospel that he proclaims. The word that stirs up faith in those whom it accosts and challenges is to be found on the lips and in the heart, i.e., close to one who would believe. See 10:17. It is not easy to determine the sense of *pistis* in this verse. It could designate the reaction to the preached word and thus be *fides qua creditur*, as Cranfield takes it (*Romans*, 526); but it could more likely be taken as the content of what is preached, *fides quae creditur*, as Bultmann (*TDNT* 6.209); Käsemann (*Commentary*, 290), Michel (*Brief an die Römer*, 258), and Schlier (*Römerbrief*, 312) have understood it.

9. *if you profess with your lips that "Jesus is Lord."* One must utter the basic Christian confession of faith and mean it. Paul proceeds to cite the credal and acclamatory, perhaps even kerygmatic, formula of the early Palestinian church: in Aramaic *mārēh Yēšûᶜ* or in Greek *Kyrios Iēsous*, "Jesus is Lord" (1 Cor 12:3; cf. 2 Cor 4:5; Phil 2:9–11). This verse begins with *hoti*. As translated above, it is understood as an explanation of "the word of faith that we preach" (10:8). But the *hoti* could mean "because, for," and simply express a further point in Paul's argument. In either case, genuine Christian faith begins for Paul with an affirmation, an assent to a basic proposition, but it does not stop there, as the rest of the verse makes clear.

The expression *Kyrios Iēsous* may be an imitation of a similar Roman acclamation, *Kyrios Kaisar*, "Caesar is Lord," used together with the vb. *diasōzesthai*, "to be saved," and quoted in *Mart. Pol.* 8:2. But it lacks the public and polemical connotation of the latter.

Some MSS (B, 81), Coptic versions, and Clement of Alexandria insert *to rhēma* and change *Kyrion Iēsoun* to *hoti Kyrios Iēsous* to make Paul's statement more precise: "if you confess the word with your mouth, that Jesus is Lord." *Rhēma* would refer to the message of the Christian gospel.

and believe in your heart that God raised him from the dead. In addition to the verbal confession, an inward faith is demanded, which will guide the whole person in dedication to God in Christ. Thus *Kyrios* becomes the title par excellence for the risen Christ. Paul once again ascribes the resurrection of Christ to the Father (see the NOTE on 4:24). His resurrection is again presented as the kernel of Christian faith, the basis of salvation; cf. 4:24; 1 Thess 4:14; 1 Cor 15:14–15; 2 Cor 5:15.

you will be saved. Salvation comes to the fore in such a Pauline formulation; see Introduction, section IX.B. Such salvation, then, depends on an affirmation of the lordship of Christ and a conviction stemming from the heart that Christ has been rasied. All thus depends on faith, which engages the whole person of the believer. Although Moses proclaims uprightness and "life" for the one who "does" the deeds of the law (10:5), Paul insists that right in the Book of Moses itself uprightness is attained by faith.

10. *Such faith of the heart leads to uprightness; such profession of the lips to salvation.* Lit., "it is believed with the heart unto uprightness, but with the mouth unto salvation." The chiastic balance stresses the different aspects of the one basic act of personal adherence to Christ and its effect. The difference between justification and salvation should not be stressed. The verse formulates rhetorically the relation of human uprightness and salvation to faith and the profession of it.

11. *For Scripture says.* See the NOTE on 4:3.

"No one who believes in him shall be put to shame." Again Paul quotes Isa 28:16, as in 9:33. He now modifies the quotation by adding *pas.* "all," thus emphasizing the universality of the application: "not . . . all" (= no one). In Isaiah the words referred to the precious cornerstone laid by Yahweh in Zion (see the NOTE on 9:33); they are again accommodated by Paul to faith in Christ and used as an assurance of salvation for all those who believe in Christ, Jews included. The addition of *pas* prepares for the quotation from Joel in v 13, and the prep. phrase *ep autō,* "in him," now clearly refers to the risen Christ. For the idiom *pisteuein epi* + dat., see BDF §187.6.

12. *No distinction is made between Jew and Greek.* All have the opportunity to share alike in the new uprightness through faith (3:22–23, 29).

the same Lord is Lord of all. At first *Kyrios* might seem to refer to Yahweh, because Paul is using Jewish titles applied elsewhere to him, and the expression to "call upon the name of" is used of Yahweh in 1 Sam 12:17–18; 2 Sam 22:7); again, v 13 refers explicitly to Joel 3:5. But in the immediate context, especially after 10:9, *Kyrios* can refer only to Jesus, who is the risen Lord of Jew and Greek (cf. 9:5; Phil 2:9–11). The risen Christ as *Kyrios* is "Lord of all" (cf. Acts 10:36). In this context (see vv 11, 13) Paul would mean by "all" not just the "Jew and Greek" of v 12a or Israel and the Gentiles of 9:30–31, but all human beings, as the OT passage to be quoted in v 13 implies.

Moreover, the title "Lord of all" is a Jewish formula, used of Yahweh in 1QapGen 20:13, *mārēh wĕšallîṭ ʿal kullāʾ*, "Lord and Master over all"; cf. Josephus, *Ant.* 20.4.22 §90 (*tōn pantōn . . . monon kai prōton hēgēmai Kyrion*, "I have considered you the first and only Lord of all"), and possibly also the disputed 11QPsᵃ 28:17: *ʾdwn hkwl*, "Lord of all" (if *ʾdwn* is to be understood as construct state, and not as absolute; see *WA*, 125; cf. P. Auffret and J. Magne, *RevQ* 9 (1977–78): 163–88, 189–96; A. Hurvitz, "Psalm 151 fom Qumran," *Eretz-Israel* 8 [1967]: 82–87, esp. 84). It has also turned up in 4Q409 1:6, [*wbrk ʾt ʾdw]n hkwl, hll*, "[and bless the Lor]d of all, praise . . ." (E. Qimron, *JQR* 80 [1990]: 341–47). It is now applied by Paul to the risen Christ.

bestowing his riches on all who call upon him. The bounteous goodness of the risen Christ is displayed to all who invoke him as "Lord."

13. *"For everyone who calls upon the name of the Lord shall be saved."* Paul quotes Joel 3:5 (2:32E) according to the LXX, which corresponds to the MT and where *sōthēsetai* renders Hebrew *yimmālēṭ*. In the original context the prophet speaks of the awesome day of the Lord, when deliverance and survival will come to those who invoke Yahweh. Paul applies the title to his *Kyrios*. In the OT those who "call upon the name of the Lord" denoted sincere and pious Israelites; in the NT it is transferred to Christians (1 Cor 1:2). Verses 12–13 thus become an eloquent witness to the early church's worship of Christ as *Kyrios*. The adj. *pas* with which the quotation begins echoes that introduced by Paul into the quotation in 10:11.

As in 7:22–8:3, Müller ("Zwei Marginalien") would rearrange the order of the verses thus: 10:13, 14, 15b, 15a, 17, 16, 18. But again, is that the way Paul would have wanted them read?

BIBLIOGRAPHY

Bieder, W., *Die Vorstellung von der Höllenfahrt Jesu Christi: Beitrag zur Entstehungsgeschichte der Vorstellung vom sog. Descensus ad inferos*, ATANT 19 (Zurich: Zwingli-Verlag, 1949), 71–75.

Black, M., "The Christological Use of the Old Testament in the New Testament," *NTS* 18 (1971–72): 1–14.

Butler, C., "The Object of Faith According to St. Paul's Epistles," *SPCIC*, 1.15–30.

Campenhausen, H. von, "Das Bekenntnis im Urchristentum," *ZNW* 63 (1972): 210–53.

Delling, G., " 'Nahe ist dir das Wort': Wort—Geist—Glaube bei Paulus," *TLZ* 99 (1974): 401–12.

Dupont, J., " 'Le Seigneur de tous' (Ac 10:36; Rm 10:12): Arrière-fond scripturaire d'une formule christologique," *Tradition and Interpretation in the New Testament: Essays in Honor of E. Earle Ellis . . .* , ed. G. F. Hawthorne with O. Betz (Grand Rapids, Mich: Eerdmans; Tübingen: Mohr [Siebeck], 1987), 229–36.

Eckstein, H.-J., " 'Nahe ist dir das Wort': Exegetische Erwägungen zu Röm 10,8," *ZNW* 79 (1988): 204–20.

Feuillet, A., *Le Christ, Sagesse de Dieu, d'après les épîtres pauliniennes*, EtBib (Paris: Gabalda, 1966), 321–27.

Führer, W., " 'Herr ist Jesus': Die Rezeption der urchristlichen Kyrios-Akklamation durch Paulus Römer 10,9," *KD* 33 (1987): 137–49.

Genung, J. F., "The Righteousness Which Is of Faith: Romans x 4–11," *JBL* 4 (1884): 29–36.

Goldberg, A. M., "Torah aus der Unterwelt? Eine Bemerkung zu Röm 10,6–7," *BZ* 14 (1970): 127–31.

Heller, J., "Himmel- und Höllenfahrt nach Römer 10,6–7," *EvT* 32 (1972): 478–86.

Hughes, M. J., "Romans x. 6–8," *ExpTim* 19 (1907–8): 524–25.

Kaiser, W. C., "Leviticus 18:5 and Paul: Do This and You Shall Live (Eternally?)," *JETS* 14 (1971): 19–28.

Langevin, P. E., "Le Salut par la foi: Rm 10,8–13," *AsSeign* 14 (1973): 47–53.

Lindemann, A., "Die Gerechtigkeit aus dem Gesetz: Erwägungen zur Auslegung und zur Textgeschichte von Röm 10,5," *ZNW* 73 (1982): 231–50.

Lyonnet, S., "Saint Paul et l'exégèse juive de son temps: À propos de Rom., 10, 6–8," *Mélanges bibliques rédigés en l'honneur de André Robert* (Paris: Bloud & Gay, 1957), 494–506; revised, *Études*, 298–309.

McNamara, M., *The New Testament and the Palestinian Targum to the Pentateuch*, AnBib 27 (Rome: Biblical Institute, 1966), 70–81.

Müller, F., "Zwei Marginalien im Brief des Paulus an die Römer," *ZNW* 40 (1941): 249–54.

Neufeld, V. H., *The Earliest Christian Confessions*, NTTS 5 (Leiden: Brill, 1963).

Seifrid, M. A., "Paul's Approach to the Old Testament in Rom 10:6–8," *TrinJ* 6 (1985): 3–37.

Stanley, D. M., *Christ's Resurrection*, 195–97.

Suggs, M. J., " 'The Word Is Near You': Romans 10:6–10 Within the Purpose of the Letter," *Christian History and Interpretation: Studies Presented to John Knox*, ed. W. R. Farmer et al. (Cambridge: Cambridge University Press, 1967), 289–312.

Vielhauer, P., "Paulus und das Alte Testament," *Studien zur Geschichte und Theologie der Reformation: Festschrift für E. Bizer*, ed. L. Abramowski and J. F. G. Goeters (Neukirchen-Vluyn: Neukirchener-Verlag, 1969), 33–62.

Vos, J. S., "Die hermeneutische Antinomie bei Paulus (Galater 3.11–12; Römer 10.5–10)," *NTS* 38 (1992): 254–70.

York, A. D., "The Dating of Targumic Literature," *JSJ* 5 (1974): 49–62.

38. ISRAEL HAS NOT RESPONDED TO THIS PREACHED WORD (10:14–21)

10 ¹⁴But how will people call upon him in whom they have not believed? How can they believe in him to whom they have not listened? How can they hear of

him unless through a preacher? [15]And how can people preach unless they are sent? As it stands written, *"How timely the arrival of those who bring good news!"* [16]Yet everyone has not heeded the gospel. But even Isaiah says, *"Lord who has believed our message?"* [17]Faith then comes from what is heard, and what is heard comes through the word of Christ. [18]But I ask, Can it be that they have not heard of it? Of course they have! *"Their voice has gone forth over all the earth, and their words to the bounds of the world."* [19]But again I ask, Can it be that Israel did not understand? First of all, Moses says, *"I shall make you jealous of those who are not a nation; and with a foolish nation shall I provoke your anger."* [20]And Isaiah made bold to say, *"I was found by those who were not seeking me; I showed myself to those who were not asking for me."* [21]Yet of Israel he says, *"All day long have I held out my hands to a disobedient and defiant people."*

COMMENT

Paul now begins the fourth subsection in this part of his argument (10:14–21): Israel has not taken advantage of this new, easy way to justification and salvation offered in the gospel and foreshadowed in the prophets of old. Hence, it is responsible for its misstep. The opportunity to believe in Christ was offered to all, but especially to Israel. It cannot claim that it did not hear this gospel. Paul's indictment of Israel in this passage is severe, especially in v 21.

Again, he argues in a form of diatribe: objections or difficulties are formulated to express an excuse for Israel's situation. They echo perhaps comments on Paul's missionary sermons among Jews or objections that he often encountered. He briefly answers each one and quotes the OT to prove his contention about the responsibility of Israel. The four objections that he takes up are (1) how can people believe such a gospel, unless it has been fully preached by messengers duly sent? (vv 14–15); (2) but it has not been accepted by everybody! (vv 16–17); (3) but perhaps Israel did not hear it! (v 18); and (4) perhaps Israel did not understand it! (vv 19–21). Another way to phrase the objections is as Nygren has formulated them (*Romans*, 385): "(1) one cannot confess him in whom one does not believe; (2) one cannot believe in him of whom one has not heard; (3) one cannot hear without a preacher; (4) no preachers come unless God sends them."

Paul stresses in this passage that God has done all that he could to bring Israel to faith. In Christ Jesus he laid the foundation for the gospel, the word to be preached. He has sent forth his heralds that Israel might hear his message. Paul insists: the gospel has been preached; the message has been heard. The voice of the heralds has gone forth to the ends of the earth. Israel has heard and has understood, but it remains in its obstinacy, while a foolish nation (Gentiles) respond to the call of the gospel.

Paul introduces this form of argument at this point in his discussion not to justify the preaching of the gospel to the Gentiles or to justify an authorized ministry of gospel preachers (though this may be the brunt of v 15), but to justify

God's own activity vis-à-vis his chosen people. God has done what he could in seeing that the gospel was proclaimed to Israel; it has had the opportunity of knowing about that gospel and of accepting it. Hence its "ignorance" (10:3) is its own responsibility. That is why he ends this section with the quotation of Isa 65:2.

John Chrysostom summed up the argument thus: "If then being saved were to come of calling upon him, and calling upon him from believing, and believing from hearing, and hearing from preaching, and preaching from being sent, and if they were sent and did preach, and if a prophet went around with them to show them, to proclaim, and to say, 'These are those whom they were making known for a long time, whose feet even they praised because of the manner of their preaching,' then it would be very clear that the disbelief is only their own fault" (*In ep. ad Romanos* hom. 18.1 [PG 60.573]).

NOTES

10:14. *how will people call upon him in whom they have not believed?* The first difficulty is multiple and begins with the assumption that the cult of Christ must be founded on belief in him. Invocation of Christ as savior and justifier presupposes faith in him, which leads to a still further question.

How can they believe in him to whom they have not listened? The question refers not to the Jews of Palestine, who might have witnessed the ministry of Jesus, but to those who had not had the opportunity to listen to him directly. The "word of faith" has to be heard. The Greek vb. *akouein* governs the gen. and means "listen to someone," not "hear about."

How can they hear of him unless through a preacher? Lit., "how can they hear apart from a herald?" Faith is founded on an authorized preaching, on the testimony of those who have been charged with the mission to make known the word of God about the new mode of salvation. Here, as in v 17, the initial step in all faith is a "hearing" of the proposed message; the object of faith, propositionally formulated, is thus first presented. The message of God's gospel must come to human beings from outside of them; it cannot rise spontaneously in their hearts or minds. They have to be accosted by it as announced by a commissioned herald. Paul is summarizing the conditions for salvation: salvation stems from calling upon the Lord, which implies faith. Faith implies knowing about the gospel, which has to be preached by someone, someone who is authorized or sent with a commission to do so.

15. *how can people preach unless they are sent?* Authoritative preaching, the basis of faith, presupposes a mission from God. Basic to Paul's view is the preacher as spokesman for another, not as someone with his own message authorized by himself; this notion explains his emphasis in 1 Cor 15:9–11; 2 Cor 4:5; 11:4 (Dunn, *Romans*, 621). In expressing the sending or mission, Paul uses the vb. *apostellein*, alluding to the "apostolic" origin of the testimony of the Christian

church and its authorized preaching of the gospel of the Christ-event: "the Christian teacher must have *Mission,* and this, not from those to whom he delivers his message, but from the Divine Monarch Whose herald he is. Hence the value placed by S. Paul on his title *apostolos,* Rom. i. 1; Gal. i. 1,12,16" (Liddon, *Explanatory Analysis,* 187). Cf. C. Gore, *Romans,* 2.56–57.

Such authorized preaching leads in the Christian tradition to the institution of ordained ministry: bishops, priests, and deacons, charged with preaching the gospel. Not long after Paul, Clement of Rome understood the principle that Paul enunciates, when he wrote,

> The apostles received the gospel for us from the Lord Jesus Christ; Jesus the Christ was sent from God. The Christ, then, is from God, and the apostles from the Christ. In both ways, then, they were rightly ordered by the will of God. Having therefore received their commands and being fully reassured by the resurrection of our Lord Jesus Christ, they were entrusted with the word of God and went forth preaching with the assurance of the holy Spirit about the kingdom of God that was to come. From place to place and city to city they preached and set up their first converts, testing them by the Spirit, to be bishops and deacons of future believers. This was no new method, for many years before bishops and deacons had been written of, for thus says Scripture somewhere, "I shall set up their bishops with uprightness and their deacons with faith." (*1 Clem.* 42.1–5 [quoting a Greek form of Isa 60:17, which does not agree with the LXX]; cf. *1 Clem.* 44.1–6)

Recall 1 Cor 1:14–17, the contrast that Paul draws between baptizing and preaching, and the emphasis that he puts on the latter.

As it stands written. See the NOTE on 1:17.

"How timely the arrival of those who bring good news!" Lit., "how timely the feet of those who evangelize good things." Paul answers the first compound objection with a quotation of Isa 52:7, in a form closer to the MT than to the LXX. In Isaiah the text lauds the herald (sg.) who brings good news as he runs on mountain ridges and announces to Jews left in ruined Jerusalem that deliverance from Babylonian captivity has come and that Jerusalem's restoration is close at hand. As used by Paul, the text takes on the overtones of his good news, the "gospel" about Christ and the salvation that is available through him, which has been announced by apostles (hence the pl.). In effect, Paul replies to the first objection by insisting that the "gospel" has indeed been preached to Israel. Such a system of authorized messengers has also been foreseen already in the OT, and the prophet's words are quoted to show that such preaching of the gospel has indeed taken place in accord with divine determination of old. Cf. Nah 2:1 (1:15E).

Some MSS (א², D, F, G, Ψ, and the *Koinē* text-tradition) add after "feet" *tōn euangelizomenōn eirēnēn,* "of those announcing peace." This is clearly a copyist's harmonization of Paul's text with the LXX of Isa 52:7.

16. *Yet everyone has not heeded the gospel.* Lit., "but not all have hearkened to the gospel." The second objection emphasizes the problem of "hearing" the good tidings. Paul uses the Greek vb. *hypakouein,* which means "listen and submit to." Cf. 1:5, "the commitment of faith" (see the NOTE there). Paul repeats in a different way what he said in 10:3, "they have not submitted to the uprightness of God." For the litotes in his formulation, "not all," see Rehkopf, "Grammatisches," 224–25.

But even Isaiah says. Paul replies to the objection by repeating the objection uttered long before by Israel's great prophet. See 9:27–28; 10:20; 15:2.

"Lord, who has believed our message?" Lit., "our report." Paul quotes Isa 53:1 according to the LXX, which adds *Kyrie,* but otherwise corresponds to the MT. In effect, Paul says that because not everyone (among the Jews) has accepted the good news, it does not mean that it has not been preached to them, because a comparable refusal to believe God's message was foreseen by Isaiah in his mission. Paul uses the noun *akoē,* which can mean (1) the faculty of hearing (1 Cor 12:7); (2) the act of hearing, "listening"; or (3) "that which is heard, report, account," hence "preaching." In using Deutero-Isaiah's words, Paul shows that a message sent by God is not always received with faith, even the one about the suffering Servant of Yahweh. Cf. John 12:38 (also quoting Isa 53:1).

17. *Faith then comes from what is heard.* Lit., "faith is from an act of hearing." See Gal 3:2, 5; 1 Thess 2:13. In other words, faith begins with listening to a proposition, e.g., "Jesus is Lord" (10:9) and with an acceptance of it as "the word of preaching." Such acceptance leads to *hypakoē pisteōs,* the "(personal) commitment of faith" (1:5; [16:26]), and such faith produces trust and hope, as it works itself out through love (Gal 5:6).

what is heard comes through the word of Christ. Lit., "the report (is) through the utterance of Christ." But this vague expression can be variously interpreted, as Käsemann (*Commentary,* 295) recognizes, and Paul does not further explain it. It could mean "through the message that Christ himself has brought" (gen. of origin); so Lagrange (*Romains,* 261). Or, more likely in this context, "through the message about Christ" or "through the message of the Messiah" (objective gen.), as Sanday and Headlam have taken it (*Romans,* 298). See 10:8, "the word of faith that we preach." Thus Christ would be speaking his message through the mouths of his authorized heralds. See Rickards, "The Translation."

This is the last time that Christ is mentioned in this part of Romans (chaps. 9–11); he will reappear in 12:5. Nor is "Jesus" or "Lord" (= the risen Christ) used in the rest of chaps. 10–11. For the significance of this silence, see the NOTES on 11:26.

Some MSS (ℵ^c, A, D^{b,c}, K, P, Ψ, 33, 614, 1241, and the *Koinē* text-tradition) change *Christou* to *theou,* but that is a copyist's harmonization of the Pauline text with *rhēma theou*, which occurs elsewhere in the NT (e.g., Luke 3:2; John 3:34; Eph 6:17; Heb 6:5; 11:3).

18. *Can it be that they have not heard of it?* Lit., "they have not heard, have they?" The third objection: Perhaps the Jews did not really hear the message about Christ! Maybe they did not have the opportunity to hear the good news; maybe apostolic preachers have not done their job.

Of course they have! Lit., "rather, on the contrary." *Menounge* is an emphatic corrective particle, "more than that." Cf. 9:20; Phil 3:8 (BAGD, 503b).

"Their voice has gone forth over all the earth, and their words to the bounds of the world." Paul replies to the third objection by quoting Ps 19:5 according to the LXX, which reads *phthongos autōn*, "their voice," instead of Hebrew *qawwām*, "their line." The psalmist sings of the works of nature proclaiming the glory of God everywhere; Paul accommodates the psalmist's words to the preaching of the gospel. It has gone forth to all the earth, to the end of the *oikoumenē*, whatever that would have meant in Paul's day. In 15:19 he will speak of himself as having preached the gospel from Jerusalem all the way around to Illyricum, and he looks forward to carrying the good news even to Spain (15:21). Thus, in effect, Paul asserts the universal character of the preaching of the gospel and denies that Israel has lacked the opportunity to believe in Christ. Like the whole world, Israel has heard the good news.

19. *But again I ask.* So Paul introduces the fourth objection of his imaginary interlocutor.

Can it be that Israel did not understand? I.e., maybe apostolic preachers spoke in an unintelligible fashion, so that Israel did not comprehend their message. Is Israel invincibly uncomprehending? The adj. *prōtos* follows the vb. *egnō*, and most commentators take it as part of the following answer to the question. But it could also modify *Israēl* in the question, meaning, Can it be that Israel as first (of all peoples) has not understood the gospel? It is so understood by Zahn; but see Cranfield (*Romans*, 538–39).

First of all, Moses says. If the adj. *prōtos* is rightly taken with this answer that Paul gives to the objection, then it may mean that Paul cites not only Isaiah (10:20), but also Moses, and him first of all. Or it may mean, "Moses was the first to say (to Israel)," i.e., as early as Moses it was said to Israel; and I (Paul) repeat it.

"I shall make you jealous of those who are not a nation; and with a foolish nation shall I provoke your anger." Paul quotes Deut 32:21 according to the LXX, which corresponds to the MT; but he changes *autous*, "them," to *hymas*, "you." He thus cites part of the Song of Moses, in which Yahweh, through Moses, tries to educate Israel and announces that it will be humiliated by heathen. Paul thus compares the present status of Israel with what its condition was at the time of its wandering in the desert. If it was humiliated then for its infidelity, how much greater should its humiliation be now; Gentiles, the "nonpeople" and "a foolish nation," understand the gospel message, yet Israel is uncomprehending. What happens to the Gentiles is meant to provoke Israel into a reaction. See 11:11, 14,

599

which is here foreshadowed. So Paul reintroduces the role of the Gentiles into his argument. Cf. 1 Cor 10:7, 22, where Paul alludes to Deut 32:21 in the light of Deut 32:6. The provocation of Israel to jealousy has recently turned up in a Qumran text, being used there in a different sense: "and making for themselves a high place on a lofty mountain to provoke Israel to jealousy" (*lhqny> >t ysr>l*; 4Q372 1:12). It seems to be said of "foreigners" (*bny n>kr*), but is possibly an allusion to the Samaritan temple on Mount Gerizim.

20. *Isaiah made bold to say.* Lit., "Isaiah grows bold and says." To the testimony of the Torah Paul adds that of one of the prophets of old in order to silence Israel about its claim that it has not understood.

"*I was found by those who were not seeking me; I showed myself to those who were not asking for me.*" Paul quotes Isa 65:1 in a form close to the LXX, but not exactly, because he reverses the verbs at the beginning of the clauses. In the original context of Trito-Isaiah, the same people are envisaged by the prophet's words in vv 1–2, be they Samaritans, apostate Jews, or simply Jews (disputed among OT commentators). But Paul, influenced by the LXX, which speaks of *ethnos*, "nation," in v 1 and of *laos* in v 2, splits up the reference in the two verses. The first is applied to Gentiles, the second to Jews. The contrast is obvious between the Gentiles, "the foolish nation," accepting Christ in faith, and the Jews, "a disobedient and defiant people." See 9:30. God chose to manifest himself to people who were not even trying to find him and who lacked all comprehension of his designs; yet he was only pursuing his goal of acquitting the godless and thereby goading his own people on to a realization of the care that he has really had for them.

21. *Yet of Israel he says.* I.e., Isaiah says. Paul continues the quotation.

"*All day long have I held out my hands to a disobedient and defiant people.*" Paul quotes Isa 65:2 to characterize the situation of Israel as he sees it. He cites Isaiah according to the LXX, but puts "all day long" at the head of the sentence for emphasis. The LXX renders Hebrew *>el 'am sorer*, "to a rebellious people," with two ptcs., *apeithounta kai antilegonta*, "being disobedient and contradictory." The clause, "held out my hands," is meant not in the sense of supplication, but in that of welcome or invitation, a gesture that Israel has refused. Thus Paul insists that God has never stopped reaching out to Israel, even in all its resistance.

So ends Paul's scathing indictment of Israel. It is surpassed in his letters only by what he says in 1 Thess 2:14–15. Cf. Acts 13:45; 28:22.

BIBLIOGRAPHY

Gewalt, D., "Die 'fides ex auditu' und die Taubstummen: Zur Auslegungsgeschichte von Gal. 3, 2 und Röm. 10, 14–17," *LB* 58 (1986): 45–64.

Keller, M. A., " 'La fe a través del mensaje' (Rom 10,17): Experiencia de fe, promulgación," *Biblia y fe* 11.31 (1985): 59–69.

Ludwig, J., "Fides ex auditu: A Meditation on Rom. 10:17," *Festschrift der Vereinigung katholischer Theologen "Aurelia," aus Anlass der 75. Stiftungsfestes,* ed. Aktivitas (Bonn: Hanstein, 1926), 69–71.

Müller, F., "Zwei Marginalien im Brief des Paulus an die Römer," ZNW 40 (1941): 249–54, esp 252–54.

Rehkopf, F., "Grammatisches zum Griechischen des Neuen Testamentes," *Der Ruf Jesu und die Antwort der Gemeinde: Exegetische Untersuchungen Joachim Jeremias . . . gewidmet . . . ,* ed. E. Lohse et al. (Göttingen: Vandenhoeck & Ruprecht, 1970), 213–25, esp. 224–25.

Rickards, R. R., "The Translation of *dia rhēmatos Christou* ('through the word of Christ') in Romans 10.17," *BT* 27 (1976): 447–48.

Whitaker, G. H., "Hebrews iv. 2 and Romans x. 16ff.," *Expos* 8.23 (1922): 239–40.

ISRAEL'S FAILURE: IT IS PARTIAL AND TEMPORARY (11:1–36)

◆

39. ISRAEL'S HARDENING IS PARTIAL (11:1–10)

11 ¹I ask then, Has God rejected his people? Certainly not! I am an Israelite myself, a descendant of Abraham, from the tribe of Benjamin. ²No, *God has not rejected his people,* whom he foreknew. Do you not know what Scripture says in the passage about Elijah, how he pleaded with God against Israel: ³*"Lord, they have killed your prophets and torn down your altars; and I am left alone, and they are seeking my life."* ⁴And what was the divine reply to him? *"I have reserved for myself seven thousand men who have not bent the knee to Baal."* ⁵So too at the present time a remnant, chosen by grace, has come into being. ⁶And if by grace, it is no longer by deeds, for grace would cease to be grace. ⁷So then what? What Israel sought, it did not achieve; the chosen ones achieved it, whereas the others were made obtuse. ⁸As it stands written, *"God granted them stupor of spirit, eyes that see not and ears that hear not—even to this day."* ⁹David too says, *"May their table be a snare and a trap, a stumbling block and a retribution for them;* ¹⁰*may their eyes be dimmed so that they cannot see! Bend their backs continually!"*

COMMENT

The picture painted thus far by Paul in chaps. 9–10 is not pleasant: Israel's misstep suits the plan of God based on his gratuitous election (chap. 9), but actually its cause rests not with God but with Israel itself (chap. 10). Yet as early as 9:27 Paul hinted at a ray of hope, when he said that "a remnant shall be saved." Now he returns to this aspect of the problem and further explains that God has not rejected his people, that Israel's disbelief is only partial (11:1–10), that it is only temporary (11:11–24), and that all Israel shall be saved; indeed, in God's plan mercy is to be shown to all, Jews included (11:25–32). At the end of this section Paul bursts into a hymn to the merciful wisdom of God that has been manifested in his dealings with his chosen people (11:33–36). So the chapter is divided by the vast majority of commentators (Barrett, Barth, Black, Cranfield, Dunn, Käsemann, Lagrange, Munck, Nygren, Sanday and Headlam, Schlier); but Johnson ("The Structure") would instead divide the chapter into three sections: (1) 11:1–16, the remnant is the adumbration of the salvation of all Israel (subdivided into vv 1–6 and 7–16); (2) 11:17–32, Israel's present and ultimate priority is maintained (subdivided into vv 17–24 and 25–32); (3) 11:33–36, the wisdom of God is praised. Such a division may indicate that one theme dominates

Paul's discussion that all Israel will be saved, but it is not in reality much better than the division commonly used.

In chap. 11 Paul formally takes up the problem of "the rejection of Israel" (v 15), the issue that has been preoccupying him since 9:1. Now he will explain in what sense that phrase is to be understood, whether "Israel" is a subjective or an objective genitive. At first (11:1–10), he is concerned with the fact that that "rejection" affects only a part of Israel. Hence Israel's plight is only partial.

In this paragraph Paul develops his argument in three ways: he cites his own experience as a Jewish Christian, he appeals to the answer given to Elijah in his struggle against Baalism, and he contrasts the "remnant" of Israel with the "others."

NOTES

11:1. *I ask then.* Lit., "I say, therefore." Paul begins this paragraph and the following (vv 11–24) with the same emphatic *legō oun.*

Has God rejected his people? Paul alludes to Ps 94:14 and frames it as a question, using the negative *mē* (which expects a negative answer) instead of *ou* of the LXX, *ouk apōsetai Kyrios ton laon autou,* "the Lord will not reject his people." The same promise is found in 1 Sam 12:22 and in MS B of the LXX of Ps 95:4. Psalm 94 is one of personal lamentation, a prayer for deliverance of an individual from enemies. Paul alludes to it to frame the question as an objection to his argument: has God, who once chose Israel as his people, now cast them off? The implied objection is that, if God's plan is one of gratuitous election and Israel has been unfaithful, and if Gentiles are now accepting the gospel, whereas Israel is not, then apparently God has repudiated those who were once his chosen people. The query reflects an attitude recorded in Jer 31:37, "Then shall I cast off the whole race of Israel because of all that they have done, says the Lord." In using "his people," Paul echoes a favorite term of the OT for Israel; cf. 1 Chr 17:21, "Is there, like your people Israel, whom you redeemed from Egypt, another nation on earth whom a god went to redeem as his people?"

Most Greek MSS read *ton laon,* as in the LXX, but MSS P[46], F, G, and some patristic writers read *tēn klēronomian,* "(his) heritage," which is found in the second part of the verse in the LXX.

Certainly not! Paul emphatically, almost indignantly, rejects the implication. How can I, a genuine Israelite, admit such a thing? See the NOTE on 3:4.

I am an Israelite myself. I.e., a member of God's holy people, a member of Israel of old, even though he has accepted Christ Jesus and his mode of uprightness. Paul can still boast of his Jewish heritage. See the NOTE on 9:4; and cf. 2 Cor 11:22. Paul argues thus not as a proof of what he has just denied, but to state its motivation, precisely as an Israelite, he understands God's dealings with his people and knows that he himself is an indication that God has not rejected Israel.

a descendant of Abraham. Lit., "of the seed of Abraham." See the NOTE on 9:7; cf. 4:16; Gal 3:29. This connection with Abraham will become crucial in the argument of chap. 11.

from the tribe of Benjamin. I.e., with no mean connections, for Benjamin was considered the most Israelite of the tribes, the "beloved of the Lord" (Deut 33:12). From it came Saul, the great warrior king and first ruler of the undivided monarchy, Paul's Hebrew namesake. See Phil 3:5. Paul and other Jewish people have been called and invited to belief in Christ. Such Jewish Christians show that God has not rejected his people, some of whom at least have been favored by his grace.

2. *No, God has not rejected his people.* Now Paul quotes Ps 94:14, changing the fut. to the aor. *apōsato* in an emphatic denial.

whom he foreknew. I.e., by God's predilection Israel has been assured a place in the divine plan of salvation. Cf. 1 Sam 12:22, "For the sake of his own great name the Lord will not cast away his people, since Yahweh himself has taken it to heart to make you a people for himself." Cf. Amos 3:2, "You have I known more than all the families of the earth." Israel has been included in God's foreknowledge; recall 8:29.

Do you not know what Scripture says. See the NOTE on 1:2. So Paul introduces two quotations from the OT that he will contrast.

in the passage about Elijah? Lit., "in Elijah," see the NOTES on 9:25; 4:3. Cf. BDF §219.1. Elijah was the ninth-century prophet from Tishbe in Gilead, the master of Elisha. His loyalty to Yahweh enabled him to take the lead in the struggle against the introduction of Baalism into the kingdom of Israel from Tyre under Jezebel. Elijah challenged the prophets of Baal to a contest on Mount Carmel to see who would be lord, Baal or Yahweh; he stood alone against 450 prophets of Baal. When their entreaty of Baal did not kindle the fire of sacrifice, Elijah successfully sought the aid of Yahweh, whose fire fell and consumed the offering (1 Kgs 18:1–46). Elijah's success and the subsequent slaughter of the prophets of Baal were reported to Jezebel, and he fled as a result to Beer-sheba, and then to Mount Horeb (1 Kgs 19:1–8).

how he pleaded with God against Israel. So Paul sums up the meaning of the Elijah story. Paul uses *entynchanein,* "intercede with, plead for"; cf. Heb 7:25; also 1 Macc 8:32; 10:61, 63; 11:25, "plead against," as here.

3. *"Lord, they have killed your prophets and torn down your altars; and I am left alone, and they are seeking my life."* Paul uses 1 Kgs 19:10 in an abridged and inverted form. He abbreviates 1 Kgs 19:9–18 to make his point: the example of Elijah is drawn from Israel's history to illustrate God's plan in the present situation. After his journey of forty days and nights to reach Horeb, the mountain of God, Elijah took shelter in a cave where he complained bitterly to Yahweh about Israel's infidelities and its opposition to him, Yahweh's prophet, now isolated in despair. Yahweh announced the coming chastisement of his people, but also the deliverance of seven thousand in Israel who had not become idolaters. In this

situation Elijah sensed himself all alone, for he had become an object of the Israelites' scorn because of his allegiance to Yahweh.

4. *And what was the divine reply to him?* I.e., to Elijah the loyal prophet. Paul uses *chrēmatismos*, "oracle, (divine) utterance, (oracular) reply"; cf. 2 Macc 2:4; 1 Clem. 17:5.

"I have reserved for myself seven thousand men who have not bent the knee to Baal." Paul quotes 1 Kgs 19:18 freely, according to neither the MT nor the LXX. He is interested in only one point: seven thousand remained faithful to Yahweh; so Israel has not been entirely repudiated. Even though Jewish Christians (like Paul) sense their isolation, they know that their status as such comes from God's favor. Paul knows that he is part of the remnant.

Paul's Greek text reads *tē Baal*, treating Baal as a fem. noun, whereas the LXX of 1 Kgs 19:18 uses the masc. *tō Baal*. The fem. article is used because the fem. Greek noun *aischynē*, equalling Hebrew *bōšet*, "abomination," was often substituted in reading for the name of a pagan god, especially for Baal (and even in writing, MT of 2 Sam 2:8; 3:8). Compare the MT and the LXX of 1 Kgs 18:25. The fem. *tē Baal* is also found in the LXX of 2 Kgs 21:3; Jer 2:8; 12:16. See BDF §53.4. See A. Dillmann, "Über Baal mit dem weiblichen Artikel," *Monatsbericht der königlichen preussischen Akademie der Wissenschaften* (1881): 601–20.

5. *So too at the present time.* See the NOTE on 3:21; cf. 3:26.

a remnant, chosen by grace, has come into being. Lit., "a remnant according to the selection of grace," i.e., without any regard for their fidelity to the law. See 9:27. In the remnant "Israel" continues to exist and to be graced by God who called it. This implies that Paul recognized that other Jews, like himself, had been drawn to Christ and that he would proclaim Christ Jesus even to his "kinsmen by race." This does not mean merely "some Jews," but Paul understands "Israel" now existing in the remnant. For the fuller OT background of the remnant idea, see Clements, " 'A Remnant' "; Hasel, *The Remnant*. The Essenes of Qumran also regarded themselves as *běhîrê rāṣôn*, "those chosen by (divine) benevolence" (1QS 8:6; cf. Vogt, "Peace among Men").

6. *if by grace, it is no longer by deeds.* See 3:24; 4:4; 9:16. The existence of such a remnant of Jewish Christians is evidence of God's benevolence rather than of human merit. It depends not on the character of the people or on their achievements or qualifications; it depends wholly on God and his grace. Not even the chosen remnant has claims on God. Cf. Gal 3:18. On "by deeds," see the NOTES on 2:15; 3:20; and 4:2.

for grace would cease to be grace. Some Greek MSS (ℵ^c, B, L, etc.) add *ei de ex ergōn ouketi esti charis epei to ergon ouketi estin ergon*, "but if it is of deeds, then it is no longer grace; otherwise a deed is no longer a deed." This is a strange addition; see TCGNT, 526. On *epei* meaning "for otherwise," see BDF §456.3.

7. *So then what?* See the NOTE on 3:1.

What Israel sought, it did not achieve. The majority of the Jewish people apart from the remnant did not attain the uprightness they pursued (9:30–31). This is the source of the sorrow that Paul expresses in 9:1–2 and 10:1.

the chosen ones achieved it. Lit., "the election," the abstract is used for the concrete, "those whom God chose," i.e., Jewish Christians, the remnant of 9:27. Although the "election" embraces both Gentiles and the Jewish remnant, Paul is thinking only of the latter, when he contrasts it with *hoi loipoi*, "the rest, the others." The Jewish remnant, in accepting God's call in the gospel, have achieved the uprightness that they pursued.

whereas the others were made obtuse I.e., by God. Paul again uses a theological passive (ZBG §236) and indulges in protological thinking, ascribing to God himself the hardening of Israel's heart and its failure to achieve what the remnant achieved. See 9:18 and the NOTE there.

8. *As it stands written.* See the NOTE on 1:17.

"God granted them stupor of spirit, eyes that see not and ears that hear not—even to this day." On the conflated OT quotations that occur here, see the NOTE on 3:10. Paul links together parts of Deut 29:3; Isa 29:10; and Ps 69:23–24. Israel lies in stupor and sees not what is before it; it sleeps and hears not the gospel that is preached over all the earth (10:18).

The words of Deut 29:3, not quoted literally, were addressed by Moses to Israel. It had witnessed all of the portents sent by God against Pharaoh on its behalf, but it had never appreciated their full significance: "But to this day Yahweh has not given you a mind to understand, or eyes to see, or ears to hear." Paul modifies his free quotation of this OT verse with an addition from Isa 29:10, "a spirit of stupor," drawn from a passage in which Isaiah spoke of the spiritual blindness and perversity of Israel. The conflated texts serve Paul's purpose of describing Israel's reaction to Christ, but one should not miss the way in which Paul uses the OT, citing it to his own purpose (see *ESBNT*, 44–45; J. Schmid, *BZ* 3 [1959]: 161–73).

9. *David too says.* David's name stands at the head of Psalm 69, which Paul now quotes.

"May their table be a snare and a trap, a stumbling block and a retribution for them." Ps 69:23–24 is quoted according to the LXX, which is close to the MT, but not exactly the same. The psalm itself is a lament for deliverance from personal tribulation and enemies, in which the psalmist invokes God's wrath against those who resist his will. By "table" is meant a tablecloth spread on the ground, over which one might trip. Paul cites these words to show that what is closest to Israel has become the source of its misstep and its stumbling. Thus he echoes what he said about Israel's unenlightened zeal (10:2). Cf. Ps 35:8.

10. *"may their eyes be dimmed so that they cannot see!"* The catchword bond is "eyes," which joins Psalm 69 to Deut 29:3 and Isa 29:10. The effect is a quotation from *Těnāk*, from the Law, the Prophets, and the Writings. One need not try to decide to what the other details refer (feasting, etc.); the main point is

the sealing by God of the situation that exists (see the NOTE on 9:18), a situation that is neither entire nor final. But it explains Israel's lack of understanding.

"Bend their backs continually!" I.e., may their backs be always weak and feeble under the burden that they bear because of their rejection of the gospel. The sense of the phrase *dia pantos* is disputed. In the LXX it translates Hebrew *tāmîd*, "continually," and often has the same meaning in extrabiblical Greek. Hence it should not be given here the meaning "forever" that it has in the LXX of Isa 57:16 or in the RSV of this passage. See Cranfield, "Significance."

BIBLIOGRAPHY

Clements, R. E., " 'A Remnant Chosen by Grace' (Romans 11:5): The Old Testament Background and Origin of the Remnant Concept," *Pauline Studies: Essays Presented to Professor F. F. Bruce . . .* , ed. D. A. Hagner and M. J. Harris (Exeter, UK: Paternoster; Grand Rapids, Mich.: Eerdmans, 1980), 106–21.

Cohen, K. I., "Paul the Benjaminite: Mystery, Motives and Midrash," *Center for Hermeneutical Studies Protocol* 60 (1990): 21–28.

Cranfield, C.E.B., "The Significance of *dia pantos* in Romans 11,10," *SE II,* TU 87 (1964), 546–50; repr. in *The Bible and Christian Life* (Edinburgh: Clark, 1985), 197–202.

Dobschütz, E. von, "Zum paulinischen Schriftbeweis," *ZNW* 24 (1925): 306–7.

Dreyfus, F., "Le Passé et le présent d'Israël (Rom 9,1–5; 11,1–24)," *Die Israelfrage,* ed. L. de Lorenzi, 131–92, esp. 140–51.

Hanson, A., "The Oracle in Romans xi. 4," *NTS* 19 (1972–73): 300–302.

Hasel, G. F., *The Remnant: The History and Theology of the Remnant Idea from Genesis to Isaiah,* 2d ed. (Berrien Springs, Mich.: Andrews University, 1974).

Huguet, M.-T., "Mise à l'écart d'Israël? Une Approche au sujet de la spécificité théologique de la 'maison d'Israël' et de sa relation à l'église," *NovVet* 60 (1985): 103–20.

Johnson, D. G., "The Structure and Meaning of Romans 11," *CBQ* 46 (1984): 91–103.

Luz, U., *Geschichtsverständnis,* 80–83, 90, 98, 286–300, 392–94.

Müller, C., *Gottes Gerechtigkeit,* 44–47.

Munck, J., *Christ & Israel,* 104–43.

Peterson, E., *Le Mystère des Juifs et des Gentils dans l'église,* Courrier des iles 6 (Paris: Desclée de Brouwer, [1935]), 51–66.

Rengstorf, K. H., "Paulus und die älteste römische Christenheit," *SE II,* TU 87 (1964), 447–64.

Rese, M., "Die Rettung der Juden nach Römer 11," *L'Apôtre Paul: Personnalité, style et conception du ministère,* BETL 73, ed. A. Vanhoye (Louvain: Leuven University/Peeters, 1986), 422–30.

Schmidt, K. L., "Die Verstockung des Menschen durch Gott: Eine lexikologische und biblisch-theologische Studie," *TZ* 1 (1945): 1–17.

Vogt, E., " 'Peace among Men of God's Good Pleasure' Lk 2.14," *The Scrolls and the New Testament*, ed. K. Stendahl (New York: Harper & Bros., 1957), 114–17.

Wilcox, M., "The Promise of the 'Seed' in the New Testament and the Targumim," *JSNT* 5 (1979): 2–20.

Zeller, D., *Juden und Heiden*, 126–33, 245–69.

40. ISRAEL'S DISBELIEF IS TEMPORARY AND PROVIDENTIAL (11:11–24)

11 ¹¹Now then I ask, Did they stumble so as to fall irremediably? Certainly not! Yet because of their trespass salvation has come to the Gentiles to make Israel jealous. ¹²Now if their trespass has meant the enrichment of the world, and their loss the enrichment of Gentiles, how much more will their full number mean! ¹³I turn now to you Gentiles: inasmuch as I am the apostle of the Gentiles, I make much of this ministry of mine ¹⁴in the hope that I may stir up my own people to jealousy and save some of them. ¹⁵For if their rejection has meant the reconciliation of the world, what will their acceptance mean? Nothing less than life from the dead! ¹⁶If the firstfruits are holy, so too is the whole batch of dough; if the root is holy, so too are the branches. ¹⁷If some of the branches have been lopped off, you, though a branch from a wild olive tree, have been grafted into their place and have come to share in the rich sap of the olive root. ¹⁸Do not boast over those branches. If you do, remember this: you do not support the root; the root supports you. ¹⁹You may indeed say, "Branches were lopped off so that I might be grafted in." ²⁰True, but they were lopped off because of a lack of faith, whereas you are there because of faith. So do not become haughty for that reason; be fearful. ²¹For if God did not spare the natural branches, perhaps he will not spare you either. ²²Consider then God's kindness and severity; severity to those who have fallen, but kindness to you, if you only remain in his kindness. For you too may be cut off. ²³And those others, if they do not remain in their lack of faith, will be grafted back in. God indeed has the power to graft them in again. ²⁴For if you were cut from an olive tree that is wild by nature and grafted contrary to nature into a cultivated one, how much more readily will these, the natural branches, be grafted back into their own olive stock!

COMMENT

Having explained Israel's misstep as affecting only part of the Jewish people, Paul now goes on to discuss other aspects of the misstep, its temporal and providential character. In this regard he understands how Israel's failure fits into the salvific plan of God. As Paul sees it, its purpose has been threefold: (1) to allow salvation to come to the Gentiles; (2) to make Israel jealous of such Gentiles;

and (3) to allow their eventual share in salvation as a sign of their coming from death to life.

In this paragraph Paul addresses the predominantly Gentile Roman Christians in his role as "the apostle of the Gentiles" (11:13). He warns them not to become smug over their situation, the status of rectitude that they have attained through faith in Christ Jesus. Their share in such justification or salvation is actually a share in the inheritance destined for Israel itself. It is not something that Gentiles have attained independently of Israel.

To develop this discussion Paul compares Gentile Christians with branches of a wild olive tree that have been cut from their own stock and grafted into a cultivated olive tree. The life that they now live as a graft is derived from the cultivated olive stock. The stock from which Gentile Christians derive their new life is that of Israel of old. Thus "the church of the Gentiles is an extension of the promises of God to Israel and not Israel's displacement" (Beker, *Paul the Apostle,* 332).

Von Harnack once thought that Paul was reintroducing an ethnic argument into his discussion by using the metaphor of the olive tree, an ethnic argument that is contrary to the sense of "Israel" in chaps. 9–10. "In chaps. ix. and x. the Apostle seems to acquiesce in the answer that the promises still remain in force because they apply to Israel *kata pneuma.* . . . in cap. xi. another entirely different view appears by the side of the first. There is fulfilment of the Divine promises also for Israel *kata sarka.* God cannot and has not rejected His people— meaning here, Israel *kata sarka!*" (*The Date of the Acts and of the Synoptic Gospels,* New Testament Studies 4 [London: Williams & Norgate; New York: Putnam, 1911], 45). Thus, Paul would have distinguished ethnic Israel from eschatological Israel (9:6), but now he has reintroduced the ethnic aspect that he had sought to refine in chap. 9. The same sort of view is espoused by Dinkler (*JR* 36 [1956]: 116–17).

Indeed, this difference has become the basis of the opinion of many interpreters, who think that Paul is inconsistent, incoherent, or even contradictory in these chapters: e.g., Räisänen, "Römer 9–11: Analyse," 2892; Watson, *Paul, Judaism,* 170; Kümmel, "Die Probleme," 32. Attempts have been made to solve this alleged contradiction by stressing that Paul, in beginning his discussion at 9:1, did not yet realize the solution to which he was to come in 11:25–32. So Noack ("Current"); similarly Hyldahl ("Jesus"); Senft ("L'Election"); Wilckens (*Römer,* 263).

Others insist that the contradiction is only apparent. From the very beginning of chap. 9 Paul has been aiming at the salvation of "all Israel." That salvation stems from the grace and mercy of God, and not from the conduct of his people. This is the Pauline thesis in chap. 9: God's word has not failed. So (with varying nuances) Kühl (*Römer,* 319–20, 403–5); Gaston (*Paul and the Torah,* 92–99); Getty ("Paul").

But the charge of inconsistency is overdrawn. As Bourke has rightly seen, what

Paul says here in 11:17–24 has to be understood against the background of what he has already affirmed in 11:16b about the "root," in Romans 4 about Abraham and his offspring, and esp. in Gal 3:29: "But if you belong to Christ, you are the offspring of Abraham, heirs according to the promise." Romans 4 inculcates that all believers are the offspring of Abraham; but it is not just faith that makes people children of the patriarch, but incorporation into Christ, without which no one can be among the offspring of Abraham, whether Jew or Gentile (A *Study*, 80–82; cf. Davies, *NTS* 24 [1977–78]: 31).

The question of coherence, moreover, has to be judged in terms of the way one understands the image Paul uses. Whom does the olive tree itself represent? For Lyonnet (*SBJ*, *Aux Galates, aux Romains* [1959], 117 n. a), it represents historic, ethnic Israel; similarly Wilckens, *Römer*, 2.246; Byrne, *Reckoning*, 203; Peterson, Tremel, Schlier (*Römerbrief*, 333–34). This view seems to depend on what Paul says in 11:28: "as far as election is concerned, they are beloved of God because of the patriarchs." But it is the interpretation that creates the incoherence. For that reason, others think that the olive tree represents eschatological Israel or spiritual Israel, the remnant and the Gentile Christians; so Nygren (*Romans*, 400); Hofius, Stuhlmacher, Refoulé (*RB* 98 [1991]: 72). The latter interpretation seems to be correct in view of 11:23, which envisages the lopping off of the branches of the cultivated olive because they "remain in their lack of faith." As Schmidt has put it (*An die Römer*, 194), "Paul insists that only the elect and those who have been graced with faith belong to the people of God; only they are the branches of the olive tree, whether they be naturally grown or subsequently grafted in. That is why there are offspring of Abraham by birth who, not being chosen, now resemble lopped off branches and pagans who as a result of being chosen have been introduced into the history of Abraham's blessing."

If the olive tree stands for the group of those who believe in Christ, the "root" of which is Abraham, who, though called as a pagan, became the person of faith, there is then no sole ethnic ground for membership. Gentile Christians and the remnant are all God's people united in the same faith; they are "Israel" in the eschatological sense. True, Paul has already accorded Israel in the ethnic sense a priority because of its historic call (1:16; 2:9–10); chronologically it has precedence over the Gentiles in God's plan. The pagan Abraham was first called by God to become the "root" of the Jewish people, and to them Jesus first announced his gospel. Thus the Jewish patriarch is the "root" of the church, Jewish and Gentile. Once again Paul singles out the Jewish people because of their historic role as the first children of Abraham and is concerned that Gentile Christians not lose sight of their connections and their roots. "In Christ there is neither Jew nor Greek and yet a continued place for the Jewish people as such" (Davies, *NTS* 24 [1977–78]: 33).

NOTES

11:11. *Now then I ask.* Lit., "I say, therefore." See 11:1. Paul poses the question with reference to those who have encountered the stumbling block.

Did they stumble so as to fall irremediably? Lit., "they have not stumbled, have they, so as to be fallen?" Is their misstep so serious that the majority of Israel has cut itself off from salvation? Paul contrasts the vbs. *ptaiein* and *piptein*. The vb. *ptaiein*, "stumble," is suggested by the *skandalon* of 11:9 and is used elsewhere in a moral sense (Deut 7:25; 2 Kgs 19:26; Jas 2:10; 3:2).

Certainly not! See the NOTE on 3:4. Israel has stumbled over Christ, but it has not fallen down completely so that it cannot regain its footing. Indeed, its stumbling has been providential in that apostles turned from them to preach the gospel to the Gentiles. Yet Paul looks forward to a time in which Israel will recover its footing, Israel's disbelief will disappear, and its trespass will be no more. Cf. Acts 13:45–48; 18:6. On Christ the stumbling block, see the NOTE on 9:33.

because of their trespass salvation has come to the Gentiles. The misstep and stumbling of Israel have become "their trespass." Paul plays on the relation of *paraptōma*, "false step, transgression," and the vb. *ptaiein*. Israel's historic "transgression" has enabled salvation to come to the Gentiles, and this result has its purpose in God's plan.

to make Israel jealous. In the long run Israel's stumbling would arouse in it a jealousy of the Gentiles, who were attaining the uprightness before God that Israel had been pursuing. Paul's motivation in seeking to make Israel "jealous" is not of the highest level; he argues from a very human consideration. See the NOTE on 10:19, which already suggested the idea of jealousy in the quotation from Deut 32:21 and cites a Qumran text that uses the same expression, "to make Israel jealous."

12. *if their trespass has meant the enrichment of the world.* I.e., what Israel has failed to do has affected even the *kosmos* (see the NOTES on 1:20; 3:19; 4:13). The *kosmos* has, consequently, come into a situation of "wealth," in being able to share in the bounty of messianic salvation. Cf. 10:12.

and their loss the enrichment of Gentiles. Lit., "their defeat." Not just the *kosmos*, but more specifically, Gentiles have come to share in the rich heritage of Israel, which it has itself been losing. The noun *hēttēma* is found in the sense of "defeat, loss" in Isa 31:8 and 1 Cor 6:7.

how much more will their full number mean! The meaning of *plērōma* is disputed, because it has several possible meanings. Its basic meaning is "fullness," but it can be used to denote (1) "that which fills up, the contents"; (2) "that which makes something full, the complement"; (3) "that which is full of something"; (4) "that which is brought to fulfillment/completion," "full number"; (5) "fulfillment, fulfilling"; (6) "the state of being full" (Gal 4:4). Here meaning (4) is most likely, "that which is brought to fullness, full number," as in 11:25. But some commentators understand it as "their fulfillment, filling" (of the divine command). See BAGD, 672. Paul hints at the untold benefits for the world that would come about with the acceptance of Jesus as Messiah by the Jewish people as a whole; if their action has so far resulted in such incredibly rich benefits, then what will the acceptance by their full number mean for all? See 11:25.

13. *I turn now to you Gentiles.* Paul passes from exposition to exhortation as he addresses the Roman Christians, regarding them as predominantly of Gentile background; see the NOTES on 1:13 and 11:25.

inasmuch as I am the apostle of the Gentiles. The epithet commonly given to Paul stems from this, his own writing (see Gal 2:7–8; cf. Acts 9:15; 22:21). Here he plays on the "grace and apostolate" mentioned in 1:5 and is fully aware of his commission to preach the gospel to Gentiles.

I make much of this ministry of mine. Lit., "I glorify this service," i.e., hold it in great esteem and do everything in my power to see that it succeeds. Paul knows that he serves the interests of Israel better by preaching to the Gentiles.

14. *in the hope that I may stir up my own people to jealousy.* Lit., "if perchance I may stir to jealousy my (own) flesh." Though a Christian, Paul still regards himself as a member of the Jewish people (11:1c–e). Calling them "my flesh," he gives vivid expression to his solidarity with them. He spends himself in the ministry of the gospel, preaching it to the Gentiles with one purpose: to stimulate his people to envy the lot of the Gentiles. See 10:19.

and save some of them. So Paul discloses his ultimate goal as an apostle of the Gentiles; see 10:1; cf. 1 Cor 9:22. Although Paul's ministry primarily concerns itself with the salvation of Gentiles, he insists that there is a deeper motivation in his mission: the salvation of Israel.

15. *if their rejection has meant.* After vv 13–14, which were a sort of parenthetical remark, Paul turns now to repeat in different language what he said in v 12.

Some commentators (e.g., Black, *Romans*, 155; Cranfield, *Romans*, 562; Murray, *Romans*, 2. 81; Nygren, *Romans*, 397; Wilckens, *Römer*, 245) understand *apobolē autōn*, "their rejection," as an objective gen., God's (temporary) "rejection of them," even comparing the gloss in Sir 10:20: "Fear of the Lord is the beginning of acceptance, but the beginning of rejection is obstinacy and arrogance." But it is better taken as a subjective gen., i.e., the Jews' rejection (of the gospel), in view of what Paul has exclaimed in 11:1, where he rejects the idea that God has rejected his own people. To introduce the idea of a temporary rejection of Israel by God is to read something into the text that is not there; it is nonetheless a very common interpretation of this phrase.

the reconciliation of the world. Although Paul does not explain this phrase here, he has already used a similar expression in 2 Cor 5:19, "God was in Christ, reconciling the world to himself," i.e., setting it at one with himself. See Introduction, section IX.B. The providential aspect of Israel's "rejection" has been the extension of reconciliation with God to all other human beings, and even a cosmic extension of that effect to the whole universe. Such a reconciliation will have the effect of making the ethnic Israel jealous and thus of drawing it closer to God's new mode of salvation.

what will their acceptance mean? I.e., their acceptance or welcoming of the gospel, as the counterpart of their "rejection" of it (v 15a). Many commentators, however, think that "acceptance" means "acceptance by God," appealing to 14:3 and 15:7; so Black (*Romans*, 155), BAGD, 717.

Nothing less than life from the dead! Cf. John 5:24. The meaning of this phrase is quite disputed.

Origen (*In ep. ad Romanos* 8.10 [PG 14.1190]), Cyril of Alexandria, many medieval commentators, Barrett (*Romans*, 215), Black (*Romans*, 144), Cranfield (*Romans*, 563), Lagrange, Lietzmann, Lyonnet, Michel, Sanday and Headlam, and Wilckens understand *zōē ek nekrōn* to refer to the general resurrection of the dead at the end of time. If the conversion of the Gentiles represents the first phase of redemption, viz., "reconciliation," then the "acceptance" of the gospel by the Jews will represent its definitive stage, "the last act of salvation history" Käsemann (*Commentary*, 307). Appeal is made to vv 25–26 to support this interpretation of "life from the dead" as the general resurrection at the parousia; commentators who use this interpretation often add that Paul is not necessarily asserting a temporal connection here. Yet this interpretation has given rise to the idea that the conversion of all Jews to Christ will precede the end of the world, a dubious conclusion at best.

Other interpreters, such as Theophylact, Photius, Euthymius, Cornely (*Commentarius*, 598), Godet (*Romans*, 2.243), and Murray (*Romans*, 2.82–84), understand *zōē ek nekrōn* in a figurative sense: "The conversion of Israel en masse will be for the Gentiles an event of great utility and happiness" (Huby, *Romains*, 390). This reading is preferred because Paul does not write *anastasis nekrōn*, the expression that he uses elsewhere for "resurrection of the dead" (6:5; 1 Cor 15:12, 13, 21, 42). Moreover, the context has nothing to do with the parousia; Paul has been talking about his own ministry, and v 15 resumes v 12 and gives the basis for what he said in vv 13–14. For the figurative sense of "life" and "death," see Luke 15:24, 32; cf. Ezek 37:3–6.

Still others, such as Leenhardt (*Romans*, 285) and Stanley (*Christ's Resurrection*, 197), consider the image to refer to the Jewish people themselves; their acceptance of the gospel will mean for them the passage from a status of death to life. There would be an allusion to the effect of their identification with Christ, as in baptism (6:4), and above all to the new life that would be theirs as a result of their "acceptance." The last interpretation seems preferable.

16. *If the firstfruits are holy, so too is the whole batch of dough.* In this verse Paul mixes his metaphors, firstfruits and root. In the first part Paul uses *aparchē* in the strict sense, as in 8:23 (see the NOTE there). Because the first portion of the meal is set aside for the Lord (i.e., given to the Temple priests [Josephus, *Ant.* 4.4.4 §70]), the whole batch acquires a legal purity, making it fit to be consumed by the people of God (cf. Lev 19:23–25; 23:14; Num 15:17–21; Philo, *De spec. leg.* 1.27–28 §131–44). Holiness denotes consecration to the awesome service of God. Paul follows up this image with that of the root.

if the root is holy, so too are the branches. See Jer 11:16–17. The nation of Israel is compared with a tree; its roots are the patriarchs and individual Israelites

613

belong to the stock of the tree and are nourished by the sap of the root. For God himself has sanctified the root by his gracious election of it as his own. But the individual branches have to remain in close connection with the stock and the root to enjoy the same holy character.

This image of the root expresses the same idea as the previous image of the firstfruits. But to what do "root" and "firstfruits" specifically refer? For Origen (*In ep. ad Romanos* 8.11 [PG 14.1193]) and Theodore of Mopsuestia, the first handful of dough and the root are Christ, whose holiness guarantees blessings for all humanity. For Barrett (*Romans*, 216), Kühl (*Römer*, 385), and B. Weiss, they refer to the converted remnant, the "elect" of v 7, an interpretation that suits the preceding context. For Cornely, Käsemann (*Commentary*, 308), Lagrange (*Romains*, 279), Michel, Pesch, Sanday and Headlam, and Wilckens, the "root" means the patriarchs, because in v 17 it will be used again to designate ancient Israel, onto which the Gentiles have been grafted.

Either of the last two interpretations is possible. Perhaps, however, it is better to divide the images between the two interpretations (with Cranfield, Leenhardt): the first handful of dough representing the "remnant," which has already accepted Christ, and the root representing the "patriarchs," especially Abraham. Thus a link is established with both the preceding and the following contexts. Cf. *1 Enoch* 93:5: "After that in the third week, at its end, a man will be chosen as the plant of upright judgment; after him will come the plant of uprightness forever" (usually understood to be Abraham and his offspring).

Some MSS (P[46], F, G, P*, 6, 1241, 1506, 1881) omit the *ei* at the beginning of this part of the verse; but it is to be retained because of the balance of the statements.

17. *If some of the branches have been lopped off, you, though a branch from a wild olive tree, have been grafted.* Paul, still addressing Gentile Christians, warns them not to be smug about their favored situation and the plight of the Jews. This verse explains how Gentile Christians have become *sperma Abraam*, "offspring of Abraham." The lopped-off branches are the individual Jews who have not accepted the gospel; the Gentiles are the wild olive shoot grafted onto the cultivated olive tree in their stead. Note how Paul diplomatically uses *tines*, "some," when he is actually speaking of the majority of the Jewish people.

Many commentators think that Paul speaks of the olive tree because it was an OT figure for Israel (see Jer 11:16–19; Hos 14:6), but Davies considers it a symbol of Greco-Roman culture ("Paul and the Gentiles").

Paul is also said to be dependent on the practice among ancient horticulturists of grafting a branch of an old, worn-out olive tree that had been giving good fruit onto a young, wild olive tree. But the grafting of which Paul speaks here has since the time of Origen (*In ep. ad Romanos*, 8.11 [PG 14.1195]) been said to be the opposite of what was the normal ancient grafting process. Indeed, it has often been thought that, in using it, Paul betrays his urban background and ignorance of the real horticultural practice. See, however, Columella, a contemporary of

Paul, who does know of a mode of grafting "a green slip taken from a wild olive tree," putting it tightly into a hole made in an old olive tree (*De re rustica* 5.9.16). Cf. Baxter and Ziesler, "Paul."

into their place. Lit., "in among them," i.e., in among the remaining branches of the old cultivated olive tree. Cf. 4:12; Gal 3:6–9. Paul does not say that the old tree has been cut down in divine providence; it still stands and is the source of vitality to the Gentiles who now share in its richness of life.

and have come to share in the rich sap of the olive root. Lit., "have become a sharer of the root, of the richness of the olive tree." I.e., Gentile Christians now draw their vitality from the Jewish stock of old.

Some MSS ($\aleph^2$, A, D², and the *Koinē* text-tradition), followed by the Vg, insert *kai,* "and," between "of the root" and "of the richness," but others (P⁴⁶, D*, F, G) omit "the root." The asyndetic phrases are found in MSS $\aleph^*$, B, C, and Ψ.

18. *Do not boast over those branches.* I.e., in your smugness, O Gentile Christian! Paul uses the 2d person sg. in his directly addressed warning. Cf. Judg 9:9.

If you do, remember this: you do not support the root; the root supports you. Lit., "if you do boast, (it is) not you (that) support the root." Paul's expression is elliptical; something like "remember this" has to be supplied (see BDF §488.2). Israel of old still occupies the privileged position of the carrier of life and salvation to the world.

19. *You may indeed say, "Branches were lopped off so that I might be grafted in."* So Paul echoes the self-complacent Gentile Christian who realizes the Jewish predicament and considers himself more important as a result.

20. *True.* Paul does not deny that the failure of Israel has made easy the conversion of the Gentiles, but Israel was not lopped off simply that Gentiles might be grafted onto the stock.

but they were lopped off because of a lack of faith. Israel's failure to accept the gospel has resulted in their being lopped off; it relied too much on its own advantages and was not disposed to react to God's grace offered to it. Yet its situation had no intrinsic connection with the election of the Gentiles actually grafted into its place. Paul uses a dat. of cause, *tē apistia,* "on account of their disbelief" (see BDF §196).

whereas you are there because of faith. Lit., "but you stand (there) because of faith." The real contrast is between faith and lack of faith. The situation of the Gentiles is owing to God's gratuitous election and their response in faith, not to any merits of which Gentile Christians can boast. Yet Gentile Christians are liable to be tempted in a similar way, to trust in the human situation in which they find themselves and fail to recognize its divine source. Cf. 1 Cor 16:13; 2 Cor 1:24.

So do not become haughty for that reason; be fearful. Lit., "do not think about haughty things, but rather (those of) reverence." So Paul counsels Gentile Christians not to become smug about their faith. Cf. 12:16; 1 Cor 10:12.

21. *if God did not spare the natural branches.* Lit., "the branches according to nature" (*kata physin*), i.e., the branches of the cultivated old olive tree. Despite the privileged position of Israel as his chosen people, some of them were lopped from their ancestral heritage because of their lack of faith.

perhaps he will not spare you either. I.e., if in your pride and smugness you too fail to recognize the source of your faith and thus prove faithless. The adv. phrase *mē pōs*, "perhaps," is read by MSS P⁴⁶, D, F, G, Ψ, the *Koinē* text-tradition, and Latin and Syriac versions; but other important MSS (ℵ, A, B, C, P, 6, 81, etc.) omit it. If omitted, then Paul's admonition becomes stronger. Cf. BDF §370.1.

22. *Consider then God's kindness and severity; severity to those who have fallen, but kindness to you.* These two qualities come closest to what has traditionally been called God's "mercy and justice," but to express them Paul uses Hellenistic terms, *chrēstotēs* and *apotomia.* Cf. Pseudo-Plutarch, *De liberis educandis* 18 §13d. Significantly, he does not use *eleos* and *dikaiosynē*, which because of their OT background have a notably different connotation. On the chiasmus used, see BDF §477.2. Paul refers here to the Jews "who have fallen," recalling v 11; the phrase means "those who have not believed."

if you only remain in his kindness. God's election, though gratuitous, is conditioned by Christians' responsible fulfillment of obligations to him. Gentile Christians persist in faith if they recognize that their condition is owing to the goodness of God.

For you too may be cut off. Again, Paul uses *epei* in the sense of "because otherwise"; see BDF §456.3. Gentile Christians can end up being in the condition of Israel, if they try to vaunt their superiority. This is the warning that Paul now sounds.

23. *And those others, if they do not remain in their lack of faith, will be grafted back in.* Finally, Paul explains how the lopped-off branches will be able to find life in the vital parent stock of Abraham and the patriarchs. What Israel is excluded from by its lack of faith in Christ it will be included in by such faith. Thus Paul expects unbelieving Israel to be grafted once again into the stock from which it has been broken off by its disbelief.

God indeed has the power to graft them in again. Paul argues a fortiori: if God were able to graft a wild olive branch onto an old cultivated olive tree, then he can also graft in again a branch lopped off from that cultivated stock. Throughout the argument based on the wild olive shoot Paul implies that the lopped-off natural branches have not yet been cast on the rubbish heap. Israel has not been definitively rejected by God (11:1). The "power" of which Paul speaks must be understood as that related to the gospel (1:16), the "power for salvation." Hence Israel's salvation cannot take place apart from the power manifested in the preaching of the gospel of Christ.

24. *For if you were cut from an olive tree that is wild by nature and grafted contrary to nature into a cultivated one, how much more readily will these, the*

natural branches, be grafted back into their own olive stock! The contrast suggests the transcendent nature of the vocation to which Gentile Christians have been called. The restoration of the Jewish people, however, will be easier than the call of the Gentiles. So Israel's rejection is not definitive, but temporary.

BIBLIOGRAPHY

Allison, D. C., "Romans 11:11–15: A Suggestion," *Perspectives in Religious Studies* (Macon, Ga.) 12 (1985): 23–30.

Bartsch, H. W., "Die antisemitischen Gegner des Paulus im Römerbrief," *Antijudaismus im Neuen Testament? Exegetische und systematische Beiträge*, ed. W. P. Eckert et al. (Munich: Kaiser, 1967), 27–43.

Baxter, A. G. and J. A. Ziesler, "Paul and Arboriculture: Romans 11.17–24," *JSNT* 24 (1985): 25–32.

Bourke, M. M., *A Study of the Metaphor of the Olive Tree in Romans XI*, Studies in Sacred Theology 2.3 (Washington, D.C.: CUA, 1947).

Dahl, N. A., *Das Volk Gottes: Eine Untersuchung zum Kirchenbewusstsein des Urchristentums*, 2d ed. (Darmstadt: Wissenschaftliche Buchgesellschaft, 1963), 237–46.

Davies, W. D., "Paul and the Gentiles: A Suggestion Concerning Romans 11:13–24," *Jewish and Pauline Studies* (London: SPCK; Philadelphia, Penn.: Fortress, 1984), 153–63, 356–60.

Haacker, K., "Das Evangelium Gottes und die Erwählung Israels," *TBei* 13 (1982): 59–72.

Hanson, A. T., "Christ the First Fruits, Christ the Tree," *Studies*, 104–25.

Hughes, P. E., "The Olive Tree of Romans XI," *EvQ* 20 (1948): 22–45.

Jegher-Bucher, V., "Erwählung und Verwerfung im Römerbrief? Eine Untersuchung von Röm 11, 11–15," *TZ* 47 (1991): 326–36.

Langevin, P.-E., "Saint Paul, prophète des Gentils," *LTP* 26 (1970): 3–16.

Linder, S., "Das Pfropfen mit wilden Ölzweigen (Röm. 11,17)," *PJ* 26 (1930): 40–43 + figs. 1–3.

Montagnini, F., "Nul ne peut faire échec au plan du salut: Rm 11,13–15.29–32," *AsSeign* n.s. 51 (1972): 9–14.

Mussner, F., "Fehl- und Falschübersetzungen von Röm 11 in der Einheitsübersetzung," *TQ* 170 (1990): 137–39, apropos of vv 12, 20, 25b, 26a, 27, and 28.

Plag, C., *Israels Wege zum Heil*, 32–48.

Quinlan, S., "The Olive Tree in the Forum—The Letter to the Romans," *Furrow* 33 (1982): 3–12.

Ramsay, W. M., "The Olive-Tree and the Wild-Olive," *Expos* 6.11 (1905): 16–34, 152–60; repr. in *Pauline and Other Studies in Early Christian History* (London: Hodder and Stoughton, 1908), 219–50.

Rengstorf, K. H., "Das Ölbaum-Gleichnis in Röm 11.16ff.: Versuch einer weiterführenden Deutung," *Donum gentilicium: New Testament Studies in Honour of David Daube*, ed. E. Bammel et al. (Oxford: Clarendon, 1978), 127–64.

Riggans, W., "Romans 11:17–21," *ExpTim* 98 (1986–87): 205–6.

Sneen, D., "The Root, the Remnant, and the Branches," *WW* 6 (1986): 398–409.

41. THE MYSTERY OF ISRAEL:
IT WILL ALL BE SAVED (11:25–32)

11   25I do not want you to be unaware of this mystery, brothers, lest you become wise in your own estimation: a partial hardening of heart has come upon Israel until the full number of the Gentiles comes in; 26and so all Israel shall be saved, as it stands written, *"From Zion shall come the deliverer; he shall turn godlessness away from Jacob. 27This is my covenant with them, when I take away their sins."* 28As far as the gospel is concerned, they are enemies for your sake; but as far as election is concerned, they are beloved of God because of the patriarchs. 29For irrevocable are God's gifts and his call. 30As you were once disobedient to God but now have been shown mercy as a result of their disobedience, 31so too they have now become disobedient so that they too may now be shown mercy as a result of the mercy shown to you. 32For God has imprisoned all people in disobedience that he might show mercy to all!

COMMENT

Paul realizes that his solution to the problem of Israel is not really satisfactory; so he begins to speak of the mystery of Israel. By this he means not that the problem is insoluble or opaque to human intelligence, but that it is part of a secret hidden in God and now revealed, even if not wholly comprehensible. For God's mercy to all human beings and his purpose, now made known, dominate Paul's perspective.

In this paragraph we come to the logical conclusion of Paul's treatment of the problem of Israel. Now he gives his main reason, for which all that preceded has been merely preparatory. It is couched in terms of a divine mystery now made know. Roman Christians, whom he is addressing, have to realize that they cannot rely only on their own speculation about Israel's relation to the plan of God now made known in Christ Jesus. For a mystery hidden in God for long ages is involved, and Paul's hymnic conclusion, lauding the wisdom of that plan and mystery, will follow in the next paragraph. Having counseled his Gentile Christian readers against smugness about their position in God's salvific plan, he stresses that Israel is not unprivileged, even though it has not fully listened to the gospel and has not fully reacted to it with faith. He hastens to emphasize that "all Israel shall be saved," because in God's plan mercy is to be shown to all, including Israel itself.

What Paul says in v 26, "and so all Israel shall be saved," has been the subject of much debate over the centuries.

Although Plag (*Israels Weg zum Heil*, 41) regards vv 25–27 as a secondary insert, which did not belong to the original context, his view is hardly correct (see Wilckens, *Römer*, 2.252; Stuhlmacher, "Zur Interpretation," 557). Rather, they form the climax of chaps. 9–11.

In what sense does Paul express his conviction about the salvation of all Israel? Two basic explanations are given today for this conviction. (1) The first is theological: the vb. *sōthēsetai*, "shall be saved," is understood as a theological passive, i.e., it will be saved "by God" (see ZBG §236). God will display an act of mercy to Israel independently of any acceptance of Jesus as Messiah or of a mass conversion to the Christian gospel. Israel would, then, be delivered from its partial hardening by a deliverer (v 26b; cf. Isa 59:20), who would be none other than Yahweh himself, bringing his covenant with Israel to its fruition. The main argument for this interpretation is the fact that Paul has not mentioned Christ in chap. 11 at all, and not even since 10:17. The "covenant" (v 27) would then be the everlasting covenant between Yahweh and Israel (2 Sam 23:5); there is no verb in v 27a, much less a future (often read into it). It is then quite different from the new covenant of Jer 31:33; God would honor that everlasting covenant by delivering Israel from its hardened position. Thus God himself would bring about the salvation of Israel—apart from Christ. Paul does not say that Israel will accept Jesus as the Messiah; "he says only that the time will come when 'all Israel will be saved' (11:26)." So Stendahl, *Paul among Jews and Gentiles*, 4; see p. 132: "it dawns on Paul that the Jesus movement is to be a Gentile movement—God being allowed to establish Israel in his own time and way"; see also his *Meanings*, 205–44. Similarly Getty, "Paul and the Salvation of Israel," 464; Lapide and Stuhlmacher, *Paul, Rabbi and Apostle*, 47–54.

(2) The second explanation is christological: the vb. *sōthēsetai* is interpreted as in 1 Cor 9:22, where it has the connotation of "be converted," and the salvation of Israel will come about through Christ, who will be the "deliverer" (v 26b), through whom God will turn all godlessness from Jacob. The christological interpretation, however, is used in two different senses.

(a) For some commentators, the reference is to the parousiac Christ (as in 1 Thess 1:10), and the "covenant" of Jer 31:33 is indeed the "new covenant" in its definitive stage. Thus, at the parousia "all Israel" would be pardoned its culpable "hardening" and would have its sins "taken away" without conversion to the gospel. God would thus provide a *Sonderweg* for the salvation of all Israel through the parousiac Christ. "The parousia Christ saves all Israel without a preceding 'conversion' of the Jews to the gospel. . . . God saves all Israel through Christ (solus Christus) and, indeed, 'through grace alone' and through 'faith alone' without the works of the Law, since Israel's *emunah* turns now totally toward the

Christ who comes again"; so Mussner, *Tractate*, 34; see also his articles. Similarly (with slightly differing nuances) Gager, *The Origins*; Gaston, *Paul and the Torah*, 92–99, 147–48; B. Mayer, *Unter Gottes Heilsrathschluss*, 290; Jocz, *The Jewish People*, 315–22.

(b) Others insist that Paul's solution to the salvation of all Israel cannot be a *Sonderweg*, in view of the thrust of Romans as a whole. For in this letter Paul insists that the justification of "all" human beings depends on faith in Christ Jesus (*panti tō pisteuonti*, 1:16), in him "who was handed over (to death) for our trespasses and raised for our justification" (4:25; cf. 10:9; 11:14). Without such faith there is no salvation. By this "all" Paul means all Jews and Gentiles alike (1:16; 3:21–22, 30), for Paul's gospel is not addressed to Gentiles only. Thus Christ has to be understood as "the deliverer" of Israel (11:26b), and the "covenant" (v 27) is that of Jer 31:33, as realized in the ministry, death, and resurrection of Jesus Christ, and not limited to the parousia, for there is nothing in the passage that refers to the parousia. So Hvalvik, "A 'Sonderweg' for Israel"; cf. Sanders, *Paul, the Law*, 192–96: "the simplest reading of 11:13–36 seems to be this: the only way to enter the body of those who will be saved is by faith in Christ" (p. 196); cf. *USQR* 33 (1978): 182–83. Similarly, Campbell, "Salvation," 70; Davies, "Paul," 23–30; Dahl, *Studies*, 153; Hübner, *Gottes Ich*, 114–20.

The latter form of the christological interpretation seems to be the only one tenable, for it is difficult to see how Paul would envisage two different kinds of salvation, one brought about by God apart from Christ for Jews, and one by Christ for Gentiles and believing Jews. That would seem to militate against his whole thesis of justification and salvation by grace for *all* who believe in the gospel of Christ Jesus (1:16). For Paul the only basis for membership in the new people of God is faith in Christ Jesus. What Paul says in 11:12 has to be related to 5:9–10, 15–17 and 2 Cor 3:7–11 so that the thrust of his entire argument is christocentric. One would also have to ask how distinct Christianity really was from Judaism in Paul's day, especially prior to A.D. 70. Hence through Christ "all Israel" will be saved.

Such modern interpretations of this passage and of v 26 in particular have to be seen against the background of older, especially patristic interpretations, which are at times strikingly different. Before Clement of Alexandria (150–215) no patristic writer apparently commented on 11:26 (see the NOTE on v 26). Those of the first three centuries who know of Paul's teaching fail to mention a coming salvation of the Jews. These writers fall into two classes: (1) those who considered the Christian church to be the new Israel, the replacement of Israel of old: So *1 Clem.* 29.1–3; 30.1; 59.4; *2 Clem.* 2.3; *Apoc. Peter* 2; Ignatius, *Magn.* 8.1–2; 10.2–3; *Barn.* 4.8; 14.1, 5; 10.12; Justin, *Dialogue with Trypho* 11.5 ("we are the true spiritual Israel" [FC 6.165]); 121.4–122.1; *Didascalia* 6.5.4–8; and (2) those who considered the Christian church to be an entity distinct from both paganism and Judaism; through it comes salvation: *Ep. Diogn.* 1 (*kainon touto genos*, "this new race"); Aristides, *Apologia* 2.

NOTES

11:25. *I do not want you to be unaware.* See the NOTE on 1:13.

of this mystery. For the first time in Romans Paul uses *mystērion*; it will appear again in the doxology added to chap. 16 (v 25). Paul employed it in 1 Cor 2:1, 7; 4:1; 13:2; 14:2; and 15:51. For him, it denotes a secret knowledge about a decision hidden in God from of old, now revealed in and through Jesus Christ for the salvation of all humanity; it is an unfolding manifestation of God's eschatological activity. What Paul means by "mystery" is part of his "gospel," an apocalyptic aspect of it. Thus Paul concludes his argument not only with logic, but also with the mention of revelation. By "mystery," Paul thinks of three things: the partial insensibility of Israel; the manner of Israel's salvation; and the salvation of not only all Israel, but of all humanity, viz., God's purpose in history, as realized in the grace given to humanity through Christ Jesus. He is concerned that the predominantly Gentile Christian community of Rome be aware of these things.

The word *mystērion* occurs in the LXX of Dan 2:18, 19, 27, etc., as a translation of Aramaic *rāz*. In meaning, it is close to the Qumran use of *rāz*, where it also denotes a secret hidden and now revealed (see 1QpHab 7:1–4, 13–14; 8:1–3). It is also found in the Deutero-Paulines (Col 1:26–27; 2:2; 4:3; Eph 1:9; 3:3, 4, 9; 5:32; 6:19). Cf. Brown, "The Semitic Background"; Vogt, " 'Mysteria' "; Coppens, " 'Mystery,' "

brothers. See the NOTE on 1:13.

lest you become wise in your own estimation. Lit., "that you may not be conceited to/in yourselves." Gentile Christians should not conclude that their view of human history is the only valid one or that their share in salvation history is owing to their own merits. Paul prefers to disclose to them aspects of the divine "mystery," of God's own purpose in history. For the expression, see the LXX of Prov 3:7.

Greek MSS ℵ, C, D and the *Koinē* text-tradition read the prep. *par*'; but others (P⁴⁶, F, G, Ψ) omit it; MSS A and B read *en*. It is hard to say which is preferable. See BDF §188.2

a partial hardening of heart has come upon Israel. Lit., "a hardening from a part (*or* in part) has come to Israel" or "a hardening has come to Israel in part." It is not easy to say with what the prep. phrase *apo merous* is to be taken, for Paul has placed it between the two nouns, "hardening" and "Israel." He uses the same modifying phrase in 1 Cor 12:27. In any case, he is thinking in terms of a partial hardening that is already in process. Paul alludes to what he called "the others" (*hoi loipoi*) in v 7, those not among "the elect" (*hē eklogē*), i.e., not part of the Jewish Christian remnant. Such a hardening is partial, because it is also temporary.

until the full number of the Gentiles comes in. Again, *plērōma* is used as in v 12 (see the NOTE there), but it is now applied to the Gentiles as a whole. Two interpretations of it are current: "until the full number (or strength) of the

Gentiles" has accepted the gospel, as foreseen by God's foreknowledge; or until the salvation of the Gentiles occurs to its "fullest extent." In either case *plērōma* would denote the full number of the "elect" from among the nations. The hardening of Israel's heart would last until the full number of Gentiles have been grafted into the stock of the patriarchs of Israel. Thus Paul stresses the inclusion of the Gentiles in the ultimate salvation promised to Israel. The salvation of the Gentiles is not something that happens apart from Israel and the stock of the patriarchs. Cf. 3:29–30; 4 Ezra 4:35–36; *T. Zeb.* 9:8.

But when will that full number be reached? Paul does not say, but from other places he seems to have thought that it would occur soon. See 13:11–12; 1 Cor 7:26–29; 1 Thess 4:15–17.

In using *eiselthē*, "comes in, enters," Paul does not say into what the Gentiles enter. It could mean entrance into the community of salvation, or even entrance into the kingdom of God (as in Mark 9:47; used absolutely in Matt 23:13). The former is more likely, because "the kingdom" is not a very operative term in Paul's writings. Cf. Luke 21:24.

That the idea of the "full number" has an OT background is plausible, as Aus ("Paul's Travel Plans," 234) has maintained, but it is another question to say, as he does, that Paul is thinking that "the 'full number of the Gentiles' in Rom. xi 25 will only 'come in' when Paul has brought Christian representatives from *Spain* to Jerusalem as a part of his collection enterprise." That is highly eisegetical.

26. *so all Israel shall be saved.* Paul's conviction about the lot of his former coreligionists is thus formalized. Indirectly, Paul repeats the conviction of Trito-Isaiah: "Your people shall all be upright; they shall all possess the land . . . ; I, the Lord, will swiftly accomplish these things in their time" (60:21–22). That conviction about a coming, final conversion of all Israel is echoed in QL: "This is the rule for all the congregation of Israel at the end of days, when they are g[a]thered [together to wa]lk according to the judgment of the sons of Zadok, the priests, and for the men of their covenant, who have turne[d from walking in] the way of the people. They are the people of his counsel who have kept his covenant in the midst of wickedness, making expi[ation for the lan]d" (1QSa 1.1–3).

Paul's introductory words, *kai houtōs*, have been understood in a temporal sense, "and then" (e.g., NABRNT, Althaus, Barrett [*Romans*, 223: "when this is done"], Käsemann [*Commentary*, 313], Michel [*Brief an die Römer*, 281]; cf. Hyldahl, "*Kai houtōs*"). This meaning introduces a sense that is related to the understanding of "life from the dead" (11:15) as a reference to the resurrection of the dead at the parousia. But this translation cannot be right, despite the allegedly similar use of *kai houtōs* in Acts 17:33; 20:11, because a temporal meaning of *houtōs* is not otherwise found in Greek, not even in 1 Thess 4:17; 1 Cor 11:28; 14:25 (*pace* Feuillet, "L'Espérance," 486). Judant ("À propos," 113) ascribes this translation to Origen and John Chrysostom, but I fail to find *tunc* in Rufinus's translation of Origen (*In ep. ad Romanos* 8.12 [PG 14.1195–98]); and Chrysostom does not even comment on this part of the verse (PG 60.591)! Again, they have been understood as correlative to *kathōs gegraptai* (Stuhlmacher, "Zur Interpretation," 560), but Paul does not so use *houtōs*; see Koch, "Beobachtungen," 186–87 n. 53; Müller, *Prophetie*, 227 n. 37. It has to be understood instead not only as referring to all that precedes (esp. vv 11–12, 15–16, 23–24 [not just to the hardening in v 25c: Paul "does not mean that Israel will be saved *because* it is hardened," Sanday and Headlam, *Romans*, 335]), but also, in a logical sense, as giving the presuppositions of what follows (as in 1 Thess 4:17; 1 Cor 11:28; 14:25). The salvation of "all Israel" can and will only occur when the full number of the Gentiles has come in (so Hofius, ZTK 83 [1986]: 315). Lagrange has explained it well: "*Kai houtōs* is not synonymous with *kai tote*, 'and then'; the conversion of the Gentiles is not only the sign that the hour has come; it will also undoubtedly have a causal connection" with the salvation of the Jews (*Romains*, 284). Paul is sure that it will happen unexpectedly and paradoxically, even as Scripture hints. Yet it is hardly likely that he is thinking about his coming evangelization of the pagans in Spain. The scope of the "full number" of the Gentiles must be larger than that.

The phrase *pas Israēl*, a Hebraism for *kol-Yiśrā᾽ēl*, occurs 148 times in the OT and always designates historic, ethnic Israel, usually in the synchronic sense of the generations of Israel contemporary with the author; but in Mal 3:22 it has a diachronic sense, "all Israel" of every generation. For Paul, *pas Israēl* means Israel in the ethnic sense and diachronically, because of the eschatological sense of the future *sōthēsetai*: the Jewish people as a whole, both "the remnant" (11:5) or "the chosen ones" (11:7) and "the others" (11:7), will be saved, just as it is promised in *T. Benj.* 10:11: "all Israel will be gathered to the Lord"; or in the later *m. Sanh.* 10:1: "All Israel will have a share in the world to come."

Pas Israēl is a corporate expression (= "whole Israel," see BDF §275.4), as in 1 Kgs 12:1; 2 Chr 12:1; Dan 9:11; hence it does not necessarily include every individual Israelite. It is contrasted with the "full number of the Gentiles," because Israel enjoyed the prerogative of election and as the chosen people was promised salvation. But it is also contrasted with "Israel in part" (11:25c) and the "remnant" (11:5). Hence "all Israel" has the same meaning as the "full number" of 11:12.

By "will be saved," Paul means that ethnic Israel will come to deliverance from the condition of hardened hearts through faith in the gospel. *Sōzein* is a missionary term associated with the goal of Paul's ministry of the gospel (see 10:9–10, 12; 11:14; 1 Cor 7:16; esp. 9:20–22; 10:33), which knows of no distinction between Jew and Greek.

Some commentators, however, have understood "all Israel" universally of "the Christian church in its final state": Calvin, *Romans* (trans. J. Owen), 437; Whiteley, *Theology*, 97; apparently also Aageson, CBQ 48 (1986): 285; Cerfaux, *Une Lecture*, 104–5; Giblin, *In Hope*, 303; Glombitza, "Apostolische Sorge," 316; Ponsot, "Et ainsi." This meaning was also found among patristic writers, who cited this Pauline text to stress that God's salvation was universal; they tended to understand *pas Israēl* as "spiritual Israel," made up of Jews and Gentiles who had been converted to the gospel, or as "the Israel of God" (Gal 6:16): so Irenaeus, *Adversus haereses* 4.2.7 (SC 100.2.410–11); Clement of Alexandria, *Excerpta ex Theodoto* 56.4–5 (GCS 17.2.126; SC 23.174); Theodore of Mopsuestia, *In ep. ad Romanos* 11.26 (PG 66.857); Theodoret of Cyrrhus, *Interpretatio ep. ad Romanos* 11.26–27 (PG 82.180). Both Origen and Augustine, however, interpret the phrase differently in different writings. Thus in *Commentarius in ep. ad Romanos* (8.13 [PG 14.1199–1200]) Origen understands "all Israel" of ethnic Israel, but in his *Commentarius in Matthaeum* (17.5 [PG 13.1485]) he thinks not of "Israel according to the flesh," but of spiritual Israel; and in *In Ieremiam* hom. 5.4 [PG 13.301]) it seems rather to mean the remnant of Israel. Similarly, Augustine in *Ep.* 149.19 (CSEL 44.365) understands it of all believers; but elsewhere of ethnic Israel: *Quaestiones evangeliorum* (2.33 [PL 35.1347]); *De civitate Dei* (20.29 [CSEL 40.503]). The understanding of "all Israel" in such a spiritual sense, however, is scarcely correct; it goes against the meaning of *Israēl* in the rest of Romans (see the NOTE on 9:6), and especially that in the immediately preceding v 25c. This is the meaning that the majority of commentators from the fifth to the twelfth centuries gave to "all Israel." Others restrict the meaning of "all Israel" to the remnant (9:27), the elect Israel (Refoulé, ". . . *ainsi*," 181; but see now *RB* 98 [1991]: 76–79).

as it stands written. See the NOTE on 1:17. The salvation to which Paul refers stands in accord with the Scriptures of Judaism itself, as Paul shows by the following quotation.

"From Zion shall come the deliverer; he shall turn godlessness away from Jacob." Paul quotes Isa 59:20–21a in a form closer to the LXX than to the MT. The MT reads, "He will come to Zion as a deliverer (*gôʾēl*), to those of Jacob who turn from transgression." Trito-Isaiah is telling of the spiritual destiny of Israel, using "Zion" and "Jacob" as literary variant names for Israel. The LXX, however, introduces a slightly different nuance when it reads, "He will come as the deliverer (*ho rhyomenos*) for the sake of Zion and will turn godlessness away from Jacob." Paul changes the prep. *heneken*, "for the sake of," to *ek*, "from," perhaps under influence from Ps 14:7 (*tís dōsei ek Siōn to sōtērion tou Israēl*, "who will grant from Zion the salvation of Israel?"); or perhaps it comes from a copyist's error, misreading *eis Siōn* (= Hebrew *lĕṢiyyôn*) as *ek Siōn*. See Schaller, "*Hēxei ek Siōn*," 201–6 (*ek Siōn* is regarded as pre-Pauline).

In the MT and the LXX the "deliverer" is Yahweh. (For a view that Paul also so understands the term, see the COMMENT.) The sixth-century Babylonian Talmud (*b. Sanh.* 98a) ascribes to Rabbi Yoḥanan, a third-century Palestinian of the second generation of Amoraim, a messianic interpretation of this "deliverer." On the basis of this late text, Cranfield (*Romans*, 578) thinks it "likely" that Paul too so understood it. At any rate, Paul does interpret the Isaian text christologically; for him *ho rhyomenos* denotes Christ as "the deliverer." Cf. 1 Thess 1:10.

Some commentators take this passage to be a reference to the parousia of

Christ (Cranfield, *Romans* 578; Wilckens, *Römer,* 2.256; Käsemann, *Commentary,* 314). Although Paul does use *ryesthai* in 1 Thess 1:10 of Christ's second coming, he uses it elsewhere in a more generic sense, referring to God (15:31; 2 Cor 1:10) or Christ (Rom 7:24). Not even the future *hēxei* necessarily implies the second coming; reference to the parousia is nowhere made in chaps. 9–11 (Koch, "Beobachtungen," 187). It may be a *futurum propheticum,* as Wilckens admits (*Römer,* 2.257 n. 1155), and as it is used in Trito-Isaiah. Paul may even understand the words as somehow having been fulfilled (see 9:33). Compare also 11:28 with 15:8.

"From Zion" may be a way of referring to Jesus' descent from David or, more generically, his origin from among the chosen Jewish people of old (see 9:5); or even to Jerusalem as the place of Christ's death and resurrection. In the Jewish tradition this verse was often cited to show how Gentiles would share eventually in the blessing of Jerusalem: *Ps. Sol.* 17:30–31; *Sib. Or.* 3:710–26.

"Jacob" is to be understood as Israel as a whole, *pace* Jeremias, "Einige," 200 (he understands "Jacob" as "all Israel," which is typological for all of the people of promise, including both Jews and Gentiles).

27. *"This is my covenant with them, when I take away their sins."* Paul quotes Isa 59:21a according to the LXX, which is close to the MT. To it he adds Isa 27:9 (LXX: *hotan aphelōmai autou tēn hamartian*), changing the object to the pl. *tas hamartias autōn.* The first part of the Isaian quotation seems to refer to Jer 31:33. Cf. 1 Cor 11:25; 2 Cor 3:6. The taking away of Israel's sins is a sign of God fulfilling his side of the new pact with it. In announcing this fulfillment of the covenant, God has reckoned with Israel's infidelity. Thus the second Isaian quotation is a message of hope: Jacob (Israel) will be blessed after all relics of its idolatry have been taken away. Thus the salvation of all Israel is for Paul a certainty and an act that will be brought about by God's grace, "the consummation of Judaism itself, despite the dislocation involved by the entry of the Gentiles into salvation before the Jews. Paul was not thinking in terms of what we normally call conversion from one religion to another but of the recognition by Jews of the final or true form of their own religion" (Davies, "Paul," 27). The "covenant" is undoubtedly a reference to the "new covenant" of Jer 31:31.

28. *As far as the gospel is concerned, they are enemies for your sake.* I.e., enemies of God, cut off from relationship with him. So Paul sums up the sense of vv 11–24 and also of vv 25–27. Verses 28–32 reveal that Paul is indeed thinking of a christological sense of the salvation of "all Israel," for here he contrasts Israel with the predominantly Gentile readers to whom he is writing. Because of its temporary and partial failure to accept the "gospel" about Jesus as the Messiah, Israel as an ethnic group has put itself in opposition to God. It does not want to know about the gospel, and this has put it in a state of enmity with God. This reaction has also been providential for Gentiles (11:11–12), and the providence of God is the underlying notion. By the phrase *di' hymas,* "for your sakes," Paul means that "you Gentiles" can share in the salvation originally promised to Israel.

Here *dia* + acc. expresses cause. Again, Paul addreses the Christians of Rome as predominantly Gentile. Implied in his statement is the idea that no one can be saved apart from Christ Jesus. See Davies, "Paul," 31; Sanders, *Paul and Palestinian Judaism*, 472–74, 489–90.

but as far as election is concerned, they are beloved of God because of the patriarchs. The election of Israel is irrevocable in human history, manifest in the favor shown to its patriarchs (Lev 26:42), a claim that Gentiles lack. The everlasting character of the election of Israel is echoed in 11QTemple 29:7–8: "They will be my people, and I shall be theirs forever; I shall dwell with them forever and ever." The phrase *kata de tēn eklogēn* is parallel to *kata men to euangelion*; hence *eklogē*, "election," does not have the same meaning as in v 5, where it referred to the "remnant." The two parts of this verse thus express the tension between the gospel and the election of Israel. The tension is reformulated in v 29. Cf. 9:5, 11, 25; 15:8. See B. Reicke, "Um der Väter willen, Röm 11,28," *Judaica* 14 (1958): 106–14. Here *dia* + acc. again expresses cause. Paul uses *pateres* globally in the sense of Israel's forebears, as he used the sg. *patēr* of Abraham (4:16) and of Isaac (9:10); see the NOTE on 9:5.

What Paul admits in this verse creates a problem for his generic thesis about justification and salvation through faith, which he is defending globally in chaps. 9–11, because he seems to admit another principle of salvation, one somehow tied to an ethnic condition and based on God's love of the patriarchs. But he phrases the matter in this way because he is interested in the contrast of Israel as "enemies" and as "beloved." Paul insists that its former condition does not wipe out the latter. Both of these elements are part of God's salvation history. Paul's explanation of the way of salvation for Israel goes through disbelief to faith, through stumbling and fall to restoration, through partial rejection to final acceptance. Thus God leads Israel through rejection to salvation.

29. *irrevocable are God's gifts and his call.* Lit., "without regret (are) the gifts and the call of God." Not only has God not repented or gone back on his promises and all of the good things that he has provided for his chosen people, but he has not gone back on his call either. That "call" refers to the initial summons of Abraham (Gen 12:1–2), which became in time the election of Israel as God's "chosen" people (Deut 7:6–7: "You are a people sacred to the Lord, your God; he has chosen you from all the nations on the face of the earth to be a people peculiarly his own"; cf. Ezek 20:5; Isa 41:8–10; Ps 135:4). But now that call must also include God's summons of Israel by the gospel. Cf. C. Spicq, "*Ametamelētos* dans *Rom.*, XI,29," *RB* 67 (1960): 210–19. See Ps 110:4.

30. *As you were once disobedient to God.* Paul addresses the Roman Christians as predominantly pagan in background, and his view of their former status agrees with what his Jewish kinsfolk would have thought: Gentile disobedience was basically disbelief in God, and because of it Gentiles were under God's wrath. The Latin Vg translates the vb. *ēpeithēsate* as *non credidistis*, "You did not believe," and *apeitheia* in v 30b as *incredulitas*, "disbelief." Paul now interprets

626

human "disobedience" as that which calls forth God's mercy (recall 3:5; 6:1). God's uprightness has been revealed to them too.

Some Greek MSS (ℵ², Ψ, and the *Koinē* text-tradition) as well as the Latin and Syriac versions add the intensive adv. *kai* before *hymeis*, which would mean "even you." It may have been added to make *kai hymeis* a parallel to *kai houtoi* in v 31a.

but now have been shown mercy as a result of their disobedience. See 11:11. The disobedience of the Jews has been an opportunity for the manifestation of divine mercy to Gentiles. It has been the occasion for God's decision to incorporate the Gentiles into the salvation promised to Israel of old. See 15:9. On *apeitheia* as a dat. of cause, see BDF §196.

31. *so too they have now become disobedient.* I.e., not by disbelief in God, but by disbelief in Christ Jesus, the agent whom he sent for their deliverance and salvation. Thus they have become "vessels of wrath" (9:22–23). See 10:21.

so that they too may now be shown mercy as a result of the mercy shown to you. Here Paul actually writes, "as a result of the mercy shown to you, so that they too may now be shown mercy." At first sight, the prep. phrase *tō hymeterō eleei* seems to modify the vb. *ēpeithēsan* in v 31a: "they have become disobedient as a result of the mercy shown to you." Indeed, it has been so taken by some commentators: Barrett (*Romans*, 226), Byrne (*Reckoning*, 201), Dunn (*Romans*, 688), Huby (*Romains*, 404 n. 3), Käsemann (*Commentary*, 316), Kuss (*Römerbrief*, 809, 817), Lagrange (*Romans*, 288), Lietzmann (*An die Römer*, 106), Schlier (*Römerbrief*, 337, 343), Wilckens (*Römer*, 2.260), and Zeller (*Juden und Heiden*, 213).

There are, however, serious reasons for thinking that Paul writes with hyperbaton, putting the phrase in a proleptic position for the sake of emphasis (see BDF §477.1; cf. Rom 11:2; 12:3; Gal 2:10; 1 Cor 3:5; 2 Cor 2:4; 3:5; also John 13:29; Acts 7:48; Col 4:16; Plato, *Meno* 71d; *Charmides* 169d). The noun *eleei* is again to be understood as a dat. of cause (BDF §196).

Two main reasons can be proposed for this interpretation: (1) the parallelism with v 30 (see Cranfield, *Romans*, 582):

v 30	*v 31*
hymeis, "you"	*houtoi*, "they"
pote, "once"	*nyn*, "now" (first one)
ēpeithēsate, "were disobedient"	*ēpeithēsan*, "have become disobedient"
nyn, "now"	*nyn*, "now" (second one)
eleēthēte, "you have been shown mercy	*eleēthōsin*, "they may be shown mercy"
tē toutōn apeitheia, "as a result of their disobedience"	*tē hymeterō eleei*, "as a result of the mercy shown to you"

627

(2) the harmony of this mode of interpretation with 11:11, 14, and 26: when the phrase *tō hymeterō eleei* is joined to the verb in the purpose clause, it repeats the same idea as in v 11: mercy shown to the Gentiles is to excite the Jews to envy; so the verse is understood by Boylan (*Romans*, 186–87), Cornely (*Commentarius*, 624), Feuillet ("L'Espérance," 487–91), Godet (*Romans*, 262), Munck (*Christ and Israel*, 140), Murray (*Romans*, 102), Sanday and Headlam (*Romans*, 338), and Zahn (*Römer*, 528).

Meyer (*Romans*, 1160) understands the dat. *tō hymeterō eleei* as the object of the vb. *epeithēsan*, "so they too have now disobeyed the mercy extended to you." Such an interpretation is rare, but it does agree with the Latin Vg, *ita et isti nunc non crediderunt in vestram misericordiam*.

Paul sees the problem as a matter of reciprocity. God's mercy and grace were originally manifested to Israel, when it became his chosen people. Those qualities continued to favor it. Sinful Gentiles have now been brought in to share in those blessings accorded to Abraham and his offspring. That mercy has now been manifested in a special way toward the Gentiles who have accepted the gospel and become "vessels of mercy." Now the mercy shown to the Gentiles becomes the basis of mercy to be displayed to Israel in its enmity. Universal salvation thus proceeds from God's mercy, but in the case of Israel it now comes after the full number of the Gentiles have come to salvation, and as a result of the mercy shown to the Gentiles. Hence the salvation of Israel does not take place apart from Christ (see Zeller, *Juden und Heiden*, 257).

Good Greek MSS (א, B, D*, 1506) read the second *nyn*, "now," in this part of the verse, whereas others (P⁴⁶, A, D², F, G, Ψ, and the *Koinē* text-tradition) omit it; and still others (33, 365) add *hysteron*, "at last." The last reading suits the idea of Israel being saved at the resurrection of the dead (recall "life from the dead," 11:15 and the translation of *kai houtōs* in 11:25 as "and then"). The omission of the second *nyn* in this part of v 31 may also be owing to the same sort of interpretation. The retention of it as the *lectio difficilior* in the text affects the meaning that is given to *houtōs* in v 26. As already indicated, it is needed for the parallelism with v 30.

32. **God has imprisoned all people in disobedience that he might show mercy to all!** Lit., "has locked up all for disobedience." Again Paul indulges in protological thinking (see the COMMENT on 1:18–32). Recall 3:19–20, 23; cf. Gal 3:22–23. All, both Jews and Greeks, have as groups been unfaithful to God, who makes use of such infidelity to manifest to all of them his bountiful mercy, to reveal about God just what he is. As v 31 makes clear, ethnic distinctions will remain, even when God does eventually display his mercy to "all." Cf. Wis 11:23; 1 Tim 2:4. It is a mystery why Zahn restricts *tous pantas* to the Jews in light of the preceding verse.

Several MSS (P⁴⁶, D*, G) and the VL change *tous pantas*, "all people," to *ta panta*, neut. "all," probably to assimilate this text to Gal 3:22.

So Paul comes to the end of his discussion about Israel's place in God's new plan of salvation for all human beings. After his firm "no" to the idea that God has rejected his people, he now has recourse to God's mercy to all. As human beings look at Israel's situation, it is its responsibility and its tragedy; but as God looks at it, it is the way to Israel's salvation (Nygren). Yet what Paul says in this verse reveals that he envisions mercy "for all" through Christ Jesus; that is the gist of vv 28–32. Hence the theological explanation of vv 25–26, as Stendahl has proposed, cannot be maintained. For Paul, God himself will bring everything to a good and proper conclusion through Christ Jesus. See the NOTE on 5:18. To this claim he adds a solemn cry of jubilation.

BIBLIOGRAPHY

Aus, R. D., "Paul's Travel Plans to Spain and the 'Full Number of the Gentiles' of Rom. xi 25," *NovT* 21 (1979): 232–62.

Brown, R. E., "The Semitic Background of the New Testament *Mysterion* (I)," *Bib* 39 (1958): 426–48; (II), 40 (1959): 70–87; repr. *The Semitic Background of the Term "Mystery" in the New Testament,* FBBS 21 (Philadelphia, Penn.: Fortress, 1968).

Coppens, J., " 'Mystery' in the Theology of Saint Paul and Its Parallels at Qumran," *Paul and The Dead Sea Scrolls,* ed. J. Murphy-O'Connor and J. H. Charlesworth (New York: Crossroad, 1990), 132–58.

Dibelius, M., "Vier Worte des Römerbriefes," *SBU* 3 (1944): 3–17, esp. 14–17.

Ellington, J., "It Is Written . . . but Where?" *BT* 38 (1987): 424–29.

Fessard, G., "Théologie et histoire: À propos du Temps de la conversion d'Israël," *Dieu vivant* 8 (1947): 37–65.

Feuillet, A., "L'Espérance de la 'conversion' d'Israël en Rm 11, 25–32: L'Interprétation des versets 26 et 31," *De la Tôrah au Messie: Études d'exégèse et d'herméneutique bibliques offertes à Henri Cazelles . . . ,* ed. M. Carrez et al. (Paris: Desclée, 1981), 483–94.

Glombitza, O., "Apostolische Sorge: Welche Sorge treibt den Apostel Paulus zu den Sätzen Röm. xi 25ff.?" *NovT* 7 (1964–65): 312–18.

Johnson, D. G., "The Structure and Meaning of Romans 11," *CBQ* 46 (1984): 91–103.

Judant, D., "À propos de la Destinée d'Israël: Remarques concernant un verset de l'épître aux Romains XI, 31," *Divinitas* 23 (1979): 108–25.

————, *Judaïsme et christianisme: Dossier patristique* (Paris: Desclée, 1969).

Koch, D.-A., *Die Schrift als Zeuge des Evangeliums: Untersuchungen zur Verwendung und zum Verständnis der Schrift bei Paulus,* BHT 69 (Tübingen: Mohr [Siebeck], 1986), 175–78.

Manns, F., "Une Tradition rabbinique réinterprétée dans l'évangile de Mt 22,1–10 et en Rm 11,30–32," *Anton* 63 (1988): 416–26.

Mayer, B., *Unter Gottes Heilsratschluss: Prädestinationsaussagen bei Paulus,* FB 15 (Würzburg: Echter-Verlag, 1974), 280–300.

Müller, U. B., *Prophetie und Predigt im Neuen Testament: Formgeschichtliche Unter-*

suchungen zur urchristlichen Prophetie, SNT 10 (Gütersloh: Mohn, 1975), 225–32.

Räisänen, H., "Römer 9–11: Analyse eines geistigen Ringens," ANRW 2.25.4 (1987), 2891–2939, esp. 2916–23.

Reicke, B., "Um der Väter willen, Röm. 11, 28," *Judaica* 14 (1958): 106–14.

Rese, M., "Die Rettung der Juden nach Römer 11," *L'Apôtre Paul: Personnalité, style et conception du ministère*, BETL 73, ed. A. Vanhoye (Louvain: Leuven University, 1986), 422–30.

Richardson, P., *Israel in the Apostolic Church*, SNTSMS 10 (Cambridge: Cambridge University Press, 1969), 126–47.

Stuhlmacher, P., "Zur Interpretation von Römer 11,25–32," *Probleme biblischer Theologie: Gerhard von Rad zum 70. Geburtstag*, ed. H. W. Wolff (Munich: Kaiser, 1971), 555–70.

Tachau, P., *"Einst" und "Jetzt" im Neuen Testament: Beobachtungen zu einem urchristlichen Predigtschema in der neutestamentlichen Briefliteratur und zu seiner Vorgeschichte*, FRLANT 105 (Göttingen: Vandenhoeck & Ruprecht, 1972), 108–12.

Talbot, E. R., *The Mystery of the Jew: As Revealed by St. Paul in Romans XI . . .* (London: Macintosh, 1872).

Vogt, E., " 'Mysteria' in textibus Qumrān," *Bib* 37 (1956): 247–57.

Windisch, H., "Die Sprüche vom Eingehen in das Reich Gottes," ZNW 27 (1928): 163–92.

On 11:25–26

Bartling, V., " 'All Israel Shall Be Saved,' Rom 11:26," CTM 12 (1941): 641–52.

Batey, R., " 'So All Israel Will Be Saved': An Interpretation of Romans 11:25–32," *Int* 20 (1966): 218–28.

Bloesch, D. G., " 'All Israel Will Be Saved': Supersessionism and the Biblical Witness," *Int* 43 (1989): 130–42.

Campbell, W. S., "Salvation for Jews and Gentiles: Krister Stendahl and Paul's Letter to the Romans," *Studia biblica 1978: Sixth International Congress on Biblical Studies, Oxford 3–7 April 1978*, 3 vols., JSNTSup 2–3, 11, ed. E. A. Livingstone (Sheffield, UK: JSOT, 1979–80), 3.65–72.

Caubert Iturbe, F. J., " '. . . et sic omnis Israel salvus fieret': Rom 11,26," SPCIC, 1.329–40.

———, " 'Et sic omnis Israel salvus fieret,' Rom 11,26: Su interpretación por los escritores cristianos de los siglos III–XII," *EstBíb* 21 (1962): 127–50.

Cooper, F. C., "Romans 11:25–26," *ResQ* 21 (1978): 84–94.

Davies, W. D., "Paul and the People of Israel," NTS 24 (1977–78): 4–39.

Dunn, J. D. G., "Paul's Epistle to the Romans: An Analysis," ANRW 2.25.4 (1987), 2867, 2872.

Gager, J. G., *The Origins of Anti-Semitism: Attitudes Toward Judaism in Pagan and*

Christian Antiquity (Oxford and New York: Oxford University Press, 1983), 261–64.

Gaston, L., *Paul and the Torah*, 92–99, 147–48.

Getty, M. A., "Paul and the Salvation of Israel: A Perspective on Romans 9–11," *CBQ* 50 (1988): 456–69.

Grässer, E., "Zwei Heilswege: Zum theologischen Verhältnis von Israel und Kirche," *Kontinuität und Einheit: Für Franz Mussner*, ed. P.-G. Müller und W. Stenger (Freiburg im Breisgau: Herder, 1981), 411–29; repr. in *Der Alte Bund im Neuen*, WUNT 35 (Tübingen: Mohr [Siebeck], 1985), 212–30.

Harrington, D. J., "Israel's Salvation According to Paul," *TBT* 26 (1988): 304–8.

Hofius, O., " 'All Israel Will Be Saved': Divine Salvation and Israel's Deliverance in Romans 9–11," *PSB* Sup 1 (1990): 19–39.

Horne, C. M., "The Meaning of the Phrase 'And Thus All Israel Will Be Saved' (Romans 11:26)," *JETS* 21 (1978): 329–34.

Hvalvik, R., "A 'Sonderweg' for Israel: A Critical Examination of a Current Interpretation of Romans 11.25–27," *JSNT* 38 (1990): 87–107.

Hyldahl, N., "*Kai houtōs* i Rom 11,26: Note til Kresten Drejergaards fortolkning," *DTT* 37 (1974): 231–34.

Jeremias, J., "Einige vorwiegend sprachliche Beobachtungen zu Röm 11. 25–26," *Die Israelfrage*, ed. L. de Lorenzi, 193–216.

Jocz, J., *The Jewish People and Jesus Christ: A Study in the Relationship Between the Jewish People and Jesus Christ* (London: SPCK, 1949), 315–22.

Koch, D.-A., "Beobachtungen zum christologischen Schriftgebrauch in den vorpaulinischen Gemeinden," *ZNW* 71 (1980): 174–91, esp. 186–89.

Lapide, P. and P. Stuhlmacher, *Paul, Rabbi and Apostle* (Minneapolis, Minn.: Augsburg, 1984), 47–54.

Mussner, F. " 'Ganz Israel wird gerettet werden' (Röm 11,26): Versuch einer Auslegung," *Kairos* 18 (1976): 241–55.

———, "Heil für alle: Der Grundgedanke des Römerbriefs," *Kairos* 23 (1981): 207–14.

———, *Tractate on the Jews: The Significance of Judaism for Christian Faith* (London: SPCK; Philadelphia, Penn.: Fortress, 1984).

Osborne, W. L., "The Old Testament Background of Paul's 'All Israel' in Romans 11:26a," *AsJT* 2 (1988): 282–93.

Osten-Sacken, P. von der, "Heil für die Juden—auch ohne Christus?" *Wenn nicht jetzt, wann dann? Aufsätze für H. J. Kraus . . .* , ed. H. G. Geyer et al. (Neukirchen-Vluyn: Neukirchener-Verlag, 1983), 169–82; repr. in *Evangelium und Tora*, 256–71.

Ponsot, H., "Et ainsi tout Israël sera sauvé: Rom., XI, 26a," *RB* 89 (1982): 406–17.

Refoulé, F., ". . . et ainsi tout Israël sera sauvé," *Tantur Yearbook* (1983–84): 39–57.

———, ". . . *et ainsi tout Israël sera sauvé*": *Romains 11.25–32* (LD 117; Paris: Cerf, 1984).

Sänger, D., "Rettung der Heiden und Erwählung Israels: Einige vorläufige Erwägungen zu Römer 11,25–27," *KD* 32 (1986): 99–119.

Schaller, B., *"Hēxei ek Siōn ho rhyomenos: Zur Textgestalt von Jes 59:20f. in Röm 11:26f," De Septuaginta: Studies in Honour of John William Wevers . . . ,* ed. A. Pietersma and C. Cox (Mississauga, Ont.: Benben, 1984), 201–6.

Schreiner, T. R., "The Church as the New Israel and the Future of Ethnic Israel in Paul," *StudBibTheol* 13 (1983): 17–38.

Stendahl, K., "Judaism and Christianity Then and Now," *Harvard Divinity Bulletin* 28 (1963): 1–9.

————, *Meanings: The Bible as Document and as Guide* (Philadelphia, Penn.: Fortress, 1984).

Tison, J.-M., "Salus Israël apud Patres primi et secundi saeculi," *VD* 39 (1961): 97–108.

42. HYMN OF PRAISE TO GOD'S WISDOM AND MERCY (11:33–36)

11 33 O the depth of the riches, of the wisdom, and of the knowledge of God!
How inscrutable are his judgments!
How untraceable his ways!

34 *Who has known the mind of the Lord?*
Who has been his counselor?

35 Who has ever given him a gift
to receive a gift in return?

36 For from him and through him and for him are all things.
To him be glory forever! Amen.

COMMENT

Paul ends his discussion of the problem of Israel with a hymnic composition, a poem to the inscrutable wisdom of God. It is a fitting conclusion to the discussion, because in v 25 Paul wisely referred the whole problem to a divine "mystery," something now made known to humanity, yet not yet wholly comprehensible. It is not a matter of a contrast between apparent injustice in God and his real justice, but of inadequate human comprehension. God's goodness is not at fault, even if he has "imprisoned all people in disobedience" (11:32). Paul ascribes everything to the designs of God's wisdom and knowledge, which are for human beings unsearchable. So he can utter his doxology, which sums up chaps. 9–11 and corresponds to the hymn uttered in 8:31–38.

As might be expected, this doxology is addressed to God, who has accomplished all of it through Christ, who, however, is not mentioned, not even in v 34, where *Kyrios* is used, referring to Yahweh, because it is in a verse quoted from Isaiah.

The key verse in this passage is 11:34, "Who has known the mind of the Lord?" It sums up all of Paul's foregoing discussion about the relationship of Israel to Christ, about the relationship of Jews to Christians ever since Paul penned these lines. One has to realize that Paul has not solved "the problem of Israel," nor have Christian theologians since then.

Yet this hymn also forms the conclusion to the whole of the doctrinal section of Romans (1:16–11:36). For not only God's dealings with Israel are unsearchable and manifest his uprightness and mercy to his chosen people, but all God's dealings with humanity are so. No one holds God in his debt. God's ways of dealing with human beings are quite different from what humans might calculate. What they receive from God is not merited; their justification and salvation stem from his grace and his mercy. Moreover, God constantly makes use of human sinfulness and disobedience to achieve his own ends. Paul also introduces a cosmic dimension in v 36.

What Paul says here about God's inscrutable judgments and untraceable ways is not a contradiction of what he wrote in 1:19–20, about what could be known about God. For there Paul did not want to say that a human being could come to a full comprehension of God. When Paul looks at the way God has treated his chosen people, and Gentiles along with them, he sees constant manifestations of divine mercy in the history of humanity, even though his chosen people could not bring itself to accept Jesus and God's gospel about him. In this inscrutability lies the mystery of God's dealing with humanity. In all of it God's uprightness, mercy, and grace triumph. In a sense, Paul is expressing not so much the conclusion of his argument as the basic reason that underlies it all. For this reason he can utter his doxology, as he meditates on the mystery of divine election.

There is no reason to think that Paul has borrowed this hymnic composition from some source, Jewish or Jewish Christian; he has composed it himself after the manner of contemporary hymns of praise. See R. Deichgräber, *Gotteshymnus und Christushymnus in der frühen Christenheit,* SUNT 5 (Göttingen: Vandenhoeck & Ruprecht, 1967), 61–64.

The structure of the doxology has been worked out by Norden (*Agnostos Theos*). It consists of nine lines. The first three are exclamations; the next four are questions (two an OT quotation); the last two are a declaration and a doxological acclamation. Again, there are three divine attributes, three questions, and three relations of things to God. The declaration has a Stoic formulation, similar to that found in Marcus Aurelius, *Meditation* 4.23: "All that is in tune with you is in tune with me! Nothing that is on time for you is too early or too late for me! All that your seasons bring, O Nature, is fruit for me! All things come from you, subsist in you, are destined for you (*ek sou panta, en soi panta, eis se panta*)!"

But instead of the pantheistic *en soi panta*, Paul uses *di' autou*, "through him," lauding the personal God whom he worships. Cf. *2 Apoc. Bar.* 14:8–9; 20:4; 21:10.

See further Lietzmann, *An die Römer*, 107; Dibelius, "Die Christianisierung"; Ogara, "Ex ipso."

NOTES

11:33. *O the depth of the riches, of the wisdom, and of the knowledge of God!* The human and weak Paul exclaims not in awe and fear, but in wonder and gratitude, at the boundless providence of God in arranging the mutual assistance of Jews and Gentiles in the attainment of salvation. Israel's role in the divine plan of salvation may never have been suspected, if God's "mystery" had not been made known. Underlying the mystery is God's wisdom: his comprehension of the relation of all things in this world; and behind the governing of human history is the wealth of God's grace and mercy; also his knowledge: his intuition of the details of all things. The three genitives (riches, wisdom, knowledge) are all dependent on *bathos*, "depth," used figuratively as in 1 Cor 2:10; Rev 2:24; Sophocles, *Ajax* 130 (where it also occurs with *ploutou*). To them correspond in reverse order the questions of v 34. See 9:23; 1 Cor 1:19–21; 2:7, 10; cf. Col 2:3; Eph 3:8, 10.

The phrase *gnōsis theou*, "knowledge of God," as a subjective gen. and an expression for God's elective knowledge has normally been without a close parallel, even in the Pauline corpus; Amos 3:2 uses the vb. *yāda'* in this sense, and Deut 9:24 the suffixal form *da'tî*. The suffixal form of the noun also occurs in QL: *wbd'tw nhyh kwl*, "and by his knowledge all (things) come to be" (1QS 11:11).

Although MS 321 and the Latin Vg omit the first *kai*, reading *O altitudo divitiarum sapientiae*, the majority of Greek MSS read it, thus making three attributes of God dependent on *bathos*.

How inscrutable are his judgments! How untraceable his ways! Compare *2 Apoc. Bar.* 14:8–9, "But who, O Lord, my Lord, can comprehend the workings of your judgment? Who can search out the depths of your way? Or who can trace the profundity of your path? Or who can describe your unfathomable counsel?" See Wis 17:1; Job 9:10; Ps 77:20; Prov 25:3. The noun *krimata* refers here not to judicial decisions, as it sometimes does (Ps 36:7), but to judgments about the world and its fullness. See *1 Clem.* 60.1. On the "ways" of the Lord, see Isa 55:8–9; Ps 95:10.

34. *Who has known the mind of the Lord? Who has been his counselor?* The answer to the questions is, of course, "No one!" See 1 Cor 2:16, where Paul asks the same question and answers it by saying, "We have the mind of Christ." Here Paul quotes Isa 40:13 according to the LXX, but with slight changes of word order. In the original context of Isaiah the words refer to the deliverance of the

Jewish people from exile by Yahweh and extol his greatness in providing for it. Neither in his plans nor in his gifts to human beings is God a debtor. All things proceed from his gracious bounty; he needs neither consultants nor research assistants. Cf. Wis 9:13; Job 15:8; Jer 23:18. "Where on earth chaos rules and human beings are perverted and go about their perverting work, only that *sophia* can hold which is in Christ alone (1 Cor 1:30)" (Käsemann, *Commentary*, 320).

35. *Who has ever given him a gift to receive a gift in return?* This may be a quotation for Job 41:3, but it does not agree with LXX of that verse, being closer to the MT (*mî hiqdîmanî waʾăšallēm*, "who has preceded me that I should repay?"). But the OT text is uncertain; others think that Paul may be alluding to Job 35:7 or 41:1. In any case, Paul realizes that God needs no one to anticipate his bounty, so rich are his gifts. God seeks no cooperation from human beings that would in any way be a condition of his bounty, though he does expect cooperation with the prevenient graces that he gives. To that prevenient grace faith and human cooperation respond. But God's goodness is not a payment for services rendered.

36. *For from him and through him and for him are all things.* Paul thus acknowledges God the Father as the creator, sustainer, and goal of the universe. The prep. *ex* denotes origin, *dia* (with the gen.) the originator of an action or condition, and *eis* (with the acc.) its end or goal. Thus the relationship of God to the whole universe is stated. Paul's prayer thus expresses the absolute dependence of all creation on God. Everything comes from him, Israel's prerogatives as well as the bounteous call of the Gentiles. Prerogatives and call continue in his providential care, and they are all destined to glorify him. See 1 Cor 8:6; 11:12; cf. Col 1:16–17; Heb 2:10.

To him be glory forever! Paul ends his hymn with a doxology to God the Father. *Soli Deo gloria!* See 1:25; 16:27; cf. Phil 4:20 and the Deutero-Pauline Eph 3:21; 1 Tim 1:17; 2 Tim 4:18c. For the Jewish background of such praise of God, see Sir 39:14b–16; 1 Esdr 4:40; 4 Macc 18:24; 1QS 11:15–17; 1QH 7:26–27; *m.ʾAbot* 6. Paul uses the phrase *doxa tou theou*, not as earlier (see the NOTES on 1:23; 3:23), but in the liturgical sense of enhancing God's glory and renown by praise, prayer, and thanksgiving, as in Gal 1:5; 1 Cor 10:31; 2 Cor 4:15; Phil 1:11).

Amen. See the NOTE on 1:25.

BIBLIOGRAPHY

Barth, M., "Theologie—ein Gebet (Röm 11,33–36)," *TZ* 41 (1985): 330–48.

Bonnard, P.-E., "Les Trésors de la miséricorde (Rm 11,33–36)," *AsSeign* 53 (1964): 13–19; revised, *AsSeign* n.s. 52 (1974): 9–14.

Bornkamm, G., "The Praise of God: Romans 11.33–36," *Early Christian Experience*, 105–11.

Dibelius, M., "Die Christianisierung einer hellenistischen Formel," *Neue Jahrbücher für das klassische Altertum* 35 (1915): 224–36; repr. in *Botschaft und Geschichte: Gesammelte Aufsätze*, 2 vols. (Tübingen: Mohr [Siebeck], 1953–56), 2.14–29.

Dion, H.-M., "La Notion paulinienne de 'richesse de Dieu' et ses sources," *ScEccl* 18 (1966): 139–48.

Harder, G., *Paulus und das Gebet*, NTF 1.10 (Gütersloh: Bertelsmann, 1936), 51–58.

Jeremias, J., "Chiasmus in den Paulusbriefen," ZNW 49 (1958): 145–56; repr. in *Abba: Studien zur neutestamentlichen Theologie und Zeitgeschichte* (Göttingen: Vandenhoeck & Ruprecht, 1966), 276–90, esp. 284.

Mehlmann, I., "*Anexichniastos* = investigabilis (Rom 11,33; Eph 3:8)," *Bib* 40 (1959): 902–14.

Norden, E., *Agnostos Theos: Untersuchungen zur Formgeschichte religiöser Rede* (Stuttgart and Berlin: Teubner, 1923; repr. Darmstadt: Wissenschaftliche Buchgesellschaft, 1956), 240–50.

Ogara, F., "Ex ipso et per ipsum et in ipso sunt omnia," VD 15 (1935): 164–71.

Pépin, J., "Le 'Conseiller' de Dieu," *Lectures anciennes de la Bible*, Cahiers de Biblia Patristica 1, ed. P. Maraval (Strasbourg: Centre d'Analyse et de Documentation Patristiques, 1987), 53–73.

Wilckens, U., "*Sophia, ktl.*," TDNT 7.465–528, esp. 517–18.

Zeller, D., *Juden und Heiden*, 267–69.

II. HORTATORY SECTION: THE DEMANDS OF UPRIGHT LIFE IN CHRIST (12:1–15:13)
A. Spirit-Guided Christian Life Must Be Worship Paid to God (12:1–13:14)

◆

43. LIFE IN THE WORLD AS WORSHIP OF GOD (12:1–2)

12 ¹I urge you, then, brothers, by God's mercy to offer your bodies as living sacrifices, holy and acceptable to God, as a cult suited to your rational nature. ²Do not conform yourselves to this present world, but be transformed by a renewal of your whole way of thinking so that you may discern what is God's will, what is good, acceptable to him, and perfect.

COMMENT

Paul now adds to the doctrinal discussion of God's uprightness and of the justification and salvation of human beings by grace through faith an exhortation addressed to the Christians of Rome, even though they are practically unknown to him. Romans 12–15 forms a catechetical unit, a paraenetic development of the consequences of justification. This hortatory part of Romans is also an expression of God's uprightness, but now in terms of concrete conduct. The unit reflects the tendency in the early church to join paraenesis to a kerygmatic or doctrinal exposé. Chapters 12–15 thus represent Paul's ethical instruction based on the kerygma of Christ crucified and raised, a form of which he has presented in chaps. 1–11. In 6:4 Paul spoke of "a new way of life"; and in 6:18 he maintained that "you have become slaves of uprightness." Now he begins to spell out what that means for one who is upright because of faith in Christ Jesus, for one who lives as a justified Christian in the new aeon.

Whether these chapters lack "an immediate relation with the circumstances of the letter," as Dibelius once maintained for the hortatory parts of Paul's letters (*From Tradition to Gospel* [New York: Scribners, n.d.], 238), may be seriously questioned. For Karris has rightly shown that there are more detailed relations in it to the doctrinal part than have usually been admitted ("Romans 14:1–15:13," 81–82), even though Paul's exhortation still often remains generic. As Stuhlmacher has put it, "Chapters 12–16 belong inextricably to the letter . . . because the apostle nowhere (and certainly not in Romans) expounds abstract theology, but always only concrete exhortation. Whether the Romans really believe in Christ as their redeemer and Lord will be evident, according to Paul, by how they

637

(as Gentile and Jewish Christians) deal with one another and how they resolve the tensions among one another in Rome" ("Theme of Romans," 341).

This hortatory section, however, is not exactly an ethical treatise, for it is quite unsystematic and somewhat rambling, *pace* Nygren (*Romans*, 411–12). As it stands in Romans, it implies that Mosaic legal prescriptions may no longer be the norm for Christian conduct, but there are demands on Christians, and the principle at work in all of them is love or charity (see 13:8–10) that flows from faith evoked by the kerygma or the gospel.

Many of the topics in this section are generalities, reflecting problems with which Paul had to cope in the past in other churches founded by him, perhaps problems even of the church of Corinth, from which he sends this letter to Rome. The discussion in 14:1–15:13 reflects, however, a situation in the Roman church of which Paul has become aware. The discussion in 13:1–7 may also reflect a situation in the empire as a whole that he realizes will affect the Christians of Rome too. When he composes these parts of the hortatory section, he is probably dependent on hearsay reports about the church in Rome. Otherwise, though the topics are not closely related, they concern in general the relation of justified Christians to one another and to the society in which they live. And yet, Paul already has in mind concrete applications of Christian life in the new aeon, how Christians are to try to discern God's will in the situations in which they find themselves.

Bahr ("Subscriptions," 38–39) is of the opinion that Paul himself would have written the hortatory section (12:1–15:33) in his own hand; an interesting hypothesis, which lacks any really convincing evidence.

In part A Paul discusses mostly the demands made on Christian living for the sake of unity. The unity and harmony of the community demand that individuals realize that they are living in the new aeon and are to strive to overcome evil with good. The common pursuit of the good is expected of those who are members of the body of Christ and whose lives are to be a sacrifice offered to God. Paul now takes up the consequences of that part of his thesis which stated that "the one who is upright shall find life through faith" (1:17).

Those commentators who consider chaps. 9–11 to be a "foreign body" in Romans (see p. 540) note how chap. 12 continues as a logical sequel to chap. 8. Indeed, this is said to be the force of the conj. *oun*, with which 12:1 begins. But it is instead a particle that introduces "the result of the whole previous argument" (Sanday and Headlam, *Romans*, 351).

The material in part A can be divided thus: (1) 12:1–2: life in the world as worship to God; (2) 12:3–8: sober existence using God's gifts for all; (3) 12:9–21: counsels for Christians living in the community; (4) 13:1–7: Christians' relations to civil authorities; (5) 13:8–10: the debt of love that fulfills the law; and (6) 13:11–14: eschatological exhortation: Christian life as vigilant conduct.

In this opening hortatory paragraph Paul's instruction consists of two sentences, the first expressing the somatic aspect of Christian life, the second the noetic, as Betz has explained ("Foundation," 61). The second is expressed by two imperatives, one negative, the other positive. The sum of the instruction is that Christians should live their lives in "this world" as if they were offering thereby worship to God. This way of life Paul regards as an expression of their very rational nature (*tēn logikēn latreian hymōn*). In this way he sees the transformation or metamorphosis of the Christian that has taken place as an effect of the Christ-event working itself out in concrete everyday life. As he says in Gal 5:25, "If we live by the Spirit, let us also walk by the Spirit."

NOTES

12:1. *brothers.* See the NOTE on 1:13. At the beginning of the hortatory section Paul again addresses the Christians of the church of Rome in this way.

I urge you, then, . . . by God's mercy to offer your bodies as living sacrifices. Paul speaks as an authorized apostle (1:5; 11:13) and does not hesitate to urge or implore the Christians of Rome. He makes use of a standard literary form called petition, with a divine authority phrase (see Mullins, "Petition," 53). Paul introduces his exhortation by using *parakalō,* "I urge," which he will employ again in 15:30; 16:17, and as he often does in other writings (1 Cor 1:10; 4:16; 2 Cor 2:8; 10:1; Phil 4:2; Phlm 10; cf. Eph 4:1; 1 Tim 2:1). See Bjerkelund, *Parakalô.*

The position of the prep. phrase *dia tōn oiktirmōn tou theou,* lit., "by the mercies of God," makes the interpretation of it problematic, because it may go with what precedes, *parakalō oun hymas,* "I urge you, then, by God's mercy." Thus it would be the motivation that Paul derives from the merciful, bounteous acts (note the pl.) manifested to Jews and Greeks, which he has discussed in chaps. 9–11, esp. in 11:30–32: "Christian morality is the response to all the mercy of God . . . set forth in the preceding chapters" (Dodd, *Romans,* 190); it is also taken in this way by Althaus, Barrett, Cranfield, and Sanday and Headlam. The pl. *oiktirmoi,* "mercies," is often found in the LXX (e.g., 2 Sam 24:14; Dan 2:18), where it translates the Hebrew pl. *raḥămîm* or Aramaic pl. *raḥmîn.* Alternatively, the phrase may go with the infin. *parastēnai,* "to offer by God's mercy." It would then refer to the offering as another manifestation of the bounteous mercy of God. The vb. *paristanai* not only means to place something at the disposition of another but also has the nuance of "offering, presenting" something as a sacrifice. It is used thus by Josephus (*Ant.* 4.6.4 §113) and Lucian (*De sacrificiis* 13); BAGD, 628. Cf. Rom 6:13, 19. Whereas the Jewish sacrifice implied the slaughter of what was offered, Paul uses the verb figuratively of Christian life and activity.

In either case, it is by God's mercy that this new Christian life is lived. It is not we who bring it about that the gospel transforms our lives, but God's mercy that transforms our lives. "It depends not on human willing or effort, but on God's mercy" (9:16).

your bodies. I.e., "yourselves." See Introduction, section IX.D. Recall 6:13,

"Do not put your members at sin's disposal as weapons of wickedness, but instead put yourselves at God's disposal as those who have come to life from death and offer your members to God as weapons of uprightness."

holy and acceptable to God. Paul implicitly compares Christians with animals slaughtered in Jewish or pagan cults, but he corrects the comparison by adding "living" and the following phrases. It is not a cult that offers dead animals to God; Christians who strive to do what is right give a cultic or sacrificial sense to their lives, as they offer themselves and their conduct to him.

as a cult suited to your rational nature. Or "a spiritual cult," i.e., worship governed by the *logos,* as befits a human being with *nous* and *pneuma,* and not merely one making use of irrational animals. This cult is a way of expressing Christian noetic dedication. Faith living itself out through love enables Christians to live according to the highest aspects of their beings. In Gal 5:24 Paul says, "Those who belong to Christ Jesus have crucified the flesh with its passions and desires." Such a view could have a cultic aspect. See also Hos 6:6; Ps 50:14, 23 (LXX). Recall too that Paul regarded his own preaching of the gospel as a cultic act (1:9); that was for him the concrete noetic and rational way he was asked by God to live his Christian life. See Phil 2:17; 4:18; 1 Pet 2:5; 3:15; *T. Levi* 3:6: "[angels of the presence] offer to the Lord a reasonable soothing odor (*osmēn euōdias logikēn*) and a bloodless offering."

Here the important thing for Paul is that such a spiritual cult, suited to one's rational nature and entailing the offering of the Christian's body, is precisely what he means by living under the uprightness of God. Spiritual worship is thus the realization of God's eschatological work, whereby he is claiming for himself the world that belongs to him. It implies the offering to God of the human body and self in an act of obedience stemming from faith. See further Käsemann, "Worship."

The phrase probably functions as adv. acc., modifying the whole preceding clause (see BDF §480.6). Käsemann (*Commentary,* 190) thinks that Paul adds these qualifications as a Hellenistic polemic against the irrational cult of folk religions. Possibly. The phrase has a counterpart in Hellenistic Greek phrases such as the *logikas thysias* of the *Corpus Hermeticum* 1.31; *logikē thysia,* 13.18 (see A. D. Nock and A. J. Festugière, *Corpus Hermeticum,* 2 vols., Coll. Budé [Paris: Éditions "Les Belles-Lettres," 1945], 19, 208). Although the word *logikos* is not found in the LXX and the phrase does not occur there, the idea of keeping the law as an act of worship or sacrifice is expressed in Sir 35:1–6.

2. *Do not conform yourselves to this present world.* This is the first imperative, negatively expressed. What Paul means by "conforming" is not explained here, but is to be understood of the contrasting transformation or metamorphosis by the Spirit of Christ, of which he speaks in 2 Cor 3:18. "This world" is passing and imperfect (1 Cor 7:31); hence the Apostle's recommendation. Paul alludes to the Jewish distinction of "this world/age/aeon" and the "world/age/aeon to come," a distinction that was adopted by the early church and given a Christian nuance.

For Paul the "world/age/aeon to come" has already begun; the "ages" have met at the start of the Christian dispensation (1 Cor 10:11). Hence Christians, though in "this world," must live for God and not be conformed to any other standard. See Phil 3:21; Gal 1:4.

be transformed. Or "let yourselves be transformed" (BDF §314), i.e., with the aid of God's grace and the holy Spirit. This is the second imperative, positively expressed: a complete metamorphosis of thinking, willing, and conduct is recommended.

by a renewal of your whole way of thinking. Lit., "by a renewal of the mind." The metamorphosis is not external but inward, involving the renewal of the *nous*, that aspect of the human being which is considered the seat of intellectual and moral judgment (see Introduction, section IX.D). This metamorphosis is brought about by the indwelling Spirit of God that "leads" those incorporated into Christ through faith and baptism and makes of them "children of God" (8:12–14; cf. Col 3:10; Eph 4:23; Titus 3:5). The "mind" or the "intellect" is to be ruled no more by the passions of the body. Cf. 1 Cor 2:15–16: "we have the mind of Christ."

Some MSS (א, D^c, L, P, and most minuscles) add *hymōn*, "your," after "mind."

so that you may discern what is God's will. Or "test what is. . . ." Knowledge of what God desires becomes the norm of Christian conduct. The Christian judges no longer according to the "present world," but according to what God wills. See Baumert, "Zur 'Unterscheidung'." See 2:18; Phil 1:10; cf. Eph 5:17.

what is good, acceptable to him, and perfect. Three adjectives sum up the transformed life of the Christian justified and living by faith in Christ Jesus. See Eph 5:10.

BIBLIOGRAPHY ON THE HORTATORY SECTION

Adams, B. E., "Responsible Living in Community Setting (Romans 12–16)," *SwJT* 19 (1976–77): 57–69.

Bahr, G. J., "The Subscriptions in the Pauline Letters," *JBL* 87 (1968): 27–41.

Candlish, R. S., *Studies in Romans 12: The Christian's Sacrifice and Service of Praise* (Grand Rapids, Mich.: Kregel, 1989).

Cerfaux, L., *Une Lecture,* 109–23.

Culpepper, R. A., "God's Righteousness in the Life of His People: Romans 12–15," *RevExp* 73 (1976): 451–63.

Daube, D., "Jewish Missionary Maxims in Paul," *ST* 1 (1947): 158–69.

Flender, H., "Weisung statt Ermahnung: Einführung in die Bibelarbeit über Römer 12," *BK* 28 (1973): 81–84.

Forell, G. W., *The Christian Lifestyle: Reflections on Romans 12–15* (Philadelphia, Penn.: Fortress, 1975).

Grabner-Haider, A., *Paraklese und Eschatologie bei Paulus: Mensch und Welt im*

Anspruch der Zukunft Gottes, NTAbh n.s. 4 (Münster in Westfalen: Aschendorff, 1968), 116–28.

Karris, R. J., "Romans 14:1–15:13 and the Occasion of Romans," *RomDeb*, 65–84.

Moiser, J., "Rethinking Romans 12–15," NTS 36 (1990): 571–82.

Richards, L. O., *The Good Life: A Study of Romans 12–16* (Grand Rapids, Mich.: Zondervan, 1981).

Roetzel, C. J., "Sacrifice in Romans 12–15," WW 6 (1986): 410–19.

Segalla, G., "Kerigma e parenesi come critica alla prassi in Rm. 12,1–15,13," *Teologia* 6 (1981): 307–29.

Schrage, W., *Die konkreten Einzelgebote*, 49–53, 163–74.

Stuhlmacher, P., "The Theme of Romans," *RomDeb*, 333–45.

Vouga, F., "L'Épître aux Romains comme document ecclésiologique (Rm 12–15)," ETR 61 (1986): 485–95.

Part A of the Hortatory Section

Cranfield, C.E.B., *A Commentary on Romans 12–13*, SJT Occasional Papers 12 (Edinburgh and London: Oliver & Boyd, 1965).

Dabeck, F., "Der Text Röm 12,1–13,10 als Symbol des Pneuma," SPCIC, 2.585–90.

Dehn, G., *Vom christlichen Leben: Auslegung des 12. und 13. Kapitels des Briefes an die Römer*, BibSN 6–7 (Neukirchen-Vluyn: Neukirchener-Verlag, 1954).

Deidun, T. J., *New Covenant Morality in Paul*, AnBib 89 (Rome: Biblical Institute, 1981), 95–103.

Dodd, C. H., "The Primitive Catechism and the Sayings of Jesus," *New Testament Essays: Studies in Memory of Thomas Walter Manson*, ed. A. J. B. Higgins (Manchester: University Press, 1959), 106–18; repr. in *More New Testament Studies* (Grand Rapids, Mich.: Eerdmans, 1968), 11–29.

Gleixner, H., "Die Relevanz des christlichen Glaubens für die Ethik," TGl 76 (1986): 307–23.

Lorenzi, L. de (ed.), *Dimensions de la vie chrétienne (Rm 12–13)*, Benedictina, Section biblico-oecuménique 4 (Rome: Abbazia di San Paolo fuori le mura, 1979).

Ortkemper, F.-J., *Leben aus dem Glauben: Christliche Grundhaltungen nach Römer 12–13*, NTAbh n.s. 14 (Münster in Westfalen: Aschendorff, 1980).

Ruler, A. A. van, *Op gezag van een Apostel* (Nijkerk: Callenbach, 1971).

Thompson, M. B., *Clothed with Christ: The Example and Teaching of Jesus in Romans 12.1–15.13*, JSNTSup 59 (Sheffield, UK: Academic Press, 1991).

Romans 12

Hamann, H. P., "The Christian Life According to Romans 12," LTJ 19 (1985): 73–79.

Käsemann, E., "Worship and Everyday Life: A Note on Romans 12," NTQT, 188–95.

Riesner, R., *Handeln aus dem Geist: Zwölf Thesen zu Römer 12* (Giessen and Basel: Brunner-Verlag, 1977).

Schelkle, K. H., "Der Christ in der Gemeinde: Eine Auslegung von Röm 12," *BK* 28 (1973): 74–81.

Schlier, H., "Die Eigenart der christlichen Mahnung nach dem Apostel Paulus," *Besinnung auf das Neue Testament*, 340–57.

Voss, G., "In Christus Gemeinschaft bilden: Eine Auslegung des 12. Kapitels des Römerbriefes," *Una Sancta* 43 (1988): 277–83, 342.

Whitaker, G. H., "The Twelfth Chapter of Romans," *ExpTim* 27 (1915–16): 475–77.

Zahn, A., *Betrachtungen über das zwölfte Kapitel des Römerbriefs* (Stuttgart: Steinkopf, 1889).

Zimmermann, H., "Grundlage und Sinn der paulinischen Ermahnung," *Catholica* 29 (1975): 20–29.

Rom 12:1–2

Asmussen, H., "Das Opfer der Gemeinde," *EvT* 1 (1934–35): 49–55.

Baumert, N., "Zur 'Unterscheidung der Geister,' " *ZKT* 111 (1989): 183–95.

Betz, H. D., "Christianity as Religion: Paul's Attempt at Definition in Romans," *JR* 71 (1991): 315–44.

————, "The Foundation of Christian Ethics According to Romans 12:1–2," *Witness and Existence: Essays in Honor of Schubert M. Ogden*, ed. P. E. Devenish and G. L. Goodwin (Chicago and London: University of Chicago, 1989), 55–72.

Bjerkelund, C. J., *Parakalô* (Oslo: Universitetsforlaget, 1967), 156–734.

Blank, J., "Zum Begriff des Opfers nach Röm 12,1–2," *Funktion und Struktur christlicher Gemeinde: Festgabe für Prof. Dr. Heinz Fleckenstein* (Würzburg: Echter-Verlag, 1971), 35–51.

Casel, O., "Die *logikē thysia* der antiken Mystik in christlich-liturgischer Umdeutung," *Jahrbuch für Liturgiewissenschaft* 4 (1924): 37–47.

Corriveau, R., *The Liturgy of Life*, 151–85.

Daly, R. J., *Christian Sacrifice* (Washington, D.C.: Catholic University of America, 1978), 243–46.

Evans, C., "Romans 12.1–2: The True Worship," *Dimensions*, ed. L. de Lorenzi, 7–49.

Gubler, M.-L., " 'Passt euch nicht den Masstäben dieser Welt an!' (Röm 12,2): Von der Zivilcourage biblischer Frauen," *Diakonia* 18 (1987): 305–16.

Harrington, D. J., "Freed for Life in the Spirit—Together: Romans 12:1–8: A Meditation," *RRel* 45 (1986): 831–35.

Hooker, M. D., "Interchange in Christ and Ethics," *JSNT* 25 (1985): 3–17.

Klauck, H.-J., "Kultische Symbolsprache bei Paulus," *Freude am Gottesdienst: Aspekte ursprünglicher Liturgie* . . . (Stuttgart: Katholisches Bibelwerk, 1983), 107–18.

Lowrie, S. T., "Romans XII.1–8: Translation and Interpretation," *Princeton Theological Review* 17 (1919): 627–43.

Lyonnet, S., "Le Culte Spirituel: Rm 12,1–2," *AsSeign* n.s. 53 (1970): 11–14.

Maher, M., "Christian Life and Liturgy," *Religious Life Review* (Dublin) 26 (1987): 46–52.

Mullins, T. Y., "Petition as a Literary Form," *NovT* 5 (1962): 46–54.

Ogara, F., " 'Rationabile obsequium vestrum,' " *VD* 15 (1935): 5–14.

Parsons, M., "Being Precedes Act: Indicative and Imperative in Paul's Writing," *EvQ* 60 (1988): 99–127.

Radl, W., "Kult und Evangelium bei Paulus," *BZ* 31 (1987): 58–75.

Rossano, P., "L'ideale del bello (*kalos*) nell'etica di S. Paolo," *SPCIC* 2.373–82.

Schlier, H., "Der Christ und die Welt," *GLeb* 38 (1965): 416–28; repr. in *Das Ende der Zeit*, 234–49.

————, "Vom Wesen der apostolischen Ermahnung nach Römerbrief 12,1–2," *Zeit der Kirche*, 74–89.

Schweizer, E., "Gottesdienst im Neuen Testament und Kirchenbau heute," *Beiträge zur Theologie des Neuen Testaments* (Zurich: Zwingli-Verlag, 1970), 249–61.

Seidensticker, P., *Lebendiges Opfer (Röm 12,1): Ein Beitrag zur Theologie des Apostels Paulus*, NTAbh 20.1–3 (Münster in Westfalen: Aschendorff, 1954), 256–63.

Smiga, G., "Romans 12:1–2 and 15:30–32 and the Occasion of the Letter to the Romans," *CBQ* 53 (1991): 257–73.

Stoessel, H. E., "Notes on Romans 12:1–2: The Renewal of the Mind and Internalizing the Truth," *Int* 17 (1963): 161–75.

Tångberg, K. A., "Romerbrevet 12,1–2 og paranesebegrepet i nytestamentlig forskning," *TTKi* 57 (1986): 81–91.

Walter, N., "Christusglaube und heidnische Religiosität in paulinischen Gemeinden," *NTS* 25 (1978–79): 422–42, esp. 436–41.

Weatherspoon, J. B., "The Consecration of Life: Romans 12:1; John 17:19," *RevExp* 23 (1926): 129–36.

Wenschkewitz, H., *Die Spiritualisierung der Kultusbegriffe: Tempel, Priester und Opfer im Neuen Testament*, Angelos Beiheft 4 (Leipzig: Pfeiffer, 1932), 110–31.

44. Sober Existence Using God's Gifts for All (12:3–8)

12 ³In virtue of the grace given to me I say to every one of you: Do not think more highly of yourself than you ought to; rather, think of yourself with sober judgment according to the measure of faith that God has apportioned each of you. ⁴For just as we have many members in one body and all of the members do not have the same function, ⁵so we, though many, are one body in Christ, and individually members of one another. ⁶We have gifts that differ according to the grace given to us. If prophecy, let it be used in proportion to one's faith; ⁷or

ministry, let it be used in service; or if one is a teacher, let him use it for instruction; [8]if one is an exhorter, for encouragement; if one is a contributor to charity, let him use it with simple generosity; if one is a leader, with diligence; if one does works of mercy, let it be with cheerfulness.

COMMENT

Everyday life is the realm in which Christians are to pay such worship to God the Father. The cult to be rendered should manifest itself concretely in a life in community or society based on humility and charity. Paul recalls to the Christians of Rome that they are not to pretend to be more than they are. "If anyone is in Christ, that one is a new creation" (2 Cor 5:17). To be in Christ is to be a member of the body of Christ.

When Paul descends to particulars, after the generic exhortation of vv 1–2, he gives advice first of all to the charismatic element in the community. They may be gifted, but they are to use their gifts for the good of all.

The lives of all Christians call for a proper, unselfish use of talents and spiritual gifts received. As an apostolic founder of Christian communities, Paul realized only too well the dangers to the community of elements in it that overestimated their worth. Hence he urges that each Christian, who lives by faith in Christ Jesus, be content with the function or role that he or she has been called to perform in the community and likewise respect the function or role of others. In doing so, Christians will display the proper respect for God himself and his gifts. For the function or role is measured by the faith that has been apportioned to each one. That faith is a gift and also calls for life together so that its full expression may work itself out in love (Gal 5:6).

NOTES

12:3. *In virtue of the grace given to me I say to every one of you.* Paul addresses the Christians of Rome as a commissioned apostle, called and graced by God himself; see 1:5; 11:13; 15:15. He seeks to motivate the Romans to a proper Christian life.

Do not think more highly of yourself than you ought to. See 1 Cor 4:6c. However gifted Christians may be, they are still members of the body of Christ, called to serve one another. Paul's comment is pertinent especially to the "strong," of whom he will speak in 14:1–15:13.

rather, think of yourself with sober judgment. Lit., "think unto sobriety." Paul plays on the vb. *phronein*, "think, be minded," and its compounds *hyperphronein* and *sōphronein*. The latter echoes the great Greek virtue of moderation, *sōphrosynē*. See BDF §488.1b. Paul urges the Roman Christians to form a modest estimate of themselves.

according to the measure of faith that God has apportioned each of you. The norm of one's thinking has to be *pistis*, "faith," dispensed by God in varying degrees. Cf. Eph 4:7. This is not the charismatic "faith" of 1 Cor 13:2 (faith that moves mountains), for the exhortation is addressed to all Christians of Rome; rather, it may be either the active response of the believer (*fides qua creditur*) or, better, the object believed in (*fides quae creditur*), which in the concrete is Christ Jesus. Paul's advice is especially pertinent if he is already thinking of the "strong" and the "weak" of 14:1–15:13. In either case, the faith they have is a gift of God. Each one, instead of thinking too highly of oneself, should measure himself or herself by the standard of what one believes according to God's gift (see Cranfield, "*Metron pisteōs*"; Birdsall, "*Emetrēsen*"). On *metron* as a "standard" (by which to measure something), see Protagoras, *Fragment* 1 (Diels, *Fragm. der Vorsokr.* 2); Plato, *Laws* 4.716c; Xenophon, *Cyropaedia* 1.3, 18.

4. *just as we have many members in one body and all of the members do not have the same function.* These Pauline words are particularly pertinent to the divided Roman community. Paul appeals to experience and draws an analogy from the human body with its many parts (feet, hands, eyes, ears, heart, etc.). See 1 Cor 12:5, 12–13, 25.

5. *so we, though many, are one body in Christ.* Paul does not say here, as he does in 1 Cor 12:27, "you are the body of Christ," to stress their mutual unity in him under the figure of the body. See also 1 Cor 6:15–20; 7:7; 10:16–17; 12:12–31; cf. Col 3:15; Eph 4:4, 15. As in 1 Cor 12:12–31, the phrase "one body" probably does not suggest anything more than a moral union of the members who work together for the common good of the whole, as in the body politic. We have to look elsewhere for further nuances of Paul's thought on the subject (see *PAHT*, §PT122–27). Nor does he mention the "one body" in any connection with the church. Christians are "one body" because they are "in Christ" (8:1; cf. Gal 3:26). See Introduction, section IX.D. One should preserve the nuances of Paul's thought in various passages. The oneness that Christians experience in Christ does not do away with their differences or their manifold gifts. Cf. Col 3:15.

individually members of one another. Paul uses *to de kath' heis*, "individually, with relation to each individual" (BDF §305). "In Christ" Christians are interrelated, and no one stands in isolation; so all their services must be in terms of the body as a unit. Cf. Eph 4:25; 5:30.

6. *We have gifts that differ according to the grace given to us.* Paul plays on the words *charismata*, "gifts, charisms," and *charis*, "grace." The charisms are the specific participation of individual Christians in grace; they are "the concretion and individuation of the Spirit" (Käsemann, *Commentary*, 335). Such participations are all rooted in what Paul himself has called *to charisma tou theou*, "the gift of God" (6:23), which is "eternal life in Christ Jesus our Lord." Christ is the prime analogate, when it comes to charisms. All others partake in the gift that is Christ Jesus. Yet there are other charisms that Christians are endowed with, and

of these Paul speaks here. They are indications of the measure of faith that God has apportioned to each one.

They are what later theology called *gratiae gratis datae*, "graces freely bestowed," in view of a function to be performed in the community. The different gifts of grace that Christians receive from the Spirit as a result of faith are destined for the benefit of the whole body. Each member must realize the social character of the God-given talents and make use of them for the common good without envy or jealousy of gifts given to other members. Gifts have been given that with them Christians might serve one another. All charisms are graces that move Christians to action on behalf of others. No one is superfluous or to be regarded as a supernumerary. See 1:11; 1 Cor 7:7; 12:4; 1 Pet 4:10.

Paul proceeds to enumerate seven such charisms, using at first abstract terms for them, and later the names of persons who possess such gifts. The septet stands symbolically for the totality of such God-given charisms. Whether they are more than charisms, e.g., specific offices in the Christian community, is a debate for dogmatic theologians. One cannot answer that question on the basis of Paul's writings.

If prophecy. The first gift is inspired Christian preaching, as in 1 Cor 12:10, 28; 13:2; 14:1, 3–6, 24, 39; 1 Tim 4:14. It is given primacy of place among the *charismata*, clearly said to be a gift of the Spirit in 1 Cor 12:10–11. It denotes not one who predicts the future, but one who speaks in God's name and probes the secrets of hearts (1 Cor 14:24–25). On the use of *eite . . . eite* to link together various charisms, see BDF §454.3.

let it be used in proportion to one's faith, Lit., "according to the analogy of faith." *Analogia* means "right relationship, proportion" (BAGD, 56). Paul's caution is to curb the charismatics and their enthusiasm; all inspired preaching must be in accord with Christian faith. Faith thus serves as a norm.

The word *pistis* is differently understood by commentators. The best interpretation is to understand it as *fides quae creditur*, the body of Christian belief, the believed-in object, as in 12:3; Gal 1:23; 3:23. This sense would mean, then, that inspired preaching must not contradict Christian faith, for there can also be false prophecy (1 Thess 5:20–21); so Bultmann (*TDNT* 6.213), Lagrange, and Schlier (*Römerbrief*, 370). Others take it in the sense of *fides qua*: inspired preaching is to be engaged in in proportion to the "apprehension of and response to the grace of God in Christ Jesus" (Cranfield, *Romans*, 621). Still others take it in the sense of charismatic faith, the faith that moves mountains (1 Cor 13:2), i.e., with respect of the limits of such a charism and without adding material from personal and subjective whims, so (with variant explanations) Gaugler, Leenhardt, and Sanday and Headlam.

From this Pauline phrase comes the later theological expression about the ecclesiastical norm or the rule of faith, "according to the analogy of faith." It was often used by patristic and medieval writers to relate the teaching of the OT to the NT as promise and fulfillment and as an integrating principle in the development of dogma. See L. Scheffczyk, "Analogy of Faith," *Sacramentum Mundi*, 6 vols. (New York: Herder and Herder, 1968–70), 1.25–27. But it often came to be misused as meanings and interpretations of later vintage were imported into the biblical text in its name. If there is any validity in such a principle for the interpretation of Scripture, it must be understood as the analogy of "biblical" faith or of "Pauline" or "Johannine" faith, depending on the writer being interpreted.

7. *or ministry*. The second gift is *diakonia*, "service." It is not easy to say just what Paul means by this term; it may be specific service, such as table service (Acts 6:2), or the administration of material aid to members of the community (15:25, 31; 1 Cor 16:15; 2 Cor 8:4); or generic, of all activity meant to build up the community, as Paul speaks of his own ministry in 11:13; 1 Cor 12:5; 2 Cor 4:1; 11:8; cf. Col 4:17; Eph 4:12. He will use cognate words in 15:25 and 31 as he speaks of the collection to be taken to Jerusalem; that is a form of *diakonia*.

let it be used in service. Peculiarly, Paul uses the same word *diakonia* to explain what *diakonia* should be or what its mode is. Undoubtedly, he means that the person who serves should really put his or her heart into such service. In 15:30–32 prayer is involved in it. Cf. 1 Pet 4:10.

or if one is a teacher. Paul now shifts to the mention of gifted persons, the third category of gifts. *Ho didaskōn* is the one who instructs, either in catechesis (1 Cor 14:19; Gal 6:6) or in the interpretation of Scripture. In either case, it has to do with the communication of knowledge about God's will. Paul considers himself at times in this capacity (1 Cor 4:17); cf. Col 1:28; 3:16. "Teachers" are mentioned in the third place in the list in 1 Cor 12:28.

let him use it for instruction. Here *didaskalia* probably means something like *hē didachē tōn apostolōn*, "the teaching of the apostles" (Acts 2:42), i.e., the teaching of Christian doctrine, a task seen as distinct from preaching and service. See 1 Cor 12:28; cf. Eph 4:11; 1 Tim 4:13.

8. *if one is an exhorter*, I.e., the "spiritual father" of the community, who by his consolation and admonition guides the members in their communal life; he possesses the fourth kind of charism.

for encouragement. By *paraklēsis* Paul probably means counsel or instruction in ethical conduct. See 1 Thess 5:11; Phil 2:1; Heb 13:22.

if one is a contributor to charity. I.e., one who "shares" private wealth, a philanthropist, an almsgiver; so Paul describes the fifth kind of God-given charism. This sense of *metadidonai* is found in Job 31:17; Prov 11:26; Luke 3:11; Eph 4:28; *T. Iss.* 7:5; *Herm. Vis.* 3.9.4. This charism is understood in this way by the majority of commentators today, but Zahn (*Römer*, 547) thought it referred to one who dispenses both spiritual gifts and material goods, a meaning that would find some support in Paul's use of *metadidonai* in 1:11 and in 1 Thess 2:8. But the spiritual gifts would seem to be part of the first three charisms. But van Unnik ("The Interpretation") insists that *metadidonai* is found elsewhere in the Greek language with a wider meaning than "giving to the poor" (e.g., 2 Macc 1:35; 8:12; Wis 7:13; Dio Chrysostom, *Oratio* 41.9) so that he would translate "if one communicates [the riches of the gospel], let him do it with simplicity," i.e., without self-exaltation, because the wealth of the gospel itself is grace.

let him use it with simple generosity. The philanthropist's giving should be characterized by *haplotēs*, "simplicity," i.e., lacking duplicity or secondary, ulterior motivation and should be done without thinking twice about it. See 2 Cor 8:2; 9:11, 13; 11:3.

if one is a leader. The sixth charism belongs to *ho proistamenos*, lit., "the one standing at the head," "the one who presides, directs, or rules." See 1 Thess 5:12; 1 Tim 5:17 (presiders in the church); 1 Tim 3:4, 5, 12 (presider over a household); cf. Josephus, *Ant.* 8.12.3 §300 ("govern"); 12.2.13 §108 ("chief officers"); Justin, *Apology* 1.67. This seems to be the meaning intended by Paul, even though he does not specify the way in which such a gifted person would preside. The word has been so understood here by Origen (*In ep. ad Romanos* 9.3 [PG 14.1217]), Calvin, Käsemann (*Commentary*, 342), and Schlatter. If the order of the gifts is significant, then the "leader's" position is noteworthy.

The *RSV*, however, translates this substantivized ptc., "he who gives aid," a meaning that BAGD, 707 tolerates. It is so understood by Cranfield (*Romans*, 626) and preferred by Schlier (*Römerbrief*, 372), because it is collocated between two other caritative charisms, *ho metadidous*, "contributor," and *ho eleōn*, "one who does works of mercy"; likewise Lagrange, Michel, and Reicke (*TDNT* 6.701). But then, what is the difference between this charism and *ho metadidous* or *diakonia*?

with diligence. Or "with zeal/dispatch." Diligent attention should characterize the leader's oversight.

if one does works of mercy. The seventh gift belongs to *ho eleōn*, the person who performs acts of mercy, the Christian social worker, the "Good Samaritan." This charism probably corresponds to what Tob 1:3 and 4:7 describe as *eleēmosynēn poiein*. But it could refer to all sorts of acts of charity (caring for the sick, burying the dead, providing for imprisoned persons). It may even refer more specifically to those who tend the sick (so Käsemann). See 2 Cor 9:7.

let it be with cheerfulness. The spirit in which the acts are done is as important as the acts themselves.

BIBLIOGRAPHY

Aune, D., *Prophecy in Early Christianity and the Ancient Mediterranean World* (Grand Rapids, Mich.: Eerdmans, 1983), 198–217.

Baumert, N., "Charisma und Amt bei Paulus," *L'Apôtre Paul: Personnalité, style et conception du ministère*, BETL 73, ed. A. Vanhoye (Louvain: Leuven University, 1986), 203–28.

———, "Zur Begriffsgeschichte von *charisma* im griechischen Sprachraum," *TP* 65 (1990): 79–100.

———, "Zur 'Unterscheidung der Geister,' " *ZKT* 111 (1989): 183–95.

Best, E., *One Body in Christ* (London: SPCK, 1955).

Birdsall, J. N., "*Emetrēsen* in Rom. xii. 3," *JTS* 14 (1963): 103–4.

Brockhaus, U., *Charisma und Amt: Die paulinische Charismenlehre auf dem Hintergrund der frühchristlichen Gemeindefunktionen* (Wuppertal: Brockhaus, 1972).

Brosch, J., *Charismen und Ämter in der Urkirche* (Bonn: Hanstein, 1951).

Chłąd, S., "Charyzmaty w Rz 12, 6–8," *Ruch Biblijny y Liturgiczny* 39 (1986): 24–32.

Cranfield, C. E. B., "*Metron pisteōs* in Romans XII.3," *NTS* 8 (1961–62): 345–51; repr. in *The Bible and Christian Life* (Edinburgh: Clark, 1985), 203–14.

Ellis, E. E., " 'Spiritual' Gifts in the Pauline Community," *NTS* 20 (1973–74): 128–44.

Friedrich, G., "Geist und Amt," *Wort und Dienst: Jahrbuch der theologischen Schule Bethel* 3 (1952): 61–85.

Grau, F., "Der neutestamentliche Begriff *charisma*, seine Geschichte und seine Theologie," Ph.D. diss., Universität Tübingen, 1946).

Greeven, H., "Propheten, Lehrer, Vorsteher bei Paulus: Zur Frage der 'Ämter' im Urchristentum," *ZNW* 44 (1952–53): 1–43; repr. in *Das kirchliche Amt im Neuen Testament*, ed. K. Kertelge, WF 189 (Darmstadt: Wissenschaftliche Buchgesellschaft, 1977), 305–61 (with Nachtrag).

Hanson, P. D., *The People Called: The Growth of Community in the Bible* (San Francisco, Calif.: Harper & Row, 1986), 438–51.

Hemphill, K. S., "The Pauline Concept of Charisma," Ph.D. diss., Cambridge University, 1976, 1640–96.

Hennen, B., "Ordines sacri: Ein Deutungsversuch zu 1 Cor 12, 1–31 und Röm 12, 3–8," *TQ* 119 (1938): 427–69.

Herten, J., "Charisma—Signal einer Gemeindetheologie des Paulus," *Kirche im Werden: Studien zum Thema Amt und Gemeinde im Neuen Testament* . . . , ed. J. Hainz (Munich and Paderborn: Schöningh, 1976), 57–89.

Käsemann, E., "Geist und Geistesgaben im NT," *RGG*, 2.1272–79.

———, "Ministry and Community in the New Testament," *ENTT*, 63–94.

———, "The Theological Problem Presented by the Motif of the Body of Christ," *Perspectives*, 102–21.

Lindeboom, L., "De analogia fidei en Rom. 12:6(7)," *GTT* 17 (1916–17): 448–57, 511–26.

McKee, E. A., "Calvin's Exegesis of Romans 12:8—Social, Accidental, or Theological?" *CTJ* 23 (1988): 6–18.

Magass, W., "Die Paradigmatik einer Paränese am Beispiel von Röm 12,3: 'er soll nicht höher von sich denken, als er denken darf': Ein Beitrag zum Häresieverdacht als *Terma*-Verdacht," *LB* 35 (1975): 1–26.

Ogara, F., " 'Habentes . . . donationes . . . differentes,' " *VD* 16 (1936): 5–13.

Porter, C. L., " 'For the Sake of the Grace Given Me,' " *Encounter* 52 (1991): 251–62.

Sánchez Bosch, J., "Le Corps du Christ et les charismes dans l'épître aux Romains," *Dimensions*, ed. L. de Lorenzi, 51–83.

Schürmann, H., "Die geistlichen Gnadengaben in den paulinischen Gemeinden," *Ursprung und Gestalt: Erörterungen und Besinnungen zum Neuen Testament* (Düsseldorf: Patmos, 1970), 236–67.

Schulz, S., "Die Charismenlehre des Paulus: Bilanz der Probleme und Ergebnisse," *Rechtfertigung: Festschrift für Ernst Käsemann . . .* , ed. J. Friedrich et al. (Tübingen: Mohr [Siebeck]; Göttingen: Vandenhoeck & Ruprecht, 1976), 443–60.

Scippa, V., "I carismi per la vitalità della Chiesa: Studio esegetico su 1 Cor 12–14; Rm 12, 6–8; Ef 4, 11–13; 1 Pt 4,10–11," *Asprenas* (Naples) 38 (1991): 5–25.

Sisti, A., "Carismi e carità (*Rom*. 12,6–16)," *BeO* 12 (1970): 27–33.

Unnik, W. C. van, "The Interpretation of Romans 12:8: *ho metadidous en haplotēti*," *On Language, Culture, and Religion: In Honor of Eugene A. Nida*, ed. M. Black and W. A. Smalley (The Hague and Paris: Mouton, 1974), 169–83.

Viard, A., "Charismes et charité: Rm 12,6–16," *AsSeign* 16 (1962): 15–31.

45. COUNSELS FOR CHRISTIANS LIVING IN THE COMMUNITY (12:9–21)

12 ⁹Love must be unfeigned. You must detest what is evil and cling to what is good. ¹⁰Be devoted to one another with brotherly love; outdo one another in showing honor. ¹¹Serve the Lord, unflagging in diligence, fervent in spirit, ¹²rejoicing in hope, patient in affliction, persistent in prayer. ¹³Contribute to the needs of God's dedicated people, and practice hospitality. ¹⁴Bless those who persecute you; bless and do not curse them. ¹⁵Rejoice with those who are rejoicing; mourn with those who are mourning. ¹⁶Think in harmony with one another. Put aside haughty thoughts and associate with the lowly. Do not become wise in your own estimation. ¹⁷Repay no one evil for evil; take thought for what is noble in the sight of all human beings. ¹⁸If it possibly lies in your power, live at peace with everyone. ¹⁹Take no revenge, dear friends, but leave room for God's wrath, for it stands written: *"Vengeance is mine; I will repay,"* says the Lord. ²⁰But *if your enemy is hungry, feed him; if he is thirsty, give him something to drink. In doing so, you will heap coals of fire upon his head.* ²¹Do not be overcome by evil, but overcome evil with good.

COMMENT

Having asserted the unity of Christians in the "one body," Paul now goes on to give a series of counsels for such Christians. They are the demands that life in the Christian community makes of them. In v 9 Paul enunciates the generic principle, that love must govern all, and that Christians must do good and avoid evil. Next, in vv 10–13 he spells out the basic obligations, listing ten generic counsels that sum up the ways in which genuine love is to be manifested without pretense. In the following verses, 14–21, Paul sets forth the Christian's obligation with respect to an enemy or a persecutor. It is remarkable how basic Paul's counsels are in this paragraph. Yet he formulates them in obvious good faith, making use of ten gnomic sayings, probably realizing from experience the need of such counsels. But before he again descends to particulars, Paul enunciates the principle that must govern all of them, the rule of love. In this regard his discussion echoes the order of 1 Corinthians 12–13. In 14:1–15:13 Paul will handle in greater detail the problems of the "weak" and the "strong" in the Roman community; what he says here in vv 9–21 is a generic preparation for that discussion.

Did Paul compose such a list himself? Or does it represent a list of instructions commonly used among early Christian preachers? Many commentators are convinced that there are in this paragraph of Romans echoes of the Jesus tradition, that Paul makes use of fragments of the sayings of Jesus that had already become part of a primitive catechesis (see vv 14, 17a, 18, 19a). Others argue from the use of participles instead of imperatives in vv 9–13 that Paul is using "a Semitic source originating in very primitive Christian circles" (Barrett, *Romans*, 240). This view has been contested by Cranfield (*Commentary on Romans 12–13*, 40 n. 3) but supported by Talbert ("Tradition"), who regards vv 9–13 as "an inherent unity." Barrett thinks that the imperatival participles disappear after v 13, but they do recur in vv 16a–c and 17–19a. Hence they raise the question whether vv 14–21 stem from "a new source." Talbert is certainly right in saying that the unique appearance of the so-called imperatival participles in this passage cannot be owing to Paul's slipping unconsciously into such a style, because it does not appear in hortatory sections of other letters. Talbert also thinks that he can detect, after the unit of vv 9b–13, traditional material in vv 16a, b, 17a, 18, 19a, and 21. D. A. Black has also shown the chiastic arrangement of vv 9–13:

A	*apostygountes to ponēron*
	kollōmenoi tō agathō
B	*tē philadelphia eis allēlous philostorgoi*
	tē timē allēlous proēgoumenoi
	tē spoudē mē oknēroi
C	*tō pneumai zeontes*
	tō kyriō douleuontes
B′	*tē elpidi chairontes*
	tē thlipsei hypomenontes
	tē proseuchē proskarterountes
A′	*tais chreiais tōn hagiōn koinōnountes*
	tēn philoxenian diōkontes

The list may be compared with a similar list, which is not as well structured, in the Qumran Manual of Discipline, 1QS 1:1–11.

NOTES

12:9. *Love must be unfeigned.* Lit., "(let) love (be) unfeigned," supplying the vb. *estō.* See 2 Cor 6:6; 1 Cor 13:7. Such love without sham or hypocrisy is further explained by a series of counsels or maxims about Christian conduct. So far Paul has used the noun *agapē* only of God's love (5:5, 8; 8:35, 39), but now he begins to use it as the expression of outgoing, selfless concern for a fellow human being. The love must not be that of pretense, of actors on a stage. Etymologically, the adj. *anypokritos* is related to the vb. *hypokrinesthai*, "answer," i.e., to reply like an actor on the stage. Affection masked as a pretense of friendship is odious, but Christian love cannot be that. Christian love has to be a reflex of the love that Christ himself showed to humanity: "Walk in love, as Christ loved us and gave himself for us" (Eph 5:2). For love is only the way that justifying faith works itself out (Gal 5:6). The adj. *anypokritos* is found in Wis 5:18 and 18:15, but only rarely in secular writings (Marcus Aurelius, *Meditations* 8.5 [as an adv.]).

You must detest what is evil and cling to what is good. Lit., "detesting," a ptc. with which the vb. *este* has to be supplied. See Amos 5:15, "Hate evil and love good"; Ps 97:10. Similarly, the Essenes of Qumran were exhorted "to love all that He has chosen and hate all that He has despised; to depart from all evil and cling to all good works" (1QS 1:4–5). Cf. *T. Benj.* 8:1, "Do away with evil (*kakian*), envy, and hatred of brothers, and cling to goodness (*agathotēti*) and love."

Paul makes use of a series of participles, which act in elliptical sentences as the equivalent of imperatives; see vv 10b–13, 16a–c, 17–19a (BDF §468.2). Whether one should call them "imperatival participles" is another question. See Daube, who so argues on the basis of rabbinical Hebrew participial usage, in a note in "Participle and Imperative." Daube is supported by Barrett, "Imperatival Participle"; Davies, *Paul and Rabbinic Judaism*, 130–33; Talbert, "Tradition"; and Kanjuparambil, "Imperatival Participles." Certainly, the data that Kanjuparambil presents from 1QS prove nothing. It seems, rather, that Meecham ("The Use of the Participle") and Salom ("The Imperatival Use") were on the right track in supporting J. H. Moulton (*A Grammar of New Testament Greek*, 3d ed. [Edinburgh: Clark, 1908], 1.180–83), that the phenomenon represents a genuine Hellenistic development of the Greek participle. Cf. E. Mayser, *Grammatik der griechischen Papyri aus der Ptolemäerzeit*, 2 multipart vols. (Berlin: de Gruyter, 1926–38), 2.1.196 n. 3 and 340–41. Mayser disagrees with some of Moulton's interpretations, and the matter is in need of further study.

10. *Be devoted to one another with brotherly love.* Unfeigned love must be shown above all to members of the Christian community. Paul uses *philadelphia* to distinguish it from wider obligations of *agapē*. See 1 Thess 4:9; Heb 13:1; 1 Pet

1:22. See C. Spicq, "*Philostorgos* (à propos de Rom., xii, 10)," *RB* 62 (1955): 497–510.

outdo one another in showing honor. The sense of this phrase is disputed. The translation used here follows that of several ancient versions; Vg: *honore invicem praevenientes.* It could mean, however, "As far as honor is concerned, let each one esteem the other more highly" (see BDF §150; BAGD, 706). See 13:7; 1 Pet 2:17.

11. *Serve the Lord.* This is the motive for all Christian conduct. Instead of *kyriō*, some MSS (D, G) read *kairō*, "serve the hour." If this were the correct reading, Christians would be urged to meet the demands of the time in which they live (see O. Cullmann, *Christ and Time* [Philadelphia, Penn.: Westminster, 1950], 42; cf. Acts 20:19; Col 3:24. The latter reading, however, is usually explained as a copyist's confusion of an abbreviation, *Kō* being read as *Krō* (= *kai* + *rō*). See B. M. Metzger, *The Text of the New Testament*, 3d ed. (New York: Oxford University Press, 1992), 187.

unflagging in diligence. Or "zeal." Roman Christians are thus urged not to allow themselves to grow slack in zeal, in the service either of other human beings or of God. The quality *spoudē*, "zeal, diligence, eagerness" is the same as that recommended to the community leader in 12:8c.

fervent in spirit. Lit., "seething in spirit/Spirit." Because this phrase stands in parallelism with several others that characterize the attitude of the Christian who serves the Lord, it is best understood of a human characteristic. The same expression is used of Apollos in Acts 18:25, who knew "only the baptism of John." In his case the expression would hardly refer to the holy Spirit; so apparently Origen (*In ep. ad Romanos* 9.9 [PG 14.1219]); John Chrysostom (*In ep. ad Romanos* hom. 21.3 [PG 60.605]).

But Theophylact (*Expositio in ep. ad Romanos* 12.11 [PG 124.508]), Calvin, and many modern interpreters (e.g., Cranfield, *Romans*, 634; Schlier, *Römerbrief*, 376) understand it as referring to the holy Spirit, which inflames the Christian: "zeal" would be understood as a gift of God, and his Spirit would responsible for the flame that makes the Christian seethe. Cf. 1 Thess 5:19, "do not extinguish the Spirit."

12. *rejoicing in hope.* See 5:2–3; 1 Pet 1:3–9. Because "hope" is the mark of Christians, they should rejoice in it and what it guarantees them; see the NOTES on 8:23–24. The phrase *tē elpidi*, "in hope," is a dat. of cause; see BDF §186.

patient in affliction. Confronted with *thlipsis*, "tribulation, distress," Christians are urged to endure. See 5:3; 8:18.

persistent in prayer. Above all, Paul recommends that Christians learn to commune with God at all times; see Phil 4:6; 1 Thess 5:17; cf. Col 4:2; Eph 6:18; 1 Tim 2:1.

13. *Contribute to the needs of God's dedicated people.* Lit., "taking an interest in the needs of the saints." Paul uses the pres. ptc. of *koinōnein*, "share," but in the more specific sense of "sharing by contributing (monetarily)," as he also does

in Gal 6:6. Recall his use of the noun *koinōnia* in the same sense (15:26; 2 Cor 8:4; 9:13; cf. Phil 4:15). See J. Hainz, *"Koinōnia,* etc.," *EDNT* 2.303–5; Campbell, *"Koinōnia,"* 367. On "saints," see the NOTE on 1:7. Paul may be hinting to the Christians of Rome that they too should think of helping the Jerusalem Christian community with alms (see 15:25).

Some MSS (D*, F, G) and some Latin versions read instead *mneiais,* "(contribute to the) memories," a clearly inferior reading.

practice hospitality. Lit., "pursue love of strangers." Cf. 1 Tim 3:2; 5:10; Titus 1:8; Heb 13:2; 1 Pet 4:9. This widespread recommendation was important for early Christians who traveled, as it would be in view of Paul's plans to visit the Roman community. It would be a special mark of their unity and harmony.

14. *Bless those who persecute you.* I.e., those who cause you trouble, sense you as a threat to themselves, or see you as a danger. This counsel echoes Jesus' words in Matt 5:44–47 and Luke 6:27–28, but the wording is not the same. The transition to the love of one's enemies may have been occasioned by the use of *diōkein,* "pursue," at the end of v 13, as that verb can also mean "persecute." But see Stuhlmacher, "Jesustradition"; Allison, "Pauline Epistles."

Although the text is broken, Abraham may be depicted praying for Pharoah the "persecutor" in 1QapGen 20:28.

Some important MSS (P⁴⁶, B, 1739) omit the obj. *hymas,* "you," thus making the sense more general, "Bless (all) persecutors." The object may have been added by copyists, seeking to conform Paul's counsel to the saying of Jesus; see *TCGNT,* 528. There is no reason to think that Paul is aware of any official persecution of Christians in Rome at this time. If *hymas* is omitted, it would be possible to translate, "Bless those who practice (it, viz., hospitality, mentioned at the end of v 13)." While possible, it is hardly likely, because of the following sentence.

bless and do not curse them. The impv. *eulogeite* is repeated in most MSS, but omitted in MSS P⁴⁶ and Ψᶜ, and in Bohairic versions. The sense is not affected by the omission. Paul thus recommends that Christians of Rome go against their natural inclination in the treatment of those who oppose them. They are not to curse, but to call down God's blessings on such persecutors.

15. *Rejoice with those who are rejoicing; mourn with those who are mourning.* Paul recommends that Christians share in one another's triumphs, joys, and successes, but also in their sorrows, troubles, and losses. Cf. Sir 7:34: "Do not avoid those who weep, but mourn with those who mourn." See Phil 2:18. Paul uses infins. *chairein* and *klaiein* as imperatives (BDF §389). Assonance also marks his formulation (§488.3).

Since John Chrysostom (*In ep. ad Romanos* hom. 22.1 [PG 60.610]), commentators have noted that it is easier to "sympathize" with those who mourn than to "congratulate" those who succeed and rejoice over their success, because the latter usually excites envy and jealousy. For that reason Paul puts rejoicing in the first place. Cf. Lagrange, *Romains,* 306.

16. *Think in harmony with one another.* Lit., "thinking the same thing toward

each other," i.e., having the same regard for one another. Paul uses a ptc., *phronountes*, which agrees with the subject of the impv. *eulogeite* in v 14. In fact, there is a series of ptcs. in the following verses that continue this construction; all of them have to be translated as impvs. (*apodidontes*, v 17; *pronooumenoi*, v 17; *eirēneuontes*, v 18; *ekdikountes*, v 19 [which may instead modify the vb. *dote* in the same verse]). In any case, Paul recommends mutual esteem for the concord of the community, but also a warning against any false self-esteem. See 15:5; 2 Cor 13:11; Phil 2:2; 4:2.

Put aside haughty thoughts. Lit., "lofty thoughts," which might mean ambition, but more likely connotes pride, which can be detrimental to community life. See 11:20; cf. 1 Tim 6:17.

associate with the lowly. I.e., "lowly people," the Greek *tapeinois* being understood as masc., as Lagrange (*Romains*, 306–7) prefers and as Leivestad ("*Tapeinos*," 45–46) insists. But in view of the preceding neut. *ta hypsēla* (not to set one's mind on lofty things), it could mean, "give yourselves to lowly tasks" (neut.), as Sanday and Headlam prefer (*Romans*, 364). In either case, it would be a recommendation to counteract pride. Bury ("Romans xii.16") would read, instead of *synapagomenoi*, "associating," the ptc. *synypagomenoi*, "subjecting yourselves," i.e., "sharing the subjection (or lowly estate) of the humble." Does this admonition suggest that Paul considers the Roman Christians to be of the upper class? To say yes would be to draw a conclusion from slim evidence.

Do not become wise in your own estimation. See 11:25. Paul's counsel against conceit may echo Prov 3:7, *mē isthi phronimos para seautō*, "Do not be wise in your own eyes." Cf. Isa 5:21. "The one who is wise in his own estimation is foolish in arrogance; the one who cherishes his own foolishness as wisdom cannot know the real wisdom of God" (Origen, *In ep. ad Romanos* 9.18 [PG 14.1222]).

17. *Repay no one evil for evil.* Paul's counsel of no retribution may echo the words of Jesus used in Matt 5:38–39, 43–44 and Luke 6:29, 35. See 1 Thess 5:15; 1 Cor 13:5–6; 1 Pet 3:9; cf. Prov 20:22; 24:29; Exod 23:4–5.

take thought for what is noble in the sight of all human beings. This counsel echoes Prov 3:4, *pronoou kala enōpion kyriou kai anthrōpōn*, "take thought for what is noble in the sight of the Lord and of human beings." See 2 Cor 8:21, where the text of Proverbs is echoed even more closely. That form of the text has affected the textual transmission of this verse in some MSS, which add *enōpion tou theou kai*, "in the sight of God and. . . ." See TCGNT, 528. The problem is, What are *kala*, "noble things" in the sight of all human beings? Paul widens his vision; he is not merely thinking of what is noble in the sight of Christians alone. It could refer to "good relations" with all people, Christians or otherwise. In the next paragraph Paul introduces civil authorities; they, then, may already be included in his use of "all." Cranfield (*Romans*, 646) rejects the idea that Paul is referring to a *sensus communis*, and identifies the *kala* with the gospel. But that is to introduce something that seems foreign to the vision of "all human beings." Paul would have mentioned the gospel explicitly if that were what he meant;

rather, in this sort of exhortation he is indulging in generalities that "all human beings" can recognize. Cf. Luke 6:27c. See Rossano, "L'ideale del Bello."

18. *If it possibly lies in your power.* Lit., "if the possible is what is from you." *live at peace with everyone.* Lit., "being peaceful with all human beings." On the ptc., see the NOTE on 12:9b. See Heb 12:14a. Some commentators would see an echo here of the Jesus tradition in Mark 9:50c.

19. *Take no revenge.* See Lev 19:18, which Paul implicitly quotes. Desire for revenge against outside enemies and the pursuit of it are excluded from the Christian purview. The right to avenge oneself is not part of the conquest of evil, despite any first impression. Charity must reign in everything.

dear friends. Lit., "beloved," a mode of address that echoes the greeting in 1:7 (see the NOTE there).

but leave room for God's wrath. Lit., "give scope to wrath." Paul uses *orgē* alone, even though he means "God's (eschatological) wrath" (see Introduction, section IX.A). Cf. 1 Thess 2:16. This meaning was used by Origen, who proposed it along with another: leave room for the wrath of an angry person (*In ep. ad Romanos* 9.22 [PG 14.1224]). John Chrysostom understood it of God's wrath (*In ep. ad Romanos* hom. 22.2 [PG 60.611]). For the idiom "leave space," see Eph 4:27; Sir 4:5; 13:22; 19:17; 38:12.

for it stands written. See the NOTE on 1:17.

"Vengeance is mine; I will repay," says the Lord. Paul quotes Deut 32:35 in a form closer to the MT (*lî nāqām wĕšillēm, lĕʿēt tāmûṭ raglām*, "vengeance is mine, and recompense, at the time when their foot slips"). But the LXX reads *en hēmera ekdikēseōs antapodōsō, en kairō, hotan sphalē ho pous autōn*, "on the day of revenge I shall repay, at the time when their foot slips." Cf. Heb 10:30, where Deut 32:35 is also quoted, exactly as Paul cites it. Both Paul and Hebrews take the first clause from the Hebrew and use the vb. *apodōsō* from the LXX. *Pace* Ellis, Paul does not modify "the Hebrew with the Targum" ("A Note," 131). The later targum is simply following the LXX tradition. The quotation of the OT makes certain the avenging application of God's wrath. Hence the Christian should leave to God the retribution of evil and pursue only good. See 2 Thess 1:6–8.

20. *if your enemy is hungry, feed him; if he is thirsty, give him something to drink. In doing so, you will heap coals of fire upon his head.* Paul cites Prov 25:21– 22a according to the LXX, MS B, which reads *psōmize*, "feed," instead of *trephe*, the reading in other LXX MSS (Did *psōmize* get into MS B of the LXX from this verse of Romans?) Paul thus makes the recommendation of Proverbs his own. Some commentators hear an echo of the Jesus tradition here (Luke 6:27a + 35; Matt 5:44a).

The meaning of Prov 25:22a, however, is quite obscure. The MT reads *kî gehālîm ʾattāh hōteh ʿal-rōʾšô.*

(1) T. K. Cheyne, Dahood ("Two Pauline Quotations"), and Ramaroson ("'Charbons ardents'") understand the prep. *ʿal* to mean "from" instead of

"upon," as it can in Ugaritic. Moreover, the ptc. *ḥōteh* means "remove" (see *HALAT*, 349: "wegnehmen"); hence, "remove coals from his head." This meaning might suit the Hebrew text of the MT, but the LXX and Paul's text clearly read *sōreuseis epi*, "heap upon" (BAGD, 800; B-A, 1595; LSJ, 1750). Hence the Greek text of 25:22a cannot tolerate such a meaning. Various explanations have been proposed for the Greek form of the verse.

(2) Origen (*In ep. ad Romanos* 9.23 [PG 14.1225]), Pelagius, Ambrosiaster (*In ep. ad Romanos* 12.20 [CSEL 81.416–17]), Augustine (*Expositio quarundam propositionum ex ep. ad Romanos* 63.3–4 [CSEL 84.44]; *De doctrina christiana* 3.56 [CSEL 80.94]), Jerome (*Ep.* 120.1 [CSEL 55.475–76]), and many who follow them (e.g., Käsemann, *Commentary*, 349) have understood the coals as a symbol of burning pangs of shame. The enemy would be moved by kindness to shame, remorse, and humiliation, which would burn like coals of fire upon his head. But such a symbolic use of burning coals is otherwise unattested, except perhaps in the fifth-century *Tg. Prov* 25:21–22: "If your enemy is famished, give him bread to eat; if he is thirsty, give him water to drink, for you will bring coals of fire upon his head, and God will deliver him to you."

(3) Morenz ("Feurige Kohlen") calls attention to a third-century Demotic text describing an Egyptian ritual in which a penitent carries on his head a dish of burning charcoal as an expression of repentance for offenses committed. Hence kindness to an enemy would make him express his repentance in this way before God. See Klassen, "Coals of Fire," for a nuanced use of Morenz's explanation.

(4) Some Greek patristic writers (e.g., Chrysostom, *In ep. ad Romanos* hom. 22.3 [PG 60.612]; Theophylact, *Expositio ep. ad Romanos* 12.20 [PG 124.512]) understood the coals to be a symbol of a more noble type of revenge: if one feeds an enemy and he remains hostile, one makes him liable to more serious punishment from God, i.e., one heaps coals of divine punishment on his head. But again, such a symbolic use is not otherwise attested, unless this is the sense meant by 4 Ezra 16:54: *Non dicat peccator non se peccasse, quoniam carbones ignis conburet super caput eius qui dicit: Non peccavi coram Deo et gloria ipsius*, "Let not the sinner say that he has not sinned, for (God) will burn coals of fire upon the head of him who says, 'I have not sinned before God and his glory.' " Cf. Ps 140:11.

(5) Stendahl ("Hate") modifies interpretation (4) by comparing Paul's general principle with statements in QL advocating the nonretaliation against evil done by enemies and the deferring of retribution to God's day of vengeance, a covert way of expressing one's "hatred" for one's enemies (see 1QS 10:17–20; 9:21–22; 1:9–11). Paul's use of Deuteronomy 32 and Proverbs 25 would, then, be a qualified way of adding to the measure of an enemy's sins and guilt in God's sight.

Whatever be the real meaning of this mysterious verse, it is clear that Paul is recommending not Stoic passive resistance to hostility, but instead the OT treatment of an enemy in order to overcome evil with positive charitable action, as the next verse suggests. Cf. 2 Kgs 6:22.

21. *Do not be overcome by evil, but overcome evil with good.* The Christian's victory over evil consists in refusing to promote evil by returning evil for evil and to become like the evil person who injures, and in accepting injury without resentment and without allowing love to be turned into hate or even weakened (Cranfield, *Romans,* 650). Cf. *T. Benj.* 4:3.

Verse 21 sums up vv 14–21, the victory of justified Christians over evil enemies, in that they have learned to live as Christians and not succumb to evildoing. Although Paul uses *kakon* and *agathon* here, there may be a sort of *inclusio* with v 9, where *ponēron* and *agathon* occur. In any case, v 21 sums up vv 9–21 as well.

BIBLIOGRAPHY

Allison, D. C., Jr., "The Pauline Epistles and the Synoptic Gospels: The Pattern of the Parallels," *NTS* 28 (1982): 1–32.

Ashe, R. P., "Romans xii.13,14," *ExpTim* 39 (1927–28): 46.

Barrett, C. K., "The Imperatival Participle," *ExpTim* 59 (1947–48): 165–66.

Bartina, S., "Carbones encendidos, ¿sobre la cabeza o sobre el veneno? (Prov 25, 21–22; Rom 12, 20)," *EstBíb* 31 (1972): 201–3.

Black, D. A., "The Pauline Love Command: Structure, Style, and Ethics in Romans 12:9–21," *FilNeot* 2 (1989): 3–22.

Bury, R. G., "Romans xii.16; I Corinthians xiii.7," *ExpTim* 49 (1937–38): 430.

Campbell, J. Y., "*Koinōnia* and Its Cognates in the New Testament," *JBL* 51 (1932): 352–80.

Cheyne, T. K., *Jewish Religious Life after the Exile* (New York: Putnam, 1898), 142.

———, "The Rendering of Romans xii. 16," *Expos* 2.6 (1883): 469–72.

Dahood, M. J., "Two Pauline Quotations from the Old Testament," *CBQ* 17 (1955): 19–24.

Daube, D., "Jewish Missionary Maxims in Paul," *ST* 1 (1947): 158–69; repr. in *The New Testament and Rabbinic Judaism* (London: Athlone, 1956), 336–51.

———, "Participle and Imperative in I Peter," in E. G. Selwyn, *The First Epistle of St. Peter,* 2d ed. (London: Macmillan, 1947), 467–88.

De Kruijf, T. C., "The Literary Unity of Rom 12,16–13,8a: A Network of Inclusions," *Bijdragen* 48 (1987): 319–26.

Dunn, J. D. G., "Paul's Knowledge of the Jesus Tradition: The Evidence of Romans," *Christus Bezeugen: Für Wolfgang Trilling,* ed. K. Kertelge et al., Erfurter theologische Studien 59 (Leipzig: St. Benno-Verlag; Freiburg im Breisgau: Herder, 1990), 193–207.

Eller, V., "Romans 13 (Actually Romans 12:14–13:8) Reexamined," *TSF Bulletin* (Madison, Wisc.) 10.3 (1987): 7–10.

Ellis, E. E., "A Note on Pauline Hermeneutics," *NTS* 2 (1955–56): 127–33.

Furnish, V. P., *Love Command,* 102–8.

Jewett, R., *Christian Tolerance,* 92–114.

ROMANS

Kanjuparambil, P., "Imperatival Participles in Rom 12:9–21," *JBL* 102 (1983): 285–88.

Klassen, W., "Coals of Fire: Sign of Repentance or Revenge?" *NTS* 9 (1962–63): 337–50.

Légasse, S., "Vengeance humaine et vengeance divine en Romains 12,14–21," *La Vie de la parole: De l'Ancien au Nouveau Testament: Études d'exégèse et d'herméneutique bibliques offertes à Pierre Grelot* . . . (Paris: Desclée, 1987), 281–91.

Leivestad, R., "*Tapeinos—Tapeinophrōn*," *NovT* 8 (1966): 36–47.

Linder, J. R., "Gedanken und Bemerkungen zu einigen Stellen des Neuen Testaments," *TSK* 35.2 (1862): 553–76, esp. 568–69 (on Rom 12:20).

Meecham, H. G., "The Use of the Participle for the Imperative in the New Testament," *ExpTim* 58 (1946–47): 207–8.

Morenz, S., "Feurige Kohlen auf dem Haupt," *TLZ* 78 (1953): 187–92.

Nestle, E., "A Parallel to Rom. xii. 11," *ExpTim* 10 (1898–99): 284.

Neirynck, F., "Paul and the Sayings of Jesus," *L'Apôtre Paul: Personnalité, style et conception du ministère*, BETL 73, ed. A. Vanhoye (Louvain: Leuven University, 1986), 265–321, esp. 295–303.

Ogara, F., " 'Noli vinci a malo, sed vince in bono malum' " *VD* 19 (1939): 11–17.

Ramaroson, L., " 'Charbons ardents': 'sur la tête' or 'pour la feu'? (Pr 25,22a—Rm 12,20b)," *Bib* 51 (1970): 230–34.

Ratschow, C. H., "Agape: Nächstenliebe und Bruderliebe," *ZST* 21 (1950–52): 160–82.

Roberton, S., "A Note on Romans xii. 21: *mē nikō hypo tou kakou*," *ExpTim* 60 (1948–49): 322.

Rossano, P., "L'ideale del Bello *(kalos)* nell'etica di S. Paolo," *SPCIC* 2.373–82.

Ruffenach, F., "Prunas congregabis super caput eius (Prov. 25, 22)," *VD* 6 (1926): 210–13.

Salom, A. P., "The Imperatival Use of the Participle in the New Testament," *AusBR* 11 (1963): 41–49.

Sauer, J., "Traditionsgeschichtliche Erwägungen zu den synoptischen und paulinischen Aussagen über Feindesliebe und Wiedervergeltungsverzicht," *ZNW* 76 (1985): 1–28.

Schnabel, E. J., *Law and Wisdom*, 299–342.

Seesemann, H., *Der Begriff koinōnia im Neuen Testament*, BZNW 14 (Giessen: Töpelmann, 1933).

Segert, S., " 'Live Coals Heaped on the Head,' " *Love & Death in the Ancient Near East: Essays in Honor of Marvin H. Pope*, ed. J. H. Marks and R. M. Good (Guilford, Conn.: Four Quarters, 1987), 159–64.

Škrinjar, A., " 'Carbones ignis congeres super caput eius' (Rom. 12,20; cf. Prov. 25,22)," *VD* 18 (1938): 143–50.

Smothers, E. R., "Give Place to the Wrath (Rom. 12:19): An Essay in Verbal Exegesis," *CBQ* 6 (1944): 205–15.

660

Spicq, C., "La Charité, volonté et réalisation de bien à l'égard du prochain (Rm 12,16–21)," *AsSeign* 17 (1962): 21–28.

Steinmetz, F.-J., " 'Weinen mit den Weinenden': Auslegung und Meditation von Lk 6,25; 1 Kor 7,30; Röm 12,15," *GLeb* 42 (1969): 391–94, esp. 393–94.

Stendahl, K., "Hate, Non-Retaliation, and Love: 1 QS x, 17–20 and Rom. 12:19–21," *HTR* 55 (1962): 343–55; repr. in *Meanings: The Bible as Document and as Guide* (Philadelphia, Penn.: Fortress, 1984), 137–49.

Stott, J. R. W., "Christian Responses to Good and Evil: A Study of Romans 12:9–13:10," *Perspectives on Peacemaking: Biblical Options in the Nuclear Age*, ed. J. A. Bernbaum (Ventura, Calif.: Regal, 1984), 43–56.

Stuhlmacher, P., "Jesustradition im Römerbrief? Eine Skizze," *TBei* 14 (1983): 140–50.

Synofzik, E., *Die Gerichts- und Vergeltungsaussagen*, 48–49.

Talbert, C. H., "Tradition and Redaction in Romans xii. 9–21," *NTS* 16 (1969–70): 83–94.

Vattioni, F., "Rom. 12,20 e Prov. 25,21–22," *SPCIC*, 1.341–45.

Walter, N., "Paulus und die urchristliche Jesustradition," *NTS* 31 (1985): 498–522, esp. 501–3.

Wenham, D., "Paul's Use of the Jesus Tradition: Three Samples," *The Jesus Tradition Outside the Gospels*, Gospel Perspectives 5, ed. D. Wenham (Sheffield, UK: JSOT, 1985), 7–37.

Wilson, W. T., *Love Without Pretense; Romans 12.9–21 and Hellenistic-Jewish Wisdom Literature*, WUNT 2.46 (Tübingen: Mohr [Siebeck], 1991).

Yonge, J. E., "Heaping Coals of Fire on the Head (Rom. xii. 20)," *Expos* 3.2 (1885): 158–59.

Zyro, [F. Fr.], "Röm. 12, 19: *dote topon tē orgē*," *TSK* 18.2 (1845): 887–92.

46. THE RELATION OF CHRISTIANS TO CIVIL AUTHORITIES (13:1–7)

13 ¹Let every person be subject to the governing authorities, for there is no authority except from God, and those which exist have been set up by God. ²Consequently, anyone who resists authority opposes what God has instituted; such opponents will bring judgment on themselves. ³For rulers are not a terror to good conduct, only to evil. Would you be free from fear of the bearer of authority? Then do what is right, and you will gain his approval. ⁴For he is God's servant working for your good. But if you do wrong, then be afraid, for he does not carry the sword for nothing. He is God's servant, an avenger, bringing wrath upon the wrongdoer. ⁵Therefore, one must be subject, not only because of such wrath, but also because of one's conscience. ⁶For this reason you also pay taxes. Authorities are God's servants, persistently devoted to this very task. ⁷Pay all of them their

due—taxes to whom taxes are due, revenue to whom revenue is due, respect to whom respect is due, and honor to whom honor is due.

COMMENT

Paul continues his exhortation addressed to the Christians of the capital of the Roman Empire with a specific instruction that must answer questions that they have had in their lives as Christians, viz., in their relation to those who govern them as civil authorities in this world. This admonition, then, represents a specific instance of what he has been talking about thus far in this hortatory section of Romans.

Although this passage of Romans is often spoken of as that in which Paul discusses the relation of Christians to the "state," there is no mention in it of the "state." Such a view of this passage reflects a modern problem that especially came to the fore in the period of Hitler and Mussolini and after the Second World War. Nor is there mention of "Rome," the important and pervasive civil authority in the world at the time in which Paul lived and wrote. We know so little of the relations of early Christians to the civil and political authorities of that time.

It may be that Paul takes up this issue, which he has not discussed in any of his other letters, because he is writing to the Christians of Rome, the capital of the empire of the time. Such a community more than others would have been conscious of imperial authority; so Käsemann, *Commentary*, 350. The Zealots had not yet emerged in Palestinian Jewish history; they can be traced only to about A.D. 66, a short time before the revolt of Palestinian Jews against Roman occupation and the eventual destruction of Jerusalem by the Romans. Diaspora Jews or Jewish Christians in Rome or elsewhere may not have shared their specific rebellious attitude against Rome. But there is no reason to think that Romans Jews would not have been affected by attitudes of Palestinian Jews; and one would have to say the same about Jewish Christians in Rome.

Up to the time that Paul wrote there had been no official persecution of Christians in Rome. Emperor Claudius (41–54) expelled Jews (undoubtedly also Jewish Christians) from Rome about A.D. 49. But the reason for that expulsion was local (see Introduction, section I); it did not reflect something common to Jews all over the Roman Empire, much less Jewish Christians outside of Rome. Yet as he wrote from Corinth (in the winter of 57–58), Paul seems to have learned something about the situation of Christians at Rome, a situation that probably grew out of that expulsion by Claudius (see 14:1–15:13). Moreover, Paul may have been aware of the reaction of people in the empire to the conduct of the *publicani* and the general tax-situation under Nero (see Introduction, section I). So he may have been moved to say something about the general background of such problems as faced the Christians of Rome. Because the basic attitude of Jews about the imperial government could have had repercussions among early Christians of either Jewish or Gentile background, he could be writing with such a situation in mind. In the eastern Mediterranean area especially, where the cult of the emperor was popular, there would also have been understandable Christian reactions to such a cult (to judge from later times). See further Bammel, "Romans 13." For such reasons Paul formulates in this passage his basic ideas about the relation of Christians to governing authorities.

Moreover, the reason Paul includes such a discussion in the hortatory section of Romans may be his desire to stress that Christians, now made "free" through the Christ-event and given the right of a heavenly citizenship (Phil 3:20, "our *politeuma* [commonwealth] is in heaven"), may not view their relation to earthly authorities with indifference, much less hostility. Though they live in the new aeon as a result of their justification through faith in Christ Jesus, they are still part of this aeon with its laws and order. In the new aeon Christ is Lord, who has granted "freedom" to Christians, but this freedom is neither license nor a right to civil anarchy. The reason is that civil authority itself comes from God, whom Christians are called to reverence and respect.

It is remarkable that Paul can discuss this topic in the absence of any christological consideration. Nor is there anything about faith in this passage, nor anything peculiarly rabbinic about Paul's mode of argument here. Käsemann (*Commentary*, 351) also finds it lacking in any eschatological motivation. Yet the mention of "wrath" (13:4–5) and of "judgment" (13:2b) surely evokes some eschatological consideration. Although there are some principles that Paul derives from the OT, the mention of "conscience" (13:5) reveals that Paul's discussion of this topic is more rational and philosophical than theological, as he gives a theistic interpretation of the relationship of citizens to the governing authorities. For he views civil authority as coming from God, without any Christian or Jewish nuance. It is not specifically the God of Israel or the Father of our Lord Jesus Christ who provides the basis of Paul's argument. It is simply "God." And it is something that he seems to address to all human beings, not just Christians, for in v 1 he speaks of "every person." Indeed, as Strobel has shown, Paul's terminology in the passage shows his acquaintance with Roman administration and constitutional law ("Zum Verständnis," 90). His peculiar emphasis is to relate it all to God.

The passage emphasizes order, authority, civil obedience, payment of taxes or revenue, and honor for civil authorities, regarded as "God's servants" (13:6). Even though Paul does argue philosophically about the relation of Christians to civil authorities, his teaching still has to be understood against the background of that about the lordship of the risen Christ (10:9; cf. 1 Cor 12:3), and especially about what he says in 1 Cor 8:6: "Though there are so-called gods in heaven or on earth, as there are many gods and many lords, yet for us there is one God, the Father, from whom are all things and for whom we exist, and one Lord, Jesus Christ, through whom are all things and through whom we exist."

Because of the lack of a christological emphasis or motivation and because of its rational and philosophical thrust, some interpreters have even raised the question whether this pericope is an interpolation; thus Barnikol ("Römer 13"), Eggenberger (*Die Quellen*), Kallas, ("Romans xiii. 1–7"), Munro ("Romans 13:1–7"), O'Neill (*Romans*, 15), Pallis (*To the Romans*, 14), and Schmithals (*Römerbrief als historisches Problem*, 185–97). Such interpreters argue for this view from the lack of a connection between the topic and the context of Romans (compare 12:21 and 13:8), from the differing nuances of some of the vocabulary, from the "subjection material" that it contains (allegedly of later date in the first Christian century), etc. The paragraph sounds much more like what one finds in 1 Pet 2:13–17 (cf. Titus 3:1). Yet, even if one admits with Käsemann (*Commentary*, 352) that it reads like "an alien body in Paul's exhortation," there is really no evidence to think that this passage has been interpolated or that it was not composed by Paul, even for this spot in the hortatory section of Romans, as Wilckens notes ("Römer 13,1–7," 215–16). By the end of the second century it is quoted by Irenaeus (*Adversus haereses* 5.24.1), and none of the Greek MSS of Romans lacks it. Moreover, de Kruijf has shown that structurally it is built by *inclusiones* into connection with chap. 12. The passage suits the context as an extension of the Pauline admonition to "live at peace with everyone" (12:18)— now including even "governing authorities." See further K. Aland, *Neutestamentliche Entwürfe*, 41. Again, if Borg is right, 13:1–7 continues the thought of 12:14–21 and is intended as a statement with particular meaning to the Roman church in its particular situation. "Why does Paul urge the Roman church to submit to Roman authority?" Because he "is convinced that what Christ does is to span the chasm between Jew and Gentile, a conviction that he expresses not only in Romans (i. 16, iii. 23–4, 29–30), but elsewhere as well" (Gal 3:28; cf. Eph 2:11–21). When Paul wrote Romans, "Judaism was on the brink of catastrophe as a result of its longstanding resistance to Roman imperialism. An emerging Christianity, founded by a Jew whom the Romans had crucified—regarded still by Rome as a Jewish sect, and inextricably implicated, by history and culture, by ideology and associational patterns, in the Jewish world—was inevitably caught up in the crisis of Jewish-Roman relations. What was the right posture to adopt toward Rome?" Paul answers that question in this paragraph ("New Context," 214–18). For a further literary analysis of the passage and its relevance to the rest of Paul's writing, see Wilckens, "Römer 13,1–7," 211–13.

Paul's discussion of the relation of Christians to civil authorities, nevertheless, remains on the level of general principles. Some commentators query whether the composition is dependent on Mark 12:13–17, the pronouncement story about rendering to Caesar the things that are Caesar's. That that story may have been current in early Christian tradition by the time Paul writes Romans can be admitted, but there is no real indication that Paul was aware of it or that it has any bearing on this passage. See Goppelt, "Die Freiheit," 217. Moreover, the composition of the Marcan Gospel is usually set about 65 at the earliest. Surely Paul would not have known that Gospel as we have it today.

The passage has created a major problem in modern theological discussion because Paul's teaching has at times been invoked to justify any sort of human government. The supposition running through vv 1–7 is that the civil authorities are good and are conducting themselves rightly in seeking the interests of the political community. Paul does not envisage the possibility of either a totalitarian or a tyrannical government or one failing to cope with the just rights of individual citizens or of a minority group. He insists merely on one aspect of the question: the duty of subjects to duly constituted and legitimate authority. He does not discuss the duty or responsibility of civil authorities to the people governed, apart from one minor reference (13:4). Moreover, the concept of legitimate civil disobedience is beyond his ken. Paul is not discussing in exhaustive fashion the relation of Christians to governing authorities; "he is silent about possible conflicts and the limits of earthly authority" (Käsemann, *Commentary*, 354).

Paul must certainly have known of the role of Pontius Pilate in the death of Jesus, hence of the connivance of a Roman governor who handed him over to be crucified. Yet that knowledge of Pilate's involvement did not deter him from recognizing the legitimate role that Pilate had as a civil authority. Through Pilate Jesus suffered the effects of wrath in this world; and through persecuting Roman emperors early Christians would also suffer such effects. They would be part of "the sufferings that we now endure" (8:18).

Again, we know little about how Paul personally got along with Roman governors or officials. His experience before Gallio (Acts 18:12–17) would not have left a bad taste in his mouth; cf. also Acts 16:19–40; 22:22–29; 25:6–12.

What Paul teaches in this passage has to be understood against the background of the OT itself, in which Israel was instructed, especially in the time of the exile, to respect governing authorities, even to pray for them: Jer 29:7 ("Seek the welfare of the city to which I have exiled you and pray to the Lord on behalf of it, for in its welfare will be your welfare"); Bar 1:11 ("Pray for the life of Nebuchadnezzar king of Babylon"); 1 Macc 7:33. Cf. *Ep. Arist.* 45; Josephus, *J.W.* 2.10.4 §197; *Ag. Ap.* 2.6 §§76–77.

NOTES

13:1. *every person.* Lit., "every soul," a Hebraism (see the NOTE on 2:9), which stresses the obligation of every individual. Paul's instruction is not restricted to Christians. In some MSS (P⁴⁶, D*, F, G) and in the VL version, "soul" is omitted, and there is the simple impv., "be subject to all higher authorities." This omission even broadens Paul's counsel.

be subject. The vb. is *hypotassein*, "be subject," and not merely *hypakouein*, "obey." In other words, Paul recommends submission in earthly matters as an expression of the Christian's relation to God and his order of things. Compare Titus 3:1; 1 Pet 2:13–14. Such submission is clearly measured by the form of human government in which one resides; it would carry nuances depending on the form of monarchic, democratic, or republican state. It is important to keep

Paul's perspective in mind, for he does not lose sight of the Christian's "freedom" in Christ Jesus. Cf. Eph 5:21.

to the governing authorities. Lit., "to authorities having power over (you)," i.e., "highly placed, governing authorities" (BAGD, 841). The noun *exousia* denotes (1) "freedom of choice, right to act or dispose of"; (2) "ability, capability" to do something; (3) "authority, absolute power" (in the abstract); (4) "an authority" (in the concrete), "a bearer of authority." In the pl. it is commonly used for human "authorities" in profane Greek (Polybius, *History* 28.4.9; 30.4.17 [= "those in high position," not only the "higher ranks," but all with authority]) and in the NT (Luke 12:11; Titus 3:1). Paul is referring to duly constituted human governing authorities. What he calls "governing authorities" here he will call "rulers" *(archontes)* in v 3. These are the Greek equivalents of the Roman *imperia* and *magistratus,* "the numerous government offices of the comprehensive state-apparatus of the worldwide empire" (Strobel, "Zum Verständnis," 79).

In medieval and Renaissance times commentators were divided over whether Paul was referring solely to civil rulers. Cajetan, Seripando, Melanchthon, and Calvin understood the phrase to refer to civil magistrates, whereas Sadoleto and Luther understood it as "spiritual rulers" and "secular princes" (LW 25.469). Luther even thought that the secular princes were carrying out their duties more successfully and better than ecclesiastical rulers (LW 25.471). This distinction rarely surfaces in the modern discussion of the text.

However, Cullmann ("Zur neuesten Diskussion") has maintained that *exousiai* denotes the "invisible angelic powers that stand behind state government," or even with a double meaning, "the empirical state *and* the angelic powers." He compares 1 Cor 2:8; 15:24; 1 Pet 3:22; Col 1:16; 2:10, 15; Eph 1:21; 3:10; 6:12, where it seems from the context that *exousia* could have such a meaning. A form of this interpretation was proposed earlier, apparently first by Dibelius (*Geisterwelt*), but he later abandoned it ("Rom"). It was then used by Karl Barth (*Church and State*), Dehn ("Engel"), and Schmidt (*TBl* 13 [1934]: 328–34), before Cullmann made it popular.

Yet in 1 Pet 2:13 *basileus,* "emperor," and *hēgemones,* "governors," are clearly human, and in this context there is nothing that clearly calls for an angelic meaning of *exousia.* Indeed, the authorities to whom taxes are paid (v 6) have to be human authorities. Again, Paul would not say that Christians are to be subject to angels; in 1 Cor 6:3 he holds that Christians will "judge angels"; see further Morrison, *Powers,* 40–54. According to Käsemann (*Commentary,* 353), the vast majority of exegetes have rejected Cullmann's interpretation. "Human authorities" is preferred as the interpretation, because Paul is using the vocabulary of Hellenistic political administration: *tetagmenai,* "set up" (13:1), *diatagē,* "institution" (13:2); *archontes,* "rulers" (13:3); *leitourgoi,* "servants" (13:6) (see *TDNT* 8.29–30). Hence Paul is referring to ordinary human civil authorities, on whom Christians are dependent and to whom they are expected to subject themselves.

In the postapostolic period Clement of Rome prays for human "rulers and governors upon the earth" to whom God has given "power of sovereignty" (*1 Clem.* 60.2–61.2). Polycarp tells the proconsul of Asia, "We have been taught to give honor to magistrates and authorities appointed by God, as is fitting" (*Mart. Pol.* 10.2). These testimonies clearly continue in the same line of Paul's thinking.

there is no authority except from God. Lit., "except by God," because the better reading is the prep. *hypo* (expressing agency); but some MSS (D*, F, G) read *apo*, "from," a correction demanded by sense. As a Christian, Paul acknowledges the Father as the source of all the welfare, prosperity, and peace brought by human civil rule. He thus states the reason for such obedience. This is fundamentally an OT teaching (see 2 Sam 12:8; Prov 8:15–16; Jer 27:5–6; Isa 45:1; Dan 2:21, 37; 4:17; Sir 4:27; Wis 6:1–3). Josephus ascribes the same teaching to the Essenes: "for not apart from God does anyone rule" (*J.W.* 2.8.7 §140); cf. 1 Enoch 46:5. As Paul formulates it, however, it sounds like a philosophical truth.

those which exist have been set up by God. In the preceding clause Paul stated the reason for his position negatively; now he does so positively. Even Rome's imperial authority comes from God, though Rome may not recognize it or may be reluctant to admit it. Civil authorities may not all agree with God's will in the governance of the world, but their authority still comes from him. It is not an arbitrary creation or invention of human beings. Recall the prayer of early Christians in Acts 4:24–28.

2. *anyone who resists authority opposes what God has instituted.* Paul now reformulates his reason differently, applying it to individuals. A general principle is deduced from what has been enunciated in the last two statements. Submission to civil authorities is a form of obedience to God himself, for the relationship of humans to God is not limited to the religious or cultic sphere of life. Hence even Christians, "freed" by Christ Jesus from the powers of this world, cannot resist the political authority that comes ultimately from God, even if that authority is at the time in the hands of heathens.

Paul uses the expression *tē tou theou diatagē*, lit., "the institution of God." Since the time of Deissmann (*LAE*, 59), the second-century inscription (*CIG* 4300.6) has been cited as a parallel: *tōn theiōn dia[tag]ōn* (so Strobel, "Zum Verständnis," 86). But it has more correctly been read recently as *tōn theiōn dia[tagma]tōn*, a way of expressing "imperial constitutions." The technical Greco-Roman expressions are either *diataxis* or *diatagma* (= Latin *edictum*).

such opponents will bring judgment on themselves. Such judgment will be exercised eschatologically at least, by God himself, if not sooner, through the human authority set up. The noun *krima* is used in the sense of *katakrima*, "judgment against, condemnation" (see the NOTE on 2:2).

3. *rulers are not a terror to good conduct, only to evil.* Paul uses the pl. *hoi archontes* because he stresses the generic character of the political situation. Here *archontes* are clearly human "rulers," as in 1 Cor 2:6–8; *Ps. Sol.* 17:36; Josephus, *Ant.* 20.1.2 §11; and in the variant reading of Titus 1:9. Those who live in accord with the regulations of legitimate civil authority have no need to fear; those who

may have to fear are those who oppose such authority by rebellious conduct. See 1 Pet 3:13; cf. 1 Tim 1:8–9.

The best Greek MSS (P⁴⁶, ℵ, A, B, D*, F⁽ᶜ⁾, P) read *tō agathō ergō*, but MS F* reads *tō agathoergō*, "to the one doing good," which Lorimer (NTS 12 [1965–66]: 389–90) insists is the more original reading.

Would you be free from fear of the bearer of authority? Lit., "do you wish not to have to fear the bearer of authority?" i.e., the human being constituted in authority.

Then do what is right. I.e., in the eyes of the person in authority.

and you will gain his approval. Fear of civil authority comes only from opposition to it.

4. *he is God's servant working for your good.* This is a reformulation of v 1, stressing two things: (1) the delegated character of civil authority, its relation to God (*theou diakonos*); "The earthly ruler is *the servant of God in the aeon of wrath*" (Nygren, *Romans*, 429 [his emphasis]); and (2) the final cause of such an institution. It envisages only a civil government properly fulfilling its functions. The phrase *eis to agathon*, "for the good," expresses the goal or purpose of civil authority, the reason why it has been set up and exists in human society. This formulation comes close to acknowledging the idea of the "common good," the aim of every proper human government.

if you do wrong, then be afraid. Opposition to legitimately constituted civil authority can only result in fear, and rightly so. Paul is not speaking about what has been called in modern times "civil disobedience." Such a notion would be anachronistic here, legitimate though it may be in the case of an unjust government, or even of a government duly constituted that acts unjustly.

for he does not carry the sword for nothing. Paul introduces the sword as the symbol of penal authority, of the power legitimately possessed by a civil authority to coerce recalcitrant citizens to maintain order and strive for the common good by obeying the law of the society. It is also used by Paul as the symbol of divine wrath combating rebellious conduct. Cf. Philostratus, *Vitae Sophistarum* 1.25.3 (*dikastou xiphos echontos*, "of a judge having the sword"). The expression *machairan phorein*, "carry a sword," could be a symbol for capital punishment (*ius gladii*, "power of the sword"), which authorities could inflict, as Michel understands it (*Brief an die Römer*, 401–2), but it must be remembered that that was a limited authority possessed by Roman provincial governors over Roman citizens who were soldiers under their command (see A. N. Sherwin-White, *Roman Society and Roman Law in the New Testament* [Oxford: Clarendon, 1963], 8–11). Paul's statement seems to be of broader scope. Or it could be a reference to police, as *machairophoroi* denotes in Pap. Tebtunis 391.20; Pap. Michigan 577.7–8. Such sword bearers could also designate civil guards and those who enforce taxation. In any case, Paul's statement is echoed in many ancient writers, as van Unnik has shown ("Lob und Strafe," 336–38).

He is God's servant. Paul repeats the description used at the beginning of the verse.

an avenger, bringing wrath upon the wrongdoer. The bearer of civil authority is thus described as an instrument of God's *orgē* (see the NOTES on 1:18 and 12:19). The "wrongdoer" is the rebellious citizen, who is punished by a civil authority and whose punishment thus becomes an expression of divine wrath.

5. *Therefore, one must be subject, not only because of such wrath, but also because of one's conscience.* Lit., "wherefore (there is) a necessity to subject oneself." Some MSS (P⁴⁶, D, G) and the VL version omit *ananke* and read the infin. as impv. *hypotassesthe*, "subject yourselves." Another motivation for submission to civil authority is introduced: Paul realizes that fear of punishment or of divine (eschatological) wrath will not always deter citizens from violating civil regulations. His appeal to conscience, then, puts the matter on a moral basis, for the obligation to obey civil laws can be more than just civil or penal. Conscience also links human reaction to civil government with the divine origin of civil authority itself. On "conscience," see the NOTE on 2:15. Bultmann considered v 5 to be an "exegetical gloss" introduced between vv 4 and 6 ("Glossen," 281–82), but few commentators follow him in this view.

6. *For this reason you also pay taxes.* Paul takes it for granted that the Christians of Rome have been paying taxes; *teleite* is to be understood as an indic., not an impv. The noun *phoros* denotes the direct tributary payment, such as property tax or poll tax. See W. Rebell, *EWNT* 3.1044–45.

Authorities are God's servants. For the third time Paul stresses the delegated nature of civil authority (see 13:1, 4), now in the matter of taxes. The basis of the right to levy them is also that of civil authority itself. See 1 Pet 2:19. Paul calls the civil authorities *leitourgoi*, a term that is composed of *laos*, "people," and *ergein*, "work for," and designates a person who performs a public service for the state. In classical Greece it was often a service performed gratis by someone in public office, especially by finance ministers (see Strobel, "Zum Verständnis," 86–87). In this neutral sense it is also used in the LXX: Josh 1:1 (MS A); 2 Sam 13:18; 1 Kgs 10:5; Sir 10:2; and by Paul himself in Phil 2:25. In time, the word came to designate a "cultic minister," someone active in God's service: see Isa 61:6 (where *leitourgoi* stands in apposition to *hiereis*); Neh 10:40; cf. Rom 15:16; Heb 8:2. Paul will use this religious sense of the word to describe himself in 15:16 as a "cultic minister" (see the NOTE there). From this religious usage of the word and its cognates developed the term "liturgy."

persistently devoted to this very task. Thus Paul expresses one of the obligations of civil authority to citizens: they rightly impose and collect taxes, for this is the reason that they have been constituted in authority. For the vb. *proskarterein*, see Xenophon, *Hellenica* 7.5.14; Polybius, *History* 1.55.4. Although *eis auto touto* might seem to refer to all that has been mentioned in vv 3–4 (so Barrett, *Romans*, 247), it is preferably taken as referring to the collection of taxes. For that too pertains to God's designs.

7. *Pay all of them their due.* Paul enunciates the principle that governs his entire discussion in vv 1–7.

taxes to whom taxes are due, revenue to whom revenue is due. Thus Paul distinguishes various kinds of taxation. See the NOTE on *phoros* in v 6. Here Greek *telos* denotes indirect taxes, excise duty like tolls, sales tax, etc., as distinct from direct taxation. Recall the words of Jesus recorded in Mark 12:17 and parallels; see the COMMENT above.

respect to whom respect is due. Lit., "awe, reverence" (*phobos*, the same word that Paul used in v 3 in a more pejorative sense). Because civil authorities are placed in a higher rank in society, they command due recognition. "Respect" would denote a higher form of reverence than *timē*, "honor," in the next clause. Cf. Prov 24:21. See Strobel, "Furcht, wem Furcht gebührt."

honor to whom honor is due. Human society reckons with differences in the social and political order, and the Christian is called on to recognize such differences and respect them. So Paul formulates the problem of life in civil and political society for a Christian, who is otherwise in Christ Jesus. Recall Gal 3:28: "There is neither Jew nor Greek, neither slave nor free, neither male nor female; for you are all one in Christ Jesus." In other words, on the basis of faith and baptism, all justified human beings are "in Christ Jesus" without distinction, but in civil or political society it is another question. Paul calls on such baptized believers to respect and honor those who are leaders in civil and political society.

BIBLIOGRAPHY ON CHAPTER 13

Beatrice, P. F., "Il giudizio secondo le opere della legge e l'amore compimento della legge: Contributo all'esegesi di Rm 13,1–10," *StudPatav* 20 (1973): 491–545.

Brouwer, A. M., "Christen en overheid volgens Rom. 13:1–10," *NThStud* 23 (1940): 150–63.

Käsemann, E., "Principles of the Interpretation of Romans 13," *NTQT*, 196–216.

Kuss, O., "Paulus über die staatliche Gewalt," *TGl* 45 (1955): 321–34; repr. in *Auslegung und Verkündigung*, 3 vols. (Regensburg: Pustet, 1963–71), 1.246–59.

Lategan, B. C., "Reception: Theory and Practice in Reading Romans 13," *Text and Interpretation: New Approaches in the Criticism of the New Testament*, NTTS 15, ed. P. J. Hartin and J. H. Petzer (Leiden: Brill, 1991), 145–69.

Meinhold, P., *Caesar's or God's: The Conflict of Church and State in Modern Society* (Minneapolis, Minn.: Augsburg, 1962).

Molnar, A., "Romains 13 dans l'interprétation de la première, Réforme," *ETR* 46 (1971): 231–40.

Rhijn, C. H. van, "Rom. XIII en Openb. XIII: Over en naar aanleiding van een rectorale oratie," *ThStud* 25 (1907): 287–97.

Riekkinen, V., *Römer 13: Aufzeichnung und Weiterführung der exegetischen Diskussion*, Annales academiae scientiarum fennicae: Dissertationes humanarum litterarum 23 (Helsinki: Suomalainen Tiedeakatemia, 1980).

Riniker, H., "Römer 13 zwischen Militärjustiz und Theologiestudenten," *KRS* 127 (1971): 146–52.

Venetz, H.-J., "Zwischen Unterwerfung und Verweigerung: Widersprüchliches im Neuen Testament? Zu Röm 13 und Offb 13," *BK* 43 (1988): 153–63.

Wells, P., "Dieu créateur et politique," *RRef* 27 (1976): 30–44.

Rom 13:1–7

Abineno, J. L. C., "The State, According to Romans Thirteen," *South East Asia Journal of Theology* 14 (1972): 23–27.

Affeldt, W., *Die weltliche Gewalt in der Paulus-Exegese: Röm. 13,1–7 in den Römerbriefkommentaren der lateinischen Kirche bis zum Ende des 13. Jahrhunderts,* Forschungen zur Kirchen- und Dogmengeschichte 22 (Göttingen: Vandenhoeck & Ruprecht, 1969).

Aland, K., "Das Verhältnis von Kirche und Staat in der Frühzeit," *ANRW* 2.23.1 (1979), 60–246.

———, "Das Verhältnis von Kirche und Staat nach dem Neuen Testament und den Aussagen des 2. Jahrhunderts," *Neutestamentliche Entwürfe,* TB 63 (Munich: Kaiser, 1979), 26–123.

Asmussen, H., *Wiederum steht geschrieben!* (Munich: Kaiser, 1939).

Bammel, E., "Ein Beitrag zur paulinischen Staatsanschauung," *TLZ* 85 (1960): 837–40.

———, "Romans 13," *Jesus and the Politics of His Day,* ed. E. Bammel and C. F. D. Moule (Cambridge: Cambridge University Press, 1984), 365–83.

Barnadas, J. M., "L'Apoliticitat de Jesús i la del cristià (Jo xviii, 28–xix, 16 = Rom xiii, 1–7)," *EstFranc* 74 (1973): 61–73.

Barnikol, E., "Römer 13: Der nichtpaulinische Ursprung der absoluten Obrigkeitsbejahung von Römer 13,1–7," *Studien zum Neuen Testament und zur Patristik: Erich Klostermann . . . dargebracht,* TU 77 (Berlin: Akademie-Verlag, 1961), 65–133.

Barraclough, R., "Romans 13:1–7: Application in Context," *Colloquium* (Auckland/Sydney) 17 (1984–85): 16–22.

Barrett, C. K., "The New Testament Doctrine of Church and State," *New Testament Essays* (London: SPCK, 1972), 1–19.

Barth, K., *Church and State* (London: Macmillan, 1939).

Bauer, G., "Zur Auslegung und Anwendung von Römer 13, 1–7 bei Karl Barth," *Antwort: Karl Barth . . .* (Zollikon-Zurich: Evangelischer-Verlag, 1956), 114–23.

Bauer, W., " 'Jedermann sei untertan der Obrigkeit,' " *Walter Bauer: Aufsätze und kleine Schriften,* ed. G. Strecker (Tübingen: Mohr [Siebeck], 1967), 263–84.

Bergmeier, R., "Loyalität als Gegenstand paulinischer Paraklese: Eine religionsgeschichtliche Untersuchung zu Röm 13,1ff. und Jos. B.J. 2,140," *Theokratia: Jahrbuch des Institutum Judaicum Delitzschianum* 1 (1967–69) [appeared 1970]): 51–63.

Bieder, W., *Ekklesia und Polis im Neuen Testament und in der Alten Kirche* (Zurich: Zwingli-Verlag, 1941).

Bielecki, S., "Rz 13,1–7 w kontekście historii zbawienia (Röm 13,1–7 im Kontext der Heilsgeschichte)," *RTK* 34 (1987): 47–56.

Blank, J., "Kirche und Staat im Urchristentum," *Kirche und Staat auf Distanz: Historische und aktuelle Perspektiven*, ed. G. Denzler (Munich: Kösel, 1977), 9–28.

———, "Die Glaubensgemeinde im heidnischen Staat," *Schriftauslegung in Theorie und Praxis*, Biblische Handbibliothek 5 (Munich: Kösel, 1969), 174–86.

Bligh, J., "Demonic Powers," *HeyJ* 1 (1960): 314–23.

Böld, W., *Obrigkeit von Gott? Studien zum staatstheologischen Aspekt des Neuen Testaments* (Hamburg: Wittig, 1962).

Bolognesi, P., "La situazione del cristiano davanti all'autorità secondo Romani 13," *RBR* 17 (1982): 9–23.

Borg, M., "A New Context for Romans xiii," *NTS* 19 (1972–73): 205–18.

Bornhäuser, K., "Paulus und die obrigkeitlichen Gewalten in Rom," *Christentum und Wissenschaft* 7 (1931): 201–21.

Bornkamm, G., *Paul*, 210–16.

Boyer, S., "Exegesis of Romans 13:1–7," *Brethren Life and Thought* 32 (1987): 208–16.

Bring, R., "Der paulinische Hintergrund der lutherischen Lehre von den zwei Reichen oder Regimenten," *ST* 27 (1973): 107–26.

Bruce, F. F., "Paul and 'The Powers That Be,'" *BJRL* 66.2 (1983–84): 78–96.

Campenhausen, H. von, "Zur Auslegung von Röm. 13: Die dämonistische Deutung des *exousia*-Begriffs," *Festschrift Alfred Bertholet*, ed. W. Baumgartner et al. (Tübingen: Mohr [Siebeck], 1950), 97–113; repr. *Aus der Frühzeit des Christentums* (Tübingen: Mohr [Siebeck] 1963), 81–101.

Carr, W., *Angels and Principalities: The Background, Meaning and Development of the Pauline Phrase "hai archai kai hai exousiai,"* SNTSMS 42 (Cambridge: Cambridge University Press, 1981), 115–18.

Cranfield, C. E. B., "The Christian's Political Responsibility According to the New Testament," *SJT* 15 (1962): 176–92.

———, "Some Observations on Romans xiii. 1–7," *NTS* 6 (1959–60): 241–49.

Cullmann, O., *Christ and Time*, rev. ed. (Philadelphia, Penn.: Westminster, 1964), 191–210.

———, *The State in the New Testament* (New York: Scribners, 1956), 50–70, 93–114.

———, "Zur neuesten Diskussion über die *exousiai* in Röm. 13,1" *TZ* 10 (1954): 321–36; trans. in *The State*, 93–114.

Dehn, G., "Engel und Obrigkeit: Ein Beitrag zum Verständnis von Römer 13,1–7," *Theologische Aufsätze, Karl Barth . . .* (Munich: Kaiser, 1936), 90–109.

Delling, G., *Römer 13,1–7 innerhalb der Briefe des Neuen Testaments* (Berlin: Evangelische Verlagsanstalt, 1962).

Deniel, R., "Omnis potestas a Deo: L'Origine du pouvoir civil et sa relation à l'église," *RSR* 56 (1968): 43–85.

Dibelius, M., *Die Geisterwelt im Glauben des Paulus* (Göttingen: Vandenhoeck & Ruprecht, 1909).

———, "Rom und die Christen im ersten Jahrhundert," *Sitzungsberichte der Heidelberger Akademie der Wissenschaften*, Phil.-hist. Kl. 2 (1941–42); repr. in *Botschaft und Geschichte: Gesammelte Aufsätze*, 2 vols. (Tübingen: Mohr [Siebeck], 1953–56), 2.177–228.

[Dibelius, O.], *Violett-Buch zur Obrigkeitsschrift von Bischof Dibelius: Dokumente zur Frage der Obrigkeit*, 3d ed. (Frankfurt am Main: Stimme-Verlag, 1963).

Draper, J. A., " 'Humble Submission to Almighty God' and Its Biblical Foundation: Contextual Exegesis of Romans 13:1–7," *JTSA* 63 (1988): 30–38.

Duesberg, H., "La Soumission aux autorités: Romains 13,1–8," *BVC* 73 (1967): 15–26.

Dunn, J. D. G., "Romans 13:1–7—A Charter for Political Quietism?" *Ex auditu* 2 (1986): 55–68.

Dyck, H. J., "The Christian and the Authorities in Romans 13:1–7," *Direction* 14.1 (1985): 44–50.

Eck, O., *Urgemeinde und Imperium*, BFCT 42.3 (Gütersloh: Bertelsmann, 1940).

Eggenberger, C., "Der Sinn der Argumentation in Röm 13,2–5," *KRS* 100 (1944): 54–70, 118–30; 101 (1945): 243–44.

———, "Die Quellen der politischen Ethik des 1. Klemensbriefes," Ph.D. diss., Universität Zurich, 1951.

Ellul, J., "Petite Note complémentaire sur Romains 13,1," *Foi et vie* 89 (1990): 81–83.

Emslie, B. L., "The Methodology of Proceeding from Exegesis to an Ethical Decision," *Neotestamentica* 19 (1985): 87–91.

Fatum, L., "Paulus og den socialpolitiske konsekvens," *DTT* 39 (1976): 106–33.

Ferrando Palacio, M. A., *La sumisión del cristiano al poder civil según Rom. 13,1–7*, Anales de la Faculdad de Teología 20.3 (Santiago: Universidad Católica de Chile, 1969).

Friedrich, J., W. Pöhlmann, and P. Stuhlmacher, "Zur historischen Situation und Intention von Röm 13, 1–7," *ZTK* 73 (1976): 131–66.

Fuchs, E., "Romains 13:1–7," *BCPE* 29 (1977): 58–62.

Furnish, V. P., *Moral Teaching*, 115–39.

Gale, H. M., "Paul's View of the State: A Discussion of the Problem in Romans 13:1–7," *Int* 6 (1952): 409–14.

Garrett, J. L., Jr., "The Dialectic of Romans 13:1–7 and Revelation 13: Part One," *JChSt* 18 (1976): 433–42; "Part Two," 19 (1977): 5–20.

Gaugusch, L., "Die Staatslehre des Apostels Paulus nach Röm 13," *TGl* 26 (1934): 529–50.

Goldstein, H., "Die politischen Paränesen in 1 Petr 2 und Röm 13," *BibLeb* 14 (1973): 88–104.

Goppelt, L., "Die Freiheit zur Kaisersteuer: Zu Mk. 12,17 und Röm. 13,1–7," *Christologie und Ethik: Aufsätze zum Neuen Testament* (Göttingen: Vandenhoeck & Ruprecht, 1968), 208–19.

———, "Der Staat in der Sicht des Neuen Testaments," ibid., 190–207.

Grant, W. J., "Citizenship and Civil Obedience: Romans xiii," *ExpTim* 54 (1942–43): 180–81.

Grosheide, F. W., "Bijdrage tot de verklaring van Rom. 13:1–7," *GTT* 48 (1948): 135–49.

Hanson, A. T., *Wrath*, 93–96.

Heiligenthal, R., "Strategien konformer Ethik im Neuen Testament am Beispiel von Röm 13. 1–7," *NTS* 29 (1983): 55–61.

Héring, J., " 'Serviteurs de Dieu': Contributions à l'exégèse pratique de Romains 13:3–4," *RHPR* 30 (1950): 31–40.

Hultgren, A. J., "Reflections on Romans 13:1–7: Submission to Governing Authorities," *Dialog* 15 (1976): 263–69.

Hutchinson, S., "The Political Implications of Romans 13:1–7," *Biblical Theology* (Belfast) 21 (1971): 49–59.

Käsemann, E., "Römer 13,1–7 in unserer Generation," *ZTK* 56 (1959): 316–76.

———, "Principles of the Interpretation of Romans 13," *NTQT*, 196–216.

Kallas, J., "Romans xiii. 1–7: An Interpolation," *NTS* 11 (1964–65): 365–74.

Kittel, G., "Das Urteil des Neuen Testaments über den Staat," *ZST* 14 (1937): 651–80.

Koch-Mehrin, J., "Die Stellung des Christen zum Staat nach Röm. 13 und Apok. 13," *EvT* 7 (1947–48): 378–401.

Kosnetter, J., "Röm 13,1–7: Zeitbedingte Vorsichtsmassregel oder grundsätzliche Einstellung?" *SPCIC*, 1.347–55.

Krodel, G., "Church and State in the New Testament," *Dialog* 15 (1976): 21–28.

Kruijf, T. C. de, "The Literary Unity of Rom 12,16–13,8a: A Network of Inclusions," *Bijdragen* 48 (1987): 319–26.

Kuss, O., "Paulus über die staatliche Gewalt," *Auslegung und Verkündigung*, 3 vols. (Regensburg: Pustet, 1963–71), 1.246–59.

Laub, F., "Der Christ und die staatliche Gewalt—Zum Verständnis der 'politischen' Paränese Röm 13,1–7 in der gegenwärtigen Diskussion," *MTZ* 30 (1979): 257–65.

Lee, P., " 'Conscience' in Romans 13:5," *Faith and Mission* 8 (1990): 85–93.

Lorimer, W. L., "Romans xiii. 3," *NTS* 12 (1965–66): 389–90.

McDonald, J. I. H., "Romans 13. 1–7: A Test Case for New Testament Interpretation," *NTS* 35 (1989): 540–49.

———, "Romans 13:1–7 and Christian Social Ethics Today," *Modern Churchman* 29.2 (1987): 19–25.

Merk, O., *Handeln*, 161–64.

Merklein, H., "Sinn und Zweck von Röm 13, 1–7: Zur semantischen und pragmatischen Struktur eines umstrittenen Textes," *Neues Testament und Ethik: Für*

Rudolf Schnackenburg, ed. H. Merklein (Freiburg im Breisgau: Herder, 1989), 238–70.

Morgenthaler, R., "Roma—Sedes Satanae: Röm. 13,1ff. im Lichte von Luk. 4,5–8," *TZ* 12 (1956): 289–304.

Morrison, C., *The Powers That Be: Earthly Rulers and Demonic Powers in Romans 13.1–7*, SBT 29 (London: SCM; Naperville, Ill.: Allenson, 1960).

Mosetto, F., "A chi le tasse, le tasse (Rm 13,7)," *Parole di vita* 31 (1986): 275–82.

Moulder, J., "Romans 13 and Conscientious Disobedience," *JTSA* 21 (1977): 13–23.

Munro, W., *Authority in Paul and Peter*, SNTSMS 45 (Cambridge: Cambridge, University Press, 1983).

———, "Romans 13:1–7: Apartheid's Last Biblical Refuge," *BTB* 20 (1990): 161–68.

Neufeld, K. H., "Das Gewissen: Ein Deutungsversuch im Anschluss an Röm 13,1–7," *BibLeb* 12 (1971): 32–45.

Neugebauer, F., "Zur Auslegung von Röm. 13,1–7," *KD* 8 (1962): 151–72.

Nürnberger, K., "Theses on Romans 13," *Scriptura* 22 (1987): 40–47.

Ogle, A. B., "What Is Left for Caesar? A Look at Mark 12:13–17 and Romans 13:1–7," *TToday* 35 (1978–19): 154–64.

Picca, J. V., *Romanos 13, 1–7 un texto discutido: Prolegómenos para su interpretación*, Biblioteca di scienze religiose 34 (Rome: Libreria Ateneo Salesiano, 1981).

Pierce, C. A., *Conscience*, 66–74.

Pohle, L., *Die Christen und der Staat nach Römer 13: Eine typologische Untersuchung der neueren deutschsprächigen Schriftauslegung* (Mainz: Grünewald, 1984).

Porter, S. E., "Romans 13:1–7 as Pauline Political Rhetoric," *FilNeot* 3 (1990): 115–39.

Preisker, H., "Das historische Problem des Römerbriefes," *Wissenschaftliche Zeitschrift der Universität Jena* (1952–53): 29–50.

Reese, T. J., "Pauline Politics: Rom 13:1–7," *BTB* 3 (1973): 323–31.

Romaniuk, K., "Il cristiano e l'autorità civile in Romani 13,1–7," *RivB* 27 (1979): 261–69.

Shear-Yashuv, A., "Römer 13,1–7 und Offenbarung 13," *Religion, Philosophy and Judaism*, vol. 1: *From Christianity to Judaism, Theological and Philosophical Articles* (Jerusalem: R. Mass, 1987), 91–115.

Schelkle, K. H., "Staat und Kirche in der patristischen Auslegung von Rm. 13,1–7," *ZNW* 44 (1952–53): 223–36.

Schlier, H., "Die Beurteilung des Staates im Neuen Testament," *Zeit der Kirche*, 1–16.

———, "Mächte und Gewalten im Neuen Testament," *TBl* 9 (1930): 289–97.

———, "The State According to the New Testament," *The Relevance of the New Testament* (New York: Herder and Herder, 1968), 215–38.

Schmidt, K. L., "Das Gegenüber von Kirche und Staat in der Gemeinde des Neuen Testaments," *TBl* 16 (1937): 1–16.

Schrage, W., *Die Christen und der Staat nach dem Neuen Testament* (Gütersloh: Mohn, 1971), 50–62.

————, *Die konkreten Einzelgebote*, 222–28.

Schweitzer, W., *Die Herrschaft Christi und der Staat im Neuen Testament*, BEvT 11 (Munich: Kaiser, 1949).

Stein, R. H., "The Argument of Romans xiii 1–7," *NovT* 31 (1989): 325–43.

Steinmetz, D. C., "Calvin and Melanchthon on Romans 13:1–7," *Ex auditu* 2 (1986): 74–81.

Stringfellow, W., *Conscience and Obedience: The Politics of Romans 13 and Revelation 13 in Light of the Second Coming* (Waco, Tex.: Word Books, 1977).

Strobel, A., "Furcht, wem Furcht gebührt: Zum profangriechischen Hintergrund von Rm 13,7," ZNW 55 (1964): 58–62.

————, "Zum Verständnis von Rm 13," ZNW 47 (1956): 67–93.

Trimaille, M., "Vivre en chrétiens et en citoyens responsables (Romains 13, 1–7)," *Cahiers Évangile* 7 (1974): 49–54.

Unnik, W. C. van, "Lob und Strafe durch die Obrigkeit: Hellenistisches zu Röm 13,3–4," *Jesus und Paulus: Festschrift für Werner Georg Kümmel . . .* , ed. E. E. Ellis and E. Grässer (Göttingen: Vandenhoeck & Ruprecht, 1975), 334–43.

Veldhuizen, A. van, "Wie zijn *leitourgoi theou* in Rom. 13:6," *ThStud* 32 (1914): 312–14.

Vonck, P., "All Authority Comes from God: Romans 13:1–7: A Tricky Text about Obedience to Political Power," *African Ecclesiastical Review* 26 (1984): 338–47.

Walker, R., *Studie zu Römer 13,1–7*, TEH 132 (Munich: Kaiser, 1966).

Webster, A. F. C., "St. Paul's Political Advice to the Haughty Gentile Christians in Rome: An Exegesis of Romans 13:1–7," *St. Vladimir's Theological Quarterly* 25 (1981): 259–82.

Wengst, K., *Pax Romana and the Peace of Jesus Christ* (London: SCM, 1987), 80–84.

Wilckens, U., "Der Gehorsam gegen die Behörden des Staates im Tun des Guten: Zu Römer 13, 1–7," *Dimensions*, ed. L. de Lorenzi, 85–150.

————, "Römer 13,1–7," *Rechtfertigung als Freiheit*, 203–45.

Wink, W., *Naming the Powers I* (Philadelphia, Penn.: Fortress, 1984), 45–47.

Winter, B. W., "The Public Honouring of Christian Benefactors: Romans 13.3–4 and 1 Peter 2,14–15," *JSNT* 34 (1988): 87–103.

Yoder, J. H., *The Politics of Jesus* (Grand Rapids, Mich.: Eerdmans, 1972), 192–214.

Zsifkovits, V., *Der Staatsgedanke nach Paulus in Röm 13,1–7 mit besonderer Berücksichtigung der Umwelt und der patristischen Auslegung*, Wiener Beiträge zur Theologie 8 (Vienna: Herder, 1964).

Zwaan, J. de, "Een trekje van Paulus' karakter," *TTijd* 47 (1913): 468–71.

47. THE DEBT OF LOVE THAT FULFILLS THE LAW (13:8–10)

13 ⁸Owe nothing to anyone, save that of loving one another; for the one who loves another has fulfilled the law. ⁹The commandments, "*You shall not commit*

adultery, You shall not kill, You shall not steal, You shall not covet"—or any other commandment—are summed up in this one, *"You shall love your neighbor as yourself."* [10]Love does no wrong to a neighbor, for love is the fulfillment of the law.

COMMENT

From the Christian's duty to civil authorities Paul moves on to the obligation of charity or love that sums up the whole Mosaic law in the new dispensation. The uprightness that must govern earthly and civil life is based on the uprightness of the new aeon, which lives itself out through love of one's neighbor. In this way the uprightness of God rules the conduct of Christian life. For Paul Christians must conduct themselves "in Christ" and "in love." This relation of the obligation of love to the Mosaic law will take on a more pronounced form when Paul comes to chap. 14, where regard for Mosaic legality has affected those who are called the "weak." So Paul's instruction here about love is indirectly preparing for what he will say in that section. In effect, he is now reassuring Roman Christians that the manifestation of love for one another is already a form of fulfilling the law.

So far Paul has spoken of God's love *(agapē)* for human beings (5:5, 8; 8:35, 37, 39; 9:13, 25) and will speak (possibly) of the Spirit's love in 15:30. He has also spoken of the love of human beings for God (8:28), but now he takes up the question of human love for other human beings (12:9; 13:8–10; 14:15), and human love may also be meant in 15:30, as the fruit of the Spirit (see Gal 5:22).

In the preceding passage Paul spoke of *tas opheilas*, "dues": taxes, revenues, respect, and honor to be paid to all civil authorities. Now he expands on what a Christian *owes (opheilete)* to all human beings, especially to one another in the Christian community. He puts it strangely, speaking of love as something that is owed, or conceived of as a debt. In doing so, he makes use of oxymoron, for love cannot be "owed." It is the open, outward concern of one person for another that does not depend on what the other has done or will do in return. Thus, love cannot be "owed" like a debt. It is not a quid pro quo. In fact, the only debt that Christians ought to incur is that which they are bound to incur, the debt of mutual love (Barrett).

Paul also sees the obligation of loving one's neighbor as the fulfillment of the Mosaic law. If love dominates human existence, then the do's and dont's of the law are fulfilled, and the law is sustained and upheld (3:31). For love is the way Pauline faith works itself out (Gal 5:6); it thus becomes "the deeds" of which Jas 2:18 speaks, "I by my deeds will show you my faith." This notion might seem to suggest, however, that the law in the long run has the last say, if love fulfills the law. What he means, however, is that the Christian living by faith that works itself out through love fulfills the aspiration of those who have tried to live by the Mosaic law. He is not proposing the fulfillment of the law as an ideal for Christian life. Paul is simply repeating in other words what he already said in 8:4.

In these few verses, which sum up the role of love in Christian life and reveal it as the fulfillment of the Mosaic law, Paul does not give an elaborate treatment of love. For that one has to consult 1 Corinthians 13, where a whole chapter is devoted to the qualities of Christian love.

NOTES

13:8. *Owe nothing to anyone, save that of loving one another.* In this counsel all of the obligations of Christian life find their summation. Paul expresses love as a debt to stress its role in all Christian conduct. It is not restricted only to fellow Christians, but embraces all human beings. Thus it conquers all rivalry within human society. The pron. *allēlous,* "one another," might seem restricted to fellow Christians, but in the next sentence Paul uses *ton heteron* generically, "another, somebody else," and in v 9 it becomes *ton plēsion sou,* "your neighbor," which has a wider extension. Cf. Col 3:14; 1 Tim 1:5; 1 John 4:11. Having spoken of *tas opheilas,* "(their) due," lit., "debts," in v 7, Paul now picks up on that idea and says *mēdeni mēden opheilete,* "owe no one a debt." The play on the words reveals once again that vv 1–7 belong, indeed, integrally to this part of Romans.

the one who loves another has fulfilled the law. As elsewhere in Romans, the Mosaic law is meant (see the NOTE on 2:12), as the subsequent quotations from the Decalogue make clear. Love thus becomes the summation of the obligations of that law; the one who expresses love does not really need the prescriptions or proscriptions of the Mosaic law. See Gal 5:14; Col 3:14; 1 Tim 1:5.

Paul uses *ho heteros,* lit., "the other," as he does in 1 Cor 6:1; 10:24, 29; 14:17; and Gal 6:4, as the equivalent of *ho plēsios,* "neighbor," the word that occurs in the OT citation in v 9. Cf. Phil 2:4; Rom 2:21. As Barrett explains (*Romans,* 250), love for a neighbor can be misinterpreted as "love for the like-minded" person who is congenial to me; love is Christian only if it can include love for the one who differs from me.

By contrast, Marxsen ("Der *heteros nomos*"), Leenhardt (*Romans,* 337 n.), and Walther ("Translator's Dilemma") take *ton heteron nomon* as a unit and translate "the one who loves has fulfilled the other law," i.e., the "second" commandment (see Mark 12:31), a specific reference to Lev 19:18, where *plēsion* is used. But that is a highly unlikely division of the words in this part of the verse. As Cranfield notes (*Romans,* 675), there has been no clear reference to any law in the preceding context; *nomos* was last used in 10:5. See also Danker, "Under Contract."

9. *The commandments, "You shall not commit adultery, You shall not kill, You shall not steal, You shall not covet."* Paul quotes what Roman Catholics call commandments 6, 5, 7, and 9 or 10 from the Decalogue of Deut 5:17, 18, 19, and 21 in the order of the LXX (MS B); cf. Exod 20:13, 14, 15, 17, which has the order 6, 7, 5, 9 or 10; the MT of Deut 5:17, 18, 19, and 21 has the order 5, 6, 7, 9, as has that of Exod 20:13, 14, 15, and 17. Cf. Luke 18:20; Jas 2:11; Philo,

De Dec. 120, 132. Some Greek MSS (א, P, 048, 81, 104) add *ou pseudomarty-rēseis,* "You shall not bear false witness," as the next to last commandment, undoubtedly a copyist's addition, harmonizing the Pauline text with the OT Decalogue.

or any other commandment. I.e., of the Decalogue; this is the immediate sense of the additional phrase, but Paul's typically rhetorical generalization has a more remote sense, which extends what he says about love to any legal system, Roman, ecclesiastical, civil, etc. See Wis 6:17–18.

are summed up in this one, "You shall love your neighbor as yourself." Paul may be echoing a saying of Jesus that sums up the Mosaic law with Deut 6:4–5 and Lev 19:18 (Mark 12:28–34 and parallels). He quotes Lev 19:18b according to the LXX, which corresponds to the MT (*wěʾāhabtā lěrēʿăkā kāmôkā*). In the context of Leviticus "neighbor" means a fellow countryman, a fellow Jew, as "the sons of your own people" indicates in the immediately preceding context (19:18a). See also Gal 5:14 and Jas 2:8, where it is called "the royal law." Such a summation of the Mosaic law is attributed to Rabbi Aqiba: *zeh kělāl gādôl battôrāh,* "This is the great summation in the Law" (Str-B, 1.357, 907–8). So rabbis summed up the 613 commands and prohibitions of the Torah and their developments. As used by Paul, "neighbor" has a wider extension than the Jewish understanding of it. It would mean a fellow human being with whom one lives. Contrast 4 Macc 2:5–6, where "reasoning" is said to sum up all: "For instance, the law says, 'You shall not covet your neighbor's wife, or anything that belongs to your neighbor.' Now since the law has said that we are not to covet, I should much more easily persuade you that reasoning can govern our coveting, just as it does the emotions which are impediments to justice."

10. *Love does no wrong to a neighbor.* Because, as Paul understands it, love is the working out of faith, the way Christian *pistis* expresses itself (Gal 5:6). See 1 Cor 13:4–6. This may seem like a rather negative achievement of love, that it does no wrong to a neighbor. It is true, however, because a faith that works through love actually pursues all that is good in life. Real faith involves a love that pursues all that is good for the neighbor. This comes about for Christians because the love of God has been poured into their hearts "through the holy Spirit given to us" (5:5).

for love is the fulfillment of the law. I.e., its *plērōma,* the full carrying out of "the requirement of the law" (8:4), what was required of those living under the Mosaic law to fulfill their covenantal obligation. Although this may seem to be only an abstract formulation of the preceding, Paul is enunciating his own basic principle. If Christ is "the end of the Law" (10:4), the goal toward which it was aimed in the history of human salvation, then "love," which motivated his whole existence and soteriological activity (8:35), can be said to be the fulfillment of the law itself. It thus becomes the norm for Christian conduct and, when properly applied, achieves all that the law stood for. Thus Paul shows how "the faith that works itself out through love" (Gal 5:6) actually "upholds the law" (3:31). But compare how Wis 6:18 puts it: "Love means the keeping of her [i.e., wisdom's] laws; the observance of her laws is the basis for incorruptibility."

BIBLIOGRAPHY

Abrahams, I., "The Greatest Commandment," *Studies in Pharisaism and the Gospels: First Series* (Cambridge: Cambridge University Press, 1917), 18–29.

Bencze, A. L., "An Analysis of 'Romans xiii. 8–10,'" *NTS* 20 (1973–74): 90–92.

Berger, K., *Die Gesetzesauslegung Jesu: Ihr historischer Hintergrund im Judentum und im Alten Testament*, WMANT 40 (Neukirchen-Vluyn: Neukirchener-Verlag, 1972), 1.50–55, 80–136.

Borgen, P., "The Golden Rule: With Emphasis on Its Use in the Gospels," *Paul Preaches Circumcision and Pleases Men* (Trondheim: Tapir, 1983), 99–114.

Bornkamm, G., "Wandlungen im alt- und neutestamentlichen Gesetzesverständnis," *Geschichte und Glaube*, 2 vols., BEvT 48, 53 (Munich: Kaiser, 1968–71), 2.73–119.

Danker, F. W., "Under Contract: A Form-Critical Study of Linguistic Adaptation in Romans," *Festschrift to Honor F. Wilbur Gingrich . . .* , ed. E. Barth and R. E. Cocroft (Leiden: Brill, 1972), 91–114, esp. 111 n. 2.

Dülmen, A. van, *Theologie*, 225–30.

Feuillet, A., "Loi ancienne et morale chrétienne d'après l'épître aux Romains," *NRT* 92 (1970): 785–805.

Fridrichsen, A., "Exegetisches zu den Paulusbriefen," *TSK* 102 (1930): 291–301, esp. 294–97.

Furnish, V. P., *Love Command*, 108–11.

Grosheide, F. W., "Romans 13:8b," *ThStud* 31 (1913): 345–48.

Hübner, H., *Law*, 66–67, 83–85.

Hughes, D. G., "Nota breve: Rom. 13,8b," *EstBíb* 2 (1943): 307–9.

Lyonnet, S., "La Charité plénitude de la loi (Rm 13,8–10)," *Dimensions*, ed. L. de Lorenzi, 151–78; repr. in his *Études*, 310–28.

Marxsen, W., "Der *heteros nomos* Röm. 13, 8," *TZ* 11 (1955): 230–37.

Merk, O., *Handeln*, 164–65.

Moule, C. F. D., "Obligation in the Ethic of Paul," *Christian History and Interpretation: Studies Presented to John Knox*, ed. W. R. Farmer et al. (Cambridge: Cambridge University Press, 1967), 389–406.

Neirynck, F., "Sayings of Jesus," 291–94.

Nissen, A., *Gott und der Nächste im antiken Judentum: Untersuchungen zum Doppelgebot der Liebe*, WUNT 15 (Tübingen: Mohr [Siebeck], 1974).

Ogara, F., " 'Nemini quidquam debeatis, nisi ut invicem diligatis,'" *VD* 15 (1935): 41–47.

Perkins, P., *Love*, 12–25, 78–88.

Piper, J., "Is Self-Love Biblical?" *Christianity Today* 21 (1976–77): 1150–53.

Räisänen, H., *Law*, 26–27, 64–66.

Schrage, W., *Die konkreten Einzelgebote*, 97–100, 249–71.

Schreiner, T. R., "The Abolition and Fulfillment of the Law in Paul," *JSNT* 35 (1989): 47–74.

Swaeles, R., "La Charité fraternelle accomplissement de la Loi: Rm 13,8–10," *AsSeign* 54 (1972): 10–15.

Viard, A., " 'La Charité accomplit la loi': Commentaire de Romains 12,9 à 13,10," *VSpir* 74 (1946): 27–34.

Walther, J. A., "A Translator's Dilemma: An Exegetical Note on Romans 13:8," *Perspective* 13 (1972): 243–46.

Wischmeyer, O., "Das Gebot der Nächstenliebe bei Paulus: Eine traditionsgeschichtliche Untersuchung," *BZ* 30 (1986): 161–87.

48. ESCHATOLOGICAL EXHORTATION: CHRISTIAN LIFE AS VIGILANT CONDUCT (13:11–14)

13 ¹¹Do this, then, realizing how critical the moment is—that it is already time for you to be roused from sleep; for our salvation is now closer than when we first believed. ¹²The night is far spent, and day has drawn near. Let us cast off, then, the deeds of darkness and don the armor of light, ¹³that we may conduct ourselves with decency as befits the daylight, not in orgies or drunkenness, not in debauchery or sexual excess, not in quarreling or jealousy. ¹⁴Put on rather the Lord Jesus Christ and give no more thought to the desires of the flesh.

COMMENT

Paul now appends to the end of part A of the hortatory section of Romans an eschatological exhortation: Roman Christians must realize that they are already living in the *eschaton*, for the two ages (that of the Torah and that of the Messiah) have met (1 Cor 10:11). Christ, by his passion, death, resurrection, exaltation, and heavenly intercession, has inaugurated the new aeon, the *eschaton*: Salvation is at hand, and Christians must respond to the time in which they live with vigilant conduct. The one who through faith is upright is to live a life in tune with the new aeon, which explains why Christians cannot conform themselves to this world (12:2), but must be in harmony with the new aeon. They must look forward to the day when salvation comes.

The only passages so far in Romans in which Paul has touched on eschatological topics (apart from the brief mention of God's "wrath") have been 2:5–11, where he reminds his readers that they will have to reckon with "God's just judgment" (*dikaiokrisia tou theou*) as he will recompense everyone "according to his deeds," quoting Prov 24:12; and 8:18–25, where he speaks of the basis of

Christian hope. Now Paul introduces eschatological motivation into the hortatory section of Romans. It will appear again briefly in 14:10c and 12.

Eschatological teaching is minimal in the passage when the content is considered. Salvation is said to be nearer, but it is still a thing of the future. The time in which Christians live is considered critical, and they are exhorted to vigilance. Note the use in these verses of apocalyptic stage-props: *kairos, hōra,* darkness versus light, sleep versus vigilance, deeds versus armor. Note too Paul's motivation by the use of the same props in an earlier letter with more pronounced eschatological teaching (1 Thess 5:1–11). See also 1 Cor 7:26–28, 30. Cf. Col 4:5; Eph 5:16.

Schlier (*Römerbrief,* 395–96) thinks that these verses, though a piece of prose, contain a rhythmic passage, possibly a baptismal hymn:

hōra ēdē hēmas ex hypnou egerthēnai.
hē nyx proekopsen, hē de hēmera ēngiken.
apothōmetha oun ta erga tou skotous,
endysōmetha de ta hopla tou phōtos.

He may be correct, but he has to omit words to obtain the cited form.

NOTES

13:11. *Do this, then.* I.e., carry out the practice of love in your Christian lives.

realizing how critical the moment is. Lit., "knowing the critical time"; cf. 3:26; 5:6; 8:18; 11:5; (12:11?). The period of Christian existence is *kairos,* a time when Christians are called upon to manifest by their actions that they are such and to conduct themselves suitably. Even though what Paul says about Israel in 11:25–26 might suggest that the definitive stage of salvation is still something of the future, nevertheless the *kairos* has begun. Now is the time for Christians to appropriate to themselves by their faith, working itself out through love, the effects of what Christ once achieved for all. See 1 Cor 7:29.

that it is already time for you to be roused from sleep. I.e., from the sleep of unconcern about one's conduct and existence. See 1 Thess 5:6; 1 Cor 15:34; cf. Eph 5:14; John 4:23. Instead of *hymas,* some MSS (P⁴⁶, ℵ, D, G, Ψ, 33, 614, 1739, and the *Koinē* text-tradition) read *hēmas,* "us." That wording, however, seems to be a harmonization of the text with "our" in the next clause.

our salvation is now closer than when we first believed. The eschatological deliverance of Christians as the fulfillment of the pledge (2 Cor 1:22) or of the firstfruits (Rom 8:23) has been guaranteed by the indwelling Spirit. It is now nearer than it was when human beings first put their faith in Christ. Paul speaks of a time lapse between the messianic period of salvation history and its consummation in the parousia. In 1 Cor 10:11 he spoke of Christians as people "upon whom the ends of the ages have met," i.e., the end of the period of Torah and the beginning of the period of the Messiah. So the *eschaton* is in progress, between Christ's resurrection and his parousia. Hence every step that Christians take brings them closer to "the day of the Lord," when the glory of the Lord will be revealed and that of the children of God (8:21).

12. *The night is far spent, and day has drawn near.* Paul implies that not too long a time separates Christians from their eschatological destiny. Compare 1 John 2:8, "the darkness is passing away, and the true light shines already."

Let us cast off, then, the deeds of darkness and don the armor of light. The old aeon was that of sin and death, and human conduct was besmirched by them; it was marked by "deeds of darkness," the deeds that are done under the cover of night. The new aeon or the eschaton is ruled by light. The dualistic contrast of day and night and of light and darkness is symbolic of good and evil, just as in 1 Thess 5:5–8 (cf. Eph 5:8–11). These pairs are commonly used in contemporary Jewish apocalyptic writings, especially in the sectarian QL (1QS 2:7; 3:20–4:1; 1QM 15:9, "in darkness are all their deeds," i.e., the deeds of the sons of darkness who are dominated by the prince of demons, Belial). Contrast Eph 6:2.

Instead of *apothōmetha*, the reading of א, A, B, C, D², Ψ, 048, and the *Koinē* text-tradition, some MSS (P⁴⁶, D*,ᶜ, F, G) as well as the VL and Vg read rather a strange *apobalōmetha*, "let us throw off," which, however, does not differ much in meaning. Again, in some Greek MSS (A, D) a copyist's correction has introduced *erga*, "deeds," in place of *hopla*, "armor," to make the pair parallel.

don the armor of light. Christians cannot afford to remain in the unprotected condition of scantily clothed sleepers at a time when the situation calls for "armor." The armor is not described here, but in 1 Thess 5:8 is it depicted as faith, charity, and hope; cf. 2 Cor 6:7; 10:4; Eph 6:13–17. Those who live in light, i.e., those justified by Christ, cannot conduct themselves as though they were still in darkness. Their deeds cannot be those "of the flesh"; recall the catalog of such deeds that Paul gives in Gal 5:19.

13. *that we may conduct ourselves with decency as befits the daylight.* Lit., "let us walk becomingly as in (the) day." See 1 Thess 4:12. Paul uses the ingressive aor. subjunct. of *peripatein*; see BDF §337.1; see also §425.4.

not in orgies or drunkenness. I.e., with conduct usually associated with the darkness of night. Paul now introduces a list of vices that are characteristic of "darkness" (see the NOTE on 1:28). When Augustine, the African teacher of rhetoric, tells of his conversion to Christianity, he describes a scene in Milan: when he heard a child singing in a nearby house, "Tolle lege, tolle lege" ("take up and read"), he picked up a scroll lying at his feet and read this verse of Romans and the next (*Confessions* 8.12 [CSEL 33.194–95]). They thus sparked the conversion of a great Christian whose writings helped shape western theology.

not in debauchery or sexual excess, not in quarreling or jealousy. See 1:29. See Lövestam, *Spiritual Wakefulness.*

14. *Put on rather the Lord Jesus Christ.* Let Christ be your armor. Through

baptism the Christian has already "put on" Christ (Gal 3:27), like armor or a heavenly garment. The baptized Christian has become another Christ. But that identification of the Christian with Christ has to bear fruit in one's conscious life; as one becomes more and more aware of Christian identity, one should withdraw more and more from sin and sinful conduct. Such a psychological outlook, once cultivated, will stifle all the desires of the Ego subject to sin. The Christian must now live *en Christō*. See 13:12. Cf. 1 Thess 5:8; Eph 6:10–20.

give no more thought to the desires of the flesh. See Gal 5:16, 19–20. As the flesh will make its own demands, there is no need to meet it halfway. Paul uses a good Greek expression, *pronoian poieisthai*, "exercise foresight, provision," an abstract noun with the middle of *poiein*, a good classical Greek idiom also found in Dan 6:19; *Ep. Arist.* 80; Josephus, *Ag.Ap.* 1.2 §9 (cf. BDF §310.1; see the NOTE on 1:9).

BIBLIOGRAPHY

Barr, J., *Biblical Words for Time* (London: SCM, 1962).

Baumgarten, J., *Paulus und die Apokalytik*, WMANT 44 (Neukirchen-Vluyn: Neukirchener-Verlag, 1975).

Dautzenberg, G., "Was bleibt von der Naherwartung? Zu Röm 13,11–14," *Biblische Randbemerkungen: Schülerfestschrift Rudolf Schnackenburg . . .* , ed. H. Merklein and J. Lange (Würzburg: Echter-Verlag, 1974), 361–74.

Grabner-Haider, A., *Paraklese und Eschatologie bei Paulus: Mensch und Welt im Anspruch der Zukunft Gottes*, NTAbh n.s. 4 (Münster in Westfalen: Aschendorff, 1968), 79–90.

Haulotte, E., "La Formule paulinienne: 'Revêtir le Christ,' " *Symbolique du vêtement selon la Bible* (Paris: Aubier, 1966), 210–25.

Lafont, G., "En État d'urgence (Rm 13,11–14)," *AsSeign* 3 (1963): 21–28.

———, "Le Temps du salut: Rm 13,11–14," *AsSeign* n.s. 5 (1969): 12–16.

Lövestam, E., *Spiritual Wakefulness in the New Testament* (Lund: Gleerup, 1963), 25–45.

Müller, U. B., "Die Proklamation der Nähe des Eschaton oder des Endes dieser Welt als Teil prophetischer Mahnrede," *Prophetie und Predigt im Neuen Testament: Formgeschichtliche Untersuchungen zur urchristlichen Prophetie*, SNT 10 (Gütersloh: Mohn, 1975), 140–75.

Ogara, F., " 'Hora est iam nos de somno surgere' (Rom. 13,11–14)," VD 14 (1934): 353–60.

Schelkle, K. H., "Biblische und patristische Eschatologie nach Röm., XIII, 11–13," *SacPag*, 2.357–72.

Sisti, A., "La salvezza è vicina (Rom. 13,11–14)," *BeO* 7 (1965): 271–78.

Vögtle, A., "Paraklese und Eschatologie nach Röm 13,11–14," *Dimensions*, ed. L. de

Lorenzi, 179–220; repr. in *Offenbarungsgeschehen und Wirkungsgeschichte: Neutestamentliche Beiträge* (Freiburg im Breisgau: Herder, 1985), 205–17.

———, "Röm 13,11–14 und die 'Nah'-Erwartung," *Rechtfertigung: Festschrift für Ernst Käsemann . . .* , ed. J. Friedrich et al. (Tübingen: Mohr [Siebeck], 1976), 557–73; repr. in *Offenbarungsgeschehen*, (see above), 191–204.

B. THE DUTY OF LOVE OWED BY THE STRONG IN THE COMMUNITY TO THE WEAK (14:1–15:13)

◆

49. CHRISTIAN SOLIDARITY: ITS EXTENT AND ITS LIMITS (14:1–12)

14 ¹Welcome among you anyone who is weak in conviction, but not to quarrel about disputable matters. ²One may be convinced that one may eat anything, but the one who is weak eats only vegetables. ³Let the one who eats not despise the one who abstains; let the one who abstains not pass judgment on the one who eats, for God has welcomed him. ⁴Who are you to sit in judgment on the servant of another? Before his own master he stands or falls. And stand he will, for the master is able to make him stand. ⁵One person regards one day as more important than another; yet another regards every day as the same. Each one, however, should be fully convinced of this in his own mind: ⁶the one who observes a set day, observes it for the Lord; and the one who eats, eats for the Lord, for he gives thanks to God. The one who abstains, abstains for the Lord and also gives thanks to God. ⁷Yet none of us lives for himself, and none of us dies for himself. ⁸If we live, we live for the Lord; and if we die, we die for the Lord. So whether we live or die, we belong to the Lord. ⁹For this reason too Christ died and came to life again in order that he might exercise lordship over both the dead and the living. ¹⁰Why then do you sit in judgment over your brother? Or why do you despise your brother? We shall all have to appear before God's tribunal, ¹¹for it stands written, *"As I live, says the Lord, to me every knee shall bend, and every tongue shall give praise to God."* ¹²Every one of us, then, will give an account of himself before God.

COMMENT

The second part of the hortatory section begins here. Although it picks up on the debt of love or charity (13:8), its tone is different, because it now extends that duty of love to the "weak" in the community. Whereas part A of the hortatory section of the epistle (12:1–13:14) contained many generic counsels, this part becomes more specific. It is immediately concerned with such questions as the eating of meat, drinking of wine, and observance of holy days. But more fundamentally it deals with the age-old problem of the scrupulous versus the enlightened conscience, or the conservative versus the progressive. Paul seems to have heard something about such a problematic group in the Roman church (see Introduction, section V), and in this part of Romans he addresses the problem. He deals with it only in generic terms, however, probably because he is not intimately acquainted with all of the details. Although the problem is not of major importance in itself, it gives Paul the opportunity to formulate prudent principles based on conviction (14:1, 22, 23), love (14:15), the example of Christ (14:9, 15; 15:3, 7–8), and the Christians' loyalty to him (15:13). Paul's discussion ends with a plea for unity based on important ideas of the doctrinal section.

The treatment of the topic in 14:1–15:13 is paraenetic; as Karris has noted, it contains thirteen imperatives or cohortatives (14:1, 3bis, 5, 13bis, 15, 16, 19, 20, 22; 15:2, 7 ["Romans 14:1–15:13," 72]). Yet it still remains generic enough that many commentators think that the harmony and accord between the "weak" and the "strong" represents a perennial problem that Paul encountered elsewhere in his evangelization of the eastern Mediterranean world. Whether the terms "weak" and "strong" are Paul's or actually terms that he has learned to be in use among Christians of Rome is hard to say. In any case, he now takes up the problem of the "weak" and the "strong." Indeed, his words can readily be applied to the need for forbearance in any form of human society, Jewish or Christian, religious or lay, monastic or clerical. It is but another form of the problem of law versus freedom. Because communal life always develops regulations, how does one cope with them? Some individuals react scrupulously, others maturely. Although Paul is, in effect, talking about "conscience," he does not use that word here. Instead, the word is "conviction" (*pistis*).

The "weak" are probably Jewish Christian members of the Roman community; the "strong," the Gentile Christian members (see Introduction, section V). Years ago, Rauer sought to identify the "weak" with Gentile Christians, individuals whose custom of abstaining from meat and wine stemmed from their background in gnostic, Hellenistic mystery religions (*Die "Schwachen"*). Part of the difficulty with this opinion is the question whether there were gnostic sects this early in history. It is known that Orphics, Dionysiac mystics, and Pythagoreans abstained from eating meat, and at times also from wine; so converts from such backgrounds might have considered the continuance of such practices to be proper.

Although there was per se no prohibition of eating meat in Judaism of the time, it is known that some Jews abstained from meat and wine, especially those who lived in pagan environments in the diaspora (see Dan 1:8, 12–16; 10:3; Jdt 8:6; 10:5; 12:1–2; Esth 14:17 [Vg]). Vegetarianism was sometimes practiced; 2 Sam 17:28 implies that such things as "wheat, barley, meal, parched grain, beans, lentils" would be used in such a practice; cf. 2 Macc 5:27. Philo tells of the Therapeutai in Egypt, who so abstained (*De vita cont.* 4 §37). The practice among Jewish Christians may stem from the fear of eating meat that was "unclean" (*koinon*) or that had been offered to idols, as in 1 Corinthians 8. Hegesippus tells of James, "the brother of the Lord, called 'the Upright,'" who abstained from wine, beer, and animal flesh (*oinon, sikera, empsychon*; Eusebius, *Historia ecclesiastica* 2.23.5). Cf. Josephus, *Life* 2 §14. Moreover, the use of *koinon* in the specific Jewish sense of "unclean" in 14:14 and of *kathara*, "clean," in 14:20, as well as the implied contrast of Jews and Gentiles in 15:7–13, makes it highly likely that Paul understands the "weak" as Christians of Jewish background. There is no evidence that the "weak" were organized formally into a community or congregation, though there may have been groups of them who lent each other mutual support. Watson has argued that Paul envisages "two congregations, separated by mutual hostility and suspicion over the question of the law" ("Two Roman Congregations," 206). That reading, however, is far from certain. The use of the OT in 15:7–13 does not necessarily mean that the differing Roman Christians, or even congregations of them, were refusing to worship together.

Whether the "weak" and the "strong" can be divided into five different groups that disagreed over doctrines and practices, as Minear (*Obedience of Faith*, 8–17) has maintained, is highly speculative. Minear's explanation has found few followers. See Wedderburn, *Reasons*, 47–49.

The subdivision of this part of Romans is not without its problems. Some commentators make no effort to subdivide it (Huby, Lagrange). The *RSV* has the maximum division: 14:1–4, 5–9, 10–12, 13–23; 15:1–6, 7–13 (six sections in all). Cranfield (*Romans*, 698–99) uses five parts: 14:1–12, 13–23; 15:1–6, 7–12, 13. Käsemann (*Commentary*, 365), the *NAB*, and Wilckens use four: 14:1–12, 13–23; 15:1–6, 7–13; Barrett (*Romans*, 255–73), three: 14:1–12, 13–23; 15:1–13. It seems best to follow the division of Käsemann.

In 14:1–12 Paul counsels the Christians of Rome to welcome fellow Christians, be they "weak" or "strong," but especially the "weak." They too stand before the Lord, no matter what they eat or what days they celebrate, for all, weak and strong alike, have one day to stand before "God's tribunal."

Again, Paul may be incorporating into his discussion in v 9 a pre-Pauline formula, in part at least.

NOTES

14:1. *Welcome among you anyone who is weak in conviction.* I.e., learn to live generously with the brother or sister who is "weak." Paul has probably heard about scrupulous Jewish Christians whose judgments are based on an insufficiently enlightened faith. Such persons have not really grasped what is meant by uprightness through faith and have sought to find assurance in added practices. Yet even such persons belong to the Christian community, and they are to be "welcomed," for God has welcomed them. See 15:1; 1 Cor 8:9; 9:22; 1 Thess 5:14.

The problem in this verse is the meaning of *pistis*; it will appear again in vv 22, 23bis. Because the vb. *pisteuein* is used in v 2 referring to a "belief," not in the sense of the essence of Christianity (i.e., not in Christ Jesus as Lord) but to a conviction that one may eat anything, *pistis* is hardly to be taken here or in vv 22–23 as meaning genuine Christian "faith" in the Pauline sense, *pace* Käsemann (*Commentary*, 365, 374, 379). Even Cranfield (*Romans*, 698, 700), who translates the phrase "weak in faith," admits that this chapter refers not to weakness in basic Christian faith, but to weakness in assurance that one's faith permits one to do certain things. Apropos of 14:22–23, BAGD (664a) says that *pistis* "gains fr. the context the mng. *freedom* or *strength in faith, conviction.*"

The vb. *proslambanesthai* means "take to oneself, take into one's household" (see 15:7), hence "welcome," accept with an open heart. See 15:7.

but not to quarrel about disputable matters. Lit., "not for the purpose of quarrels about opinions," i.e., debates about inconsequential matters that undermine confidence and trust on all sides. Thus Paul insists on the duty of Christians to welcome into their midst even "weak" fellow members. No one should try to impose his point of view on others. Cf. 1 Cor 10:25, 27.

2. *One may be convinced that one may eat anything.* I.e., strong or mature and enlightened Christians may be sure of themselves and the freedom they have to eat anything, meat or other food. The vb. *pisteuei* does not mean "believe" here, but "to have the confidence to risk, to feel equal to" (BDF §397.2).

but the one who is weak eats only vegetables. Paul's first example involves vegetarianism or a food taboo. Whereas the "strong" eat food of all sorts, the "weak" eat only vegetables, undoubtedly because of their pre-Christian background.

3. *Let the one who eats not despise the one who abstains; let the one who abstains not pass judgment on the one who eats.* Once it is seen that such an issue is not related to the essentials of Christian faith, the obligation of mutual charity for all becomes clear. Sameness of view in such indifferent matters is not a Christian ideal. Paul enunciates his principle: eating and abstaining are *adiaphora*, indifferent matters. Hence one's conduct should not lead one to criticize a fellow Christian. See 14:10; 1 Cor 10:25–27. There is room in the Christian community for both sorts of people.

for God has welcomed him. This is the motivation for Paul's principle, and for his counsel in v 1 as well. God has introduced both the weak and the strong into his household.

4. *Who are you to sit in judgment on the servant of another?* The *oiketēs*, "household servant," is responsible only to his own *kyrios*, "master." The warning is addressed to the "weak" Christian, who might regard as lax a person who is actually a member of God's household. See 2:1; cf. Col 2:16. When one begins to judge another Christian, one is undertaking to do what God has reserved to himself or to Christ.

Before his own master he stands or falls. God alone, as that person's master, will judge his servant's failure or success. From God too will come the acceptance of the weak and the status of the strong. See 1 Cor 10:12, where "standing" or "falling" symbolize success in responsible conduct or failure. The image is that of one standing before a judge's tribunal. The "servant" is expected to serve his master and to be "judged" accordingly.

And stand he will, for the master is able to make him stand. Paul plays on the sense of *kyrios*, "master" of a household, and God as *Kyrios.* Instead of *dynatei gar*, "for (the master) is able," the reading of MSS A, B, C, D*, F, G, 6, and 104, some MSS (P⁴⁶, Dᵇ·ᶜ, L, P, 623*, 1739) read *dynatos gar (estin)*, an obvious substitute for the unusual vb. *dynatein.* Again, instead of *kyrios*, the reading in MSS P⁴⁶, ℵ, A, B, and P, some MSS (D, F, G) read *theos*, probably under the influence of *ho theos* in v 3.

5. *One person regards one day as more important than another.* Paul's second example of scrupulosity involves sabbatarianism or celebration of holy days and fast days. Such days as sabbaths, new moons, feasts, and jubilee years are probably meant; they were assiduously observed by Palestinian Jews (see Zech 7:5; 8:19). The "days," however, could also be fast days, as Karris suggests ("Romans 14:1–15:13," 77), following Dederen and Rauer. For instance, the *Yôm hak-kippûrîm* (Lev 16:29; 23:27–32); in NT times, Mondays and Thursdays (Luke 18:12; *Did.* 8:1; *m. Taʿan.* 2:9). Judaism also developed in time a text called *Megillat Taʿanit,* "Scroll of Fasting," which listed days on which it was not permitted to fast or to mourn. In time, early Christians too came to fast on Wednesdays and Fridays (*Did.* 8:1; *Herm. Sim.* 5.3.7). In any case, "weak" Christians of Rome continued to distinguish such days from ordinary days, whereas the "strong" were not so concerned about them. See Gal 4:10.

yet another regards every day as the same. I.e., the attitude of the "strong" in the Roman community. There is no evil in entertaining different convictions about such matters, and Paul resolutely excludes disputes or critical judgment about them.

Each one, however, should be fully convinced of this in his own mind. The conviction is expressed in the following verse. On the vb. *plērophoreisthō*, see Becker, "Quid *plērophoreisthai.*" Cf. 4:21.

6. *the one who observes a set day, observes it for the Lord.* Lit., "esteems the Lord," who in this context is God (see v 6c). This is the motivation for the "weak." What matters here is motivation, whether the days be observed or not, as long as the Lord is served thereby. For a member of the Lord's household is expected to serve his Lord. The *Koinē* text-tradition adds, *kai ho mē phronōn tēn hēmeran kyriō ou phronei*, "the one who does not observe a set day, does not observe it for the Lord." This, however, is an obvious addition made to balance *kai ho mē esthiōn*, "and the one who abstains," at the end of the verse.

the one who eats, eats for the Lord. The same motivation is found for the "strong." For Christians no longer live for themselves; they live for God, and Christ lives in them.

for he gives thanks to God. Not just by saying grace over the meal, but by the very act of eating other than vegetables. That too is a form of thanking God for his bounty to humanity. Cf. 1 Cor 10:30.

The one who abstains, abstains for the Lord and also gives thanks to God. Paul applies the same logic to the "weak" as he had to the "strong." For the weak, in abstaining from eating meat, also thank the Lord by such abstention. The important aspect in eating or abstaining is the motivation, to honor and thank the Lord God. Ever since v 4 Paul has been speaking of *Kyrios*, and one may wonder whether he means God or Christ. In view of the parallelism in this verse, it seems best to understand *Kyrios* in the OT sense of God. This reading is suggested too by v 11, where Paul uses Isa 49:18. In v 9, however, Paul extends this lordship to Christ, and in v 14 it becomes clear that by *Kyrios* he means Christ Jesus.

7. *Yet none of us lives for himself, and none of us dies for himself.* Paul moves the discussion to a more basic level, that of life and death itself. One has come into life in order to live for God; and even in death, the supreme ending of that life, one dies as a way of honoring and thanking God. So the sustenance that one takes, whether it be vegetables or meat, helps to preserve life, but self-preservation should not be the major preoccupation in life. The purpose of life and death is something entirely different. The liberating act of Christ, who lived and died himself in order to free human beings from bondage to law, sin, and death itself (8:2), has enabled them to live for God (6:10–11; Gal 2:19–20).

8. *If we live, we live for the Lord; and if we die, we die for the Lord.* This passage implies the service of God in all things, and it is the basis of life in the true Christian sense. In life and in death, the Christian exists *tō Kyriō,* i.e., to praise, honor, and serve God, the creator and maker of all. Failure to do so was the basis of Paul's indictment of the pagan in 1:21.

So whether we live or die, we belong to the Lord. Cf. Gal 2:20. Christians belong to and must acknowledge their relation to God as *Kyrios* (see 1 Cor 6:20b; 7:23–24; 8:6a). Sometimes Paul centers this motivation on Christ too; see 8:9b; 1 Cor 3:23.

9. *For this reason too Christ died and came to life again in order that he might exercise lordship over both the dead and the living.* Thus Paul formulates the finality of the passion, death, and resurrection of Christ, stressing his sovereignty and lordship over the dead and the living. It is a universal dominion proper to the *Kyrios* of all (cf. 1 Thess 5:10; Phil 2:11). The first part of the verse echoes traditional (possibly pre-Pauline) terminology about the death and resurrection of Christ. Hence the problems of eating and abstaining or of observing set days or not are pitted against the fundamental Christian belief that Christ died and was raised to be the Lord of history. All such minutiae must be judged in their proper perspective. The Christian, who shares in that redemption by faith and baptism, will eventually share the glory of the risen Lord himself. See 1 Thess 4:14; 2 Cor 5:14–15. Influenced perhaps by 1 Thess 4:14, some MSS (F, G, 629) read *anestē,* "rose," instead of *ezēsen,* "came to life," the reading of the better MSS (א*, A, B, C, 1739, 2127).

10. *Why then do you sit in judgment over your brother?* The Christian must

691

not pass critical judgment over other Christians, be they weak or strong. This verse repeats, in effect, v 4.

Or why do you despise your brother? Paul realizes that such judgment can lead even to the deprecation of a fellow Christian, and he emphasizes the fraternal relationship of all Christians, which forbids anyone to criticize or despise another.

We shall all have to appear before God's tribunal. See 2 Cor 5:10, where it is called "the tribunal of Christ." Another argument for Paul's view is thus introduced, echoing the sentiments of 14:4. All Christians without distinction will have to be judged by God; and if so, there is no reason for one to judge another for conducting oneself freely in an indifferent matter, whether that conduct be liberal or restrictive. Some Greek MSS ($\aleph^c$, C^2, Ψ, 048, 0209, and the *Koinē* text-tradition) read *Christou* instead of *theou*, which is the reading of the majority of the best MSS ($\aleph^*$, A, B, C^*, D, F, G, 630, 1506, 1739). It may be a copyist's attempt to harmonize this text with 2 Cor 5:10.

11. *for it stands written.* See the NOTE on 1:17.

"*As I live, says the Lord, to me every knee shall bend, and every tongue shall give praise to God.*" Paul supports his contention by conflating Isa 49:18 (*zō egō, legei Kyrios*) and 45:23 (quoting it according to the LXX, but with a minor change of word order). The latter Isaian text has been used in Phil 2:10–11 in a form quite close to the meaning of the original, as Paul extends its meaning to acknowledge Christ as *Kyrios*. But here the vb. *exomologēsetai* is taken in the sense of "admitting, confessing" what one has done before God as Judge: bending the knee and confessing sins are what Christians do before God. If so, then they should not presume to judge someone else. Cf. Jer 22:24; Ezek 5:11–12. See Black, "Christological Use," 8.

12. *Every one of us, then, will give an account of himself before God.* So Paul formulates an eschatological motivation for proper Christian conduct of both the weak and the strong. Some Greek MSS (B, F, G, 6, 630, 1739, etc.) omit the last prep. phrase, *tō theō*.

BIBLIOGRAPHY ON PART B OF THE HORTATORY SECTION

Cambier, J., "La Liberté chrétienne est et personnelle et communautaire (Rm 14,1–15,3)," *Freedom and Love*, ed. L. de Lorenzi, 57–126.

Cranfield, C. E. B., "Some Observations on the Interpretation of Romans 14,1–15,13," *ComViat* 17 (1975): 193–204.

Dupont, J., "Appel aux faibles et aux forts dans la communauté romaine (Rom 14,1–15,13)," *SPCIC*, 1.357–66.

Gaertner, C. A., "Instructions to the Weak and the Strong According to Romans 14," *CTM* 21 (1950): 659–73.

Giblin, C. H., *In Hope of God's Glory*, 231–36.

Karris, R. J., "Romans 14:1–15:13 and the Occasion of Romans," *RomDeb*, 65–84.

Lorenzi, L. de (ed.), *Freedom and Love: The Guide for Christian Life (1 Co 8–10; Rm*

14–15), Benedictina, series biblico-oecumenica 6 (Rome: Abbazia San Paolo fuori le mura, 1981).

Meeks, W. A., "Judgment and the Brother: Romans 14:1–15:13," *Tradition and Interpretation in the New Testament: Essays in Honor of E. Earle Ellis . . .* , ed. G. F. Hawthorne with O. Betz (Grand Rapids, Mich.: Eerdmans; Tübingen: Mohr [Siebeck], 1987), 290–300.

——— , "The Polyphonic Ethics of the Apostle Paul," *Annual of the Society of Christian Ethics* (1988): 17–29.

Murray, J., "The Weak and the Strong," *WTJ* 12 (1949–50): 136–53.

Nababan, A. E. S., "Bekenntnis und Mission in Römer 14 und 15," Ph.D. diss., Universität Heidelberg, 1963.

Omanson, R. L., "The 'Weak' and the 'Strong' and Paul's Letter to the Roman Christians," *BT* 33 (1982): 106–14.

Rauer, M., *Die "Schwachen" in Korinth und Rom nach den Paulusbriefen,* BibSF 21.2–3 (Freiburg im Breisgau: Herder, 1923).

Reasoner, M., "The 'Strong' and the 'Weak' in Rome and in Paul's Theology," Ph.D. diss., University of Chicago, 1990.

Riggenbach, E., "Die Starken und Schwachen in der römischen Gemeinde," *TSK* 66 (1893): 649–78.

Watson, F., "The Two Roman Congregations: Romans 14:1–15:13," *RomDeb,* 203–15.

Wette, W. M. L. de, "Exegetische Bemerkungen—2. Ueber Römer 14," *TSK* 3 (1830): 351–52.

Rom 14:1–12

Baarda, T., "Jes 45:23 in het Nieuwe Testament (Rm 14,11: Flp 2,10v)," *GTT* 71 (1971): 137–79.

Baulès, R., "Le Chrétien appartient au Seigneur: Rm 14,7–9," *AsSeign* n.s. 55 (1974): 10–15.

Becker, J., "Quid *plērophoreisthai* in Rom 14, 5 significet," *VD* 45 (1967): 11–18.

——— , "Zu *plērophoreisthai* in Röm 14,5," *Bib* 65 (1984): 364.

Black, M., "The Christological Use of the Old Testament in the New Testament," *NTS* 18 (1971–72): 1–14.

Carson, D. A. (ed.), *From Sabbath to Lord's Day: A Biblical, Historical, and Theological Investigation* (Grand Rapids, Mich.: Zondervan, 1982).

Dederen, R., "On Esteeming One Day Better than Another," *AUSS* 9 (1971): 21–23, 29–30.

Dunn, J. D. G., "Jesus and Ritual Purity: A Study of the Tradition History of Mk 7, 15," *À Cause de l'Évangile: Études sur les Synoptiques et les Actes offertes au P. Jacques Dupont, O.S.B. . . .* , LD 123 (Paris: Cerf, 1985), 251–76.

Furnish, V. P., *Love Command,* 115–18.

Jezierska, E. J., " 'Zyjemy dla Pana, umieramy dla Pana . . .': Św. Pawel o proegzystencji chrześ cijanina w 2 Kor 5, 15 i Rz 14, 7–8," *CollTheol* 59.3 (1989): 27–33.

Kreitzer, L. J., *Jesus and God in Paul's Eschatology*, JSNTSup 19 (Sheffield, UK: Academic Press: 1987), 107–12.

Lacey, D. R. de, "The Sabbath/Sunday Question and the Law in the Pauline Corpus," *From Sabbath*, ed. D. A. Carson, 159–95.

Lincoln, A. T., "From Sabbath to Lord's Day: A Biblical and Theological Perspective," *From Sabbath*, ed D. A. Carson, 343–412.

Merk, O., *Handeln*, 167–73.

Minear, P. S., *The Obedience*, 6–35.

Moule, C. F. D., "Death 'to Sin', 'to Law', and 'to the World': A Note on Certain Datives," *Mélanges bibliques en hommage au R. P. Béda Rigaux*, ed. A. Descamps and A. de Halleux (Gembloux: Duculot, 1970), 367–75.

Nieder, L., *Die Motive*, 71–77.

Rongy, H., "Les Faibles et les forts dans la communauté romaine," *RevEcclLiége* 30 (1938–39): 313–17.

Rordorf, W., *Sunday: The History of the Day of Rest and Worship in the Earliest Centuries of the Christian Church* (London: SCM; Philadelphia, Penn.: Westminster, 1968), 87, 137–38.

Theissen, G., *The Social Setting of Pauline Christianity: Essays on Corinth* (Philadelphia, Penn.: Fortress; Edinburgh: Clark, 1982), 121–43.

Thüsing, W., "Leben für den Kyrios (Röm 14,4–12)," *Per Christum in Deum*, 30–39.

Wolf, E., "Trauansprache über Römer 14,7–9," *EvT* 31 (1971): 507–10.

Zeller, D., *Juden und Heiden*, 218–23.

50. THE MARKS OF CHRIST'S RULE IN THE COMMUNITY (14:13–23)

14 [13]So let us no longer pass judgment on one another. Make rather this decision, never to put a stumbling block or an obstacle in your brother's way. [14]As one who is in the Lord Jesus, I know and am convinced that nothing is unclean in itself; but for the one who considers something to be unclean, that becomes so for him. [15]If your brother is indeed distressed because of what you eat, you are no longer conducting yourself in love. Let not the food you eat bring ruin to such a one for whom Christ died. [16]Do not let what is good for you be reviled as evil. [17]For the kingdom of God is not eating and drinking, but uprightness, peace, and joy in the holy Spirit. [18]Anyone who serves Christ is this way is pleasing to God and esteemed among human beings. [19]Let us then pursue what makes for peace and for mutual edification. [20]Do not demolish the work of God for the sake of food. All things are indeed clean, but it is wrong for a human being to eat something that creates a stumbling block for another. [21]It is better not to eat meat

or drink wine, or do anything that causes your brother to trip, to stumble, or to be weakened. [22]The conviction that you have keep to yourself before God. Blessed, indeed, is the one who does not condemn himself for what he approves. [23]But the one who has doubts is already condemned if he eats, because the eating does not proceed from conviction. For whatever proceeds not from conviction is sin.

COMMENT

The main part of Paul's exhortation is now addressed to the "strong," even though that term has not yet appeared, as it will in 15:1. Paul insists that, though the "strong" know that "nothing is unclean in itself" (14:14), yet he summons them to live up to the demand of Christian faith that "works itself out through love" (Gal 5:6). The strong do not exist alone in this world; besides them are the weak brothers and sisters. Love and the example of Christ are proposed to them as motivation for their conduct and attitude. If Christ rules in the community, then all will be as it should be. The strong may be tempted to judge and criticize the weak; but Paul has already addressed that attitude in the preceding paragraph. Now the strong may be tempted to disregard the weak and act in virtue of their conviction; thus they run the risk of misleading the weak to imitate them and act against their own consciences. In this situation Paul calls for conduct governed by love and the example of Christ. Once again, the principles that Paul enunciates in this passage are generic and can be applied to all Christians.

At the end of this paragraph the doxology that now appears in 16:25–27 has been inserted in MSS A, L, P, Ψ, 0209, 5, 33, 104, 181, 326, 330, 614, and 1175; in some cases it appears both here and after 16:23. In some MSS of the VL and the Vg the blessing of 16:24 is added after 14:23 before the doxology. See Introduction, section III; cf. *TCGNT,* 533–36; Aland, "Glosse," 18–22 or 46–49.

NOTES

14:13. *So let us no longer pass judgment on one another.* The transitional opening of this passage in chap. 14 is really a conclusion from vv 1–2; it is introduced by the illative particle *oun.* A critical spirit ill suits the Christian. So Paul sums up what he has just spelled out in detail in the preceding paragraph.

Make rather this decision, never to put a stumbling block or an obstacle in your brother's way. By what they do, the "strong" should not cause others to take offense or entice others to act against their own convictions. The strong and the weak are not to live side by side without concern for each other; instead, the strong are asked to do nothing that will make the weak brother or sister stumble. Cf. 1 Cor 8:9.

14. *As one who is in the Lord Jesus, I know and am convinced.* Paul appeals to his own status as a Christian and to his association with the risen Christ as a

basis for his conviction. Cf. Gal 5:10, where Paul appeals to his confidence; cf. Phil 1:14; 2:24.

nothing is unclean in itself. Lit., "common," i.e., something that comes into contact with anything and everything. The adj. koinon became the designation of food ceremonially impure (non-kāšēr) among Greek-speaking Jews (1 Macc 1:47, 62). Compare the use of kathara, "pure," in 14:20; cf. Titus 1:15; Acts 10:14–15; 11:8; Josephus, Ant. 11.8.7 §346 (koinophagia, also called miarophagia, 4 Macc 5:27; 7:6). See Pascher, Rein und Unrein, 165–68. Cf. the Qumran distinction between ṭāmēʾ, "impure," and ṭāhôr, "clean" (CD 6:17; 12:20). This verse is somewhat parenthetical and sets forth a principle that is operative in the rest of the discussion in this paragraph. The principle is similar to what Paul said in 1 Cor 8:4: "we know that an idol has no real existence"; hence meat offered to it is not really contaminated. Yet it may be so regarded by some Christians. Hence such a principle has to be properly understood. It may be related to that in 14:6; it may also echo Jesus' saying about the Pharisaic distinction between "clean" and "unclean" ("common" and "uncommon") things (Matt 15:11). Cf. Lev 17:15; Str-B 1.718. The created thing in itself is neither clean or unclean, because it comes from God (see 1 Cor 10:26; Ps 24:1). That is the basis of the conviction of the strong. Because Paul uses koinon in its specific Jewish sense, this is one of the best arguments for interpreting the "weak" Christians as Jewish Christians in this part of Romans.

but for the one who considers something to be unclean, that becomes so for him. The subjective reaction of a person colors the conviction about it. Hence one's estimate of such a thing can take on an importance that it does not have in se.

15. If your brother is indeed distressed because of what you eat, you are no longer conducting yourself in love. I.e., your faith is not working itself out through love (Gal 5:6). This verse resumes the idea of v 13, but Paul now introduces the prime consideration, charity or love. Though to the strong no food is unclean, concern for a "brother" (= fellow Christian) will make the strong consider the social aspects of judgment, conduct, and actions. For it is easier for the strong to be concerned about the weak than vice versa. The strong can do two things: they can either exercise their freedom toward the indifferent things or refrain from doing so. In either case they are free. That is why Paul calls upon the strong to act freely and responsibly.

Let not the food you eat bring ruin to such a one for whom Christ died. Lit., "do not destroy by your food that one for whom Christ died." Paul thus challenges fellow Christians to greater heights by putting the matter of indifferent things in the perspective of the redemption wrought by Christ Jesus. The vicarious character of Christ's death is clearly asserted; recall 5:6, 8; cf. 1 Cor 8:11. The weak "brother," who follows the dictates of his conscience, may be distressed at the sight of Christians partaking of certain kinds of food. The strong, in vaunting their enlightened or emancipated consciences before the weak, are not making profession of charity. Paul calls on Christians to relinquish their legitimate claims of freedom for the sake of those who are weak (14:20).

16. *Do not let what is good for you be reviled as evil.* Lit., "let not your good be blasphemed," i.e., be taken as evil. The "good" is the strength of conviction that such a person has, i.e., Christian liberty itself. This Paul admits, but he refuses to allow such freedom to be asserted at the expense of distress to another. It might lose its esteemed quality and be brought into disrepute. Cf. 1 Cor 10:29b–30. Instead of *hymōn*, "you," MSS D, F, G, Ψ read *hēmōn*, "us."

17. *the kingdom of God is not eating and drinking, but uprightness, peace, and joy in the holy Spirit.* The essence of the kingdom does not consist in freedom from such things as dietary regulations, but in the freedom of the Christian to react to the promptings of the indwelling Spirit. Cf. 1 Cor 8:8. Three qualities, two of which echo key ideas of the doctrinal section of Romans, uprightness (chaps. 1–4) and peace (5:1; 8:6), proceed from the Spirit's promptings and are conditions of Christian conduct in the kingdom or, better, are eschatological gifts that characterize the kingdom. In Gal 5:13 Paul counsels Christians to be slaves to one another in love because of their newfound Christian freedom (see 1 Cor 8:1; 10:23). Paul here speaks of "the kingdom of God," a topic frequently on the lips of Jesus in the Synoptic Gospels (e.g., Mark 1:15; 4:11, 16, 30). But it never becomes a vital topic in Paul's preaching; reference is made to it only in 1 Thess 2:12; 1 Cor 4:20; 15:24, and in catechetical summaries that Paul probably inherited from traditional teaching before him (Gal 5:21; 1 Cor 6:9, 10; 15:50 [in these cases, the phrase is anarthrous, *basileia theou*]). Now he refers to it as a way of characterizing Christian existence and conduct, meaning that the present manifestation of the kingdom among Christians cannot tolerate disputes about food, drink, and calendaric observances. Its characteristics are, rather, uprightness, peace, and joy, things that mark Christ's rule among Christians, things that make for mutual upbuilding. See 1 Cor 4:20, where Paul makes a similar statement: "The kingdom of God consists not in talk, but in power." The "holy Spirit" is to be understood with each of the three characteristics; see Gal 5:22 (so Käsemann, but Cranfield restricts it to joy alone). Cf. 1 Thess 1:6. For a similar Pauline attitude about food, see 1 Cor 8:8. His formulation here in Romans is not to be understood as a strict definition of the kingdom, but it is part of his didactic teaching about it. Codex 4 adds after "uprightness" *kai askēsis*, "and asceticism," a remarkable addition.

18. *Anyone who serves Christ in this way is pleasing to God and esteemed among human beings.* See 2 Cor 5:9; 10:18; Heb 12:28b. Service of Christ in uprightness, peace, and joy is the basis of acceptance by God and recognition by other human beings.

19. *Let us then pursue what makes for peace and for mutual edification.* See 15:2; Heb 12:14. Paul echoes a thought from Ps 34:15, "seek peace and pursue it." Some MSS (ℵ, A, B, F, G, 048) read the indic. *diōkomen*, "we are pursuing,"

instead of the subjunc. *diōkōmen*, read by MSS C, D, and the *Koinē* text-tradition. See 1 Thess 5:11.

20. *Do not demolish the work of God for the sake of food.* Paul substantially repeats what he counseled in v 15. Of more importance than the right to eat or drink or celebrate feasts is the Christian's obligation not to destroy the "work of God" by making a weak Christian stumble. For the weak are what they are by God's favor; he has brought them to this status, and as Christians they are of his fashioning. In the context, "the work of God" probably refers to the weak Christian; but it may refer to the unity of the Christian community, which could be undone by insistence on extravagant claims of freedom without respect for others (cf. 1 Cor 3:9).

All things are indeed clean. Paul repeats the principle enunciated in v 14. They are clean because they come from God, who has made them part of his bounty to humanity and the created universe. See Titus 1:15.

but it is wrong for a human being to eat something that creates a stumbling block for another. Lit., "it is wrong/evil for a human being who eats with an (attending) obstacle." The prep. phrase *dia proskommatos* may express an attendant circumstance (so BAGD, 180a); but it may also express cause, "because of offense" (BAGD, 180b–181a). Paul now strongly condemns the scandal done to weak Christians. Christians who inconsiderately use their freedom without wondering whether it tempts others and causes them to fall are not walking in love (14:15). Cf. 1 Cor 8:9–10.

21. *It is better not to eat meat or drink wine, or do anything that causes your brother to trip, to stumble, or to be weakened.* This verse is, in effect, a repetition of v 13. Paul means that in this way unity, harmony, and love among Christians will be achieved. See 1 Cor 8:11–13; 10:31. The best Greek MSS (P⁴⁶, ℵ², B, D, F, G, Ψ, 0209, and the *Koinē* text-tradition) and the Latin and Syriac versions read three verbs here, *proskoptei ē skandalizetai ē asthenei*, whereas MSS ℵ*, A, C, 048, etc. read only the first verb, probably as a result of the copyist's eye jumping from the ending -*ei* on *proskoptei* to that on *asthenei*.

22. *The conviction that you have keep to yourself before God.* Lit., "as for you, keep the conviction you have to yourself in the sight of God," i.e., the conviction about food, drink, and the observance of feast days. The relation of a Christian to God should not be paraded in quarrels and disputes about food and drink. The clear insight and the firm conviction that the strong Christian has of the moral goodness of a certain deed should guide him or her whenever one scrutinizes one's conduct in the sight of God. This is the norm, when an action is considered between oneself and God. But social considerations may compel one to modify one's conduct before others. Here it is clear that *pistis* cannot mean essential Christian faith; it expresses a conviction about food, drink, and calendaric observances. Essential Christian faith, rather, is something that one may, and sometimes may have to, parade before humanity; but this is not true of conviction about indifferent matters. Some MSS (ℵ, A, B, C,) read the rel. pron.

hēn, which is translated here, but MSS D, F, G, Ψ, and the *Koinē* text-tradition omit it. Without the pron., the text could be read as a question, "Do you have a conviction? Keep it. . . ."

Blessed, indeed, is the one who does not comdemn himself for what he approves. A beatitude is uttered over the one who has no qualms of conscience for a practical decision, whether to eat or not to eat. Cranfield (*Romans*, 727) would limit the beatitude to the "strong Christian" as one truly possessing the inner freedom to do those things of which he approves, hence untroubled by the scruples that afflict a weak Christian.

23. *But the one who has doubts is already condemned if he eats.* The "weak" Christian, who has not yet acquired the inner liberty of the "strong," would be led astray by following the example of the "strong," because he or she would really be acting against the dictates of conscience. If weak Christians were to eat meat or drink wine to spare themselves the criticism or scorn of the strong, then they suffer condemnation (lit., "have been condemned," the pf. tense is used to express the condition in which they find themselves).

because the eating does not proceed from conviction. The basis of any moral act is the dictate of conscience. If to eat meat were not governed by the dictate of conscience, then sin would be involved.

For whatever proceeds not from conviction is sin. Lit., "all that is not of conviction is sin." Paul ends his discussion with a maximlike utterance. The statement encounters three difficulties: (1) How generic is *pan*, "all"? (2) What is the sense of *pistis?* and (3) What is the sense of *hamartia?*

(1) As Augustine (*Contra Iulianum* 4.32 [PL 44.755]) understood it, *pan* applies to everything, "in every case." Augustine was applying Paul's dictum to the controversy with the Pelagians and was really going beyond Paul's meaning. By contrast, John Chrysostom (*In ep. ad Romanos* hom. 26.3 [PG 60.640]) rightly understood *pan* to refer to all such indifferent matters as those instanced in the preceding context (vv 2–3, 5): all dietary and calendaric observances.

(2) As Augustine understood *pistis*, it would refer to basic Christian faith, as in 1:17 and 3:25, 28. He took it thus in his controversy with the Pelagian Julian, maintaining that all deeds of pagans prior to justification were sinful (*Contra Iulianum* 4.32). Again, he went beyond Paul's context, in which it is a question of Christian "weak" and "strong," not of pagans. But with other medieval commentators, Thomas Aquinas (*Summa theologiae* I–II, q. 19, a. 5 [Parma ed 2.77]) understood *pistis* as meaning "conscience" ("omne quod est contra conscientiam"; cf. *In ep. ad Romanos* 14.3 [Parma ed. 13.145]). See also F. Suarez, *De bonitate et malitia humanorum actuum*, disp. 12, sect. 1.3 (*Opera* 4.437). This interpretation of *pistis* as *conscientia* has been attributed to Origen (*In ep. ad Romanos* 10.5 [PL 14.1255]), Ambrosiaster (*In ep. ad Romanos* 14.23 [CSEL 81.453]), and other patristic writers, who use the word "conscience," but it is debated whether these early writers really meant the same thing as the philosophical idea of *conscientia*. See Araud, "Quidquid." Luther (*Commentary on Ro-*

mans, ad loc. [LuthW 25.507–8]) realized that *pistis* could be interpreted "in a double sense," as "opinion and conscience," but preferred "the absolute sense in the fashion of the apostle, as identical with faith in Christ." So too Käsemann (*Commentary*, 379); Dunn (*Romans*, 829); and Wilckens (*Römer*, 3.97). Yet many modern commentators (Bardenhewer, Best, Black, Cranfield, Gutjahr, Lietzmann, and Sanday and Headlam) have realized the problem that this interpretation creates, in that it disregards the neutrality of many human acts, and have therefore understood *pistis* to mean "conviction," a meaning acknowledged by BAGD (664), i.e., a confidence that proceeds from Christian faith, which is distinct from it and manifests itself as liberty with regard to indifferent matters (*adiaphora*), as in vv 1b, 22, 23a.

(3) *Hamartia* would denote not the power controlling human beings (3:9b) or indwelling sin (7:17), but the basic idea of *hamartanein*, "miss the mark": the Christian would miss the mark by conduct in a specific case that proceeds not from inner freedom or from a conviction about the act to be done.

Clearly, one has to respect the full Pauline context of 14:1–15:13, and the utterance in v 23, maximlike though it sounds, should not be made into an absolute. The "maxim" is not applicable to all Christian conduct as such; it has to do with "all" indifferent matters, such as eating meat, drinking wine, and observing feasts. It is not a rule governing the basic relation of a Christian believer to God, much less the conduct of unbelieving pagans. See Sanday and Headlam, *Romans*, 393–94.

BIBLIOGRAPHY

Aland, K., "Glosse, Interpolation, Redaktion und Komposition in der Sicht der neutestamentlichen Textkritik: Eine Randbemerkung," *Apophoreta: Festschrift für Ernst Haenchen* . . . , BZNW 30 (Berlin: Töpelmann, 1964), 7–31; repr. in *Studien zur Überlieferung des Neuen Testaments und seines Textes*, ANTF 2 (Berlin: de Gruyter, 1967), 35–57.

Araud, R., "Quidquid non est ex fide peccatum est: Quelques interprétations patristiques," *L'Homme devant Dieu: Mélanges offerts au Père Henri de Lubac*, 3 vols. (Paris: Aubier, 1963–64), 1.127–45.

Corsani, B., "Hor tutto ciò che non è di fede, è peccato: Saulo da Tarso (Ai Romani, XIV,23)," *Protestantesimo* 34 (1979): 65–81.

M. D., "Twenty Misused Scripture Texts: VII. 'Whatsoever Is Not of Faith Is Sin.' Rom. xiv. 23," *ExpTim* 6 (1894–95): 568.

Donfried, K. P., "The Kingdom of God in Paul," *The Kingdom of God in Twentieth-Century Interpretation*, ed. W. Willis (Peabody, Mass.: Hendrickson, 1987), 175–90.

Evans, O. E., "Paul's Certainties III: What God Requires of Man—Romans xiv. 14," *ExpTim* 69 (1957–58): 199–202.

Fridrichsen, G. W. S., "The Gothic Text of Rom. xiv 14 *(ti koinon einai)* in Cod. Guelferbytanus, Weissenburg 64[1]," *JTS* 38 (1937): 245–47.

Haufe, G., "Reich Gottes bei Paulus und in der Jesustradition," *NTS* 31 (1985): 467–72.

Hünermann, P., "Zeit zum Handeln: 'Lasst uns also nach dem streben, was zum Frieden und zum Aufbau (der Gemeinde) beiträgt' (Röm 14,19)," *TQ* 172 (1992): 36–49.

Johnston, G., " 'Kingdom of God' Sayings in Paul's Letters," *From Jesus to Paul: Studies in Honour of Francis Wright Beare*, ed. P. Richardson and J. C. Hurd (Waterloo, Ont.: Wilfred Laurier University, 1984), 143–56.

Lindeboom, C., "Hoe moeten zij wederlegt worden, die zeggen, dat Matth. 10:32 en Rom. 14:22 met elkander in strijd zijn?" *GTT* 5 (1904): 28–29.

Nösgen, [K. F.], "Eine kleine paulinische Studie über Römer 14, 17. 18," *NKZ* 16 (1905): 546–61.

Pascher, W., *Rein und Unrein: Untersuchung zur biblischen Wortgeschichte*, SANT 24 (Munich: Kösel, 1970), 165–68.

Peterson, E., " *Ergon* in der Bedeutung 'Bau' bei Paulus," *Bib* 22 (1941): 439–41.

51. CHRIST IS OUR MODEL IN ALL CONDUCT (15:1–6)

15 [1]We who are strong ought to bear with the failings of those who are weak and not merely suit our own pleasure. [2]Each of us should please his neighbor for his good, to build him up. [3]For not even Christ suited his own pleasure, but as it stands written, *"The insults of those who insult you have fallen upon me."* [4]And what was written of old was written for our instruction that through endurance and the encouragement of the Scriptures we might have hope. [5]May God, the source of such endurance and encouragement, grant you a spirit of mutual harmony in accord with Christ Jesus, [6]so that with one mind and one voice you may glorify the God and Father of our Lord Jesus Christ.

COMMENT

The example of Christ is now proposed by Paul to the "strong" who are mentioned for the first time, even though the exhortation to them began at 14:13. Paul identifies himself with them and urges them to think of the encouragement that comes to them from the example of Christ himself and from the Scriptures, which have been entrusted to them for this very purpose. Christ has already shown how Christians should relate to one another, how the strong should bear with the failings of the weak. In his life on earth he did not consult his own interests, but the interest of all humanity that he came to serve. Thus he gave all Christians an example of how they ought to conduct themselves toward one another.

NOTES

15:1. *We who are strong.* Paul uses *hoi dynatoi*, "the capable, powerful ones," as a description of the mainly Gentile Christians of the Roman church. Although he himself is a Jewish Christian, he here identifies himself with the strong.

ought to bear with the failings of those who are weak. Paul calls the weak *adynatoi*, thus introducing a term that is the counterpart of *dynatoi*, "strong," in the first part of this verse. Up to this point he has referred to the "weak" as *astheneis* (14:1–2; cf. 14:12). The verb that he uses, *bastazein*, means either "bear" (a burden) or "endure, put up with" (BAGD, 137). The former would imply that the strong are called upon to help the weak in shouldering the burden of their scruples; the latter would counsel patient endurance or forbearance in the face of the immature attitude of the weak. See Gal 6:2. Cf. 1 Cor 9:2.

and not merely suit our own pleasure. Selfish concern, even based on strong conviction and inner freedom, should not be the motivation of Christians. They should not follow their own ideas or their personal tastes, for all are bound, one to the other.

2. *Each of us should please his neighbor for his good, to build him up.* Lit., "let each one of us please the neighbor for (his) good unto upbuilding," i.e., for the building up of his spiritual life and through him that of the community. The good of all Christian activity is a manifestation of love, and love of the neighbor was already inculcated in Lev 19:18, in the sense of love of a fellow Jew, a compatriot. Now the pleasing of one's neighbor contributes to making him or her a better Christian, and thus contributes to the good of all. See 14:19. The phrase *pros oikodomēn* is often taken to mean "to edify" in some pietistic or sanctimonious sense, but Paul means by it spiritual growth, understanding it corporately as a contribution to Christian solidarity. See 1 Thess 5:11; 1 Cor 10:23 (" 'All things are lawful'; but all things are not helpful; 'All things are lawful'; but all things do not build up"); 14:4–5, 7–8, 12, 26. Cf. G. W. MacRae, AER 140 (1959): 361–76.

3. *not even Christ suited his own pleasure.* See Phil 2:6–8 (but suffered death for all, even death on a cross); 2 Cor 8:9. Christ's giving of his life was motivated by his love for human beings (8:32–35). Love, then, should motivate Christians to please others and to contribute to the upbuilding of all. Life in the body of Christ means that Christians must learn to "bear one another's burdens" (Gal 6:2). Cf. 1 Cor 11:1 ("Be imitators of me, as I am of Christ").

as it stands written. See the NOTE on 1:17.

"The insults of those who insult you have fallen upon me." Paul quotes Ps 69:10 according to the LXX, which corresponds to the MT. Psalm 69 is a lament of individual upright sufferers who recognize in their personal tribulations that the reproaches leveled against God, to whom they pray for deliverance, have actually come to fall on themselves. Their tribulations stem from revilement

coming from those who even revile God himself. As applied to Christ, the words mean that he willingly accepted his sufferings and bore the reproaches uttered against God by the enemies of God. Both in the psalm and in Romans the second pers. pron. *se* refers to God, but the original sense of the psalm is not too pertinent to the situation envisaged by Paul; therefore he tries to justify the accommodated sense that he gives to it, as he seeks to apply it to Christians. Paul invokes here the classic psalm that the early church used to describe the passion of Jesus. For him it has become a Scriptural passage with significance for Christian disciples in their dealings with one another.

4. *what was written of old was written for our instruction.* See 4:23, which makes the same point that the OT Scriptures have meaning for Christians of today. Paul realizes that the Scriptures come to us from the past and were often composed directly for people of old, but they are not merely a document from the past, because they were intended by God to continue to address Jews and Christians generation after generation. As a Christian, Paul did not think, as Marcion later would, of rejecting the OT, for he recognizes the validity of the oracles entrusted by God to Israel of old as pertinent even for Christians. See 1 Cor 9:10; and especially how Paul interprets the events of the Exodus in 1 Cor 10:1–6. Cf. 2 Tim 3:16.

that through endurance and the encouragement of the Scriptures we might have hope. When Jesus' suffering is viewed against sacred history, it takes on a deeper meaning. Seen in this larger perspective, it gives Christians a basis for endurance *(hypomonē)*, that character that gives strength in persecution and suffering. It also supplies a basis for their hope (recall 5:3–4). On the encouragement of Scripture, see 1 Macc 12:9, where the letter of Jonathan makes known to the Spartans the "consolation" that the Jewish people find in their "holy books." Cf. Heb 3:6. Thus the goal of steadfast Christian conduct, encouraged by the Scriptures, is ultimately hope. With the aid of the Scriptures Paul exhorts his readers to endurance and constancy.

5. *May God, the source of such endurance and encouragement, grant you a spirit of mutual harmony in accord with Christ Jesus.* Thus Paul prays for the harmony of the Christian community of Rome, realizing that such unanimity is itself a gift of God, as is the understanding of Scripture. Recall 12:16; cf. 2 Cor 13:11; Phil 2:2; 4:2. Christ Jesus is again proposed as the model of Christian solidarity. When Christians live not only for themselves, but for others, then that solidarity is achieved. God himself is seen as the source of such harmony, because he supplies the grace of endurance and encouragement.

6. *so that with one mind and one voice you may glorify the God and Father of our Lord Jesus Christ.* Paul too prays for that harmony of Christian life, which is to redound to the glory of God, the goal of all Christian existence. See 2 Cor 1:3. Again Paul prays to God the Father through Christ Jesus. See 1:7. Cf. Wiles, *Paul's Intercessory Prayers*, 77–90.

BIBLIOGRAPHY ON CHAPTERS 15 AND 16

Lucht, H., *Ueber die beiden letzten Kapitel des Römerbriefes: Eine kritische Untersuchung* (Berlin: Heuschel, 1871).

Millies, H. C., *Historisch-kritisch onderzoek naar de echtheid van Rom. XV en XVI* (Utrecht: Beijers, 1866).

Schumacher, R., *Die beiden letzten Kapitel des Römerbriefes: Ein Beitrag zu ihrer Geschichte und Erklärung*, NTAbh 14.4 (Münster in Westfalen: Aschendorff, 1929).

Smith, W. B., *Unto Romans: XV. and XVI.* (Norwood, Mass.: no publ., 1902).

Straatman, J. W., "Het slot van den brief van Paulus aan de Romeinen: Een kritisch onderzoek," *TTijd* 2 (1868): 24–57.

Rom 15:1–6

Congar, Y., "La Consolation des Écritures (Rom 15,2–6)," in *La Bible, chemin de l'unité?* ed. G. Casalis and F. Refoulé (Paris: Cerf, 1967), 69–84.

Dupont, J., "Accueillants à tous: Rm 15,4–9," *AsSeign* n.s. 6 (1969): 13–18.

———, "Imiter la charité du Christ (Rm 15,1–13)," *AsSeign* 4 (1961): 13–34.

George, A., "Les Écritures, source d'espérance (*Romains*, 15, 1–6)," *BVC* 22 (1958): 53–57.

Hanson, A. T., "The Interpretation of the Second Person Singular in Quotations from the Psalms in the New Testament: A Note on Romans XV,3," *Hermathena* 73 (1949): 69–72.

Rosman, H., "Tolle, lege," *VD* 20 (1940): 116–23, esp. 116–18.

Spitta, F., "Zu Röm. 15, 4. 7. 8," *TSK* 86 (1913): 109–12.

Thüsing, W., "Das herrscherliche Wirken Christi als Verherrlichung Gottes (Rom 15,3.5–12)," *Per Christum in Deum*, 39–45.

Wiles, G. P., *Paul's Intercessory Prayers: The Significance of the Intercessory Prayer Passages in the Letters of St Paul*, SNTSMS 24 (Cambridge: Cambridge University Press, 1974).

Worley, D., " 'He Was Willing,' " *ResQ* 18 (1975): 1–11.

52. WELCOME ALL WHO TURN TO CHRIST AS LORD, JEW AND GENTILE (15:7–13)

15 ⁷Welcome one another, then, as Christ welcomed you, for the glory of God! ⁸For I tell you, Christ became a servant to the circumcised to show God's fidelity, to confirm the promises made to the patriarchs, ⁹and Gentiles have glorified God for his mercy, as it stands written,

"Therefore, I will proclaim you among the Gentiles
and sing praise to your name."

¹⁰Again it says,

"Rejoice, you Gentiles, along with his people."
11   *"Praise the Lord, all you Gentiles,*
and let all peoples sound his praise."

¹²Once again Isaiah says,

"There shall appear the Root of Jesse,
the one who rises to rule the Gentiles;
in him the Gentiles shall find hope."

¹³So may the God of hope fill you with all joy and peace in believing, so that you may abound in hope by the power of the holy Spirit.

COMMENT

These verses stress the mutual acceptance of Jews and Gentiles in the Christian community that is governed by the rule of Christ. Again, Paul appeals for unity and harmony based on the model of Christ. The motivation of it is the glory of God; the pattern is what Christ did; and the purpose is threefold: to manifest God's fidelity, to confirm the promises made to the patriarchs, and to relate the Gentiles to the goal of Israel's existence, viz., the glory of God.

With this paragraph Paul comes to the end of what he has to say about the weak and the strong and their mutual relations. He appeals again to the example of Christ, through whom God has gathered a united people destined to praise him with one voice. We come now to see how the gospel of God's uprightness unleashed in the world of humanity can seep down even into the relation of Jewish and Gentile Christians in one community.

To bolster his contention, Paul again appeals to the OT, as an example of what he said in vv 4–5, and introduces a *testimonia* list into his concluding exhortation; see the COMMENT on 3:10–20. He will quote the Torah, the Prophets, and the Writings, and in each case the catchword bond is "Gentiles" *(ethnē)* or "peoples" *(laoi)*. Käsemann *(Commentary*, 384) thinks that the tensions and debates of the preceding paragraphs vanish completely from view in this climactic paragraph, in which Paul cites Scripture to aid his argument. But the tensions and debates are still implicit, especially when the OT passages mention "Gentiles." For it is precisely here that one finds the contrast of Jew and Gentile that is the basis for interpreting the "weak" as mainly Jewish Christians.

The paragraph forms the conclusion to the hortatory section (12:1–15:13) and is the logical conclusion to the letter as a whole (1:16–15:13). The epistolary conclusion will follow in 15:14–16:24.

NOTES

15:7. *Welcome one another.* See the NOTE on 14:1. Cf. Phlm 17.

as Christ welcomed you. Paul repeats his basic exhortation of 14:1 in a more generic form. Whereas in 14:3c it was God's welcome, it is now Christ's welcome that becomes the pattern of Christian conduct. This is Paul's conclusion, echoing a similar instruction of the Johannine Jesus (John 13:34; 15:12). MSS B, D*, P, 048, 104, 614, 629, 1506 read *hēmas,* "us," instead of *hymas,* "you."

for the glory of God! The motive behind all of Christ's activity becomes the motivation for the conduct and mutual embrace of all Christians; see also Phil 1:11; 2:11. Cf. 1Q19 13:1; 1QSb 4:25; 1QS 10:9. Paul again uses *doxa tou theou* in the liturgical sense; see the NOTE on 11:36.

8. *Christ became a servant to the circumcised.* Lit., "a servant of (the) circumcision." See Gal 2:8–9 for the same way of designating the Jewish people. Jesus had to be a Jew and minister to them in order to confirm God's promises and thereby give evidence of God's truth and fidelity *(alētheia)*; see the NOTE on 3:4. Recall the saying of the Matthaean Jesus, "sent only to the lost sheep of the house of Israel" (Matt 15:24).

to show God's fidelity. Lit., "for the sake of the fidelity of God." This is the first purpose that Paul sees in the ministry of Jesus.

to confirm the promises made to the patriarchs. The second purpose. See Mic 7:20; Gen 12:1–3; 17:6–8; Acts 2:39; 3:25. As Paul understands these promises, both Jews and Gentiles share in them (recall 11:13–24). On this confirmation of the promises Paul bases his appeal for the unity of Jewish and Gentile Christians despite their ethnic backgrounds. See 11:28–29.

9. *Gentiles have glorified God for his mercy.* This is an indirect expression of the third purpose: that Gentiles may praise God for the mercy he has manifested to them. They too were included in the promises made to the patriarchs of Israel, as the Scripture texts to be cited will show. Although Jesus' ministry was directed to the Jews of Palestine, Gentiles were to be included eventually in God's kingdom, as even the OT promises indicate. See 11:30. As a result they too have been called to glorify God. "Vases of wrath" have become "vases of mercy" (9:22–23), and they are now called to glorify God for the manifestation of his mercy to them.

as it stands written. See the NOTE on 1:17.

"Therefore, I will proclaim you among the Gentiles and sing praise to your name." Paul begins a *testimonia* list as he quotes Ps 18:50 (= 2 Sam 22:50) according to the LXX, which corresponds to the MT, but he omits *Kyrie.* Psalm 18 is a royal thanksgiving psalm, in which a king on the Davidic throne thanks God for victory in battle over his enemies, the "nations." In Paul's use of the verse, "nations" become the "Gentiles," and the OT quotation supports Paul's

contention that Jewish Christians are to praise God along with Gentile Christians. Just as of old "nations" or "Gentiles" were called upon to glorify the God of Israel and thus join Israel in its worship of Yahweh, so now too Gentile Christians are called to join Jewish Christians in a united and harmonious glorification of God.

10. *"Rejoice, you Gentiles, along with his people."* Paul quotes a form of Deut 32:43, which differs somewhat from both the LXX and the MT. The latter reads *harnînû gôyīm ʿammô kî dam ʿăbādāyw yiqqôm*, "Praise his people, you nations, for he avenges his servants' blood." The LXX, however, reads *euphranthēte, ouranoi, hama autō, kai proskynēsatōsan autō pantes huioi theou*, "Rejoice, O heavens, along with him, and let all the sons of God adore him." This LXX form is now seen as a translation of a Hebrew *Vorlage* attested in 4QDeut^q as *hrnynw šmym ʿmw whšthww lw kl ʾlhym*, "Sing praise with him, O heavens" (or possibly, "Praise his people, O heavens"), "and let elohim adore him." See Skehan, "A Fragment." The Pauline form of the verse agrees with none of these earlier forms. The words are taken from the Song of Moses, its last verse, which is an invitation to the heavens (LXX 43a) and to the nations (43b) to break out in song and praise God along with his people. Paul applies this invitation to Gentile Christians too, recommending that they praise God along with Jewish Christians.

11. *"Praise the Lord, all you Gentiles, and let all peoples sound his praise."* Paul quotes Ps 117:1, almost according to the LXX, which has two parallel 2d pl. impvs., as does the MT. Some Greek MSS (F, G, and the *Koinē* text-tradition) as well as Latin and Syriac versions read the second verb here as a 2d pl. impv. too, *epainesate*, an obvious copyist's harmonization of Paul's text with the LXX. Paul quotes a doxological psalm with a slight change of word order. Its purpose was to summon the praise of all peoples to the worship of Yahweh, and the universality of such praise is stressed. Paul's purpose, in quoting it, is to recommend the praise of God to all, Gentile as well as Jewish Christians in the Roman community.

12. *Once again Isaiah says.* See vv 10, 11; Heb 1:5; 2:13.

"There shall appear the Root of Jesse, the one who rises to rule the Gentiles; in him the Gentiles shall find hope." Paul quotes Isa 11:10, slightly abridging the Greek text of the LXX, which differs from the MT. The latter reads *wĕhāyāh bayyôm hahûʾ šōreš yišay ʾăšer ʿōmēd lĕnēs ʿammîm; ʾēlāyw gôyīm yidrōšû*, "and on that day, (about) the Root of Jesse, which rises as a sign for the nations, the nations will inquire." The LXX introduces the idea of the Root of Jesse "ruling" the nations, which will find their "hope" in him: *kai estai en tē hēmera ekeinē hē riza tou Iessai kai ho anistamenos archein ethnōn. epʾ autō ethnē elpiousin*, "and on that day the Root of Jesse will also be the one who rises to rule the nations; for him the nations will hope." In the Isaian context the "Root" refers to an individual king of the Davidic dynasty, which is referred to as "Jesse" (the father of David). This king of the Davidic line is to be a rallying point for "Gentiles." He would arise like a signal or standard before them. This description of the messianic age Paul accommodates, understanding Jesus as the anointed king, the Messiah,

welcoming Jew and Gentile alike. Thus Jesus, sprung from the root of Jesse, has become the source of hope for both Jewish and Gentile Christians.

13. *So may the God of hope fill you with all joy and peace in believing.* Paul's exhortation ends with a prayer for the weak and the strong Christians of the Roman community. The final blessing, which concludes the hortatory section, employs key ideas of the OT passages just cited; in addition, it echoes those of the doctrinal and hortatory sections, alluding to 14:17 and 8:23–25. The "God of hope" is the one in whom both Jews and Gentiles believe and find their justification and salvation. Paul prays that God may be the source of joy and peace for all believers in Christ Jesus. The Greek MSS D, F, and G omit the prep. phrase *en tō pisteuein,* "in believing." Cf. BDF §404.1.

so that you may abound in hope by the power of the holy Spirit. Paul puts the prep. phrase "by the power of the holy Spirit" in the final, emphatic position in his prayer, thus stressing once again the role of the Spirit in Christian life. As in 8:23–27, Paul roots Christian hope in the gift of the Spirit.

BIBLIOGRAPHY

Bieder, W., *Die Verheissung der Taufe im Neuen Testament* (Zurich: EVZ Verlag, 1966).

Frid, B., "Jesaja och Paulus *versus* Bibelkommissionen i Rom. 15.12," *STK* 58 (1982): 11–16.

———, "Jesaja und Paulus in Röm 15:12," *BZ* 27 (1983): 237–41.

Hahn, F., *Mission in the New Testament,* SBT 47 (London: SCM; Naperville, Ill.: Allenson, 1965), 97–110.

Ljungman, H., *Pistis,* 48–54.

Ponthot, J., "L'Expression cultuelle du ministère paulinien selon Rom 15,16," *L'Apôtre Paul: Personnalité, style et conception du ministère,* BETL 73, ed. A. Vanhoye (Louvain: Leuven University/Peeters, 1986), 254–62.

Reichrath, H. L., "Juden und Christen—Eine Frage von 'Ökumene?' Was uns Römer 15,7–13 dazu lehrt," *Judaica* 47 (1991): 22–30.

Schulz, A., *Nachfolgen und Nachahmen: Studien über das Verhältnis der neutestamentlichen Jüngerschaft zur urchristlichen Vorbildethik,* SANT 6 (Munich: Kösel, 1962), 270–89.

Skehan, P. W., "A Fragment of the 'Song of Moses' (Deut. 32) from Qumran," *BASOR* 136 (1954): 12–15.

Wynne, G. R., "Mercy and Truth," *ExpTim* 21 (1909–10): 405–7.

Zeller, D., *Juden und Heiden,* 218–23.

III. PAUL'S PLANS, COMING TASK, AND REQUEST FOR PRAYERS (15:14–33)

◆

53. PAUL'S MISSIONARY PRINCIPLE IN HIS WORK SO FAR; HIS DESIRE TO VISIT THE ROMANS EN ROUTE TO SPAIN (15:14–24)

15 [14]I myself am convinced about you, brothers, that you are full of goodness, equipped with all knowledge, and capable of admonishing one another. [15]Yet I write to you quite boldly, partly to remind you in virtue of the grace given to me by God [16]to be a minister of Christ Jesus to the Gentiles, with the priestly duty of preaching God's gospel, so that the offering of the Gentiles might become acceptable and consecrated by the holy Spirit. [17]Therefore, in what pertains to God I have this boast in Christ Jesus. [18]For I shall not dare to speak of anything save what Christ has accomplished through me for the commitment of the Gentiles, either in word or in deed, [19]by the power of signs and wonders, or by the power of God's Spirit. So I have fully preached the gospel of Christ from Jerusalem all the way around to Illyricum. [20]Thus it has been my ambition to preach the good news where Christ has not been named, lest I build on the foundation of someone else. [21]But as it stands written, *"Those who have had no news of him will see, and those who have not heard of him will understand."* [22]This is why I have so often been hindered from coming to you. [23]But now since I no longer have room for work in these regions and have been longing for many years to come to you, (I plan to do so) [24]as I proceed on my way to Spain. I hope to see you as I travel along and be sped on my way there by you, once I have enjoyed your company for a while.

COMMENT

Now that Paul has finished the exposé of his gospel and set forth its implications for upright Christian life, he adds the epistolary conclusion to his letter to the Romans. In it he sends news about himself, his future apostolic plans, his need to go to Jerusalem with the collection that he has taken up in Macedonia and Achaia, and his desire to come to the west. His labors in the east have come to an end, and after the visit to Jerusalem, he wants to come to Rome on his way to Spain, where he hopes to undertake further evangelization. Paul takes the occasion of recounting his plans to compliment the Roman Christians on the good things that he has heard about them; he is proud to write to them as "the apostle of the Gentiles," even though he has had so far no influence on them or on their belief in Christ. Yet this part begins with a semiapologetic tone, because Paul realizes that at times he has formulated some ideas rather sharply. He is convinced that there is still room for exhortation, even in the church of Rome, the faith of which is well known (1:8).

In vv 14–33 Paul composes a passage that in form and content deals with what has been called his apostolic *parousia*. In such a passage Paul usually expresses his intention to send a representative or to come personally to a Christian community; in this way he becomes present to it, even though in this case he speaks of his projected "presence." Other such passages dealing with his *parousia* can be found in Phlm 21–22; 1 Cor 4:14–21; 1 Thess 2:17–3:13; Phil 2:19–24 (see Funk, "The Apostolic *Parousia*").

This epistolary conclusion may be subdivided into three parts: (1) 15:14–24; (2) 15:25–29; and (3) 15:30–33. In the first part Paul states the disposition in which he writes (vv 14–19a) and elaborates on his coming apostolic relation to the Roman community (vv 15b–24).

NOTES

15:14. *I myself am convinced about you.* Although he has just finished exhorting the Roman Christians to unity and harmony (15:7–13), Paul points out his abiding and satisfying conviction (using the perf. tense to express the continuance of it) that he has of their goodness and their understanding of Christian faith and life. To stress his personal conviction about them, Paul uses *kai autos egō*, "and I myself"; the phrase stands in contrast to *kai autoi*, "you yourselves," in the following clause.

brothers. Again Paul so hails the Christians of Rome; see the NOTE on 1:13. Some MSS (א, A, B, C, D², Ψ, and the *Koinē* text-tradition), the Vg, and Syriac versions read "my brothers," a slight variant. The pron *mou* is omitted in MSS P⁴⁶, D*, F, G, 1739.

that you are full of goodness, equipped with all knowledge, and capable of admonishing one another. Thus Paul expresses his confidence in the Roman Christians and echoes what he wrote in 1:8. He notes their qualities: goodness, knowledge, and ability to admonish or correct one another. Thus he foreshadows what he will say in vv 23b and 32 and engages in a final *captatio benevolentiae*. See 1 Cor 1:5; Phil 1:9. How Paul came to know these things about the Christians of Rome he does not say. Recalling such qualities, he clearly flatters them with his rhetoric.

15. *Yet I write to you quite boldly.* Lit., "more boldly, rather boldly," the adv. being actually in the comparative degree: Paul may mean that he is writing more freely and more strongly than the goodness and knowledge, which he has just praised, may warrant. He is aware that some of the things about which he writes to the community of Rome, which he has not founded, may seem a bit audacious

and provocative. And so, he utters a quasi-apology, as he did in 1:5 and 13. He uses the epistolary aor. *egrapsa*; see BDF §334.

MSS P⁴⁶, ℵ², D, F, G, Ψ, and the *Koinē* text-tradition add *adelphoi*, "brothers," after *hymin*, "to you." If it is to be retained, see the NOTE on 1:13.

partly to remind you in virtue of the grace given to me by God. I.e., the God-given charism (= *gratia gratis data* of later theology) to preach the gospel and to summon Gentiles to faith in Christ. He will explain as much in the following verse. But see 1:5, where he has already spoken of "the grace of apostleship" that he has received. Also 12:3, "in virtue of the grace given to me I say. . . ." Cf. 12:6; Gal 2:7–9; 1 Cor 3:10; 4:6; cf. Eph 3:2, 7–8. Paul is explaining to the Christians of Rome that he is justified in writing to them as he does, because he is the Apostle to the Gentiles. As such, he is concerned that his ministry serve all Gentiles, wherever they may be. But he insists that he is only reminding them of what they already know. What he has written is nothing other than the usual instruction of the church, which must have been known to the community. Here his "reminder" consists only in the sharpening of the catechesis. So he avoids introducing into his letter anything new or foreign to such a tradition (Michel, *Brief an die Römer*, 456). What Paul thus writes makes it unlikely that he thinks that Christianity in Rome is still in need of apostolic foundation, *pace* G. Klein (see Introduction, section V).

16. *to be a minister of Christ Jesus to the Gentiles.* See 11:13. Paul describes his role in liturgical language, using neither *diakonos*, "servant," as in 2 Cor 3:6, nor *oikonomos*, "steward," as in 1 Cor 4:1, but *leitourgos*, "cultic minister" (see the NOTE on 13:6). Though *leitourgos* theoretically could have no more than a secular meaning, as sometimes in the LXX, it takes on the religious nuance from the context in which Paul uses it. As such a cultic minister, Paul offers his evangelization of the Gentiles to God as a form of worship. Recall the way Paul formulated this idea in 1:9: "the God, whom I worship with my spirit in the evangelization of his Son, is my witness. . . ." Cf. Col 1:25.

with the priestly duty of preaching God's gospel. In his mission to the Gentiles Paul sees his function to be like that of a Jewish priest dedicated to the service of God in his Temple. If all Christian life is to be regarded as a worship paid to God (12:1), the spreading of Christ's gospel is easily compared to the role of a sacred minister in such worship. Paul implies that the preaching of the word of God is a liturgical act in itself. He uses of it the vb. *hierourgein*, "function as a priest." This verb is a hapax legomenon in the NT; in the LXX it occurs only in one MS of 4 Macc 7:8, meaning "to minister (to the law) as a priest." Josephus and Philo normally use it without an object in the sense of "offer sacrifice" (*Ant.* 14.4.3 §65; 17.6.4 §166; *De cherub.* 28 §96). If Clement of Rome (*1 Clem.* 8:1) can look on OT prophets as cultic ministers of God's grace (*hoi leitourgoi tēs charitos tou theou*), this term can be applied even more to the apostles, prophets, and teachers of the NT (cf. 2 Cor 3:3). The service of the priests in the Jerusalem Temple provides the background of Paul's metaphorical language (cf. Exod 28:35,

43; 29:30, where Aaron and his sons are referred to as "priests" and the vb. *leitourgein* is used of their cultic service); but the language could also refer to service in pagan temples. Cf. the figurative use of *leitourgein* in Acts 13:2.

Nevertheless, one cannot deduce from this Pauline view of his role as a preacher of the gospel that he was aware of himself as a Christian "priest," *pace* L. Shehan, "The Priest," 13. The problem is not the question whether Paul ever functioned as a Christian "priest," a minister of sacraments; he may well have been such, for he admits that he baptized Crispus, Gaius, and the household of Stephanas (1 Cor 1:14–16). Although he never says so, he probably did preside at the Christian celebration "the Lord's Supper" (1 Cor 11:20; possibly Luke so depicts him in Acts 20:11). The name of the Christian "priest," however, develops in some modern languages from Greek *presbyteros*, "elder," a title that Paul never uses of himself. The name for the cultic "priest" of the Old Law, *hiereus*, is used in the NT only of Christ (Heb 5:6; 7:1–23, etc.) and never of any of his apostles or disciples. The frame of reference for Paul's designation of himself in this passage as *leitourgos* or *hierourgōn* is that of the Jewish priesthood of the Jerusalem Temple, or, as Cranfield has shown, that of the Levites (*Romans*, 755). Cf. W. Pesch, "Zu Texten"; Schelkle, "Der Apostel als Priester"; Weiss, "Paulus—Priester"; Wiéner, "*Hierourgein.*"

so that the offering of the Gentiles might become acceptable. *Tōn ethnōn* is best taken as an objective gen.; it thus denotes the evangelized Gentiles who are consecrated and offered to God as an acceptable sacrifice through Paul's evangelization of them. Because the *finis* of all sacrifice is to bring about in some way the return of sinful human beings to God, Paul looks on his work among the Gentiles as a form of sacrifice, for their conversion has achieved that very purpose. The Apostle of the Gentiles offers to God not slaughtered animals, but repentant human beings, and this is the *prosphora* acceptable to God. See 12:1; cf. Isa 66:20. Compare Phil 2:17, where Paul sees himself as a libation poured over "the sacrificial offering of your faith," i.e., over the faith of the predominantly Gentile Philippian church that he has evangelized. By contrast, Denis prefers to understand the gen. *tōn ethnōn* as subjective, "the offering that the Gentiles make" ("Fonction apostolique," 405–6). Paul's ministry would then be to bring the Gentiles to offer their cult to God. This is a possible meaning, but in view of Phil 2:17 it is less suitable. Does this verse mean that Paul never so offered Jewish converts? Hardly, though appeal has been made to this statement to maintain that Paul never regarded it as his responsibility to convert Jews as such (Sanders, *USQR* 33 [1978]: 178).

consecrated by the holy Spirit. The evangelized Gentiles thus share in an effect of the Christ-event; they have been "sanctified" (see Introduction, section IX.B), and this dedication to God and his service is made possible by the gift of the holy Spirit.

17. in what pertains to God I have this boast in Christ Jesus. Paul's pride and boast are rooted where they should be, in Christ (see 5:2). Such an expression of

his self-confidence comes from Paul's awareness of the ministry that he has carried out among the Gentiles so far. He is not expressing it because he expects any opposition in Rome from the Christians there. Rather, he knows that his ministry is God-inspired and that it has been carried out with the help of divine grace. So he "boasts" in Christ Jesus, i.e., in what he has accomplished for Christ Jesus and in the grace that has come to him from Christ enabling him to accomplish it. His self-confidence parallels the confidence that he has already expressed in the Roman Christians in v 14. Such expressions of self-confidence can be found in other ancient Greek writings; see Dio Chrysostom, *Oratio* 41.1; Thucydides, *Peloponnesian War* 2.60.5; Heb 2:17. Cf. Olson, "Epistolary Uses." The phrase *ta pros ton theon* is used as an adv. acc., "in what pertains to God"; see BDF §160.

18. *I shall not dare to speak of anything save what Christ has accomplished through me for the commitment of the Gentiles.* Paul indirectly admits his success in evangelizing the Gentiles; it is a source of his pride, his boast (*kauchēsis*). Yet he knows that it has been accomplished "through" him by Christ Jesus; he is only an instrument in the conversion of the Gentiles and has not achieved it by his own powers or merits. For Christ has really brought about their turning to God. See 2 Cor 13:3.

either in word or in deed. This phrase is further explained in the following verse.

19. *by the power of signs and wonders.* Paul thus admits that some miracles have been wrought through him; see 2 Cor 12:12. The Lucan account depicts some (Acts 16:18, 26; [20:10?]; 28:6). Paul uses traditional language, *sēmeia kai terata* for miraculous deeds; cf. Dan 6:28 (Theod.); 2 Thess 2:9; Heb 2:4; Acts 2:22, 43; 4:30; 14:3; 15:12. See Stolz, "Zeichen."

by the power of God's Spirit. Paul implies that the Spirit was behind all of his words, deeds, signs, and wonders. See 1 Cor 2:4; 1 Thess 1:5. In MS B *theou* is omitted, and in MSS A, D*, F, G, 33, etc. *hagiou*, "holy," is added, an obvious copyist's correction. The earliest textual witnesses (P⁴⁶, ℵ, D¹, Ψ, and the *Koinē* text-tradition) read *pneumatos theou*, "God's Spirit."

So I have fully preached the gospel of Christ from Jerusalem all the way around to Illyricum. Lit., "so that I have filled up the (preaching of the) gospel of Christ from Jerusalem even in a circle as far as Illyricum." The clause is not well formulated. Paul is describing the ambit of his evangelization of the eastern Mediterranean world from a geographic, not a historical point of view, from Jerusalem as far as Illyricum. He is thinking of his ministry in the towns of southern and northern Galatia, in the provinces of Asia, Achaia, and Macedonia. Rhetorically, he exaggerates, because one may wonder what he means by "fully preached." This term, however, gives us an inkling of the way he conceived of his apostolate during the preceding twelve years or so; he was called as a pioneer preacher of the gospel, to establish new communities of believers in the gospel among the Gentiles, as he will explain in v 20. Did he also preach to Jews at times in the eastern area? There is no reason to think that he did not. Otherwise how is one to explain 2 Cor 11:24 (the thirty-nine lashes experienced at the hands of the Jews) or 1 Cor 9:10 ("to the Jews I became as a Jew in order to win Jews").

Jerusalem. Jerusalem is the matrix of Christianity, its mother church, because there the Christ-event took place. Paul regards it also as the starting point of his ministry, even though his call to be the Apostle to the Gentiles occurred near Damascus (Gal 1:17c). Jerusalem was for Paul the place where he met those who were "apostles before me" (Gal 1:17a), where he learned from Cephas (Gal 1:18), and where his gospel met with approval (Gal 2:2). Here and elsewhere in Romans 15 Paul writes *Ierousalēm*, whereas in Gal 1:17–18 and 2:1 he uses the form *Hierosolyma.*

Illyricum. This area would correspond to modern Albania and southern Yugoslavia. It had become an imperial province of the Roman Empire in 11 B.C., but its indigenous populace revolted against Rome in time, and it was reconquered in A.D. 6–9 by Tiberius. In A.D. 9 it was divided into two imperial provinces, known at first as Illyricum Superius and Illyricum Inferius, but later as Pannonia and Dalmatia. It is not easy to say in what sense Paul would be using the name Illyricum. For him it almost certainly designated the area north of Macedonia (see Strabo, *Geography* 7.7.4; Appian, *Roman History* 10.1.6).

Actually, we never learn from Paul's letters of his preaching the gospel in either Jerusalem or Illyricum. Although Luke describes Paul's evangelical ministry in three blocks of texts (Acts 13:3–14:28; 15:37–18:22; and 18:23–21:17), he does not depict Paul preaching there either, but he does make Paul say that he preached repentance to "those at Damascus and Jerusalem first" (Acts 26:20). Paul was in Macedonia during his third missionary journey (54–58) and may have gone from there to Illyricum (whence he may even have written part of 2 Corinthians; see *PAHT,* §P43). Part of the problem is the meaning of the phrase *kai kyklō.* The dat. *kyklō* was often used adverbially in classical Greek in the sense of "in a circle, round about" (BAGD 456–57; cf. LXX Gen 23:17; Exod 19:12). As used here, it hardly refers to the environs of Jerusalem, as older commentators once understood it. It is, rather, used rhetorically to suggest the sweep of Paul's evangelization. There is no need to think, with Hahn (*Mission,* 96 n. 8), that Paul was considering Illyricum as "the ancient boundary separating the eastern and western halves of the empire." There is no evidence for that interpretation here or elsewhere in Paul's letters. Rather, with a rhetorical flourish he looks back on his evangelization of Syria, Cilicia, Asia Minor (especially Ephesus and Troas), Macedonia, and Achaia, adding Illyricum because it designated for him the country on the Adriatic Sea across from Italy, to which he hopes to travel and is now writing.

In the phrase "the gospel of Christ," *tou Christou* would be an objective gen., i.e., the gospel about Christ, and *euangelion* apparently has here the active sense of the "preaching of the gospel," as in 1:9 and Phil 4:15. As Paul thus writes to the Romans, he is developing his missionary theology: "He argues theologically in order to make the missionary congregations understand their own place within the divine economy, what God has granted and promised to them and therefore what he expects of them" (Dahl, "Missionary Theology," 71). The sweep of his evangelization stresses the conviction that Paul had of his vocation, not to baptize, but to preach the gospel (1 Cor 1:17). His apostolate "to the Gentiles" was thus being accomplished.

20. *Thus it has been my ambition to preach the good news.* Lit., "thus considering it an honor to preach. . . ." The function of this verse is contested. Sanday and Headlam (*Romans*, 408), Cranfield (*Romans*, 763), and Dunn (*Romans*, 865) understand it as an explanation or qualification of what was said in v 19b: Paul has completed his mission in the east, but not in an absolute sense. He has viewed himself as a "pioneer preacher." There were areas in the east where he did not preach, because he did not want to build on the work of others. In this view, the adv. *houtōs* modifies the infin. *euangelizesthai*, "it has been my ambition so to preach." It thus serves to explain why Paul has not yet been to Rome. Because his field in the east is covered, he is desirous to proceed to the west, to Rome and to Spain. Lagrange (*Romains*, 353) and Käsemann (*Commentary*, 395), however, understand the verse as a transition to the plans to be announced in vv 22–24. It thus continues Paul's "boast" in a new sense and formulates a sort of principle. The former interpretation seems preferable, but it is not easy to decide.

where Christ has not been named. Lit., "not where Christ has been named." What Paul really means is, "where Christ has not yet been named." "Named" has to be understood in the sense of acknowledgment, worship, or reverence (cf. Isa 26:13; Amos 6:10), and not just "known," as BAGD (574) would interpret it.

lest I build on the foundation of someone else. Paul is not, then, thinking of Christ as the sole foundation of Christian life (1 Cor 3:11), but of the work of other apostles and prophets who have founded churches. His ambition has been to carry the gospel of Christ's name to areas where it has not been heard. What he says is in part explained by what he wrote in 2 Cor 10:14–16: "We are not overextending ourselves, as though we did not reach you; we were the first to come to you with the gospel of Christ. We boast not beyond limit, in the work of other persons; rather our hope is, that as your faith increases, our field among you may be greatly enlarged, so that we may preach the gospel in lands beyond you, without boasting of work already done in another's field." It may seem puzzling why Paul would have made that his overriding ambition. Why should he have been reluctant to build upon the foundation that someone else had laid? This statement may seem to create a problem with what he says in 1:13 and 15, where he expresses his eagerness "to preach the gospel also to you who are in Rome," when it is clear that he did not found the Roman church and that some other Christians must have done so. Yet what seems like a principle that he enunciates here may have been true of his activity in the east and may also explain why he is desirous now to go to Spain. Clearly, Paul is not saying that he absolutely avoids preaching where Christ is already known. His principle cannot be so interpreted as to contradict his desire to preach to the Romans too. The two ideas are compatible. In any case, the differences do not create the basis for the dividing of Romans, as Schmithals has advocated (see Introduction, section IV). What Paul says here is simply another way of formulating the commission given to him to establish Christian communities. In 1 Cor 3:5–9 Paul recognizes that he and Apollos are both servants of God, commissioned to do different things to build up God's field or God's building, as occasion offers.

21. *as it stands written.* See the NOTE on 1:17. It is not easy to explain why Paul introduces at this point in his statement of plans a quotation from the OT.

"Those who have had no news of him will see, and those who have not heard of him will understand." Paul quotes Isa 52:15 according to the LXX, which introduces "of him" into its translation of the MT. The Hebrew simply says, "What they have not been told, they see, and what they have not heard, they understand." The "they" refers to the "nations" and "kings" mentioned in the first part of the verse. By introducing *peri autou,* the LXX makes the verse refer to the Servant of Yahweh and his sufferings. It is thus more suited than the MT to Paul's use of the verse with reference to Christ. Paul implies that through his ministry those who had not previously heard about Christ have come to knowledge about him and belief in him.

Because the "of him" in this verse has to refer to Christ, it is puzzling why some commentators have tried to understand it as if Paul were referring to himself as the Servant of the Lord and to his ministry as a commission like that of the Isaianic Servant. Dunn (*Romans,* 966) tries to argue for it. If there is any validity for this view of Paul as another Servant of the Lord, it does not depend on this passage in Romans.

22. *This is why I have so often been hindered from coming to you.* Because Paul has been so busy evangelizing the eastern Mediterranean area, from Jerusalem around to Illyricum, he has not yet been able to travel to Rome, the capital of the empire. See 1:13, the ideas of which Paul now resumes. He implies that his concern for place after place in that eastern area preoccupied him so that he could not come to Rome, no matter how often he thought of doing so. To express how often that was, he says *ta polla,* "many times." Paul does not mention Satan as the hindrance, as he does in 1 Thess 2:18. Cf. Acts 16:6. On the omission of the adv. *mē* before the articular infin. with a vb. of hindering, see BDF §400.4.

23. *now since I no longer have room for work in these regions and have been longing for many years to come to you, (I plan to do so).* Paul knows, of course, that he has not yet converted all of the Gentiles in the eastern Mediterranean area, but he regards his function as that of pioneer preacher who must lay foundations. He has established representative communities and churches in the eastern Mediterranean that will, with God's help, be able to cope with matters and prepare for the day of the Lord. Others may build upon what he has done (1 Cor 3:6, 10). See 1:10–11.

24. *as I proceed on my way to Spain.* As in 15:28, we learn only now of Paul's plans to visit Spain. The Iberian peninsula was at that time part of the Roman Empire, noted for its silver and gold mines (1 Macc 8:2). Spain was apparently discovered by Phoenicians from Tyre in the early part of the first millennium B.C. In the third century it came under the Carthaginian domination of Hamilcar Barca and Hannibal. The eastern coast of Spain was subjected to Roman control after the Carthaginians were subdued by Scipio Africanus in 206 B.C. Two Roman provinces were set up in 197 B.C. (Hispania Citerior and Hispania Ulterior), but it was not until the time of Augustus that the whole peninsula came under Roman domination and three provinces were established, the senatorial province of Baetica and the imperial provinces of Lusitania (roughly what is now Portugal) and Tarraconensis. For Paul Spain represents the unconverted world of the west, the pagans in a remote part of the Roman Empire, where, it seems, Latin was the dominant language.

It is often thought that Paul's interest in going to Spain stemmed from his knowledge that Jews dwelled there. Käsemann (*Commentary*, 398) confidently asserts, "Spain was a common place of travel. . . . There were certainly some synagogues there." Similarly Michel, *Brief an die Römer*, 463 n. 3. Yet though Jews from Libya, Cyrene, and Rome are depicted by Luke (Acts 2:10) as present in Jerusalem for the feast of the Assembly (what Josephus calls *Asartha* [= Aramaic ʿăṣartāʾ, "gathering"] or Pentecost, *Ant.* 3.10.6 §252), none are mentioned as coming from Spain. Moreover, there is thus far no evidence of Jewish habitation in Spain prior to the third century A.D. (see Bowers, "Jewish Communities"; S. W. Baron, A *Social and Religious History of the Jews* [New York: Columbia University Press], 1 [1952]. 170; E. Schürer, *HJPAJC* 3.84–85). So Josephus's statement that there is no city "Greek or barbarian" or "a single nation" to which Jewish customs had not spread (*Ag. Ap.* 2.39 §282) may have to be taken with a grain of salt. Paul's interest in Spain undoubtedly stemmed from having heard about that part of the Roman Empire as well as from his conviction about himself as "the apostle of the Gentiles" (11:13). From something of this kind emerged his desire to find an area in the west where "Christ has not been named" (15:20). —Did Paul ever get to Spain? See *PAHT* §§P50–54.

On the conj. *hōs an* with the subjunct., see BDF §455.2. Greek MS ℵ² and the *Koinē* text-tradition try to remedy the anacoluthon that is found in the best MSS (P⁴⁶, ℵ*, A, B, C, D, F, G, etc.), adding after "Spain" the words *eleusomai pros hymas*, "I shall come to you." The sentence in most MSS lacks a main verb, which accounts for the clause added in my translation of v 23.

I hope to see you as I travel along. I.e., to the west. See 1 Cor 16:6.

and be sped on my way there by you. I.e., to be dispatched at least with their prayers and good wishes, if not also with their alms. Paul uses the vb. *propempein*, as in 1 Cor 16:6, 11; 2 Cor 1:16. He expects the Christians of Rome to be involved in his effort to carry the gospel of Christ ever farther abroad.

once I have enjoyed your company for a while. Lit., "if I am first partly filled with your company." Recall 1:11–12. While there, Paul would almost certainly be able to get information about Spain from Romans familiar with that country.

BIBLIOGRAPHY

Aus, R. D., "Paul's Travel Plans to Spain and the 'Full Number' of the Gentiles of Rom 11:25," *NovT* 21 (1979): 232–62.

Barnikol, E., *Spanienreise und Römerbrief* (Halle an der Saale: Akademischer Verlag, 1934).

Borse, U., "Paulus in Jerusalem," *Kontinuität und Einheit: Für Franz Mussner*, ed. P.-G. Müller and W. Stenger (Freiburg im Breisgau: Herder, 1981), 43–64.

Bowers, W. P., "Jewish Communities in Spain in the Time of Paul the Apostle," *JTS* 26 (1975): 395–402.

Brunner, P., "Zur Lehre vom Gottesdienst der im Namen Jesu versammelten Gemeinde," *Leiturgia*, 5 vols., ed. F. K. Müller and W. Blankenburg (Kassel: Johannes Stauda, 1954–70), 1.83–364.

Dabelstein, R., *Die Beurteilung der 'Heiden' bei Paulus*, BBET 14 (Bern and Frankfurt: Lang, 1981), 111–14.

Dahl, N. A., "The Missionary Theology in the Epistle to the Romans," *Studies in Paul* (Minneapolis, Minn.: Augsburg, 1977), 70–94.

Denis, A.-M., "La Fonction apostolique et la liturgie nouvelle en Esprit: Étude thématique des métaphores pauliniennes du culte nouveau," *RSPT* 42 (1958): 401–36, 617–56.

Eckert, J., "Die Kollekte des Paulus für Jerusalem," *Kontinuität und Einheit* (see above under Borse), 65–80.

Funk, R. W., "The Apostolic *Parousia*: Form and Significance," *Christian History and Interpretation: Studies Presented to John Knox*, ed. W. R. Farmer et al. (Cambridge: Cambridge University Press, 1967), 249–68.

Gaugusch, L., "Untersuchungen zum Römerbrief: Der Epilog (15, 14–16, 27), eine exegetische Studie," *BZ* 24 (1938–39): 164–84, 252–66.

Geyser, A. S., "Un Essai d'explication de Rom. xv. 19," *NTS* 6 (1959–60): 156–59.

Hahn, F., *Mission in the New Testament*, 96–97.

Hengel, M., "Die Ursprünge der christlichen Mission," *NTS* 18 (1971–72): 15–38.

Holl, K., "Der Kirchenbegriff des Paulus in seinem Verhältnis zu dem der Urgemeinde," *Gesammelte Aufsätze zur Kirchengeschichte*, vol. 2: *Der Osten* (Tübingen: Mohr [Siebeck], 1928; repr. Darmstadt: Wissenschaftliche Buchgesellschaft, 1964), 44–67; repr. in *Das Paulusbild in der neueren deutschen Forschung*, WF 24, ed. K. H. Rengstorf (Darmstadt: Wissenschaftliche Buchgesellschaft, 1964), 144–78.

Jewett, R., "Paul, Phoebe, and the Spanish Mission," *The Social World of Formative Christianity and Judaism: Essays in Tribute to Howard Clark Kee*, ed. J. Neusner et al. (Philadelphia, Penn.: Fortress, 1988), 142–66.

Klauck, H.-J., "Kultische Symbolsprache bei Paulus," *Freude am Gottesdienst: As-*

pekte ursprünglicher Liturgie . . . (Stuttgart: Katholisches Bibelwerk, 1983), 107–18.

Knox, J., "Romans 15:14–23 and Paul's Conception of His Apostolic Mission," *JBL* 83 (1964): 1–11.

Krieger, N., "Zum Römerbrief," *NovT* 3 (1959–60): 146–48.

Meinardus, O. F. A., "Paul's Missionary Journey to Spain: Tradition and Folklore," *BA* 41 (1978): 61–63.

Michelsen, M., "Über einige sinnverwandte Aussprüche des Neuen Testaments: . . . Röm. 15,16," *TSK* 46 (1873): 128–35.

Müller, P., "Grundlinien paulinischer Theologie (Röm 15, 14–33)," *KD* 35 (1989): 212–35.

Munck, J., *Paul*, 49–53, 282–308.

Olson, S. N., "Epistolary Uses of Expressions of Self-Confidence," *JBL* 103 (1984): 585–97.

———, "Pauline Expressions of Confidence in His Addressees," *CBQ* 47 (1985): 282–85.

Pedersen, S., "Theologische Überlegungen zur Isagogik des Römerbriefes," *ZNW* 76 (1985): 47–67.

Pesch, W., "Zu Texten des Neuen Testamentes über das Priestertum der Getauften," *Verborum veritas: Festschrift für Gustav Stählin* . . . , ed. O. Böcher und K. Haacker (Wuppertal: Brockhaus, 1970), 303–15.

Ponthot, J., "L'Expression cultuelle du ministère paulinien selon Rom 15,16," *L'Apôtre Paul: Personnalité, style et conception du ministère*, BETL 73, ed. A. Vanhoye (Louvain: Leuven University, 1986), 254–62.

Radl, W., "Alle Mühe umsonst? Paulus und der Gottesknecht," ibid. 144–49.

———, "Kult und Evangelium bei Paulus," *BZ* 31 (1987): 58–75.

Robinson, D. W. B., "The Priesthood of Paul in the Gospel of Hope," *Reconciliation and Hope: New Testament Essays on Atonement and Eschatology Presented to L. L. Morris* . . . , ed. R. Banks (Exeter, UK: Paternoster; Grand Rapids, Mich.: Eerdmans, 1974), 231–45.

Roloff, J., *Apostolat—Verkündigung—Kirche: Ursprung, Inhalt und Funktion des kirchlichen Apostelamtes nach Paulus, Lukas und den Pastoralbriefen* (Gütersloh: Gütersloher-Verlag, 1965), 94–96.

Schelkle, K.-H., "Der Apostel als Priester," *TQ* 136 (1956): 257–83.

Schlier, H., "Die 'Liturgie' des apostolischen Evangeliums (Römer 15,14–21)," *Martyria, Leiturgia, Diakonia: Festschrift für Hermann Volk* . . . , ed. O. Semmelroth et al. (Mainz: Grünewald, 1968), 247–59; repr. in *Das Ende der Zeit*, 169–83.

Shehan, L., "The Priest in the New Testament: Another Point of View," *Homiletic and Pastoral Review* 76.2 (1975–76): 10–23.

Stolz, F., "Zeichen und Wunder: Die prophetische Legitimation und ihre Geschichte," *ZTK* 69 (1972): 125–44.

Stuhlmacher, P., "Erwägungen zum Problem von Gegenwart und Zukunft in der paulinischen Eschatologie," *ZTK* 64 (1967): 423–50.

———, *Das paulinischen Evangelium*, vol. 1: *Vorgeschichte*, FRLANT 95 (Göttingen: Vandenhoeck & Ruprecht, 1968), 100–5.

Thornton, T. C. G., "St Paul's Missionary Intentions in Spain," *ExpTim* 86 (1974–75): 120.

Trocmé, E., "L'Épître aux Romains et la méthode missionnaire de l'apôtre Paul," *NTS* 7 (1960–61): 148–53.

Weiss, K., "Paulus—Priester der christlichen Kultgemeinde," *TLZ* 79 (1954): 355–64.

Wenschkewitz, H., "Die Spiritualisierung der Kultusbegriffe Tempel, Priester und Opfer im Neuen Testament," *Angelos* 4 (1932): 71–230, esp. 192–93.

Wiéner, C., "*Hierourgein* (Rm 15,16)," *SPCIC* 2.399–404.

Zeller, D., *Juden und Heiden*, 64–74, 222–29.

54. His Coming Task Before that Visit: To Carry a Collection to the Poor of Jerusalem (15:25–29)

15 ²⁵At present, however, I am making my way to Jerusalem to bring aid to God's dedicated people there. ²⁶For Macedonia and Achaia kindly decided to make some contribution for the poor among these people in Jerusalem. ²⁷They kindly decided to do so, and indeed they are indebted to them. For if Gentiles have come to share in the spiritual blessings of Jerusalem Christians, they ought to be of service to them in material things. ²⁸So when I have completed this task and have delivered this contribution under my own seal, I shall set out for Spain, passing through your midst. ²⁹I know that, when I arrive among you, I shall be coming with the full blessing of Christ.

COMMENT

Paul continues to recount his plans, indicating that, before he will be able to come to Rome, he has to travel to Jerusalem to transmit a collection, which the churches that he has founded in Achaia and Macedonia have taken up for the poor among the Christians of the Jerusalem church. He senses an urgency in this matter; he does not think that he can send it to Jerusalem in the care of someone else. He must go there himself. In the following paragraph (15:30–33), he will hint at the reasons for this decision. Paul has attached much importance to this collection, intended to establish good relations between the Jewish Christian mother-community of Jerusalem and the newly founded Gentile Christian churches. The collection was intended to be a token of their solidarity with the mother church. His preoccupation with this collection will thus cause a delay in his coming to Rome and to Spain. Moreover, he undoubtedly regarded this gesture toward Jerusalem as a sign not only of solidarity, but also of the love of his Gentile Christian communities for those who were really in need of their assistance. He thus sees himself carrying out the recommendation that was made to him at the time of his visit to Jerusalem in A.D. 49 (for the so-called Council), at which he was asked "to remember the poor," a thing that he was eager to do (Gal 2:10). Now he sees a concrete way in which he himself will be able to carry that out. The collection is thus neither a form of temple tax nor a diaspora donation; "it is a sign of the Gentiles' recognition and respect for Jerusalem as the mother congregation" (J. Jervell, "Letter to Jerusalem," 58).

By means of such a collection, Paul educated the communities that he founded to Christian concern and harmony, especially between the mother church of Jerusalem and his new foundations. In this way "he made an essential contribution, both theological and practical, to the formation of a common consciousness of the Church as a whole. One of the chief reasons, humanly speaking, why the Church, which was quickly growing in extent, did not split up, is to be found in Paul's theology, which made all the faithful vividly conscious of the unity conferred on them by God and which imperatively called for concord" (R. Schnackenburg, *The Church in the New Testament* [New York: Herder and Herder, 1965], 82).

NOTES

15:25. *At present, however, I am making my way to Jerusalem.* Paul contemplates a return to the mother church, the place whence he said his evangelization of the eastern Mediterranean area began (15:19). See Acts 19:21; 20:22. He writes *poreuomai*, using the pres. indic. to convey that he is on the point of departure for Jerusalem.

to bring aid to God's dedicated people there. Lit., "serving the saints." The collection taken up in the Gentile churches founded in Galatia, Achaia, and Macedonia (Gal 2:10; 1 Cor 16:1–4; 2 Cor 8:1–9:15) must be carried by Paul personally to Jerusalem, despite his desire to head west. He regards the taking of this collection to Jerusalem as *diakonōn*, the performance of an act of *diakonia*, "service," the term he uses in 2 Cor 8:4, as well as 9:1, 12, and 13 for such aid. Recall his comment about this sort of activity in the body of Christ in 12:7. The pres. ptc. *diakonōn* is best understood in a final sense, in place of the classical fut. ptc., as elsewhere in Hellenistic Greek (see O'Rourke, "The Participle"; cf. ZGB §283–84; BDF §339.2c); cf. the similar use of the pres. ptc. in Matt 20:20; 22:16; Acts 3:26; 15:27; 17:13. On "saints," see the NOTE on 1:7.

26. *Macedonia.* This area in the lower Balkans and northern Greece became an important political, military, and economic entity under Philip II and his son, Alexander the Great, in the fourth century B.C. After Alexander it was ruled by the Macedonian Diadochoi (Antipater, Cassander, and Lysimachus) and finally

came under Roman domination in 167 B.C., becoming a province in 146 B.C. Its capital was Thessalonica, and it included the towns of Pella, Heracles, Philippi, Neapolis (the port of Philippi), Amphipolis, Apollonia, and Beroea (see Acts 16:11; 17:1, 10). Paul himself evangelized much of this province and founded churches at least in Philippi and Thessalonica, to which he also wrote letters (see 1 Thess 1:7–8; 4:10; Phil 4:15; 1 Cor 16:5; 2 Cor 1:16; 2:13; 7:5; 8:1; 11:9). Cf. J. Finegan, "Macedonia," *IDB*, 3.216–17.

Achaia. The Roman province in the southern peninsula of Greece, the capital of which was Corinth. It also included Athens and most of Greece south of Macedonia. It became a senatorial province of Rome in the reorganization of the empire by Augustus in 27 B.C. and was ruled by a proconsul (see Acts 18:12). Paul wrote several letters to the church of Corinth, which he apparently founded (see *PAHT*, §§P41–43). Cf. J. Finegan, "Achaia," *IDB*, 1.25.

kindly decided to make some contribution for the poor among these people in Jerusalem. Lit., "to make some sharing for the poor of the saints in Jerusalem." Paul makes mention of the "poor" in Gal 2:10; they are probably the same. Paul now grows silent about his own role in setting up the collection in these churches (see 1 Cor 16:1–32; 2 Cor 8:1–4, 6; 9:2, 12–14, where he writes about the matter). He ascribes their contribution to their own willingness. On *koinōnia*, see the NOTE on 12:13; cf. Seesemann, *Der Begriff "koinōnia."* Mention is also made in Acts 11:29 (cf. 12:25) of Christians of Antioch sending aid to "the brethren who lived in Judea," but they are not called either *hagioi* or *ptōchoi* by Luke.

Hoi ptōchoi, "the poor," designates the needy among the Jewish Christians of Jerusalem; *pace* Holl ("Kirchenbegriff"), Lietzmann (*An die Römer*, 123), it is not a title for that community as a whole, such as the Hebrew term *>ebyônîm* seems to have been for the Qumran sectarians (4QpPs[a] 1–2 ii 9; 1, 3–4 iii 10; but cf. Keck, "'The Poor . . . Qumran," 75–77). It denotes, rather, the real needy among those who were Jerusalem Christians, whom Paul otherwise calls "saints." *Tōn hagiōn* is to be regarded as a partitive genitive (BDF §164.1), of which "the poor" form a part.

27. *They kindly decided to do so, and indeed they are indebted to them*. Pace Holl, the collection was not the payment of a legal levy imposed by Jerusalem on the daughter churches. Paul even repeats the vb. *eudokēsan* to stress the voluntary nature of the contribution made by the Macedonians and Achaians. The collection was the result of freewill offerings given by these Gentile Christians to the poor of the Jerusalem church in an effort to relieve their distress. But the Gentile Christians are also acknowledging thereby their indebtedness to the mother church of Jerusalem. It is a charitable act that expresses their solidarity with it.

For if Gentiles have come to share in the spiritual blessings of Jerusalem Christians. Lit., "in their spiritual things." Paul uses *pneumatika*, as he did in 1:11 to designate heaven-sent gifts.

they ought to be of service to them in material things. Lit., "they owe it to minister to them also in things of the flesh." Paul now uses the contrast of *pneumatika* and *sarkika* in a very distinctive way (cf. 1 Cor 9:11). The Gentile Christians have shared in the spiritual benefits of Jewish Christians, the first converts to Christ; so they now have felt obliged to share their material benefits with the poor of Jerusalem. See 1 Cor 9:11; Gal 6:6. Underlying this sharing is the recognition that "salvation comes from the Jews" (John 4:22; cf. Rom 9:4–5). Paul may also be hinting delicately to the Romans that they too should think similarly of their indebtedness to the mother church.

28. *when I have completed this task and have delivered this contribution under my own seal.* Lit., "having completed it and having sealed the fruit (of the collection) for them." Paul uses two ptcs. *epitelesas* and *sphragisamenos.* The former is to be taken in the sense in which the verb *epitelein* is used in Phil 1:6; 2 Cor 8:6, 11a, "bring to an end" (BAGD, 302); the latter is a figure drawn from tenant farming. When the tenant farmer delivered the harvested fruit or produce to the owner, the sacks were marked with the farmer's seal as an identification of its source. The seal was an official mark of ownership used in deliveries, and sealing was the last act before delivery (cf. MM, 617–18). In effect, it connotes delivery. Paul uses such a figure because he wants the collection to be known as the *karpos,* "fruit," coming from the churches founded by him in the Lord's harvest. Hence he will deliver the proceeds himself to Jerusalem, figuratively under his own seal. He may be implying thereby that he senses himself to be still under suspicion in Jerusalem. See further Radermacher, *"Sphragizesthai";* Deissmann, *Bible Studies,* 2d ed. (Edinburgh: Clark, 1909), 238–39. The view of Bartsch (ZNW 63 [1972]: 95–107) that the Macedonians and the Achaians are themselves to be understood as the "fruit" and the seal of the union of Paul's churches with the mother church is surely farfetched. See now the support for Deissmann's view given by Horsley, *NDIEC* 2.191.

I shall set out for Spain, passing through your midst. Lit., "I shall go off through you to Spain." Having finished his digression explaining the collection, Paul restates his intention to come to Rome en route to Spain.

29. *I know that, when I arrive among you, I shall be coming with the full blessing of Christ.* Lit., "with the fullness of the blessing of Christ." Recall what Paul said in 1:11 about passing on some spiritual gift to the Christians of Rome. MSS ℵ², Ψ, and the *Koinē* text-tradition insert *tou euangeliou tou,* "(blessing) of the gospel of (Christ)," an addition that does not help much.

BIBLIOGRAPHY

Barnikol, E., *Römer 15: Letzte Reiseziele des Paulus: Jerusalem, Rom und Antiochien: Eine Voruntersuchung zur Entstehung des sogenannten Römerbriefes,* Forschungen zur Entstehung des Urchristentums, des Neuen Testaments und der Kirche 4 (Kiel: Mühlau, 1931).

Bartsch, H. W., "Die Kollekte des Paulus," *Kirche in der Zeit* 20 (1965): 555–56.

————, ". . . wenn ich ihnen diese Frucht versiegelt habe. Röm 15.28: Ein Beitrag zum Verständnis der paulinischen Mission," *ZNW* 63 (1972): 95–107.

Berger, K., "Almosen für Israel: Zum historischen Kontext der paulinischen Kollekte," *NTS* 23 (1976–77): 180–204.

Cerfaux, L., " 'Les Saints' de Jérusalem," *ETL* 2 (1925): 510–29; repr. in *Recueil L. Cerfaux*, 2.389–413.

Dölger, F. X., "Zu *sphragizesthai* Rom 15,28," *Antike und Christentum: Kultur- und Religionsgeschichtliche Studien*, 6 vols. (Münster in Westfalen: Aschendorff, 1929–50), 4 (1934). 280.

Georgi, D., *Die Geschichte der Kollekte des Paulus für Jerusalem*, Theologische Forschung 38 (Hamburg-Bergstedt: Reich, 1965).

Holl, K., "Der Kirchenbegriff des Paulus in seinem Verhältnis zu dem der Urgemeiende," *Sitzungsberichte der preussischen Akademie der Wissenschaften* (Berlin: Akademie der Wissenschaften, 1921), 920–47; repr. in *Gesammelte Aufsätze zur Kirchengeschichte*, vol. 2: *Der Osten* (Tübingen: Mohr [Siebeck], 1928; repr. Darmstadt: Wissenschaftliche Buchgesellschaft, 1964), 44–67.

Jervell, J., "The Letter to Jerusalem," *RomDeb*, 53–64.

Keck, L. E., " 'The Poor among the Saints' in Jewish Christianity and Qumran," *ZNW* 57 (1966): 54–78.

————, "The Poor among the Saints in the New Testament," *ZNW* 56 (1965): 100–29.

Munck, J., *Paul*, 282–308.

Nickle, K. F., *The Collection: A Study in Paul's Strategy*, SBT 48 (London: SCM; Naperville, Ill.: Allenson, 1966).

O'Rourke, J. J., "The Participle in Rom 15,25," *CBQ* 29 (1967): 116–18.

Radermacher, L., "*Sphragizesthai*: Rm 15,28," *ZNW* 32 (1933): 87–89.

Stuhlmacher, P., *Evangelium*, 100–5.

Zeller, D., *Juden und Heiden*, 229–36, 279–84.

55. Paul's Request for Prayers that His Mission to Jerusalem May Succeed; His Concluding Blessing (15:30–33)

15 ³⁰I urge you, then, brothers, by our Lord Jesus Christ and by the love of the Spirit, to join me in my struggle by praying to God on my behalf, ³¹that I may be delivered from unbelievers in Judea and that my service in Jerusalem may be acceptable to God's dedicated people, ³²and that by God's will I may come to you with joy and be refreshed together with you. ³³May the God of peace be with all of you! Amen.

COMMENT

At this point in his concluding message of the letter Paul reveals that he is apprehensive about the trip to Jerusalem and the reception that he will find there. He suspects that he will encounter difficulty from "unbelievers," probably from Jews who regard him as an apostate, but also from Jewish Christians who may be suspicious of him because of his work among the Gentiles and of the gospel that he preaches about justification by grace through faith in Christ Jesus apart from deeds of the law. For this reason Paul requests that the Christians of the Roman community pray to God on his behalf, that he may find a proper welcome in Jerusalem and that the collection that he is bringing may not be misunderstood. He asks the Roman Christians to pray for three things: that no danger may befall him from unbelievers in Judea, that his collection may be received by the saints in the proper spirit, and that he may eventually come to Rome with a joyous heart. Finally, he concludes this part of his letter with a blessing on the Christians of Rome.

Jervell ("Letter to Jerusalem") thinks that neither Paul's trip to Spain nor his stay in Rome makes this letter necessary or explains its content. The clue to why Paul writes Romans is found in these verses: the help and moral support that he needs from the Romans at this time. Yet that is to allow the tail to wag the dog. This may be a minor preoccupation as Paul composes the letter, but the collection to be taken to Jerusalem cannot explain the major thrust of his letter or be the chief "clue" to its interpretation.

The letter, however, is not yet at an end. After this section he begins the final part of his epistolary conclusion (16:1–23).

NOTES

15:30. *brothers.* See the NOTE on 1:13.

I urge you, . . . by our Lord Jesus Christ and by the love of the Spirit. Both the Lord and the Spirit motivate Paul's request for prayers. The "love of the Spirit" may be the charity that the Spirit pours out, the Spirit's love, or possibly the love that the Christians of Rome have of the Spirit. The subjective gen., however, is more likely, because Paul is probably referring to the Spirit as the source and inspiration of Christian prayer (see 8:26–27). Cf. Col 1:8; Eph 6:18. Paul again uses *parakalō*, "I urge" (see the NOTE on 12:1); on the mediation of Christ, see the NOTE on 1:8.

to join me in my struggle. The "struggle" will be explained in the following clauses (v 31). Cf. Col 4:12. See Pfitzner, *Paul and the Agon Motif,* 109–29.

by praying to God on my behalf. Lit., "in your prayers on my behalf to God." Favored though he is as an apostle of the Gentiles, Paul is not too proud to ask for the prayers of fellow Christians. He realizes that the success of his mission to Jerusalem depends on such prayer. See 1 Thess 5:25; 2 Cor 1:11; cf. Col 4:3; 2 Thess 3:1–2; Heb 13:18.

31. *that I may be delivered from unbelievers in Judea.* Paul's description of his possible adversaries is generic enough that one cannot be certain whom he has in mind. He is probably referring to former Jewish acquaintances who have not accepted the Christian gospel and may resent his becoming a Christian evangelist. For this reason he calls them *apeithountes,* "unbelievers," lit., "those not convinced" (of the Christian gospel). See 2:8; cf. 1 Thess 2:15; Acts 14:2; 19:9.

Ioudaia, "Judea," is the southern part of Palestine, in which Jerusalem (15:19, 26), the goal of Paul's journey, was located. It was distinct from Samaria and Galilee (to the north) and from Idumaea (farther to the south). It coincided roughly with the old kingdom of Judah. With the conquest of Pompey in 63 B.C., it came under Roman domination and, along with Samaria, Galilee, and Idumaea, became part of the province of Syria. It was known as Syria Palaestina and at first was governed by princes or kings. In A.D. 6 Judea became a Roman province of minor rank, governed by prefects at first, later by procurators. After the destruction of Jerusalem (70) it became a regular province ruled by a praetorian legate, who commanded a legion withdrawn from Syria. Its coins bore the legend *Iudaea Capta.* At the time of Paul's projected visit to Jerusalem, Judea would have been governed by M. Antonius Felix (Acts 23:24), who had been the procurator since 52.

that my service in Jerusalem may be acceptable to God's dedicated people. Lit., "that my service unto Jerusalem may be acceptable to the saints." Instead of *diakonia,* "service," some Greek MSS (B, D*, F, G) read *dōrophoria,* "gift bringing." Paul has already explained why he considers this collection a service (see 15:27), but now he expresses his apprehension about its reception. Was it accepted by the Jerusalem poor? Dunn (*Romans,* 880) is inclined to argue from the silence about the collection in Acts 20:4–5 that it was not accepted. But that is drawing a conclusion that probably goes beyond the evidence. See Acts 24:17, which implies just the opposite, as Bruce ("Romans Debate," 192) maintains. In effect, Paul is here asking indirectly that the Roman Christians, with their special ties to Jerusalem Christians, may intercede with them on his behalf. It may even be for this reason that Paul is writing such a lengthy exposé of the gospel to the Christians of Rome: that they might have a good idea of what he preaches and how he has understood his mission (see Dahl, "Missionary Theology," 77).

32. *by God's will I may come to you with joy.* Paul thus relates his whole trip, to Jerusalem and to Rome, to the will (*thelēma*) of God. See 1:10; 12:2. He uses this motif often; see 1 Cor 1:1; 2 Cor 1:1; 8:5; Gal 1:4. By it he alludes to the divine plan of salvation, seeing his own plans related to it. Cf. Acts 18:21. But MSS ℵ*, B, D* read some form of *thelēmatos Iēsou Christou,* "the will of Jesus Christ," a form that Paul never uses elsewhere. It is clearly a copyist's modification of the text.

be refreshed together with you. Recall the correction that Paul introduced into the statement of his plans in 1:12. He now reformulates it differently. Instead of *synanapausōmai hymin,* the reading of MSS ℵ*, A, C, 6, 33*, 81, and 365, some MSS (P⁴⁶, B) omit this phrase, whereas others (D, F, G) replace it with *kai anapsyxō meth'* *hymōn,* "I shall be refreshed together with you."

33. *May the God of peace be with all of you!* This is an unusual ending for Paul; cf. Phil 4:9. It is hardly the ending of the letter; hence the fifteen-chapter form of Romans is scarcely plausible. Contrast 1 Thess 5:23; 1 Cor 16:23; Gal 6:18; Phil 4:23; 2 Cor 13:13; cf. 2 Thess 3:16. In a sense, it corresponds to the greeting of 1:7 at the beginning of the letter. Paul now mentions God as the source of such peace that he wishes for the Christians of Rome, i.e., the God who grants peace to all human beings. On "the God of peace," see 16:20; 1 Thess 5:23; 1 Cor 14:33; 2 Cor 13:11; Heb 13:20; *T. Dan* 5:2.

Amen. See the NOTE on 1:25. *Amēn* is omitted in MSS A, G, 330, 436, 451, 630, 1739, and 1881. It is also omitted in P⁴⁶, the oldest text of Romans, but that is undoubtedly because the doxology (16:25–27) occurs here. See Introduction, section III.

BIBLIOGRAPHY

Dahl, N. A., "The Missionary Theology in the Epistle to the Romans," *Studies in Paul,* 70–94.

Delling, G., "Die Bezeichnung 'Gott des Friedens' und ähnliche Wendungen in den Paulusbriefen," *Jesus und Paulus: Festschrift für Werner George Kümmel . . . ,* ed. E. E. Ellis and E. Grässer (Göttingen: Vandenhoeck & Ruprecht, 1975), 76–84.

Schmithals, W., "The Collection of the Contributions," *Paul and James,* SBT 46 (London: SCM; Naperville, Ill.: Allenson, 1965), 79–84.

IV. CONCLUSION: LETTER OF RECOMMENDATION FOR PHOEBE AND GREETINGS TO ROMAN CHRISTIANS (16:1–23)

◆

56. PAUL RECOMMENDS PHOEBE, A MINISTER OF CENCHREAE (16:1–2)

16 ¹I commend to you our sister Phoebe, a minister of the church of Cenchreae. ²Please receive her in the Lord in a manner worthy of God's dedicated people and help her in whatever she may require of you; she has been a patroness of many here, and of myself too.

COMMENT

Paul has concluded the discussion of his plans and now ends his letter to the Christians of Rome with a letter of recommendation for Phoebe, a minister of the church of Cenchreae, a port serving the town of Corinth, from which he writes. For the relation of this chapter to the letter as a whole, see Introduction, sections III and IV. In the letter Paul also sends greetings to Christians of Rome, saluting at least twenty-six persons, twenty-four of them by name. After an admonition, companions of Paul also send their greetings. The chapter ends with a doxology.

Chapter 16 may be divided thus: (1) 16:1–2, the recommendation for Phoebe; (2) 16:3–16, greetings to many persons in the Roman community; (3) 16:17–20, warning about those who create dissension; (4) 16:21–23, greetings from the scribe and Paul's fellow workers; and (5) 16:25–27, doxology.

Verse 24 is omitted in the best Greek MSS; in the MSS where it occurs, it is undoubtedly a copyist's addition, borrowed from 16:20b. MS Ψ and the *Koinē* text-tradition read: "The grace of our Lord Jesus Christ be with you all! Amen." See also 2 Thess 3:18; Rev 22:21.

According to Michel (*Brief an die Römer*, 472), "numerous Semitisms" mark off the style of chap. 16 from the rest of the letter, but he does not specify them.

Verses 1–2 show how a letter of recommendation would have been written in the early church, supply us with the name of an early Christian for whom one has been composed, and reveal how one early Christian functioned in a local church.

NOTES

16:1. *I commend to you.* Paul uses *synistēmi de hymin*, the technical epistolary expression to introduce a friend to other acquaintances (see Chio, *Ep.* 8

728

[*hopōs auton systēsaimi soi*]; 2 Macc 9:25), even though this verb is not common in many Greek letters of introduction from antiquity. See Keyes, "Greek Letter," 39; cf. Kim, *Form*, 132–34. Also Acts 18:27; 2 Cor 3:1; 4:2; 5:12; 10:12; 12:11. Note the particle *de*, which implies that something has preceded; hence chap. 16 is hardly an independent composition, unless we are to suppose that whoever would have added it to Romans 1–15 deliberately inserted it to give the impression that chap. 16 was originally part of the letter.

our sister. Paul uses *adelphē* of a fellow Christian; see the NOTE on 1:13; cf. 1 Cor 7:15; 9:5; Phlm 2; Jas 2:15. In so referring to her, Paul assures the Romans that she is not an impostor. In Acts 23:16 Paul is said to have a sister in the sibling sense, but she is unnamed. Thus "our" means the Christians of Corinth as a whole. MSS P⁴⁶, A, F, G, P, etc. read instead *hymōn*, "your," which would have to be understood in a generic sense, something like "your fellow Christian," for there is no reason to think that Phoebe originally came from Rome.

Phoebe. An otherwise unknown Gentile Christian woman, who is undoubtedly the bearer of this letter to the Christians of Rome. The name *Phoibē* suggests her pagan background and probably connotes her status as a freed slave (so Schlier, *Römerbrief*, 441). The name was of mythological origin, that of a Titaness, daughter of Heaven and Earth (Hesiod, *Theognis* 136), wife of Coeus, and mother of Leto, grandmother of Apollo (Phoebus) and Artemis. The name means "shining, beaming, bright"; it was commonly used in the Greco-Roman world of the time (Dittenberger, *Sylloge*³, 805.10 [ca. A.D. 54]; *Pap. Florentina* 50:61 [third century A.D.]).

a minister. Or perhaps "also a minister," for the adv. *kai* is read in MSS P⁴⁶, ℵ², B, C*, and 81. In the Greco-Roman world *diakonos* denoted a "waiter" at table (Xenophon, *Memorabilia* 1.5.2), a royal "servant," or even a holder of a religious (non-Christian) office (see *IGRom* 4.474.12; 4.824.6). Paul calls Phoebe *diakonos*, which may designate her generically as an "assistant" or "minister" in the church or specifically as a "deacon," a member of a special group in the church. There is no way of saying whether the term refers at this time to the diaconate, an "order," which clearly emerged in the church by the time of Ignatius of Antioch (*Eph.* 2:1; *Magn.* 6:1). For the generic use, see 1 Thess 3:2; 2 Cor 3:6; 11:23. By contrast, Phil 1:1; Titus 1:9; and 1 Tim 3:8, 12 begin to point in the direction of a specific group or function. Paul does not call Phoebe *diakonissa*, a term that eventually emerges in ecclesiastical tradition in the patristic period (*Constitutiones Apostolicae* 3.7). He calls her *diakonos*, using a word of common gender, as do a sixth-century Cappadocian inscription of a certain married Maria (*NDIEC* 2 §109.4) and a fourth-century Jerusalem inscription of Sophia, who is also called "a second Phoebe" (*NDIEC* 4 §122.3–4). In 1 Tim 3:11 *gynaikes*, "women," are mentioned in the instructions given to *diakonoi*, but it is not clear whether these *gynaikes* are themselves *diakonoi* or the "wives" of deacons. W. Michaelis (*ZNW* 25 [1926]: 146) denies that Phoebe holds any official standing in the church of Cenchreae, but that is not clear. See Gibson, "Phoebe."

of the church. For the first time in the letter to the Romans Paul uses the word *ekklēsia.* Here it designates a local organized Christian community, probably one that could gather in a house. The word occurs only in this chapter, and only in the sense of a local congregation (vv 1, 4, 5, 16, 23). There is no connotation of a universal church, as in some passages in 1 Corinthians (or in Colossians and Ephesians). Nor does Paul ever refer to "the church in Rome," as he has often done with other localities (1 Thess 1:1; 1 Cor 1:2; 2 Cor 1:1; cf. Gal 1:2).

of Cenchreae. Lit., "at Cenchreae." Six places or towns with the name *Kenchreai* are known in antiquity: (1) a place in Argeia in the eastern Peloponnesus; (2) a town in the Troas in Asia Minor, the legendary birthplace of Homer; (3) a town near Lindos (modern Archipolis) on the island of Rhodes; (4) a place near the town of Mitylene on the island of Lesbos; (5) a place near Lampsakos in the Troas; and (6) one of the two ports of Corinth (PW 11.1.165–70). Of these places the most important was the last; it has been mentioned by ancient writers (Strabo, *Geography* 8.6.4 §369; 8.6.22 §380 [called a *kōmē,* "village"]; Pausanias, *Descriptio Graeciae* 2.1.5; 2.2.3; 7.6.7; Philo, *In Flacc.* 19 §155: *to Korinthion epineion,* "the port of Corinth"). It is thus undoubtedly the one to which Paul refers. It was situated seven kilometers southeast of Corinth, on the Saronic Gulf, serving trade with Asia, whereas Lechaion was the port three kilometers north of Corinth on the Gulf of Corinth, serving trade with Italy. Both Cenchreae and Lechaion were on the Isthmus of Corinth, which funneled traffic to and from northern Greece and the Peloponnesus. Apuleius (*Metamorphoses* 10.35) calls Cenchreae "the famous town of the most noble colony of the Corinthians," with a very secure harbor, frequented by ships of many nations. "In Cenchreae there are a temple of Artemis and a wooden statue of her; also . . . a bronze image of Poseidon, and at the opposite end of the harbor sanctuaries of Asclepius and Isis" (Pausanius, *Descriptio Graeciae* 2.2.3). The feast of Isis celebrated at Cenchreae is described by Apuleius (*Metamorphoses* 11.8–11, 16–17). It seems to be the same place as that mentioned in Acts 18:18. The letter of recommendation was probably written from Corinth, not from Cenchreae, even though Phoebe was from there. Legend has it that a bishopric was established there under Lucius (16:21), a disciple consecrated by Paul (*Constitutiones apostolicae* 7.46.10 [ed. F. X. Funk]). See Scranton, *Kenchreai;* J. Murphy-O'Connor, *St. Paul's Corinth,* 17–21.

But Michaelis would instead identify Cenchreae as the town in Troas (number 2 above), because Stephanus of Byzantium mentions it first, even before the Corinthian Cenchreae: *Kenchreai, polis Trōados en hē dietripsen Homēros manthanōn ta kata tous Trōas,* "Cenchreae, a town of Troas in which Homer spent time learning about the Trojans" (see A. Meineke, *Stephani Byzantii Ethnicorum quae supersunt* [Berlin: Reimer, 1849], 371). Michaelis prefers this identification because of his view that Paul wrote Romans from Philippi. Cenchreae in Troas would then be more logical as a place from which Phoebe would come. She would be carrying a letter of recommendation to the church of Ephesus, and then would travel farther to Rome to carry Romans 1–15 there. But even though we know that Paul visited and worked in Troas (2 Cor 2:12), this location of Cenchreae is hardly to be preferred to that of the Corinthian port.

2. *Please receive her in the Lord.* Phoebe is to be welcomed into the community as one of its members. "In the Lord" occurs again in vv 8, 11, 12, 13, and 22; it is an abbreviation of the fuller form used at 6:23 and 8:39, "in Jesus Christ our Lord." It has probably become an expression of close relationship. In this instance it would connote the mode of Christian hospitality.

in a manner worthy of God's dedicated people. Lit., "of the saints"; see the NOTE on 1:7. Paul flatters his readers by associating them with the "holy ones," formerly called and chosen, and with the early mother church of Jerusalem, which enjoyed this title par excellence (see 1 Cor 6:1; 16:1; 2 Cor 8:4; 9:1).

help her in whatever she may require of you. Lit., "in whatever affair she may need (you or your help)." This is the usual epistolary expression of conditional need in a letter of recommendation; see Kim, *Form*, 79. The noun *pragma*, "deed, matter, affair, business" is per se not specific, but it occurs in 1 Cor 6:1 in the sense of "lawsuit," and may have that connotation here. It may then suggest that Phoebe was going to Rome as a litigant; so Michel and Dunn. Paul uses the impv. *parastēte*, "help," and has perhaps chosen this verb because of a relationship it may have to Phoebe's own role of *prostatis*, expressed in the next clause.

she has been a patroness of many here. Although many commentators have understood this title *prostatis* figuratively, as "helper, support," it actually denoted a person of prominence in the ancient Greco-Roman world (PWSup 9.1287–1302; TDNT 6.703; EWNT 3.426–27; Theissen, "Soziale Schichtung," 250–52). On *prostatis* as equal to Latin *patrona*, see BDF §5.3. In giving Phoebe this title, Paul acknowledges the public service that this prominent woman has given to many Christians at Cenchreae. *Prostatis* may be related to *proistamenos* (12:8 [see the NOTE there]; cf. 1 Thess 5:12); so Phoebe was perhaps a superior or at least a leader of the Christian community of Cenchreae, as some commentators suggest (Kühl, Leenhardt, Lietzmann, Murray, Schulz [who would translate it "president"]). She probably owned a house there and, as a wealthy, influential person involved in commerce, was in a position to assist missionaries and other Christians who traveled to and from Corinth. We can only speculate about the kind of assistance she gave: hospitality? championing their cause before secular authorities? furnishing funds for journeys? Cf. NDIEC 4.242–44.

and of myself too. Paul thus acknowledges the debt he owes Phoebe. She perhaps played hostess to him when he visited Cenchreae at times during his three-month stay in Corinth. MSS D, F, and G read *kai emou kai allōn* (+ *pollōn*, D²) *prostatis*, "patroness of me and of (many) others."

731

BIBLIOGRAPHY ON CHAPTER 16

See also the bibliography on the integrity of Romans, Introduction, section IV.

Albertz, M., *Die Botschaft des Neuen Testaments*, 4 vols. (Zollikon-Zurich: Evangelischer-Verlag, 1947–57), 1.2.70–86.

Keyes, C. W., "The Greek Letter of Introduction," *American Journal of Philology* 56 (1935): 28–44.

Kim, C.-H., *Form and Structure of the Familiar Greek Letter of Recommendation*, SBLDS 4 (Missoula, Mont.: Scholars Press, 1972).

Lampe, P., "Die römischen Christen von Röm 16," in *Die stadtrömischen Christen in den ersten beiden Jahrhunderten*, WUNT 2.18 (Tübingen: Mohr [Siebeck], 1987; 2d ed. 1989), 124–53.

Ollrog, W.-H., "Die Abfassungsverhältnisse von Röm 16," *Kirche: Festschrift für Günther Bornkamm* . . . , ed. D. Lührmann and G. Strecker (Tübingen: Mohr [Siebeck], 1980), 221–44.

Richardson, P., "From Apostles to Virgins: Romans 16 and the Roles of Women in the Early Church," *TorJT* 2 (1986): 232–61.

Roenneke, E., *Das letzte Kapitel des Römerbriefs im Lichte der christlichen Archäologie* (Leipzig: Klein, 1927).

Schüssler Fiorenza, E., "Missionaries, Apostles, Coworkers: Romans 16 and the Reconstruction of Women's Early Christian History," *WW* 6 (1986): 420–33.

Sihler, E. G., "A Note on the First Christian Congregation at Rome," *CTM* 3 (1932): 180–84.

Rom 16:1–2

Adinolfi, M., "Le collaboratrici ministeriali di Paolo nelle lettere ai Romani e ai Filippesi," *BeO* 17 (1975): 21–32.

Arichea, D. C., "Who Was Phoebe? Translating *diakonos* in Romans 16.1," *BT* 39 (1988): 401–9.

Brooten, N., *Women Leaders in the Ancient Synagogue: Inscriptional Evidence and Background Issues*, Brown Judaic Studies 36 (Chico, Calif.: Scholars Press, 1982; repr. [Atlanta, Ga.], 1990).

Caddeo, L., "Le 'Diaconesse,' " *RBR* 7 (1972): 211–25.

Finger, R. H., "Phoebe: Role Model for Leaders," *Daughters of Sarah* 14.2 (1988): 5–7.

Gibson, M. D., "Phoebe," *ExpTim* 23 (1911–12): 281.

Goodspeed, E. J., "Phoebe's Letter of Introduction," *HTR* 44 (1951): 55–57.

Heine, S., "Diakoninnen—Frauen und Ämter in den ersten christlichen Jahrhunderten," *IKZ* 78 (1988): 213–27.

———, *Frauen der frühen Christenheit* (Göttingen: Vandenhoeck & Ruprecht, 1986); *Women and Early Christianity: A Reappraisal* (London: SCM, 1987; Minneapolis, Minn.: Augsburg, 1988).

Kearsley, R. A., "Women in Public Life in the Roman East: Iunia Theodora, Claudia

Metrodora and Phoibe, Benefactress of Paul," *Ancient Society, Resources for Teachers* (North Ryde, NSW) 15 (1985): 124–37.

Michaelis, W., "Kenchreä (Zur Frage des Abfassungsortes des Rm)," *ZNW* 25 (1926): 144–54.

Montevecchi, O., "Phoebe prostatis (Rom. 16,2)," *Miscel.lània papirològica Ramon Roca-Puig en el seu vuitantè aniversari*, ed. S. Janeras (Barcelona: Fund. S. Vives Casajuana, 1987), 205–16.

————, "Una donna 'prostatis' del figlio minorenne in un papiro del II^a," *Aeg* 61 (1981): 103–15.

Murphy-O'Connor, J., *St. Paul's Corinth* (Wilmington, Del.: Glazier, 1983), 17–21.

Ollrog, W. H., *Paulus und seine Mitarbeiter: Untersuchungen zu Theorie und Praxis der paulinischen Mission*, WMANT 50 (Neukirchen-Vluyn: Neukirchener-Verlag, 1979), 25–26, 31, 37–38, 50–51, 55–58, 75–79, 120, 192–94, 240.

Paul, C., "A Plethora of Phoebes," *Faith and Culture* 15 (1989): 75–86.

Romaniuk, K., "Was Phoebe in Romans 16,1 a Deaconess?" *ZNW* 81 (1990): 132–34.

Scholer, D. M., "Paul's Women Co-Workers in the Ministry of the Church," *Daughters of Sarah* 6.4 (1980): 3–6.

Schulz, R. R., "A Case for 'President' Phoebe in Romans 16:2," *LTJ* 24 (1990): 124–27.

Scranton, R. et al., *Kenchreai: Eastern Port of Corinth*, vol. 1: *Topography and Architecture*, American School of Classical Studies in Athens 1 (Leiden: Brill, 1978).

Spaeth, A., "Phebe, the Deaconness," *LCR* 4 (1885): 210–22, 260–81.

Theissen, G., "Soziale Schichtung in der korinthischen Gemeinde: Ein Beitrag zur Soziologie des hellenistischen Urchristentum," *ZNW* 65 (1974): 232–72.

Trebilco, P., "Women as Co-Workers and Leaders in Paul's Letters," *Journal of th Christian Brethren Research Fellowship* 122 (1990): 27–36.

Zappella, M., "A proposito di Febe *prostatis* (Rm 16,2)," *RivB* 37 (1989): 167–71

57. PAUL'S GREETINGS TO VARIOUS PERSONS (16:3–1

16 ³My greetings to Prisca and Aquila, fellow workers of mine in C^.
⁴They risked their necks for me; not only am I, but all Gentile c^y
grateful to them. ⁵Greet too the church that meets at their house. Gr^o
dear friend Epaenetus, the first convert to Christ in Asia. ⁶Greetings^y-
has worked hard for you. ⁷Greetings to Andronicus and Junia, my ^s.
men, who were imprisoned with me and who are outstanding am^ in
They were in Christ even before me. ⁸Greetings to Ampliatus, ^ear
the Lord. ⁹Greetings to Urbanus, my fellow worker in Christ^ to
friend Stachys. ¹⁰Greetings to Apelles, who is approved in Chr^

the household of Aristobulus. [11]Greetings to my fellow countryman Herodion, and to those who belong to the Lord in the household of Narcissus. [12]Greetings to those workers in the Lord, Tryphaena and Tryphosa. Greetings to my dear friend Persis, who has toiled hard in the Lord. [13]Greetings to Rufus, the chosen one of the Lord, and to his mother—whom I call mother too. [14]Greetings to Asyncritus, Phlegon, Hermes, Patrobas, Hermas, and the brothers who are with them. [15]Greetings to Philologus and Julia, Nereus and his sister, Olympas, and all God's dedicated people who are with them. [16]Greet one another with a holy kiss. All of the churches of Christ send you their greetings.

COMMENT

Paul now includes in his letter of recommendation for Phoebe greetings to various persons in the Roman church, mentioning at least twenty-four people by name. Indirectly, Paul is commending himself on his coming visit to Rome. Some of them are people whom Paul has known and with whom he has worked; others are those whose names have come to his attention. This may be the case at least for the last ten named, in vv 14–15. The way he speaks of twelve others suggests that he knew them personally: Prisca, Aquila, Epaenetus, Andronicus, Junia, Ampliatus, Stachys, Apelles, Urbanus, Persis, and Rufus and his mother. Of those singled out as active in the service of the gospel, seven are women (Prisca, Mary, Junia, Tryphaena, Tryphosa, Persis, and the mother of Rufus) and five are men (Aquila, Andronicus, Urbanus, Apelles, Rufus).

Among those named, some have Greek names: Andronicus, Apelles, Aristo- bulus, Asyncritus, Epaenetus, Erastus, Hermes, Jason, Narcissus, Nereus, Olym- pas, Patrobas, Persis, Philologus, Phlegon, Sosipater, Stachys, Timotheos, Try- phaena, Tryphosa; some have Latin names: Ampliatus, Aquila, Caius, Julia, Junia, Lucius, Quartus, Rufus, Tertius, Urbanus; a few may have Hebrew names: Mary (but *Maria* may be the fem. form of Latin *Marius*) and Herodion (this name at least borne by Jews, if it is not really Semitic). Mary, Rufus, and Julia ur in Roman Jewish inscriptions. Some names denote prominent persons, rs not so prominent. Many are the names of slaves, freedmen, craftsmen, and e folk, what we would call today the lower middle class. The persons greeted letter of recommendation supply Phoebe with a list of persons on whom ld call in Rome for hospitality and assistance.

he letters that Paul has written to churches that he himself founded he eets individuals as he does here. That may have been because he did not ingle out some individuals and neglect others. In any case, the difference notes now undoubtedly comes from the fact that this letter is being sent to a congregation that he did not found personally, but in which he a number of Christian friends now reside.

NOTES

16:3. *Prisca and Aquila.* See 1 Cor 16:19; Acts 18:1–3, 18–19, 22 (v.1.), 26–27; 2 Tim 4:19. In Acts 18 Luke uses the diminutive form of the name *Priskilla*, "Priscilla," which is also found here in some minuscule MSS of Romans (81, 365, 614, 629, 630, 945) and in some ancient versions (Vg, Syr) as the result of copyists' harmonization. These persons are identified in Acts 18 as Jewish Christians, husband and wife, who had recently come to Corinth after being banished from Italy as a result of the decree of the emperor, Claudius (see p. 31; *PAHT* §P10). Aquila was originally from Pontus and was a tentmaker (*skēnopoios*), which probably means that he made not military leather tents, but linen tents and awnings for private citizens (see Lampe, "Paulus—Zeltmacher"). Having left Italy and at first settled in Corinth, he and his wife engaged in tentmaking and eventually moved to Ephesus, where they took up residence and instructed among others Apollos, the Alexandrian rhetor (Acts 18:26). When Paul wrote 1 Corinthians from Ephesus, he sent greetings to the Corinthian church from the Christians who gathered in the house church of Prisca and Aquila there (1 Cor 16:19). This notice in Romans implies that they have returned to Rome. In both Pauline and Lucan writings the name *Priska/Priskilla* precedes *Akylas*, and Harnack deduced therefrom that she was the more prominent figure in the early Christian community of the time (*SPAW* [1900]: 7–83). They are undoubtedly Paul's source of information about the contemporary situation in the Roman community. They are mentioned again in 2 Tim 4:19, which Lampe regards as "another example of the historical flaws in the Pastoral Letters" ("Roman Christians," 221).

The mention of Prisca and Aquila creates a problem. Were they among Jewish Christians already in Corinth before Paul first arrived there? So Acts 18:1–2 implies. But if so, who then founded the Christian church of Corinth? Paul is usually regarded as the founder; but then that would have to be understood as apart from Prisca and Aquila, who were already Christians. But *pace* Devis ("Aquila," 395), it is far from clear that they "received all their Christian formation from Paul." Lampe plausibly suggests that it was Paul who urged them to return to Rome as a "vanguard" to assemble a house church and prepare for his arrival ("Roman Christians," 220).

fellow workers of mine in Christ Jesus. I.e., either at Corinth (Acts 18:3) or at Ephesus (1 Cor 16:19; Acts 18:26). Paul calls them *synergoi*, "coworkers," i.e., those who shared in the Pauline mission of evangelization. See also 16:9, 21; 1 Thess 3:2; Phil 2:25; 4:3; 1 Cor 3:9; 2 Cor 1:24; 8:23; Phlm 1:24.

4. *They risked their necks for me.* Paul gratefully recalls some intervention of Prisca and Aquila on his behalf which endangered them as well, either at Ephesus (perhaps at the riot of the silversmiths, Acts 19:23) or during some Ephesian imprisonment, to which Paul may refer in 1 Cor 15:32 and 2 Cor 1:8–9. They may have attempted to use some of the influence that their wealth and social position gave them (Dunn, *Romans*, 892). Cf. Acts 15:26.

not only am I, but all Gentile churches are grateful to them. Prisca and Aquila were probably remembered for the support and generosity they extended to Gentile Christian communities in Corinth or near Ephesus and elsewhere.

5. *Greet too the church that meets at their house*. Lit., "also the church according to their house." The word *oikon* is ambiguous; it could mean either "(according to their) household," i.e., made up of members of the household of Aquila and Prisca, or it could refer to their physical "house," in which they and other Christians met for worship, i.e., a house church. The latter seems to be more likely, because there is evidence of such *domus ecclesiae* in later times at Rome itself (see Petersen, "House-Churches"). For the expression *hē kat' oikon ekklēsia*, see 1 Cor 16:19; Phlm 2; cf. Col 4:15; Ps.-Clem. *Recognitions* 10.71 (GCS 51.371). These are then the earliest references to groups of Christians who met together in individual houses; undoubtedly, in the bigger cities and towns there would have been more than one such house. Christians would have made use of such meetings in houses as they began to break away from the Jerusalem Temple and local Jewish synagogues to conduct their own (Christian) prayer services and liturgies. They may also have been necessitated as a result of the prohibition of assembly decreed by Claudius against the Jews (Cassius Dio, *Historia Romana* 60.6.6; see p. 32), which may have affected not only Jews, but Jewish Christians as well. Besides the group that meets at the house of Aquila and Priscilla, Paul seems to imply that there were other such groups: possibly those of the household of Aristobulus (16:10) or of the household of Narcissus (16:11); the Christians associated with Asyncritus et al. (16:14), and those associated with Philologus et al. (16:15).

Mention of such house churches also implies the centrality of the home in early Christian life. The household (*familia*) was the unit, and at times it was converted as a whole (cf. Acts 16:33). Cf. Col 4:15; Acts 12:12, 17; 1 *Clem.* 1.3. The Pseudo-Clementine *Recognitions* 10.71 tells of Theophilus of Antioch, who consecrated "the massive palace of his house with the name of a church" (GCS 51.371). For reports on excavated house churches, see Kraeling, *The Christian Building*; von Gerkan, "Zur Hauskirche"; Wiegand and Schrader, *Priene*.

Greetings to my dear friend Epaenetus. An otherwise unknown male Gentile Christian. The name *Epainetos* is found in Greek inscriptions and in Diodorus Siculus (19.79.2).

the first convert to Christ in Asia. Lit., "the firstfruits of Asia for Christ," Paul's first convert in the Roman province of Asia (the western end of Asia Minor, with its gubernatorial seat at Ephesus). Paul now regards the conversion of Epaenetus as the one that sparked the conversion of many others in the province. His turning to Christ "consecrated" the rest of Asia to Christianity (see the NOTE on 11:16). See 1 Cor 16:15 for a similar statement about Stephanas and his household in Corinth. Being mentioned immediately after Prisca and Aquila, Epaenetus may have traveled to Rome with them (so Lampe, "Roman Christians," 221). According to later legends, Epaenetus became a bishop in Carthage. MSS

D[1], Ψ, and the *Koinē* text-tradition read *Achaias* instead of *Asias*, undoubtedly under the influence of 1 Cor 16:15.

6. *Greetings to Mary.* An otherwise unknown (Jewish?) Christian woman. Instead of *Marian*, the acc. sg. of *Maria*, read in MSS A, B, C, P, Ψ, 104, 365, and 1739, the more Semitic form *Mariam* is found in MSS P[46], ℵ, D, F, G, and the *Koinē* text-tradition. *Maria(m)* is developed from *Miryām*, "Miriam" (the name of Moses' sister, Exod 15:20); it was originally a Semitic name of Canaanite origin, related to the Hebrew and Ugaritic noun *mrym*, "height, summit." As the name of a woman, it probably connoted something like "Excellence." The name *Maria* is also found on Roman inscriptions (*CIL* 6.4394, 22223; *NDIEC* 4 §115) and has been explained as the fem. form of *Marius*, or a name related to the *gens Maria*. So it is not certainly a Semitic name.

who has worked hard for you. The vb. *kopian* denotes hard work, toil, struggle. It is Paul who gives this word a Christian connotation, designating by it voluntary, laborious activity on behalf of the gospel (see A. von Harnack, "Kopos"). Here Paul attributes it to Mary without specifying in what regard she so worked. He may not have known her personally, but only heard about her. Yet the fact that he singles her out for such toil reveals how highly he thought of the work of such Christian women on behalf of the gospel.

7. *Greetings to Andronicus and Junia.* Apart from the identification that Paul himself gives in the following phrases, they are otherwise unknown converts to Christianity. *Andronikos* was a common enough Greek masculine name, used also in Diodorus Siculus 19.59.2; Appian, *Macedonica* 16. It was borne by a member of the imperial household (*CIL* 6.5326: C. Iulius Andronicus) and is the name of a Hellenized Jew in Josephus, *Ant.* 13.3.4 §§75, 78. Cf. *CIL* 6.5325–26 (name of a freedman); 6.11626 (name of a slave). In the *Acts of John* 31 (*HSNTA* 2.222), a praetor, a leading citizen of Ephesus, is named Andronicus. Those who think that chap. 16 was originally addressed to the Ephesian church have cited the name Andronicus and identified this person with this well-known Andronicus of Ephesus. But the *Acts of John* is not certainly dated before the third century A.D., so the occurrence of the name in this text is coincidental.

Paul writes *Iounian*, which could be the acc. sg. of the fem. name *Iounía*, -*as*, "Junia," or the acc. sg. of the masc. name *Iouniâs*, -*â*, "Junias." MS P[46] and some versions (Vg, Bohairic, Ethiopic) read instead *Ioulian*, "Julia" (influenced by 16:15?). Many ancient commentators up to the twelfth century understood either *Iounian* or *Ioulian* to be the wife of Andronicus: Rufinus (Origen), *In ep. ad Romanos* 10.21 (PG 14.1280), but "Junias" in 10.39 (PL 14.1089) [Is it original? See the quotation of Origen in Rabanus Maurus below, where "Junia" is used]; Ambrosiaster, *Commentarius in ep. ad Romanos* 16.7 (CSEL 81.480: *Iuniam* [*Iuliam*]); Jerome, *Liber interpretationis hebraicorum nominum* 72.15 (CCLat 72.150); *Expositio in ep. ad Romanos* 16.7 (PL 30.744); Theodoret of Cyrrhus, *Interpretatio ep. ad Romanos* 16.7 (PG 82.219–20); Ps.-Primasius, *Commentarius in ep. ad Romanos* 16.7 (PL 68.505); John Damascene, *In ep. ad*

Romanos 16.7 (PG 95.565); Haymo, *In ep. ad Romanos* 16.7 (PL 117.505); Rabanus Maurus, *In ep. ad Romanos* (PL 111.1607–8); Hatto, *In ep. ad Romanos* 16: "Virum et uxorem intellegere debemus" (PL 134.282); Oecumenius, *Commentarius in ep. ad Romanos* 16 (PG 118.629); Lanfranc of Bec, *Ep. ad Romanos* 41 (PL 150.154); Bruno the Carthusian, *In ep. ad Romanos* 16 (PL 153.119); Theophylact, *Expositio in ep. ad Romanos* 114: *kai tauta gynaika ousan tēn Iounian*, "especially since Junia is a woman" (PG 124.551–52); Peter Abelard, *Commentarius in ep. ad Romanos* 16.7 (CCConMed 11.330); Peter Lombard, *In ep. ad Romanos* (PL 191.1528). Indeed John Chrysostom even said of Junia, "How great the wisdom of this woman that she was even deemed worthy of the apostles' title" (*In ep. ad Romanos* 31.2 [PG 60.669–70]). The tenth-century menology of Emperor Basil Porphyrogenitus records for 17 May the feast of Saints Andronicus and Junia: *consortem secum habens atque adiutricem divinae praedicationis, admirabilem feminam Juniam, mundo et carni mortuam, soli Deo vivam, ac munere suo fungentem*, "having with him as consort and helper in godly preaching the admirable woman Junia, who, dead to the world and the flesh, but alive to God alone, carried out her task" (*Acta Sanctorum, Maii* 4, ed. Bollandists [Rome and Paris: V. Palmé, 1866], 4). Among modern commentators, Barrett, Cranfield, Dunn, Huby, Lagrange, and Wilckens have interpreted *Iounian* as feminine.

The masc. name *Iounias* is attested nowhere else (see Lampe, *Die stadtrömischen Christen*, 124–53; "Roman Christians," 223), but it is often claimed to be a shortened form of the Latin name Junianus, Junianius, or Junilius (see BDF §125.2). If this claim were right, such a name would indicate that he was at first a slave, then freed by a *dominus* named "Junius."

Giles of Rome (1247–1316) is said to have been the first to break with the patristic tradition and to interpret Andronicus and Julia(!) as two men *(viri)*; see *Aegidii Columnae Romani in epistulam Pauli ad Romanos commentaria*, 97. Ninth-century minuscule MSS, fitted with accents, already bear the masc. form *Iouniân*, and never the fem. form *Iounían* (see Lampe, "Iunia/Iunias").

Yet B-A (771) still query whether the feminine name suits the context, following Lietzmann (*An die Römer*, 125): "muss wegen der folgenden Aussagen einen Mann bezeichnen." Ever since the second edition of the Nestle critical NT text, masc. *Iouniân* has been read, even in N-A²⁶, and "Junias" is the form preferred in the *RSV, NEB, NIV*, and *NJB*, as well as by the majority of modern commentators. Now, however, the *NABRNT, REB*, and *NRSV* finally read "Junia."

my fellow countrymen. Or possibly, "my relatives." But the word *syngenēs*, lit., "related, akin to," is used in 9:3 to refer to fellow Jews (see the NOTE there). The two so designated here would have been of Jewish background, converted to Christianity before Paul. Phil 4:22 reveals that Paul had dealings with slaves or *liberti* of the imperial *oikia* in Ephesus; Andronicus and Junia could have been of such a background. For Watson ("Two Roman Congregations," 210–11), they were "the most important members of the Jewish Christian group" in Rome, "shared the Jerusalem church's deep suspicion of Pauline 'freedom from the law,' " and probably were "the founders of the Roman congregation."

who were imprisoned with me. Lit., "my fellow prisoners." Kittel (*TDNT* 1.196–97) thinks that *synaichmalōtoi* is to be understood figuratively because, when Paul elsewhere speaks of coimprisonment, he uses *syndesmios*. But Kittel does not say in what sense this figure would be meant, and Sanday and Headlam and Käsemann rightly insist on the literal meaning of the term. We do not know the place of such imprisonment; it could have been Ephesus (1 Cor 15:32), or Philippi (Acts 16:23), or someplace else (2 Cor 11:23). Clement of Rome (*1 Clem.* 5:6) speaks of Paul being imprisoned seven times, yet never says where. Paul uses the same term in Phlm 23 (Col 4:10), where it is predicated of Epaphras (Aristarchus). Again, Castel S. Pietro ("*Synaichmalōtos*") seeks instead to translate *synaichmalōtos* as "conquered along with me," i.e., in the war waged by Christ himself to take converts captive; so the term would again be understood figuratively. This reading is, however, hardly convincing, even though Origen had already considered it (*In ep. ad Romanos* 10.21 [PG 14.1280]). It is possible, however, that Paul does not mean that Andronicus and Junia were imprisoned with him at the same time or in the same place; his mode of expression could mean only that they too (at some time) had been imprisoned for the faith; so Sanday and Headlam, *Romans*, 423; and Schlier, *Römerbrief*, 444.

who are outstanding among the apostles. The prep. phrase *en tois apostolois* may mean "those of mark (numbered) among the apostles" or "those held in esteem by the apostles." Barrett, Cranfield, Lagrange, Lietzmann, Michel, Rengstorf, Schlatter, Schlier, Schnackenburg, Zeller, and BAGD take it in the former sense, as did most of the patristic interpreters. Cornely and Zahn prefer the latter sense.

The former sense would mean that Andronicus and Junia were *apostoloi*. This title is not to be confused with *hoi dōdeka*, "the Twelve" (note the distinction of the two groups in 1 Cor 15:5, 7). The title "apostle" was given in the early church not only to the Twelve, but to others as well who were understood as commissioned itinerant evangelists (e.g., commissioned by a church, Acts 13:1–3). At least sixteen persons are called "apostles" in the NT: the Twelve plus Barnabas and Paul (Acts 14:4, 14), unnamed persons (1 Cor 9:5; 12:28; 2 Cor 8:23; 11:13; Eph 4:11), as well as possibly Andronicus and Junia here. See further *Did.* 11.3–6; *Herm. Vis.* 3.5.1; and *Herm. Sim.* 9.15.4; 9.16.5; 9.25.2. Thus Paul would be sending greetings to a male and a female apostle, to some of those who probably carried the Christian message to Rome before him. They could be considered paired messengers of the gospel, even if husband and wife, and not necessarily two male emissaries (see J. Jeremias, "Paarweise Sendung"); compare Aquila and Prisca. They would then have been Jewish Christian "apostles," probably from among the Jerusalem Hellenists, as their names suggest, who would have been heralds of the gospel before Paul, "without being able to lay claim to an appearance of the risen Lord" (Schnackenburg, "Apostles," 294).

They were in Christ even before me. I.e., converts to Christianity before Paul was called. The text reads thus in MSS א*, A, B, C, P, Ψ, 33, 81, 1739, and in the *Koinē* text-tradition. But MSS D, G read *tois pro emou,* which, being in the dat. case, would agree with *tois apostolois* and would mean that "the apostles" were Christians before Paul. It would not then be a description of Andronicus and Junia. This is obviously a strange correction, perhaps influenced by Gal 1:17. Although P⁴⁶ reads the peculiar sg. *gegonen,* it otherwise supports the text tradition of the better MSS.

8. *Greetings to Ampliatus, my dear friend in the Lord.* Otherwise unknown. Instead of the full form *Ampliaton,* some MSS (B², D, Ψ) read the shortened *Amplian.* The name was frequently used for slaves (*CIL* 6.4899, 15509) or freedmen (*CIL* 6.14918).

9. *Greetings to Urbanus, my fellow worker in Christ.* Otherwise unknown; it was a common Roman slave name, used even in the imperial household in Rome (*CIL* 6.4237). Indeed, along with Persis (16:12), Asyncritus, and Phlegon (16:14), this name does not occur in any of the many inscriptions found at Ephesus, whereas they all appear in Roman inscriptions (Lampe, "Roman Christians," 216). On *synergon* "fellow worker," see the NOTE on 16:3. Cf. 2 Cor 8:23.

and to my dear friend Stachys. Otherwise unknown. A not too common Greek name (*IGRom* 3.1080.37; 3.1095a.19), also used in Latin for a slave of the imperial household at Rome (*CIL* 6.8607).

10. *Greetings to Apelles.* Otherwise unknown. The name was often used in Greek (see W. Dittenberger, *Orientis graeci inscriptiones selectae,* 2 vols. [Hildesheim: Olms, 1960], §§265.12, 444.7; Philo, *Leg. ad Gai.* 30 §§203–5), frequently by Jews (Horace, *Satires* 1.5.100).

who is approved in Christ's service. Lit., "the tested one in Christ," i.e., one who has proved himself a genuine Christian.

and to the household of Aristobulus. Lit., "those from among (the people) of Aristobulus," i.e., "the (brethren) from among the (slaves, freedmen, freedwomen) of Aristobulus" (see BDF §162.5). Paul does not greet Aristobulus himself, but only the Christian part of his household. He may have been a pagan, otherwise unknown, for the name Aristobulus was widely used; it could refer to a slave of the imperial household.

But an Aristobulus, grandson of Herod the Great and son of Aristobulus and Bernice (*J.W.* 2.11.6 §221 end) was the brother of Herod Agrippa I, a friend and confidant of Emperor Claudius (*Ant.* 20.1.2 §12), long resident in Rome. Some commentators think that members of the household of this Aristobulus could be referred to as *hoi ek tōn Aristoboulou,* even though he himself would have died by this time. If he brought Christians with him in his household, this could have been the way Christianity first came to Rome.

11. *Greetings to my fellow countryman Herodion.* Or possibly "my relative";

see the NOTE on 16:7. Herodion is an otherwise unknown Jewish Christian. His name suggests that he was a freedman of the Herodian line.

and to those who belong to the Lord in the household of Narcissus. Lit., "those who belong to the Lord from among (the people) of Narcissus." The construction is almost the same as that in v 10b. The name Narcissus was often used for slaves and freedmen (see Suetonius, *Claudii vita* 28; Cassius Dio, *Roman History* 64.3.4). Again, Paul does not greet Narcissus, but the Christians of his household; hence he may also be a pagan.

Sanday and Headlam (*Romans,* 425–26) think that this Narcissus was possibly the well-known freedman of that name, former secretary of Emperor Claudius. At the murder of Claudius (A.D. 54) he was arrested and was forced to commit suicide by Agrippina shortly after the accession of Nero. See Tacitus, *Annals* 31.1; Cassius Dio, *Roman History* 60.34. Although he was no longer alive, Paul would be sending greetings to the Christians of his household.

12. *Greetings to those workers in the Lord, Tryphaena and Tryphosa.* I.e., laborers in the cause of the Lord. They are otherwise unknown, but are probably to be regarded as sisters. Paul's description of them may mean that he does not know them personally. The names are found in both Greek and Latin inscriptions (*CIG* 2.3092 2819, 2839, 3348; *CIL* 6.15622–26, 4866, 15241).

Greetings to my dear friend Persis, who has toiled hard in the Lord. Otherwise unknown. Persis was a name often used for a female slave (*IGRom* 7.2074; *CIL* 5.4455).

13. *Greetings to Rufus.* Is he possibly the same as the Rufus, son of Simon of Cyrene, mentioned in Mark 15:21? The suggestion is often made because of the likely origin of the Marcan Gospel in Rome or Italy, but it may be sheer speculation. Rufus was a commonly used Latin name for slaves, and is found even in the Greek spelling *Rouphos* (Diodorus Siculus, 11.60.1; 14.107.1; Josephus, *Ant.* 17.10.3 §266; 17.10.9 §294). According to later legends, this Rufus became the bishop of Thebes.

the chosen one of the Lord. Lit., "elect in the Lord." Not, however, merely in the sense of "called to be a Christian" (that would not single him out), but someone whose career as a Christian was "select" or distinguished.

and to his mother—whom I call mother too. Lit., "also of me." But it is not immediately clear in what sense Paul means this. Possibly on some occasion and in some place in the eastern Mediterranean area she had shown him a special gesture of motherly kindness, which Paul now recalls.

14. *Greetings to Asyncritus, Phlegon, Hermes, Patrobas, Hermas.* Otherwise unknown. In *CIL* 6.12565 a freedman of Augustus bears the name Asyncritus, "Incomparable"; cf. *NDIEC* 2.85. Phlegon was a name used by slaves (*CIL* 2.2017; 14.2008a) and by a freedman of Hadrian, the historian of Tralles (C. Müller, *Fragmenta historicorum graecorum,* 5 vols. [Paris: F. Didot, 1885], 3.602–3). Hermes may be the name of the Greek god given to a human being or else an abbreviated form (as also the subsequent Hermas) of names like Herma-

741

goras, Hermodorus, Hermogenes. Hermes was commonly used for slaves (*CIL* 6.8121), whereas Hermas was less so. Patrobas is an abbreviated form of *Patrobios*, a name borne by a famous freedman and confidant of Nero, who was in charge of the emperor's theatrical events (Suetonius, *Neronis vita* 45.1; Cassius Dio, *Roman History* 63.3.1–2) and who was executed by Galba (Tacitus, *Histories* 1.49.1; 2.95.2).

Both Origen (*Comm. in ep. ad Romanos* 10.31 [PG 14.1282]) and Eusebius (*Historia ecclesiastica* 3.3.6) identify the Hermas of this verse with the author of the writing, *The Shepherd*, but modern scholars tend to regard that work as a composition of the mid-second century, following the testimony of the Muratorian Canon §7: it was written "most recently, in our own times, in the city of Rome by Hermas, while his brother Pius occupied the see as bishop of the Roman church." See A. Carlini, "Erma."

and the brothers who are with them. This addition may suggest that those just named and other Christians were known to Paul as a group that met together, perhaps in some house church.

15. *Greetings to Philologus and Julia, Nereus and his sister, Olympas.* *Philologos* was a common name for slaves and freedmen (*CIL* 5.7462; 6.4116; 9.5120). Julia is probably to be understood as his wife, and Nereus and Olympas may be their children. Julia was a very common female name, especially among the female slaves of the imperial household (*CIL* 6.20416, 20715–17). Nereus was an old mythical name (for the god of the sea) often given to boys; it was also commonly used for slaves and freedmen. Olympas was an abbreviated form of names beginning with *Olymp-*; it is found in *IGRom* 3.1080.28 and *CIL* 14.1286. The copyists of MSS C* and Gᵍʳ replaced "Julia" with "Junia," thus reversing the reading of P⁴⁶ in v 7.

and all God's dedicated people who are with them. Lit., "and all the saints who are with them." See the NOTE on 1:7. Again, this may be a reference to a house church.

16. *Greet one another with a holy kiss.* See 1 Thess 5:26; 1 Cor 16:20; 2 Cor 13:12. Paul often ends a letter in this way, using in an epistolary context what was perhaps a liturgical gesture at the celebration of the Lord's Supper (Justin, *Apology* 1.65.2). Cf. 1 Pet 5:14. See Benko, "The Kiss"; Hofmann, *Philema hagion.*

All of the churches of Christ send you their greetings. I.e., from Corinth, Cenchreae, and elsewhere in the eastern Mediterranean, from Jerusalem to Illyricum. Thus Paul greets the Christians of Rome in the name of churches in the area that he has founded. It is a fitting global greeting for the church that he is about to visit for the first time. Indirectly, Paul recommends himself thereby to the church of Rome. Cf. 1 Cor 16:19–20. This greeting is omitted in MSS D, F, and G, where it occurs instead in v 21.

BIBLIOGRAPHY

See also the bibliography on pp. 65–67.
Bacon, B. W., "Andronicus," *ExpTim* 42 (1930–31): 300–4.

Barton, G. A., "Who Founded the Church at Rome?" *ExpTim* 43 (1931–32): 359–61.

Benko, S., "The Kiss," *Pagan Rome and the Early Christians* (Bloomington, Ind.: Indiana University, 1984), 79–102.

Brooten, B., " 'Junia . . . Outstanding among the Apostles' (Romans 16:7)," *Women Priests: A Catholic Commentary on the Vatican Declaration*, ed. L. and A. Swidler (New York: Paulist Press, 1977), 141–44.

Carlini, A., "Erma (*Vis.* II 3,1) testimone testuale di Paolo?" *Studi classici e orientali* (Pisa) 37 (1987): 235–39.

Castel S. Pietro, T. da, "*Synaichmalōtos*: Compagno di prigionia o conquistato assieme? (Rom. 16,7; Col. 4,10; Filem. 23)," *SPCIC* 2.417–28.

Devis, M., "Aquila et Priscille," *L'Anneau d'or* 65 (1955): 393–97.

Erbes, K., "Die Bestimmung der von Paulus aufgetragenen Grüsse, Röm. 16,3–15," *Zeitschrift für Kirchengeschichte* 22 (1901): 224–31.

———, "Zeit und Ziel der Grüsse Röm 16,3–15 und der Mitteilungen 2 Tim 4,9–21," *ZNW* 10 (1909): 128–47, 195–218, esp. 128–47.

Fàbrega, V., "War Junia(s), der hervorragende Apostel (Röm. 16,7), eine Frau?" *JAC* 27–28 (1984–85): 47–64.

Filson, F. V., "The Significance of Early House Churches," *JBL* 58 (1939): 105–12.

Gerberding, K. A., "Women Who Toil in Ministry, Even as Paul," *CurTM* 18 (1991): 285–91.

Gerkan, A. von, "Zur Hauskirche von Dura-Europos," *Mullus: Festschrift Theodor Klauser*, *JAC* Ergänzungsband 1, ed. A. Stuiber and A. Hermann (Münster in Westfalen: Aschendorff, 1964), 143–49.

Gielen, M., "Zur Interpretation der Formel *hē kat' oikon ekklēsia*," *ZNW* 77 (1986): 109–25.

Gnilka, J., "Die neutestamentliche Hausgemeinde," *Freude am Gottesdienst: Aspekte ursprünglicher Liturgie* . . . (Stuttgart: Katholisches Bibelwerk, 1983), 229–42.

Hainz, J., *Ekklesia*, 192–98.

Harnack, A. von, "*Kopos (kopian, hoi kopiōntes)* im frühchristlichen Sprachgebrauch," *ZNW* 27 (1928): 1–10.

———, "Über die beiden Recensionen der Geschichte der Prisca und des Aquila in Act. Apost. 18,1–27," *SPAW* (1900): 2–13.

Hauke, M., *Die Problematik um das Frauenpriestertum vor dem Hintergrund der Schöpfungs- und Erlösungsordnung* (Paderborn: Bonifatius, 1986), 352–54; *Women in the Priesthood? A Systematic Analysis in the Light of the Order of Creation and Redemption* (San Francisco, Calif.: Ignatius, 1988), 357–59.

Hofmann, K.-M., *Philema hagion*, BFCT 2.38 (Gütersloh: Bertelsmann, 1938).

Jeremias, J., "Paarweise Sendung im Neuen Testament," *New Testament Essays: Studies in Memory of Thomas Walter Manson 1893–1958* . . . , ed. A. J. B. Higgins (Manchester: Manchester University Press, 1959), 136–43, esp. 139; repr. in *Abba*, 132–39, esp. 136.

Klauck, H. J., *Hausgemeinde und Hauskirche im frühen Christentum*, SBS 103 (Stuttgart: Katholisches Bibelwerk, 1981).

Kraeling, C. H., *The Christian Building*, The Excavations at Dura-Europos . . . Final Report 8.2, ed. C. Bradford Welles (Locust Valley, N.Y.: J. J. Augustin, 1967), 127–55.

Kraemer, R. S., "Women in the Religions of the Greco-Roman World," *Religious Studies Review* 9 (1983): 127–39.

Lampe, P., "Iunia/Iunias: Sklavenherkunft im Kreise der vorpaulinischen Apostel (Röm 16,7)," ZNW 76 (1985): 132–34.

———, "Paulus—Zeltmacher," BZ 31 (1987): 256–61.

———, *Die stadtrömischen Christen*, 124–53.

Meeks, W. A., *First Urban Christians*, 23–25.

Mullins, T. Y., "Greetings as a New Testament Form," *JBL* 87 (1968): 418–26.

Petersen, J. M., "House-Churches in Rome," VC 23 (1969): 264–72.

Refoulé, F., "À Contre-courant: Romains 16,3–16," RHPR 70 (1990): 409–20.

Rhijn, C. H. van, "Rom. XVI,4," ThStud 23 (1905): 378–79.

Rouffiac, J., "Remarques sur les noms propres de Romains xvi," *Recherches sur les caractères du grec dans le Nouveau Testament d'après les inscriptions de Priène*, Bibliothèque de l'École des Hautes Études, Sciences religieuses 24.2 (Paris: Leroux, 1911), 87–92.

Schnackenburg, R., "Apostles Before and During Paul's Time," *Apostolic History and the Gospel: Biblical and Historical Essays Presented to F. F. Bruce . . .* , ed. W. W. Gasque and R. P. Martin (Exeter, UK: Paternoster; Grand Rapids, Mich.: Eerdmans, 1970), 287–303.

Schulz, R. R., "Romans 16:7: Junia or Junias?" *ExpTim* 98 (1986–87): 108–10.

Schumacher, R., "Aquila und Priscilla," TGl 12 (1920): 86–99.

Sevenster, J. N., "Waarom spreekt Paulus nooit van vrienden en vriendschap? (naar aanleiding van Rom. 16:1–16)," NedTTs 9 (1954): 356–63.

Swidler, L., *Biblical Affirmations of Women* (Philadelphia, Penn.: Westminster, 1979).

Wiegand, T. and H. Schrader, *Priene: Ergebnisse der Ausgrabungen und Untersuchungen in den Jahren 1895–1898 . . .* (Berlin: G. Reimer, 1904), 480–81.

58. Paul's Admonition about False Teachers; His Concluding Blessing (16:17–20)

16 [17]I urge you, brothers, to watch out for those who create dissension and scandal in opposition to the teaching you have learned. Keep away from them. [18]For such people do not serve our Lord Christ, but their own appetites; for by smooth talk and flattery they deceive the minds of the simple. [19]Your commitment, however, is known to all; so I am happy about you. But I want you to be wise

about what is good, and innocent about what is evil. ²⁰The God of peace will soon crush Satan under your feet. The grace of our Lord Jesus be with you!

COMMENT

Paul now adds a personal admonition, perhaps even writing it in his own hand. Whereas in 1 Cor 16:21–24 the added note was one of encouragement, here it is monitory.

It is strange that Paul, writing to a community that he did not found or evangelize, would undertake to admonish it. It is, however, only a half-admonition, because he also commends the Roman Christians for their faith commitment (16:19), as in 1:8 and 15:14. Above all, Paul desires that the Christians of Rome continue the pursuit of what is good, because their "faith is proclaimed in all the world" (1:8), so he urges them to avoid what evil may be coming their way from another source. Finally, he calls down upon them the blessing of the God of peace and of the Lord Jesus.

Paul's warning to the community against the influence of strangers who would introduce dissension and scandal differs much from the tone and style of the rest of Romans. There is nothing in the immediately preceding context that calls for it. Yet Paul did say in 15:15 that he has written "quite boldly"; and this would be a good instance of such writing. The polemical tone interrupts the greetings sent in vv 3–16 and those in vv 21–23. The introductory vb. *parakalō de,* "I urge you," makes clear the break between v 16 and v 17. After v 16 one would expect the final greeting of v 20b. The paragraph has, moreover, nothing to do with the problem addressed in 14:1–15:13. Indeed, it sounds much like that of Gal 6:12–17 or Phil 3:2–21. It is not easy, then, to identify the people to whom Paul refers. The similarity of this paragraph to Phil 3:17–19 makes one think that these verses could have come from another fragment of Pauline epistolary correspondence such as that used to make up the composite letter to the Philippians. Yet there is no reason to think that this paragraph is a non-Pauline interpolation, as Erbes ("Zeit") and Ollrog ("Die Abfassungsverhältnisse," 230–34; *Paulus,* 226–34) have maintained, for it is integral to the letter to the Romans, as Wilckens rightly saw (*An die Römer,* 3.140).

NOTES

16:17. *brothers.* See the NOTE on 1:13.

I urge you, . . . to watch out for those who create dissension and scandal. Unfortunately Paul does not further specify who these people are. Bammel ("Romans 13," 370) thinks that Paul refers to "Zealot inclinations in the Christian community at Rome." But were there Zealots at this early period? The art. *tous* implies that the Roman readers of Paul's letter would understand to whom he is referring. Paul used *dichostasia,* "dissension," in the catalog of vices in Gal 5:20.

"Scandal" would refer to the attempt to trip Christians up in their convictions. Instead of *parakalō*, read by the majority of Greek MSS, MS D and Latin versions read *erōtō*, "I ask." On *parakalō*, see the NOTE on 12:1.

in opposition to the teaching you have learned. See 6:17, "the standard of teaching to which you have been entrusted." This phrase would refer to the kerygmatic and paraenetic teaching that other missionaries had passed on to them (1 Cor 15:1–3). Cf. Gal 5:20; 2 Thess 2:14–15. To be compared are 1QS 5:7–13 and CD 20:25–34.

Keep away from them. Lit., "bend away from them." The Roman Christians are urged to avoid all false teachers who come to them from abroad. Cf. 1 Thess 3:6; 1 Cor 5:9, 11.

18. *such people do not serve our Lord Christ.* See Phil 3:18–19. The opposition that such dissenters create is not in the service of the risen Lord. To "serve Christ" (12:11; 14:18) means to lead a Christian life in an ecclesial, everyday setting (cf. Col 3:24; Eph 6:7; Titus 3:10–11; 2 Tim 3:5).

but their own appetites. Lit., "slaves of their own belly," i.e., themselves. See Phil 3:19; Gal 5:7–12 for similar strong language used by Paul. "Belly" may be a sarcastic reference to dietary regulations that such false teachers are trying to impose. See 2 Cor 11:20. Cf. Origen, *Commentarius in ep. ad Romanos* 10.34 (PG 14.1283). W. Schmithals ("Die Irrlehrer von Rm 16,17–20," ST 13 [1959]: 51–69) would identify these strangers as Jewish-Christian gnostics. But were there any such gnostics in the days of Paul? Gnostics emerged in the mid-second century, not earlier.

by smooth talk and flattery they deceive the minds of the simple. Lit., "the hearts of the nonevil." The innocent can easily be led astray by such persons. Cf. Eph 5:6; Col 2:4; 2 Pet 2:3; Titus 1:10.

19. *Your commitment, however, is known to all.* Lit., "your obedience," i.e., your commitment to the faith; cf. 1:5, 8; 15:18; 16:26. Paul emphasizes commitment and contrasts it with the dissent that does not serve the Lord. Although he had to warn Roman Christians about false teachers, he now heaps lavish praise on them.

so I am happy about you. On the vb. *chairō*, see the NOTE on 12:12.

I want you to be wise about what is good, and innocent about what is evil. Paul expresses his joy about the well-known ethical conduct of the Christians of Rome. He wants them to be *akeraioi*, "guileless, unsophisticated," when it comes to evil.

20. *The God of peace will soon crush Satan under your feet.* On the God of peace, see the NOTE on 15:33. The blessing that Paul uttered there is now recast. Paul alludes to Gen 3:15, as he interprets the serpent of Genesis as Satan, the personification of all evil, disorder, dissension, and scandal in the community. God, who shapes human ways in peace, will do away with such dangers that threaten the community. Paul implies that the false teachers are under the

influence of Satan, as in 2 Cor 11:14–15. Some Greek MSS (A, 365, 630) read the opt. *syntripsai,* which would mean, "May the God of peace crush."

The grace of our Lord Jesus be with you! The usual Pauline final greeting (see 1 Cor 16:23; 1 Thess 5:28; cf. 2 Thess 3:18). In 2 Cor 13:33 the formula becomes triadic. MSS A, C, P, Ψ, 33, 81, 1739 and the *Koinē* text-tradition add *Christou* after *Iēsou,* whereas MSS D, F, G, and the Vg omit this final blessing and add it as v 24 after v 23.

BIBLIOGRAPHY

Baumgarten, J., *Paulus,* 213–16.

Franzmann, M. H., "Exegesis on Romans 16:17ff.," *ConcJourn* 7 (1981): 13–20.

Jewett, R., *Christian Tolerance,* 17–22.

Koehler, E. W. A., *Romans 16:17–20* (Milwaukee, Wisc.: Northwestern Publ. House, 1946).

Kraemer, R. W., *The Interpretation of Romans 16:17–20 in Ecclesiology* (St. Louis: Concordia Seminary, 1968).

Kretzmann, P. E., "Zu Röm. 16, 17f.," *CTM* 4 (1933): 413–24.

Lutheran Church—Missouri Synod, *Exegesis on Romans 16:17ff.* (no place: no publ., 1950).

Müller, K., *Anstoss und Gericht: Eine Studie zum jüdischen Hintergrund des paulinischen Skandalon-Begriffs,* SANT 19 (Munich: Kösel, 1969), 46–67.

Müller, U. B., *Prophetie und Predigt im Neuen Testament: Formgeschichtliche Untersuchungen zur urchristlichen Prophetie,* SNT 10 (Gütersloh: Mohn, 1975), 175–90, 201–14.

Schmithals, W., "The False Teachers of Romans 16:17–20," *Paul and the Gnostics,* 219–38.

Trevijano, R., "*Eulogia* in St. Paul and the Text of Rom. 16,18," *SE* VI, TU 112 (1973), 537–40.

59. GREETINGS FROM PAUL'S COMPANIONS AND THE SCRIBE TERTIUS (16:21–23)

16 [21]Timothy, my fellow worker, and Lucius, Jason, and Sosipater, my fellow countrymen, send their greetings to you. [22]I, Tertius, who write this letter, also greet you in the Lord. [23]Gaius, my host, and the whole church here, send greetings too. Erastus, the treasurer of this city, and Quartus, our brother, also greet you.

COMMENT

Paul ends his letter to the Christians of Rome with greetings to them from eight Christians who are with him. Those named are all men, and significantly no women. The greetings are perhaps formulated by Paul, but the scribe Tertius, who identifies himself, writes them. They are appended to Paul's farewell blessing of v 20. They form a postscript and have really nothing to do with the theme or subject of chaps. 1–15. Once this fact is recognized, it is seen how unfair it is to castigate Paul for ending the letter with "a confused jumble of ideas which displace one another and avoid any order" (Käsemann, *Commentary*, 419).

In 15:26 Paul implied that he was writing from the vicinity of "Macedonia and Achaia," a detail that fits well with Acts 20:1–5, at the end of his Mission III. Here in 16:21–23 he is still based in Corinth (Achaia), and mentions Timothy, So(si)pater, and Gaius as being with him; they are also named in Luke's independent report of Acts 20:4.

Bahr ("Subscriptions," 38–40) is of the opinion that Paul would have taken the pen from Tertius (see the COMMENT on 12:1–2) and appended chap. 16, the letter of recommendation and greetings, even adding the greetings in his own name. Yet none of this is clear, even if it is an interesting hypothesis.

NOTES

16:21. *Timothy*. This coworker was taken by Paul from Lystra on his second missionary journey. According to Acts 16:1–3 he was the son of a Jewish-Christian woman (named Eunice, according to 2 Tim 1:5) and a Greek (Gentile) father. The Lucan Paul had him circumcised "because of the Jews in those places." He accompanied Paul on many of his missionary journeys and went to Corinth to try to smooth out relations between that church and Paul (2 Cor 1:1, 19). He was well known in Ephesus (1 Cor 4:17; 16:10). Now he is in Corinth with Paul and sends his greetings along to the Christians of Rome. Timothy is listed as the cosender of four of Paul's letters: 1 Thess 1:1; 2 Cor 1:1; Phil 1:1; Phlm 1; cf. 2 Thess 1:1; Col 1:1. In 2 Tim 1:2 he is addressed as the bishop of Ephesus. Cf. Heb 13:23.

my fellow worker. See the NOTE on 16:3. Would Paul have had to add this description, if chap. 16 were a letter of recommendation addressed to the Ephesian church?

Lucius. Not necessarily the Lucius of Cyrene (Acts 13:1), and even less likely Luke the evangelist, who is otherwise called *Loukas* (Phlm 24; cf. Col 4:14; 2 Tim 4:11), even though Origen (*In ep. ad Romanos* 10.39 [PL 14.1288]) and some modern commentators have so considered him (e.g., Dunn, *Romans*, 909). Cranfield (*Romans*, 805) even toys with the idea that the We Passage of Acts 20:5–15 may imply that the author of Acts was with Paul at this time. Yet it is unlikely, for the very We Passage, taken at face value, suggests instead that the author joined Paul in Philippi, after he had left Corinth, where he would have written Romans during the "three months" spent there according to Acts 20:3. See *The Gospel According to Luke*, 35–51. Legend has it that Paul consecrated this Lucius the first bishop of Cenchreae (*Constitutiones apostolicae* 7.46.10).

Jason. Possibly the same as Jason of Thessalonica, Paul's host there (Acts 17: 5–9). The Greek name *Iasōn* often served as a substitute for *Iēsous* (see BDF §53.2d), and possibly for this reason Paul regards him along with Sosipater, though they come from Greece, as *syngeneis mou*.

Sosipater. Undoubtedly the same as *Sōpatros* of Beroea, the one who is said to accompany Paul on his last journey to Jerusalem in Acts 20:4. The name is also known from 2 Macc 12:19, 24. In contradistinction to Timothy, who is called *synergos*, Lucius, Jason, and Sosipater, now resident in Corinth, may be delegates from Achaia who will accompany Paul to Jerusalem as he takes the collection there.

my fellow countrymen. See the NOTE on 16:7.

send their greetings to you. I.e., along with Paul and Timothy.

22. *I, Tertius, who write this letter.* Paul's Christian scribe, who is adding these few verses in his own name. Other passages in Paul's letters suggest that he was again using a scribe: 1 Cor 16:21; Gal 6:11; cf. 2 Thess 3:17; Col 4:18. Apart from this reference, *Tertios* is not a Latin name often attested, though the fem. Tertia is known (*NDIEC* 4 §94). The name is attested in an inscription in the Roman cemetery of Priscilla; see G. Edmundson, *The Church*, 22 n. 1. The Latin name may suggest that Paul's scribe in Corinth had some connection with the Roman community. According to later legends, Tertius became the bishop of Iconium.

also greet you in the Lord. On *en Kyriō*; see the NOTE on 16:2. The position of this prep. phrase at the end of the sentence leaves open the question of what it modifies. As translated, it is taken to modify *aspazomai*, "I greet," i.e., I send you greetings as a Christian, or send you my Christian greetings, or as Goodspeed translates it, "I, Tertius . . . , wish to be remembered to you as a fellow Christian." But it could also modify *ho grapsas tēn epistolēn*. Then it would mean, "who write this letter in the Lord," i.e., I as a Christian write or, as Origen took it, Tertius writes for the glory of God (*In ep. ad Romanos* 10.40 [PG 14.1289]). Bahr (*CBQ* 28 [1966]: 465) toys with the possibility that *en kyriō* refers not to Christ, but to Paul himself as *kyrios*, "I, Tertius, who write the letter in the service of (my) master [Paul], greet you." Theoretically, such an interpretation might be possible; but it is not very likely, as Bahr has to add an implied *mou*, "my," to make it intelligible.

23. *Gaius, my host.* This undoubtedly means Paul's, not Tertius's, host. He is probably the same person as Gaius of Corinth (1 Cor 1:14), whom Paul admits he baptized. The Corinthian Christian community may have met in his house. Michaelis would identify him instead with the Gaius of Macedonia who was with Paul in Ephesus (Acts 19:29), because he thinks that Paul wrote Romans from Philippi; see *Die Gefangenschaft des Paulus in Ephesus* (Gütersloh: Bertelsmann, 1925), 92–93.

and the whole church here, send greetings too. Again *ekklēsia* is used in the local sense. Paul may mean that this church met at Gaius's house. See the NOTE on 16:1.

Erastus. The name Erastus is well attested in inscriptions (see *SIG* 838.6). *Pace* Lietzmann (*An die Römer,* 128), the one named here is almost certainly the same as the person mentioned in Acts 19:22 and 2 Tim 4:20. Paul names him now because of his prominence in the Corinthian community. This city treasurer or chamberlain is undoubtedly the same as the aedile Erastus, who paved a square in first-century Roman Corinth, according to a Latin inscription still partly in situ in the square near the eastern parados of the theater:

ERASTVS PRO AEDILIT[AT]E
S P STRAVIT

"Erastus, in return for his aedileship, laid the pavement at his own expense." (*S. P. = sua pecunia.*) See J. H. Kent, *The Inscriptions 1926–1950,* Corinth 8.3 (Princeton, N.J.: American School of Classical Studies at Athens, 1966), 17–31, 99–100, pl. 21, no. 232 (dated to the time of Nero); *Ancient Corinth: A Guide to the Excavations,* 6th ed. (Athens: American School of Classical Studies at Athens, 1954), 74; cf. Murphy-O'Connor, *St. Paul's Corinth,* 37.

the treasurer of this city. Lit., "steward of the city." The expression *oikonomos tēs poleōs* is often found as a title on Greek inscriptions (*CIG* 2512, 2717, 6837) and usually denoted a slave or, more often, a freedman, the *servus arcarius* of a town, or *arcarius rei publicae.* Although Cadbury ("Erastus"), Roos ("De titulo"), and Lane Fox (*Pagans,* 293) have been reluctant to identify the Erastus of the Corinthian inscription with the Erastus of Paul's letter, Mason (*Greek Terms,* 71) has not hesitated to equate *oikonomos* and *aedilis coloniae* (see *IGRom* 4.813; 4.1435; 4.1630). This equivalence of *oikonomos* and *aedilis* is not universally accepted. Theissen (*Social Setting*) thinks that it corresponds instead to Latin *quaestor,* but much of his evidence comes from a later period in the empire (ibid., 78). Yet Broneer, Furnish, Kent, and Murphy-O'Connor have seen no difficulty in accepting the likelihood of the Erastus of this inscription as the same person as Paul's friend. Kent himself noted that the pavement dates from the mid-first century A.D., that the name Erastus is not otherwise found at Corinth, and that *oikonomos* describes with reasonable accuracy the function of a Corinthian aedile.

A second Corinthian inscription mentioning an Erastus has recently been found (see Clarke, "Another"), but it scarcely refers to the same person as mentioned by Paul or by the earlier Corinthian inscription, for it is dated to the second century A.D.

Quartus, our brother. I.e., fellow Christian; see the NOTE on 1:13. The Latin name is attested in *CIL* 2.1270; 10.859.23. This Quartus is otherwise unknown, but his Latin name, like that of Tertius, may link him with Roman Christians or suggest that he is known to them. Lagrange (*Romains,* 277), following earlier interpreters, thinks that he may even have been the brother of Tertius, the third and fourth sons of the same parents. According to later legends, Quartus became the bishop of Berytus (modern Beirut).

24. The best MSS of Romans omit this verse, but MSS D, G, and some MSS of the VL add the blessing of v 20 here.

BIBLIOGRAPHY

Bahr, G. J., "The Subscriptions in the Pauline Letters," *JBL* 87 (1968): 27–41.

Broneer, O., "Corinth: Center of St. Paul's Missionary Work in Greece," *BA* 14 (1951): 78–96.

Cadbury, H. J., "Erastus of Corinth," *JBL* 50 (1931): 42–58.

Clarke, A. D., "Another Corinthian Erastus Inscription," *TynBul* 42 (1991): 146–51.

Edmundson, G., *The Church in Rome in the First Century* (London and New York: Longmans, Green, 1913).

Ellis, E. E., "Paul and His Co-workers," *NTS* 17 (1970–71): 437–52.

Furnish, V. P., "Corinth in Paul's Time: What Can Archaeology Tell Us?" *BARev* 15[read 14].3 (1988): 14–27.

Gill, D. W. J., "Erastus the Aedile," *TynBul* 40 (1989): 293–301.

Goodspeed, E. J., "Gaius Titius Justus," *JBL* 69 (1950): 382–83.

Harrison, P. N., "Erastus and His Pavement," *Paulines and Pastorals* (London: Villiers, 1964), 100–5.

Lane Fox, R., *Pagans and Christians* (Harmondsworth, UK: Penguin, 1988), 293.

Longenecker, R. N., "Ancient Amanuenses and the Pauline Epistles," *New Dimensions in New Testament Study*, ed. R. N. Longenecker and M. C. Tenney (Grand Rapids, Mich.: Zondervan, 1974), 281–97.

McDonald, W. A., "Archaeology and St. Paul's Journeys in Greek Lands: Part III— Corinth," *BA* 5 (1942): 36–48.

Mason, H. J., *Greek Terms for Roman Institutions: A Lexicon and Analysis*, American Studies in Papyrology 13 (Toronto: Hakkert, 1974), 71.

Miller, W., "Who Was Erastus?" *BSac* 88 (1931): 342–46.

Pölzl, F. X., *Die Mitarbeiter des Weltapostels Paulus* (Regensburg: Manz, 1911), 263–415.

Roos, A. G., "De titulo quodam latino Corinthi nuper reperto," *Mnemosyne* 58 (1930): 160–65.

Shear, T. L., "Excavations in the Theatre District and Tombs of Corinth in 1929," *AJA* 33 (1929): 515–46, esp. 525–26, fig. 9 (photo).

Theissen, G., *Social Setting*, 75–83.

Waele, F. J. de, "Erastus, Oikonoom van Korinthe en vriend van St. Paulus," *Mededeelingen van het Nederlandsch Historisch Instituut te Rome* 9 (1929): 40–48.

———, "Die korinthischen Ausgrabungen 1928–1929," *Gnomon* 6 (1930): 54; 10 (1934): 226.

Weerd, H. van de, "Een nieuw opschrift van Korinthe," *Revue belge de philologie et d'histoire* 10 (1931): 87–95.

Woodward, A. M., "Archaeology in Greece, 1928–1929," *Journal of Hellenic Studies* 49 (1929): 220–39, esp. 221.

———, "Greek Archaeology and Excavation," *The Year's Work in Classical Studies 1928–1929* (Amsterdam: J. Benjamins, 1930, repr. 1970), 105–18, esp. 110.

V. DOXOLOGY (16:25–27)

♦

60. GLORY TO THE GOD OF WISDOM THROUGH JESUS CHRIST (16:25–27)

16 ²⁵Now to him who is able to strengthen you according to my gospel and the preaching of Jesus Christ, in accord with the revelation of the mystery kept secret for long ages, ²⁶but now disclosed and made known by command of the eternal God in prophetic writings so that all of the Gentiles may come to the commitment of faith—²⁷to the only wise God, be glory forever through Jesus Christ! Amen.

COMMENT

In its present form the letter to the Romans in many MSS (P⁶¹, ℵ, B, C, D, 81, 1739) and versions (VL, Vg, Coptic, Syriac, Ethiopic) ends with a doxology or an ascription of praise uttered to God. On the position of this doxology in various Greek MSS, see Introduction, section III. It is probably not an authentic Pauline composition, but a doxology that was added to the letter at the time of the formation of the Pauline corpus of letters. Yet some interpreters have regarded it as a Pauline composition (so Bacon, Fahy, Gatzweiler, Nygren), and occasionally one argues for its authentic relation to this letter (e.g., Walkenhorst). In any case, though the vocabulary and tone of this paragraph sometimes differ from the rest of Romans, it does echo some of the themes of the letter.

Paul has doxologies elsewhere in his letters (11:36; Gal 1:5; Phil 4:20; cf. Eph 3:21; 1 Tim 1:17). But none of them is so long or so solemnly composed as this one. See also Heb 13:20–21; Jude 24–25; *1 Clem.* 65; *Mart. Pol.* 20.

Even if not authentically Pauline or originally part of Romans, it forms a fitting conclusion to the letter, for it catches the spirit of the Pauline message of the letter: from of old God in his wisdom has bound up salvation with Christ Jesus, and the mystery of this wise decision has now been disclosed. The God who rules over human beings of all ages has now caused his gospel to be proclaimed among the nations to bring about the commitment of faith among them: "To the only wise God be glory forever through Jesus Christ." The doxology seems to be derived from a liturgical setting. In using it, "Paul" invites the Christians of Rome to praise God for the revelation of the gospel and the realization of God's salvific plan, the divine "mystery" rooted in silence until recently in human history, but now made known in and through Christ Jesus. In thus relating the Christian "gospel" and "preaching" to "mystery" and to the silence of God, the doxology acknowledges once again God's wisdom. In its own

753

way it echoes the hymn to the wisdom of God in 11:33–36. For the OT and Jewish background of "mystery," see *PAHT* §PT33–34.

NOTES

16:25. *to him who is able to strengthen you*. "Paul" blesses God the Father, who is the source of Christian revelation and the author of the salvific plan that has come to realization in the work of Christ Jesus. He thus praises God as the one who is the source of strength and constancy for Christian people. See 14:4; cf. Eph 3:20; Jude 24. The strange rel. pron. *hō* is read in important MSS (P⁴⁶, ℵ, A, C, D, Ψ, 33, 88, 181, 326, 330, 614, 1729, and the *Koinē* text-tradition), but omitted in MSS B and 630 and by Origen. It obviously creates an anacoluthon, and probably for that reason was omitted.

according to my gospel and the preaching of Jesus Christ. "Paul" acknowledges that the gospel that he has been preaching not only stems from Jesus Christ but also proclaims him as the source of such strength and constancy for all believers. In using "my," he refers to his personal way of announcing the good news. Thus "Paul" recognizes that his preaching of Christ is the "good news" (see pp. 109–10). Cf. 2:16; 11:28; cf. Gal 1:16; 2 Tim 2:8. *Kērygma* is probably used of the "preaching" of the gospel, the good news about Jesus Christ (objective gen.), but it could also be "the preaching of Jesus Christ" (subjective gen., as the Vg understands it). See 10:8; 1 Cor 1:21, 23; 2:4; 15:1; 2 Cor 1:19; Gal 2:2.

in accord with the revelation of the mystery kept secret for long ages. Lit., "according to the mystery kept silent for eternal ages." See the NOTE on 11:25. Here the "gospel" and the "mystery" are more or less equated. See 1 Cor 2:6, 7, 10; cf. Col 1:26–27; 2:2; Eph 1:9; 3:3–4, 9. This thought underlies much of the argument of chaps. 9–11 and is also implied in the first eight chapters (Sanday and Headlam, *Romans*, 434). On the silence of God, see Isa 64:11; Pss 28:1; 35:22; 39:13; 50:3; Wis 18:14–16; Ignatius, *Magn.* 8:2; *Eph.* 19:1. *Pace* Lührmann (*Offenbarungsverständnis*, 122–23), the notion of "the silence of God" is not gnostic. Cf. Dewailly, ("Mystère"), who supplies its OT background.

26. *but now disclosed and made known*. I.e., through the gospel and the preaching of Jesus Christ. Cf. Eph 3:5; 1 Pet 1:20; 2 Tim 1:9–10.

by command of the eternal God. This may be an allusion to Paul's commission as an apostle to the Gentiles so that he could make known this mystery, now revealed, not only to Israel, but to all nations. On the phrase "eternal God," see the LXX of Gen 21:33; Isa 16:4; 40:28; Bar 4:8; Suz 35; 3 Macc 7:16; 1QapGen 19:8.

in prophetic writings. I.e., the OT and the Jewish apocalyptic writings that bear on this "mystery." See 1:1–2; 3:21. The ideas summed up in this verse are found throughout Romans: the continuity of the OT with Christianity, the fact that Christ Jesus came in accordance with the Scriptures, that the new mode of salvation and justification was witnessed by the prophets of old, and that God has thus brought to realization his plan of salvation.

so that all of the Gentiles may come to the commitment of faith. An appositional gen., the commitment that is faith; see the NOTE on 1:5. Cf. 15:18; Acts 6:7; 1 Pet 1:22. Thus the Gentiles are envisaged as included in the "mystery" that once concerned Israel (11:25).

27. *to the only wise God.* This is the climax of the doxology. See 11:33–36; cf. 1 Tim 1:17; Jude 24; Rev 15:4. God is one, the God of both Jews and Greeks (3:29–30), and infinitely wise (11:33). He leads and guides human beings, even when his paths are inscrutable. The OT background of the "only God" can be found in 2 Kgs 19:15; Pss 83:19; 86:10; Isa 37:16, 20; Neh 9:6; 2 Macc 7:37; LXX Dan 3:45. For the use of *monos* with deities of various sorts in antiquity, see Delling, *"Monos Theos."* See also Dupont, *("Monō")*, who insists that "Paul" is deriving his formula about the wise God not from a Platonic background, but from the OT. Cf. Fitzmyer, *"Monos," EDNT* 2.440–42.

be glory forever through Jesus Christ! Praise is paid once again to God the Father through his Son, Jesus Christ. Similar endings of doxologies can be found in Gal 1:5; Phil 4:20; Eph 3:21; 1 Tim 1:17; 2 Tim 4:18; Heb 13:21; 1 Pet 4:11; 2 Pet 3:18; Jude 25; Rev 1:6; 4 Macc 18:24. MSS P61, ℵ, A, D, P, 81, and the VL, Vg, and Coptic, Ethiopic, and Syriac versions add *tōn aiōnōn* after *eis tous aiōnas,* "(for ages) of ages."

Some MSS (P, 33, 104, 256, 263, 436, 1319, 1837) place the blessing of v 20 after this doxology, thus ending the letter with a benediction.

Amen. See the NOTE on 1:25.

In the best MSS (ℵ, A, B*, C, D*) the subscription is merely *pros Rhōmaious,* "To the Romans," but in a number of MSS it is recorded more fully: *pros Rhōmaious egraphē apo Korinthou,* "It was written to the Romans from Corinth" (B1, D2, P). MS L adds *tou hagiou Paulou,* "of Saint Paul." The *Koinē* text-tradition reads *tou hagiou Paulou epistolē pros Romaious egraphē dia Phoibēs tēs diakonou tēs en Kenchreiais ekklēsias,* "The letter of Saint Paul to the Romans was written through Phoebe the deacon of the church in Cenchreae." The meaning, however, must be "was sent" through Phoebe, unless one prefers to regard this subscription as a contradiction of 16:22. But MS 337 finally gets it straight: *egraphē hē pros Rhōmaious epistolē dia Tertiou. epemphthē de dia Phoibēn apo Korinthiōn,* "The letter to the Romans was written through Tertius; it was sent from Corinth through Phoebe."

BIBLIOGRAPHY

Aland, K., "Der Schluss und die ursprüngliche Gestalt des Römerbriefes," *Neutesta-mentliche Entwürfe,* TB 63 (Munich: Beck, 1979), 284–301.

Bacon, B. W., "The Doxology at the End of Romans," *JBL* 18 (1899): 167–76.

Bishop, E. F. F., "Some New Testament Occurrences of *Monos* with *Theos,*" *Muslim World* 51 (1961): 123–27.

Champion, L. G., "Benedictions and Doxologies in the Epistles of Paul," Ph.D. diss., Universität Heidelberg, 1934.

Deichgräber, R., *Gotteshymnus*, 25–40.

Delling, G., "*Monos Theos,*" *TLZ* 77 (1952): 469–76.

Dewailly, L.-M., "Mystère et silence dans Rom. xvi. 25," *NTS* 14 (1967–68): 111–18.

Dupont, J., "*Monō sophō theō (Rom.*, xvi,27)," *ETL* 22 (1946): 362–75.

Elliott, J. K., "The Language and Style of the Concluding Doxology of the Epistle to the Romans," *ZNW* 72 (1981): 124–30.

Fahy, T., "Epistle to the Romans 16:25–27," *ITQ* 28 (1961): 238–41.

Gatzweiler, K., "Gloire au Dieu sauveur: Rm 16,25–27," *AsSeign* 8 (1972): 34–38.

Goldammer, K., "Der KERYGMA-Begriff in der ältesten christlichen Literatur," *ZNW* 48 (1957): 77–101.

Hurtado, L. W., "The Doxology at the End of Romans," *New Testament Textual Criticism: FS Metzger*, ed. E. J. Epp and G. D. Fee (Oxford: Clarendon, 1981), 185–99.

Kamlah, E., "Traditionsgeschichtliche Untersuchungen zur Schlussdoxologie des Römerbriefes," Ph.D. diss., Universität Tübingen, 1955.

Knox, J., "A Note on the Text of Romans," *NTS* 2 (1955–56): 191–93.

Lührmann, D., *Das Offenbarungsverständnis*, 113–40.

Mowry, L., "The Early Circulation of Paul's Letters," *JBL* 63 (1944): 73–86.

Schmithals, W., "On the Composition and Earliest Collection of the Major Epistles of Paul," *Paul and the Gnostics*, 239–74.

Walkenhorst, K.-H., "The Concluding Doxology of the Letter to the Romans and Its Theology," *Katorikku Kenkyu* 27 (1988): 99–132; in Japanese, with English summary.

INDEX OF SUBJECTS

◆

757

INDEX OF COMMENTATORS AND MODERN AUTHORS

◆